Third Edition

W9-DCJ-420

Women's Lives

A PSYCHOLOGICAL EXPLORATION

Claire A. Etaugh
Bradley University

Judith S. Bridges
*University of Connecticut
at Hartford, Emerita*

PEARSON

Boston   Columbus   Indianapolis   New York   San Francisco   Upper Saddle River
Amsterdam   Cape Town   Dubai   London   Madrid   Milan   Munich   Paris   Montreal   Toronto
Delhi   Mexico City   Sao Paulo   Sydney   Hong Kong   Seoul   Singapore   Taipei   Tokyo

To my grandchildren, Anthony and Isabel,
who enrich my life and embody my hopes for the future. —C.E.

To my grandsons Nick, Benjamin, and Devin,
who reflect the promise of a more gender-neutral tomorrow. —J.S.B.

Editorial Director: Craig Campanella
Editor in Chief: Jessica Mosher
Executive Editor: Susan Hartman
Director of Marketing: Brandy Dawson
Executive Marketing Manager: Jeanette Koskinas
Marketing Manager: Nicole Kunzmann
Production Project Manager: Elizabeth Gale Napolitano

Manager, Cover Design: Jayne Conte
Editorial Production and Composition Service:
　Revathi Viswanathan/PreMediaGlobal
Cover Designer: Suzanne Behnke
Cover Image: Image Source/Alamy
Printer/Binder/Cover Printer: Courier Companies, Inc.
Text Font: Garamond 10/12

Credits and acknowledgments borrowed from other sources and reproduced, with permission, in this textbook appear on the appropriate page within text or on page 490.

Library of Congress Cataloging-in-Publication Data

Etaugh, Claire.
　Women's lives : a psychological exploration / Claire A. Etaugh, Judith S. Bridges. — 3rd ed.
　　p. cm.
　Includes bibliographical references and index.
　ISBN-13: 978-0-205-25563-4
　ISBN-10: 0-205-25563-9
　1. Women—Psychology. 2. Women—North America—Social conditions. I. Bridges, Judith S. II. Title.
　HQ1206.E883 2012
　155.3′33—dc23

　　　　　　　　　　　　　　　　　　　　　　　　　　　2011051405

10 9 8 7 6 5 4 3 2 V092 14

ISBN-10: 0-205-25563-9
ISBN-13: 978-0-205-25563-4

CONTENTS

Preface   xviii

Chapter 1   Introduction to the Psychology of Women   1
Definitions: Sex and Gender   2
Women and Men: Similar or Different?   2
    Similarities Approach   2
    Differences Approach   2
Feminism   3
History of Women in Psychology   4
    ■ **GET INVOLVED 1.1:** How Do People View Feminism?   5
    Women and the American Psychological Association   5
    Women's Contributions   6
History of the Psychology of Women   7
    The Early Years   7
    The Recent Years   7
Studying the Psychology of Women   8
    Bias in Psychological Research   8
    ■ **GET INVOLVED 1.2:** Are Samples in Psychological Research Biased?   11
    Feminist Research Methods   13
    ■ **EXPLORE OTHER CULTURES 1.1:** Doing Cross-Cultural Research on Gender   14
    Drawing Conclusions From Multiple Studies   14
    ■ **LEARN ABOUT THE RESEARCH 1.1:** Principles of Feminist Research   15
Themes in the Text   16
    Theme 1: Intersectionality: The Diversity of Women's Identities and Experiences   16
    Theme 2: Gender Differences in Power   17
    ■ **WHAT YOU CAN DO 1.1:** Help Empower Girls and Women   18
    Theme 3: Social Construction of Gender   18
        Summary   19   •   Key Terms   20
        What Do You Think?   20   •   If You Want to Learn More   20
        Websites   21

Chapter 2   Cultural Representation of Gender   22
Stereotypes of Females and Males   23
    The Content of Gender Stereotypes   23
    ■ **GET INVOLVED 2.1:** How Do You View Typical Females and Males?   24

The Perceiver's Ethnicity and Gender Stereotypes   25

The Target's Characteristics and Gender Stereotypes   25

Stereotypes of Girls and Boys   27

Bases for Gender Stereotypes   27

Stereotypes Based on Identity Labels   29

Sexism: Experiences and Attitudes   30

Experiences With Sexism   30

Changes in Sexist Attitudes Over Time   31

Modern Sexism   31

Ambivalent Sexism   31

■ **GET INVOLVED 2.2:** Who Holds Modern Sexist Beliefs?   32

■ **EXPLORE OTHER CULTURES 2.1:** Benevolent Sexism Is a Global Phenomenon   32

Representation of Gender in the Media   33

Pattern 1: Underrepresentation of Females   33

■ **GET INVOLVED 2.3:** How Are Females and Males Portrayed on Prime-Time Television?   34

Pattern 2: Underrepresentation of Specific Groups of Females   34

■ **GET INVOLVED 2.4:** Media Advertisements and the Double Standard of Aging   37

Pattern 3: Portrayal of Gender-Based Social Roles   37

Pattern 4: Depiction of Female Communion and Male Agency   38

Pattern 5: Emphasis on Female Attractiveness and Sexuality   39

Impact of Gender-Role Media Images   40

■ **LEARN ABOUT THE RESEARCH 2.1:** Are Babies Portrayed Stereotypically in Birth Congratulations Cards?   41

■ **WHAT YOU CAN DO 2.1:** Increase Girls' and Women's Awareness of the Effects of Media   41

■ **GET INVOLVED 2.5:** Are Both Women and Men Persons?   42

Representation of Gender in the English Language   42

Language Practices Based on the Assumption That Male Is Normative   42

Negative Terms for Females   44

Significance of the Differential Treatment of Females and Males in Language   45

Summary   45   •   Key Terms   46
What Do You Think?   46   •   If You Want to Learn More   47
Websites   47

Chapter 3   **Gender Self-Concept and Gender Attitudes   48**

Gender Self-Concept   49

Prenatal Development   49

Stages of Prenatal Sex Differentiation   50

Intersexuality   51

■ **EXPLORE OTHER CULTURES 3.1:** Multiple Genders   52

Theories of Gender Typing   54

Psychoanalytic Theory   54

Social Learning Theory   56

Cognitive Developmental Theory   57

Gender Schema Theory   58

■ **WHAT YOU CAN DO 3.1:** Ways to Minimize Gender Schemas in Children   59

Gender-Related Traits   60

Changes in Gender-Related Traits Over Time   60

■ **GET INVOLVED 3.1:** What Are Your Gender-Related Traits?   61

Gender-Related Traits and Psychological Adjustment   62

Evaluation of the Concept of Androgyny   62

■ **LEARN ABOUT THE RESEARCH 3.1:** A Real-Life Approach to Androgyny   63

Gender Attitudes   63

■ **GET INVOLVED 3.2:** What Are Your Gender Attitudes?   64

■ **EXPLORE OTHER CULTURES 3.2:** Gender Attitudes in Global Context   65

Individual Differences in Gender-Related Attitudes   65

■ **GET INVOLVED 3.3:** Ethnic Variations in Gender Attitudes   67

Perceived Value of Female Versus Male Gender-Related Attributes   67

■ **GET INVOLVED 3.4:** Would You Rather Be a Female or a Male?   68

*Summary   69   •   Key Terms   70
What Do You Think?   70   •   If You Want to Learn More   71
Websites   71*

Chapter 4   Infancy, Childhood, and Adolescence   72

Children's Knowledge and Beliefs About Gender   73

Distinguishing Between Females and Males   73

Gender Identity and Self-Perceptions   73

Gender Stereotypes   74

■ **LEARN ABOUT THE RESEARCH 4.1:** Gender Stereotypes About Occupations   75

Gender-Related Activities and Interests   76

Physical Performance and Sports   76

■ **EXPLORE OTHER CULTURES 4.1:** How Do Children Develop Gender Stereotypes in Other Cultures?   76

Toys and Play   77

Gender Segregation   78

■ **GET INVOLVED 4.1:** Play Patterns of Girls and Boys   78

Influences on Gender Development   80

Parents   80

■ **LEARN ABOUT THE RESEARCH 4.2:** Learning Gender-Related Roles at Home and at Play   81

Siblings   83

School   84

Peers   84

Media   85

Puberty   85

■ **GET INVOLVED 4.2:** Influences on Gender Development   85

Events of Puberty   86

Menarche   86

Gender Differences in Puberty   89

Early and Late Maturation in Girls   89

Psychosocial Development in Adolescence   90

Identity Formation   90

Self-Esteem   91

Gender Intensification   92

■ **WHAT YOU CAN DO 4.1:** Empowering Girls to Lead Social Change   93

Body Image   93

■ **GET INVOLVED 4.3:** Perceptions of Actual and Desirable Physique   96

Summary   97   •   Key Terms   98
What Do You Think?   98   •   If You Want to Learn More   98
Websites   99

Chapter 5   **Gender Comparisons   100**

Gender-Related Social Behaviors and Personality Traits   100

Aggression   101

Prosocial Behavior   102

Influenceability   102

Emotionality   103

Moral Reasoning   104

Communication Style   104

Verbal Communication   104

■ **GET INVOLVED 5.1:** "Troubles Talk": Effects of Gender on Communication Styles   106

Nonverbal Communication   108

Gender Comparison of Cognitive Abilities   108

Verbal Ability   109

Visual–Spatial Ability   109

Mathematics Ability   112

■ **EXPLORE OTHER CULTURES 5.1:** Gender Differences in Mathematics Achievement Around the World   113

■ **LEARN ABOUT THE RESEARCH 5.1:** Factors Linked to Women's Perspectives on Math   114

■ **LEARN ABOUT THE RESEARCH 5.2:** Gender, Computers, and Video Games   115

■ **WHAT YOU CAN DO 5.1:** Encouraging Girls in Math and Science   118

Summary   118   •   Key Terms   119
What Do You Think?   119   •   If You Want to Learn More   119
Websites   120

Chapter 6 **Sexuality   121**

Sexuality   122

Sexual Anatomy and Sexual Response   122

Sexual Attitudes   123

Sexual Behaviors   124

Sexual Problems   125

Lesbians, Gay Men, Bisexuals, and Transgender Individuals   128

■ **GET INVOLVED 6.1:** Attitudes Toward Lesbians   128

Bisexuals   129

Attitudes Toward Sexual Minorities   130

■ **EXPLORE OTHER CULTURES 6.1:** Sexual Minorities Around the World   130

Explanations of Sexual Orientation   132

■ **WHAT YOU CAN DO 6.1:** Supporting Rights of Sexual Minorities   132

Sexual Activity During Adolescence   133

Frequency of Sexual Activity   133

■ **LEARN ABOUT THERE SEARCH 6.1:** Hook-Ups and Friends With Benefits   134

Factors Associated with Sexual Activity   134

The Double Standard   135

Sexual Desire   135

Sexual Activity in Midlife   136

Physical Changes   136

Patterns of Sexual Activity   136

Sexual Activity in Later Life   137

Benefits of Sexual Activity in Later Life   137

■ **GET INVOLVED 6.2:** Attitudes Toward Sexuality in Later Life   138

Sexual Behavior of Older People   138

Factors Affecting Sexual Behavior   139

Enhancing Sexuality in Later Life   139

Summary   140   •   Key Terms   141
What Do You Think?   141   •   If You Want to Learn More   141
Websites   142

Chapter 7   **Reproductive System and Childbearing   143**

Menstruation   144

The Menstrual Cycle   144

Menstrual Pain   144

Attitudes Toward Menstruation   145

Menstrual Joy   146

Premenstrual Syndrome   146
■ **GET INVOLVED 7.1:** Menstrual Symptoms   147

Contraception   148

Contraception in Adolescence   148

Methods of Contraception   149

Abortion   151

Incidence   151

Methods   152

Consequences of Abortion   152
■ **EXPLORE OTHER CULTURES 7.1:** Women's Reproductive Lives Around the World   153

Pregnancy   153

Pregnancy: Physical and Psychological Changes   153
■ **EXPLORE OTHER CULTURES 7.2:** Female Genital Cutting   154
■ **WHAT YOU CAN DO 7.1:** Help Increase Reproductive Choices of Girls and Women   154
■ **EXPLORE OTHER CULTURES 7.3:** Pregnancy-Related Deaths Around the World   155

Miscarriage   156

Teenage Pregnancy   157
■ **EXPLORE OTHER CULTURES 7.4:** Why Is the Teen Pregnancy Rate So High in the United States?   157

Childbirth   159

Stages of Childbirth   159

Methods of Childbirth   159

Childbearing After 35   160

Childbearing in the Later Years   161
■ **GET INVOLVED 7.2:** Pregnancy and Childbirth Experiences   161

Postpartum Distress   162

Infertility and Assisted Reproductive Technology   163

Reproductive Functioning in Midlife and Beyond   164

Menopause   164
■ **LEARN ABOUT THE RESEARCH 7.1:** Childfree by Choice   165

■ **EXPLORE OTHER CULTURES 7.5:** Menopause: Symbol of Decline or of Higher Status?   167

Hormone Replacement Therapy   167
*Summary   168   •   Key Terms   169
What Do You Think?   170   •   If You Want to Learn More   170
Websites   170*

Chapter 8   **Relationships   171**

Friendships   172

Friendship in Adolescence   172

Friendship in Adulthood   172

Friendship in Later Life   173

Romantic Relationships   174

Desirable Qualities in a Partner   174

Perception of Sexual Interest   175

■ **EXPLORE OTHER CULTURES 8.1:** What Do People in Other Cultures Look for in a Mate?   175

Dating   176

■ **LEARN ABOUT THE RESEARCH 8.1:** Dating Issues for Women With Physical Disabilities   176

■ **GET INVOLVED 8.1:** Dating Scripts of Women and Men   178

Committed Relationships   179

Marriage   179

Cohabitation   180

Lesbian Relationships   181

Single Women   182

Divorced Women   182

Never-Married Women   184

Widowed Women   185

Women Who Have Lost a Same-Sex Partner   187

Motherhood   188

Stereotypes of Mothers   188

Single Mothers   189

■ **WHAT YOU CAN DO 8.1:** Help Address Issues of Parenting and Work–Family Balancing   189

Lesbian Mothers   190

Mothers With Disabilities   191

The "Empty Nest" Period   191

■ **LEARN ABOUT THE RESEARCH 8.2:** Adult Children of Lesbian Mothers   192

Relationships in the Later Years   193

■ **GET INVOLVED 8.2:** Women's Experiences During the Empty Nest Period   193

Siblings   194

Adult Children   194

■ **EXPLORE OTHER CULTURES 8.2:** Living Arrangements of Older Women and Men   195

Grandchildren   196

■ **EXPLORE OTHER CULTURES 8.3:** Grandmothers: The Difference Between Life and Death   197

Parents   198

■ **GET INVOLVED 8.3:** Interview With Older Women   199

Summary   200   •   Key Terms   201
What Do You Think?   201   •   If You Want to Know More   202
Websites   202

Chapter 9 **Education and Achievement   203**

Women's Educational Goals, Attainments, and Campus Experiences   204

Educational Goals   204

Educational Attainments   204

■ **LEARN ABOUT THE RESEARCH 9.1:** Is There a "Boy Crisis" in Education?   205

■ **EXPLORE OTHER CULTURES 9.1:** Educating Girls Worldwide: Gender Gaps and Gains   206

Campus Climate   207

■ **EXPLORE OTHER CULTURES 9.2:** The Oppressive Educational Climate under Taliban Rule   207

■ **WHAT YOU CAN DO 9.1:** Promote Education of Girls Worldwide   208

Women's Work-Related Goals   210

■ **GET INVOLVED 9.1:** Does Your Campus Have a Hospitable Environment for Women?   210

Career Aspirations   211

Career Counseling   212

Work–Family Expectations   213

Work–Family Outcomes   213

Salary Expectations   214

Influences on Women's Achievement Level and Career Decisions   214

Orientation to Achievement   214

Personal Characteristics   216

Sexual Orientation   217

Social and Cultural Factors   217

■ **GET INVOLVED 9.2:** Family and Cultural Values About Education and Career Goals   219

Job-Related Characteristics   219

Summary   220   •   Key Terms   220
What Do You Think?   221   •   If You Want to Learn More   221
Websites   221

Chapter 10   **Employment   222**

Women's Employment Rates and Occupational Choices   223

Employment Rates   223

Occupational Choices   224
■ **LEARN ABOUT THE RESEARCH 10.1:** Job Retention and Advancement Among Low-Income Mothers   224

Gender Differences in Leadership and Job Advancement   225

Leadership Positions   226

Barriers That Hinder Women's Advancement   227

Women as Leaders   231

Gender Differences in Salaries   231

Comparative Salaries   231

Reasons for Differences in Salaries   232
■ **WHAT YOU CAN DO 10.1:** Effectively Negotiate Your Salary   234
■ **EXPLORE OTHER CULTURES 10.1:** Girls and Women in the Global Factory   235
■ **GET INVOLVED 10.1:** Gender-Based Treatment in the Workplace   236

Women's Job Satisfaction   236

Gender Differences in Satisfaction   236

Job Satisfaction of Sexual Minorities   237

The Older Woman Worker   238

Employment Rates   238

Why Do Older Women Work?   238

Entering the Workforce in Later Life   239

Age Discrimination in the Workplace   239

Changing the Workplace   239

Organizational Procedures and Policies   239

Strategies for Women   240
■ **GET INVOLVED 10.2:** Ways to Make the Workplace Better for Women   241

Retirement   241

The Retirement Decision   242
■ **GET INVOLVED 10.3:** Interview With Older Women: Work and Retirement   242

Adjustment to Retirement   243

Leisure Activities in Retirement   244

■ **GET INVOLVED 10.4:** Leisure Activities of Older and Young
Women   245

Economic Issues in Later Life   247

Poverty   247

Retirement Income: Planning Ahead   248

■ **EXPLORE OTHER CULTURES 10.2:** Economic Status of
Older Women   249

■ **WHAT YOU CAN DO 10.2:** Start Planning for Retirement   249

*Summary   251   •   Key Terms   252
What Do You Think?   252   •   If You Want to Learn More   253
Websites   253*

Chapter 11   **Balancing Family and Work   254**

Women's Family and Employment Roles: Perceptions and
Attitudes   255

Perceptions of Working and Stay-at-Home Mothers   255

■ **LEARN ABOUT THE RESEARCH 11.1:** Are Women "Opting Out"
of Careers?   256

■ **EXPLORE OTHER CULTURES 11.1:** Attitudes Toward Married Women's
Employment: A Cross-Cultural Perspective   257

Factors Influencing Attitudes Toward Women's Multiple
Roles   257

Division of Family Labor   258

■ **GET INVOLVED 11.1:** How Do College Students Evaluate Mothers Who Are
Full-Time Students?   258

Housework and Child Care   259

Caring for Aging Parents   260

Leisure Time   260

Women's Perceptions of the Division of Family Labor   260

Explanations of the Division of Family Labor   261

Family–Work Coordination   262

Balancing Family and Work: Costs and Benefits   262

■ **GET INVOLVED 11.2:** What Psychological Experiences Do You Think You Will
Have If You Combine Employment and Motherhood?   263

Effects of Mothers' Employment   264

Solutions to Family–Work Balancing Challenges   266

■ **EXPLORE OTHER CULTURES 11.2:** Parental Leave Policies Around
the World   267

■ **LEARN ABOUT THE RESEARCH 11.2:** How Do Tag-Team Parents Reconcile
Their Own Roles With Their Traditional Gender Attitudes?   269

Midlife Transitions in Family and Work Roles 270
■ **GET INVOLVED 11.3:** Women's Experiences in Coordinating Family and Work Roles 270
■ **WHAT YOU CAN DO 11.1:** Advocate for Family-Friendly Work Policies 271
Satisfaction with Life Roles 271
Regrets About Life Direction 272
Making Changes 272
Midlife Transitions: A Cautionary Note 272
Summary 273 • Key Terms 274
What Do You Think? 274 • If You Want to Learn More 275
Websites 275

Chapter 12 **Physical Health 276**
Health Services 277
The Physician–Patient Relationship 278
Type and Quality of Care 278
Ethnicity, Poverty, and Health Care 279
Women with Disabilities and Health Care 280
Sexual Minority Women and Health Care 280
Health Insurance 280
Sexually Transmitted Infections (STIs) 281
■ **GET INVOLVED 12.1:** What Women Say About Their Health 282
Overview of STIs 282
AIDS 283
■ **LEARN ABOUT THE RESEARCH 12.1:** Knowledge and Communication About STIs 284
■ **EXPLORE OTHER CULTURES 12.1:** The Global AIDS Epidemic 285
Reproductive System Disorders 286
Benign Conditions 286
Cancers 287
Hysterectomy 288
Osteoporosis 288
Risk Factors 289
Prevention and Treatment 289
Heart Disease 290
Gender Differences 290
Risk Factors 291
Diagnosis and Treatment 292
Psychological Impact 293
Breast Cancer 293
Risk Factors 294

■ **GET INVOLVED 12.2:** Assessing Your Risk Breast Cancer   295

Detection   295

■ **WHAT YOU CAN DO 12.1:** Doing a Breast Self-Examination   296

Treatment   297

Psychological Impact   297

Lung Cancer   298

Risk Factors   298

Detection and Treatment   298

Physical Health in Later Life   298

Gender Differences in Mortality   298

Social Class and Ethnic Differences   300

■ **EXPLORE OTHER CULTURES 12.2:** Health Report Card for Women Around the World   301

Gender Differences in Illness   302

Disability   302

Promoting Good Health   303

Physical Activity and Exercise   303

■ **LEARN ABOUT THE RESEARCH 12.2:** Good Health Habits and Longevity   303

Nutrition   305

Summary   305   •   Key Terms   307
What Do You Think?   307   •   If You Want to Learn More   307
Websites   308

Chapter 13   **Mental Health   309**

Factors Promoting Mental Health   310

Social Support   310

Optimism: "The Power of Positive Thinking"   311

Mental Health in Childhood and Adolescence   311

Internalizing Disorders in Girls   311

Externalizing Disorders in Girls   311

Eating Disorders   312

Types of Eating Disorders   312

Causes of Eating Disorders   313

Treatment of Eating Disorders   314

■ **EXPLORE OTHER CULTURES 13.1:** Cultural Pressure to Be Thin   315

Substance Use and Abuse   315

Alcohol   315

Illegal Substances   317

Anxiety Disorders and Depression   317

Anxiety Disorders   317

Depression   318
■ **GET INVOLVED 13.1**: How Do Women and Men Respond to Depression?   320
Suicide   321
■ **EXPLORE OTHER CULTURES 13.2**: Gender Differences in Suicide:
A Global Phenomenon   322

Mental Health of Sexual Minority Women   323
Stresses and Problems   323
Coping Mechanisms   323

Mental Health of Older Women   324
Gender Differences   324
The Vital Older Woman   324

Diagnosis and Treatment of Psychological Disorders   325
Gender Bias in Diagnosis   325
■ **WHAT YOU CAN DO 13.1**: Ways to Manage Stress and Promote Good
Mental Health   325
Gender Bias in Psychotherapy   326
■ **LEARN ABOUT THE RESEARCH 13.1**: What Is "Normal"? Gender
Biases in Diagnosis   326
Therapy Issues for Women of Color and Poor Women   327
Types of Therapy   327
Summary   328   •   Key Terms   329
What Do You Think?   329   •   If You Want to Learn More   329
Websites   330

Chapter 14   **Violence Against Girls and Women   331**
Sexual Harassment at School   332
Elementary and Secondary School   332
The College Campus   333
■ **GET INVOLVED 14.1**: What Constitutes Sexual Harassment on Campus?   334
Sexual Harassment in the Workplace   335
■ **WHAT YOU CAN DO 14.1**: Reducing Sexual Harassment on Campus   336
Incidence   336
Consequences   338
Explanations   338
Women's Responses   339
Stalking   339
What Is Stalking?   339
Perpetrators, Victims, and Effects   339
Violence Against Girls   340
Child Sexual Abuse   340

Infanticide and Neglect   342

■ **EXPLORE OTHER CULTURES 14.1:** Where Are the Missing Girls in Asia?   342

■ **EXPLORE OTHER CULTURES 14.2:** Girls for Sale: The Horrors of Human Trafficking   343

Dating Violence   344

Incidence   344

Who Engages in Dating Violence?   344

Rape   345

Incidence   345

Acquaintance Rape   345

Factors Associated with Acquaintance Rape   346

■ **GET INVOLVED 14.2:** Gender and Rape Myths   347

■ **EXPLORE OTHER CULTURES 14.3:** Attitudes Toward Rape Victims Around the World   348

Effects of Rape   348

Rape Prevention   349

■ **LEARN ABOUT THE RESEARCH 14.1:** Positive Life Changes Following Sexual Assault   349

Theories of Rape   350

Intimate Partner Violence   351

Incidence   351

Role of Disability, Social Class, and Ethnicity   352

Risk Factors   352

■ **EXPLORE OTHER CULTURES 14.4:** Intimate Partner Violence Around the World   353

Effects of Intimate Partner Violence   353

Leaving the Abusive Relationship   353

Theories of Intimate Partner Violence   354

Interventions   354

Elder Abuse   354

■ **EXPLORE OTHER CULTURES 14.5:** A Global View of Elder Abuse   355

Who Is Abused and Who Abuses?   356

What Can Be Done?   356

■ **WHAT YOU CAN DO 14.2:** Working to Combat Violence   356

Summary   357   •   Key Terms   358
What Do You Think?   358   •   If You Want to Learn More   359
Websites   359

Chapter 15 **A Feminist Future**   360

Feminist Goals   361

Goal One: Gender Equality in Organizational Power   361

Goal Two: Gender Equality in Relationship Power   361

Goal Three: Gender Equality in Power for All Groups of Women   362

Goal Four: Greater Flexibility in the Social Construction of
   Gender   362

Actions to Achieve These Goals   363

Research and Teaching   363

Socialization of Children   364

■ **LEARN ABOUT THE RESEARCH 15.1:** Why and How Should We Raise
Feminist Children?   364

Institutional Procedures   365

Individual Actions   366

Collective Action   366

■ **WHAT YOU CAN DO 15.1:** Become an Advocate   367

■ **EXPLORE OTHER CULTURES 15.1:** Women's Movements Worldwide   368

■ **GET INVOLVED 15.1:** A Perfect Future Day   369

Feminist Beliefs   369

■ **GET INVOLVED 15.2:** How Do You View Feminism?   370

Feminist Identification   370

Emergence of Feminist Beliefs   371

Men and Feminism   372

■ **GET INVOLVED 15.3:** How Involved in Feminist Activism Are You?   373

Postscript   373

Summary   374   •   What Do You Think?   375
If You Want to Learn More   375   •   Websites   376

References   377

Name Index   466

Subject Index   483

Photo Credits   490

PREFACE

Over the last few decades, the burgeoning interest in psychology of women has been reflected in a rapidly expanding body of research and a growing number of college-level courses in the psychology of women or gender. The third edition of *Women's Lives: A Psychological Exploration* draws on this rich literature to present a broad range of experiences and issues of relevance to girls and women. Because it does not presuppose any background in psychology, this book can be used as the sole or primary text in introductory-level psychology of women courses and, with other books, in psychology of gender or interdisciplinary women's studies courses. Additionally, its presentation of both current and classical research and theory makes it a suitable choice, along with supplementary materials, for more advanced courses focused on the psychology of women or gender.

Every chapter in this textbook reflects substantial changes in this field during the past few years. We have made several changes based on the extremely helpful comments from reviewers and the many students and faculty who have used the two life span editions and the two topical editions of this book. This new topical revision includes the following highlights:

- Over 2,100 new references emphasize the latest research and theories, with more than half from 2010 to the present.
- *What You Can Do*, a new boxed feature in each chapter, provides students with hands-on activities to both empower themselves and help promote a more egalitarian society.
- *Explore Other Cultures*, another boxed feature in each chapter, gives students an understanding of the role of cultural, social, and economic factors that shape women's lives around the world.
- *Get Involved* is a set of activities in each chapter that promotes active student participation in research.
- The unique life span approach of two previous chronological editions is embedded within topical chapters on sexuality, reproduction and childbearing, education and achievement, employment, physical health, mental health, and violence against girls and women.
- Coverage of the lives of women in the middle and later years is far more extensive than in any other textbook in the field.
- An updated list of Websites and current books at the end of each chapter provides students with resources for additional study and research.
- Expanded use of vignettes and quotes from women adds richness to the data and helps students personally connect with the material.
- New and expanded coverage of many topics reflects scientific and social developments of the second decade of the new millennium.

These changes are broken down by chapter and include:

- Chapter 1:
  New organizing theme: Intersectionality
  New material on ethnic women psychologists
- Chapter 2:
  Updated information on stereotypes related to gender, age, class, ethnicity, ableness, and sexual orientation
  New research on representation of diverse groups of women in the media
- Chapter 3:
  Updated information on multiple genders
  New material on women leaders of Native American nations

- Chapter 4:
  Expanded section on children's gendered occupational choices
  New material on the social construction of menarche, self-esteem in adolescent girls, and factors that influence body image
- Chapter 5:
  Updated findings on relational aggression
  Expanded section on cultural factors affecting girls' math achievement
- Chapter 6:
  New section on hook-ups and friends with benefits
  Expanded coverage of lesbian, gay, bisexual, and transgender individuals
  New research on sexual activity of women throughout the life span
- Chapter 7:
  Current trends in birthrates of teens and women over 35
  Updated information on assisted reproductive technology, menopause, and hormone replacement therapy
  New material on attitudes toward pregnancy in employed women and in women with disabilities
- Chapter 8:
  Recent trends in dating
  Expanded sections on marital satisfaction, cohabitation, and single mothers
  Updated information on same-sex marriages and civil unions in the United States and abroad
- Chapter 9:
  Expanded section on the educational and occupational goals and achievements of girls and young women
  Updated material on the education of the girls in developing nations
  New material on the academic environment for women of color and for low-income women
- Chapter 10:
  New coverage of workplace issues for women with disabilities, immigrant women, low-income women, and sexual minority women
  Updated information on challenges for women in leadership roles
- Chapter 11:
  Expanded coverage of dual-income couples and the "opting out" controversy
  Updated research on the benefits and costs of work–family balancing
- Chapter 12:
  New section on lung cancer in women
  New section of health care issues for women with disabilities
  Expanded coverage of health care issues for sexual minority women, ethnic minority women, low-income women, and immigrant women
  The latest information on heart disease, breast cancer, and sexually transmitted infections in women
- Chapter 13:
  Expanded coverage on reducing stress and promoting good mental health
  Updated research on mental health issues of lesbian, gay, bisexual, and transgender individuals
- Chapter 14:
  New section on stalking
  Expanded coverage of sexual harassment on college campuses and in the workplace, and on intimate partner violence in the United States and abroad
  Updated information on human trafficking, acquaintance rape, and elder abuse

- Chapter 15:
  Updated coverage of women's movements worldwide
  Additional information on men and feminism

SPECIAL FEATURES RELATED TO CONTENT AND ORGANIZATION

LIFE SPAN APPROACH EMBEDDED WITHIN TOPICAL CHAPTERS. Virtually all textbooks on the psychology of women or psychology of gender use a topical approach and also include two or three chronological chapters. Typically, there is a chapter or two on childhood and adolescence and one on women in the middle and later years. Almost all coverage of midlife and older women is contained in that one chapter. The result is that many of the issues and experiences relating to women in midlife and beyond are barely touched on or simply are not covered at all. These older women remain relatively invisible.

Our approach is different. We have taken the unique life span approach of our two earlier chronologically focused texts and have embedded this approach within almost all chapters, including topical chapters on sexuality, reproduction and childbearing, education and achievement, employment, physical health, mental health, and violence against girls and women. Midlife and older women are discussed in all chapters except the one on infancy, childhood, and adolescence.

INTERSECTIONAL APPROACH THAT INTEGRATES WOMEN'S DIVERSE IDENTITIES. The text provides extensive coverage of women of color, women in other cultures around the world, and sexual minority women. Although there is less information available, we have also included material on low-income women and women with disabilities whenever possible. New to this edition, we have used an intersectional perspective that integrates women's diverse identities within each chapter rather than examining subgroups of women in separate chapters. We emphasize that women's identities are shaped not simply by adding the effects of their class, ethnicity, age, sexual orientation, physical ability, religion, and nationality, but by a complex combination of all these characteristics in which the whole is greater than the sum of its parts.

THOROUGH EXAMINATION OF BALANCING FAMILY AND WORK. It is clear that the balancing of family and work has become a major issue facing families around the globe. We have devoted an entire chapter to this timely topic in order to thoroughly explore the theories, challenges, benefits, and solutions associated with this worldwide reality of the twenty-first century.

PEDAGOGICAL FEATURES

INTRODUCTORY OUTLINE. Each chapter begins with an outline of the material, thus providing an organizational framework for reading the material.

OPENING VIGNETTES. To grab students' attention and connect the material to real life, each chapter begins with one or two actual or hypothetical experiences illustrating one or more issues discussed in the chapter.

WHAT YOU CAN DO. A new boxed feature in this edition provides students with experiential activities that help them to both empower themselves and help promote a more egalitarian society.

WHAT DO YOU THINK? The text includes critical-thinking questions in every chapter. The end-of-the-chapter questions foster skills in synthesis and evaluation by asking the student to apply course material or personal experiences to provocative issues from the chapter.

GET INVOLVED.   As a means of providing firsthand involvement in the material, each chapter contains a number of student activities. Some require collecting data on a small number of respondents and others focus solely on the student. Furthermore, each exercise is accompanied by critical-thinking questions that focus on explanations and implications of the activity's findings.

The active learning involved in these activities serves several purposes. First, it reinforces the material learned in the text. Second, those exercises that involve surveys of other people or analyses of societal artifacts introduce students to the research process, which, in turn, can stimulate interest in research, increase familiarity with a variety of assessment techniques, and provoke critical evaluation of research techniques. Third, the Get Involved activities demonstrate the relevance of the course material to students' experiences or to the experiences of important people in their lives.

EXPLORE OTHER CULTURES.   In order to provide students with a deeper appreciation of women in a global context, each chapter contains between one and five boxed features highlighting the role of cultural, social, and economic factors in shaping women's lives around the world.

LEARN ABOUT THE RESEARCH.   To stimulate students' interest in and appreciation of research as a source of knowledge about girls and women, each chapter has one or two boxed sections that focus on research. These Learn About the Research sections either highlight an interesting recent study or present an overview of recent findings in an intriguing research area. We expose students to a variety of research techniques (content analysis, interviews, questionnaires) without requiring that they have any background in psychological research methods. Furthermore, to highlight the importance of diversity in research samples, our selections include studies of underrepresented populations.

Following the research presentation are What Does It Mean? questions. These provoke more critical thinking by asking the student to consider a variety of issues related to the research, such as explanations and implications of the findings.

KEY TERMS.   Terms in bold and definitions in italics within the text help students preview, understand, and review important concepts. These terms appear again at the end of each chapter, along with the page number on which the term appears.

SUMMARY.   The point-by-point end-of-the-chapter summary helps students synthesize the material.

IF YOU WANT TO KNOW MORE.   Recommended readings at the end of each chapter facilitate more extensive examination of the material. This edition includes more than 100 new and current recommended books to stimulate students to expand their knowledge.

WEBSITES.   An updated list of Websites at the end of each chapter provides students with additional resources.

WRITING STYLE

In order to engage the student and construct a nonhierarchical relationship between ourselves and the student, we use a nonpedantic first-person writing style. To reinforce this relationship in some of the opening vignettes and within the text, we have also presented our own experiences or those of our friends, families, and students.

SUPPLEMENTS

Pearson is pleased to offer the following supplements to qualified adopters.

Instructor's Manual and Test Bank (0205866204). The Instructor's Manual and the Test Bank contain a variety of activities to stimulate active learning. The Instructor's Manual includes critical thinking discussion topics and offers exercises that the instructor can use instead of, or supplementary to, the Get Involved activities incorporated within the text. In addition, the manual includes new film and video listings as well as updated additional Internet Websites. Finally, it contains multiple-choice and essay questions for each chapter, many of them new to this edition of the book.

PowerPoint Presentation (0205866190). The PowerPoint presentation contains outlines of key topics for each text chapter, presented in a clear and visually attractive format.

MySearchLab (0205860575). MySearchLab (www.mysearchlab.com) is an engaging online experience that personalizes learning for students. Features include the ability to highlight and add notes to the eText online or download changes straight to the iPad. Chapter quizzes and flashcards offer immediate feedback and report directly to the grade book. A wide range of writing, grammar, and research tools and access to a variety of academic journals, census data, Associated Press newsfeeds, and discipline-specific readings help students hone their writing and research skills.

ACKNOWLEDGMENTS

We owe a great deal to the many reviewers whose expert suggestions and insights were invaluable in the development of this book. Our sincere thanks to all of you who reviewed the text for the third edition specifically: Sara Buday, University of Missouri, St. Louis; Mary Dolan, California State University, San Bernardino; Jenelle Fitch, Texas Women's University; Ann Fuehrer, Miami University; Bree Kessler, Hunter College; Robin Kowalski, Clemson University; Joyce Quaytman, University of California, Chico; Jennifer Taylor, Humboldt State University.

It has been a pleasure to work with the publishing professionals at Pearson. In particular, we acknowledge the invaluable support and assistance of Susan Hartman, our editor for this book. We also are deeply indebted to Trish Blattenberger, who flawlessly and cheerfully carried out the mind-boggling tasks of locating and keeping track of over 2,100 new references, recording hundreds of track changes, securing permissions, proofreading, and carrying out numerous other tasks essential to the production of this book. In addition, kudos to Pat Campbell and Patti Hall for their help with the author index. We are grateful as well for the assistance of Robert Ray of the Chicago Public Library.

Thanks also to the students in our Psychology of Women courses who provided excellent editorial suggestions on earlier versions of the manuscript and for whom, ultimately, this book is written.

Finally, the book could not have been completed without the loving support of our families. Judith thanks her mother, Ruth; mother-in-law, Hilde; and children, Rachel and Jason, and their spouses, Gray and Nora, for providing support and inspiration throughout this project. Also, her deepest appreciation goes to her husband Barry for his unwavering patience, understanding, and encouragement. Claire's heartfelt thanks go to the women and men who have enriched her life and have been an endless source of encouragement and support: her parents, Martha and Lou; siblings, Paula, Bonnie, and Howard; children, Andi and Adam; grandchildren, Anthony and Isabel; and "extended family" of friends, Peggy, Pat, Pat, Barbara, Kevin, Pam, Suzanne, and Janis.

CHAPTER 1

Introduction to the Psychology of Women
History and Research

Definitions: Sex and Gender

Women and Men: Similar or Different?
   Similarities Approach
   Differences Approach

Feminism

History of Women in Psychology
   Women and the American Psychological Association
   Women's Contributions

History of the Psychology of Women
   The Early Years
   The Recent Years

Studying the Psychology of Women
   Bias in Psychological Research
   Feminist Research Methods
   Drawing Conclusions From Multiple Studies

Themes in the Text
   Theme 1: Intersectionality: The Diversity of Women's Identities and Experiences
   Theme 2: Gender Differences in Power
   Theme 3: Social Construction of Gender

In 1965 when I (Judith) was applying to graduate schools, the chair of one psychology department informed me that my college grades met the criterion for male, but not female, admission into the program. That department (and others) had two sets of standards, and obviously, fewer women than men were admitted. When I look back at that time it is amazing to me to realize that I quietly accepted this pronouncement. I was disappointed but not outraged. I rejoiced at my acceptance by a comparable department but never thought to protest discriminatory admission policies (which were not unique to that department). A generation ago I did not identify this issue or any other gender inequality in institutional, legal, or interpersonal practices as a problem. However, over the last several decades my awareness and concern about these issues dramatically changed. Claire and I are deeply committed to gender equality in all areas of life and hope that this text will help illuminate both the progress women have made and the challenges that remain in the attainment of this important goal.

I n this chapter we set the groundwork for the study of the psychology of women. We present major definitions, explore relevant history, examine research issues, and discuss the themes of the book. We begin with a look at the difference between sex and gender.

DEFINITIONS: SEX AND GENDER

Psychologists do not agree completely on the definitions of the words *sex* and *gender*. *Sex* is used to refer either to whether a person is female or male or to sexual behavior. This ambiguity of definition sometimes can cause confusion. For example, Claire offered a course several years ago entitled "The Psychology of Sex Differences." The course dealt with behavioral similarities and differences of females and males. After the first day of class, some students approached her with a puzzled look on their faces. The course title had led them to believe that the subject matter of the course was human sexuality.

The words *sex* and *gender* have often been used interchangeably to describe the differences in the behaviors of women and men. One example is the term *sex roles,* which is sometimes used to refer to culturally prescribed sets of behaviors for men and women. *Sex Roles* is even the name of a highly respected journal. Yet many psychologists believe that the term **gender roles** is more appropriate to describe the concept of *cultural beliefs applied to individuals on the basis of their socially assigned sex* (Wood & Eagly, 2010).

To avoid confusion, we will use the term **gender** to refer to *the meanings that societies and individuals give to female and male categories* (Wood & Eagly, 2010). We use the term **sex** to refer to *the classification of individuals as female or male based on their genetic makeup, anatomy, and reproductive functions.* Even this definition may be too simple: Recent research on intersex individuals indicates that there are more than two sexes (Russo & Tartaro, 2008). See Chapter 3 for further discussion of that issue.

WOMEN AND MEN: SIMILAR OR DIFFERENT?

Scholars who study sex and gender issues usually take one of two approaches. Either they emphasize the similarities between women and men or they focus on the differences between them.

Similarities Approach

Those who adhere to the similarities viewpoint seek to show that *men and women are basically alike in their intellectual and social behaviors. Any differences that do occur are small and inconsistent, and produced by socialization, not biology* (Blakemore et al., 2009; Eagly et al., 2004). This approach, also called the **beta bias**, has its origins in the work of early twentieth-century women psychologists. As we shall see later in the chapter, a number of these psychologists carried out research that challenged the prevailing belief that women are different from (and inferior to) men. Most feminist theory and research dealing with gender differences has retained this similarities approach (Bohan, 2002).

Differences Approach

The differences viewpoint, also known as the **alpha bias**, *emphasizes the differences between women and men.* Historically, these differences have been thought to arise from *essential qualities within* *the individual that are rooted in biology* (Charles & Bradley, 2009; England, 2010). This concept is known as **essentialism**.

The differences perspective has origins in both ancient Western and Eastern philosophies, which associate men with reason and civilization and women with emotion and nature (Hare-Mustin & Marecek, 1990). As we have seen, early psychologists often equated women's differences from men with inferiority and "otherness." Men set the standard whereas women were seen as deviations from that standard (Caplan & Caplan, 2009). For example, Sigmund Freud stated that because women do not have a penis, they suffer from penis envy. Using the same logic, one could argue just as persuasively that men experience uterus envy because they cannot bear children. (Karen Horney [1926/1974], a psychoanalyst who challenged many of Freud's views, made this very proposal.)

Contemporary feminists regard female–male differences as arising from a culture's expectations of how individuals should behave. In other words, behavioral differences between the genders are not inborn but are socially constructed (Kinser, 2010; Marecek et al., 2004). As we shall see at the end of this chapter, the social construction of gender is one of the three major themes of this book.

Some feminists have added still another twist to the differences approach. They embrace cultural feminism, a view that celebrates those positive qualities historically associated with women, such as a sense of human connection and concern for other people (Jordan et al., 2003; Kinser, 2010; Miller, 2008). The theories of Nancy Chodorow (1994) and Carol Gilligan (1982, 1993) illustrate the cultural feminist approach. According to Chodorow, early childhood experiences forever set females and males down different paths in their development of identity, personality, and emotional needs. Girls develop an early attachment to their mother, whom they perceive as similar to themselves. This leads girls to develop relational skills and a desire for close emotional connections. Boys, on the other hand, reject their emotional attachment to their mother, who is perceived as dissimilar. Boys instead identify with male figures who are often more distant. In the process, they become more invested in separation and independence and develop a more abstract and impersonal style (Blakemore et al., 2009). Gilligan (1982, 1994) also sees women's identity as based on connections and relationships to others. She believes that women reason and make moral judgments in a "different voice," a voice concerned with caring and responsibility. Men, on the other hand, are more concerned with abstract rights and justice. These different patterns of reasoning are equally valid and sophisticated, according to Gilligan. We shall discuss moral reasoning in females and males in greater detail in Chapter 5.

Regardless of one's approach to gender comparisons, the study of gender and the psychology of women is rooted in a feminist perspective. Therefore, let's now examine the meaning of feminism.

FEMINISM

A feminist is

someone who believes in equality in the workforce

a person who fights for women's rights

someone who protests about controversial issues, such as abortion or sexual harassment

a big, bra-burning, man-hating woman

(College students' view of feminism, from Houvouras & Carter, 2008, pp. 246–249)

Do any of these definitions reflect your own view of feminism? Although the term *feminism* is frequently used by the media, in opinion polls, and in casual conversation, people obviously differ in their conceptions of its meaning. There is even diversity among feminists. Although united in their belief that women are disadvantaged relative to men, feminists differ in their beliefs about the sources of this inequality and the ways to enhance women's status (Hemmings, 2011; Lorber, 2010). Let's examine five different types of feminism embraced by feminist scholars.

Liberal feminism is *the belief that women and men should have the same political, legal, economic, and educational rights and opportunities* (Kirk & Okazawa-Rey, 2010; Lorber, 2010). Liberal feminists advocate reform; their goals are to change attitudes and laws that are unfair to women and to equalize educational, employment, and political opportunities. For example, they seek the creation of an educational environment that encourages women's growth in all academic fields, removal of barriers to full participation and advancement in the workplace, and more political leadership positions for women. Liberal feminists stress the similarities between females and males and contend that gender differences are a function of unequal opportunities.

In contrast, **cultural feminism** reflects *the belief that women and men are different and that women's special qualities, such as nurturance, concern about others, and cooperativeness, should be valued* (Lorber, 2010). Cultural feminists are concerned about destructive outcomes related to masculine traits, such as aggressiveness and lack of emotional expressiveness, and want to empower women by elevating the value attached to their interpersonal orientation.

Another type of feminism, **socialist feminism**, reflects *the attitude that gender inequality is rooted in economic inequality* (Kirk & Okazawa-Rey, 2010; Lorber, 2010). Socialist feminists believe that various inequalities based on gender, ethnicity, and social class interact with one another and cannot be eliminated until the capitalistic structure of North American society is changed.

Radical feminism, on the other hand, is *the belief that gender inequality is based on male oppression of women* (Kirk & Okazawa-Rey, 2010; Lorber, 2010). Radical feminists contend that **patriarchy**, *male control over and dominance of women*, has existed throughout history and must be eliminated to achieve gender equality. In other words, different from socialist feminists, radical feminists see men, rather than capitalism, as the source of women's oppression. Consequently, they are concerned not only about inequality in societal institutions, such as the workplace, but also about power differential in the family and other types of intimate relationships.

Many women of color have argued that the feminist movement is concerned primarily about issues that confront White women (Hill Collins, 2008; Nix-Stevenson, 2011). Consequently, they often embrace **women of color feminism** (also known as womanism), which is *the belief that both* **racism**, *bias against people because of their ethnicity, and* **classism**, *bias based on social class, must be recognized as being as important as* **sexism**, *gender-based bias* (Lorber, 2010).

Clearly, there is no reason why a feminist perspective has to be limited to one viewpoint. Many individuals combine two or more into their personal definition of feminism. Now, perform the exercise in Get Involved 1.1 to more closely examine each of these types of feminism.

HISTORY OF WOMEN IN PSYCHOLOGY

The first women in psychology faced a number of obstacles, especially in establishing their credentials, because many universities in the late 1800s and early 1900s did not welcome women who sought advanced degrees (Johnson, 2009; Milar, 2000). Judith's experience described at the beginning of this chapter indicates that overt sexist policies toward women in psychology continued well into the twentieth century. Nevertheless, several women overcame the odds to become pioneers in the field (Kimmel & Crawford, 2001). Margaret Floy Washburn was the first woman to receive a Ph.D. in psychology in America in 1894. It took another 40 years before doctorates in psychology were awarded to Black women: Inez Beverly Prosser and Ruth Winifred Howard ("February Is Black History Month," 2004).

GET INVOLVED 1.1
How Do People View Feminism?

Answer the following questions and then ask several female and male acquaintances to do the same. Save your own answers but do not refer back to them after completing this chapter.

First, indicate which of the following categories best characterizes your identity as a feminist: I

1. consider myself a feminist and am currently involved in the Women's Movement
2. consider myself a feminist but am not involved in the Women's Movement
3. do not consider myself a feminist but agree with at least some of the objectives of feminism
4. do not consider myself a feminist and disagree with the objectives of feminism.

Second, on a scale from 1 (strongly disagree) to 6 (strongly agree), indicate the extent to which you disagree or agree with each of the following statements.

1. Women should be considered as seriously as men as candidates for the presidency of the United States.

2. Although women can be good leaders, men make better leaders.
3. A woman should have the same job opportunities as a man.
4. Men should respect women more than they currently do.
5. Many women in the workforce are taking jobs away from men who need the jobs more than women.
6. Doctors need to take women's health concerns more seriously.
7. Women have been treated unfairly on the basis of their gender throughout most of human history.
8. Women are already given equal opportunities with men in all important sectors of their lives.
9. Women in the United States are treated as second-class citizens.
10. Women can best overcome discrimination by doing the best they can at their jobs, not by wasting time with political activity.

WHAT DOES IT MEAN?

Before computing your scores for the 10 items, reverse the points for statements 2, 5, 8, and 10. That is, for a rating of 1 (strongly disagree), give 6 points, for a rating of 2, give 5 points, and so on. Then sum the points for all 10 items. Higher scores reflect greater agreement with feminist beliefs.

1. Are there differences in the feminist labels and/or feminist attitude scores between your female and male respondents?
2. For each respondent, including yourself, compare the feminist attitude score to the selected feminist category. Did you find that individuals who gave themselves a feminist label (i.e., placed themselves in category 1 or 2) generally agreed with the feminist statements and

obtained a score of 40 or higher? Similarly, did the individuals who did not label themselves as feminists (e.g., category 3 or 4) tend to disagree with the feminist statements and receive a score below 40? If there was no correspondence between the feminist identity label and the feminist beliefs, give possible reasons.
3. Do you think that individuals who vary in ethnicity and social class might hold different attitudes about feminism? If yes, explain.

Source: "Putting the feminism into feminism scales: Introduction of a liberal feminist attitude and ideology," *Sex Roles*, 34, pp. 359–390, © 1996.

Women and the American Psychological Association

One year after the founding of the American Psychological Association (APA), in 1893, 2 of the 14 new members admitted were women: Mary Whiton Calkins and Christine Ladd-Franklin (Hogan & Sexton, 1991). Calkins went on to become the first woman president of the APA

Twelve women have been elected president of the American Psychological Association. In chronological order, they are Mary Whiton Calkins, Margaret Floy Washburn, Anne Anastasi, Leona Tyler, Florence Denmark, Janet Spence, Bonnie Strickland, Dorothy Cantor, Norine Johnson, Diane Halpern, Sharon Stephens Brehm, and 2011 president, Melba Vasquez (shown here).

in 1905. Margaret Floy Washburn was elected the second woman president in 1921 (Scarborough, 2010). It would be 51 years before the APA had another female leader.

Since the early 1970s, the number of women in APA leadership roles has increased notably and 12 women have become president (Azar, 2011; Brehm, 2007). In 2005, women represented 53 percent of the APA members, 49 percent of the council of representatives, and 38 percent of the board of directors, although only 26 percent of APA fellows, the most prestigious membership category. More than one-third of the reviewers and nearly half of the associate editors of APA journals (but only 28 percent of the editors) are women (American Psychological Association, 2006).

Women's Contributions

Women have been relatively invisible in psychology; their contributions to the field have often been overlooked or ignored (Scarborough, 2005). Coverage of gender-related topics has also been limited. However, the situation has been improving. Florence Denmark (1994) examined undergraduate psychology textbooks from 1982 and 1993 for the inclusion of women's contributions and of gender-related topics. The books printed in the 1990s showed progress in both areas. Claire and her students (Etaugh et al., 1995) similarly found that coverage of gender-related topics in introductory psychology textbooks increased by nearly 40 percent between the early 1970s and the early 1990s.

Even when the works of women psychologists are cited, they may still be overlooked. There are two related reasons for this apparent invisibility of many women psychologists. First, the long-standing practice in psychology books and journal articles is to refer to authors by their last name and first initials only. (Ironically, even if this practice were to change, some women authors still might choose to use their initials in order to avoid possible gender-biased devaluation of their scholarly work [Walsh-Bowers, 1999].) Second, in the absence of gender-identifying information, people tend to assume that the important contributions included in psychology books and articles have been carried out by men. When Claire learned about the Ladd-Franklin theory of color vision in introductory psychology, she assumed that two men named Ladd and Franklin had developed the theory. Only later did she discover that it was the work of Christine Ladd-Franklin. Similarly, most people assume that it was *Harry* Harlow who established the importance of touch in the development of attachment. How many individuals know that his wife, psychologist Margaret Kuenne Harlow, was his research partner and a codeveloper of their groundbreaking theory? In order to make the contributions of women psychologists more visible in this book, we frequently use first names when identifying important researchers and theorists.

HISTORY OF THE PSYCHOLOGY OF WOMEN

Ignorance about women pervades academic disciplines in higher education, where the requirements for the degree seldom include thoughtful inquiry into the status of women as part of the human condition.

(Carolyn Sherif, cited in Denmark et al., 2000, p. 1)

How has the psychology of women developed as a field since Carolyn Sherif wrote this sentence about 30 years ago? Let us turn to a brief history of the feminist approach to the study of gender.

The Early Years

Rachel Hare-Mustin and Jeanne Marecek (1990) call the early years of psychology "womanless" psychology. Not only were there few women psychologists, but also women's experiences were not deemed important enough to study. Concepts in psychology were based on the male experience. For example, as we shall see in Chapter 3, Sigmund Freud formulated his views of the Oedipus complex and penis envy from a male perspective but applied them to both genders. The same is true of Erik Erikson's notion of the development of identity during adolescence, as we shall see in Chapter 6.

In addition, early psychologists viewed women as different from and inferior to men (Denmark et al., 2008). For example, to explain their premise that women are less intelligent than men and thus unfit for higher education, male psychologists claimed that women's brains were smaller than men's (Bem, 2008; Caplan & Caplan, 2009; Fine, 2010). This theory seemed to be discredited by the discovery that *relative* brain size—the weight of the brain relative to the weight of the body—is actually greater in women than in men. But stereotypes are not that easily erased. Scientists began comparing various segments of the brain in the two genders in an attempt to find the cause of women's purported inferior intelligence. No differences were found (Fine, 2010). Yet the search continued. In 1982, the prestigious journal *Science* published a study claiming that the corpus callosum (the connection between the two hemispheres of the brain) is larger in women than in men. The researchers stated that this difference might account for women's supposedly inferior spatial skills. (See Chapter 5 for a detailed discussion of this topic.) The study had many flaws, including the fact that only nine males' brains and five females' brains had been examined. Ruth Bleier, a neuroanatomist, and her colleagues did a study that corrected the flaws and used a much larger sample. They found no gender differences. Yet *Science* refused to publish their findings on the grounds that they were too "political" (Caplan & Caplan, 2009).

The first generation of women psychologists carried out research that challenged assumptions of female inferiority (Rutherford et al., 2010). Helen Thompson Woolley found little difference in the intellectual abilities of women and men. Leta Stetter Hollingworth tackled the prevailing notion that women's menstrual cycles were debilitating, rendering women unfit to hold positions of responsibility. She demonstrated that intellectual and sensory-motor skills did not systematically vary across the menstrual cycle (Denmark et al., 2008). Many of these ideas lay dormant, however, because few women were able to obtain academic positions where they could study and teach about these topics (Unger, 2010).

The Recent Years

A number of events in the 1960s signaled the beginning of the second wave of the feminist movement in the United States, including the publication of Betty Friedan's (1963) book *The Feminine Mystique,* the passage of the Equal Pay Act (see Chapters 10 and 15), and the formation of the

National Organization for Women (NOW). In each case, the spotlight turned on glaring economic, social, and political inequities between women and men.

During these years, the psychology of women emerged as a separate field of study. In 1969, the Association for Women in Psychology was founded, followed in 1973 by the APA Division (now Society) of the Psychology of Women. Several textbooks on the psychology of women were written, journals such as *Psychology of Women Quarterly* and *Sex Roles* were established, and college courses on the topic began to appear. Feminist theorists and researchers demonstrated the sexist bias of much psychology theory, research, and practice. They set about expanding knowledge about women and correcting erroneous misinformation from the past (Basow, 2010a; Rutherford & Yoder, 2011). Today, women make up nearly half of the psychologists in the workforce. This percentage is very likely to increase because almost three out of four doctoral degrees in psychology are now awarded to women ("The Nation," 2010).

STUDYING THE PSYCHOLOGY OF WOMEN

With a basic understanding of the history of the psychology of women, we now turn to an examination of issues involved in performing psychological research. As you probably learned in introductory psychology, our understanding of human behavior stems from research conducted by psychologists and other scientists who use the scientific method to answer research questions. Although you might have learned that this method is value free, that it is not shaped by researchers' personal values, feminist scholars (Sechzer & Rabinowitz, 2008) argue that values can influence every step of the research process. Let's turn now to a brief discussion of these steps to see how researchers' own ideas about human behavior can influence our understanding of the psychology of women.

Bias in Psychological Research

SELECTING THE RESEARCH TOPIC.   The first step in any scientific investigation is selecting the topic to examine. Just as your personal preferences lead you to choose one term paper topic over another, scientists' personal interests influence the topics they decide to investigate. Throughout the history of psychology, most psychologists have been males; thus, for many years, topics related to girls and women were rarely investigated (Sechzer & Rabinowitz, 2008). Since 1970, however, the increasing number of female psychologists and the growth of the psychology of women as a discipline have resulted in an explosion of research devoted to the psychology of woman and/or gender (Lips, 2010). For example, an estimated 50–70 new scientific publications on sex differences appear each week (Ellis et al., 2008).

Another influence on topic selection is the researcher's assumptions about gender characteristics. For example, a psychologist who believes leadership is primarily a male trait is not likely to investigate the leadership styles of women. To give another example, aggressive behavior is typically associated with males. Consequently, relatively little is known about the relationship between aggressive behavior in girls and their adjustment in adulthood (Fontaine et al., 2008). Bias in topic selection is even more evident when one focuses on women of color. Not only are there relatively few psychologists of color but researchers, influenced by the biased assumption that people of color are deviant, deficient, and helpless, have examined ethnic minority women in relation to only a narrow range of topics, such as poverty and teen pregnancy (Tucker & Herman, 2002; Reid, 1999). The tendency to treat women of color as helpless deviates reinforces a negative image of ethnic minority females and denies their full personhood as women with a wide breadth of concerns and experiences.

FORMULATING THE HYPOTHESIS.   Once the topic is selected, the researcher generally formulates a hypothesis (a prediction) based on a particular theoretical perspective. Consequently, the researcher's orientation toward one theory or another has a major influence on the direction of the research. To better understand this effect, consider the link between two theories of rape and related research hypotheses. One theory proposes that rape has evolved through natural selection, which leads to the hypothesis that rape is present in nonhuman animals (Thornhill & Palmer, 2000). A very different theory contends that rape stems from a power imbalance between women and men. One hypothesis stemming from this theory is that regions of the country with more gender inequality of power should have higher rates of rape than regions with less power imbalance (Ullman & Najdowski, 2011). As we see in the next section, these different hypotheses lead to very different kinds of research on rape.

Theoretical perspectives about ethnicity can similarly influence the hypotheses and direction of research. As Pamela Trotman Reid and Elizabeth Kelly (1994) noted, many studies on women of color are designed to "illuminate deficits and deviance from White norms" (p. 483). Rather than examining strengths of women of color, this deviance perspective leads to research that focuses on ethnic minority women as powerless victims.

DESIGNING THE STUDY.   Because the methods used to gather data stem from the underlying predictions, hypotheses based on disparate theories lead to different procedures. This, in turn, affects the type of knowledge researchers gain about the topic under investigation. Returning to our rape example, the hypothesis that rape is not unique to humans has led to investigations of forced copulation in nonhuman species (McKibben et al., 2008), which would not be appropriate to the investigation of a power hypothesis. The prediction that rape is linked to the degree of gender inequality in society has led to studies of the relationship between a city's rape rate and its occupational and educational gender inequality (Whaley, 2001). Each of these procedures provides very different kinds of information about rape that can lay the foundation for different attitudes about this form of violence (see Chapter 14). Examining specific aspects of research design will show us the ways bias can also affect the choice of procedures.

SELECTING RESEARCH PARTICIPANTS.   One of the consistent problems in psychological research has been the use of samples that do not adequately represent the general population. A **sample** refers to *the individuals who are investigated in order to reach conclusions about the entire group of interest to the researcher* (i.e., the **population**). For example, a researcher might be interested in understanding the emotional experiences of first-time mothers in the first months following childbirth. It would be impossible, however, to assess the experiences of all new mothers (*population*). Instead, the investigator might seek 100 volunteers from among mothers who gave birth in any one of three hospitals in a specific geographical area (*sample*).

Unfortunately, research participants are not always representative of the larger population. Throughout most of the history of psychology, psychologists have focused primarily on young, White, middle-class, heterosexual, able-bodied males (Russo & Landrine, 2010; Unger, 2010). This procedure can lead to unfortunate and incorrect generalizations about excluded groups. It would be inappropriate, for example, to draw conclusions about women's leadership styles by examining male managers. Furthermore, focusing on selected groups can lead to the disregard of excluded groups.

A related issue is whether and how researchers specify the gender composition of their samples. One problem is that a sizable minority of authors do not report this information. For example, between 30 percent and 40 percent of studies published in 1990 in a large variety of major psychology journals failed to mention the gender makeup of their participants (Ader & Johnson, 1994;

Zalk, 1991). Therefore, the reader does not know whether the findings are applicable to both genders. Interestingly, the failure to report gender in the title of the article or to provide a rationale for sampling only one gender was more common in studies with male-only participants than in studies with female-only participants. Furthermore, discussions based on male participants were more likely to be written in general terms, whereas those based on only female participants were likely to be restricted to conclusions about females. These practices suggest that males are considered normative, and results obtained from them generally applicable, whereas females are somehow "different." That is, it appears that males are considered the standard against which all behavior is measured.

Although there has been improvement in the gender balance of participants in psychological research, samples have been limited in other ways. One problem is the relative invisibility of people of color (Huang & Coker, 2010; Hurtado, 2010). Even psychologists critical of the male bias in traditional psychology have erred by using primarily samples of Whites (Hall, 2003). For example, between 1989 and 1991, only about 10 percent of the articles published in journals that focus on women and gender roles examined the ethnicity of the participants (Reid & Kelly, 1994). A positive development is that these journals now require a description of the ethnicity of the sample even if it is restricted to White participants. Note, however, that specifying the ethnic composition of the sample does not mean that the researcher actually examined the relationship between the participant's ethnicity and the behavior under investigation. On a positive note, the growing recognition of the need to integrate findings related to ethnic, class, and cultural differences into mainstream theory, practice, and research has led in the past 25 years to an explosion of research on and by ethnic women psychologists, including Jean Lau Chin, Fanny Cheung, Lillian Comas-Diaz, Oliva Espín, Cynthia de las Fuentes, Beverly Greene, Aída Hurtado, Gwendolyn Puryear Keita, Teresa LaFromboise, Carolyn Payton, Pamela Trotman Reid, Janis Sanchez-Hucles, and Melba Vasquez (pictured earlier) (Hurtado, 2010; "Revisiting Our Roots," 2010).

Samples have been restricted, additionally, in their socioeconomic status: Most participants have been middle class, and poor women, until recently, have been nearly invisible (Henderson & Tickamyer, 2009; Lott, 2010; Reid, 2011). As a result, problems that have a much greater impact on poor women than on middle-class women are rarely studied. For example, very little is known about the sexual harassment of low-income women by their landlords, even though this is unfortunately a common occurrence (Bullock et al., 2010; Perry-Jenkins & Claxton, 2009). In addition, most studies of employed women have focused on those in professional jobs. Moreover, when researchers do study poor and working-class individuals, they tend to focus on people of color, perpetuating a biased assumption about ethnicity and social class as well as limiting our understanding of both poor White women and middle-class women of color (Henderson & Tickamyer, 2009; Reid 1999).

Pick up any psychology journal and you will see that many of the middle-class individuals who serve as research participants are college students. Because this group is restricted in age, education, and life experiences compared to the general population, numerous findings based on these samples cannot be generalized to other types of people.

Other groups, such as lesbian, gay, bisexual, and transgender individuals and people with disabilities, are underrepresented in psychological research, and less research has focused on older women than on younger women or girls (Garnets, 2008; Gergen, 2008; Olkin, 2008; Quinlan et al., 2008). What can explain researchers' narrow focus on White, middle-class, heterosexual, able-bodied, young individuals? One possibility is that psychologists are more interested in understanding the experiences of people like themselves, and the majority of investigators fit the characteristics of the typical participants. Another possibility is that psychologists might use these individuals in their research because it is easier to recruit them. These are the people most likely to be located within the situational contexts—such as academic or professional environments—inhabited by

GET INVOLVED 1.2
Are Samples in Psychological Research Biased?

In this exercise you are to compare descriptions of samples published in journals oriented toward women or gender to mainstream psychological journals. At your campus library, select one recent issue of *Psychology of Women Quarterly* or *Sex Roles*. Also select a recent issue of one of the following: *Journal of Personality and Social Psychology, Developmental Psychology,* or *Journal of Consulting and Clinical Psychology*. For each article in these issues, read the brief section that describes the participants. This is found in the Method section of the article and is usually labeled Participants, Sample, or Subjects. As you read these sections, note the following information:

1. Is the gender of the participants specified? If yes, does the sample include females only, males only, or both?
2. Is the ethnicity of the participants specified? If yes, does the sample include predominantly or exclusively Whites, predominantly or exclusively individuals of another single ethnic group, or a balanced mixture of individuals from two or more ethnic groups?
3. Is the social class of the participants specified? If yes, is the sample predominantly or exclusively middle class, predominantly or exclusively working class or poor, or a mixture of social classes?
4. Are any other characteristics of the participants (e.g., sexual orientation, presence of a disability) given? If yes, specify.

After recording the information for each article from one journal, add up the number of articles that specified the gender of the sample, the number that specified ethnicity, and so on. Similarly, sum the articles that included both genders, those that included more than one ethnic group, and so forth. Follow the same procedure for the other journal.

WHAT DOES IT MEAN?

1. Which participant characteristic was described most frequently? Explain why.
2. Which participant characteristic was represented in the most balanced way? Explain why.
3. Which participant characteristic was specified least often? Explain why.
4. Did the two journals differ in their descriptions of their samples? If yes, explain.
5. What are the implications of your findings?

Source: Morgan (1996).

researchers (Quinlan et al., 2008). Also, due to cross-group mistrust and/or misunderstanding, it is sometimes more difficult for nonminority investigators to recruit minority individuals (Huang & Coker, 2010). Whatever the causes, the exclusion of certain groups of people from psychological examination not only devalues their experiences but can also lead to inaccurate conclusions about them based on faulty generalizations. To get firsthand knowledge about the extent of biased samples in recent psychological research, complete the exercise in Get Involved 1.2.

SELECTING THE MEASURES. Another step in the design of a study is the selection of procedures to measure the behaviors or characteristics under investigation. These procedures can determine the results that researchers find. For example, in their review of aggression in girls and boys, Jamie Ostrov and Stephanie Godleski (2010) note that different findings are obtained depending on how aggressive behavior is measured. Boys are more likely than girls to show physical aggression (e.g., pushing, hitting) whereas girls are more apt to show relational aggression (e.g., spreading malicious gossip). As you can see, relying on only one of these measures would have led to misleading conclusions.

ANALYZING AND INTERPRETING THE FINDINGS.   Once the data have been collected, the researcher performs statistical analyses to discover whether the findings support the hypotheses. Although there are numerous types of statistical tests, they all provide information about the **statistical significance** of the results, which means that *the findings are not due to chance alone.* For example, in a study of college students' belief in rape myths (Girard & Senn, 2008), respondents rated the degree to which they agreed with 20 false statements often used to justify rape, such as "many women secretly desire to be raped." The rating scale for each item ranged from 1 (not agree) to 7 (strongly agree). Females had an average rating of 32.6 and males had a rating of 42.0. These numbers have no meaning in themselves. However, a statistical analysis applied to these data indicated that the difference of 9.4 between the male and female averages was not due to chance alone; males, more than females, believed in rape myths.

Once statistical tests have been applied to the data, the researcher must interpret the findings. Statistical analyses inform us only about the likelihood that the data could have been produced by chance alone. Now, the researchers must discuss explanations and implications of the findings. One type of bias occurring at this stage is interpreting the findings in a way that suggests a female weakness or inferiority. For example, studies have shown that females use more tentative speech than males do (see Chapter 5). They are more likely than men to say, "I *sort of* think she would be a good governor" or "She *seems* to be a strong candidate." Some researchers (e.g., Lakoff, 1990) have suggested this is an indication of females' lack of confidence—an interpretation pointing to a female deficit. Another equally plausible and more positive interpretation is that females use more tentative speech as a means of encouraging other people to express their opinions (DeFrancisco & Palczewski, 2007). Susan Fiske, past president of the Association for Psychological Sciences, offers another example of how a trait can be labeled to suggest female inferiority. She cites the "field independence–field dependence" continuum. Men have been described as "field independent" (not being influenced by a surrounding context), considered a favorable attribute, whereas "field *depen*dence" was a deficit that women had (Fiske, 2010b). What about being labeled field *sensitive,* clearly a more positive term, she asks?

A second problem related to the interpretation of findings is generalizing results based on one group to other groups. As discussed earlier in this chapter, psychologists frequently examine narrowly defined samples, such as White, male, middle-class college students, and sometimes they generalize their findings to other people, including females, people of color, and working-class individuals. Linda Gannon and her associates (1992) examined evidence of generalization from one gender to the other found in several major psychology journals published from 1970 to 1990. Although there was improvement since the 1970s, when inappropriate gender generalizations occurred in 19 percent to 76 percent of the articles, these researchers found that even in 1990, percentages ranged from 13 percent to 41 percent.

A third bias in the interpretation of data has been the assumption that the presence of gender differences implies biological causes (Caplan & Caplan, 2009; Fine, 2010). For example, some researchers have assumed that the preponderance of men in the sciences is due to their higher levels of fetal testosterone, despite a lack of consistent supporting data (Fine, 2010; Valla & Ceci, 2011).

COMMUNICATING THE FINDINGS.

Publishing.   The primary way that psychologists communicate their research findings to others is by publishing their studies, usually in psychological journals. Unfortunately, editors and reviewers who make decisions about which studies are worthy of publication tend to favor those that report statistical significance over those that do not. This publication bias can affect the body of our knowledge about gender. Studies that show a statistically significant gender difference are more likely to be published than those that do not and can lead to exaggerated conclusions about the differences between females and males (Caplan & Caplan, 2009).

Another type of publication bias exists as well. Victoria Brescoll and Marianne LaFrance (2004) found that politically conservative newspapers were more likely than liberal newspapers to use biological explanations for gender differences. Moreover, readers tended to believe whatever bias was represented in these news stories. Let the reader beware!

Gender-Biased Language.   The language that researchers use in their research papers is another possible source of gender bias in the communication of findings. Gender-biased language, such as the use of the male pronoun to refer to both genders, can lead to serious misinterpretation. As is discussed in Chapter 2, male pronouns tend to be interpreted as males only, not as males and females (DeFrancisco & Palczewski, 2007). Fortunately, although this practice was prevalent in the 1970s and 1980s, the *Publication Manual of the American Psychological Association* (American Psychological Association, 2010) now specifies that gender-biased language must be avoided. Research is now more likely to be reported using nonsexist language (Sechzer & Rabinowitz, 2008).

Another, more subtle type of biased language is the use of nonparallel terms when writing about comparable female and male behaviors, thus implying an essential difference between the genders. For example, much of the research on gender and employment refers to women who work outside the home as "employed mothers" but refers to men who work outside the home as simply "employed" (Gilbert, 1994). This distinction carries the implicit assumption that the primary role for women is motherhood whereas the primary role for men is the provider.

Conclusion.   Although it is unlikely that most researchers attempt to influence the research process in order to support their preconceived ideas about a topic, the biases they bring to the research endeavor can affect their choice of topic, hypotheses, research design, interpretation of findings, and communication about the study. Given that researchers have very human personal interests, values, and theoretical perspectives, they do not fit the image of the objective scientist (Caplan & Caplan, 2009).

Despite these inherent biases, we do not want to give the impression that psychological research is unduly value laden or that it provides no useful information about the psychology of women. Most researchers make a concerted attempt to be as unbiased as possible, and research from psychology and other social scientific disciplines has provided a rich body of knowledge about females' experiences. However, one must read these studies critically, with an understanding of their possible limitations—especially their failure to focus on the diversity of girls and women. For a look at doing gender research around the world, see Explore Other Cultures 1.1.

Feminist Research Methods

Traditional psychological research emphasizes objectivity, control, and quantitative measures as a means of understanding human behavior, and some feminist psychologists advocate adherence to this general methodology. Others, however, contend that more accurate representations of women's lives are achieved with qualitative procedures, such as women's accounts of their experiences (Crabtree et al., 2009; Gergen, 2010; Hesse-Biber et al., 2010; Lykes et al., 2010; Unger, 2011). For example, a qualitative investigation of women's friendships might ask participants to describe, in their own words, the most important friendships they have had. In contrast, an objective measure might ask them to complete a questionnaire written by the researcher in which participants indicate how often they have experienced a variety of feelings and interactions in their most important

---

EXPLORE OTHER CULTURES 1.1
Doing Cross-Cultural Research on Gender

Cross-cultural research has made important contributions to our understanding of gender development (Best & Thomas, 2004). Nevertheless, there are methodological pitfalls that need to be avoided in order to draw meaningful conclusions from such research. Judith Gibbons (2000) gives an example of how similar findings may have different meanings depending upon the culture being studied. She and her colleagues studied adolescents' drawings of the ideal woman. In a variety of cultures, many adolescents drew the ideal woman as working in an office. However, when the drawings were then presented to peers in the same culture for interpretation, adolescents gave responses that were both similar across cultures, but also culturally specific. For instance, in all countries studied, women working in offices were

described as hardworking. However, Guatemalan adolescents also viewed them as working for the betterment of their families, Filipino teenagers described them as adventurous and sexy, and U.S. teens saw them as bored with the routine of office work.

Another formidable methodological challenge in cross-cultural research is the issue of sampling. In studying gender issues, samples are often drawn from a certain setting, such as colleges and universities, as a way to ensure equivalent samples. But college or university students do not reflect the population similarly in different countries because the proportion of the population attending university differs widely internationally.

Sources: Best and Thomas (2004); Gibbons (2000).

---

friendships. Whereas the qualitative approach attempts to capture each participant's unique perspective, the quantitative approach compares participants' responses to a standard situation. For a more detailed examination of principles of feminist research, look at Learn About the Research 1.1.

Drawing Conclusions From Multiple Studies

Researchers use one of two procedures to draw conclusions about gender differences on the basis of large numbers of published studies. This section examines these two techniques.

NARRATIVE APPROACH. The traditional way of examining psychological gender differences has been to sift through dozens or even hundreds of studies on a particular topic and to form an impression of the general trends in their results. The first major attempt to synthesize the research on gender differences in this narrative fashion was carried out by Eleanor Maccoby and Carol Nagy Jacklin in 1974. In this massive undertaking, they tallied the results of over 1,600 published and unpublished studies appearing in the 10 years prior to 1974. Gender differences were declared to exist when a large number of studies on a given topic found differences in the same direction. Although the contribution of this pioneering work is enormous, a major drawback is its use of a simple "voting" or "box-score" method, which gave each study the same weight regardless of sample size or magnitude of the reported difference (Eagly et al., 1995). In addition, the possibility of subtle biases is always present in any narrative review.

META-ANALYSIS. A more sophisticated and objective technique of summarizing data has been developed in recent years. **Meta-analysis** is *a statistical method of integrating the results of several studies on the same topic*. It provides a measure of the magnitude, or size, of a given gender difference rather than simply counting the number of studies finding a difference (Cumming, 2011).

LEARN ABOUT THE RESEARCH 1.1
Principles of Feminist Research

Although feminists have a variety of opinions about the most effective methods for studying girls and women, they agree that such research should increase our understanding of females and help change the world for them (Lykes et al., 2010; Sechzer & Rabinowitz, 2008). Thus, feminists, like all researchers, bring a set of values to the research process, values that can direct the nature and interpretation of the research. Claire and her colleague Judith Worell (Worell & Etaugh, 1994) have articulated a set of principles that are based on the values of feminist research. These are summarized as follows:

1. Challenging the traditional scientific method.
   a. Correcting bias in the research process.
   b. Expanding samples beyond White, middle-class participants.
   c. Acknowledging the legitimacy of both quantitative and qualitative methods.
2. Focusing on the experiences of women.
   a. Examining diverse categories of women.
   b. Investigating topics relevant to women's lives.

   c. Attending to women's strengths as well as their concerns.
3. Considering gender imbalances in power.
   a. Recognizing that women's subordinate status is a sign of power imbalance, not deficiency.
   b. Attempting to empower women.
4. Recognizing gender as an important category for investigation.
   a. Understanding that a person's gender can influence expectations about and responses to that person.
5. Recognizing the importance of language.
   a. Changing language to be inclusive of women.
   b. Understanding that language can both influence thought and be influenced by thought.
6. Promoting social change.
   a. Creating a science that benefits women.
   b. Guiding action that will lead to justice for women.

WHAT DOES IT MEAN?

1. Assume you are a feminist researcher interested in examining how women handle employment and family obligations. Using the feminist principles outlined earlier, describe the characteristics of the sample you might wish to study and the research methods you would use in collecting your data.
2. A hypothetical study of the educational expectations of White, Mexican American, and Vietnamese American eighth-grade girls found that the White girls expect to complete more years of schooling than the other groups. The researcher concluded that Latina and Asian American girls have lower educational expectations than White girls. Critique this conclusion, using feminist research principles.

Source: Based on Worell and Etaugh (1994).

Gender researchers using meta-analysis first locate all studies on the topic of interest. Then they do a statistical analysis of each study that measures the size of the difference between the average of the men's scores and the average of the women's scores. This difference is divided by the standard deviation of the two sets of scores. The standard deviation measures the variability or range of the scores. For example, scores ranging from 1 to 100 have high variability, whereas scores ranging from 50 to 53 show low variability. Dividing the difference between men's and women's scores by the standard deviation produces a d statistic. Finally, the researchers calculate the average of the d statistics from all the studies they located. The resulting d is called the **effect size**. *It indicates not only whether females or males score higher but also how large the difference is.* This is one of the major advantages of meta-analysis over the traditional narrative method of summarizing research (Cumming, 2011).

The value of d is large when the difference between means is large and the variability within each group is small. It is small when the difference between means is small and the variability within each group is large (Cumming, 2011). Generally a d of 0.20 is considered small, 0.50 is moderate, and 0.80 is large. However, these guidelines still do not settle the debate of whether a particular difference is *meaningful* or important. In cancer research, for example, even a very small effect size can have powerful consequences. Suppose a treatment was discovered that completely cured a small number of women with a highly lethal form of cancer. Although the effect size might be quite small, this discovery would be hailed as a major medical breakthrough. As we discuss later in the book, the effect sizes for some psychological gender differences are greater than those found in most psychological research whereas others are close to zero.

Now that we have explored the historical and methodological framework for understanding the psychology of women, we focus on the major themes that characterize this book.

THEMES IN THE TEXT

Science is not value free. As we have seen, the evolving belief about the importance of women has had a powerful impact on topics and methods of psychological research. Similarly, this text is not value neutral. It is firmly rooted in a feminist belief system, which contends (1) that the diversity of women's identities and experiences should be recognized and celebrated; (2) that men hold more power than women; and (3) that gender is shaped by social, cultural, and societal influences. These beliefs are shared by many feminist psychologists and are reflected throughout this book.

Theme 1: Intersectionality: The Diversity of Women's Identities and Experiences

As we saw in the discussion of research biases, minimal attention given to females throughout most of the history of psychology not only devalues women's experiences but also often leads to incorrectly generalizing men's experiences to include women. Similarly, a psychology of women restricted to White, middle-class, heterosexual, able-bodied, young females in North America minimizes the importance of women of color; poor and working-class women; lesbian, bisexual, and transgender women; women with disabilities; older women; and women in other cultures, and it can lead to the false conclusion that the experiences of the majority are applicable to all (Kimmel, 2011).

Consequently, this text examines the heterogeneity of females' experiences. We do so within a lens of **intersectionality**, which means that *people exist in a framework of multiple identities that interact with each other to determine an individual's experiences and that cannot be understood separately from each other because they are integral parts of a whole* (Hurtado, 2010; Kinser, 2010; Meem et al., 2010). These identities include one's gender, ethnicity, class, sexual orientation, age, ableness, marital status, and nationality (Cole, 2009; Dill & Zambrana, 2009b; Ferree, 2010; Spade & Valentine, 2011). Intersectionality implies that to understand a woman's identity, you do not simply *add* one feature to another, as in woman + Black + heterosexual + middle-aged, but rather multiply them (Enns & Byars-Winston, 2010). As an example, compare two women born in New York City some years ago. One is Claire Etaugh, who is a White, college-educated, heterosexual, able-bodied psychology professor. The other is Audre Lorde, who was a Black, college-educated, lesbian, less able-bodied, renowned feminist writer and poet. To label both of us as educated, female New Yorkers is true, but ignores our very different life experiences shaped by the several intersecting identities that we did not share. In this text, the authors discuss both similarities and differences in the attitudes, emotions, relationships, goals, and behaviors of girls and women who have a diversity of backgrounds. For example, we explore interpersonal relationships of heterosexual and lesbian women (Chapter 8); physical and mental health concerns of White women and women of color (Chapters 12 and 13); problems on campus and in the workplace faced by women with disabilities (Chapters 9 and 10); and health, employment, and interpersonal issues of older women (Chapters 8, 10, and 12). However, because most of the research to date on the psychology of women has been based on restricted samples, it is important to note that our presentation includes a disproportionate amount of information about young, middle-class, heterosexual, able-bodied, White women and girls living in the United States.

When referring to cultural variations among people, we use the term *ethnicity* rather than *race*. **Race** is *a biological concept that refers to physical characteristics of people* (Lott, 2010). However, experts disagree about what constitutes a single race, and there is considerable genetic variation among people designated as a single race. **Ethnicity**, on the other hand, refers to *variations in cultural background, nationality, history, religion, and/or language* (Lott, 2010), a term more closely associated with the variations in attitudes, behaviors, and roles that we discuss in this book.

Unfortunately, there are no universally acceptable labels that identify a person's ethnicity. Some terms are based on geographical origin as in *African American* and *Euro-American* whereas others are based on color, such as *Black* and *White*. Furthermore, each major ethnic category encompasses a diversity of ethnic subtypes. For example, Americans with Asian ancestry, regardless of their specific origin (e.g., China, Japan, Korea, Vietnam), are generally grouped into a single category of Asian Americans. Similarly, Whites from countries as diverse as Ireland, Germany, and Russia are combined into one ethnic group. Along the same lines, the label *Latina/o* refers to individuals from Mexico, Cuba, and Puerto Rico, and others of Hispanic origin (Burton et al., 2010; Zinn & Wells, 2008). With the hope that our usage does not inadvertently offend anyone, ethnic group labels used in this book are Asian American, Black, Latina/o, Native American, and White, recognizing that each of these broad ethnic categories actually encompasses a diversity of cultures.

Theme 2: Gender Differences in Power

In no known societies do women dominate men. . . . Men, on average, enjoy more power than women, on average, and this appears to have been true throughout human history.

(Pratto & Walker, 2004, p. 242)

Two interlocking ideas characterize our power theme. One is that the experiences of women in virtually all cultures are shaped by both **organizational power**, *the ability to use valuable resources to dominate and control others,* and **interpersonal power**, *the ability to influence one's partner within a specific relationship.* The greater organizational power of males compared to that of females is evident in our discussion of numerous topics, including gender differences in salary (Chapter 10), the underrepresentation of women in high-status occupations (Chapter 10), and sexual harassment (Chapter 14). Additionally, gender differences in interpersonal power are clearly reflected in our discussions of interpersonal violence (Chapter 14), rape (Chapter 14), and the allocation of household responsibilities (Chapter 11).

Both of these power differentials reflect an undesirable imbalance in a form of power, called **power-over**, *a person's or group's control of another person or group.* This type of power is

> ## WHAT YOU CAN DO 1.1
> ### Help Empower Girls and Women
>
> One theme of this book is that men hold more power than women. Many national organizations that work to empower girls and women have local chapters, such as the NOW, the Girl Scouts, the YWCA (Young Women's Christian Association), and the American Association of University Women. Volunteer for one of these organizations in your community.

distinguished from **power-to**, *the empowerment of self and others to accomplish tasks* (Chrisler, 2008c). Whereas the former is a negative type of power that restricts opportunities and choices of members of the less powerful group, the latter allows for personal growth for all. Thus, feminist psychologists want to eliminate the former and increase the latter (Denmark & Klara, 2007).

A second component of our theme of power differences is that many women experience more than one type of power imbalance. In addition to a gender difference in power, women can experience power inequities as a function of their ethnicity, social class, sexual preference, age, and physical ability (Burn, 2011; Lott, 2010). Furthermore, the effects of these imbalances are cumulative. For example, women of color experience greater discrimination in the workplace than do White women (Chapter 10). As bell hooks (1990) stated, "By calling attention to interlocking systems of domination—sex, race, and class—Black women and many other groups of women acknowledge the diversity and complexity of female experience, of our relationship to power and domination" (p. 187).

One consequence of gender differences in power is that women and women's issues receive less emphasis and visibility than men and men's issues. In this chapter, for example, we saw that women's contributions to psychology have often been overlooked. We examine other instances of this problem in our discussion of specific topics, such as the underrepresentation of females in the media (Chapter 2) and the exclusion of women from major studies of medical and health issues (Chapter 12). See What You Can Do 1.1 for ways you can help empower girls and women.

Theme 3: Social Construction of Gender

As indicated at the beginning of this chapter, social scientists differentiate between sex, the biological aspects of femaleness and maleness, and gender, the nonbiological components. Our third theme is the **social construction of gender**, which points out that *the traits, behaviors, and roles that people associate with females and males are not inherent in one's sex; they are shaped by numerous interpersonal, cultural, and societal forces.* Even if some aspects of being a female or a male are biologically based, we live in a society that emphasizes gender, and our development as women and men—as well as our conceptions of what it means to be a female or a male—is significantly influenced by cultural and societal values (Charlebois, 2011; Kimmel, 2011; Lott, 2010; Wood & Eagly, 2010). We do not exist in a sterile laboratory; instead, we are continually affected by an interlocking set of expectations, pressures, and rewards that guide our development as women and men.

Furthermore, our experience and conceptions of femaleness and maleness cannot be viewed as separate from our ethnicity and social class (Charlebois, 2011) or from our sexual orientation and physical ability/disability (Lorber, 2010). Each of these identities is also socially constructed. Lesbians, for example, are affected not only by societal expectations about what women are like, but also by people's beliefs about and attitudes toward lesbianism. To put it another way, studying women without looking at the intersections of their socially constructed multiple identities results in a limited and incomplete understanding of women's lives (Dill & Zambrana, 2009a; White, 2011).

The social construction of gender is discussed in relation to several topics in the text. For example, we examine theories that explain how children develop their ideas about gender (Chapter 3); explore the processes of instilling a child with expectations about what it means to be a girl or boy (Chapter 4); and look at social influences on gender in our discussion of gender differences in aggression (Chapter 5), friendship (Chapter 8), and the division of household labor (Chapter 11).

Summary

DEFINITIONS: SEX AND GENDER

- *Sex* refers to the classification of females and males based on biological factors. *Gender* refers to social expectations of roles and behaviors for females and males.

WOMEN AND MEN: SIMILAR OR DIFFERENT?

- The similarities approach (beta bias) argues that women and men are basically alike in their behaviors and that any differences are a product of socialization.
- The differences approach (alpha bias) emphasizes that women and men are different and that these differences are biologically based.

FEMINISM

- Liberal, cultural, socialist, radical, and women of color feminism all posit that women are disadvantaged relative to men. They differ in their assumptions about the sources of this inequality.

HISTORY OF WOMEN IN PSYCHOLOGY

- For many years, women attained few leadership positions and awards in the APA, but gains have been made in recent years.
- Women's contributions to psychology have often been overlooked or ignored, but that situation is improving.

HISTORY OF THE PSYCHOLOGY OF WOMEN

- In the early years of psychology, women were viewed as inferior to men and their experiences were rarely studied.
- Early women psychologists carried out research that challenged the assumptions of female inferiority.
- In the 1970s, the psychology of women emerged as a separate field of study.

STUDYING THE PSYCHOLOGY OF WOMEN

- Psychological research is not value free. Throughout most of its history, psychology did not pay much attention to the experiences of girls and women in either the topics investigated or the participants studied.
- Since 1970, there has been an increase in research focus on females; however, most of this research has been carried out on White, middle-class, heterosexual, able-bodied women.
- Generalizing results based on one type of participant to other types of people can lead to inaccurate conclusions.
- The researcher's theoretical perspective influences the hypothesis examined in the research, which in turn affects the type of information learned from the research.
- The measures used to study the research topic can influence the findings of the research.
- Due to publication bias, published studies are more likely to present gender differences than gender similarities.
- Very few studies use blatantly biased gender language, but a more subtle bias can be detected in the use of nonparallel terms for comparable female and male behaviors.
- Some feminists advocate the use of traditional objective, quantitative research methods, while others favor qualitative procedures.

- There are several principles that characterize most feminist research.
- The narrative approach and meta-analysis are two methods of integrating results of several studies on the same topic.
- Meta-analysis is a statistical method that provides a measure of the magnitude of a given difference, known as the effect size.

THEMES IN THE TEXT

- Three themes are prominent in this text.
- First, psychology must examine the intersecting identities and experiences of diverse groups of women.

- Second, the greater organizational and interpersonal power of men compared to women negatively shapes and limits women's experiences. Women of color, poor and working-class women, sexual minority women, and women with disabilities experience additional power inequities, with cumulative effects.
- Third, gender is socially constructed; it is shaped by social, cultural, and societal values.

Key Terms

gender roles *2*	patriarchy *4*	intersectionality *16*
gender *2*	women of color feminism *4*	race *17*
sex *2*	racism *4*	ethnicity *17*
beta bias *2*	classism *4*	organizational power *17*
alpha bias *2*	sexism *4*	interpersonal power *17*
essentialism *3*	sample *9*	power-over *17*
liberal feminism *4*	population *9*	power-to *18*
cultural feminism *4*	statistical significance *12*	social construction of
socialist feminism *4*	meta-analysis *14*	gender *18*
radical feminism *4*	effect size *16*	

What Do You Think?

1. Do you prefer the similarities approach or the differences approach to the study of gender issues? Why?
2. Which definition of *feminism* or combination of definitions best reflects your own view of feminism? Why?
3. Do you think it would be desirable for women and/or men if more people identified themselves as feminists? Explain your answer.

4. We noted a few experiences of women that are influenced by a gender imbalance in power, and we will cover other examples throughout the text. However, can you now identify any behaviors or concerns of women that you think are influenced by a power imbalance?

If You Want to Learn More

Berger, M. T., & Guidroz, K. (2011). *The intersectional approach: Transforming the academy through race, class, and gender.* Chapel Hill, NC: University of North Carolina Press.

Caplan, P. J., & Caplan, J. B. (2009). *Thinking critically about research on sex and gender* (3rd ed.). Boston, MA: Pearson.

Chrisler, J. C., & McCreary, D. R. (Eds.). (2010). *Handbook of gender research in psychology.* New York: Springer.

Dill, B. T., & Zambrana, R. E. (Eds.). (2009). *Emerging intersections: Race, class, and gender in theory, policy, and practice.* New Brunswick, NJ: Rutgers University Press.

Fine, C. (2010). *Delusions of gender: How our minds, society, and neurosexism create difference.* New York: W. W. Norton.

Hesse-Biber, S. N. (2010). *Mixed methods research: Merging theory with practice.* New York: Guilford.

Hill Collins, P. (2008). *Black feminist thought: Knowledge, consciousness, and the politics of empowerment* (2nd ed.). New York: Routledge.

Jordan, J. V., Walker, M., & Hartling, L M. (Eds.). (2004). *The complexity of connection: Writings from the Stone Center's Jean Baker Miller Training Institute.* New York: Guilford.

Knight, G. P., Roosa, M. W., & Umaña-Taylor, A. J. (2009). *Studying ethnic minority and economically disadvantaged populations: Methodological challenges and best practices.* Washington, DC: American Psychological Association.

Lott, B. (2010). *Multiculturalism and diversity: A social psychological perspective.* Maiden, MA: Wiley-Blackwell.

Meezan, W., & Martin, J. I. (Eds.). (2004). *Research methods with gay, lesbian, bisexual, and transgender populations.* Binghamton, NY: Harrington Park Press.

Mills, S., & Mullany, L. (2011). *Language, gender, and feminism: Theory, methodology, and practice.* New York: Routledge.

O'Connell, A. N. (2001). *Models of achievement: Reflections of eminent women in psychology* (Vol. 3). Mahway, NJ: Erlbaum.

Rudman, L. A., & Glick, P. (2008). *The social psychology of gender: How power and intimacy shape gender relations.* New York: Guilford.

Ryle, R. (2012). *Questioning gender: A sociological exploration.* Thousand Oaks, CA: Sage

White, J. W. (2011). *Taking sides: Clashing views in gender* (5th ed.). New York: McGraw-Hill.

Websites

Feminism
feminist.com
http://www.feminist.com/

CHAPTER 2

Cultural Representation of Gender

Stereotypes of Females and Males
   The Content of Gender
     Stereotypes
   The Perceiver's Ethnicity and
     Gender Stereotypes
   The Target's Characteristics and
     Gender Stereotypes
   Stereotypes of Girls and Boys
   Bases for Gender Stereotypes
   Stereotypes Based on Identity
     Labels

Sexism: Experiences and Attitudes
   Experiences With Sexism
   Changes in Sexist Attitudes Over
     Time
   Modern Sexism
   Ambivalent Sexism

**Representation of Gender in
the Media**
   Pattern 1: Underrepresentation
     of Females
   Pattern 2: Underrepresentation of
     Specific Groups of Females
   Pattern 3: Portrayal of Gender-
     Based Social Roles
   Pattern 4: Depiction of Female
     Communion and Male Agency
   Pattern 5: Emphasis on Female
     Attractiveness and Sexuality
   Impact of Gender-Role Media
     Images

**Representation of Gender in the
English Language**
   Language Practices Based on the
     Assumption That Male Is
     Normative
   Negative Terms for Females
   Significance of the Differential
     Treatment of Females and
     Males in Language

In September 1970, on the day I (Judith) began my academic career, there was a meeting of the faculty at my campus. As was the custom, the campus director introduced me and another new professor to the rest of the faculty and staff. His introduction of my male colleague was both unsurprising and appropriate; he identified him as "Dr. Lantry Brooks" and then provided his academic credentials. Although my educational background was also given, the director introduced me, quite awkwardly, as "Dr., Mrs. Judith Bridges."

What images of women's and men's roles does this dual title suggest? Is there a power difference implied by the different forms of address used for my male colleague and me?

Leap ahead to 2011. At that time, a colleague of Claire's went through a lengthy decision-making process about the surname she would use after her forthcoming marriage. She knew her fiancé was not going to change his name, and she considered taking his name, retaining her birth name, or hyphenating their names. She decided to hyphenate.

Does this colleague's decision have any effect on people's impressions of her? When students read her name in the course schedule, when she applies for grants, or when she is introduced to new acquaintances, does her hyphenated name suggest a different image than her alternative choices would have? Why do people associate different characteristics with different surname choices; that is, what social experiences help shape these images?

In this chapter, we explore these issues and similar ones as we examine stereotypes of females and males, the nature of sexism, and the representations of gender in the media and in language.

STEREOTYPES OF FEMALES AND MALES

Before we begin, think about your conception of the *typical* adult woman and the *typical* adult man. Then indicate your ideas in Get Involved 2.1.

The Content of Gender Stereotypes

The characteristics shown in Get Involved 2.1 reflect **gender stereotypes**, that is, *widely shared beliefs about the attributes of females and males.* These views are present in virtually all cultures that have been studied (Ruspini, 2011; Webster & Rashotte, 2009). As this sample of traits indicates, *personality characteristics associated with women, such as sympathy, kindness, and warmth, reflect a concern about other people.* Social scientists call this cluster of attributes **communion**. *The group of instrumental traits associated with men, including achievement orientation and ambitiousness,* on the other hand, *reflects a concern about accomplishing tasks* and is called **agency** (Eagly & Sczesny, 2009).

Consistent with the tendency to associate communal traits with females and agentic traits with males is people's tendency to expect different roles for women and men (Kite et al., 2008). For example, although most women are employed (U.S. Census Bureau, 2010b), many individuals continue to expect that women will be the primary caregivers of both children and older parents and that men will be the primary providers (Steinberg et al., 2008). In addition, people perceive female family members (i.e., mothers, grandmothers, sisters, aunts) to be more communal toward them than male family members (Monin et al., 2008).

Interestingly, some of these stereotypes have remained relatively unchanged since the 1970s, especially those involving experiencing and expressing emotion and caring as more typical of women and those involving assertiveness, independence, and activity as more typical of men (Kite et al., 2008; Nesbitt & Penn, 2000; Pierce et al., 2003). However, as women have gained status in Western culture in the last few decades, they have increasingly been viewed as having stereotypically masculine traits (Twenge, 2009). The typical woman is no longer considered to be less logical, direct, ambitious, or objective than the typical man or to have greater difficulty in making decisions or separating ideas from feelings. These traits constitute agentic characteristics having to do with competence and the capacity to be effective (Nesbitt & Penn, 2000).

You might have noted that the attributes comprising the male stereotype are more highly regarded in North American society and are more consistent with a powerful image and a higher status than those comprising the female cluster (Gerber, 2009). In Western culture, with its strong emphasis on the value of hard work and achievement, people tend to associate agentic qualities, such as ambition and independence, with power and prestige and to evaluate these traits more

GET INVOLVED 2.1
How Do You View Typical Females and Males?

Indicate which of the following characteristics reflect your conception of a *typical* adult woman and a *typical* adult man. Write *W* next to each characteristic you associate with women and *M* next to each characteristic you associate with men. If you think a particular trait is representative of both women and men, write both *W* and *M* next to that trait.

_____ achievement oriented	_____ emotional
_____ active	_____ gentle
_____ adventurous	_____ independent
_____ affectionate	_____ kind
_____ aggressive	_____ people oriented
_____ ambitious	_____ pleasant
_____ boastful	_____ rational
_____ charming	_____ softhearted
_____ daring	_____ sympathetic
_____ dominant	_____ warm

WHAT DOES IT MEAN?

Did your conceptions of a typical woman and a typical man match those reported by samples of university students from the United States and 28 other countries? These students described the typical woman with traits including affectionate, charming, emotional, gentle, kind, people oriented, softhearted, sympathetic, and warm; they described the typical man with characteristics such as achievement oriented, active, adventurous, ambitious, boastful, daring, independent, and rational.

1. If your impressions of the typical woman and the typical man did not agree with the descriptions reported by these samples of college students, give possible reasons.

2. What was the ethnic identity of the typical woman and man that you considered when performing this activity? If you thought about a White woman and man, do you think your conceptions would have varied had you been asked to specifically consider Blacks, Latinas/os, Asian Americans, or Native Americans? If yes, what are those differences and what can explain them?

3. Similarly, did you think of a middle-class woman and man? Would your impressions have varied had you thought about working-class or poor females and males? Explain any possible differences in gender stereotypes based on social class.

Sources: Based on De Lisi and Soundranayagam (1990) and Williams and Best (1990).

positively than communal attributes, such as gentleness and emotionality. In fact, highly competent and agentic women often are disliked, especially by men (Eagly & Sczesny, 2009). Thus, gender stereotypes are the first indication of the power imbalance discussed in Chapter 1.

Gender stereotypes are relevant to another theme, introduced in Chapter 1, the social construction of gender. Regardless of their accuracy, gender-related beliefs serve as lenses that guide one's expectations and interpretations of other people (Halpern et al., 2011). They can elicit stereotypic behaviors from others. For example, a high school teacher who believes that females are more nurturing than males might ask female students to volunteer in a day-care center run by the school. This activity would provide females but not males the opportunity to develop their caregiving traits. Thus, the teacher's stereotype about the communal characteristics of girls and women might actually contribute to the construction of feminine traits in her female students.

The importance of gender stereotypes in the social construction of gender is also evident in the choices individuals make about their own behavior. For example, based on gender-related beliefs, more adolescent females than males might be likely to seek out babysitting experiences and, thus, more strongly develop traits such as nurturance and compassion.

The traits we have examined thus far are those that North Americans see as *representative* of most women and men. However, these stereotypes differ from people's views of the *ideal* woman and man. Sue Street and her colleagues (Street, Kimmel et al., 1995; Street, Kromrey et al., 1995) studied college students' and faculty's conceptions about the *ideal* woman and the *ideal* man, as well as beliefs about *most* women and *most* men. They found that both students and faculty perceived most women as communal and most men as agentic. However, they viewed the ideal woman as very high in both female-related and male-related traits; that is, they believed she should be caring, sensitive, gentle, and compassionate as well as logical, intelligent, achievement oriented, and assertive. Additionally, although these respondents saw the ideal man as highest in agentic traits, they believed he should be relatively high in compassion as well. Thus, both students and faculty believe ideal persons of both genders should have both types of characteristics.

The Perceiver's Ethnicity and Gender Stereotypes

When you performed Get Involved 2.1, did your selection of traits for females and males match those found in previous research? Alternatively, did you find that you either were less restrictive than the samples investigated in these studies or that you used different stereotypes? Possibly you indicated that some of these characteristics were reflective of both females and males or that some were more representative of the gender not usually associated with the stereotype. Although there is considerable consistency among people in their gender stereotypes, all individuals do not think alike.

In fact, there is evidence that people from different ethnic backgrounds vary in the degree to which they believe the ideal characteristics for females are different from the ideal traits for males, with Blacks less stereotypic in their views than Latinas/os or Whites (Kane, 2000; Leaper, 2002). In one study, for example, it was found that Black adults were less likely than the Whites or Latinas/os to associate specific personality characteristics with each gender; instead they considered a larger variety of traits as desirable for both females and males (Harris, 1994). For example, Blacks rated assertiveness, independence, and self-reliance as equally desirable for Black women and men, whereas the other two ethnic groups evaluated these traits as more desirable for men than women in their cultural groups. Also, Blacks viewed eagerness to soothe hurt feelings as equally desirable for individuals of both genders, but Whites and Latinas/os perceived it as more desirable for women than men. The results of this and other studies indicate that among these three ethnic groups, Blacks are the least likely to adhere to rigid gender stereotypes for women and men.

The Target's Characteristics and Gender Stereotypes

We have seen that people with diverse ethnic backgrounds differ somewhat in their perception of stereotypes of women and men. Now let's examine how these stereotypes vary as a function of the characteristics of the person who is the object, or target, of the stereotype. These characteristics include a woman's age, ethnicity, social class, sexual orientation, and ableness.

AGE.   One of the challenges facing older people in North America and many other parts of the world is the presence of stereotypes (mostly negative) that many people hold about older people (Antonucci et al., 2010; Staudinger & Bowen, 2010). Both children and adults express stereotyped views about older people, some positive (warm, kind, friendly, wise) and others negative (incompetent, inactive, unattractive, feeble, sick, cranky, forgetful, obstinate) (Fingerman & Charles, 2010; Fiske, 2010a; Hummert, 2011; Irni, 2009). Such negative stereotypes are part of a concept known as **ageism,** *a bias against older people.* Ageism resembles sexism and racism in that all are forms of prejudice that limit people who are the object of that prejudice. Unlike sexism and racism, however, everyone will confront ageism if they live long enough (Hurd Clarke, 2011).

Ageism seems to be more strongly directed toward women than men. For centuries, unflattering terms have been used to describe middle-aged and older women: shrew, crazy old lady, crone, hag, wicked old witch, old maid, dreaded mother-in-law (Have you ever heard any jokes about fathers-in-law?) (American Psychological Association, 2007a; Bugental & Hehman, 2007; Grant & Hundley, 2007; Sherman, 2001). Another example of negative attitudes toward older women is the double standard of aging that we will examine later in the chapter.

Psychologists seem to share society's negative views of older women. They are more likely to rate older women as less assertive, less willing to take risks, and less competent than younger women (American Psychological Association, 2007a). Moreover, feminists are not free of ageism and have paid very little attention to older women (Antonucci et al., 2010). For example, even though textbooks on the psychology of women and psychology of gender note the invisibility of older women in the media, these texts themselves give only minimal coverage to midlife and older women (Etaugh et al., 2010). In addition, coverage of eating disorders and sexually transmitted infections in these textbooks focuses almost exclusively on younger women, even though these conditions affect women of all ages. Elder abuse also is ignored by most of the books.

Although aging women have traditionally been viewed less positively than aging men, there is some indication that attitudes toward older women may be improving. One positive sign is what psychologist Margaret Matlin (2001) calls the "Wise and Wonderful Movement." In the twenty-first century, there has been an explosion of books on women who discover themselves in middle or old age. The books present a positive picture of the challenges and opportunities for women in their later years. Three of these books, by Joan Chittister (2008), Laura Hurd Clarke (2011) and Suzanne Levine (2009), are listed as recommended readings at the end of this chapter.

ETHNICITY.   Research has found that women are viewed differently according to their ethnicity. Latinas, for example, are described in relatively positive or neutral terms: pleasant, caring, family-oriented, and passive (Mindiola et al., 2002; Niemann et al., 1994). Asian American women are often perceived as soft-spoken and subservient, but also as hard-working and highly educated, a "model minority" (Khang & Heller de Leon, 2006).

Black women tend to be viewed in terms of the cultural matriarchal stereotype: tough, direct, aggressive, dominant, and strong (Donovan et al., 2005; Mindiola et al., 2002). This somewhat negative stereotype indicates that individuals may overlook the harsh realities of racial and gender oppression in the lives of many Black women and may perceive Black women through a racist lens, a problem experienced by other ethnic minority women as well (Chisholm & Greene, 2008).

SOCIAL CLASS.   Studies have found that individuals of lower socioeconomic status are typically characterized as dishonest, dependent, lazy, stupid, uneducated, promiscuous, drug using, and violent (Cozzarelli et al., 2001). One study found that women from a poor, White community in Appalachia were perceived as dirty, uncouth, "white trash," and unfit mothers (Jones, 2007). Similarly, women who receive public aid are subjected to demeaning, hostile attitudes and treatment by workers in the welfare system (Lott, 2010).

SEXUAL ORIENTATION.   Lesbian, gay, bisexual, and transgender (LGBT) individuals experience widespread social stigmatization that either renders them invisible or causes them to be viewed as sick, immoral, or evil (Fassinger et al., 2010; Herek, 2010). Moreover, many gays and lesbians claim that the labels "masculine" and "feminine" represent efforts of the heterosexual community to pigeonhole LGBTs in traditional ways (Rathus et al., 2010).

ABLENESS.   People attribute more negative characteristics to women with disabilities than to able-bodied women. This bias against people because of their disability is known as **ableism** (Chisholm & Greene, 2008). Women with disabilities, unlike able-bodied women, are frequently stereotyped as unattractive, asexual, unfit to reproduce, helpless, weak, and overly dependent (Banks, 2010; Martin, 2008b; Nosek, 2010; Nario-Redmond, 2010).

In summary, we can see that gender stereotypes are not applied uniformly to all women. A woman's age, ethnicity, social class, sexual orientation, and ableness influence how she is perceived.

Stereotypes of Girls and Boys

We have seen that people have different expectations of the traits and behaviors of adult females and males. Now let's examine adults' gender-stereotypic expectations of children.

As early as the first few days of life, newborn girls and boys are perceived differently. Parents rate newborn daughters as finer featured, less strong, and more delicate than newborn sons, despite medical evidence of no physical differences between them (Karraker et al., 1995). Thus, it is apparent that adults hold gender stereotypes of the physical characteristics of children immediately after the child's birth.

Adults' gender stereotypes of children are not restricted to early infancy. When Canadian college students were asked to rate typical characteristics of 4- to 7-year-old girls and boys, they rated 24 out of 25 traits as being more typical for one gender than the other (Martin, 1995). Additionally, the traits seen as typical for girls versus boys reflected the communion–agency stereotypes evident in gender stereotypes of adults. For example, these students rated girls, compared to boys, as more gentle, sympathetic, and helpful around the house, and they rated boys as more self-reliant, dominant, and competitive than girls.

Bases for Gender Stereotypes

Our exploration of the origins of gender stereotypes focuses on two related issues: (1) the reasons why people stereotype on the basis of gender and (2) the reasons why these stereotypes center on communal traits for females and agentic attributes for males. In other words, we will consider explanations for both the *process* and the *content* of gender stereotyping.

SOCIAL CATEGORIZATION.   Because individuals are bombarded daily with diverse types of people, behaviors, situations, and so on, they simplify their social perceptions by *sorting individuals into categories,* a process called **social categorization**. They focus on the characteristics people share with other members of that category. As an example, in a hospital individuals might categorize the health professionals they encounter as doctors and nurses. Then, the differential set of characteristics they associate with physicians versus nurses serves as a behavior guide when they interact with them, enabling them to ask questions appropriate to their skills and knowledge.

Although individuals use a variety of cues for the sorting process, social categorization is frequently based on easily identified characteristics, such as ethnicity, age, and gender (Dovidio & Gaertner, 2010). The process of gender stereotyping begins with the categorization of individuals as females or males with the implicit assumption that the members of each gender share certain attributes. Then, when one meets a new individual, he/she attributes these gender characteristics to this person.

Although the social categorization and stereotyping processes help simplify a person's understanding of and interactions with other people, they can lead a person astray, because neither all females nor all males are alike. Individuals are most likely to rely on stereotypes when they have little differentiating information about the person. Once more details about a person are available, they use that information in addition to the person's gender to form their impressions and guide their interactions (Kite et al., 2008). For example, when evaluating an individual's level of ambition, people might make use of the person's gender if no other information were available. However, this information would be much less important if they knew the individual was the CEO of a major corporation.

SOCIAL ROLE THEORY.   Given that people divide others into gender categories and attribute similar characteristics to all members of a category, we turn now to the question of why people associate communion with females and agency with males. One possibility is that these stereotypes stem from people's observations of the behaviors individuals typically perform in their social roles. According to **social role theory** (Diekman & Schneider, 2010; Wood & Eagly, 2010), *stereotypes of women and men stem from the association of women with the domestic role and men with the employee role.* Thus, because individuals have observed women primarily in the domestic role, they assume women have the nurturing traits characteristic of that role. Similarly, because more men than women have traditionally been seen in the employment role, people perceive men as having the agentic traits displayed in the workplace.

Support for this theory of gender stereotypes comes from studies that show the influence of a person's social role on the application of gender-related traits to her/him. For example, social roles can override gender when assigning communal or agentic characteristics to others. Specifically, when participants are asked to describe a woman and a man who are homemakers, they view them as equally communal. Similarly, when asked to describe a full-time female and male employee, they perceive both as agentic. In addition, women and men who are employed are viewed as more agentic than those who are not (Coleman & Franiuk, 2011), mothers are seen as more communal than nonmothers (Bridges et al., 2000; Etaugh & Poertner, 1992), and married women are perceived as more communal than unmarried women (Etaugh & Nekolny, 1990; Etaugh & Poertner, 1991). Clearly, when people are aware of an individual's social role, their stereotypes of the person are influenced by that role information.

The influence of social roles on gender stereotypes is evident even when people are asked to describe women and men in both the past and the future. When both college students and students after college were asked to rate the average woman and the average man in 1950, 1975, 2025, and 2050, they viewed females as becoming dramatically more masculine over time and males as becoming somewhat more feminine (Diekman & Eagly, 1997). What accounts for these perceptions? In support of social role theory, the researchers found that the decreasing degree of gender stereotyping was related to the belief that the occupational and domestic roles of women and men during this time period have become and will continue to become increasingly similar.

Keep in mind, however, the evidence presented earlier in this chapter—that stereotypes have remained relatively constant, at least since the 1970s. What can explain the discrepancy between the increased participation of women in the labor force and the consistency of gender stereotypes over time? Although more women are employed now than in the past, they are more likely than men to be employed in caregiving occupations, such as nursing and early childhood education. Also, regardless of their employment role, women still have the primary caregiving responsibility in their families. Although social roles are gradually changing, women remain the primary nurturers and men the primary providers around the world (Cabrera et al., 2009; Chuang & Su, 2009; Tamis-LeMonda et al., 2009). Consequently, it is not surprising that people's stereotypes of females and males have been resistant to change.

Stereotypes Based on Identity Labels

Recall the experience Judith described at the beginning of the chapter when she was introduced as "Dr., Mrs. Bridges." The fact that the campus director introduced her this way but did not present her male colleague as "Dr. Lantry Brooks who happens to be married" implies he believed that a woman's identity, more than a man's, is shaped by her marital role. Although his use of a dual title was unusual, his belief about a woman's identity is consistent with the long-standing cultural norm that a woman is defined in terms of her relationship to a man (Gooding & Kreider, 2010). Given that a woman's title of address can signify her marital role and that her marital status has been viewed as an important aspect of her identity, people might expect different stereotypes of women who use different titles for themselves. Consider the woman who chooses not to use the conventional "Miss" or "Mrs." labels that announce her marital status but instead identifies herself with the neutral "Ms." Kelly Malcolmson and Lisa Sinclair (2007) replicated older studies that had found that women who prefer the title Ms. are perceived as more agentic but less communal than traditionally titled women. Thus, the Ms. title remains a powerful cue eliciting a stereotype consistent with male gender–related traits and inconsistent with female gender–related traits. Other research by Carol Lawton and her colleagues (Lawton et al., 2003) found that *Ms.* was often defined as a title for unmarried women, especially by younger adults. Older unmarried women were more likely to prefer *Ms.* as their own title than were younger unmarried women, whereas married women overwhelmingly preferred the use of *Mrs.*

Given that people's impressions of a woman are influenced by her preferred title, a related question is whether these stereotypes vary according to another identity label, a woman's choice of surname after marriage. Similar to the preference for *Ms.* as a title of address, a woman's choice of a surname other than her husband's, such as her birth name or a hyphenated name, is a nontraditional practice that separates the woman's personal identity from her identity as a wife. Nowadays, about 20 percent of college-educated brides do not take their husbands' last names, compared with only 4 percent in 1975 (Grossman, 2007). The more education a married woman has, the more likely she is to use a nonconventional surname. Compared to women with bachelor's degrees, those with professional degrees (i.e., lawyers, physicians) are five times more likely to choose a nontraditional name, and those with doctorates are nearly ten times more likely to do so (Gooding & Kreider, 2010). Thus, it is not surprising that studies by Claire, Judith, and their students (Etaugh et al., 1999; Etaugh & Conrad, 2004; Etaugh & Roe, 2002) showed that college women and men view married women who use a nontraditional surname as more agentic and less communal than women who follow the patriarchal practice of taking their husbands' names after marriage.

Why do a woman's preferred title and surname influence the characteristics attributed to her? One possibility is that individuals have observed more women with nontraditional forms of address (i.e., title and/or surname) in the workplace than in the domestic role and, thus, attribute more agentic traits to her. Indeed we've just seen that married women who use nonconventional surnames are often highly educated and have prestigious occupations (Gooding & Kreider, 2010). Thus, consistent with social role theory (Wood & Eagly, 2010), stereotypes of women who prefer nontraditional forms of address might be due to the belief that they are in nontraditional roles.

SEXISM: EXPERIENCES AND ATTITUDES

The definition of *sexism* as bias against people because of their gender can be directed at either females or males. However, because women have a power disadvantage relative to men, they are more likely to be targets of sexism (Glick & Fiske, 2007). Therefore, our discussion focuses on the more specific definition of **sexism** as *stereotypes and/or discriminatory behaviors that serve to restrict women's roles and maintain male dominance.* For example, stereotypes such as "women should be the primary caregivers" and "women are not competent to be police officers or university presidents" serve to shape women's role choices. *Violating these gender stereotypes can result in social and economic reprisals*—a phenomenon referred to as the **backlash effect** (Swim & Hyers, 2008). For example, a highly qualified female job applicant may be viewed as socially deficient, leading to hiring discrimination and ultimately the maintenance of male dominance in the culture at large.

Consider the real-life case of Ann Hopkins, a highly accomplished manager at Price Waterhouse, a prestigious accounting firm. In 1982, Hopkins was one of 88 candidates for partner and the only female candidate. At that time, she had more billable hours than any other contenders, had brought in $25 million worth of business, and was highly regarded by her clients. However, Ann Hopkins was turned down for the partnership. She was criticized for her "macho" style and was advised to "walk more femininely, talk more femininely, dress more femininely, wear makeup and jewelry" (Hopkins, 2007, p. 62).

Hopkins filed a lawsuit, asserting that her promotion had been denied on the basis of her gender. Although she won this suit, her employer appealed the decision all the way up to the Supreme Court. The Court decided in Ann Hopkins's favor, concluding that gender-based stereotyping had played a role in the firm's refusal to promote her to partner. After this decision, Ann Hopkins did become a partner and was awarded financial compensation for her lost earnings (Hopkins, 2007).

Experiences With Sexism

Sadly, almost all girls and women experience sexism at one time or another (Moradi & DeBlaere, 2010). For example, in a study of 600 teenage girls of varied socioeconomic and ethnic backgrounds (Leaper & Brown, 2008), it was found that half of the girls reported hearing discouraging, sexist comments about their abilities in science, math, or computer usage. Three-fourths had received disparaging comments about their athletic abilities and sports involvement. Male peers were the most common perpetrators of academic and athletic sexist remarks. Such disapproval may lead some girls to downplay their interests and competencies in sports or academic areas, which can ultimately diminish their later achievements in these areas. Even more troubling, perhaps, teachers were a frequent source of discouraging remarks about girls' academic abilities, as were fathers. (More about this in Chapter 5.)

The perception of sexism depends, in part, on a woman's interpretation (Moradi & DeBlaere, 2010). To one woman a joke that sexually degrades women is sexist, but to another woman that joke is simply funny. Women also differ from one another in their willingness to acknowledge their own experience with discrimination. For example, college women who have a strong desire for social approval are less likely to acknowledge they had experienced sexist discrimination than are those willing to risk disapproval (Kobrynowicz & Branscombe, 1997). According to these researchers, claiming sexism might be perceived as socially undesirable for women who are greatly concerned about the amount of approval they receive from others.

Changes in Sexist Attitudes Over Time

In the past few decades, the endorsement of traditional gender roles and overt sexism has decreased in many countries especially within North America and Europe (Swim, Becker, 2010). It is likely that the reduction in overt sexism is due, in part, to legislative actions (e.g., 1960s legislation prohibiting education and workplace discrimination on the basis of sex) and other social changes (e.g., the significant influx of married women into the workplace in the last few decades). However, some of the decline in overt sexism might reflect the decreased social acceptability of blatantly sexist views, rather than a real weakening of beliefs that serve to maintain traditional roles and power differences. Several theorists have suggested that more subtle types of sexism have emerged: modern sexism and ambivalent sexism.

Modern Sexism

Modern sexism (Swim, Becker et al., 2010) is based on the coexistence of conflicting attitudes. According to this perspective, some people hold egalitarian values but, at the same time, harbor negative feelings toward women. The resulting ideology is *characterized by the belief that gender discrimination is no longer a problem in society and is manifested by harmful treatment of women in ways that appear to be socially acceptable.* For example, a modern sexist might argue that policies that foster gender equality, such as affirmative action, should not be implemented. Thus, it is possible for a person to espouse sexist beliefs such as these but not appear to be prejudiced against women.

Do you know anyone who endorses modern sexism? See Get Involved 2.2 for examples of modern sexist beliefs.

Ambivalent Sexism

Generally, people consider sexism to comprise *negative* stereotypes about women, such as the beliefs that women are fragile, submissive, and less competent than men. And, of course, we can see how stereotypes such as these are detrimental to women. Interestingly, however, Peter Glick and Susan Fiske (2007; Lee et al., 2010) have proposed that sexism can be **ambivalent**, encompassing both **hostile sexism**, or *negative stereotypes of women,* and **benevolent sexism**, or *the seemingly positive view that idealizes women as pure objects of men's adoration and protection.*

Although hostile sexist beliefs are overtly demeaning, benevolent sexist views are usually accompanied by genuine affection, and the holder of these attitudes might be unaware of their implicit sexist bias. For example, a husband who shields his wife from the family's financial difficulties might be unaware of the biased assumptions implicit in his desire to protect her. According to Glick and Fiske (2007), hostile and benevolent sexism both imply that women are weak and best suited for traditional gender roles. Both serve to justify and maintain patriarchal social structures. Some aspects of benevolent sexism may appeal to some women. For example, beliefs that women are less physically strong or more emotionally sensitive allow women to not engage in distasteful activities ranging from taking out the garbage to fighting in wars (Goodwin & Fiske, 2001). Moreover, some women may endorse benevolent sexism in order to avoid antagonizing their male partners (Expósito et al., 2010). However, research shows that benevolent sexism actually has a more harmful effect than hostile sexism on women's performances on cognitive tasks. In one study, patronizing statements read before task performance led to feelings of self-doubt and decreased self-esteem, which undermined performance. Hostile sexist statements did not have this negative effect (Dardenne et al., 2007). For a look at ambivalent sexism around the world, see Explore Other Cultures 2.1.

GET INVOLVED 2.2
Who Holds Modern Sexist Beliefs?

On a scale from 1 (strongly disagree) to 7 (strongly agree), indicate the extent to which you disagree or agree with each of the following statements. Also, ask several female and male acquaintances who vary in age to respond to these statements.

1. It is rare to see women treated in a sexist manner on television.

2. Society has reached the point where women and men have equal opportunities for achievement.

3. Over the past few years, the government and news media have been showing more concern about the treatment of women than is warranted by women's actual experiences.

4. Discrimination against women is no longer a problem in the United States.

5. Women's requests in terms of equality between the sexes are simply exaggerated.

6. Universities are wrong to admit women in costly programs such as medicine when, in fact, a large number will leave their jobs after a few years to raise their children.

7. Due to social pressures, firms frequently have to hire underqualified women.

WHAT DOES IT MEAN?

Sum the ratings you gave to these seven statements. Do the same for each of your respondents. Note that each statement reflects a sexist belief; therefore, the higher the score, the greater the sexism.

1. Are there differences between the views of your female and male respondents? Explain your finding.

2. Are there differences between the views of respondents who vary in age? Explain your finding.

3. Do you think it is possible that a person could endorse one or more of these beliefs but not be supportive of traditional roles and male dominance? Why or why not?

Sources: Based on Swim et al. (1995) and Tougas et al. (1995).

EXPLORE OTHER CULTURES 2.1
Benevolent Sexism Is a Global Phenomenon

Peter Glick, Susan Fiske, and their colleagues (2000) measured ambivalent sexism in over 15,000 participants in 19 countries in Africa, the Americas, Asia, Australia, and Europe. Although both hostile and benevolent sexism were prevalent in all cultures, these attitudes were strongest in Africa and Latin America and weakest in Northern Europe and Australia. Without exception, men showed more hostile sexism than women. In contrast, women in about half the countries endorsed benevolent sexism as much as or even more than men did (Figure 2.1). What accounts for these cross-cultural differences? The key factor appears to be the degree to which gender inequality exists in the various nations. Gender inequality is measured by such things as women's (relative to men's) participation in a country's economy and political system, their life expectancy, educational level, and standard of living. In countries with the greatest gender inequality (i.e., in Africa and Latin America), both men's and women's sexism scores were highest. Furthermore, the more hostile sexism the men showed, the more likely women were to embrace benevolent sexism, even to the point of endorsing it more strongly than men. How can this be explained? According to Glick and Fiske (2007), the greater the threat of hostile sexism from a society's men, the stronger the incentive for women to adopt benevolent sexism's protective nature.

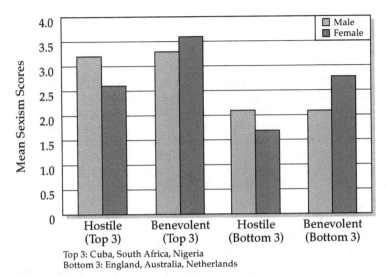

Top 3: Cuba, South Africa, Nigeria
Bottom 3: England, Australia, Netherlands

FIGURE 2.1 Hostile and Benevolent Sexism Across Countries: The Top Three in Gender Equality Versus the Bottom Three

REPRESENTATION OF GENDER IN THE MEDIA

We have seen that North American adults have different conceptions of females and males. We turn now to the depiction of these stereotypes in the media. People are bombarded daily with differential images of females and males on television, in the movies, in books, and in magazines. Are these images consistent with gender stereotyping? Try the exercise in Get Involved 2.3 to examine television portrayals of gender.

Numerous investigations of the depiction of females and males in both electronic and print media have revealed several consistent patterns: the underrepresentation of females, the underrepresentation of specific groups of females, the portrayal of gender-based social roles, the depiction of female communion and male agency, and the emphasis on female attractiveness and sexuality. Our first task is to examine these patterns. Then we consider the effects of media images on gender stereotypes and attitudes.

Pattern 1: Underrepresentation of Females

As we have previously seen, women are perceived as less powerful and less important than men. This imbalance of power and value is reflected in the underrepresentation of females in media around the world. For example, the proportion of females has changed little since the 1990s. Currently, between 32 and 38 percent of characters on television shows for both children and adults are female (Hether & Murphy, 2010; Media Awareness Network, 2010). Similarly, the percentage of female characters in television commercials (Das, 2011; Paek et al., 2011) and movies (APA Task Force, 2007; Lauzen, 2003) ranges from approximately 20 to 45 percent. Recent studies of G-rated films found that nearly three out of four characters were male (Lamb, 2006; Smith et al., 2010). This underrepresentation is also mirrored in video games (Yao et al., 2010), Sunday morning news analysis shows (Brazile, 2007), computer clipart images (Milburn et al., 2001), coloring books (Fitzpatrick & McPherson, 2010), and even cereal boxes (Black et al., 2009).

GET INVOLVED 2.3
How Are Females and Males Portrayed on Prime-Time Television?

Watch five different prime-time shows and record the following information: (1) the number of major female and male characters; (2) the ethnicity of these characters; (3) the employment status and occupation, if employed, of each major female and male character; (4) the marital and parental status of these characters; (5) the approximate age of each of these characters (e.g., 20s, 30s); and (6) whether or not each character's physical appearance was mentioned or otherwise appeared to be an important characteristic of that person. After recording this information, examine commonalities and differences in the depiction of females and males and in the portrayal of different age groups. Also, if these shows featured women and/or men of color, compare portrayals of characters of varying ethnicities.

WHAT DOES IT MEAN?

1. Are your findings consistent with those presented in this chapter? If not, what might explain any differences you observed?

2. Do your findings indicate that members of each gender are depicted similarly, regardless of their ethnicity or age? If you found differences related to ethnicity or age, explain them.

3. Do you think that media images of gender, as described in this chapter and as shown by your analysis, help shape people's construction of gender? Explain your answer.

This situation has improved in recent years in certain types of children's reading material. For example, picture books are more likely to feature males and females equally in titles, as central characters, and in pictures (Gooden & Gooden, 2001; Lane & Etaugh, 2001). Children's school textbooks are less gender biased then they were 30 years ago, but male characters continue to outnumber female ones in basic readers and math materials (Meece & Scantlebury, 2006).

Pattern 2: Underrepresentation of Specific Groups of Females

ETHNICITY. The invisibility of females is most evident when considering females in less powerful social categories. Women and girls of color, especially Latinas, Asian Americans, and Native Americans, are featured very infrequently in children's and adult's television shows, commercials (Coltrane & Messineo, 2000; Van Evra, 2004), movies (Lauzen, 2003; Smith et al., 2010), and video games (Williams et al., 2009). When they do appear, they are highly stereotyped (Berry, 2007; Gill, 2007; Martin & Kazyak, 2009). For example, Latina characters are often shown in low-status occupations such as maids (Navarro, 2002). On prime-time television shows, Black women and men, compared to Whites, are portrayed as more passive, are dressed in more provocative and less professional manner, and are judged to be the laziest and least respected ethnic group (Mastro & Greenberg, 2000). Ethnic minority women are also underrepresented in advertisements in a wide variety of periodicals (Lipkin, 2009; Sengupta, 2006).

AGE. Although older adults of both sexes are generally underrepresented in the media, this is especially true for women (Cole & Sabik, 2009; Hurd Clarke, 2011; Kessler et al., 2010; Prieler et al., 2011). Joan Chrisler (2007) notes that the scarcity of images of women over 50 in the media conveys the message that women should either hide the signs of aging or stay hidden. The few older women who appear on television shows are portrayed less favorably than older men. They are often depicted as comic or eccentric figures, asexual, burdensome, dependent, interfering, gossipy, or downright villainous (Gill, 2007; Hant, 2011; Wilkinson & Ferraro, 2002). Whereas prime-time male characters aged 65 and older are depicted as active, middle-aged, mature adults, women of that age are more likely to be designated as elderly (Signorielli & Bacue, 1999). In the movies (Lauzen, 2003), female characters are younger than male characters, with most women under age 35. In fact, women over 50 are portrayed in only 12 percent of the roles in popular movies, and among the top actors aged 50 or older, only 20 percent are women (Haskell & Harmetz, 1998). Older women of color are rarely seen (Robinson et al., 2004).

Older women in popular films are portrayed as more unfriendly, unintelligent, unattractive, scary, or wicked (Bazzini et al., 1997; Sobchack, 2009). In the popular animated Disney films, for example, evil older women abound: the wicked queen in *Snow White and the Seven Dwarfs*, Cinderella's stepmother, Maleficent (*Sleeping Beauty*), Ursula (*The Little Mermaid*), Cruella DeVille (*101 Dalmatians*), the Red Queen (*Alice in Wonderland*), and Mother Gothel (*Tangled*). Attractive actresses such as Meryl Streep, Jessica Lange, and Diane Keaton are labeled "geezer babes"—and thus too old for romantic parts—whereas male actors many years their senior are paired with young ingenues (Chrisler, 2007; Genzlinger, 2004; Haskell, 1998). Along the same lines, women over the age of 39 accounted for only 27 percent of all Academy Award winners for Best Actress from 1927 to 1990, whereas men in the same age category won 67 percent of Best Actor awards (Markson & Taylor, 1993). Hollywood's long-standing tendency to add years to actresses and subtract them from actors has led to some interesting—and biologically impossible—movie relationships. For example, 29-year-old Angelina Jolie played the mother of 28-year-old Colin Farrell in the 2004 film *Alexander* (Beumont, 2005).

Print media are no exception. In magazines targeting 40- and 50-year-old women, for example, most of the models are in their 20s and early 30s (Bessenoff & Del Priore, 2007). Readers of these magazines are bombarded with ads for antiaging products (Hurd Clarke, 2011). Those older women who do appear in the media are praised for their youthful appearance and for hiding the signs of aging (Hant, 2011). Internet ads for antiaging products send the message that older women are worthwhile only to the extent that they revert to middle-aged and even youthful norms of female beauty (Calasanti, 2007). In the words of Susan Bordo,

> *I'm 56. The magazines tell me that at this age, a woman can still be beautiful. But they don't mean me. They mean Cher, Goldie, Faye, Candace. Women whose jowls have disappeared as they've aged, whose eyes have become less droopy, lips grown plumper, foreheads smoother with the passing years. "Aging beautifully" used to mean wearing one's years with style, confidence, and vitality. Today, it means not appearing to age at all.*

(2004, p. 246)

In the present youth-oriented society, the prospect of getting older is generally not relished by either sex. For women, however, *the stigma of aging is much greater than it is for men.* Susan Sontag (1997) has labeled this phenomenon the **double standard of aging**. The same gray hair and wrinkles that enhance the perceived status and attractiveness of an older man diminish the attractiveness and desirability of an older woman. Some researchers account for this by noting that a woman's most socially valued qualities—her ability to provide sex and bear children—are associated with the physical beauty and fertility of youth. As she ages, she is seen as less attractive because her years of social usefulness as childbearer are behind her. Men, however, are seen as possessing qualities—competence, autonomy, and power—that are not associated with youth but rather increase with age (Brooks, 2010; Cole & Sabik, 2010; England & McClintock, 2009). Before going further, try Get Involved 2.4.

Older men are often portrayed as powerful and distinguished, but older women are perceived as losing their attractiveness.

SEXUAL ORIENTATION.   Lesbians and gay men have been another underrepresented group in the media. As recently as the early 1990s, there were few visible gay characters, and they were usually portrayed as unattractive, sad, and suicidal, or unstable and psychopathic (D'Erasmo, 2004; Meem et al., 2010). But as gays and lesbians have become more accepted in recent years, sexual minority characters are increasingly being featured in mainstream television shows, films, and theater (Meem et al., 2010). In 1997, the sitcom *Ellen* became the first prime-time television show to have an openly gay lead character (DeFrancisco & Palczewski, 2007). Shows such as *Will and Grace*, *Queer Eye for the Straight Guy*, and *Queer as Folk* were mainstream hits (Kirk & Okazawa-Rey, 2010; Slagle & Yep, 2007), and a reality show spinoff, *The Real L-Word*, had its debut in 2010 (Karpel, 2010). In 2005, a long-time character on *The Simpsons* came out of the closet, and Homer Simpson conducted dozens of same-sex weddings to boost tourism in his town (Waxman, 2005). Also in that year, MTV

GET INVOLVED 2.4
Media Advertisements and the Double Standard of Aging

Look through newspapers and magazines for advertisements that include middle-aged adults. Then answer the following questions:

1. Are there differences in the appearance of the women and the men?

WHAT DOES IT MEAN?

1. Do the advertisements show evidence of a double standard of aging?

2. What can advertisers do to minimize differences in the portrayal of middle-aged females and males?

2. Do females and males advertise different products?

3. In advertisements with two or more people, what is the role of the principal male or female in relationship to others?

3. How do media images of midlife adults help shape people's perceptions of middle-aged women and men?

Source: Berk et al. (1998).

---

started the first cable television channel directed at gay and lesbian viewers (Carter & Elliott, 2004). The trend-setting *New York Times* began publishing same-sex wedding and commitment ceremony announcements in 2002. And a 2003 issue of the popular magazine *Brides* had a feature on what to wear to a same-sex wedding (Toussaint, 2003).

Pattern 3: Portrayal of Gender-Based Social Roles

Females and males are portrayed differently in the media not only in terms of their numbers but also in relation to their social roles. Over the last few decades there has been an increase in the percentage of prime-time television shows that feature female characters who are employed, with 60 percent of female characters depicted as working in the 1990s. Furthermore, their range of jobs has broadened; by the 1990s, only one quarter were shown in traditional female jobs, such as secretary or nurse (Signorielli & Bacue, 1999). But although women lawyers, doctors, and police officers appear on television, many of these depictions are unrealistic. For example, not all women in these professions are young and beautiful (Van Evra, 2004)! And working-class employees such as Roseanne have almost vanished (Douglas, 2010).

On the other hand, consistent with the stereotypical association of men in the worker role and women in the family role, popular television shows (Lauzen et al., 2008), commercials (Nassif & Gunter, 2008; Robinson & Hunter, 2008; Royo-Vela et al., 2008; Valls-Hernandez & Martinez-Vicente, 2007), movies (Smith et al., 2010), children's readers (Etaugh et al., 2007), and Sunday comics (LaRossa et al., 2001) still show more men than women with jobs and more women than men in traditional family roles. In the movies, women are more likely than men to hold powerless occupations, such as retail clerk, and they are rarely shown in leadership roles (Lauzen, 2003). Even in movies with a strong, successful, independent woman character, the woman's life is more constrained than the man's, and traditional cultural patterns triumph in the end (Dowd, 2007). Sophisticated, successful, single career women, such as Ally McBeal and the four women of *Sex and the City,* expend considerable energy looking for Mr. Right (Gill, 2007). Thus, despite the presence of several positive employed-female role models on television and the fact that the majority of American married women are employed (U.S. Census Bureau, 2010a), there is little depiction of women who successfully combine a career and marriage. The media send a message that successful women professionals cannot have rewarding home lives, if indeed they have any at all (Douglas, 2009; Gill, 2007).

In the leading teen magazine for girls, *Seventeen,* the world of work is dominated by powerful men, and fashion modeling is presented as the pinnacle of "women's work" (Massoni, 2004). Moreover, stereotyped depictions of women in both general interest and fashion magazine advertisements have decreased only slightly over the past 50 years (Lindner, 2004; Mager & Helgeson, 2011).

Despite the increasing participation of women in sports, female athletes continue to be underrepresented in the media (Media Awareness Network, 2010). Moreover, those who participate in traditional feminine sports such as tennis, golf, or gymnastics get more coverage than women who compete in more masculine team sports such as basketball or softball (Fink & Kensicki, 2002; Tuggle et al., 2002). In the 2000 Olympics, women who competed in sports involving power or hard physical contact—discus throw, javelin throw, shot put, weightlifting, martial arts—received almost no television coverage (Tuggle et al., 2002). Moreover, the athleticism of female athletes tends to be underplayed. For example, in the official media guide of the National Collegiate Athletic Association, female athletes are more likely than male athletes to be shown in passive and nonathletic poses (Buysse & Embser-Herbert, 2004). In addition, sports announcers and writers highlight female athletes' femininity, minimize their athletic ability, and use comments that imply that female athletes are more vulnerable than their male counterparts (Media Awareness Network, 2010; Parker & Fink, 2008).

Pattern 4: Depiction of Female Communion and Male Agency

Consistent with the depiction of females and males in different social roles, the communion stereotype for females and the agency stereotype for males are both evident in the media. Despite the growing body of movies and television shows featuring women fighting and committing mayhem—*Survivor, Fear Factor, Buffy the Vampire Slayer, Kill Bill, Charlie's Angels,* and *Terminator,* among others (Greenwood, 2007; Solomon, 2005)—boys and men are depicted as more active, assertive, aggressive, and powerful than females in a range of media (Basow, 2008). These include adult films (Gilpatric, 2010), children's cartoons (APA Task Force, 2007), print advertisements (Mager & Helgeson et al., 2011), toy commercials (Kahlenberg & Hein, 2010), Disney-Pixar films (Gillam & Wooden, 2011), children's literature (Basow, 2010a; Etaugh et al., 2003), and even coloring books (McPherson et al., 2007). Furthermore, consistent with their greater power, males are presented as narrators in approximately 70 to 90 percent of commercials that use voice-overs (e.g., Das, 2011; Paek et al., 2011; Valls-Fernández & Martinez-Vicente, 2007), thus projecting an image of authority and expertise. In addition, men are two to three times more likely than women to be used as news sources both in newspapers (Schwartz, 2011) and on television news (Desmond & Danilewicz, 2010).

On the other hand, the media portray females as communal, that is, oriented toward other people. Even when a woman is depicted as an action hero—such as Xena, the warrior princess—she is liked best when she embodies traditionally valued feminine traits such as nurturance, compassion, and using the mind over the sword (Calvert et al., 2001). Over half of the violent female action figures in contemporary American films are portrayed in a submissive role to the male hero and nearly half are romantically linked to him (Gilpatric, 2010). Similarly, even the most feisty of the more recent Disney "princesses," including Ariel, Belle, Jasmine, Mulan, Pocahontas, Rapunzel, and Tiana, are kind, obedient (or punished if they are not), and love-struck (Barnes, 2010; England et al., 2011; Gillam & Wooden, 2008; Martin & Kazyak,

2009). Most mothers in children's literature are nurturers. Many are homemakers, whereas others are in traditional female nurturing occupations such as teaching, nursing, or social work (Lehr, 2001). Similar gender messages even permeate Girl Scout and Boy Scout handbooks, with the former providing girls with more other-oriented activities, and the latter providing boys with more self-oriented activities (Denny, 2011).

Pattern 5: Emphasis on Female Attractiveness and Sexuality

The media define females, more than males, by their looks and sexuality. For example, commercials show more women than men in suggestive clothing (APA Task Force, 2007). In addition, commercials, television shows, and movies portray women as more likely than men to receive comments about their appearance (Lauzen & Dozier, 2002). In pursuit of physical perfection, women routinely risk their health to undergo extensive plastic surgery on television reality shows such as *Extreme Makeover*.

Females in video games frequently are hypersexualized and scantily clad (Behm-Morawitz & Mastro, 2009; Yao et al., 2010). The lyrics to popular music often contain explicit sexual references that are degrading to women (Harris, 2008; Weitzer & Kubrin, 2011). Moreover, music videos emphasize women's sexuality rather than their musical talent (Zhang et al., 2010), featuring men performing and provocatively dressed, young women dancing suggestively (S. L. Smith et al., 2009; Turner, 2011; Wallis, 2011). Although female sexuality is highlighted by the media, women often pay a heavy price if they actually engage in sexual activity. Two recent studies of women in the James Bond movies (Neuendorf et al., 2010) and in slasher horror films (Welsh, 2010) found that women who engaged in sexual behavior often were harmed or killed.

This emphasis on female appearance and sex appeal is apparent in print as well as in electronic media. Mainstream magazines targeted at teenagers and young women stress the importance of improving one's physical attractiveness through diet, exercise, fashion, and use of beauty products (Gill, 2007; Murray, 2011). These magazines prey on women's insecurities to get them to buy the advertisers' wares (Lipkin, 2009). Moreover, the depiction of women is more sexualized than that of men. Sexual imagery in women's magazine advertising has, in fact, increased in recent years (Frith et al., 2005; Nelson & Paek, 2005; Reichert & Carpenter, 2004). Women are depicted as sex objects in two-thirds of the ads appearing in women's fashion magazines and in magazines for teen girls (Stankiewicz & Rosselli, 2008). Sexualized images of female athletes abound in women's sports and fitness magazines (Hardin et al., 2005). A typical example is a photograph from *Shape* magazine showing four women members of the U.S. Olympic swim team standing naked behind a strategically draped American flag. Sports announcers and writers frequently refer to a female athlete's attractiveness and heterosexuality, thus conveying to the audience that her looks are more salient than her athletic role (APA Task Force, 2007; Billings et al., 2002; Fink & Kensicki, 2004; Knight & Giuliano, 2001).

Not only is a woman's attractiveness portrayed as highly important but that attractiveness is also depicted as overly thin (Dworkin & Wachs, 2009; Grabe et al., 2008; Zhang et al., 2010). For example, most *Playboy* centerfold models are underweight, and approximately one-third are so thin that they meet the World Health Organization's standard for anorexia nervosa, a severe eating disorder (see Chapter 13). Magazines focusing on sports that emphasize thinness—gymnastics, ice skating, dancing—are more likely to feature overly thin cover models than are magazines dealing with sports such as running, tennis, and swimming (Ginsberg & Gray, 2006). Gregory Fouts and Kimberley Burggraf (2000) found that over 25 percent of female characters in Canadian situation comedies were underweight. They also observed that the thinner

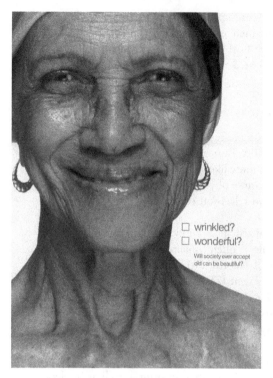

□ wrinkled?
□ wonderful?

Will society ever accept
old can be beautiful?

Irene Sinclair, age 96, in a Dove commercial
challenging traditional stereotypes of beauty.

the female, the more positive comments she received from male characters, and the heavier the woman, the more derogatory remarks she got. On the show *America's Next Top Model,* dangerously underweight young women reaped praise for their looks, whereas normal-weight contestants at 5 feet 8 inches and 130 lbs were mocked as "plus-sized" (Pozner, 2004). Overweight women not only are underrepresented on television and considered less attractive, but are also less likely to interact with romantic partners (Greenberg et al., 2003).

Thus, the media still portray appearance and sexuality as two highly valued aspects of a woman's identity. More specifically, they present the message that it is White beauty that is valued (Baker, 2005; Dworkin & Wachs, 2009). Black actresses and models who are depicted as physically desirable are likely to be light-skinned and to possess White facial features (Dworkin & Wachs, 2009; Harrison & Thomas, 2009), thus informing the Black viewer that not just beauty but White beauty is important (Townsend et al., 2010). Even popular children's fairy tales, such as Cinderella, Snow White, and Sleeping Beauty, highlight youthful feminine beauty, which often is associated with being White, virtuous, and economically privileged (Baker-Sperry & Grauerholz, 2011).

The media's portrayal of women's appearance does have some bright spots. In 2004, for example, Dove launched the "Dove Campaign for Real Beauty," a global effort intended to act as a catalyst for widening the definition and discussion of beauty. The campaign targeted the United States and Great Britain and featured billboard images of six women of various ages, sizes, types, and shapes (Gill, 2007). Each photograph showed a woman whose appearance challenges traditional stereotypes of beauty and asked viewers to judge her looks by casting votes and joining a discussion of beauty issues at the campaign's Website. For example, "Oversized? Outstanding?" were the choices next to Tabatha Roman, 34, a plus-size woman, and "Wrinkled? Wonderful?" appeared next to the photo of Irene Sinclair, 96.

Impact of Gender-Role Media Images

We have seen that the media portray a world more heavily populated by males than by females, a world in which males are more likely than females to have jobs and be active and assertive and where beauty and romantic relationships are central to females' identity. Research shows that media not only reflect and transmit existing stereotypes but also have a socializing effect (APA Task Force, 2007; Pecora et al., 2007; Reichert & Lambiase, 2005). For example, exposure to music videos leads to and is associated with stronger endorsement of traditional gender roles and greater acceptance of dating violence (Ward, 2002; Ward et al., 2005), as well as lowered body esteem and decreased confidence in math ability in women (Grabe & Hyde, 2009). Thus, the media can play an important role in shaping people's construction of gender and in providing them with expectations of what females and males are like—their personality traits, social roles, and value to society. In addition, the very limited depiction of non-White or older females can reinforce perceptions of the powerlessness of these groups and communicate that their experiences are not important (Van Evra, 2004).

Consider other types of media that might portray females and males stereotypically. See, for example, Learn About the Research 2.1 to find out about stereotypes in greeting cards. Then read What You Can Do 2.1 to see how you can help to increase girls' and women's awareness of the effects of media.

LEARN ABOUT THE RESEARCH 2.1
Are Babies Portrayed Stereotypically in Birth Congratulations Cards?

We have seen that girls and boys are portrayed stereotypically in virtually all media. To explore how infant girls and boys are portrayed, Judith and her students examined the visual images and verbal messages present in 61 birth congratulations cards for girls and 61 cards for boys.

Not surprisingly, pink was the most common color used on the cards for girls and blue on the cards for boys. Boys were more likely to be shown performing physical activities, such as walking or building, whereas girls were pictured passively sitting or lying down. Similarly, more of the cards for boys featured toys, such as sports equipment and vehicles, that require considerable action, whereas girls were pictured with baby toys, such as rattles and mobiles, that required less physical involvement. Larger animals, including bears and dogs, were more common on the cards for boys, and smaller, less aggressive birds and rabbits were shown on the cards for girls.

Although there were few gender-specific verbal messages in the cards, there were several interesting differences. Girls, more than boys, were described as "little" and "sweet," whereas the happiness of parents or the child was included more often in the verbal message to boys than in the message to girls.

WHAT DOES IT MEAN?

1. The pictures on the cards for girls and boys differed in terms of the types of activities the children were doing and the types of toys and animals presented. How do these differential images fit in with gender stereotypes of females and males?

2. Do any of the study's findings suggest that one gender is more culturally valued than the other? Explain your answer.

3. When buying a birth congratulations card for a friend or relative, do you look for a gender-stereotypic or a nonstereotypic card? Why?

Source: Bridges (1993).

WHAT YOU CAN DO 2.1
Increase Girls' and Women's Awareness of the Effects of Media

1. Contact About-Face (about-face.org), whose mission is to equip girls and women with tools to understand and resist harmful media messages that affect self-esteem and body image.

2. Contact the Girls, Women + Media Project (mediaandwomen.org), which works to increase awareness of how media represent and affect girls and women.

After receiving information from either organization, make a presentation to a class, residence hall, sorority meeting, or Girl Scout troop.

GET INVOLVED 2.5
Are Both Women and Men Persons?

Ask two acquaintances of each gender to help you with this activity. Tell them you are studying people's choices about grammatical structure; that is, you are examining students' selections of specific words in a sentence. Therefore, you would like them to fill in the blank in each of the following:

1. Debra Cook won the raffle at the charity fund-raising event. The event organizers will send the prize to this _____ in two weeks.

    person   woman

2. Dave Sherman moved to a new town and went to the Town Hall to register to vote. The registrar of voters gave this _____ the application form.

    person   man

WHAT DOES IT MEAN?

Examine the selections made by your respondents.

1. Did they select different terms depending on the gender of the person?
2. Were there any differences between the answers of the females and males?

3. Did these answers correspond to the findings of Hamilton, as discussed in this chapter?
4. What interpretation can you offer for your findings?

_____

Source: Hamilton (1991).

REPRESENTATION OF GENDER IN THE ENGLISH LANGUAGE

The previous section demonstrated how communication via the mass media portrays different images of females and males. Now we examine the different ways females and males are depicted in the English language itself, and how this differential portrayal can shape conceptions of gender. *Language that unnecessarily differentiates between females and males or excludes and trivializes members of either sex* is called **sexist language**. Let's consider different types of sexist language.

Language Practices Based on the Assumption That Male Is Normative

Numerous language practices reflect the assumption that **male is normative**; that is, *male behaviors, roles, and experiences are the standards (i.e., norms) for society.* Integral to this perspective are the assumptions that males are more important than females and that female behaviors, roles, and experiences deviate from the norm (Fiske, 2010a; Holtgraves, 2010). One indication of these assumptions is that adults tend to think of males as persons, as standard or normative individuals in society. For example, Mykol Hamilton (1991) found that college students were more apt to describe typical persons as males than as females and to refer to a male as a *person* but a female as a *woman*. Try Get Involved 2.5 and see if your findings match those reported by Hamilton. Even animals, flowers, and inanimate objects tend to be conceived as male when their sex is unspecified (Lambdin et al., 2003).

Now let's examine some of the language practices that reflect this belief of male as normative.

MASCULINE GENERIC LANGUAGE.   Consider the following situation:

> At the first session of a training program called "Reducing Man's Addictions,"
> the program's director informed participants that they would be divided into small

groups for discussion of the material and that each group should appoint a chairman to facilitate its discussion. Also, the director indicated that at the end of the training program each participant would have sufficient knowledge so that he could work at a drug rehabilitation center.

Describe your image of this event. Does the program deal with addiction problems of both women and men or men only? Will the chairs of the groups be men or women? What is the gender of the participants? Are these gender images clear?

Now substitute *woman's* for *man's*, chairwoman for *chairman*, and *she* for *he*. Ask yourself the same questions.

Regardless of your own interpretations of these two verbal descriptions, note that the latter was written using gender-specific (i.e., female) terms whereas the former was written in **masculine generic language**, which is *language that uses male terms but purports to be inclusive of females and males*. Both male pronouns, such as *he* and *his*, and male nouns, such as *chairman, freshman, businessman, man-hours, and forefathers*, are used not only in reference to males but also as inclusive of both genders (reflecting the assumption that male is standard).

Are these masculine generic terms interpreted as gender neutral; that is, are they as likely to elicit images of females as males? Research suggests they are not. Rather, these terms tend to be exclusionary, connoting just what they directly indicate, that is, men and boys (DeFrancisco & Palczewski, 2007; Holtgraves, 2010; Miller & James, 2009). For example, in one study (Switzer, 1990), first- and seventh-grade children listened to the following story:

Pretend that [teacher's name] told you that a new student is coming to be a part of your class. Tomorrow will be _____ first day. Describe how you think _____ will feel on the first day. (p. 74)

Students heard the story with one of the following pronouns inserted in the blanks: *he, he or she*, or *they*. The results showed that *he* is not assumed to mean both females and males. Its exclusionary interpretation was demonstrated by the finding that 93 percent of the children who heard the *he* story, wrote that the student was a boy. On the other hand, when the pronouns were the inclusive *he or she* or *they*, the girls were more apt to write about a girl than a boy and the boys were more likely to write about a boy than a girl.

Given that male pronouns are evidently not gender neutral, it is not surprising that the use of male nouns as gender neutral similarly connotes male images. In one study (McConnell & Fazio, 1996), college students rated a *chairman* as more masculine than either a *chair* or a *chairperson*, suggesting that the former leads to more male-related mental imagery than the other two. Therefore, it is not surprising that the newer, gender-neutral terms, *chair* and *chairperson*, are more likely used in reference to women whereas the traditional term, *chairman*, is more often used to indicate a man (Romaine, 1999).

SPOTLIGHTING. Spotlighting refers to *the practice of emphasizing an individual's gender*, as in "*Female* professor receives prestigious grant" or, as in a headline about a spy who for decades had handed British atomic secrets to Russia, "Grandma led two lives" (Knightley, 1999). Consistent with the male as normative perspective, this practice of highlighting a woman's gender reinforces the notion that males are the standard (Bem, 2008). That is, although spotlighting does give recognition to specific females, it also conveys the message that these females are exceptions.

One investigation of gendered spotlighting examined televised broadcasts of the 1989 women's and men's National Collegiate Athletic Association final four basketball tournaments (Messner et al., 1993). The researchers observed spotlighting an average of 26 times per game during the women's tournament with commentary, such as ". . . is a legend in *women's* basketball" or "this NCAA *women's* semifinal is brought to you by . . ." (p. 125). However, there was no evidence of spotlighting during the men's games.

DIMINUTIVE SUFFIXES FOR FEMALE TERMS.   The English language sometimes differentiates genders by using a root word to designate a male and an added suffix to specify a female. This language feature, like others discussed in this section, is based on the assumption of the male as the standard. A suffix is needed to indicate the nonnormative exception, the female (Fiske, 2010a). Examples of this include *actor/actress* and *poet/poetess*. In fact, according to Suzanne Romaine (1999), the only English words where the female term is the root word with a male suffix added are *widower* and *bridegroom*. Why do these words have female roots? Perhaps the term *widower* reflects the fact that women generally outlive men and *bridegroom* might be based on the traditional expectation that women's roles are linked to marriage and the family. Romaine (1999) contends that this practice of marking the female with a suffix added to the male root is one way the English language signifies that a woman is a "lesser man" (p. 140).

Negative Terms for Females

Another language practice that reflects the differential treatment of females and males is the greater number of negative terms depicting women than men.

PARALLEL TERMS.   There are numerous pairs of words in the English language in which the objective meanings of the female and male terms are comparable, but the female word has a negative connotation. Consider, for example, *bachelor* and *spinster* or *old maid*. All three refer to unmarried persons, but the female terms connote an undesirable state reflecting rejection and old age. Another example is *master* versus *mistress*. Originally these referred to a man and woman in charge of a household, a usage that still pertains to *master*. *Mistress,* however, has developed a sexual connotation with negative overtones (DeFrancisco & Palczewski, 2007).

CHILDLIKE TERMS.   Have you ever heard the term *girl* in reference to an adult woman? Perhaps you have noted a male manager say something like the following to one of his associates: "I'll have my *girl* phone your *girl* to schedule a lunch meeting for us." Given that neither of the secretaries to whom he is referring is likely to be "a female child," the term *girl* is not appropriate. However, it is more common for people to refer to adult women as *girls* than to adult men as *boys* (DeFrancisco & Palczewski, 2007). For example, in the investigation (Messner et al., 1993) of televised commentary of women's and men's sports discussed earlier, the researchers found that, although the female athletes were not younger than their male counterparts, the broadcasters referred to female basketball and tennis players as *girls* but never called the male athletes *boys*.

Other childlike terms that are applied more to women than to men include *baby, babe,* and *sweetie*. Although these terms might be perceived as signs of affection in an intimate relationship, their use by nonintimates reflects the childlike quality of many terms used to identify women.

ANIMAL AND FOOD TERMS.   Researchers of the gender biases of language (e.g., Wood, 1994) point to the heavy use of animal names and food products in reference to women as another example of the negative depiction of females. Examples of these include the animal labels *fox, chick, bitch,* and *cow,* and the food-related terms *honey, cookie, dish,* and *feast for the eyes.*

SEXUALIZATION OF WOMEN.   As discussed earlier in this chapter, the media treat a woman's sexuality as an important aspect of her identity. American English also places a strong emphasis on a woman's sexuality. In one study (Grossman & Tucker, 1997), college students were asked to list all of the slang words they could think of for either a woman or a man. Although there was no difference in the number of terms associated with each gender, approximately 50 percent of the terms used for females were sexual (e.g., *slut*), whereas less than 25 percent of those used for males were. Furthermore, there are far more negative sexual terms for women than for men (DeFrancisco & Palczewski, 2007).

In Grossman and Tucker's study of slang, the terms used for women were more negative than those used for men. For example, among the most frequently listed terms were *bitch* and *slut* for women but *guy* and *dude* for men.

Significance of the Differential Treatment of Females and Males in Language

We have examined several indications that English depicts males as the societal standard and that many language conventions portray females in negative terms. Do these practices matter? According to Janet Swim and her colleagues (Swim et al., 2003, 2004), they certainly do. Sexist language reinforces and perpetuates gender stereotypes and status differences between women and men. Whether or not the speaker or writer intends harm, sexist language can have a negative effect on how girls and women perceive themselves (Enander, 2010).

The words of Jessica, a 25-year-old college senior, make this point vividly:

> *Using animal and food terms to refer to women is obviously degrading, and hazardous to a woman's self-esteem. If a woman hears herself being called a cow or bitch enough, she will believe that she is one. I didn't think it could happen if you were a strong person; I mean, I know I'm not a bitch, right? Wrong. After five years of hearing it from a significant other, I actually found myself calling myself these names aloud! It's powerful.*

Summary

STEREOTYPES OF FEMALES AND MALES

- Based on the tendency to sort others into gender categories, people assume that certain characteristics, behaviors, and roles are more representative of females and others of males. These are called gender stereotypes.
- Stereotypes vary according to the ethnicity of the person holding the stereotype and the age, ethnicity, social class, sexual orientation, and ableness of the target person.

- Stereotypes of women with disabilities differ from stereotypes of able-bodied women.
- According to social role theory, because people associate females with the domestic role and males with the employment role, female stereotypes tend to center on communion and male stereotypes on agency.
- Women who choose to be called "Ms." or who use a nontraditional name after marriage are perceived as more agentic and less communal than women who prefer conventional titles of address.

SEXISM

- Large numbers of women have experienced either minor or major sexist incidents.
- Several different forms of sexism have been proposed by scholars. Modern sexism is a subtle form of sexism, based on egalitarian values combined with underlying negative feelings toward women. Ambivalent sexism includes both hostile and benevolent attitudes.

REPRESENTATION OF GENDER IN THE MEDIA

- Females are underrepresented in the media.
- Certain groups of women are particularly underrepresented, including ethnic minority women, older women, and sexual minority women.
- The stigma of aging is greater for women than men. This double standard is based on society's emphasis on youthful physical beauty for women.
- Although the media do depict women in occupational roles, television features few women who successfully combine family and work roles.

- Similarly, various media present messages consistent with the importance of the domestic role for women and the provider role for men.
- Many forms of media portray males as more agentic than females and show females as being relationship oriented.
- Media images emphasize the importance to females of physical attractiveness and sexuality.
- The media both reinforce and contribute to stereotypes of gender.

REPRESENTATION OF GENDER IN THE ENGLISH LANGUAGE

- Numerous English language practices, including using the masculine generic, spotlighting, and diminutive suffixes for female terms, are based on the assumption that the male is normative.
- Other practices that deprecate women include the use of parallel terms, childlike terms, animal and food terms, and sexual terms.
- The differential treatment of females and males in language both reflects and helps shape gender images.

Key Terms

gender stereotypes 23	social role theory 28	benevolent sexism 31
communion 23	sexism 30	double standard of aging 35
agency 23	backlash effect 30	sexist language 42
ageism 26	modern sexism 31	male is normative 42
ableism 27	ambivalent sexism 31	masculine generic language 43
social categorization 27	hostile sexism 31	spotlighting 43

What Do You Think?

1. We have seen that women who use the title Ms. or who do not take their husbands' surnames after marriage are perceived as more agentic and less communal than women who use Miss or Mrs. or who take their husbands' names. One explanation for this is provided by social role theory. Can you think of any other possible explanations?

2. Consider the work by Glick and Fiske on ambivalent sexism.
   a. Do you agree that positive stereotypes of women can serve to maintain patriarchal roles and relationships? Why or why not?
   b. Do you believe that benevolent and hostile sexism are equally detrimental to women? Why or why not?

3. We have examined numerous sources of societal representations of gender, such as greeting cards, children's books, and television commercials. What other types of media might reflect gender stereotypes?

4. Which of the various language features that treat females and males differently do you think has the most detrimental effect on girls and women? Why?

5. Provide evidence, from the chapter or from your own experience, that language influences one's perceptions of gender.

If You Want to Learn More

Benshoff, H. M., & Griffin, S. (2009). *America on film: Representing race, class, gender, and sexuality at the movies* (2nd ed.). Malden, MA: Wiley-Blackwell.

Chittister, J. (2008). *The gift of years: Growing old gracefully.* New York: Bluebridge.

Cole, E., & Daniels, J. H. (2005). *Featuring females: Feminist analyses of media.* Washington, DC: American Psychological Association.

Cortese, A. J. (2008). *Provocateur: Images of women and minorities in advertising* (3rd ed.). Lanham, MD: Rowman & Littlefield.

DeFrancisco, V. P., & Palczewski, C. H. (2007). *Communicating gender diversity: A critical approach.* Newbury Park, CA: Sage.

Dines, G., & Humez, J. E. (Eds.). (2011). *Gender, race, and class in media: A critical reader* (3rd ed.). Thousand Oaks, CA: Sage

Douglas, S. J. (2010). *Enlightened sexism: The seductive message that feminism's work is done.* New York: Times Books.

Durham, M. G. (2008). *The Lolita effect: The media sexualization of young girls and what we can do about it.* New York: Overlook Press.

Hurd Clarke, L. (2011). *Facing age: Women growing older in an anti-aging culture.* Lanham, MD: Rowman & Littlefield.

Lamb, S. (2006). *Packaging girlhood: Rescuing our daughters from marketers' schemes.* New York: St. Martin's Press.

Levine, S. B. (2009). *Fifty is the new fifty: Ten life lessons for women in second adulthood.* New York: Penguin.

Lind, R. A. (2009). *Race/gender/media: Considering diversity across audiences, content, and producers* (2nd ed.). Boston, MA: Pearson.

Reichert, T. (Ed.). (2008). *Investigating the use of sex in media, promotion and advertising.* Binghamton, NY: Haworth Press.

Sunderland, J. (2011). *Language, gender, and children's fiction.* New York: Continuum International Publishing Group.

Zaslow, E. (2009). *Feminism, Inc.: Coming of age in girl power media culture.* New York: Palgrave Macmillan.

Websites

The Media

Media Watch
http://www.mediawatch.com

Representation of Gender in Language

Gender-Neutral Language
http://dir.yahoo.com/society_and_culture/gender/gender_neutral_language/

CHAPTER 3

Gender Self-Concept and Gender Attitudes

Developmental Processes and Individual Differences

Gender Self-Concept

Prenatal Development
  Stages of Prenatal Sex
    Differentiation
  Intersexuality

Theories of Gender Typing
  Psychoanalytic Theory
  Social Learning Theory
  Cognitive Developmental
    Theory
  Gender Schema Theory

Gender-Related Traits
  Changes in Gender-Related
    Traits Over Time
  Gender-Related Traits
    and Psychological
    Adjustment
  Evaluation of the Concept
    of Androgyny

Gender Attitudes
  Individual Differences
    in Gender-Related
    Attitudes
  Perceived Value of Female
    Versus Male Gender-
    Related Attributes

In 1965, soon after starting graduate school, Judith was discussing graduate student issues with her eight male classmates. During this conversation, much to her surprise and dismay, one of the men stated that she lacked femininity. When asked to explain, he said, "Judith is too highly achievement oriented to be feminine."

The comment by Judith's classmate suggests that, in his mind, people cannot combine female-stereotypic and male-stereotypic characteristics. Do you see problems with this type of thinking?

Now consider the lighthearted mockery of gender-expected behaviors shown by Judith's daughter and son-in-law during their wedding ceremony. On the one hand, the setting was traditional with the bride in a long white gown, the groom

in a tuxedo, and an entourage of bridesmaids and ushers. On the other hand, inconsistent with tradi-
tional expectations, at the end of a beautiful and serious service, the officiator concluded with "Now
you may kiss the groom!"

Do you know people who, like Judith's daughter and son-in-law, believe their behaviors should not be
dictated by their gender? Do you know others who see value in separate roles for women and men?

In this chapter, we focus on issues like these as we examine the integration of gender into one's
personal identity. After a brief look at the components of gender self-concept, we look at prenatal sex development and its influence on these gender concepts. Then we explore theoretical
perspectives of gender learning and conclude with an examination of variations among people in
their gender attitudes.

GENDER SELF-CONCEPT

One component of gender self-concept is **gender identity**: *one's self-definition as a female or male*
(Ryle, 2012). This identity generally develops between the ages of 2 and 3. Most individuals establish
a gender identity in accordance with their external reproductive organs. **Transgender individuals**,
however, do not. They have a *gender identity inconsistent with their reproductive organs*. They firmly
believe they were born with the body of the wrong sex and identify with the other sex (American
Psychological Association, 2009; Connell, 2010).

Despite the usual consistency between anatomy and gender identity, there are variations in the
degree to which people incorporate gender stereotypes into their own personalities and attitudes. As
we saw in Chapter 2, there are numerous commonly held expectations about the appropriate traits and
roles for females and males. However, these gender stereotypes reflect *beliefs* about individuals; they do
not tell what anyone is *actually* like. Although these stereotypes are descriptive of some people, they
are not representative of all. Instead, individuals differ in the extent to which their traits, behaviors,
interests, and roles conform to those expected for their gender. Moreover, they differ in their **gender
attitudes**, their *beliefs about the appropriate traits, interests, behaviors, and roles of females and males.*

Are various domains of an individual's gender self-concept associated with one another?
Although most people's gender identity is consistent with their anatomy, that does not imply a connection between gender identity and gender-related attributes. A person can feel that she is a female
but have masculine-typed traits, such as ambition and independence, or engage in occupations generally associated with men, such as construction worker or engineer. Furthermore, a person's gender-
related attributes are not linked to her or his **sexual orientation**. *Preference for a same- or other-gender
sexual partner* does not reflect the individual's gender-related traits, behaviors, interests, or roles
(Zucker, 2001).

PRENATAL DEVELOPMENT

Our journey toward understanding the development of a personal sense of gender begins with
an examination of **prenatal sex differentiation**, that is, *the biological processes that influence the
making of one's physical sex.* The first step in this complex set of processes is the joining of the sex
chromosomes in the fertilized egg, followed by several other events that collectively contribute
to the determination of sex (see Table 3.1). As you can see, biological sex is multidimensional;
it is defined by one's chromosomes, hormones, reproductive organs, and brain organization
(Roughgarden, 2009).

TABLE 3.1   Stages of Prenatal Sex Differentiation of Females and Males

Stages	Females	Males
1. Chromosomes	XX	XY
2. Gonads and hormones	Ovaries (estrogens)	Testes (androgens)
3. Internal reproductive organs	Uterus, fallopian tubes, and upper vagina	Vas deferens, seminal vesicles, and prostate
4. External genitalia	Clitoris, labia, and vaginal opening	Penis and scrotum
5. Brain differentiation	Female differentiation of the hypothalamus	Male differentiation of the hypothalamus

Stages of Prenatal Sex Differentiation

The stages of prenatal sex differentiation begin with the sex chromosomes, followed by the development of the gonads and hormones, internal reproductive organs, external genitalia, and differentiation of the brain. Let us examine each of these steps in greater detail.

CHROMOSOMES.   Sex differentiation begins with the combining of the sex chromosomes at conception. Normally individuals inherit 23 pairs of chromosomes from their parents. Twenty-two of these pairs contain genes that determine the general nature of the human species and the individual's specific characteristics (e.g., eye color), and one pair consists of the sex chromosomes, containing the genetic material that begins the process of sex differentiation. Genetic females have two X chromosomes, one received from each parent, and genetic males have one X chromosome received from their mother and one Y from their father (Blakemore et al., 2009).

GONADS AND HORMONES.   Until the sixth week of development there are no anatomical differences between XX and XY embryos. In fact, all embryos contain the same undifferentiated tissue that will later develop along sexual lines (Fine, 2010). However, during the sixth week, the Y chromosome in XY embryos directs the previously undifferentiated gonadal tissue to develop into testes, the male sex glands. In XX embryos, gonadal development begins at approximately the twelfth week after conception; the previously undifferentiated gonadal tissue develops into ovaries, the female sex glands. Evidence suggests that the X chromosome might direct this development (Tobach, 2001).

Once the gonads develop, the remaining process of sex differentiation is regulated by the sex hormones. Prenatal male differentiation requires the presence of the *male sex hormones*, collectively known as **androgens**. Until recently, it was believed that no gonadal hormones were necessary for female development and that differentiation of female sex organs would proceed in the absence of androgens. Now there is evidence that the *female sex hormones*, collectively known as **estrogens**, play a more active role in female development than previously believed (Jordan-Young, 2010).

INTERNAL REPRODUCTIVE ORGANS.   The female and male internal reproductive organs develop from the same previously undifferentiated tissue. Both XX and XY fetuses contain two sets of tissues, the Müllerian ducts and the Wolffian ducts. The **Müllerian ducts** are *the foundation for female structures.* The **Wolffian ducts** serve as *the basis for male internal reproductive structures.* In XX individuals, the Müllerian ducts differentiate into the uterus, fallopian tubes, and upper vagina and the Wolffian tissue degenerates. In XY development, two substances produced by the testes govern the process of developing male internal reproductive structures. **Testosterone**, *an androgen*, is needed to transform the Wolffian ducts into the male organs, including the vas deferens, seminal vesicles, and prostate; and the **Müllerian-inhibiting substance** is *necessary for the degeneration of the Müllerian ducts* (Eliot, 2009).

EXTERNAL GENITALIA. Similar to the development of the internal reproductive structures, the external structures develop from previously undifferentiated tissue present in both XX and XY individuals. In XX fetuses, estrogen differentiates this tissue as the clitoris, labia, and vaginal opening. In XY development, testosterone transforms the tissue into the penis and the scrotum (Blakemore et al., 2009).

BRAIN DIFFERENTIATION. Sex differences in the brain are less observable and more controversial than sex differences in reproductive organs. Experimentation on animals and studies of humans whose prenatal exposure to androgens was abnormal for their genetic sex shows that there is a critical period of time during which exposure to sex hormones can affect the hypothalamus and thus influence the threshold for subsequent behaviors. For example, in both animals and humans, this early exposure to androgens organizes the hypothalamus so that it becomes relatively insensitive to estrogen (Hines, 2010). The result is the elimination of the normal hormonal cyclical pattern associated with the menstrual cycle. We explore behavioral and sexual effects in humans in the next section, as we examine the outcomes of certain variations in prenatal sex differentiation.

Intersexuality

The pattern of sex differentiation just described is the typical one that characterizes the prenatal development of most individuals. However, several variations can occur, and an examination of these can help one understand the role of the chromosomes and hormones in gender identity and gender-related attributes.

    Intersexuality, *the intermingling of female and male sexual characteristics*, occurs in as many as 1.7 percent of births. In some cases, the baby has ambiguous genitalia that look like an enlarged clitoris or a mini-penis. In other cases, the external genitalia are at odds with the baby's gonads (Davidson, 2011b). In Western cultures, which recognize only two genders, the typical course of action has been early genital surgery, coupled with gender reassignment (Diamond, 2010). (See Explore Other Cultures 3.1 for a different view.) But genital surgery can lead to loss of fertility, reduced sexual functioning, urinary difficulties, and psychological problems, without providing the individual with any firmer sense of gender identity or increased quality of life (Golden, 2008; Minto et al., 2003). The Accord Alliance (formerly, the Intersex Society of North America), along with an increasing number of researchers, recommends that any surgery be postponed until adolescence, when the individual can make an informed choice (Diamond, 2010; Meem et al., 2010). Let us take a closer look at some of the varieties of intersexuality.

TURNER SYNDROME. **Turner syndrome** is *a condition in which the individual has a single X chromosome rather than a pair of sex chromosomes.* The missing chromosome could have been an X or a Y but is defective or lost. Because two chromosomes are necessary for the development of the gonads, the individual has neither ovaries nor testes. Externally, the genitalia are female and the individual is reared as a girl. Estrogen therapy at puberty enables girls with Turner syndrome to develop female secondary sex characteristics, such as breasts and pubic hair (Davenport, 2008; Eliot, 2009; Sybert & McCauley, 2004).

EXPLORE OTHER CULTURES 3.1
Multiple Genders

All societies recognize female and male genders and roles, although there is considerable cross-cultural variability in how these roles are expressed. The United States and virtually all Western nations formally recognize only two genders, and any variations from these are considered abnormal (Schilt & Westbrook, 2009). Recent efforts to be more flexible in recognizing additional gender categories (e.g., Fausto-Sterling, 2000; Girshick, 2008; Parker, 2007; Roughgarden, 2009) are highly controversial. A number of non-Western cultures, however, recognize third and fourth genders. These are women and men who do not fit typical gender identities and roles. Often, these individuals are considered spiritually enlightened by having an alternative gender, and they may be respected and accepted (American Psychological Association, 2009; Sellers, 2008). The Hijras of India are male-to-female transgender individuals, often castrated, who are viewed as a third gender embodying the spirits of both females and males. Frequently called upon to bless new babies, they dress as females, live in Hijra communities, and some maintain a monogamous relationship with a man (Borck, 2011; Meem et al., 2010; Nanda, 2011). In Indonesia, transvestites known as "waria"—a combination of the words for woman and man—have been welcomed for centuries as entertainers and beauticians (Perlez, 2003). Similarly, Polynesians recognize two-spirited people called "mahu," which means half-man, half-woman. These individuals include feminine men and masculine women, and they usually work in female-dominated occupations (Roughgarden, 2009). Many native North American societies recognize two-spirit individuals (Borck, 2011; Meem et al., 2010; Nanda, 2011). Biological female two-spirits typically were found west of the Rockies among the Apache, Cheyenne, Mohave, Navajo, Tlingit, and Zuni. The "manly hearted woman," for example, wore men's clothes, led war parties, and was completely accepted in that role. As native societies assimilated European beliefs, however, third- and fourth-gender roles often disappeared, changed, or came to be viewed negatively (Adams & Philips, 2009; Girshick, 2008; Roughgarden, 2009).

CONGENITAL ADRENAL HYPERPLASIA (CAH). **Congenital adrenal hyperplasia** is *an inherited disorder in which the adrenal glands of a genetic female malfunction and produce abnormally high levels of androgens* (Hines, 2010). Because this hormone is not produced until after the internal reproductive organs develop, these individuals have a uterus. However, the disorder causes either a partial or complete masculinization of the external genitals with the formation of an enlarged clitoris or a penis. Usually CAH is diagnosed at birth and the baby is reared as a girl, receiving some degree of surgical feminization of the genitals. Additionally, because this condition does not cease at birth, the individual generally needs hormonal therapy to prevent continued masculinization of her body (Hines, 2010).

ANDROGEN-INSENSITIVITY SYNDROME. The **androgen-insensitivity syndrome** is *an inherited disorder in which the body of a genetic male cannot utilize androgen* (Eliot, 2009; Garrett & Kirkman, 2009). Analogous to CAH, in which prenatal exposure to androgen masculinizes the external genitals of a genetic female, this inability of body tissue to respond to androgen feminizes the external genitals of a genetic male. Usually, the feminization of the external genitalia is complete and there is no suspicion that the baby is a genetic male. Similarly, the inability of the body to respond to androgen prevents the Wolffian ducts from differentiating into the internal male reproductive structures. However, because of the presence of the Müllerian-inhibiting substance, the Müllerian ducts do not develop into the internal female organs. Consequently, the individual has no internal reproductive organs.

5 ALPHA-REDUCTASE DEFICIENCY. The **5 alpha-reductase deficiency** is *an inherited condition in a genetic male that prevents the prenatal differentiation of the external genital tissue into a penis* (Brinkmann, 2009). In other ways, prenatal development follows a male blueprint; testes and male internal reproductive organs develop. At birth, these genetic males appear to be girls and are labeled as such. However, the surge of testosterone at puberty causes a belated masculinization of the external genitals and the development of male secondary sex characteristics, such as a deepening voice and facial hair. Thus, these genetic males, generally raised as girls, now develop the body of a male. In the Dominican Republic, where certain communities have a high frequency of the disorder, it is known as *guevedoces,* or "eggs (i.e., testicles) at twelve" (Jordan-Young, 2010).

DEVELOPMENT OF INTERSEXUALITY. The relative influence of prenatal and postnatal experiences on gender-related development has been the focus of considerable controversy. Studies of intersexuals have examined the role of prenatal hormones in the development of nonsexual gender-related attributes, gender identity, and sexual orientation, and have produced inconsistent findings. Some researchers contend that prenatal biological factors are highly influential, whereas others conclude that experiences after birth are more significant in shaping individuals' gender-related attributes.

First, let's examine the effects of prenatal hormones on gender-related interests and activities. On the one hand, higher levels of testosterone in pregnant women are related to more masculine-typed toy choices and activities in their young daughters (Hines, 2010). In addition, girls with CAH, who were exposed to androgens prenatally, show stronger-than-average preferences for boys' toys and activities and for boys as playmates (Hines, 2010; Jordan-Young, 2010). They report themselves to be more aggressive and less maternal. But most of the affected women are heterosexual, and their sexual identity and gender identity are almost always female (Hines, 2010).

Investigations on the effects of prenatal estrogen suggest that it might not be necessary for the development of female gender-related interests or role expectations. For example, girls with Turner syndrome, who lack prenatal estrogen, are similar to matched controls in their preferences for female playmates and female-style clothing, satisfaction with the female gender role, and interest in marriage and motherhood. Similarly, androgen-insensitive (XY) individuals raised as females tend to have female-related interests, although they too lack prenatal estrogen. Such individuals are generally romantically and sexually attracted to males. On tests of verbal and spatial skills, they also perform more like females than males (Lippa, 2005; Sybert & McCauley, 2004).

Turning to the development of gender identity, research similarly provides inconsistent findings. Some investigators have pointed to the importance of the gender of rearing, that is, experiences after birth, in gender identity (Zucker, 2008). Others, such as Milton Diamond (2009), contend that prenatal experiences predispose individuals toward a female or male identity. He further suggests that prenatal processes influence some intersexuals to switch from the gender of rearing to an identity with the other gender. One study, for example, examined genetic males with normal male hormones but who were born without a penis and subsequently underwent early sex-reassignment surgery and were raised as girls. Nearly half still developed male gender identity by adolescence (Reiner & Gearhart, 2004). Studies of individuals who have experienced the female-to-male body change caused by 5 alpha-reductase deficiency show similar results. In the Dominican Republic, 16 of 18 who were raised as girls elected to reverse their gender identity at puberty and become males (Imperato-McGinley, 2002). In New Guinea also, 13 out of 16 individuals with this condition changed their gender identity (Roughgarden, 2009).

Finally, studies of intersexual individuals have led some researchers to contend that sexual orientation has its origins in prenatal development. Melissa Hines (2010), for example, points to a slightly increased lesbian or bisexual orientation among women with CAH and suggests that prenatal exposure to androgen may serve as one influence on sexual orientation. However, based on their review of research on the topic, Amy Banks and Nanette Gartrell (1995) conclude that atypical prenatal hormone exposure is not related to increased same-gender sexual orientation.

What can researchers conclude about this controversial issue? Unfortunately, it is difficult to evaluate the relative contribution of biological and environmental factors because the relevant variables cannot be adequately controlled. For example, it is difficult to separate effects of the atypical exposure to prenatal hormones of CAH girls from the psychological and interpersonal reactions they might experience after birth. Both CAH girls and their parents are aware of these girls' masculinization, and this knowledge might serve as a powerful influence on the girls' gender-related self-concept and on their parents' treatment of them (Jordan-Young, 2010). At this time, the most accurate conclusion to be drawn appears to be that gender is both a biological and a social phenomenon. The challenge for researchers is to examine how biological processes interact with social influences from the earliest years onward (Best, 2010; Hines, 2010).

THEORIES OF GENDER TYPING

Now we turn to an exploration of the major theories that attempt to explain *the acquisition of the traits, behaviors, and roles that are generally associated with one's gender,* a process known as **gender typing**. Although these theories propose different processes involved in the learning of gender, only one (psychoanalytic theory) contends that the development of gender-related attributes is rooted in biological sex differences. The other perspectives share the assumption that gender traits, behaviors, and roles are socially constructed; that they develop from children's interactions with others; and that they are not inherent in humans' biology. Even psychoanalytic theory emphasizes the perceived significance of anatomical differences, rather than the effect of hormonal or other biological sex differences on gender development. For a summary of the major theories of gender typing, see Table 3.2.

Psychoanalytic Theory

Psychoanalytic theory, developed by Sigmund Freud (1925/1989), proposes that *gender typing stems from children's awareness of anatomical differences between females and males combined with their strong inborn sexual urges.* According to this theory, during the so-called phallic stage of development (between ages 3 and 6) two experiences occur that have dramatic consequences for gender typing. The first is the child's discovery of the anatomical differences between females and males and the second is the child's love for the parent of the other gender.

The boy's sexual attraction for his mother, known as the **Oedipus complex**, is accompanied by a belief that his father is a rival for his mother's affections. The boy's growing awareness of the anatomical differences between males and females leads him to assume that females have been castrated, and that he, too, will be castrated by his powerful rival, his father. *The boy's fear of castration by his father,* called **castration anxiety**, induces him to give up his Oedipal feelings for his mother and *form a close emotional bond with his father,* called **identification**. Through this identification process, the boy adopts his father's masculine behaviors and traits and incorporates his father's values into his superego (the moral component of personality), thus developing a strong sense of morality.

The phallic stage follows a different course for the little girl. Her discovery of the anatomical distinction between females and males does not resolve the Oedipus complex, as in boys, but rather

TABLE 3.2   Theories of Gender Typing

Theory	Major Theorist	Sources of Learning	Motive	Sequence of Events
Psychoanalytic theory	Sigmund Freud	Parents; emotional bond with same-sex parent is critical	Internal: reduce fear and anxiety; no reinforcement necessary	(Same-sex) parental attachment → identification (modeling) → gender identity
Social learning theory	Walter Mischel	Parents, larger social system provide models; child is relatively passive	External: reinforcements. Internal: Expected reinforcements. "I want rewards. I am rewarded for doing girl things. Therefore, I want to be a girl."	(Same-sex) parental attachment (due to rewards) → modeling (identification) → gender identity
Social cognitive theory	Albert Bandura	Parents, larger social system provide models; child is more active than in social learning theory in evaluating social standards; cognition plays a greater role	Similar to social learning theory	Similar to social learning theory
Cognitive developmental theory	Lawrence Kohlberg	Parents and larger social system interacting with child's cognitive system	Internal: desire for competence. "I am a girl. Therefore, I want to do girls things. Therefore, doing girl things is rewarding."	Gender identity → modeling (same-sex parent) → (same-sex) parental attachment
Gender schema theory	Sandra Bem	Parents and larger social system interacting with child's cognitive system. Society dictates that gender is an important schema, so child organizes information around this schema.	Similar to cognitive developmental theory	Because child learns that gender is an important schema, child develops gender identity. Sequence then proceeds as in cognitive developmental theory.

sets it in motion. Sometimes referred to as the Electra complex, the girl develops **penis envy**, *a desire to possess the male genitals*, and blames the mother for her "castrated" state. Her desire for a penis is replaced by a desire for a child and she turns to her father to fulfill that wish. Because the girl does not fear castration (having already been castrated), the chief motive for resolving the Oedipus complex is absent. Later, realizing that she will never possess her father, the girl gives up her Oedipal feelings, identifies with her mother, and begins to acquire her mother's feminine traits and behaviors. However, her superego development is weak because it is not driven by the powerful motivator of castration anxiety.

EVALUATION.   First, Freud's theory clearly is highly male-biased as shown by his use of the male term *phallic* to label the critical stage of gender development, his emphasis on the superiority of the male organ, and his assumption that females are doomed to feelings of inferiority because they lack a penis. For these reasons, psychoanalytic theory is not widely embraced by feminist scholars (Bem, 2008). Second, key psychoanalytic concepts, such as penis envy and castration anxiety, are conceptualized as unconscious; thus, they cannot be measured empirically. Third, Freud has been criticized for emphasizing the anatomical foundations of gender development to the virtual exclusion of societal influences. For Freud, gender is constructed from the presence or absence of a penis and not the societal value attached to males. Later, psychoanalytic thinkers placed greater emphasis on the psychological and sociocultural aspects of gender development. Others, including Karen Horney, Clara Thompson, Nancy Chodorow, Jessica Benjamin, and Ellen Kaschak, have proposed psychoanalytic views that minimize the masculine orientation of Freud's theory (Bell, 2004; Casey, 2002; Denmark et al., 2008).

Social Learning Theory

Whereas psychoanalytic theory envisions the growing child as driven by inborn desires, **social learning theory**, originally proposed by Walter Mischel (1966), views *gender development as influenced by the social environment.* Based on learning theory principles, this perspective proposes that *children acquire behaviors associated with their gender because those behaviors are more likely to be imitated and to be associated with positive reinforcement.*

OBSERVATIONAL LEARNING.   One mechanism through which gender-related behaviors are acquired is **observational learning** (also called imitation or modeling); that is, *the acquisition of behaviors by observing role models.* Children are continually exposed to both real-life and media models who engage in gender-stereotypic behaviors. Children are more likely to imitate same-sex than other-sex models, and this is especially true for boys (Hines, 2010). By observing these models, children learn which behaviors are considered appropriate for their gender. For example, 5-year-old Jenny sees her mother bake cookies and then pretends to bake in her play kitchen. And, because the nurses in her pediatrician's office are females, Jenny believes that only women can be nurses. Jenny also learns that it is important for women to be pretty because she sees women on television who are often concerned about their appearance.

REINFORCEMENT AND PUNISHMENT.   Social learning theory maintains that even though children may initially engage in both cross-gender and same-gender imitation, they are increasingly likely to perform gender-appropriate behaviors. The mechanisms that explain this phenomenon are reinforcement and punishment. If people expect a positive reinforcement (reward) for performing the behavior, children will likely engage in that behavior. Similarly, if children anticipate a negative consequence (punishment), they are not likely to perform that act. Thus, children learn, both through observing the consequences to models and through the consequences of their own behaviors, that girls are more likely to be rewarded for certain actions and boys for others. A girl playing "dress-up" might be praised for her beauty as she parades around wearing her mother's old dress and high heels. If her brother wears the same outfit, however, his parents might scold or ridicule him.

COGNITION. A modification of social learning theory, known as **social cognitive theory**, states that *observational learning and rewards and punishments following behavior alone cannot account for gender typing; thought processes (cognitions) also play a role.* As children develop, they not only receive rewards and punishments from others but also begin to internalize standards about appropriate gender-related behavior (Bussey & Bandura, 2004; Olson & Dweck, 2008). Thus, children initially engage in gender-appropriate behaviors because they anticipate rewards from others. Later, their internalized standards about gender-related behavior motivate them to engage in gender-appropriate activities in order to gain self-satisfaction and avoid self-censure. Thus, Pablo might refuse to play with his sister's dolls because doing so would violate his personal standard of appropriate behavior for boys.

EVALUATION. Unlike psychoanalytic theory, the concepts of the social learning perspective are clear and observable. Numerous studies that have examined the theory's assumptions have provided support for some aspects of the theory and are inconclusive about others.

One assumption of social learning theory is that girls and boys receive encouragement and reinforcement for different behaviors. In support of this perspective, studies show that parents do treat their daughters and sons differently in regard to some behaviors. For example, parents buy their daughters and sons different types of toys, encourage different play activities, and assign them different chores (see Chapter 4).

According to social learning theory, the other process in gender typing is observational learning. Although children do imitate same-gender role models, observational learning is not restricted to the behaviors of individuals of the same gender as the child (Martin et al., 2002). Other characteristics, such as a model's power, can influence the selection of role models.

Cognitive Developmental Theory

Cognitive developmental theory, originally formulated by Lawrence Kohlberg (1966), contends that *children are neither pushed by their biological desires nor pulled by external rewards and punishments. Instead, children are active learners, attempting to make sense of the social environment.* They actively search for patterns and rules that govern the functioning of females and males and then follow these in an attempt to best adapt to social demands.

By approximately 3 years of age, children can correctly label their own gender (that is, they have gender identity). However, they do not yet know that gender is unchangeable, that neither time nor behavioral and appearance modifications can alter one's gender. For example, Kohlberg (1966) reported that most 4-year-olds believe that a girl if wanted to could become a boy, if she engaged in boy-related activities or if she wore a boy's clothes.

This is because the young child relies on superficial physical characteristics, such as clothing or hair length to determine gender. Preschool children do not recognize that changes in an object's visible characteristics do not necessarily alter its fundamental nature.

Cognitive developmental theory contends that gender typing cannot take place until children develop the concept of **gender constancy**, *the belief that gender is permanent regardless of changes in age, behavior, or appearance.* Once children acquire that understanding, between the ages of 4 and 7, they seek out information about which behaviors are gender-appropriate and which are not. To learn which behaviors are performed by females and which are performed by males, children actively observe parents and other role models. Then they engage in the gender-appropriate behaviors because behaving in a gender-consistent manner is, in itself, rewarding.

Cognitive developmental theory argues that rewards for gender-consistent behavior merely inform the child what is gender appropriate but do not serve to strengthen those behaviors, as in the social learning theory view. Rather, children engage in these behaviors because acting in a gender-consistent manner is, in itself, rewarding. Let's look at an example to clarify the distinction. Six-year-old Caitlin has been praised for helping her mother cook dinner. According to social learning theory, she then wants to cook again because she anticipates positive reinforcement from others (and possibly from herself) for cooking. Attaining gender constancy is not necessary, because her desire to cook stems from her expectation of reward, not because cooking is defined as a female activity. According to cognitive developmental theory, however, the praise given to Caitlin serves as information that cooking is a female activity. If she has attained gender constancy, she now wants to cook because behaving in a gender-consistent manner is, in itself, rewarding.

EVALUATION.   The concepts of cognitive developmental theory, like those of social learning theory, are clearly defined and easily measured and have generated considerable research. One key assumption of this perspective is that gender typing depends on an awareness of the unchangeability of gender. This assumption has received mixed support (Ruble et al., 2007). Studies have shown that gender constancy precedes some, but not all, aspects of gender development (Galambos et al., 2009).

A second assumption of cognitive developmental theory, that children value same-gender activities once they attain gender constancy, receives considerable support. Numerous studies show that children value their own gender more highly than they value the other gender (e.g., Powlishta, 2001).

A major criticism of cognitive developmental theory is that it does not specify why children use gender as a classifying concept. Kohlberg (1966) asserts that children want to adhere to social rules in order to master the social environment, but his theory does not explain why these rules are structured around gender rather than other attributes such as race or eye color.

Gender Schema Theory

Gender schema theory, proposed by Sandra Bem (1993), incorporates elements of cognitive developmental and social learning theories. Like the first, it proposes that *children develop an interrelated set of ideas, or schema, about gender that guides their social perceptions and actions.* However, unlike cognitive developmental theory, gender schema theory postulates that the use of gender as an organizing principle does not naturally stem from the minds of children. Similar to social learning theory, it assumes that *gender schema development stems from learning the gender norms and practices of society.*

The theory proposes that children form notions of the traits and roles associated with females and males on the basis of societal expectations. They then use this information to regulate their own behavior, and their self-esteem becomes contingent on their adherence to these gender schemas.

A significant difference between gender schema and cognitive developmental theories lies in the basis for gender schema development. Whereas Kohlberg (1966) assumes that the development of cognitive conceptualizations about gender is a natural process, Bem contends that children use gender to process social information because societal norms and practices emphasize its importance. Thus, children do not organize the social environment on the basis of physical attributes, such as handedness or hair color, because society does not give these characteristics the same significance it applies to gender. Bem argues that children cannot avoid noticing that different toys, activities, jobs, and chores are deemed acceptable for girls and boys by their parents, peers, and teachers. Elementary school teachers do not line up children separately by race because they do not want to emphasize race as a distinguishing characteristic. They often, however, group children by sex, thus increasing its perceived importance as a distinguishing characteristic. Indeed when preschool teachers make gender salient by doing such things as lining up children by gender and using gender-specific language (e.g., "I need a girl to hand out the markers"), children show increased gender stereotypes and decreased play with other-sex peers (Hilliard & Liben, 2010).

Bem (1998) claims that individuals vary in the degree to which they use gender schemas to understand and evaluate others and to guide their own behavior. According to Bem, people who have strong gender schemas consider a narrower range of activities as acceptable for individuals of each gender, including themselves. For example, boys have more powerful gender schemas than girls (Gelman et al., 2004). This finding is consistent with research showing that boys are more likely than girls to maintain gender boundaries (Blakemore et al., 2009).

Even within a given sex, some individuals have stronger, less flexible gender schemas than do others, perhaps due to individual differences in exposure to gender as an organizing characteristic. Consequently, Bem (1998) proposes several strategies parents can use to minimize the development of gender schemas and thus reduce the development of gender-stereotypic attitudes and behavior. Read What You Can Do 3.1 and share Bem's ideas with others.

EVALUATION.   One strength of gender schema theory is that, unlike cognitive developmental theory, it explains why children structure their social perceptions around gender rather than other attributes. In addition, considerable research supports the theory (Casey, 2002; Martin & Dinella, 2001). For example, one of the theory's assumptions is that gender schemas help individuals organize memories, thus facilitating the recollection of gender-consistent information. Consistent with this view, individuals remember material consistent with their own gender better than they remember material consistent with the other gender (Ganske & Hebl, 2001; Martin et al., 2002; Susskind, 2003). For example, when adults were asked to recall items that had been in a room, women were better able to remember female-related items, such as a makeup kit, a cookbook, and a purse, whereas men were better at recalling male-related objects, including aftershave, a sports video, and a necktie (Cherney & Ryalls, 1999).

WHAT YOU CAN DO 3.1
Ways to Minimize Gender Schemas in Children

1. Eliminate gender stereotyping from your behavior. For example, share household duties instead of dividing them along gender lines.
2. Eliminate gender stereotyping from the choices you give your children. Offer toys, activities, and clothing associated with both females and males.
3. Define *femaleness* and *maleness* along anatomical and reproductive lines only, thus reducing your children's tendency to organize the social world according to gender. The following anecdote from Bem about her 4-year-old son Jeremy illustrates the limitations of a cultural definition of gender and the greater flexibility of a biological definition:

One day Jeremy decided to wear barrettes to school. Another little boy told Jeremy that he must be a girl because "only girls wear barrettes." After explaining to this child that "wearing barrettes doesn't matter" and that "being a boy means having a penis and testicles," Jeremy finally pulled down his pants to make his point more vividly. The other child was not impressed. He simply said, "Everybody has a penis; only girls wear barrettes." (1998, p. 109)

Source: Bem (1998).

GENDER-RELATED TRAITS

We have explored a variety of theories that explain gender typing. Now let's examine variations in individuals' conformity to stereotyped expectations about their gender.

The most commonly measured variation has been in the gender-related traits individuals ascribe to themselves, that is, in their personal identification with female-related and male-related characteristics. Historically, these two sets of traits were viewed as bipolar, that is, as opposite extremes of a single continuum. In the chapter opening vignette, Judith's classmate believed she could not be both feminine and achievement oriented, reflecting the bipolar view that a person cannot have characteristics stereotypically associated with both females and males.

In the 1970s, there was a change in this characterization of female-related and male-related traits. Psychologists began to conceptualize the two dimensions as independent, rather than opposite, of one another. Unlike a bipolar dimension, such as tall–short, in which it is impossible to be described by both traits, the new perspective posited that individuals can exhibit any combination of female-stereotypic and male-stereotypic characteristics. That is, a high degree of one does not imply a low degree of the other.

In 1974, Sandra Bem proposed that femininity and masculinity should be assessed independently and developed the Bem Sex Role Inventory (BSRI) to accomplish that goal. The BSRI includes one set of traits viewed as more desirable for females than for males and another set of items seen as more desirable for males than for females. Soon after, Janet Spence and Robert Helmreich (1978) developed and published the Personal Attributes Questionnaire (PAQ), which also has two separate dimensions to measure gender-related personality characteristics. On both instruments, the female-related scale comprises communal traits and the male-related scale reflects agentic traits (see Chapter 2); however, when used as measures of gender-related trait identification, they have typically been labeled either "femininity" and "masculinity" or "expressiveness" and "instrumentality."

The BSRI and the PAQ evaluate femininity/expressiveness and masculinity/instrumentality as independent dimensions. Respondents receive a score on each dimension, and the combination of the two indicates which of four categories best describes their gender-related traits. These categories are (1) **femininity**, *a high score on the femininity/expressiveness scale and a low score on the scale for masculinity/instrumentality;* (2) **masculinity**, *a high score on the masculinity/instrumentality scale and a low score on the femininity/expressiveness scale;* (3) **androgyny** (derived from the ancient Greek words for male—*andro*—and female—*gyn*), *high scores on both scales;* and (4) **undifferentiation**, *low scores on both scales.* Any individual, regardless of gender, can be characterized by any of these categories.

To assess your own gender-related traits, try Get Involved 3.1.

Changes in Gender-Related Traits Over Time

College women and high school girls' . . . assertiveness . . . increased from 1931 to 1945, decreased from 1946 to 1967 and increased from 1968 to 1993. . . . Why did women's assertiveness scores switch twice over the century?

(Twenge, 2001, pp. 133, 141)

In the 1970s, studies showed that more female than male college students scored high on femininity, whereas more males than females scored high on masculinity and approximately one-third of both genders were androgynous (e.g., Spence & Helmreich, 1978). To determine whether there has been any change over time, Jean Twenge (1997b) performed a meta-analysis of femininity and masculinity scores based on samples from over 50 different college campuses since the 1970s. Interestingly, the most notable change found by Twenge was the dramatic increase in masculinity scores of women. Also, there was a significant increase in androgyny among women

GET INVOLVED 3.1
What Are Your Gender-Related Traits?

The following is a partial set of characteristics from the PAQ. For each item, choose the letter that best describes where you fall on the scale. Choose A if you feel the characteristic on the left strongly describes you, and choose E if the trait on the right is strongly descriptive of you. Choose C if you are in the middle, and so on. Also, ask a friend to rate you on these characteristics.

1. Not at all independent	A B C D E	Very independent
2. Not at all emotional	A B C D E	Very emotional
3. Very rough	A B C D E	Very gentle
4. Not at all competitive	A B C D E	Very competitive
5. Not at all helpful to others	A B C D E	Very helpful to others
6. Not at all kind	A B C D E	Very kind
7. Not at all self-confident	A B C D E	Very self-confident
8. Gives up very easily	A B C D E	Never gives up easily
9. Not at all understanding of others	A B C D E	Very understanding of others
10. Goes to pieces under pressure	A B C D E	Stands up well under pressure

WHAT DOES IT MEAN?

To score yourself, give 0 points for a response of **A**, 1 point for **B**, and so on. Then add up your points for items 2, 3, 5, 6, and 9; this comprises your femininity/expressiveness score. Similarly, sum your points for items 1, 4, 7, 8, and 10; this comprises your masculinity/instrumentality score. Use the same procedure to score your friend's ratings of you.

1. Are your two scores similar to each other or is one much higher than the other? Does your pattern of scores reflect the gender-related trait category you think best describes you? Why or why not?

2. Is your pattern of scores similar to the pattern based on your friend's ratings? If not,

describe the differences. Also, explain why your friend views your gender-related traits differently than the way you perceive them.

3. Although the PAQ is widely used today, it was based on 1970s' perceptions of traits more typical of either females or males. Are there any characteristics presented here that no longer seem to be more representative of one gender than the other? Which ones?

_____

Source: From _Masculinity and femininity: Their psychological dimensions, correlates, and antecedents_ by Janet T. Spence and Robert L. Helmreich. Copyright © 1978. By permission of the University of Texas Press.

and a weaker increase among men. Other research (Harper & Schoeman, 2003; Spence & Buckner, 2000; Twenge, 2001) has found that women and men no longer differ on a number of items long considered to be masculine. These include being active, independent, self-reliant, ambitious, assertive, acting as a leader, and defending one's beliefs. When compared to their own mothers, today's college women show more masculine-typed and less feminine-typed behaviors (Guastello & Guastello, 2003).

Jean Twenge, Janet Spence, and Camille Buckner suggest that these changes in gender-related traits may be accounted for by societal changes that have occurred in recent years. Girls have been encouraged to become more assertive, to stand up for their rights, to be independent, and to have high occupational goals. They have been given more opportunities to develop their agentic skills, especially in the educational, vocational, and sports arenas.

Similarly, women were expected to be self-sufficient during the Great Depression and World War II, in the early-to-middle years of the twentieth century, whereas passive domesticity was encouraged in the 1950s and early 1960s. These shifts in women's status and roles closely parallel the changes in women's assertiveness over the course of the century (Twenge, 2001).

Thus, today's young women are more likely than their counterparts in the 1970s to have witnessed or experienced roles that involve male-stereotypic characteristics. This could have contributed to the development of their greater masculinity and, in turn, their greater androgyny. So, consistent with the view that gender is socially constructed, changes in women's personal sense of gender seem to be related to their social experiences.

Gender-Related Traits and Psychological Adjustment

Once psychologists started to conceptualize gender-related traits as being more complex than a single dimension of femininity–masculinity, they began to examine the psychological well-being of individuals who varied in their pattern of gender-stereotypic traits. For example, Bem (1975) hypothesized that because androgynous individuals are comfortable engaging in both feminine and masculine behaviors, they can adapt more adequately to various situational demands and should report greater well-being than nonandrogynous individuals. Research shows, however, that it is high masculinity, and not the specific combination of high masculinity and high femininity, that is strongly related to well-being and self-esteem (Lefkowitz & Zeldow, 2006; Moore, 2007; Russo & Tartaro, 2008). Predictably, it is the positive aspects of masculinity (e.g., independence, mastery), not its negative components (e.g., aggressiveness, selfishness), that are linked with psychological health (Woodhill & Samuels, 2003).

What can explain the positive relationship between masculinity and psychological adjustment? As we saw in Chapter 2, masculine-typed traits are more highly valued in North America than feminine-typed traits. Therefore, people with masculine-typed traits perhaps feel better about their ability to function effectively. Derek Grimmell and Gary Stern (1992) found support for this explanation when they compared college students' BSRI self-ratings, their BSRI ratings of the ideal person, and their psychological well-being. The higher students' own masculinity was in relation to their perception of ideal masculinity, the higher their own self-esteem and the lower their anxiety and depression. Thus, it appears that the degree to which individuals feel they possess highly valued masculine traits is a good predictor of their psychological adjustment.

However, before we conclude that androgyny is not related to psychological well-being, let's consider a different conceptualization of androgyny. See Learn About the Research 3.1 for another approach to androgyny measurement and its psychological benefits.

Evaluation of the Concept of Androgyny

When the psychological measurement of androgyny was introduced in the 1970s, it was received enthusiastically by feminist scholars. It replaced the notion that psychological health required that females be feminine and males be masculine. By embodying socially desirable traits for both females and males, androgyny seemed to imply the absence of gender stereotyping. Furthermore, by incorporating both feminine and masculine behaviors, it appeared to broaden the scope of behaviors that can be used to handle different situations and, thus, lead to more flexible and adaptive behaviors.

Although androgyny continues to be viewed by feminist scholars as more positive than restrictions to either femininity or masculinity, several feminist criticisms have been leveled against this concept. One is that the notion of androgyny, similar to the bipolar differentiation of femininity–masculinity, is based on the division of gender into female-stereotypic and male-stereotypic

> ## LEARN ABOUT THE RESEARCH 3.1
> ### A Real-Life Approach to Androgyny
>
> We have seen that masculinity, and not the coexistence of masculinity and femininity, best predicts psychological adjustment. Jayne Stake, however, argues that the psychological benefits of androgyny are best demonstrated when communal and agentic behaviors are given in response to expectations demanded by specific life situations.
>
> Stake focused on individuals' responses to job demands that required both communal and agentic behaviors. She wondered if people who use both types of behaviors in these situations experience benefits compared to those who rely on one type or neither type. To study this, undergraduate students were individually asked to describe a work situation in which they were expected to behave with both "sensitivity and caring" (e.g., "Be sensitive to the needs of others," "Show others you care about them") and "mastery and independence" (e.g., "Always show that
>
> you can handle things on your own—without the help of others," "Show you have technical know-how"). Then they were asked to describe the behaviors they used to cope with these dual expectations. These coping strategies were coded into one of the four categories generally used to classify gender-related traits. Students also indicated to what extent their well-being was affected by work situations that expected both types of behaviors.
>
> The results showed that individuals who used androgynous responses to dual expectations in job situations experienced more rewards and fewer negative outcomes than those using other types of strategies. Thus, examining gender-related attributes as behavioral responses to specific situations and not just as general personality traits may be a fruitful approach to understanding the beneficial effects of various gender-related orientations.
>
> ### WHAT DOES IT MEAN?
>
> 1. Stake examined expectations for communal and agentic behaviors in the workplace. What other situations might make simultaneous demands?
> 2. Identify a job experience you had where both types of demands were made. Describe
>
> how you handled it and how you felt in this situation. Was your experience consistent with the results reported here?
>
> _____
>
> *Source:* Stake (1997).

characteristics (Bem, 1993; Hoffman & Youngblade, 2001). Rather than making traits *gender neutral*, androgyny involves the combination of *gender-specific* orientations. A second concern is that androgyny might be erecting unrealistic goals for individuals—the requirement that people be competent in both the communal and agentic domains. Third, according to Bem (1993), the concept of androgyny does not deal with masculinity and femininity in their unequal cultural context. It neither acknowledges nor attempts to eliminate the greater cultural value placed on male activities. Last, Bem is concerned that androgyny will not lead to the elimination of gender inequality, a goal that requires *societal* rather than *personal* change. That is, the mere existence of individuals with both feminine and masculine traits does not alter the patriarchal power structure in society.

GENDER ATTITUDES

Let's turn now to an examination of variations in gender attitudes. People differ in the degree to which they believe that gender should dictate females' and males' roles. Some individuals hold a **traditional gender attitude**, *the belief that females should engage in communal behaviors and roles and males should engage in agentic behaviors and roles.* They might believe, for example, that women

GET INVOLVED 3.2
What Are Your Gender Attitudes?

On a scale from 1 (strongly agree) to 7 (strongly disagree), indicate the degree to which you agree or disagree with each of the following statements:

1. The husband should be the head of the family.
2. Keeping track of a child's out-of-school activities should be mostly the mother's responsibility.
3. Home economics courses should be as acceptable for male students as for female students.

4. A person should generally be more polite to a woman than to a man.
5. It is more appropriate for a mother rather than a father to change their baby's diaper.
6. It is wrong for a man to enter a traditionally female career.
7. Things work out best in a marriage if a husband leaves his hands off domestic tasks.
8. Women can handle pressures from their jobs as well as men can.
9. Choice of college is not as important for women as for men.

WHAT DOES IT MEAN?

Before computing your score, reverse the points for statements 3 and 8. That is, if you answered "1" (strongly agree) to these two questions, give yourself 7 points, if you answered "2," give yourself 6 points, and so on. Then sum the points for the 9 items. Note that higher scores reflect more nontraditional or egalitarian gender attitudes.

1. These statements come from the Sex-Role Egalitarianism Scale, developed in the 1980s. Are there questions that you think are no longer adequate measures of egalitarian gender beliefs? If yes, explain.
2. Look at your answers to Get Involved 3.1. Is there any consistency in the extent to which you describe yourself as communal and/or agentic and your beliefs about appropriate gender-related behaviors and roles? For

example, if you received high scores on both communion and agency, reflecting an androgynous identity, did your answers to the questions in this activity indicate egalitarian beliefs? Explain why a person's gender-related traits might not be associated with her or his gender attitudes.

3. If most North Americans were to endorse egalitarian gender beliefs, what positive outcomes might be experienced by women and girls? By men and boys? Would there be any negative consequences for either gender? Explain.

Source: From the Sex-Role Egalitarianism Scale, by King & King (1990). Reproduced by permission of Sigma Assessment Systems, Inc.

should be the primary rearers of children whereas men should be the primary financial providers or that women are better suited than men to nursing whereas men are better suited than women to corporate management. Others adhere to a **nontraditional or egalitarian gender attitude**, *the belief that behaviors and roles should not be gender specific.* To get more familiar with the meaning of gender attitudes, take the test in Get Involved 3.2.

The Sex-Role Egalitarianism Scale (King & King, 1990), shown in part in Get Involved 3.2, illustrates the multidimensional nature of gender attitudes. This scale comprises beliefs about appropriate roles within five life domains: marital, parental, employment, social–interpersonal, and educational. There is considerable evidence that gender attitudes are not uniform across these dimensions. Instead, individuals in Western industrialized nations tend to have less traditional beliefs about women's employment roles than they do about women's combined family and work roles

EXPLORE OTHER CULTURES 3.2
Gender Attitudes in Global Context

Deborah Best and her colleagues (Best, 2001; Best & Thomas, 2004) have conducted studies of the gender attitudes of university students in 14 different countries. Their research indicates that gender attitudes range from traditional to more egalitarian both across and within cultures. For example, the most egalitarian attitudes were found in northern European countries (England, Finland, Germany, the Netherlands). The United States was in the middle of the distribution, and the most traditional attitudes were found in Africa and in Asian countries (India, Japan, Malaysia, Nigeria, Pakistan). Other studies have found that Muslim nations in the Middle East and North Africa are the least likely of all nations to endorse gender equality (Norris & Inglehart, 2004). Across countries, women hold more egalitarian views than men. Within a given country, however, the gender attitudes of women and men correspond highly (Best & Thomas, 2004; Olson et al., 2007). Now go back to Chapter 2, and compare these results with those of Glick and Fiske (2000) on hostile and benevolent sexism across cultures.

(Anderson & Johnson, 2003; Treas & Widmer, 2000). For example, Judith Treas and Eric Widmer (2000) found that individuals in 23 developed nations overwhelmingly supported full-time employment for married women with no children. Mothers of preschoolers, however, were expected to stay home or work only part time. For a look at gender-role attitudes in other countries, read Explore Other Cultures 3.2.

Individual Differences in Gender-Related Attitudes

As we have seen, gender attitudes can vary from traditional to egalitarian. What demographic and personality characteristics are related to differences in gender attitudes?

GENDER.   Not surprisingly, one characteristic is gender. Dozens of studies using mostly samples of Whites have shown that males have more traditional beliefs about the appropriate roles for women than females (Corrigal & Konrad, 2007; de Valk, 2008; Levant et al., 2007; Nierman et al., 2007; Riggio & Desrochers, 2005). Similarly, Black men (Kane, 2000) and Asian men (Anderson & Johnson, 2003; Ui & Matsui, 2008) hold more traditional gender-role attitudes than their female counterparts.

ETHNICITY.   Another demographic characteristic that is related to gender attitudes is ethnicity. As we saw in Chapter 2, Black women are less likely than White or Latina women to adhere to gender stereotypes. Correspondingly their attitudes about gender-related behaviors and roles also are less traditional. For example, Black women hold more egalitarian views about women's employment and political roles than White women do (Davis & Greenstein, 2009; Harris & Firestone, 1998). Also, Black college women, compared to White college women, perceive less conflict in the combination of the provider and domestic roles (e.g., Bridges & Etaugh, 1996), a difference possibly due to Black women's longer history of combining work and family roles.

What about gender attitudes of Latinas? Traditionally, Latina/o families have been characterized as patriarchal, with a dominant, powerful husband/father and a submissive, self-sacrificing wife/mother. Thus, it is not surprising that Latina women have been found to hold more traditional views about women's employment and political roles than either Black or White women (Davis & Greenstein, 2009; Harris & Firestone, 1998). However, the views held by Latina women have become less traditional over time. For example, Donna Castañeda (1996) notes that second- and third-generation Latinas/os are less likely than first-generation women and men to believe that the husband should be the sole provider and decision maker within the family and that females should do all of the housework and obey the husband's/father's demands. Thus, the degree of acculturation of Latina women and Latino men seems to be strongly related to their gender attitudes.

Research on Native Americans has focused on their actual gender-related behaviors and roles rather than on their attitudes and has shown great variations over time and across tribal groups. According to scholars such as Devon Mihesuah (2004) and Stephanie Sellers (2008), women's behaviors and roles in traditional Native American life included caregiving, spiritual continuation of their people, and transmission of cultural knowledge. Many Native American societies were characterized by complementary but equally powerful roles for some women and men whereas other groups institutionalized alternative female roles. For example, within several Plains tribes, women's roles included masculine ones, such as the "warrior woman" and the "manly-hearted woman" (aggressive and independent) in addition to the traditional role of the hard working wife. Other tribes, such as the Hopi, Iroquois, Navajo, Pawnee, and Seminole, were matrilineal; women owned the material goods and passed these on to their daughters and sisters and played important economic, political, and spiritual roles (Sellers, 2008; Smith, 2007; Weaver, 2009).

Scholars contend that colonization by Europeans and the increasing acculturation of Native Americans into the dominant White culture have contributed to a breakdown in complementary female–male roles and to an increase in male dominance and the subjugation of women in several Native American societies (Sellers, 2008; Weaver, 2009). However, in many tribes, women continue to have considerable political power because of their traditional roles of caretakers for the community and transmitters of the culture. Today, women increasingly are assuming positions of tribal leadership. For example, women head over 20 percent of tribal governments in California, the state with the highest Native population ("Woman Named Mohegan Tribal Chief," 2010). Two of the most influential recent female tribal leaders are Wilma Mankiller and Lynn Malerba. Mankiller, who died in 2010, was elected and served as the first woman principal chief of the Cherokee Nation, leading her people to increased economic independence and cultural renewal (Plec, 2011). Malerba was selected in 2010 as chief of the Mohegans, one of the best known and most prosperous Native American Nations ("Woman Named Mohegan Tribal Chief," 2010). In order to learn more directly about the gender attitudes of women of different ethnicities, perform the interviews described in Get Involved 3.3.

OTHER FACTORS.   Gender attitudes are also related to religious factors. Among college students, Jews tend to have the least traditional gender beliefs and conservative Protestants the most, with mainline Protestants and Catholics somewhere in between (Davis & Greenstein, 2009; Harville & Rienzi, 2000). Moreover, the more strongly individuals embrace religion in their lives, the more traditional their gender attitudes are (Bang et al., 2005; Brewster & Padavic, 2002; Cunningham, 2008).

Other demographic characteristics related to gender attitudes are social class, political ideology, age, year in college, academic performance, and college major. Specifically, nontraditional views about gender tend to be associated with attaining higher social and educational level (Brewster & Padavic, 2002), having liberal political views (Apparala et al., 2003; Cichy et al., 2007), being a younger adult (Apparala et al., 2003; Cunningham, 2008), being a senior in college as opposed to a first-year student (Bryant, 2003), having a high GPA (Bryant, 2003), and, for women, majoring in a male-dominated field (Karpiak et al., 2007).

GET INVOLVED 3.3
Ethnic Variations in Gender Attitudes

Interview two college women of approximately the same age (i.e., both traditional-age students or both older adults) from each of two different ethnic groups. Ask the following questions:

1. Do you think there should be different roles for women and men in the family? In dating relationships? In the workplace? If your respondent answered "yes" to any of these, ask her to be specific.

2. How important is your future/current career to your personal identity?
3. Do you plan to marry and have children? If yes, do you anticipate any difficulty balancing your family and work roles?
4. Who do you think should be the primary provider in your family?
5. How do you think you and your spouse/partner will divide up the household and child care responsibilities?

WHAT DOES IT MEAN?

1. Although your sample is very small, did you observe any ethnic differences? Did these differences match those discussed in the text? If yes, show the connections. If no, explain why your results might differ from those reported in past research.

2. You interviewed women college students. Do you think your findings might have been different had your respondents been college graduates? Working-class or poor women without a college education? Explain your answers.

In addition, gender attitudes are related to a personality characteristic known as authoritarianism, which is characterized by intolerance of ambiguity and is strongly related to prejudice toward members of perceived out-groups such as Blacks, Jews, sexual minorities, and people with disabilities. As you might guess, both women and men who are high in authoritarianism endorse traditional societal roles for women and men (Swim et al., 2010). Traditional attitudes about gender are also associated with the belief that gender differences are caused by biological or religious (divine) causes as opposed to differences in socialization or opportunities (Neff & Terry-Schmitt, 2002).

Perceived Value of Female Versus Male Gender-Related Attributes

Given the greater power held by males in most societies, is it more advantageous to be a male than to be a female? Alternatively, are gender-related advantages and disadvantages equally distributed between the genders or, perhaps, balanced in favor of females? To examine this question, try the exercises in Get Involved 3.4.

When Arnie Cann and Elizabeth Vann (1995) asked college students to list as many advantages and disadvantages as they could associate with being the other gender, they found that, overall, both women and men associated more advantages with being male. Specifically, these students considered differences in physical appearance requirements and actual physical differences as more disadvantageous to females than to males. For example, they believed that females are under more pressure than males to focus on their appearance and that biological differences, such as pregnancy and menstruation, are disadvantageous to females. Interestingly, these students did not perceive males to have more social-role advantages than females. Although females were seen to be limited by workplace discrimination and the expectation to be subordinate in their relationships, males were viewed as hurt by the social pressure on them to be successful and to play a leadership role.

GET INVOLVED 3.4
Would You Rather Be a Female or a Male?

Have you ever considered what life would be like if you were the other gender? Think about any advantages and/or disadvantages that would occur if you were the other gender. For each of the following two categories, list any advantages and/or disadvantages of being the other gender: (1) *social roles,* that is, opportunities that are not equally available to the two genders and/or behaviors that are considered more appropriate for one gender than the other; and (2) *physical differences,* for example, reproductive, size, or strength differences. Also, ask an other-gender friend to perform the same exercise. Discuss your answers with your friend.

WHAT DOES IT MEAN?

1. Did you imagine more advantages and/or disadvantages in one category than the others? If yes, how can you explain the pattern of perceived advantages and disadvantages?
2. Are your friend's perceptions of the advantages of being your gender consistent with your perceptions of the disadvantages of being your friend's gender? Why or why not?
3. Examine the number of advantages relative to disadvantages that you associated with being the other gender. Do the same for your friend's responses. Do you and/or your friend attach greater value to one gender or the other? If yes, explain.
4. If you or your friend perceive a relative advantage of one gender over the other, discuss some societal changes that would have to occur to reduce this discrepancy?

Source: Cann and Vann (1995).

Thus, these students seemed to be aware that the gender imbalance in power puts women at a disadvantage and that the social construction of the agentic, achievement-oriented male role establishes potentially difficult expectations for men.

Given the evidence that males are seen as having more advantages than females, it is not surprising that males who violate gender expectations are evaluated more negatively than females who do so (Risman & Seale, 2009; Swearer et al., 2008). Scholars have proposed two possible explanations for this difference. The **social status hypothesis** contends that *because the male gender role is more highly valued than the female role is, a male is seen as lowering his social status by engaging in female-stereotypic behaviors, whereas a female performing male-stereotypic behaviors is perceived as raising her status* (Kite, 2001; Twenge, 2009). Consequently, males who engage in cross-gender behaviors are viewed more negatively than are females who deviate from gender expectations. The social status hypothesis receives some support from the finding that people believe that occupations with higher prestige require skills associated with masculine characteristics and that these jobs should pay more than those requiring feminine characteristics (Kite, 2001).

The other explanation of the more negative evaluation of male gender-role violation is the **sexual orientation hypothesis** (Kilianski, 2003; Kite 2001). This perspective argues that *cross-gender behavior in boys but not girls is considered a sign of actual or potential same-sex sexual orientation.* Several investigations have provided support for this perspective. For example, Emily Kane (2006) found that parents of preschoolers accepted gender nonconformity in their daughters but not in their sons. Two-thirds expressed negative reactions to their sons' dressing up in feminine attire, wearing nail polish, or playing with Barbie dolls, and several expressed fears that such activity meant that the son either was gay or would be perceived as gay.

Summary

GENDER SELF-CONCEPT

- Gender self-concept includes gender identity and gender attitudes.

PRENATAL DEVELOPMENT

- Prenatal sex differentiation is a multistage process. The joining of the sex chromosomes at conception is followed by the differentiation of the gonads, the development of the internal and external reproductive organs, and the organization of the hypothalamus.
- After the gonads develop, the presence or absence of androgens influences the development of the reproductive organs and the brain.
- Estrogens appear to play a role in female development.
- Some individuals experience variations in their prenatal development known as intersexuality.
- Turner syndrome is a chromosomal disorder in which the individual has a single X chromosome. These individuals are raised as girls and have female gender expectations, although they have no sex glands and no prenatal estrogen.
- Genetic females with CAH are usually reared as girls, although they have a partial or complete masculinization of their external genitals.
- Genetic males with the androgen-insensitivity syndrome have feminized external genitals and are reared as girls.
- Genetic males with a 5 alpha-reductase deficiency experience a female-to-male body transformation at puberty.
- Studies of intersexuals provide mixed evidence regarding the influence of prenatal biological factors on nonsexual gender-related attributes, gender identity, and sexual orientation. Some researchers claim that gender-related development is dependent on prenatal factors, and others point to the importance of the gender of rearing.

THEORIES OF GENDER TYPING

- Psychoanalytic theory proposes that gender typing stems from the child's identification with the same-gender parent, a process that occurs when the child resolves the Oedipus complex. For boys, the resolution stems from fear of castration by the father. For girls, it stems from the realization that she will never possess her father.
- Social learning theory proposes that children acquire gender behaviors via imitation of same-gender models and positive reinforcement of their own gender-consistent behaviors. Social cognitive theory stresses the added role of cognition.
- Cognitive developmental theory contends that once children attain gender constancy, they are motivated to behave in gender-appropriate ways. Thus, they actively seek out the rules that characterize female behavior and male behavior. They then engage in gender-consistent behaviors because it enables them to competently adjust to the social environment.
- Gender schema theory proposes that children develop an interrelated set of ideas about gender. They learn the societal norms and practices that signify the importance of gender. They then organize the social world on the basis of gender and guide their own actions accordingly.

GENDER-RELATED TRAITS

- On the basis of their gender-related traits, individuals can be categorized as feminine, masculine, androgynous, or undifferentiated.
- Research has shown an increase in masculinity and androgyny in women over time.
- Masculinity is related to psychological adjustment.
- Androgyny was once considered to be highly desirable, but recently feminist scholars have criticized it.

GENDER ATTITUDES

- Gender attitudes are multidimensional.
- College students have less traditional beliefs about the value of the employment role for women but more traditional views about the combination of women's employment and family roles.
- Among Whites, women are generally more nontraditional in their beliefs than men are.
- Among women, Blacks hold more traditional views about domestic responsibilities than Whites, but have more nontraditional views about the combination of women's employment and family roles.
- The roles of Latina/o women and men have become more egalitarian over time, but Latinas have more traditional views than Black and White women.
- The gender-related behaviors and roles of Native American women vary greatly across tribes and in several societies increased acculturation has been accompanied by greater male dominance.
- Traditional gender attitudes are linked to being older, more religious, less educated, of lower social class, politically conservative, and authoritarian.
- College women and men associate more advantages with being male than with being female.
- Males, compared to females, are more negatively evaluated for engaging in cross-gender behavior.

Key Terms

gender identity *49*
transgender individuals *49*
gender attitudes *49*
sexual orientation *49*
prenatal sex differentiation *49*
androgens *50*
estrogens *50*
Müllerian ducts *50*
Wolffian ducts *50*
testosterone *51*
Müllerian-inhibiting
    substance *51*
intersexuality *51*

Turner syndrome *51*
congenital adrenal hyperplasia *52*
androgen-insensitivity
    syndrome *52*
5 alpha-reductase deficiency *53*
gender typing *54*
psychoanalytic theory *54*
Oedipus complex *54*
castration anxiety *54*
identification *54*
penis envy *55*
social learning theory *56*
observational learning *56*

social cognitive theory *57*
cognitive developmental theory *57*
gender constancy *57*
gender schema theory *58*
femininity *60*
masculinity *60*
androgyny *60*
undifferentiation *60*
traditional gender attitude *63*
nontraditional or egalitarian
    gender attitude *64*
social status hypothesis *68*
sexual orientation hypothesis *68*

What Do You Think?

1. If you gave birth to an intersexual child, would you decide on surgical restructuring of the child's reproductive system and genitalia early in life, or would you wait until closer to puberty when your child could participate in the decision? Give reasons for your answer.

2. Evidence indicates that boys, more than girls, select role models who are powerful. Explain this finding.

3. As discussed in Chapter 2, it is possible that the media not only reflect gender stereotypes but also help shape them. Now that you are familiar with theories of gender typing, use one of these theories to explain how the media might contribute to an individual's acquisition of gender stereotypes.

4. Which gender-typing theory or theories best explain(s) the development of gender-related traits, behaviors,

and roles? Explain. To help you develop your reasons, critically think about the evaluations presented in the text. Additionally, if you have had any contact with young children, try to provide anecdotal support for some of the theoretical concepts.

5. Discuss the advantages and disadvantages to girls/women and boys/men of gender-related trait identifications consistent with stereotypes, that is, femininity

in females and masculinity in males. Can you think of the advantages and disadvantages of an androgynous identity?

6. There is some evidence that individuals who internalize their religious beliefs and attempt to live by them hold more traditional gender attitudes than individuals who do not. Consider possible explanations for this finding.

If You Want to Learn More

Anselmi, D. L. (2010). *Questions of gender: Perspectives and paradoxes.* New York: McGraw-Hill.

Becker, J. B. (2008). *Sex differences in the brain: From genes to behavior.* New York: Oxford University Press.

Blakemore, J. E., Berenbaum, S. A., & Liben, L. S. (2009). *Gender development.* New York: Psychology Press.

Colapinto, J. (2000). *As nature made him: The boy who was raised as a girl.* New York: HarperCollins.

Fausto-Sterling, A. (2000). *Sexing the body: Gender politics and the construction of sexuality.* New York: Basic Books.

Harper, C. (2007). *Intersex.* Oxford, England: Berg Publishers.

Karkazis, K. (2008). *Fixing sex: Intersex, medical authority, and lived experience.* Durham, NC: Duke University Press.

Reis, E. (2009). *Bodies in doubt: An American history of intersex.* Baltimore, MD: Johns Hopkins University Press.

Samons, S. L. (2009). *When the opposite sex isn't: Sexual orientation in male-to-female transgender people.* New York: Routledge.

Weill, C. L. (2009). *Nature's choice: What science reveals about the biological origins of sexual orientation.* New York: Routledge.

White, J. W. (2011). *Taking sides: Clashing views in gender* (5th ed.). New York: McGraw-Hill.

Websites

Gender Identity

Border Crossings
http://www.uiowa.edu/-commstud/resources/bordercrossings/

Women's Studies Links

http://dir.yahoo.com/health/diseases_and_conditions/intersexuality

CHAPTER 4

Infancy, Childhood, and Adolescence

Children's Knowledge and Beliefs About Gender
- Distinguishing Between Females and Males
- Gender Identity and Self-Perceptions
- Gender Stereotypes

Gender-Related Activities and Interests
- Physical Performance and Sports
- Toys and Play
- Gender Segregation

Influences on Gender Development
- Parents
- Siblings
- School
- Peers
- Media

Puberty
- Events of Puberty
- Menarche
- Gender Differences in Puberty
- Early and Late Maturation in Girls

Psychosocial Development in Adolescence
- Identity Formation
- Self-Esteem
- Gender Intensification
- Body Image

I was 6 when I realized there were different expectations for boys and girls. My brother and I used to play dress up at home all the time. It was an Easter Sunday and I wanted to wear the tie and my brother wanted to wear the dress. My father got really mad and my mom told us that since we were going to church I had to wear the dress and my brother had to wear the suit. I had a fit about the hose itching and my father told me to get used to it because girls were supposed to dress like girls and boys like boys. (Traci, a 23-year-old college senior)

My mom wanted me to wear pink and my brother blue. At Christmas all of the granddaughters were given makeup and Barbie dolls whereas the boys were given GI Joe or hunting gear. My mother raised me to know how to cook, clean, budget, and do all of the work to take care of children and a household. However, my brother has never even washed a dish. (Jamie, a 20-year-old college junior)

Both my parents encouraged me to do well in school, but while my brother was signed up for karate lessons at the YMCA I was signed up for things like jazz dance. When I joined girls' football in high school, my mother cringed every time I left the house in a jersey or came back with a bloody lip. She kept telling me she would "never understand." I was teased constantly, mostly by boys. They told me I would never be good enough at football, but I kept my head high and ignored them. (Erika, a 20-year-old college junior)

An old nursery rhyme declares that little girls are made of "sugar and spice and everything nice," while little boys are made of "frogs and snails and puppy dogs' tails."

Are girls and boys really as different as the nursery rhyme suggests? Is there even a kernel of truth in these age-old stereotypes? And if so, what factors might be responsible? The childhood recollections of Traci, Jamie, and Erika indicate the important contributions made by family members. In this chapter, we focus on the development of girls in infancy, childhood, and adolescence and examine both similarities and differences between girls and boys during these years. We also explore factors that influence gender development, including the roles played by parents, siblings, schools, peers, and the media. We then look at the physical transformations of adolescence, examining puberty and individual differences in rates of physical maturation. Finally, we turn to psychosocial development in adolescence, exploring identity, self-esteem, gender intensification, and body image.

CHILDREN'S KNOWLEDGE AND BELIEFS ABOUT GENDER

Early childhood is a time when much of the social construction of gender takes place. Let's examine some of these processes more closely. For a summary of the major milestones of gender stereotyping and gender-role adoption, see Table 4.1.

Distinguishing Between Females and Males

"Is it a girl or a boy?" is typically the first question asked following a child's birth (unless of course, the parents chose to learn the answer from a sonogram months earlier!). From the moment babies enter the world, they are surrounded by abundant cues signifying gender. They are given gendered names and are outfitted in color-coded clothing, diapers, and blankets (Hines, 2010). It is not surprising that children learn to differentiate between females and males at an early age. Infants as young as 3–4 months of age can tell the difference between pictures of adult female and male faces, and 6-month-olds are able to distinguish between their voices. By the age of 12 months, children can match the face and voice of men and women (Zosuls et al., 2008). Between the ages of 2 and 2½ years, they can accurately label pictures of girls and boys (Etaugh et al., 1989; Etaugh & Duits, 1990). Young children who learn to identify females and males early show more gender-typical preferences for toys and peers than children of the same age who do not make this distinction (Zosuls et al., 2009).

Gender Identity and Self-Perceptions

As we saw in Chapter 3, children develop gender identity between 2 and 3 years of age. By that time, they can accurately label their own gender and place a picture of themselves with other same-gender children (Campbell et al., 2002; Zosuls et al., 2008). As children become more aware of their membership in a particular gender category, they begin to view their own gender more favorably than the other gender (Powlishta, 2001; Susskind et al., 2005). In one study of children in second through tenth grade, for example, girls believed that girls were nicer, harder workers, and less selfish than

TABLE 4.1   Milestones of Gender Typing

Age	Gender Stereotyping and Gender-Role Adoption	Gender Identity
1–5 years	• "Gender-appropriate" toy preferences emerge. • Gender stereotyping of activities, occupations, and behaviors appears and expands. • Gender segregation in peer interaction emerges and strengthens. • Girls' preference for play in pairs, boys' for play in larger groups, appears.	• Gender constancy develops in a three-stage sequence: gender labeling, gender stability, and gender consistency.
6–11 years	• Gender segregation reaches a peak. • Gender-stereotyped knowledge expands, especially for personality traits and achievement areas. • Gender stereotyping peaks between ages 5 and 7, then becomes more flexible.	• "Masculine" gender identity strengthens among boys; girls' gender identity becomes more androgynous.
12–18 years	• Gender-role conformity increases in early adolescence and then declines. • Gender segregation becomes less pronounced.	• Gender identity becomes more traditional in early adolescence ("gender intensification"), after which highly stereotypic self-perceptions decline.

Note: These milestones represent overall age trends. Individual differences exist in the precise age at which each milestone is attained and in the extent of gender typing.

Source: Adapted from Berk (2009).

boys. Boys, on the other hand, felt that *they* were nicer, harder workers, and less selfish than girls (Etaugh et al., 1984).

Gender Stereotypes

In Chapter 2, we discussed how gender stereotypes are formed. This process begins early in life. Rudimentary knowledge about gender-typical objects and activities develops during the second year. Children as young as 24 months know that certain objects (e.g., ribbon, dress, purse) and activities (e.g., putting on makeup, rocking a baby, vacuuming) are associated with females and that other objects (e.g., gun, truck, screwdriver) and activities (e.g., fixing a car, shaving) are associated with males (Levy et al., 1998; Poulin-Dubois et al., 2002). By age 3, children also display knowledge of gender stereotypes for occupations (Campbell et al., 2004; Zosuls et al., 2008). Gender-stereotyped knowledge of activities and occupations increases rapidly between ages 3 and 5 and is mastered by age 6 or 7 (Leaper & Friedman, 2007; Miller et al., 2006; Zosuls et al., 2008). For a closer look at how occupational stereotypes develop throughout childhood, read Learn About the Research 4.1.

In addition, preschoolers demonstrate a rudimentary awareness of gender stereotypes for personality traits. Traits such as "cries a lot," "gets feelings hurt easily," "needs help," "likes to give hugs and kisses," and "can't fix things" are applied to girls, whereas "hits people," "likes to win at

LEARN ABOUT THE RESEARCH 4.1
Gender Stereotypes About Occupations

The stereotype that certain occupations are more appropriate for one gender than the other emerges early in childhood (Paludi, 2008a). Even children as young as 2 and 3 years of age make a distinction between "women's jobs" and "men's jobs" (Betz, 2008). Not surprisingly, girls are more interested than boys in feminine-typed occupations, and boys are more interested than girls in masculine-typed occupations (Weisgram et al., 2010). However, girls generally are less rigid in their occupational stereotypes than boys and are more likely to have nonstereotyped career aspirations for themselves (Blakemore et al., 2009; Fulcher, 2005). For example, when ethnically diverse children from kindergarten through eighth grade are asked what they want to be when they grow up (Bobo et al., 1998; Etaugh & Liss, 1992), younger girls often choose traditional feminine occupations such as teacher and nurse, although a few list traditionally male occupations, such as doctor and pilot. Older girls, however, are more likely than younger ones

to choose a traditionally masculine career and are less likely to pick a feminine one. Boys, on the other hand, aspire to masculine careers at all ages and almost never choose a feminine occupation. These results may stem from several factors: (a) By fourth grade, children view stereotypical feminine occupations less favorably than masculine occupations (Bukatko & Shedd, 1999); (b) as early as first grade, children perceive that few feminine jobs are high in status (Teig & Susskind, 2008); and (c) children's occupational stereotypes are less restrictive for females who engage in counterstereotypic occupations (e.g., Mary, who is a doctor) than for males who engage in counterstereotypic occupations (e.g., Henry, who is a nurse) (Wilbourn & Kee, 2010). This is another example of evaluating males more negatively than females when they violate gender expectations (see Chapter 3). Interestingly, children of both sexes are more likely to have nontraditional occupational aspirations when their mothers hold nontraditional gender attitudes (Fulcher, 2011).

WHAT DOES IT MEAN?

1. Why are girls more flexible in their career aspirations than boys?

2. Why are male-dominated careers more attractive to both girls and boys than are female-dominated careers?

3. What are some ways that gender stereotypes about occupations can be reduced?

---

playing games," "is not afraid of scary things," and "fixes things" are seen as characteristics of boys (Bauer et al., 1998; Ruble & Martin, 1998). Preschoolers are also more likely to label an ambiguous emotional display by boys as anger, but as sadness when displayed by girls (Parmley & Cunningham, 2008). In general, knowledge of gender-typical personality traits emerges later than other stereotypical information (Eisenberg et al., 1996) and increases rapidly throughout elementary school (Best, 2010). But as early as age 6, children are aware that men generally have higher social status than women (Martin & Ruble, 2010).

The gender stereotypes learned in the toddler and preschool years become quite rigid between 5 and 7 years of age. They then become more flexible until early adolescence when they begin to become more traditional again (Crouter et al., 2007; Galambos et al., 2009; Trautner et al., 2005). In one study (Alfieri et al., 1996), children 9 to 16 years old were given 12 trait-related terms, half of them feminine and half masculine, and were asked whether the items described males, females, or both. Gender-trait flexibility, indicated by choosing the "both" option, peaked at ages 11 and 12 and declined thereafter. Boys showed less flexibility than girls, particularly regarding masculine traits. Similarly, research by Elaine Blakemore (2003) and by Lisa Serbin and her colleagues

(Serbin et al., 1993) has found that 11-year-olds know more about stereotypes than younger children but are also more aware of gender-role exceptions, such as girls using tools and sports equipment and boys engaging in domestic chores. Although these older children retain the broad stereotypes, their increasing cognitive maturity allows them to recognize the arbitrary aspects of gender categories, and they are more willing to accept and even try behaviors that are typical of the other gender (Etaugh & Rathus, 1995; Katz & Walsh, 1991). How do gender stereotypes develop in other cultures? Read Explore Other Cultures 4.1.

GENDER-RELATED ACTIVITIES AND INTERESTS

We have seen that children acquire gender stereotypes at an early age. Are these stereotypes reflected in the interests children develop and the play activities they choose? Let's now examine this question.

Physical Performance and Sports

In the preschool and elementary school years, girls and boys are fairly similar in their motor skills. Boys are slightly stronger, and they can typically run faster, throw a ball farther, and jump higher (Mondschein et al., 2000). Their activity levels also tend to be greater, at least in some settings (Blakemore et al., 2009). Girls are better at tasks requiring overall flexibility, precise movement, and coordination of their arms and legs. This gives them an edge in activities such as jumping jacks, balancing on one foot, and gymnastics (Etaugh & Rathus, 1995).

Gender differences in motor skills favoring boys become increasingly pronounced from childhood through adolescence (Blakemore et al., 2009). What might account for this change? It appears that childhood gender differences in motor skills (with the exception of throwing) are more likely a result of environmental factors, such as practice and gender role socialization, than biological ones (Blakemore et al., 2009). Boys receive more opportunities, encouragement, and support for participating in sports (R. L. Hall, 2008). So it is not surprising that by middle childhood, boys in most cultures spend more time than girls in vigorous, competitive, athletic activities, particularly in team sports (Colley et al., 2005).

During puberty, hormonal changes increase muscle mass for boys and fat for girls, giving boys an advantage in strength, size, and power. But hormones are only part of the story. Social pressures on girls to act more feminine and less tomboyish intensify during adolescence, contributing

EXPLORE OTHER CULTURES 4.1
How Do Children Develop Gender Stereotypes in Other Cultures?

Deborah Best and John Williams (see Best, 2009; Best & Thomas, 2004) developed a Sex Stereotype Measure to assess children's knowledge of gender stereotypes. When they gave it to 5-, 8-, and 11-year-olds in 25 countries, they found that stereotype learning in all countries accelerated during the early school years and was completed during adolescence and early adulthood. Girls and boys learned these stereotypes at the same rate. There was a tendency for male-typed traits to be learned somewhat earlier than female-typed traits. However, female-typed traits were learned earlier than male traits in Latin/Catholic cultures (Brazil, Chile, Portugal, Venezuela) where, according to Best and Williams, the female stereotype is more positive than the male stereotype. In predominantly Muslim countries, children learned the stereotypes at an earlier age than in non-Muslim countries, perhaps reflecting the greater divide between female and male roles in Muslim cultures.

to girls' declining interest and participation in athletic activities (Colley et al., 2005; McHale, Shanahan et al., 2004). This trend is troubling, given that involvement in sports is associated with a number of positive traits in girls and women, including higher self-esteem, better body image, enhanced sense of competence and control, reduced stress and depression, less risky sexual activity, lessened likelihood of smoking and substance abuse, better academic performance, and higher college graduation rates (Brake, 2010; DeBate et al., 2009; Findlay & Bowker, 2009; Fox et al., 2010; Greenleaf et al., 2009; Martin, 2010; Pearson et al., 2009; Women's Sports Foundation, 2009). Girls' sports participation has benefits that last well into adulthood, including greater likelihood of employment (Stevenson, 2010) and healthier activity and weight levels (Kaestner & Xu, 2010). The good news is that the participation of girls and young women in sports has increased dramatically since the passage in 1972 of Title IX of the Education Amendments Act. This federal legislation bars discrimination in all educational programs, including athletics. The number of girls and women in high school and college athletic programs is at least 10 times greater now than before Title IX. Currently, 43 percent of U.S. college athletes are women, with the percentage being highest in larger institutions (Women's Sports Foundation, 2009). Canada has seen a similar rise in female student athletes (Hoeber, 2008). The bad news is that schools still spend disproportionately more money on recruiting, and operating expenses for men's sports and on the salaries of coaches (mostly White males) of men's teams (Cunningham, 2008; Lipka, 2007; Women's Sports Foundation, 2009). Moreover, since the passage of Title IX, the percentage of college women's teams coached by female head coaches has dropped from 90 percent to 43 percent (Acosta & Carpenter, 2008; 2010). Only 8 percent of Division I college programs have women as athletic directors (Acosta & Carpenter, 2010; Sander, 2011). Furthermore, Black women have made fewer gains than White women, both as players and as coaches (Brake, 2010; R. L. Hall, 2008; Lapchick, 2010).

Toys and Play

Gender differences in children's play activities and interests are more evident than they are in other areas such as personality qualities or attitudes (McHale et al., 1999). Girls and boys begin to differ in their preference for certain toys and play activities early in life, and at times these interests are quite intense (DeLoache et al., 2007). By the time they are 12 to 18 months old, girls prefer to play with dolls, cooking sets, dress-up clothes, and soft toys, whereas boys choose vehicles, sports equipment, and tools (Hines, 2010; Leaper & Friedman, 2007; Serbin et al., 2001). By 3 years of age, gender-typical toy choices are well established and these differences persist throughout childhood (Cherney & London, 2006; Golombok et al., 2008; McHale, Kim et al., 2004, 2009). However, girls are more likely than boys to display neutral or cross-gender toy choices and activities (Cherney & London, 2006; Galambos et al., 2009; Green et al., 2004). For example, girls are more likely to request transportation toys and sports equipment as gifts than boys are to ask for dolls (Etaugh & Liss, 1992).

Why are girls more likely to depart from the stereotype? In most cultures, masculine activities have greater prestige than feminine ones. Thus, according to the social status hypothesis (see Chapter 3), a girl who plays with "boys'" toys will be viewed more positively than a boy who plays with "girls'" toys, who will be seen as lowering his status. As we shall see later, girls who prefer boys' company and activities do, in fact, receive more peer and parental acceptance than boys who prefer the company and activity of girls (Carr, 2007). Moreover, children generally find boys' toys more interesting and appealing than girls' toys (Blakemore & Centers, 2005). You can do lots more fun and exciting things with Legos than with a tea set!

Because of their preferences, girls and boys experience very different play environments (Edwards et al., 2001). During the preschool and elementary school years, boys in a variety of cultures spend more time than girls in vigorous physical outdoor activities such as playing with large vehicles, climbing, exploratory play, sports, and **rough-and-tumble play,** which consists of *playful chasing, tumbling, hitting, and wrestling, often accompanied by laughter and screaming* (Blakemore et al., 2009; McIntyre & Edwards, 2009; Hines, 2010). Boys are more likely to engage in competitive activities, to play in large groups that are organized around dominance, and to take more physical risks in their play (Blakemore et al., 2009; Galambos et al., 2009; Weinberger & Stein, 2007). Their fantasy play focuses on action and adventure themes (Leaper & Friedman, 2007). Girls' play preferences, on the other hand, include dolls, domestic play, reading, and arts and crafts. They also engage in more symbolic (i.e., "pretend") play than boys (Cote & Bornstein 2009; McHale, Crouter, & Tucker, 2001). Girls' play is more sedentary, more cooperative and egalitarian, more socially competent, and more supervised and structured by adults. Also, girls are more likely than boys to play with a small group of children or just one other child (Blakemore et al., 2009; Galambos et al., 2009; Poulin & Chan, 2010). To take a closer look at play patterns of girls and boys, try Get Involved 4.1.

Gender Segregation

Around 2 years of age, children begin to prefer playing with children of the same gender (Lee et al., 2007; McIntyre & Edwards, 2009; Mehta & Strough, 2009). Gender segregation increases during childhood and is especially strong in middle childhood (Blakemore et al., 2009; Mehta & Strough, 2009). It is found across cultures and settings (Galambos et al., 2009). Even when children choose seats in the lunchroom or get into line, they frequently arrange themselves in same-gender groups. Peer pressure can be a powerful motivator, as illustrated in Barrie Thorne's (1993) observation of second graders seating themselves in the lunchroom. One table was filling with both boys and girls, when a high-status second-grade boy walked by. He commented loudly, "Too many girls," and headed for another table. The boys at the first table picked up their trays and moved, leaving no boys at the first table, which had now been declared taboo. Children who cross the "gender boundary"

GET INVOLVED 4.1
Play Patterns of Girls and Boys

Observe preschool-aged children in a day-care center or preschool during a free-play session. Keep a record of the following behaviors:

1. The toys that girls choose and those that boys choose.

2. The activities girls engage in and those that boys engage in.

3. How often (a) girls play with other girls; (b) boys play with other boys; and (c) girls and boys play with each other.

WHAT DOES IT MEAN?

1. Did boys and girls show different patterns of toy choice and activity preference? If so, describe these patterns. How do you account for any differences you observed?

2. Which toys in general were most in demand? Were these "girl" toys, "boy" toys, or gender-neutral toys?

3. Did boys prefer to play with same-gender peers more than girls did, was it the other way around, or were there no differences? How do you account for any differences you observed?

are unpopular with their peers, although there are certain conditions under which contact with the other gender is permissible. Often these overtures involve playful teasing, pushing, and grabbing (Pellegrini, 2001), as seen in Table 4.2.

Why do children play primarily with children of their own gender? According to Eleanor Maccoby (1998), girls may avoid boys for two reasons. One is that they don't like the rough, aggressive, dominant play style of boys. A second is that boys are unresponsive to their polite suggestions. Analogously,

Girls' play is quieter, more symbolic, and more socially competent than is boys' play.

boys may avoid girls because girls are not responsive to their rough play (Eisenberg et al., 1996). An alternative view is that rather than actively trying to avoid children of the other gender, children simply prefer the company of their own gender because they share a preference for gender-typed toys and activities (Zosuls et al., 2008).

TABLE 4.2	Knowing the Rules: Under What Circumstances Is It Permissible to Have Contact With the Other Gender in Grade School?
Rule:	The contact is accidental.
Example:	You're not looking where you are going, and you bump into someone.
Rule:	The contact is incidental.
Example:	You go to get some lemonade and wait while two children of the other gender get some. (There should be no conversation.)
Rule:	The contact is in the guise of some clear and necessary purpose.
Example:	You may say "pass the lemonade" to persons of the other gender at the next table. No interest in them is expressed.
Rule:	An adult compels you to have contact.
Example:	"Go get that map from X and Y and bring it to me."
Rule:	You are accompanied by someone of your own gender.
Example:	Two girls may talk to two boys though physical closeness with your own partner must be maintained and intimacy with the others is disallowed.
Rule:	The interaction or contact is accompanied by disavowal.
Example:	You say someone is ugly or hurl some other insult or (more commonly for boys) push or throw something at them as you pass by.

Source: Sroufe, L. A., Bennett, C., Englund, M., Urban, J., and Shulman, S. (1993), The Significance of Gender Boundaries in Preadolescence: Contemporary Correlates and Antecedents of Boundary Violation and Maintenance. *Child Development,* 64: 455–466. Copyright © 1993 The Society for Research in Child Development, Inc. Reprinted by permission of John Wiley & Sons, Inc.

INFLUENCES ON GENDER DEVELOPMENT

Socialization refers to *the process by which each generation passes along to children the knowledge, beliefs, and skills that constitute the culture of the social group.* Because societies prescribe somewhat different social roles for adult females and males, girls and boys are typically socialized differently in order to prepare them for the adult roles they will play (Basow, 2008; Reid et al., 2008). This is a restatement of the third theme of our book, namely, that much of gender is socially constructed. A variety of sources help shape the behaviors and interests of boys and girls. These include parents, siblings, teachers, peers, and the media. In Chapter 3, we briefly mentioned the role of these influences when we discussed theories of gender typing. In this section, we examine these factors in greater detail.

Parents

When I was 4 or 5, my father asked me what I wanted to be when I grew up.

ME: *I'll be a carpenter and make furniture.*
HIM: *Oh, no, Holly, girls can't be carpenters. Only boys can.*
ME: *Okay, then I'll be a fisherman.*
HIM: *No, girls can't be fishermen either. They aren't strong enough.*

(Holly, a 50-year-old middle-school teacher)

Children's gender-typed views about themselves and others are closely linked to the gender self-concepts and attitudes of their parents (Mendelsohn & Perry-Jenkins, 2007; Tenenbaum & Leaper, 2002). How do parents transmit their views on gender to their children? One of the most obvious ways is by providing their sons and daughters with distinctive clothing, room furnishings, and toys. Infant girls are likely to be dressed in a ruffled pink outfit (sometimes with a bow attached to wisps of hair), whereas baby boys typically wear blue (Pomerleau et al., 1990; Shakin et al., 1985). The bedrooms of infant and toddler girls contain dolls, dollhouses, and domestic items and are decorated in pastel colors, frills, and flowery patterns. Baby boys' rooms feature animal themes, sturdy furniture, blue bedding, and a variety of sports equipment, vehicles, military toys, and educational materials (Basow, 2008). Clearly, infants are too young to express their preference in these matters.

Could it be that infant girls and boys give off subtle cues that influence their parents' gender-typed behavior? Research suggests that this is not the case. For example, in some studies, adults are asked to play with an unfamiliar infant who has a girl's name and is dressed in girls' clothing. Other adults play with an infant who wears boys' clothes and has a boy's name. (In fact, it is actually the same baby, who is dressed and named according to whether it is introduced as one gender or another.) Adults who believe the child is a boy are more likely to offer "him" a football or hammer and to encourage physical activity. Those who think the baby is a girl are more apt to offer a doll (Etaugh & Rathus, 1995; Stern & Karraker, 1989).

Although there are very few sex differences in the physical and behavioral characteristics of infant girls and boys, parents perceive their babies in gender-stereotyped ways as soon as they are born. Compared to girls, infant boys are viewed as less emotional, more competent, larger, stronger, and more athletic (Blakemore et al., 2009). Both mothers and fathers play more roughly with their little boys than with their little girls, and fathers, in particular, roughhouse with their young sons (Bronstein, 2006; Lindsey & Mize, 2001).

Moreover, parents in virtually all cultures expect their young children to adhere to traditional gender roles and they react negatively to those who do not do so. As we saw in Chapter 3, this is especially true for boys (Blakemore & Hill, 2008; Iervolino et al., 2005; Yu & Xie, 2010). For example, parents and other adults are less likely to purchase cross-gender toys than to purchase gender-typical toys for children, even when children request the cross-gender toy (Etaugh & Liss, 1992; Karraker & Hartley, 2007). Boys are even less likely than girls to receive such toys (Fisher-Thompson et al., 1995). Parents, especially fathers, also tend to offer gender-typical toys to children during free play and are more supportive when children engage in gender-typical activities than in cross-gender activities (Basow, 2008; Blakemore & Hill, 2008). It is no wonder that more than one of Claire's male students has confided in her that as a child he longed to play with his sister's Barbies, but would do so only when no one else was home. Given that fathers treat children in more gender-typical ways than mothers do, it is not surprising that children's gender-typical activity preferences are more closely linked to their father's gender-related attitudes than to their mother's (McHale et al., 1999).

One way in which parents foster gender stereotypes in their children is through conversation. Susan Gelman and her colleagues (Gelman et al., 2004) videotaped mothers and their daughters or sons (ages 2, 4, or 6) discussing a picture book that focused on gender. Although mothers rarely expressed gender stereotypes directly, they emphasized gender concepts indirectly. For example, they provided gender labels (e.g., "That's a policeman"), contrasted males and females (e.g., "Is that a girl job or a boy job?"), and gave approval to their children's stereotyped statements (e.g., "Ballet dancers are girls!").

Parents also shape their children's environment by assigning chores based on gender (Lloyd et al., 2008; McHale & Crouter, 2008; Raley & Bianchi, 2008). In many cultures around the world, girls are more likely to be given domestic and child care tasks centered around the home, whereas boys typically are assigned outside chores such as yard work and taking out trash. In addition, girls spend more time on housework than boys do (Best, 2010; East, 2010; Gager et al., 2009; "The State of the Kid," 2009; Tudge, 2008). For a closer look at the relationship between toy giving, chore assignments, and children's gender-related development, read Learn About the Research 4.2.

LEARN ABOUT THE RESEARCH 4.2
Learning Gender-Related Roles at Home and at Play

Are the toys children request and receive and the chores adults assign them related to gender differences in play activities and occupational goals? To study this question, Claire Etaugh and Marsha Liss (1992) gave questionnaires to 245 children of ages 5 to 13, before and after Christmas, asking which gifts they requested and which ones they received.

The children also were asked to name their friends, play activities, assigned chores, and occupational aspirations. Children generally requested and received gender-typical toys. They were less likely to receive requested cross-gender toys (such as a girl asking for a baseball glove). Children who wanted and received gender-typical toys were also more likely to be assigned gender-typical chores, to engage in gender-typical play activities, and to have same-gender friends. Girls preferred masculine toys and jobs more than boys preferred feminine ones. As they got older, both girls and boys increasingly preferred masculine toys, and girls increasingly chose masculine occupations.

WHAT DOES IT MEAN?

1. Why do you think parents and other adults are more likely to give children a requested gender-typical toy than a requested cross-gender toy? What message does this send? Did you ever ask for a gender-atypical toy? Did you get it?

2. Why do girls prefer masculine toys and jobs more than boys like feminine ones? Explain.

3. How might the assignment of gender-typical chores help influence the formation of gender roles?

Isabel or Isaac? Adults are more likely to offer a doll to "Isabel" and a football to "Isaac." (In fact, both babies are Claire's granddaughter, Isabel.)

Parents treat daughters and sons differently in other ways than encouraging activities or assigning chores. For example, mothers talk more to their daughters than to their sons as early as 6 months of age (Clearfield & Nelson, 2006). They also use warmer, more supportive speech with daughters than with sons (Gleason & Ely, 2002). Earlier, we saw that mothers also talk more about emotions with their daughters. Even in early childhood, mothers talk more to girls about relationships, the workings of reproductive bodies, and moral issues involving sexuality (Martin & Luke, 2010). Parents also emphasize prosocial behaviors and politeness more with their daughters than their sons (Eisenberg & Fabes, 1998) and act more warmly toward their daughters (Zhou et al., 2002). Furthermore, cross-cultural research in Argentina, Italy, and the United States shows that mothers are more emotionally involved with their toddler daughters than with their toddler sons, and that the daughters, in turn, are more responsive than the sons (Bornstein et al., 2008; Lovas, 2005).

In addition, parents control their daughters more than their sons, while granting their sons greater autonomy and greater opportunities to take risks (Leaper & Friedman, 2007; Morrongiello & Hogg, 2004; Smetana & Daddis, 2002). For example, parents are more likely to make decisions for girls and to give them help even if it is not requested. Boys, on the other hand, are encouraged to make their own decisions and to solve problems on their own (Blakemore et al., 2009). Moreover, mothers expect more risky behaviors from sons than from daughters and consequently intervene less frequently to stop boys' injury-risk behavior in play settings (Morrongiello & Dawber, 2000; Morrongiello & Hogg, 2004).

Parents also respond differently to the emotions expressed by girls and boys. Starting in infancy, they are more likely to control the emotions of their sons. We have seen that parents talk more about emotions to daughters. They are also more tolerant of expressions of fear and sadness in their daughters, whereas they are more permissive of anger in their sons (Blakemore et al., 2009).

Parents not only directly instruct their children about gendered behaviors, but they also serve as role models of these behaviors (Blakemore et al., 2009; Sutfin et al., 2008). Take the case of maternal employment. More mothers work outside the home today than ever before. Also, although to a lesser degree, more fathers are participating in child care and household chores (see Chapter 11). Not surprisingly, researchers have found that maternal employment is associated with less stereotyped gender-related concepts and preferences in boys and girls (Galambos et al., 2009; Hoffman & Youngblade, 2001; Riggio & Desrochers, 2005; Schuette & Killen, 2009). Children also show less stereotyping in their activity preferences if their fathers are highly involved in sharing child care and housework and if their mothers frequently engage in traditional "masculine" household tasks such as washing the car and doing yard work (Etaugh & O'Brien, 2003; Murray & Steil, 2000).

Children growing up in single-parent homes tend to be less traditional in their gender stereotypes and activities than those from two-parent homes (Leaper, 2000). One reason for this is that a single parent engages in activities normally carried out by both parents, such as housework, child care, home repairs, and going to work. In addition, the absent parent is most often the father, who usually encourages children's adherence to gender norms more strongly than the mother does (Kane, 2006).

Siblings

The role of siblings in gender role socialization has received less attention than that of parents and peers. Yet siblings are the most frequent out-of-school companions for children and young adolescents (Parke & Buriel, 2006). Not surprisingly, siblings make significant positive contributions to each other's development (Caspi, 2011; Hines, 2010; Padilla-Walker et al., 2009;

Wright & Cassidy, 2009). Consistent with social-learning predictions about the importance of role models (see Chapter 3), older siblings appear to play a role in the gender socialization of their younger siblings (Caspi, 2011; Crouter et al., 2007). For example, a longitudinal study in England (Rust et al., 2000) found that both girls with older sisters and boys with older brothers were more gender-typed than only children of their gender. These only children, in turn, were more gender-typed than children with other-gender older siblings.

School

Schools convey powerful messages to children about gender typing. For one thing, the school social structure is biased. Women hold most of the low-paying elementary school teaching positions, while men more often occupy the higher-paying high school teaching jobs. Additionally, men are more often in the leadership positions of principal and superintendent (Meece & Scantlebury, 2006). This sends a clear signal that men hold more power than women, one of the themes of this book.

In the classroom, girls and boys are often treated unequally by their teachers (Basow, 2010b). A meta-analysis of empirical studies (Jones & Dindia, 2004) showed that teachers pay far less attention to girls than to boys. This finding has been strikingly documented by Myra and David Sadker (1994; Sadker & Zittleman, 2009). The Sadkers found that teachers call on boys more often and give them more time to answer questions. Boys are more likely to be praised, corrected, helped, and criticized constructively, all of which promote student learning. Girls are more likely to receive a bland and ambiguous "okay" response. Black girls are the least likely to be given clear feedback. Teachers are more likely to accept calling out from boys, whereas girls are reprimanded for the same behavior. Boys are rewarded for being smart, but girls are rewarded for being neat, pretty, and compliant. In addition, teachers are likely to give girls the answer when they ask for help but tend to help boys use strategies to figure out the answer themselves (DeZolt & Hull, 2001; Meece & Scantlebury, 2006). Unfortunately, teachers are generally unaware that they are treating boys and girls differently. Later in the chapter, we will see how such unequal treatment may contribute to the declining self-esteem of adolescent girls.

African American girls may encounter unique educational perceptions and obstacles. A recent two-year study at a predominantly Black and Latino middle school found that Black girls performed well academically, but that teachers often questioned their manners and behavior. Many teachers perceived the Black girls as "loud and confrontational" and tried to mold them into displaying more "ladylike" behaviors, such as being quieter and more passive (Morris, 2007).

Peers

Children exert strong pressures on each other to engage in gender-appropriate behavior. As early as the preschool years, they modify their activity and toy preferences to conform to the patterns their peers reward. This seems especially true for boys who have many male friends (Ewing Lee & Troop-Gordon, 2011). The mere presence of other children inhibits gender-inappropriate play (Eisenberg et al., 1996; Lott & Maluso, 2001). Children who show gender-typical behavior are accepted by their peers (Yunger et al., 2004). Boys who display traditionally feminine activities are teased, rejected, and disliked by both boys and girls, whereas girls who engage in traditionally masculine activities generally are accepted by children of both sexes (Pronk et al., 2010; Rubin et al., 2006). Even the label given to boys who show cross-gender behavior—"sissy"—has negative overtones, whereas the term used for girls who display cross-gender behavior—"tomboy"—does not. It is thus not surprising that gender-atypical boys have more social adjustment problems than gender-atypical girls (Kreiger, 2005).

Media

We saw in Chapter 2 that females are underrepresented in the media and that females and males are portrayed in stereotyped ways. What is the impact of these media messages on children's gender-related learning? Most of the research has focused on television. Children's television viewing averages 2–5 hours a day for preschoolers and peaks at about 4 hours a day at age 11 (Fabes & Martin, 2003), but there are large individual differences in viewing. Children who are heavy viewers have greater knowledge of gender stereotypes (Ward & Harrison, 2005; L. M. Ward, 2007). In these correlational studies, it is difficult to know the direction of influence. Television may cause children to develop stronger stereotypes. On the other hand, children with stronger stereotypes may choose to watch more television because it shows images that are consistent with their beliefs (Van Evra, 2004). A third alternative is that both factors are involved.

Stronger evidence of the impact of television comes from experiments that examined whether television can undo or counter the stereotypic messages. Studies have found that exposure to characters who engage in nontraditional behaviors and roles (nurturing boys and girl auto mechanics, for example) reduces children's gender stereotypes about activities, domestic roles, and occupations (Ward & Harrison, 2005).

For a closer and more personal look at influences on gender role development, try the exercise in Get Involved 4.2.

PUBERTY

I think what is happening to me is so wonderful, and not only what can be seen on my body, but all that is taking place inside [. . .] Each time I have a period (and that has only been three times) I have the feeling that in spite of all the pain, discomfort, and mess, I have a sweet secret, and that is why, although it is nothing but a nuisance to me in a way, I always long for the time that I shall feel that secret within me again.

(Frank, 1995, pp. 158–159)

GET INVOLVED 4.2
Influences on Gender Development

Describe your own gender socialization. Focus on specific things that were said, done, or modeled by (a) your parents and other family members; (b) your teachers; (c) your peers; and (d) television, books, and other media. Then ask two female friends and two male friends to do the same.

WHAT DOES IT MEAN?

Include your own responses when answering the following questions:

1. Did the females and the males you interviewed describe different kinds of socialization experiences? If so, what were they?

2. Identify aspects of your own socialization and that of your friends that are consistent with the material presented in the chapter.

3. When did you realize there were social expectations for your gender?

4. What happened in situations when you crossed gender lines?

5. How have your socialization experiences affected your current choices in activities, friends, major, career, and so on?

_____

Source: Based on Gilbert and Scher (1999).

One of the most moving accounts of a young woman's entry into adolescence was written by Anne Frank, a Jewish girl who lived in Nazi-occupied Holland during World War II. Anne kept a diary during the two years she and her family hid from the Nazis in an attic. Anne wrote about her sudden physical growth, commenting on the shoes that no longer fit her and the undershirts that became "so small that they don't even cover my stomach" (Frank, 1995, p. 101). She also grew concerned about her appearance and asked her sister "if she thought I was very ugly" (p. 55). A few months before she and her family were discovered and sent to die in a concentration camp, Anne wrote the above entry about the "wonders that are happening to [my] body."

In this section, we will explore the physical transformations of adolescence. First we describe the events of puberty. We then discuss gender differences in these events. Finally, we examine individual differences in rates of physical maturation.

Events of Puberty

Puberty is the *period of life during which sexual organs mature and the ability to reproduce emerges.* Increasing levels of sex hormones stimulate the development of primary and secondary sex characteristics. **Primary sex characteristics**—in girls, the ovaries, fallopian tubes, uterus, and vagina—*are structures that make reproduction possible.* **Secondary sex characteristics** are *visible signs of sexual maturity that are not directly involved in reproduction,* such as breast development and the appearance of pubic and underarm hair (Rathus et al., 2010; Shirtcliff et al., 2009). Table 4.3 summarizes these changes.

Most White girls begin to show signs of puberty by the age of 10, and Black girls do so about a year earlier (Butts & Seifer, 2010; Susman et al., 2010). Other studies confirm that feelings of sexual attraction, one of the behavioral hallmarks of puberty, also first appear between the ages of 9 and 10 (Marano, 1997). However, some research shows that many girls start puberty far earlier than previously thought. For example, Marcia Herman-Giddens and her colleagues (1997, 2004) found that by the age of 8, more than 10 percent of White girls and about one-third of Black girls have some breast development, pubic hair, or both.

Menarche

Menarche, *the first menstrual period,* is a dramatic and meaningful event in women's lives, symbolizing the end of childhood and the start of adulthood. Many women have vivid memories of their first menstrual period and, even years later, can describe details of the experience (Chrisler, 2008a; Nalebuff, 2009). (If you, the reader, are female, can you?)

The average age of menarche in the United States is about 12.2 years for Black and Latina girls and 12.8 years for White girls, although it is quite normal for a girl to begin to menstruate any time between 9 and 15 (Butts & Seifer, 2010; Hillard, 2008; McDowell et al., 2007). *Over the past 150 years, the onset of puberty and the attainment of adult height and weight have occurred at progressively earlier ages in the United States and western Europe* (Susman & Dorn, 2009). This **secular trend** is most likely a result of better nutrition and medical care. The onset of puberty seems to be triggered when individuals reach a certain body weight. Improved nutrition, health, and living conditions have led to the achievement of that weight at a younger age (Butts & Seifer, 2010). The rise in obesity among American children may play a role as well, because girls with a high percentage of body fat in early childhood show earlier onset of puberty (DiVall & Radovick 2008; Susman & Dorn, 2009). Another more controversial hypothesis is that early puberty is triggered by eating the meat of livestock whose growth was sped up by giving them sex hormones (Mendle et al., 2007).

TABLE 4.3   Stages of Pubertal Development in Females

Beginning sometime between ages 8 and 11

Pituitary hormones stimulate ovaries to increase production of estrogen.

Internal reproductive organs begin to grow.

Pubic hair begins to appear.

Breast development begins.

Beginning sometime between ages 9 and 15

First the areola (the darker area around the nipple) and then the breasts increase in size and become more rounded.

Pubic hair becomes darker and coarser.

Growth in height continues.

Body fat continues to round body contours.

A normal vaginal discharge becomes noticeable.

Sweat and oil glands increase in activity, and acne may appear.

Internal and external reproductive organs and genitals grow, which makes the vagina longer and the labia more pronounced.

Beginning sometime between ages 10 and 16

Areola and nipples grow, often forming a second mound sticking out from the rounded breast mound.

Pubic hair begins to grow in a triangular shape and to cover the center of the mons.

Underarm hair appears.

Menarche occurs.

Internal reproductive organs continue to develop.

Ovaries may begin to release mature eggs capable of being fertilized.

Growth in height slows.

Beginning sometime between ages 12 and 19

Breasts near adult size and shape.

Pubic hair fully covers the mons and spreads to the top of the thighs.

The voice may deepen slightly (but not as much as in males).

Menstrual cycles gradually become more regular.

Some further changes in body shape may occur into the early 20s.

Note: This table is a general guideline. Changes may appear sooner or later than shown, and not always in the indicated sequence.

Source: Rathus, Spencer A., Nevid, Jeffrey S., Fichner-Rathus, Lois, *Human Sexuality in a World of Diversity*, 8th edition, © 2011. Reprinted by permission of Pearson Education, Inc., Upper Saddle River, NJ.

Environmental stress is also linked to an earlier onset of puberty. For example, girls from divorced families or families high in parent–parent or parent–child conflict or girls who have suffered physical or sexual abuse begin to menstruate earlier than other girls (Belsky et al., 2010; Mendle et al., 2009; Short & Rosenthal, 2008). One explanation for these findings is that stress may lead to overeating, which increases body weight, which then triggers the onset of puberty. An alternative explanation for the family stress findings is that mothers who matured early tend to have early-maturing daughters, possibly because of genetic factors (Belsky et al., 2007; Ellis & Essex, 2007). Early maturers become sexually active, marry, and give birth at younger ages than others. But early marriages are more likely to end in divorce. So, girls whose parents divorce may reach puberty early not because of parental conflict and divorce, but simply because their own mothers matured early (Mustanski et al., 2004).

In many countries around the world, girls report mostly negative feelings about menarche (Bobel, 2010). In North America, girls have mixed feelings about the event with Black and Latina girls reporting more negative attitudes than White girls (Chrisler, 2008a). On the one hand, menstruation is an eagerly awaited sign of growing up (Orringer & Gahagan, 2010; Stubbs, 2008). In the words of one adolescent girl, "It's a great feeling knowing that one day when you want to have a baby, that you can do it. To me that's just amazing" (Commonwealth Fund, 1997, p. 39). Still, some girls also believe that menstruation is embarrassing, frightening, or disgusting and worry about having an "accident" (Chrisler, 2008a; Kissling, 2006). "I was terribly worried about staining"; "It was gross. I felt very dirty" (Lee, 2008, pp. 615, 620).

Feminine hygiene advertisements reflect and reinforce these concerns by focusing on the discomfort and messiness of menstrual periods and the potential embarrassment of "showing" (Bobel, 2010; Lee, 2008; Stubbs, 2008). Women are taught to conceal the fact that they are menstruating. Even within the family household, menstruation is often a sensitive topic that is not openly discussed (Orringer & Gahagan, 2010). One of Claire's students shared the following experience: "When I started my period, I didn't tell a soul. I wrote down 'pads' on my parents' grocery list and they showed up in the bathroom closet. That was the extent of the 'birds and bees' talk in my family." Cultural pressure to hide menstrual cycles and marketing pitches for products that keep a woman clean and deodorized during her menstrual cycles send a clear message to women that their bodies are unacceptable in their natural state. Moreover, with the recent availability of contraceptives that eliminate menstrual periods, ads for these drugs emphasize the debilitating effects of periods and the joys of menstrual suppression (Bobel, 2010; Hitchcock, 2008). Not surprisingly women who place a great deal of emphasis on their appearance and body image have more negative attitudes and emotions, including disgust and shame, toward their menstrual cycles (Fahs, 2011).

A negative attitude toward menstruation before menarche is associated with greater menstrual discomfort (Yeung et al., 2005). For example, girls whose mothers lead them to believe that menstruation will be uncomfortable or unpleasant later report more severe menstrual symptoms. Moreover, girls who begin to menstruate earlier than their peers, or who are otherwise unprepared and uninformed about pubertal changes, find menarche especially distressing (American Psychological Association, 2002; Reid et al., 2008). Those with more positive early experiences and good preparation, on the other hand, hold more positive attitudes and are more satisfied with their bodies (Stubbs, 2008). When 14- and 15-year-old girls were asked what advice they would give to younger girls about menarche, they recommended emphasizing the normalcy of menstruation, providing practical information on handling menstrual periods, and discussing what menarche actually feels like (American Psychological Association, 2002). Today's mothers seem to be following this advice. In one study (Lee, 2008), for example, most college women recalled mothers who were supportive and helpful when they started menstruating. This finding may reflect the increasing openness in society about menstruation as well as the attitudes of a generation of mothers who have grown up with feminism (Lee, 2008).

Gender Differences in Puberty

Besides the obvious differences in secondary sex characteristics, girls and boys differ in other ways as they move through puberty. For one thing, girls begin and finish puberty about two years before boys, on average (Susman & Dorn, 2009). The **adolescent growth spurt,** *a rapid increase in height and weight,* also starts earlier in girls, at about age 9, whereas boys start their spurt at about age 11. The period of peak growth occurs at age 12 for girls and 14 for boys, on average, and then tapers off for two years or so. Boys grow more than girls during their spurt, adding an average of 12 inches to their height, whereas girls grow slightly over 11 inches. Boys also gain more weight than girls do during their growth spurt (Susman & Rogol, 2004).

Body shape changes in puberty as well. Girls gain twice as much fatty tissue as boys, largely in the breasts, hips, and buttocks, whereas boys gain almost twice as much muscle tissue as girls (DeRose & Brooks-Gunn, 2006). These changes produce the more rounded shape of women as compared to men. As the growth spurt begins to slow down, adolescents reach sexual maturity. In girls, the most obvious sign is menarche. We shall discuss other aspects of menstruation in Chapter 7.

Early and Late Maturation in Girls

I remember when I got my first period. It was the summer between fourth and fifth grades—I guess I was 10 . . . By sixth and seventh grades, I had this intense desire to hang out with older kids, usually older boys. I tried pot for the first time when I was 12. I could usually convince people I was 15 when I was in seventh grade and I started hanging out with other girls who looked older . . . Sometimes we would go off with older boys. Often we were drinking or smoking pot . . . Overall, I was pretty unhappy during the teen years; at times, I guess, depressed. I had a hard time fitting in at school even though I got good grades. I was always looking for a group where I belonged. It wasn't until college that I really found my niche.

(Graber & Brooks-Gunn, 2002, p. 35)

The timing of the events of puberty vary considerably from one girl to another (Short & Rosenthal, 2008), as shown in Table 4.3. Early-maturing girls may feel awkward and self-conscious because they begin the physical changes of puberty earlier than their peers. Boys may tease them about their height and developing breasts, which can lead to feelings of body shame (Lindberg et al., 2007; Summers-Effler, 2004). In addition, because they look older than they actually are, others may place sexual and other expectations on them that are difficult to meet. No wonder that early maturers tend to have lower self-esteem, higher levels of depression and anxiety, and a poorer body image than girls who mature later (Mendle et al., 2007; Natsuaki et al., 2009; Rudolph & Troop-Gordon, 2010; Yuan, 2007).

Early-maturing girls tend to associate with older peers (Poulin & Pedersen, 2007; Short & Rosenthal, 2008). This may explain why they begin sexual activity at an earlier age and are more likely to engage in risky behavior such as smoking, drinking, substance abuse, and delinquent behavior (Hayatbakhsh et al., 2008; Richards & Oinonen, 2011; Susman & Dorn, 2009). But not all early-maturing girls suffer negative consequences. Instead, early maturation seems to accentuate behavioral problems in girls who had already shown adjustment difficulties earlier in childhood (Susman & Dorn, 2009).

Once early-maturing girls reach high school, they come into their own socially. They may serve as advisors to their late-maturing girlfriends on such increasingly important topics as makeup, dating, and sex. By late adolescence, early-maturing girls seem to be as well adjusted as other girls (Lien et al., 2010). By age 30, they appear to be more self-possessed and self-directed than their late-maturing peers. Perhaps learning to cope with the stresses of puberty at an early age prepares early-maturing girls to deal effectively with later stressful events (Weichold et al., 2003).

Late-maturing girls may have relatively low social status during the middle school and junior high school years. They look and are treated like "little girls" and are often excluded from boy–girl social activities. Late-maturing girls often are dissatisfied with their appearance and lack of popularity. By tenth grade, however, they are noticeably showing the physical signs of puberty. They often wind up more popular and more satisfied with their appearance than early-maturing girls. One reason for this may be that late maturers are more likely to develop the culturally valued slender body shape than early maturers, who tend to be somewhat heavier (Simmons & Blyth, 1987).

PSYCHOSOCIAL DEVELOPMENT IN ADOLESCENCE

How much do I like the kind of person I am? Well, I like some things about me, but I don't like others. I'm glad that I'm popular since it's really important to me to have friends. But in school I don't do as well as the really smart kids. That's OK, because if you're too smart you'll lose your friends. So being smart is just not that important. But what's really important to me is how I look. If I like the way I look, then I really like the kind of person I am. I've also changed. It started when I went to junior high school. I got really depressed. There was this one day when I hated the way I looked, and I didn't get invited to this really important party, and then I got an awful report card, so for a couple of days I thought it would be best to just end it all. I was letting my parents down, I wasn't good-looking anymore, and I wasn't that popular and things were never going to get better. I talked to Sheryl, my best friend, and that helped some.

(adapted from Harter, 1990, pp. 364–365)

This self-description from a 15-year-old girl illustrates some of the psychological characteristics of adolescent females. Notice how important physical appearance is to her self-esteem. Note also that she discloses her private thoughts to her best friend. Can you recall what was important to you at age 15?

Adolescence is a time of learning more about oneself and others. Two key issues are developing a sense of who you are and how you feel about yourself. Adherence to traditional gender roles often becomes stronger and girls begin to focus a great deal on their appearance. In this section, we explore four aspects of psychosocial development in the adolescent girl: identity formation, self-esteem, gender intensification, and body image.

Identity Formation

One of the most important tasks of adolescence is to develop a sense of **identity,** that is, *deciding who we are and what we want to make of our lives.* According to Erik Erikson (1968, 1980), adolescent identity formation involves commitment to a vocation and a philosophy of life. In order to do so, adolescents must **individuate,** that is, *see themselves as separate and unique.* Carol Gilligan (1982), Sally Archer (1992), Ruthellen Josselson (1996), and others maintain that this model describes the traditional identity development of males better than that of females. They believe that achieving identity for both female and male adolescents requires an interplay between separateness (meeting one's own needs) and connectedness (satisfying the needs of those one cares for) (Arseth et al., 2009).

Research supports the view that adolescent females and males take similar paths in their quest for identity (Beyers & Seiffge-Kronke, 2010). Elements of career choice, personal competence, and interpersonal relationships are central to the identity of both genders (Aronson, 2008; Giesbrecht, 1998; Murray, 1998). For one thing, adolescent girls' educational and career aspirations have increased in recent years and now parallel those of boys (Denmark, 1999). In addition, an increasing number of teenagers (83 percent of females and 72 percent of males) say that having a good marriage and family life is extremely important to them as a life goal (Popenoe & Whitehead, 1999). However, whereas most adolescent girls see interconnections between their career goals and family goals, most adolescent boys perceive no connection between the two. For example, young women place greater emphasis than young men do on flexible working hours that facilitate the coordination of employment and childrearing (see Chapter 11). Still, it appears that, nowadays, individual differences in identity development may be more important than gender differences (Klimstra et al., 2010; Waterman, 1999).

Studies conducted on the identity formation of ethnic minority adolescent girls have found that one key factor in this process is the family unit, often an extended kinship network, which is a highly valued part of life among Asian Americans, Blacks, Latinas/os, and Native Americans. Identity with the family and community seems to provide strength and resources for adolescent girls of color as they strive to integrate their ethnicity and their femaleness within a larger society that devalues both (Rhodes et al., 2007; Vasquez & de las Fuentes, 1999).

Self-Esteem

The two really blonde girls in our class dressed better than the rest of the girls, and I always felt like I couldn't compete with them. This feeling carried on throughout high school. Even though I felt like I was smarter than the boys, I didn't feel better because I didn't look nice enough to impress them. Basically, I grew up not really caring for boys and thinking that they were stupid, but that it was important to impress them by looking nice. I was so confused. I felt superior, but not. And I felt anxious around both males and females, but probably more anxious around males.

(Jamie, a 25-year-old college senior)

Self-esteem is *the sense of worth or value that people attach to themselves.* High self-esteem has long been associated with healthy psychological adjustment and good physical health (Stern, 2008; Stinson et al., 2008; Trzesniewski et al., 2006). Beginning in early adolescence, self-esteem diminishes for both genders, with girls showing lower self-esteem than boys (Cambron et al., 2008; Galambos et al., 2009; McLean & Breen, 2009; Orth et al., 2008). A meta-analysis of over 97,000 respondents by Kristen Kling and her colleagues (1999) shows that this gender gap becomes greatest in late adolescence, with a small-to-moderate effect size of 0.33 (see Chapter 1). This gender difference continues throughout adulthood, narrowing only in old age (Malanchuk & Eccles, 2006). Black girls have higher self-esteem than White, Latina, and Asian American girls during late adolescence (Buchanan & Selmon, 2008; Galambos et al., 2009; Gray-Little & Hafdahl, 2000; Greene & Way, 2005; Gutman & Eccles, 2007; Twenge & Crocker, 2002). Compared to White adolescent girls, Black girls have more confidence in their physical attractiveness, sports ability, femininity, popularity, and social relations (Malanchuk & Eccles, 2006).

What causes girls' self-esteem to decline in adolescence and why do Black girls remain more self-confident than others? For one thing, focusing on one's physical appearance is closely linked to self-esteem (Barker & Bornstein, 2007; Impett et al., 2011; Mercurio & Landry, 2008). Girls are more dissatisfied with their appearance than boys, a difference that increases during adolescence (Gentile et al., 2009; Vaughan & Halpern, 2010). But Black girls, as we shall see, are less concerned about body shape and size than White girls, and physical appearance is less important to their sense of self-worth (Boroughs et al., 2010; Jones-DeWeever, 2009). Upon entering adolescence, for example, the self-esteem of obese Latina and White girls drops more than that of nonobese girls, but obese Black girls do not show this decline (Strauss, 2000).

In addition, we saw earlier in this chapter that schools shortchange girls in ways that undermine girls' perceptions of their competence and importance (Sadker & Zittleman, 2009). Black girls, however, seem less dependent on school achievement for their self-esteem. In fact, they are less accepted by their peers than are White girls when they do well in school (Fuller-Rowell & Doan, 2010). Black girls' view of themselves is more influenced by their community, family, and sense of ethnic identity (Buchanan & Selmon 2008; Jones-DeWeever, 2009; Thomas et al., 2011). Black females are socialized early in life by their mothers and other female relatives and mentors to be strong, independent women who can cope with a society in which racism, sexism, and classism can be barriers to the development of a positive identity (Costigan et al., 2007; Rhodes et al., 2007; Settles et al., 2008; Sharp & Ispa, 2009; Townsend, 2008).

Several theorists, including Carol Gilligan (1993, 2002) and scholars at the Stone Center (e.g., Jordan, 1997), maintain that as girls make the transition to adolescence, they become aware of growing up in a patriarchal society that devalues women and views the desirable stereotype of the "good woman" as being nice, pleasing to others, and unassertive. This places girls in conflict with their view of themselves as self-sufficient, independent, and outspoken. Many girls respond to this conflict by losing confidence in themselves and by suppressing their thoughts, opinions, and feelings, that is, by "losing their voice."

However, research by Susan Harter and her colleagues (Harter, 1998, 1999) found that adolescent boys and girls did not differ with respect to the loss of voice. About a third of young people of both genders said they disguised their true feelings and thoughts in dealing with certain categories of individuals, but a large majority of these females and males did not report doing so. Harter and her colleagues found that *gender role identity,* not gender itself, predicted the level of voice, a finding since confirmed by other researchers (e.g., Smolak & Munstertieger, 2002). Masculine and androgynous adolescents of both genders reported higher levels of voice and higher self-esteem than those with a feminine orientation. Although the feminine girls in Harter's study reported loss of voice in public contexts, such as school and group social situations, this did not occur with parents or close friends. Support, approval, and acceptance from parents and teachers appear critical to the development of high esteem and to the expression of one's thoughts and feelings (Harter, 1998).

See What You Can Do 4.1 to help girls "raise their voice" by empowering them to lead social change.

Gender Intensification

All through grade school, I had been very active in sports. Basketball was my favorite and I was really good at it. Basketball gave me self-esteem. When I was 13, I set my life's goal—to one day coach the Boston Celtics. I will never forget the reactions I got when I told people this. Everyone—my friends, my parents' friends, other adults—all said the same thing: A girl could never coach a professional men's team. Until then, it hadn't occurred to me that gender mattered. I just thought you needed talent and desire, which I had. I was totally heartbroken. Then I began to question whether women were as good as men in basketball. If not, why was I playing? I didn't ever again want people to tell me I couldn't do something because I was a girl. So I quit basketball and became a cheerleader. I didn't really want to, but I felt people wouldn't like me unless I became a "complete and total girl."

(Liz, a 21-year-old college senior)

> ### WHAT YOU CAN DO 4.1
> **Empowering Girls to Lead Social Change**
>
> Girls for a Change (GFC; girlsforachange.org) is a national organization that empowers teen girls to create and lead social change by providing role models and leadership training. Become a volunteer or start a GFC team in your community.

Gender differences in value orientation become pronounced at the onset of adolescence. For example, a study by Kimberly Badger and her colleagues (1998) of geographically diverse American adolescents found that as early as sixth grade, girls were more likely than boys to place a high value on (1) compromising; (2) being kind and forgiving; (3) expressing feelings; (4) wanting to know what people are like inside; (5) enjoying people; (6) getting along with others; and (7) having friends, cooperating, and helping. In addition, early adolescent girls, compared to boys, are more agreeable, open, and conscientious (Klimstra et al., 2009). Early adolescence is also marked by an increase in the rigidity of gender-role stereotypes, although girls continue to remain more flexible than their male peers (Bartini, 2006; Basow, 2010b). This *increasing divergence in gender-related behaviors and attitudes of girls and boys that emerges in early adolescence* is known as **gender intensification** (Galambos et al., 2009). At this age, perceiving oneself to be a typical member of one's same-sex peer group is important to a sense of psychological well-being (Carver et al., 2003; Yunger et al., 2004).

Several factors contribute to the development of gender intensification. For one thing, the physical changes of puberty accentuate gender differences in appearance. Peers, parents, and other adults, especially those with traditional views of gender, apply increasing pressure on girls to display "feminine" behaviors (Carr, 2007; Crouter et al., 2007; Raffaelli & Ontai, 2004), as illustrated poignantly by Liz's experience. This magnification of traditional gender expectations is stronger for girls than for boys, probably because girls have been given more latitude than boys have to display cross-gender behaviors in middle childhood (Crockett, 1991). In addition, when adolescents begin to date and enter romantic relationships, they may increase their gender-stereotypical behavior in order to enhance their appeal to the other gender. For example, girls become intensely interested in appearing physically attractive to boys and spend long hours focusing on their clothes, hairstyles, complexions, and weight (Hilbrecht et al., 2008; Maccoby, 1998). Furthermore, cognitive changes make adolescents more aware of gender expectations and more concerned about what others think of them (Crockett, 1991). The resulting adherence to a traditional construction of gender seems at least partly responsible for the gender differences in self-esteem, friendship patterns, dating behaviors, and cognitive skills that we discuss in this chapter and in Chapters 5 and 8.

Gender intensification starts to decrease by middle to late adolescence. Gender-related occupational stereotypes (see earlier in this chapter) become more flexible, and sexist attitudes (see Chapter 2) become less pronounced. Also, the understanding that gender-related traits, behaviors, and roles are culturally created and modifiable increases (Crockett, 1991).

Body Image

I was always heavier than other females my age, but was very healthy and athletic as a child and into high school. I played basketball, soccer, tennis, and softball. My weight was never an issue for me until I reached adolescence. I suddenly became very conscious of my weight. Boys in my class would make comments. It took me several years before I could become comfortable with my weight and grow to like my body.

(Becky, a 22-year-old senior)

The weight gain associated with puberty occurs within a cultural context that emphasizes a female beauty ideal of extreme thinness (Evens et al., 2008; Moradi, 2010). According to some feminist theorists (Smolak, 2009; Swim et al., 2010; Tylka & Sabik, 2010), girls and women in Western culture internalize the masculine view of the body as a sexualized object to be looked at and evaluated, a process termed *self-objectification* (Calogero et al., 2011). As girls internalize the "thin ideal" body image of Western society, which is unattainable for most women, they become intensely dissatisfied with their weight and shape (Choma et al., 2009; Clark & Tiggemann, 2008; Moradi & Huang, 2008). Girls as young as age 3 already favor a thin body ideal (Harriger et al., 2010). Girls' body image starts to decrease in the early grade-school years, and substantial numbers of preteen girls diet to control their weight (Colton et al., 2007; Wertheim et al., 2009). By adolescence, girls are much more concerned with body weight and appearance than are males of the same age. They have a less positive body image, are less satisfied with their weight, and are more likely to be dieting (Galambos et al., 2009; Gentile et al., 2009; Petrie et al., 2010; Slater & Tiggemann, 2010; von Soest & Wichstrom, 2009; Warren et al., 2010; Wertheim et al., 2009). American adolescent girls and women often view themselves as too heavy even at average weight levels, and many of them have a negative view of their overall appearance (Perrin et al., 2009; Vaughan & Halpern, 2010; Yuan, 2007). Body image concerns and disordered eating behaviors have been documented in females around the world (Anderson-Frye, 2009; Frisén & Holmqvist, 2010; Jung et al., 2009). For example, a survey in Great Britain found that only 8 percent of the teenage girls responding were happy with their bodies. Even though 58 percent said they were of normal weight, two-thirds of the entire sample thought they needed to lose weight. A quarter of the respondents admitted that they already suffered from an eating disorder (Barton, 2005). Similarly, research with German teens found that half the girls in the normal-weight category described themselves as being too fat (Parker-Pope, 2008).

The importance of body image to adolescent females is indicated by the close association between teenage girls' body image and their self-esteem. The more negative their body image, the lower their self-esteem. For adolescent boys, however, evidence for a relationship is mixed (Dohnt & Tiggemann, 2006; Kashubeck-West et al., 2005; Ricciardelli et al., 2009; Wertheim et al., 2009). Being overweight is associated with having a poorer self-image and greater body image dissatisfaction with one's body in girls as young as age 6 (Goldfield et al., 2010; Petrie et al., 2010; Stephens et al., 2007).

Body dissatisfaction among Western girls and women has increased sharply over the last 50 or so years (Feingold & Mazzella, 1998; Jung & Forbes, 2010). Men's body image, however, has remained relatively stable over time (Cash et al., 2004). Along these same lines, Joan Jacobs Brumberg (1997), after reviewing 150 years of girls' diaries, concluded that the focus of adolescent girls has shifted from developing their talents, interests, character, and contributions to society to worrying about their weight, shape, and appearance. According to one therapist who works with teenage girls (Netburn, 2002, pp. ST1, ST7), " 'Who am I?' has been replaced by 'What image should I project?' and part of that image involves for many girls engaging in unhealthy behaviors: dieting, tanning, smoking to keep your weight down." We will discuss the unhealthy weight control behaviors known as eating disorders in Chapter 13.

A major factor contributing to the increase in poor body image is the increasing emphasis in Western culture on thinness as the ideal female body shape (Grabe et al., 2008; Kolata, 2007). Studies of *Playboy* centerfolds, fashion models, and even cartoon characters have found that the average size and shape of the idealized woman has become thinner and more boyish over the last few decades (Grabe et al., 2008; Grogan, 2008; Smith, 2008). Twenty years ago, the average model weighed 5 percent less than the average woman, but today's models weigh 23 percent less (Media Awareness Network, 2010). Magazines designed for women or girls are far more likely than magazines aimed at men or boys to focus on becoming slim, trim, and beautiful through diet, exercise, and cosmetic surgery (APA Task Force, 2007). Furthermore, as mentioned in Chapter 2, thin central women characters are overrepresented in television situation comedies, and the thinner they are, the more positive comments they receive from male characters (Fouts & Burggraf, 2000). So powerful is the cultural emphasis on slenderness in adolescent girls and young women that simply viewing photographs or media images of physically attractive women with idealized physiques is associated with diminished body-image satisfaction, lower self-esteem, increased anger, anxiety, depressed mood, eating disorder symptoms, and approval of surgical body alteration (Aubrey, 2010; Grabe et al., 2008; Krahé & Krause, 2010; Roberts et al., 2009; Schooler, 2008; Strahan et al., 2008; Tiggemann & Miller, 2010; Tiggemann & Polivy, 2010). Even girls as young as 5 experience heightened body dissatisfaction after exposure to Barbie doll images (Dittmar et al., 2006). In addition, adolescent girls who read beauty and fashion magazines and articles about dieting are more likely to use unhealthy dieting methods (Utter et al., 2003; Van den Berg et al., 2007). In the words of one adolescent girl:

There's such pressure. I look at movie stars and I'm like, "Oh, my God. She's so pretty. She's so thin. I want to look like that." I'm not a small person. I am never going to be like a size 2. I should be happy with what I am and just accept that. But inside I'm freaking out because I can't eat.

(Commonwealth Fund, 1997, p. 67)

Pressure from family and friends to be thin and to look good also can undermine girls' body images (Anschutz et al., 2009; Ata et al., 2007; Girl Scouts, 2010; Kluck, 2010; Mackey & LaGreca, 2008; Rodgers et al., 2009). Overweight teenagers are more likely than normal-weight children to be physically bullied by their peers, teased, or excluded from social activities (Janssen et al., 2004; Taylor, 2011). Furthermore, girls whose peers tease them about their weight and pressure them to lose weight have more body dissatisfaction and engage in more disordered eating behaviors (Frisen & Holmqvist, 2010; Menzel et al., 2010). Even simply having conversations with peers about appearance lowers body satisfaction in girls (Jones, 2004). In addition, exposure to other girls of similar weight who are dieting increases dieting behavior in adolescent girls (Mueller et al., 2010). Within the family, mothers and sisters both exert considerable influence on the body image of girls (Coomber & King, 2008). Mothers are much more likely to identify weight as a problem in daughters than in sons. In some cases, parents will talk in their daughter's presence about her need to lose weight (Cox et al., 2006; Goode, 2003). Teasing—especially by girls' fathers and brothers—is also emerging as a powerful influence on those who feel bad about their bodies (Eisenberg et al., 2003; Thompson, in Berger, 2000). Marla Eisenberg and her colleagues (2003) found that adolescents who were teased by family members or peers about their weight were more likely than other teenagers to be depressed and to think about or attempt suicide.

In their search for the "perfect look," more teenage girls are desiring and choosing to undergo cosmetic surgery (Calogero et al., 2010; Henderson-King & Brooks, 2009). Moreover, the procedures requested are changing from a generation ago. Although nose reshaping is still the most popular surgery, girls are increasingly choosing breast augmentation, liposuction, and tummy tucks (American Society of Plastic Surgeons, 2009; Sarwer et al., 2009). Preteen girls, or "tweens" as they are now called, get manicures, pedicures, and facials (Tyre & Pierce, 2003). More than half of 5- to 9-year-old girls report using lipstick or lip gloss, and nearly two-thirds use nail polish (Sweeney, 2008). It's not unusual to see girls age 12 or younger trying to look like pop stars with skimpy tube tops, strappy high-heeled shoes, and revealing shorts. Marketers call it K.G.O.Y., or Kids Getting Older Younger (Orenstein, 2011; Paul, 2010).

Black women, especially those with a strong cultural identity, are more satisfied with their bodies and are less concerned about weight loss and dieting than are White females (Carter-Edwards et al., 2010; De Braganza & Hausenblas, 2010; Grabe & Hyde, 2006; Hesse-Bieber et al., 2010; Hollander, 2010; Kronenfeld et al., 2010; Perrin et al., 2009). Standards of beauty and attractiveness in Black culture place less emphasis on thinness than in White culture (Edwards George & Franko, 2010; Overstreet et al., 2010). However, even though females of color may be more satisfied with their bodies than their White counterparts, they still have more body dissatisfaction and are more likely than males of color to be dieting (Dohm et al., 2010; Eaton et al., 2010). Moreover, cosmetic surgery is gaining in popularity among Black, Latina, and Asian women. Both body dissatisfaction and eating disorders have been reported among Asian, Black, Latina, and Native American girls and women, and among the urban poor as well as the sub-urban middle class (Bisaga et al., 2005; Edwards George & Franko, 2010; Forbes & Frederick, 2008; Regan & Cachelin, 2006; Warren, 2010). The more that American ethnic minority women and non-Western women adopt the values of mainstream U.S. society, the more they may suffer

GET INVOLVED 4.3
Perceptions of Actual and Desirable Physique

For this exercise, survey four young adult females, two Black and two White. Show each woman the following nine figure drawings and ask her the following questions:

1. Using the numbers under the figures, which represents your perception of *your current body*?

2. Which represents your perception of *your ideal body*?

3. Which is the body you feel *men find the most attractive*?

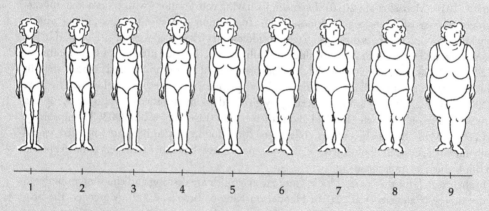

| 1   2   3   4   5   6   7   8   9 |

WHAT DOES IT MEAN?

1. How did the women's perceptions of their current body compare with their perception of their ideal body?

2. How did women's perceptions of their current body compare with what they feel men find most attractive?

3. Were there any differences in the perceptions of Black and White women?

from body dissatisfaction and eating problems (Dohm et al., 2010; Swim et al., 2010). Try Get Involved 4.3 for a closer look at the body images of Black and White women.

Lesbians are less preoccupied with weight and dieting and have higher levels of body self-esteem than heterosexual women and gay men (Ålgars et al., 2009; Grogan, 2008), but they have still more weight concerns than heterosexual men (Morrison et al., 2004; Rothblum, 2002; Share & Mintz, 2002; Slevin, 2010; Wrench & Knapp, 2008). Why are lesbians more comfortable with their bodies? According to Judith Daniluk (1998), society views lesbians as sexually unappealing because of their sexual orientation, no matter how slender and beautiful they might be. This decoupling of physical attractiveness and sexual appeal may help protect lesbians from developing a negative body image. Another explanation (Farr & Degroult, 2008; Polimeni et al., 2009) is that lesbian subculture downplays or actively resists the dominant cultural value placed on beauty for women (see Chapter 8).

Summary

CHILDREN'S KNOWLEDGE AND BELIEFS ABOUT GENDER

- Children are able to distinguish females and males as early as 3–4 months of age.
- By age 2 or 3, they can label their own gender and show some awareness of gender- typical objects, activities, and occupations.
- Awareness of gender stereotypes for personality traits emerges later in the preschool years.
- Stereotypes become more flexible after age 7.

GENDER-RELATED ACTIVITIES AND INTERESTS

- Preschool girls and boys are similar in their motor skills.
- Differences favoring boys become more pronounced in adolescence as a result of both environmental and biological factors.
- Participation in sports is associated with positive traits in females. Their participation has soared since the passage of Title IX.
- By age 3, gender differences in toy choices and activities are well established.
- Gender segregation, the preference for same-gender children, emerges by age 3 and increases during childhood.

INFLUENCES ON GENDER DEVELOPMENT

- Both parents, but fathers more than mothers, encourage gender-typical toys, play activities, and chore assignments for their children.

- Parents talk more to their daughters, give them less autonomy, and encourage their prosocial behaviors.
- Maternal employment is associated with less stereotyped gender-related concepts and preferences in sons and daughters.
- Older siblings influence the gender development of younger siblings.
- Boys receive more attention from teachers than girls do. They are more likely to be called on, praised, and criticized constructively.
- Girls are also shortchanged in school textbooks.
- Children exert strong pressures on each other to engage in gender-typical behavior.
- Boys are viewed more negatively than girls when they engage in cross-gender activity.
- Children who are heavy television viewers are more aware of gender stereotypes.
- Exposure to characters who show nontraditional behaviors reduces children's gender stereotypes.

PUBERTY

- During puberty, sexual organs mature and secondary sex characteristics appear.
- Menarche is a major event of puberty.
- Girls who mature early tend to adjust less easily than late-maturing girls.

PSYCHOSOCIAL DEVELOPMENT IN ADOLESCENCE

- Adolescent girls and boys show similar patterns of identity development, focusing on both occupational choices and interpersonal relationships.
- Girls begin to show lower self-esteem than boys in early adolescence, and the gender gap widens during adolescence. Explanations include girls' dissatisfaction with their physical appearance, shortchanging of girls in school, and girls' "losing their voice." Black girls have higher self-esteem than other girls.
- Early adolescents show an increasing divergence in gender-related behaviors and attitudes, known as gender intensification.
- Adolescent girls, compared to boys, have a more negative body image and are more likely to diet. Cultural pressures for slimness are partly responsible.

Key Terms

rough-and-tumble play *78*
socialization *80*
puberty *86*
primary sex characteristics *86*

secondary sex characteristics *86*
menarche *86*
secular trend *86*
adolescent growth spurt *89*

identity *90*
individuate *90*
self-esteem *91*
gender intensification *93*

What Do You Think?

1. Should parents attempt to raise their children in gender-neutral ways? If so, why? What would be the advantages? What would be the disadvantages? Incorporate material from Chapters 2 and 3 into your answers.
2. Why do you think teachers pay more attention to boys than to girls? What can be done to ensure more equal treatment of girls in the classroom?
3. In your opinion, why are boys who engage in feminine activities viewed more negatively than girls who engage in masculine activities?
4. Lois Gould (1990), in her fictional *X: A Fabulous Child's Story*, wrote about Baby X, whose gender was concealed from everyone except its parents. This created considerable consternation among relatives and family friends. Why do you think that was?
5. The earlier onset of puberty in the United States and western Europe has not been accompanied by earlier gains in social and emotional development that would help children successfully manage their sexuality. What are the implications for individual adolescents and for society?
6. What actions can parents and teachers take to help enhance the self-esteem of adolescent girls?
7. How does the social construction of gender influence women's body images versus men's body images?

If You Want to Learn More

Bettis, P. J., & Adams, N. G. (2005). *Geographies of girlhood: Identities in-between.* Mahwah, NJ: Erlbaum.

Bordo, S. (2004). *Unbearable weight: Feminism, western culture, and the body.* Los Angeles: University of California Press.

Brake, D. L. (2010). *Getting in the game: Title IX and the women's sports revolution.* New York: New York University Press.

Denner, J., & Guzman, B. L. (Eds.). (2006). *Latina girls: Voices of adolescent strength in the United States.* New York: New York University Press.

Eliot, L. (2009). *Pink brain, blue brain: How small differences grow into troublesome gaps—and what we can do about it.* New York: Houghton Mifflin Harcourt.

Fingerson, L. (2006). *Girls in power: Gender, body, and menstruation in adolescence.* Albany, NY: State University of New York Press.

Harris, A. (Ed.). (2004). *All about the girl: Culture, power, and identity.* New York: Routledge.

Leadbeater, B. J., & Way, N. (Eds.). (2007). *Urban girls revisited: Building strengths.* New York: New York University Press.

Levin, D. E., & Kilbourne, J. (Eds.). (2008). *So sexy so soon: The new sexualized childhood and what parents can do to protect their kids.* New York: Ballantine Books.

Lipkin, E. (2009). *Girls' studies.* Berkeley, CA: Seal Press.

Nalebuff, R. K. (Ed.). (2009). *My little red book.* New York: Twelve.

Paechter, C. (2007). *Being boys, being girls: Learning masculinities and femininities.* Berkshire: Open University Press.

Sadker, D., & Zittleman, K. (2009). *Still failing at fairness: How gender bias cheats girls and boys in school and what we can do about it.* New York: Scribner.

Sax, L. (2010). *Girls on the edge: The four factors driving the new crisis for girls.* New York: Basic Books.

Straus, M. B. (2007). *Adolescent girls in crisis: Intervention and hope.* New York: Norton.

Weitz, R. (2010). *The politics of women's bodies: Sexuality, appearance, and behavior* (3rd ed.). New York: Oxford University Press.

Websites

Sports

Empowering Women in Sports
http://www.feminist.org/sports

http://www.girlpower.gov
http://www.girlsinc.org/
http://www.nedic.ca/

CHAPTER 5

Gender Comparisons
Social Behavior, Personality, Communication, and Cognition

Gender-Related Social Behaviors and Personality Traits
- Aggression
- Prosocial Behavior
- Influenceability
- Emotionality
- Moral Reasoning

Communication Style
- Verbal Communication
- Nonverbal Communication

Gender Comparison of Cognitive Abilities
- Verbal Ability
- Visual–Spatial Ability
- Mathematics Ability

In high school, I once struggled with some concepts in my advanced algebra class. My teacher did not help me much. He kept telling me not to worry about it; that I would not be using algebra in my future. I excelled in that class, and kept taking math courses, which surprised him. (Nathalie, a 22-year-old college senior)

GENDER-RELATED SOCIAL BEHAVIORS AND PERSONALITY TRAITS

In Chapter 2, we examined numerous gender stereotypes. How accurately do these stereotypes reflect actual differences in the social behaviors, personality characteristics, communication style, and cognitive abilities of females and males? In this chapter, we review all four of these areas. As we shall see, some stereotypes have at least a grain (or more) of truth to them, whereas others are not supported by the evidence. Two cautionary notes: First, even when gender differences are found, they are typically small. Second, there is considerable overlap in the characteristics of females and males (Caplan & Caplan, 2009; White, 2011). For example, girls are generally more nurturant toward younger children than boys are, but some boys show greater nurturance than some girls.

Aggression

She talks about you.
You talk about her.
She glares at you.
You stare at her.
Is it a rumor, or is it the truth?
She lies to you, you lie right back.
You need a friend, but for sure not her.
She takes your guy.
You want him back.
Too much stress, too much pressure.
But I guess this is life.

(Kelsey, 12 years old)

Aggression is behavior that is intended to hurt someone, either physically or verbally. By age 2, boys show higher levels of physical aggression than girls, and during the preschool period, the differences become striking (Alink et al., 2006; Asendorpf et al., 2008; Baillargeon et al., 2007; Miner & Clarke-Stewart, 2008). Boys continue to be more physically and verbally aggressive than girls into adulthood (Bushman & Huesmann, 2010; Campbell et al., 2010; Card et al., 2008; Faris & Felmlee, 2011; Ostrov & Godleski, 2010). The differences hold across socioeconomic groups and across cultures (Archer, 2004; Eliot, 2009; Gershoff et al., 2010). Beginning in preschool, however, girls are somewhat more likely than boys to use **relational aggression**, which involves *harming others through nonphysical hurtful manipulation of their peer relationships*. For example, girls might exclude a peer from their play group, or spread malicious rumors and gossip about her, as illustrated in Kelsey's poem in the beginning of this section and in movies such as *Heathers* and *Mean Girls* (Murray-Close & Ostrov, 2009; Ostrov & Godleski, 2010; Pepler et al., 2008; Wiseman, 2009). Moreover, girls are more likely than boys to perceive relationally aggressive acts as mean and hurtful and to be more distressed by such behaviors (Coyne et al., 2006; Crick et al., 2009). This gender difference in how children display aggression is so striking that even preschool children are aware of it (Giles & Heyman, 2005).

Interestingly, although aggression is typically associated with rejection by peers, girls who use relational aggression tend to be both popular and powerful within their peer group (Brown & Larson, 2009; Closson, 2009; Dijkstra et al., 2009). What might account for this unexpected finding? According to Suzanna Rose and her colleagues (2004), strategic use of relational aggression may serve to maintain social dominance as well as to display superiority.

Both biological and environmental influences may contribute to gender differences in aggression (Bushman & Huesmann, 2010; Hines, 2010). On the biological side, it has been noted that the gender difference emerges early and appears across most cultures. In addition, the sex hormone testosterone appears to play a role, at least in animal aggression. Research on the relationship between aggressive behavior and testosterone in humans, however, has produced mixed results (Bushman & Huesmann, 2010; Frieze, 2005). A meta-analysis by Angela Book and her colleagues (2001) yielded a weak, positive correlation between testosterone and aggressive behavior in humans. However, this correlation is difficult to interpret because the causal direction can go either way. That is, increasing testosterone levels can lead to aggression, but it is also the case that acting aggressively (such as winning a sports contest) leads to a rise in testosterone levels (Bushman & Huesmann, 2010; Galambos et al., 2009; McIntyre & Edwards, 2009). Jacquelyn White and Robin Kowalski (1994) suggest that studies showing a connection between aggression and testosterone may be unduly emphasized because they are consistent with the stereotype of the aggressive male and the submissive female.

Environmental factors are probably even more important than biological ones in producing gender differences in aggression. For one thing, parents are less tolerant of aggressive acting-out behaviors in girls (Blakemore et al., 2009; Chaplin et al., 2005; Martin & Ross, 2005). Consequently, girls expect more guilt, more peer and parental disapproval, and fewer material gains for aggression than boys do (Eisenberg et al., 1996). In addition, parents' encouragement of boys' rougher, dominance-oriented physical play and their use of gender-typical toys such as guns may serve to promote and maintain aggression. Furthermore, the rougher, dominance-oriented play of boys' groups may contribute to the maintenance of higher aggression levels in boys (Hines, 2010).

Prosocial Behavior

Prosocial behavior is *voluntary behavior intended to benefit someone else.* It includes helping, comforting and caring for others, sharing, and cooperating (Eisenberg et al., 2009). The stereotype is that females are more nurturant, supportive, and helpful than males (Frieze & Li, 2010). Are they?

Most studies of children have found gender differences in prosocial behavior favoring girls (Eisenberg et al., 2009; Knafo & Plomin, 2006). For example, toddler girls under the age of 2 are more likely than boys to comfort someone in distress (Kiang et al., 2004). Girls also are kinder and help others more than boys do (Caprara et al., 2001; Eisenberg et al., 2009). This tendency of girls to be more prosocial has been found in a variety of cultures (Eisenberg et al., 2009).

Studies with adults, however, paint a different picture, with men helping more than women. This is partly because studies with adults frequently involve instrumental and chivalrous assistance, such as rescuing strangers, sometimes in potentially dangerous situations (e.g., helping to change a tire or picking up a hitchhiker). Women, on the other hand, are more likely to offer psychological support and help to friends and family members (Rankin & Eagly, 2008; Sprecher et al., 2007; Wood & Eagly, 2010). Unfortunately, this aspect of helpfulness has largely been overlooked by researchers. In one extremely dangerous real-world situation—the rescuing of Jews during the Holocaust—women helped as often as men. They are also more likely to donate kidneys, volunteer for the Peace Corps, and serve as medical volunteers in dangerous settings (Wood & Eagly, 2010).

Gender differences in helping styles are consistent with stereotyped expectations for males and females. How do the differences arise? In many societies, girls are expected to be more nurturant, kind, and emotionally supportive than boys, and they are rewarded for these behaviors. Boys, meanwhile, are more often rewarded for helping behaviors that involve rescuing, risk taking, and chivalry (Eagly, 2009; Eisenberg et al., 2009).

Influenceability

Females tend to be stereotyped as more easily influenced and more conforming than males. Is there any evidence to support this view? Again, the answer depends on several factors, such as the type of measure used and the gender composition of the group being studied (Carli, 2010). The two major types of tasks used to measure the ability to influence are persuasion studies and group pressure conformity studies. In **persuasion studies**, *participants indicate their position on a controversial topic.*

A different position supported by arguments is presented by another individual and the participant's position is again measured. **Group pressure conformity studies** are similar, except that *a group of people, not just one individual, supports a position discrepant with the participant's.*

Alice Eagly and Linda Carli (1981) performed a meta-analysis on both kinds of studies and found that women were more easily influenced than men. The gender difference was greater for the conformity studies, but all differences were small. Females were influenced more when masculine topics, such as technology or sports, were used. The gender difference was also greater when the researchers were male.

Several factors may account for these findings. For one thing, females are socialized to yield to social influence whereas males are trained to do the influencing. Remember also that from an early age, females show more cooperation and less conflict in group settings. Accepting the views of others can be viewed as a mechanism for maintaining social harmony and avoiding conflict. In addition, consistent with the theme that females have less power than males, women are accorded a lower status than men in most societies. Individuals of lower status generally learn to conform to the wishes of higher-status individuals (Eagly et al., 2000; Hogg, 2010).

Emotionality

In most societies, females are thought to be more emotional than males: more fearful, anxious, easily upset, and emotionally expressive. Males are viewed as more likely to express anger and pride and to hide or deny their emotions (Brody & Hall, 2008; Kagan, 2010). Even preschool children, when read stories in an emotionally ambiguous context, are more likely to perceive boys as angry and girls as sad (Parmley & Cunningham, 2008). Is there any truth to these stereotypes?

Preschool girls express less anger and more fearfulness than boys. They are also better at labeling emotions and understanding complex emotions such as pride (Bosacki & Moore, 2004). In elementary school, boys start to hide negative emotions such as sadness whereas girls begin to hide negative emotions, such as disappointment, that might hurt others' feelings. By adolescence, girls report more sadness, shame, and guilt, whereas boys deny experiencing these feelings. Girls and women also report more fear and anxiety than boys and men (Else-Quest et al., 2006; McLean & Anderson, 2009). In addition, they report experiencing emotions more intensely and more readily (Blakemore et al., 2009; Simon & Nath, 2004). Note that these findings do not answer the question of whether females are actually more emotional than males or whether they simply are more likely to report their feelings.

Another aspect of emotionality is **empathy**, which involves *feeling the same emotion that someone else is feeling.* The stereotype is that women are more empathic than men. Are they in reality? The answer depends on how you measure empathy. When individuals are asked to report how they feel in certain situations (e.g., "Does seeing people cry upset you?"), females show more empathy than males (Bekker & van Assen, 2008; Eisenberg et al., 2006; Wentzel et al., 2007). However, when individuals' behaviors are observed unobtrusively or when their physiological reactions are measured, no gender differences in empathy are found (Eisenberg et al., 2006). These findings suggest that when people know what is being measured and can control their reactions, they may act in the socially acceptable gender-typical manner.

Socialization seems to be an important factor in the development of differences in emotionality (or in the willingness to report emotions). We saw in Chapter 4 that parents are more accepting of fear and sadness in girls and anger in boys. Mothers focus more on emotions, particularly sad emotions, when talking to their daughters (Fivush et al., 2000; Gleason & Ely, 2002). In addition, parents put more pressure on sons to control their emotions, while encouraging their daughters to be emotionally expressive (Blakemore et al., 2009). Parents also emphasize closer emotional relationships with daughters than with sons. As early as preschool, mothers and daughters are already closer emotionally than mothers and sons (Benenson et al., 1998).

A series of studies by Penelope Davis (1999) on adults' memories of childhood events provides an interesting illustration of the apparent social construction of gender differences in emotionality. She found that, in general, females and males did not differ either in the number of memories recalled or in how quickly they recalled them. However, females consistently recalled more childhood memories of events associated with emotion and were faster in accessing these memories. Furthermore, this difference was observed across a wide range of emotions experienced by both the individuals and others.

Moral Reasoning

Are there gender differences in moral reasoning? The question has been hotly debated ever since Lawrence Kohlberg (Kohlberg & Puka, 1994) proposed that males show higher levels of moral reasoning than females. In his research, Kohlberg asked individuals to respond to moral dilemmas. In one dilemma, a druggist refuses to lower the price of an expensive drug that could save the life of a dying woman. Her husband, who cannot afford the drug, then steals it. Was he right or wrong in doing so, and why? Kohlberg reported that males' answers emphasized abstract justice and "law and order," which he believed to be more advanced than the emphasis on caring and concern for others expressed by females. As we saw in Chapter 1, Carol Gilligan (1982, 1994) argued that females' moral reasoning is just as advanced as that of males, but that females speak "in a different voice" that emphasizes personal connections rather than abstract legalities.

Research, however, generally fails to support Kohlberg's and Gilligan's view that there are gender differences in the underlying basis of moral reasoning (Turiel, 2006). For example, a meta-analysis of 113 studies by Sara Jaffee and Janet Hyde (2000) found only slight differences in the care orientation favoring females and in the justice orientation favoring males. In some studies, in fact, women are more likely than men to show both a care response *and* a justice response (Mainiero et al., 2008). In addition, extensive literature reviews (Gibbs et al., 2007; Walker, 2006) find no consistent gender differences in moral reasoning across a variety of cultures. And, among college students in the United States, women are more concerned with moral issues than are men (Skoe et al., 2002).

Moral reasoning appears to be more dependent on the context of the situation than on the gender of the individual (Turiel, 2006). For example, both women and men are more likely to use a care-based approach when interacting with a friend than with a stranger, or when interacting with a member of their in-group as opposed to someone outside their group (Fine, 2010).

COMMUNICATION STYLE

> In short, feminine talk is a lot of polite talk about silly things; whereas masculine talk is a little blunt talk about important things.

> (Spender, 1979, quoted in Popp et al., 2003)

People believe that men have demanding voices, swear, are straight to the point, are forceful, and boastful. Women, on the other hand, are thought to talk a lot, speak politely and emotionally, enunciate clearly, use good grammar, talk about trivia, and gossip (Popp et al., 2003). According to a bestselling book, women and men are so different in their communication styles that it is as if *Men Are From Mars, Women Are From Venus* (Gray, 1992). What does research tell us about differences between the communication styles of females and males?

Verbal Communication

Evidence supports a number of gender differences, and one of these is, indeed, the difference in talkativeness. Interestingly, however, the talking behavior of females and males is the opposite of the stereotype. In many situations studied by researchers, including online discussion groups, males talk more than females, more frequently, and for longer periods of time. Furthermore, this gender difference is apparent as early as the preschool years and continues throughout adulthood (Cameron, 2007; Carli & Bukatko, 2000; Gleason & Ely, 2002; Leaper & Ayers, 2007).

Given the gender difference in talkativeness, one might expect that males also interrupt others more than females do. Research indicates that gender differences in the number of interruptions depend on the situations and also that women and men have different goals when they interrupt others (Gleason & Ely, 2002). One purpose of an interruption is *to show interest and affirm what the other is saying*—an **affiliative interruption**—for example, by saying "uh-huh." A second reason for interrupting is *to usurp the floor and control the conversation*—an **intrusive interruption**. This might be accomplished by taking over the conversation even though the previous speaker shows no signs of relinquishing the floor. It might not surprise you to learn that females are more likely to engage in affiliative interruption and males, in intrusive interruption (Athenstaedt et al., 2004; Eckert & McConnell-Ginet, 2003; Leman et al., 2005). These differences are consistent with both the social construction of females as other-directed and caring, and the gender inequality in power. Affiliative interruptions are one way to express an interest in other people, and females might have learned through their socialization that this was one means of showing concern about and reinforcing others. On the other hand, both intrusive interruptions and talkativeness are associated with the desire to maintain dominance and with the power to do so. More powerful individuals are seen as having the right to dominate the conversation and to usurp the floor. This connection between power and communication behavior is illustrated in a study by Elizabeth Cashdan (1998), who observed female and male college students in group discussions and asked them to rate their housemates on characteristics of power. The more powerful students were found to talk the most.

Gender differences have also been found in conversational style. Consistent with communal and agentic stereotypes, studies show that females use more emotional, polite, affiliative, soothing, and supportive speech, whereas males use more direct, goal-oriented, assertive, domineering, and abrupt speech (DeFrancisco & Palczewski, 2007; Leaper & Ayers, 2007; Leman & Lam, 2008; Shinn & O'Brien, 2008). For example, women are more likely than men to refer to emotions and use intensive adverbs ("She is *really* friendly"), whereas men tend to use directives ("Think about this") and judgmental adjectives ("Working can be a drag") more than women do.

Another gender difference in conversational style is that females use speech that is sometimes referred to as more tentative. Such speech may contain uncertainty verbs (e.g., "It *seems* that the class will be interesting"), hedges (e.g., "*I kind of feel* you should not be too upset about this"), tag questions ("It's hot in here, *don't you think*?"), and disclaimers of expertise ("*I may be wrong, but . . .*") (Basow, 2008; Leaper & Robnett, 2011).

One explanation for this gender difference in speech is that females have lower self-esteem than males and, consequently, speak more tentatively (Lakoff, 1990). Another interpretation is that women's tentativeness results not from their uncertainty but from their lower status (DeFrancisco & Palczewski, 2007; Speer & Stokoe, 2011). Less powerful individuals are more likely to use more tentative speech, regardless of their own confidence in what they are saying, and, as we have noted throughout this text, women have less power than men. In support of this explanation, research suggests that females use more tentative language in their conversations with men but not in their interactions with other women (Carli & Bukatko, 2000).

Still another perspective on this gender difference in conversational style is that the language features used by women do not reflect tentativeness at all but instead are due to women's communal orientation—their desire to leave open the lines of communication and encourage the participation of others (Speer & Stokoe, 2011). Research has found that tag questions in fact serve a variety of functions depending on the situation. For example, in one study (Cameron, in LaFrance, 2001), both women and men in powerful roles used tag questions to generate talk from other participants. However, women and men in less powerful roles used them to seek reassurance for their opinions. This finding indicates that gender differences in verbal communication depend in part on the situation. For example, conversational style is generally more gender-stereotyped in same-sex groups than in mixed-sex groups (Athenstaedt et al., 2004; Leaper, 2004). In the latter groups, women and men tend to adjust their behaviors to each other. Whatever the explanation for women's greater use of so-called tentative speech, such speech makes people seem less credible, powerful, or persuasive (Brownlow et al., 2003). Can you think of how this perception might be problematic for women in leadership positions?

Another aspect of conversational style is the way people respond to a friend's troubles. Shari Michaud and Rebecca Warner (1997) found that women were more likely than men to offer sympathy in response to a friend's problems, whereas men were more likely to change the subject. In addition, women were more likely than men to appreciate receiving advice or sympathy, whereas men were more likely to resent it. On the other hand, research by Erina MacGeorge and her colleagues (2004) found only slight differences in the way women and men responded. Both sexes preferred to listen, sympathize, and give thoughtful advice. Men were only slightly more likely to give advice, and women were slightly more likely to provide support. Similarly, both women and men appreciated advice that was relevant to their problems and was given in a respectful, kind manner. MacGeorge and her colleagues concluded that women and men do not come from two different communication cultures but are instead from the same "planet." Do Get Involved 5.1 to see whether your findings support the view of Gray or MacGeorge.

Like Erina MacGeorge, Anthony Mulac (1998) argues that gender differences in communication style are subtle and that it is difficult to identify the gender of speakers simply from their words. Mulac and his colleagues performed several studies in which college students were asked to determine the gender of a communicator after reading a written communication, such as a transcription of a speech from a public speaking class or an essay describing landscape photos. In none of these situations were respondents able to guess accurately the gender of the communicator. Mulac

GET INVOLVED 5.1
"Troubles Talk": Effects of Gender on Communication Styles

Give the following two-part survey to two female and two male traditional-aged college students.

PART I. Imagine your friend is upset because of having one of the PROBLEMS listed here. For each problem, indicate how likely you would be to make each of the listed RESPONSES.

PROBLEM A: *Your friend says "I'm upset because I may be breaking up with my dating partner."* *What do you do?*

Offer sympathy	very unlikely	1	2	3	4	5	very likely
Change the subject	very unlikely	1	2	3	4	5	very likely

PROBLEM B: *Your friend says "I'm upset because I may fail a course."* *What do you do?*

Offer sympathy	very unlikely	1	2	3	4	5	very likely
Change the subject	very unlikely	1	2	3	4	5	very likely

PART II. Now imagine that you have each of the problems cited earlier. Indicate how you FEEL when your friend makes the indicated RESPONSES.

> **PROBLEM A:** *You tell your friend "I'm upset because I may be breaking up with my dating partner." Your friend offers SYMPATHY. How much do you feel the following?*

Grateful	not at all	1	2	3	4	a lot
Resentful	not at all	1	2	3	4	a lot

> **PROBLEM B:** *You tell your friend "I'm upset because I may fail a course." Your friend gives ADVICE on solving the problem. How much do you feel the following?*

Grateful	not at all	1	2	3	4	a lot
Resentful	not at all	1	2	3	4	a lot

Source: Adapted from Michaud and Warner (1997). With kind permission from Springer Science+Business Media: *Sex Roles*, 37, 527–540, Michaud, S. L., & Warner, R. M. (1997). "Gender differences in self-reported response to troubles talk." Copyright © 1997, Springer Netherlands.

WHAT DOES IT MEAN?

For Part I, compare the scores of your female and male respondents on the "sympathy" scale of the two problems. Do the same for the "change the subject" scale. For Part II, compare the female and male respondents in terms of how grateful or resentful they are for receiving sympathy (Problem A), and how grateful or resentful they are for receiving advice (Problem B).

1. Did you find the same results as Michaud and Warner (1997) for Parts I and II of the survey? If not, give reasons.

2. As described in the chapter, John Gray theorizes that women and men come from two different cultures of communication, whereas Erina MacGeorge disagrees. Do your findings support the view of Gray or MacGeorge? Explain.

3. Your data, like those of Michaud and Warner (1997), were collected from traditional-aged college students. Do you think that middle-aged women and men would respond differently? (You would, of course, have to make the problems age-appropriate by, for example, substituting "spouse" for "dating partner," and "get a poor job performance evaluation" instead of "fail a course.") Explain your answer.

---

concluded that "spoken and written language used in everyday communication by women and men, as well as girls and boys, displays a high degree of similarity" (p. 131).

Similar to conversational style, there are some differences in the actual content of females' and males' conversations. Women are more likely than men to talk about personal topics and social-emotional activities, whereas men are more likely to discuss impersonal topics and task-oriented activities (Newman et al., 2008). For example, Ruth Anne Clark (1998) asked college students to list all the topics discussed in a recent conversation with a same-gender close friend and to indicate the dominant topic. Not surprisingly, given the importance of romantic relationships to young adults, both females and males talked about the other gender. However, women's conversations were more likely than men's to be dominated by interpersonal issues whereas men were more likely to focus on sports and other leisure activities.

Nonverbal Communication

Consistent with the communal stereotype, people believe that females are more likely than males to engage in nonverbal behaviors that demonstrate interpersonal interest and warmth. Are these beliefs accurate? Considerable evidence shows that they are. For one thing, girls and women are more likely than boys and men to engage in mutual eye contact with another individual for longer periods of time, particularly if that individual is female (Ambady & Weisbuch, 2010; Hall, 2006). This gender difference in gazing behavior is not present at birth but appears as early as 13 weeks of age and continues through adulthood (Leeb & Rejskind, 2004). Females also are more likely to smile, nod, lean forward, and approach others more closely (Basow, 2008; Hall, 2006; LaFrance et al., 2003). Girls and women across cultures are also more sensitive to the meanings of nonverbal messages portrayed by others and more accurately interpret their emotions (Ambady & Weisbuch, 2010; Brody & Hall, 2000). In addition, research on interpersonal sensitivity indicates that females are better than males at initially getting to know the personality traits, emotional states, and behavioral tendencies of other people. They are also more accurate at recalling the appearance and behaviors of social targets (Hall & Schmid Mast, 2010).

One explanation for these gender differences is the differential socialization of females and males, with females receiving greater societal encouragement for being socially concerned (Basow, 2008; Leaper & Ayers, 2007). Smiling and gazing communicate interest and involvement in another person. In addition, women's ability to accurately decipher other people's emotional states might stem from their greater interest in others and their more extensive experience with emotional communication.

A different explanation of females' superior sensitivity skills lies in their subordinate status within society. Less powerful individuals are good interpreters of the nonverbal cues of more powerful people (Keltner & Lerner, 2010; Kraus et al., 2010). This ability to decipher the nonverbal behavior of others allows lower-status individuals, including women, to anticipate the reactions of those in power and thus respond appropriately (Basow, 2008; Krause et al., 2010).

Touch is another form of nonverbal communication. Nancy Henley (1995) contended that there is an unwritten societal rule that high-status individuals can touch low-status individuals, but those of low status cannot touch those of high status. For example, it is more likely that the president of a corporation will pat a janitor on the back than the reverse. Henley concluded that because males have more power than females, there is more male-to-female touching than the reverse.

Studies show that males do show more touching associated with instrumental goals such as asserting power or showing sexual intent. On the other hand, women exhibit more touching in the form of hugs or other cues of social support (Hall, 2006). And in established heterosexual relationships, both women and men are found to initiate touch (DeFrancisco & Palczewski, 2007). Obviously, gender and status differences in touching are more complex than were originally believed.

GENDER COMPARISON OF COGNITIVE ABILITIES

Research into questions about sex differences and similarities in intelligence is fraught with political minefields and emotional rhetoric from all ends of the political spectrum. But research is the only way we can distinguish between those stereotypes that have some basis in fact and those that don't.

(Diane Halpern, president-elect of the American Psychological Association, cited in Kersting, 2003)

Although females and males do not differ in general intelligence, they do vary in certain cognitive skills. Some differences emerge in childhood but others do not appear until adolescence (Halpern, 2007; Hines, 2010). No doubt some of these differences have a bearing on the career choices made by females and males. Remember our cautionary notes from the beginning of this chapter. Gender differences, where they exist, are generally small. Females and males are much more alike in cognitive abilities than they are different. Even when there is a small average difference favoring one gender on a test of a particular cognitive skill, many individuals of the other gender will score well above the average. Also recall from Chapter 1 that the presence of a gender difference does not tell us anything about the causes of the difference. Finally, keep in mind that cognitive skills, like the social behaviors and personality traits we discussed earlier in this chapter, develop within a social context. As we shall see throughout this section, attitudes and expectations about the cognitive performance of females and males play an important role in socially constructing that performance.

Verbal Ability

Verbal abilities include a variety of language skills such as vocabulary, reading comprehension, writing, spelling, grammar, and word fluency. Females show superior performance on most verbal tasks, although the differences are small (Halpern et al., 2007; Hines, 2010; Hyde, 2007). Gender differences in verbal ability appear earlier than other cognitive gender differences. Girls are more vocal than boys during infancy, talk at an earlier age, produce longer utterances, have larger vocabularies, and are more fluent (Leaper & Smith, 2004; Statistics Canada, 2006; Stoner et al., 2005; Tamis-LeMonda et al., 2004). They also are less likely to have developmental delays involving language (Sices et al., 2004).

Girls continue to show an edge in verbal skills throughout the grade school years. They achieve higher scores on tests of reading comprehension and are less likely to display reading problems such as reading disability (dyslexia) and reading below grade level (Mullis et al., 2007; U.S. Department of Education, 2007a,b). In adolescence, girls continue to outperform boys in reading, writing, language achievement, and speech production (OECD, 2009; U.S. Department of Education, 2007a,b; Van de gaer et al., 2009; Wai et al., 2010).

Some researchers have suggested that gender differences in verbal skills and other cognitive abilities are becoming smaller (Hyde & McKinley, 1997; Lippa, 2005) but others conclude that these differences are not diminishing and have remained relatively stable for decades (Nowell & Hedges, 1998; Voyer et al., 1995).

What might account for the greater verbal ability of girls? In Chapter 4, we saw that parents vocalize more to their infant daughters than to their infant sons (Clearfield & Nelson, 2006). This may lead to increased vocalization by female infants, which may in turn encourage parents to talk even more to their young daughters. Girls' early advantage with language may lead them to rely more on verbal approaches in their interactions with others, further enhancing their verbal ability. In addition, playing with stereotypically feminine toys such as dolls and stuffed animals may encourage pretend play and the development of verbal skills (Cherney & London, 2006).

Parental expectations also may play a role in girls' superior verbal skills. Studies in Finland, Japan, Taiwan, and the United States find that as early as first grade, children and their mothers generally believe that girls are better than boys at language and reading (Lummis & Stevenson, 1990; Räty & Kasanen, 2010). In addition, girls whose mothers think that girls are better readers receive higher scores on reading comprehension and vocabulary than girls whose mothers think girls and boys read equally well.

Visual–Spatial Ability

Visual–spatial ability refers to skill in visualizing objects or shapes and in mentally rotating and manipulating them. Visual–spatial skills are used extensively in engineering, architecture, surgery, and navigation and in everyday activities such as doing jigsaw puzzles or reading maps (Tzuriel & Egozi, 2010).

TYPES OF VISUAL–SPATIAL ABILITY.   Gender differences in visual–spatial ability are larger and more consistent than in other cognitive skills, with males outperforming females in many, although not all, areas (Hines, 2010; Schoenfeld et al., 2010; Titze et al., 2008). The pattern of differences depends on the spatial ability being measured. For example, females consistently excel in remembering the spatial location of objects (Halpern, 2007). Three other facets of visual–spatial ability have been identified by Marcia Linn and Anne Petersen (1985). Tasks used to measure these three components are shown in Figure 5.1.

a. **Mental Rotation**
Choose the responses that show the standard in a different orientation.

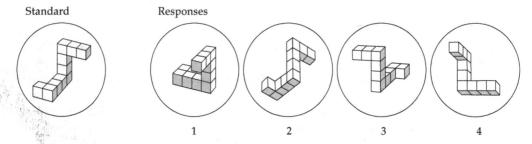

b. **Spatial Perception**
Pick the tilted bottle that has a horizontal water line.

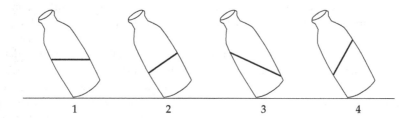

c. **Spatial Visualization**
Find the figure embedded in the complex shape below.

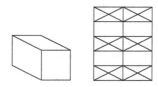

FIGURE 5.1 • Types of spatial tasks. Large sex differences favoring males appear on mental rotation, and males also do better than females on spatial perception. In contrast, sex differences on spatial visualization are weak or nonexistent.   *Source:* From "Emergence and Characterization of Sex Differences in Spatial Ability: A Meta-Analysis," M. C. Linn and A. C. Peterson, 1985, *Child Development, 56.* © The Society for Research in Child Development, Inc. Reprinted by permission.

Mental rotation involves *the ability to rapidly manipulate two- or three-dimensional figures* (see Figure 5.1a). Meta-analyses (see Chapter 1) show that the largest gender difference in spatial skills occurs on tests of this ability, with an overall *d* value of 0.60 (Voyer et al., 1995). Boys begin to outperform girls as early as 3 to 5 months of age (Moore & Johnson, 2008; Quinn & Liben, 2008). The gender difference continues in childhood and increases in adolescence and adulthood (Ehrlich et al., 2005; Hines, 2007; Vuoksimaa et al., 2010).

Tests of **spatial perception** involve the *ability to locate the vertical or the horizontal while ignoring distracting information*. For example, individuals may be asked to identify a horizontal water line in a tilted bottle (see Figure 5.1b). Gender differences on spatial perception tests like this are smaller than those found on mental rotation tasks (overall *d* = 0.40) (Hines, 2007; Vasilyeva, 2010; Voyer et al., 1995). Boys begin to perform better than girls by age 9, and this difference gets larger during the adolescent and adult years (Hines, 2010).

Tasks measuring **spatial visualization** include *finding simple shapes hidden within larger, complex shapes* (see Figure 5.1c). Gender differences favoring males are much smaller or absent on these tasks (overall *d* = 0.20) (Voyer et al., 1995).

The size of gender differences on spatial visualization and spatial perception tasks has been decreasing over time (Feingold, 1993; Voyer et al., 1995). Differences on mental rotation tests, however, have remained stable or even increased (Ruble & Martin, 1998; Voyer et al., 1995).

EXPLANATIONS OF GENDER DIFFERENCES. Several biological and environmental theories have been proposed to account for gender differences in visual–spatial abilities. Biological theories focus on genes, hormones, or the organization of the brain. According to one theory, visual–spatial ability is influenced by sex-linked recessive genes on the X chromosome. Research does not support this view, however (Newcombe, 2007a).

Another biological theory is that sex hormone levels affect visual–spatial skills in either of two ways (Hines, 2007; Vasilyeva, 2010). One possibility is that hormones circulating in the bloodstream might directly affect visual–spatial performance (Halpern et al., 2007). Studies have shown that women with higher testosterone levels achieve better spatial scores than women with lower testosterone levels, whereas the reverse is true in men (Puts et al., 2008). Keeping in mind that women's testosterone levels, on average, are lower than those of men, these findings suggest that the optimal level of testosterone for certain spatial skills is in the low male range (Hampson & Moffat, 2004). Other research, however, finds that actively circulating sex hormones do not affect spatial performance in adolescent girls and boys (Liben et al., 2002).

Another possibility is that prenatal sex hormones might irreversibly organize the brain to enhance certain spatial functions (Valla & Ceci, 2011). Evidence for this view comes from studies of girls with congenital adrenal hyperplasia (CAH) (see Chapter 3), which exposes them to high levels of prenatal androgens. At birth, the hormone imbalance is corrected and they are raised as girls. A meta-analysis found that CAH girls display better visual–spatial skills than unaffected girls (Puts et al., 2008). Some psychologists (e.g., Jordan-Young, 2010), however, point out that parents' awareness of the possible masculinizing effects of androgens may influence their treatment of and expectations for their daughters. Additional evidence for the possible role of prenatal androgens is that women with male twins outperform women who have female twins on mental rotation tasks (Vuoksimaa et al., 2010). Can you think of an alternative explanation? (Hint: Think of the different sex-typed activities that girls with a boy twin versus a girl twin would experience.)

Some theorists have attributed gender differences in visual–spatial skills to differences in the lateralization of female and male brains. **Lateralization** refers to the *specialization of the cerebral hemispheres of the brain to perform different cognitive functions*. For most individuals, the left hemisphere is involved in language and mathematical computation, whereas the right hemisphere is more involved in processing visual and spatial information (Fine, 2010). Evidence is mixed on whether male brains are more completely lateralized or specialized than female brains (Fine, 2010), but in any case, it is not clear that lateralization leads to better performance in visual–spatial or other cognitive skills (Newcombe, 2007a).

Numerous environmental theories have been proposed to explain gender differences in visual–spatial skills. Most of these focus on the impact of cultural gender stereotypes, observational learning, and encouragement of gender-typed activities and interests on shaping the experiences and attitudes of females and males. Participation in spatial activities fosters the development of spatial abilities in both girls and boys (Cherney, 2008; Hines, 2010; Liben & Christensen, 2011; Vasilyeva, 2010), yet females engage in fewer spatial activities than males. Why is this? For one thing, gender-stereotyped "boys'" toys, such as blocks, Erector Sets, Legos, and model planes and cars, provide more practice with visual–spatial skills than gender-stereotyped "girls'" toys (Vasilyeva, 2010). In addition, boys are also encouraged more than girls to participate in sports, which often involves moving balls and other objects through space (Etaugh & Rathus, 1995). Action video games, which are especially popular with boys, also appear to develop spatial skills (Cherney, 2008; Feng et al., 2007; Terlecki & Newcombe, 2005). If experience enhances the development of visual–spatial skills, then appropriate training ought to improve these skills. Research indicates that it does, for both females and males (Hines, 2010). Some training procedures have reduced or eliminated gender differences (Cherney, 2008; Newcombe, 2009, Terlecki et al., 2008; Tzuriel & Egozi, 2010; Vasilyeva, 2010).

The stereotyping of visual–spatial activities as masculine also influences performance. Studies have found that females and males with more masculine self-concepts perform better on visual–spatial tasks than those with less masculine self-concepts (Hines, 2010; Nori et al., 2009). However, if females are led to believe they will do well on these tasks, their scores improve dramatically. For example, prior to giving high school students the mental rotations test, Angelica Moe (2009) told one group that men were better than women on the test, and told another group that women were better on the test. A control group received no gender information. Men performed better than women in the control and the "men are better" groups. But women in the "women are better" group outperformed all other women, and did just as well as men.

Mathematics Ability

In 1990, Janet Hyde and her colleagues did a meta-analysis of 100 studies that compared gender differences in mathematics performance. They found that girls and boys did equally well at understanding mathematical concepts at all ages but that boys did better than girls in problem solving, starting at age 15. In studies that sampled from the general population, females showed a slight edge over males. However, in highly select samples (for instance, college students or mathematically precocious youth), differences in mathematics performance were larger and favored males (Else-Quest & Hyde, 2008).

Gender differences in mathematics performance have decreased since that time (Else-Quest & Hyde, 2008). One striking example is the change in the number of mathematically gifted girls and boys who score 700 on the math section of the SAT exam at age 13. Twenty-five years ago, there were 13 boys for every girl at that high level, achieved by only 1 out of every 10,000 students. Now, the ratio is only 3.8 to 1 (Wai et al., 2010). In addition, gender differences in mathematics performance no longer exist among U.S. elementary or high school students and girls earn better grades in math than boys (AAUW, 2010; Ceci & Williams, 2010; Lindberg et al., 2010). The magnitude of the gender difference in mathematics is not the same in all cultures, however, as shown in Explore Other Cultures 5.1.

EXPLORE OTHER CULTURES 5.1
Gender Differences in Mathematics Achievement Around the World

Differences between cultures in mathematics performance are much greater than the sex differences in performance. If one looks at the recent averages of boys' and girls' scores over several dozen countries, boys performed slightly better than girls (Else-Quest et al., 2010; Guiso et al., 2008). Results for individual countries, however, tell a different tale. Girls performed as well as boys in two of the three countries with the highest eighth-grade math scores (Chinese Taipei and Korea) and did better than boys in the third country (Singapore). Moreover, girls in all three countries scored much higher than boys in many other nations, including the United States (Hines, 2010).

Another indicator of the critical role of culture in fostering math talent in girls comes from recent research on the most difficult math competitions for young people, including the USA and International Mathematical Olympiads and the Putnam Competition. What is striking is that the majority of the top-scoring U.S. girls are immigrants or children of immigrants from countries where mathematics education is a priority for all children (Hyde & Mertz, 2009). Similarly, of the dozen top-ranked countries in the International Mathematical Olympiad, nearly all are in Eastern Europe or Asia (e.g., Bulgaria, Korea, Romania, Ukraine) and many have several prize-winning girls on their teams (Andreescu et al., 2008; Hyde & Mertz, 2009). Once again, these are countries with rigorous math curricula and cultures that encourage both girls and boys to excel in math.

A related finding is that gender differences in math performance and attitudes are smaller in countries with greater gender equality. More specifically, girls perform better in countries where females have equal access to education and where more women have careers in scientific research (Else-Quest et al., 2010). Together, these results indicate the powerful role of culture in the social construction of mathematics achievement.

Let us now examine more closely some of the factors associated with women's math performance.

FACTORS ASSOCIATED WITH MATH PERFORMANCE.   The single best predictor of scores on mathematics achievement tests is the number of mathematics courses an individual has taken. High school girls are now as likely as boys to take advanced mathematics and advanced biology and chemistry courses (National Science Foundation, 2008; Snyder & Dillow, 2010).

In college, however, some women avoid choosing math and science courses and careers even when they are gifted in mathematics (Ceci & Williams, 2010; Watt, 2008). This is troubling, because mathematics is a critical factor in career development, paving the way to high-status and high-salary careers in the sciences, medicine, engineering, and business (AAUW, 2010). Why, then, do many young women begin to avoid math and science in college?

One important clue is found in the attitudes and feelings that females and males develop toward mathematics. **Mathematics self-efficacy**, *one's beliefs concerning one's ability to successfully perform mathematical tasks,* is related to actual math performance (Betz, 2008; Williams & Williams, 2010). Researchers have found that males around the world have greater mathematics self-efficacy than females (Else-Quest et al., 2010; Martin et al., 2009; Nagy et al., 2010; Penner, 2008). Compared to males, females are more anxious about math and have less confidence in their ability to learn it, despite their equal or superior performance on tests and in the classroom. This self-perception emerges as early as elementary school, when girls begin to view math and science as part of the male domain, and it continues into adolescence (Cvencek et al., 2011; Galambos et al., 2009; Kurtz-Costes et al., 2008; Lindberg et al., 2008). The more that girls endorse this stereotype, and the lower their self-confidence in math, the poorer their math performance (Beilock et al., 2010; Ceci & Williams, 2010; Steffens & Jelenec, 2011), and the less interest they have in continuing math studies (Denissen et al., 2007; Kiefer & Sekaquaptewa, 2007). Adolescent girls are also less likely than adolescent boys to view mathematics and science as interesting and useful for their future careers (Frenzel et al., 2010). Keep in mind, however, that many girls and women have positive views about math. For a more detailed look at factors that are associated with women's perspectives on math, see Learn About the Research 5.1.

LEARN ABOUT THE RESEARCH 5.1
Factors Linked to Women's Perspectives on Math

Women's experiences with math and their attitudes toward it differ greatly. Debra Oswald and Richard Harvey (2003) set out to identify college women's differing perspectives on and experiences regarding math. They used a technique called the Q-method, which is considered a useful tool for feminist research (Kitzinger, 1999). In the first phase of the Q-method, women are interviewed about their thoughts, experiences, and attitudes regarding a topic, in this case, math. Researchers then select a large number of statements, called Q-sort items, and ask a new group of women to sort the items on a scale ranging from *strongly disagree* to *strongly agree*. Finally, participants with shared viewpoints are grouped together. Oswald and Harvey identified three groups of college women who differed in their experiences, attitudes, and awareness of stereotypes about math. Over half the women, labeled the "successfully encouraged" group, had high self-perceived math ability, found math to be personally relevant, and had positive attitudes toward it. They had been encouraged by parents and teachers and were relatively unaware of negative

stereotypes. About 20 percent of women were in the "mathematically aversive" group. They did not like math, had negative perceptions of their ability, and were somewhat aware of negative stereotypes about women and math. Although not directly discouraged in math, neither were they encouraged to pursue it. Nearly 20 percent of women belong to the "stereotypically discouraged" group, consisting of women who were very aware of negative gender stereotypes regarding math, lacked parental and teacher support, and had negative experiences in math. These women were fairly neutral in their attitudes toward math and in their own math abilities.

This study clearly shows that a number of variables, including self-perceived ability, experience with math, encouragement (or discouragement), and degree of awareness of stereotypes, are key factors linked to women's perspectives on mathematics. The authors were encouraged that their largest group consisted of successfully encouraged women. They saw this as a possible indicator that women may become better represented in math-related fields in the future.

WHAT DOES IT MEAN?

1. The stereotypically discouraged group was keenly aware of gender stereotypes about math. Do you think these women might be experiencing *stereotype threat?* (See next section.) Explain your answer.

2. Do you think the results of this study would have been different if the participants had

been a group of noncollege women? Explain your answer.

3. Into which of the three groups would you place yourself? Explain your answer.

EXPLANATIONS OF GENDER DIFFERENCES.   Several theories have been proposed to account for gender differences in math performance and attitudes. One viewpoint is that genetic, hormonal, and/or structural brain differences underlie gender differences in mathematical ability (Geary, 2007; Kimura, 2007). Critics have argued that research fails to support this interpretation (Newcombe, 2007a; Spelke, 2005), and the biological approach remains controversial.

Most researchers who study gender differences assert that whatever biological factors might exist are dwarfed by social forces that steer girls and young women away from mathematics. For starters, mathematics and science are stereotyped as male domains around the world (Nosek et al., 2009). As early as first grade, parents in China, Finland, Great Britain, Japan, and the United States believe that boys are better than girls in mathematics (Furnham et al., 2002; Lindberg et al., 2008; Lummis & Stevenson, 1990; Räty & Kasanen, 2010). These beliefs and expectations influence parents' perceptions and behaviors toward their children and also the children's own perceptions and behaviors (Hines, 2000). For example, a series of studies by Jacquelynne Eccles and her colleagues (e.g., Eccles et al., 2000) found that parents with stronger stereotypes about the abilities of girls and boys in math, English, and sports had different expectations of their own daughters' and sons' abilities in these areas. These expectations, in turn, were linked to their children's performance and self-perceptions of competence regardless of their actual ability levels.

How are parents' expectations transmitted to their children? Among other things, parents provide different experiences for their daughters and sons. For example, they are more likely to buy their sons science-related toys and computer materials (Bleeker, 2003; Simpkins et al., 2005). (See Learn About the Research 5.2 for a discussion of gender, computers, and video games.) In addition, when parents take their young children to interactive science exhibits at museums, they

LEARN ABOUT THE RESEARCH 5.2
Gender, Computers, and Video Games

Girls and boys both like to play video games, but boys spend more time playing them (Downs & Smith, 2010; Hilbrecht et al., 2008; Padilla-Walker et al., 2010; Willoughby, 2008). Why is this? One major reason is that girls find fewer games that appeal to them (Winn & Heeter, 2009). For one thing, most games have violent themes (Tafalla, 2007). The few females who appear in the games are often young, White, and hypersexualized (Williams et al., 2009; Yao et al., 2010). They are more likely than male characters to be shown partially nude or engaging in sexual behaviors (Burgess et al., 2007; Dill & Thill, 2007; Downs & Smith, 2010; Jansz & Martis, 2007; Miller & Summers, 2007). In addition, the females portrayed in video games are thinner than the average American woman, and those shown in games for children are thinner than those in games for adults (N. Martin et al., 2009). Playing video games that contain such unrealistically thin women lowers body esteem in young women players (Barlett & Harris, 2008), possibly decreasing the attractiveness of these games for girls and young women, and thus their time commitment. Girls and women prefer educational, action, and adventure-type games to those with violence and sports themes (Cherney & London, 2006; Gotlib, 2011). In recent years, the number of games designed for girls has increased sharply, but girls' games are as stereotyped as those designed for boys, featuring Barbies, makeovers, jewelry, and cooking (Rabasca, 2000; Seedyk & de Laet, 2005). When Mattel released the Barbie PC, a pink Barbie-themed computer for girls, it came with just a little more than half of the educational software found on Mattel's companion computer for boys (blue, of course), the Hot Wheels PC. Omitted were programs dealing with logic, human anatomy, and spatial visualization (Headlam, 2000).

(continued)

The gender gap in video-game usage has important implications for girls' experience with computers because video games often provide a child's introduction to the computer. By the time children enter school, and well into adulthood, males have more positive attitudes toward computers than females and have greater confidence in their computer skills (Beyer, 2006; Johnson et al., 2008; Misa, 2010). Although overall computer and Internet use rates for girls and boys are now about the same, boys are using computers to program, create Web pages, and solve problems, whereas girls dominate the blogosphere and social networking sites (Bennett & Yabroff, 2010; Pan, 2008).

How can girls' attitudes toward computing be improved? Here are some other suggestions (Jenkins & Cassell, 2008; Messersmith et al., 2008; Scheckler, 2011):

- Design more gender-neutral educational games.
- Use computers throughout the school curriculum, including areas in which girls excel.
- Make efforts to combat girls' popular stereotype that computer work is masculine, nerdy, and antisocial.
- Encourage computer clubs and summer computer classes for girls.

WHAT DOES IT MEAN?

1. Why are most video games and educational software dominated by themes of violence and adventure?
2. What do you think accounts for gender differences in computer-related attitudes?
3. What can be done to minimize or eliminate these differences?

---

are more likely to explain the science to their sons than to their daughters (Crowley et al., 2001). Similarly, both mothers and fathers are more likely to use scientific concepts and vocabulary when explaining a physics task to a son than to a daughter (Tenenbaum & Leaper, 2003; Tenenbaum et al., 2005).

Children receive the same message in the math and science classroom, as illustrated in Nathalie's comments at the start of the chapter. High school math and science teachers believe boys to be more interested, more confident, and higher achievers in these subjects than girls (Plucker, 1996). Teachers not only expect boys to do better but also overrate male students' capacity to do math (Lindberg et al., 2010). Because expectations often guide behavior, it is not surprising to find that math teachers spend more time instructing, interacting with, and giving feedback to boys than to girls (Blakemore et al., 2009). Even the former president of Harvard University, Lawrence Summers, asserted a few years ago that women may be innately inferior to men in mathematics, highlighting the prejudice women scientists face at every stage of their careers (Kantrowitz, 2005). And who knows how many young women are discouraged by such remarks from pursuing math and science careers in the first place? Recent research (AAUW, 2010; Brown & Leaper, 2010; National Academies of Sciences, 2007) indicates that negative stereotypes continue to discourage women from entering math and science careers and interfere with retention and advancement in these areas.

These prejudices provide another explanation for the poorer performance of females in math and in other masculine-stereotyped areas, such as visual–spatial tests, namely, the concept of **stereotype threat**. According to this view, developed by Claude Steele and his colleagues, *members of stereotyped groups (e.g., women and ethnic minorities) sometimes perform more poorly on tests because they are distracted and anxious about whether their performance will confirm a negative stereotype held about* *the group's ability* (Blascovich & Mandes, 2010; Schmader, 2010; Shapiro & Neuberg, 2007; C. M. Steele et al., 2002). Stereotype threat theory further predicts that performance suffers only when stereotype threat is activated but not when it is reduced or removed. To illustrate, researchers asked college students one of three questions before performing a mental rotation test, a task in which males usually excel (McGlone & Aronson, 2006). One group of students was asked about living in a single-sex or coed dorm, a question that activates gender stereotypes. A second group was asked why they chose to attend a selective private college. This primes students to focus on their intellectual talent. The control group was asked an irrelevant question about living in the northeastern United States. In the control group, men outperformed women on the mental rotation test, as in research discussed earlier in the chapter. In the group primed to focus on gender, the women did even worse, and the men did better. In the group cued to think about their status as students at a selective college, however, the gender gap closed dramatically. Women's scores increased but men's stayed the same, wiping out the gender difference in performance.

Similar results have been found in many academic settings, from elementary school through college, using various manipulations to either activate or minimize stereotype threat (Armenta, 2010; Campbell & Collaer, 2009; Gervais et al., 2011; Logel et al., 2009; Nguyen & Ryan, 2008; Rydell et al., 2010; Walton & Spencer, 2009; Zhang et al., 2009). The good news is that the pressures associated with negative stereotypes can be overcome by teaching students ways to reduce stereotype threat. For example, Catherine Good and her colleagues (Good et al., 2003) assigned college students to mentor seventh graders in a low-income ethnically diverse school district. Some children were told that intelligence developed over time and that they could overcome challenges and achieve academic success. Others were given unrelated information about drug use. Girls given the positive message about their academic skills scored higher on a standardized math test than girls given the unrelated message. Similarly, minority and low-income students given the positive academic message did better on a standardized reading test than those in the unrelated message group.

GENDER EQUITY IN SCIENCE AND MATH EDUCATION.   In recent years, increasing emphasis has been given to establishing gender equity in the fields of science, mathematics, and engineering education. The National Science Foundation and the AAUW Educational Foundation alone have funded hundreds of projects aimed at increasing the participation of girls and women in these fields. The publication "Under the Microscope" (AAUW, 2004) provides a summary of some of these efforts. Many of the funded projects involve extracurricular activities such as field trips and museums; a large number include mentoring activities; and others provide workshops for teachers. In addition, the AAUW is working with the National Girls Collaborative Project to link over 1,500 projects that give girls positive science and math experiences (Britsch et al., 2010).

What are some things teachers can do to make the math and science classroom more "girl friendly"? Females respond more positively to math and science instruction if they are taught in a cooperative, student-centered, group-oriented manner, using an applied perspective and a hands-on approach rather than in the traditional competitive manner using a theoretical perspective and a book-learning approach (Hartman & Hartman, 2008; Osborne et al., 2008). When the former practices are used, both girls and boys are more likely to continue taking courses in math and science and to consider future careers in these fields (Eccles & Roeser, 1999). In addition, having one or more faculty mentors, male or female, is a key factor in attracting high school and college women to science careers (Blackwell, 2010; Carrell et al., 2009).

See What You Can Do 5.1 for ways in which you can encourage girls' interest in math and science.

WHAT YOU CAN DO 5.1
Encouraging Girls in Math and Science

To encourage girls' interest and achievement in math and science, here are four things to share with educators and parents in your community and with the women and girls in your life.

1. **Teach children that intellectual skills, including spatial skills, are acquired.**
   Encourage children to play with construction toys, take things apart and put them back together, and work with their hands.
2. **Fight negative stereotypes about girls' math and science abilities.**
   Expose students to successful female role models in math and science.

3. **Help girls recognize their career-relevant skills.**
   Encourage girls to see their success in high school math and science as an indicator that they have the skills to succeed in science and engineering careers.
4. **Encourage high school girls to take calculus, physics, chemistry, and computer science.**
   These classes keep career options open.

Source: St. Rose (2010).

Summary

GENDER-RELATED SOCIAL BEHAVIORS AND PERSONALITY TRAITS

- Girls and boys are more alike than different in their social behaviors and personality traits. Gender differences, when found, are generally small.
- Boys are more physically aggressive than girls whereas girls are more likely to use relational aggression.
- Girls and boys are similar in prosocial behavior, but the few observed differences favor girls.
- Females are somewhat more easily influenced than males in certain situations.
- Girls are more likely than boys to express their emotions and report feeling empathy. Whether this reflects actual differences in emotionality or in the willingness to report feelings remains an open question.
- Research does not support Kohlberg's and Gilligan's claim of gender differences in the underlying basis of moral reasoning. Both females and males show caring and justice concerns in resolving moral conflicts.

COMMUNICATION STYLE

- Gender differences in verbal communication include males' greater talkativeness and intrusive interruptions and females' greater affiliative interruptions and their use of speech characterized as tentative. When responding to friends' troubles, women are more likely than men to give support and less likely to give advice.
- Both college women and men like to talk to their friends about the other gender. However, women's conversations focus on interpersonal issues more than do men's.
- Females smile and gaze at their conversational partner more than males do. They are also better able to interpret nonverbal messages. These differences might reflect the communal socialization of females. Another possibility is that women's ability to understand others is an adaptive mechanism that stems from their lower societal status.
- Explanations for these gender differences focus on females' interpersonal orientation and the gender imbalance in power.

GENDER COMPARISON OF COGNITIVE ABILITIES

- Females and males do not differ in general intelligence but show some differences in certain cognitive skills.
- Girls have a slight advantage in verbal skills beginning in infancy. Girls outperform boys in reading, writing, and speech production and are less likely to have reading problems.
- On visual–spatial tests, gender differences favoring boys are greatest in mental rotation, less in spatial perception, and smaller or absent in spatial visualization.
- Girls are better than boys in mathematics computation skills and get better grades in mathematics courses. Boys are better at problem solving starting in mid-adolescence and perform better on standardized mathematics tests. These differences have been decreasing.
- Biological explanations for gender differences in cognitive skills focus on genetics, hormones, and brain structure or organization.
- Environmental explanations include differential socialization of girls and boys by parents and teachers, gender typing of activities as feminine or masculine, gender differences in attitudes toward various cognitive skills, and stereotype threat.

Key Terms

relational aggression *101*
prosocial behavior *102*
persuasion studies *102*
group pressure conformity studies *103*

empathy *103*
affiliative interruption *105*
intrusive interruption *105*
mental rotation *111*
spatial perception *111*

spatial visualization *111*
lateralization *111*
mathematics self-efficacy *113*
stereotype threat *116*

What Do You Think?

1. Why do you think girls are more likely than boys to engage in relational aggression?
2. Adolescent girls report feeling more sadness, shame, and guilt than adolescent boys do. Do you think that females are actually more emotional than males or are simply more likely to report their feelings? Explain your answer.
3. Explanations for gender differences in verbal communication style focus on females' interpersonal orientation and the gender imbalance in power. Which of these explanations do you favor? Explain your answer.
4. What can parents do to maximize girls' potential for learning and liking math?

If You Want to Learn More

Anthony, M., & Lindert, R. (2010). *Little girls can be mean: Four steps to bully-proof girls in the early grades.* New York: St. Martin's Griffin.

Burger, C. J., Creamer, E. G., & Meszaros, P. S. (Eds.). (2007). *Reconfiguring the firewall: Recruiting women to information technology across cultures and continents.* Wellesley, MA: A. K. Peters, Ltd.

Cameron, D. (2007). *The myth of Mars and Venus: Do men and women really speak different languages?* New York: Oxford University Press.

Chatman, L., Nielsen, K., Strauss, E. J., & Tanner, K. D. (2008). *Girls in science: A framework for action.* Arlington, VA: NSTA Press.

Chesler, P. (2009). *Woman's inhumanity to woman.* Chicago, IL: Lawrence Hill Books.

Goetz, S. G. (2007). *Science for girls: Successful classroom strategies.* Lanham, MD: Scarecrow Press.

Hamilton, C. (2008). *Cognition and sex differences.* New York: Palgrave Macmillan.

Hanson, S. L. (2008). *Swimming against the tide: African-American girls and science education.* Philadelphia, PA: Temple University Press.

Jelenec, P. (2008). *Girls and the leaky math pipeline: Implicit math-gender stereotypes and math withdrawal in female adolescents and women.* Saarbrücken, GER: VDM Verlag.

Misa, T. J. (2010). *Gender codes: Women and men in the computing professions.* Hoboken, NJ: Wiley.

Petersen, A. R. (2005). *Engendering emotions.* New York: Palgrave Macmillan.

Speer, S. A., & Stokoe, E. (Eds.). (2011). *Conversation and gender.* Cambridge, UK: Cambridge University Press.

Trauth, E. (Ed.). (2006). *Encyclopedia of gender and information technology.* Hershey, PA: Idea Group, Inc.

Websites

Association for Women in Mathematics
http://www.awm-math.org/

Engineer Girl!
http://engineergirl.org/

Girl Tech: Getting Girls Interested in Computers
http://math.rice.edu/~lanius/club/girls.html

Women in Engineering: ProActive Network
http://wepan.org/

CHAPTER 6

Sexuality

Sexuality
  Sexual Anatomy and Sexual
      Response
  Sexual Attitudes
  Sexual Behaviors
  Sexual Problems
**Lesbians, Gay Men, Bisexuals,
and Transgender Individuals**
  Bisexuals
  Attitudes Toward
      Sexual Minorities
  Explanations of Sexual
      Orientation
**Sexual Activity During
Adolescence**
  Frequency of Sexual
      Activity
  Factors Associated with
      Sexual Activity
  The Double Standard
  Sexual Desire
Sexual Activity in Midlife
  Physical Changes
  Patterns of Sexual
      Activity
Sexual Activity in Later Life
  Benefits of Sexual Activity
      in Later Life
  Sexual Behavior of Older
      People
  Factors Affecting Sexual
      Behavior
  Enhancing Sexuality in
      Later Life

*I don't want to be forced to take care of a child that I'm not
ready for or get an STD . . . As for sex, it'll happen someday,
but just not today.* (a 17-year-old female high school senior;
in Villarosa, 2003, p. D6)

*We didn't have the choice of time when the kids were
young. Now we have time during the day. We seldom make
love at nighttime. Now we can choose. It might be 10 A.M.
or 2 P.M.—whenever we're feeling turned on.* (a 65-year-old
woman; in Doress-Worters & Siegal, 1994, p. 85)

Did these opening vignettes surprise you? Both of
them run counter to the popular stereotypes of the
hormonally driven, sexually active teenager on the
one hand and the sexually disinterested older woman on
the other. In this chapter, we explore the fascinating diversity of women's sexuality throughout the lifespan, including
sexual attitudes, behaviors, problems, and orientations.

SEXUALITY

We start with a discussion of women's sexual anatomy and sexual response. Then we look at sexual attitudes, behaviors, and problems.

Sexual Anatomy and Sexual Response

EXTERNAL FEMALE SEXUAL ANATOMY.   The *external female sexual organs,* collectively called the **vulva**, are shown in Figure 6.1. Women can get a clear view of their own vulva by squatting and looking into a hand mirror. The **mons pubis** (also *mons veneris,* mountain of Venus) is *a pad of fatty tissue covering the pubic bone.* During puberty, it becomes covered with coarse hair. The hair continues between the legs and around the anus, the opening of the large intestine. The *fatty hair-covered area between the legs forms flaps called* the **labia majora** (outer lips). They surround *soft hairless flaps of skin,* the **labia minora** (inner lips). Between the inner lips and the anus lies the perineum (Rathus et al., 2010). Spreading the inner lips apart reveals that they join at the upper end to form a fold of skin, or *hood* over the **clitoris**. *This highly sensitive organ, whose only known function is sexual pleasure, consists of erectile tissue that swells during sexual stimulation* (somewhat like the penis). Although smaller than the penis, the clitoris has more than twice as many nerve fibers (Schulman, 2003). Right below the clitoris is the urethral opening, through which urine passes. Below that is the larger vaginal opening. The **vagina** is *the canal leading to the uterus.* The menstrual blood passes through it and it is the birth canal during childbirth (Rathus et al., 2010).

THE SEXUAL RESPONSE CYCLE.   Women and men respond similarly during the four phases of the **sexual response cycle**, *the physiological responses of individuals to sexual stimulation from any source* (sexual intercourse, masturbation, etc.) (Donatelle, 2012). Here we discuss women's responses.

In the *excitement phase,* a major response is **vasocongestion**, *the swelling of genital tissues with blood.* Vasocongestion produces vaginal lubrication shortly after stimulation. The clitoris and labia swell with blood. The inner two-thirds of the vagina expand, the uterus elevates, the breasts enlarge, the nipples become erect, and the skin becomes flushed. Heart rate, breathing rate, and muscle tension increase.

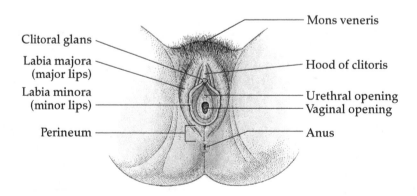

Mons veneris

Clitoral glans

Labia majora (major lips)

Labia minora (minor lips)

Perineum

Hood of clitoris

Urethral opening
Vaginal opening

Anus

FIGURE 6.1 Female External Sex Organs
Source: Rathus, Spencer A., Nevid, Jeffrey S., and Fichner-Rathus, Lois, *Human Sexuality in a World of Diversity*, 8th edition, © 2010. Reprinted by permission of Pearson Education, Inc., Upper Saddle River, NJ.

During the *plateau phase,* the clitoris, now extremely sensitive, shortens and withdraws under the clitoral hood. *The low third of the vagina becomes engorged with blood, forming the* **orgasmic platform**. Heart rate, blood pressure, and breathing rate continue to rise.

In the *orgasmic phase,* the orgasmic platform, uterus, and anal sphincters contract strongly several times, at intervals of less than a second. These contractions constitute the orgasm.

During the *resolution* phase, the *body returns to its pre-arousal state* within 15 to 30 minutes. Blood is released from engorged areas; the clitoris, vagina, uterus, and labia return to normal size; and muscle tension dissipates. Heart rate and breathing rate return to pre-arousal levels.

MULTIPLE ORGASMS.　Alfred Kinsey and his colleagues (Kinsey et al., 1953) reported that 14 percent of the women they interviewed experienced multiple orgasms. Although a few studies have reported higher percentages, most report figures of about 5 percent, more in line with Kinsey's research ("Women Can Have," 2007). Unlike women, few men are physiologically capable of multiple orgasms. This is one of the major gender differences in sexual response, the other being that men but not women ejaculate during orgasm. Although having multiple orgasms can be a good thing, some women now feel that they are sexually inadequate if they don't. One orgasm can be quite satisfying, as can sex that does not culminate in orgasm.

ONE OR TWO KINDS OF ORGASM?　Freud (1938) proposed that there were two types of female orgasm: clitoral and vaginal. Clitoral orgasms were achieved through clitoral stimulation during masturbation. This form of orgasm, practiced by young girls, was considered immature and sexually inadequate in adult women. Women were expected to shift to vaginal orgasms, brought on by sexual intercourse. Research, however, has demonstrated that there is only one kind of orgasm, physiologically, whether it is brought on by clitoral or vaginal stimulation. Furthermore, the clitoris is indirectly stimulated even in vaginal intercourse. Although orgasms resulting from clitoral and vaginal stimulation are physiologically the same, there may be psychological or subjective differences (Rathus et al., 2010). For example, the context of sexual intercourse includes a partner to whom one may be emotionally attached, whereas masturbation is often (but not always) done without the presence of a partner. Sexual pleasure is also possible without orgasm. Expressing sexual feelings for another person involves a number of pleasurable activities, of which intercourse and orgasm may be only a part (Donatelle, 2012).

Sexual Attitudes

THE SEXUAL DOUBLE STANDARD.　Historically, women's sexuality was discouraged and denied, especially outside of marriage. The social construction of norms about female and male sexuality is nowhere seen more clearly than in this **sexual double standard**, *which allowed and even encouraged premarital sex for men, but not for women.* As premarital sex became more acceptable, the double standard has evolved into a belief that casual sexual activity is acceptable for men, but that women's sexual experiences should occur only in the context of a serious relationship (Diamond & Savin-Williams, 2009). As examples of the double standard, young women are judged more negatively than young men when they provide a condom for protection (Fassinger & Arseneau, 2008) or when they have a sexually transmitted infection (Smith et al., 2008).

GENDER DIFFERENCES IN ATTITUDES.　Women generally have less permissive attitudes toward sexual behavior than men (Fisher, 2010; Petersen & Hyde, 2010). In a recent meta-analysis of research in several countries on sexual attitudes and behavior, Jennifer Petersen and Janet Hyde (2010) found that women reported more negative attitudes than men about casual sex. Women were somewhat more likely to feel anxious or guilty about sex and to emphasize relationships as a context for sex, and were less likely to endorse the double standard. No gender differences were found in attitudes toward masturbation, extramarital sex, and premarital sex when couples are committed or engaged. In general, gender differences in attitudes toward sexual behavior overall narrowed as people got older. These differences also diminished from the 1970s into the twenty-first century (Petersen & Hyde, 2010). A recent survey of Americans aged 45 and older found that although women continued to hold less permissive attitudes toward sex than men, attitudes of both groups have become more permissive. For example, women were still more likely than men to say that nonmarital sex is wrong (28 vs. 17 percent), but this opposition was down by half compared to 10 years ago (Fisher, 2010). Other studies show that men from countries around the world are more likely than women to rate sex as important and to report greater physical and emotional pleasure from it (Angier, 2007; Fisher, 2010).

ATTITUDES TOWARD WOMEN WITH DISABILITIES. Girls and young women with disabilities may face particular challenges in developing a healthy sexuality (Donatelle, 2012; Maxwell et al., 2007). A common assumption is that women with disabilities are asexual beings who have no sex life and who are unsuitable as romantic partners (Banks, 2010; Chrisler & Garnett, 2010; Groh & Serowsky, 2009; Nosek, 2010). Many women with disabilities have spoken out about the unavailability of adequate counseling on sexuality, birth control, pregnancy, and childbirth. Women with disabilities engage in less sexual activity and are less satisfied with their sex lives than able-bodied women (Groh & Serowsky, 2009; Nosek, 2010). Whereas able-bodied women often resent being treated as sex objects, some women with disabilities resent being treated as asexual objects (Nosek, 2010). The view of women with disabilities as asexual is based on misconceptions about their sexual desires and abilities. Most individuals with disabilities have the same sexual desires as able-bodied persons. Their ability to perform sexually depends on their adjustment to the physical limitations of their disability and the availability of a helpful partner (Nosek, 2010; Rathus et al., 2010).

Sexual Behaviors

The recent National Survey of Sexual Health and Behavior (NSSHB), the most comprehensive study of sexuality in the United States, surveyed a representative sample of nearly 5,900 individuals from ages 14 to 94. The researchers found that both women and men engaged in diverse solo and partnered sexual activities. Masturbation, oral sex, and vaginal intercourse were prevalent in both sexes. The proportion of women and men engaging in these behaviors peaked in the 20s and decreased with age. Being in good health and having a partner were related to higher levels of sexual activity for both sexes (Herbenick et al., 2010a,b; Reece et al., 2010).

GENDER DIFFERENCES. A number of gender differences in sexual activity were reported both in the NSSHB and in the recent meta-analysis by Petersen and Hyde (2010). Men, compared to women, had a higher incidence of intercourse and oral sex, more frequent intercourse, a greater number of partners, first intercourse at a younger age, and more extramarital sex. Women appear to be narrowing the adultery gap in recent years, however, with younger women being unfaithful to their spouses nearly as often as men (Parker-Pope, 2010).

Letitia Anne Peplau (2002) sums up these differences as indicating that men are more interested in sex than are women. She also contends that assertiveness and dominance are more closely linked to male sexuality than to female sexuality. For example, she notes that men tend to initiate sex in heterosexual relationships and that men are more likely than women to use intimidation or physical force to get an unwilling partner to engage in sex (see Chapter 14). Another gender difference proposed by Peplau (2002) and by Lisa Diamond (2007) is that women have greater sexual plasticity, that is, their sexual beliefs and behaviors are more capable of being shaped and changed by cultural, social, and situational factors. For example, women are more likely than men to engage in sexual behavior that runs counter to their established pattern of sexual desire, that is, heterosexual women having sex with women and lesbians engaging in sex with men (Diamond, 2003b). Women's sexual attitudes and behaviors also seem to be affected more by their education level and by the views of their culture than are men's attitudes and behaviors (Fassinger & Arseneau, 2008; Peplau, 2002).

Although gender differences in sexuality are well documented, one must also keep in mind that there are tremendous variations in sexual expression among women of different ages, marital statuses, educational levels, religions, and races/ethnicities. Women who are younger, White, and well educated, and who have no religious affiliation have more varied sexual practices than other women. For example, they are more likely to have experienced oral and anal sex and to find these acts appealing (Laumann & Mahay, 2002).

Two limitations of research on sexual attitudes and behaviors must be kept in mind. One is the problem of volunteer bias. Many people refuse to participate in surveys of their sexual views and practices. Thus, samples are biased because they include the responses only of those individuals who are willing to discuss their intimate behavior. Such individuals tend to be more sexually permissive and to have more liberal attitudes toward sexuality than nonvolunteers. Therefore, survey results based on volunteer samples may not be representative of the population at large (Rathus et al., 2010).

A second problem is that all the results are based on self-reports, not on direct observations of behavior. It is possible that there are gender differences in reporting behaviors, but few, if any, differences in actual sexual behaviors or attitudes. Women may underreport their sexual experiences and men may exaggerate theirs (Jonason & Fisher, 2009). As a result of these two problems, one must take findings regarding gender differences in sexuality with a grain of salt.

Sexual Problems

What constitutes a sexual problem or dysfunction for women? How frequently do such problems occur? These issues are currently topics of vigorous debate among researchers. Some scholars have defined anything interfering with orgasm as a sexual problem. Others, however, argue that emphasizing orgasm reflects the male perspective that sex ends with ejaculation, whereas for many women, orgasm is not the goal or the most important part of sexual activity (Fassinger & Arseneau, 2008; Tolman et al., 2003). In this section, we examine changing views of women's sexual problems.

Researchers who study sexual problems have typically employed the widely used system for classifying sexual dysfunction from the *Diagnostic and Statistical Manual of Mental Disorders IV* (*DSM-IV*) of the American Psychiatric Association (1994). Four categories are recognized: sexual desire disorders, sexual arousal disorders, orgasmic disorders, and sexual pain disorders. Feminist scholars have criticized this categorization, as we shall see shortly, because it is overly genital and neglects issues of relationships and social context (Tiefer, 2008).

Large-scale studies have used the *DSM-IV* categories to examine sexual problems in U.S. adults ages 18–85 (Laumann et al., 1999, 2008). These studies have found that the most frequently reported sexual problem among women is *a lack of desire for sexual activity,* or **inhibited sexual desire**. About 25 percent of younger women and up to 40 percent of older women report having this problem. (Persons who have little interest in sex, but are not concerned by it, are not considered to have the disorder.) About one in seven younger women and over one in three older women report **sexual arousal disorder**, which involves *insufficient lubrication or a failure to be aroused*. Nearly one in four younger women and one in three older women report **female orgasmic disorder**, defined as *experiencing the excitement phase of the sexual response cycle but not achieving orgasm*. (If a woman is satisfied with this situation, she is not considered to have an orgasmic disorder.) About 7 percent of younger woman and 18 percent of older women report **dyspareunia**, or *painful intercourse*. Often a physical condition, such as a sexually transmitted infection (STI), lack of lubrication, or a structural problem, is involved. Psychological factors such as anxiety about sex or prior sexual trauma may also be responsible (Rathus et al., 2010). Another sexual pain disorder documented by Laumann and his colleagues is **vaginismus**, the *involuntary contraction of vaginal muscles*, making intercourse painful or impossible. Vaginismus is often caused by factors such as childhood sexual abuse, rape, a family upbringing that included negative attitudes toward sex, and a history of painful intercourse (Rathus et al., 2010).

Laumann and his colleagues (2008) also found that factors such as age, marital status, ethnicity, education, and economic status were related to the incidence of sexual dysfunction. For women, the prevalence of sexual problems declined until about age 60 and then leveled off, except for those who reported trouble lubricating. Men, on the other hand, had more problems with age, particularly erectile dysfunction and inability to achieve orgasm. Single, divorced, separated, and widowed individuals showed an elevated risk of sexual problems. Ethnicity also was associated with sexual problems. For example, among younger women, White women were more likely to report sexual pain, whereas Black women more often experienced low levels of desire and pleasure. Latinas, on the other hand, reported lower rates of sexual problems than other women.

Women and men with less education and lower income reported more sexual problems than more highly educated and affluent individuals. What might account for this social class difference in sexual problems? Poorer physical and mental health in individuals of lower social status may be a factor because diminished health is related to problems with sex (Laumann et al., 2008). Underlying physical conditions that can cause sexual dysfunction include diabetes, heart disease, neurological disorders, side effects of medications, alcoholism, drug abuse, and heavy smoking. Psychological causes of sexual problems include stress or anxiety from work, concern about poor sexual performance, marital discord, or depression. Some of these problems are all too common in the lives of poor women and men (Heiman, 2008). Unfortunately, the sociocultural predictors of sexual problems studied by Laumann and his associates have often been given little attention in the popular and professional media. Instead, media focus on the high incidence of physiological problems, and the need for drug companies to develop medical treatments, such as female Viagra, to treat women's sexual "illnesses" (IsHak et al., 2010; Moynihan & Mintzes, 2010; Singer, 2010).

A NEW VIEW OF WOMEN'S SEXUAL PROBLEMS.   Recently, however, a group of therapists and sex researchers has developed a new view of women's sexual problems that focuses on the sociocultural, political, psychological, social, and relational bases of women's sexual problems (Groh & Serowsky, 2009; Tiefer, 2008). These researchers define sexual problems as discontent or dissatisfaction with any emotional, physical, or relational aspect of sexual experiences that may arise in one or more of four interrelated aspects of women's sexual lives (see Table 6.1). This view focuses on the *prevention* of women's sexual problems through tackling the economic, political, and sociocultural root causes of the problems, and not on medical treatment alone (Castañeda & Ulibarri, 2010; Tiefer, 2008).

TABLE 6.1 Women's Sexual Problems: A New Classification

Sexual problems, defined as discontent or dissatisfaction with any emotional, physical, or relational aspect of sexual experience, may arise in one or more of the following four interrelated aspects of women's sexual lives.

I. Sexual Problems Due to Sociocultural, Political, or Economic Factors

A. Ignorance or anxiety due to inadequate sex education, lack of access to health services, or other social constraints:
   1. Lack of vocabulary to describe physical or subjective experience.
   2. Lack of information about sexual biology and life-stage changes.
   3. Lack of information about how gender roles influence men's and women's sexual expectations, beliefs, and behaviors.
   4. Inadequate access to information about and services that could provide contraception and abortion, STI prevention and treatment, and counseling for sexual trauma and domestic violence.
B. Sexual avoidance or distress due to perceived inability to meet cultural norms regarding correct or ideal sexuality, including:
   1. Anxiety or shame about one's body, sexual attractiveness, or sexual responses.
   2. Confusion or shame about one's sexual orientation or identity, or about sexual fantasies and desires.
C. Inhibitions due to conflict between the sexual norms of one's subculture or culture of origin and those of the dominant culture.
D. Lack of interest, fatigue, or lack of time due to family and work obligations.

II. Sexual Problems Relating to Partner and Relationship

A. Inhibition, avoidance, or distress arising from betrayal, dislike, or fear of partner; partner's abuse or couple's unequal power; or partner's negative patterns of communication.
B. Discrepancies in desire for sexual activity or in preferences for various sexual activities.
C. Ignorance or inhibition about communicating preferences or initiating, pacing, or shaping sexual activities.
D. Loss of sexual interest and reciprocity as a result of conflicts over commonplace issues such as money, schedules, or relatives, or resulting from traumatic experiences, such as infertility or the death of a child.
E. Inhibitions in arousal or spontaneity due to partner's health status or sexual problems.

III. Sexual Problems Due to Psychological Factors

A. Sexual aversion, mistrust, or inhibition of sexual pleasure due to:
   1. Past experiences of physical, sexual, or emotional abuse.
   2. General personality problems with attachment, rejection, cooperation, or entitlement.
   3. Depression or anxiety.
B. Sexual inhibition due to fear of sexual acts or of their possible consequences, such as pain during intercourse, pregnancy, STI, loss of partner, or loss of reputation.

IV. Sexual Problems Due to Medical Factors

A. Pain or lack of physical response during sexual activity despite a supportive and safe interpersonal situation, adequate sexual knowledge, and positive sexual attitudes. Such problems can arise from:
   1. Numerous local or systemic medical conditions affecting neurological, neurovascular, circulatory, endocrine, or other systems of the body.
   2. Pregnancy, STIs, or other sex-related conditions.
   3. Side effects of many drugs, medications, or medical treatments.
   4. A medical treatment or diagnostic procedure, such as a hysterectomy or other necessary procedure.

Source: From the Manifesto of the New View Campaign. Copyright © 2000 Leonore Tiefer. Reprinted by permission of the author. www.newviewcampaign.org/manifesto5.asp.

LESBIANS, GAY MEN, BISEXUALS, AND TRANSGENDER INDIVIDUALS

Before reading this section, try the exercise in Get Involved 6.1. Compare your findings with the information that follows.

Sexual orientation consists of three components: sexual/romantic attraction, sexual behavior, and sexual identity (Jordan-Young, 2010). In the past, women's sexual orientation was divided into two categories: lesbian and heterosexual. Later, the bisexual category was added. Recently, a "mostly straight" identity has been proposed to describe women who fall between homosexuality and heterosexuality (Thompson & Morgan, 2008). A **lesbian** is a woman who is *emotionally and sexually attracted to other women*, a **gay man** is *attracted to other men*, and a **bisexual** person is *attracted to both men and women* (Meem et al., 2010). A **transgender** person is an individual whose gender identity differs from the gender she or he was assigned at birth (Schilt & Westbrook, 2009). It is difficult to estimate the number of women who are lesbian, bisexual, or transgender because negative attitudes toward sexual minorities discourage some individuals from reporting this behavior. In addition, sexual identities of women may change over time. Whereas many gay men recall their same-sex attraction as beginning before puberty, many lesbians report not feeling same-sex attractions until adulthood (Diamond, 2007). In the NSSHB mentioned earlier, 7 percent of American women *identified* themselves as having a lesbian or bisexual sexual orientation; but twice that number reported *engaging in sexual behavior* with women during their lifetime (Herbenick et al., 2010b,c). However, a 10-year longitudinal study of lesbian and bisexual women found that two-thirds of the participants had changed sexual minority identities at least once in their lives and over one-third had done so more than once (Diamond, 2008). In addition, the comprehensive National Longitudinal Study

GET INVOLVED 6.1
Attitudes Toward Lesbians

Ask two female and two male friends to complete the following exercise:

Our society views some groups of unmarried women as having higher social status or acceptability than other groups of unmarried women. Give each group below a social status score based on how you think these groups are viewed in society. Assign each group a score ranging from 1 to 100, with *high* scores indicating *high* status and *low* scores indicating *low* status.

Social Status Score

divorced heterosexual women	_____
never-married lesbians	_____
widowed heterosexual women	_____
never-married heterosexual women	_____

WHAT DOES IT MEAN?

1. In what ways are your female and male respondents' answers alike? In what ways are they different? Explain the differences and similarities.
2. How does the social status of lesbians compare to that of the three groups of heterosexual women?
3. How would you account for the differences in social status of these four groups of women?

_____

Source: Etaugh and Fulton (1995).

of Adolescent Health found a great deal of fluidity in romantic attractions and relationships over an 18-month period. For example, of the 4 percent of girls who reported bisexual attraction at the beginning of the study, only one-fourth did so 18 months later; the majority of them later reported attraction to and relationships with males (Russell & Seif, 2002). Findings like these suggest that, as noted earlier in the chapter, female sexual orientation is more "fluid" than that of males, meaning that it is more sensitive to situational and contextual factors (Diamond & Savin-Williams, 2009).

Bisexuals

Because most people view sexual orientation as consisting of two categories—heterosexual and homo-sexual—many bisexual individuals feel misunderstood or invisible (Burn, 2011; Hequembourg & Brallier, 2009). Bisexual women and men are often viewed as going through a transitional stage between heterosexuality and homosexuality, denying their true sexuality, or avoiding commitment to a particular lifestyle or partner (Bowles, 2011; Hequembourg & Brallier, 2009; Rust, 2009). Furthermore, bisexuality is often criticized by both heterosexuals and homosexuals as indicating promiscuity, indecisiveness, or immaturity (Meem et al., 2010; Rust, 2009). The dilemma faced by a bisexual woman was expressed this way:

> *Invisibility is a problem. Few people know we exist because we don't "fit" into either the het-erosexual or the lesbian world. When we are open, both worlds judge us.*

(Boston Women's Health Book Collective, 1992, p. 214)

One of Claire's bisexual students described the following experience in her journal:

> *If I hear "The lesbian's dating a boy?!" one more time . . . So I met a boy and we've started dating, not a big deal to me but obviously to others. My main issue here is pigeon-holing. "I thought you were supposed to be gay," as if I have become a caricature of a human.*

(Angelique, age 22)

Research shows that some individuals feel attracted to both sexes simultaneously and may carry on relationships with both men and women at the same time (Rust, 2009). This is more likely to occur in women than in men (Chandra et al., 2011; Diamond & Savin-Williams, 2009). Large-scale surveys have found that among women, bisexual attractions are much more common than exclusive attractions to women (Chandra et al., 2011), and many bisexuals are more attracted to one gender than the other (Rust, 2001). Currently, more women are experimenting with bisexual-ity or at least feel more comfortable reporting same-sex encounters than was the case in the 1990s: 12 percent in 2005 versus 4 percent in 1998 (Mosher et al., 2005).

Same-sex sexuality thus is a matter of degree for many women, who do not clearly fit into any one category. In the words of Susan:

> *I'm in a physical/sexual sense 60 percent heterosexual and 40 percent gay . . . My sexual fantasies are often with a man but my romantic ones are with a woman . . . In the emo-tional realm I'm 30 percent heterosexual and 70 percent gay. I can't imagine spending my life with a guy! Sex wouldn't be enough. I want to take long trips with girls. I want to exchange lipstick colors and compare Hillary [Clinton] stories . . . I'm attracted to certain types of males, both the really femme girly boys and the really masculine studs . . . and the really feminine girls with powdered faces. The butch ones can be a Friday night fantasy. Don't think about writing down that I'm a lesbian, or even bisexual. I hate both words!*

(Savin-Williams, 2006, p. 316)

Attitudes Toward Sexual Minorities

Heterosexism is *the view that heterosexuality is the norm and that homosexuality is abnormal.* Sexual minority individuals may themselves internalize heterosexist attitudes (Szymanski & Owens, 2008). This view often leads to **homophobia**, *negative reactions to homosexuality and irrational fear of homosexuals.* Such reactions are pervasive not only in American society (Herek, 2009a; Kantor, 2009; Pew Research Center, 2007c) but also in many other parts of the world (see Explore Other Cultures 6.1). In a 2010 survey of American adults, for example, 75 percent of individuals aged 65 and over felt that sex between adults of the same sex is always wrong, although on a positive note, only 43 percent of young adults felt this way (Pew Research Center, 2010a). Although heterosexual men are more negative than women toward gay men, there are small or no gender differences in attitudes toward lesbians (Gallagher, 2008; Moskowitz et al., 2010; Petersen & Hyde, 2010). This finding is consistent with the research we discussed in Chapters 3 and 4 showing that men who violate gender roles are judged more harshly than women who do so. Although about one-half of older Americans oppose gay marriage, civil unions, and same-sex couples rearing children, only about one-third of young adults feel that way (Pew Research Center, 2007c; 2010a; "The Nation," 2010). Homophobic views are especially strong among males, political conservatives, people with a high degree of religious commitment, those with less education, and individuals who hold traditional gender-role attitudes and authoritarian right-wing views. These individuals are less likely to have family members or friends who are openly gay or lesbian, and they are more

EXPLORE OTHER CULTURES 6.1
Sexual Minorities Around the World

Sexual minorities are discriminated against in varying degrees by laws and social policies around the world (Bakirci, 2011; Fumia, 2011; Hooghe et al., 2010; Štulhofer & Rimac, 2009). Same-gender sexual behavior is still illegal in dozens of countries, including many African and predominantly Muslim nations. In these countries, homosexuality may be punishable with prison sentences (for example, in Nicaragua), beatings (Malaysia), and death (Afghanistan, Iran, Sudan, and Yemen [Burn, 2011]). Even where homosexuality is not illegal, lesbians and gay men often do not "come out" for fear of losing their children, jobs, and social status, or becoming the target of physical or verbal attack (Burn, 2011).

Although Americans have become more accepting of homosexuality in the past few decades, they are less tolerant than citizens of most other advanced democracies in western Europe and North America. In France, Britain, Italy, Germany, Czech Republic, and Canada, 75 percent or more believe society should accept homosexuality. Americans, by comparison, are evenly divided on this issue, similar to the views in Latin American countries.

Lesbianism was acceptable in a number of Native American cultures before Western colonization. For instance, women from the Mohave, Maricopa, Cocopa, Klamath, and Kaska tribes could marry other women and make love with other women without stigma (Burn, 2011). However, contemporary attitudes of Native Americans, which have been influenced by the dominant American culture, may be less accepting (Amaro et al., 2002). Similarly, in the African country of Lesotho, it is not unusual for women to have romantic relationships with each other before and even during heterosexual marriage (Burn, 2011). However, these relationships occur less often in Lesotho women exposed to Western ideas.

The experiences of sexual minorities vary not only among countries but also within them. San Francisco, for example, has an active sexual minority community, but in many places in the United States, sexual minorities are more likely to remain closeted.

likely to believe that a homosexual orientation is freely chosen (Herek, 2009b; Hooghe et al., 2010; Lipka, 2010; Morrison et al., 2009; Nagoshi et al., 2008; Petersen & Hyde, 2010; Saad, 2010; Schwartz, 2010; Smith et al., 2009; Whitley, 2007). On the other hand, about 75 percent of Americans feel that sexual minorities should have equal rights in housing, and 60 percent support equal rights in employment and health benefits for lesbian and gay partners (Lax & Phillips, 2009).

WOMEN OF COLOR. Black individuals hold somewhat more negative attitudes toward sexual minorities than do Whites (Pew Research Center, 2009; Vincent et al., 2009; Whitley et al., 2011). Thus, Black lesbian and bisexual women are confronted with the intersecting societal barriers of sexism, racism, and homophobia, placing them in "triple jeopardy" (Bowleg, 2008; Fassinger & Israel, 2010). In some ethnic minority cultures, women who do not adhere to traditional gender roles or who are not subordinate to men are often ostracized or mistreated. For example, "two spirit" Native American women experience disproportionate levels of sexual and physical violence (Lehavot, 2009). Sexual minority women in these communities may be more reluctant to "come out," choosing to remain invisible rather than be rejected (Castañeda, 2008; Cole & Guy-Sheftall, 2003; Parks et al., 2004).

DISCRIMINATION.   Discrimination against sexual minorities can take many forms. The most virulent form of homophobia is expressed in violent "hate crimes" often committed against gay men by groups of adolescent or young adult males (Federal Bureau of Investigation, 2009; Herek, 2009a). One national study found that 38 percent of gay men had experienced crimes against their person or property, compared with about 13 percent of lesbians and bisexual women and 11 percent of bisexual men. Gay men were also more likely than other sexual minorities to be verbally harassed (Herek, 2009a). Sadly, homophobia and prejudice are daily experiences for many sexual minority students during the school day (Biegel, 2010; Russell et al., 2010). In one nationwide survey of more than 6,200 lesbian, gay, bisexual, and transgender middle and high school students, nearly nine out of ten were called names or threatened because of their sexual orientation. Almost half had been physically harassed and nearly one-quarter had been assaulted. More than half felt unsafe in school and one-third missed at least a day of school because of feeling unsafe (Kosciw et al., 2008). Transgender students are even more likely than their lesbian, gay, and bisexual peers to experience harassment and assault (Greytak et al., 2009). Another recent study found that sexual minority college students and employees were twice as likely as heterosexuals to report experiencing harassment. The incidence was even higher among sexual minority students of color (Rankin et al., 2010). Sexual minority youth are also more likely to be harshly punished by schools and courts than their straight peers, even though they are less likely to engage in serious misdeeds (Himmelstein & Bruckner, 2011).

Home may not be a safe haven either. Sexual minority teens and adults who "come out"—that is, declare their sexual orientation to others—may be rejected by their families. In some cases, they are compelled to leave home and seek survival in the streets (Goldman, 2008; Grossman, 2006, Herek & Garnets, 2007). Such experiences, not surprisingly, can lead to a reluctance to reveal one's sexual orientation (Fassinger & Arseneau, 2008; Rosenfeld, 2009) and to increased levels of emotional stress and psychological problems among harassed individuals (Hatzenbuehler et al., 2010; Plöderl & Fartacek, 2009; Wylie et al., 2010). We shall explore some of these problems more fully in Chapter 13. Despite the stress faced by many lesbian, gay, bisexual, and transgender youth, the good news is that most display strength and resiliency and are often involved in antihomophobia advocacy efforts (Russell et al., 2010).

Although some states have laws that ban discrimination on the basis of sexual orientation in employment, credit, housing, and public accommodation, more than half do not (Meyer, 2011). Same-sex marriage is specifically banned in most states; as of this writing, it is legal in only Connecticut, the District of Columbia, Iowa, Massachusetts, New Hampshire, New York, and Vermont, although California, Colorado, Delaware, Hawaii, Illinois, Maine, Maryland, Nevada, New Jersey, Oregon, Rhode Island, Washington, and Wisconsin give same-sex couples spousal rights (Patterson, 2009). Argentina, Belgium, Canada, Iceland, Mexico City, the Netherlands, Norway, Portugal, South Africa, Spain, and Sweden allow same-sex marriages, and several other countries permit same-sex couples to register as partners (Barrionuevo, 2010; Cole, 2010; Human Rights Campaign, 2011). Courts in slightly more than half the states in the United States allow lesbian or gay individuals to adopt their partner's child (Patterson, 2009), a right endorsed by the American Academy of Pediatrics.

See What You Can Do 6.1 for ways in which you can help support the rights of sexual minorities.

Explanations of Sexual Orientation

The origins of homosexuality are complex and controversial (Hines, 2010; Werhun, 2011). A number of psychological and biological theories have been proposed. According to Sigmund Freud (1925/1989), all individuals are initially bisexual. The mother is the original love object for both girls and boys. In heterosexual development, the father becomes the girl's love object, and she substitutes other males for him as she gets older. When the mother remains the love object, lesbian development occurs. Little evidence exists in support of this theory, however (Werhun, 2011). From a learning theory point of view, early positive sexual activity with members of one's own gender or negative sexual experiences with members of the other gender could lead to homosexuality. However, many lesbians and gay men are aware of their sexual orientation before they have engaged in any sexual activity (Carver et al., 2004).

Biological theories focus on genetic or hormonal factors. In one study, 48 percent of identical twin sisters of lesbians were also lesbians, compared with just 16 percent of fraternal twin sisters, and 6 percent of adopted sisters (Bailey et al., 1993). So, sexual orientation appears to be at least partly genetic. But if genetics were the whole story, 100 percent of the identical twin sisters would be lesbian.

Is sexual orientation influenced by sex hormones? In adulthood, there is no link between levels of female and male sex hormones and sexual orientation (Veniegas & Conley, 2000). *Prenatal* sex hormones may be a factor, however. Studies of intersexuality discussed in Chapter 3

WHAT YOU CAN DO 6.1
Supporting Rights of Sexual Minorities

1. If your school has a gay–straight alliance, get involved. If not, start one. Ideas can be found at www.glsen.org.
2. Volunteer for Parents and Friends of Lesbians and Gays (PFLAG). For information, contact www.pflag.org.
3. Volunteer for the Trevor Project, www.thetrevorproject.org, a suicide prevention hotline that supports sexual minority youth.

Source: Burn (2011).

pointed to the prenatal influence of androgen on the development of females' sexual orientation (Berenbaum et al., 2009; Hines, 2010). For example, the finger-length patterns in lesbians resemble those of men more than those of heterosexual women (Breedlove, 2010; Meem et al., 2010; Werhun, 2011). This finding and others suggest that high levels of androgens (male sex hormones) during the prenatal period may partially masculinize certain physiological and anatomical characteristics of lesbians, including the brain structures responsible for sexual orientation (Hines, 2010; Honekopp & Watson, 2010).

Most likely, complex interactions among biological, psychological, and environmental factors determine sexual orientation, and different causal mechanisms may operate for different individuals (Donatelle, 2012; Jordan-Young, 2010).

SEXUAL ACTIVITY DURING ADOLESCENCE

Why does it seem that all boys want is sex? (Brenda, age 14)

What happens when I have a boyfriend who wants to have sex and I don't? (Ruth, age 13)

Why is it that when a guy has sex with a girl, he is called a "stud," but the girl is considered a "slut"? (Veronica, age 13; all in Zager & Rubenstein, 2002)

Although most teenagers have their first sexual intercourse in their mid-to-late teens (Guttmacher Institute, 2011a), the experience is quite different for females and males. Women, compared to men, describe their first experience as less positive and more negative, and they are less likely to report physical pleasure and orgasm. Women are also more likely to indicate an emotional connection with their partners and partner pressure as reasons for their sexual initiation (Walsh et al., 2011). In fact, nearly one out of four girls who first have sex at age 14 or younger report that the act was nonvoluntary (Hoffman, 2008). Let's take a closer look at sexual activity during adolescence. We'll discuss teenage pregnancy in Chapter 7.

Frequency of Sexual Activity

Males become sexually active at younger ages than females. Among females, Black girls show the earliest onset of sexual activity and Asian Americans the latest ("Facts on American Teens," 2010; Zimmer-Gembeck & Helfand, 2008). In addition, adolescent boys, compared to adolescent girls, have more sex (including same-sex behavior) and more sex partners (Chandra et al., 2011). Rates of teenage sexuality reached near-record highs in the late 1980s, but have declined since the early 1990s. For example, the percentage of high school students who had intercourse decreased from 54 percent in 1991 to 46 percent in 2009 (Eaton et al., 2010). The decline has been most noticeable among Black females and among males of all ethnicities. Efforts to educate young people about safe sex and about the risks of pregnancy and STIs such as AIDS have played a key role in reducing these numbers. Still, by the time they graduate from high school, about two-thirds of girls will have engaged in sex ("Facts on American Teens," 2010; Kirby & Laris, 2009).

Two forms of sexual activity that are growing in popularity among college students and young adults are the "hook-up" and "friends with benefits." For a more detailed look at these sexual encounters, see Learn About the Research 6.1.

Another trend in teenage sexuality involves using the Internet to interact with others (Denizet-Lewis, 2004). The term **cybersex** has several meanings but is often defined as a *social interaction between at least two persons who exchange computer messages for purposes of sexual arousal and satisfaction* (Döring, 2000). There are two feminist views of cybersex, quite different from each other.

LEARN ABOUT THE RESEARCH 6.1
Hook-Ups and Friends With Benefits

Among both female and male college students and young adults, one increasingly common form of sexual activity is the **hook-up**, a *one-time casual unplanned sexual encounter that can range anywhere from kissing to intercourse* (Bogle, 2008; Regnerus & Uecker, 2011; Stepp, 2007). Another form of sexual intimacy is known as **friends with benefits**. In this arrangement, the *partners start out as friends and decide to periodically engage in sexual behavior but not become a couple* (Diamond, 2010). Paula England and her colleagues (England et al., 2007) found that over 70 percent of the students they surveyed had hooked up, usually after consuming alcohol. One in five of these students had hooked up with ten or more different partners during their college years. Men are more likely than women to prefer hooking up to dating while the reverse is true for women (Bradshaw et al., 2010; Rhoads et al., 2010). Why is this? Women view hooking up as less likely to lead to a relationship and as more likely to produce feelings of distress, shame, or regret (Eshbaugh & Gute, 2008; Fielder & Carey, 2010; Hamilton & Armstrong, 2009; Owen et al., 2010; Regnerus & Uecker, 2011; Smith et al., 2008).

WHAT DOES IT MEAN?

1. Discuss concerns that young people who have hook-ups or friends with benefits don't learn to build emotional intimacy before they get physically intimate and may fail to know how to connect with future partners on an intimate level. Are these concerns valid? Why or why not?

2. When, if at all, do you consider it to be acceptable to have a hook-up or a "friend with benefits"? What level of physical intimacy do you think is appropriate between people who don't have an emotional relationship?

The victimization perspective focuses on how women and girls as individuals and as a group are harmed by online harassment and virtual rape. In contrast, the liberation perspective argues that cybersex benefits girls and women by allowing them to explore their sexuality freely and more safely (Döring, 2000). Which view do you agree with, and why?

Factors Associated with Sexual Activity

Many factors affect the onset of sexual activity, the number of sexual partners, and the risk of becoming pregnant or causing a pregnancy. These include the effects of puberty, family, and peers, as well as individual characteristics. As we noted in Chapter 4, early-maturing girls tend to initiate sexual activity sooner than other girls (Lansford et al., 2010; Zimmer-Gembeck & Helfand, 2008). One likely reason for this is that the development of breasts, curves, and other secondary sex characteristics may attract sexual attention from males (Zabin & Cardona, 2002).

You may be surprised to learn that parents are the biggest influence on teenagers' decisions about whether to have sex and that friends are next (National Campaign to Prevent Teen Pregnancy, 2003). Parents, however, underestimate their own influence and believe that teenagers' friends play a more important role. Unfortunately, fewer than half of older teen women and just over one-fourth of men this age say that they have talked with a parent about birth control and how to say "no to sex" (Centers for Disease Control and Prevention, 2011). And although many teens look up sexual health information online, these Websites often contain inaccurate information (Guttmacher Institute, 2011b).

Teenagers who delay the onset of sexual activity, who have fewer partners, and who are at lower risk of pregnancy are close to their parents, see them as supportive, and communicate well with them (Kan et al., 2010; Parera & Surís, 2004; Parkes et al., 2011; Roche et al., 2005). Their parents are more likely to be married, are better educated, have a higher income level, use firm, consistent discipline, and are aware of their teen's friends and activities (Dupéré et al., 2008; East et al., 2006; Manlove et al., 2009; Roche & Leventhal, 2009; Zimmer-Gembeck & Helfand, 2008). Teenagers who begin sexual activity at a later age are also more apt to be religious; have better grades in school, higher educational aspirations, greater social maturity, and lower levels of alcohol, cigarette, and drug use; and, in the case of girls, are more apt to participate in sports (Collins & Steinberg, 2006; Gold et al., 2010).

An early onset of sexual activity, a greater number of partners, and increased risk of pregnancy are linked to having sexually active or pregnant siblings and peers, having had a single teenage mother, having parents who are permissive about sex but do less monitoring of their teen's behavior, and being in a committed dating relationship (Bersamin et al., 2008; East, 2009; Hawes et al., 2010; Hofferth & Goldscheider, 2010; Lansford et al., 2010; Manlove et al., 2009; McHale et al., 2009; Siebenbruner et al., 2007; Uecker, 2008). Girls who have sexual intercourse at an early age, as well as those who fail to use contraceptives, tend to be depressed and have low self-esteem, negative body image, and little sense of control over their lives (APA Task Force, 2007; Meier, 2007; Rubin et al., 2009; Spencer et al., 2002). Sexual and physical abuse in childhood, which may contribute to these negative feelings about oneself, also increase the likelihood of both early sexual activity and early pregnancy (Hendrick & Reddy, 2007; Logsdon-Conradsen, 2011; Tyler & Johnson, 2006).

The Double Standard

Despite the relaxing of sexual prohibitions over the past few decades, the double standard of sexuality in society—acceptable for boys, but not girls—remains alive and well (Schalet, 2010). Parents may be willing to condone sexual experimentation in their sons ("Boys will be boys") but rarely sanction it in their daughters. Girls, more than boys, are encouraged to express their sexuality only within the context of a committed, socially approved relationship. Consequently, it is not surprising to find that adolescent girls are more likely than adolescent boys to focus on the emotional aspect of sex (Tiegs et al., 2007) and to consider affection a prerequisite for sexual intimacy (Walsh et al., 2011). As one example, a survey of nearly 300,000 first-year college students found that 60 percent of males but only 35 percent of females agreed with the statement, "If two people really like each other, it's all right for them to have sex even if they've known each other for only a very short time" ("This Year's Freshmen," 2005).

Sexual Desire

Girls and young women receive powerful societal messages that it is *their* responsibility to suppress desire and serve as sexual gatekeepers (Diamond & Savin-Williams, 2009). Perhaps for this reason, the sexual desire of teenage girls is rarely studied (Bay-Cheng et al., 2009). When Deborah Tolman (2002) interviewed adolescent, low-income girls of color and middle-income White girls, all reported feelings of powerful sexual desire. At the same time, the girls feared the potential of negative consequences of expressing these desires: pregnancy, STIs, losing respect and reputation, and limiting educational opportunities. The ethnic minority girls were more afraid of physical violation, and encountered stereotypes that they are oversexualized. White girls felt physically safer but faced a different troublesome stereotype, that of the "good girl" who is supposed to show no evidence of sexuality. Individual girls resolved these "dilemmas of desire" in different ways. Some suppressed their sexual desires, others avoided situations that could arouse sexual feelings, and still others arranged conditions in which they could safely express desire.

SEXUAL ACTIVITY IN MIDLIFE

Sexual activity and satisfaction vary among midlife women just as they do among young women. Women who in their earlier years found sexual expression to be fulfilling typically continue to enjoy sex in their middle years and beyond. Other women, whose sexual desires were not strong earlier, may find that their interest diminishes further during middle age. In this section, we examine the sexuality of women in midlife.

Physical Changes

Most women experience a number of physical changes as they enter menopause, some of which may affect sexual activity (Seiden & Bilett, 2007; Wroolie & Holcomb, 2010). Decline in the production of estrogen is responsible for many of these changes. The vaginal walls become less elastic, thinner, and more easily irritated, causing pain and bleeding during intercourse. Decreases in vaginal lubrication can also lead to painful intercourse (Herbenick et al., 2010a).

Various lubricants and moisturizers can ease vaginal dryness. Paradoxically, one of the best remedies is to have more sex! Sexual activity increases blood flow to the vagina, which makes the tissues fuller, and also triggers lubrication (Brody, 2009a). Signs of sexual arousal—clitoral, labial, and breast engorgement and nipple erection—become less intense in midlife, and sexual arousal is slower. Most menopausal women, however, experience little or no change in *subjective* arousal. Although the number and intensity of orgasmic contractions are reduced, few women either notice or complain about these changes. Furthermore, slower arousal time for both women and men may lengthen the time of pleasurable sexual activity (Etaugh, 2008).

Patterns of Sexual Activity

Whereas some midlife women report a decline in sexual desire and the capacity for orgasm during these years, others report the opposite pattern (Birnbaum et al., 2007; Brody, 2009a; Tracy & Junginger, 2007; Woods et al., 2010). Some women report an increased desire for nongenital sexual expression such as cuddling, hugging, and kissing (Block, 2008; Groh & Serowsky, 2009). The extent of sexual activity in middle-aged women is strongly influenced by past sexual enjoyment and experience. Years of sexual experience can more than make up for any decrease in physical responsiveness (Rathus et al., 2010). Women who have been sexually responsive during young adulthood are most likely to be sexually active as they get older (Etaugh, 2008). In addition, both heterosexual and lesbian women who communicate openly with their partners and make changes in their sexual activities to adapt to menopausal changes are more likely than other women to report active and satisfying sex lives (Winterich, 2003).

Many postmenopausal women find that their sexual interest and pleasure are heightened. Books such as *Sex and the seasoned woman* (Sheehy, 2007) and *Prime* (Schwartz, 2007) sing the praises of the sexual passions of midlife women. What are some possible reasons for this renewed sexual interest? One is freedom from worries about pregnancy (Torpy, 2007). This factor may be especially relevant for older cohorts of women for whom highly effective birth control methods were unavailable during their childbearing years. A second reason is the increase in marital satisfaction that often develops during the postparental ("empty nest") years (Etaugh, 2008).

Sexual activity decreases only slightly and gradually for women in their 40s and 50s. Greater declines in activity and in sexual satisfaction may result from physical or psychological changes, however (Fisher, 2010; Lindau & Gavrilova, 2010). Physical causes include various medical conditions, certain medications, and heavy drinking (Brody, 2007). Medical procedures such as mastectomy and hysterectomy do not impair sexual functioning. In fact, many women experience improved sexual function, including greater sexual desire, an increase in orgasms, and a drop in painful intercourse following a hysterectomy (Hartmann et al., 2004; Wroolie & Holomb, 2010). For those women who feel that their ability to enjoy sex after a hysterectomy is diminished, counseling can be helpful (Block, 2008). Similarly, mastectomy does not interfere with sexual responsiveness, but a woman may lose her sexual desire or her sense of being desired. Talking with other women who have had a mastectomy often helps. One resource is the American Cancer Society's Reach to Recovery program (American Cancer Society, 2011).

Sexual activity and contentment during middle age are more likely to diminish for individuals who have lost their partners (Fisher, 2010; Lindau & Gavrilova, 2010). For example, in a recent nationally representative study of sexuality in Americans aged 45 and over, only one in ten who had no partner, but six in ten of those with sexual partners, were satisfied with their sex lives (Fisher, 2010). Although about three-fourths of men of all ages have a sexual partner, only two-thirds of young and middle-aged women do. Among women aged 75 and over, only four in ten have a partner (Lindau & Gavrilova, 2010).

SEXUAL ACTIVITY IN LATER LIFE

Before reading this section, try Get Involved 6.2. See how your attitudes and those of your friends compare to the information in the chapter.

Sexual activity can be as gratifying in the later years as in the younger years (Alexander et al., 2010). Unfortunately, as Get Involved 6.2 demonstrates, there are a number of myths and stereotypes about sexuality in later life. Most of today's older Americans grew up at a time when attitudes toward sexuality were more restrictive than they are today, particularly for women (Kontula & Haavio-Mannila, 2009; Mares & Fitzpatrick, 2004). Unlike men, many women were taught that they should not enjoy sex and should not initiate it. This "double standard" of sexuality for women and men mentioned earlier in the chapter exists for adults of all ages. Older women also are subjected to the double standard of aging discussed in Chapter 2. Thus, compared to older men, women in their later years are perceived as sexually inactive and sexually unattractive (Antonucci et al., 2010; Lai & Hynie, 2011). Men tend to choose younger women or women who look young as their sexual partners and mates (Daniluk, 1998; Rathus et al., 2010). A few years ago, in a special issue of the *Journal of Social Issues* devoted entirely to sexuality, there was not a single word about the sexuality of older women (Goodchilds, 2000). Many older women themselves are self-conscious about their aging bodies (Henig, 2004a). Let us examine older women's sexuality—the benefits of sexual activity in later life, sexual behaviors and the factors affecting them, and enhancement of sexual experience in the later years.

Benefits of Sexual Activity in Later Life

Sexual activity can have physical, psychological, and emotional benefits for older adults (Kontula & Haavio-Mannila, 2009; Lindau & Gavrilova, 2010). The physical benefits include improving circulation, maintaining a greater range and motion of joints and limbs in arthritic persons, helping one sleep, and controlling weight gain (Butler & Lewis, 2002; Doress-Worters & Siegal, 1994,

GET INVOLVED 6.2
Attitudes Toward Sexuality in Later Life

On a scale from 1 (strongly disagree) to 7 (strongly agree), indicate the extent to which you disagree or agree with each of the following statements. Also, ask three female and three male acquaintances who vary in age to respond to these statements.

1. Older people lose their interest in sex and no longer engage in sexual activity.

2. Changes in hormone levels that occur during and after menopause cause women to find sex unsatisfying and unpleasant.

3. Women who are beyond the childbearing years lose their sexual desire and their sexual desirability.

4. In order to have a full and satisfying sex life, a woman must have a male partner.

5. Older women who still enjoy sex were probably nymphomaniacs when they were younger.

6. Older people with chronic illness or physical disabilities should cease sexual activity completely.

WHAT DOES IT MEAN?

Add up the ratings you gave to these six statements. Do the same for each of your respondents. Note that each statement reflects a myth based on folklore and misconceptions. Therefore, the higher the score, the more the respondent holds unfounded beliefs about sexuality in later life.

1. Are there differences between the views of your female and male respondents? Explain your answer.

2. Are there differences between the views of respondents who vary in age? Explain your answer.

3. In what way might society's attitudes toward aging and older people be related to the persistence of these myths about sexuality in later life? Explain your answer.

Sources: Doress-Worters and Siegal (1994); Gibson (1996).

Leitner & Leitner, 2004). Sexual activity among older people has psychological and emotional benefits as well. It can improve one's sense of well-being, increase life satisfaction, enhance a woman's feeling of femininity and desirability, offer an outlet for emotions, and provide a shared pleasurable experience (Leitner & Leitner, 2004). In the later years, sexual activities other than intercourse—oral sex, manual stimulation, caressing—bring pleasure with or without orgasm (Burgess, 2004; Rathus et al., 2010).

Sexual Behavior of Older People

Interest in sexual activity remains fairly high throughout adult life, especially for men, declining only gradually in the later years (Fisher, 2010; Herbenick et al., 2010b; Lindau & Gavrilova, 2010). In a recent national survey, 40 percent of men but only 11 percent of women aged 75–85 reported still having sexual desires (Lindau & Gavrilova, 2010).

Still, some women find sex more satisfying and their attitudes toward sex more positive and open in later life. In one nationwide survey of Americans over age 60, 70 percent of sexually active women said they were as satisfied, or even more satisfied, with their sex lives than they were in their 40s (Leary, 1998). Once grown children have left the nest, couples may experience a "second honeymoon" as marital satisfaction increases (Aubin & Heiman, 2004; Connidis, 2010). (See the second vignette at the beginning of the chapter.)

In the earlier mentioned survey (Lindau & Gavrilova, 2010), over 80 percent of men aged 57–64, two-thirds of those aged 64–75, and 40 percent between age 75 and 85 had engaged in sexual behavior within the past year. Many of them had done so on a weekly basis. The corresponding figures for women were 60 percent, 40 percent, and 17 percent, respectively. Women at all ages were less likely than men to be sexually active, in part because more of them lacked a partner. In addition, good health is related to sexual interest and activity, and older women are less likely than men to report being in good or excellent health (Lindau & Gavrilova, 2010; Schick et al., 2010). Decreased sexual desire of one's partner is another reason for a decline in sexual activity among older people (McHugh, 2007).

Factors Affecting Sexual Behavior

A number of both physical and psychological factors influence sexual behavior in older women.

PHYSICAL FACTORS.   The physical changes in the reproductive system that begin in midlife (see Chapter 7) become more pronounced in the later years, as estrogen levels continue to decline. Physical changes, illness, chronic disabilities, and medication can affect sexuality in later life (Lindau & Gavrilova, 2010). However, even the most serious conditions should not stop women and men from engaging in satisfying sexual activity (Butler & Lewis, 2002). Heart disease, especially if one has had a heart attack, leads many older adults to give up sex, fearing it will cause another attack. But the risk of this is low. Most people can resume sexual activity in 12 to 16 weeks. Stroke rarely damages sexual function and it is unlikely that sexual exertion will cause another stroke. Arthritis, the most common chronic disability, causes joint pain that can limit sexual activity (Read, 2004). Surgery and drugs can relieve the pain, but in some cases, medications decrease sexual desire. Exercise, rest, warm baths, and changing the positions or timing of sexual activity can be helpful. Medications such as certain antidepressants and tranquilizers can also reduce a woman's sexual desire. However, a physician can often prescribe a different medication without this side effect.

PSYCHOSOCIAL FACTORS.   A person's attitudes toward sex-related physical changes can interfere with sexual activity more than the actual changes themselves. A major psychosocial constraint is the societal view that sexual desire in older adults, especially older women, is abnormal (Block, 2008). As a result, older adults who want to fulfill their sexual desires may feel apprehensive and guilty. In addition, many older women feel unattractive and thus may avoid sexual activity with a partner or decide not to seek a new partner if they become widowed or divorced (Burgess, 2004).

Another constraint for residents of nursing homes is that the attitudes of nursing home staff are often not supportive of sexual behavior. Although more nurses are respecting the wishes of their clients for sexual freedom and privacy (Johnson & Scelfo, 2003), many nursing home administrators feel that sexual activity on the part of residents "causes problems," even if the individuals are married. Even masturbation may be strongly discouraged (Beers & Jones, 2004; Butler & Lewis, 2002; Villarosa, 2002).

Enhancing Sexuality in Later Life

Sexual activity can be more rewarding for older adults if people come to realize that sexual expression is a normal part of life regardless of age. Sex counseling can help remove inhibitions restricting an older person's sexual behavior. Emphasizing the quality of the sexual relationship rather than performance can make sexual experiences more enjoyable for older people (Hillman & Stricker, 1994; Leitner & Leitner, 2004). Those who are in supervised living arrangements need to be given opportunities to have private time together for intimate contact (Alexander et al., 2010). Health care professionals should provide information and counseling to older people regarding the impact of both normal physical changes and medical conditions on sexual functioning, yet doctors rarely address sexual concerns in older adults, particularly in women (Lindau & Gavrilova, 2010).

The many older women who are not in an ongoing physical relationship need to feel it is permissible to express their sexuality in whatever way is comfortable for them, whether it be enjoying their fantasies, engaging in masturbation, using a vibrator, or accepting an asexual lifestyle (Block, 2008; Butler & Lewis, 2002; Seiden & Bilett, 2007). Although some older women are celibate because they lack the opportunity to meet partners, others choose to be celibate but still enjoy sensuous experiences:

> In Colette's novel, Break of Day, I discovered celibacy as a strategy for older women who too often see themselves as stripped of identity without a partner. Colette sees age fifty-five as the end of having lovers, but the beginning of an aloneness that is joyous and drenched in sensuality—particularly for the artist in all of us. It is a great gift to be one's self at last.
>
> (Marilyn Zuckerman, a poet in her 60s, in Doress-Worters & Siegal, 1994, p. 88)

Summary

SEXUALITY

- The external female organs (vulva) consist of the mons pubis, labia majora, labia minora, and clitoris.
- The four phases of the sexual response cycle are excitement, plateau, orgasm, and resolution.
- Women, more so than men, are capable of multiple orgasms.
- Orgasms resulting from clitoral and vaginal orgasm are physiologically the same.
- The sexual double standard condones casual sexual activity for men but not for women.
- Women have less permissive attitudes toward sexual behavior than men and emphasize relationships as a context for sex.
- Women are less likely than men to engage in most sexual behaviors.
- The four major types of sexual dysfunction are sexual desire disorders, sexual arousal disorders, orgasm disorders, and sexual pain disorders.
- The new view of women's sexual problems focuses on sociocultural, psychological, and relational factors.

LESBIANS, GAY MEN, BISEXUALS, AND TRANSGENDER INDIVIDUALS

- Lesbians and gay men are attracted to same-sex persons; bisexuals are attracted to both sexes. The gender identity of transgender persons differs from the one assigned at birth.
- Sexual identities of some sexual minority individuals change over time.
- Homophobia is pervasive in American society. It is most commonly found in older, less educated, politically conservative males who hold traditional gender-related attitudes and fundamentalist religious beliefs.
- Complex interactions among genetic, hormonal, and environmental factors appear to determine sexual orientation.

SEXUAL ACTIVITY DURING ADOLESCENCE

- Rates of teenage sexuality have been decreasing.
- The onset of sexual activity is influenced by pubertal development and individual characteristics as well as by family and peers.

SEXUAL ACTIVITY IN MIDLIFE

- Postmenopausal physical changes can lead to painful intercourse.
- Some women show a decline in sexual interest and capacity for orgasm whereas others show the opposite pattern.

SEXUAL ACTIVITY IN LATER LIFE

- Sexual activity can have physical, psychological, and emotional benefits for older individuals.
- Interest in sexual activity remains fairly high throughout adulthood, declining gradually in the later years.
- Sexual interest and activity are greater for older men than for older women. One reason for decreased sexual activity, especially for women, is the lack of a partner.
- Physical changes, illness, disability, and psychosocial factors influence sexual behavior in older women.
- Sexuality may be enhanced through counseling, changes in societal attitudes, and greater opportunities for intimate contact.

Key Terms

vulva *122*

mons pubis *122*

labia majora *122*

labia minora *122*

clitoris *122*

vagina *122*

sexual response cycle *122*

vasocongestion *122*

orgasmic platform *123*

sexual double standard *123*

inhibited sexual desire *125*

sexual arousal disorder *126*

female orgasmic disorder *126*

dyspareunia *126*

vaginismus *126*

lesbian *128*

gay man *128*

bisexual *128*

transgender *128*

heterosexism *130*

homophobia *130*

cybersex *133*

hook-up *134*

friends with benefits *134*

What Do You Think?

1. Why do you think women generally have less permissive attitudes toward sexual behavior than men do?
2. Why do you think that society holds negative attitudes toward gay men and lesbians?
3. If you were to design a school-based or community-based sex education program, what would you include?
4. What is your position on programs that provide contraceptives to teenagers?

If You Want to Learn More

Block, J. D. (2008). *Sex over 50*. New York: Penguin.

Bogle, K. (2008). *Hooking up: Sex, dating, and relationships on campus*. New York: New York University Press.

Brill, S., & Pepper, R. (2008). *The transgender child: A handbook for families and professionals*. San Francisco, CA: Cleis Press.

Carpenter, L. M. (2005). *Virginity lost: An intimate portrait of first sexual experiences*. New York: New York University Press.

Carroll, J. L. (2010). *Sexuality now: Embracing diversity*. Belmont, CA: Wadsworth.

Daniluk, J. C. (2003). *Women's sexuality across the life span: Challenging myths, creating meanings*. New York: Guilford.

Diamond, L. (2009). *Sexual fluidity: Understanding women's love and desire*. Cambridge, MA: Harvard University Press.

Meem, D. T., Gibson, M. A., & Alexander, J. F. (2010). *Finding out: An introduction to LGBT studies*. Thousand Oaks, CA: Sage.

Parker, R., & Aggleton, P. (2007). *Culture, society, and sexuality: A reader*. New York: Routledge.

Rathus, S. A., Fichner-Rathus, L., & Nevid, J. S. (2010). *Human sexuality in a world of diversity* (8th ed.). Upper Saddle River, NJ: Prentice Hall.

Regnerus, M., & Uecker, J. (2011). *Premarital sex in America: How young Americans meet, mate, and think about marrying*. New York: Oxford University Press.

Resh, E. K. (2009). *The secret lives of teen girls: What your mother wouldn't talk about but your daughter needs to know.* New York: Hay House.

Rose, T. (2003). *Longing to tell: Black women talk about sexuality and intimacy.* New York: Picador.

Schwartz, P. (2007). *Prime: Adventures and advice on sex, love, and the sensual years.* New York: HarperCollins.

Sheehy, G. (2006). *Sex and the seasoned woman: Pursuing the passionate life.* New York: Ballantine.

Tolman, D. L. (2002). *Dilemmas of desire: Teenage girls talk about sexuality.* Cambridge, MA: Harvard University Press.

Zaslau, S. (2012). *Dx/Rx: Sexual dysfunction in men and women.* Sudbury, MA: Jones & Bartlett.

Websites

Disability

Disabled People's International
http://www.dpi.org

Sexual Minorities

American Civil Liberties Union—LGBT Rights
http://www.aclu.org/lgbt-rights

CHAPTER 7

Reproductive System and Childbearing

She was placed on my chest and I began to cry from the overwhelming sense of emotions I felt. I was feeling so many things simultaneously: relief, love, excitement, awe, astonishment, pride, and achievement. It was truly a momentous occasion, very surreal and very beautiful. When I looked deeply into my newborn daughter's eyes for the very first time, I kissed her softly and whispered: "Hi, baby, welcome to the world, we've been waiting for you." (Boston Women's Health Book Collective, 2008, p. 182)

Menstruation
    The Menstrual Cycle
    Menstrual Pain
    Attitudes Toward
        Menstruation
    Menstrual Joy
    Premenstrual Syndrome

Contraception
    Contraception in Adolescence
    Methods of Contraception

Abortion
    Incidence
    Methods
    Consequences of
        Abortion

Pregnancy
    Pregnancy: Physical and
        Psychological Changes
    Miscarriage
    Teenage Pregnancy

Childbirth
    Stages of Childbirth
    Methods of Childbirth
    Childbearing After 35
    Childbearing in the Later
        Years
    Postpartum Distress
    Infertility and Assisted
        Reproductive Technology

**Reproductive Functioning in
Midlife and Beyond**
    Menopause
    Hormone Replacement
        Therapy

Giving birth to a child can be one of the major events of a woman's life. Childbirth typically (although not exclusively) occurs during late adolescence and young adulthood. In this chapter, we focus on women's reproductive system functioning throughout the life span, including menstruation, contraception, abortion, pregnancy, and childbirth. We conclude with an exploration of reproductive functioning in midlife and beyond, looking at menopause and hormone replacement therapy.

MENSTRUATION

The menstrual cycle involves the release of a mature egg or ovum from its surrounding capsule or follicle. The cycle, which occurs in four phases, averages 28 days in length. (*Menstruation* is derived from the Latin word for *month*.) The menstrual cycle is governed by a feedback loop involving two brain structures—the hypothalamus and the pituitary gland—and the ovaries and uterus (Donatelle, 2012; Hawkins & Matzuk, 2008). In this section, we explore the biological, psychological, and cultural aspects of menstruation.

The Menstrual Cycle

In the *follicular* phase of the menstrual cycle, days 4 to 14, low levels of estrogen and progesterone cause the hypothalamus to stimulate the pituitary gland to secrete follicle-stimulating hormone (FSH). This causes the ovaries to increase estrogen production and bring several follicles and their eggs to maturity. Estrogen stimulates development of the endometrium (uterine lining) in order to receive a fertilized egg. Estrogen also signals the pituitary to stop producing FSH and to start producing luteinizing hormone (LH). The LH suppresses development of all but one follicle and egg.

In the second or *ovulatory* phase, about day 14, LH level peaks, causing rupture of the follicle and release of the egg near a fallopian tube. This is called **ovulation**. A woman is most likely to become pregnant on the three days before or on the day of ovulation (Office on Women's Health, 2009). During ovulation, some women experience *mittelschmerz* ("middle pain") on the side of the abdomen where the egg has been released.

During the *luteal* phase, LH stimulates the follicle to form a yellowish group of cells called the *corpus luteum* ("yellow body"), which produces large amounts of progesterone and estrogen. These hormones, which reach their peak around day 20 or 21 of the cycle, cause the endometrium to secrete nourishing substances in the event the egg is fertilized and implanted in the uterine lining. If fertilization does not occur, high progesterone levels cause the hypothalamus to stop the pituitary's production of LH. This causes decomposition of the corpus luteum and a sharp drop in levels of estrogen and progesterone through day 28.

The fourth phase, *menstruation* (days 1 to 4), occurs when the low levels of estrogen and progesterone can no longer maintain the uterine lining, which is shed and exits through the cervix (the lower end of the uterus) and vagina as menstrual flow. The low hormone levels trigger the beginning of another cycle. Should the egg be fertilized, however, the hormone levels remain high, and a new cycle does not occur (Donatelle, 2012).

Changes in the levels of the ovarian and pituitary hormones over the menstrual cycle are shown in Figure 7.1.

Menstrual Pain

Menstrual pain, or **dysmenorrhea**, includes painful abdominal cramps and lower back pain during menstruation. About 55 to 73 percent of adolescent girls and women report experiencing menstrual pain each month (Harel, 2008). Women who report higher levels of menstrual pain and discomfort are also more likely to report high levels of psychological stress in their lives, and poorer health. They are also more likely to smoke and to consume alcohol (Alexander et al., 2010; Harel, 2008; D. Miller, 2010; Woolven, 2008).

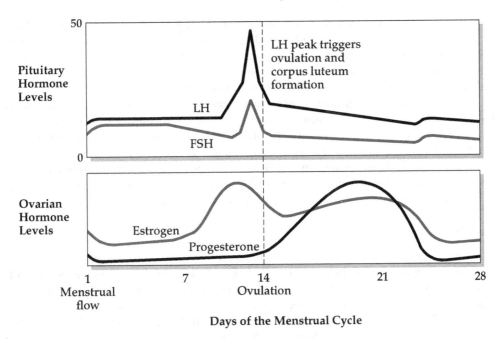

FIGURE 7.1 Changes in Hormone Levels During the Menstrual Cycle
Source: Excerpt pp. 530–532 from *Access to Health,* 5th ed. by Rebecca J. Donatelle and Lorraine G. Davis. Copyright © 1998 by Allyn & Bacon. Reprinted by permission of Pearson Education, Inc.

The cause of menstrual discomfort is thought to be **prostaglandins**, *hormonelike chemicals secreted by the uterine lining and other tissues as menstruation approaches.* These substances cause uterine contractions, decreased blood flow, and increased sensitivity to pain, which lead to cramping. Women who suffer from severe menstrual pain often have unusually high levels of prostaglandins (Pruthi, 2010). Over-the-counter antiprostaglandin drugs such as ibuprofen and naproxen help relieve menstrual pain in many women (Donatelle, 2012; Office on Women's Health, 2009b). A warm bath or heating pad may be beneficial as well. Also helpful is a low-fat vegan diet, which includes whole grains, legumes, vegetables, and fruits, but no eggs or dairy products (Harel, 2008; Northrup, 2010; Physicians Committee, 2007).

Attitudes Toward Menstruation

> *On a recent TV show, the plot involved a man intent on killing a group of female medical students. He wore a T-shirt that read "Don't trust anybody who bleeds for five days and doesn't die." That chilling statement said volumes about a mind-set going back millennia.*

> (Pam, a 49-year-old school teacher)

Throughout history, menstruation has had "bad press." Menstrual blood has been viewed as having magical and often poisonous powers. Menstruating women have been isolated and forbidden to prepare food or to engage in sexual activity (Bobel, 2010; Fahs, 2011). Menstrual myths and taboos still exist, although in a somewhat less extreme form. For example, some adolescent girls and women believe that menstruating women should not exercise, swim, or wash their hair (Chrisler, 2008a). In addition, many euphemistic terms are used to avoid the word *menstruation:* "period," "that time of the month," "I've got my friend," "she's on the rag," "the curse," "Aunt FLO is visiting" (Fahs, 2011; Fingerson, 2006). Have you heard or used other expressions? How many are positive? Many Americans believe that a woman cannot function normally when menstruating, but there is little evidence that athletic performance, academic performance, problem solving, memory, or creative thinking show meaningful fluctuations over the menstrual cycle (Chrisler, 2008b).

Still, negative attitudes toward the menstruating woman remain strong. In one study (Forbes et al., 2003), for example, college men and women both perceived a menstruating woman, compared to the "average woman," as being more irritable, angry, and sad, and as less energized and less sexy. Men, but not women, also saw her as annoying, unreasonable, "spacey," less nurturing, less reliable and dependable, less creative and intellectually curious, and more disagreeable and spiteful than other women. Women found some redeeming features in the menstruating woman, viewing her as more maternal, strong, and trustworthy than the average women.

Menstrual Joy

Despite the prevalence of negative attitudes toward menstruation, some women experience their menstrual periods as self-affirming, creative, and pleasurable, and as signifying femininity and fertility (Kissling, 2006; Lorber, 2010). Negative expectations about menstruation may influence many women to focus more on its associated unpleasant symptoms. But what would happen if menstruation were portrayed in a more positive light? Researchers in the United States (Chrisler et al., 1994) and in Great Britain (Aubeeluck & Maguire, 2002) studied the effects of presenting positive and negative views on women's reported responses to menstruation. The researchers administered both the Menstrual Joy Questionnaire (MJQ) and the Menstrual Distress Questionnaire (MDQ) to college women (see Get Involved 7.1). The MJQ lists positive feelings that might be experienced before or during menstruation, such as self-confidence, creativity, and power. The MDQ lists negative feelings that might occur at these times, such as irritability, anxiety, and fatigue. The researchers found that women who completed the MJQ before they were given the MDQ reported less menstrual distress and more favorable attitudes toward menstruation than those who received the questionnaires in reverse order. It appears that the way menstruation is portrayed can affect the way women react to their menstrual cycles. Try the questionnaires in Get Involved 7.1 and see whether you find the same results.

Interestingly, the findings that menstruation actually has some positive aspects did not generate a lot of media publicity or subsequent research. According to Margaret Matlin (2003), this illustrates the **women-as-problem bias**, that is, *psychologists' preference for studying negative aspects of women's lives rather than positive ones.*

Premenstrual Syndrome

For me, menstrual distress is very real. Every month, the week before my period started, I became a different person. I felt such rage and could not control it. My husband and children suffered verbal and physical abuse for years. I thought I was going insane. In the last 3 years, I have been taking medication and am doing better. I feel like I can take back my life.

(Sharah, 35 years old)

For most women, mild-to-moderate physical and emotional fluctuations are part of the normal menstrual cycle experience. Women may experience breast tenderness, bloating, anxiety, or irritability that may be annoying but do not disrupt their daily lives (Chrisler & Rose, 2011; Donatelle, 2012). A small minority of women experience *symptoms so severe that their normal functioning is*

GET INVOLVED 7.1
Menstrual Symptoms

Ask four female friends or relatives to complete both parts of the following questionnaire. Give half of them Part I, followed by Part II. Give the other half Part II first, then Part I. The instructions are: *Rate each item on a 5-point scale, using 1 if,* *shortly before and during your menstrual period, you do not experience the feeling at all; 2, if you experience the feeling slightly; 3, if you experience it moderately; 4, if you experience it quite a bit; and 5, if you experience it intensely.*

Part I Menstrual Joy		Part II Menstrual Distress	
Energetic	_____	Irritated	_____
Affectionate	_____	Sad	_____
Cheerful	_____	Tense	_____
Creative	_____	Moody	_____
Powerful	_____	Fatigued	_____
Self-confident	_____	Out of control	_____
Active	_____	Anxious	_____
Sense of well-being	_____	Angry	_____

Add the score for the menstrual joy feelings. Do the same for the feelings of menstrual distress.

WHAT DOES IT MEAN?

1. Did individuals who completed the menstrual joy part first report less menstrual distress than those who completed the menstrual distress part first? If so, why?

2. Why do you think some women have more positive feelings than others before and during their menstrual periods?

3. Why have the negative aspects of menstruation been emphasized much more than the positive aspects?

4. What might be done to focus more on the positive side of menstruation?

Source: From *The Curse: A Cultural History of Menstruation.* Copyright 1976, 1988 by Janice Delaney, Mary Jane Lupton, and Emily Toth. Used with permission of the University of Illinois Press.

impaired for a week each month preceding menstruation, as illustrated in Sharah's comments. These women are considered to suffer from **premenstrual syndrome (PMS)** (Donatelle, 2012). Although the prevalence of PMS does not appear to be dependent on cultural or ethnic differences (Casper & Yonkers, 2010; Miller, 2010), it is not experienced the same way around the world. For example, women in China are much more likely to report temperature changes than emotional changes (Chrisler & Rose, 2011).

WHAT IS PMS?   For years, controversy has swirled around the validity of PMS as a disorder because scientists have not agreed upon its definition. Since 1987, the American Psychiatric Association has included PMS in its diagnostic handbook, labeling its most severe form **Premenstrual Dysphoric Disorder (PMDD)**. To be diagnosed with PMDD, *a woman must experience at least five symptoms during the week before her menstrual period, including depression, anxiety, mood swings, or anger/irritability.*

The symptoms must interfere markedly with work or social relationships and must be present only in the premenstrual phase of the cycle (Chrisler, 2008b). About 3 to 9 percent of women of reproductive age meet these strict criteria although 12 to 18 percent have symptoms sufficient to cause monthly distress and impairment (Kiesner, 2009; Potter et al., 2009). Some theorists feel that the diagnosis of PMDD validates the experiences of a group of women and is thus empowering (Chen, 2009). But others object to treating normal reproductive system functioning in women as a disease. Some feminist psychologists believe that classifying PMDD as a psychiatric disorder stigmatizes women as mentally ill, undermines their self-esteem, and feeds into socially constructed stereotypes about women (Bobel, 2010; Caplan, 2008; Chrisler, 2008b).

For example, a widely held stereotype in North America is that women experience negative moods before their menstrual periods (Chrisler et al., 2008b). Thus, if a woman feels anxious, sad, irritable, or moody and believes she is in the premenstrual phase of her cycle, she may attribute her feelings to PMS. Differences in the life circumstances of individual women may also influence their experiences with menstrual symptoms. For example, women with high levels of stress report increased severity of symptoms before and during their menstrual periods (Gollenberg et al., 2010; Sadler et al., 2010). Genetic factors appear to be involved as well (Chrisler & Rose, 2011).

TREATING PMS.   Whether PMS/PMDD is a mental disorder or not, it is important to give help to women who seek it. Some women report that dietary changes or progesterone supplements provide some relief, but these approaches may be effective for only a small subset of women (Miller, 2010). Taking vitamins E and B and calcium with vitamin D reduces the symptoms of PMS in many women (Miller, 2010; O'Grady & Lori, 2009). Antidepressants, including Prozac and Paxil, that raise levels of serotonin in the brain relieve emotional and often physical symptoms of PMS (Cohen, 2008). Exercise also helps to reduce symptoms (Daley, 2009).

CONTRACEPTION

The typical American woman marries at age 25 and achieves her desired family size of two children by age 31. She then spends the next 20 years until menopause trying to avoid an unintended pregnancy (Dailard, 2003). In this section, we look at the use of contraception, starting with the teen years.

Contraception in Adolescence

Girls make the decision [to use condoms] because males don't really care if you have a condom or not. . . . Just as long as he gets to [do] it. . . . He doesn't get pregnant.

(A sexually active teenage girl, in Denner & Coyle, 2006, p. 290)

The use of contraceptives, both condoms and long-acting hormonal methods, has increased among sexually active adolescents, especially girls, in recent years, due in part to the growing awareness of the danger of AIDS and other sexually transmitted infections (STIs) (Centers for Disease Control and Prevention, 2011; Manning et al., 2009). In one study, a large majority of teenagers—69 percent of girls and 80 percent of boys—said they had used a condom the last time they had intercourse, compared with well under half of adults (Fortenberry et al., 2010; Sanders et al., 2010). Still, a substantial number of adolescents do not use contraceptives consistently. About one-fourth of teenage girls do not use contraceptives every time they have sexual intercourse ("Facts on American Teens," 2010). Unfortunately, a sexually active teen who does not use contraception has a 90-percent chance of becoming pregnant within a year (Guttmacher Institute, 2011a).

Many adolescent girls and women resist initiating use of condoms or other contraceptives. Why is this? Some women do not have enough power and control in their relationship with a male partner to be able to persuade him to wear a condom, particularly if he is reluctant to do so (Stevens & Galvao, 2007; Woolf & Maisto, 2008). In some cases, an abusive male may deliberately interfere with the woman's attempt to use birth control methods, in order to promote a pregnancy unwanted by the woman (Miller et al., 2010). Women may also reject condom use because they believe it diminishes sexual pleasure, disrupts intimacy, and suggests that the woman does not trust her partner (Regnerus & Vecker, 2011). For others, taking control of a sexual situation—even if just to introduce a condom—may disrupt their feminine sexual identity and threaten potential rewards they expect in the form of love and protection (Gavey & McPhillips, 1999). Other factors that contribute to lack of contraceptive use in women include reluctance to acknowledge one's own sexual activity, a sense of invincibility ("*I* won't get pregnant"), misconceptions regarding use of contraception, and cost (Devi et al., 2009; Diamond & Savin-Williams, 2009; Huber & Ersek, 2009).

Which individuals are most likely to practice contraception? The older teenagers are when they begin sexual activity, the more likely they are to use contraception. Other factors associated with contraceptive use in high school and college students include being in a committed relationship, having high educational aspirations and achievement, having knowledge about sex and contraception, desiring to avoid STIs and pregnancy, being minimal users of alcohol and drugs, having good communication and a supportive relationship with parents who monitor their activities, discussing contraceptive use with parents and with one's partner, having supportive friends who use contraceptives, waiting a longer time between the start of a relationship and having sex with that partner, and having high self-esteem and feelings of control over one's life (DiClemente et al., 2008; Holcombe et al., 2008; Richards et al., 2008; Ryan et al., 2007; Salazar et al., 2009; Van Home et al., 2009).

Teenagers who attend schools that distribute condoms, compared to teens in schools that don't, are less likely to have ever had sex or less likely to have had sex recently. Moreover, sexually active youth whose schools give out condoms are twice as likely to use condoms as those who can't get condoms at school (Blake et al., 2003). They are also less likely to get pregnant (Blank et al., 2010). Unfortunately, however, few high schools in the United States make contraceptives available (Guttmacher Institute, 2011a).

Methods of Contraception

The one totally foolproof method of contraception is abstinence. Today, increasing numbers of teenagers are pledging not to have sex before marriage. However, a majority of those who take this virginity pledge do not live up to their vows (Brody, 2004a). Moreover, those teenagers who have taken a virginity pledge are *less* likely to use contraception when they do engage in sexual activity (Bearman, 2004; Manlove et al., 2003). In addition, sex education programs based on abstinence are generally ineffective; they do not delay the onset of sexual activity nor decrease the number of teenagers having sex and becoming pregnant (Boonstra, 2009a; Diamond & Savin-Williams, 2009; Lamb, 2010). In fact, there is evidence that such programs are linked to an *increase* in STIs and teen pregnancies (Guttmacher Institute, 2011b; Yang & Gaydos, 2010).

A wide variety of contraceptive choices are available in addition to abstinence (see Table 7.1). As women's reproductive goals change during their childbearing years, the type of contraception they choose also changes. Birth control pills are most often used by women in their teens and 20s, by unmarried women, and by those with some college education. Tubal ligation is more commonly used by women who are over 34, who have previously been married, or who have no more than a high school education. Tubal ligation for women is far more common than vasectomy is for their

TABLE 7.1   Effectiveness Rates of Contraceptive Methods

Method	Effectiveness Percentage		Disadvantages
	Correct Use	**Typical Use**	**Disadvantages**
Birth control pills	99.7	92.0	Risk of blood clots in smokers over 35
Condom (sheath placed over penis)	98.0	85.0	Need to put on before intercourse; may lessen male's sensations; may tear or slip off
Depo-Provera (injection)	99.7	97.0	Menstrual bleeding
Diaphragm (cup placed in vagina)	94.0	84.0	Need to insert before intercourse; unreliable without spermicide
Essure (microcoil inserted in fallopian tubes)	99.8	99.8	Possible cramps
Hormonal vaginal ring (placed in vagina)	99.7	92.0	May slip out; must change monthly
Implants (Implanon)	99.9	99.0	Irregular menstrual periods
Intrauterine device (placed in uterus)	99.4	99.2	Heavy menstrual flow; cramps; inflammation
Rhythm method (fertility awareness)	95.0	75.0	High failure rate
Skin patch	99.7	92.0	Risk of blood clots in smokers over age 35
Spermicide	82.0	71.0	Need to insert before intercourse; not reliable when used alone
Sponge (placed in vagina)	91.0	84.0	Need to insert before intercourse; high failure rate; vaginal infection
Tubal ligation (cutting and tying fallopian tubes)	99.5	99.5	Slight surgical risk; not usually reversible
Vasectomy (cutting and tying sperm-carrying ducts)	99.9	99.8	Slight surgical risk; not usually reversible
Withdrawal (of penis before ejaculation)	96.0	73.0	High failure rate

Sources: Curtis (2010); Donatelle (2012); Pruthi (2010); and Rathus et al. (2010).

male sexual partners (Mosher & Jones, 2010). Of all methods, the condom is the only one providing any protection against STIs. Unfortunately, many women have difficulty preventing unintended pregnancy because they cannot afford the more effective prescription methods of contraception. Not surprisingly, uninsured women are less likely than insured women to use contraceptives. One in ten women who have not used contraception regularly in the past year report that difficulty in accessing methods was responsible for their nonuse (Frost et al., 2008).

In addition to these methods, emergency contraception, the so-called morning after pill (or "plan B"), was approved in the United States in 2009 (Devi et al., 2009). This method is typically used when regular contraception ("plan A") either fails or is skipped. Plan B involves taking high doses of birth control pills within 72 hours of having sex, and then again 12 hours later. A newer version of plan B, name Ella, is effective up to five days after sex (Harris, 2010a,b). These procedures work by delaying ovulation or blocking fertilization of the egg. They do not affect a pre-existing pregnancy (Barot, 2010; Pruthi, 2010). Contrary to popular belief, providing emergency contraception in advance to teenagers does not result in riskier sex practices or switching to less reliable contraceptive methods (Meyer et al., 2011). In the United States, 17-year-olds can purchase plan B over the counter, but younger teens in most states must have a prescription (Devi et al., 2009; Donatelle, 2012). Do you think plan B should be available without prescription for all adolescents? Why or why not?

ABORTION

Abortion is one of the most commonly performed medical procedures and also one of the most controversial. In the United States, the debate over abortion centers around two opposing views: abortion as a right and a means for attaining individual freedom and equity for women versus abortion as a threat to morality, the family, and society. These differing attitudes toward abortion in turn stem from different socially constructed beliefs, attitudes, and values about gender roles and female sexuality (Alexander et al., 2010; Henderson & Jeydal, 2010).

The 1973 landmark Supreme Court decision in *Roe v. Wade* gave women the legal right to terminate pregnancy by abortion during the first trimester (three months) of pregnancy. The Court allowed individual states to set conditions for second-trimester abortions and ruled third-trimester abortions illegal except when the mother's life was endangered (Jones et al., 2008; "Laws, Lies," 2010; Rathus et al., 2010). Since then, a number of restrictions on abortion have been enacted. For example, as of this writing, over two-thirds of the states in the United States require parental consent or notification for minors seeking abortion (Dennis et al., 2009; Guttmacher Institute, 2011c). The U.S. Congress has barred the use of federal Medicaid funds to pay for abortion except when the mother's life is endangered or in cases of rape or incest. Because poor families rely on Medicaid for health care and few have private health insurance, low-income women are less able to afford abortion (Guttmacher Institute, 2011b; Whelan, 2010). In addition, the U.S. Supreme Court recently upheld a congressional ban of a specific type of late-term abortion known as *dilation and extraction* and referred to by critics as "partial birth" abortion (Guttmacher Institute, 2011d).

Nationwide polls conducted more than 35 years after the *Roe v. Wade* ruling have found that public opinion has shifted away from general acceptance of legal abortion toward a more ambivalent acceptance, favoring choice but only under certain conditions (Gallup, 2010; Pew Research Center, 2010a). The proportion of first-year college students believing that abortion should be legal was 58 percent in 2009, a drop of 5 percentage points since 1990 ("The Nation," 2010).

Incidence

Nearly half of the pregnancies among American women are unplanned, and four in ten of these are terminated by abortion (Guttmacher Institute, 2010a). In 2007, nearly 830,000 women in the United States had abortions (Pazol et al., 2011). Not surprisingly, over 90 percent of abortions take place within the first trimester (Pazol et al., 2011; Sulik & Heath, 2010). In recent years, the abortion rate has steadily been declining, especially among teens; data show a 13-percent decrease between 1998 and 2001.

Three-fourths of women undergoing abortions are under 30. Four out of five are unmarried, over half are already mothers, and close to half have had a previous abortion. White women account for nearly 40 percent of all abortions, but their abortion *rate* is below that of women of color. Black women are more than three times as likely as White women to have an abortion and Latinas are twice as likely (Pazol et al., 2011; Sulik & Heath, 2010). Why are abortion rates higher for women of color? Research suggests that they are more likely than White women to become pregnant unwillingly. Cultural pressures may disadvantage ethnic minority women in negotiating sexual and contraceptive choices with their male partners (Stevens & Galvao, 2007).

Abortion rates are similar in countries where it is legal and in those where it is outlawed (Burn, 2011). This suggests that banning abortion does not deter women who seek the procedure. In addition, although abortion is safe in countries where it is legal, it is more dangerous in nations where it is illegal and is often performed under unsafe conditions (Burn, 2011; Cohen, 2009; Poltera, 2011).

Methods

The safest and most common method of abortion is **vacuum aspiration**, in which *the contents of the uterus are removed by suction* (Pazol et al., 2011). Although most American women prefer this surgical procedure, those up to eight weeks pregnant can choose to take certain drugs to induce abortion. Women take mifepristone, the pill known as RU-486, and one to three days later take the drug misoprostol. This procedure, known as a medical abortion, is highly effective when used within the first eight weeks of pregnancy (Feminist Women's Health Center, 2009). Women who choose medical abortion prefer its privacy, sense of empowerment, naturalness, and avoidance of surgery (Feminist Women's Health Center, 2009; Sulik & Heath 2010; Upadhyay & Murthy, 2010). Currently, more than half of the early abortions in France, Scotland, and Sweden, but only 13 percent in the United States, are done with pills rather than surgically (Guttmacher Institute, 2010a; Kolata, 2002; Pazol et al., 2011).

Consequences of Abortion

Abortion is one of the safest medical procedures available. The risk of death from childbirth (1 in 10,000) is about ten times higher than the risk of death from abortion performed within the first 12 weeks by a health professional (1 in more than 100,000) (David & Lee, 2001; Donohoe, 2005). What about the psychological consequences of abortion? Because abortion is a planned response to an unwanted pregnancy, the woman may experience positive emotions to it, such as feelings of relief or of having made a good decision. On the other hand, negative emotions such as anxiety, regret, or guilt may also arise because of moral and social sanctions against abortion. Brenda Major and her colleagues (Major et al., 2000, 2009) found that a woman's reaction to abortion is affected by her particular circumstances, including her coping skills and the degree of social support she has. For example, a woman is more likely to experience postabortion stress if she has little social support from her partner, family, and friends; if she has poorer coping skills; if she blames herself for the pregnancy; and/or if she has a prior history of mental health problems. The most negative feelings occur *before* the abortion. Although some women report mild distress afterward—guilt, anxiety, and regret—the strongest feeling is one of relief (Major et al., 2009). Research on the long-term psychological aftereffects of abortion has found no link between abortion and subsequent poor mental health, especially when the abortion is conducted during the first trimester (Charles et al., 2008; Major, et al., 2009; Munk-Olsen et al., 2011; Steinberg & Finer, 2011; J. T. Warren et al., 2010). When women seek but are *denied* abortions (as is the case in some eastern European countries), their children are more likely to feel neglected or rejected, to drop out of school, and to have social problems at work and with friends than children of mothers who did not seek abortion (David & Lee, 2001).

So far in this chapter, we have focused on the reproductive lives of young women in the United States. For a more global picture, turn to Explore Other Cultures 7.1 and 7.2. Then, read What You Can Do 7.1 to learn some ways you can help increase reproductive choices of girls and women.

EXPLORE OTHER CULTURES 7.1
Women's Reproductive Lives Around the World

In order for women throughout the world to best fulfill their future roles as mothers, workers, and leaders, they need improved access to education and to reproductive health services. How are their reproductive health needs currently being met? (We look at education in Chapter 9.) Researchers have gathered information on this question from virtually all countries around the globe (Boonstra, 2009b; Guttmacher Institute, 2010b,c; Hampton, 2010; Logsdon-Conradsen, 2011; UNICEF, 2008). Here are some of the key findings:

- Up to 60 percent of adolescent births throughout the world are unplanned.

- Contraceptive use by married and unmarried women is greater than in the past, but in most of the world is still low. In most Latin American and Caribbean countries, for example, 30–50 percent of young unmarried women do not use contraceptives. In sub-Saharan Africa, these figures range from 25 to 60 percent.

- Adolescent childbearing is declining in countries where it had been common, as access to education increases and the advantages of delayed childbearing are recognized. Still, in much of South Asia and sub-Saharan Africa,

between 45 and 70 percent of women marry before age 18, and as many as one in ten women have their first child before age 16, when pregnancy and childbirth are risky for both mother and child.

- STIs that threaten the lives and health of young women and their newborns are on the rise, particularly in the developing world (see Chapter 12).

- Sexual relationships that result from force, coercion, and abuse; cultural practices such as female genital cutting (see Explore Other Cultures 7.2); and sexual exploitation of young girls and adolescents for commercial gain endanger the reproductive and mental health of young women.

In most countries, the poorest young women are at greatest risk of poor sexual and reproductive health. In developing countries of Asia, Latin America, and sub-Saharan Africa, they are more likely than wealthier women to be married and to have a child by age 18 and are less likely to use contraceptives, use maternal health services, or know how to protect themselves from HIV (Guttmacher Institute 2010c; Kristof & WuDunn, 2009).

PREGNANCY

For much of history, a woman's life was dominated by pregnancy and childbirth. A hundred years ago, death associated with pregnancy and childbirth was a serious threat for women around the globe. In the twentieth century, the risk dropped significantly for women in developed nations, but it continues to pose a major risk for those in developing countries (Kristof & WuDunn, 2009; Sai, 2010). For a closer look at this issue, see Explore Other Cultures 7.3.

In the past several decades, the advent of the birth control pill, widespread contraceptive use, and legalized abortion have allowed individuals to plan and control the size of their families (Propp, 2003). The marvels of modern technology make it possible to monitor pregnancy virtually from the moment of conception and render it possible for infertile couples to bear children. In this section, we explore pregnancy, miscarriage, and pregnancy in teenagers.

Pregnancy: Physical and Psychological Changes

Pregnancy begins when an egg and a sperm cell unite in the fallopian tube. The fertilized egg begins to divide as it travels toward the uterus, a three- or four-day journey. When it arrives, it implants itself into the thick lining of the uterus. Pregnancy typically lasts 40 weeks and is divided into three trimesters of three months each. A missed menstrual period is often the first indication of pregnancy

EXPLORE OTHER CULTURES 7.2
Female Genital Cutting

Female genital cutting (FGC), *the surgical removal of parts of the external female genitalia,* is a major source of reproductive health problems for girls and women in 27 African countries, parts of the Middle East, and East Asia, as well as for immigrants of those nations who live in Europe, Australia, and North America (Burn, 2011; Fourcroy, 2010; Henderson & Jeydel, 2010). An estimated 3 million girls and women per year undergo this procedure, usually in early childhood or adolescence. The mildest and most common form of FGC involves removing the clitoris, but usually both the clitoris and labia minora are removed. The most extreme form, known as **infibulation** or pharaonic circumcision, consists of *removing the clitoris, labia minora, and the inner two-thirds of the labia majora, which are then sewn together.* A tiny pencil-sized hole is left for the passage of urine and menstrual flow (Alexander et al., 2010; Burn, 2011; Fourcroy, 2010). The procedure is usually performed by women, often using crude, unsterilized instruments and without anesthesia. Resulting medical problems range from pain and infection through long-term difficulties with urination, menstruation, sexual intercourse, fertility, and childbirth (Amnesty International 2010; Burn, 2011; Shah & Batzer, 2010).

Why does this practice persist when it is so obviously harmful to women? Girls in these cultures are considered unmarriageable without undergoing FGC (Lorber, 2010). Some people mistakenly believe that the Islamic religion requires it. Others argue that eliminating the source of women's sexual sensations ensures female chastity. The practice is banned in the United States, and it is condemned by the United Nations and World Health Organization. Women's organizations in Africa are actively involved in efforts to eradicate FGC, which is now outlawed in most African nations although it is still practiced (Kristof & WuDunn, 2009; Odoi-Agyarko, 2010).

WHAT YOU CAN DO 7.1
Help Increase Reproductive Choices of Girls and Women

1. Volunteer at a family planning clinic.
2. Work with a campus or community organization to create a program designed to help young women develop the skills to request that male sexual partners use condoms.

Present your program at residence hall and sorority meetings, or to at-risk teen girls.

_____

Source: Burn (2011).

although simple tests that are available in any drugstore can detect pregnancy within days after conception (Boston Women's Health Book Collective, 2008; Pruthi, 2010).

PHYSICAL CHANGES.   During pregnancy, the blood volume in the body doubles and the breasts generally increase two bra sizes. The most dramatic change occurs in the uterus, which grows from less than two ounces to almost two pounds, not including the placenta or the baby (Alexander et al., 2010; Curtis & Schuler, 2004). Early signs of pregnancy include breast tenderness, more frequent urination, fatigue, and nausea. Nausea and vomiting are usually confined to the first trimester, and despite being called "morning sickness," they can occur anytime during the day (Boston Women's Health Book Collective, 2008; Paykel, 2010). Claire and Judith can vouch for the value of eating crackers or toast slowly in the morning before getting up. Ginger and vitamin B6 are also good for reducing nausea (Simkin et al., 2010). Food aversions and cravings may also develop (Pruthi, 2010; Tassone & Landherr, 2009). For example, Claire couldn't stand coffee or onions, which she normally loved. Many women describe the second trimester as the easiest stage of pregnancy. During

EXPLORE OTHER CULTURES 7.3
Pregnancy-Related Deaths Around the World

Women in developed countries rarely die of complications of pregnancy nowadays, but these complications remain the number one cause of death and disability of young women in less developed parts of the world (Foster-Rosales, 2010; Sai, 2010). For example, the maternal mortality rate is 364 times higher for sub-Saharan Africa than for industrialized nations (1 maternal death for every 22 live births in sub-Saharan Africa versus 1 in 8,000 in industrialized nations) (UNICEF, 2008). Even within the same geographic area, striking differences exist. Haitian women, for instance, are nearly 5 times more likely to die in pregnancy than Dominican women, who live on the same island. And the maternal mortality rate for Russian women is more than 10 times higher than that of their Finnish neighbors (Burn, 2011). Women at greatest risk around the world are those who are young and poor, live in rural areas, and are members of minority groups. For example, Black women in the United States are almost 4 times more likely to die of pregnancy complications than are White women (Logsdon-Conradsen, 2011). In Canada, Native women are at greater risk than White women (Maine & Chavkin, 2002). A key factor in these differences in maternal mortality is access to good-quality health care. Black Americans receive poorer health care than White Americans, even when they are of the same socioeconomic status (Saftlas et al., 2000). In developing countries, the low social status of women hampers their access to existing health care services (Cohen, 2010; Foster-Rosales, 2010; Hausmann et al., 2009). Women's lack of power in families and communities gives them little say over decisions to seek care that could save their lives (Sai, 2010; UNIFEM, 2008). For example, even where low-cost transportation has been arranged by charitable organizations to increase access to emergency facilities, some husbands refuse to spend scarce resources on their wives, even though they would do so for themselves or their sons (Liljestrand & Gryboski, 2002).

Women in war zones are at especially high risk. In Afghanistan, for example, one woman dies out of every eight who give birth. Currently, this is the highest maternal death rate in the world (Burn, 2011; Henderson & Jeydel, 2010).

this phase, most of the nausea and fatigue disappear. By the end of the fifth month, women begin to feel fetal movements ("quickening"). During the third trimester, weight gain and protrusion of the abdomen become quite noticeable. Some of the activities of daily living, such as tying one's shoes, may become a challenge. The expanding uterus exerts increasing pressure on the other internal organs, which may lead to shortness of breath, heartburn, and a need for frequent urination (Boston Women's Health Book Collective, 2008; Simkin et al., 2010).

In the past, pregnancy was viewed as an illness, but that is less true today. Most women feel that their pregnancy is a normal and healthy—if somewhat inconvenient—experience. Regular exercise along with good nutrition reduces or eliminates many discomforts (Donatelle, 2012; Simkin et al., 2010). Claire played pool well into her first pregnancy, until her bulging abdomen made it too difficult to bend over the pool table. During her pregnancy with her second child, a summer baby, she swam until the day she gave birth.

PSYCHOLOGICAL CHANGES.   A woman's feelings during pregnancy vary tremendously depending on such factors as her economic circumstances, her desire to be pregnant, her physical condition, and her childhood experiences (Halbreich, 2005; Simkin et al., 2010). At each stage, women sometimes feel positive and sometimes negative. Feelings of being more sensual, potent, creative, and loving may occur. Negative feelings include loss of individuality, worries about whether the baby will be normal, distress at gaining weight and looking awkward, concerns about changes in the couple's relationship, and anxieties about coping with the responsibilities of parenting (American College of Obstetricians and Gynecologists, 2010; Wenzel, 2010).

REACTIONS TO PREGNANT WOMEN.   A pregnant woman elicits a variety of reactions from those around her. Many women have had the experience of having their pregnant abdomen patted by people who would not consider such a gesture with a nonpregnant woman (Neiterman, 2007; Zimmerman, 2009). Pregnant women may also be targets of hostility (Hebl et al., 2007) and perceived as irritable, emotional, and suffering from physical maladies (Lips, 1997). Even when viewed as equally qualified, dependable, committed, and fit for the position, a pregnant applicant receives lower hiring recommendations than a nonpregnant candidate from both female and male raters (Cunningham & Macan, 2007; Masser et al., 2007). Discrimination toward pregnant working women is, unfortunately, all too common. Many have been denied training opportunities, experienced criticism of their performance, had their work hours reduced, or been dismissed without good reason after announcing their pregnancy (Gross & Pattison, 2007; Mäkelä, 2011; McDonald et al., 2008).

WOMEN WITH DISABILITIES.   Women with disabilities are sometimes discouraged from getting pregnant, under the misconception that they cannot have a safe pregnancy, have a healthy baby, and be a good mother (Maxwell et al., 2007; Meekosha, 2010). Depending on the nature of the disability, some women may in fact have special considerations to discuss with their health care providers. For these women, as with any other woman, regular prenatal care and a birth plan are important to ensure favorable pregnancy, birth, and postbirth outcomes (Alexander et al., 2010).

Miscarriage

Miscarriage is the *spontaneous loss of a pregnancy before the 20th week of gestation* (Jaffe & Diamond, 2011). At least one in seven known pregnancies result in miscarriage. However, the actual rate is considerably higher because about half of very early pregnancies are lost before a woman realizes that she is pregnant (Tassone & Landherr, 2009).

Most early miscarriages are a result of major genetic defects in the embryo or fetus. Others are caused by hormonal imbalances in the mother, structural problems in the uterus or cervix, or diseases of the immune system (American College of Obstetricians and Gynecologists, 2010; Branch et al., 2010; Mitchell, 2009). Following one miscarriage, a woman's chances of having a subsequent normal pregnancy remain quite high. Even after three miscarriages, her chances of maintaining the next pregnancy are still about 60 percent (Tassone & Landherr, 2009).

Until recently, it was assumed that miscarriages were not very stressful to the parents because the embryo or fetus was not yet a "real child." Well-meaning friends and relatives, even to this day, say things such as "It was meant to be" or "You can always have another child." Worse yet, others may say nothing, as though the event had not happened (Brier, 2008; Parsons, 2010). But, in fact, parents start anticipating the birth of their child very early in pregnancy, so a miscarriage produces grieving and a sense of loss (American College of Obstetricians and Gynecologists, 2010; Moss, 2008; Swanson et al., 2009). In addition, women may feel guilty and somehow responsible for the pregnancy loss. They may also feel angry and jealous toward other pregnant women. These feelings may be mingled with anxiety about the possibility of problems occurring in a future pregnancy (Boston Women's Health Book Collective, 2008). Women who have been struggling for years with infertility problems and women who have delayed parenthood into their 30s may be especially devastated when they experience a miscarriage. Fathers grieve too, of course, but their grief is typically of shorter duration and less intense than that of mothers (Brier, 2008; Jaffe & Diamond, 2011).

Listening and responding supportively to the grieving parents can be very helpful (Boston Women's Health Book Collective, 2008). Speaking with others who have been through the same experience is often beneficial for the parents. For example, when Claire's daughter Andi miscarried during her first pregnancy at age 39, she found it comforting to talk to her cousin, who had had two consecutive miscarriages before giving birth to a healthy baby.

Teenage Pregnancy

In an AAUW (American Association of University Women) survey of teenage girls, Blacks and Latinas mentioned pregnancy as a concern in their lives more than White and Asian American girls and did so at a younger age. Black and Latina girls described pregnancy as a "choice," which they counseled their peers not to make at an early age. Asian American and White girls described pregnancy as an "accident" and cautioned against the "risks" and "dangers" of sex (Haag, 1999).

Nevertheless, almost 750,000 American girls aged 15 to 19 become pregnant each year, and most of these pregnancies are unplanned (Guttmacher Institute, 2010a). Substantial ethnic disparities exist among birth rates for adolescents. In 2008, the birth rate per 1,000 females, ages 15–17, was 7 for Asian Americans, 11 for Whites, 31 for Native Americans, 32 for Blacks, and 41 for Latinas. Since 1990, the birth rate for U.S. teens has declined, reaching a 70-year low in 2009 (Hamilton et al., 2010). The biggest decrease has occurred for Black adolescents. Among those teens who have had babies, however, the proportion who are unmarried has jumped from 15 percent in 1960 to 87 percent in 2008 (Hamilton et al., 2010). The decrease in teenage births is not a result of abortion, which has declined among teenagers starting in the 1990s. Rather, young people are delaying sex until they are older; having sex less frequently; using birth control, especially condoms, more often and more responsibly; and choosing more effective contraceptive methods, such as long-lasting hormonal implants (Guttmacher Institute, 2011b; Hoffman, 2008a). The most recent drop is also attributed, in part, to the economic recession (Hamilton et al., 2010).

Interestingly, although the percentage of all births to unwed mothers reached an all-time high of 41 percent in 2009, nearly four in five of these mothers were not teenagers, but rather were 20 or older (Hamilton et al., 2010). As we shall see in Chapter 8, more single women in their 30s and 40s are choosing to have children. And many co-habiting couples are having children as well, as the stigma of having a child out of wedlock declines (Pew Research Center, 2007a). How do pregnancy rates in the United States compare to those in other industrialized nations? For answer, see Explore Other Cultures 7.4.

EXPLORE OTHER CULTURES 7.4
Why Is the Teen Pregnancy Rate So High in the United States?

Despite the decline in births among American teenagers, the United States still has one of the highest teen pregnancy rates among industrialized nations. The U.S. rate is twice that of Canada, Great Britain, and Sweden, at least four times the rates of France and Germany, and ten times the rate of Japan (Guttmacher Institute, 2011b; Raley, 2008). What could account for this big difference? Are U.S. teenagers more sexually active? Do they begin having sex at an earlier age? Research has found that levels of sexual activity and the age at which teenagers initiated sex do not, in fact, vary appreciably across the countries. The major reason that teen pregnancy is higher in the United States is that teens' use of contraceptives is higher in other countries, where teenage sexual activity is more accepted and contraceptive services are much more widely available (Darroch et al., 2001; Guttmacher Institute, 2011b). The differing attitudes toward teenage sexuality in the United States and Europe are reflected in their sex education policies. An "abstinence-only" policy is often emphasized in sex education in the United States, whereas Europeans emphasize informed choice and responsibility (National Campaign, 2003). Many European countries have been providing comprehensive sex education to all school children for many years. These programs encourage abstinence but also provide information about birth control methods and free access to contraceptives (Papalia, 2005).

CONSEQUENCES OF TEENAGE PREGNANCY.   The consequences of unplanned teenage pregnancy are often adverse for both mother and child. Teenage mothers are likely to live in poverty and to suffer from a lack of psychological and social support. In addition, they typically drop out of school, have less stable employment patterns, and are more likely to be on welfare. Their marriages are less apt to be stable, they are more depressed, and they are more likely to have additional children out of wedlock (Fletcher & Wolfe, 2009; Hofferth & Reid, 2002; Hoffman, 2008b; Kalil & Kunz, 2002). The impact of early childbearing continues well into adulthood for both women and men. At midlife, compared to delayed childbearers, teenage mothers have less schooling, less prestigious, lower-paying occupations, more unstable marriages, and poorer physical health (Taylor, 2009).

Children born to teenagers have an increased risk of prematurity, birth complications, or death during infancy (Ventura et al., 2011). This may result partly from the young age of the mother and partly from inadequate prenatal care (Logsdon-Conrads, 2011). Pregnant teenagers and teenage mothers are more likely than other women to engage in behaviors that put their unborn babies and young infants at risk. For example, these women are more likely to drink and smoke during pregnancy and are less likely to put their infants in the back-sleep position, which helps prevent sudden infant death syndrome (Phares et al., 2004; Sonfield, 2010). The children of young mothers are also more apt to have emotional, behavioral, and cognitive difficulties, most likely as a result of their impoverished caregiving environment (Federal Interagency Forum, 2007; Hofferth & Reid, 2002), and they are more likely to be abused or neglected (Goerge et al., 2008; Sonfield, 2010). In adolescence, children of teenagers show higher rates of school failure, delinquency, and earlier sexual activity and pregnancy than children born to older mothers (Centers for Disease Control and Prevention, 2011; Manlove et al., 2008; Maynard & Hoffman, 2008).

SUPPORT FOR PREGNANT TEENAGERS.   Support programs for pregnant teenagers have met with some success in improving the lives of teenage parents and their children (Cherry et al., 2009; Seitz, & Apfel, 2010). Programs include one or more of the following components: family planning services, child-care provisions, education about parenting and job skills, and welfare reform incentives. Teenage mothers who participate in comprehensive programs have fewer children in the long run and are more likely to complete high school and become economically self-sufficient. Their children are healthier, suffer less abuse, have fewer developmental problems, and do better in school (Schellenbach et al., 2010; Seitz & Apfel, 2010).

PREVENTING TEENAGE PREGNANCY.   Programs aimed at preventing teen pregnancy have taken various approaches: providing knowledge of sexuality and contraception, teaching abstinence, building decision-making job and social skills, enhancing gender and ethnic pride, and discussing life options (Oringanje et al., 2009; Sullentrop, 2011). Programs that combine elements of these approaches are the most successful in delaying sexual activity, increasing contraceptive use, and reducing pregnancy (Drew, 2011; Robin et al., 2004; Sullentrop, 2011). Although an overwhelming majority of American parents favor sex education in school, there is considerable debate on what should be taught, when, and by whom. In recent years, many school-based programs focused only on abstinence because the schools were prohibited from mentioning contraception in order to receive federal funding (Lewin, 2010; Lindberg et al., 2006). Unfortunately, as we saw earlier, this approach has little effect on reducing sexual activity or pregnancy (Diamond & Savin-Williams, 2009).

CHILDBIRTH

The birth of one's first child can be a physically and psychologically transforming experience (Pruthi, 2010; also see the vignette at the beginning of the chapter). In Chapter 8, we will examine some of the psychological aspects involved in making the transition to motherhood. In this section, we focus on the biological aspects of childbirth. We also examine postpartum distress, infertility, and assisted reproductive technology.

Stages of Childbirth

In the first stage, the cervix becomes dilated to 10 centimeters (about 4 inches) in diameter, a process that may last from a few hours to a day or more. The *cervix* also *becomes flatter and thinner*, a process known as **effacement**. In the second stage, which lasts from a few minutes to several hours, uterine contractions move the baby through the vagina. At the end of this stage, the woman often feels the urge to push, and usually within minutes (sometimes hours), the baby is born. During the third stage, which lasts from five to thirty minutes, the placenta detaches from the uterine wall and is expelled. Progesterone and estrogen levels drop dramatically during the second and third stages (Boston Women's Health Book Collective, 2008; Pruthi, 2010; Simkin et al., 2010).

Methods of Childbirth

Throughout most of the twentieth century, and into the twenty-first, women have given birth in hospitals, attended by obstetricians using surgical instruments and anesthetics. Although use of these medical procedures has saved lives and reduced pain, it has also depersonalized childbearing. Feminists argue that it has taken from women control over their own bodies and, through drugs, denied many women the experience of giving birth (Boston Women's Health Book Collective, 2008; Kennedy, 2010; Northrup, 2010).

One example of the "medicalization" of the birth process is the **cesarean section** (or C-section). *Incisions are made in the abdomen and uterus and the baby is surgically removed.* C-sections are performed if vaginal delivery is expected to be difficult or threatens the health of the mother or baby—as when the mother's pelvis is small or misshapen, the baby is very large, or the baby is not in the normal birth position. But more pregnant women in the United States and Canada are choosing to deliver this way even when there is no medical need (Alexandre, 2011; Grady, 2010; Plante, 2009). In the United States, the rate of C-sections rose from 5 percent in 1970 to a record high of 33 percent of all births in 2009 (Menacker & Hamilton, 2010). This increase in unnecessary C-sections may be driven in part by busy mothers wanting to schedule their deliveries, as well as by obstetricians seeking to avoid potential malpractice suits (Caughey, 2009; Grady, 2010).

Another example of the medicalization of childbirth is the induction of labor for practical (rather than medical) reasons, such as the convenience of the doctor, hospital, or parents. Although the procedure is relatively safe, it increases the risk of C-sections, especially in first-time mothers, because the cervix may not dilate quickly enough (Boston Women's Health Book Collective, 2008). In the United States, the rate of labor-induced births doubled from 10 percent in 1990 to 22 percent by 2005, causing some experts to speak out against the practice (Martin et al., 2009).

Parents can now choose among more family-centered approaches to childbearing. The most popular method in the United States is prepared child birth, or the **Lamaze method**. *Prelabor classes are conducted to teach the mother to control her pain through relaxation, breathing techniques, and focusing exercises.* A labor coach (usually the husband or partner) provides moral support and coaches techniques of breathing and relaxation during childbirth (Alexander et al., 2010; Boston Women's Health Book Collective, 2008). Others also may serve as a labor coach: a woman's mother, sister, friend, or *an experienced and knowledgeable female labor and birth coach* known as a **doula**. *Doula* comes from the Greek word meaning "woman who serves a woman" (Tassone & Landherr, 2009). The continuous labor support provided by doulas has been shown to reduce C-section rates, decrease the need for pain medication, decrease the length of labor, increase maternal satisfaction, and improve breastfeeding success (Davidson, 2011a; Paykel, 2010).

Home birth also has increased in recent years, providing mothers with familiar settings and enhancing the feeling that the woman and her family are in control. More women are also choosing to deliver in homelike birthing centers outside a hospital. Family members and friends may be present during labor and delivery. Many hospitals now provide family-friendly birthing rooms (Boston Women's Health Book Collective, 2008; MacDorman et al., 2010). Other aspects of family-centered birth include minimizing the use of anesthesia, using the more natural (and gravity-assisted) sitting position to give birth and eliminating practices such as enemas, shaving of the genital area, and performing an episiotomy, an incision that widens the vaginal opening to allow passage of the baby's head (Boston Women's Health Book Collective, 2008; Kuhn, 2005).

Using certified nurse-midwives for prenatal care and delivery has also become increasingly popular in Canada, Europe, and the United States (Craven, 2010; MacDorman et al., 2010; Mortenson, 2011b). Certified nurse-midwives attended only 1 percent of U.S. births in 1975 but now perform about 10 percent of deliveries (Martin et al., 2011; Pérez-Peña, 2004). Mortality rates are lower and birth weights are higher for infants delivered by nurse-midwives than for those delivered by physicians even though nurse-midwives tend to serve traditionally higher-risk women such as teenage mothers and those with lower income and less education (Lydon-Rochelle, 2004). Women using midwives are also less likely to request pain-reducing medication, more likely to have a vaginal delivery, and more likely to breastfeed (Paykel, 2010; Sandall et al., 2010). The most likely explanation for this is that nurse-midwives, compared to physicians, spend more time with patients during prenatal visits, provide more patient education and counseling, and are with their patients throughout labor and delivery (Boston Women's Health Book Collective, 2008; Strong, 2000).

Childbearing After 35

Although 75 percent of mothers of newborns in the United States are 20–34 years old, a growing number of women are having babies at age 35 and older. In 2009, 14 percent of babies had a mother who was at least 35, and at least 3 percent (over 113,000) were born to women aged 40 and over (Hamilton et al., 2010).

Over 7,000 women between ages 45 and 49 gave birth in 2010, a record high (Hamilton et al., 2009). But because fertility begins to decline after age 27, older women have a harder time conceiving. Among women over 40, half will require medical assistance in order to conceive (Brody, 2004b). About 15 to 20 percent of women aged 40 to 42 can become pregnant using their own eggs, compared with fewer than 3 percent of women over 44, as an increasing percentage of their eggs become abnormal (Gibbs, 2002; St. John, 2002). Women over 35 have more miscarriages; more preterm, low-birth-weight and stillborn babies; higher levels of complications during pregnancy; and more chromosomal abnormalities (such as Down syndrome), and are more likely to have C-sections than younger women (American College of Obstetricians and Gynecologists, 2010; Delpisheh et al., 2008; Holzman et al., 2009; March of Dimes, 2009; McIntyre et al., 2009). The good news is that almost all older mothers, like their younger counterparts, have healthy babies and that infant mortality rates are comparable for the two groups (Berkowitz et al., 2006; Etaugh, 2008).

A lesser-known fact about midlife pregnancy is that about half of the pregnancies of women over 40 are unintended—a rate second only to teenagers. During perimenopause, the years prior to the end of menstruation, women may grow lax about birth control because they think there is little risk of pregnancy and may believe they have reached menopause. However, a woman's menstrual cycle becomes less regular in perimenopause and she may go several months without a period before having one (North American Menopause Society, 2011).

To find out more about individual women's experiences with pregnancy and childbirth, try Get Involved 7.2.

Childbearing in the Later Years

An amusing comic strip several years ago featured an elderly couple sitting in rocking chairs. The woman, knitting a tiny sweater, was obviously pregnant. Looking at her husband with an irritated expression on her face, she exclaimed "You and your 'once more for old times' sake!'" The humor of the situation was based on the then impossibility of an elderly woman's becoming pregnant. But this is no longer a laughing matter.

Late in 2006, Carmen Bousada gave birth in Spain to healthy twin boys. News of the event spread like wildfire around the globe. What made this birth so special? Carmen Bousada was 67 years old (James, 2007). Donated sperm fertilized a young woman's donor eggs in a test tube, and the resulting embryos were implanted in Bousada's hormonally readied uterus. Most fertility clinics set an age limit of 50 to 55 for a woman seeking in vitro fertilization, but Bousada lied about her age. Recent successes in transplanting frozen ovarian tissue and in freezing eggs and embryos further raise the possibility that women may be able to bear children well into their postmenopausal years (Chrisler & Garrett, 2010; Ernst et al., 2010).

Controversy swirls around the issue of whether postmenopausal women should be denied help in becoming pregnant (Chrisler & Garrett, 2010; Deech & Smajdor, 2007; Gross & Pattison, 2007; James, 2007; Peterson, 2005). Those who support this view cite several reasons: (1) Such

GET INVOLVED 7.2
Pregnancy and Childbirth Experiences

1. Briefly interview two women in their 20s, two middle-aged women, and two older women about their experiences with pregnancy and childbirth. It will be helpful, but not essential, if you know your respondents fairly well. You may interview your sisters, cousins, friends, mother, aunts, grandmothers, and so on. Keep a record of your respondents' comments.

2. Compare and contrast the responses of the women in the three age groups.

WHAT DOES IT MEAN?

1. In what ways are the pregnancy experiences of the three groups of women different? In what ways are they alike?

2. In what ways are the childbirth experiences of the three groups different? In what ways are they alike?

3. What social and historical conditions may have influenced the pregnancy and childbirth experiences of these three generations of women?

pregnancies risk the mother's health; (2) an older mother is less likely than a younger one to live long enough to raise her child to adulthood; (3) it is unnatural and a perverse use of technology that has been widely accepted for younger women for over 30 years.

These arguments have been rebutted by others (Deech & Smajdor, 2007; Peterson, 2005) who claim that (1) The complications that could affect the older mother's health also occur in younger women, although less frequently, and are treatable; (2) Any responsible mother, regardless of age, should make provisions for the care of her child in the event that she dies before the child is grown. Some younger women with severe medical conditions have babies. Should they also be barred from reproducing? (3) If the reproductive technology exists, why shouldn't an older woman take advantage of it? Should older women be denied other medical advances such as coronary bypass surgery? (Claire's mother-in-law had this procedure when she was in her early 80s and lived another 20 years in robust health. She did not, however, contemplate having another child.)

Some scholars believe that both age discrimination and gender discrimination are at the root of society's discomfort about older women's having babies (Deech & Smajdor, 2007). Think of people's reactions to the news of men becoming fathers in their 60s and beyond: comedian Charlie Chaplin, actor Tony Randall, singer Rod Stewart, and former U.S. senator Strom Thurmond, to mention but a few. Rather than disapproval, there is acceptance and even admiration of the sexual prowess of these older men.

Postpartum Distress

During the postpartum period, the first weeks after birth, many women experience some psychological distress. The mildest and most common form, called **maternity blues** or baby blues, is experienced by up to 75 percent of new mothers. *This mood state, characterized by crying, anxiety, and irritability, typically begins three to four days after childbirth and lasts for a few days or weeks.* Maternity blues are more common following a first birth and may reflect the mother's adjustment to the stresses of new parenthood (Shelton, 2011; Stevens, 2010).

One out of eight women have *severe feelings of depression that last for weeks or months after delivery.* These changes, called **postpartum depression**, are characterized by anxiety or panic attacks, loss of interest in daily activities, despair, feelings of worthlessness and guilt, sleep and appetite disturbances, fatigue, difficulty in concentrating, and thoughts of harming oneself or the baby (Stevens, 2010). The peak period for experiencing postpartum depression is three to six months after the birth (Paulson & Bazemore, 2010). One or 2 in 1,000 women experience postpartum psychosis, a serious condition that often includes delusions, hallucinations, and thoughts (or deeds) of hurting oneself or the infant (Abrams & Curran, 2009; Jones et al., 2010). Andrea Yates, convicted of drowning her five young children in the bathtub, suffered from postpartum psychosis. She explained that Satan told her this was the only way to save the children, because she was a bad mother (Vallance, 2011).

Women are more likely to develop postpartum depression if they are young, poor, less educated, and first-time mothers. Risk factors also include a history of mental illness, previous depression, marital difficulties or other stressful life events, and lack of support from family and friends (Abrams & Curran, 2009; Alexander et al., 2010; Davé et al., 2010; Jones et al., 2010). In interviews with 35 British and American mothers with postpartum depression, Natasha Mauthner (2002) found that many of the women held idealized cultural constructions of the "perfect mother" that contrasted sharply with their perception that they were not measuring up. It is unclear whether the drastic drop in levels of estrogen and progesterone after birth also plays a role because symptoms of postpartum depression also occur in mothers of newly adopted children (Boston Women's Health Book Collective, 2008; Whiffen, 2001), and in fathers (Davé et al., 2010; Friedman, 2009; Paulson & Bazemore, 2010).

Social support and various psychological interventions play an important role in reducing the risk of postpartum depression (Dennis et al., 2009; Shelton, 2011; Turjanski, 2010). Although support and therapy clearly help prevent and treat postpartum depression, most women recover from the condition within three to six months without any treatment (Cuijpers et al., 2008).

Infertility and Assisted Reproductive Technology

Infertility is *the failure to conceive a child after a year of trying* (Greil et al., 2010). About one in ten Americans in their reproductive years experience infertility, and the likelihood of being infertile increases with age for both women and men. In 40 percent of the cases, the difficulty is traced to the woman, in 40 percent of the cases, the problem originates with the man, and in the remaining cases, the origin is combined or unknown (Ford, 2009). Causes of infertility in women include blockage of the fallopian tubes, failure of the ovaries to produce eggs, uterine fibroids, and **endometriosis**, *the presence of uterine lining tissue in abnormal locations* (Mitchell, 2009). A leading cause of infertility in women is polycystic ovary syndrome (PCOS), in which high levels of the hormone testosterone interfere with ovulation. Clues that a woman may have PCOS are the presence of facial hair, acne, obesity, and infrequent or irregular periods (Ford, 2009; "Polycystic Ovary Syndrome," 2010). Lifestyle factors also play a role in infertility. If a woman is obese, has an eating disorder, or is a heavy smoker, or if she or her partner drink heavily, the risk of infertility increases (ESHRE Task Force, 2010; Freizinger et al., 2010).

About 15 percent of infertile couples have tried recently developed assisted reproductive technologies (Rebar & DeCherney, 2004). In 72 percent of those cases, couples use IVF or **in vitro fertilization** in which *the couple's own sperm and egg are fertilized in a glass laboratory dish ("in vitro" means "in glass") and the resulting embryo is transferred into the woman's uterus* (Ford, 2009). Louise Brown, born in England in 1978 as a result of IVF, was the first of these so-called test-tube babies, now numbering nearly 4 million strong worldwide (Daar & Brzyski, 2009; Henig, 2010). In 16 percent of infertility treatments, the couples' frozen embryos are used, and in 12 percent, donor eggs are used (Sunderam et al., 2009). Donated eggs are typically used for older women who do not produce eggs or whose eggs are damaged. Older women who use donor eggs from young women can have successful pregnancies at least until their mid-50s (Heffner, 2004; Orenstein, 2007). In the United States, egg selling is big business. So-called Ivy League eggs are in great demand, and ads in campus newspapers offer tens of thousands of dollars for the eggs of college women (Levine, 2010; Tuller, 2010).

The "success rate," that is, the percentage of times a live birth results, is about 35 percent for freshly fertilized embryos from the woman's own eggs, 34 percent for IVF, 54 percent for freshly fertilized embryos from donor eggs, and 33 percent for frozen embryos from donor eggs (Sunderam et al., 2009). Babies born after fertility treatments have higher rates of stillbirth, prematurity, low birth weight, and birth defects, although most are healthy (Van Steirteghem et al., 2010). Depending on the procedure used and on the mother's age, anywhere from about 10 percent to 40 percent are multiple births (Sunderam et al., 2009). In addition, the treatments are expensive. For example, the average cost of a single IVF effort in the United States ranges from $12,000 to $25,000, but insurance usually covers little or nothing of the procedure (Saul, 2009a; Smock & Greenland, 2010).

Another approach to infertility, **surrogate motherhood**, involves *paying a woman who agrees to become pregnant and deliver a child for a couple.* Twenty years ago, the surrogate mother was almost always the baby's biological mother. Her egg was fertilized through artificial insemination by sperm from the man of the couple who hired the surrogate. In most surrogate pregnancies today, however, the couple's own embryo is carried by the surrogate mother, who is thus biologically unrelated to the baby (Brody, 2009b). In a few instances, women have served as surrogates for their daughters who were unable to carry pregnancies to term, thus giving birth to their own grandchildren (Christ, 2008). Close to 1,000 infants are born through surrogacy every year in the United States (Horowitz et al., 2010; Saul 2009b). This practice raises a number of social, legal, and financial questions (Cahn, 2009). Can a contract signed before a baby's conception be legally binding after birth? Who are the legal parents? Should the surrogate mother be paid for her services? Some critics are concerned about the potential economic exploitation of poor women as surrogate mothers. Yet overall, surrogacy appears to be a positive experience for surrogate mothers. Most surrogates are married, often have completed a family of their own, enjoy being pregnant, and find it rewarding to help an infertile couple become parents. They generally have a good relationship with the commissioning couple and have few problems handing over the baby, and many maintain contact with the couple and the child (Beckman, 2006; Brody, 2009; Gross & Pattison, 2007; Jadva et al., 2003).

In addition, fears about the impact of surrogacy on the well-being of children and families appear to be unfounded (Golombok et al., 2004). In fact, mothers of children born via a surrogacy arrangement show more warmth toward their babies and are more emotionally involved than in families where the child is conceived naturally. Both the commissioning mother and father have better parenting skills than do the parents in nonsurrogate families, and the babies themselves show no differences in their temperament and behavior, when compared with nonsurrogate babies. Nor do there seem to be problems when the surrogate mothers hand over the babies to the mothers who have commissioned the surrogacy.

Whereas some couples wish to have children but cannot, others make a choice not to have children. For a fuller discussion of this issue, see Learn About the Research 7.1.

REPRODUCTIVE FUNCTIONING IN MIDLIFE AND BEYOND

Menopause is a normal and natural part of aging, and each woman experiences it in her own way (Hudson, 2010). The decline in hormone levels that occurs during menopause sometimes is treated medically with hormone replacement therapy. In this section, we examine both of these topics.

Menopause

Menopause is the *cessation of menstrual periods for a full year.* For most American women, menopause occurs between the ages of 44 and 58, with an average age of 51. Smokers reach menopause up to two years earlier than nonsmokers (Edelman, 2010; Sammel et al., 2009). Compared with White women, menopause occurs somewhat earlier in Black women and somewhat later in Asian American women (Butts & Seifer, 2010; Sammel et al., 2009). Menopause occurs because of the decline in the number of ovarian follicles (egg-producing cells), which results in a decline in the production of both estrogen and progesterone. Some estrogen continues to be produced after menopause by the adrenal glands and fat cells (Edelman, 2010). *The five to seven years preceding the beginning of menopause,* known as the **perimenopause**, are marked by increasing irregularity of the menstrual cycle and variations in the amount of menstrual flow (Wroolie & Holcomb, 2010). As we shall see, the way in which a woman experiences menopause reflects a host of physiological, psychological, and cultural factors (Edelman, 2010; Im et al., 2008).

PHYSICAL SYMPTOMS.   The frequency and severity of physical symptoms associated with menopause vary widely among women. In North America, the most commonly reported symptom is the **hot flash**, *a sudden feeling of heat that spreads over the body with mild or profuse sweating, which usually lasts one to five minutes and may occur several times daily* (Wingert & Kantrowitz, 2009). Surveys

LEARN ABOUT THE RESEARCH 7.1
Childfree by Choice

At a certain point, we had decided we weren't going to have kids . . . My mom was kind of hopeful that I would change my mind. She would say things like "Well, when you're done with your education, we'll talk about it again." There was a lot of resistance, people saying "Oh, you wouldn't want a baby? But they're so cute." The people who've just recently had kids say things like "Oh, it's awesome. It's the greatest gift. You're really missing out."

(Tara, age 27, in Scott, 2009, p. 63)

More than at any other time in history, women and men in the industrialized world are deciding not to have children. Europe's population has been falling since 1998 as the birth rate there has continued to decline. Between 10 and 20 percent of western European women who are now in their 50s and 60s have no children (Hayden, 2011; Rowland, 2007). Similarly, in 2008, one in five U.S. women in their early 40s had no children (U.S. Department of Commerce, 2011). Although some of these women ultimately will have a child, most will not.

The decision to not have children is facilitated by the availability and legality of effective forms of birth control, the feminist emphasis on women's right to make choices in their lives, and the wider participation of women in the labor force (Koropeckyj-Cox et al., 2007). However, the decision not to have children—to be childless or "childfree"—goes against the traditional gender norms of almost all cultures. Women who make this choice are often perceived negatively (Vinson et al., 2010). They are criticized as shallow, deviant, cold, self-indulging, immature, materialistic, irresponsible, and unfeminine (Dykstra & Hagestad, 2007a,b; D. M. Hall, 2008; Hayden, 2011; Scott, 2009). They may be marginalized, pitied, given unsolicited advice, and pressured by others to have children (Simon, 2008; Walker, 2011).

Why do women choose not to have children? The reasons are many. Some women want autonomy, economic independence, and increased career prospects. Other women simply do not enjoy children, believe that they would not make good parents, or want a flexible lifestyle that would be hampered by children. Still others perceive motherhood to be a sacrifice and a burden, involving loss of time, energy, leisure and, ultimately, identity (Connidis, 2010; Gilbert, 2008; Hayden, 2011; Walker, 2011). In some cases, their own mothers were dissatisfied or ambivalent about their parental role (Baker, 2003). In addition, adults today view children as less central to marital happiness than was the case in the past. Only 41 percent of adults in the United States now believe that children are important to a happy marriage, down from 65 percent in 1990 (Pew Research Center, 2007b). Consistent with this finding, couples who have never had children report greater emotional well-being than parents, even empty nesters (Simon, 2008). In addition, women who have never had children report higher levels of autonomy and self-realization than women with children (Read & Grundy, 2011).

WHAT DOES IT MEAN?

1. Are the terms *childless* and *childfree* exact synonyms? In what ways do they differ in meaning?
2. In what way could a mother's dissatisfaction or ambivalence about parenting influence her daughter's decision about whether to have children?
3. What can be done to increase society's acceptance of women who decide not to have children?

report that up to 80 percent of menopausal women experience hot flashes. Some women will have hot flashes for a few months, some for a few years, and some not at all (North American Menopause Society, 2011; Wroolie & Holcomb, 2010). Hot flashes at night (sometimes called *night sweats*) can interfere with the sleep of some menopausal women, but most women find hot flashes to be only a minor inconvenience (Wingert & Kantrowitz, 2009).

Loss of estrogen also causes thinning of the vaginal lining and decreased vaginal lubrication. These changes can lead to painful sexual intercourse and also make the vagina more prone to infection. Headaches and joint and muscle pains are other physical symptoms that are occasionally reported (Chrisler & Almond, 2011; O'Grady & Lori, 2009; Thacker, 2009). Women who smoke experience more severe symptoms (Ziv-Gal & Flaws, 2010). The most serious physical consequence of menopause, osteoporosis, is discussed in Chapter 12.

Women in different ethnic and cultural groups vary in the kinds and degree of menopausal symptoms they report. For example, hot flashes are most prevalent in Black women, followed by Latinas and White women, and are least common in Asian American women (Butts & Seifer, 2009; DeAngelis, 2010a; Im, 2009; Ziv-Gal & Flaws, 2010).

PSYCHOLOGICAL REACTIONS.   It is popularly believed that menopausal women are more likely to display such psychological symptoms as depression, irritability, or mood swings. There is no evidence, however, that these or other psychological symptoms are associated with hormone levels during menopause (Nosek et al., 2010). Some women may feel irritable or tired, but these feelings may be linked to disruptions in sleep caused by hot flashes (North American Menopause Society, 2011). In fact, the majority of postmenopausal women report that the happiest and most fulfilling time of their lives was between the ages of 50 and 65 (North American Menopause Society, 2008).

Even if some women do show heightened psychological distress during the menopausal years, this cannot be attributed to solely biological processes. Stressful life events that occur in middle age (see Chapters 8 and 11) may be largely responsible for increased distress. Women not only are confronting their own aging during this time but may also be coping with stressful changes in the family: the illness or death of a spouse, divorce or separation, difficult teenagers, children who are preparing to leave home, and/or aging parents who require care (Dare, 2010; Nosek et al., 2010; Wroolie & Holcomb, 2010).

ATTITUDES TOWARD MENOPAUSE.   Popular images and stereotypes of menopausal women are overwhelmingly negative in North America, especially among younger, premenopausal women (Ayers et al., 2010; Marván et al., 2008). Menopause continues to be described in the medical literature by a long list of negative symptoms and terms such as "estrogen deprivation" and "ovarian failure" (Wingert & Kantrowitz, 2009). The popular press reinforces the notion of menopause as a condition of disease and deterioration that requires treatment by drugs (DeAngelis, 2010b; Harris, 2008; Singer & Wilson, 2009).

Many women, however, view menopause as a positive life transition (Hvas, 2006; Im et al., 2008; Perz & Ussher, 2008). In fact, most middle-aged American women minimize the significance of menopause as only a temporary inconvenience. Many look forward to menopause as marking the end of menstruation and childbearing (Chrisler & Versace, 2011). In one survey, the majority of postmenopausal women reported feeling "only relief" when their menstrual periods stopped whereas only 2 percent said they experienced "only regret" (Rossi, 2004).

Not surprisingly, women express more positive attitudes toward menopause when it is described as a normal life transition than when it is described as a medical problem (Ayers et al., 2010). Similarly, a woman who expects menopause to be unpleasant is apt to focus on its negative aspects. For example, women with more negative attitudes toward menopause are more likely to report vaginal dryness, headaches, and irritability (Ayers et al., 2010), and greater symptom intensity (Nosek et al., 2010).

EXPLORE OTHER CULTURES 7.5
Menopause: Symbol of Decline or of Higher Status?

Women in non-Western cultures often have menopausal experiences and attitudes very different from those reported by Western women, indicating that menopausal symptoms are at least in part socially constructed (Chrisler & Versace, 2011; Lerner-Veva et al., 2010). For example, Chinese, Indian, Japanese, and Indonesian women are much less likely than women in Western cultures to report hot flashes or other physical symptoms (Ayers et al., 2010; Wingert & Kantrowitz, 2009). Women of high social castes in India and Lakota Sioux women in the United States report very few negative symptoms, and for them, menopause is in fact an eagerly anticipated event. Why might that be? When these women reach menopause, they are freed from menstrual taboos, treated with increased respect and authority, and able to participate more fully in society (Chrisler & Versace, 2011; Edelman, 2010). No wonder they experience few negative menopausal symptoms! In Western cultures, on the other hand, aging does not confer higher status on a woman but rather lowers it. It is thus not surprising that there are more complaints about "symptoms" in such a youth-oriented culture (Godfrey & Low Dog, 2008).

Attitudes toward menopause also differ according to a woman's ethnic and cultural background. Studies of Asian American, Black, Latina, and White women found that Black women reported the most positive attitudes toward menopause whereas Asian American women were least positive (Dillaway et al., 2008; Wroolie & Holcomb, 2010). Across ethnic groups, better-educated women held more positive views.

What are women's experiences with and attitudes toward menopause in non-Western societies? Take a look at Explore Other Cultures 7.5.

Hormone Replacement Therapy

Hormone replacement therapy (HRT) is *a medical treatment that replaces hormones in women whose levels drop after menopause.* Women who have had their uterus removed can take estrogen alone whereas those who still have their uterus are advised to take a combination of estrogen and synthetic progesterone (progestin) in order to be protected against uterine cancer (Alexander et al., 2010).

The combined estrogen–progestin pill relieves the menopausal symptoms of hot flashes, night sweats, insomnia, and vaginal dryness. It also helps prevent osteoporosis and reduces the risk of colon cancer. However, recent large-scale studies have found that it also increases the risk of heart attack, stroke, blood clots, breast and ovarian cancer, gallbladder disease, and urinary incontinence (Bach, 2010; Heiss et al., 2008; Farquhar et al., 2009; Thacker, 2009; Welton et al., 2009). Women who started HRT early in menopause are less likely to have these risks than women who began the therapy 10–15 years later (Bach, 2010; Brinton et al., 2010; Edelman, 2010; Jungheim & Colditz, 2011).

Which women should use HRT after menopause? That decision must be based on each woman's evaluation of the benefits and risks to herself (see Table 7.2) given her personal and family medical history. Some women whose quality of life suffers because of extreme hot flashes or vaginal atrophy elect to use HRT. However, they are now advised to take the lowest dose that provides relief, and for the shortest time possible (Chrisler & Almond, 2011; North American Menopause Society, 2011). Women should definitely *not* use hormones if they have a history of, or are at a higher risk for, heart disease, stroke, cancer of the breast or uterus, chronic liver disease, or diabetes. Women should *consider* avoiding hormones if they have migraine headaches, gallbladder disease, uterine fibroid tumors, high blood pressure, seizure disorders, or blood clots (Deborah Grady, 2006; Edelman, 2010).

TABLE 7.2   Benefits and Risks of Combined HRT

Benefits	Risks
Ends hot flashes	Increases risk of heart attack and stroke
Relieves vaginal dryness and atrophy	Increases risk of ovarian cancer
Delays bone loss	Increases risk of uterine cancer if estrogen is taken without progesterone
Increases bone density	
Decreases risk of colon cancer	Increases risk of gallbladder disease
May decrease risk of Parkinson's disease	Increases risk and severity of breast cancer
May delay cognitive decline if given at menopause	Increases risk of urinary incontinence

Sources: Bach (2010); Dumas et al. (2008); Farquhar et al. (2009); Ovarian Cancer National Alliance (2010); and Thacker (2009).

ALTERNATIVES TO STANDARD HRT.   The usual dose of estrogen given in HRT is 0.625 milligram. However, lower doses may confer similar benefits in building bones and relieving hot flashes and vaginal dryness while lowering risks (Thacker, 2009). An alternative approach is the use of synthetic estrogens that have some of the benefits but fewer of the risks of natural estrogen. One such hormone, raloxifene, also *reduces* the risk of breast cancer and bone loss. Certain antidepressants also reduce hot flashes in recently menopausal women (Edelman, 2010; Freeman et al., 2011; Hudson, 2010).

Lifestyle modifications, especially those involving regular exercise and dietary modifications, may be beneficial in reducing menopausal symptoms. Limiting or eliminating caffeine, alcohol, smoking, and spicy foods reduces the frequency of hot flashes (Edelman, 2010; North American Menopause Society, 2011). Consuming foods and herbs that contain estrogen-like substances, such as soy products, flaxseed, and black cohosh, may be helpful as well, although the evidence is mixed (Chrisler & Almond, 2011; Edelman, 2010; Michelfelder, 2009; Ricci et al., 2010). Known as **phyto-estrogens**, these *plant foods do not contain estrogen but affect the body in a similar manner.* Phyto-estrogens are many times weaker than pharmaceutical estrogens and may not alleviate severe menopausal symptoms or provide the same benefits against osteoporosis that estrogen provides (North American Menopause Society, 2003).

Summary

MENSTRUATION

- The menstrual cycle is regulated by hormones, brain structures, and reproductive organs.
- Attitudes toward menstruation remain somewhat negative, despite evidence that physical and psychological performances do not change meaningfully over the menstrual cycle.
- Some women experience menstrual joy, a feeling of heightened creativity and energy.
- A small minority of women experience the symptoms of premenstrual syndrome (PMS).

CONTRACEPTION

- Contraceptive use has increased among adolescents, but many use contraceptives sporadically or not at all.
- The type of contraception chosen by women changes as their reproductive goals change.

ABORTION

- Most abortions occur within the first trimester by means of the vacuum aspiration method.
- Early abortion is physically safe and generally has no negative psychological aftereffects.

PREGNANCY

- Physical effects of pregnancy include nausea, fatigue, and weight gain.
- Women have both positive and negative feelings during pregnancy.
- People may react negatively to a pregnant woman.
- Most miscarriages result from genetic defects in the embryo or fetus.
- The teenage pregnancy rate is higher in the United States than in most industrialized nations, but the teenage birth rate is declining, probably due to increased condom use.
- Teen pregnancy has serious economic, social, and medical costs.
- Programs stressing a combination of abstinence, contraception, and life skills can delay sexual activity and reduce pregnancy rates.

CHILDBIRTH

- The three stages of childbirth are dilation of the cervix, birth of the baby, and expulsion of the placenta.
- Rates of cesarean delivery and induction of labor are high in the United States.

- Family-centered approaches to childbearing include the Lamaze method, home birth, birthing rooms and centers, and use of midwives.
- Older women have more difficulty conceiving but generally have healthy babies.
- Many women experience maternity blues shortly after giving birth. A small percentage of women experience the more severe postpartum depression and postpartum psychosis.
- About 15 percent of infertile couples have tried reproductive technologies, such as in vitro fertilization, frozen embryos, donor eggs, and surrogate motherhood.

REPRODUCTIVE FUNCTIONING IN MIDLIFE AND BEYOND

- Menopause, caused by a decrease in estrogen production, causes hot flashes and vaginal dryness but is not linked to heightened psychological distress.
- Menopausal experiences and attitudes differ across ethnic and cultural groups.
- Middle-aged women usually have positive attitudes toward menopause.
- Benefits of hormone replacement therapy (HRT) include decrease in menopausal symptoms and decrease in the risk of osteoporosis and colon cancer.
- Risks of HRT include increased risk of heart attack, stroke, breast and ovarian cancer, gall bladder disease, and urinary incontinence.
- Alternatives to HRT include synthetic estrogens and phyto-estrogens.

Key Terms

ovulation *144*
dysmenorrhea *144*
prostaglandins *145*
women-as-problem bias *146*
premenstrual syndrome (PMS) *147*
premenstrual dysphoric disorder (PMDD) *147*
vacuum aspiration *152*

female genital cutting *154*
infibulation *154*
miscarriage *156*
effacement *159*
cesarean section *159*
Lamaze method *159*
doula *160*
maternity blues *162*
postpartum depression *162*

infertility *163*
endometriosis *163*
in vitro fertilization *163*
surrogate motherhood *163*
menopause *164*
perimenopause *164*
hot flash *164*
hormone replacement therapy *167*
phyto-estrogens *168*

What Do You Think?

1. If a friend of yours unexpectedly became pregnant, what factors might influence her decision about whether or not to terminate the pregnancy?

2. Why do you think that even though many college students have heard about the risks of sexually transmitted diseases, including HIV infection, they fail to use condoms regularly or to engage in other self-protecting behaviors? What actions could be taken to make more of your friends engage in "safer sex" practices?

3. Do you favor or oppose school-based education programs that provide contraceptives to teenagers? Support your answer.

4. Who is the baby's real mother—the surrogate mother who conceived and carried the baby or the wife of the man who fathers the baby? Is motherhood primarily a biological or psychological concept? Explain your answers.

5. Should women in their 50s and 60s have babies? Why or why not?

6. In your opinion, why do young women have more negative views of menopause than middle-aged women?

If You Want to Learn More

Baumgardner, J. (2008). *Abortion and life*. New York: Akashic Books.

Boston Women's Health Book Collective. (2008). *Our bodies ourselves: Pregnancy and birth*. New York: Touchstone.

Crockin, S. L., & Jones, H. W. (2009). *Legal conceptions: The evolving law and policy of assisted reproductive technologies*. Baltimore, MD: Johns Hopkins University Press.

De Jonge, C. J., & Barratt, C. L. (Eds.). (2011). *Assisted reproductive technology: Current accomplishments and new horizons*. Cambridge, UK: Cambridge University Press

Edelman, L. S. (2010). *Menopause matters: Your guide to a long and healthy life*. Baltimore, MD: Johns Hopkins University Press.

Maizes, V., & Low Dog, T. (Eds.). (2010). *Women's integrative health*. New York: Oxford University Press.

Mitchell, D. (2009). *The concise encyclopedia of women's sexual and reproductive health*. New York: St. Martin's Press.

Scott, L. (2009). *Two is enough: A couple's guide to living childless by choice*. Berkeley, CA: Seal Press.

Stein, E., & Kim, S. (2009). *Flow: The cultural story of menstruation*. New York: St. Martin's Press.

Tassone, S. A., & Landherr, K. M. (2009). *Hands off my belly: The pregnant woman's survival guide to myths, mothers, and moods*. New York: Prometheus.

Thacker, H. L. (2009). *The Cleveland Clinic guide to menopause*. New York: Kaplan.

Venis, J. A., & McCloskey, S. (2007). *Postpartum depression demystified: An essential guide for understanding and overcoming the most common complication after childbirth*. New York: Marlowe.

Websites

Sexuality and Reproductive Health
About Go Ask Alice!
http://www.goaskalice.columbia.edu/

Contraception
About Go Ask Alice!
http://www.goaskalice.columbia.edu/
Planned Parenthood: Your Contraceptive Choices
http://www.plannedparenthood.org/pp2/portal/medicalinfo/birthcontrol/

Pregnancy and Childbirth
Reproductive Health
http://www.cdc.gov/reproductivehealth/index.htm

Childbirth
http://www.childbirth.org
Pregnancy & Child Health Resource Centers
http://www.mayoclinic.com/findinformation/healthylivingcenter/index.cfm

Infertility
Infertility Resources
http://www.ihr.com/infertility

Menopause
North American Menopause Society
http://www.menopause org

CHAPTER 8

Relationships

Friendships
  Friendship in Adolescence
  Friendship in Adulthood
  Friendship in Later Life
Romantic Relationships
  Desirable Qualities in a
    Partner
  Perception of Sexual Interest
  Dating
Committed Relationships
  Marriage
  Cohabitation
  Lesbian Relationships
Single Women
  Divorced Women
  Never-Married Women
  Widowed Women
  Women Who Have Lost a
    Same-Sex Partner
Motherhood
  Stereotypes of Mothers
  Single Mothers
  Lesbian Mothers
  Mothers with Disabilities
  The "Empty Nest" Period
**Relationships in the Later
Years**
  Siblings
  Adult Children
  Grandchildren
  Parents

A middle-aged lesbian couple had been together for 15 years when their daughter was born. To celebrate the joyous occasion, they held a naming ceremony for their friends. The nonbiological mother held the baby and presented her with her full name consisting of her given name and each parent's surname. Then each parent lit a candle and made a wish for their baby girl. Following this, they expressed their feelings for one another and for their new family. (Muzio, 1996)

Last Sunday, Ashley and I went over to my mom's house and we made applesauce together. It was really fun because it was all three of us and I used to do that with my mom when I was a kid . . . And we were just working together doing all the different parts of the applesauce and conversing. We were all acting like friends, but at the same time there was that bond there—that grandmom, mom, daughter thing. It was neat. (Denise, age 38, in Fingerman, 2003, p. 66)

These vignettes portray women's experiences with interpersonal relationships in different parts of the life cycle. In this chapter, we explore the nature of women's close relationships—including friendships, romantic relationships, marriage and other long-term relationships, unattached lifestyles, and motherhood. We end the chapter by examining women's relationships in the later years with their siblings, adult children, grandchildren, and parents.

FRIENDSHIPS

Close relationships are essential to good mental health and well-being. Friends, in particular, are a major source of support and self-esteem throughout an individual's life (Castañeda & Burns-Glover, 2008). Let's take a closer look at gender differences in friendships, starting in adolescence and moving through the adult life span.

Friendship in Adolescence

Starting in childhood and throughout life, a person's closest friends tend to be people of the same gender. Even though romantic attachments increase during adolescence, in general, most teenagers around the world still choose members of their own gender as friends and as best friends (Chen & Wang, 2010; Mehta & Strough, 2010; Nelson et al., 2010; Pinquart & Silbereisen, 2010). Starting in early adolescence, girls report greater satisfaction with their same-gender friendships than do boys (Thomas & Daubman, 2001). They also report higher levels of affection nurturance, trust, security, and closeness (Rose & Rudolph, 2006; Valkenburg & Peter, 2007).

Intimacy, the sharing of thoughts and feelings with someone else, is a key characteristic of adolescent friendships, especially those of girls (Brown & Larson, 2009; Poulin & Chan, 2010). Girls show greater increases in intimacy from early to late adolescence, they report more self-disclosure and emotional support, and they spend more time with their friends than do boys (Collins & Steinberg, 2006; Rose & Smith, 2009; Rueger et al., 2008).

Girls tend to have close, intimate, one-on-one friendships characterized by self-disclosure and emotional support. In the words of one adolescent girl,

> I've had a best friend for about five years now, and she pretty much knows everything about me. I'd probably turn to her for all of my problems because she's always helped me out and always gave me the right answers for everything.

> (Commonwealth Fund, 1997, p. 19)

Boys are more likely to have larger, less intimate friendship groups that focus on shared group activities, mostly sports and competitive games (Blakemore et al., 2009; Lee et al., 2007; Rudolph et al., 2007).

Studies of ethnically and socioeconomically diverse adolescents have found friendship patterns that differ somewhat from those commonly seen among White, middle-class adolescents (Rubin et al., 2010). For example, Julia Duff (1996) found that 95 percent of middle-class White girls reported competition as an aspect of their friendships, whereas only 38 percent of low-income girls of color did so. Similarly, White girls were five times as likely to report feeling "used" by a close friend and were nearly three times as likely to indicate that jealousy was an issue.

Friendship in Adulthood

Although both women and men highly value their friendships, women's friendships, as in adolescence, are more intimate and emotionally supportive than men's (Rose, 2007; Whitbourne, 2009).

This greater desire for intimacy may lead young women to hold higher expectations and standards for their same-sex friends than young men do (Benenson et al., 2009). Women and men achieve closeness with their friends somewhat differently. Women are described as operating "face to face," by sharing thoughts and feelings, whereas men develop closeness "side by side," by sharing activities (Sanchez-Hucles, 2003).

The emotional support shown in heterosexual female friendships is a particularly important quality of sexual minorities' friendships as well. The reinforcement and empathy that are part of close relationships in this "family of choice" can help sexual minority individuals cope with prejudice from the broader society and support the development of a positive sexual identity (Galupo 2007, 2009; Ueno et al., 2009; Weinstock, 2009).

How can one account for gender differences in emotional intimacy and expressiveness in friendships? Consistent with the general assumption that gender is socially constructed, experiences and attitudes shape orientations toward friendship. As we saw in Chapter 4, parents are more likely to encourage emotional expression in their daughters and discourage it in their sons, and females and males carry these messages into their peer relationships. Furthermore, because emotional expression is viewed as a feminine trait and many males think of gay men as having feminine traits, males might associate emotional closeness between males with homosexuality. This perceived connection can be threatening and might steer boys and men away from expressing emotions to their male friends (Castañeda & Burns-Glover, 2008).

Although most of the research on adolescent and adult friendship has focused on same-sex friends, some recent studies have examined cross-sex friendships (Baumgarte & Nelson, 2009; Galupo, 2009; McDougall & Hymel, 2007; Monsour, 2002; Weger & Emmett, 2009). These friendships are similar in many ways to same-sex friendships but also offer some unique benefits. Female–male friends provide each other with insider perspectives and other-sex companionship and also sensitize each other to gender differences in communication style. Men report more cross-sex friendships than do women (Galupo, 2009). In addition, feminine men have more cross-sex friendships than masculine men, and masculine women have more cross-sex friendships than feminine women (Reeder, 2003).

Friendship in Later Life

Friends provide the emotional support and companionship that sustain women as they meet the challenges, changes, and losses of later life (Antonucci et al., 2010). Because many married women eventually lose their spouses through death or divorce, most women grow old in the company of other women (Mehta & Strough, 2009). In later life, women are more engaged with friendships and social networks than are men and are more likely both to give and to receive emotional support (Arber, 2004; Canetto, 2003). Older women's close friends tend to be about the same age and socio-economic status, have the same social and ethnic background, and live close to each other (Rawlins, 2004). Friendships among older women enhance physical and mental health and contribute to continued psychological growth (Gergen & Gergen, 2006; Moreman, 2008). Long-term friends contribute to a sense of continuity and connection with the past. Over time, friends can come to be considered as family, further increasing one's sense of connectedness (Hall, 2007).

Social class influences the way in which friendships are made and maintained. Older middle-class women often make friends through membership in an association. The main basis of such friendships is shared interest of the group and its activities. Working-class and poor women are more likely to choose relatives as close friends and to provide practical assistance to each other, including helping one another with transportation, shopping, and running errands (Moreman, 2008; Sanchez-Hucles, 2003).

For many sexual minority individuals, friendships function as an extended family (Connidis, 2010; Heaphy, 2009; Oswald & Masciadrell, 2008). Many midlife and older lesbians who came out during a period that was more hostile toward sexual minorities than is true today were not accepted by their families. For them, and for other sexual minority individuals who have been rejected by their families of origin, friendships serve this familial role (De Vries & Megathlin, 2009; Heaphy, 2009; Witten, 2009). And because most lesbians have not been married and have not created a traditional family, these social networks of friends can be an important source of support to midlife and older women (Calasanti, 2009; Rose, 2007; Weinstock, 2009).

ROMANTIC RELATIONSHIPS

The process of looking for a suitable partner preoccupies many individuals during their teen and young adult years. In this section, we look at some features of this process. What qualities do women and men look for in a potential partner? How do they act in dating situations? How do they gauge their partner's interest in having sex?

Desirable Qualities in a Partner

What qualities do individuals look for in a romantic partner or mate? Both in heterosexual and same-sex relationships, people are often attracted to those whom they perceive as loving, supportive, extroverted, agreeable, and intelligent (Felmlee et al., 2010; Klohnen & Luo, 2003). Women prefer men who display self-assurance and stand up for themselves with other men, but who also exhibit warmth and agreeableness (Gangestad et al., 2004). Women are more likely than men to value love, faithfulness, and commitment (Meier et al., 2009). Although both sexes also value physical attractiveness, men put more emphasis on looks than women do, whereas women put a higher priority on status and resources (Brabeck & Brabeck, 2006; Eastwick & Finkel, 2008; Sheldon, 2007). In online profiles, for example, women are more likely to offer physical attractiveness and ask for financial stability whereas men are more apt to ask for physical attractiveness and offer financial security (Conkle, 2010; Glasser et al., 2009; Sears-Roberts Alterovitz & Mendelsohn, 2009). Not surprisingly, women are more likely than men to misrepresent their weight in online profiles, and men are more likely to misrepresent their financial assets (deBacker et al., 2008; Hall et al., 2010). Lesbians are less likely than heterosexual females to offer attractiveness as an attribute, perhaps because they are less likely to base their relationships on physical appearance (Kimmel, 2002; Smith & Stillman, 2002b).

This great value placed on physical appearance has unfortunate consequences for heterosexual women. Not only can it contribute to a distorted body image and eating disorders (see Chapters 4 and 13), but it also denigrates women by placing more importance on superficial characteristics than on behaviors and accomplishments. Best-selling books such as *Looking Younger* (Jones, 2008) and *How Not to Look Old* (Krupp, 2008) play on women's fears of losing not only their sexual allure, but their edge in the workforce as well. Emphasis on physical appearance has a particularly negative impact on women with disabilities. These women are less likely than able-bodied women to be perceived as attractive and desirable and may even evoke reactions of repulsion and rejection. Not surprisingly, the resulting poor self-image and fear of rejection can lead women with disabilities to avoid social and intimate relationships (Banks, 2010; Nosek, 2010).

Given the double standard of aging (see Chapter 2), it is not surprising that body dissatisfaction is high in midlife women, especially those who place great importance on their appearance (Hurd Clarke, 2011; McLean et al., 2010; Mellor et al., 2010). One study, for example, found that nearly half of a group of women with a median age of 51 were dissatisfied with their bodies

(Grippo & Hill, 2008). Midlife women are more dissatisfied with their appearance than midlife men (Algass et al., 2009; Donaghue & Smith, 2008; Slevin, 2010). Consequently, they are more likely than men to diet ("QuickStats," 2008) and to use age concealment techniques, such as liposuction, breast and face lifts, tummy tucks, and injectable wrinkle fillers such as Botox (American Society of Plastic Surgeons, 2009; Baker & Gringart, 2009; Hurd Clarke, 2011; Muise & Desmarais, 2010; Slevec & Tiggemann, 2010). In addition, the demand for cosmetic genital surgery is increasing in the United States and western Europe, as more women seek to have "designer vaginas" (Braun, 2010; Liao et al., 2009). Even young mothers are increasingly getting "mommy makeovers"—including a breast lift, tummy tuck, and liposuction—intended to reduce postpartum stretch marks and abdominal fat (Singer, 2007). Moreover, women feel pressured to seek out surgery at younger ages than a decade ago, often beginning with their eyelids in their mid- or late 30s, and moving through a series of cosmetic surgeries over the next few decades (Merkin, 2004). Whereas the vast majority of cosmetic surgeries are performed on White women, ethnic minority women are increasingly seeking these procedures (Dolnick, 2011). The good news is that as women move into their 50s and beyond, many become more satisfied with and accepting of their bodies (Donaghue & Smith, 2008; Liechty & Yarnal, 2010).

The results reported in this section were based on U.S. samples. What do females and males in other cultures look for in a romantic partner or prospective mate? See Explore Other Cultures 8.1.

Perception of Sexual Interest

How do young adults determine sexual interest of their partners? In heterosexual relationships, both males and females interpret certain nonsexual behaviors as cues that one's partner is interested in sex. For example, some young adults believe that asking someone out on a date indicates the requester is interested in having sex (Mongeau et al., 1998). Also, some assume that how much a partner spends on a date influences how far things go sexually (Basow & Minieri, 2011).

In general, men are more likely than women to perceive sexual interest in nonsexual behaviors (Lindgren et al., 2008). For example, college men are more likely than college women to misperceive flirting (Henningsen, 2004), friendliness (Farris et al., 2008), or even a brief conversation

---

EXPLORE OTHER CULTURES 8.1
What Do People in Other Cultures Look for in a Mate?

David Buss (1994) and his colleagues have studied the characteristics that adults in 37 cultures prefer in potential mates. In all cultures, men valued physical attractiveness more highly than did women. They also preferred younger mates and mates with domestic skills. Women in 36 of 37 cultures, however, valued "good earning capacity" more than men did and they preferred older mates. Still, there was a great degree of consistency in the preferences of women and men. Both ranked "kind and understanding" as most important, followed by "intelligent," "exciting personality," and "healthy." Despite these overall similarities, cultural differences occurred on almost all items. The largest cultural difference was found for chastity, which was considered to be unimportant by northern Europeans, but very important in China, India, and Iran. What might account for these cultural differences? Alice Eagly and her colleagues (Wood & Eagly, 2010) reexamined the 37 cultures as well as a subset of 9 of these cultures. They found that women's preference for older mates with resources and men's preference for younger women with domestic skills and intact virginity were most pronounced in societies in which women's status was low. These differences decreased as societies became more egalitarian. In other words, gender differences in the characteristics that people prefer in mates reflect the extent to which women and men occupy different roles in a given society.

(Henningsen et al., 2006; Levesque et al., 2006) as indicating sexual interest. Explanations of these gender differences range from differential socialization to greater readiness toward sexual arousal in men (Lindgren et al., 2008). Whatever the cause, can you identify problems stemming from the cues men use to perceive sexual interest? Unfortunately, the sexual meaning men give to many nonsexual behaviors can lead to a misunderstanding of women's desires and to possible sexual aggression.

Dating

Almost all of the research on dating has focused on able-bodied women and men. Persons with disabilities face other issues in dating relationships. To examine some of the issues for women with disabilities, see Learn About the Research 8.1.

ONSET OF DATING.   The mixed-gender friendship and peer groups that start to form during early adolescence are central to the emergence of dating and romantic relationships that begin to blossom at this time (Sassler, 2010; Tuval-Mashiach et al., 2008; Underwood & Rosen, 2009). Dating not only serves as a courting ritual that can lead to serious commitment and

---

LEARN ABOUT THE RESEARCH 8.1
Dating Issues for Women With Physical Disabilities

Because previous research had shown that women with physical disabilities are considered asexual and not acceptable as romantic partners, Diana Rintala and her colleagues examined dating issues experienced by women with and without disabilities. Their national sample included 475 women with disabilities (average age, 41.5) and 425 able-bodied women (average age, 38). These women responded to mailed questionnaires.

The researchers found that women who were disabled before their first date began dating approximately two-and-one-half years later than able-bodied women. However, there was no difference in the percentage of women with or without disabilities who had ever had sex with a man, although somewhat fewer women with disabilities reported having had sex with a woman.

Compared to able-bodied women, the women with disabilities were less satisfied about

their dating frequency and perceived more problems trying to attract dating partners. They were also more concerned about both physical obstacles in the environment and societal barriers to dating, including people's assumptions that women with disabilities are uninterested in or unable to have sexual intimacy. Last, women with disabilities experienced more personal barriers to dating, such as pressure from family members not to date and low frequency of getting out of the house to socialize.

Based on these findings, the researchers suggest several interventions that might improve the dating experiences of women with disabilities. Some of these are (1) removal of physical barriers in public places, (2) educating the public about disability and sexuality, and (3) educating families about the appropriateness of dating for women with disabilities.

WHAT DOES IT MEAN?

1. What specific strategies could be used to educate the public about disability and sexuality and to change families' feelings about the appropriateness of dating? What solutions other than those presented here might improve the dating situation for women with disabilities?

2. This investigation focused on women only. Do you think men with disabilities experience similar problems? Explain your answer.

Source: Rintala et al. (1997).

marriage, but also as an opportunity for sexual experimentation, enhancement of a teenager's social status and popularity, and development of a sense of identity (Connolly & McIsaac, 2009; Simon et al., 2008).

Over the last several decades, the age when U.S. adolescents start dating has decreased. Many girls now begin to date at age 12 or 13, and many boys at 13 or 14. Some girls report dating as early as age 8, with parents as chaperones (Myers & Raymond, 2010). About one-quarter of 12-year-olds have been involved in a romantic relationship, compared to 70 percent of 18-year-olds (Connolly & McIsaac, 2009).

Many of the factors that are related to the initiation of sexual activity (see Chapter 6) are also related to the age at onset of dating. For example, Black teenagers begin both dating and sexual activity earlier than White and Latina/o adolescents. Other factors related to early dating include early age at puberty, associating with older peers, and belonging to a divorced or stepparent family (Connolly & McIsaac, 2009).

Young people usually bring to their early dating encounters a set of beliefs regarding how they should behave in order to appeal to the other gender and maintain the relationship. The advice passed along to girls by girlfriends, mothers, older siblings, and the media frequently includes such helpful hints as massaging the boy's ego, bringing up subjects that he enjoys talking about, admiring his accomplishments (but not mentioning yours), and being understanding, but not too assertive or confrontational. A boy, on the other hand, learns to "take care" of a girl he dates by making the arrangements, being chivalrous (opening the door, helping her put her coat on), paying for the date, and taking her home (Boynton, 2003; Maccoby, 1998; Rose, 2000). Notice how traditionally gender-typed these dating expectations are.

DATING SCRIPTS. Suzanna Rose and Irene Hanson Frieze (1993) explored this subject in greater detail by studying the expected **dating scripts** and actual dating behavior of college students on a first date. A dating script is a *culturally developed sequence of expected events that guides an individual's behavior while on a date.* (The task the researchers used is described in Get Involved 8.1. Try it with some of your friends.) Students' expected dating behaviors and their actual behaviors were very similar. Some aspects of the dating script were the same for females and males. These included worrying about one's appearance, talking, going to a show, eating, and kissing good-night. Many of the elements of the date, however, were strongly gender-stereotypical. Males were the initiators. They asked for and planned the date, drove the car and opened doors, and started sexual interaction. Females, on the other hand, reacted to what men did: being picked up, having doors opened, and responding to sexual overtures. They also focused more on the private domain, such as concern about appearance and enjoying the date (Rose & Frieze, 1993). More recent research has confirmed that these dating scripts continue to operate in the twenty-first century (Bartoli & Clark, 2006; Morr Serewicz & Gale, 2008). Dating scripts of lesbians and gay males are similar in many respects to those of heterosexuals, but they are not as strongly gender-typed (Rose & Zand, 2002).

Dating scripts reflect not only the stereotype of the communal female and the agentic male but also suggest that heterosexual romantic relationships are characterized by a power imbalance between women and men (Laner & Ventrone, 1998). Does research support this assumption of greater male power? Studies of late adolescents and young adults find that some dating couples view their relationships as egalitarian, at least in terms of certain types of power, whereas others perceive a power imbalance (Galliher et al., 1999; Sprecher & Felmlee, 1997). When there is inequality, couples are more likely to view males than females as the powerful partner, consistent with males' greater power in society (Sprecher & Felmlee, 1997).

GET INVOLVED 8.1
Dating Scripts of Women and Men

Complete the following task from the study by Rose and Frieze (1993, p. 502). Then ask two unmarried female and two unmarried male undergraduates to do the same.

From the perspective of your own gender, list the actions that a woman (use the word "man" *for male participants) would typically do as she (he) prepared for a first date with someone new, then met her (his) date, spent time during the date, and ended the date. Include at least 20 actions or events that would occur in a routine first date, putting them in the order in which they would occur.*

WHAT DOES IT MEAN?

1. What elements of a dating script were shared by your female and male respondents?
2. In what ways were the dating scripts gender-stereotypical?
3. How do your results compare to those of Rose and Frieze (1993) described in the text?
4. Based on your knowledge of gender stereotypes, gender-related attitudes, and socialization experiences, what might account for the differences in the dating scripts of females and males?
5. Do you think that the degree of traditional gender-stereotypical behavior in dating scripts would be the same on a fifth date as on a first date? Explain your answer.

RECENT TRENDS IN DATING.   As more individuals remain single for longer periods of time, or become single as a result of divorce, elaborate partnering "markets" have developed in major cities. Edward Laumann and his colleagues (2004) interviewed over 2,000 adults in four Chicago neighborhoods, including those with largely Black, Latino/a, or gay populations. They found that the partnering markets operate differently for women and men. Women, for example, were less likely than men to meet a partner through institutions such as work or church as they got older, in part because men in their 40s often sought women who were at least five to eight years younger. Neighborhoods and cultures also influenced the ways in which people found partners. In Latino/a neighborhoods, for example, family, friends, and the church played a more important role in meeting partners than in other areas. Young, upper-income individuals on the city's north side were more apt to find partners at school or work. Gay men were more likely to look for short-term relationships whereas lesbians usually sought long-term partners.

A more modern way to meet a potential partner is to visit online dating sites (Conkle, 2010). Specialized sites for singles of various ages, religions, ethnicities, and disabilities have proliferated in recent years (Barrow, 2010; Conkle, 2010). Millions of singles have gone on a date someone they met through such a service (Sprecher et al., 2008). Online dating has shed its image as a last resort for losers or a meeting ground for casual sex, as word spreads of successful long-term relationships that began online (Conkle, 2010). Not surprisingly, traditional dating scripts still apply, at least in the sense that men usually send the first e-mail message and often do not respond when a woman does so (Harmon, 2003). Still another recent dating phenomenon is speed-dating, in which 10–12 couples sit around a room, exchanging information with potential dates in six- to eight-minute segments (Conkle, 2010; Finkel & Eastwick, 2008; Houser et al., 2008).

Not only are there more single Americans than ever before, but more of them are middle-aged or older. Many older singles are either dating or looking for someone to date (AARP, 2003).

Interestingly, one-third of the women (like most men) prefer to date younger individuals. Older singles have more realistic dating expectations than younger ones. Few of them expect or want dating to lead to marriage. Instead, they are looking for someone to talk to and do things with. And, like their younger single counterparts, many older adults are looking for partners or companions online (Sidener, 2004).

COMMITTED RELATIONSHIPS

Committed relationships can take several different forms. Among heterosexuals, the most common type of committed relationship by far is marriage. Cohabitation (i.e., living together) has increased in recent years, often as a prelude to marriage. Lesbians and gay men also form committed relationships, although they are unable to legally marry in most of the United States. In this section, we examine these forms of committed relationships.

Marriage

Although nearly all Americans hold marriage as an ideal, powerful social and cultural forces have made marriage increasingly optional in the twenty-first century (Bianchi et al., 2008; Connidis, 2010; Pew Research Center, 2010b; Regnerus & Uecker, 2011; Smock & Greenland, 2010). Most women view marriage positively, although some variation occurs across ethnic groups. Latinas place a higher value on marriage than other groups (Kaufman & Goldscheider, 2007), which might reflect the strong value placed on family in Latina/o culture. Black women show less interest in marriage than do women of other ethnic groups, perhaps because they see marriage as less important to their individual success (Kaufman & Goldscheider, 2007).

MARRIAGE RATES.   High marriage rates indicate the continuing value placed on marriage in society. In 2008, 80 percent of White, 73 percent of Latina, 80 percent of Asian American, and 60 percent of Black women 18 years or older were married or had been married at some point, with percentages for men at 74, 63, 70, and 58, respectively (U.S. Census Bureau, 2010c). The median age at first marriage has been increasing. In 2009, it was 26 for women and 28 for men, an increase of approximately five years since 1970 (U.S. Census Bureau, 2009). This increase in age of marriage is due in part to changes in economic conditions, leading both women and men to desire some degree of financial security before embarking on a long-term commitment. In addition, as more women pursue higher education and careers, they tend to marry later (Cherlin, 2010; Stevenson, 2010). College-educated women typically marry at age 30 (U.S. Department of Commerce, 2011). Women with disabilities are less likely to marry and are more likely to marry later in life than men with disabilities or able-bodied women (Olkin, 2008). The vast majority of Americans marry individuals of their own race. However, during the past 25 years, the number of interracial marriages has increased, comprising 3.9 percent of all married couples in 2008 (U.S. Census Bureau, 2010c).

MARITAL SATISFACTION.   Couples who report high levels of marital satisfaction use active, problem-focused coping strategies; hold similar attitudes, goals, and values; and communicate well with each other (Cavanaugh & Blanchard-Fields, 2011; Gilbert & Rader, 2008). Women are more involved than men in maintaining such communication, consistent with the social construction of females as concerned about the feelings of others. For example, wives provide better support on days when their husbands experience greater stress. By contrast, when wives experience more stress, their husbands display a mixture of support and negativity (Neff & Karney, 2005). Wives also tend to be happier and more satisfied when their husbands are emotionally engaged and spend time with them (Wilcox & Nock, 2007) and when they perceive that they and their spouses contribute equally to the marriage (DeMaris, 2010).

One of the biggest determinants of marital satisfaction is the presence of children. Marital satisfaction declines over time for women and men whether or not they have a child (Bradbury & Karney, 2010; Doss et al., 2009; Hirschberger et al., 2009; Mitnick et al., 2009). Couples who become parents, however, show steeper declines in satisfaction than those who do not (Dew & Wilcox, 2011; Lawrence et al., 2008). When children leave home, couples experience an increase in marital satisfaction (Parker-Pope, 2009). What do you think accounts for these changes?

Most studies show that men report greater marital satisfaction than women (Bulanda, 2011; Lasswell, 2002; Lemme, 2006), although a few find no gender difference (Lucas et al., 2003). It is clear, however, that marriage provides women and men with many benefits. Both married women and men are happier than their unmarried counterparts, a relationship found around the globe (Corra et al., 2009; Diener et al., 2000; Joutsenniemi et al., 2006; Sbarra & Nietert, 2009). Moreover, married individuals, especially those in good relationships, are mentally and physically healthier and better able to deal with work-related stress (Aumann & Galinsky, 2009; Diamond et al., 2010; Dupre & meadows, 2007; Fincham & Beach 2010; Hughes & Waite, 2009; Koball et al., 2010; Liu, 2009; Liu & Umberson, 2008). They also show a lower incidence of risky and antisocial behavior and greater financial success and stability (Johnson et al., 2004). However, this "marriage benefit" is smaller for women than for men, and may not exist, according to some researchers (Diamond et al., 2010; Felder, 2006). People in strained, unhappy relationships usually fare worse medically than happily married individuals (Parker-Pope, 2010). Furthermore, marital stress affects women's health and sense of well-being more than men's (Fincham & Beach, 2010; Proulx et al., 2007).

Why are people in good marriages happier and healthier than single individuals? One obvious answer is the care and support they receive from their spouses, although women provide more care and support than they receive. Second, married couples often benefit financially because they have a combined household and, frequently, two incomes. Third, spouses tend to encourage health-promoting behaviors in one another (Antonucci et al., 2009; Connidis, 2010; Hughes & Waite, 2009; Jin & Christakis, 2007). It is also possible, of course, that individuals with positive personality traits and healthier lifestyles are more likely to attract a mate in the first place (Johnson et al., 2004).

Cohabitation

Cohabitation, *the state in which an unmarried couple lives together*, has dramatically increased in the United States over the last several decades. An estimated 50 percent or more of couples in the United States live together before marriage, with a higher incidence occurring among those with less education (Cherlin, 2010; Regan, 2008). Cohabitation is even more common in Europe (Comerford, 2011).

Many adolescents view living together as a way to test compatibility before marriage (Sassler, 2010), and for many couples, cohabitation indeed serves as a trial marriage (Stanley et al., 2011; Syltevik, 2010). For some couples, however, especially divorced or widowed persons, cohabitation is seen as an alternative to marriage that is driven by finances, convenience, and housing considerations (Hardie & Lucas, 2010; Rhoades et al., 2009).

Despite its popularity, not all people are in favor of cohabitation. Not surprisingly, middle-aged and older adults are more opposed than are young adults (Pew Research Center, 2010b). Traditionally religious individuals also are less willing to cohabit (Jose et al., 2010; Stanley et al., 2011), perhaps because cohabitation is counter to the teachings of many religions. Furthermore, individuals who hold more liberal sexual views and less traditional gender and political attitudes have more positive views of cohabitation (Hardie & Lucas, 2010; Jose et al., 2010; Pew Research Center, 2007a). Clearly, this lifestyle is inconsistent with traditional views about premarital chastity for women and is less likely than marriage to enable fulfillment of traditional gender roles.

Cohabiters report lower levels of affection and higher levels of conflict than married couples (Soons & Kalmijn, 2009). Interestingly, even after marriage, individuals who previously lived with each other have lower marital satisfaction, have higher levels of domestic violence, and are more likely to get divorced than married couples who had not lived together before marriage (Diamond et al., 2010; Jose et al., 2010; Kulik & Havusha-Morgenstern, 2011; Stanley et al., 2010, 2011). This does not necessarily mean that cohabitation fosters marital instability. Rather, these findings could result from a **selection effect** whereby *the attitudes of individuals who cohabit are more accepting of divorce and less committed to marriage than the attitudes of noncohabiters* (Stanley et al., 2010).

Lesbian Relationships

Contrary to popular stereotypes, lesbians are as likely as heterosexual women to be part of a couple and are more likely than gay men to be in a lasting, marriage-like relationship (Carpenter & Gates, 2008; Cherlin, 2010; Reczek et al., 2009). For example, the majority of sexual minority couples who have married in Massachusetts or formed civil unions in Vermont or had domestic partnerships in California have been women (Bellafante, 2005; Rothblum et al., 2008).

Lesbian relationships tend to be egalitarian, with household activities and other relationship behaviors determined through negotiation and based more on individual skills and interests than on rigid gendered conceptions of appropriate behaviors. In fact, lesbian relationships are characterized by more equality of power and a more equal division of paid and unpaid labor than are either heterosexual or gay relationships (Diamond et al., 2010; Esmail, 2010; Goldberg, 2010). Interestingly, bisexual women who have had relationships with partners of both genders report more conflicts over power in their heterosexual than in their same-gender relationships, in part because of dissatisfaction with the power balance in heterosexual relationships (Weinberg et al., 1994).

Lesbian couples are more likely than gay men to be in a lasting, marriage-like relationship.

Most lesbians are involved in sexually exclusive relationships (Goldberg, 2010). Although they may engage in less frequent sex than either heterosexuals or gay men (Farr et al., 2010a; Goldberg, 2010), they engage in considerable nongenital physical expression, such as hugging and cuddling, and are as satisfied with their sexual relationships as are heterosexual and gay couples (Littlefield et al., 2000; Patterson, 2000).

Although lesbians are generally satisfied with their relationships, lesbian couples experience a variety of unique stressors. First, conflicts can arise when one partner is more open about her sexual orientation than the other partner (Patterson, 2000). Second, lesbians must cope with the frequent lack of societal acceptance of their relationship (Diamond et al., 2010). Third, lesbian couples frequently face economic difficulties, in part because their income is based on the earnings of two women and women tend to earn less than men (see Chapter 10) and because many lesbian couples are denied domestic partner insurance and Social Security benefits typically awarded to married individuals (OWL, 2010). Finally, lesbian women are sometimes denied custody of their children or the right to adopt their partner's child (Rothblum, 2007).

On a more positive note, lesbians show higher levels of relationship quality over time than either heterosexual couples or gay men (Kurdek, 2008). In addition, lesbian couples report feeling less lonely than heterosexual married women (Grossman et al., 2001). Some writers suggest that lesbian couples are advantaged compared with heterosexual wives because they are more likely to share similar life expectancy, to be less threatened by changes in physical appearance, and to have accumulated their own financial resources through employment (Huyck, 1995).

Aging sexual minority women must confront the triple obstacles of sexism, ageism, and homophobia (OWL, 2010; Witten, 2009). Older lesbians who faced prejudice and discrimination during more hostile times often hid their identities and their relationships with other women (Connidis, 2010; Kuyper & Fokkema, 2010; Read, 2009). Even now, because of social constraints, they may not openly acknowledge the nature of their relationship. Unfortunately, this secrecy has led to the near invisibility of the older lesbian and gay population, and to their reduced access to health services.

As is true for heterosexuals, being in a committed relationship increases life satisfaction for older lesbians (Connidis, 2010). Moreover, after spending many years coping with the social stigma of their sexual orientation, lesbians and gay men have developed the inner resilience and social networks that may make them better prepared than heterosexuals to cope with the stigma of aging (MetLife Mature Market & the Lesbian and Gay Issue Network, 2010; Witten, 2009).

SINGLE WOMEN

When people marry, they don't always live happily ever after. Some divorce, others lose their spouses or same-sex partners through death. A small percentage of women never marry at all. In this section, we examine women who are divorced, never married, widowed, or who have lost a same-sex partner.

Divorced Women

Couples do not walk down the aisle with expectations of splitting up. Nevertheless, approximately 40 percent of all American marriages end in divorce, although divorce rates have decreased somewhat in recent years (Pew Research Center, 2007b). Although first marriages that end in divorce last for about eight years, marriages can dissolve at any point in the life cycle (U.S. Census Bureau, 2010c) and for numerous reasons—including incompatibility, communication problems, infidelity, substance abuse, and physical violence.

Although divorce occurs throughout the population, divorce rates differ depending on one's ethnic group, educational level, and age at marriage. African Americans are the most likely to divorce, followed by Whites and Latinos/as and then Asian Americans (Amato, 2010; Regan, 2008). College-educated individuals are less likely to divorce than those without college degrees (Amato, 2010; Conger et al., 2010). In addition, as the age of marriage rises through the late 20s, the divorce rate falls and then levels off (Shellenbarger, 2008).

Women with disabilities are more likely than able-bodied women or men with disabilities to be divorced (Olkin, 2008). Not surprisingly, both financial pressure and interpersonal problems can be contributing factors. If the spouse with a disability is unable to continue working, or if the able-bodied partner must quit work to care for her or his spouse, the couple might experience considerable financial strain. In addition, psychological reactions, such as anger or moodiness, on the part of either spouse or stress stemming from an overload of responsibilities for the able-bodied partner can damage the quality of the relationship. Consistent with the social construction of females as caregivers, wives are less likely than husbands to leave a spouse who has a disability (Etaugh, 2008).

EFFECTS OF DIVORCE ON WOMEN AND THEIR CHILDREN. Although divorced mothers view themselves as better parents than do mothers in high-conflict marriages, single parenting after a divorce can be highly stressful (Hetherington & Kelly, 2002). The breakup of a marriage produces numerous stressors for custodial parents and their children. Not only must both deal with strong emotional reactions, such as grief, anger, and guilt, but also their daily routines often involve major adjustments. Financial pressures can require the mother to begin or extend her employment, there can be major modifications in household responsibilities, and the family might have to change residence.

Given these and other stressors associated with parental divorce, children tend to experience a variety of emotional, academic, and behavioral problems in the immediate aftermath (Amato & Cheadle, 2008; Hetherington, 2004; Hetherington & Kelly, 2002; Potter, 2010), but most rebound within two years and are as psychologically healthy as children from two-parent homes. In fact, research comparing children from divorced and nondivorced families finds that differences are very small and that children in conflict-ridden intact families experience lower levels of psychological well-being than do children in divorced families (Amato, 2005; Lansford, 2009). Moreover, children in joint-custody arrangements following divorce are as well-adjusted as children in two-parent families (Bauserman, 2002).

Divorced women also experience initial problems followed by satisfactory adjustment. Immediately following the breakup, it is common for divorced women to experience higher levels of depression and distress than married women. These negative reactions are greatest in the first few years after the divorce and diminish over time (Amato, 2010), with few long-term effects on women's psychological adjustment (Etaugh, 2008; Lee & Gramotnev, 2007). Even if divorced women remarry, they are somewhat more likely to have chronic physical health problems than women who have been continuously married (Cornwell & Waite, 2009). Ethnicity also can affect a woman's adjustment to divorce. For example, studies suggest that Latinas experience more distress than White women, perhaps due to the strong emphasis on marriage in Hispanic culture (Pew Research Center, 2007a). However, Black mothers show a greater sense of personal mastery following divorce than White mothers (McKelvey & McKenry, 2000), possibly because African American culture provides these women with greater coping skills to deal with the adversities of divorce.

Many women experience a dramatic decline in family income after divorce, which places them in a significantly worse financial situation than divorced men (Diamond et al., 2010; McLanahan & Percheski, 2008). Divorced mothers are twice as likely as divorced fathers to live in poverty.

Fewer than two-thirds of divorced mothers with children under 21 years of age are awarded child support, and less than half of these receive full child support on a regular basis (U.S. Census Bureau, 2007). Not surprisingly, divorced women with low income and low occupational status are at greater risk for distress and depression (Etaugh, 2008).

Despite the problems resulting from a breakup, divorce can represent a positive means of reacting to a neglectful, conflict-ridden, or abusive relationship, and women do not feel more upset after a divorce than they did in their high-conflict marriages. Although initially they experience depression and distress, women tend to be happier two years postdivorce than they were during the last year of their marriage. Further, divorced women are likely to be less depressed than women in unhappy marriages (Hetherington & Kelly, 2002).

In addition to relief from leaving a conflict-laden marriage, many women report a variety of positive psychological outcomes—greater feelings of independence and freedom, the ability to meet the challenges of living without a spouse and functioning as a single parent, which can produce a new sense of competence (Hetherington & Kelly, 2002).

COPING WITH DIVORCE.   What factors help women cope with the strains of divorce? Employment is one factor that can facilitate adjustment (Amato, 2000). It provides an identity outside of women's marital role, is an avenue for productivity and income, and is a source of positive distraction and social support for divorced women. A divorced teacher stated, "Work filled my time and diverted my mind . . . It kept my mind off things for a while" (Bisagni & Eckenrode, 1995, p. 581). And a clerical worker noted, "My coworkers really do care. Like when I was going through the divorce, they really wanted to know if I was okay, without trying to pry. . . . if I couldn't talk to my coworkers, I probably would've gone to professional help a lot longer" (Bisagni & Eckenrode, 1995, p. 580).

Social support from family and friends is also vitally important in helping divorced women cope. Women who have a social network of friends and relatives to help them deal with the ramifications of divorce are less depressed and show more positive adjustment in the years following the marital breakup (Jenkins, 2003; Krumrei et al., 2007). Having a stable, new partner is another source of support that can have beneficial effects in postdivorce adjustment (Rice & Else-Quest, 2006).

Never-Married Women

Although some women become single at least for a period of time as a result of the end of a marriage, some never marry. Approximately 4 percent of women and 4 percent of men in the United States aged 75 and over have never married (U.S. Census Bureau, 2010c). Women with disabilities are more likely to remain single than able-bodied women or men with disabilities (Olkin, 2008).

Although marriage is still viewed as the expected lifestyle, today there is more freedom in, acceptance of, and support for single lifestyles than in the past in both the United States and Canada (Connidis, 2010). In one survey, 83 percent of American women and 73 percent of men said a woman can lead a complete and happy life if she is single (Pew Research Center, 2007b). Still, single women continue to be portrayed negatively in the media and are widely perceived as odd, social outcasts or selfish, commitment-phobic career women who lead barren, disappointing lives (DePaulo & Morris, 2006; Reynolds et al., 2007; Simpson, 2011). How do never-married heterosexual women feel about being single? Evidence shows that many are ambivalent about their marital status. On the one hand, they miss the benefits of steady companionship and feel sad about growing old alone, but at the same time, they enjoy their freedom, independence, and opportunities for personal growth (DePaulo, 2006; Reynolds, 2008; Sharp & Ganong, 2007; Trimberger, 2005). Increasing numbers of single women are signing up for housewarming and birthday registries, having decided not to wait for marriage to request the china, crystal, and appliances they wish to own (Zernike, 2003). Some are not only purchasing a home instead of renting but are also buying a second, vacation home (Cohen et al., 2003). A Website, SingleEdition.com, celebrates singlehood and offers shopping, financial, and other advice to singles (Newman, 2007).

The absence of a marital partner does not mean that single women are lacking social relationships. As we have seen, some date or are in committed romantic relationships, and many have strong ties to their extended families, network of friends, and community (Bookwala & Fekete, 2009; DePaulo et al., 2007; Schachner et al., 2008). Moreover, an increasing number of middle-aged never-married women are choosing to become mothers via adoption or sperm donation (Bazelon, 2009; Etaugh, 2008; Jones, 2007). In the words of one woman, "It would be nice to be in a relationship, but I don't really need that. My life is fine the way it is. And my life is full of love" (Boston Women's Health Book Collective, 1998, p. 187).

One disadvantage of being a single woman in midlife is that single women, more than their married sisters, are expected to, and in fact do, provide caregiving for aging parents, even at the expense of their own careers (DePaulo, 2009). On the plus side, never-married women typically have developed skills in independent living and in building support systems that stand them in good stead as they get older (Connidis, 2010). Compared with married women, the never-married older woman is better educated, has a higher income, is less likely to be depressed and commit suicide, values her freedom and autonomy, and has close connections with siblings, cousins, nieces and nephews, and friends and other interpersonal supports (Dykstra & Hagestad, 2007b; Etaugh, 2008; Wenger et al., 2007). Never-married older women also have fewer chronic health problems than those who are divorced or widowed (Hughes & Waite, 2009). The workplace is a significant source of friends for single women, and in retirement, these women go on to form new friendships with neighbors or members of organizations to which they belong (Doress-Worters & Siegal, 1994). Single older women have also learned to cope in their earlier years with the "stigma" of not being married and so are better able to deal with the effects of ageism in their later years. Most older, single women are satisfied with their lives and seem at least as happy as married women (Newtson & Keith, 2001; Paradise, 1993).

Widowed Women

Despite the increasing divorce rate, most marriages are terminated not by divorce, but by the death of a spouse. Around the world, women are more likely to become widowed than men, because women not only have a longer life expectancy but also tend to marry men older than themselves (Connidis, 2010; England & McClintock, 2009). In the United States, women 65 years and older are three times as likely as men of the same age to be widowed: 42 percent versus 14 percent (U.S. Census Bureau, 2010c).

Remarriage rates are much higher for widowers than for widows in most nations (Walter, 2003). In the United States, for example, the ratio is eight to one (Brody, 2010c). Consequently, older women are nearly twice as likely as older men to live alone (Pew Research Center, 2010c).

One obvious reason for the much lower remarriage rate of women is that unmarried older women greatly outnumber unmarried older men. For instance, unmarried women aged 65 and over in the United States outnumber unmarried men in that age category by more than two to one (Federal Interagency Forum, 2009). Furthermore, because men tend to marry women younger than themselves, the pool of potential mates expands for an older man but shrinks for an older woman. In addition, widowed women are much less likely than widowed men to be interested in forming a new relationship (Connidis, 2010; Sassler, 2010). Widows point out that they value their independence and enjoy their freedom. Moreover, they are not eager to resume the domestic responsibilities of a long-term relationship. Many do not relish the idea of becoming a caregiver for an older man, having, in some cases, already experienced the stresses of caring for a terminally ill partner (Chambers et al., 2009; Roark, 2009; Sweeney, 2010). Widowers, on the other hand, typically want someone to organize their households and social lives and provide companionship (Olson, 2006).

> *Four months after her husband of 42 years died, Verna hit an emotional low. "I told myself I have two choices. I can sit home, mourn, complain and cry, or make a new life in which I would learn to smile and be happy again in my own activities such as volunteering and starting a social life with new friends who aren't couples."*

(Arney, 2001)

REACTION AND ADJUSTMENT TO WIDOWHOOD.   Widowhood is one of the most stressful of all life events. The surviving spouse must not only cope with the loss of one's life partner but also adjust to a new status as a widowed person (Connidis, 2010). During the first year after their husband's death, widows show poorer mental and physical health than longer-term widows (Manzoli et al., 2007; Wilcox et al., 2003). Women who provided long-term care to their spouse prior to his death are more likely to be depressed than those who provided care on a short-term basis or not at all (Keene & Prokos, 2008). Most older widowed individuals adjust to their spouse's death within two to four years, although feelings of loneliness, yearning, missing their partner, and lowered life satisfaction remain for extended periods of time (Lucas et al., 2003). As many as 10 to 20 percent of widows, however, experience long-term problems, including clinical depression, abuse of alcohol and prescription drugs, and increased susceptibility to physical illness. Among these are women with a prior history of depression, those whose marriages were less satisfactory, those whose husbands' deaths followed the deaths of other close relatives and friends, and those who depended on their husbands for most social contacts (Etaugh, 2008).

Other factors—age; the degree of forewarning of the spouse's death; and financial, social, and personal resources—also affect a woman's reaction to widowhood (Bradsher, 2001; Michael et al., 2003). Studies comparing the mental and physical health of older widows and older married women have not generally found any differences between these groups (Etaugh, 2008). Younger widows, on the other hand, initially experience greater difficulties in coping with their situation (Michael et al., 2003). One reason for the greater distress experienced by young widows may be the greater likelihood that the husband's death was unexpected. Although younger individuals experience greater distress following their partner's death, the length of recovery is greater for older people (Michael et al., 2003).

Widowhood often results in a substantial reduction in financial resources for women, not only because the husband's income or pension ceases, but also because considerable expenses may be incurred during the husband's final illness (Carr & Ha, 2006; van den Hoonaard, 2011). Loneliness is another problem faced by widows. About 70 percent of older widows live alone (Fields & Casper, 2001). Having the social support of family, friends, and neighbors to stave off loneliness helps to alleviate the psychological and physical effects of loss-related stress (Antonucci et al., 2010; Chambers et al., 2009; Cicirell, 2010; Guiaux et al., 2007; Rook, 2009; Silverstein & Giarrusso, 2010). Interestingly, research has found more loneliness among women who have lived with a spouse for many years than among women who live alone (Etaugh, 2008).

The death of a spouse takes a heavier toll on men than on women. Widowed men suffer more psychological depression, psychiatric disorders, and physical illnesses, and have higher death rates and suicide rates than widowed women (Baiardi & Wolf, 2009; Elwert & Christakis, 2008;

Jin & Christakis, 2009; Manzoli et al., 2007). This may be due to the fact that women are more apt than men to admit a need for social support, to benefit from that support, and to have broad social networks with relatives and friends, including other widows (Aldwin et al., 2010; Baiardi & Wolf, 2009; Chambers et al., 2009; Cicirelli, 2010; Ha, 2008).

The experiences of widowhood were vividly portrayed in a longitudinal study of over 4,300 older Australian widows by Susan Feldman and her colleagues (2000). The concerns of the widows were not restricted just to the experience of bereavement and loss but also involved the challenges of daily life, including financial and social matters. Recent widows worried about managing their personal finances and coping with financial hardship. Another common theme was the need to keep busy. Relationships to family, friends, neighbors, and social groups became especially important. Many women displayed an attitude of courage, strength, and resilience as they coped with the challenges of their new life. In the words of one woman, who had been widowed for four years,

> *I felt desolate and despairing [when he died] . . . I have managed to survive and lead a comfortable and quite interesting (albeit at times a rather lonely) life. I am pleased that I have adjusted, and I handle all of my affairs. I shall never get over the loss, but I have lived to see the day.*

> (Feldman et al., 2000, p. 164)

Widows learn to enjoy living alone and derive a sense of competence from learning new, and some traditionally masculine, tasks (van den Hoonaard, 2011). Moreover, the realization that they have withstood an event that seemed insurmountable enhances their self-esteem (Carr, 2004a).

Keep in mind that this knowledge of widows has been obtained primarily from older women, most of whom had traditional marriages. When the young women of today become widows, they will be more likely to have had a different set of life experiences than the current population of widows, including a college education and a job or career that may better prepare them for a healthy adjustment to widowhood (Etaugh, 2008).

Women Who Have Lost a Same-Sex Partner

Lesbians and gay men may encounter unique problems when their partner dies. They may not be eligible for survivor benefits, and in the absence of a will, they may have no claim to the partner's estate that they have helped to build (Broderick et al., 2008; OWL, 2010). Loss of a same-sex partner is especially stressful if the relationship was not publicly acknowledged, but even when the relationship is open, friends, family, and work colleagues may not comprehend the severity and nature of the loss (Connidis, 2010; Walter, 2003; Whipple, 2006).

> *Recently, I vacationed with friends who had been friends also with my deceased partner-in-life. A guest arrived with slides of earlier vacations, including pictures of my lover. I objected that if I had been a man who had been recently widowed, they surely would have asked if I would object to showing the pictures. One friend responded she wanted very much to see them. She blanched when I suggested that she might feel differently after the death of her husband. Clearly, she thought that my relationship to Karen differed from her marriage; she evidently also thought my love differed from her friendship with Karen only by degree. Heterosexuals really do not understand what lesbians feel for their partners, even when they know us well. All of these friends had known Karen and me as lovers and had sent me bereavement condolences when Karen died.*

> (Doress-Worters & Siegal, 1994, p. 145)

MOTHERHOOD

One of the most intimate relationships a woman can experience is her relationship with her child. Consistent with the assumption that motherhood serves as a major source of fulfillment for women, many women view their relationship with their children as the most meaningful experience of their lives surpassing even their relationship with their spouses (Pew Research Center, 2007b). In the words of one mother, "For the first time I cared about somebody else more than myself, and I would do anything to nurture and protect her" (Boston Women's Health Book Collective, 1992, p. 488).

Although "the joy of having children" is by far the most important reason parents give for having children (Livingston & Cohen, 2010), this does not mean that parenting leads exclusively to positive emotions. Instead, mothers experience a swirl of opposing feelings. Motherhood can bring a great sense of love, connection, and joy accompanied by a tremendous burden of responsibility and guilt (Brabeck & Brabeck, 2006; Coyle, 2009; Simon, 2008). As one woman said, "The first month was awful. I loved my baby but felt apprehensive about my ability to satisfy this totally dependent tiny creature. Every time she cried I could feel myself tense up and panic" (Boston Women's Health Book Collective, 1998, p. 511). Motherhood can produce an expansion of personal identity as well as the loss of self. Mothers can feel exhilarated by their new role yet resent or mourn the loss of other aspects of their lives that might now diminish, such as involvement in work or community activities (Almond, 2010; Johnson & Rodgers, 2006). For many professional women, becoming pregnant for the first time leads to a restructuring of their professional identity to include identity as a working mother (Ladge et al., 2011). In addition, as we have seen, the transition to parenthood often has a negative impact on marital satisfaction (Doss et al., 2009; Lawrence et al., 2007).

Stereotypes of Mothers

The "good mother" is socially constructed as a warm, forgiving, generous, nurturing person who is easily able to meet all her children's needs and who puts their needs before her own (Dillaway & Paré, 2008; Kinser, 2010; Wolf, 2011). Unfortunately, no mother is able to consistently meet either her own standards or the standards of others, and all mothers suffer at least occasional feelings of inadequacy and guilt because of this idealized image (Karlyn, 2011; Milkie, 2011; Nelson, 2010). One mother complained, "I didn't know how to change a diaper any more than my husband did. In fact, I may have been more nervous about it, since I was 'supposed' to know how" (Boston Women's Health Book Collective, 1998, p. 511). Popular childrearing books do little to dispel this notion. One study examined the degree to which 23 current popular childrearing books portrayed the "new image" of the involved father (Fleming & Tobin, 2005). Only 4 percent of paragraphs mentioned fathers. In addition, the father's role was portrayed as predominantly ancillary to the mother's and was often depicted as voluntary and negotiable.

The good mother image can also lead people to blame mothers for their children's problems (Hall, 2008; Kinser, 2010; Wolf, 2011) because the social construction of the mother role, more than the father role, assumes an all-knowing, self-sacrificing, always-caring parent. This may explain why a man who harms or even kills his own children receives relatively little media coverage, whereas when Andrea Yates drowned her five children (see Chapter 7), she received international attention (Barash, 2002). Moreover, media speculate that the mothers are the culprits when mothers of murdered or missing children do not act exactly as the public thinks they should. The tears of Patsy Ramsey, mother of murdered Jon Benet Ramsey, were labeled "an act," whereas Kate McCann was criticized for seeming too cool and composed about the disappearance of her young daughter in 2007 (Yabroff, 2007).

The good mother stereotype illustrates the **motherhood mandate,** *the societal belief that women should have children and that they should be physically available at all times to tend to their young children's needs* (Russo, 1979). This view of motherhood was prevalent in North America in the 1960s and 1970s. With the dramatic increase in the employment of mothers in recent decades (see Chapter 11), has the motherhood mandate waned? Many scholars believe it has come back in a different form in the twenty-first century (Collins, 2009; Kinser, 2010; Richards, 2008), as the media glorify middle-class mothers who leave the workplace to become full-time homemakers, but simultaneously criticize women on welfare who stay home with their children (Macdonald, 2010; Springer, 2010). Susan Douglas (2010) criticizes this "new momism" in which the mother is expected to devote her entire being, all the time, to raising the perfect child.

In addition to communal qualities, numerous demographic characteristics are included in the societal image of the good mother (Kinser, 2010). She is expected to be middle-class, heterosexual, married, not too old, and also to have a job that does not prevent her from spending "adequate" time with her children. The more a mother deviates from this image, the more devalued she is and the less likely her own mothering practices and experiences are seen as valid (Breheny & Stephens, 2009; Rolfe, 2008). Many mothers who are employed full time struggle with tension between their worker identity and intensive mothering expectations (Drago, 2007; Johnston & Swanson, 2007).

A content analysis of contemporary women's magazines by Deirdre Johnston and Debra Swanson (2003) found mixed messages that could undermine the confidence of both employed and stay-at-home mothers. Women were almost always portrayed as full-time homemakers, but these women were frequently shown as overwhelmed, confused, and interested only in superficial topics. When employed mothers were portrayed, magazines focused only on whether employment jeopardized family relationships.

See What You Can Do 8.1 to help address issues related to parenting and work–family balancing.

Single Mothers

In the last several decades, there has been a significant increase in the percentage of single-parent, mother-headed families. The proportion of infants born to unmarried women rose to 38 percent in 2008 (Dye, 2010). Although many single mothers are in their 20s and have no more than a high school education, an increasing number of unmarried mothers are in their 30s, 40s, and 50s and are college-educated. This is the group of women we discussed earlier in the section on "never-married women," who are choosing in early middle age to become mothers via adoption or sperm donation (Bazelon, 2009; Etaugh, 2008). Whereas in 1970 approximately 12 percent of families were maintained by a mother only, this figure increased to 25 percent in 2008, including 55 percent of Black, 26 percent of Latina, 18 percent of White, and 12 percent of Asian families. By comparison, only 4 percent of households are maintained by a single father (U.S. Census Bureau, 2010c). Who are these single mothers? Nearly two-thirds are White, and most have one or two children. About one in three of these women are cohabiting; the large majority, however, are heading a single-parent household.

WHAT YOU CAN DO 8.1
Help Address Issues of Parenting and Work–Family Balancing

Join, volunteer, or attend an event sponsored by the National Association of Mothers' Centers (motherscenters.org). Through its public policy initiative entitled MOTHERS (Mothers Ought to Have Equal Rights), it addresses many areas related to parenting, maternal health, child development, and work–family integration.

TABLE 8.1   Poverty Status of Single-Parent Families in 2007

Ethnicity	Single-Mother Families % Below the Poverty Level	Single-Father Families % Below the Poverty Level
All ethnic groups	28	14
Black	37	26
Latina/o	38	15
White	25	12
Asian	16	8

Source: U.S. Census Bureau (2010c).

Nearly half of all households below the poverty line are headed by single mothers (U.S. Census Bureau, 2010c). As Table 8.1 shows, about one-third of female-headed families with dependent children live in poverty, and this number is significantly greater among Black and Latina families than White families. Note that single-father families of all ethnicities are much less likely to be poor, another illustration of the intersection of gender, class, and ethnicity. *The increasing percentage of women living below the poverty line* is referred to as the **feminization of poverty** and is found across affluent Western democracies (Brady & Kall, 2008; Burn, 2011).

How do women cope with the responsibilities of single motherhood? One important factor is social support from family and friends (Olson & Ceballo, 1996; Shanok & Miller, 2007). This support can be both emotional and instrumental, such as helping when there is an emergency, assisting with transportation to and from day care, and caring for a child while the mother is at work.

Several strengths of Black families and communities can help Black single mothers cope more effectively. Because Blacks have a long history of maternal employment, single mothers have numerous role models for managing the stressors of coordinating these roles. **Extended families**, in which *at least one other adult family member resides in the same household as the mother and her children,* and **augmented families,** in which *adult nonrelatives live with the mother and her children,* are family structures in the Black community that can be helpful to single mothers (Belgrave & Allison, 2010). These families offer additional role models for the children and provide substitute caregivers when the mother is at work or is tending to other responsibilities outside of the home. Because extended families are frequently involved in childrearing in Latina/o and Native American as well as Black families (Coll & Pachter, 2002; Dalla et al., 2010; Gerstel & Sarkisian, 2008), they can be helpful to single mothers in these communities as well.

Lesbian Mothers

Until quite recently, most Americans viewed families from a heterosexual perspective. Now, however, a majority say their definition of family includes same-sex couples with children, as well as married same-sex couples (Powell et al., 2010). About one-third of lesbians and one-fifth of gay men are parents (Tavernise, 2011). Many of their children were born into previous heterosexual marriages. However, a growing number of lesbians choose to have children after they have identified as lesbians, by means of artificial insemination, maternal surrogacy, or adoption (Biblarz & Savci, 2010; Ehrensaft, 2008; Gates, 2008; Mitchell & Green, 2008).

Because custody battles involving lesbian mothers frequently focus on their psychological adjustment and parenting styles, numerous studies have examined lesbians in their motherhood role. These studies show that lesbian mothers are similar to heterosexual mothers in self-esteem and psychological adjustment (Goldberg, 2010). This similarity between lesbian and heterosexual mothers is particularly noteworthy considering that lesbian mothers face stressors such as social disapproval not experienced by heterosexual mothers. In addition, some lesbians face rejection by their families of origin when they decide to parent (Goldberg, 2010; Johnson & O'Connor, 2002).

Although lesbian women do not differ from heterosexual women in nurturance or commitment to their children, they do raise their daughters and sons in a less gender-stereotypic manner (Patterson, 2006; Sutfin et al., 2008; Tasker, 2010). As models of gender-related behavior, they are less traditional than heterosexual mothers (Biblarz & Stacey, 2010). For example, partners are more likely to equally share financial and family responsibilities and be involved in feminist activities. Lesbian mothers are also less likely to purchase gender-stereotyped toys for their children and have less traditional gender-related expectations for their daughters.

Research on lesbian donor insemination families shows that the quality of children's relationship with the social mother is comparable to that with the biological mother (Vanfraussen et al., 2003). Moreover, unlike fathers in heterosexual families, the social mother is as involved in the child's activities as is the biological mother.

Just as the research on lesbian mothers finds few differences from heterosexual mothers, scores of studies show few differences between children raised by lesbian mothers and those raised by heterosexual mothers. Reviews of this research conclude that children from lesbian and heterosexual families are similar in psychological well-being, self-esteem, social and behavioral adjustments, and cognitive functioning (Bos & Sand Fort, 2010; Farr et al, 2010a,b; Patterson, 2009; Van Gelderen et al., 2009; Wainright & Patterson, 2008). Since, lesbian mothers raise their children in a less gender-stereotypic manner than heterosexual parents, their children, especially daughters, are less likely to have stereotyped notions of masculine and feminine behavior. These children are more tolerant of gender nonconformity and other forms of diversity in peers (Fulcher et al., 2008; Mortenson, 2011a), and are more likely to aspire to occupations that cross traditional gender lines (Bos & Sand Fort, 2010; Fulcher et al., 2003; Stacey & Biblarz, 2001). Also, adult children of lesbian parents, like those of heterosexual parents, have a gender identity and sex-typed behaviors and preferences consistent with their biological sex. They are not more likely than the adult children of heterosexual parents to have a lesbian, gay, or bisexual orientation (Dominus, 2004; Fulcher et al., 2008; Tasker, 2005). See Learn About the Research 8.2 to examine the psychological and social outcomes of adults raised by lesbian mothers.

Mothers With Disabilities

The traditional view held by society is that women with disabilities are psychologically unable to cope with the demands of pregnancy, childbirth, and childrearing (Drew, 2009; Maxwell et al., 2007; Olkin, 2008). However, there is no evidence that mothers with disabilities are less capable parents than able-bodied women. In fact, studies have demonstrated the ingenuity of mothers with disabilities in developing their own adaptive methods of baby care and mothering (Olkin, 2008). Through the Looking Glass is a nonprofit organization that provides services and training to prospective and new parents with disabilities (lookingglass.org).

The "Empty Nest" Period

Since my boys left, I have started dedicating my time to worthy causes that I enjoy. I volunteer at the hospital, spend a few hours a week at a retirement home, and I joined a women's group. My husband and I also are planning a vacation. We haven't done that—just the two of us— in a long time. These changes are good for me. Sure I still miss the boys, but they're growing up now. It's part of life, so you make the best of it.

(a 55-year-old woman)

LEARN ABOUT THE RESEARCH 8.2
Adult Children of Lesbian Mothers

Most of the research on the effects of lesbian mothers on children has focused on school-age children. Fiona Tasker and Susan Golombok expanded on this research by comparing the experiences of young adults who had been raised by lesbian mothers and those raised by heterosexual mothers. The researchers restricted the heterosexual sample to adults whose mothers had been single for some period while raising them in order to compare two groups of children whose mothers differed in sexual orientation, but not in the presence of a man in the household.

The findings showed no difference in the psychological well-being of the two groups of adult children. Moreover, adults raised by lesbian mothers were no more likely than those in heterosexual families to have experienced same-gender sexual attraction. However, there was a difference in sexual experimentation. Of those who reported some same-gender interest, children raised by lesbian mothers were more likely than children in heterosexual families to have had a same-gender sexual experience ranging from a single incident of kissing to cohabitation. All of the respondents in both groups had also experienced at least one heterosexual relationship. Having a lesbian mother may thus broaden the adolescent's view of acceptable sexual behavior possibilities. However, the finding that almost all of the young adults raised by lesbian mothers identified themselves as heterosexuals suggests that having a same-gender sexual experience does not lead to a lesbian or gay sexual identity.

WHAT DOES IT MEAN?

1. Do you think that differences between the two groups would have been more pronounced if the adult children of heterosexual mothers had come from homes with both a mother and a father? Explain your answer.

2. Prepare an argument in support of or in opposition to lesbian motherhood. Refer to the findings of this study, other materials from this chapter, theories of gender typing (see Chapter 3), and any other information that you believe is relevant.

3. Do you think that adults raised by lesbian mothers versus those reared by heterosexual mothers differ in the way they raise their own children? Explain your answer.

Source: Tasker and Golombok (1997).

Motherhood, as we have seen, is an important aspect of identity for most women. How do mothers experience the **empty nest period**, that is, *the period of a parent's life when children no longer live in the parents' home?* Most women react quite positively and seek opportunities to pursue new careers, further their education, or provide service to their communities (Dare, 2010; Mitchell & Lovegreen, 2009). And because children can be a source of tension in any marriage, women often report higher marital satisfaction once their children have left home (Bradbury & Karney, 2010).

The empty nest period is not experienced the same way by all women. Women who are reluctant to let go of their parenting role may perceive this period as stressful and as a time of loss (Dare, 2010; Mitchell & Lovegreen, 2009). However, mothers who are employed during the childrearing years establish an identity in addition to their motherhood role, and this can ease the difficulty of relinquishing parenting responsibilities.

Of course, mothers do not stop being parents when their children move out, but rather remain involved in their children's lives in somewhat different ways. Although their contacts are generally less frequent, they continue to offer advice and encouragement and often provide financial assistance (Cherlin, 2010; Fingerman et al., 2010; Kahn et al., 2011; Proulx & Helms, 2008). Although most mothers experience the departure of their children at some point during midlife, there are variations in children's age of departure, and a significant number return home for some period of time after leaving, for financial or personal reasons (Henig, 2010; Roberts, 2009; Smits et al., 2010). Over half of men 18 to 24 years old and nearly half of women that age still live with their parents, or have moved back home. Moreover, 10 percent of U.S. adults younger than age 35 recently reported moving home because of the economic recession (Roberts, 2009). Perhaps even more surprising is that 10 percent of Americans between ages 35 and 44 are living with parents or in-laws (Wadler, 2009). Parents' reaction to their children's return is related to the degree to which the return is characterized by a continued dependence on the parents. The greater the children's financial dependency and the lower their educational attainment, the greater the parent–child strain. Furthermore, parents' satisfaction with the living arrangement is positively related to their child's self-esteem, possibly because low self-esteem signals difficulty in assuming independent adult roles. These findings suggest that parents are most satisfied with the parent–child relationship when they perceive their children as assuming the normative roles of adulthood (Etaugh, 2008; Swartz, 2009). To find out more about experiences during the empty nest period, try Get Involved 8.2.

RELATIONSHIPS IN THE LATER YEARS

As women get older, they experience several changes in their family relationships. Earlier in the chapter, we saw that marriages may end as a result of divorce or a spouse's death. Bonds with siblings often become stronger as one gets older. In addition, new life enters the family in the form of grandchildren and great-grandchildren. Role reversal often occurs as aging women become caregivers for their even older parents. In this section, we will explore these changes.

GET INVOLVED 8.2
Women's Experiences During the Empty Nest Period

Interview two midlife women whose children have left home. Choose any women available to you, such as relatives, neighbors, classmates, and the like. However, if possible, select one woman whose last child left home within the year and another whose children have been gone for several years. Ask each to (1) identify any positive and/or negative experiences; (2) indicate any changes in her employment role (e.g., started a new job, increased her work hours), community service, and/or leisure activities as a result of her children's departure; and (3) indicate whether she perceives these changes as primarily positive or primarily negative.

WHAT DOES IT MEAN?

1. How would you characterize the experiences of your two interviewees? Did they mention more positive or negative experiences? How do their experiences compare to the empty nest experiences in the text?

2. What changes, if any, did they make in their life roles? How did they feel about these changes?

3. Were there any differences in the experiences of the woman whose children recently left home and the woman whose children left years earlier? If yes, how do you explain these differences?

4. Do you think the empty nest experiences of these midlife women will differ from the future experiences of today's young adults? Why or why not?

Siblings

Sisters and brothers play a unique role in the lives of older people, drawing on the shared experiences of childhood and most of the life span (Aldwin et al., 2010; Chambers et al., 2009). Feelings of closeness and compatibility among siblings increase throughout the course of adulthood and are generally strong in later life (Aldwin et al., 2010; Conger & Little, 2010). Types of sibling support vary across ethnic groups, with Blacks and Latinas/os relying more on siblings for practical assistance than do their White counterparts (Bedford, 1995; Conger & Little, 2010). Relationships with sisters are emotionally closer than those with brothers, and the bond between sisters is particularly close (Conger & Little, 2010; Galambos et al., 2009; Voorpostel et al., 2007). Older adults who have close relationships with their siblings are more likely to have high morale, a sense of emotional security, and a lower incidence of depression than those who do not (Chambers et al., 2009; Thomas, 2010). Older rural women have higher life satisfaction if they simply have a sister living nearby, regardless of the amount of contact they have (Bedford, 1995).

The closeness of the sibling bond in later life is illustrated in the following comment:

> *I have two sisters who live upstairs. People are always surprised that we get along so well, living in the same house. My sisters never go out without coming by to ask me if they can get me anything. We weren't always like that. We were too busy with our own lives. Now we try hard to help each other.*
>
> (a 70-year-old widow, in Doress-Worters & Siegal, 1994, p. 134)

Adult Children

Women are typically described as the family **kinkeepers**, *those who maintain the bonds between and within generations.* Their adult children are more apt to confide in them than their fathers (Kalmijn, 2007; Laursen & Collins, 2009; Sarkisian & Gerstel, 2008). Adult daughters maintain closer ties to their parents than do sons, and unmarried daughters tend to have more intense ties to their parents than married daughters (Fingerman & Birditt, 2011; Sarkisian & Gerstel, 2008). During adolescence, the mother–daughter relationship is often characterized by both closeness and emotional conflict. Closeness typically increases once the daughter leaves home to attend college (Smetana et al., 2004). Adult daughters continue to have more harmonious relationships with their mothers than with their fathers (Connidis, 2010; Swartz, 2009). The close ties between grown daughters and their mothers, as shown in surveys of older women and their middle-aged daughters (Fingerman, 2003; Lefkowitz & Fingerman 2003; Miller-Day, 2004), are characterized by satisfying interactions, a history of little conflict, few control issues, and many opportunities for informal contact. In the words of four mothers:

> *She has been awfully good to me in every way, when I'm sick and when I'm well, when I'm in a good humor and when I'm in a bad humor.*
>
> *I can reason with [my daughter] and she understands me. We just sit down and talk it over. We never have an argument. Not that we're perfect, but it's just not necessary.*
>
> *We go for lunch. We go shopping . . . I may go three or four days or a week and not see her, but we talk. I feel like that starts my day.* (all three quotes from Blieszner et al., 1996, pp. 13–18)
>
> *She tells me about her work and sometimes her problems, which includes me in her world. It makes me happy.* (Fingerman, 2003, p. 60)

Although some older Americans live with their adult children, they strongly prefer living alone in their own home even when in declining health (Connidis, 2010; Older Women's League, 2006). Most would rather have "intimacy at a distance" than live with relatives (Chambers et al., 2009). Three-quarters of older parents do, however, have an adult child living within a half-hour drive, and 40 percent of adult children see a parent at least once a week (Swartz, 2009). Older women who live alone report high levels of psychological well-being and appear to be doing as well as, or even better than, older women who live with a spouse (Michael et al., 2001). Informal and formal caregiving systems in the community contribute to this well-being by enabling older persons to remain at home longer. When the informal system of family, friends, and neighbors cannot meet their needs, older individuals turn to the services of organizations and professionals, such as Meals on Wheels, van service for the disabled, home aides, and visiting nurses (OWL, 2006).

Nearly one in ten older men and two in ten older women reside with their adult children, siblings, or other relatives (Etaugh, 2008), usually because of increasing infirmity. Living with or close to an adult child is more prevalent among ethnic minority older people than among Whites in the United States, and this living arrangement is also common in developing countries (Bongaarts & Zimmer, 2002; Dorius & Wray-Lake, 2008; Goldner & Drentea, 2009; Pew Research Center, 2010c). (For a closer look, see Explore Other Cultures 8.2.)

In the United States, older Asian Americans are most likely to live with their children and other relatives, followed by Blacks and Latinas/os. Whites are least likely to live with their children (Bianchi et al., 2008; Federal Interagency Forum, 2009). As we saw earlier, older ethnic minority women play key roles in their family networks by providing economic, social, and emotional support to their adult children and grandchildren. Black households are often organized around women, with older women at the center. Males are more directly involved in Latina/o and Native American households and families. Still, women in these groups enjoy greater prestige, respect, and domestic authority as they grow older (Armstrong, 2001; Padgett, 1999).

EXPLORE OTHER CULTURES 8.2
Living Arrangements of Older Women and Men

In the United States, nearly half of all women aged 75 and older live alone, in contrast to about one-fifth of men in the same age category. Looked at another way, close to 80 percent of all U.S. adults aged 75 and over who live by themselves are women (He et al., 2005). Figures for Canada and Great Britain are comparable to those for the United States, and a similar pattern is found in most other developed countries. In most Asian countries, however, the situation is quite different. About 75 percent of older women and men live with relatives, many of them in three-generation households (Koropeckyj-Cox & Call, 2007; Ofstedal et al., 2003). Multigenerational families also remain common in the southern European countries of Italy, Greece, and Spain (Billari & Liefbroer, 2008) and in rural parts of Eastern Europe, including Russia,

Poland, and Romania. Even so, older women in these countries are more likely than older men to live alone (Mercer et al., 2001).

In developing countries, older adults often live with their adult children (Ruggles & Heggeness, 2008). In some of these countries, it is traditional for an older woman to live with her eldest son. This arrangement is commonly found in some African countries and in several Asian nations, including China, India, Pakistan, and Bangladesh (Arnett, 2008; U.S. Census Bureau, International Database, 1997, 1995). We saw in Chapter 7 that these Asian countries place a much higher value on sons than daughters, resulting in abortion of female fetuses and greater neglect of female children. Can you see the link between these practices and the sons' obligation to care for parents in their old age?

Grandchildren

The greatest gift I ever received was my grandmother. My grandmother has been the backbone of my life since I was 18 months old, when I began living with her. My grandmother put her life on hold so that I could become the best I could be.

(Sharoia Taylor, age 16, in AARP, 2004, p. 11)

The stereotyped portrayal of a grandmother is often that of an older, white-haired woman providing treats for her young grandchildren. However, grandmothers do not fit into any one pattern. Although more than 80 percent of Americans and Canadians over age 65 are grandparents (Connidis, 2010), some people become grandparents by the time they are 30. About half of women experience this event before age 50, and some spend half of their lives as grandmothers (Etaugh, 2008; Livingston & Parker, 2010). Nowadays, many middle-aged grandmothers are in the labor force and may also have responsibilities of caring for their older parents (Etaugh, 2008; Hank & Buber, 2009). Thus, they may have less time to devote to grandparenting activities. On the other hand, more grandmothers are taking on the responsibility of raising their grandchildren, as we will see later in the chapter. Grandmothers' involvement with their grandchildren depends on a number of factors, including geographical distance, the grandmother's relationship with her grandchild's parents, the grandmother's physical and mental health, and the mother's employment status (Chambers et al., 2009; Tan et al., 2010).

Earlier in the chapter, we noted that the ties between family generations are maintained largely by women. One example of this is that grandmothers tend to have warmer relationships with their grandchildren, especially their granddaughters, than do grandfathers (Sheehan & Petrovic, 2008). They are also more likely to value time spent with grandchildren (Livingston & Parker, 2010). The maternal grandmother often has the most contact and the closest relationship with grandchildren (Chambers et al., 2009; Lussier et al., 2002; Silverstein, 2008). Children living with a single mother tend to be especially close to their maternal grandmother (Bridges et al., 2007). Moreover, strong relationships with maternal grandmothers may help grandchildren adjust to the divorce of their parents (Henderson et al., 2009). In some parts of the world, the presence of a grandmother may literally spell the difference between life and death for her grandchildren (see Explore Other Cultures 8.3).

PROVIDING CARE AND SUPPORT FOR GRANDCHILDREN. During their grandchildren's infancy and childhood, nearly half of the grandparents in the United States and Europe provide the children's parents with considerable emotional support, information, help with child care and household chores, and, to a lesser degree, financial support (Hank & Buber, 2009; Livingston & Parker, 2010; Mutchler & Baker, 2009). For example, almost one-third of all preschoolers whose mothers work or are in school are looked after by their grandparents, usually a grandmother (J. Lee, 2007; U.S. Census Bureau, 2010d). Some baby-boomer grandmothers (such as Claire and her sister) are retiring or taking time off from their careers to become nannies for their grandchildren (Alexander, 2004; J. Lee, 2007). The grandmother's role in lending economic, social, and emotional support for her children and grandchildren is more active in many ethnic minority groups than among Whites. For example, Black and Latina/o grandparents are more likely than White grandparents to care for their grandchildren while the children's parents are at work (Connidis, 2010). Native American, Latina and Black grandmothers are significant figures in the stability and continuity of the family (Haxton & Harknett, 2009; Johnson et al., 2003; Nadeem & Romo, 2008; Pittman, 2007). In one study of low-income multiracial Hawaiian children who had an absent or incapacitated parent, the nurturance and guidance of grandparents was a key factor in the children's well-being as they grew

EXPLORE OTHER CULTURES 8.3
Grandmothers: The Difference Between Life and Death

According to researchers (Coall & Hartwig, 2011; Opie & Power, 2008; Sear & Mace, 2008), grandmothers have helped ensure the survival and fitness of their grandchildren since prehistoric times. These women, no longer reproductively active themselves, are able to invest their energies in providing for the physical and psychological health of grandchildren and other young relatives. Kristen Hawkes (2010) studied the present-day Hadza hunter-gatherers of Northern Tanzania and found that older women gather more edible plant foods than any other members of the group. Nursing Hadza women, unable to provide for their older children while tending their infants, rely not on their mates but on these postmenopausal women relatives—their mothers, aunts, or older cousins—to

make sure that the older children are well fed. The presence or absence of a grandmother often makes the difference between life or death for grandchildren in other subsistence cultures as well (Coall & Hertwig, 2011). Anthropologists Rebecca Sear and Ruth Mace (2008) found that in rural Gambia, the presence of a maternal grandmother increased the survival rate of her toddler grandchildren. However, the presence of a paternal grandmother (the father's mother) made no difference in the children's survival. Even more surprisingly, the presence of the father didn't either! Similar results have been found in parts of rural India and Japan as well (Angier, 2002). Why do you think the role of the maternal grandmother is especially important?

to adulthood (Werner, 2010; Werner & Smith, 2001). Similarly, research in the United States and the United Kingdom has found that close, supportive relationships with grandparents are linked with better mental health in adolescents and young adults raised in single-parent families (Attar-Schwartz et al., 2009; Ruiz & Silverstein, 2007). But even in two-parent, middle-income families, grandmothers' involvement is related to children's positive social adjustment (Barnett et al., 2010).

For some children, grandparents are part of the family household. In the United States, the number of grandparents living in homes with grandchildren has doubled since 1970 to 6.2 million in 2007 (U.S. Census Bureau, 2010c). Some of the increase results from an uncertain economy and the growing number of single mothers, which has sent young adults and their children back to the parental nest (Baker & Mutchler, 2010). In other cases, older adults are moving in with their adult children's families when they can no longer live on their own. New immigrants with a tradition of multigenerational households have also swelled the number of such living arrangements (Navarro, 2006). The arrangement benefits all parties. Grandparents and their grandchildren are able to interact on a daily basis. The grandparents often assume some parenting responsibilities, which makes it possible for young single mothers to stay in school (Gordon et al., 2004; Navarro, 2006). In some cases, living with a single mother and a grandmother is associated with improved cognitive outcomes for the child (Dunifon & Kowaleski-Jones, 2007).

RAISING GRANDCHILDREN.   Increasing numbers of grandparents now find themselves raising their grandchildren on their own. Of the 6.2 million grandparents living in a household with a grandchild, over 40 percent *are raising their grandchildren without a parent present*. Nearly two-thirds of these **skip-generation parents** are grandmothers (U.S. Census Bureau, 2010c). Grandparents become full-time caregivers for their grandchildren for a number of reasons: parental illness, child abuse or neglect, substance abuse, psychological or financial problems, divorce, incarceration, and military deployment (Connidis, 2010; Dorius & Wray-Lake, 2008; Lumpkin, 2008; Patrick & Goedereis, 2009). In some developing countries, parents migrate to urban areas to work, while grandparents remain behind and raise the grandchildren (Yardley, 2004). The AIDS epidemic has also increased the number of grandparents who are raising grandchildren in many nations, including the United States (Altman, 2006; Baker & Mutchler, 2010; Parker & Short, 2009). Children reared by their grandparents fare well relative to children in families with one biological parent. They also show little difference in health and academic performance relative to children raised in traditional families (Thomas et al., 2000).

The belief that caregiving grandmothers are primarily poor ethnic women of color is a myth. Parenting grandmothers can be found across racial and socioeconomic lines (Edwards & Sterne, 2008). Over half of the grandparents raising grandchildren are White, 24 percent are Black, 19 percent are Latina/o, 3 percent are Asian American, and 2 percent are Native American (U.S. Census Bureau, 2010c). Black women who are raising their grandchildren, compared to White women, report feeling less burdened and more satisfied in their caregiving role, even though they are generally in poorer health, dealing with more difficult situations, and dealing with them more often alone (Pruchno, 1999).

Rearing a grandchild is full of both rewards and challenges (Erbert & Alemán, 2008; Patrick & Godereis, 2009; Swartz, 2009). Although parenting a grandchild is an emotionally fulfilling experience, there are psychological, health, and economic costs. A grandmother raising the young child of her troubled adult daughter may concurrently feel ashamed of her daughter; anxious about her own future, health, and finances; angry at the loss of retirement leisure; and guilt about her own parenting skills (Erbert & Aleman, 2008; Linsk et al., 2009). Moreover, grandparents primarily responsible for rearing grandchildren are more likely than other grandparents to suffer from a variety of health problems, including depression, diabetes, high blood pressure, heart disease, and a decline in self-rated physical and emotional health. Furthermore, they tend to delay seeking help for their own medical problems (Linsk et al., 2009; Lumpkin, 2008; Patrick & Godereis, 2009; Silverstein & Giarusso, 2010; Umberson et al., 2010).

Grandparents raising grandchildren are often stymied by existing laws that give them no legal status unless they gain custody of the grandchild or become the child's foster parents. Each of these procedures involves considerable time, effort, and expense. Yet, without custody or foster parent rights, grandparents may encounter difficulties in obtaining the child's medical records, enrolling the child in school, or becoming eligible for certain forms of financial assistance (Sumberg, 2007). For example, the welfare grant that a low-income grandmother collects on her grandchild's behalf is only a fraction of what she would receive if she were to become the child's foster parent (Bernstein, 2002). In most instances, grandchildren are ineligible for coverage under grandparents' medical insurance, even if the grandparents have custody (Ellin, 2004a). In some cases, states ignore the significant expenditures made by caretaker grandparents when calculating the grandparents' eligibility for Medicaid ("Grandparents Raising Grandchildren," 2002). Consequently, many grandparent caregivers face significant financial challenges (Patrick & Godereis, 2009).

Parents

Although more women are becoming caregivers of their grandchildren, others are providing care for their aging parents, spouses, or other relatives (Kahn et al., 2011). Nearly half of all caregivers of the older people are daughters. Daughters-in-law and granddaughters play a substantial role as well (Connidis, 2010; National Alliance for Caregiving, 2009).

The older caregiver may herself have some health problems ("Characteristics and Health," 2007; Godfrey & Warshaw, 2009; Older Women's League, 2006) and is facing her own aging. The sight of her parent becoming more frail and dependent may conjure up a frightening and saddening vision of what is in store for her. Older daughters sometimes feel angry and guilty at the sacrifices involved in looking after a parent (Connidis, 2010).

My grandmother lived to be almost one-hundred-and-two years old, and my mother cared for her until she was ninety-seven and had to go into a nursing home. Now my mother obviously feels it is her turn, which it is. I am the real problem here, for I have led a very active life and cannot seem to adjust to this demanding and devastating situation. I am almost overcome with the inevitable guilt at my resentment and anger.

(a 72-year-old woman, in Doress-Worters & Siegal, 1994, p. 208)

Ethnic minority groups provide more care for aging family members than Whites do, possibly as a result of strong cultural norms of filial responsibility among these groups, as well as financial considerations (Goldner & Drentea, 2009). Among Asian Americans, 42 percent care for older relatives, compared to 34 percent of Latinos/as, 28 percent of Blacks, and 19 percent of Whites (AARP, 2001).

We have been discussing older women's relationships with family and friends. To explore this topic on a more personal level, try Get Involved 8.3.

GET INVOLVED 8.3
Interview With Older Women

Interview two women aged 65 or older. It is helpful, but not essential, if you know your respondents fairly well. You may interview your mother, grandmothers, great-aunts, great-grandmothers, and so on. Keep a record of your respondents' answers to the questions given here. Compare and contrast the responses of the two women.

1. What is one of the nicest things to happen to you recently?

2. How would you describe your relationship with your children?

3. Do you have any sisters and brothers? How would you describe your relationship with them?

4. What do you like about being a grandparent? (if applicable)

5. What types of activities do (did) you enjoy with your grandchildren?

6. Tell me about your best friends and the kinds of things you enjoy doing together.

7. What do you like about your current living situation?

8. What do you dislike about it?

9. In general, what are your feelings on nursing homes?

10. How do you feel about the life you've led?

11. As an experienced woman, what tidbit of wisdom could you pass on to me?

WHAT DOES IT MEAN?

1. How would you characterize the relationships of your interviewees with their adult children? Do they appear to be closer to their daughters than to their sons? If so, why?

2. What kinds of relationships do your interviewees have with their grandchildren? Have either or both participated in child care activities with their grandchildren? How do their experiences compare to those reported in the text?

3. Were there any differences in the relationships of these women with their sisters as compared to their brothers? If yes, how do you explain these differences?

4. How does the discussion in this chapter help you understand your respondents' attitudes toward their current living situation and toward nursing homes?

Summary

FRIENDSHIPS

- Girls' friendships are more intimate than those of boys. Girls tend to have a few close friendships whereas boys have larger, less intimate friendship groups.
- Both college women and men like to talk to their friends about the other gender. However, women's conversations more than men's focus on interpersonal issues.
- Emotional closeness is important to the friendships of both heterosexual and lesbian women but is more central to women's than men's friendships.
- Gender socialization and heterosexual males' perceived connection between emotional closeness and homosexuality are two explanations for the gender difference.
- Friendships among older women enhance physical and mental health.

ROMANTIC RELATIONSHIPS

- Heterosexual women are more likely than heterosexual men to value a romantic partner's financial stability and less likely to place importance on physical attractiveness. Similarly, lesbian women put less emphasis on physical attractiveness than gay men do.
- Heterosexual and gay men put more emphasis on the physical attractiveness of a potential partner than heterosexual and lesbian women.
- Middle-aged women are more likely than middle-aged men to be dissatisfied with their appearance.
- Romantic relationships are commonly characterized by traditional gender-related behaviors and roles. When there is a power imbalance, the male is generally viewed as the more powerful partner.
- The age when adolescents start to date has decreased.
- Many dating behaviors are strongly gender-stereotypical.

- Men are more likely than women to perceive nonsexual behaviors, such as a female asking out a male, as indicative of sexual interest.
- Current dating trends include development of urban "partnering markets," online dating services, speed-dating, and dating among older singles.

COMMITTED RELATIONSHIPS

- Most women and men marry, but the age of marriage has gone up in recent years.
- High levels of marital satisfaction are related to problem-focused coping strategies, similarity of goals, values, and attitudes, and good communication.
- Marital satisfaction decreases when children are born and increases when they leave home.
- Women and men who are married are happier and healthier than their unmarried counterparts.
- More men than women are married in later life.
- Cohabiters who do not intend to marry tend to be less satisfied with their relationships than married individuals.
- Married couples who previously cohabited are more likely to get divorced. This might be accounted for by a selection effect.
- Most lesbians are in committed, egalitarian, sexually exclusive relationships. Although many experience stressors not encountered by heterosexuals, they are similar to their heterosexual counterparts in their relationship satisfaction.
- Older lesbians in committed relationships provide each other with a mutual support system and shared economic benefits.

SINGLE WOMEN

- About 40 percent of U.S. marriages end in divorce.

- Divorce is associated with stressors for both women and their children.
- Despite initial emotional problems, both women and children tend to effectively adjust.
- Divorced women are generally less depressed than those in unhappy marriages.
- Employment and social support help women cope during the postdivorce period.
- Single women report mixed feelings about being unattached. Some regret the absence of a steady partner, some are satisfied living alone, and some become involved in romantic relationships. Many are highly involved in social networks of relatives, friends, and neighbors.
- Single women have skills in independent living and in building support systems.
- Women are more likely than men to be widowed but are much less likely to remarry.
- Reaction to widowhood depends on several factors including age, degree of forewarning of the spouse's death, and financial and social resources.
- Loss of a same-sex partner may be very stressful.

MOTHERHOOD

- The good mother stereotype can lead to mothers being blamed and mothers' self-blame if something goes wrong or if the mothers deviate from the ideal stereotype.
- Many single mothers face financial problems. Social support, as well as extended and augmented families, can help single mothers cope.
- Lesbian and heterosexual mothers are similar in mothering style and adjustment. Children reared in lesbian and heterosexual families are similar in their psychological and social adjustment and their sexual orientation.
- Most women report positive feelings about the "empty nest" period. Women who were employed during the childrearing years find it easier to relinquish the parental role.

RELATIONSHIPS IN THE LATER YEARS

- Feelings of closeness among siblings increase during adulthood, and the sister–sister bond is especially strong.
- Older women generally have positive relationships with their adult daughters.
- Unmarried older adults, most of whom are women, prefer living alone. Living with an adult child is the least popular choice, especially among Whites.
- The closeness of the grandparent–grandchild relationship depends on many factors.
- More grandparents than ever live in multigeneration households, particularly in ethnic minority groups.
- Increasing numbers of grandmothers are rearing their grandchildren.
- Growing numbers of older adults, especially women, are caregivers of their parents.

Key Terms

dating scripts *177*
cohabitation *180*
selection effect *181*
motherhood mandate *189*

feminization of poverty *190*
extended families *190*
augmented families *190*
empty nest period *192*

kinkeepers *194*
skip-generation parents *197*

What Do You Think?

1. The text discusses several negative consequences of the strong emphasis placed by men on a romantic partner's appearance. What kind of societal changes might contribute to a de-emphasis on physical attractiveness in romantic attraction?

2. Letitia Peplau (1998) contends that research on lesbian and gay couples can help dispel biased stereotypes. What are some common stereotypes about lesbian couples? How can scientific research be made public and accessible so that these stereotypes can be altered? Do you think there should be an attempt to eradicate these stereotypes as well as other unfavorable attitudes? Explain your answer.

3. Gail Collins (2009) and Amy Richards (2008) contend that there has been a resurgence of praise for women who give up their careers for full-time motherhood. Do you agree? If so, how can society reconcile the contradictory assumptions that full-time motherhood is desirable for middle-class mothers, but that poor mothers should combine employment with parenthood? How do you think people react to middle-class mothers who choose to continue their employment? How do they react to fathers who opt for full-time parenting? Explain your answers.

4. What are the advantages and disadvantages of grandparents rearing their grandchildren?

5. Are older widows better off living alone? With family members? In a retirement community? Why?

6. More single women are deliberately choosing to have and rear children on their own. Are they being selfish? Explain your answer.

If You Want to Know More

Amato, P. R., Booth, A., Johnson, D. R., & Rogers, S. J. (2007). *Alone together: How marriage in America is changing*. Cambridge, MA: Harvard University Press.

Chambers, P., Allan, G., Phillipson, C., & Ray, M. (2009). *Family practices in later life*. Bristol, UK: Policy Press.

Coontz, S., Raley, G., & Parson, M. (Eds.). (2008). *American families: A multicultural reader*. New York: Routledge.

DePaulo, B. (2006). *Singled out: How singles are stereotyped, stigmatized, and ignored, and still live happily ever after*. New York: St. Martin's Press.

Engels, R., Kerr, M., & Stattin, H. (Eds.). (2007). *Friends, lovers, and groups: Key relationships in adolescence*. West Sussex, UK: Wiley.

Fincham, F. D., & Cui, M. (Eds.). (2011). *Romantic relationships in emerging adulthood*. New York: Cambridge University Press.

Goldberg, A. E. (2010). *Lesbian and gay parents and their children: Research on the family life cycle*. Washington, DC: American Psychological Association.

Hayslip, B., & Kaminski, P. (Eds.). (2008). *Parenting the custodial grandchild: Implications for clinical practice*. New York: Springer.

Kinser, A. E. (2010). *Motherhood and feminism*. Berkeley, CA: Seal Press.

McAdoo, H. P. (2007). *Black families*. Thousand Oaks, CA: Sage.

Morrissette, M. (2008). *Choosing single motherhood: The thinking woman's guide*. New York: Houghton Mifflin.

Neff, M. (2009). *From one widow to another: Conversations on the new you*. Chicago, IL: Moody.

Regan, P. C. (2008). *The mating game: A primer on love, sex, and marriage* (2nd ed.). Thousand Oaks, CA: Sage.

Thornton, A., Axinn, W., & Xie, Y. (2007). *Marriage and cohabitation*. Chicago, IL: University of Chicago Press.

Websites

Lesbian Mothers
Lesbian Mothers Support Society
http://www.lesbian.org/lesbian-moms/

Living Arrangements
Senior Living Alternatives
http://www.senioralternatives.com/

Caregiving
National Alliance for Caregiving
http://www.caregiving.org

Grandparents
http://www.aarp.org/relationships/grandparenting/
http://www.grandparents.com/gp/home/index.html

CHAPTER 9

Education and Achievement

Women's Educational Goals, Attainments, and Campus Experiences
    Educational Goals
    Educational Attainments
    Campus Climate

Women's Work-Related Goals
    Career Aspirations
    Career Counseling
    Work–Family Expectations
    Work–Family Outcomes
    Salary Expectations

Influences on Women's Achievement Level and Career Decisions
    Orientation to Achievement
    Personal Characteristics
    Sexual Orientation
    Social and Cultural Factors
    Job-Related Characteristics

You might recall from the opening vignette in Chapter 1 that when Judith applied to graduate school in 1965, she was told that several psychology graduate programs had higher admission standards for women than for men. The unofficial explanation for this discriminatory practice was the need to limit the number of female students because they were more likely than men to drop out of graduate programs for marriage and/or childrearing. This view that women would or should not pursue both family life and a career also was evident in the comment of a male graduate student who asked why Judith wanted a Ph.D. given that she hoped to marry and have children. Similarly, when she did get married, a female cousin suggested she give up her Ph.D. aspirations and become a mother instead.

    This perceived dichotomy between career and family might seem strange today. The cultural milieu has changed dramatically since the 1960s. Today, the majority of college women want to have it all—both a career and a family (Hoffnung, 2004).

In this chapter, we first examine females' educational goals, attainments, and college experiences. Next, we explore young women's career aspirations, issues related to career counseling, and women's plans regarding coordination of their careers with family life. Finally, we turn to influences on their career choices.

WOMEN'S EDUCATIONAL GOALS, ATTAINMENTS, AND CAMPUS EXPERIENCES

As we discuss in more detail in Chapter 10, men earn higher salaries than women and are more likely to hold leadership positions in domains such as politics, and professions (U.S. Census Bureau, 2010c). Do these discrepancies indicate, as some have suggested, that women, compared to men, place a lower value on education and have a lower level of educational attainments? In this section, we examine women's educational goals, attainments, and experiences on the college campus.

Educational Goals

Research (Frank et al., 2008; Massey et al., 2008; Mello, 2008; Perry & Vance, 2010; Sax, 2008; Wang & Pomerantz, 2009) shows that across ethnicities, adolescent girls endorse higher educational and occupational goals than do boys. For example, Judith Kleinfeld (2009) interviewed high school seniors, differing in ethnicity and social class, about their future plans. Regardless of social class, female students were more apt than males to have well-developed plans to attend college, based on their view that education is a crucial investment toward pursuing an occupation that would allow them to contribute to society. Middle-class males, in contrast, saw college as just the expected path, which would provide a job with a good income. Most working-class males did not view college as necessary for their future success and did not plan on attending.

Let us now look at how women's educational goals translate into educational attainments.

Educational Attainments

In the United States, 93 percent of females and 90 percent of males graduate from high school (U.S. Census Bureau, 2010c). Until the mid-1980s, men earned the majority of bachelor's degrees each year, but since 1985, women have surpassed men (Snyder & Dillow, 2010). As of 2009, women earned 53 percent of all bachelor's degrees (King, 2010). Some critics view this situation as a "boy crisis" in education. For more on this issue, see Learn About the Research 9.1.

You can see in Table 9.1 that within each ethnic group, women obtain the majority of associate's, bachelor's, master's, and doctoral degrees. Asian American, Black, and Latina women earn half or more of professional (e.g., medical, dental, law) degrees. Both doctoral and professional levels of education have experienced a dramatic change in the participation of women in the past few decades. For example, in 1965, women obtained only 12 percent of doctoral and 4 percent of professional degrees (U.S. Census Bureau, 2003b), compared to the 2007–2008 figures of 54 percent and 50 percent, respectively. Today, women earn more than three-fourths of degrees in veterinary medicine and nearly three-fourths of degrees in pharmacy, formerly male-dominated fields. They also earn nearly half of law and medical degrees (Snyder & Dillow, 2010).

LEARN ABOUT THE RESEARCH 9.1
Is There a "Boy Crisis" in Education?

Girls, nowadays, are more likely than boys to do well in school, graduate high school, and get college degrees. Some critics in the United States, Canada, Europe, and Australia suggest that as girls have progressed, boys have fallen behind (Kanner & Anderson, 2010; Leathwood & Read, 2009). A few even claim that there is a "boy crisis" or a "war against boys" in which resources have been lavished on female students at the expense of male students (Benjamin, 2010; Rosin, 2010; Tyre, 2008; Whitmire, 2010). Some colleges are pushing hard to recruit more male students, even going so far as giving men "special consideration." Jennifer Delahunty Britz, dean of admissions and financial aid at Kenyon College, refers to this as "the dirty little secret of admissions." She and others note that some outstanding female applicants are being denied entrance to top colleges, whereas males with lesser credentials are admitted (Kahlenberg, 2011; Whitmire, 2007; Wilson, 2007a,b).

Two studies (AAUW, 2008b; Mead, 2006), however, cast serious doubt on the existence of a boy crisis in education. The studies used data from the National Assessment of Educational Progress, a survey of student achievement in the United States since 1971, as well as SAT and ACT college entrance exam scores, and other measures of educational achievement. Both studies find that, in the words of study-author Sara Mead, "the real story is not bad news about boys doing worse; it's good news about girls doing better" (Mead, 2006, p. 3). Boys actually are scoring higher on standardized tests and achieving more than ever before. But girls have improved their performance even more. The same is true of college enrollments, which are on the rise for both sexes. Once again, women's enrollment rates are increasing faster than men's.

Some groups of boys *are* falling behind, particularly African American and Latino boys and boys from low-income families (Langhout & Mitchell, 2008). The gender gap is greatest among low-income students of all races but disappears among students whose families are at the top of the economic ladder (AAUW, 2008b; Espenshade & Radford, 2009; King, 2010; Mead, 2006). In fact, a recent nationwide study found that high-income men of all races are slightly *more* likely than high-income women to be in college (King, 2010). The results from these studies suggest that social class is a better predictor of school success than is gender. Several writers note that the educational crisis among low-income, ethnic minority boys will not be solved by blaming the preponderance of female teachers at the lower grades, or educational reforms that allegedly favor girls' learning styles. These reforms, including better trained teachers and more co-operative, group-oriented and hands-on learning approach, help both boys and girls learn (Kimmel, 2008). In addition, teaching boys skills that will better prepare them for classroom success will help them in learning to pay attention, listening, and cooperating with peers (Basow, 2008; Brown, 2006; Jacobson, 2006).

WHAT DOES IT MEAN?

1. Why do you think women's college-going rates are exceeding those of men?
2. Sara Mead, author of one of the studies discussed here, states that "the idea that women might actually surpass men in some areas . . . seems hard for many people to swallow. Thus, boys are routinely characterized as falling behind even as they improve in absolute terms" (2006, p. 3). Do you agree or disagree with this statement? Support your answer.
3. What can be done to ensure that all students have the education and opportunities they need to realize their potential?

TABLE 9.1   Degrees Conferred by Ethnicity and Gender, 2007–2008

Type of Degree	Asian Americans		Blacks		Latinas/os		Native Americans		Whites	
	Women	Men	Women	Men	Women	Men	Women	Men	Women	Men
Associate's	59%	41%	69%	31%	61%	39%	66%	34%	61%	39%
Bachelor's	55	45	66	34	61	39	61	39	56	44
Master's	54	46	72	28	64	36	66	34	62	38
Doctorate	57	43	68	32	56	44	56	44	53	47
Professional	56	44	63	37	53	47	48	52	48	52

Source: Snyder and Dillow (2010).

This high level of educational attainments by women is, unfortunately, more true of able-bodied women than of women with disabilities. Women with disabilities also have less education than men with disabilities and are less likely to graduate from high school or attend college (Beckles & Truman, 2011; Nosek, 2010). Furthermore, they are less likely than males with disabilities to receive occupationally oriented vocational training that can provide them with the skills needed in the job market (Schur, 2004). Not only must students with disabilities cope with physical barriers in educational settings (e.g., access to buildings, availability of appropriate instructional materials), but they also must contend with isolation, prejudice, and discrimination (Nosek, 2010; Olkin, 2010).

So far, we have been discussing educational attainments of girls and women in the United States. In developing societies, many girls are unable to attend school at all, or attend for just a few years before they drop out (Burn, 2011; Henderson & Jeydel, 2010). For a closer look at this serious problem, see Explore Other Cultures 9.1 and 9.2. Then read What You Can Do 9.1 to learn how you can help promote education of girls worldwide.

EXPLORE OTHER CULTURES 9.1
Educating Girls Worldwide: Gender Gaps and Gains

What is the state of education for girls around the world? Studies in developing and developed nations (Grant & Behrman, 2010; Hausmann et al., 2009) report both good news and bad news. The good news is that between 1985 and 2009, access to education improved worldwide. For example, nearly two-thirds of countries studied now have no gender gap at the primary school level (Grant & Behrman, 2010).

The bad news is that several countries still have serious gender gaps, with 16 million fewer girls than boys in primary school (Kristof & WuDunn, 2009). Gender disparities are greatest in South Asia, the Middle East, and sub-Saharan

Africa, where male literacy rates far surpass those of females (UNICEF, 2011; UNIFEM, 2010). In most countries, girls from poor families are less likely to attend school than those from wealthier households (Kristof & WuDunn, 2009; Leathwood & Read, 2009). In Africa and Latin America, increasing numbers of unmarried girls are dropping out of school because of unplanned pregnancy or forced early marriage (Davis, 2011). School policies often require the expulsion of pregnant girls. Another reason that girls leave school earlier than boys is to work the land. In Africa, girls and women do 80 percent of the agricultural work, although they own just a small fraction of the farmland (Smith, 2005;

UNIFEM, 2010). Moreover, the AIDS epidemic in Africa is forcing many girls to leave school to support the family and care for the sick (see Chapter 12).

Educating girls has many benefits. The more years of education, the fewer, healthier, and better educated are their subsequent children. Empowering women through literacy also enhances their voice in family affairs and reduces gender inequality in other areas (Burn, 2011; Henderson & Jeydel, 2010). How can girls' enrollment in school be increased? Strategies (Davis, 2011; Hausmann et al., 2009; Kristof & Wudunn, 2009; Nussbaum, 2010) include the following:

Build more schools, especially in rural areas of developing countries.

Lower families' costs of educating daughters by providing stipends or even free lunch.

Educate parents about the importance of educating daughters as well as sons.

Provide programs to prevent teenage pregnancy.

Encourage teen mothers to stay in school.

Attach day-care centers to schools to look after young children, allowing their older sisters to attend school.

Provide toilets and menstrual supplies at schools.

Provide flexible school hours.

Recruit more female teachers.

Campus Climate

Julie Zeigler arrived at Duke University in 2003 to work on a doctorate in physics. Instead, she left in 2004 with only a master's because of a hostile atmosphere towards women that female graduate students and faculty say has existed for years. These women report that male physicists have kissed and grabbed them, ignored them, refused to take them seriously and greeted their comments and questions with hostility.

(Wilson, 2004a)

The gender biases in elementary and high school (Chapter 4) continue into college and graduate school. Female students often experience a **chilly climate** in the classroom and elsewhere on campus, in which *faculty members, staff, or students display different expectations for women students, or single them out or ignore them* (Betz, 2008; Vaccaro, 2010). Some faculty members use sexist language,

EXPLORE OTHER CULTURES 9.2
The Oppressive Educational Climate Under Taliban Rule

In 1996, the ultraconservative Taliban regime took over in Afghanistan, promptly banning education for girls and women. This was a severe blow in a country where fewer than 20 percent of women can read compared to a literacy rate of 50 percent for males (Burn, 2011). For the five years of Taliban rule, almost no females saw the inside of a classroom, although some courageous women secretly taught small groups of girls in their homes, and some girls were home-schooled by their parents (Dominus, 2002). With the end of Taliban rule, women and girls eagerly flocked back to the classroom, despite attempts by Islamic militants to damage or destroy some of their schools (Henderson & Jeydel, 2010). Yet even in the "new" Afghanistan, the educational picture still is far from rosy. Because a rise in banditry and rape has made roads unsafe even in daylight, many girls do not dare go to school. In addition, Taliban attacks on girls' schools have escalated and hundreds of schools have been closed down (Burn, 2011; Henderson & Jeydel, 2010). Some Afghan families go as far as to disguise a daughter as a boy so that she can more easily receive an education and work outside the home (Nordberg, 2010).

WHAT YOU CAN DO 9.1
Promote Education of Girls Worldwide

A number of organizations are devoted to helping girls in developing countries obtain an education. Two of them are Girls Global Education Fund (ggef.org) and Camfed International (us.camfed.org). Contact one of these organizations and see how you can help.

tell sexist jokes, suggest that women are less able to learn the material, ignore women's comments, or focus on women's appearance and sexuality rather than their intellectual competence. Eventually, this chilly atmosphere can negatively affect women's feelings of self-worth and confidence. The impact may be even greater for ethnic minority women, sexual minority women, and women with disabilities. These women may be the target of blatant sexist, racist, homophobic, and other prejudicial acts, such as placing signs on residence hall room doors that bar members of certain groups. Or they may experience more *subtle forms of humiliation and bias* called **microaggressions**. These can include sexual or racist humor, social exclusion, or making assumptions about intelligence on the basics of race or sex (Bush et al., 2009; Morrison, 2010; Sue et al., 2009).

The chilly climate for women is another reflection of the gender inequality of power in North American society. Sexist treatment of women on campus, whether blatant or subtle, reflects a greater value attached to males and serves to maintain an already existing power imbalance. Furthermore, this treatment reinforces constructions of women as inferior or less valued than men.

THE ACADEMIC ENVIRONMENT FOR WOMEN OF COLOR. Some women of color experience primarily White campuses as occasionally unwelcoming and unsupportive (Winkle-Wagner, 2009). Some Black and Latina female students have reported instances in which they were ignored, devalued, and assumed to be less intelligent by their peers or professors (Navarro et al., 2009; Panter et al., 2008; Winkle-Wagner, 2009; Zambrana & MacDonald, 2009). The only Black female in a business class with White male students commented that when the class made a group presentation, "I was kind of ignored . . . whenever there was a question or something like that . . . It is hard to feel competent with them like that" (Winkle-Wagner, 2009; p. 117).

Stereotype threat (discussed in Chapter 5 in relation to women) can also seriously affect the college experience of students of color. According to this view, students of color must deal with the possibility that their poor performance will confirm the inferiority of their ethnic group. In an attempt to feel less vulnerable, they may downplay the importance of achievement to their self-esteem.

Another problem for some students of color is that they experience the individualism prominent in academic life as inconsistent with the collectivistic values of their culture. The individualistic value system of Western, primarily North American and European, cultures emphasizes personal achievement, independence, and individual uniqueness. The collectivistic values of Asian, Native American, and Latina/o cultures, on the other hand, stress the importance of the group, including the family, the community, and the work team. The competitive style of college education can be uncomfortable for these students. Native Americans, for example, have difficulties adjusting to the competitive climate (Canabal, 1995). As one Native American college senior stated, "When I was a child I was taught certain things, 'don't stand up to your elders,' 'don't question authority,' 'life is precious,' 'the earth is precious,' 'take it slowly,' 'enjoy it.' And then you go to college and you learn all these other things and it never fits" (Canabal, 1995, p. 456).

Although the clash between individualism and collectivism can produce conflicts for some students, Angela Lew and her colleagues (Lew et al., 1998) note that these value systems can coexist.

These researchers found that some Asian American students adopted both sets of values, viewing individual achievement as a way to fulfill both personal and family goals. Lew and her associates suggest that internalization of both value systems can help the student to function effectively in two different cultural environments. Of course, it may be easier for some students than for others to integrate and reconcile the disparate sets of values.

THE ACADEMIC ENVIRONMENT FOR WORKING-CLASS AND POOR WOMEN.   Research on working-class and poor women's adjustment to college life is very limited. One interesting study (LePage-Lees, 1997) of high-achieving women from working-class or poor families found that many of these women felt they had to hide their backgrounds from others in order to achieve during undergraduate and graduate school. These women also felt that other students were better prepared and more intelligent. One respondent said, "People now think the only issue is ethnicity, and I still think that economic level is an important issue regardless of ethnicity. Economics doesn't explain everything but it explains a lot" (p. 380).

As Erika Kates (2007) points out, low-income women with young children who decide to improve their lives through higher education face numerous challenges as they cope with limited finance, child care responsibilities, and juggling job and school schedules. The story of Pauline illustrates the obstacles and the ultimate benefits. This Black woman attended college at age 17 but dropped out after falling in love. After having three children, she was deserted by the children's father. Once her youngest child was in child care, she began community college as a welfare recipient. Pauline successfully overcame several obstacles, completed college, and found a job in her town's school department (Kates, 1996, p. 550).

SINGLE-SEX INSTITUTIONS.   Given the existence of an uncomfortable climate on some mixed-gender campuses, it is not surprising that scholars have been studying the benefits of single-sex high school and college environments for women's academic and personal development.

Some educators believe that women's colleges provide a more effective educational environment for female students.

The 54 women's colleges operating today in the United States are among the more ethnically and socioeconomically diverse liberal arts colleges, providing generous financial aid packages to underserved groups of women (Calefati, 2009). Women's high schools and colleges provide more leadership opportunities for women students, higher achievement expectations for them, and more female role models within the faculty and administration (Mansfield, 2011; Women's College Coalition, 2008). Students at women's colleges have higher career goals, participate more actively in class, collaborate more frequently with other students, both in and out of class, and report higher levels of support than women at co-educational schools (Kinzie et al., 2007; Massey et al., 2008). Other benefits of women's high schools and colleges are the greater likelihood of close student–faculty relations, increased self-confidence and self-esteem, and less sexism (Mansfield, 2011; Pankake, 2011; Salomone, 2007). Also, women's college graduates are more likely than graduates of mixed-gender institutions to pursue male-dominated fields, such as the physical sciences and mathematics, to reach high levels of achievement in their careers and, for both reasons, to earn higher salaries (Reid & Zalk, 2001; Wolf-Wendel et al., 2000).

Use the survey in Get Involved 9.1 to assess the academic climate on your campus.

WOMEN'S WORK-RELATED GOALS

In an address to the graduating class of a women's college, feminist author Gloria Steinem noted a major difference between the goals of her generation of female college graduates in 1956 and those of young women today: "I thought we had to marry what we wished to become. Now you are becoming the men you once would have wanted to marry" (Goldberg, 1999, p. G3). This quote suggests that college women are striving for, and attaining, high-achievement goals and are no longer

---

GET INVOLVED 9.1
Does Your Campus Have a Hospitable Environment for Women?

Answer the questions presented here and ask three female students the same questions. If possible, select interviewees who vary in ethnicity, physical ability/disability, and/or sexual orientation.

1. Did you ever hear a professor tell a sexist or racist "joke" during or outside of class?

2. Did you ever hear a professor make a derogatory comment about a student's gender, ethnicity, physical disability, or sexual orientation? If yes, indicate the nature of that comment.

3. Do you feel that women and men receive the same degree of encouragement and support from their instructors? If not, explain.

4. Do you feel that women of color, women with disabilities, and sexual minority women receive the same degree of encouragement and support from their instructors as White, able-bodied, heterosexual women? If not, explain.

WHAT DOES IT MEAN?

1. Did you find any evidence of bias against women based on sex, ethnicity, disability, or sexual orientation? If yes, do you think these experiences affect the education process of students who are targets of these behaviors? Why or why not?

2. Did you find any evidence of differential support for students because of their gender, ethnicity, physical ability, or sexual orientation? If yes, do you think this can affect the educational process of students who receive less support? Explain.

living vicariously through the accomplishments of their husbands. In the following section, we discuss women's career aspirations and some differences in the career goals of females and males.

Career Aspirations

There are few differences in the career aspirations of women with and without disabilities (DeLoach, 1989) and among women of different ethnicities (Fouad & Byars-Winston, 2005). However, there is some evidence that Black college women expect success more than White women do (Ganong et al., 1996). In addition, Asian American college women are more likely than White college women to aspire toward male-dominated and more prestigious occupations (Leung et al., 1994). One explanation is that although Asian culture values traditional gender roles, Asian American families encourage their daughters to pursue nontraditional prestigious occupations associated with social recognition (Leung et al., 1994).

As we have seen, high school girls and college women generally have higher educational and career aspirations than their male counterparts (Perry & Vance, 2010; Snyder & Dillow, 2010). Some women, however, lower their aspirations during high school and college; major in less prestigious, often female-dominated, career fields; and, therefore, eventually end up in lower-level careers (Betz, 2008; Frome et al., 2008; Paludi, 2008a). Let us take a closer look at factors that influence young women's career aspirations.

Women are more likely to seek and earn degrees in academic disciplines that focus on people, such as education, psychology, and health sciences (Evans & Diekman, 2009; Kessel & Nelson, 2011; Su et al., 2009) (see Table 9.2). Interestingly, girls who believe in the altruistic value of math and science have more interest in, and more positive attitudes toward, these fields than do other girls (Weisgram & Bigler, 2006). What might account for this? One explanation is that, as we saw in Chapter 4, girls are socialized toward communal behaviors. Consistent with the social construction of women as caring and nurturant, they are encouraged to develop a strong interest in and

TABLE 9.2   Bachelor's, Master's, and Doctoral Degrees, 2007–2008, in Selected Fields by Gender

Educational Field	Bachelor's Degree		Master's Degree		Doctorate	
	Women	Men	Women	Men	Women	Men
Biological/life sciences	60%	40%	58%	42%	51%	49%
Business and management	49	51	45	55	40	60
Computer and information sciences	18	82	27	73	22	78
Education	79	21	77	23	67	33
Engineering	18	82	23	77	21	79
English	68	32	67	33	64	36
Health professions	83	17	81	19	64	36
Mathematics	44	56	43	57	31	69
Physical sciences	41	59	38	62	30	70
Psychology	77	23	80	20	73	27
Social sciences and history	49	51	51	49	43	57
Visual and performing arts	61	39	58	42	51	49

Source: "The Nation: Student Demographics" (2010).

concern for other people, and as a consequence, they develop career and life goals that focus on communion and caregiving (Evan & Diekman, 2009).

Table 9.2 also shows that relatively few female students aspire toward the high-paying fields of computer and information sciences, engineering, and physical sciences. Even those qualified college women who venture into these science and engineering areas are more likely than college men to drop out of these programs (Ceci & Williams, 2010; Hartman & Hartman, 2008; Koput & Gutek, 2011). Moreover, whereas men tend to stick with their science and engineering studies if their grades are average, women do so only if they earn high grades (C. C. Miller, 2010).

What accounts for women's continued low participation rate in these academic areas? As we saw in Chapter 5, the possibility that females are less mathematically or scientifically skilled can be ruled out. We also noted in that chapter that parents and teachers are less likely to encourage the development of math or science skills in girls than boys. We saw that gender differences in attitudes toward and interest in science emerge early with girls becoming less confident of their ability to do math and science (Betz, 2008). In fact, many college women perceive themselves as "different" from individuals in science fields (Cheryan & Plaut, 2010). In addition, stereotypes of scientists as "nerds" who are obsessed with technology, but who have little interest in people, conflict more with the gender roles of women than of men (Cheryan et al., 2009; C. C. Miller, 2010; Selwyn, 2007; Stross, 2008). So it is not surprising that women who are interested both in science and in helping others tend to avoid engineering in favor of the biological and medical sciences (Newcombe et al., 2009). Moreover, female students who do choose to major in math, science, and engineering report higher levels of discrimination than either women in female-dominated majors—such as arts, education, humanities, and social sciences—or men in any major (J. Steele et al., 2002). Such negative experiences may lead to expectations of discriminatory hiring and promotion practices in these fields, causing some women to reconsider their career choices (Messersmith et al., 2008). The dearth of female role models and insufficient faculty encouragement may be other factors that play an important role in steering women away from careers in the sciences (AAUW, 2010). Indeed, when bright female college students have female professors in math and science courses, they do better in their classes and are more likely major in science or math (Carrell et al., 2009).

Career Counseling

During the 1950s and 1960s, women were largely invisible to career counselors because women were not viewed as interested in pursuing careers (Betz, 2008). Starting in the 1960s and 1970s, career counselors tended to steer girls and women toward traditionally female careers (Farmer, 2006). Although there is now much greater acceptance of females' pursuit of traditionally male occupations, some counselors, teachers, and parents continue to show gender-biased attitudes toward career choices. Many girls are discouraged from taking advanced math and science courses or from choosing high-status professions dominated by males (Fassinger & Asay, 2006). Gender bias also permeates vocational interest inventories and aptitude testing (Lonborg & Hackett, 2006).

What can career counselors do to support, encourage, and expand the career aspirations of young women? Nancy Betz (2008) suggests that counselors should help women in the following areas: (1) advocating for family–friendly work policies, such as flex time; (2) locating support systems and mentors; (3) encouraging husbands or partners to participate fully in housework and child care; (4) developing effective cognitive and behavioral coping strategies; and (5) obtaining necessary education, training, and job-hunting skills. Career counselors also need to become aware and understand that both women's and men's views and needs are shaped by culture, ethnicity, social class, sexual orientation, and ableness (Gysbers et al., 2009; Hook & Bowman, 2008; Kosciulek, 2009).

Work–Family Expectations

> *My plan is to get a job after graduate school and hopefully marry. After a few years of establishing myself in my career, I plan to have two children. After a short maternity leave, I plan to work part time, and hope my husband will too, so one of us can always be home. When I told my boyfriend this, he said he hasn't even considered how to balance work and family, and he was astonished that my plans for the future are all mapped out.*

(Erika, a 21-year-old college senior)

The vast majority of college women nowadays desire marriage, motherhood, and a career. For example, in Michele Hoffnung's (2004) survey of senior women at five different American colleges, 96 percent planned to have a career, 86 percent planned to marry, and 98 percent planned to have children. If you are interested in both employment and parenthood, have you considered how you would like to combine these? Research shows that most college women, like Erika, want to work before they have children and interrupt their employment for some period during their children's early years (e.g., Bridges & Etaugh, 1996). The majority of male students, however, are like Erika's boyfriend and are much less likely to think about connections between career and family goals (Betz, 2008; Friedman & Weisbrod, 2005; Konrad, 2003).

Although most college women want to interrupt their employment for childrearing, Black college women want to discontinue their employment for a shorter period of time than White women do. For example, Judith and Claire found that Black women want to return to employment when their first child is approximately 2 years old, whereas White women want to delay employment until their child is approximately 4 (Bridges & Etaugh, 1996).

Why do Black college women prefer an earlier return to employment after childbirth? For one thing, their own mothers return to work sooner after child birth than do mothers of White college women (Hoffung, 2004). This finding is consistent with Black women's long history of combining the roles of mother and provider (Boushey, 2009). The earlier return to work of Black mothers may account for the fact that their college-going daughters are less likely than White college women to believe that continuous maternal employment produces negative outcomes for children, such as low self-esteem, feelings of neglect, and lack of maternal guidance (Bridges & Etaugh, 1996). Similarly, Audrey Murrell and her colleagues (Murrell et al., 1991) found that college-educated Black women had a stronger work orientation and a more intense commitment to professional goals than White women. Along these same lines, evidence suggests that college-educated Black women are more likely than their White counterparts to be encouraged by their parents to consider an occupation as essential to success (Higginbotham & Weber, 1996). Together, this body of research indicates that employment may be a more integral aspect of Blacks' construction of women's roles than it is for Whites.

Some educated women of color face another role-related problem: finding an appropriate mate within one's ethnic group. For example, Black college women express the desire to marry a person of equal or greater educational and occupational status. However, because they earn a higher proportion of every type of higher education degree than Black men, they may be frustrated in this desire (Clark et al., 2011).

Work–Family Outcomes

In the previous section, we saw that the great majority of college women expect to "have it all": career, marriage, and motherhood. How do these expectations relate to actual career and family outcomes? In order to explore this question, Michele Hoffnung (2004) surveyed some women as college seniors and again seven years later.

Career remained the major focus for the women throughout their 20s. Not quite half had married, and most had not yet started a family. Marital status was unrelated to educational attainment and career status seven years out from college graduation. The few women who had become mothers, however, had fewer advanced degrees and lower career status than other women. They typically chose more traditional careers that took less time to train for, such as teacher or physical therapist. These women also held more traditional attitudes toward women's rights, roles, and responsibilities and were more likely to come from families with lower socioeconomic status.

In college, women of color had lower expectations for marriage than White women did, and in fact, they were less likely to be married seven years later. Their educational attainments were equal to those of White women and their careers had higher status. These findings are consistent with research we looked at in the previous section suggesting that college-educated women of color have very high career motivation (Bridges & Etaugh, 1996; Murrell et al., 1991).

Salary Expectations

Consistent with a tendency to have less prestigious career aspirations than men do, women expect lower salaries in their jobs. However, even among students majoring in the same field, women have lower salary expectations than men (Taylor, 2007). What might account for this? One possibility is that women know that females earn lower salaries than males and base their own salary expectations accordingly (Williams et al., 2010). Another possibility is that women lower their salary expectations because they place importance on making accommodations in their jobs to fulfill their family obligations (Heckert, 2002). A third possibility is that women are more likely than men to underestimate their worth (Ellin, 2004b) (see Chapter 10).

INFLUENCES ON WOMEN'S ACHIEVEMENT LEVEL AND CAREER DECISIONS

Although this chapter focuses on women's education and achievement, it is essential to note that achievement goals can be satisfied in diverse ways. Raising a well-adjusted and loving child, providing emotional and physical support to a spouse recovering from a stroke, and helping the homeless in one's community are only a few of the numerous forms achievement can take that are independent of education and occupation. However, despite the diversity of achievement directions, researchers have focused primarily on the traditional areas of education and occupation, and if one defines achievement in this manner, it appears that women have achieved less than men. As we noted at the beginning of this chapter, more men than women, aspire to the most prestigious careers, and hold high positions within their occupational fields. Now we examine possible internal and external influences on women's achievement levels and occupational decisions. First, we look at their orientation to achievement in general and the personal traits that might be related to their career decision making. Then, we explore social and cultural influences on young women's educational and occupational pursuits.

Orientation to Achievement

For several decades, psychologists attempted to explain women's lower achievement compared to men's as due, in part, to their orientation to achievement.

ACHIEVEMENT MOTIVATION.   One explanation was that females' **achievement motivation**, that is, their *need to excel,* was lower than males'. However, early studies by David McClelland and others on which this conclusion was based used a male-biased theoretical framework. Achievement was defined primarily in ways applicable to men's lives and emphasized competition and mastery in such areas as school, jobs, and sports. But as we have seen, achievement can also occur in other domains, such as the personal or interpersonal areas (Mednick & Thomas, 2008).

At the present time, researchers believe that women and men are similarly motivated to achieve (Hyde & Kling, 2001). However, gender socialization practices of families, peers, teachers, and others teach youngsters not only the importance of achievement but also the "gender-appropriate" direction it should take. For example, girls tend to learn that, if they have children, they should be the primary caregiver. Consequently, they may adjust their achievement goals in order to meet this expectation.

FEAR OF SUCCESS. Another view of women's lower achievement in comparison to men's came from Matina Horner (1972), who proposed that women want to achieve but have a **fear of success**, that is, *a motive to avoid situations of high achievement.* Horner contended that women were concerned about the negative social consequences that can result from success, especially social rejection and loss of femininity. This suggestion might seem strange as you read this book in the twenty-first century. However, in the 1970s and 1980s, this idea was embraced by many scholars who studied females' fear of success.

To test her concept of the fear of success, Horner devised the following statement: *After first-term finals, Anne/John finds herself/himself at the top of her/his medical school class.* She asked college women to write a paragraph about Anne and college men to write about John. Approximately two-thirds of the women wrote negative stories with themes such as Anne's physical unattractiveness, her inability to have romantic relationships, rejection by her peers, and her decision to transfer into a less prestigious occupation. Most of the stories told by the men about John, on the other hand, reflected positive outcomes.

Although Horner believed these results indicated a motive to avoid success on the part of women, subsequent research points to a different conclusion. It now appears that these stories did not reflect women's fear of high-achieving situations in general, but rather their awareness of negative consequences that can occur when individuals violate gender stereotypes. Medicine, especially in the 1970s when Horner performed her study, was strongly dominated by men. Thus, it is likely that females' negative stories reflected their concern about the problems individuals face in gender-atypical occupations, rather than their desire to avoid a high level of achievement (Hyde & Kling, 2001). Later studies showed that both women and men wrote negative stories about a successful woman in medicine *and* a successful man in nursing (Engle, 2003). Years of subsequent research on this topic have failed to find reliable gender differences in fear of success (Mednick & Thomas, 2008). Consequently, psychologists today do not believe that women's lower level of educational or occupational achievement can be accounted for by their fear of success.

ACHIEVEMENT ATTRIBUTIONS. A third explanation given for gender differences in levels of achievement is that females and males make different **achievement attributions**, that is, *explanations about their good and poor performance.* In general, people are *more likely to attribute positive performance to their own internal traits, such as their ability or effort, whereas they tend to attribute negative performance to external causes, such as task difficulty or bad luck.* This **self-serving attributional bias**, like self-esteem (see Chapter 4), is linked to healthy psychological adjustment and happiness (Mezulis et al., 2004). In other words, taking responsibility for good performance (e.g., "I did well on the test because I know the material"), but attributing poor performance to external factors (e.g., "I failed the test because it was unfair"), enables a person to maintain a good self-image. On the other hand, the reverse pattern—blaming yourself for failure and not taking credit for your successes—could lead to an unwillingness to persevere in a challenging situation and to low self-esteem.

A meta-analysis by Amy Mezulis and her colleagues (2004) shows that females, but not males, show a marked decline in the self-serving attributional bias starting in early adolescence. (Reread the section on self-esteem in Chapter 4, and note the similar, and possibly related, decline.) These gender differences in attributions of performance are small, however (see review by Mednick & Thomas, 2008), and are associated with the type of performance situation. For example, in male-stereotyped domains, such as mathematics, males attribute success to ability more than females do, but in female-stereotyped domains, such as languages or English, the reverse pattern occurs (Beyer, 1997; Birenbaum & Kraemer, 1995). Similarly, women are more likely to blame their lack of ability for failing a math test than for failing a verbal test, whereas men show the reverse tendency (Kiefer & Shih, 2004).

ACHIEVEMENT SELF-CONFIDENCE.   Another internal barrier that has been used to explain women's lower achievement in comparison to men's is their lower self-confidence. Many studies show that males are more self-confident in academic situations than females. For example, even though girls get higher grades in school than boys (Buchanan & Selmon, 2008), they tend to underestimate their grades, as well as their overall intelligence, and class standing whereas boys tend to overestimate theirs (Furnham et al., 2006; Smith, 2006; Steinmayr & Spinath, 2009; Wigfield et al., 2006). Mary Crawford and Margo MacLeod (1990) also found that when asked why they don't participate in class discussion, college women's responses reflected questionable confidence in their abilities, such as "might appear unintelligent in the eyes of other students" and "ideas are not well enough formulated" (p. 116). Men's reasons, on the other hand, focused on external factors, as in "have not done the assigned reading" or participation might "negatively affect [their] grade" (p. 116). Other research suggests that even among high achievers in the sciences, fewer women than men believe their scientific ability to be above average (Sonnert & Holton, 1996).

Females do not show lower levels of confidence in all situations, however. Studies indicate that females' confidence is lower than males' in male-linked tasks, such as mathematics, and spatial skills but is higher in female-linked tasks, such as reading and English, arts and music, and social skills (Byrne, 2008; Nagy et al., 2008; Steinmayr & Spinath, 2009; Watt, 2004; Wigfield et al., 2006). Females' confidence is also higher when performance estimates are made privately rather than publicly (e.g., Daubman et al., 1992). Research (Daubman & Sigall, 1997; Heatherington et al., 1993) suggests that in some situations, what appears to be lower self-confidence (e.g., publicly predicting lower grades for oneself) might really reflect women's desire to be liked or to protect others from negative feelings about themselves.

CONCLUSION.   Early conclusions that women have lower aspirations than men because they are not as highly motivated to excel and because they fear the negative consequences of success have not been supported. Although some evidence exists for gender differences in achievement attributions and self-confidence, these differences are not observed in all situations. Furthermore, as is the case with all types of psychological gender differences, the differences are small and do not apply to all females and males. Thus, most social scientists point to other factors to help explain different career aspirations and attainment levels of women and men.

Personal Characteristics

Are personal characteristics related to women's career aspirations? The answer is "yes." For example, women who work full time are more likely to support egalitarian roles for women than are women who work part time (Cunningham et al., 2005). Also, women who choose male-dominated careers are more likely than those who pick female-dominated careers to be competitive, autonomous, and instrumental and to have less traditional gender attitudes and more liberal social and political attitudes (Betz, 2008; Martin, 2008b; Sax & Bryant, 2006).

Another factor related to career choice is the individual's **self-efficacy**, that is, *the belief that one can successfully perform the tasks involved in a particular domain*. Individuals with high self-efficacy for a particular field are more likely to aspire toward and succeed in that field as a career (Sax & Bryant, 2006; Stern, 2008; Wigfield et al., 2006). For example, although females tend to have lower self-efficacy in mathematics and science than males (Betz, 2008) (see Chapter 5), those women who select and persist in careers in science or engineering have high self-efficacy for mathematics (Larose et al., 2008). Furthermore, females, compared to males, have higher self-efficacy for health-related professions and other female-dominated, skilled labor occupations such as social work and teaching. These gender differences, in turn, correspond to differences in occupational choices.

Sexual Orientation

Many lesbians and bisexual women become aware of their sexual identity during late adolescence or adulthood (Glover et al., 2009), at the same time that they are selecting a career. The overlap of these two processes can influence career development (Hook & Bowman, 2008; Lippa, 2008; Lyons et al., 2010). Sexual minority women might put career selection on hold as they explore their sexuality and intimate relationships (Bieschke & Toepfer-Hendey, 2006; Lyons et al., 2010). Also, as a result of coming out, many lose the family support that can be beneficial to the career-selection process.

In addition, lesbians' career choices might be directly affected by their perception of the occupational climate for lesbians and gay men. Whereas some sexual minority individuals select occupations they perceive as employing large numbers of lesbians and gay men in order to experience an environment in which there is safety in numbers, those who are closeted or anxious about their sexual identity might avoid these occupations (Colgan et al., 2008; Croteau et al., 2008; Hook & Bowman, 2008).

On the positive side, Fassinger (1995) notes that lesbians tend to be less traditional in their attitudes about gender than are heterosexual women. Consequently, they tend to consider a broader range of occupational options and are more likely to choose jobs in male-dominated fields (Peplau & Fingerhut, 2004). These jobs, as we shall see, pay more than jobs in the female-dominated areas.

Social and Cultural Factors

Although some individual characteristics are related to individuals' career choices, career decisions are made within a sociocultural context in which the attitudes of significant people and the values of one's culture contribute to career selection as well. Support and encouragement from parents are very important for women of all ethnicities (Betz, 2008; Fouad & Kantamneni, 2008; Hanson, 2007; Hellerstein & Morrill, 2011; Li & Kerpelman, 2007). Parental support and availability influence career aspirations and achievements in Black (Hanson, 2007; Higginbotham, 2009; Jackson & Dorsey, 2009), Native American (Juntunen et al., 2001), and Latina (Ojeda & Flores, 2008) women. High-achieving Black and White women report receiving considerable family support for pursuing highly prestigious careers and being strongly influenced by their families. For example, a Black female scientist commented, "I was always encouraged to do the things I wanted to do and was told by my grandmother that I could be whatever I wanted to be if I committed myself to it and did not lose my focus on the objective" (Hanson, 2007, p. 25). A same-sex parent often has the greatest effect on career expectations and outcome of adolescents (Schoon et al., 2007; Whiston & Keller, 2004). One longitudinal study of female high school seniors, for example, found that attachment to the mother contributed to high career aspirations five years later (O'Brien et al., 2000). Another longitudinal study showed that mothers' high expectations for their 10-year-old daughters predicted the latter's earnings in adulthood (Flouri & Hawkes, 2008). Among female college students, those with plans for a nontraditional career are more likely than other women to have a highly educated mother with a nontraditional career and parents who support their career choices (Schoon et al., 2007; Whiston & Keller, 2004).

In addition to social support, cultural values play a role in women's career development. According to McAdoo (in Higginbotham & Weber, 1996), many Black families believe that college education and professional attainments are family, as well as individual, goals. Moreover, there is evidence that high-achieving Black women who move up from their working-class backgrounds feel a sense of obligation to their families. In one study (Higginbotham & Weber, 1996), almost twice as many Black as White upwardly mobile women expressed this sense of familial debt. A Black occupational therapist said, "I know the struggle that my parents have had to get me where I am. . . . I feel it is my responsibility to give back some of that energy they have given to me" (p. 139).

Another cultural value shown by Black women is their concern for their communities. Many successful Black women are committed to ending both sexism and racism in the workplace and community (Jackson & Dorsey, 2009) and using their achievements to inspire and mentor other people of color (Osborne, 2008; Robinson & Nelson, 2010). As expressed by a high-ranking Black female city official, "Because I have more opportunities, I've got an obligation to give more back and to set a positive example for Black people and especially for Black women. I think we've got to do a tremendous job in building self-esteem and giving people the desire to achieve" (Higginbotham & Weber, 1996, p. 142). Similarly, many Latina adolescents from working-class families realize that their parents work long hours at multiple, dead-end jobs. They aspire to fulfilling careers that will allow them to create better lives for themselves and their families, and that will also enable them to make a positive contribution to their community (Marlino & Wilson, 2006). Many high-achieving Latina women receive family encouragement and have a supportive social network. However, some experience a conflict between traditional, cultural values that guide them toward family-oriented goals and other socialization factors that encourage high educational and career attainments (Flores et al., 2006; Gomez et al., 2001).

Conflicting values are also evident in the experiences of educated Native American women (McCloskey & Mintz, 2006). Although research on Native Americans' achievement goals is sparse, it suggests that family and community members sometimes try to discourage Native women from attending college. Consequently, those who persist in seeking a college education may feel they are going against their culture (Kidwell, in LaFromboise et al., 1990).

To more directly learn about family and cultural influences on women's career goals, perform the interviews described in Get Involved 9.2.

In addition to cultural variations across ethnic groups, values associated with social class can influence career decisions. According to Constance Flanagan (1993), working-class families, who hold more traditional gender attitudes than middle-class families, also see less value in academic achievement. Thus, working-class women who have an interest in school and a willingness to be independent of their families are likely to become invested in employment immediately after high school, whereas middle-class women with those attributes are apt to seek higher education.

GET INVOLVED 9.2
Family and Cultural Values About Education and Career Goals

Interview two female students who vary in ethnicity. Select your interviewees from any two of the following ethnic groups: Asian American, Black, Latina, Native American, and White. Inform them you are exploring connections between women's family and cultural values and their education and career goals.

First, ask each respondent to indicate her college major, career goal, and expected educational attainment (i.e., highest educational degree). Second, ask her to evaluate the degree to which her family's values support her specific educational aspirations and career goals. Third, ask her to evaluate the degree to which her specific educational aspirations and career goals were influenced by her ethnic or national cultural values.

WHAT DOES IT MEAN?

1. Did you find any differences among respondents in the extent to which they received support from their families? If yes, refer to information presented in the text or to your own ideas and explain these differences.

2. Did your respondents report that their goals were influenced by their values? Is the information you obtained consistent with the material presented in the text? If not, explain the discrepancies.

Job-Related Characteristics

Individuals vary in the benefits they want from working in a particular job, and these benefits can play a role in guiding career selections. Research shows that college women and men differ little in the importance they place on pay, job qualities, or factors related to promotions and job perks (Heckert et al., 2002).

However, women and men differ in the importance they attach to other job-related attributes, which can account for some of the differences in their occupational choices. For high school and college students (Konrad et al., 2000; Staff et al., 2009) and successful women and men (Ferriman et al., 2009; Schwartz & Rubel-Lifschitz, 2009; Su et al., 2009), differences are generally consistent with gender roles and stereotypes. For example, males are somewhat more likely to value material success, earnings, promotions, freedom, risk taking, challenge, leadership, and power. Females are more apt to value interpersonal relationships, helping others, respecting colleagues, working with people, and striking a balance between professional achievement and personal relationships.

Another gender difference in job values is the greater emphasis women place on good, flexible working hours and ease of commuting, especially if they have children (Corrigall & Konrad, 2006; Ferriman et al., 2009; Heckert et al., 2002). This gender difference probably reflects women's belief that mothers should stay home and care for infants, a value that is expressed during many stages of females' lives. For example, twelfth-grade girls who place a high value on having a family-friendly job are more likely to change their career aspirations from male-dominated fields (e.g., science) to female-dominated occupations (Frome et al., 2008).

Regardless of the type of job, women's ratings of the importance of several job characteristics rose during the 1980s and 1990s. These include job security, power, prestige, feelings of accomplishment, task enjoyment, and using one's abilities. It is possible that as gender barriers to opportunity declined, women's aspirations rose to obtain previously unavailable job attributes (Konrad et al., 2000).

Summary

WOMEN'S EDUCATIONAL VALUES, ATTAINMENTS, AND CAMPUS EXPERIENCES

- Across ethnicities, adolescent girls endorse higher educational and occupational goals than do boys.
- Women obtain the majority of associate's, bachelor's, master's, and doctoral degrees, and half of all professional degrees.
- The campus climate can be problematic for some women. They may experience sexism in the classroom, and many perceive the academic environment as hostile and demeaning.
- Women of color, poor women, and women with disabilities experience additional problems on campus.

WOMEN'S WORK-RELATED GOALS

- College women generally aspire to less prestigious careers than college men. Few women decide to enter the physical sciences or engineering.
- Career counselors can do several things to support and expand women's career aspirations.
- Most college women envision their futures as involving employment, marriage, and motherhood. Many plan to interrupt their employment for childrearing.
- Women have lower salary expectations than men. Possible explanations are women's knowledge that females earn less than males, their willingness to accommodate their jobs to their family lives, and their belief that they deserve less.

INFLUENCES ON WOMEN'S ACHIEVEMENT LEVEL AND CAREER DECISIONS

- There is no evidence that women have less motivation to achieve than men do or that women stay away from high-achieving situations because they fear success.
- Gender differences in attributions for performance are very small and are more likely to occur when making attributions in gender-stereotypic domains.
- Women display less self-confidence than men, especially in relation to male-linked tasks and when estimates of one's performance are made publicly.
- Women with nontraditional gender-related traits or attitudes are more likely to aspire toward male-dominated careers.
- Women's feelings of self-efficacy for particular occupational fields are related to their aspirations for those fields.
- Career decisions of sexual minority individuals are sometimes influenced by their perceptions of the job climate for lesbians and gay men.
- Family support and family and cultural values can influence women's career development.
- Job-related characteristics valued more highly by males include a good salary, promotions, and opportunity for advancement.
- Characteristics valued more strongly by females are interpersonal relationships and helping others. However, women in male-dominated occupations highly value masculine-typed job qualities.

Key Terms

chilly climate *207*
microaggressions *208*
achievement motivation *214*

fear of success *215*
achievement attributions *215*
self-serving attributional bias *215*

self-efficacy *217*

What Do You Think?

1. Discuss your opinion about the relative advantages and disadvantages for women of attending a women's college versus a mixed-gender college.
2. This chapter discusses several issues faced by women of color and women with disabilities on college campuses. Select two or three of these concerns and suggest institutional procedures that could address these problems and improve the academic climate for these groups.
3. Many women who desire both employment and motherhood want to interrupt their employment for childrearing. What can explain this? As part of your answer, discuss the extent to which gender differences in power (see Chapter 1) and gender socialization (see Chapter 4) explain this.
4. The traditional conception of achievement as the attainment of high academic and occupational success has been criticized as reflecting the achievement domains of men more than of women. Do you agree with this criticism? Give a rationale for your answer. Also, if you agree, suggest other indices of success that would reflect women's achievement more accurately.
5. Discuss the relationship between gender stereotypes and common career choices of young women and men. Also, several changes have occurred in the educational attainments and career aspirations of women over time. Show how a changing social construction of gender has contributed to this.

If You Want to Learn More

American Council on Education. (2005). *Leadership through achievement: Women of color in higher education.* Washington, DC: Author.

Bonham, G. W. (Ed.). (2006). *Women on campus: The unfinished liberation.* Piscataway, NJ: Transaction.

Ceci, S.J., & Williams, W.M. (Eds.). (2007). *Why aren't there more women in science? Top researchers debate the evidence.* Washington, DC: American Psychological Association.

Grogan, M., & Shakeshaft, C. (2011). *Women and educational leadership.* San Francisco, CA: Wiley.

Leathwood, C., & Read, B. (2009). *Gender and the changing face of higher education: A feminized future?* Berkshire, England: Open University Press.

Maslak, M.A. (Ed.). (2007). *The structure and agency of women's education.* Albany: State University of New York Press.

Papadimitriou, M. (2006). *What girls say about their science education: Is anybody really listening?* Victoria, B.C., Canada: Trafford.

Salomone, R. (2005). *Same, different, equal: Rethinking single-sex schooling.* New Haven, CT: Yale University Press.

Sax, L. J. (2008). *The gender gap in college: Maximizing the developmental potential of women and men.* San Francisco, CA: Jossey-Bass.

Touchton, J. (2008). *A measure of equity: Women's progress in higher education.* Washington, DC: Association of American Colleges and Universities.

Walsh, W. B., & Heppner, M. J. (Eds.). (2006). *Handbook of career counseling for women* (2nd ed.). Mahwah, NJ: Erlbaum.

Watt, H. M., & Eccles, J. S. (Eds.). (2008). *Gender and occupational outcomes: Longitudinal assessment of individual, social, and cultural influences.* Washington, DC: American Psychological Association.

Winkle-Wagner, R. (2009). *The unchosen me: Race, gender, and identity among Black women in college.* Baltimore, MD: Johns Hopkins Press.

Websites

Education

American Association of University Women
http://www.aauw.org

Women with Disabilities

Disabled People's International
http://www.dpi.org

CHAPTER 10

Employment

Women's Employment Rates and Occupational Choices
Employment Rates
Occupational Choices

Gender Differences in Leadership and Job Advancement
Leadership Positions
Barriers That Hinder Women's Advancement
Women as Leaders

Gender Differences in Salaries
Comparative Salaries
Reasons for Differences in Salaries

Women's Job Satisfaction
Gender Differences in Satisfaction
Job Satisfaction of Sexual Minorities

The Older Woman Worker
Employment Rates
Why Do Older Women Work?
Entering the Workforce in Later Life
Age Discrimination in the Workplace

Changing the Workplace
Organizational Procedures and Policies
Strategies for Women

Retirement
The Retirement Decision
Adjustment to Retirement
Leisure Activities in Retirement

Economic Issues in Later Life
Poverty
Retirement Income: Planning Ahead

When I got my offer, I was so thrilled and honored, I accepted my job immediately. I didn't even think to bargain. Maybe we lack self-confidence, so we undersell ourselves. (Martha West, law professor, in Fogg, 2003, p. A14)

When a man leaves, he is getting the golden parachute to enjoy the good life. When a woman leaves of her own accord, they say "Well, she couldn't take the pressure" . . . I'll say the unspoken: A lot of companies are still more comfortable with a White man in the job. (John Challenger, chief executive of Challenger, Gray, & Christman, a Chicago firm that tracks chief executives, in Stanley, A., 2002)

A couple of times in my career, someone would tell me that I couldn't do something. I would just tell myself that I wasn't going to talk to that person anymore, and I went ahead and did it anyway . . . I tell other women that persistence pays, and that if you can't work through a problem, to go around it. (Christine King, chief of AMI Semiconductor, in King & Olsen, 2002)

We're still climbing Mount Everest, and we're maybe halfway up . . . There are pockets [of success], and there always have been. And what's exciting is there are more pockets of success now. (Megan Smith, MIT graduate, former chief executive of a dot-com, now in business development at Google, in Hafner, 2003)

In this chapter, we examine the nature of women's employment. We begin with an overview of how many women work, what kinds of jobs they have, the challenges they face in job advancement and becoming leaders, the salaries they receive, and their job satisfaction. We then focus on the status of older women workers. Next, we consider procedures and policies that can improve the work environment for women. Finally, we turn to retirement and economic issues facing older women.

In our exploration of these topics, we use the terms *employment* and *work* interchangeably, so it is important that we clarify their meaning. According to Irene Padavic and Barbara Reskin (2002), the term *work* refers to *activities that produce a good or a service*. Thus, it includes all sorts of behaviors, such as cooking dinner, mowing the lawn, writing a term paper, teaching a class, fixing a car, volunteering in a nursing home, or running a corporation. The kind of work that we cover in this chapter is employment, that is *work for pay*, a major focus of the lives of women (and men) in terms of both time and personal identity. However, our focus on paid employment does not imply that this form of work is more valuable than other types of productive activities. Society would not function without the unpaid labor that contributes to family and community life.

WOMEN'S EMPLOYMENT RATES AND OCCUPATIONAL CHOICES

What percentage of women are employed? What occupations do they choose? Let's discuss each of these issues.

Employment Rates

Women's labor force participation has increased dramatically in recent decades, especially among mothers of young children. Women now comprise half of the work force (English et al., 2010). Whereas in 1970 only 30 percent of married women with children under age 6 were in the labor force, by 2007 this number had increased to 62 percent (U.S. Census Bureau, 2010b). Among all individuals aged 16 years and older, 59 percent of White and Asian women and 61 percent of Black women are employed compared to 74 percent of White men, 75 percent of Asian men, and 67 percent of Black men (U.S. Census Bureau, 2010b). Women with disabilities have lower employment rates than either men with disabilities or able-bodied women (Banks, 2010; Goodley, 2011; Nosek, 2010), and many are employed in menial jobs (Patwell, 2010). Women with disabilities may confront several barriers in the workplace, including little or no accessible parking or public transportation nearby, inaccessible work environments, and a need for adaptations to workstations (Alexander et al., 2010).

What accounts for the influx of women into the workplace? Several factors have contributed (Cotter et al., 2008). First, the women's movement provided encouragement for women to consider other role options in addition to the homemaker role. Second, women's current higher level of educational attainment (see Chapter 9) has better prepared them for careers that provide greater challenge, stimulation, and a sense of accomplishment. Women with higher levels of education are more likely to be employed and to return to work more rapidly after giving birth (Cebula & Coombs, 2008; England, 2010; Johnson & Downs, 2005). Third, many women must work for financial reasons. Today, few middle-class families can afford home ownership, adequate health insurance, and a middle-class lifestyle on one income (Boushey, 2009). In working-class families, two incomes are often needed to remain above the poverty line (Christensen & Schneider, 2010b).

Currently, two-thirds of women are either the primary or co-breadwinner for their families (AAUW, 2010). Economic necessity is particularly great for women who are single heads of households, and these women comprise more than half of all families living in poverty in the United States (U.S. Census Bureau, 2010c). In 2008, 25 percent of all families with children were headed by an unmarried mother, and 78 percent of these mothers with school age children were employed (U.S. Census Bureau, 2010b). Unfortunately, for poor women who are heads of household, the employment opportunities are greatly limited, and numerous obstacles block the way to employment. Read Learn About the Research 10.1 for an exploration of employment issues for low-income mothers.

Occupational Choices

One way to examine the occupational choices of women and men is to look at the occupations that employ the fewest number of women and those that employ the greatest number of women. The 20 occupations with the lowest percentage of women are in just four major groups, sometimes

---

LEARN ABOUT THE RESEARCH 10.1
Job Retention and Advancement Among Low-Income Mothers

The passage of welfare reform programs in 1996 increased employment rates and reduced poverty rates among poor mothers. However, earning enough to support a family continues to be problematic for these women and their employment options remain limited. A low-wage earner who has left the welfare system may earn too much to be eligible for benefits such as Medicaid and food stamps, yet be too poor to afford health insurance or adequate food. Thus, many former welfare recipients are more financially strapped than before (S. Lee, 2007). In addition, much of the low-income work available occurs in evening or night shifts, creating scheduling and child care problems for families (Crosnoe & Cavanagh, 2010).

In order to understand influences on the job retention and advancement of poor mothers, Sunhwa Lee (2007) studied over 2,600 low-income mothers. Half of these women were White, 25 percent were Black, and nearly 20 percent were Latina.

Over half had never been married, and they had an average of two children.

Nearly 40 percent of the sample worked in service occupations, primarily food, health, and cleaning services. This figure is higher than the overall percentage of women in these occupations. Because these jobs are often of limited duration, pay low wages, provide little opportunity for advancement, and offer limited benefits, they do not readily lead to self-sufficiency.

The study found that having at least some college education, a regular source of child care, and employer-provided health insurance were critical factors for mothers' job retention and advancement. However, two-thirds of the women had neither any college education nor employer-provided health insurance. The author concluded by emphasizing the need for a more comprehensive support system for low-wage women workers to help them more successfully navigate the current employment environment (S. Lee, 2007).

WHAT DOES IT MEAN?

1. How can some of the problems raised by this study be addressed by government, the private sector, educational institutions, or other societal institutions? Be specific.

2. Most of the research on women's achievement and career aspirations has focused on middle-class women. Which factors examined in Chapter 9 are less relevant to the lives of poor women? Explain your answer.

_____

Source: S. Lee (2007).

called "hard hat" occupations: construction; installation, maintenance, and repair; production; and transportation and material moving. The 20 occupations with the greatest concentration of women are similarly clustered in just a few groups, principally health care, office and administrative work, teaching, and caring for young children (U.S. Census Bureau, 2010c).

Occupational segregation has declined considerably in the past 35 years (Leicht, 2008). Women have increased their numbers in both managerial and professional jobs, and now hold half of these positions. However, when women and ethnic minorities hold managerial positions, they tend to be concentrated in positions with lower pay and less authority and are more likely to manage workers of their own sex and ethnicity (Hirsh & Kornrich, 2008; U.S. Department of Commerce, 2011). Moreover, significant differences still remain in the types of occupations pursued by women and men (Gruenfeld & Tiedens, 2010). In 2009, women accounted for over 95 percent of all kindergarten teachers and dental assistants and 92 percent of registered nurses, but only 20 percent of computer programmers and 7 percent of civil engineers (Hegewisch et al., 2010). In addition, although more women have entered the relatively high-paying skilled trades (e.g., as carpenters, plumbers, and electricians), they still comprise less than 3 percent of these workers (Hegewisch et al., 2010; U.S. Census Bureau, 2010b). Women remain segregated in so-called pink-collar fields. About 30 percent of female employees work in just 10 occupations. Most of these are low-status, low-paying service jobs such as secretary, cashier, restaurant server, nursing aide, home health worker, and cook (Eagly & Sczesny, 2009). Thus, the workplace continues to be characterized by significant sex segregation, with men tending to dominate the most high-paying and prestigious occupations such as medicine, engineering, and banking (England, 2010). This situation persists all around the globe (Burn, 2011).

Furthermore, more employers today are cutting costs by hiring part-time or temporary workers, who are paid less and have minimal or no benefits. Women are more likely than men to hold these jobs, whose flexibility may fit well with a woman's family obligations (Christensen & Schneider, 2010b).

The workplace is segregated not only by gender but also by ethnicity. Whites are more likely than Blacks and Latinas/os to hold high-status and high-paying managerial or professional jobs and ethnic minorities are more likely than Whites to hold service jobs (U.S. Census Bureau, 2010c). Immigrant women, regardless of ethnicity, also tend to be employed in low-paying, low-status occupations such as nanny, housekeeper, and farm worker. Their employment, especially in the first two of these jobs, have played a critical role in allowing middle- and upper-income women to participate in the workforce (Echaveste, 2009).

GENDER DIFFERENCES IN LEADERSHIP AND JOB ADVANCEMENT

Nearly half of all law school graduates and nearly half of the new associates in law firms are women. Yet, women represent only 17 percent of partners at law firms.

(O'Brien, 2006)

Half of the students in divinity school now are women. But in the mainline Protestant churches that have been ordaining women for decades, they account for just 3 percent of pastors of large congregations that average over 350 per service . . . Many women clergy call this the stained-glass ceiling.

(Banerjee, 2006)

Women constitute only 17 percent of opinion writers at the New York Times, *10 percent at the* Washington Post, *28 percent at* U.S. News & World Report, *23 percent at* Newsweek, *and 13 percent at* Time. *Overall, only 24 percent of nationally syndicated columnists are women and they tend to be White and right wing.*

(Ashkinaze, 2005)

Leadership Positions

First, some good news. Within the past few years, the U.S. government has registered some historic firsts: first woman House speaker (Nancy Pelosi); first woman to make a serious run at the U.S. presidential race (Hillary Clinton); first Republican woman to run for vice president (Sarah Palin); first Supreme Court to have three female justices (Ruth Bader Ginsburg, Sonia Sotomayor, and Elena Kagan).

But the picture isn't all rosy. In virtually every nation, women are less likely than men to hold positions of authority (Catalyst, 2010; Center for American Women and Politics, 2011; Wood & Eagly, 2010; Yaish & Stier, 2009). For example, although 40 percent of managers in the United States are women (Center for American Women and Politics, 2011), women become scarcer the higher one goes in an organization. Women constitute only 14 percent of Fortune 500 executive officers, 16 percent of board directors of these companies, 17 percent of U.S. senators, 17 percent of congressional representatives, 16 percent of state governors, 23 percent of college and university presidents, and 3 percent of chief executives at Fortune 500 firms. The situation for women of color is even worse (Broadbridge & Hearn, 2008; Catalyst 2010a,b; Center for American Women and Politics, 2011). Although the United States has yet to elect a woman as president, other countries such as Pakistan (Benazir Bhutto), Israel (Golda Meir), India (Indira Gandhi), and Great Britain (Margaret Thatcher) have been elevating women to the role of chief executive for decades (Foster, 2011). In the twenty-first century alone, several women have risen to lead their countries. These include Ellen Johnson Sirleaf of Liberia, Africa's first female president; Michelle Bachelet of Chile, the first woman to lead a major Latin American country; Dilma Rousseff, Brazil's first woman president; and Angela Merkel, the first female chancellor of Germany. In 2010, out of 192 member countries of the United Nations, 8 had female presidents, 9 had women prime ministers, and 3 had queens (Chin, 2010). Out of 145 countries, the United States ranks 69th—tied with Turkmenistan—in women's participation in the lower or single legislative body of the country. Women make up just 17 percent of the U.S. House of Representatives. Sweden is near the top of the list, with 45 percent, whereas Saudi Arabia and Qatar are at the bottom with no women (Inter-Parliamentary Union, 2011). Even in female-dominated fields, such as nursing, social work, and education, *men are likely to earn more and get promoted faster,* a phenomenon known as the **glass escalator** (Harvey Wingfield, 2009; Williams, 2010). For example, over 80 percent of grade school teachers are women, but 85 percent of school superintendents are men (Melendez de Santa Ana, 2008; U.S. Census Bureau, 2010b). While being a **token** (i.e., *a sole representative of one's group*) thus clearly benefits men, it often is disadvantageous for women. The token woman in a male-dominated workplace is often perceived negatively, excessively scrutinized, treated unfairly, and isolated (Clayton et al., 2010; King et al., 2010, Schmitt et al., 2009).

The concept of the **glass ceiling** refers to *invisible but powerful barriers that prevent women from advancing beyond a certain level* (Barreto et al., 2009). One variation on this concept is the "stained glass ceiling" for female clergy (Fiedler, 2010). Another is the "concrete ceiling" for ethnic minority women, in reference to the difficulties these women face in moving into higher positions because of the intersecting effects of sexism and racism (Martin, 2008). Women who do pass through the glass ceiling are more likely than men to be assigned to a **glass cliff** position, which involves *leading a unit that is in crisis and has a high risk of failure* (Bruckmüller & Branscombe, 2010; Ryan et al., 2009). There is also a **sticky floor** in traditional women's jobs, meaning *women have little or no job ladder, or path, to higher positions* (Henderson & Jeydel, 2010). Clerical work and the garment industry are examples of occupations with little room for growth. Furthermore, some women experience a **maternal wall**, in which they *get less desirable assignments, lower salaries, and more limited advancement opportunities once they become mothers* (Faraday-Brash, 2010).

Even the best and brightest women find progress to be frustratingly slow. For example, a recent study of the careers of high-potential graduates from elite MBA programs found that women lagged behind men in advancement and compensation, starting from their first job, and were less satisfied with their careers (Carter & Silva, 2010).

Barriers That Hinder Women's Advancement

What prevents women from reaching positions of leadership? We now turn to the role of mentors, social networks, and discrimination.

MENTORS AND SOCIAL NETWORKS. A **mentor** *is a senior-level person who takes an active role in the career planning and development of junior employees.* Mentors help their mentees develop appropriate skills, learn the informal organizational structure, meet key people, and have access to opportunities that enable them to advance. Consequently, mentoring has positive effects on job satisfaction, promotion, and career success (Cheung & Halpern, 2010; O'Brien et al., 2010). This is especially true for women in male-dominated businesses (Ramaswami et al., 2010).

Women employees may have difficulty in identifying an appropriate mentor. The limited number of women in senior-level positions, especially in male-dominated fields, makes it hard for a woman to find a female mentor (Bernstein et al., 2010). In addition, men may be reluctant to mentor young women for a variety of reasons, including fear of gossip about an affair or a possible sexual harassment suit (Foust-Cummings et al., 2008; Nolan et al., 2008; Paludi et al., 2010).

A second vehicle for advancement that is limited for women and people of color is access to informal social networks (Rayburn et al., 2010). These networks can provide information about job opportunities, informal workplace norms and behaviors, and opportunities to meet important members of the organization (Sabattini & Dinolfo, 2010). Furthermore, they offer social support and can serve as an important step in developing a mentoring relationship with a senior-level person. However, male reluctance to deal

Liberian President Ellen Johnson Sirleaf, Africa's first female president, is shown shortly before receiving the 2007 U.S. Presidential Medal of Freedom in Washington, DC. More women around the world are assuming positions of political power, although their numbers remain small.

with women means women are less likely than men to be invited to informal social events (e.g., golf outings, after-hours drinking group, strip club) or to be included in informal communication networks (Bernstein & Russo, 2008; Fine, 2010; Foust-Cummings et al., 2008; Kolb & McGinn, 2009; Leathwood & Read, 2009). Such social opportunities are especially likely to be lacking for women who work in male-dominated occupations (Koput & Gutek, 2011; C. Taylor, 2010). Women with child care responsibilities right after work also are limited in opportunities for after-hours socializing (Allen, 2004). One way for women to become part of a network is to join local or national organizations such as the National Association for Female Executives or the American Association of University Women (AAUW), attend events, and meet people (Eddleman et al., 2003; Miles-Cohen et al., 2010).

DISCRIMINATION.   Another factor limiting the job advancement of women is sex discrimination, that is, unfavorable treatment based on gender. Such discrimination occurs despite the existence of laws that prohibit using gender (as well as ethnicity, national origin, or age) as a determinant in hiring or in other employment decisions (Crosby, 2008). One factor that influences evaluation of job applicants is the gender dominance of the occupations, with females favored for female-dominated jobs and males favored for male-dominated jobs (Davison & Burke, 2000). In addition, employers are less likely to hire mothers than nonmothers. Fathers, however, are not disadvantaged in the hiring process (Correll et al., 2007). Moreover, gender discrimination in hiring is most likely to occur when little information is provided about the candidate's qualifications. In this case, the applicant's gender is highly salient and can give rise to stereotyped impressions and decisions. However, when the applicant's academic and employment records are presented, these materials strongly influence the evaluator's impressions (Davison & Burke, 2000).

Discrimination also operates after the point of hiring. Recently settled and ongoing lawsuits against major corporations and brokerage firms including Wal-Mart, Morgan Stanley, Merrill Lynch, Boeing, and Novartis reveal major sex and ethnic inequities in pay and promotion (Anderson, 2007; Greenhouse, 2010; Liptak & Greenhouse, 2010; "Novartis," 2010). For example, brokerage firms have been found to take away women's clients and commissions, give them pay cuts and demotions following maternity leave, and assign lucrative accounts to male cronies (Anderson, 2007). A more subtle form of discrimination is **patronizing behavior**, in which *supervisors give subordinates considerable praise while withholding valued resources such as raises and promotions.* Such behavior has a more negative effect on the performance of female workers than male workers (Fiske, 2010a; Nadal, 2010; Sue, 2010).

Gender discrimination is alive and well in higher education as well. For example, among faculty with children, women are less likely than men to be granted tenure (COACHE, 2010). In addition, the more prestigious the university, the fewer women it has on the faculty and in tenured positions (Wilson, 2004b). Those women who do get hired at major research universities often experience discrimination. For example, studies in 1999 and 2002 at the Massachusetts Institute of Technology (MIT), a top science and engineering university, found that women were disadvantaged not only in promotions and salary but also in research grants, appointments to important committees, types of teaching assignments, and even in the size of their research laboratories. Furthermore, not one woman had ever served as head of a science department. As discussed in Chapter 9, these small inequities, or microaggressions, are subtle forms of marginalization that accumulate over time to create an unfair and hostile environment for women (Nadal, 2010; Sue, 2010; Vaccaro, 2010). MIT responded by instituting several steps to improve the status of women faculty. By 2011, the number of women in science and engineering had doubled, pay and other resources were more equitably distributed, and more women were serving in senior leadership positions, including MIT's first woman president.

The downside is a growing perception on campus that correcting earlier biases has meant hiring less qualified women. In addition, letters of recommendation for tenure written for male faculty focus on their intellect, whereas those written for women emphasize their temperament (MIT, 2011).

Experiences of gender discrimination at work are related to more negative relationships with supervisors, and coworkers, along with lower levels of organizational commitment and job satisfaction (Bernstein & Russo, 2008; Bond et al., 2004). For women, perceiving and experiencing discrimination are associated with negative psychological symptoms, such as increased anxiety and depression, and lowered self-esteem. Among men, however, the perception and experience of discrimination are unrelated to well-being (Schmitt et al., 2002).

Let's now look at three factors that help explain why women experience discrimination in the workplace: stereotypes, ingroup favoritism, and perceived threat.

STEREOTYPES. One important factor is the operation of gender stereotypes. The successful manager is seen as having male gender-stereotypic traits, such as ambition, decisiveness, self-reliance, ability to handle stress, and strong commitment to the work role. This "think manager–think male" mindset leads to the conclusion that a woman is less qualified (Billing, 2011; Eagly & Chin, 2010; Rezvani, 2010). Across a wide variety of settings, women are presumed to be less competent than men and less worthy to hold leadership positions (Eagly & Carli, 2007; Mavin, 2008; Ridgeway & England, 2007). A review of studies in the United States, Germany, Spain, Australia, the United Kingdom, China, and Japan reveals that individuals in these nations, especially men, perceive men to be more qualified managers (Burn, 2011). Madeline Heilman's (2001) review of research on leadership in organizations shows that the success of female managers is devalued or is attributed to external factors rather than to the woman's competence. When women are perceived to be as competent as men, they are often viewed as violating gender stereotypes that require women to be communal. As a consequence, people, especially males, often dislike and dismiss the contributions of highly competent women who speak and act decisively and assertively (Ayman et al., 2009; Denmark et al., 2008; Eagly & Sczesny, 2009; Okimoto & Brescoll, 2010). Women are also more negatively evaluated when they adopt less pleasant aspects of masculine style of leadership, that is, an autocratic, angry, punitive, nonparticipative approach (Brescoll & Uhlmann, 2008; Ridgeway, 2011; Tapia, 2008; Wood & Eagly, 2010). In the words of a male corporate vice president, "With a male executive there's no expectation to be nice. He has more permission to be an ass. But when women speak their minds, they're seen as harsh" (Banerjee, 2001). In order to be influential, women therefore must combine agentic qualities such as competence and directness with communal qualities such as friendliness and warmth (Eagly & Carli, 2007; Heilman & Okimoto, 2007).

Racial stereotypes also include attributes that are viewed as not conducive to leadership. For example, Blacks are stereotyped as antagonistic, Latinos/as as unambitious, and Asian Americans as unassertive (Eagly & Chin, 2010). These stereotypes constitute an additional barrier confronting ethnic minority women who aspire to leadership roles.

Unfavorable gender stereotypes of women are most likely to operate when the evaluators are men (Duehr & Bono, 2006; Jackson et al., 2007; Uhlmann & Cohen, 2005). Given that more than half of all managers and administrators are men and that men dominate higher-level management positions, many female workers are evaluated by men and, therefore, face the possibility of similar stereotype-based judgments and decisions. Negative gender stereotypes also are more likely to operate when women perform in a male domain. In such settings, women are less likely than men to be selected as leaders, be promoted, receive positive evaluations for their leadership, or be liked (Ayman & Korabik, 2010; Eagly & Chin, 2010; Heilman & Okimoto, 2007; Kumra & Vinnicombe, 2008; Strauss, 2008). Even a small mistake can be damaging to their status (Brescoll et al., 2010). You may have heard the saying that women or ethnic minorities must be "twice as good" as men or White individuals to receive the same level of respect or status. (Interestingly, a biography of Condoleeza Rice, the first Black female U.S. secretary of state, has this exact title [Mabry, 2007].) The concept that *standards are higher for groups stereotyped as less competent, known as the* **shifting standards hypothesis**, has in fact been supported in a series of studies by Monica Biernat and her colleagues (Biernat et al., 2010).

The operation of negative stereotyping when women work in male-related jobs or use masculine styles is clearly illustrated by the experience of Ann Hopkins (see Chapter 2). Hopkins, a high-performing manager, was denied promotion to partner because her employers claimed she was not sufficiently feminine. Apparently Ann Hopkins was punished for her masculine style in a male-dominated field (Hopkins, 2007). A recent study of thousands of women and men working in the fields of science, engineering, and technology portrays a pervasive macho culture where women are outsiders (Hewlett et al., 2008). The study reported that the culture within these fields is at best unsupportive and at worst hostile to women. The statistics in the report paint a grim picture: Nearly two-thirds of the women said they experienced sexual harassment on the job; over half said that in order to succeed, they had to "act like a man"; half of the women engineers lacked a mentor; and 40 percent of technology workers said they needed to be available 24/7, hours that put greater strain on working mothers than on working fathers. Given such a culture, it is not surprising that by age 40, half of the women respondents had left science, engineering, and technology for other fields, a rate twice that of their male colleagues.

INGROUP FAVORITISM. Ingroup favoritism (i.e., liking those who resemble us) can reinforce biases that stem from cultural stereotypes (Eagly & Chain, 2010). Differences between White male managers and females or people of color can create tension that managers attempt to avoid. In the words of one corporate manager, "What's important is comfort, chemistry, relationships, and collaborations. That's what makes a shop work. When we find minorities and women who think like we do, we snatch them up" (Federal Glass Ceiling Commission, 1995a, p. 28). His need to emphasize minorities and women suggests that he thinks achieving rapport with these groups is less likely to occur than rapport with other White men. Women of color may be particularly marginalized and are often viewed as affirmative action hires (DeFour, 2008).

PERCEIVED THREAT. A third factor influencing discrimination in the workplace is the perception of threat. Many White male managers view the career progression of women or people of color as a direct threat to their own advancement. "If they are in, there's less of a chance for me. Why would I want a bigger pool? White men can only lose in this game. I'm endangered" (Federal Glass Ceiling Commission, 1995a, p. 31). In one study, male managers were more likely to perceive women as a threat when their department contained more female managers (Beaton et al., 1996). As you might expect, women view women's gains in power more positively than men do (Diekman et al., 2004). Similarly, current progress toward gender equality seems more substantial to men than to women (Eibach & Ehrlinger, 2010). Not surprisingly, groups that are disadvantaged by the present hierarchy are more likely to approve of social change and also view such change as occurring more slowly (Davis & Greenstein, 2009; Eibach & Ehrlinger, 2010).

What do all of the barriers against the advancement of women have in common? Consistent with one of the major themes of this book, these obstacles are clear reflections of power differences in the workplace. Men have higher status and more resources; that is, they have higher organizational power. Although there has been progress in recent years, men continue to have the ability to control opportunities and decisions that have major impact on women (Burn, 2011; Reskin, 2010). On the positive side, however, as more and more women and people of color enter higher-status occupations and gradually advance within these fields, they will acquire greater organizational resources, thus contributing to a reduction in this power inequality.

Women as Leaders

We have seen that women face more barriers to becoming leaders than men do, especially in male-dominated fields (Eagly & Carli, 2007). How do women and men actually behave once they attain these positions? In other words, what are their leadership styles? And are women and men equally effective as leaders?

Alice Eagly (2007) has identified three types of leadership styles: **transformational**, **transactional**, and **laissez-faire**. Transformational leaders *set high standards and serve as role models by mentoring and empowering their subordinates.* They focus on the success of the group and the organizations. Transactional leaders *clarify workers' responsibilities, monitor their work, reward them for meeting objectives, and correct their mistakes.* They focus on the individual power of the leader. Laissez-faire leaders *take little responsibility for managing* (Duff-McCall & Schweinle, 2008; Eagly, 2007).

Studies indicate that women are more transformational and that men are more transactional (Chrisler & Clapp, 2008; Eagly & Chin, 2010; Haddad & Schweinle, 2010). Male managers are less likely than female managers to reward good performance and are more likely to pay attention to workers' mistakes, wait until problems become severe before attending to them, and be absent and uninvolved in critical times.

Recent research shows that women's more transformational style and greater use of rewards for good performance are linked to higher ratings of effectiveness (Eagly, 2007). For example, a five-year study of the leadership skills of over 2,400 female and male managers found that female managers were rated significantly better than their male counterparts by their supervisors, themselves, and the people who worked for them (Pfaff & Associates, 1999). These differences extended both to the communal skills of communication, feedback, and empowerment and to agentic skills such as decisiveness, planning, and setting standards.

GENDER DIFFERENCES IN SALARIES

> *Women, want to earn more than men? Here's how: Be a science technician, baker, teacher's assistant, cafeteria attendant, or bartender's helper! Otherwise, forget it.*

This clearly fictitious job ad is based on real data released recently by the U.S. Census Bureau on the salaries of hundreds of jobs ("Gender Wage Gap," 2010). In the jobs mentioned here, women earned slightly more than men, on average. In all other occupations, women earned less.

In this section, we look at the gender gap in salaries and explore reasons for this difference.

Comparative Salaries

Although the earnings gap between women and men in the United States has declined over the last few decades, in 2009, women still earned only 77 cents for each dollar men earned (U.S. Department of Commerce, 2011). Similar gender gaps in salary exist in the European Union countries (Caprile & Pascual, 2011). In the United States, men who worked full time in 2008 earned a median annual salary of $47,127 compared with $36,278 for women (Institute for Women's Policy Research, 2010). Full-time employed women of color fare even more poorly than White women, except for Asian American women who earn 80 percent of what White men earn, compared to 78 percent for White women. Black women earn 62 percent of what White men earn and Latinas earn just 53 percent (Institute for Women's Policy Research, 2011). Similarly, women with disabilities have lower earnings than either their male counterparts or able-bodied women (Schur et al., 2009). In addition, the gender gap in pay increases with age. In 2008, full-time women workers aged 55 to 64 earned 75 percent of the weekly salary of men in the same age group. Women aged 20 to 24, on the other hand, were paid 92 percent of the weekly wages of men of comparable age (U.S. Bureau of Labor Statistics, 2010b). Why are older women's earnings depressed? For one thing, older women have spent less time in the labor force than younger women. Also, many started working when employers were free to discriminate in pay between women and men doing the same work. Even now, 50 years after the passage of the 1963 Federal Equal Pay Act, the legacy of once-legal salary discrimination remains (Bosworth et al., 2001).

Although Black women make less than White women on average, Black women with bachelor's degrees earn slightly more than similarly educated White women (U.S. Census Bureau, 2010c). What are the possible reasons for these differences? For one thing, minority women, especially Blacks, are more likely to hold two jobs or work more than 40 hours per week. In addition, Black professional women tend to return to the work force earlier than others after having a child. Also, employers in some fields may give extra financial incentives to hire young, Black, professional women in order to diversify their workforce.

Given that the majority of employed women provide at least half of their families' income and that a sizable minority of families are headed by employed single women, the gender gap in wages has important implications for families. Not only is it detrimental to the financial well-being of many families, both two-parent and single-parent, but it also places more women than men at risk of poverty (AAUW, 2008a).

To get a more detailed picture of the gender gap, let's examine wage differentials within selected occupations. In 2008, the ratio of female-to-male earnings was 87 percent for software engineers, 80 percent for lawyers, 86 percent for pharmacists, and 83 percent for physicians (Institute for Women's Policy Research, 2009; Lo Sasso et al., 2011). Even in occupations that employ primarily women, women's salaries are lower than men's. In 2008, female nurses earned 87 percent as much as male nurses, female elementary and middle-school teachers earned 83 percent of what male teachers earned, and among secretaries and administrative assistants, women earned 83 percent of what men earned (Institute for Women's Policy Research, 2009). As we saw earlier, these wage discrepancies are smaller for younger women than for older ones (Luciano, 2003).

The cumulative effect of the gender pay gap is far from trivial. For the average woman with a bachelor's degree, the wage gap translates into $1.2 million over the course of a lifetime. A woman with a professional degree (e.g., law or medicine) loses $2 million during her life (WAGE Project, 2007). For poor, single mothers, the earnings gap poses additional problems. Many employed unmarried women do not earn enough to support their families (AAUW, 2011). Analyses indicate that if single mothers were paid the same as men with comparable education and work hours, the poverty rate for their families would be reduced by 50 percent (Jones-DeWeever et al., 2009; Meyer & Herd, 2007). Not surprisingly, most studies show that women believe their salaries are not commensurate with the value of their work or their abilities and experience. Regardless of their age, ethnicity, occupation, or income, nine out of ten say that equal pay for equal work is a priority (AAUW, 2011).

Reasons for Differences in Salaries

Several factors have been offered as explanations of the pay differential. In considering these reasons, keep in mind the societal power differential in the workplace.

GENDER DIFFERENCES IN INVESTMENTS IN THE JOB.   According to the **human capital perspective**, *salaries reflect investments of human capital (e.g., education and work experience). Because of their family responsibilities, women, relative to men, reduce their investment in their education and jobs and so are paid less* (Burn, 2011; Walby, 2011). Does the evidence support this viewpoint?

Let's look first at the influence of education. If educational differences could explain salary differences, females and males with comparable levels of education should earn similar wages. The reality is that at every level of educational attainment, from high school to master's degree, Asian, Black, Latina, and White women earn less than men in the same ethnic group (U.S. Census Bureau, 2010b). It is disheartening that male high school graduates earn more than women with an associate's degree and that the average salary of women with a college degree is $30,000 less than that of male college graduates (U.S. Census Bureau, 2010b).

What about investment of time on the job? Women spend an average of 7.73 hours per day at work compared to men's 8.27 hours (U.S. Census Bureau, 2010b), and time at work does play some role in the wage gap (Fairfield, 2009; Keaveny et al., 2007; Rose & Hartmann, 2008). Another indicator of time investment is the interruption of employment. Because of their childbearing, childrearing, and eldercare responsibilities, women are more likely than men to temporarily leave employment (Hewlett, 2010; Lovejoy & Stone, 2011). However, employment interruptions are becoming less common because there is a greater dependence on two incomes, thus shortening parental leaves, and also because women are having fewer children. Currently, nearly two-thirds of American women return to work within one year of giving birth to their first child, compared to fewer than 17 percent in the 1960s (Johnson, 2008).

So, do differences in investment help explain pay differences? Studies have found that human capital factors such as differences in educational background and time commitment explain only a portion of the gender wage gap (Keaveny et al., 2007; Travis et al., 2009). Let's look at other possible factors.

OCCUPATIONAL SEGREGATION.   A major factor contributing to both gender and ethnic differences in pay is the difference in jobs held by women and men and by individuals in different ethnic groups (AAUW, 2009; Boushey, 2009; Hegewisch et al., 2010). We saw earlier in this chapter that women and people of color are less likely than White men to attain higher-level, higher-paying positions. Women tend to be congregated in female-dominated occupations, and these occupations are at the low end of the salary scale. Moreover, the greater the number of women in an occupation, the lower the wages (Hegewisch et al., 2010; Keaveny et al., 2007). As an example, child care workers earn a lower hourly wage than janitors, car washers, or parking lot attendants (Meyer & Herd, 2007; Weinberg, 2004).

Why do occupations employing mostly women pay less than those employing mostly men? One answer is that women's occupations are devalued relative to men's (Boushey, 2009). In Chapter 3, we saw that people more highly value males and male-related attributes. In the workplace, this value difference gets translated into employers' higher evaluation of male-dominated jobs and job-related skills associated with men (Cohen & Huffman, 2003). For example, physical strength, which characterizes men more than women, is highly valued and well compensated in metal-working jobs. Nurturance, a trait associated with females, on the other hand, is not highly valued. Consequently, occupations in which nurturance is more important, such as child care, are on the low end of the pay scale (Dodson & Zincavage, 2007).

SALARY NEGOTIATIONS.   Another reason for the gender gap in salaries is that women are less likely than men to initiate salary negotiations and are more willing to accept whatever salary is offered by their employers (Babcock & Laschever, 2008; Stuhlmacher, 2009). For example, in Linda Babcock's survey of Carnegie Mellon graduates who had master's degrees, it was found that only 7 percent of the women but 57 percent of the men had negotiated their salaries. Moreover, those who negotiated raised their salaries by an average of about $4,000 (Babcock & Laschever, 2008). Even when women do negotiate, they don't fare as well as men. When negotiating a starting salary or a raise, men receive an average of 4.3 percent more than the initial offer, whereas women receive only 2.7 percent more (Eddleman et al., 2003). By failing to negotiate for their starting salary, women can lose half a million dollars or more by the time they retire (Babcock & Laschever, 2008).

Why are women less likely to bargain when setting their starting salaries or raises? One factor is that women are generally less comfortable than men with self-promotion. Starting in childhood, boys are encouraged to talk about their achievements, whereas girls are taught to be polite, compliant, and modest, and not to brag (AAUW, 2007; Eagly & Carli, 2007). This makes some women feel that negotiating brands them as overly aggressive and pushy, thereby violating gender norms (Amanatullah & Morris, 2010). Indeed, women who initiate salary negotiations are judged more harshly than men who do so (Bowles et al., 2007). In addition, women are more likely to believe that employers will notice and reward good performance without being asked (Fogg, 2003; Katz & Andronici, 2006). Another factor is that women often underestimate their worth whereas men may overestimate theirs (Hogue et al., 2007). For example, a study of business students by Lisa Barron (cited in Ellin, 2004b) found that 71 percent of the men indicated they were entitled to more money than other job applicants, whereas 70 percent of women believed they were entitled to a salary equal to that of other candidates. For tips on negotiating your salary, see What You Can Do 10.1.

WAGE DISCRIMINATION.   One key factor in the gender gap in salaries is **wage discrimination**, *differential payment for work that has equal or substantially similar value to the employer* (AAUW, 2008a; Castilla, 2008; Fairfield, 2009). Unequal pay scales were once considered justifiable by employers on the basis that women work only for "extras" or "pocket money" or that women can function with less money than men can (Paludi et al., 2010). Since passage of the 1963 Federal Equal Pay Act, however, unequal pay for equal work has been illegal. Nevertheless, because wage discrimination laws are poorly enforced, equal pay legislation has not guaranteed equality (Burn, 2011). It should not be surprising, therefore, that thousands of women have filed discrimination claims (Padavic & Reskin, 2002), and settlements have been made for women employed in a range of occupations.

WHAT YOU CAN DO 10.1
Effectively Negotiate Your Salary

1. Find out salary information for comparable jobs by using Websites, contacting professional associations, talking to colleagues, using your college's placement office.

2. Assess the value of your skills and work experience using the same resources mentioned in item 1.

3. During negotiations, indicate that salary is important to you.

4. Negotiate things other than salary: benefits, perks, job title, responsibilities, and so on.

5. Be persistent and willing to compromise. If the hiring individual says "no," don't simply accept this. Ask "How close can you come to my offer?"

6. Role-play salary negotiations with experienced colleagues, or job counselors at your college.

Sources: Babcock and Laschever (2008); Ellin (2004b); and Frankel (2004).

Another troubling finding is that *women with children earn significantly less than childless women, even when they have comparable education, work experience, and job characteristics.* This phenomenon, known as the **motherhood wage penalty** or maternal wall, averages up to an 18-percent reduction in salary per child in the United States and Europe (Bernard & Correll, 2010; Cheung & Halpern, 2010; Gangl & Ziefle, 2009; Loughran & Zissimopoulos, 2009). By contrast, men with children enjoy a **fatherhood wage premium**, *earning more than men without children* (Cheung & Halpern, 2010; Glauber, 2008; Hodges & Budig, 2010). What can account for the motherhood penalty? Researchers suggest two possibilities. One is that mothers may be less productive on the job than nonmothers because the latter can spend more of their nonemployment time in refreshing leisure, rather than in exhausting housework and child care. Alternatively, employers may discriminate against mothers in terms of job placement, promotion, or pay levels within jobs (Gangl & Ziefle, 2009; Lips & Lawson, 2009). In support of this view, even outstanding employees who are mothers are perceived as less professionally competent than those who have no children (Cuddy et al., 2004). They are also viewed as less competent, less committed, and less available for work than employed fathers and are held to higher performance and punctuality standards (Correll et al., 2007; Güngör & Biernat, 2009; Heilman & Okimoto, 2008; King, 2008). Once again, as we saw in Chapter 2, social roles influence gender stereotypes.

What are wages and working conditions like for women in developing nations? For a closer look, read Explore Other Cultures 10.1.

Now that you are familiar with some of the problems experienced by women in the workplace, perform the interviews in Get Involved 10.1 to gain firsthand knowledge about women's experiences with wage or promotion discrimination, and with other forms of gender-biased treatment.

EXPLORE OTHER CULTURES 10.1
Girls and Women in the Global Factory

The fact that women's work worldwide is frequently unpaid or underpaid is closely linked to women's lower power and status (Burn, 2011). In many developing countries in Africa, Central America, and Asia, thousands of women and girls as young as 8 work for low wages 15 or more hours a day, everyday, in **sweatshops**—*businesses that violate safety, wage, and child labor laws* (Burn, 2011; Kristof & WuDunn, 2009). Health problems are common in these factories due to harsh working conditions such as poor ventilation, exposure to chemicals, and repetitive motion. Most of the clothes, shoes, toys, and electronics purchased by North Americans were likely manufactured by women working in sweatshops in nations such as Bangladesh, Burma, China, the Dominican Republic, Haiti, Honduras, Indonesia, Guatemala, Malaysia, Mexico, Nicaragua, the Philippines, and Vietnam (Burn, 2011; Lorber, 2010). In El Salvador, for example, the young female workers are paid an average of 94 cents for each $165 jacket that they sew for North Face (Burn, 2011). In addition, thousands of women and girls are trafficked from poor countries to wealthy ones, where they are forced to work against their will in factories, in restaurants, on farms, and in people's homes (Henderson & Jeydel, 2010; Lorber, 2010). These women laborers seldom question their working conditions, having grown up in male-dominated households where they have learned to be subservient and dutiful (Freeman, 2010). In addition, they are often unaware of their rights and afraid of losing their jobs if they assert themselves (Henderson & Jeydel, 2010; Lorber, 2010). The efforts of the International Labour Organization, along with women's increasing union membership and the work of women activists around the world, have produced some progress in passing laws to improve women's work conditions, producing greater implementation of these laws, and educating women about their rights (Burn, 2011).

GET INVOLVED 10.1
Gender-Based Treatment in the Workplace

Interview two employed women. If possible, select full-time employees, but if they are not available, include any working women, including students with part-time jobs. Ask each respondent to discuss her experiences with the following: (1) discrimination in salary, (2) discrimination in promotion, (3) gender stereotyping by coworkers or supervisors, and (4) any other types of gender-based unfair treatment.

WHAT DOES IT MEAN?

1. Compare the reported experiences of your respondents with the information reported in the chapter. Describe both the differences and similarities between your findings and the material presented in the text. Give possible reasons for the differences, if any.

2. What kinds of changes do you think could be instituted so that the specific problems your respondents identified would be eliminated or greatly reduced?

WOMEN'S JOB SATISFACTION

Earlier in this chapter, we saw that women and men congregate in different jobs and that the most prestigious occupations employ more men than women. We also noted that women's job levels and salaries are generally lower than men's. Do these gender differences in occupational dimensions correspond to differences in job satisfaction?

Gender Differences in Satisfaction

Research generally finds either no gender differences in overall job satisfaction or higher satisfaction in women (Clayton et al., 2010; Martinez, 2005). *Situations in which women are as satisfied as men with their jobs despite having lower pay and status* have been labeled the **paradox of the contented female worker** (Clayton et al., 2010). In such cases, women may be comparing themselves to other women rather than to men, which is more likely to occur in a female-dominated work setting. The fact that women are often as satisfied as men suggests that many factors other than job and salary level contribute to the overall satisfaction gained from one's job. One such factor is social support from peers and supervisors (Bond et al., 2004; Settles et al., 2007). Ellen Auster (2001) and Wendy Campione (2008) have identified a number of other factors that are associated with women's mid-career satisfaction:

1. Having children, which seems to serve as a counterbalance to work pressures (see Chapter 11);
2. For ethnic minority women, developing a broad social network that crosses racial/ethnic boundaries;
3. Having employment gaps (e.g., parental leave) that are voluntary and supported by the organization;
4. Using flexible options, such as job sharing and flextime (see Chapter 11);
5. Having mentors in one's career;
6. Networking (i.e., developing relationships that have the potential to assist in one's career);
7. Having balanced proportions of women and men within one's work unit;
8. Experiencing lower levels of sex bias and discrimination;
9. Having family-friendly organizational policies such as parental leave, day care, and fitness activities (see Chapter 11);

Many of the clothes, shoes, toys, and electronics purchased by North Americans are manufactured by women working in Asian or Latin American sweatshops.

10. Having opportunities for autonomy, creativity, training, development, and advancement within the context of job security;
11. Having lower stress levels;
12. Having a recent meaningful promotion;
13. Being in a supervisory capacity.

Job Satisfaction of Sexual Minorities

Increasing numbers of organizations have adopted antidiscrimination policies that include sexual orientation, although these are still in the minority (Winfield, 2005). In 2010, for example, President Obama repealed the "don't ask, don't tell" policy, the U.S. military's longstanding ban on service by openly gay women and men (Stolberg, 2010). Unfortunately, many lesbian, gay, and bisexual employees continue to experience workplace discrimination based on their sexual orientation (Chung et al., 2009; Fassinger et al., 2010; Kwon & Hugelshofer, 2010). Such discrimination is related to lower levels of job satisfaction and organizational commitment and higher levels of psychological distress, absenteeism, and job turnover (Brenner et al., 2010; Fassinger et al., 2010). Thus, the decision of whether or not to come out is a major concern for lesbian workers (Goldberg, 2010; Read, 2009). Potential benefits of coming out include enhanced self-esteem, reduced role stress, and closer interpersonal relationships (Croteau et al., 2008; Goldberg, 2010; Read, 2009). On the negative side, lesbian and bisexual women fear that sexual identity disclosure might precipitate workplace discrimination. This fear is not without some basis. In fact, lesbian, gay, and bisexual individuals have been fired or passed over for promotion because of their sexual orientation (Croteau et al., 2008; "Lesbian Teacher," 2010; Meyer & Wilson, 2009). And it is legal to do so in over 60 percent of the states in the United States (Fassinger, 2008). Lesbian women of color experience an extra burden because they risk adding homophobia to the gender or ethnic prejudice which they might already experience. Given the possible risks of coming out in the workplace, it is not surprising that lesbian and gay employees are less likely to disclose their sexual orientation in workplaces in which they have observed or experienced discrimination related to sexual orientation (Brenner et al., 2010; Fassinger et al., 2010).

THE OLDER WOMAN WORKER

After Helen Martinez's children were grown, she worked as an executive secretary with a large corporation for several years. Helen decided to retire when her husband did. When he died eight years later, Helen found that her Social Security benefits and the income from her pension were barely enough to support her. At the age of 70, she went back to work for her old firm. She works 2½ days a week, running a job bank. Now 79, she does not plan to retire again unless forced to by poor health.

Brenda Milner, at age 93, has been a dedicated neuroscientist for nearly 60 years. Her many accomplishments include her groundbreaking research on the localization of memory in the brain. Milner, a professor at McGill University's Montreal Neurological Institute, continues to work five days a week teaching medical students and doing research on brain activity.

(Birchard, 2011)

Helen Martinez is typical of many women workers who enter or reenter the labor force in later life. Brenda Milner, on the other hand, is an example of older women workers who have been employed continuously throughout their adult lives. In this section, we examine the varying experiences of older women workers.

Employment Rates

Labor force participation of middle-aged and older women has increased sharply over the past 35 years. Over two-thirds of married women and more than 70 percent of unmarried women aged 45 to 64 are now in the labor force. Over the age of 65, 21 percent of single women, 14 percent of married women, and 12 percent of widowed and divorced women are employed (U.S. Census Bureau, 2010c). During the same 35-year period, by contrast, men have been retiring earlier. By 2008, only 84 percent of 45- to 64-year-old married men were in the workforce, compared to 91 percent in 1970. Similarly, the participation rate of married men aged 65 and over dropped from 30 to 23 percent (U.S. Census Bureau, 2010c). As a consequence of these changes, which hold across all ethnic groups, the proportion of paid women workers aged 45 and over is higher than ever before.

Why Do Older Women Work?

Older women work for most of the same reasons as younger women. Economic necessity is a key factor at all ages. In addition, feeling challenged and productive and meeting new coworkers and friends give women a sense of personal satisfaction and recognition outside the family (Choi, 2000; Etaugh, 2008). Healthier, better educated women are more likely than other older women to work (Haider & Loughran, 2010). In turn, active involvement in work and outside interests in women's later years appear to promote physical and psychological well-being. Work-centered women broaden their interests as they grow older and become more satisfied with their lives. Employed older women have higher morale than women retirees, whereas women who have never been employed outside the home have the lowest (Perkins, 1992).

Entering the Workforce in Later Life

Many older women have been employed throughout adulthood. For some—working-class women, women of color, and single women—economic necessity has been the driving force. But for many women, a more typical pattern has been movement in and out of the labor force in response to changing family roles and responsibilities. Some women, for example, decide to reenter the labor force after their children are grown, or following divorce or the death of their spouses (Etaugh, 2008). The recent economic recession also has pulled older women in the employment either because their husbands have lost their jobs or because they are concerned about their retirement security (Boushey, 2009). The prospects of entering or reentering the labor force after 25 or 30 years may be daunting to some women who wonder if they have the skills to be hired. Older women should not overlook the wealth of relevant experience they have accumulated through their homemaking, childrearing, and volunteer activities.

Age Discrimination in the Workplace

Earlier in the chapter, we discussed gender discrimination in employment. As women get older, they, like men, also confront age discrimination in the workplace (Gèe et al., 2007; Walker et al., 2007). The reasons for age discrimination and the age range during which it occurs differ for women and men. Women's complaints filed with the Equal Employment Opportunity Commission primarily concern hiring, promotion, wages, and fringe benefits. Men more often file on the basis of job termination and involuntary retirement (Etaugh, 2008).

Women also experience age discrimination at a younger age than men (Rife, 2001). This is another example of the double standard of aging discussed in Chapter 2. Women are seen as becoming older at an earlier age than men (Kite & Wagner, 2002; Sherman, 2001). Society's emphasis on youthful sexual attractiveness for women and the stereotype of older women as powerless, weak, sick, helpless, and unproductive create obstacles for older women who are seeking employment or who wish to remain employed. In addition, age discrimination is associated with higher psychological distress and lower positive well-being, especially for women (Yuan, 2007).

CHANGING THE WORKPLACE

We have seen that women continue to be more heavily concentrated in lower-status occupations, to have limited opportunities for advancement, to earn lower salaries than men, and to be targets of biased behavior. What can be done to continue improvements in the work environment that have begun during the last few decades?

Organizational Procedures and Policies

PAY EQUITY. We have seen that equal pay legislation has not eliminated the gender or ethnicity wage gaps. As long as women and men or Whites and people of color are segregated in different occupations, it is legal to pay them different wages. One way of narrowing these earnings gaps is **pay equity**, *pay policies based on workers' worth and not their gender or ethnicity* (AAUW, 2011). Pay equity would require that employees in different jobs that are similar in skill, effort, and responsibility receive comparable wages.

AFFIRMATIVE ACTION. Think of what affirmative action means to you. To what extent do you characterize affirmative action as a set of procedures that ensures equitable treatment of underrepresented individuals or, alternatively, as a policy that fosters preferential treatment and reverse discrimination?

Affirmative action goals and procedures are highly misunderstood. Let's examine the legal conception of affirmative action as well as typical misconceptions of its meaning.

Affirmative action in employment refers to *positive steps taken by an employer that facilitate the recruitment and advancement of historically underrepresented workers in order to ensure equal opportunity for all* (Crosby, 2008). To achieve equity, these procedures involve weighing candidates' qualifications as well as group membership. Is this definition consistent with your conception of affirmative action?

Perceptions of affirmative action are often unfavorable (Crosby, 2008). Both women and men view the beneficiaries of affirmative action as less competent employees who are less entitled to their positions (Iyer, 2009). Thus, according to Jennifer Eberhardt and Susan Fiske (1998), men and women think that affirmative action results in reverse discrimination that hurts qualified White males in favor of unqualified women or people of color. Contrary to these misperceptions, Eberhardt and Fiske claim that the recruitment and promotion of unqualified individuals and the reliance on group membership only, without consideration of qualifications, are highly unusual and illegal practices. Furthermore, the U.S. Department of Labor (n.d.) reports that accusations of reverse discrimination comprised less than 2 percent of the 3,000 discrimination cases filed in federal courts between 1990 and 1994 and that few of these were upheld as legitimate claims.

Despite criticisms of its practices, affirmative action has played an important role in reducing gender inequity in the workplace (Crosby, 2008; Iyer, 2009), and there is evidence that it has done so without negatively affecting performance, productivity, or company profits (Iyer, 2009). Its success in bringing more women into the workplace and increasing the gender similarity in occupations, job levels, and salaries is likely to result in even further reductions in gender imbalances in the future.

What kind of actions would be most effective in improving the workplace for women? The exercise in Get Involved 10.2 explores this issue.

OTHER ORGANIZATIONAL PROCEDURES.   Improvements for women and other underrepresented groups must also involve changes in the workplace itself. It is essential for employers to develop a work environment that values diversity and to back up this attitudinal climate with well-publicized antidiscrimination policies. Managers and other workers can be sensitized about both subtle and blatant forms of prejudice and discrimination in the work environment and can learn that the employer will not tolerate any form of discrimination. This can be accomplished through workshops aimed at increasing awareness of how stereotypes operate in evaluating and treating less powerful individuals, including women, people of color, sexual minorities, and people with disabilities (Walsh & Heppner, 2006).

Another strategy, recommended by the Federal Glass Ceiling Commission (1995b), is for organizations to identify employees with high potential, including women and people of color, and provide them with career development opportunities, such as specialized training, employer-sponsored networks, and job assignments that expand their experience and organizational visibility. Equally important, the commission stresses, is that senior management clearly communicate throughout the organization its firm commitment to a diverse workforce.

In order to facilitate reporting of complaints, organizations should also make use of clear, well-publicized procedures for filing and evaluating claims of discrimination. Organizations that enact such procedures and ensure that claims can be filed without fear of recrimination produce more favorable work environments for women (Russell, 2006).

Strategies for Women

Although organizational efforts have more far-reaching effects, there are several actions that women can take as they either prepare themselves for employment or attempt to improve their own situation

GET INVOLVED 10.2
Ways to Make the Workplace Better for Women

Following are six factors that can improve women's opportunities and experiences at work. Indicate how important you think each would be to making the workplace better for women in the future by rank ordering these from 1 to 6. Give 1 to the factor you think would be most beneficial to improving future conditions for women, give a 2 to the factor you consider would be next most helpful, and so on. Also, ask a woman who differs from you in ethnicity to do the same.

__1. Women's hard work

__2. Efforts of feminists to improve conditions for women

__3. Women's past contributions that demonstrate their value as workers

__4. Laws that make it less likely for employers to discriminate

__5. Greater number of women who know how to succeed in the workplace

__6. A workplace that is more responsive to women's needs

WHAT DOES IT MEAN?

Factors 1, 3, and 5 (set A) point to actions on the part of working women. Factors 2, 4, and 6 (set B) reflect adaptations resulting from political/social activism, legal mandates, and adaptations within the workplace. Determine the number of items in each set that you included among your top three items. Do the same for your other respondent.

Carol Konek and her colleagues asked a large number of career women to rank these influences and found that these women ranked the items in set A higher than those in set B. The researchers interpreted this as an emphasis on individualism, a belief that one's success is due to one's own efforts.

1. Did your answers match the responses of the study's respondents? If yes, was the reason the same? That is, do you value self-reliance and hard work more than external changes that provide increased opportunities?

2. Make the same comparison for your other respondent. Do her answers reflect an emphasis on individualism?

3. Did you notice any differences between the answers given by you and your other respondent? If yes, is it possible that these differences reflect a different emphasis on individualism versus collectivism?

Source: Based on Konek et al. (1994).

in the workplace (Babcock & Laschever, 2008; Walsh & Heppner, 2006). Women can benefit from workshops or work-related social networks that arm them with information that can help them better understand and fight against discriminatory practices in the workplace.

A useful strategy for women who experience discrimination is to join together with others who are experiencing similar inequities. Reporting a shared problem can, in some situations, receive both attention and a commitment to institutional change. Remember how a collective effort by women at MIT led to improvements in salary, research money, and laboratories.

RETIREMENT

Much of what is known about the effects of retirement is based on studies of men, despite the steady increase in women in the workplace over the past 70 years. This bias reflects the assumption that retirement is a less critical event for women than for men because of women's lesser participation in the labor force and their greater involvement in family roles. But half of workers now are women

(English et al., 2010), and retirement has equally important consequences for them. In this section, we examine factors that influence women's decision to retire, their adjustment to retirement, and their leisure pursuits in retirement. Conduct the interviews in Get Involved 10.3 to learn about the work and retirement experiences of individual older women.

The Retirement Decision

The decision to retire depends upon many factors including health, income, occupational characteristics, and marital and family situations (Wang & Schultz, 2010). When men retire, they are leaving a role that has typically dominated their adult years. They are more likely than women to retire for involuntary reasons, such as mandatory retirement, poor health, or age. Women, on the other hand, are more apt to retire for voluntary, family-related reasons, such as the retirement of one's husband or the ill health of a relative (Canetto, 2003; Hyde, 2003).

Compared to men, women arrive at the threshold of retirement with a different work and family history, less planning for retirement, and fewer financial resources (Kail et al., 2009; Moen et al., 2006; Wang & Schultz, 2010). As noted earlier, women typically experience greater job discontinuity. They may have had fewer opportunities to obtain personal career goals and may therefore be more reluctant to retire. Given their more discontinuous employment history and their employment in lower-paid jobs, women are not as likely as men to be covered by pension plans, and their Social Security benefits are lower (Henderson & Jeydel, 2010; Jacobs & Gerson, 2008; Shacklock et al., 2009). Many older women workers with low salaries choose to continue to work as long as they can. These women may not be able to afford the luxury of retirement because of economic pressures, such as inadequate retirement income or sudden loss of a spouse. Widowed and divorced women are more apt than married women to report plans for postponed retirement or plans not to retire at all

GET INVOLVED 10.3
Interview With Older Women: Work and Retirement

Interview two women, aged 65 or older. It is helpful, but not essential, to know your interviewees fairly well. You may interview your mother, grandmothers, great-aunts, great-grandmothers, and so on. Keep a record of your interviewees' responses to the following questions. Compare and contrast the responses of the two women.

1. (If employed) How are things going in your job?

2. Have you reached most of the goals you set for yourself in your life?

3. When do you plan on retiring? (or when did you retire?)

4. What are some of the day-to-day activities that you look forward to after retirement (or that you've enjoyed since retirement)?

5. How will (did) retirement change you and your lifestyle?

6. How will you adjust (or how have you adjusted) to these changes?

7. In general, how would you describe your current financial situation?

8. What do you think of the Social Security system?

WHAT DOES IT MEAN?

1. How do the work and/or retirement experiences of these women compare with the experiences of older women reported in this book?

2. Are the financial situations of your respondents similar or different to those of older women described in the text? In what ways?

(Brougham & Walsh, 2005). A growing number of women continue to work after their husbands retire. In 2000, 11 percent of all couples involving a man of 55 or over consisted of a retired husband and an employed wife (Leland, 2004).

In addition, women and men who have strong work identities have more negative attitudes toward retiring than those with weaker work identities (Frieze et al., 2011; Topa et al., 2009). Professional women and those who are self-employed, who presumably have strong work identities, are less likely than other women to retire early. Martha Graham, for example, danced until age 76 and then kept choreographing for another 20 years. Georgia O'Keeffe continued to paint into her 90s (Springen & Siebert, 2005). Older professional women do not often make systematic plans for their retirement, nor do they wish to do so (Etaugh, 2008; Heyl, 2004). Working-class women and men, on the other hand, are more likely to view retirement as a welcome relief from exhausting or boring labor, and desire to retire earlier than other workers (Gilbert, 2008; Wang & Schultz, 2010).

We have seen why some women may delay their retirement. Why do others retire early? Poor health is one of the major determinants of early retirement (Austen & Ong, 2010; Topa et al., 2009). Because aging Black women and men tend to be in poorer health than aging Whites, they are likely to retire earlier (Bound et al., 1996). Health is a more important factor in the retirement decision for men than for women, among both Blacks and Whites (Etaugh, 2008). This gender difference may result from the fact that, unlike married men, married women in poor health may withdraw early from the labor force or do not enter it in the first place. Early withdrawal or nonparticipation in the workforce is enabled by having a provider husband and by societal expectations that employment is optional for women.

Women's role as primary caregiver is another factor contributing to their early retirement. Women provide the majority of unpaid home care to frail older individuals (Stephens et al., 2009). Eldercare responsibilities often result in increased tardiness and absenteeism at work, as well as health problems for the caregiver. Because most businesses do not offer work flexibility to workers who care for older relatives, women caregivers reduce their hours or take time off without pay. Others are forced to retire earlier than planned (Austen, 2010; Etaugh, 2008; Family Caregiver Alliance, 2003).

Some women, of course, simply want to retire, whether to spend more time with a partner, family, or friends; to start one's own business; to pursue lifelong interests; or to develop new ones.

> *I haven't regretted retiring. I didn't quit my job through any dissatisfaction with the job or the people but I just felt that my life needed a change. I noticed that after working an eight-hour day I didn't have much steam left for a social life and fun. It's been pleasant spending these years doing what I want to do because I spent so many years accommodating myself to other people's needs and plans.*
>
> (a woman in her 70s, in Doress-Worters & Siegal, 1994, p. 183)

Adjustment to Retirement

Retirement has long been seen as an individual—primarily male—transition. But now, couples must increasingly deal with two retirements, according to Phyllis Moen and her colleagues (2001). In their study of 534 retired couples, these researchers found that retirement was a happy time for the couples. But the transition to retirement, defined as *the first two years after leaving a job,* was a time of marital conflict for both women and men. Wives and husbands who retired at the same time were happier than couples in which the spouses retired at different times. Marital conflict was highest when husbands retired first, perhaps because of uneasiness with the role reversal of a working wife and a stay-at-home husband. Not only does the situation pose a potential threat to the husband's role as provider, but it can also lead to disagreements over the division of household labor (Davey & Szinovacz, 2004; Mares & Fitzpatrick, 2004).

Although both genders typically adjust well to retirement, women may take longer to get adjusted (Etaugh, 2008). Newly retired women report lower morale and greater depression than newly retired men (Coursolle et al., 2010; Moen et al., 2001). Men seem to enjoy the freedom from work pressure when they retire whereas women appear to experience the retirement transition as a loss of roles. Because women are not under the same socially prescribed pressures to be employed as are men, those who *do* work, whether out of financial need or commitment to their job, may find it more difficult to stop working (Szinovacz, 1991).

For both men and women, a high level of life satisfaction in retirement is generally associated with having good health, adequate income, and active participation in leisure pursuits (Heo et al., 2010; Schwartz & Campagna, 2008; Wang & Schultz, 2010; Wong & Earl, 2009). Lower income and poorer health may account for the fact that Black retirees have lower levels of life satisfaction than White retirees (Kim & Moen, 2001). Marital status also contributes to retirement satisfaction. Married people have more positive retirement attitudes and higher retirement satisfaction than unmarried retirees (Wang et al., 2011). Retired women, particularly unmarried ones, are more involved with friends, family, organizations, and volunteer work than are retired men or lifelong housewives (Carp, 2001; Etaugh, 2008; McDonald & Mair, 2010). These social contacts are important for the life satisfaction of retired women, particularly those who are unmarried (Dorfman & Rubenstein, 1993; Reeves & Darville, 1994). For women who have never married, retirement can represent an especially significant transition. Although work assumes a greater importance in their lives than in the lives of never-married men and other women, most never-married women appear to be satisfied with retirement. Still, many pursue second careers after retirement, or continue to work part time (Rubinstein, 1994).

We shall see in Chapter 11 that multiple roles often have positive consequences for women who are employed. What is the effect of multiple role identities among older retired women? Pamela Adelmann (1993) compared Black and White women aged 60 and over who considered themselves retired only, homemakers only, or both. Women who called themselves both retired and homemakers had higher self-esteem and lower depression than women identified with only one role, especially the homemaker role. Apparently, multiple-role identities continue to benefit women even after retirement.

Leisure Activities in Retirement

Leisure or free time in later life is a fairly recent social phenomenon. In 1900, the average work week was over 70 hours. Most adults died by their mid-40s, and worked until their death. Until the Social Security Act of 1935, retirement was not a reality for most Americans. The economic safety net provided by Social Security, along with increased life expectancy, has given older Americans the opportunity for retirement and, consequently, an increased amount of free time (Lemme, 2006; Schultz & Wang, 2011).

GENDER DIFFERENCES.   Women and men, regardless of age, vary in the nature of leisure activities they prefer. Older women are more likely than older men to participate in social activities, domestic crafts (e.g., baking, quilting), and reading. Older males are more likely to engage in physical activity and spectator sports (Mobily, 1992; Shaw et al., 2010). In retirement, women are more apt than men to integrate their spheres of leisure activity, bringing together their worlds of friends, home, and hobbies (Hanson & Wapner, 1994).

Much of the research on leisure activities for older people has focused on middle-class Whites and has been studied largely from a male perspective. Very little is known about the context and meanings of leisure for aging, usually poor, minority women. Katherine Allen and Victoria Chin-Sang interviewed 30 retired Black women whose average age was 75. Work had largely dominated the lives of these women. Most of them had worked in domestic and service jobs. When asked how their experience of leisure had changed since retirement, most women replied that they had none in the past. The women considered leisure time in older age to be time to relax or to work with and for others as they chose. The church and the senior center provided important contexts for their leisure activities (Allen & Chin-Sang, 1990).

FACTORS AFFECTING LEISURE ACTIVITY.   One factor influencing participation in leisure activity is age. A longitudinal study of women and men at age 54 and again at 70 found that women's leisure activity involvement was less likely than that of men to be affected by increasing age. Men's participation in all categories of leisure activity declined between the ages of 54 and 70. On the other hand, women's informal social, home, spectatorship, travel, and hobbies/crafts activities showed no change over the 16-year period (Stanley & Freysinger, 1995). For another look at the relationship between age and leisure activity, try the exercise in Get Involved 10.4.

GET INVOLVED 10.4
Leisure Activities of Older and Young Women

1. Make three columns with the following headings:

Young Women's Current Activities	Older Women's Current Activities	Older Women's Past Activities

2. Briefly interview three young adult females about their current leisure activities. List the most common activities in the first column.

3. Briefly interview three women aged 65 or older about their current leisure activities and about their leisure activities when they were in their early 20s. List their most common current activities in the second column, and their most common leisure activities when they were young adults in the third column.

WHAT DOES IT MEAN?

1. How do the leisure activities of the older women compare with the leisure activities of older women reported in this book?

2. How similar are the current leisure activities of the older women to those when they were young women?

3. Are the leisure activities of the older women when they were young adults more similar to their current activities, or to the activities of the young adult females you interviewed? In what way?

4. Based on this exercise, would you predict that young women's leisure activities in later life would be more similar to their present activities or to those of today's older women? Explain your answer.

Source: From Leitner and Leitner (2004). Reprinted with permission from Haworth Press.

Other variables affecting leisure involvement are the amount of free time, transportation, information on and availability of leisure programs, and health status (Cavanaugh & Blanchard-Fields, 2011). Caring for ill family members, a responsibility usually assumed by women, can severely curtail the amount of available free time. Women may also be more affected than men by the lack of transportation services, lack of information about programs, and physical difficulties (Britain et al., 2011; Buchner, 2010). Because those over 85 (a majority of them women) are the fastest growing segment of the population, greater emphasis will need to be given to providing leisure services for older people who are physically impaired (Leitner & Leitner, 2004).

VARIETIES OF LEISURE ACTIVITY.   There are many paths to fulfilling leisure activities for women in later life. Some older women devote themselves to pursuits that they had little time for in their younger years. Think of Grandma Moses, for example, who took up painting late in life and became an internationally acclaimed artist. Then there are the increasing number of older adults who are taking college courses and participating in elderhostels and Lifelong Learning Institutes (Novak, 2008). Some older women join civic-minded social clubs, such as the Red Hat Society (Son et al., 2010). Other older women and men do volunteer work in a wide variety of community settings: schools, hospitals, museums, churches, and service organizations, including the Peace Corps (Kulik, 2010). Devotion to volunteering remains strong well into old age (Cavanaugh & Blanchard-Fields 2011; Novak, 2008). Volunteer service provides a number of benefits for the older people, including increased life satisfaction (Bowen et al., 2011; National Institute on Aging, 2010) and psychological well-being (Morrow-Howell, 2010; Tang et al., 2010), and is associated with increased longevity (Okun et al., 2010). In one study, for example, older African American women who volunteered as tutors in elementary schools showed improved physical activity, social interaction, and cognitive stimulation compared to a control group of nonvolunteers (Fried et al., 2004).

Whatever a woman's situation as she ages, there is usually some way in which she can serve as an **advocate**, *a person who plays an active role in making changes in her life, in the lives of others, and in society* (Dowling, 2001). For example, women can and do join and actively participate in any number of organizations that advocate for the rights of older persons or specifically for older women. AARP (formerly the American Association of Retired Persons), with over 24 million members, is a powerful advocacy group. The Gray Panthers, a smaller, more activist group, was founded by Maggie Kuhn following her forced retirement at age 65. The Older Women's League (OWL) focuses on social policies affecting midlife and older women (Doress-Worters & Siegal, 1994). Another advocacy organization, the Raging Grannies, consists of groups of feisty older women who dress as "grannies" while altering the words of traditional songs to communicate political messages at organized protests (Sawchuk, 2009). Some older women have been political and social activists for most of their lives and do not let their age slow them down. For example, Doris "Granny D" Haddock walked across the United States when she was 90 to raise awareness of finance reform. In 2004, at age 93, she undertook a 15,000 mile road trip to encourage working women to vote (Bridges et al., 2003/2004). Then there are sisters Carrie and Mary Dann, elders of the western Shoshone nation, who, well into their 70s, continued their 30-year fight to keep the U.S. government from seizing tribal lands (Bridges et al., 2003/2004).

Becoming an activist can transform the life of an older woman. Take the case of Rosemary Bizzell, a widow and grandmother of eight. Prior to joining OWL, she had never been involved in community affairs. Within three years, she had risen to prominence in the city council and in state government. In her words,

My self-image as an older woman has improved tremendously in spite of much rejection in job hunting. Apparently I was supposed to count my blessings and not expect to advance. Well, becoming involved in OWL has certainly challenged me. I cannot thank the OWL enough for opening up a whole new world for older women. I am proud of the opportunity to be part of it.

(Doress-Worters & Siegel, 1994, p. 436)

ECONOMIC ISSUES IN LATER LIFE

After I've paid the rent, I pay the phone bill. . . . Then there's my health. My doctor refused Medicaid—after 15 years—and now I have to pay him $27 out of every check. Then it takes $2.50 to do the laundry—you've got to keep your linens clean. I try to buy the cheapest things. I always make my own milk from powder. I only buy bread and chicken, and those no-name paper articles, but it still adds up. If I need clothes, I go across the street to the thrift shop. I watch for yard sales—if you see something for half a buck, there's a Christmas present. . . . But the last two weeks of the month are always hard. You just can't make it. I'm down to my last $10, and I've got more than two weeks to go.

(a woman in her 70s, cited in Doress-Worters & Siegal, 1994, pp. 191–192)

At every age, women are more likely to live in poverty than men, and poverty rates are higher for ethnic minority women than for their White counterparts (Calasanti, 2010; Henrici et al., 2010). But financial insecurity can be an even greater problem for older women, who are twice as likely as older men to live in poverty (Administration on Aging, 2011; OWL, 2010). In this section, we examine reasons for the precarious financial condition of many older women. We then turn to actions that young women can take to ensure a more secure financial future when they retire.

Poverty

What factors account for the relatively high poverty rates of older women? Their lower lifetime earnings and reduced time in the labor force adversely affect eligibility and benefits from Social Security and pensions (Hayes et al., 2010; Henderson & Jeydel, 2010). Women are also less likely to have accumulated income from savings and investments. The net result is that the income gap between women and men increases in retirement. U.S. women aged 65 and older have an average income of only a little more than half that of men the same age (Hayes et al., 2010).

Another factor associated with poverty is marital status. Nearly 20 percent of single older women in the United States who live alone live in poverty and are poorer than their counterparts in other industrialized nations (Fleck, 2007; Hayes et al., 2010). Formerly married women (i.e., widows or divorced women) are worse off financially than older women who have never married (Women's Institute for a Secure Retirement [WISER], 2011). Among married women, however, only 5 percent are below the poverty line (Hayes et al., 2010; Lee & Shaw, 2008). But a married woman is just a heartbeat away from widowhood. The income from a husband's pension is usually reduced considerably or eliminated when he dies, greatly increasing his widow's risk of plunging into poverty. Because women usually marry older men and outlive them, there is a high likelihood that they will live alone on a meager income as they grow older. The costs of a husband's illness and burial may seriously deplete the couple's savings, leaving the widow in a precarious economic state (Canetto, 2003). The longer an older woman lives, the further her assets must stretch. This situation helps explain why the very oldest women have the highest poverty rates (Meyer & Herd,

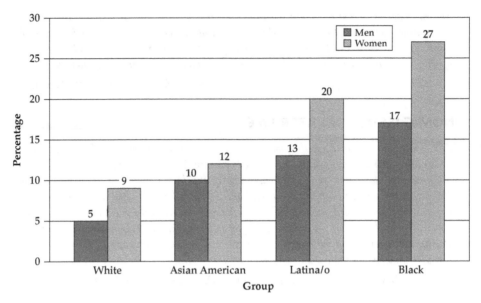

FIGURE 10.1 Percentage of Older Black, Latina/o, Asian American, and White Women and Men Below the Poverty Level, 2007.
Source: Federal Interagency Forum (2009).

2007; Society of Actuaries, 2010). Figure 10.1 illustrates a recent analysis of the percentage of older unmarried women and men who live below the poverty level.

For a closer look at the economic status of older women in other parts of the world, read Explore Other Cultures 10.2.

Retirement Income: Planning Ahead

Young women often find it hard to visualize their retirement years. However, information in this chapter makes it clear that women must take steps early in their adult life to make plans to improve their financial security in retirement. Until fairly recently, retirement planning and money management were thought to be best left to husbands (WISER, 2007). As a result, many women of all ages have relatively little understanding of what retirement planning entails. It is never too early to start thinking about the issues involved. See What You Can Do 10.2 for guidelines on how to start planning for retirement *now*.

First, you need to know that a secure retirement is based on a three-legged stool consisting of Social Security, pension income, and savings and investments. As we have seen, all three are linked to a woman's lifetime earnings, work history, and marital status (McDonnell, 2010).

SOCIAL SECURITY. Social Security benefits are the major source of income for most older women, especially those who are poor. Social Security provides about half of the income for women 65 years and older (AAUW, 2006) and keeps over two-thirds of older women from sinking into poverty. Almost 25 percent of all older women rely on Social Security as their *only* source of income (AAUW, 2008c). But heavy reliance on Social Security can be a financial nightmare. For example, the average Social Security benefit for retired women workers in 2008 was $10,757 a year, only slightly above the federal poverty threshold for older adults (Hayes et al., 2010).

EXPLORE OTHER CULTURES 10.2
Economic Status of Older Women

In richer (i.e., developed) countries, older people can more easily afford to retire because of Social Security systems or pensions. In the United States, for example, only about 14 percent of married women and 20 percent of single women aged 65 and over are in the labor force (U.S. Census Bureau, 2010b). However, these retirement benefits are often inadequate for women because they penalize the female-dominated activities of homemaker, part-time employee, domestic worker, and agricultural worker. In several countries, even women who have worked for much of their adult lives receive smaller pensions than men. In one study, women's benefits as a proportion of men's were 64 percent in the United States, 77 percent in France and Switzerland, and 85 percent in Sweden. However, at least five developed countries provide equal benefits for women and men: Australia, New Zealand, Great Britain, Germany, and the Netherlands (Mercer et al., 2001).

In developing nations, the economic situation for older women is much starker than in developed countries. Social Security and pension plans are often nonexistent. Therefore, older women and men must continue working. In Rwanda, for example, nearly three-quarters of women between ages 65 and 69 remain economically active (Kinsella & Velkoff, 2001). The low status of women in developing countries can have devastating effects in later life. For example, in most of sub-Saharan Africa, women do not have land rights or property rights. A husband typically allocates his wife a plot of land to work on to produce food for the family. But if he dies, she no longer has the right to that land or even to the family's house. The land and house are taken over by the husband's family, and she often is evicted and left destitute ("Africa's Homeless Widows," 2004; LaFraniere, 2005).

The Social Security system was designed to serve the typical family of the mid-1930s, which included a breadwinner father, a homemaker mother, and children. Most of today's families do not fit that mold because the majority of women are in the labor force. Women's different work patterns mean that they are disadvantaged by a Social Security system designed to reward male work histories that often include many uninterrupted years in relatively high-paying jobs (Kail et al., 2009).

Ethnic minority women, who tend to be concentrated in lower-paying jobs and to have higher unemployment rates, receive even lower benefits than White women (Calasanti, 2010). Because they

WHAT YOU CAN DO 10.2
Start Planning for Retirement

1. Establish your own savings and checking accounts.
2. Learn about your job benefits, such as health insurance, pension plan, and Social Security.
3. Minimize your credit card debt.
4. Set up an emergency fund worth three to six months' salary.
5. Learn about financial planning by taking a course or finding a financial advisor.
6. Consider setting up an IRA (individual retirement account).

7. Carry enough insurance to cover loss of life, health, home, and earning power.
8. Make a will.
9. Set up a **durable power of attorney,** a *document that authorizes someone to manage your financial affairs should you become incompetent.*

Sources: MetLife (2010b); Orman (2010); and WISER (2008).

are more likely than White women to be employed "off the books" where benefits do not accrue, their benefits are the lowest of all, whereas those of White men are the highest. Moreover, many women apply for their benefits early, at age 62, because they need the income. But doing so reduces their benefits (Social Security Administration, 2009).

Spousal Benefits.   A lifelong homemaker has no Social Security protection in her own name. She is eligible to receive a spousal benefit equal to half of her husband's benefit if they have been married for at least 10 years. A divorced woman is also eligible to receive half of her ex-husband's benefit if they were married for at least 10 years. If she remarries, she forfeits her right to her former husband's benefit. A widow becomes eligible to receive a portion of her husband's benefit at age 60, but she must wait until age 65 for full benefits (Social Security Administration, 2009). Cohabiting couples receive no Social Security benefits as a family unit, nor do married same-sex couples, even in states that recognize their marriage (O'Leary & Kornbluh, 2009).

Dual Entitlement.   Married women who are wage earners have **dual entitlement** but are, in effect, penalized as well. *They qualify for Social Security benefits based on both their own and their husband's work history.* But they receive only the higher of the two benefits to which they are entitled. Most dually entitled women draw benefits based on their husbands' work records because the husband's benefits are greater than theirs (Social Security Administration, 2009). These women would have been entitled to these benefits even if they had never worked a day in their lives! Thus, the Social Security contributions that married women make as workers seem unnecessary and unfair (Gilbert, 2008).

PENSION INCOME.   The second leg of the retirement stool—private pensions—can be an important source of income for women. Although about half of both older men and older women have income from pensions, the average pension benefit paid to women is less than that paid to men (Calasanti, 2010). Black and less-educated women are less likely than White and better-educated women to receive any pension income (Calasanti, 2010). Why do so few women receive pension benefits? Let us briefly examine some reasons for this.

Work Patterns.   As with Social Security, private pension plans are designed for the traditional male work pattern of long continuous years of employment in higher-paying jobs. Women not only work less continuously and in lower-paying jobs, but are also more likely to work at jobs that have either low pension coverage (service jobs, nonunion jobs, small businesses) or in part-time or temporary jobs, which have little or no coverage (AAUW, 2008c; Henderson & Jeydel, 2010; OWL, 2010).

Vesting.   Women's shorter job tenure also makes it more difficult for them to receive pensions because of a practice known as **vesting.** *The vesting period is the number of years of participation in a company plan that is required to be eligible for a pension.* Most plans require 5 years on the job in order to be vested. However, the average job tenure for a woman is only 3.8 years compared with 5.0 years for men (Hounsell, 2008).

Nonportability.   Women also are disadvantaged because of **nonportability** of pension plans. This means that *most traditional pension plans cannot be taken from one job to another.* This practice affects women more than men, because women are more likely to change jobs frequently (WISER, 2000–2010).

Spousal Benefits.   As with Social Security benefits, a woman is more likely to receive spousal pension benefits as a wife, widow, or divorcée than she is from her own experience as a worker. A widow typically receives a benefit of half the amount the couple received when the husband was alive. A divorced woman can receive similar survivor's pension benefits when her former husband dies. Although, she does not automatically receive any of his pension benefits following divorce, divorce settlements can be written to include a share of the husband's pension (Hoffman, 2002; Uchitelle, 2001).

SAVINGS AND INVESTMENTS.   The third leg of the retirement stool is income from savings and investments. Today's older women have little income from savings, and their lower earnings leave them with few resources to invest (WISER, 2006b).

Women who do invest generally are more cautious investors than men (Little, 2005). They are more wary of risk (Carr & Steele, 2010), and so are more likely to invest in conservative options such as bonds, certificates of deposit, and money-market accounts that pay lower returns than stocks. Although women tend to take fewer risks in the stock market, they do slightly better than men. Why? According to financial expert Jane Bryant Quinn (2001), women trade less, and those who trade less do better.

Summary

WOMEN'S EMPLOYMENT RATES AND OCCUPATIONAL CHOICES

- More than 60 percent of women 16 years and older, including those who are married and have young children, are employed. Economic necessity is a major reason for women's employment.
- Although the last several decades have seen a decrease, gender and ethnic segregation in the workplace continue to be highly prevalent. The most prestigious occupations are dominated by White men.

GENDER DIFFERENCES IN LEADERSHIP AND JOB ADVANCEMENT

- Women and people of color are less likely than White males to attain high positions in their occupations.
- Barriers that hinder women's advancement include the glass ceiling, shorter job ladders, limited availability of mentors, exclusion from informal social networks, and discrimination.
- Discriminatory treatment is due, in part, to the operation of gender stereotypes, ingroup favoritism, and White males' perception of threat.

- Women are presumed to be less capable leaders than men. Males often express dislike for highly competent and agentic women.
- As leaders, women tend to be more transformational and less transactional than men.

GENDER DIFFERENCES IN SALARIES

- Women earn 77 percent of what men earn. The gender discrepancy is even greater between women of color and White men. These income differences result from several factors, including gender differences in job investments, in occupations, in job levels, and in salary negotiation, as well as discrimination.
- Women generally believe their salaries are not commensurate with their work value, ability, and experience.

WOMEN'S JOB SATISFACTION

- Women are as satisfied as or more satisfied than men with their jobs.
- One factor contributing to job satisfaction for sexual minorities is the organizational climate for lesbian, gay, bisexual, and transgender workers.

THE OLDER WOMAN WORKER

- Increased numbers of middle-aged and older women are in the labor force. Economic necessity is a key reason.
- Employment among older women promotes physical and psychological well-being.
- Women face age discrimination in the workplace at a younger age than men.

CHANGING THE WORKPLACE

- Organizational strategies that can improve the workplace for women and people of color include implementation of pay equity, establishment of clearly defined affirmative action policies and procedures, and maintenance of an organizational environment characterized by sensitivity to diversity.

RETIREMENT

- Women's retirement decisions depend on many factors.
- Women earning low wages tend to delay retirement, as do professional and self-employed women. Older women with caregiving responsibilities tend to retire early.

- The decision to retire is influenced by individual, family, economic, and occupational factors.
- The transition to retirement is a time of marital conflict, especially when husbands retire first.
- Satisfaction in retirement is associated with having good health, adequate income, high activity level, and contact with friends and relatives.
- Older women and men differ in the nature of their preferred leisure activities.

ECONOMIC ISSUES IN LATER LIFE

- Older women, especially minorities, are more likely than older men to be poor or near-poor.
- The poverty rate is greater for very old women and for unmarried women.
- Because women, compared with men, spend less continuous time in the workforce, and are in more low-paying jobs, their eligibility for and benefits from Social Security and pensions suffer. Women also have less income from savings and investments than do men.
- Preretirement planning in young adulthood can improve women's financial security during later life.

Key Terms

glass escalator *226*
token *226*
glass ceiling *226*
glass cliff *227*
sticky floor *227*
maternal wall *227*
mentor *227*
patronizing behavior *228*
shifting standards hypothesis *230*

transformational *231*
transactional *231*
laissez-faire *231*
human capital perspective *233*
wage discrimination *234*
motherhood wage penalty *235*
fatherhood wage
   premium *235*
sweatshops *235*

paradox of the contented
   female worker *236*
pay equity *239*
affirmative action *240*
advocate *246*
durable power of attorney *249*
dual entitlement *250*
vesting *250*
nonportability *250*

What Do You Think?

1. What kinds of rewards, other than financial, are provided by employment? How does gender socialization affect the particular values women attach to work? Explain your answers.

2. Why do you think many people have negative impressions, including misconceptions, of affirmative action? Incorporate information about stereotypes, gender socialization, gender differences

in power, and/or any other material related to this course.

3. This chapter discussed several procedures for improving the workplace for women and people of color. What other actions can be undertaken by employers or individuals in these groups to decrease gender and ethnicity inequities in the work environment?

4. How might greater gender equity in the workplace change the current social construction of gender? Would this, in turn, influence the gender acquisition of gender-related traits, behaviors, roles, and/or career goals of future generations of females? Explain your answers.

5. Given the substantial influx of women into the labor force in the past several decades, the proportion of retired working women to lifelong homemakers will continue to increase among older women. What are the implications of this?

6. What can be done to help ease the "feminization of poverty"?

7. What are some implications of the older woman's greater economic insecurity?

8. What is meant by the statement that older minority women are in "triple jeopardy." Provide and discuss examples.

If You Want to Learn More

Barreto, M., Ryan, M. K., & Schmitt, M. T. (Eds.). (2009). *The glass ceiling in the 21st century: Understanding barriers to gender equality.* Washington, DC: American Psychological Association.

Borooah, V., & Hart, M. (2011). *Women and the labor market.* New York: Routledge.

Bratter, B., & Dennis, H. (2008). *Project Renewment: The first retirement model for career women.* New York: Scribner.

Chin, J. L., Lott, B., Rice, J. K., & Sanchez-Hucles, J. (Eds.). (2007). *Women and leadership: Transforming visions and diverse voices.* Maiden, MA: Blackwell.

Crosby, F. J., Stockdale, M. S., & Ropp, S. A. (Eds.). (2007). *Sex discrimination in the workplace.* Maiden, MA: Blackwell.

Eagly, A. H., & Carli, L. L. (2007). *Through the labyrinth: The truth about how women become leaders.* Boston, MA: Harvard Business School Press.

Fiedler, M. E. (2010). *Breaking through the stained glass ceiling: Women religious leaders in their own words.* New York: Seabury Books.

Greene, J. A. (2006). *Blue-collar women at work with men: Negotiating the hostile environment.* Westport, CT: Praeger.

Hewlett, S. A. (2007). *Off-ramps and on-ramps: Keeping talented women on the road to success.* Boston, MA: Harvard Business School Press.

Heymann, J., & Earle, A. (2010). *Raising the global floor: Dismantling the myth that we can't afford good working conditions for everyone.* Stanford, CA: Stanford University Press.

Johnson, J. (2002). *Getting by on the minimum: The lives of working-class women.* New York: Routledge.

Kellerman, B., & Rhode, D. L. (Eds.). (2007). *Women and leadership: The state of play and strategies for change.* San Francisco, CA: Wiley.

Palmer, B., & Simon, D. (2008). *Breaking the political glass ceiling: Women and congressional elections.* New York: Routledge.

Paludi, M. A. (Ed.). (2008). *The psychology of women at work: Challenges and solutions for our female workforce* (Vols. 1–3). Westport, CT: Praeger.

Parker, P. S. (2005). *Race, gender, and leadership: Reenvisioning organizational leadership from the perspectives of African-American women executives.* Mahwah, NJ: Erlbaum.

Websites

Women in the Workplace

Women's Bureau of the U.S. Department of Labor
http://www.dol.gov/wb/

Lesbians in the Workplace

Human Rights Campaign: Workplace
http://www.hrc.org/issues/workplace.asp

Pay Equity

AFL-CIO: Working Women Working Together
http://www.aflcio.org/women

Retirement and Economic Issues

AARP (formerly, the American Association of Retired Persons)
http://www.aarp.org
Gender and the Social Security System
http://www.socialsecuritymatters.org/

CHAPTER 11

Balancing Family and Work

**Women's Family and
Employment Roles:
Perceptions and Attitudes**
Perceptions of Working
and Stay-at-Home
Mothers
Factors Influencing
Attitudes Toward
Women's Multiple Roles

Division of Family Labor
Housework and Child Care
Caring for Aging Parents
Leisure Time
Women's Perceptions
of the Division of
Family Labor
Explanations of the
Division of Family Labor

Family–Work Coordination
Balancing Family and
Work: Costs and
Benefits
Effects of Mothers'
Employment
Solutions to Family–Work
Balancing Challenges

**Midlife Transitions in Family
and Work Roles**
Satisfaction With Life Roles
Regrets About Life
Direction
Making Changes
Midlife Transitions:
A Cautionary Note

My daughter was less than 1 year old when I started working as an assistant professor of psychology and my son was born two years later. Although I adored my children, and got enormous satisfaction from my career, juggling the two roles was often stressful. To this day, I can vividly recall the anxiety that erupted when my daughter or son woke up too sick to go to their caregiver's home or when both were of school age and school was canceled because of snow (a frequent occurrence in our New England community). I was plagued by worry that my commitment to my children was preventing me from devoting sufficient time and energy to my career and that my employment was somehow hurting my children. Interestingly, however, I don't recall ever feeling that my husband's job was damaging our children or that being a father was hindering his job advancement. (Judith Bridges)

Historically, women and men had different roles within the family. Men were the economic providers and women the caregivers and homemakers. However, the traditional family consisting of a provider-father, a stay-at-home mother, and their children is relatively rare today. Whereas 57 percent of U.S. children in 1960 were raised in this type of household, only one in five children in married-couple families now have a stay-at-home mother (O'Leary & Kornbluh, 2009; U.S. Census Bureau, 2010c). Compared with employed mothers, those staying at home tend to be younger, less well-educated, and Latina or foreign-born (U.S. Census Bureau, 2010c).

As we saw in Chapter 10, the majority of women, including married women with children, are now employed. Not only are more married women working, but they are also working longer hours than women did a generation ago (Williams & Boushey, 2010). Women now constitute half of the American labor force, a trend fueled by the recent recession, which resulted in more men than women losing their jobs. As a result, four out of five couples are now dual-earner couples. The women in these couples contribute nearly half of the family income (Aumann & Galinsky, 2009). As a consequence of this major transformation in women's roles, today's young women are involved in a challenging balancing act between the demands of completing their education, beginning their work lives, finding a partner, and having children. Some women postpone or even forego marriage and/or children in favor of work or career, others leave the workplace or choose part-time employment while their children are young, and still others combine family and full-time careers. Women balance these roles of worker, wife, and mother in different combinations over the course of their lives (Amato & Kane, 2011; Gerson, 2010). Stories in high-profile media have been asserting that highly educated mothers are "opting out" of careers to stay home with their children. In Learn About the Research 11.1, we examine the evidence for and against this assertion.

This chapter explores issues related to the coordination of women's multiple responsibilities in the domestic and employment domains. We begin with a look at perceptions of and attitudes toward their family and employment roles. Then we examine the impact of women's employment on the division of labor in the home as well as the challenges, costs, and benefits of balancing family and work. We explore employer resources that facilitate this coordination and consider strategies women use to manage family and work responsibilities. We conclude with a discussion of midlife transitions in family and work roles.

WOMEN'S FAMILY AND EMPLOYMENT ROLES: PERCEPTIONS AND ATTITUDES

Although the traditional view of the male provider–female homemaker was once seen as the expected and desirable family type, most adults today do not perceive it as ideal. In 1977, 64 percent of American adults believed that husbands should be providers and wives full-time homemakers. In 2008, that figure dropped to 41 percent (Galinsky et al., 2009). Let us examine how working and stay-at-home mothers are perceived. We'll then look at factors that influence attitudes toward women's multiple roles.

Perceptions of Working and Stay-at-Home Mothers

Remember from Chapter 2 that, according to social role theory, women are assumed to be higher than men in warmth and nurturance, whereas men are assumed to be higher than women in agency and competence. Consistent with social role theory, mothers who go back to work or school immediately after birth or following a brief maternity leave are viewed as less warm and communal than mothers who cut back to part-time work or school or stay at home (Bridges & Etaugh,

LEARN ABOUT THE RESEARCH 11.1
Are Women "Opting Out" of Careers?

Some headlines in national media such as the *New York Times,* the *Wall Street Journal, Newsweek,* and *Time* claim that mothers are increasingly opting out of their careers to stay home with their children (Boushey, 2009; Kuperberg & Stone, 2008). How accurate is this assertion? Two widely cited *New York Times* articles in 2003 and 2005 making this claim used small, nonrandom samples of atypical women to prove their point. One was a group of Princeton graduates whose husbands' incomes were large enough to support them and their children. The other was a small sample of Yale students responding to a survey about their future plans. Social scientists were highly critical of these anecdotal data, some collected from women who were years away from even joining the workforce (Barnett, 2007).

Studies based on large, representative samples show that women are, in fact, *not* opting out, and that working mothers are more likely than ever to pursue jobs and careers while raising their families (Percheski, 2008). It is true that mothers' labor force participation rates declined between 2000 and 2004, but so did the rates of childless women, childless men, and fathers, due to an economic recession (Boushey, 2009; Cotter et al., 2008; Day & Downs, 2009). Highly educated mothers aged 25–45 are as likely to be in the labor force as women without children, a trend that started in the mid-1980s and continues to this day (Percheski, 2008). Only two groups of women are opting out in any meaningful numbers. The larger group consists of mothers whose earnings are so low that they cannot afford child care. This group tends to be younger, less educated, and Latina or foreign born. The other group consists of women whose husbands earn extremely high salaries (Day & Downs, 2009; U.S. Census Bureau, 2011; J. Warner, 2009). Given this evidence, what might account for the myth that the best and brightest American women are dropping out of the workplace? Harvard economist Claudia Goldin (2006) suggests that some people find it hard to believe that women can both contribute to their profession and participate meaningfully in raising children. Psychologist Rosalind Barnett (2007) similarly notes that the social construction of women as the primary caregivers seems to take precedence over the evidence that most women today intend to combine family and employment, and in fact thrive on it.

WHAT DOES IT MEAN?

1. How does the debate on whether women are opting out of the workforce illustrate how different research methods can lead to very different conclusions?

2. During an economic recession, women and men with and without children are more likely to leave the labor force. Why has the focus been largely on *mothers* who leave the workforce?

3. What social and economic conditions of the past few decades have led to an increase in the percentage of women who are combining work and family roles?

1995; Coleman & Franiuk, 2011; Etaugh & Folger, 1998; Etaugh & Moss, 2001; Mottarella et al., 2009). For a closer look at attitudes toward maternal employment in other industrialized nations, see Explore Other Cultures 11.1.

In addition, mothers who are employed full time are judged more harshly than nonmothers who are employed full time. They are viewed as both less nurturing *and* less professionally competent (Etaugh & Folger, 1998; Livengood, 2010). Along the same lines, mothers are judged as less likely to be hired than are nonmothers with the same credentials (an example of the "maternal wall"). Fathers, on the other hand, are judged to be as hirable as nonfathers (Fuegen et al., 2004).

EXPLORE OTHER CULTURES 11.1
Attitudes Toward Married Women's Employment: A Cross-Cultural Perspective

Judith Treas and Eric Widmer (2000) examined attitudes toward married women's employment in 23 largely Western and industrial countries. Recall from Chapter 3 that almost everyone agreed that married women should work, preferably full time, before they had children. Support for full-time work was almost as high after children were grown. However, mothers of preschoolers were expected either to stay home or work only part time. Those with school-age children were expected to work only part time. Despite this general consensus, nations also showed some difference in attitudes. Basically, three different nation clusters were identified: the "work-oriented," "family accommodating," and "motherhood-centered." The work-oriented cluster consisted of Canada, East Germany, Israel, the Netherlands, Norway, Sweden, and the United States. Whatever the life-course stage, this cluster's respondents were the least likely to recommend that married women

stay home. Unlike other clusters, they favored part-time employment for mothers of preschoolers. These countries had more egalitarian gender-role attitudes than the other nations in the study and perceived fewer conflicts between women's work and family roles. The "family accommodating" cluster (Australia, Austria, West Germany, Great Britain, Italy, Japan, New Zealand, Northern Ireland, and Russia) put less emphasis on maternal employment. They expected mothers to stay at home with pre-schoolers and work only part time not only when their children reached school age, but even after they were grown. The "motherhood centered" cluster (Bulgaria, the Czech Republic, Hungary, Ireland, Poland, Slovenia, and Spain) endorsed full-time employment before and after marriage, but staying at home with preschoolers and, even to some extent, with school-age children. Not surprisingly, this group had the most traditional gender-role attitudes.

Factors Influencing Attitudes Toward Women's Multiple Roles

One factor that affects attitudes toward women's multiple roles is age. Only 25 percent of younger adults believe that it is a bad thing for mothers of young children to work outside the home, compared to nearly 40 percent of older adults (Pew Research Center, 2010a). Ethnicity also plays a role in attitudes toward working mothers. Historically, poor and working class women of color have been in the labor force in order to help support their families (Holvino, 2008). Thus, it is not surprising that, as we saw in Chapter 9, Black female college students plan to return to work sooner than White female students following a child's birth (Bridges & Etaugh, 1996). Still, sizable minority of Black and Latina/o adults, especially recent immigrants, believe that men should maintain the primary financial responsibility for their families. Possibly, this belief is an attempt to maintain male dignity in a society that makes it difficult for ethnic minority men to fulfill their provider role responsibility (Taylor et al., 1999).

Gender, as you might expect, also influences attitudes toward women's family and work roles. In one survey of first-year college students, women were less likely than men (17 percent versus 28 percent) to agree that married women should be full-time homemakers ("This Year's Freshmen," 2005). But the large majority of today's college students—two-thirds of both women and men—say that balancing work and family is a priority for them (Miller et al., 2009).

Another key factor that influences views on working mothers is the employment history of one's own mother. Adolescent and young adult children whose mothers were employed during their childhood do not feel they were neglected and appreciate the effort their mothers undertook to help provide for the family (Gerson, 2002). Moreover, women and men whose mothers worked all or most of the time while they were growing up are more likely than those whose mothers worked little or not at all to strongly agree that working mothers can have relationships with their children that are just as good as mothers who stay at home (Galinsky et al., 2009). Working women's grown-up daughters are even more likely than their grown-up sons to strongly agree with this statement. Thus, consistent with the assumption that gender is constructed in part from interpersonal experiences, it seems that positive experiences with an employed mother early in their childhood lead women to view the combination of motherhood and employment as acceptable female role choices that are not harmful to children. Try the Get Involved 11.1 activity to examine attitudes toward mothers who are in school full time.

DIVISION OF FAMILY LABOR

Increasing numbers of women and men have substantial household and child care obligations along with major work responsibilities. What is the relative importance of work and spousal and parental roles in the lives of women and men? Do the husbands of employed women contribute more to child

---

GET INVOLVED 11.1
How Do College Students Evaluate Mothers Who Are Full-Time Students?

For this activity, based on a study by Karen Mottarella and her colleagues (2009), ask four traditional-aged (18–21-year-old) female students to read a brief description of a mother and indicate their impression of her on rating scales. Give two participants description A, followed by the rating scales, and two participants description B, followed by the same scales.

Description A: Emily is a 31-year-old married mother. She was a full-time college student before her child was born and returned to school full time at the end of her six-week maternity leave.

Description B: Emily is a 31-year-old married mother. She was a full-time college student before her child was born and returned to school full time when her child was in first grade.

Now indicate how much you like and respect Emily by completing the following two rating scales:

like her very little	1 2 3 4 5 6 7	like her very much
respect her very little	1 2 3 4 5 6 7	respect her very much

WHAT DOES IT MEAN?

Calculate the average rating for each respondent. A high score reflects a positive evaluation of the mother and a low score shows a negative evaluation. Next, average the responses given by the two respondents who read the description of the mother who stayed in school (description A) and average the scores of the two who read the paragraph about the mother who interrupted her education (description B).

1. Similar to studies in the text, this study found that mothers who take a brief maternity leave are more negatively evaluated than those who interrupt their education. Did you find the same results? If yes, give reasons for this finding.

2. Describe socialization experiences that might influence young women's personal beliefs about a brief maternity leave versus interrupted employment or education.

3. This study and others presented in the text examined attitudes of traditional-aged college students. Do you think that older women would have different impressions? Explain your answer.

Source: Based on Mottarella et al. (2009).

care or housekeeping labor than the husbands of nonemployed women? Has this changed over time? Are women and men satisfied with this division of labor? We now explore these questions and others related to the division of family responsibilities.

Housework and Child Care

Studies published in the 1970s and the 1980s showed that husbands increased their household labor very little when their wives were employed. Although husbands have increased their housework participation somewhat since then and wives have reduced theirs, men's contribution to household labor in the United States, Canada, Australia, and Europe still does not equal that of women (Bianchi & Milkie, 2010; Craig & Mullian, 2010; Devetter, 2009; Heisig, 2011; Hook, 2010; Judkins & Presser, 2008; Knudsen & Waerness, 2008).

In 1965, American women did 35 hours of housework a week, compared to 5 hours for men. By 2005, women averaged 19 hours and men averaged 11 hours (Eagly & Carli, 2007). The division of housework between women and men is more egalitarian in countries with progressive gender ideologies (Hook, 2010). For example, women in Japan, which has relatively traditional gender attitudes, perform 90 percent of the housework, compared to 67 percent in Denmark and Finland, where gender ideologies are more egalitarian (Knudsen & Waerness, 2008). Among employed couples with no children in the United States, wives spend about 5 more hours per week performing housework than their husbands do, but among employed couples with children, the combined housework and child care gap jumps to 17 hours (Goldstein, 2000). Also, although Black and Latino husbands are more involved in household and child care duties than White husbands (Kimmel, 2009; Lang & Risman, 2006), employed women still perform a disproportionate share of these responsibilities in these families (Pinto & Coltrane, 2009; U.S. Bureau of Labor Statistics, 2010a). Women still assume the main responsibility for traditional female chores such as cooking, cleaning, and shopping, whereas men have more responsibility for traditional male chores such as yard work, repairs, and car maintenance (Schiebinger & Gilmartin, 2010; U.S. Bureau of Labor Statistics, 2010a). Note that the tasks done by women are generally performed one or more times per day or week, while those by men are done only periodically.

Regardless of their employment role, women continue to perform most child care activities, including feeding and bathing young children, attending school conferences and sports events, helping with homework, disciplining, organizing leisure activities, taking children to the doctor, and providing or arranging for substitute care when there is a school vacation or when a child is sick (Baxter et al., 2008; Bianchi & Wight, 2010; Drago, 2009; Hartmann et al., 2010; Hook, 2010; Lareau & Weininger, 2008; Maume, 2008; Sasaki et al., 2010). Fathers, on the other hand, tend to focus more on play activities with their infants and young children (Featherstone, 2010). In lesbian families, couples are more likely to share both child care and household tasks (Biblarz & Savci, 2010; Goldberg & Perry-Jenkins, 2007).

Because employed women perform the bulk of child care and housework duties, it is no surprise that one of their major concerns is simply finding the time to adequately fulfill all their responsibilities (Cornelius & Skinner, 2008; DeGroot & Fine, 2003). Another primary issue is arranging for good child care. "If I did not find good care, I simply would not work" (Snyder, 1994, p. 166). "I honestly do think that if Lizzie hadn't been there to take care of her then things would have been different because I don't think I would have been able to leave her with somebody I didn't know" (Leach et al., 2006, p. 483). Comments like these illustrate the central importance of child care for employed women. Not surprisingly, worries about child care can lead to high levels of stress for employed mothers (Leach et al., 2006; Press et al., 2006).

Caring for Aging Parents

Increasing numbers of midlife women are part of the "sandwich generation," caring simultaneously for their children and their aging parents (and in some cases, grandparents) who need assistance with daily activities such as cooking, bathing, financial matters, transportation to doctors, and shopping. Although men also provide assistance, especially to their own parents (Szinovacz & Davey, 2008), women perform the bulk of eldercare both in the United States and in other nations (Duxbury et al., 2009; Glenn, 2010; Hanratty et al., 2007; Henz, 2010; National Alliance for Caregiving, 2009; Silverstein & Giarusso, 2010; Stephens et al., 2009). In fact, it has been estimated that women can expect to spend 18 years providing care to an older parent, a period of time roughly comparable to that devoted to childrearing (Godfrey & Warshaw, 2009).

The average female caregiver is aged 48 and married, and works outside the home. We saw in Chapter 8 that she is likely to be a daughter, daughter-in-law, or granddaughter (Henz, 2009; National Alliance for Caregiving, 2009; Stephens et al., 2009). The financial impact of caring for older relatives is considerable. About half of employed caregivers have reported rearranging work schedules, decreasing working hours, or taking an unpaid leave (Stephens et al., 2009). Still others pass up promotions, quit their jobs, or retire early (Connidis, 2010). The same pattern is also found in other nations. For example, European and Australian women who provide extensive care for older relatives are also more likely to cease employment than women who are not providing such care (Austen & Ong, 2010; Masuy, 2009). Taking time out of the labor force for caregiving places a strain on women's income (MetLife, 2010a; Meyer & Herd, 2007). In addition, caregivers of older parents may also have less time for family and friends, further increasing emotional strain (National Alliance for Caregiving, 2009). No wonder caregivers of older relatives are more likely than noncaregivers to show higher levels of depression, anxiety, hostility, stress, exhaustion, and family tension ("Characteristics and Health," 2007; MetLife, 2010a; Meyer & Herd, 2007; Pinquart & Sörensen, 2006; Rubin & White-Means, 2009).

Leisure Time

With all the time women are spending on child care, eldercare, and employment, it is no surprise that employed mothers have less leisure time than either employed fathers (Arnold & Lang, 2007; Beck & Arnold, 2009; Milkie et al., 2011; Sayer, 2005) or nonemployed mothers (Miller & Brown, 2005). Feminists point out that the concept of leisure is different for women and men, with women experiencing less time for leisure in their lives than men. A common focus of women's leisure, according to this perspective, is the combining of family obligations with leisure opportunities. A woman may perceive the family's leisure as her leisure and vice versa. The home is the most common place in which women's leisure occurs. In this way, leisure can sometimes be combined with household chores. Women often multitask and may, for example, engage in a leisure activity, such as watching television, while at the same time doing housework, such as cooking or mending. Thus, much of women's leisure time may be fragmented rather than occurring in large blocks of time (Beck Arnold, 2009; Bianchi & Wight, 2010; Offer & Schneider, 2010). Even after retirement, women have less time for leisure than men because they continue to remain more occupied with domestic chores and family responsibilities (U.S. Bureau of Labor Statistics, 2010a). For example, we saw in Chapter 8 that many older women have caregiving responsibilities for grandchildren, ailing spouses, or parents.

Women's Perceptions of the Division of Family Labor

Although women perform about two-thirds of the total household labor, only a small percentage rate their division of labor as unfair (Gager, 2008; Greenstein, 2009; Sardadvar, 2011). What might account for this apparent paradox between women's heavier workload and their satisfaction with the allocation of domestic responsibilities? Possibly, women's gender socialization has led them to believe that both childrearing and household work are in women's domain. This construction of the female role may produce no discrepancy between what they expect and what they experience. Moreover, pressures to adhere to their socially prescribed maternal role make it difficult for some women to relinquish caregiving duties to their spouses or partners (Kenney & Bogle, 2009; Mannino & Deutsch, 2007). Additionally, some women, especially those holding traditional gender ideologies, might compare their own household responsibility to that of other women, rather than to their husband's responsibility and, therefore, not see themselves as unfairly burdened (Greenstein, 2009).

For those women who feel that the division of domestic labor is unfair, the perceived inequity does not stem from the amount of time they spend on household tasks, but from their *share* of the total time spent by the couple. In research involving Asian American, Black, Latina, Middle Eastern American, and White wives, the more time wives spent relative to their husbands', the more likely they were to view the allocation of family responsibilities as unfair and to feel dissatisfied with it (Stohs, 2000; Van Willigen & Drentea, 2001). On the other hand, the more a wife believes she matters to her husband, the more likely she is to report that the division of housework is fair, regardless of the share of housework she performs (Kawamura & Brown, 2007).

Explanations of the Division of Family Labor

What accounts for women's disproportionate share of child care and housekeeping duties? At least three explanations have been offered.

TIME AVAILABILITY. One explanation for the unequal division of household labor is that domestic responsibilities are allocated on the basis of each spouse's time availability (Burn, 2011). Consistent with this view, full-time homemakers, who have more time available, spend more time in household tasks than do employed women (Burn, 2011; Hook, 2010; Pinto & Coltrane, 2009). Furthermore, the more hours women and men spend in paid work, the less time they expend in housework (Poortman & Van der Lippe, 2009).

However, some patterns of domestic involvement are inconsistent with this explanation. For example, even when comparing spouses with comparable work hours, mothers spend more time than fathers caring for their children and doing household tasks (Institute for Women's Policy Research, 2007; Lachance-Grzela & Bouchard, 2010). Thus, although time availability plays some role, it alone cannot explain the allocation of domestic responsibilities.

RELATIVE POWER. Another possible explanation is that women's disproportionate share of household labor results from their lower degree of marital power (Burn, 2011). According to this view, power in marriage depends, in part, on work-related resources, such as income. The more resources one partner has in relation to the other, the greater that partner's influence (i.e., power) over the other. Because people tend to dislike household chores, the person with greater resources will use his or her power to limit engagement in these tasks. Does research support this view? Evidence indicates that it is not the *difference* in husbands' and wives' income that explains women's participation in household labor, but rather how much she earns herself (Gupta, 2007). For every $7,500 in additional income, a woman's share of housework declines by one hour per week. Yet, even when women bring greater work resources to the marriage, men retain higher status and power. For example, Veronica Tichenor (2005) found that even when wives earned significantly more than their husbands, neither husbands nor wives evaluated her career as more important than his. Furthermore, despite their lower income, husbands maintained greater financial decision-making power. Thus, even when men have fewer occupational resources than their wives, they apparently maintain other forms of power.

GENDER ATTITUDES.   A third explanation for the division of household labor is that the unequal distribution reflects spouses' beliefs about appropriate gender roles (Burn, 2011; Poortman & Van der Lippe, 2009; Powell & Greenhaus, 2010; Sasaki et al., 2010). According to this view, many couples have internalized the traditional gender beliefs that managing children and the home is primarily the wife's responsibility and that husbands should be the main financial providers. Thus, they may feel uncomfortable if they deviate from these strong societal norms (Bianchi & Milkie, 2010; Drago, 2007).

Consistent with this explanation, men who have nontraditional attitudes about family roles spend more time doing housework than those with traditional views (Lachance-Grzela & Bouchard, 2010), whereas women with nontraditional beliefs spend less time in household labor than women who have traditional attitudes (Davis et al., 2007; Davis & Greenstein, 2009; Mannino & Deutsch, 2007). Moreover, college students with traditional gender-role attitudes find it more acceptable for a man to contribute less to household chores (Swearingen-Hilker & Yoder, 2002).

FAMILY–WORK COORDINATION

Balancing Family and Work: Costs and Benefits

What kind of costs and benefits might stem from juggling family and work roles? Consider these questions, then try Get Involved 11.2 to explore your personal expectations of this issue. When Judith and Claire (Bridges & Etaugh, 1996) asked White and Black college women to respond to the items presented in Get Involved 11.2, they found that these students estimated that the benefits would be greater than the costs (70 percent versus 55 percent). Although both White and Black students had similarly viewed the probability of benefits, White students estimated a higher likelihood of negative outcomes from working during motherhood than did Black students. The long history of Black women's employment (Boushey, 2009) may contribute to their more positive attitude toward maternal employment. These different views held by Black and White women show that these attitudes are socially constructed from individuals' experiences and do not simply arise from one's gender.

In actuality, the effects of performing family and work roles are complex and encompass both positive and negative aspects. Because of this, it is important to examine women's actual experiences associated with these roles as well as explanations of these outcomes.

COSTS.   As might be expected, many employed women, especially mothers, experience **role strain**, that is, *stress stemming from one's roles* (Perrone et al., 2009). In the words of one employed mother of an infant, "Everything was a compromise. When I went to work, I felt like I should be at home. And when I was at home, I thought [about that] I left in the middle [of] all of these management meetings. And everybody's looking around like, 'Where's she going?'" (Hattery, 2001, p. 58). Role strain can stem from **role overload**, *role demands that exceed one's available time and/or energy*, and/or **interrole conflict**, *incompatible demands stemming from two or more roles* (Duxbury et al., 2008). Role overload can occur, for example, when, after 9 hours of work and commuting, a mother does her family's laundry, cooks dinner, washes the dishes, and supervises her children's homework. Interrole conflict, on the other hand, would occur if a mother wants to attend her child's band concert at school but has an important business meeting scheduled for the same time. Women in two-career families often experience the dual pressures of performing well in fast-paced demanding careers and performing well in their roles as mothers, increasing their risk of stress and exhaustion (Cocchiara & Bell, 2009). The more role strain women experience, the greater their depression and stress and the lower their job and life satisfaction (Glynn et al., 2009; Jang & Zippay, 2011).

What produces role strain? According to the **scarcity hypothesis**, *excessive role responsibilities deplete the individual's limited supply of time and energy and, consequently, can lead to stress.* When

GET INVOLVED 11.2
What Psychological Experiences Do You Think You Will Have If You Combine Employment and Motherhood?

Pretend that you have two children and a spouse/partner employed full time outside of the home. Given these circumstances, think about the experience you might have if you, also, were employed full time outside the home throughout your childrearing years. For each of the following possible consequences of employment during parenthood, estimate the probability, from 0 percent to 100 percent, that you would experience that outcome.

___**1.** higher self-esteem

___**2.** more guilt feelings

___**3.** greater feeling of missing out on your children's developmental progress (e.g., first steps)

___**4.** greater self-fulfillment

___**5.** greater number of conflicting demands

___**6.** greater intellectual stimulation

___**7.** more resentment from spouse/partner

___**8.** more anxiety about your child

___**9.** more mental exhaustion

___**10.** greater degree of pride

___**11.** more social stimulation

___**12.** more irritability

___**13.** more conflict with your spouse/partner

___**14.** more approval from other people

WHAT DOES IT MEAN?

Items 2, 3, 5, 7, 8, 9, 12, and 13 are possible costs and items 1, 4, 6, 10, 11, and 14 are possible benefits of employment for mothers. For each of these two sets of outcomes, calculate the average probability that you reported. First, add up the eight probabilities you specified for the costs and divide that total by 8. Then, sum the probabilities you estimated for the six benefits and divide that total by 6. After calculating your averages, read the text's presentation of the findings of this study.

1. Compare your expectations to those reported in the text. Are they similar? If not, can you think of reasons for any observed differences?

2. Do you think your expectations will influence your decision about the timing of your employment and childbearing?

3. Do you think your answers would have differed if you were the other gender? Refer to material on gender attitudes and gender socialization to explain your answer.

_____

Source: Based on Bridges and Etaugh (1996).

individuals have more responsibilities than they have time or energy for handling them, or when they are overwhelmed by conflicts between their role responsibilities, they can experience frustration, fatigue, or other indications of stress (Duxbury et al., 2008; Stephens et al., 2009).

Experiences related to family–work balancing can be influenced by numerous factors, not the least of which is the presence of children. The wife and worker roles alone are not related to role overload or conflict. It is the addition of the mother role to the worker role that creates women's role strain (Evenson & Simon, 2005). Having a young child, particularly one who is disabled or difficult, is particularly likely to increase role strain (Bianchi & Milkie, 2010; Martinengo et al., 2010).

Employed married women are more likely than employed married men to experience both role overload and interrole conflict and this gender difference holds across ethnic groups (Jang & Zippay, 2011; Roehling et al., 2005). The social construction of women as the major caregivers and homemakers and the construction of men as the primary providers means that women's employment is seen as *addition to* their family role, whereas men's employment is viewed as *part of* their family role (Jang & Zippay, 2011; Sachs-Ericsson & Ciarlo, 2000).

In addition to role strain, sexual minority role jugglers must face other problems as well. For example, their coworkers and/or supervisors might disapprove of their sexual orientation, making the work environment uncomfortable. Furthermore, the lack of insurance benefits available for many sexual minority families can produce economic pressures (Dilley, 2010).

BENEFITS.   Juggling family and work can lead to role overload and interrole conflict, but it can also bring numerous rewards, including higher self-esteem, better physical health, greater respect from others, and greater economic security (Kostianen et al., 2009; Steinberg et al., 2008; Teachman, 2010). Indeed, even though employed mothers are more likely than unemployed mothers to report they "always feel rushed," they are also more likely to say that they get "a great deal" or "a very great deal" of satisfaction from their family lives (Cherlin & Krishnamurthy, 2004). Employed women with nontraditional gender attitudes are more likely than those with traditional attitudes to report benefits from working (Marshall & Barnett, 1993).

The benefits of multiple role coordination are explained by the **enhancement hypothesis** (Crosby & Sabattini, 2006; Greenhaus & Powell, 2006). According to this perspective, *each additional role provides a new source of self-esteem, social approval, social status, and other benefits.* Successfully applying the different skills required by different roles can lead to achievements in many areas. Consequently, family–work balancers can develop competence in numerous domains and experience greater personal pride and fulfillment.

Aside from any rewards associated with managing several roles, women can benefit by using one role to buffer strains associated with another (Crosby & Sabattini, 2006); that is, positive events in one role can reduce the psychological impact of negative events in another role. A 35-year-old professional woman describes it like this: "Sometimes I have a really rough day at work and then I come home and these two little kids run to the door. My older daughter says 'I'm really glad you got picked to be my mother.' Then, I forget the day at work" (Crosby, 1991, p. 103). Similarly, women who enjoy their jobs are less likely to feel stressed by the demands of caring for an ailing parent than are women whose work is less satisfying (Martire & Stephens, 2003).

Faye Crosby and Laura Sabattini (2006) discuss three reasons why buffering helps psychological well-being. First, involvement in more than one role allows the family–work juggler to distance herself from the problems in one role while she engages in another role. For instance, a mother who is upset about her child's school performance can put that worry aside while she focuses on her job responsibilities.

Second, challenges in one role help put into perspective worries associated with another role. For example, a woman who is bothered about conflicts with her coworkers might view this problem as less important when faced with her husband's serious illness. When his health improves, she might continue to view the interpersonal tension at work as minor.

Third, positive events in one role can bolster self-esteem that has been damaged by negative events in another role. Thus, the disappointment of not receiving a promotion at work can be eased by a mother's feelings of competence as she helps her child successfully cope with a bully at school.

In addition to immediate benefits earned while juggling family and work roles, there is evidence of long-term positive outcomes. Longitudinal follow-up of women who graduated from college in the 1960s found that those who combined family and employment roles in early adulthood have more positive role experiences in middle age and experience greater midlife well-being than do other women (Vandewater et al., 1997).

Effects of Mothers' Employment

What are the effects of maternal employment on a woman's children and on her spouse or partner? Let us now examine these questions.

EFFECTS ON CHILDREN.   Nearly 6 in 10 first-time mothers now return to work by the sixth month after giving birth (U.S. Census Bureau, 2010b). As a result, nearly two-thirds of infants and preschool children in the United States spend time in the care of nonparental caregivers (Federal Interagency Forum, 2007). Indeed, access to child care is a key factor in women's decision to work (Herbst & Barnow, 2008). Unlike many members of their parents' and grandparents' generations, today's young adults largely accept and approve of the reality of mothers of young children working outside the home (Pew Research Center, 2010a).

Decades of research has demonstrated that high-quality day care, as measured by characteristics such as appropriate group size, favorable staff-to-child ratio, teacher training, and caregivers' commitment to children, does not adversely affect children's social, academic, or emotional development (Ahnert et al., 2006; Baker & Milligan, 2010; Brooks-Gunn et al., 2010; Burchinal et al., 2010; Goldberg et al., 2008; NICHD Early Child Care Research Network, 2006). In fact, high-quality child care provides significant socioemotional and behavioral benefits to children, especially those from economically disadvantaged homes (Camilli et al., 2010; Clarke-Stewart & Miner, 2008; Fukkink & Lont, 2007; Galinsky, 2006; Pianta et al., 2009; Votruba-Drzal et al., 2010; Watamura et al., 2011). Long-term benefits for children from low-income families include higher rates of educational attainment and employment and lower rates of criminal offenses in adulthood (Crosnoe & Cavanagh, 2010; Peters et al., 2010; Pianta et al., 2009; Vandell et al., 2010).

Maternal employment provides other benefits as well. For example, research has found that preschoolers with employed mothers were more prosocial, less anxious, and less hyperactive than children whose mothers were not employed (Nomaguchi, 2006). Girls and boys whose mothers are employed develop less stereotypical attitudes about gender roles than children with nonemployed mothers (Davis & Greenstein, 2009; Goldberg & Lucas-Thompson, 2008; Riggio & Desrochers, 2005). Because employment is seen as an agentic role and because maternal employment frequently leads to nonstereotypical structuring of household responsibilities among parents, employed mothers often serve as less traditional role models than do full-time homemakers. So it is not surprising that both female and male college students with employed mothers have more egalitarian views toward sharing household and child care tasks than students with nonemployed mothers (Cunningham, 2001; Riggio & Desrochers, 2006; Treas & Tai, 2007). Moreover, sons of employed women, compared to sons of nonemployed women, perceive females as more competent, and view men as warmer and more expressive (Parke & Buriel, 2006). In addition, daughters of working mothers show greater self-efficacy and have higher educational and career aspirations than daughters of nonemployed mothers (Buchanan & Selmon, 2008). Along the same lines, a recent meta-analysis spanning 50 years of research found that maternal employment early in children's lives was linked with higher achievement (Lucas-Thompson et al., 2010). Moreover, the great majority of young adults (almost 8 of 10) who grew up with an employed mother are pleased with their mother's working (Gerson, 2010). And today's school-age children find it equally acceptable for both mothers and fathers to work full time (Sinno & Killen, 2009).

Our exploration of the benefits that can result from maternal employment does not imply that full-time homemaking is detrimental to children's development. What is important is the consistency between a mother's role (employed or not employed) and her belief about the value of maternal employment for her children. Mothers whose roles match their own attitudes are likely to be more effective parents. A mother who is dissatisfied with her role is less likely to display the type of positive parenting characteristics that can lead to good outcomes for her children (Goldberg & Lucas-Thompson, 2008; Hoffman & Youngblade, 2001; Lerner et al., 2002).

Interestingly, most research on the effects of parental employment on children has focused on maternal employment. The social construction of gender leads us to conceptualize parenting as part of women's role and to frame child care as a women's issue rather than as a family issue (Newcombe, 2007b).

EFFECTS ON THE SPOUSE/PARTNER.   Because employment of wives and mothers represents a departure from traditional gender roles, does it have implications for the woman's relationship with her spouse or partner? The comprehensive National Survey of Families and Households found that women's employment does not affect the likelihood of divorce among couples who are happily married. However, it is a factor in ending unhappy marriages (Schoen et al., 2002; Shellenbarger, 2008). Can you think of a reason for this? According to the economic opportunity hypothesis, employment gives women the resources to leave an unhappy marriage (Teachman, 2010). How about the alternative hypothesis that a woman's employment *causes* a rift in the marital relationship? Let us examine some of the research that relates women's employment to the marital satisfaction of both wives and husbands.

Terri Orbuch and Lindsay Custer (1995) compared Black and White men married to homemakers, career-oriented wives, or job-oriented wives. (A job is work for pay; a career is a long-term series of connected work opportunities [Zichy, 2007].) They found that husbands of homemakers had the lowest well-being and husbands of women who viewed their employment as a job had the highest. According to Orbuch and Custer, it may be that husbands of job-oriented wives benefited from the financial support of a working wife but didn't experience the challenge to their traditional role associated with a career-oriented spouse. Consistent with this explanation, men experience a decline in well-being when their wives' share of the family household income increases (Rogers & DeBoer, 2001).

Turning to wives' feelings about their marriages, satisfaction is related, in part, to the consistency between wives' roles and their gender-related attitudes. Maureen Perry-Jenkins and her colleagues (1992) found that employed women who were uncomfortable about their work role experienced less marital satisfaction than those who wanted to work outside the home, and were less satisfied than full-time homemakers. It appears that positive outcomes can result from either full-time homemaking or from combining family and work. What is more important than the actual roles is the attitude toward those roles.

Studies of the relationship between women's employment and wives' and husbands' sexual satisfaction show parallel findings. Janet Hyde and her colleagues (2001) found that both women and men reported greater sexual satisfaction when they had more rewarding work experiences. This could be because positive experiences in the workplace help couples more fully enjoy their sexual relationship or because a satisfactory sex life contributes to enjoyment on the job. Or, it may be that neither domain influences the other, but that well-adjusted adults lead lives that are satisfying in many domains, including work and sexual relationships.

Solutions to Family–Work Balancing Challenges

As we have seen, the numerous rewards that can result from combining family and work roles do not eliminate the challenges jugglers face in managing their roles. What approaches can help reduce these challenges?

PARENTAL LEAVE.   Although some young college women would like to discontinue their employment for some period of time after the birth of a baby, most women do not follow that pattern. In 2006, 57 percent of married women with infants 1 year or under were employed (U.S. Census Bureau, 2011).

The high employment rate of mothers with infants points to the importance of adequate parental leave policies that provide sufficient time to adjust to parenthood and allow biological mothers to recuperate from the physical stresses of pregnancy and birth. Incredibly, the United States is one of the few countries in the world without a national policy requiring paid parental leave. (See Explore Other Cultures 11.2.) There is a stark contrast between Canada, which provides 17 weeks of paid leave, and the United States, which has no federal legislation governing leave with

EXPLORE OTHER CULTURES 11.2
Parental Leave Policies Around the World

Paid and job-protected maternity leaves from work were first established over a century ago in Europe to protect the health of mothers and their infants. Beginning in the 1960s, these policies expanded to also cover paternity leaves in most industrialized nations and several developing countries (Heymann et al., 2007). Of the 169 countries providing paid leaves, including many developing nations in Africa, Asia, and Latin America, 98 offer at least 14 weeks of paid leave (Heymann et al., 2007). Germany and Sweden provide the most fully paid leave: 47 weeks. Five other countries offer at least six months at full pay: Canada, Finland, Greece, Japan, and Norway (Burn, 2011; Gornick, 2010; Ray et al., 2009). The United States offers the briefest leave of any industrialized nation (12 weeks) and is among only five countries with an unpaid leave, the others being Australia, Lesotho, Papua New Guinea, and Swaziland (Burn, 2011). Even Australia offers a full year of leave, although unpaid, and a substantial "baby bonus" regardless of whether the parents take a leave (Ray et al., 2009). Why do you think the United States lags so far behind other nations?

pay. The only federal law mandating parental leave in the United States is the Family and Medical Leave Act, which is applicable only to workplaces with 50 or more employees, thus covering only about 60 percent of the workforce. The act allows workers (women and men) who have been employed for a year in those companies to take up to 12 weeks of *unpaid* leave for medical conditions or family responsibilities, including the birth or adoption of a child (Christensen & Schneider, 2010b; Jang & Zippay, 2011). Only 8 percent of American workers receive paid family leave benefits through policies of their employer or state (Lovell et al., 2007). Many women thus take shorter leaves than they would like to take because their families cannot afford the loss of their income. Not surprisingly, women with the lowest incomes return to work most quickly. Low-income Native American and Asian American women take the shortest leaves of any ethnic group (Manuel & Zambrana, 2009).

Nowadays, four out of five first-time mothers work until one month or less before giving birth. Over half return to work within six months and more than four in five return within a year (U.S. Census Bureau, 2010b). Women with higher levels of education work later into their pregnancies, return to work more rapidly after giving birth, and are more likely to return to work full time than women with less education (Aisenbrey et al., 2009; Johnson & Downs, 2005). Other factors associated with women's earlier planned return to work after childbirth include having more positive attitudes about combining employment and parenting and perceiving one's employer as supportive of employees' family needs (Lyness et al., 1999). Possibly, the belief that the employer is sensitive to work–family issues contributes to a greater comfort at work and an expectation that family responsibilities will be accommodated.

How does parental leave affect women's employment? The evidence suggests that using family leave may, in fact, be harmful to the work lives of both men and women. Mothers who take even a short time off after giving birth are more likely to experience negative career consequences than those who do not (Aisenbrey et al., 2009). Men who take leave for childbirth or care of a sick parent are viewed as less committed to the organization than men who do not take leave or women who take leave for the same reason (Wayne & Cordeiro, 2003). Stay-at-home fathers often find a stigma attached to their decision, especially when they return to the workforce after a period at home. As a result, fathers are much less likely than mothers to use family-friendly benefits (Belkin, 2010; Craig & Sawrikar, 2009). As long as workplace norms penalize individuals who use such benefits, workers will be reluctant to take advantage of them (Minnotte et al., 2010; Pedersen et al., 2008; Sabattini & Crosby, 2009).

"FAMILY-FRIENDLY" WORKPLACE POLICIES. Employers can play a key role in helping parents coordinate their family and work roles by being supportive and providing a family-friendly culture (Galinsky et al., 2010; Hutchens & Nolen, 2010; Lerner, 2010). One way to do this is by offering paid family leave, discussed earlier.

A second family-friendly benefit is flexible work hours (Galinsky et al., 2010; Lerner, 2010; Lundberg-Love & Faulkner, 2008). **Flextime,** *flexible work scheduling that allows the employee to choose the arrival and departure time within a set of possible options offered by the employer,* can enable parents to better accommodate their work hours to their children's regular child care or school schedules and to deal with unforeseen and unscheduled family demands. One recent poll of over 1,000 organizations found that one-third of them offered flextime and 10 percent offered compressed work weeks (Galinsky, et al., 2010). Flexible benefits such as these are associated with increased employee retention and engagement, reduced work–family conflict, lower absenteeism, greater job satisfaction, and higher productivity (Christensen & Schneider, 2010a; Craig & Sawrikar, 2009; Hill et al., 2010; Jang & Zippay, 2011), benefiting both employees and employers.

A third option that helps many workers is telecommuting. The increasing use of technology in the labor force makes this option to work from home attractive to certain types of workers (Steinberg et al., 2008). In 2006, 45 million Americans telecommuted at least some of the time. As with flextime, telecommuting is linked to greater job satisfaction, increased performance, and reduced work–family conflict (Gajendran & Harrison, 2007).

Fourth, employer help with child care would ease a major burden faced by employed parents. Child care assistance programs can include referral services and day care subsidies as well as on-site day care and backup day care when families have emergencies (Jang & Zippay, 2011). Given that child care is one of employed parents' greatest worries (Galinsky et al., 2008; Weigt & Solomon, 2008), it is not surprising that workers who have child care benefits show greater commitment to their employers (Wang & Walumbwa, 2007). Parents also need assistance with care of older children (Galinsky et al., 2008). School programs that provide before- and after-school care would not only provide safe and stimulating activities for children but also would reduce parental worry and eliminate the need for parents to coordinate multiple daily child care arrangements.

Finally, eldercare services would help many of the millions of workers who provide care for older relatives. But very few companies in the United States provide such benefits, claiming that they are too costly (Galinsky et al., 2008; Paludi et al., 2010).

Unfortunately, family-friendly benefits such as flexible hours, telecommuting, on-site child care, and eldercare benefits are offered primarily by large companies, yet the majority of workers are employed by small companies. Furthermore, companies that employ better-educated, highly skilled workers are more likely to offer these benefits than companies with a primarily unskilled labor force (Harrington & Lodge, 2009; Hutchens & Nolen, 2010; O'Leary & Kornbluh, 2009; Williams, 2010). Interestingly, employers with more women and minorities in top-level positions offer more family-friendly benefits (Galinsky et al., 2008).

SUPPORT FROM OTHER PEOPLE. Enlisting the aid of others to reduce their domestic burden can be effective for some family–work jugglers (Frone, 2003; Stuenkel, 2005). Families who have the financial resources can purchase services such as housecleaning and meal preparation, although women still remain responsible for arranging the execution and management of these services (Charlebois, 2011). Other women rely on the assistance of friends, family, and neighbors (Cheung & Halpern, 2010; Williams, 2010). Women's well-being is positively related to their husbands' greater participation in child care and housework (Edwards, 2007). Keep in mind, however, that support from husbands or male partners is frequently construed as "help," not as a shared responsibility, underscoring the social construction of different and unequal roles for women and men.

Some employed couples work alternating shift schedules in order to share the child care duties, thus reducing or eliminating the need for nonparental care. For a close look at the gender attitudes of some working-class couples who use this strategy, turn to Learn About the Research 11.2.

LEARN ABOUT THE RESEARCH 11.2
How Do Tag-Team Parents Reconcile Their Own Roles With Their Traditional Gender Attitudes?

We saw in Chapter 10 that nonstandard shift work often creates scheduling and logistical problems for families (Crosnoe & Cavanagh, 2010). Nonstandard schedules are linked with lower marital satisfaction and with marital instability, especially in families with children (Kalil et al., 2010; Mills & Tàht, 2010; Perry-Jenkins et al., 2007).

When two parents work different shifts, this creates transitions termed **tag-team parenting** (Lerner, 2010) in which *parents hand off the child care responsibilities to each other as they come and go from work.* This arrangement clearly represents a departure from traditional gender roles. How do working-class couples with alternating shifts reconcile these more fluid roles with their traditional gender attitudes?

Francine Deutsch and Susan Saxon (1998) interviewed 23 primarily White working-class couples who had traditional views about parental, marital, and employment roles. These couples alternated their work shifts so that one parent was home with the children while the other parent worked. Husbands worked an average of 46 hours per week in blue-collar jobs, such as custodian or electrician, and wives worked an average of 33 hours per week in occupations such as clerical or food service worker.

Some couples handled the inconsistency between their gender attitudes and their own roles by modifying their traditional views. As one woman said, "When we first married, Larry felt like I was there . . . to do the dishes, to clean the house, to take care of the kids. Things have changed since then. We're more equals. It's more like I'm his wife, not his slave" (Deutsch & Saxon, p. 344).

Other ways that couples handled inconsistencies between their attitudes and roles was to maintain the belief that their family roles still reflected three core elements of traditional gender roles. First, they viewed the husband as the primary provider. As one husband said, "I have to work and I have to be the breadwinner" (Deutsch & Saxon, p. 349). Second, the couples, especially the husbands, did not view the worker role as a primary aspect of the mother's identity, but rather it as a financial necessity. One husband said, "I think it would be great if she could be home all the time. . . . Right now she's really got no choice because we need the money." Third, the couples saw the mother as the primary caregiver. One mother noted, "As much as we try to do everything 50/50, if Jimmy gets hurt and he cries, I think I'm the one that should take care of him" (p. 356).

The authors conclude that these couples reconciled potentially discrepant attitudes and role behaviors by viewing their roles as constrained by financial considerations and maintaining their beliefs that the husband was still the primary breadwinner and the wife, the primary caregiver.

WHAT DOES IT MEAN?

1. The couples in this study were primarily White and working class. Do you think middle-class couples or couples with different ethnicities might respond differently? Explain your answer.

2. What are the advantages and disadvantages to the children of parents who work alternating shifts?

3. What are the advantages and disadvantages of alternating shifts to a couple's marriage?

Source: From Deutsch and Saxon (1998).

PERSONAL COPING STRATEGIES.   Unfortunately, some women receive no support from others, or the help they do receive is insufficient. Under these circumstances, women use several personal strategies to manage their numerous role responsibilities. One is to negotiate with their employers about reduced hours (Hewlett, 2007). Women who reduce their work hours as a means of coping with family and work responsibilities report both benefits and costs. They experience greater satisfaction at home and less work–family conflict than women employed full time. However, they report less career opportunity and work success (Hewlett, 2007).

Another strategy for women is to change their perceptions of their responsibilities (Chrisler, 2008c). They might, for example, lower their standards for housecleaning or accept the possibility that a promotion might take longer to achieve. Many employed women utilize this strategy at least to some extent. As we saw earlier in this chapter, employed mothers spend fewer hours doing housework than do stay-at-home mothers.

A third approach women use to coordinate family and work roles is to cut back on other activities such as sleep and leisure pursuits in order to handle all role responsibilities (Chrisler, 2008c; Dillaway & Paré, 2008; Higgins et al., 2010). This approach can be difficult and exhausting, and women who use it are sometimes referred to as "supermoms." A fourth strategy used by some college-educated women is to devote themselves to their careers and then take time off to be stay-at-home mothers while their children are young. This option, however, is seldom realistic for single mothers or for women whose husbands do not earn a sizable income (Hewlett, 2007). The exercise in Get Involved 11.3 will help you gain firsthand information about women's experiences in balancing family and work roles. Then see What You Can Do 11.1 to become an advocate for family-friendly work policies.

MIDLIFE TRANSITIONS IN FAMILY AND WORK ROLES

Many women who currently are in their middle adult years go through a process of life review, that is, an intensive self-evaluation of numerous aspects of their lives (Etaugh, 2008). They reexamine

GET INVOLVED 11.3
Women's Experiences in Coordinating Family and Work Roles

Interview two employed mothers who have children under 6 years of age. Ask each to talk about the following experiences: (1) time problems, if any, in performing all of their responsibilities; (2) conflicts, if any, between demands from different roles; (3) problems, if any, in arranging for child care; (4) psychological benefits they receive from their mother role; (5) psychological benefits they receive from their worker role; (6) personal coping strategies and/or employment benefits that have helped them deal with any time problems, conflicts, or child care difficulties; and (7) additional employer benefits they would find beneficial.

WHAT DOES IT MEAN?

1. What new information did you learn from these mothers' experiences that you did not learn from the text?
2. Did the responses of these women enhance your understanding of the costs and benefits of balancing motherhood and employment? Explain your answer.
3. Which solution do you think is the most effective for dealing with family–work balancing? Explain your answer.
4. Which family–work balancing hypothesis best accounts for these mothers' experiences? Explain your answer.

WHAT YOU CAN DO 11.1
Advocate for Family-Friendly Work Policies

Contact or join MomsRising (www.momsrising .org), a grassroots campaign devoted to making employment policies more family friendly (e.g., paid family leave, paid sick days, increased support for high-quality child care). Make a presentation on this topic to a class, residence hall meeting, or campus organization.

_____

Source: Kinser (2010).

their family and occupational values and goals, evaluate their accomplishments, and sometimes consider new career directions. Some make transitions to different jobs during their middle adult years whereas others begin their paid work role at this point in their lives.

Because of the many societal gender-role messages encountered by the current cohort of midlife women, some have followed traditional roles early in adulthood and continued these roles at midlife whereas others began their adult lives committed to traditional roles but made changes in their middle adult years. Still others deviated from traditional expectations by committing themselves to careers in early adulthood. Because each of these patterns of choices can be fulfilling, many women are satisfied with their life paths and, therefore, make no changes at midlife (Stewart & Vandewater, 1999; Zucker et al., 2002).

Given changing societal standards about appropriate roles for women, it is not surprising that one characteristic theme in the life reviews of midlife women today has been the search for an independent identity. Ravenna Helson (1992) has noted that for many women, the need to rewrite the life story in middle age is related to the lessening of the dependence and restriction associated with marriage and motherhood as children grow up. Thus, many heterosexual women attempt to affirm their own being, independent of their husbands, through graduate education, beginning a career, or switching careers (Burns & Leonard, 2005; Helson, 1992; Shellenbarger, 2004; Stewart & Vandewater, 1999). Sexual minority women, however, generally do not experience major transitions at midlife. Many are not mothers and have not experienced the role constraints characteristic of traditional heterosexual marriages. Therefore, they are not aiming to redefine themselves as separate from significant others. Furthermore, they already have a strong sense of self due to years of defining themselves independently of others' expectations and fighting hostility directed toward sexual minorities, and most have considered work an important part of their identity throughout their adult lives (Etaugh, 2008).

Satisfaction With Life Roles

For both young and midlife women, paid work is a significant predictor of psychological and physical well-being (Klumb & Lampert, 2004). Middle-aged women who are involved in either beginning or building their career are both psychologically and physically healthier than women who are maintaining or reducing their career involvement (Etaugh, 2008). Women who have attained the occupational goals they set for themselves in young adulthood also have a greater sense of life purpose and are less depressed in midlife than those who fall short of their expectations (Carr, 1997). Furthermore, satisfaction with work predicts a general sense of well-being: The more satisfied women are with their jobs, the better they feel in general (Vandewater et al., 1997).

For other women, being a full-time homemaker or student can be associated with the same degree of psychological well-being as that experienced by women who are employed (McQuaide, 1998). Midlife homemakers whose life goal was a domestic role have a comparable sense of purpose in life to women who aspired toward and achieved an occupational role. Not surprisingly, however, women who are involuntarily out of the workforce, due to forced early retirement or layoff, are not as satisfied with midlife as women with a chosen role (Etaugh, 2008). Thus, there are multiple routes to well-being in midlife, and it appears that a key factor influencing midlife role evaluation is not a woman's *role* per se but fulfillment of her *preferred role* (Carr, 1997).

Regrets About Life Direction

Although some midlife women are satisfied with traditional roles, others are distressed about missed educational or occupational opportunities (Torges et al., 2005). Some middle-class women, who as young adults devoted themselves solely to marriage and motherhood, voice regrets in midlife about their earlier traditional decisions. Abigail Stewart and Elizabeth Vandewater (1999) examined regrets experienced by women who graduated from college in the mid-1960s. These women reported disappointments about not pursuing a more prestigious career, marrying before establishing a career, and not returning to work after having children. The women who made changes based on these regrets experienced greater psychological well-being at midlife than those who had regrets but did nothing to alter their life direction.

Why did some women have regrets but not act on them? Interestingly, it was not external constraints, such as the number of children they had, that seemed to prevent these women from making goal-related changes. Instead, it was the tendency to ruminate on negative life events and engage in self-pity. Thus, these women seem to have been constrained by personality characteristics rather than external obstacles.

Making Changes

Pursuing a new direction at midlife involves making significant changes in one's life role during the middle adulthood years (McAdams & Cox, 2010). A midlife woman who chooses to switch direction at this point must be willing to leave one long-term role (e.g., full-time homemaking or career) that has been a significant part of her identity and proceed down a new and unfamiliar path. In so doing, she is leaving a role to which she has devoted considerable time and energy during her adult years. What are the psychological experiences of women who begin a work role or alter occupational directions in midlife?

Let's take a closer look at Stewart and Vandewater's (1999) sample of 1,964 college graduates who made major work-related changes in midlife. After an earlier, full-time commitment to the traditional roles of wife and mother or to traditional female jobs, such as elementary or secondary school teaching, these women realized there was a broader set of options available to them and decided to follow a new career interest or return to an earlier interest that they had never pursued. What precipitated their new directions? For many, the women's movement made a strong impact on their midlife development by raising their awareness of the increasing possibilities open for women and, consequently, changing the way they constructed the female role. As they described it, "[The] women's movement taught me that I could be a doer and not a helper" and "[The] women's movement and political activism of the '60s led me to law school" (p. 404). These women were happy about the changes they made and felt a sense of accomplishment and pride. However, despite new directions suggested by the increasing societal acceptance and encouragement of women's diverse roles, making these significant life changes was often difficult.

Midlife Transitions: A Cautionary Note

We saw in Chapter 1 that generalization based on one type of respondent can lead to false conclusions about individuals who are not represented in the sample. For at least two reasons, the research findings presented here are relevant to a specific group of midlife women and should not be extended to other women. First, the respondents in these studies were primarily White, highly educated, middle-class women. The midlife experiences of ethnic minority, less educated, and poor women are vastly different (Allen & Walker, 2009). For example, many of them have been both breadwinners and caregivers throughout their adult lives. They have not had the luxury of being able to choose one role or the other. Large variations in the options available to different groups of women can affect their aspirations and opportunities during both early adulthood and at midlife. For example, poor women may feel so constrained by poverty that significant change and growth at midlife appears outside the realm of possibility.

Second, the midlife experiences discussed here must be placed in historical context. As social constructions of gender have evolved over time, women have experienced differing perceptions of their options. Women examined in the studies reported here were in their middle adult years in the late twentieth and early twenty-first centuries. Consequently, the gender-based social climate that shaped their development was different from the societal attitudes influencing the lives of future generations of midlife women (Settersten & Trauten, 2009). For example, today's midlife women were exposed to both traditional and flexible gender-role expectations at different points in their lives. Thus, it is likely that they experienced more regrets about previous traditional choices than future generations of midlife women will. Because there are greater options for young women today than there were when current midlife women were making life choices, fewer young women today may feel the need to make significant revisions in their life paths during middle age (Stewart & Ostrove, 1998). Today's older women have also experienced different constructions of women's roles than have current midlife women. Because they were in midlife before the major societal role changes discussed here, they did not experience the career and role opportunities encountered by today's midlife women and, consequently, were not faced with decisions about major role changes.

Summary

WOMEN'S FAMILY AND EMPLOYMENT ROLES: PERCEPTIONS AND ATTITUDES

- Four out of five U.S. couples are dual-earner couples.
- The two groups of mothers who tend to opt out of the labor force are poor single women and women with high-earning husbands.
- Most North Americans now approve of employment among mothers of young children.
- Mothers who continue full-time employment after childbirth are evaluated more negatively than those who stay home or work part time.

DIVISION OF FAMILY LABOR

- Women perform most of the child care and housekeeping duties in the family even if they are employed. This pattern exists across ethnic groups, and around the world.
- Women provide the majority of care for aging parents and other older relatives.
- Much of women's leisure time is fragmented into small blocks of time.
- Women tend to be satisfied with the division of labor, although they perform the greater share.
- One reason may be that women have been socialized to view household duties as their domain. They might also view their obligations as fair compared to those of other women.
- Explanations for the unequal division of labor focus on time availability, relative power, and gender attitudes.

FAMILY–WORK COORDINATION

- Women across ethnic groups experience role strain as well as numerous benefits from multiple role juggling.
- Role strain can be explained by the scarcity hypothesis; benefits, such as self-esteem and approval from others, can be explained by the enhancement hypothesis.
- Another benefit of engaging in both family and work roles is that one role can buffer strains associated with the other.
- High-quality day care, even during infancy, does not hinder the child's social, academic, or emotional development. Furthermore, it can help improve school performance and reduce the social problems of children from low-income homes.
- Children with employed mothers have less stereotypical attitudes about gender roles than children of full-time homemakers.
- Positive psychological feelings, good parenting, and marital satisfaction are more likely when a woman feels comfortable about her role, whether as a full-time homemaker or employed wife and mother.
- The United States is one of the few industrialized countries that do not have federal legislation mandating paid parental leave.
- Women take shorter parental leaves if they are more highly educated, have nontraditional attitudes toward combining employment and parenting, and perceive their employers as family-friendly.
- Employer resources, such as flextime, telecommuting, and child care assistance, and husbands' participation in family responsibilities and provision of emotional support can help women more effectively manage their multiple demands.
- Personal adjustments, such as altering one's role definitions, changing one's perceptions of responsibilities, and attempting to perform all role duties, are types of strategies women use to balance their family and work roles.

MIDLIFE TRANSITIONS IN FAMILY AND WORK ROLES

- Many women go through a life review during their middle adult years.
- Because those who are in midlife at the beginning of the twenty-first century were exposed to traditional gender-role expectations during their early years and to flexible gender roles later, many women now seek an identity independent of their husbands'.
- Some midlife women are satisfied with either the career or traditional paths they have followed.
- Other women experience regrets about previous traditional role choices, and some of these women choose to make significant changes in their life direction.

Key Terms

role strain *262*
role overload *262*
interrole conflict *262*

scarcity hypothesis *262*
enhancement hypothesis *264*
flextime *268*

tag-team parenting *269*

What Do You Think?

1. Use any theory of gender typing (see Chapter 3) to explain the current division of household labor as presented in the text. Would this theory predict a greater equality of child care and household responsibility in the future? Explain your answer.

2. Recall that women seem to be satisfied with an unequal division of household labor. Do you agree with the explanations given in the text? Are there other factors that can account for this phenomenon? Explain your answer.

3. Explain why young Black women, compared to White women, desire an earlier return to employment after they have children. Refer to material in previous chapters and any other information that addresses the question.

4. Women experience more role strain than men. Do you think this will change in the future? Explain your answer.

5. Does any of the material in this chapter have public policy implications related to parental leave? That is, does it point to the need for new parental leave legislation? Explain your answer.

6. Discuss the origins and implications of the widespread conceptualization of parenting as a female role. What benefits to mothers, fathers, and children would stem from a more inclusive view of parenting?

If You Want to Learn More

Christensen, K., & Schneider, B. (Eds.). (2010). *Workplace flexibility: Realigning 20th-century jobs for a 21st-century workforce.* Ithaca, NY: Cornell University Press.

Gerson, K. (2010). *The unfinished revolution: How a new generation is reshaping family, work, and gender in America.* New York: Oxford University Press.

Gilbert, N. (2008). *A mother's work: How feminism, the market, and the policy shape family life.* New Haven, CT: Yale University Press.

Halpern, D. F., & Cheung, F. M. (2008). *Women at the top: Powerful leaders tell us how to combine work and family.* Malden, MA: Wiley-Blackwell.

Korabik, K., Lero, D. S., & Whitehead, D. L. (Eds.). (2008). *Handbook of work–family integration: Research, theory, and best practices.* San Diego, CA: Academic Press.

Lerner, S. (2010). *The war on moms: On life in a family-unfriendly nation.* Hoboken, NJ: Wiley.

Lewis, J. (2009). *Work–family balance, gender, and policy.* Northampton, MA: Edward Elgar Publishing.

Marcus-Newhall, A., Halpern, D. F., & Tan, S. J. (Eds.). (2008). *The changing realities of work and family.* Malden, MA: Wiley-Blackwell.

Mason, M. A., & Ekman, E. M. (2007). *Mothers on the fast track: How a new generation can balance family and careers.* New York: Oxford University Press.

Muhlbauer, V., & Chrisler, J. (Eds.). (2007). *Women over 50: Psychological perspectives.* New York: Springer.

Paludi, M. A., & Neidemeyer, P. E. (Eds.). (2009). *Work, life, and family imbalance: How to level the playing field.* Westport, CT: Praeger.

Shifrin, K. (Ed.). (2009). *How caregiving affects development: Psychological implications for child, adolescent, and adult caregivers.* Washington, DC: American Psychological Association.

Vachon, M., & Vachon, A. (2011). *Equally shared parenting: Rewriting the rules for a new generation of parents.* New York: Penguin.

Websites

Family–Work Coordination

Catalyst
http://www.catalystwomen.org/
Institute for Women's Policy Research
http://www.iwpr.org/
Work and Family: National Partnership for Women and Family

http://www.nationalpartnership.org/
Work and Family Connection
http://www.workfamily.com
Sloan Work and Family Research Network
http://www.bc.edu/wfnetwork

CHAPTER 12

Physical Health

Health Services
    The Physician–Patient Relationship
    Type and Quality of Care
    Ethnicity, Poverty, and Health Care
    Women With Disabilities and
        Health Care
    Sexual Minority Women and
        Health Care
    Health Insurance

Sexually Transmitted Infections (STIs)
    Overview of STIs
    AIDS

Reproductive System Disorders
    Benign Conditions
    Cancers
    Hysterectomy

Osteoporosis
    Risk Factors
    Prevention and Treatment

Heart Disease
    Gender Differences
    Risk Factors
    Diagnosis and Treatment
    Psychological Impact

Breast Cancer
    Risk Factors
    Detection
    Treatment
    Psychological Impact

Lung Cancer
    Risk Factors
    Detection and Treatment

Physical Health in Later Life
    Gender Differences in Mortality
    Social Class and Ethnic Differences
    Gender Differences in Illness
    Disability

Promoting Good Health
    Physical Activity and Exercise
    Nutrition

Several years ago, Dr. Annette Stanton, a professor of psychology at the University of Kansas, attended a university reception with a colleague. She reacted strongly when her colleague referred to a recent study concerning the connection between heart disease and caffeine consumption, which had received a great deal of media coverage. "I guess our hearts are safe if we have a cup of coffee," he said. "Your heart may be safe; I have no idea about the safety of my heart! That study was conducted on over 45,000 men," retorted Dr. Stanton. (adapted from Stanton, 1995, p. 3)

Physical health is not just a biological phenomenon, but a psychosocial one as well. It involves both individual behaviors and lifestyles and societal systems. There is a growing realization that women's health and health care are linked to inequalities in assessment, treatment and access to care, and lack of research on health topics relevant to women in general and to ethnic minority women (Bird & Rieker, 2008; Moore, 2008; Rondon, 2010; White, 2011) in particular. As a result, gender-sensitive health care has been increasingly moving into the mainstream of health policy (Kuhlmann & Annandale, 2010).

In this chapter, we examine issues in women's health and health care. We start by focusing on health services. Next, we turn to sexually transmitted infections, including AIDS, which has become the scourge of adolescent and young women worldwide. We then explore disorders that tend to affect women in the middle and later years: reproductive system disorders, osteoporosis, heart disease, breast cancer, and lung cancer. We continue with a discussion of women's health later in life. We close by focusing on ways to promote good health.

HEALTH SERVICES

Only two decades or so ago, little was known about many aspects of women's health. Women were routinely excluded as research participants in large studies designed to examine risk factors and potential treatments for various diseases, as shown in the chapter-opening vignette. Even the first clinical trials to examine the effects of estrogen on heart disease were conducted solely on men! Scientists gave two principal reasons for confining medical experiments to men. First, women's monthly hormonal fluctuations "complicated" research results. Second, potential ethical and legal problems might arise from experimenting on women who would later bear children (Goldkind et al., 2010; Low Dog & Maizes, 2010). The "male is normative" assumption (see Chapter 2) played a role as well (Bird & Rieker, 2008; Lorber, 2010).

The growing recognition that women have a number of poorly understood medical problems and that diseases sometimes affect women and men in radically different ways has increasingly led health researchers to include women in their studies (Alexander et al., 2010; Bairey Merz et al., 2010; Foody et al., 2010). Under the leadership of the first woman director of the National Institutes of Health, Bernadine Healy, the federal government established an Office of Research on Women's Health, and the National Institutes of Health mandated the inclusion of women in federally funded medical research (Garcia et al., 2010). However, although more women are being studied, many medical studies still exclude them. For example, men continue to be the focus for much of the research on the leading cause of death among both women and men: heart disease (WomenHeart, 2011). Few of these studies include older women, even though heart disease is common in this group (Kitzman & Rich, 2010; Mosca et al., 2004). In addition, women, older people, and ethnic minorities are underrepresented in recent research on three of the leading causes of cancer death: lung cancer, breast cancer, and colorectal cancer (Badgwell et al., 2008; Given & Given, 2008; Grann, 2010; Herrera et al., 2010; Muss et al., 2009). Other health issues of ethnic minority women and poor rural women (Bowleg, 2008; Leach et al., 2011) have also not been sufficiently explored.

Moreover, medical researchers often ignore the requirement that they analyze their data to see if women and men respond differently to a given treatment (WHO, 2010a). In addition, women are still underrepresented in studies to establish standard doses of new medications (Gochfeld, 2010; Nieuwenhoven & Klinge, 2010). This omission can have serious consequences because women, especially older women, may have adverse effects from unnecessarily high drug doses, which have been established using male body weight as the standard (Groh, 2009; Whitley & Lindsey, 2009).

In addition, gender biases still exist within the health care delivery system, leading to differences in the way health professionals interact with women and men and to differences in the care women and men receive (Bairey Merz et al., 2010; White, 2011). In this section, we examine issues of gender discrimination in health services.

The Physician–Patient Relationship

Sexism in the physician–patient interaction is well documented (White, 2011). Feminist analyses describe the interaction between female patients and male physicians as paternalistic, with women patients treated as subordinates. Male physicians frequently trivialize women's experiences by interrupting female patients and making jokes in response to their concerns. Physicians may belittle women's health complaints by attributing them to psychosomatic factors (Wilkinson & Ferraro, 2002). For example, women's pain reports are taken less seriously than men's, and they receive less aggressive treatment for it. Women's pain reports are more likely to be dismissed as "emotional" and thus not "real" (Wartik, 2002). This stereotype may account for the fact that women consistently receive more prescriptions for tranquilizers, antidepressants, and anti-anxiety drugs than men (Correa-de-Araujo et al., 2005; Curtis et al., 2004; Rice & Russo, 2010).

Sexist views of women are perpetuated in medical journal advertisements and medical textbooks as well. For example, anatomy and physical diagnosis textbooks have considerably fewer illustrations of women than men, and most of these are in the sections on reproduction (Mendelson, in Levison & Straumanis, 2002). Similarly, 80 percent of cardiovascular drug ads in medical journals feature men only, even though heart disease is the number one killer of both women and men. When women are included, they tend to be younger than the average age of women with heart disease. In addition, the women are predominantly White, even though the rate of heart disease for African American is 72 percent higher than for White women (Ahmed et al., 2004). Moreover, most physicians depicted in medical journal ads are White males whereas most of their patients are portrayed as White women. Female patients are also much more likely than male patients to be shown nude or provocatively dressed (Hawkins & Aber, 1993; Metzl, 2003).

A nationwide survey of women's health (Commission on Women's Health, 2003) found that women were twice as likely as men to report negative feelings about the patient–physician relationship. One in four women (compared to one in eight men) reported that they were "talked down to" by a physician. Moreover, 17 percent of women (compared to 7 percent of men) have been told that a medical condition they felt they had was "all in their head." Female physicians are more likely than male physicians to establish interpersonal rapport with their patients and to provide them with information and preventive services (Bertakis, 2009; Chen, 2010; Reid et al., 2010; Sandhu et al., 2009). They also spend more time with their patients and tend to focus on them as people rather than on the procedures they need (Olfson et al., 2009). Moreover, women with heart disease risk factors and patients with diabetes receive higher quality care from female physicians than from male physicians (Carvajal, 2011; Schmittdiel et al., 2009). Patients of female physicians report a greater willingness to reveal personal problems such as family violence or sexual abuse (Clancy, 2000). Not surprisingly, both women and men express more satisfaction with women physicians (Bean-Mayberry et al., 2006; Bertakis, 2009; Coulter et al., 2000).

Type and Quality of Care

Discrimination based on gender affects not only interpersonal aspects of health care but also the type and quality of care that women receive. When one looks at medical conditions that affect both women and men, women often receive less adequate care even when the severity of the condition is the same for both. As we shall see later in this chapter, women with heart disease receive less aggressive treatment than men (Bairey Merz et al., 2010; Ng et al., 2010). Women are also not as likely as men to receive kidney dialysis, a kidney transplant, or knee replacement surgery (Borkhoff et al., 2008).

Biases exist even in childhood. For example, girls who are growing too slowly are referred to specialists only half as often as boys (Grimberg et al., 2005). Although it is true that boys tend to suffer greater social consequences if they are short, slow growth may be a sign of underlying disease. The failure of doctors to send small girls for closer examination can mean that serious problems go undetected.

Ageism presents older women with a double whammy. For one thing, health care professionals often emphasize older women's dependence, reinforcing women's perceptions of low self-efficacy and decreasing their active health care behaviors (Alexander et al., 2010). Moreover, older women are less likely than younger women to receive Pap smears, mammograms, or tests for colon cancer ("QuickStats," 2008; Yankaskas et al., 2010). In addition, physicians often attribute an older woman's chronic ailments to natural aging, and consequently, they are less apt to treat her for these conditions. For example, despite the fact that urinary incontinence and arthritis, which affect more women than men, can be treated effectively using medical or behavioral means, many health professionals dismiss it as an inevitable part of the aging process (Lachs, 2010; Pruthi, 2010).

Ethnicity, Poverty, and Health Care

Women of color are more likely than White women to be poor and uninsured. Latinas have the highest uninsurance rate of any group of women, followed by Native American women (Kogan et al., 2010; Moonesinghe et al., 2011). Because the lack of health insurance is often a financial barrier to seeking preventive health care, women of color and poor women are less likely to get the medical care they need (Boehmer & Bowen, 2010; Muennig et al., 2010; Peterson & Yancy, 2009; Weitz, 2010; Wilper et al., 2009). In particular, women of color have often lacked access to preventive health care services such as Pap smears, mammograms, and cholesterol screening (Borrayo et al., 2009; Clark et al., 2009; Gorin et al., 2008; Low Dog & Maizes, 2010). Furthermore, experiences with prejudice or culturally inappropriate health care cause many women of color to visit the doctor less frequently than White women do and to forego or delay follow-up and treatment after a medical test indicates an abnormality (Kilbourne et al., 2006; Press et al., 2008; Riall et al., 2010). Immigrant women, in addition to facing the obstacles just mentioned, must often contend with language barriers (Comas-Díaz, 2010b). In the words of one lower-income Latina woman, "They don't understand my language, my culture, my issues" (Clemetson, 2002, p. A12).

The good news is that the number of poor and ethnic minority women receiving mammograms and Pap smears has risen substantially during the past decade (American Cancer Society, 2009; Henley et al., 2010). The bad news is that even when their insurance and income are the same, racial and ethnic minorities in the United States often receive health care of lower quality than Whites (Bowleg, 2008; Robbins & Padavic, 2007). In addition, poor women receiving Medicaid assistance have different reproductive health benefits than women with employment-based health insurance. Poor women on Medicaid receive mandated coverage of contraceptives, unlike working- and middle-class women. On the other hand, working- and middle-class women often have mandated coverage for infertility treatments, which Medicaid does not cover. The result is a policy that discourages poor women from having children (Lott & Bullock, 2001).

White women use prescription medications at a somewhat higher level than women of color (National Center for Health Statistics, 2007). One possible reason for this is that ethnic minority women may be more likely to encounter special difficulties procuring and using medications. Language differences and cultural differences in perceptions of illness can make communicating with the doctor especially problematic for immigrant women and men, resulting in greater difficulty following a prescribed regimen (Flores, 2006; Groh, 2009).

Women With Disabilities and Health Care

About 20 percent of all women in the United States have some level of disability. Black women have the highest incidence of severe disability, followed by White women and Latinas (Groh, 2009). Women with disabilities are faced with several barriers to health, including limited information, lack of transportation, physical inaccessibility to medical offices and equipment, and discrimination by health care providers, who may focus on the women's disability, rather than on basic routine health care needs (Alexander et al., 2010). Women with disabilities are more likely than other women to be poor, which further limits access to needed medical care (Groh, 2009).

Sexual Minority Women and Health Care

Sexual minority women may be at increased risk for certain health problems because of certain life-style factors. For example, lesbian and bisexual women may face heightened risks of breast and ovarian cancers because they are less likely than heterosexual women to experience the hormonal changes associated with pregnancy and because they are more likely to smoke and consume alcohol (Conron et al., 2010; Zaritsky & Dibble, 2010).

The social stigma attached to homosexuality also contributes to increased health risks for lesbians by reducing access to health care (Boehmer & Bowen, 2010; Buchmueller & Carpenter, 2010; Dilley et al., 2010; Kitts, 2010; McNair et al., 2011; Tracy et al., 2010). Many sexual minority women avoid going to the doctor for routine checkups—especially gynecological exams—because they feel uncomfortable talking about issues that may reveal their sexual orientation and consequently elicit negative reactions from the physician (National Women's Health Information Center, 2011). In the words of one young woman, "If you lie, then you may not get the information you need to take care of yourself. And if you come out, your doctor may become really uncomfortable with you" (Thompson, 1999, p. A25). Lesbians and bisexual women may also limit their visits to doctors because they are less likely to have health insurance as same-sex partners often cannot share spousal benefits. Even for those who do have coverage, managed health care plans often limit women's ability to choose lesbian-friendly health care providers. The reduced access to health care that results from fear of discrimination and from financial barriers elevates health risks for lesbians and bisexual women (Mayer et al., 2008; National Women's Health Information Center, 2011; Wallace et al., 2011). Organizations that can help locate health professionals who are sensitive to the needs of female sexual minorities are listed in the Websites at the end of this chapter.

Health Insurance

We have seen that women of color are more likely than White women to lack health insurance. Another group with a high rate of uninsurance is women in their late 50s and early 60s. Millions of these midlife women do not receive employer-based health insurance and are not yet eligible for Medicare benefits, which begin at age 65. Currently, one in seven women aged 60–64 has no health insurance (OWL, 2007).

What kinds of insurance programs are available to U.S. adults and how do they affect women? These programs can be grouped into government plans (Medicare, Medicaid) and private plans (fee-for-service and managed care).

GOVERNMENT PLANS.   **Medicare** is the *federal program designed to provide medical care for those who are over 65 or permanently disabled, regardless of income.* Medicare covers less than half of medical costs and it does not cover most long-term care or home and supportive care. These limitations affect women disproportionately because they not only have more medical concerns but also have more complex medical conditions than men. In addition, some physicians do not accept Medicare patients because the reimbursement is low (AARP, 2006; Alexander et al., 2010; Donatelle, 2012).

Medicaid is a *combined state and federal program designed to provide medical care for the needy of any age* (Iglehart, 2010). As with Medicare, many health care providers refuse to see Medicaid recipients because of low reimbursement rates. These patients have to rely on clinics and emergency rooms. Individuals with high medical bills who do not qualify for Medicaid *ultimately become eligible once they have depleted most of their financial resources and assets*. This process, called **spending down**, is most common among residents of nursing homes, most of whom are women (Beers & Jones, 2004; O'Brien, 2005).

Women rely more heavily than men on both Medicaid and Medicare because they are more likely to be poor and because they live longer (U.S. Department of Health and Human Services, 2009). Moreover, women are less likely than men to have insurance through their own employers because they are more likely to work in temporary or part-time jobs or in occupations that do not provide health insurance benefits (Meyer & Herd, 2007). A woman who is covered under a spouse's plan risks losing coverage in the event of divorce, the spouse's death, or his retirement (Office on Women's Health, 2007).

PRIVATE INSURANCE PLANS.   Most of Americans are covered by private health insurance provided by their own employers or the employer of a family member. One of the two types of private plans is **fee-for-service insurance**. *The insurer pays part of the cost (usually 80 percent) for specified services, including hospitalization (up to a certain limit) and diagnostic services, but not preventive care.* The second type of private insurance is **managed care**, which has become the leading means of financing health care (Donatelle, 2012). Managed care *provides services to members for a flat fee and emphasizes preventive care and early detection of disease more than fee-for-service plans do.* Health maintenance organizations (HMOs) and preferred provider organizations (PPOs) are the most common types of managed care (Donatelle, 2012). Providing inexpensive screening procedures such as mammograms and Pap tests makes the services affordable for many women. However, managed care often limits access to specialists and reduces treatment options for many women, particularly older women who frequently have many chronic ailments requiring treatment by different specialists. Limited finances often prevent older women from seeing the physicians or purchasing the medications not covered by their managed care insurance (Older Women's League, 2004). Moreover, women enrolled in HMOs are more likely than those not in HMOs to report not getting needed care and being less satisfied with their physicians (Davis et al., 2000).

Older women may view health and health care differently than younger women. To compare how these two groups view health issues, try Get Involved 12.1.

SEXUALLY TRANSMITTED INFECTIONS (STIs)

Sexually transmitted infections (STIs) have reached epidemic proportions around the world (Rogstad, 2011). Of the more than 19 million new cases of STIs diagnosed in the United States each year, nearly half occur in teens and young adults ("Facts on Sexually Transmitted Infections," 2009; Rogstad, 2011). At least one in four American teenage girls and nearly half of African American

GET INVOLVED 12.1
What Women Say About Their Health

Answer the following questions and ask two young adult women and two women aged 65 or older to answer the same questions.

1. Whom would you trust more to be your doctor, a woman or a man, or would you trust them equally?

2. Which presents the more serious risk: heart disease or breast cancer?

3. How would you describe your health: excellent, good, fair, or poor?

4. In general, who has more health problems: men or women?

5. Who handles being sick better: women or men?

6. Whose complaints do doctors take more seriously: men's, women's? Or do they give equal consideration to both?

7. How often do doctors talk down to you: most of the time, some of the time, hardly ever, or never?

8. Where do you get most of your medical information: doctors, television, newspapers and magazines, or the Internet?

WHAT DOES IT MEAN?

1. How do the responses of the older women compare with the information presented in the chapter?

2. How do the responses of the older women compare with the responses of your college-age friends? How can age account for these differences?

3. Can you think of any factors other than age that might account for any differences between the responses of the two groups of women?

Source: Elder (1997).

teenage girls are infected (Altman, 2008). We will first give an overview of STIs (see Table 12.1) and then turn to AIDS, the most life-threatening of the STIs.

Overview of STIs

If untreated, STIs can have serious consequences. For example, chlamydia, the most commonly reported STI in the United States today, can lead to chronic pain, pelvic inflammatory disease, and infertility ("Facts on Sexually Transmitted Infections," 2009; Rogstad, 2011). In addition, the human papillomavirus (HPV), found in nearly half of young American women, increases the risk of cervical cancer (Centers for Disease Control and Prevention, 2010a; "Facts on Sexually Transmitted Infections," 2009; Rogstad, 2011). People with syphilis, gonorrhea, chlamydia, or herpes are more likely than others to become infected with the AIDS virus, in part because they have open sores that allow the virus to enter the body ("Facts on Sexually Transmitted Infections," 2009; Rogstad, 2011; Teitelman et al., 2009).

STIs have a disproportionate impact on women. They are transmitted more easily to women than to men and are more difficult to diagnose in women (Crepaz et al., 2009; Upadhyay & Murphy, 2010). In addition, women may be at high risk of STIs because of social and cultural norms that dictate that women do not decline sexual intercourse with their partners or insist on the use of condoms (Crepaz et al., 2009; Teitelman et al., 2009). Factors that enhance a woman's risk for contracting STIs include being under 25, using condoms inconsistently, being sexually active at an early age,

TABLE 12.1   Major Sexually Transmitted Infections (STIs)

STI	Mode of Transmission	Symptoms	Treatment
Chlamydia	Sexual contact; from mother to baby during birth	Painful urination and intercourse, vaginal discharge; often no symptoms	Antibiotics, e.g., doxycycline, azithromycin
Genital herpes	Sexual contact; most contagious during active outbreaks	Painful blisters near vagina, buttocks; often no symptoms	No cure. Antiviral drugs help healing
Gonorrhea	Sexual contact; from mother to baby during birth	Vaginal discharge, painful urination, bleeding between periods; often no symptoms	Antibiotics, e.g., cephalosporins
Hepatitis B	Sexual contact	Jaundice, loss of appetite	Interferon; preventive vaccine
HIV/AIDS	Sexual contact; infected blood transfusions; from mother to baby during birth or breastfeeding	Flu; weight loss; fatigue; opportunistic infections such as thrush, shingles, herpes	No cure. Antiretroviral drugs delay progress of the disease
HPV/Genital warts	Sexual contact	Painless warts in vagina; often no symptoms	No cure. Wart removal by laser or burning; preventive vaccine
Syphilis	Sexual contact when sores are present; mother to fetus	Initially, hard, painless chancre (sore)	Penicillin
Trichomoniasis	Sexual contact	Yellow odorous vaginal discharge; itching, burning in vulva	Antibiotics, e.g., metronidazole

Sources: Donatelle (2012); Pruthi (2010); Rathus et al. (2010); and Zenilman and Shahmanesh (2012).

and having sex frequently and with multiple partners (Centers for Disease Control and Prevention, 2010a). Because the risk of woman-to-woman sexual transmission of STIs is small, the prevalence of STIs in lesbians and bisexual women is fairly low but is not zero (Groh & Serowky, 2009; National Women's Health Information Center, 2011).

One factor behind the rapid increase in STIs is that the majority of American women have relatively little knowledge of STIs and even less concern about contracting one (Friedman & Bloodgood, 2010). For more on this subject, see Learn About the Research 12.1.

AIDS

Acquired immunodeficiency syndrome (AIDS), *caused by the human immunodeficiency virus (HIV)*, is the most devastating of all the STIs. AIDS-related illnesses remain one of the leading causes of death worldwide (UNAIDS, 2009). Although the overall number of AIDS cases in the United States began to drop in the mid-90s, cases of HIV infection and AIDS among individuals of color have continued to increase. Women—particularly women of color—are the fastest-growing group

LEARN ABOUT THE RESEARCH 12.1
Knowledge and Communication About STIs

In 2007–2008, individual interviews were conducted in 10 metropolitan areas with Black, Latina, and White females of ages 15–25 to determine their knowledge of and communication about STIs (Friedman & Bloodgood, 2010). Most of the young women were not knowledgeable about chlamydia, its asymptomatic nature, its potential to cause infertility, or its screening. One in five thought the Pap test screened for all STIs. Moreover, most felt uncomfortable discussing STIs with parents, partners, or friends. Nearly one in three had never discussed STIs with a health care provider, mentioning barriers such as having a male provider, feeling rushed during the visit, or having their mothers present.

WHAT DOES IT MEAN?

1. What actions can be taken to better educate women about STIs? What should school children be taught on this topic?

2. What can be done to increase communication between a young woman and her reproductive health care provider?

of Americans infected with HIV. Heterosexual sex has become the leading method of transmission for women both in the United States and abroad (Rosenthal & Levy, 2010; Simoni et al., 2010). For a closer look at the global AIDS epidemic, see Explore Other Cultures 12.1.

Women accounted for nearly 30 percent of new HIV infections in the United States in 2006 (Hessol et al., 2009). Although many are young, low-income women of color who live in urban areas, the incidence of HIV-infected rural White women is also on the rise (Rural Center, 2009). Black women, who constitute just 12 percent of American women, make up nearly two-thirds of women with AIDS in the United States ("Disparities in Diagnoses," 2011). In 2006, their HIV rate was 15 times higher than that of Whites and nearly 4 times higher than that of Latinas (El-Bassel et al., 2009). Why are Black women at heightened risk for AIDS? Poverty, inadequate access to HIV prevention services, and a dearth of information about safe sex are major reasons (Kalb & Murr, 2006). In addition, the lower number of economically viable and available Black men may lead Black women to take more sexual risks in order to attract and keep a partner (El-Bassel et al., 2009; Simoni et al., 2010). Moreover, low-income women may be economically dependent on a partner and thus not in a position to negotiate safer sex (El-Sadr et al., 2010; Konkel, 2010).

Women, especially Black women, are sicker at the time of diagnosis with HIV or AIDS and die more quickly than men with the disease (Alexander et al., 2010; Rubin et al., 2009). Why are women often diagnosed at a later stage of HIV than men? For one thing, women are generally viewed as being at low risk for the disease and so they and their physicians may overlook signs of HIV infection that they exhibit. Second, women usually serve as caregivers for family members and, increasingly, as breadwinners. As a result, they may delay seeking health care for themselves until they are very ill. Finally, as noted earlier, many HIV-infected women live in poverty and do not have access to health care (Behforouz & Chung, 2010; El-Bassel et al., 2009).

Decisions about childbearing can be difficult for HIV-infected women (Sandelowski et al., 2009). Without any intervention, the chances of passing the virus to their children are 25 percent (Wilson, 2011). In industrialized countries, an infected woman who takes antiretroviral drugs during pregnancy, has a cesarean delivery, avoids breastfeeding and whose newborn is given antiretroviral drugs has only about a 1- to 2-percent chance of infecting her child (Vandermaelen et al., 2009). But in developing countries, complex antiretroviral drug regimens are often unavailable, and avoidance of breastfeeding is not a realistic

EXPLORE OTHER CULTURES 12.1
The Global AIDS Epidemic

An estimated 33 million people worldwide, more than half of them women, are infected with HIV (UNAIDS, 2010). Sub-Saharan Africa, with 10 percent of the world's population but over two-thirds of the world's HIV/AIDS sufferers, is the most severely affected region. There, 60 percent of those infected are women (UNAIDS, 2010). In Swaziland, one of the hardest hit countries, over 25 percent of adults have the virus (UNAIDS, 2010).

Adolescent girls and young women of childbearing age in Africa are two to five times more likely to develop HIV/AIDS than their male counterparts for a variety of biological, social, and economic reasons (UNAIDS, 2010). Many adolescent women marry older men, who have likely had several previous sexual partners. At the same time, cultural resistance to condom use is high. Moreover, many adolescents in sub-Saharan Africa have limited knowledge of how to protect themselves from AIDS (Boonstra, 2009b; Dodoo & Frost, 2008; Dugassa, 2009; UNICEF, 2011). These factors result in high rates of STIs, which increase chances of HIV transmission. In addition, poverty, economic dependency, and low status render women powerless to protect themselves against unsafe or unwanted sex. Sadly, the proportion of infected women is rapidly expanding in other parts of the world as well, particularly Eastern Europe and central and southeast Asia (UNAIDS, 2010). In countries such as India, where the vast majority of females with HIV are infected by their husbands, women are unable to negotiate condom use without risking physical violence (Burn, 2011). Women who contract HIV from their husbands may be abandoned by their families. Some then become sex workers to survive, further spreading the disease (Marton, 2004). Even those girls and women who do not contract HIV are deeply affected by the epidemic, because the burden of caring for the sick usually falls on them. Girls are often withdrawn from school to care for ailing parents or younger siblings, or to earn an income (Henderson & Jeydel, 2010; Mukherjee et al., 2010; United Nations Children's Fund, 2007).

Several developing countries have had some recent success in slowing the spread of HIV through AIDS education and condom promotion, and in providing greater access to HIV treatment for those who are infected. In sub-Saharan Africa, for example, Botswana and Kenya appear to be reversing their widespread epidemics (UNAIDS, 2010).

option for most women (International Treatment Preparedness Coalition, 2009). Consequently, many women with HIV must wrestle with the fact that their children may be infected and may also be motherless at a young age (Ciambrone, 2003). It is helpful for HIV-infected women to share dilemmas such as this in a support group or HIV workshop (Rural Center, 2009). Many of these women feel isolated and have not disclosed their illness out of fear of rejection and ostracism (Rural Center, 2009). Often, a support group may be a woman's first opportunity to meet other women with HIV or AIDS and to receive help in locating government-subsidized sources of anti-HIV medication (Cowley & Murr, 2004).

The best way to prevent AIDS is to practice "safer sex," that is, avoid unprotected sex with multiple partners and always use latex or polyurethane condoms during sexual intercourse (Donatelle, 2012; Moore, 2009). The good news is that, in recent years, American teenagers have shown improvement in these HIV-related sexual risk behaviors (Gavin et al., 2009). Unfortunately, many young people, including college students, still fail to engage in safer sex practices. Factors underlying these risky sexual behaviors include a perceived low risk of infection and negative attitudes toward condom use (Rathus et al., 2010).

AIDS IN OLDER WOMEN. Whatever a woman's age, if she is sexually active, she is at risk for contracting sexually transmitted diseases, including HIV. Today, about 1,300 new cases of HIV/AIDS among women aged 55 and older are diagnosed in the United States each year, and this number is growing (Prejean et al., 2006). In the mid-1980s, most AIDS cases among women in that age group were caused by blood transfusions. Now, heterosexual contact is the leading cause ("The Body," 2008). One factor increasing older women's risk during heterosexual contact is the thinning of the vaginal tissues and the decrease in lubrication after menopause, which can cause small skin tears or abrasions during intercourse, thus increasing the chance of HIV entering the bloodstream (National Institute on Aging, 2009). Another factor in the rise of HIV in older people is the increase in sexual activity fueled by Viagra, but without a corresponding increase in condom use (Schick et al., 2010; Smith & Christakis, 2009). Many of today's aging baby boomers grew up before the HIV epidemic and didn't learn how to negotiate condom use with their partners. The result is that most sexually active older singles report having unprotected sex (Rabin, 2010a; Smith & Christakis, 2009).

Older women who have HIV infection may have a harder time than infected younger women in obtaining a correct diagnosis and treatment. Because older women are generally viewed as sexually disinterested and inactive, they are less likely to be given information about safer sex practices (Jacobs & Thomlison, 2009). Few educational and prevention programs target this age group ("The Body," 2008; Jacobs & Kane, 2009). Moreover, physicians do not expect to see AIDS in older women, and therefore, they are more likely to make a late diagnosis or a misdiagnosis ("The Body," 2008). Also, women of this age group are less likely to think of themselves as being at risk for AIDS, and so they may not think to ask for an HIV test (Jacobs & Thomlison, 2009; National Institute on Aging, 2009). Failure to diagnose HIV early can have serious consequences at any age because it is harder to arrest the disease when it becomes more advanced. But older adults with HIV are even more likely to deteriorate rapidly because of their already weakened immune system ("Aging and HIV," 2010).

HIV infection takes an enormous emotional toll on older women, many of whom live alone and are already trying to cope with physical, economic, and personal losses. Whereas today's younger women are used to talking more freely about sexual problems, this is difficult for many older women. They feel ashamed and may suffer alone, avoiding telling friends and family ("The Body," 2008; Jacobs & Kane, 2009). Some avoid intimate contact with grandchildren, such as kissing on the lips, for fear of endangering the youngsters. Therapy groups are an important source of emotional support for these women (Ciambrone, 2003).

REPRODUCTIVE SYSTEM DISORDERS

STIs are not the only diseases that can affect the reproductive system. We now turn to other disorders including benign (noncancerous) conditions such as endometriosis and fibroid tumors, as well as various cancers.

Benign Conditions

Endometriosis is a chronic and sometimes painful condition in which the *lining of the uterus (endometrium) migrates and grows on pelvic structures, such as the ovaries, fallopian tubes, and bladder.* Over 5 million women in the United States are diagnosed with this condition each year. Endometriosis can cause pelvic and menstrual pain and heavy bleeding. Severe endometriosis is a major cause of infertility (Bulun, 2009; Cole, 2010).

Up to two out of three women will develop **fibroid tumors**, which are *noncancerous growths of the uterus,* at some time in their lives. Fibroids are not dangerous, but they can cause severe pelvic and menstrual pain, heavy bleeding, and possibly infertility and miscarriage. They occur more often in Black women than in White women (Hildreth, 2009c; Perron, 2010).

Cancers

Endometrial or uterine cancer is the most common cancer of the female reproductive tract and is often characterized by vaginal bleeding. Risk factors include estrogen replacement therapy (without use of progestin), obesity, early menarche, late menopause, and never having children (Donatelle, 2012). Although it is more common in White women than in Black women, Black women are more likely to die from it. Because most cases are detected early, this is one of the most curable cancers of the reproductive system, with a five-year survival rate of over 90 percent for localized uterine cancer (American Cancer Society, 2010b; Buchanan et al., 2009).

Cancer of the **cervix**, *the lower end of the uterus,* is the third most common cancer of the female genital system, after uterine and ovarian cancers (Alexander et al., 2010). In the United States, more than 90 percent of those who have developed cervical cancer have a five-year survival rate if the cancer is detected in its earliest stages (American Cancer Society, 2010c). Black, Latina, and Native American women, however, have a much higher death rate, probably because their more limited access to medical care prevents early diagnosis and treatment (Boehmer & Bowen, 2010). Factors that increase the risk of cervical cancer include smoking, early age at first intercourse, multiple sex partners, extended use of oral contraceptives, and infection with HPV, the common virus that causes genital warts (American Cancer Society, 2010c). The **Pap smear**, *an inexpensive and effective screening technique,* has been used for several decades to identify precancerous changes in the cervix. Over the past 30 years, the test has slashed cervical cancer deaths by 50 percent and saved tens of thousands of lives (Alschuler, 2010). In the United States, of those women who develop cervical cancer, about 60 percent have never had a Pap smear (Runowicz, 2007). Women should start getting an annual Pap test by age 21 or three years after the onset of sexual activity, whichever comes first. If a woman aged 30 or older has had three normal test results in a row, the interval can be increased to every two to three years (American Cancer Society, 2010c). Unfortunately, only 80 percent of women have Pap smears at least once every three years. Women who are poor, uninsured, less educated, and older are least likely to get regular Pap tests (Leach & Schoenberg, 2007; "QuickStats," 2010b). The good news is that the recently developed vaccine that protects women against HPV could drastically reduce the incidence of cervical cancer worldwide over the next several decades (Schiffman & Wacholder, 2009). Some parents, however, object to their daughters being given the preventive vaccine, fearing that doing so might send the subtle message that premarital sex is acceptable (Charo, 2007). What is your view on this issue?

Ovarian cancer is a major killer of women, causing more deaths than any other cancer of the female reproductive system. It is a so-called silent killer because its symptoms usually do not appear until the cancer is in an advanced stage. At that stage, the five-year survival rate is under 30 percent (Roett & Evan 2009; Trivers et al., 2009). Risk factors include having immediate family members with ovarian, breast, or colon cancer; having early menarche and late menopause; using hormone replacement therapy; being obese; and smoking. However, bearing children, breastfeeding, taking birth control pills, and eating a low-fat diet are protective factors (Davidson, 2011b; Hannaford et al., 2010; Ovarian Cancer National Alliance, 2010). Early symptoms of ovarian cancer include bloating, pelvic or abdominal pain, difficulty eating or feeling full quickly, and frequent or urgent urination. Women with these symptoms for more than a few weeks are advised to see their doctors (Ovarian Cancer National Alliance, 2010). A recently developed screening procedure shows promise for detecting ovarian cancer at earlier, more treatable, stages. It involves a blood test for the CA 125 tumor marker, followed by a transvaginal ultrasound (Sulik & Heath, 2010).

Hysterectomy

Each year, over 600,000 women in the United States undergo a **hysterectomy**, the *removal of the uterus*. By age 60, more than one in four American women have had their uterus removed, one of the highest rates in the world (Alexander et al., 2010). For years, many critics have questioned the high rate of hysterectomy in this country. Although removal of the uterus is considered appropriate in cases of cancer of the uterus, cervix, or ovaries, these situations account for only a small fraction of the total hysterectomies done in the United States. Endometriosis, heavy menstrual bleeding, and chronic pelvic pain are other common reasons for hysterectomy (Pruthi, 2010). But the most common reason is the presence of fibroid tumors (Goodwin & Spies, 2009). Because Black women are more likely than White women to have fibroid tumors, their hysterectomy rates are also higher (Bower et al., 2009). Other less invasive procedures include **fibroid embolization**, which *blocks blood flow to the fibroids*, and **myomectomy** the *surgical removal of the fibroids* (Goodwin & Spies, 2009).

These less invasive procedures may have fewer negative psychological effects than hysterectomy. For example, Jean Elson (2004) interviewed 44 women, ages 24 to 69, whose uterus had been removed for benign conditions. All the women reflected on their gender identity following surgery. Their reactions ranged all the way from "Now I feel like a fake woman" to "I have always been . . . the same person" (Ayoub, 2004, p. A18). Most of the women did not miss menstruation much, but they missed the potential to have children. This was true whether or not they already had children and even if they never intended to have them (Ayoub, 2004). In spite of feelings of loss, however, many women view their hysterectomy positively as relieving chronic pain and enabling them to regain control over their bodies (Markovic et al., 2008).

Another common practice, which has been heavily criticized, is the removal of the ovaries along with the uterus, even when the ovaries are normal and healthy. Physicians who carry out such surgery contend that when a women is in her mid-40s or older, the ovaries' major function is over and that removing them forestalls the possibility of ovarian cancer (Parker et al., 2009). Can you see the sexist bias in this argument? Could one not equally argue that the prostate and testes of middle-aged men should be removed to prevent cancer of these organs? Recent evidence (Parker et al., 2009) shows that women who keep their ovaries actually live *longer* than those whose ovaries are removed during a hysterectomy. This is due largely to the heart-protective effects of estrogen.

OSTEOPOROSIS

Osteoporosis is an *excessive loss of bone tissue in older adults, which results in the bones becoming thinner, brittle, and more porous.* Osteoporosis affects about 10 million Americans, 80 percent of them women (National Osteoporosis Foundation, 2010). But the seeds of osteoporosis are sown in adolescence, when bone building is most rapid (Misra, 2008). By their middle to late 20s, women reach their peak bone mass. Around age 30, gradual bone loss begins. The rate of bone loss accelerates sharply for five to seven years after the onset of menopause, as estrogen levels drop (Gagné, 2010; National Osteoporosis Foundation, 2010). Each year, 1.5 million fractures related to osteoporosis occur in the United States. Half of all women over 50 years of age will have a fracture during their lifetime because of osteoporosis. These fractures can be crippling and painful and can cause permanent loss of mobility. Moreover, 20 percent of patients with a hip fracture die of complications such as blood clots and pneumonia (Brauer et al., 2009; National Osteoporosis Foundation, 2010).

Risk Factors

Some women are more likely to develop osteoporosis than others. For a list of risk factors, see Table 12.2. Postmenopausal women with one or more of these risk factors, and all women over 65, should consider getting a bone density test, which can detect even a small loss of bone mass (National Osteoporosis Foundation, 2010).

Prevention and Treatment

A look at Table 12.2 suggests several ways to build and keep as much bone as possible. Increasing calcium and vitamin D intake during childhood, adolescence, and young adulthood is the most effective way of building denser bones and reducing risk of bone fracture (National Osteoporosis Foundation, 2010). In order to suppress bone loss, experts recommend consumption of 1,300 milligrams of calcium per day for adolescents, 1,000 milligrams for women aged 19 to 50, and 1,200 milligrams for postmenopausal women. Good sources of calcium include low-fat and nonfat milk, cheese, and yogurt; tofu and other soy products; dark-green leafy vegetables such as kale and spinach; almonds; and canned sardines and salmon (Brody, 2011).

Unfortunately, adolescents consume far less calcium than they should. Their calcium intake has been declining for decades, as their intake of soft drinks has increased and their milk consumption has decreased (Brody, 2011). In addition, most women consume only about half the daily amount of calcium they need. Calcium supplements are good additional sources, especially those containing calcium carbonate (found in Tums and Rolaids) or calcium citrate (found in Citracal). Calcium cannot be absorbed without vitamin D. In order to keep bones strong, women under age 50 need 400–800 international units per day of vitamin D, and older women need 800–1,000 international units (National Osteoporosis Foundation, 2010). Milk fortified with vitamin D and

---

TABLE 12.2   Risk Factors for Osteoporosis

Biological Factors
- Gender: women's risk is greater because their bones are smaller and lighter
- Age: after age 30, bone loss begins
- Menopause: drop in estrogen levels increases bone loss
- Thin, small-framed body
- Ethnicity: White and Asian women, who have lower bone density, are at greater risk
- Family history of osteoporosis or older relatives with fractures

Lifestyle Factors
- Diet low in calcium and vitamin D
- High intake of sodium, animal protein, caffeine
- Lack of physical activity
- Smoking
- Alcohol intake of two or more drinks a day

Medical Factors
- Rheumatoid arthritis, diabetes, celiac disease, lactose intolerance
- Eating disorders
- Certain medications: diuretics, steroids, anticonvulsants

Sources: Gagné (2010); National Institutes of Health (2009); National Osteoporosis Foundation (2010); and Templeton (2010).

sunlight are two of its best sources. Although as little as 15 minutes per day in the sun helps the body produce Vitamin D, most adults may need dietary supplements in order to prevent vitamin D deficiency (Brody, 2010d).

Diet is only part of the equation, however. Exercise is very important in increasing bone mass during adolescence and young adulthood and in slowing bone loss after menopause (Bocalini et al., 2009; Kemmler et al., 2010; Tolomio et al., 2010). The exercise should be weightbearing, such as brisk walking, low-impact aerobics, or lifting weights. Even everyday activities such as climbing stairs, walking the dog, doing yard work, dancing, or playing with children can be beneficial. It is never too late to start exercising and a little bit of physical activity is better than none (Brody, 2010b; Donatelle, 2012). Not only decreasing or eliminating smoking and decreasing consumption of alcohol and most sources of caffeine (except for green tea) are good for strong bones but they may also confer many other health benefits, as we shall see later in the chapter (Gagné, 2010).

Estrogen helps build and maintain strong bones. Estrogen replacement therapy starting in perimenopause and continuing after menopause slows bone loss, increases bone mass, and reduces the incidence of fractures (National Osteoporosis Foundation, 2010). However, because hormone replacement therapy is now known to increase the risk of heart attack, stroke, and breast cancer (see Chapter 7), it is no longer considered an option for preventing osteoporosis. Fortunately, other medications can help a woman strengthen her bones. Drugs called bisphosphonates (sold as Fosamax, Actonel, Reclast, and Boniva) decrease the risk of hip and spinal fractures. **Raloxifene**, a *synthetic estrogen* marketed as Evista, decreases bone loss in postmenopausal women and reduces the risk of spinal fractures and also breast cancer (Khosla, 2011; National Osteoporosis Foundation, 2010; Veloski, 2008).

HEART DISEASE

Heart disease is the leading cause of death for both women and men around the world. More women in the United States die of heart disease than from all forms of cancer combined, including breast cancer (Kominos, 2010; Lavie & Milani, 2009; Rutledge et al., 2012). Specifically, over one in three women will eventually die from heart disease compared to only one in thirty from breast cancer. Yet many women are not aware of the risks of heart disease (Foody et al., 2010) and perceive breast cancer as a far greater threat to their health. Although awareness that heart disease is the top killer of women has grown since the late 1990s, awareness of risk factors for the disease remains low, particularly for women under age 35 and for ethnic minority women (Brinton et al., 2010; Mosca et al., 2010; Muñoz et al., 2010).

Gender Differences

Important gender differences in heart disease affect the onset, diagnosis, and treatment of the disease in women and men (Bairey Merz et al., 2010). Heart disease in women becomes apparent about 10 years later than in men. Illness and death from heart disease increase dramatically in women after menopause, partly due to declining estrogen levels. By her 70s, a woman has a greater risk of heart attack and heart disease than a man her age (Bairey Merz et al., 2010; Brinton et al., 2010; Pruthi, 2010). Women are more likely than men to die after a heart attack. If they survive, they are more likely to have a second attack (Berger et al., 2009; Gulati & Torkos, 2011). Because women are older than men when they develop heart disease, their prognosis is poorer (Reibis et al., 2009). But women are more likely than men to die after treatment for heart disease, even when they are equally old and ill (American Heart Association, 2009).

Risk Factors

Some risk factors for heart disease are unchangeable. In addition to gender and age, these include income level, ethnicity, and family history. Women from low-income households are more likely to have heart attacks and to die from them (Rutledge et al., 2012). Because Black women are disproportionately represented at the low end of the income scale, this may partly explain why they are more likely to die from heart disease than are White women (Chan et al., 2009). This is only part of the story, however, because Latina and Native American women have lower death rates from heart disease than White women, even though their average income is lower (Lloyd-Jones et al., 2009; Torpy, 2009). The risk of heart disease and stroke also increases if close family members have had these diseases (Gulati & Torkos, 2011; Kominos, 2010).

Major risk factors over which women have control include physical inactivity, smoking, being overweight, having a poor diet, and using hormone replacement therapy (Brown & O'Connor, 2010; Pruthi, 2010). Women who have none of these factors have a much lower risk of heart disease than other women. Even young women, who have a low rate of heart disease, should begin controlling these risk factors early in life (Folta et al., 2009).

Inactivity is a major risk factor in heart disease and stroke. Sedentary women are much more likely to die from cardiovascular disease than women who are very active. Women benefit from vigorous exercise such as aerobics, running, biking, or swimming for at least 30 minutes, most days of the week. But even moderate everyday activities such as a brisk walk, gardening, household chores, and climbing stairs provide health benefits (Donatelle, 2012; Govil et al., 2009; Gulati & Torkos, 2011; Monda et al., 2009). Unfortunately, more than 40 percent of American women are sedentary or do not engage in any regular physical activity. In addition, women become even less active as they get older, when they most need the cardiovascular benefits of exercise (U.S. Department of Health and Human Services, 2010).

High blood pressure (hypertension) is another major risk factor for heart attack and the most important risk factor for stroke (Gulati & Torkos, 2011; Wijeysundera et al., 2010). The incidence of high blood pressure increases with age, especially among Black women (Mather, 2008). Reducing intake of salt and red and processed meats, losing weight (if overweight), exercising, eating a fiber-rich diet, and taking medication (if needed) can bring blood pressure under control and reduce risk of stroke (Forman et al., 2009; Myint et al., 2009). Best of all, eating one square of dark chocolate a day lowers blood pressure (Buijsse et al., 2010; Heiss & Kelm, 2010). Who says if it's good for you it must taste bad?

Women with *diabetes* are more likely to have a heart attack or stroke than are nondiabetic women. Diabetes may be delayed by controlling blood sugar, eating less saturated fat, not smoking, limiting alcohol consumption, and staying physically active (Lloyd-Jones et al., 2009). Being *overweight* also increases the risk of heart attack, stroke, high blood pressure, high cholesterol levels, and diabetes (Lloyd–Jones et al., 2009; Pruthi, 2010).

Smoking also is a powerful risk factor for heart disease and stroke in women (Donatelle, 2012). Smoking is especially harmful in women because it decreases estrogen's protective effects and can cause menopause to occur about two years early. The vast majority of women who develop heart disease before age 50 are smokers. The good news is that quitting smoking cuts heart attack risk by nearly two-thirds within five years (Kenfield et al., 2008).

Diet is important in reducing the risk of heart disease and stroke. A heart-healthy diet—sometimes called "the Mediterranean diet"—is rich in vegetables and fruits, whole grains, nuts, soy, monounsaturated oils (olive, canola), and protein derived from fish, beans, low-fat or nonfat dairy products, lean meats, and poultry (Michelfelder, 2009; Moore, 2009). Drinking green tea appears to protect against heart disease as well, especially in women (Kominos, 2010; Schneider & Segre, 2009). In addition, women who consume one alcoholic drink per day are less likely to suffer a heart attack or stroke than women who do not drink (Gulati & Torkos, 2011). Moreover, one baby aspirin (81 mg) per day lowers the risk of both heart disease and cancer in women (Hildreth, 2009b; Kominos, 2010).

Hormones also affect heart disease. *Birth control pills* decrease women's risk of heart disease and stroke (Hannaford, 2010). As noted in Chapter 7, however, *hormone replacement therapy* increases the risk of heart disease if not started early in menopause.

Men and women with aspects of so-called Type A personality—particularly anger and hostility—are more prone to develop heart disease (Chida & Steptoe, 2009). Depression is another risk factor for developing heart disease and dying from it (Carney et al., 2009; Kronish et al., 2009; Nabi et al., 2008; Rutledge et al., 2012; Whang et al., 2009; Whooley et al., 2008). Because women are more likely than men to be depressed (see Chapter 13), this factor increases women's risk. Social factors play a role in heart disease as well. For example, loneliness and low levels of social support are associated with an increased risk of heart disease for women, but not for men (Czajkowski et al., 2012; Thurston & Kubzansky, 2009). In addition, women who are divorced, widowed, or unhappily married have a higher risk of heart disease than women who are satisfied with their marriages (Orth-Gomer, 2009; Troxel et al., 2005). Job stress also increases women's risk of heart disease (Rabin, 2010b).

Diagnosis and Treatment

The management, diagnosis, and treatment of heart disease in women are poorly understood and often carried out in an inconsistent manner. The result is that women receive poorer care (Bairey Merz et al., 2010; Donatelle, 2012; Ng et al., 2010). Women with heart disease often do not receive the aggressive treatment from physicians that men do (Concannon et al., 2009; Pregler et al., 2009). For one thing, physicians often miss the signs of heart disease and heart attack in women because women are less likely to show the "classic" male symptom of crushing chest pain and are more apt than men to show symptoms such as nausea, dizziness, shortness of breath, profuse sweating, chest pressure or heaviness, extreme fatigue, sleep disturbance, back or abdominal pain, heartburn, heart palpitations, or just an odd, unwell feeling. Women may be misdiagnosed as simply suffering from indigestion, muscle pain, stress, or anxiety (Alexander et al., 2010; Bönte et al., 2008; Maserejian et al., 2009; O'Connor, 2009). In addition, many health care providers do not realize that heart disease is a woman's number one health threat (American Heart Association, 2009). In one survey of 500 randomly selected physicians, women at risk of developing heart disease were more likely than men to be assigned to a low-risk category. They were less likely to be advised to change their living habits and to take medications to help prevent heart attacks (Brody, 2005). Even when women experience the classic symptoms of chest pain, they are more likely than men to delay getting medical care (Gulati & Torkos, 2011). Women with heart attack symptoms are also more likely to delay going to the hospital if they lack adequate medical insurance (Smolderen et al., 2010). Sometimes, women ignore the symptoms because they do not want to trouble or burden their family members (Moser et al., 2012).

But even when women do call 9-1-1 after experiencing heart attack symptoms, they are much less likely than men to receive prompt medical care, losing precious minutes before the onset of treatment (Concannon et al., 2009). When women show up at the emergency room with heart attack symptoms, they are less likely than men to be admitted for evaluation (Washington & Bird, 2002). Furthermore, they are not as likely as men to receive one of the most important diagnostic heart tests, the angiogram, which can show blockage in coronary arteries. Women heart patients also are less likely to be treated by a specialist and are less likely to receive cholesterol-lowering drugs, devices such as stents (to open clogged arteries), and treatments such as coronary bypass surgery, pacemakers, and implantable defibrillators. And in the critical hours following a heart attack, fewer women are given clot-dissolving drugs (Donatelle, 2012; Gulati & Torkos, 2011; Redberg, 2007; Spurgeon, 2007), and they wait longer than men to receive an emergency angioplasty to open blocked arteries ("Women and Heart Health," 2005). Moreover, they are less often given aspirin, which aids in dissolving blood clots, or beta-blockers, which protect against future heart attacks (Cho et al., 2008; Lloyd-Jones et al., 2009). Women also get fewer referrals for cardiac rehabilitation programs following heart attacks, even though they benefit from therapy at least as much as men do (Ayala et al., 2008; Rutledge et al., 2012). Even if they are referred, women are more likely than men to experience various barriers to participation in cardiac rehabilitation. Because women are poorer and are older when they have a heart attack, they are less likely to have access to a car to transport them to the rehab site. Moreover, they are more often family caregivers, leaving less time to look after their own health. Finally, women more often have other medical conditions, such as osteoporosis and urinary incontinence, which can serve as deterrents to exercise in rehab programs because of fear of falling and leakage accidents, respectively (Grace et al., 2009; Stephens, 2009). Finally, women are often underrepresented in studies designed to test the effectiveness of cardiac rehabilitation programs (American Heart Association, 2009).

Psychological Impact

The psychosocial health of women following a heart attack or coronary bypass surgery is worse than that of men (Doering et al., 2007; Ford et al., 2008; Garavalia et al., 2007). Women are more anxious and depressed, return to work less often, take longer to recuperate physically, and resume their sex lives later than men. In spite of their poorer health, women resume household activities sooner than men and are more likely to feel guilty that they cannot quickly resume the chores they once did (Packard, 2005; Prentice, 2008). Women's poorer psychosocial functioning after heart attack and heart surgery can take a toll on their well-being, productivity, and quality of life (Husser & Roberto, 2009). In addition, the greater depression experienced by women after heart attack or heart surgery is associated with a greater risk of death and of second heart attack. Health care providers need to become aware of the potential difficulties faced by women with heart disease and to take steps to enhance the recovery of their female patients (Rosenfeld, 2006).

BREAST CANCER

As we noted earlier, women fear breast cancer more than any other disease including heart disease, the top killer of women. Yet breast cancer is not even the number one cancer killer of women. That dubious distinction belongs to lung cancer (American Cancer Society, 2010a). One out of every eight women will develop breast cancer at some time in her life. Although this statistic sounds frightening, it represents a lifetime risk. At age 40, only 1 in 229 women develops breast cancer. At age 50, the risk increases to 1 in 42 women, and at age 70, it rises to 1 in 27 (American Cancer Society, 2009).

The majority of women in whom breast cancer is diagnosed—80 percent—do not die of the disease. Moreover, the death rate from breast cancer has been dropping in recent years as a result of earlier detection, improved treatments, and a decrease in the use of hormones to treat menopause (American Cancer Society, 2010a). The five-year survival rate for women with localized breast cancer is 98 percent. Even if the cancer has spread to lymph nodes, 84 percent of women will be alive five years later. If it invades bones or other organs, the rate drops to 23 percent (American Cancer Society, 2009).

Why is the prospect of getting breast cancer so terrifying? According to Jane Brody (1999a) and Ellen Ratner (1999), both breast cancer survivors and authors, the extensive publicity given to the disease in recent years in order to stimulate research and raise women's awareness has created the misleading impression that breast cancer is more common and more deadly than it actually is. In addition, although only a small number of women in their 30s and 40s die of breast cancer, their untimely deaths may trigger greater alarm than the heart attack deaths of a far greater number of women later in life.

Risk Factors

Age, as we have just seen, is the greatest risk factor for breast cancer. Four in five breast cancers are diagnosed in women over 50 and the average age when diagnosed is 64 (Love, 2010).

Ethnicity and *social class* are also risk factors. White women are slightly more likely than Black women to get breast cancer overall, but Black women are far more likely to die from it (American Cancer Society, 2010a). One reason is that Black women are poorer. Low-income women, regardless of race, are diagnosed later, receive lower quality of care, and are more likely to die of breast cancer than other women (American Cancer Society, 2010a; Vona-Davis & Rose, 2009). But in addition, the tumors of Black women appear to be faster growing and more malignant (American Cancer Society, 2010a).

Family history of breast cancer—especially in one's mother, sister, or daughter—is another risk factor, accounting for 5 to 10 percent of breast cancers. A small percentage of women with a family history of breast cancer have unusually high risk—50 to 85 percent—as a result of inheriting one of two breast cancer genes, BRCA1 and BRCA2. Inherited breast cancer occurs at younger ages, is more likely to affect both breasts, and often appears in multiple family members, including men, over several generations. The genes are more common in Jewish women of Eastern European origin than in other groups (Jardines, 2008; Love, 2010).

Age, ethnicity, and family history are risk factors women cannot change. Other factors over which they have little or no control include *early age at menarche, late age at menopause, late age at first birth* (after 30), and *having no or few children.* All these events lengthen the amount of time women's breast tissue is exposed to high levels of estrogen, which can stimulate growth of breast cancer cells (American Cancer Society, 2010a).

Women can reduce their risk of breast cancer by making certain lifestyle choices. One of these choices is not *smoking* (Croghan et al., 2009; Xue et al., 2011). Another is cutting down on alcohol or avoiding it altogether, as even one drink per day increases the risk of developing breast cancer (American Cancer Society, 2010a).

The same diet recommended for heart health, one that is high in vegetables, fruits, whole grains, and legumes and low in red meat and processed foods, is also linked to a reduction in breast cancer (American Institute for Cancer Research, 2010; Larson et al., 2009). Drinking green tea also reduces breast cancer risk (Love, 2010). It is unclear whether fat consumption is a breast cancer risk. But high-fat diets can lead to being overweight, which is a risk factor (American Cancer Society, 2010a). Body fat produces estrogen, which can help breast cancer grow. Engaging in *physical activity* reduces breast cancer risk, most likely because it reduces body fat (McTiernan, 2010; Porter, 2008). Recent use of *birth control pills* and *hormone replacement therapy* both increase risk of breast cancer (American Cancer Society, 2010a; Krieger et al., 2010). To assess your risk of breast cancer, try Get Involved 12.2.

GET INVOLVED 12.2
Assessing Your Risk of Breast Cancer

Put a check mark next to each risk factor listed here. The total number of checks gives a general indication of your relative risk. Remember that some women have many risk factors but never get breast cancer. Others have few or no factors but do get the disease.

After you assess your relative risk, give the questionnaire to female friends and relatives, including both young and older women.

BREAST CANCER RISK FACTORS

- Increasing age
- BRCA1 or BRCA2 gene mutation
- Family history of breast cancer
- High breast density
- Personal history of breast, uterine, colon, or ovarian cancers
- Menopause after age 55
- Not having children

- Having first child after age 35
- Never breastfeeding
- Being overweight after menopause
- More than one alcoholic drink per day
- Younger than 12 at first period
- Recent postmenopausal hormone replacement therapy

Total: _____

WHAT DOES IT MEAN?

1. How did breast cancer risk vary with the age of your respondents?
2. What advice can you give to your respondents who have moderate to high risk of breast cancer?

_____

Sources: American Cancer Society (2009); and Love and Mills (2010).

Detection

The American Cancer Society recommends that women aged 20 and older do a monthly breast self-examination about a week after their menstrual period ends (during menstruation breasts have normal lumps) (American Cancer Society, 2010a). See What You Can Do 12.1 for instructions. Many women do not examine their breasts, partly out of fear of finding a lump. (Keep in mind that nine out of ten lumps are noncancerous.) This is unfortunate, because a substantial portion of breast cancers are found during self-examination, particularly among women under 40 years (Ferraro, 2006). A major reason for this is that mammograms are less effective at detecting tumors in dense young breast tissue. Women with dense breast tissue and those with high risk of breast cancer are encouraged to use ultrasound, digital mammograms, or magnetic resonance imaging (MRI) to help detect early breast cancer (American Cancer Society, 2011). All women should also have a clinical breast exam by a health professional every three years from ages 20 to 39 and annually from age 40 onward (American Cancer Society, 2010a).

A **mammogram**, *a low-dose X-ray picture of the breast,* detects small suspicious lumps up to two years before they are large enough to be felt. The American Cancer Society and the National Cancer Institute recommend a yearly mammogram for women, starting at age 40 (American Cancer Society, 2009). Nationwide, the number of women who are screened has increased since 1990. Now, two-thirds of women aged 40 and over have had a mammogram in the last two years (American

WHAT YOU CAN DO 12.1
Doing a Breast Self-Examination

How to Examine Your Breasts

Lie down on your back and place your right arm behind your head. The exam is done while lying down, not standing up. This is because when lying down the breast tissue spreads evenly over the chest wall and is as thin as possible, making it much easier to feel all the breast tissue. Use the finger pads of the 3 middle fingers on your left hand to feel for lumps in the right breast. Use overlapping dime-sized circular motions of the finger pads to feel the breast tissue.

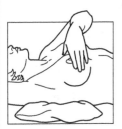 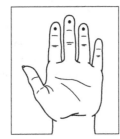

Use 3 different levels of pressure to feel all the breast tissue. Light pressure is needed to feel the tissue closest to the skin; medium pressure to feel a little deeper; and firm pressure to feel the tissue closest to the chest and ribs. It is normal to feel a firm ridge in the lower curve of each breast, but you should tell your doctor if you feel anything else out of the ordinary. If you're not sure how hard to press, talk with your doctor or nurse. Use each pressure level to feel the breast tissue before moving on to the next spot.

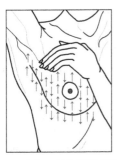

Move around the breast in an up and down pattern starting at an imaginary line drawn straight down your side from the underarm and moving across the breast to the middle of the chest bone (sternum or breastbone). Be sure to check the entire breast area going down until you feel only ribs and up to the neck or collar bone (clavicle). There is some evidence to suggest that the up-and down pattern (sometimes called the vertical pattern) is the most effective pattern for covering the entire breast without missing any breast tissue.

Repeat the exam on your left breast, putting your left arm behind your head and using the finger pads of your right hand to do the exam.

While standing in front of a mirror with your hands pressing firmly down on your hips, look at your breasts for any changes of size, shape, contour, or dimpling, or redness or scaliness of the nipple or breast skin. (The pressing down on the hips position contracts the chest wall muscles and enhances any breast changes.) Examine each underarm while sitting up or standing and with your arm only slightly raised so you can easily feel in this area. Raising your arm straight up tightens the tissue in this area and makes it harder to examine.

This procedure for doing breast self-exam is different from previous recommendations. These changes represent an extensive review of the medical literature and input from an expert advisory group. There is evidence that this position (lying down), the area felt, pattern of coverage of the breast, and use of different amounts of pressure increase a woman's ability to find abnormal areas.

Source: American Cancer Society. Reprinted with permission.

Cancer Society, 2009). However, women with low income or less education, who have more limited access to affordable health care, are less likely to be screened (Borrayo et al., 2009; Clark et al., 2009; Richardson et al., 2010). In addition, older women are screened less often than those in midlife (Federal Interagency Forum, 2009; Gorin et al., 2008). Some women avoid mammograms because they fear the pain or discomfort of the procedure itself, whereas others fear receiving a breast cancer diagnosis (Consedine et al., 2004; Magai et al., 2007).

Because breast cancer typically strikes after age 50, some women and their doctors may ignore early warning signs, such as a self-detected small lump, assuming it's only a benign cyst. Consequently, young women tend to be diagnosed when their disease has progressed further (Leibson-Hawkins, 2004).

Treatment

When breast cancer is diagnosed, several treatment options are available. For many years, the standard treatment was **radical mastectomy**, *the removal of the breast, underlying chest wall, and underarm lymph nodes.* Because of disfigurement and side effects, it is rarely done now. **Modified radical mastectomy** involves *removal of the breast and underarm lymph nodes* and **simple mastectomy** involves *removal of the breast only.* In **lumpectomy**, also known as partial mastectomy or breast-conserving surgery, only *the lump and some surrounding tissue are removed.* Lumpectomy is almost always followed by several weeks of radiation. For small tumors in the early stages of disease, lumpectomy followed by radiation is as effective in terms of 20-year survival as mastectomy (American Cancer Society, 2009; Love, 2010). Black women are less likely than White women to receive radiation after lumpectomy. It is unclear whether this disparity occurs because fewer Black women are offered the therapy, because they are more likely to decline it, or because they are unable to complete the entire treatment due to other barriers (Hampton, 2008). In addition, older and poorer women are less likely to receive appropriate treatment for breast cancer (Boehmer & Bowen, 2010).

Chemotherapy may be used to kill cancer cells that the surgeon was not able to remove. Other drugs that cut rates of breast cancer occurrence include the estrogen blockers raloxifene and tamoxifen and drugs called aromatase inhibitors. Another drug, Herceptin, shrinks tumors in women who have a certain type of fast-growing cancer or whose advanced breast cancer is not responsive to other treatments (American Cancer Society, 2010a; Love, 2010).

Psychological Impact

The diagnosis of breast cancer and the surgery that often follows cause fatigue, depression, anxiety, and anger in many women (American Cancer Society, 2009; Love, 2010). If the cancer recurs at some point after treatment, women may experience even higher levels of distress. Concerns about bodily appearance can be substantial for women who have had breast surgery (Ericksen, 2008).

Individual differences in reactions to breast cancer vary considerably. Young women appear to be affected more negatively than middle-aged or older women. They are more likely to have to deal with disruptions in family life and careers, as well as problems with fertility and sexual functioning. Consequently, they show greater declines in social functioning, mental health, and quality of life (Kroenke et al., 2004). But regardless of age, women with a "fighting spirit" and higher levels of hostility and those who voice their fears and anxieties survive breast cancer longer than those who show passive acceptance, stoicism, emotional inhibition, feelings of hopelessness, or denial of facts about the cancer (Compas & Luecken, 2002; Ray, 2004; Revenson, 2001).

Support groups are important in helping women cope with cancer. David Spiegel (2011) and his colleagues found that among breast cancer patients who had a poor prognosis, those who were randomly assigned to attend weekly group therapy sessions lived longer than women in the control group. Similarly, a recent study by Barbara Andersen and her colleagues (2008) found that after 11 years, women with breast cancer who participated in a group-based psychological intervention program were 45 percent less likely to have had their cancer return and 56 percent less likely to have died of the disease. Moreover, breast cancer patients who have friends, close relatives, and adult children live longer than patients who lack these sources of social support (Kroenke et al., 2006). Although social support does not always improve survival rates, it can enhance quality of life, mood, energy levels, and tolerance of chemotherapy and reduce depression and pain (Boehmer & Bowen, 2010; Spiegel, 2011). Psychosocial interventions that focus on reducing stress, increasing knowledge, and improving coping skills give breast cancer patients a greater sense of control, improved body image and sexual functioning, reduced distress, and greater adherence to their prescribed course of therapy (Dittmann, 2003; Taylor et al., 2003).

LUNG CANCER

Lung cancer is the leading cause of cancer deaths in women, killing more women each year than breast, uterine, and ovarian cancers combined.

Risk Factors

Although fewer men have been dying of lung cancer in the past several years, women have shown the opposite trend. Women's lung cancer death rates began to increase in the mid-twentieth century, finally leveling off in 2003. This increase is most likely linked to women's increased cigarette smoking during these years because cigarette smoking is responsible for more than 80 percent of lung cancer cases (Alexander et al., 2010; American Cancer Society, 2010b). Other risk factors include exposure to second-hand smoke, asbestos, and radon (Alexander et al., 2010).

Lung cancer develops differently in women and men. For example, women are at greater risk than men for developing lung cancer among individuals who have never smoked. Women also tend to develop lung cancer at younger ages than men ("Out of the Shadows," 2010). Although the reasons for these differences are not completely understood, one factor appears to be women's high levels of naturally occurring estrogen (Brody, 2010a).

Detection and Treatment

Women are more likely than men to be diagnosed with lung cancer at an earlier stage. Early detection is difficult, however, because symptoms, such as persistent coughing, chest pain, and voice hoarseness, do not appear until the disease has reached an advanced stage. Treatment typically includes surgery, followed by radiation and chemotherapy (Alexander et al., 2010). Women with lung cancer tend to survive longer than men at all stages of the disease ("Out of the Shadows," 2010). Sadly, the five-year survival rate for women with lung cancer is only 16 percent, compared with a 90 percent survival rate for breast cancer (American Cancer Society, 2010b).

PHYSICAL HEALTH IN LATER LIFE

In this section, we examine factors contributing to women's health in later life. We also explore gender differences in **mortality** (*death rates*) and in **morbidity** (*illness*), look at disability in old age and, finally, discuss the conditions that promote good health.

Gender Differences in Mortality

Women are sicker; men die quicker. This old saying sums up what is often referred to as the **gender paradox**: *women live longer than men, but in poorer health* (Aumann & Galinsky, 2009; Bird et al., 2010; Schüz et al., 2009). Women outlive men in all but a few countries that are ravaged by war, disease, and extreme poverty (Bird et al., 2010).

The female–male mortality gap begins before birth. Although as many as 170 males are conceived for every 100 females, the rate of miscarriage and stillbirth is higher for males. Although about 105 live males are born for every 100 live females (Bird et al., 2010), more male babies die in infancy and thereafter throughout life. Starting at age 42, women outnumber men (U.S. Census

Bureau, 2008). Between ages 65 and 69, only 81 males survive for every 100 females. Between ages 80 and 84, the ratio is down to 53 to 100, and by age 100, women outnumber men four to one (Cavanaugh & Blanchard-Fields, 2011; Godfrey & Warshaw, 2009).

At the turn of the twentieth century, life expectancy in the United States was 49 years for women and 46 years for men (Society of Actuaries, 2010). Since then, the gender gap has widened. Life expectancy at birth now is about 80 for women and 5.0 years less for men. The gender gap exists for all ethnicities. For example, White women tend to outlive White men by five years (80.8 versus 75.9) and Black women, on average, outlive Black men by nearly seven years (76.8 versus 70.0) (J. Xu et al., 2010). Why do women outlive men? Some explanations focus on biological factors, others on lifestyle behavioral differences.

BIOLOGY.   Several biological factors have been proposed to account for gender differences in mortality. One is that male fetuses are attacked by their mothers' immune systems because of male proteins that are foreign to the mothers' bodies. Another is the slower maturation of male fetuses, possibly making them more vulnerable (Eliot, 2009). An additional biological explanation is that females' second X chromosome protects them against certain lethal diseases—such as hemophilia and some forms of muscular dystrophy—that are more apt to occur in individuals (i.e., males) who have only one X chromosome (Seeman, 2009). Another biological reason for women's greater longevity involves their higher estrogen levels, which seem to provide protection against fatal conditions such as heart disease (Kajantie, 2008). In addition, women have a lower rate of metabolism, which is linked to greater longevity. There also is evidence that women's immune systems are more robust than men's, making men more susceptible to contracting certain fatal diseases (Yeretssian et al., 2009).

LIFESTYLE BEHAVIORS.   One lifestyle factor accounting for the gender gap in mortality is that males are more likely than females to engage in potentially risky behaviors such as smoking, drinking, violence, and reckless driving. They also may be exposed to more hazardous workplace conditions and are more likely to be injured at work (Berdahl, 2008; Chen et al., 2009; Estes et al., 2010; Kvaavik et al., 2010; Q. Xu et al., 2010). Table 12.3 shows that accidents and unintentional injuries are the third leading cause of death of males, but the sixth leading cause for females. Men are twice as likely

TABLE 12.3   Ten Leading Causes of Death for Females and Males in 2007

Rank	Women	Men
1	Heart disease	Heart disease
2	Cancer	Cancer
3	Cerebrovascular diseases (stroke)	Unintentional injuries
4	Chronic lung disease (asthma, bronchitis)	Chronic lung disease (asthma, bronchitis)
5	Alzheimer's disease	Cerebrovascular diseases (stroke)
6	Unintentional injuries	Diabetes
7	Diabetes	Suicide
8	Pneumonia and influenza	Pneumonia and influenza
9	Kidney disease	Kidney disease
10	Septicemia (infection of the blood)	Alzheimer's disease

Source: National Center for Health Statistics (2011).

as women to die of cirrhosis, caused largely by excessive drinking. In addition, homicide claims the lives of nearly four times as many men as women (Logan et al., 2011).

SMOKING.   As women's lifestyles have become more similar to men's, so have some of their health behaviors. For example, although the frequency of men's smoking has declined over the past 40 years, that of women increased from the 1930s through the 1990s before starting to decline. Tobacco use remains high among women aged 18–24 (American Society of Clinical Oncology, 2009). Nearly one in five women in the United States currently smoke, close to the rate for men (Centers for Disease Control and Prevention, 2010b). The prevalence of smoking varies widely across educational levels and ethnic groups. For example, one in ten women college graduates smoke, compared with nearly one in three who have not completed high school (Centers for Disease Control and Prevention, 2010c). Among women, Asian Americans have the lowest rates of smoking (4 percent) followed by Latinas (8 percent), Blacks (16 percent), Whites (20 percent), and Native Americans (31 percent).

The result of women's increase in smoking and men's decrease, as we have seen, is that smoking-related deaths from lung cancer have declined for men but have soared for women (Alexander et al., 2010; American Society of Clinical Oncology, 2009), surpassing breast cancer as the leading cause of cancer deaths among women. Smoking is also a key factor in the rise of chronic lung disease, heart disease, and stroke as a cause of death in women (Donatelle, 2012).

In the United States, and in half of the 151 countries recently surveyed by the World Health Organization, teenage girls are as likely to smoke as boys (Eaton et al., 2010; Garrett et al., 2011; National Center for Health Statistics, 2011; World Health Organization, 2010b). Teenage girls are drawn to smoking for many reasons, including an attempt to express independence, curb appetite, reduce stress, and display "adult" behavior (Chassin et al., 2009; Johnson et al., 2009; Park, 2009). Young women, especially women of color, are heavily targeted by the tobacco industry, which has intentionally designed cigarette ads to promote smoking in women (Smith, 2010; "Tobacco Company," 2011; World Health Organization, 2010b). In response to one advertiser's slogan, "You've come a long way baby," Claire reminds her students, "Yes, your rates of lung disease are getting closer to men's."

Another behavioral difference contributing to women's longevity is that women make greater use of preventive health services and are more likely to seek medical treatment when they are ill (Hunt et al., 2010). This may help explain why women live longer than men after the diagnosis of a potentially fatal disease. Women's greater tendency to visit the doctor's office suggests that they are more health conscious than men. Women generally know more than men about health, do more to prevent illness, are more likely to look up health information on the Internet, are more aware of symptoms, are more likely to talk about their health concerns, and ask doctors more questions during visits (Levine, 2004; "QuickStats," 2010a).

Women also outlive men because of their more extensive social support networks involving family, friends, and formal organizational memberships. Involvement in social relationships is related to living longer, perhaps because social ties reduce the impact of life stresses or convince individuals to increase their health-producing behaviors (Agahi & Parker, 2008; Ertel et al., 2009; Fitzpatrick, 2009; McLaughlin et al., 2011; Uchino, 2009).

Social Class and Ethnic Differences

Women live longer than men regardless of social class and ethnic membership. Nevertheless, there are differences in longevity among women of different social classes and ethnic groups, as well as across cultures (see Explore Other Cultures 12.2).

EXPLORE OTHER CULTURES 12.2
Health Report Card for Women Around the World

Women outlive men in almost every nation. In industrialized nations, where life expectancy is relatively high, women live an average of five to eight years more than men (National Center for Health Statistics, 2004). In developing countries, on the other hand, where life expectancy is low, women outlive men by only three years (Sanchez, 2010; World Health Organization, 2009). Women live longest in Japan—an average of 86 years—but live only until 42 years, on average, in Afghanistan. Longevity has increased for both sexes in almost all nations, with the exception of some African countries that have been devastated by HIV/AIDS (Hausmann et al., 2009). Death in childbirth partially accounts for the smaller female advantage in longevity in developing countries, mostly in sub-Saharan Africa and south Asia (World Health Organization, 2009). In many of these countries, women often delay seeking health care because of their limited time and access to money, their restricted mobility, and the need to get their husbands' permission to seek care. In some countries, however, the smaller difference is also a result of female infanticide and neglect of female children (see Chapter 14). Access to better health care helps account for the larger longevity differences between females and males in developed countries (Sen, 2010).

SOCIAL CLASS.   Around the world, women and men with higher incomes and more education have longer life expectancies and better health (Bowen & Gonzalez, 2010; Cutler & Lleras–Muney, 2008; Elo, 2009; Halleröd & Gustafsson, 2011; Koh et al., 2010; Sanchez, 2010; Shankar et al., 2010). Some of this difference can be accounted for by a higher incidence of risk factors such as smoking, unhealthy diet, obesity, high blood pressure, and physical inactivity among the poor and working class (Stringhini et al., 2010). People with lower incomes are less able to afford decent medical care or even adequate food and experience higher levels of chronic stress as a result of such experiences as financial difficulties and job loss. The combination of all these factors shortens life expectancy and increases rates of illness and disease (Herd et al., 2008; Khare et al., 2009; Weitz, 2010).

ETHNICITY.   Health risks and mortality rates for women vary by ethnic group (see Table 12.4). Mortality rates from all of the major causes of death (except car accidents, chronic lung disease, and suicide) are higher for Black women than for White women. White women are less likely than

TABLE 12.4   Leading Causes of Death for Females by Ethnicity, 2011

Rank	White	Black	Native American	Asian/Pacific Islander	Latina
1	Heart disease	Heart disease	Cancer	Cancer	Heart disease
2	Cancer	Cancer	Heart disease	Heart disease	Cancer
3	Stroke	Stroke	Unintentional injuries	Stroke	Stroke
4	Chronic lung disease	Diabetes	Diabetes	Diabetes	Diabetes
5	Alzheimer's disease	Kidney disease	Stroke	Unintentional injuries	Unintentional injuries

Note: Native American includes American Indian and Alaskan Native females.
Source: National Center for Health Statistics (2011).

women in other ethnic groups to die of diabetes. Asian American women, compared to White women, have lower mortality rates from heart disease; stroke; lung, breast, and cervical cancers; cirrhosis; and chronic lung disease. Black women have the shortest life expectancy of any group and Asian Americans the longest (Heron, 2010). Differences in mortality rates for women of different ethnic groups are related to their economic status throughout their lives. Blacks and Native Americans, for example, have high mortality rates and low lifetime family incomes, whereas Asian Americans have some of the highest family incomes and lower mortality rates (Meyer & Herd, 2007; Torrez, 2001). Racial discrimination is an additional stressor linked to poor health outcomes among Black individuals (Green & Darity, 2010).

Gender Differences in Illness

Although they live longer than men, women have more chronic conditions that cause suffering but do not kill. This is true in every country in which these statistics have been gathered, including developing nations (Alexander et al., 2010; Mannheim Research Institute, 2005; Pruchno et al., 2010; Sanchez, 2010). Women have higher rates of asthma, chronic fatigue syndrome, fibromyalgia, thyroid conditions, migraine headaches, anemia, urinary incontinence, and more than 80 auto-immune disorders such as rheumatoid arthritis, multiple sclerosis, and lupus (Moore, 2009; U.S. Department of Commerce, 2011; Whitley & Lindsey, 2009). American and Canadian women are less likely than their male counterparts to rate their health as excellent and more likely to describe it as good or fair (Adams et al., 2008; "QuickStats," 2011; Sanmartin et al., 2004).

These statistics do not mean, however, that women are more likely than men to develop health problems. Women spend 71 of their years in good health and free of disability, compared with only 67 years for men. But because women live longer than men, it is women who more often live many years with chronic, often disabling, illnesses (He et al., 2005). Keep in mind that a person may have one or more chronic diseases without being disabled. The key issue is whether the chronic condition restricts daily life or reduces the ability to take care of oneself (Bjorklund & Bee, 2008).

Disability

The degree of disability resulting from chronic conditions is assessed by measuring how well individuals can carry out two groups of activities: (1) **activities of daily living (ADLs)**, which include *basic self-caring activities such as eating, bathing, toileting, walking, and getting in and out of a bed or chair*; and (2) **instrumental activities of daily living (IADLs)**, which *go beyond personal care to include preparing meals, doing housework, shopping, doing laundry, attending social activities, using the telephone, taking medications, and managing money* (National Institute on Aging, 2007). As you might expect, the chances of developing a disability increase with age. For example, about two in ten White women in their 50s and four of ten in their 70s have some difficulty with ADLs (Holmes et al., 2009). By their early 90s, the frequency rises to seven in ten (Berlau et al., 2009). Older women are more likely than older men to have functional limitations that affect both ADLs and IADLs (Adams et al., 2008; Berlau et al., 2009; Crimmons & Beltrán-Sánchez, 2010).

African American women are more likely than other women to report chronic and/or disabling conditions, followed by Native American, Latina, and White women. Asian American women are only half as likely as other women to suffer from disabilities (Federal Interagency Forum, 2010; He et al., 2005; Seeman et al., 2010). Life satisfaction is often lower for women who have disabilities than for other women. They are more likely to be depressed, to have elevated stress levels, and to rate their health as only fair or poor (Chevarley et al., 2006; Goodley, 2011; Nosek, 2010). But chronic illness need not prevent a woman from enjoying her life. In the Women's Health and Aging Study,

35 percent of women with moderate to severe disabilities reported a high sense of happiness and personal mastery and low levels of anxiety and depression (Unger & Seeman, 2000).

PROMOTING GOOD HEALTH

Aging is not a disease but a natural process in a woman's life cycle. Throughout life, women can take active steps to maintain good health and decrease the impact of any health problems that develop. Lifestyle choices involving physical activity, good nutrition, not smoking, and moderate alcohol use can promote longevity and good health (Mackenzie & Rakel, 2010; van Dam et al., 2008).

In this section, we examine practices that promote good health. For a closer look at some of these factors in older women, see Learn About the Research 12.2.

Physical Activity and Exercise

Most people are pantywaists. Exercise is good for you. (Emma "Grandma" Gatewood, age 67, the first person to hike the entire 2,170 miles of the Appalachian Trail three times, quoted in Snell, 2002)

PHYSICAL BENEFITS. The numerous health benefits of physical activity have been well documented. Regular physical exercise controls weight gain (Hankinson et al., 2010) and is linked to improved overall health and quality of life (Dechamps et al., 2010; Lee et al., 2010; Sun et al., 2010). More

LEARN ABOUT THE RESEARCH 12.2
Good Health Habits and Longevity

The relationship between good health habits and longevity was demonstrated dramatically in a large-scale longitudinal investigation conducted in California. At the beginning of the study, the researchers asked each of the nearly 7,000 randomly chosen adults about their health practices. In a follow-up study done 18 years later, five good health behaviors were found to predict lower rates of death among the participants: keeping physically active, not smoking, drinking moderately, maintaining normal weight, and sleeping seven to eight hours a night. The most unexpected finding was that being involved in close relationships was as powerful a predictor of life expectancy as good health practices. Individuals who followed the greatest number of good health practices and who were most involved in social networks were least likely to die or develop disabilities over the 18 years of the study. A recent longitudinal study of nearly 5,000 adults from the United Kingdom found strikingly similar results. Individuals who kept physically active, did not smoke, drank moderately, and ate a healthful diet including fruits and vegetables lived an average of 12 years longer than people with poorer health habits (Kvaavik et al., 2010).

Another longitudinal study of older Canadian adults suggests that both social activities and productive activities such as cooking, gardening, and volunteering may be just as important as physical activity in helping older people live longer (Menec, 2003).

WHAT DOES IT MEAN?

1. In this chapter, we learned that women are more health conscious than men. Why do you think that is?
2. Young adults are less likely to engage in good health practices than are older adults. What might account for this difference?
3. How can more young adults be encouraged to develop good health habits?
4. Why do you think social and productive activities increase longevity?

specifically, physical activity is associated with decreased incidence of heart disease; stroke; breast, colon, and ovarian cancers; hypertension; diabetes; respiratory and kidney diseases; and osteoporosis (Brody, 2010b; Godfrey & Nelson, 2009; Williamson & Pahor, 2010). Even among individuals who do not achieve ideal weight, exercise reduces the risk of health decline (Dalleck et al., 2009; Fulton, 2009).

In the later years, physical activity helps maintain the muscle strength, balance, and flexibility needed to perform activities of daily living, provide mobility, and decrease falls (Ansehl et al., 2010; Elsawy & Higgins, 2010; Eynon et al., 2009; Godfrey & Studenski, 2010; Kemmler et al., 2010).

PSYCHOLOGICAL BENEFITS. Regular exercise promotes a sense of well-being, feelings of accomplishment, happiness, and increased self-esteem. It also decreases tension, anxiety, depression, and anger (Ansehl et al., 2010; Donatelle, 2012; Lebensohn, 2010; Lee & Park, 2008; Walsh, 2011). Furthermore, physically active older adults outperform sedentary older people on tests of memory, reaction time, reasoning, attention, planning ability, mental speed, and mental flexibility. They are also less likely to develop dementia. These findings suggest that regular participation in exercise improves cognitive functioning in later life (Erickson et al., 2011; Etgen et al., 2010; Kåreholt et al., 2011; Lam et al., 2009; Liu-Ambrose et al., 2010; Plassman et al., 2010). An alternative explanation, of course, is that smart people may exercise more because they are aware of its benefits!

FACTORS LINKED TO WOMEN'S ACTIVITY LEVELS. Although inactivity increases with age for both sexes, women of all ages are less apt to exercise than men (Ansehl et al., 2010; Kern et al., 2010; "Prevalence," 2008; U.S. Census Bureau, 2010a). The proportion of American women who say they never exercise almost doubles with age, from 36 percent for those under 25 to 65 percent for those 75 and older.

White women are more likely to exercise on a regular basis than women of other ethnicities, with Black women exercising least (Clarke et al., 2009; Eaton et al., 2010; Heath, 2009; U.S. Department of Health and Human Services, 2010). Much of this ethnic difference may be accounted for by differences in educational and income levels. Ethnic minority women are more likely to live in poverty and have lower income and educational levels than White women. Their neighborhoods often lack adequate and safe facilities that enable and promote physical activity (Carlson et al., 2010; Powell et al., 2006). The proportion of women who engage in exercise rises as educational and income levels increase (Lee et al., 2010; "QuickStats," 2009; U.S. Department of Health and Human Services, 2010).

Several barriers prevent individuals with disabilities from engaging in proper amounts of physical activity. These include limitations resulting from the disability itself, lack of transportation to exercise facilities, the perception (or reality) that these facilities are not disability friendly, and social attitudes that people with disabilities cannot or do not need to exercise (Ansehl et al., 2010; Rolfe et al., 2009).

One explanation for the low levels of physical activity among older women is the stereotype that exercise is increasingly seen as inappropriate as a person ages. This stereotype applies even more strongly to women than to men because of the societal expectation that, at all ages, women are less physically active than men (Travis & Compton, 2001). In addition, the social construction of gender dictates that women are the primary caregivers and managers of home and family. Taking time away from domestic responsibilities to indulge in personal leisure may cause some women to feel selfish, guilty, or overwhelmed (Ansehl et al., 2010; Godfrey & Nelson, 2009). In addition, the caregiving duties that many older women perform may make them too tired to be physically active (Ansehl et al., 2010; Reichert et al., 2007).

Older women must not only overcome sexist and ageist views about appropriate physical activity in later life but must also combat chronic health problems that inhibit many older people from exercising. Arthritic pain and urinary incontinence, chronic conditions that are more prevalent in older women than in older men, may serve as deterrents to physical activity. Other barriers include the absence of a companion and the lack of convenient transportation to a safe and affordable exercise facility (Britain et al., 2011; Buchner, 2010; Chiang et al., 2008). In addition, some women feel that they are too sick or too old to improve their physical condition, or fear that exercise may lead to injury (Ansehl et al., 2010; Bird et al., 2009; Reichert et al., 2007; Stephan et al., 2010). Unfortunately, older women are less likely than young women or older men to receive exercise counseling from their physicians ("Estimated Percentage," 2007). Moreover, the issue of attractive exercise programming for older women has been largely overlooked by exercise specialists, yet another example of the relative invisibility and lack of power of older women (Travis & Compton, 2001).

Nutrition

As we have seen, good nutrition is a key factor in promoting health. Regardless of age, a healthful diet includes lots of vegetables, fruits, and whole grains; moderate amounts of protein; and sparing use of red and processed meat, fats, oil, and sugar (Kohatsu, 2010; Sinha et al., 2009; Skerrett & Willett, 2010).

But a woman's nutritional needs also vary over her life span. During puberty, for example, calorie requirements rise to at least 2,200 per day for the average girl, and more if she is physically active. Calcium intake is especially important to ensure maximum bone growth. Pregnant women need about 300 extra calories a day to attain the recommended weight gain of 22 to 27 pounds. Breastfeeding women require extra fluids, calcium, protein, and 500 more calories per day than prior to pregnancy. By menopause, women need only about two-thirds of the calories required when they were 20, plus increased consumption of calcium, vitamin B_{12}, and vitamin D (Carlson et al., 2004; Lichtenstein et al., 2008; Simkin et al., 2010).

Many older women who live independently do not consume sufficient amounts of one or more essential nutrients. The reasons for this include difficulty getting to stores, insufficient income to buy wholesome foods, medications that interfere with absorption of nutrients, chronic conditions that restrict people to bland diets low in certain nutrients, problems with chewing, and loss of appetite. Poor appetite can result from illness, inactivity, diminished senses of taste and smell, depression, or eating alone (Brody, 2001; Wellman et al., 2007). Adequate intake of calcium and vitamin D is very important for older women in order to minimize the onset and severity of osteoporosis (Brody, 2011; Pruthi, 2010). But only few women consume the 1,200 milligrams of calcium and the 800 units of vitamin D recommended during the menopausal and postmenopausal years (Brody, 2010; Kolata, 2010; Plawecki et al., 2009). In addition, older people do not absorb vitamin D as readily as they did when younger (Templeton, 2010). Thus, nutritionists recommend that older women take vitamin supplements to make sure that their dietary needs are met (Moore, 2009).

Summary

HEALTH SERVICES

- Women are increasingly being included in health research. Unfortunately, they continue to be treated with less respect within the health care system and receive poorer medical care than men.

- Women of color are more likely than White women to be poor, uninsured, and lack medical care.
- Sexual minority women may have elevated health risks, in part due to reduced access to health care.
- Women rely more heavily than men on Medicare and Medicaid.
- Managed care insurance plans have both advantages and disadvantages for women.

SEXUALLY TRANSMITTED INFECTIONS (STIs)

- Sexually transmitted infections (STIs) are transmitted more easily to women than to men and are harder to diagnose in women.
- Women, especially those of color, are the fastest-growing group of Americans with HIV.
- HIV infection in older women is less often diagnosed and treated correctly than in younger women.

REPRODUCTIVE SYSTEM DISORDERS

- Benign disorders of the reproductive system include endometriosis and fibroid tumors.
- Uterine and cervical cancers have higher survival rates than ovarian cancer.
- The Pap smear is an effective screening device for cervical cancer.
- American women have one of the highest hysterectomy rates in the world.

OSTEOPOROSIS

- Osteoporosis, the loss of bone tissue, increases after menopause and can lead to disabling and even fatal fractures.
- Building and maintaining bone mass is enhanced by increasing calcium intake; decreasing use of alcohol, caffeine, and tobacco; increasing physical activity; and taking estrogen or certain medications.

HEART DISEASE

- Heart disease, the leading killer of women, increases dramatically after menopause.

- Women develop heart disease later than men and are twice as likely to die of it.
- Risk factors for heart disease include gender, age, ethnicity, family history, smoking, physical inactivity, high cholesterol levels, high blood pressure, diabetes, and being overweight.
- Women with heart disease receive less aggressive treatment than men.

BREAST CANCER

- One in eight women will develop breast cancer, but survival rates have been increasing.
- Risk factors include age, ethnicity, family history, drinking, smoking, weight gain, and inactivity.
- Many women do not perform monthly breast self-exams or get regular mammograms.
- For small early tumors, lumpectomy with radiation is as effective as mastectomy.
- Support groups help women cope with cancer.

LUNG CANCER

- Lung cancer is the leading cause of cancer deaths in women.
- The increase in lung cancer deaths in women is likely linked to an increase in smoking.
- Lung cancer develops differently in women and men, and women survive longer with the disease.

PHYSICAL HEALTH IN LATER LIFE

- At every age, women report more illness and use of health care services than men, yet women consistently outlive men.
- Both biological factors and lifestyle differences are responsible for women's greater longevity.
- Health risks and mortality rates for women differ by social class and ethnic group.
- Older women are more likely than older men to have some difficulty with various activities of daily living.

PROMOTING GOOD HEALTH

- Practices that promote good health include physical activity and good nutrition.

Key Terms

Medicare *280*

Medicaid *281*

spending down *281*

fee-for-service insurance *281*

managed care *281*

acquired immunodeficiency
   syndrome (AIDS) *283*

endometriosis *286*

fibroid tumors *286*

cervix *287*

Pap smear *287*

hysterectomy *288*

fibroid embolization *288*

myomectomy *288*

osteoporosis *288*

raloxifene *290*

mammogram *295*

radical mastectomy *297*

modified radical mastectomy *297*

simple mastectomy *297*

lumpectomy *297*

mortality *298*

morbidity *298*

gender paradox *298*

activities of daily living
   (ADLs) *302*

instrumental activities of daily
   living (IADLs) *302*

What Do You Think?

1. Why do you think women's heart disease risks were largely ignored until fairly recently? What actions can individuals take to help improve this situation? What actions can members of the medical community take?

2. How can knowledge of risk factors for diseases in older White women and older women of color help individuals in prevention and early detection of these diseases? How can high risk factors be reduced for both groups?

3. Why do you think there is a difference between mammogram screening rates for women who differ in socioeconomic status? What actions could be taken to change these disparities?

4. Of the health conditions mentioned in this chapter, which ones can you prevent? Which ones can you delay? What actions can you take now to protect yourself from these problems? Which of these are you currently doing, and why?

If You Want to Learn More

Alexander, L. L., LaRosa, J. H., Bader, H., Garfield, S., & Alexander, W. J. (2010). *New dimensions in women's health* (5th ed.). Sudbury, MA: Jones and Bartlett.

American Heart Association. (2009). *American Heart Association complete guide to women's heart health: The Go Red for Women way to well-being and vitality.* Dallas, TX: Author.

Bird, C. E., & Rieker, P. P. (2008). *Gender and health: The effects of constrained choices and social policies.* New York: Cambridge University Press.

Gulati, M., & Torkos, S. (2011). *Saving women's hearts: How you can prevent and reverse heart disease with natural and conventional strategies.* Missisauga, Ontario, Canada: John Wiley.

Horn, J., & Miller, R. H. (2008). *The smart woman's guide to midlife and beyond: A no-nonsense approach to staying healthy after 50.* Oakland, CA: New Harbinger.

Love, S. M. (2010). *Dr. Susan Love's breast book* (5th ed.). Philadelphia, PA: Da Capo Press.

Maxwell, J., Belser, J. W., & David, D. (2008). *A health handbook for women with disabilities.* Berkeley, CA: Hesperian Foundation.

Meyer, I., & Northridge, M. (Eds.). (2010). *The health of sexual minorities: Public health perspectives on lesbian, gay, bisexual, and transgender populations.* New York: Springer.

Moore, D. (Ed.). (2009). *Women's health for life.* New York: DK Publishing.

O'Leary, A., & Jemmott, L. S. (2010). *Women and AIDS: Coping and care.* New York: Plenum.

Pruthi, S. (2010). *Women's health encyclopedia: An integrated approach to wellness for every season of a woman's life.* London, UK: Marshall Editions Ltd.

Websites

Health Care and Health Issues: General
The AMA Women's Health Information Centre
http://www.ama-assn.org/
The New York Times articles on women's health and
excerpts from the *Harvard Guide to Women's Health*
and the *American Medical Women's Association
Women's Complete Health Book*
http://topics.nytimes.com/topics/reference/
timestopics/subjects/w/women/index.html
The National Women's Health Information Center
http://www.4woman.gov
Iris Cantor Women's Health Center
http://www.cornellwomenshealth.com
The Society for Women's Health Research
http://www.womenshealthresearch.org/
http://www.fda.gov/womens/tttc.html
http://www.womensorganizations.org/
http://www.nwhn.org/
http://www.cdc.gov/women/

Disability
Disabled People's International
http://www.dpi.org
National Organization on Disability
http://www.nod.org
American Association of People With Disabilities
http://www.aapd-dc.org

Heart Disease
American Heart Association
http://www.heart.org/HEARTORG/

Cancer
American Cancer Society
http://www.cancer.org
National Ovarian Cancer Coalition (NOCC)
http://www.ovarian.org
Susan G. Komen for the Cure
http://www.komen.org
Foundation for Women's Cancer
http://www.foundationforwomenscancer.org/

Arthritis
Arthritis Foundation
http://www.arthritis.org
National Institute of Arthritis and Musculoskeletal
and Skin Diseases
http://www.niams.nih.gov

Diabetes
American Association of Diabetes Educators
http://diabeteseducator.org
National Institute of Diabetes and Digestive and
Kidney Diseases
http://www2.niddk.nih.gov/

Sexual Minority Health
Lesbian Health & Research Center
http://www.lesbianhealthinfo.org
Gay and Lesbian Medical Association
http://www.glma.org
American and Public Health Association
http://www.apha.org/about/Public+Health+Links/
LinksGayandLesbianHealth.htm

CHAPTER 13

Mental Health

Factors Promoting Mental Health
> Social Support
> Optimism: "The Power of Positive Thinking"

Mental Health in Childhood and Adolescence
> Internalizing Disorders in Girls
> Externalizing Disorders in Girls

Eating Disorders
> Types of Eating Disorders
> Causes of Eating Disorders
> Treatment of Eating Disorders

Substance Use and Abuse
> Alcohol
> Illegal Substances

Anxiety Disorders and Depression
> Anxiety Disorders
> Depression
> Suicide

Mental Health of Sexual Minority Women
> Stresses and Problems
> Coping Mechanisms

Mental Health of Older Women
> Gender Differences
> The Vital Older Woman

Diagnosis and Treatment of Psychological Disorders
> Gender Bias in Diagnosis
> Gender Bias in Psychotherapy
> Therapy Issues for Women of Color and Poor Women
> Types of Therapy

I was diagnosed with anorexia nervosa in my sophomore year of high school. I was always the bigger one of my friends and my boyfriend at the time would always tell me he liked the fact that I was chubby. I would see all the stick-skinny models and actresses on TV and feel completely disgusted with myself. At one point during my fight with anorexia, I weighed about 35 pounds less than what was healthy for my height and I was very sick. It is so scary to look in a mirror and see fat when you are actually skin and bones. It ruined my relationship with so many loved ones and I still don't have regular menstrual cycles. (Stephanie, college junior, age 20)

    It happened one Saturday night [at] a Greek restaurant . . . Suddenly I began to feel as if the walls were edging in. My palms grew damp, my heart drummed, my stomach churned. I had only one thought: If you don't get out of this restaurant immediately, you are going to faint or die. I mumbled that

I didn't feel well and raced for the door . . . I began to avoid restaurants, but then my panic [appeared] in other venues . . . My world shrank to a thin corridor of safe places. (Anndee Hochman, 2004, pp. 99–100)

Overall, rates of mental illness are almost identical for women and men. There are, however, striking gender differences in the prevalence of specific mental disorders. Women have higher rates of eating disorders, depression, and anxiety disorders. Men are more likely to have impulse-control, antisocial, and substance abuse disorders (Becker et al., 2010; Office on Women's Health, 2009a; Rondon, 2010; Russo, 2010). In this chapter, we focus not only on pathology but also on mental *health* and the factors that promote it. We begin the chapter by looking at two key factors that are associated with good mental health: social support and optimism. We then explore mental health in childhood and adolescence, followed by a discussion of eating disorders and substance abuse. Next, we explore anxiety disorders, depression, and suicide. We then discuss mental health issues of sexual minority women and of older women. We close with a look at the diagnosis and treatment of psychological disorders.

FACTORS PROMOTING MENTAL HEALTH

Social Support

A substantial body of research indicates that both receiving and giving social support play an important role in maintaining good physical and mental health and helping people cope with stressful life events (Brown et al., 2008; Cornwell & Waite, 2009; Golden et al., 2009; McLaughlin et al., 2011; Mechakra-Tahiri et al., 2009; S. Taylor, 2010; Thomas, 2010). This association is especially strong for females. For example, girls are more likely than boys to seek social support following stressful events, and this support appears to play a more protective role for girls than for boys (Eschenbeck et al., 2007; Jackson & Warren, 2000; Rose & Rudolph, 2006). Similarly, studies have found that women who feel more loved and supported by their friends, relatives, and children are at less risk for major depression. Among men, however, level of social support is less strongly related to the risk of depression (Wareham et al., 2007).

TEND AND BEFRIEND. Women also use social support as a coping aid more readily than men do. Shelley Taylor (2000, 2010) and her colleagues have proposed that women often respond to stress by tending to themselves and their children and by forming ties with others (the "tend and befriend" response). Men, in contrast, are more likely to show aggression or escape. This so-called fight or flight response was proposed by psychologists 60 years ago to explain how both men and women react to stress. That view, however, was heavily based on studies of males (Goode, 2000) and was just assumed to apply to females (yet another example of the "male as normative"). But Taylor and her colleagues found many studies that supported their model. For example, Rena Repetti's research (cited in Taylor et al., 2000) showed that mothers returning home after a stressful day at the office were more caring and nurturant toward their children, while stressed fathers were more likely to withdraw from their families or incite conflict. What stimulates these different behaviors in females and males? Taylor and her colleagues suggest that hormonal differences are partly responsible, but they and others are quick to reject the idea that gender stereotypes are biologically hard-wired. Alice Eagly (cited in Goode, 2000), for example, points out that the gender difference could be a result of cultural conditioning that prepares females from an early age for the role of caregiver and nurturer.

Optimism: "The Power of Positive Thinking"

Question: "Do you know the difference between an optimist and a pessimist?"

Answer: The first one sees the glass as half full, while the second sees it as half empty.

You may have heard this saying before, but did you also know that optimism can actually be good for your health? An optimistic outlook—the expectation that good rather than bad things will happen—has been linked to a variety of positive mental and physical health outcomes, including longer life (Barefoot et al., 2011; Chida & Steptoe, 2008; Dockray & Steptoe, 2010; Ong, 2010; Tindle et al., 2009). Pessimism, on the other hand, is associated with poorer health outcomes and higher mortality (Chida et al., 2008; Grossardt et al., 2009; Roy et al., 2010; Rutledge et al., 2009). What accounts for the beneficial effects of optimism? One reason is that optimists are more likely than others to deal actively with or find solutions to problems (Sechrist, 2010). Another reason is that optimism appears to protect women from some of the health risks associated with depression (Jones et al., 2004).

MENTAL HEALTH IN CHILDHOOD AND ADOLESCENCE

Compared to boys, girls show fewer adjustment problems in childhood. Girls, however, are more likely than boys to first manifest psychological difficulties during the adolescent years (Blakemore et al., 2009; Butler, 2008; Röhner & Schütz, 2011). Stress levels increase for both genders during these years. However, the patterns of stress girls encounter may leave them more vulnerable to emotional disorders, such as anxiety and depression, than do those experienced by boys (Broderick & Korteland, 2002; Butler, 2008; Rudolph & Troop-Gordon, 2010). We shall explore these stresses later in the chapter.

Internalizing Disorders in Girls

Adjustment problems that are more common in girls and women, such as depression, anxiety, and social withdrawal, are often labeled "internalizing problems" (American Psychological Association, 2007a; Russo, 2010). Later in the chapter, we discuss these disorders in greater detail. Internalizing disorders are harder to detect and thus are more often overlooked than the externalizing problems shown by boys and men: aggression, conduct disorders, antisocial behaviors, and attention deficit hyperactivity disorder (American Psychological Association, 2007a; Karreman et al., 2009; Renk, 2008; Röhner & Schütz, 2011; Zhou et al., 2007). Early socialization of girls and boys into gender-typed behaviors may be responsible for these differences in the expression of distress (Andreasen, 2005).

Externalizing Disorders in Girls

Boys are more likely than girls to show externalizing behavior such as hyperactivity and aggression (Terzian et al., 2011). Unfortunately, girls with externalizing disturbances are rarely studied because of the notion that these are "male" problems (Fontaine et al., 2008; Prinstein & La Greca, 2004). This stereotype of the masculine nature of externalizing disorders persists despite the fact that the percentage of violent crimes committed by teenage girls, such as aggravated assault, is on the increase (U.S. Department of Justice, 2009). Girls who show externalizing problems exhibit deficits in social, emotional, and communication skills and elevated rates of substance use, anxiety, and risky sexual behavior (Bierman et al., 2004; Obradovic & Hipwell, 2010; Prinstein & La Greca, 2004; Wasserman et al., 2005). Moreover, these girls are more likely to have difficulties as adults.

For example, longitudinal studies in Sweden (Wangby et al., 1999), New Zealand (Fergusson & Woodward, 2000), Canada (Serbin et al., 2004), and the United States (Molnar et al., 2005; Silver et al., 2007) found that girls with externalizing problems in childhood and early adolescence were at greater risks of all types of maladjustment in late adolescence and adulthood than were those without such problems. They had higher rates of educational failure, juvenile crime, substance abuse, mental health problems, pregnancy, and poor parenting skills. On the other hand, there was little or no relationship between having internalizing problems during adolescence and later maladjustment (Wangby et al., 1999).

EATING DISORDERS

The prevalence of eating disorders among women has increased dramatically over the past few decades in North America, Europe, Australia, and New Zealand (Darby et al., 2009; Zerbe, 2008), paralleling the increase in girls' and women's body dissatisfaction that we discussed in Chapter 4. In this section, we examine types of eating disorders, their likely causes, and their treatment.

Types of Eating Disorders

Three major types of eating disorders have been identified. They are anorexia nervosa, bulimia nervosa, and binge eating disorder. Stephanie, one of Claire's students, described her battle with anorexia in the first vignette at the beginning of this chapter.

ANOREXIA NERVOSA. The defining characteristics of **anorexia nervosa** are *a refusal to maintain a minimal normal body weight (defined as 85 percent of ideal weight), intense fear of gaining weight, a distorted body image (feeling fat even when too thin), and amenorrhea* (lack of menstruation) in females. Anorexic individuals diet, fast, and exercise excessively in order to lose weight (Keel & McCormick, 2010). Unlike "normal" dieters, anorexics may lose 25 percent of their original body weight. Many of them share self-starvation tips and "thinspiration" messages on so-called pro-ana Websites (Alexander et al., 2010; Borzekowski et al., 2010; Martijn et al., 2009; Parker-Pope 2009; Riley et al., 2009). Unfortunately, dramatic weight loss can cause osteoporosis, fertility problems, hormone abnormalities, dangerously low blood pressure, and damage to vital organs (Attia & Walsh, 2009; Freizinger et al., 2010; Maxwell et al., 2010). Anorexic individuals have a nearly 10-fold greater risk of death from all causes and a 57-fold greater risk of death by suicide than their peers (Button et al., 2009; Zucker et al., 2007).

Girls and women account for more than 95 percent of cases of anorexia nervosa. About 1 percent of female adolescents and young adults suffer from the disorder in the United States and western Europe (DeBate et al., 2010). While anorexia is often thought of as a White, middle- or upper-class disease, its incidence is increasing among women of color and poor women (Dohm et al., 2010; Franko et al., 2007). Although the peak period for anorexia is adolescence (DeBate et al., 2010), females can become anorexic at virtually any age. Increasing numbers of girls as young as 6 have been diagnosed (Donatelle, 2012). In addition, a growing number of women in midlife and beyond are developing or continuing to have eating disorders. Many of these women have likely been overly concerned with weight and body image throughout their lives (Epstein, 2009; Parker-Pope, 2011; Scholtz et al., 2010). The midlife trigger for the eating disorder may be the 10- to 15-pound weight gain that typically occurs during menopause. Fear of aging, losing a spouse, dealing with a troubled child, or even having a child leave for college can set off eating problems (Mangweth-Matzek et al., 2006; McKinley, 2006; Parker-Pope, 2011; Zerbe, 2008).

Young women with physical disabilities also have an elevated risk of developing symptoms of eating disorders. These women may be more vulnerable because their disabilities often involve body-image disturbances, they feel lack of control resulting from needing assistance from others, and they may focus on weight maintenance to sustain mobility (Gross et al., 2000).

BULIMIA NERVOSA.   The primary features of **bulimia nervosa** are *recurrent episodes of uncontrolled binge eating, followed by purging activities aimed at controlling body weight.* Purging activities include self-induced vomiting, exercise, extreme dieting or fasting, and the abuse of laxatives, diuretics, or enemas (Pruthi, 2010). One young woman, bulimic since the age of 9, graphically describes her binge–purge cycles:

> *At my lunch break, I would eat a quarter-pounder with cheese, large fries, and a cherry pie. Then I would throw up in the antiseptic-scented bathroom, wash my face, and go back on the floor, glassy-eyed and hyper. After work, I would buy a quarter-pounder with cheese, large fries, and a cherry pie, eat it on the way home from work, throw up at home with the bathtub running, eat dinner, throw up, go out with friends, eat, throw up, go home, pass out.*

(Hornbacher, 1998, p. 91)

Individuals with bulimia seem to be driven by an intense fear of weight gain and a distorted perception of body size similar to that seen in anorexics. Unlike anorexics, however, bulimics often maintain normal weight (Mehler, 2011). Although usually not life-threatening, bulimia can cause gastrointestinal problems, as well as extensive tooth decay because of gastric acid in the vomited food. Bulimia may also result in an imbalance of electrolytes, the chemicals necessary for the normal functioning of the heart (Mehler, 2011).

As with anorexia nervosa, young women account for more than 90 percent of the cases of bulimia. Across the United States and western Europe, about 1 percent of females in late adolescence and early adulthood have bulimia (DeBate et al., 2010).

BINGE EATING DISORDER.   This disorder is characterized by recurrent binge eating in the absence of compensatory weight-control efforts. It is the most common of the eating disorders, has a later onset, and is often associated with obesity (DeBate et al., 2010). Although sex differences are less pronounced for this disorder, the female-to-male ratio is still 3:1 (Maine et al., 2010).

Causes of Eating Disorders

Biological, psychological, and cultural factors all seem to play a part in the development of eating disorders (Keel & McCormick, 2010; Sargent et al., 2009). Let us consider each of these in turn.

BIOLOGICAL FACTORS.   One line of biological evidence comes from comparing identical twins (who share the same genetic material) with fraternal twins (who share only half). An identical twin is much more likely than a fraternal twin to develop an eating disorder if her co-twin also has the disorder (Keel & McCormick, 2010; Klump et al., 2010). While this research suggests the existence of a genetic predisposition toward eating disorders, these findings could also reflect identical twins' highly similar social and cultural environments. Another biological consideration is that anorexics have disturbances in their levels of serotonin, a mood- and appetite-regulating chemical in the brain. However, these chemical imbalances may result *from* the eating disorder rather than cause it (Attia & Walsh, 2009; Smolak, 2009).

PSYCHOLOGICAL FACTORS. Certain psychological characteristics also put young women at higher risk for eating disorders. These include low self-esteem, high levels of anxiety, depression, perfectionism, conscientiousness, competitiveness, obsessive-compulsive thoughts and behaviors, difficulty in separating from parents, strong need for approval from others, and perceived lack of control in one's life (Altman & Shankman, 2009; Clouse, 2008; DeBate et al., 2010; Mitchell & Mazzeo, 2009; Sim et al., 2009; Watson et al., 2011). Eating disorders may also reflect family problems (Latzer et al., 2009). For example, parents of anorexics are overly nurturant and overprotective and place undue emphasis on achievement and appearance (Sim et al., 2009). Parents of bulimics tend to be highly critical and controlling, overprotective, and low in nurturance and support (Salafia et al., 2008). Another risk factor for eating disorders is sexual or physical abuse (Mazzeo et al., 2008; Sanci et al., 2008).

CULTURAL FACTORS. Some scholars view eating disorders as drastic attempts to attain the reed-thin ideal of beauty that has been socially constructed by a patriarchal society (e.g., Jung & Forbes, 2010; Malson & Burns, 2009; Sargent et al., 2009). The impact of the media in transmitting this message is illustrated dramatically in Anne Becker's study of adolescent girls living in Fiji. For details, read Explore Other Cultures 13.1.

In North America, the effect of cultural pressures to be thin is perhaps seen most vividly among girls and young women who are involved in sports. The incidence of disordered eating among female athletes is far greater than the estimate of 2 to 5 percent among the general population of girls and young women (Warren & Chua, 2008). *The combination of disordered eating accompanied by amenorrhea and premature bone loss, or osteoporosis* (discussed in Chapter 12), is sometimes called the **female athlete triad** (Joy et al., 2009). The prevalence of this condition appears to have grown along with girls' participation in dance and performance sports such as gymnastics, distance running, diving, cheerleading, and figure skating, activities that favor a lean body shape (Female Athlete Triad Coalition, 2008–2010; Klein, 2008). Varsity athletes, especially those competing at highly competitive levels, are at greatest risk (Holm-Denoma et al., 2009; Mehler & MacKenzie, 2009). Claire's student Betsy, who spent several years at a strict, elite ballet academy, described the pressure to stay thin:

> Standing at the barre, the ballet master would poke and pull at your body. The professionals would stand outside between rehearsals always holding a cigarette. All the young students concluded that smoking, in replacement of food, made you thinner. Although I never started smoking, I started consuming orange juice . . . and that's all. At slumber parties on the weekends, I made sure that my friends thought I loved food, and saw me devour the pizza. I also made sure that they didn't see me get rid of it in the bathroom afterward.

Treatment of Eating Disorders

Eating disorders are difficult to cure. Cognitive behavioral therapy, which helps people to change both their behaviors and the way they think about themselves and others, seems to be the most effective therapy for bulimia and binge eating disorder. Antidepressants are also of use in treating these disorders (Baker et al., 2008; DeBate et al., 2010; Lowe et al., 2010; Sperry et al., 2009; Wilson et al., 2010). Family therapy, which elicits the parents' aid in getting the client to eat and then gradually returns control of eating to the client, shows promise in the treatment of anorexia in adolescents (DeBate et al., 2010; Lock et al., 2010; Rosen et al., 2010). Cognitive behavioral therapy also may be helpful in improving outcomes and preventing relapse (Pike et al., 2010). Antidepressants sometimes help prevent relapse once the anorexic client returns to normal. They are not effective in reversing anorexic symptoms, however (Rosen et al., 2010; Sargent et al., 2009).

EXPLORE OTHER CULTURES 13.1
Cultural Pressure to Be Thin

Numerous studies suggest that young women in populations undergoing Westernization and modernization may be at increased risk for disordered eating (Anderson-Frye, 2009; Dunkel et al., 2010). A major reason for this association may be exposure to the modern Western cultural body ideal of thinness. In one striking example, Anne Becker interviewed girls in Fiji, a small Pacific island, just as television was introduced in 1995. Only 3 percent of girls reported they vomited to control their weight. In 1998, 15 percent reported the behavior. Similarly, 29 percent scored highly on a test of eating-disorder risk in 1998 compared with just 13 percent in 1995. The more television the girls watched, the more likely they were to diet and to report feeling "too big or fat." Several girls mentioned that they wanted to look like the Western women they saw on television shows (Becker et al., 2007). The study does not conclusively prove that television helps cause eating disorders. Still, Becker notes that the increases are dramatic in a culture that traditionally has equated a robust, nicely rounded body with health and that considers considerable weight loss ("going thin") a sign of illness.

A similar cultural shift is taking place in west and central Africa where the big, voluptuous woman has been considered the ideal of female beauty. In Nigeria, for example, brides are sent to fattening farms before their weddings. But in 2001, tall, slim, Agbani Darego of Nigeria won the Miss World title. Since then, many Nigerian girls and young women have come to favor a thinner appearance (Onishi, 2002).

Anorexia is particularly resistant to a wide range of interventions. While long-term outcomes vary by study, typically fewer than half of the clients fully recover, 20 to 30 percent show some improvement, 10 to 20 percent remain chronically ill, and 5 to 10 percent are deceased (Keel & McCormick, 2010; Sargent et al., 2009). Treatment for bulimia tends to be more successful. About three-fourths of women diagnosed as bulimic show full recovery 20 years later, while 5 percent still have an eating disorder (Keel et al., 2010). Binge eating disorder has a more favorable prognosis than either anorexia or bulimia, with a recovery rate of about 80 percent five years after treatment and a low relapse rate (Mehler, 2010; Sargent et al., 2009).

SUBSTANCE USE AND ABUSE

Until recently, substance use was considered primarily a male problem, and much of the research dealing with abuse of alcohol and other drugs was carried out on males. This oversight has led to inadequate diagnosis and treatment of women with substance abuse disorders (Reed & Evans, 2009). In this section, we concentrate on substance abuse issues in women.

Alcohol

INCIDENCE.   Starting in adolescence and into old age, females are less likely than males to use alcohol and to be heavy drinkers (St. John et al., 2009; U.S. Department of Health and Human Services, 2010; Weyerer et al., 2009; Wilsnack et al., 2009). Over their lifetime about 8 to 10 percent of women and 15 to 20 percent of men will develop alcohol problems, a male-to-female ratio of over 2:1 (Butler, 2008). *However, while women's alcoholism starts later than men's alcoholism, it progresses more quickly,* a pattern called **telescoping** (Baird et al., 2009; Roche et al., 2010). White women have higher rates of alcohol use than women in other ethnic groups; they are followed by Native American women, Black women, and Latinas. Asian American women have the lowest rates of alcohol use (U.S. Department of Health and Human Services, 2010).

Problem drinking in young women has been increasing at an alarming rate both in the United States and abroad (Eaton et al., 2010; Rúdólfsdóttir & Morgan, 2009). For example, U.S. college women are now almost as likely as college men to engage in **binge drinking**, defined as *having five drinks in a row for men or four in a row for women at least once in the last two weeks* (Kanny et al., 2011). Nearly one in two college men and one in three college women are binge drinkers ("Binge Drinking," 2008; Slon, 2008). Heavy drinking is especially prevalent among sorority women and fraternity men (Mignon et al., 2009) and others whose peers drink heavily (Danielsson et al., 2011). Sadly, the gender gap in drinking has disappeared among young adolescents: Female and male high schoolers are equally likely to drink (both at 45 percent) and females are almost as likely to binge drink (23 versus 25 percent) (Eaton et al., 2010; Johnston et al., 2010a; Kanny et al., 2010). One possible explanation is an increase in alcohol advertising targeting teenage girls. In the past few years, advertising for low-alcohol drinks such as wine coolers and alcoholic iced teas has increased in national magazines, especially in those read primarily by adolescent girls (Center on Alcohol Marketing and Youth, 2010).

HEALTH CONSEQUENCES.   Women have more body fat, less water, and less of the enzyme that breaks down alcohol than men do. As a result, they have higher levels of alcohol in their blood even when they consume the same amount of alcohol per unit of body weight (Roche et al., 2010; Whitley & Lindsey, 2009). For example, 3 ounces of alcohol consumed by a 120-pound woman has a greater effect on her than the equivalent 6 ounces of alcohol consumed by a 240-pound man has on him. As women age, they have even greater physiological susceptibility to alcohol's effect and, thus, experience impairment or intoxication after fewer drinks (Mignon et al., 2009; Slon, 2008). Another consequence is that women develop cirrhosis of the liver, hepatitis, heart disease, and brain damage at lower levels of alcohol intake than men. Prolonged heavy drinking also increases the risk of breast cancer, osteoporosis, and infertility (Mignon et al., 2009; Slon, 2008).

Drinking alcohol during pregnancy can lead to **fetal alcohol syndrome (FAS)**, *a disorder characterized by mental retardation, growth deficiencies, facial deformities, and social, emotional, learning and behavioral problems* (O'Leary et al., 2009; Zilberman, 2009). FAS is the leading preventable cause of mental retardation in the United States (Thomas, 2011). Even light drinkers risk having children with **fetal alcohol effect (FAE)**, *a milder but still serious form of FAS* (Mignon et al., 2009; Sayal et al., 2007). Unfortunately, more than half of the women of childbearing age drink occasionally, and 12 percent report that they binge drink at least once a month, potentially exposing fetuses early in the first trimester before the women realizes she is pregnant (Slon, 2008).

RISK FACTORS.   Children of alcoholic parents or siblings have increased rates of alcoholism. Genetic factors appear to play about as strong a role for daughters as for sons (Schulte et al., 2010). Adolescents whose parents and peers consume alcohol and tolerate its use are more likely to start drinking at an early age, which places them at higher risk for later alcohol-related problems (Brown & Rinelli, 2010; Slon, 2008). Divorced and single women are more likely than married or widowed women to drink heavily and to have alcohol-related problems. Women who are depressed and anxious and report stressful life events such as physical or sexual abuse also are more likely to be heavy drinkers (Butler, 2008; Mignon et al., 2009).

TREATMENT.   Society has set up several double standards for women and men. The double standard of aging was described in Chapter 2 and the double standard of sexuality was discussed in Chapter 6. There is also a double standard with regard to drinking. Heavy drinking in men is often expected and seen as normal, whereas heavy drinking in women is strongly criticized (Schulte et al., 2010). As a result, women tend to hide or deny their alcohol use, making them less likely to seek help and to be more seriously ill before the disease is diagnosed (Mignon et al., 2009; Stewart et al., 2009). Moreover, physicians are less likely to counsel female patients than male patients on alcohol or drug use (Bertakis & Azari, 2007; Chan et al., 2006). Alcohol problems in older women often are mistaken for other aging-related conditions, and thus are missed and untreated by health care providers (Marsh & Keith, 2011; National Institute on Alcohol Abuse and Alcoholism, 2008). Twelve-step alcoholism treatment programs such as Alcoholics Anonymous have been criticized for being based exclusively on research with alcoholic men. Alternative programs, such as Women for Sobriety, focus on the special issues and needs of women with drinking problems (Mignon et al., 2009; Pettinati & Plebani, 2009). These programs have shown some success in treating alcohol disorders in women (Stewart et al., 2009). However, treatment options for older women remain limited (Epstein et al., 2007).

Illegal Substances

INCIDENCE. Use of illegal substances such as marijuana, cocaine, heroin, hallucinogens, and steroids varies by gender and ethnic group. Among women, use is highest among Native Americans, followed by White, Latina, Black, and Asian American women. Regardless of ethnicity, however, males generally have higher rates of illegal drug use than females both in adolescence and in adulthood. Males also use illegal drugs more heavily than females do (Chassin et al., 2009; Conner et al., 2009; Eaton et al., 2010; Johnston et al., 2011). A possible reason for the gender gap is that drug use among girls and women is less acceptable in society. Recently, however, 8th and 10th grade girls have shown higher rates of drug use than males for some drugs, including inhalants, amphetamines, and tranquilizers (Johnston et al., 2010b). Another disturbing trend is the use of anabolic (muscle-building) steroids by preteen and adolescent girls (Donatelle, 2012). According to health experts, some teenage girl athletes are moving away from a preoccupation with thinness toward a lean, more muscular look, a trend labeled "reverse anorexia" (Nyad, 2004). Unfortunately, not only does steroid use expose females to the same severe health risks as boys (e.g., heart, liver, kidney, and skin diseases), but it also may interfere with their ability to bear children (Donatelle, 2012; National Institute on Drug Abuse, 2009).

Typically, individuals who use illegal substances use more than one substance and also use or abuse alcohol. In girls and women, the problem is compounded because they are more likely than men to both use and misuse prescription drugs, such as tranquilizers, antidepressants, and sleeping pills (Merline et al., 2004; Smith, 2011).

TREATMENT. As with treatment for alcohol problems, women in drug abuse treatment programs have different needs than men in treatment. Consequently, a successful program often depends on meeting these different needs (Briggs & Pepperell, 2009; Grella, 2009). Data comparing outcomes from women-only versus mixed-gender treatments show some advantages for the women-only programs (Greenfield & Pirard, 2009).

ANXIETY DISORDERS AND DEPRESSION

More than one in four Americans will have an anxiety disorder in their lifetime and nearly one in five will develop major depression (Bourne, 2010; Kessler et al., 2005). Women are at greater risk than men for both disorders in virtually every nation studied (McLean & Anderson, 2009; Seedat et al., 2009). In this section, we first review anxiety disorders. We then turn to depression and its all-too-frequent outcome: suicide.

Anxiety Disorders

Almost everyone feels anxious now and again. When you have to give a speech in class, for instance, it is normal to feel anxious. But when anxiety is irrational, excessive, and persists over several months, it is called an anxiety disorder (Kavan et al., 2009). Most anxiety disorders occur two to three times as frequently in women as in men (Aune & Stiles, 2009; Graber & Sontag, 2009; Kirmizioglu et al., 2009).

Generalized anxiety disorder is characterized by *excessive worry and anxiety about a variety of life situations or events.* Many people experience physical symptoms as well. It is one of the most common anxiety disorders, with about 8 percent of women developing it at some time in their lives (Butler, 2008). The difference between ordinary worrying and generalized anxiety disorder is that the level of concern is excessive, resulting in distress and interfering with everyday functioning (Torpy, 2011; Urbancic & Moser, 2009).

Panic disorder is marked by *sudden unpredictable attacks of intense anxiety accompanied by a pounding heart, dizziness, sweating, shortness of breath, and trembling.* A person having an attack has a sense of impending doom, losing control, or dying (Urbancic & Moser, 2009). About 6 percent of women and 3 percent of men will develop this disorder at some time (Church & Lucey, 2010). As shown in the second vignette at the beginning of the chapter, panic disorder can lead to **agora-phobia,** a *fear of being in public places where escape might be difficult if one were suddenly incapacitated* (*agora* is the Greek word for marketplace) (Church & Lucey, 2010). Agoraphobia will be experienced by about 7 percent of women and 4 percent of men during their lifetime (Russo & Tartaro, 2008).

Agoraphobia is just one of a group of anxiety disorders known as a **specific phobia**, a *fear of a specific object, such as a spider, or a specific situation, such as being in public places, or flying.* Roughly 16 percent of women develop a specific phobia at some time in their life (Church & Lucey, 2010). Specific phobias usually start in childhood. Social construction of gender-specific attitudes and behaviors may account for the higher prevalence of these phobias in females than in males. Expression of fear and anxiety is more socially acceptable in girls and women than in boys and men, who are discouraged from displaying these emotions (McHugh, 2008).

Depression

> *I have been immobilized, unable to formulate thought or action. Can't get out of bed most of the time. I feel terrible—hopeless, joyless, exhausted, lost.*
>
> (Sondra, age 48, cited in "Depression & Women," 2003, p. 1)

INCIDENCE. Depression is *characterized by prolonged sadness or irritability and loss of pleasure in most activities often accompanied by fatigue and feelings of worthlessness* (Torpy, 2010a). Higher rates of depression among females first appear in early adolescence and continue into adulthood (Adkins et al., 2009; Botticello, 2009; González et al., 2010; Lewin, 2010; Ozer & Irwin, 2009). As many as one in four late adolescents has experienced an episode of major depression (Galambos et al., 2004; Zahn-Waxler et al., 2008). Women with disabilities have higher rates of depression than able-bodied women (Olkin, 2006), and ethnic minority women have higher rates than White women (Anderson & Mayes, 2010). Across many nations, cultures, and ethnicities, women are about twice as likely as men to suffer from depression (Eaton et al., 2010; Fan et al., 2009; Heo et al., 2008; Van de Velde et al., 2010). Moreover, women are more likely than men to suffer an anxiety disorder along with their depression (Rice & Russo, 2010).

What are the stresses of adolescence that are linked to higher rates of depression in girls than in boys? Lisa Flook (2011) and Karen Rudolph (2009) and her colleagues found that girls experience considerable stress from relationship problems, including fights with peers, siblings, or friends. Because girls have closer, more intimate relationships with family and friends than boys do, disruptions and conflicts in these relationships can lead to depression and distress (Bakker et al., 2010; Hammen, 2009; Hutcherson & Epkins, 2009; Rudolph, 2009). Just being in a romantic relationship is associated with depression in early adolescent girls (Davila, 2008). Another stressor linked to girls' depression is concern about weight and body image (Vaughan & Halpern, 2010).

THEORIES.   Many theories have been offered to explain the gender difference in depression. Gender differences in help-seeking behavior or willingness to report symptoms have been ruled out as possible reasons (Urbancic, 2009). One explanation is biological, linking depression to hormonal changes that occur during the menstrual cycle, the postpartum period, and menopause (Lewin, 2010). As we saw in Chapter 7, however, menopause is not associated with an increase in depression. In Chapter 7, we also noted that direct relationships between menstrual and postpartum hormonal changes and depression are weak, temporary, and far from universal (Nolen-Hoeksema, 2002). One biological factor that *is* strongly linked to depression is having a low level of the neurochemical serotonin (Zavos et al., 2011). Women produce less serotonin than men do, which makes them more susceptible to depression (Cahill, 2005).

A second explanation for the gender difference in depression is that girls and women are more likely than boys and men to experience stresses that are linked to depression. We have seen that relationship stresses are linked to increased depression for adolescent girls. In addition, women are more likely than men to have low social status, undergo economic hardship, face sexism and discrimination in the workplace and elsewhere, experience marital and family strains, and be subjected to intimate partner violence, sexual abuse, and sexual harassment (Edin & Kissane, 2010; Kasen et al., 2010; Markward & Yegidis, 2011; McLaughlin et al., 2010; Pascoe & Smart Richman, 2009; Russo, 2010; Wilbur et al., 2009).

A third proposed explanation is that the feminine role makes women more vulnerable to depression by making them feel helpless and powerless to control aspects of their lives (Russo & Tartaro, 2008). Females are expected to be less competent and more in need of help than males. Their efforts and achievements are more likely to be ignored or devalued. The sense that one's actions do not count can lead to a feeling of "learned helplessness," which in turn is linked to depression. In support of this view, girls and women with more masculine behavior traits are less likely to experience depression than those with more feminine traits (Lengua & Stormshok, 2000).

A fourth theory known as *silencing the self* (Jack, 2003; Jack & Ali, 2010) is based on the assumption that women are socialized to place a high value on establishing and maintaining close relationships. According to this view, women defer to the needs of others, censor their self-expression, repress anger, and restrict their own initiatives, which increase their vulnerability to depression.

Susan Nolen-Hoeksema (Hilt & Nolen-Hoeksema, 2009; Nolen-Hoeksema et al., 2008) has proposed a fifth theory based on the way that females and males respond when they are depressed. She and other researchers (e.g., Grabe et al., 2007; Rood et al., 2009) have found that when adolescent girls and women are depressed, they *focus on their inner feelings and try over and over again to analyze the causes and consequences of their depression*. This so-called **ruminative style** may be accompanied by **corumination**, which involves *extensively discussing one's problems with another person* (Hankin et al., 2010). Both rumination and corumination lead to more severe and longer-lasting depressed moods. Adolescent boys and men, on the other hand, tend to engage in activities to distract themselves when they are depressed (Hankin, 2008; Nolen-Hoeksema, 2007; Rood et al., 2009). Try Get Involved 13.1 to see whether you find differences in the way women and men respond when they are depressed.

GET INVOLVED 13.1
How Do Women and Men Respond to Depression?

For this activity, ask one young adult woman, one young adult man, one middle-aged woman, and one middle-aged man to complete the following survey.

WHAT DO YOU DO WHEN YOU'RE FEELING DEPRESSED?

Instructions: Everyone gets depressed—sad, blue, down in the dumps—some of the time. People deal with being depressed in many different ways. For each item, please circle the number that best describes what you *generally* do when you are *depressed*. Choose the most accurate response for *you*, not what you think "most people" would say or do. There are no right or wrong answers.

	Never or Almost Never	Sometimes	Often	Always or Almost Always
1. I try to figure out why I am depressed	1	2	3	4
2. I avoid thinking of reasons why I am depressed	1	2	3	4
3. I think about how sad I feel	1	2	3	4
4. I do something fun with a friend	1	2	3	4
5. I wonder why I have problems that others do not	1	2	3	4
6. I think about all my short-comings, faults, and mistakes	1	2	3	4
7. I think of something to make myself feel better	1	2	3	4
8. I go to a favorite place to distract myself	1	2	3	4
9. I think about why I can't handle things better	1	2	3	4
10. I do something that made me feel better before	1	2	3	4

WHAT DOES IT MEAN?

Before adding up each respondent's scores for the ten items, reverse the points for items 2, 4, 7, 8, and 10. That is, for a rating of 1 (never or almost never), give 4 points; for a rating of 2, give 3 points, and so on. Then sum the points for the ten items for each respondent. Higher scores reflect greater rumination.

1. Are there differences between your female and male respondents in how they react when they are depressed? If so, how do you account for differences?

2. Did your young adults respond differently from your middle-aged adults? Account for any differences.

3. Did your results support Susan Nolen-Hoeksema's findings regarding how women and men respond when they are depressed? Account for any differences.

Source: Adapted from Butler and Nolen-Hoeksema (1994).

These explanations of depression are not mutually exclusive. Indeed, several of these factors most likely are involved (Abela & Hankin, 2009; Russo & Tartaro, 2008). For example, one large-scale study of adults suggests that women are more likely than men to get caught in a cycle of despair and passivity because of a lower sense of control over important areas of life, compounded by more chronic strain caused by women's lesser social power. In the study, chronic strain led to more rumination, which in turn increased feelings of powerlessness and depression (Nolen-Hoeksema et al., 1999).

DEPRESSION IN LATER LIFE. Clinical depression affects 10 to 15 percent of older adults in the United States and Great Britain (Kuchment, 2006). Higher rates of depression are found among medically ill, unmarried, socially isolated, homebound, or functionally impaired older adults (Fiske et al., 2009; Luanaigh & Lawlor, 2008; Mechakra–Tahiri et al., 2009). Interestingly, having an ill spouse is linked to depression for women, but not for men (Ayotte et al., 2010). Depression, in turn, can contribute to heart disease and earlier onset of death (Fiske et al., 2009; Schoevers et al., 2009).

These statistics may be underestimates, however, because many depressed older people are undiagnosed and untreated (Unützer, 2007). Studies of older adults who committed suicide have found that the majority had visited a doctor within a month before their deaths (Chapman & Perry, 2008). Unfortunately, even when older patients clearly are depressed, most physicians do not adequately diagnose or treat the condition (Groh et al., 2009; Lachs, 2010). Older adults do not always experience the classic symptoms of depression, such as sleeplessness, fatigue, low energy, loss of appetite, guilt feelings, and depressed mood, but rather may show anxiety, confusion, and physical complaints (Fiske et al., 2009; Kenna et al., 2010). Sometimes, these symptoms are side effects of medications taken for other health conditions, and changing the medication removes the symptoms. Some symptoms, such as irritability and fault finding or pessimism and little hope for the future, may be dismissed as typical personality changes that accompany aging. Even the classic symptoms of low energy, loss of appetite, or loss of interest in former sources of enjoyment may be viewed incorrectly by doctors as a "normal" consequence of medical, financial, or family difficulties or the losses that come with age (Groh et al., 2009; Segal et al., 2011). While it is true that health problems among older adults may contribute to symptoms of depression (Groh et al., 2009), most older people confront their problems without becoming clinically depressed. In fact, older adults have a lower prevalence of depression than younger adults (Chapman & Perry, 2008).

Depression is highly treatable in older adults (Cuijpers et al., 2006; Fiske et al., 2009; Snowden et al., 2008). Unfortunately, older women are less likely than younger women to receive psychotherapy, and women aged 75 and over are more likely to receive no treatment at all (Glied, 1998).

Suicide

INCIDENCE. Across all ages and ethnic groups in the United States, boys and men are four times more likely than women to commit suicide, whereas girls and women are two to three times more likely than men to attempt it (Eaton et al., 2010; Harrocks & House, 2010; Wolitzky-Taylor et al., 2010). White and Native American women and men have higher suicide rates than individuals in other ethnic groups, and Black women have the lowest. Older White males have the highest rate of all (Crosby et al., 2011; Karch et al., 2010). This group, probably the most privileged earlier in life, experiences the greatest loss of status in old age, contributing to ill health and depression (Roark, 2009). The lower suicide rates among Black women, on the other hand, are thought to be related to the protective factors of extended family and community networks and religious faith (Chaudron & Caine, 2004; Goldston et al., 2008). For a look at gender differences in suicide across cultures, see Explore Other Cultures 13.2.

SUICIDE IN ADOLESCENCE AND YOUNG ADULTHOOD. Nearly half of all suicides among females occur between the ages of 15 and 44. Suicide is the fourth leading cause of death for women of these ages (Ortega & Karch, 2010). Risk factors for suicide in both sexes include depression, exposure to suicide or suicide attempts by family or friends, stressful life events such as interpersonal loss or disciplinary crises, substance or alcohol abuse, and having guns in the home (Jacobson & Gould,

EXPLORE OTHER CULTURES 13.2
Gender Differences in Suicide: A Global Phenomenon

In most countries, men are more likely than women to commit suicide. In industrialized nations, the male-to-female suicide ratio ranges from 2:1 in the Netherlands to 5.4:1 in the Russian Federation (Chaudron & Caine, 2004). The ratio for the United States is about 4:1 (Range, 2006). In one study of 29 nations (Lester & Yang, 1998), higher divorce rates were associated with higher suicide rates. Interestingly, this association was stronger for men than for women, in line with findings that marriage seems more beneficial for men than for women (see Chapter 8). Across cultures, unemployment is also more strongly associated with suicide and acceptance of suicide among men than among women (Helgeson, 2005). For women, suicide is more closely linked to their social and economic status. In nations where women's status is low, such as China, India, the Pacific Island countries, and parts of Turkey, their suicide rates are higher than that of boys and men (Frantz, 2000; Kim & Singh, 2004; Milner & DeLeo, 2010; Raj et al., 2008). One of the

differences between women's suicide in the West and in developing countries is the method used. Women in Western countries usually swallow pills or slash their wrists, which are treatable events. In Asia, however, women ingest highly lethal insecticides, hang themselves, or set themselves on fire (Milner & DeLeo, 2010; Raj et al., 2008).

Why are young Asian women committing suicide at such a high rate? A major factor seems to be cultural and gender conflicts that are made more intense as these traditional agricultural societies are transforming themselves into industrial societies. Many girls are still forbidden to go to school or to work and they are forced into arranged marriages, which may be abusive or unhappy (Kristof & WuDunn, 2009; Moreau & Yousafzai, 2004; Raj et al., 2008). At the same time, they are exposed through movies and television to a more prosperous, egalitarian life, which is denied to them. Such lack of control of one's life may lead to despair and suicide (Frantz, 2000; Milner & DeLeo, 2010).

Maggie Kuhn, who founded the Gray Panthers after her forced retirement at age 65, illustrates the active role older women can play as advocates for social change.

2009; Ortega & Karch, 2010; Reviere, 2011; Thompson & Light, 2011). Social factors are more strongly associated with having suicidal thoughts for girls than for boys. In particular, girls who are socially isolated from peers are more likely to think about suicide than are girls with strong social networks (Bearman & Moody, 2004).

SUICIDE IN LATER LIFE. Risk factors associated with suicide in older people are the death of a loved one; physical illness; uncontrollable pain; the specter of dying a prolonged death that harms family members emotionally and financially; fear of institutionalization; social isolation; loneliness; elder abuse; and major changes in social roles, such as retirement. As in adolescence, those who abuse alcohol and other drugs, are depressed, or suffer from other mental disorders are also at high risk (Conwell et al., 2010; Groh et al., 2009; Kenna et al., 2010; Manthorpe & Iliffe, 2010; Segal et al., 2011).

On a positive note, remember that most older people with health and other problems cope well with the changes of later life and do not become depressed or suicidal (Beers & Jones, 2004). Many continue to lead active and productive lives. In the words of Maggie Kuhn, an older woman activist,

Old age is not a disaster. It is a triumph over disappointment, failure, loss, illness. When we reach this point in life, we have great experience with failure. I always know that if one of the things that I've initiated falters and fails, it won't be the end. I'll find a way to learn from it and begin again.

(Kuhn, 1991, p. 214)

MENTAL HEALTH OF SEXUAL MINORITY WOMEN

Until 1973, the American Psychiatric Association classified homosexuality as a mental disorder (Herek, 2010). It took nearly another 30 years for the American Psychological Association to adopt guidelines for psychotherapy with gay, lesbian, and bisexual clients ("Guidelines," 2000), and nearly 10 more to issue a report on transgender individuals (American Psychological Association, 2009). These guidelines urge psychologists to understand how prejudice, discrimination, and violence pose risks to the mental health and well-being of lesbian, gay, bisexual, and transgender (LGBT) clients. Let us look at stress-related difficulties faced by the LGBT community and some helpful coping mechanisms.

Stresses and Problems

In Chapter 6, we discussed the widespread nature of prejudice and discrimination against LGBT individuals. Such homophobia can cause considerable stress in the lives of sexual minorities and increase their risk of physical and psychological problems (American Psychological Association, 2009; Dilley et al., 2010; Fassinger et al., 2010; Kantor, 2009; Riggle et al., 2009; Stotzer, 2009; Ueno & McWilliams, 2010; Wilkinson & Pearson, 2009).

Compared to heterosexual teens, lesbian, gay, and bisexual adolescents have higher rates of substance abuse, poor school adjustment, truancy, running away from home, risky sexual behavior, conflicts with the law, depression, and suicidal thoughts (Bos et al., 2008; Busseri et al., 2008; Kitts, 2010; Mustanski et al., 2010; Teasdale & Bradley-Engen, 2010). In adulthood, sexual minorities report higher rates of alcohol and substance abuse than heterosexuals (Maguen & Shipherd, 2010; McCabe et al., 2010; McNair et al., 2011; Mignon et al., 2009; Talley et al., 2010; Wallace et al., 2011). They also show poorer mental health, and higher rates of anxiety disorder, depression, suicide attempts, and suicide (Aleman & Doctor, 2010; Hatzenbuehler et al., 2010; Plöderl & Fartacek, 2009; Schultz & Beals, 2010). Bisexual women and men show the highest rates of mood and anxiety disorders of all groups (Bostwick et al., 2010; Fredriksen-Goldsen et al., 2010).

Coping Mechanisms

On a more positive note, many sexual minority individuals develop effective coping responses that are linked to good mental health. These include accepting one's sexual orientation, having a good social support network, being in a satisfying relationship, and actively participating in the lesbian and gay community (Kuyper & Fokkema., 2009; McLaren, 2009; Read, 2009; Schultz & Beals, 2010). Having family and friends who acknowledge and support their sexual identity is another key factor linked to the well-being of LGBT individuals (Beals & Peplau, 2005). LGBT individuals are also more likely than heterosexuals to seek psychological counseling (Bieschke et al., 2007; Croteau, Bieschke et al., 2008; Wallace et al., 2011). However, sexual minorities may be especially vulnerable to misdiagnosis and other forms of bias, which can serve as a barrier to seeking treatment (American Psychological Association, 2007a; Shipherd et al., 2010). Not surprisingly, sexual minority individuals are more likely to seek counsel from therapists who have been trained to work with their needs and issues (Irwin, 2009; Oswald et al., 2010).

MENTAL HEALTH OF OLDER WOMEN

As my hair grays, my skin wrinkles, and my fat redistributes, I can't take it all too sorrowfully. I have had a productive youth and have accomplished enough during it to provide a dozen people with material for my birthday roast. Milestone birthdays of middle age are wonderful when you have made positive choices, managed the unexpected, learned from the storms and sorrows, but still find yourself emotionally and physically whole.

(Pam, on the occasion of her 50th birthday)

In this section, we look at the mental health of women as they get older. First we focus on gender differences. We then concentrate on the vital older woman.

Gender Differences

The psychological health of women tends to improve as they get older (Antonucci et al., 2010; Herman-Stahl et al., 2007; Stone et al., 2010; U.S. Department of Health and Human Services, 2009; Q. Xu et al., 2010). For example, older women show fewer negative emotions, greater well-being, and more emotional control than younger women. Still, older women, compared to older men, are more depressed (Barry et al., 2008; Luijendijk et al., 2008; U.S. Department of Commerce, 2011) and report more stress, worry and sadness, more frequent negative emotions, poorer mental health, and a lower sense of well-being (George, 2010; Lawlor & Sterne, 2007). However, gender differences in depression decline or even disappear by age 80 because men's depression rates increase after age 60, while those of women remain the same or decrease (Barefoot et al., 2001; Canetto, 2001; Kenna et al., 2010). Similarly, rates of frequent anxiety decline as women age, but this is not the case for men (Srivastava et al., 2003; U.S. Department of Health and Human Services, 2009). In addition, the gender difference in self-esteem that emerges in adolescence (boys' are higher) narrows and disappears in old age (Orth et al., 2010; Robins & Trzesniewski, 2005).

The Vital Older Woman

In my sixties, I found my first taste of freedom. My earlier life was spent living according to other people's expectations of me: my parents, my husband, my family. When your family doesn't need you anymore, that's frightening, but freeing. There's time to explore and contemplate what you've learned so far. And there's a duty to send out some of those messages so that other people can benefit from all the difficult lessons you've learned. (Anna Kainen, 1995, age 82, writer)

Women, speak out. Stand up for what you believe. Go back to that teenage person you were, who wanted something very badly, then go out and get it. This is a time in your life when there's nothing and no one standing in your way. (Elizabeth Watson, 1995, age 82, theologian and environmental activist)

We have examined a number of challenges faced by many older women: declining health, financial problems, and the loss of loved ones. But this does not mean that the later years of a woman's life are filled with frustration and despair. Many older women cope successfully with the challenges that old age brings. They don't just *endure* old age; they *enjoy* it.

Most older women maintain a positive outlook and high levels of life satisfaction (Majerovitz, 2006). In some cases, positive changes in family or work situations occur as a result of women's actions. In other cases, stress relief comes about through role changes and the passage of time. Finally, some women continue to lead lives that have always been relatively satisfying (Antonucci et al., 2010; Burns & Leonard, 2005). Key components of a purposeful life for older women include caring family and friends, independence, meaningful activities, and spirituality (Hedberg et al., 2009). Older Black women express significantly more contentment with their lives than older White women, even though Blacks are more disadvantaged socioeconomically and perceive their health as worse than Whites do (Johnson, 1994). How can we explain this? Many aging ethnic minority women are able to draw on psychological, social, and cultural strengths that ease their transition to old age. They have spent their lives marshaling scarce resources to cope with everyday demands, and these coping strategies pay off later on as self-reliance. Strengths also arise from family, church, community networks, and shared ethnic identity (Antonucci et al., 2010a; Mattis, 2002; Yoon & Lee, 2004). In addition, White women may have expectations of life in the later years that are unrealistically high.

See What You Can Do 13.1 for ways to manage stress and promote mental health. Practice these methods yourself and share with others.

DIAGNOSIS AND TREATMENT OF PSYCHOLOGICAL DISORDERS

The diagnosis and treatment of psychological disorders in women have often been topics of controversy. Feminist researchers and theorists point out that diagnosis and treatment are conducted by a predominantly male psychiatric culture, using a medical model of psychological illness and viewing many aspects of female behavior as pathological (Brown, 2010). In recent times, gender bias has become more covert, but still remains a powerful force in psychological practice (American Psychological Association, 2007a). Let's take a closer look at diagnosis and treatment of women's psychological disorders.

Gender Bias in Diagnosis

Is there a double standard of mental health for women and men? In a classic study, Inge Broverman and her colleagues (1970) reported that mental health professionals gave similar descriptions for a "healthy" adult (gender unspecified) and a "healthy" male. A "healthy" woman, however, was seen as

WHAT YOU CAN DO 13.1
Ways to Manage Stress and Promote Good Mental Health

- Identify the major stressors in your life.
- Think of ways you can reduce these stresses and take appropriate actions.
- Learn to delegate and share.
- Learn to say "no."
- Communicate with support groups: friends, family, and counselors.
- Use meditation, yoga, or prayer.
- Use visualization to imagine yourself in a peaceful, relaxing place.
- Exercise.
- Spend time with a pet.
- Get a massage.
- Make time for activities you enjoy: hiking, gardening, reading, and so on.

Sources: Alexander et al. (2010) and Donatelle (2012).

less healthy in several ways: more submissive, more excitable in minor crises, more emotional, more illogical, more easily hurt, more sneaky, and less independent. Over the years, other researchers have found that gender bias in diagnosis remains alive and well. A later study, for example, found that counselors-in-training continue to have different standards of mental health for women and men, and that "healthy women" are viewed differently than "healthy adults" (Seem & Clark, 2006).

Although gender bias has become more covert, it still exists. For example, disorders that conform to gender stereotypes (e.g., anxiety in women, antisocial behavior in men) may be overdiagnosed and overtreated (Russo & Tartaro, 2008). One meta-analysis of 42 studies (McGorty et al., 2003), for example, found that professionals were more likely to diagnose and treat anxiety when it occurred in women and were more likely to diagnose and treat antisocial behavior when it occurred in men. By the same token, misdiagnosis can occur when a client's problem behaviors are inconsistent with societal expectations, such as when a woman exhibits antisocial symptoms (American Psychological Association, 2007a). For more about gender biases in diagnosis, see Learn About the Research 13.1.

Gender Bias in Psychotherapy

Gender bias also exists in psychotherapy. One classic study (American Psychological Association, 1975) documented bias in the form of fostering traditional gender roles (e.g., "be a better wife"), telling sexist jokes, not taking violence against women seriously, and seducing female clients (American Psychological Association, 1975). In another study (Fowers et al., 1996), over 200 clinical psychologists were asked to recommend strategies that would best help hypothetical females and males with identically described problems. The psychologists indicated that male clients could best be helped

LEARN ABOUT THE RESEARCH 13.1
What Is "Normal"? Gender Biases in Diagnosis

Some psychologists (e.g., Worell & Johnson, 2001) argue that the definitions of "normal" that guide psychological diagnoses are socially constructed by the dominant cultural group (i.e., White heterosexual males) and reflect stereotypical notions of gender, race/ethnicity, and sexuality. To test this view, Jill Cermele and her colleagues (2001) analyzed the depiction of women and men in the Casebook that accompanies the **Diagnostic and Statistical Manual of Mental Disorders, IV,** the *standard classification system used in the United States.* The researchers found that the Casebook (Spitzer et al., 1994), which provides case studies to guide the clinician, does indeed contain stereotyped descriptions of women and men. Men's personality traits were much more likely to be described in positive ways (e.g., charming, friendly, engaging) than in negative ways, whereas females were more often described negatively (e.g., frightened, sad, helpless). In addition, there were more than three times as many negative physical descriptions of women (e.g., disheveled, pale, obese) than of men, who were more often described positively (e.g., tall, handsome, healthy). Women were also more apt to be infantilized (e.g., described as tiny, childlike, frail, and girlish). In addition, they were more often referred to in terms of sexual behavior (e.g., seductive, flirtatious), even when these behaviors had nothing to do with the diagnosis.

WHAT DOES IT MEAN?

1. How might constructing women as different from men influence clinicians in diagnosing mental illness?

2. What can psychologists do to address biases in their notions of what constitutes normalcy and mental illness?

by increasing their instrumental (traditionally masculine) actions, whereas females could benefit more by enhancing their expressive (traditionally feminine) behaviors. Moreover, therapists are more likely to see women's emotional problems as internally caused (intrapsychic) than they are to regard men's emotional problems in this way, and they may fail to perceive the external stresses of women's lives (Russo & Tartaro, 2008; Worell, 2001).

Some therapists expect a more positive outcome with male clients than with female clients. These therapists may have even lower expectations of outcomes for ethnic minority women, sexual minority women, and women with disabilities (American Psychological Association, 2007a). In order to increase the likelihood of positive outcomes when working with women clients, therapists need to understand the challenges, strengths, intersecting identities, and social contexts of these clients (Nutt & Brooks, 2008).

Therapy Issues for Women of Color and Poor Women

Women of color and poor women face a number of external stresses that can cause or intensify mental health problems: racism, poverty, culturally approved subordinate status, and living in contexts of violence and chronic strain (McLaughlin et al., 2010; Primm et al., 2010; Safran et al., 2009). Unfortunately, financial constraints, lack of insurance, and time and transportation problems prevent many poor and ethnic minority women from seeking help (González et al., 2010; U.S. Department of Health and Human Services, 2009). In addition, people of color are underrepresented in the mental health professions so that members of these groups often have a therapist who does not know their culture or speak their language (Juckett & Rudolph-Watson, 2010; Lehti et al., 2010; Primm et al., 2010). Nonminority providers may apply racial stereotypes to their minority patients instead of seeing them as individuals. Moreover, they can be insensitive to the social and economic conditions in which women of color and poor women live (Comas-Diaz, 2010a; Lott, 2010; Markward & Yegidis, 2011; Safran et al., 2009). One reason for this is that clinical psychology literature does not contain adequate coverage of ethnically diverse populations. For example, an analysis of the leading clinical psychology journals in the 1980s and 1990s found that only 29 percent of the articles included ethnic minority populations, and only 5 percent focused specifically on these populations (Iwamasa et al., 2002).

Types of Therapy

TRADITIONAL THERAPIES.   Traditional psychotherapies are based on a medical model in which emotional pain is viewed as a "disease," which must be "treated" by an expert. This leads to a therapeutic relationship marked by an imbalance of power between therapist (often male) and patient (often female). In addition, the individual's emotional problems are seen as having internal, not external, causes. The goal of therapy is to promote the person's adjustment to existing social conditions (Brown, 2010).

FEMINIST THERAPIES.   **Feminist therapy**, on the other hand, *emphasizes the role of social, political, and economic stresses facing women as a major source of their psychological problems* (Brown, 2010; Rice & Russo, 2010). Feminist therapists focus on issues of oppression, such as sexism, racism, classism, ableism, and heterosexism. A key goal of feminist therapy is to empower clients in all spheres of life: physical, psychological, social, and spiritual (Brown, 2010; Enns & Byars-Winston, 2010). Clients are encouraged to become psychologically and economically independent and to try to change a sexist society rather than adjust to it. Another principle of feminist therapy is that therapists should not be more powerful than their clients but should build egalitarian, respectful, and collaborative relationships with them (Brown, 2010; Gentile et al., 2008; Hill & Jeong, 2008; Roffman, 2008). One vehicle for doing so is **counselor self-disclosure**, *the imparting of personal information about the life experiences of the therapist to the client* (Brown, 2010; Moore, 2010). In addition, feminist therapy stresses awareness of possible identity differences between client and therapist in terms of culture, class, sexual orientation, religion, and so on (Barrett & Ballou, 2008; Gentile et al., 2008; Greene, 2010). Feminist therapy is a philosophy underlying therapy rather than a specific therapeutic technique, and it can be integrated with other treatment approaches (Brown, 2010).

Summary

FACTORS PROMOTING MENTAL HEALTH

- Social support enhances mental health.
- Females seek and use social support more than males do.
- In reaction to stress, women more often show the "tend and befriend" response, whereas men are more likely to exhibit "fight or flight" behavior.
- Optimism is linked to positive mental and physical health.

MENTAL HEALTH IN CHILDHOOD AND ADOLESCENCE

- Stress levels increase for girls and boys during adolescence. Much of girls' stress stems from relationship problems and is linked to higher rates of depression.
- Externalizing problems in girls are less common than internalizing problems, but are more likely to be associated with adult maladjustment.

EATING DISORDERS

- Anorexia nervosa is marked by severe weight loss and fear of being overweight.
- Bulimia nervosa is characterized by cycles of binging and purging.
- Biological, psychological, and cultural factors are involved in these disorders, which occur most often in adolescent girls.

SUBSTANCE USE AND ABUSE

- Women are less likely to be heavy drinkers than men, but binge drinking is on the increase in college women.

- Women's alcoholism starts later than men's, progresses more quickly, and is diagnosed at a more advanced stage.
- Drinking in pregnancy can cause FAS or FAE.
- Females are less likely than males to use most illegal drugs.

ANXIETY DISORDERS AND DEPRESSION

- Anxiety disorders are more common in women than men. These include panic disorders and specific phobias.
- Depression is twice as common in women as in men. Possible explanations for this difference include biological factors, stressful life events, learned helplessness, self-silencing, and women's ruminative style in responding to depression.

MENTAL HEALTH OF SEXUAL MINORITY WOMEN

- Homophobia can cause considerable stress in the lives of lesbians, gays, bisexuals and transgender individuals, resulting in a variety of psychological problems.
- Effective coping mechanisms include accepting one's sexual orientation, having social support and a satisfying relationship, and participating in the LGBT community.

MENTAL HEALTH OF OLDER WOMEN

- The psychological health of women improves as they get older.
- Older women who cope successfully with aging tend to integrate agency and communion.

- Some older women continue their careers; others become volunteers or advocates for social causes.

DIAGNOSIS AND TREATMENT OF PSYCHOLOGICAL DISORDERS

- Gender bias exists in diagnosis and treatment of psychological disorders.
- Women of color face external stresses, which can intensify mental health problems and prevent them from seeking help.

- Traditional psychotherapies are marked by a power imbalance between therapist and client, and focus on internal causes of emotional problems.
- Feminist therapy is nonsexist, encourages equal power between therapist and client, and focuses on societal causes of women's problems.

Key Terms

anorexia nervosa *312*
bulimia nervosa *313*
female athlete triad *314*
telescoping *315*
binge drinking *316*
fetal alcohol syndrome (FAS) *316*

fetal alcohol effect (FAE) *316*
generalized anxiety disorder *318*
panic disorder *318*
agoraphobia *318*
specific phobia *318*
depression *318*

ruminative style *319*
corumination *319*
Diagnostic and Statistical Manual of Mental Disorders, IV 326
feminist therapy *327*
counselor self-disclosure *328*

What Do You Think?

1. If you become aware that a friend of yours has an eating disorder, what steps could you take to try to help?
2. Why do you think that society is less tolerant of drinking in women than in men?
3. In your opinion, why are women more likely than men to suffer from anxiety disorders and depression?

4. Why do you think that U.S. males are more likely to commit suicide than females, whereas females are more likely to attempt it?
5. How might stereotypes about women and men affect the way psychotherapists work with female and male clients?

If You Want to Learn More

Bieschke, K. J., Perez, R. M., & DeBord, K. A. (Eds.). (2007). *Handbook of counseling and psychotherapy with lesbian, gay, bisexual, and transgender clients* (2nd ed.). Washington, DC: American Psychological Association.

Brown, H. (2010). *Brave girl eating: A family's struggle with anorexia.* New York: William Morrow.

Brown, L. (2010). *Feminist therapy.* Washington, DC: American Psychological Association.

Chandra, P. S., Herrman, H., Fisher, J. E., Kastrup, M., Niaz, U., Rondon, M. et al. (2009). *Contemporary topics in women's mental health: Global perspectives in a changing society.* West Sussex, UK: Wiley-Blackwell.

Erickson Cornish, J. A., Schreier, B. A., Nadkarni, L. I., Henderson Metzger, L., & Rodolfa, E. R. (Eds.). (2010). *Handbook of multicultural counseling competencies.* Malden, MA: Wiley.

Fernando, S., & Keating, F. (Eds.). (2009). *Mental health in a multiethnic society: A multidisciplinary handbook.* New York: Routledge.

Kohen, D. (Ed.). (2010). *Oxford textbook of women and mental health.* Oxford, UK: Oxford University Press.

Levin, B. L., & Becker, M. A. (2010). *A public health perspective of women's mental health.* New York: Springer.

Malson, H., & Burns, M. (Eds.). (2009). *Critical feminist approaches to eating dis/orders.* New York: Routledge.

Mirkin, M. P., Suyemoto, K. L., & Okun, B. F. (Eds.). (2005). *Psychotherapy with women: Exploring diverse contexts and identities.* New York: Guilford.

Smolak, L., & Thompson, J. K. (2009). *Body image, eating disorders, and obesity in youth: Assessment,* *prevention, and treatment.* Washington, DC: American Psychological Association.

Strauman, T. J., Costanzo, P. R., & Garber, J. (Eds.). (2011). *Depression in adolescent girls: Science and prevention.* New York: Guilford.

Urbanck, J., & Groh, C. (2009). *Women's mental health: A clinical guide for primary care providers.* Philadelphia, PA: Lippincott Williams & Wilkins.

Worell, J., & Goodheart, C. (Eds.). (2006). *Handbook of girls' and women's psychological health.* New York: Oxford University Press.

Websites

Mental Health

Mental Health Net: Self-Help Resources Index
http://www.mentalhelp.net/selfhelp/
National Mental Health Association
http://www.nmha.org
Suicide Prevention Action Network
http://www.spanusa.org

Eating Disorders

http://www.mirror-mirror.org/
National Eating Disorders Association (NEDA)
http://nationaleatingdisorders.org/

Alcohol and Substance Abuse

National Institute on Drug Abuse
http://www.nida.nih.gov

Vital Older Women

Older Women's League (OWL)
http://www.owl-national.org/
Center for Healthy Aging
http://www.healthyagingprograms.org/

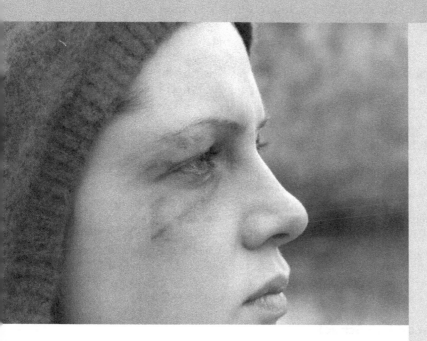

Violence Against Girls and Women

Sexual Harassment at School
    Elementary and Secondary School
    The College Campus

Sexual Harassment in the Workplace
    Incidence
    Consequences
    Explanations
    Women's Responses

Stalking
    What Is Stalking?
    Perpetrators, Victims, and Effects

Violence Against Girls
    Child Sexual Abuse
    Infanticide and Neglect

Dating Violence
    Incidence
    Who Engages in Dating
      Violence?

Rape
    Incidence
    Acquaintance Rape
    Factors Associated With
      Acquaintance Rape
    Effects of Rape
    Rape Prevention
    Theories of Rape

Intimate Partner Violence
    Incidence
    Role of Disability, Social Class,
      and Ethnicity
    Risk Factors
    Effects of Intimate Partner
      Violence
    Leaving the Abusive Relationship
    Theories of Intimate Partner
      Violence
    Interventions

Elder Abuse
    Who Is Abused and Who Abuses?
    What Can Be Done?

Ronnie Falco, a computer science graduate of Stanford University, began a successful career as a software designer, work that she loved. Unfortunately, due to the frustrating interactions she had with her male colleagues, her computer career was short-lived. Her coworkers did not look at her when they spoke to her, directed questions at male colleagues even when she had greater expertise, and seemed to resent her successful solutions to problems. Consequently, after 10 years in the computer industry, Ronnie Falco left and went into the health field. (Piller, 1998)

I suffered at home for over 20 years watching my father try to kill my mother. It was unbelievably frightening to me, and I feel it's taken a terrible toll on me, which is still going on. I'm talking about depression, relationship problems, you name it, my life feels like a mess. Living in that situation was horrific. I used to see the carving knife on the landing, and my father would chase my mother upstairs with it. I would hide her in my bedroom and put the chest of drawers against the door, and I'd tell her to get into my bed. Then I'd go out of my bedroom to take the knife off him. That happened dozens and dozens of times in my life. It's beyond words to describe this situation. My father never actually killed my mother, but the constant threat was almost as bad because I never knew what he'd do. I felt I could never go out—that I had to stay at home with my mother because who knew what would happen if I went out and left her alone. To put this on a child destroys you. (Susan, mid-30s, in Russell, 2001, p. 132)

Harassment and violence are serious public health problems that transcend demographic, social, and national boundaries. In this chapter, we focus on harassment and violence experienced by girls and women in personal relationships, at school, and on the job. We start by exploring sexual harassment at school and in the workplace and then focus on stalking. We then turn to a bleak aspect of childhood for all too many girls: sexual abuse and others forms of violence and neglect. Next, we look at the disturbing violent side of some relationships, with an examination of dating violence, rape (including acquaintance rape), and intimate partner violence. We conclude with an examination of elder abuse.

SEXUAL HARASSMENT AT SCHOOL

Sexual harassment in an educational setting includes *unwelcome verbal or physical behavior of a sexual nature when (a) submission to or rejection of the behavior forms the basis for decisions about the student (e.g., admission, grades); or (b) the behavior creates an intimidating, hostile, or offensive study environment.* Sexual harassment at school unfortunately is widespread in the United States and elsewhere (Basow, 2010b; Morgan & Gruber, 2011). In most cases, boys harass girls, rather than the other way around. Ethnic minority girls, students with disabilities, and lesbian, gay, bisexual, and transgender students are more likely to be sexually harassed than their peers (Gruber & Fineran, 2010; Wessler & De Andrade, 2006). Sexual harassment by peers is much more common than sexual harassment committed by teachers, but students are much more distressed when the harasser is a teacher (Hill & Silva, 2005; Timmerman, 2003).

Elementary and Secondary School

Reports of student sexual harassment are on the rise among junior and senior high school students. In one survey (AAUW, 2001), about half of the girls said they had received sexual comments or looks (see Figure 14.1). Nearly half reported being touched, grabbed, or pinched in a sexual way. Two-thirds of girls, but less than one-third of boys, said they were upset after being harassed. Nearly one-third of the girls reported that the unwanted activity made them not want to go to school or talk in class. Girls who are harassed are also more likely to experience academic difficulties, physical symptoms (e.g., headache, digestive upset), interpersonal relationship problems, and negative psychological outcomes such as feeling self-conscious, embarrassed, anxious, afraid, less confident, and unpopular (Basow, 2010b; Duffy et al., 2004; Felix & McMahon, 2006; Nishina & Juvonen, 2005). Sadly, teachers rarely intervene, even when they are aware of serious incidents of sexual harassment. Instead of considering sexual harassment to be serious misconduct, school authorities too often treat it as harmless instances of "boys will be boys" (AAUW, 2001).

A recent study (Ormerod et al., 2008) found that girls still experience high rates of peer sexual harassment in high school and somewhat lower rates of harassment from school personnel. These experiences continue to be more stressful for girls than for boys. Just as disturbing, however, was the finding that harassment has damaging effects even on those who do not directly experience it, by

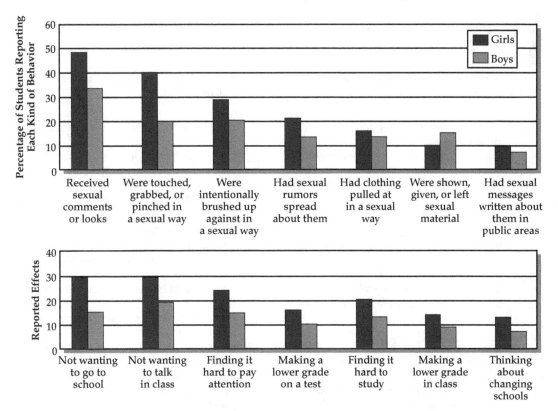

FIGURE 14.1 Percentage of Junior and Senior High School Students Who Reported Experiencing Unwelcomed Sexual Behavior at School "Often" or "Occasionally," and Its Effects   *Source:* American Association of University Women (AAUW, 2001).

creating a school climate that appears to tolerate harassment. Those girls and boys who perceived that sexual harassment was accepted at school also felt unsafe at school, tended to withdraw from school, and had lower self-esteem. Later in the chapter, we shall examine a closely related phenomenon, organizational tolerance of harassment, which has a similar chilling effect on women in the workplace.

The College Campus

Although sexual harassment in an educational setting was legally defined earlier in the chapter, there are wide variations in people's conceptions of harassing behaviors. Before reading this section, perform the exercise in Get Involved 14.1 to examine the behaviors and situations that you and your acquaintances classify as sexual harassment.

Research shows that there are gender differences in the tendency to classify behaviors such as those listed in Get Involved 14.1 as sexual harassment. Women perceive more situations as harassing than men do (Isbell et al., 2005; Lonsway et al., 2008; Smirles, 2004), and they are harsher in their judgments of the harasser (Sigal et al., 2005). Whether an individual perceives a behavior as harassment also depends, in part, on the role relationship between the harasser and the target. When students are targets, behaviors are more likely to be seen as harassment if they are performed by a professor than by another student (e.g., Bursik, 1992). Did you find these two patterns when you performed the Get Involved activity?

GET INVOLVED 14.1
What Constitutes Sexual Harassment on Campus?

Check each of the following items that you believe is a form of sexual harassment if experienced by a student. Then ask one female student and one male student to do the same.

_____ comments on personal appearance by a student

_____ comments on personal appearance by a professor

_____ unwanted letters or phone calls of a sexual nature from a student

_____ unwanted letters or phone calls of a sexual nature from a faculty member

_____ unwanted sexually suggestive looks or gestures from a student

_____ unwanted sexually suggestive looks or gestures from a faculty member

_____ offensive sexually suggestive stories or jokes told by a student

_____ offensive sexually suggestive stories or jokes told by a faculty member

_____ inappropriate staring by a student that causes discomfort

_____ inappropriate staring by a faculty member that causes discomfort

_____ unwelcome seductive remarks or questions by a student

_____ unwelcome seductive remarks or questions by a faculty member

_____ unwanted pressure for dates by a student

_____ unwanted pressure for dates by a faculty member

_____ unwanted leaning, touching, or pinching by a student

_____ unwanted leaning, touching, or pinching by a faculty member

_____ unwanted pressure for sexual favors by a student

_____ unwanted pressure for sexual favors by a faculty member

_____ nonforced sexual relationship between a faculty member and a student

_____ nonforced sexual relationship between two students

_____ forced sexual intercourse by a student

_____ forced sexual intercourse by a faculty member

WHAT DOES IT MEAN?

Separately sum the behaviors you classified as sexual harassment if performed by a student and those seen as sexual harassment if performed by a faculty member. Do the same for each of your respondents.

1. Compare the number of behaviors seen as harassment if performed by a student to those if performed by a faculty member. Is there a difference in your answers or in those of your respondents? Explain any differences

you found. Are these differences consistent with the evidence presented in the text?

2. Is there any difference in the number of behaviors seen as harassment by your female and male respondents? If yes, does it match the difference presented in the text? What might explain this?

Source: Based on Shepela and Levesque (1998).

The questions in Get Involved 14.1 raise two controversial issues related to power. One is whether sexual harassment, by definition, is restricted to behaviors performed by a person with authority (e.g., a professor) over a target (e.g., a student). The other is whether a sexual relationship between individuals who differ in power, as in a professor–student relationship, constitutes sexual harassment even if the student gives consent. In the first issue, the crucial criteria are (1) the target perceives the behavior as unwelcome, and (2) the unwanted behavior creates a hostile or an offensive atmosphere for the target. If these conditions are met, it is not necessary that the perpetrator have power over the target (Fitzgerald, 1996).

There is greater controversy surrounding the second issue. Does a romantic relationship between a professor and student constitute sexual harassment, regardless of whether it is consensual? One view is that as long as the student is an adult and expresses willingness to enter into a sexual relationship with a professor, that relationship is acceptable. Male students are more likely than female students to subscribe to this view (L'Armand et al., 2002). Another perspective is that whenever a formal power differential between two people is present, a sexual relationship involves some degree of coercion because the target is not really in a position to freely consent or refuse. According to this viewpoint, *any* sexual behavior directed at a student by a professor is harassment (Fitzgerald, 1996). Some schools have gone so far as to forbid any consensual sexual relationship between students and faculty, whereas others merely suggest that such relationships are a bad idea (Bartlett, 2002). What is the policy at your school?

INCIDENCE OF SEXUAL HARASSMENT.   The frequency of sexual harassment on college campuses is hard to assess for a number of reasons. Not only do few students submit formal complaints of harassment, but surveys of harassment experiences also show that the incidence varies from campus to campus. Also, the frequency of sexual harassment varies according to the specific type of unwanted conduct and the nature of the power relationship between the harasser and the target. Despite these problems, however, one can draw certain conclusions from surveys. First, females are more likely than males to be sexually harassed (Banyard et al., 2007; Hill & Silva, 2005). Second, women are more likely to experience subtle forms of harassment, such as unwanted sexually suggestive jokes or body language, than they are to encounter more blatant forms, such as unwanted sexual advances, although the latter do occur (Hill & Silva, 2005). Third, students are more likely to experience unwanted sexual behaviors by other students than by faculty members (Hill & Silva, 2005). Fourth, the incidence of sexual harassment is higher for certain groups of women students: those who are poor, are socially isolated, have disabilities, are ethnic or sexual minorities, or are majors in male-dominated fields such as engineering (Paludi, 2008). Fifth, sexually harassing events are more distressing for women than for men (Brinkman & Rickard, 2009). Sixth, women who identify as feminists are more likely to confront their harassers (Ayres et al., 2009).

RESPONSES TO SEXUAL HARASSMENT.   What do college students do when they experience sexual harassment? The most common response is to ignore the behavior (Swim et al., 2010b). Avoidance of the harasser and talking to others about the harassment are other common reactions. Few file a formal complaint (Hill & Silva, 2005). Unfortunately, this lack of formal response hinders attempts to reduce the frequency of harassment. See What You Can Do 14.1 for actions you can take to reduce sexual harassment on campus.

SEXUAL HARASSMENT IN THE WORKPLACE

Analogous to the definition of sexual harassment in academic settings, the legal definition of **sexual harassment in the workplace** is *unwelcome verbal or physical behavior when (a) submission to or rejection of the behavior forms the basis for work-related decisions* (**quid pro quo harassment**), *or (b) the behavior creates an intimidating, hostile, or offensive work environment* (**hostile environment**) (Morgan & Gruber, 2011; Nadal, 2010; Solberg, 2010). Examples of quid pro quo harassment would be the offer of a promotion in exchange for sex and the threat of a layoff if sex were refused. The hostile environment form of harassment is illustrated by the experience of Ronnie Falco, the software engineer described

WHAT YOU CAN DO 14.1
Reducing Sexual Harassment on Campus

There are several actions students can take to ensure that a campus environment is free of sexual harassment. Here is a sampling of what you can do:

1. Find out whether your campus has policies and procedures for dealing with sexual harassment.
2. Establish a Sexual Harassment Awareness Week during which campuswide activities related to sexual harassment take place.

These events can include activities such as plays, movies, and group discussions about sexual harassment.

3. Establish a peer educators program. Peer educators can provide both information to the campus community at large and support to those who have been harassed.

Source: Based on Paludi (2008).

in the vignette at the beginning of the chapter. In Louise Fitzgerald's widely used three-part model of sexual harassment, *quid pro quo* harassment is labeled **sexual coercion**. She divides the *hostile environment* category into two types of behavior: **Gender harassment** is insulting, hostile, and degrading behavior, but not for the purpose of sexual activity (i.e., "the put down"); **unwanted sexual attention** is unwelcome and offensive behavior of a sexual nature (i.e., "the come on") (Street et al., 2003).

Incidence

How common is sexual harassment in the workplace? Studies conducted around the world have concluded that a large proportion of women experience some form of sexual harassment at work (Burn, 2011; Henderson & Jeydel, 2010; Rospenda et al., 2009; Woods & Buchanan, 2008). Most commonly, harassment takes the form of sexual remarks and jokes (Burn, 2011; Pina et al., 2009). Although sexual coercion is relatively rare, it does occur. Frequently, the victims are relatively uneducated, and desperately in need of work. Several particularly disturbing cases have involved Latina immigrant farm workers, food packers, and merchandise stockers in the United States who have been forced to have sex with their supervisors or risk being fired, being deported, being given more physically demanding work, or receiving a cut in pay (Clarren, 2005; Greenhouse, 2007).

Although any woman in any work situation might experience harassment, there are certain factors associated with the greater likelihood of its occurrence. We now turn to an examination of these.

OCCUPATIONAL CHARACTERISTICS RELATED TO SEXUAL HARASSMENT.   Sexual harassment is more common in male-dominated blue-collar occupations, such as auto work, manufacturing, firefighting, law enforcement, coal mining, construction, and transit, than in other male-dominated, female-dominated, or gender-balanced jobs (Berdahl, 2007; Ericksen & Schultheiss, 2009; Morgan & Gruber, 2008; Woods & Buchanan, 2008).

Women in these jobs have been subjected to isolation, work sabotage, severe verbal abuse, physical violence, and intentional exposure to hazardous work conditions (Baker, 2008). For example, women officers in the New Jersey State Police Department in the early 2000s reported deer testicles put in one officer's locker, nails in another's tires, and an obscene valentine from yet another's commanding officer (Schuppe, 2007). Similarly, women in the building trades have reported sledgehammers dropped on them, being thrown off scaffolding, and having obscenities written on their equipment (Eisenberg, 2010).

Another historically male-dominated field associated with a high incidence of sexual harassment and sexual abuse is the military (McKenzie & Rozee, 2010; Turchik & Wilson, 2010). In one glaring example, almost a quarter of the female cadets who graduated from the U.S. Air Force Academy in 2003 were sexually assaulted at the academy, 12 percent were victims of attempted rape, and nearly 70 percent reported experiencing sexual harassment. Many cadets did not initially report the incidents because they feared ostracism, humiliation, and reprisals (Young, 2003). Female cadets were warned by older students about a culture of rape and harassment that victims had to accept without complaint if they wanted to remain at the academy. Other studies report that 20 to 30 percent of women soldiers were raped while serving in the military (Benedict, 2008). In 2009 alone, over 2,900 U.S. servicewomen reported being sexually assaulted by fellow troops. This figure is undoubtedly low, given that about 80 percent of military rapes go unreported (Brazile, 2010).

Why is sexual harassment of women more common in male-dominated blue-collar occupations and the military than in other jobs? One explanation is that men resist women in these jobs because the ability to do hard physical labor symbolizes their masculinity, which is threatened by hiring women (Crawley, 2011). In fact, managers in blue-collar occupations may be reluctant to hire women because they are concerned about reducing the cohesion of the male employee group, lessening productivity, and possibly creating a crisis situation (Bergmann, 2011).

WHO IS HARASSED?   Sexual harassment tends to target certain groups more than others. Women are far more likely than men to be targets and are more likely to report finding these experiences distressing (DeSouza, 2008; Magley et al., 2010; Sears et al., 2011; Woods & Buchanan, 2008). Women are more apt to feel frightened and degraded, whereas men more often feel flattered by these behaviors (Berdahl & Moore, 2006; Magley & Shupe, 2005). Younger or unmarried women are more likely than older or married females to be harassed (Rospenda et al., 2009; Stockdale & Bhattacharya, 2009), possibly because they are seen as more powerless and vulnerable than their older or married counterparts. Sexual minority women are another group at higher risk (Bowleg et al., 2008). If their sexual identity is not known, they are seen as single women and their risk goes up for that reason. Alternatively, if they are open about their identity, anti-gay prejudice can increase the likelihood that they will be harassed.

In addition, women of color are more likely to experience sexual harassment than are White women, especially in blue-collar and other male-dominated settings (Buchanan & West, 2010; Rospenda et al., 2009). When Janice Yoder and Patricia Aniakudo interviewed Black female firefighters, they found that nearly all the women received unwanted sexual behaviors including teasing and jokes, suggestive looks, touching, and pressure for dates. The women also reported isolation, lack of support, hostility, and hypercritical training, as well as racism. Consider one woman's experience: "I was basically alone. I'd walk in and everything would get quiet. I'd go to eat; everybody leaves the room . . . I've been on the job now 7 years, and there're still guys that don't talk to me" (Yoder & Aniakudo, 1999, p. 141). Another woman noted that in her first day on the job, her White male captain told her: "I don't like you. Number one, I don't like you cuz you're Black. And number two, cuz you're a woman" (Yoder & Aniakudo, 1999, p. 140). Susan Martin (2010) found similar instances of isolation and harassment of Black female police officers: "I was at the precinct 10 days before I knew I had a partner 'cause . . . (the men) called in sick" (p. 266); "There was a cutout arrow taped to the window [of my patrol car]. The word 'N____' was written on the arrow pointing to my seat" (p. 268).

CHARACTERISTICS OF OFFENDERS.   The picture that emerges from research on harassers is that the way these men construct gender might serve as a foundation for their harassing behaviors. Specifically, harassers tend to have negative attitudes toward women, hold traditional gender attitudes, and perceive sexual relationships as manipulative and exploitative (Lonsway et al., 2008). That is, the most likely offenders appear to be traditional men who do not view women as equals.

Consequences

Across ethnic groups, sexual harassment is associated with psychological and physical consequences for women, including decreased self-esteem, lowered life satisfaction, anger, fear, depression, anxiety, post-traumatic stress disorder, interpersonal difficulties, headaches, gastrointestinal problems, sleep disturbances, high blood pressure, disordered eating, substance abuse, and sexual problems. Additionally, women can experience undesirable job-related outcomes, including reduced job satisfaction, decreased morale, increased absenteeism, and a decline in organizational commitment (Buchanan & West, 2010; DeSouza, 2008; Fineran & Gruber, 2008; Hoobler et al., 2010; Leskinen et al., 2011; Rodríguez-Muñoz et al., 2010; Stockdale & Bhattacharya, 2009; Willness et al., 2007; Woods & Buchanan, 2010). Even if a woman has not experienced sexual harassment herself, just working in an organizational environment that is hostile toward women or overhearing a sexiest remark made to someone else can have negative effects on her sense of well-being (Chaudoir & Quinn, 2010; DeSouza, 2008; Fineran & Gruber, 2008). As you might expect, the more frequent and ongoing the sexual harassment, the more distressing it is (Langhout et al., 2005).

In addition, women who experience unwelcome sexual behaviors have negative psychological and physical reactions, whether or not they label their experience as harassment (Munson et al., 2001; Woodzicka & LaFrance, 2005). Women might not realize certain behaviors fit the definition of *harassment* or, alternatively, they might want to avoid the label of victim. Whatever the case, it is the experiencing of these behaviors, and not the labeling of them as harassment, that leads to unpleasant psychological and physical outcomes (Magley & Shupe, 2005).

Explanations

Why does sexual harassment in the workplace occur? According to **sex-role spillover theory** (Burn, 2011), *in occupations with few women, men's traditional gender roles spill over into the workplace and influence their interactions with female workers.* The high incidence of sexual harassment among blue-collar workers supports this theory and points to the importance of an employment context in which male-related physical attributes are very prominent (Crawley, 2011; Denmark et al., 2008). In this type of situation, harassment reflects a restrictive construction of gender that results in viewing women not as competent workers but as targets of male–female interactions.

The **power theory** of sexual harassment states that *sexual harassment is an abuse of power to gain sexual favors or to reinforce men's sense of power and privilege in the workplace.* Men generally have more power in the workplace, and some men abuse this power for sexual ends (Burn, 2011; Lockwood et al., 2011). Consistent with this theory, power increases the erroneous perception that one's subordinates have a sexual interest in the powerful person (Kunstman & Maner, 2011). The male-dominated blue-collar occupations, where sexual harassment is most frequent, provide a good example of power theory. Men in these occupations hold most of the power for several reasons. First, men historically view the blue-collar workplace as their own territory. Second, they are in the majority. Third, they view the few women who enter these occupations as being on probation. Fourth, the generally male supervisors support male workers' power. Fifth, men's overall greater physical strength is an important attribute for most blue-collar jobs. Sixth, men have higher status in society in general (Bergmann, 2011; Crawley, 2011).

These factors not only maintain a power imbalance in which men are more likely to harass but also contribute to an **organizational tolerance** in which *the negative effects of sexual harassment tend to be minimized and complaints about harassment are not taken seriously* (Burn, 2011).

Women's Responses

> *After we, a mostly female staff, facilitated the removal of our harassing principal, we had a long group lunch together. We all shared our personal experiences with that man. The shocking thing was that most of the staff had been targeted at one time or another over an 18-year period, and that each of us thought we were the only one and that it was our fault.*
>
> (Holly, a 50-year-old school teacher)

How do women respond to sexual harassment? Louise Fitzgerald and her colleagues (2001) classify responses to sexual harassment as either internally focused or externally focused. **Internally focused responses** are *responses that attempt to manage the emotions and cognitions associated with the incident(s).* Examples include ignoring the situation, minimizing the event, or blaming oneself. **Externally focused responses**, on the other hand, are *responses that attempt to solve the problem.* Examples are avoiding the harasser, asking him to stop, or seeking organizational assistance. Filing a complaint or lawsuit are rare responses (Beiner & O'Connor, 2007).

Most women who are sexually harassed do not confront the perpetrator or report the event, as in Holly's example at the beginning of this section. Why is this? For one thing, sexually harassed women frequently experience guilt, shame, and embarrassment as a result of their harassment (Beiner & O'Connor, 2007). They also desire to maintain harmony in the workplace (Yagil et al., 2006). In addition, they fear retaliation from the perpetrator (Solberg, 2010). These fears are often justified. Women who report their harassment often experience negative outcomes, such as lowered job evaluations, humiliation, and both physical and psychological health problems (Beiner & O'Connor, 2007; Cortina & Magley, 2003).

Latina women are more likely than White women to avoid or not report the harasser. This may stem from several elements in Hispanic culture, including respect for individuals of higher status, emphasis on harmonious in-group relations, and a greater adherence to traditional gender roles, which fosters more tolerance of sexual harassment and discourages women from discussing sexual topics (Cortina, 2004).

STALKING

Like sexual harassment, stalking is a crime of power and control.

What Is Stalking?

Stalking can be described as *unwanted and repeated actions toward an individual that induce fear or concern for safety* (Sigal, 2008). Stalking behaviors include attempts to contact the individual and/or place the person under surveillance (e.g., following the person, waiting outside or driving by the person's home or workplace). About one in four stalking victims report some form of cyberstalking via e-mail or instant messaging (Baum et al., 2009).

Perpetrators, Victims, and Effects

The overwhelming majority of stalkers are male, and the majority of their victims, about one million women a year, are female (Logan & Walker, 2009; Martin, 2008a). Up to one in four women, especially younger women, report being stalked, often by former partners (Jordan et al., 2010). The unpredictable nature of stalking, combined with fear of violence, can produce harmful psychological effects such as anxiety, depression, fear, and extreme stress (Baum et al., 2009; Logan & Walker, 2010; Spitzberg & Cupach, 2007). Some victims feel compelled to change jobs or schools, move to a new residence, or seek counseling. One in four victims considers suicide (Martin, 2008a).

VIOLENCE AGAINST GIRLS

> *Violence against women is a problem that encompasses physical and sexual abuse perpetrated against a woman or female child by persons known or unknown to her . . . At least one woman in three globally is beaten, coerced into sex, or otherwise abused in her lifetime. . . . Because women represent 85% of the victims of incidents of nonfatal intimate assaults that occur each year in the U.S. . . . violence is a women's health concern, a human rights issue, and a major public health problem.*

(Herrera et al., 2006, p. 458)

Tragically, both girls and women are victims of violence around the globe and often face multiple types of abuse (Alhabib et al., 2010; Chowdhary & Patel, 2010; Jordan et al., 2010). In this section, we focus on two forms of violence that are especially likely to be perpetrated against girls: child sexual abuse and infanticide or neglect.

Child Sexual Abuse

Sexual abuse of children is viewed by many as among the most heinous of crimes (Rathus et al., 2010). Although definitions vary, a typical definition of **child sexual abuse** *includes both contact and noncontact sexual experiences in which the victim is below the age of consent and the abuser is significantly older or in a position of power over the child* (Barnett et al., 2005; Briggs et al., 2011). Sexually suggestive language or exhibitionism are examples of noncontact experience, whereas contact abuse may range from kissing, fondling, and sexual touching to oral sex and vaginal or anal intercourse. The most recent development in child sexual abuse is exploitation through the Internet. Children may be propositioned online for sexual activity, may be exposed to various forms of sexually explicit material, or may experience online harassment (Barnett et al., 2005).

Incest, a form of child abuse, may be defined narrowly as *sexual contact between a child and a close relative or other family member.* Incest may be particularly devastating emotionally to a child. It involves a loss of trust in and deep sense of betrayal by the abuser and perhaps other family members—especially the mother—whom the child may perceive as failing to provide protection (Rathus et al., 2010).

The most frequently reported and publicized type of incest is between a daughter and her father or stepfather, but surveys indicate that brother–sister incest is at least twice as common. Sibling incest is highly underreported, perhaps because it is sometimes viewed as "sexual curiosity" rather than as sexual abuse (Monahan, 2010; Thompson, 2009).

INCIDENCE. The incidence of child sexual abuse is difficult to pinpoint precisely. In the United States, approximately 240,000 children annually are victims of *substantiated* sexual abuse (Barnett et al., 2005). Because many cases of abuse are never reported, this figure is unfortunately quite conservative (Bynum et al., 2010). It is estimated that one in four girls and one in six boys are abused during childhood (National Center for Victims of Crime, 2008). Asian American, Black, Latina,

Native American, and White women report similar rates of child sexual abuse (Elliott & Urquiza, 2006; White & Frabutt, 2006). Children with disabilities are more likely to be sexually and physically abused than able-bodied children (Chu et al., 2011; Hooper, 2010).

For both females and males, most sexual abuse is committed by a family member or a family friend, takes place at home, and occurs more than once. The large majority of cases involve a female victim and a male perpetrator (Hooper, 2010; Lalor & McElvaney, 2010; Peter, 2009), a blatant illustration of the power differential between females and males. In the recent scandal involving child sexual abuse by Catholic clergy, the focus has been on priests who abused boys (Bennhold et al., 2010). But in fact, it is far more common for priests to commit sexual acts with girls and women than with boys and men (Dillon, 2002; Flynn, 2008).

Few children tell anyone about being sexually abused. Girls are more likely than boys to confide in others about the experience, especially a friend or a parent, usually the mother (Hunter, 2009; London et al., 2007). Why do so few children talk about being sexually abused? For one thing, they are relatively powerless and may fear retaliation from the abuser. Second, the offender is often a trusted and beloved adult whom the youngster may be reluctant to accuse. In addition, the child may feel embarrassed, humiliated, and responsible for encouraging or allowing the abuse to occur (Freyd et al., 2005; Hooper, 2010). Claire knows this from personal experience. As she walked home from school one day at age 12, a nicely dressed man who introduced himself as a doctor began chatting with her about the possibility of baby-sitting for his two young sons. He became increasingly graphic about the details of bathing them. When they reached her apartment building, he began fondling her breasts ("My boys don't have anything like this") until she broke away and ran upstairs, flushed with shame and guilt. It was days before she was able to tell her best friend and weeks before she told her mother. Until writing this book, she had told no one else, and even decades after the incident, it was difficult for her to write these words.

CONSEQUENCES. Sexual abuse can result in devastating consequences for children, not only in the short term, but throughout their adult lives (Briere & Hodges, 2010; Cicchetti et al., 2010; Maniglio, 2009; K. Walsh et al., 2010). Girls are more likely than boys to be sexually abused and they are more adversely affected by it (Lalor & McElvaney, 2010; Olff et al., 2007; Whealin et al., 2007). Sexually abused children are more likely than other children to be depressed, anxious, or angry; have behavioral, sexual, and school problems; show aggression and bullying; feel ashamed; have low self-esteem; and show symptoms of post-traumatic stress disorder (PTSD) including fears, nightmares and sleep disturbances, and "flashbacks" of the traumatic event (Briggs et al., 2011; *Understanding and Coping*, 2010; White et al., 2011).

Adolescents who were sexually abused in childhood show earlier sexual activity, have more sex partners, and are more likely to engage in risky sexual behaviors and to become pregnant (Hendrick & Reddy, 2007; Lemieux & Byers, 2008; Priebe & Svedin, 2009; Wilson & Widom, 2008). They are also more likely than other teenagers to have eating disorders, be depressed, use drugs and alcohol, begin drug use at an early age, and try to injure themselves or commit suicide (Briere & Hodges, 2010; K. Walsh et al., 2010).

In adulthood, victims of child sexual abuse continue to be more anxious, depressed, and angry; have relationship and marital problems and impaired self-concept; feel isolated, stigmatized, and distrustful; have sexual and substance-abuse problems; have medical problems such as chronic pain, headaches, and neurological, musculoskeletal, and gastrointestinal problems; and show more suicidal and self-injurious behavior. They are also more likely to have experienced further sexual assault or physical abuse as adults (Briere & Hodges, 2010; Easton et al., 2011; Fargo, 2009; Fortier et al., 2009; T. D. Hill et al., 2010; Hillberg et al., 2011; Klonsky & Moyer, 2008; Paras et al., 2009;

Swaby & Morgan, 2009; Ullman et al., 2009; Wegman & Stetler, 2009). Childhood abuse is also associated with violent criminal behavior in adulthood. For example, up to 75 percent of incarcerated women have been sexually or physically abused as children (Herrera et al., 2006). The effects of sexual abuse are greatest when the abuser was someone close to the child; the abuse was frequent, severe, and continued over a long period of time; force was used; vaginal, oral, or anal penetration occurred; and little social support was available after disclosure of the abuse (Cutajar et al., 2010; O'Leary et al., 2010; Reyes, 2008; Ullman, 2007).

TREATMENT. Healing from childhood incest and other forms of sexual abuse is a long and arduous process. Group or individual psychotherapy helps adult survivors break their silence, gain perspective and realize they are not alone, and relinquish feelings of responsibility for the abuse (Harvey & Taylor, 2010; Hébert & Bergeron, 2007; Jepsen et al., 2009; Martsolf & Draucker, 2005; S. Warner, 2009). Ultimately, therapy can improve survivors' self-esteem and their ability to have intimate relationships.

Therapy programs for sexually abused children and adolescents are also available. A comprehensive approach is usually recommended. This may involve play therapy or art therapy for very young children; group therapy for adolescents; individual therapy for the child and each parent; marital therapy for the parents; and family therapy (Rathus et al., 2010). Cognitive behavioral therapy that specifically focuses on the abuse appears more effective than other treatments.

PREVENTION. Increasing numbers of schools are offering sexual-abuse prevention programs. According to one survey, about two-thirds of children in the United States have participated in such programs (Wurtele, 2009). In these programs, children are taught to distinguish between "good" touching (such as an affectionate pat on the back) and "bad" touching, to say "no," to leave risky situations, and to tell a trusted adult about "secrets" concerning touching (Eckenrode, 2011). Children who participate in comprehensive school-based programs are more likely to use effective strategies such as refusing, running away, or yelling when confronted by a potential abuser, and they are more apt to report incidents to adults (Gidycz et al., 2011; Rathus et al., 2010; Wurtele, 2009).

In addition, all 50 states have enacted laws designed to inform communities of the presence of known sex offenders who have been released from prison. These laws are collectively referred to as Megan's Law, after a 7-year-old girl who was raped and murdered in 1994 by a male neighbor who had recently completed a prison sentence for child sexual abuse (Smith & Li-Ching, 2011).

Infanticide and Neglect

Sadly, cultural attitudes that devalue females in many parts of the world lead to practices that have harmful and even deadly effects on female infants and girls. To learn more, see Explore Other Cultures 14.1 and 14.2. You also may wish to reread Explore Other Cultures 7.2 on female genital cutting.

EXPLORE OTHER CULTURES 14.1
Where Are the Missing Girls in Asia?

Women around the world normally give birth to about 105 boys for every 100 girls. But according to recent census figures, there are 120 boys born in China for every 100 girls (LaFraniere, 2009). In India, the ratio is 115 boys born for every 100 girls. In some areas, the sex ratio is even more skewed (Fontes & McCloskey, 2011). An estimated 100 million girls and women who should be alive in these two countries today are simply "missing" (Glenn, 2004; Kristof & WuDunn, 2009). In societies where the preference for sons is strong, such as China, India, and Pakistan, discrimination and abuse toward female children can take extreme forms such as infanticide, in which the newborn girl is suffocated, drowned, poisoned, or abandoned (Fontes & McCloskey, 2011; Guilmoto, 2009; Porter & Gavin, 2010). In addition, girls in India, Pakistan, and China are often victims of neglect, not fed as well, vaccinated as often, or taken to the doctor as quickly when ill (Murthy et al., 2010b; Sen, 2010; World Health Organization, 2010a). Poor families in China and India often view their daughters as a burden, leading them to abandon or sell their baby girls for a small fee (Burn, 2011). With the advent of ultrasound, abortion rates of female fetuses have soared in India, Korea, and rural China, even though elective-sex abortions are now illegal in these countries (Guilmoto, 2009; Xinran, 2011).

The extreme preference for sons in these countries stems from the tradition that sons, not daughters, care for aging parents, perform religious rituals, and carry on the family name and occupation (Burn, 2011; Henderson & Jeydel, 2010; Wheeler, 2011). In China, the pressure for sons is intensified by family planning laws that limit couples to one or two children (Jacobs, 2009; Xinran, 2011). In India, a girl is viewed as a burden who requires a costly dowry when she marries, leaving her parents in debt (Viswanathan, 2010). If her dowry is deemed insufficient, the husband's family may resort to "bride burning," a hideous form of domestic violence in which the woman is doused with kerosene and set on fire (Kristof & WuDunn, 2009).

What are the consequences of having a disproportionate number of males in the population? The surplus of unattached men has already triggered sex-related crimes such as rape, prostitution, abduction of women, and forced marriages in India and China (Shelley, 2010). Scholars fear that other violent crimes and social disorder also may occur (Fontes & McCloskey, 2011; LaFraniere, 2009).

EXPLORE OTHER CULTURES 14.2
Girls for Sale: The Horrors of Human Trafficking

Over 1 million women and girls worldwide are lured into leaving their homeland each year and forced into prostitution or menial work in other nations (van de Glind & Kooijmans, 2008). Many are duped with the promise of good jobs as nannies, models, or exotic dancers in wealthier countries, only to find themselves bound by contracts that immediately place them in enormous debt. Some are forced into unpaid and often inhumane servitude as domestics or child laborers (Blagbrough, 2008; Logan et al., 2009; McKenzie & Rozee, 2010; Murthy et al., 2010a). But most are forced to work as prostitutes, literally as sexual slaves, in order to pay off their debt (Burn, 2011). Countries that are poor, have high unemployment, and lack women's rights show the most **human trafficking**, defined as *the practice of buying and selling people for profit*. Heavy trafficking occurs in Asia, Africa, central and eastern Europe, Latin America, and the Middle East (van de Glind & Kooijmans,

2008; Henderson & Jeydel, 2010; Simkhada, 2008; United Nations Office on Drugs and Crime, 2009). Sex trafficking is not just a problem of poor countries, however. Primary destinations for trafficked individuals often are relatively prosperous nations, including those in western Europe and North America (Duquaine-Watson, 2011). The United States, for example, has become a major importer of sex slaves with an estimated 30,000 to 50,000 in captivity at any given time, many from Thailand, Malaysia, Mexico, Russia, and Ukraine (Murthy et al., 2010a; Pearce et al., 2011; Pérez, 2008). Sadly, the typical age of trafficking victims is dropping. It is not uncommon to find girls as young as 13—or even 8 or 9—caught in the tragic net of sexual slavery (Landesman, 2004; Shelley, 2010). One reason is that men who seek out prostitutes are looking for young girls in order to minimize their risk of exposure to HIV (Kristof & WuDunn, 2009; Murthy et al., 2010a).

DATING VIOLENCE

A darker and rarely mentioned side of dating relationships is physical aggression toward a dating partner. Dating violence cuts across socioeconomic boundaries and is occurring with alarming frequency.

Incidence

Studies show that up to 80 percent of adolescents report having had at least one experience of physical aggression in a dating relationship, ranging from being hit, shoved, and slapped to being punched, choked, threatened with a weapon, and forced to engage in sexual activity (Crooks et al., 2011; Eaton et al., 2010). Females typically engage in milder forms of aggression, such as hitting and slapping, whereas males engage in more serious acts of violence (Foshee et al., 2009; Sigal & Novitskie, 2010). Most studies, perhaps surprisingly, find that males are more likely than females to report being victims of dating aggression (Foshee et al., 2009; Jain et al., 2010; Olsen et al., 2010; Williams et al., 2008).

One possible explanation of these findings is that females underreport aggression and/or that males overreport it. Males might overreport their victimization in order to rationalize their own aggression (e.g., "She hits me, so I hit her back"). Another possibility is that females *are* actually more aggressive in their dating relationships, using violence as self-defense (Allen et al., 2009; Noonan & Charles, 2009; Teten et al., 2009).

Who Engages in Dating Violence?

Certain factors increase the likelihood of dating violence. One of the strongest predictors is being the recipient of dating violence (Crooks et al., 2011; Miller, 2011; Teten et al., 2009). This finding supports the self-defense explanation. Believing that dating violence is justifiable is another strong predictor for both females and males (Manganello, 2008). (Interestingly, both genders are more accepting of dating violence in females.) Holding traditional gender-role attitudes is also linked to dating violence for both sexes (Crooks et al., 2011; Flood & Pease, 2009; Vézina & Hébert, 2007; White & Frabutt, 2006). In addition, dating violence is more prevalent among individuals who were abused as children and who were exposed to family or community violence (Edwards et al., 2009; Miller et al., 2010; Olsen et al., 2010; Wolfe et al., 2009).

Female victims of dating violence are more likely than nonvictims to show risky sexual behavior, depression, low self-esteem, attempted suicide, disordered eating behavior, substance abuse, and binge drinking (Eaton et al., 2007; Maas et al., 2010; Olsen et al., 2010; Raiford et al., 2007; Yan et al., 2010). These findings suggest that teen dating violence can lead to a host of negative health consequences (Dingfelder, 2010). Other warning signals that a young couple's relationship may turn violent include possessiveness, controlling behavior, low relationship satisfaction, unpredictable mood swings, humiliating one's partner, and antisocial behavior (Bentley et al., 2007; Furman, 2002; Schnurr et al., 2010). Sadly, these factors continue to be involved in violent adult relationships, as we shall see later in the chapter. The fact that young women who experience dating violence in high school are at greater risk for sexual victimization during the college years and beyond highlights the need to implement programs early in the teen years to curtail such violence (Black et al., 2006; Vézina & Hébert, 2007). High school interventions such as the Safe Dates and Expect Respect programs reduce the incidence and severity of dating violence (Crooks et al., 2011; Teten et al., 2009).

RAPE

During spring break of my senior year in high school, I went to San Padre Island with my girlfriends. One night, we went to a bar and somehow got split up. I had no money and didn't know the way back. Some guys said they'd take a cab with me. They got off at their hotel and told me to come to their room while they called my friends. I was scared to go in but I did. One big guy started to force himself on me. I fought him off and he finally stopped. He didn't actually rape me but he violated my body and my trust. He walked me to my hotel acting like nothing had happened. I never told anyone what went on. I felt people would blame me for losing my friends at the bar and being stupid.

(Melinda, a 20-year-old college junior)

The definition of **rape** varies across states. However, a common legal definition is *sexual penetration of any bodily orifice against the victim's will, obtained by physical force, the threat of force, or while the victim is incapable of giving consent because of mental illness, mental disability, or intoxication* (Cook et al., 2011; Post et al., 2011). The term "sexual assault" is increasingly used to represent a broader spectrum of sexually violating acts, up to and including rape (Campbell & Townsend, 2011). The incident described earlier by Melinda fits the definition of an attempted rape. First, she clearly communicated her nonconsent and, second, the size differential between her and the perpetrator provided him with the physical force necessary to proceed against her will.

Incidence

In the United States, one out of six women has been a victim of rape or attempted rape. Nearly half of these victims are under 18 and four in five are under 30 (Ahrens et al., 2008; Hamby, 2008; Rape, Abuse & Incest National Network, 2009). Women with disabilities have an elevated risk of being sexually assaulted (Seidman & Pokorak, 2011). One of the difficulties in obtaining a "true" rate of rape is that the measurement of sexual victimization is not consistent. For example, studies have found that behaviorally specific questions (e.g., "Has anyone ever put his penis in your vagina by using force or threatening to harm you?") yield more rape disclosures than more broadly worded questions (Cook et al., 2011).

Few studies have included large numbers of people of color. Furthermore, methodological problems, such as ethnic differences in willingness to report rape, make ethnic comparisons difficult (Koss et al., 2011; Tillman et al., 2010). Given these limitations, the available evidence suggests that the rape rate is highest among Native Americans, followed by Blacks, Whites, Latinas, and Asian Americans, who have the lowest rate (Bryant-Davis et al., 2009; Hamby, 2008; Rape, Abuse & Incest National Network, 2009).

Acquaintance Rape

Often he would rape me while I was still sleeping in my bedroom. I would wake with him inside me. He wouldn't stop even after I asked him to.

(Peacock, 1998, p. 229)

Many people view "real rape" as being attacked violently by a stranger in a dark alley. But, in fact, about 9 out of 10 cases of rape are **acquaintance rape**, in which *the perpetrator and victim know each other* (Fisher et al., 2010; Seidman & Pokorak, 2011). Although marital rape has been illegal in the United States since 1993, an estimated 10–14 percent of women each year are raped by their husbands (Ferro et al., 2008). The reported frequency of such sexual aggression is highest in Black couples, followed by Latina/o and White couples (Ramisetty-Mikler et al., 2007).

Although a large proportion of women have had incidents consistent with the legal definition, most do not label their experience as rape, especially if they are raped by an acquaintance (Clements & Ogle, 2009; Cook et al., 2011; Fisher et al., 2010; Temkin & Krahé, 2008). Why is this? One view is that the woman blames herself for the experience, and also feels responsible for protecting her partner. She therefore reframes the situation as being not violent or abusive. In addition, many women (as well as men) are not aware of the broad range of behaviors that constitute rape. When the assault involves a boyfriend, if the act involves oral or manual sex, or if the woman is verbally rather than physically coerced, she is less likely to label the situation as rape (Clements & Ogle, 2009; Fisher et al., 2010; Peterson & Muehlenhard, 2011). Because this scenario deviates from the typical view of "real rape," women may downplay the experience, viewing it as miscommunication or seduction (Littleton et al., 2009).

Victims of rape are less likely to report incidents to the police than victims of other violent crimes. In addition, like Melinda in the vignette opening this section, women are even less likely to report acquaintance rape than rape committed by strangers (Chen & Ullman, 2010). Why is this? Few crimes elicit as much skepticism and victim-blaming as do allegations of rape (Belknap, 2010; Weiss, 2009). Fear of receiving negative responses from legal authorities and being labeled as promiscuous or a troublemaker may discourage sexual assault victims from reporting their experience. In addition, victims may blame themselves for getting into a dangerous situation or for not communicating their intentions more clearly (Ahrens et al., 2008; Donatelle, 2012).

Factors Associated With Acquaintance Rape

What accounts for the high incidence of acquaintance rape?

SEXUAL SCRIPT.   A number of psychologists (e.g., Wiederman, 2005) contend that the social construction of the roles of men and women in male–female sexual situations provides a social context in which acquaintance rape can occur. This traditional **sexual script** is *a socialized set of expected behaviors characterized by an aggressive male who initiates and pushes for sexual activity and a gatekeeping female who sets the limits*. Interpreting roles in this sexual script can lead to rape for a number of reasons. First, some men take the initiator role to the extreme and engage in sexual aggression. Second, as discussed in Chapter 8, men frequently infer sexual interest when it is not intended (Farris et al., 2008; Lindgren et al., 2008), which can fuel their sexual aggressiveness (Bondurant & Donat, 1999). Third, the differing roles within the sexual script can set the framework for misunderstanding because the male assumes the female will attempt to limit sexual activity as part of her role (Humphreys, 2007; O'Byrne et al., 2008). If a woman does not resist a man's sexual advances, both women and men assume that she is agreeing to have sex (Anderson et al., 2004). But if she says "no," a man may misinterpret this response as token resistance that really means "yes," leading him to disregard her objections to sex (Clark & Carroll, 2008). Research indicates that, in fact, a large majority of women who say "no" really do mean "no" (Muehlenhard, 2011; Muehlenhard & Rodgers, 1998). Thus, all refusals should be taken seriously.

CHARACTERISTICS OF SEXUALLY AGGRESSIVE MEN.   Sexually aggressive men are more likely than nonaggressive men to have witnessed or experienced family violence, hold stereotypical attitudes about gender roles, feel hostility toward women, and be physically aggressive in other situations.

They are also more likely to believe in **rape myths** (Chapleau & Oswald, 2010; Flood & Pease, 2009; Suarez & Gadalla, 2010; Weiss, 2009; Zurbriggen, 2010). These are *false beliefs about rape that are widely held and that serve to justify male sexual aggression against women.* The four most prevalent rape myths are that forced sex by an intimate partner is not really rape; that women lead men on and therefore deserve to be raped; that women often make false accusations of rape; and that women secretly want to be forced and can prevent it if they really want to (Suarez & Gadalla, 2010).

As might be expected, men tend to endorse these myths more than women do (Earnshaw et al., 2011; Ferro et al., 2008; Flood & Pease, 2009; Newcombe et al., 2008; Suarez & Gadalla, 2010). Moreover, college men who participate in athletics or belong to fraternities are more likely to have rape-supportive attitudes than other college men (Earnshaw et al., 2011; Ferro et al., 2008; Flood & Pease, 2009; Newcombe et al., 2008; Suarez & Gadalla, 2010). Among both women and men, rape myth acceptance is associated with greater sexism, racism, homophobia, ageism, classism, and religious intolerance (Flood & Pease, 2009; Suarez & Gadalla, 2010). To get firsthand knowledge about rape myth acceptance, try Get Involved 14.2. Then, to learn more about attitudes toward rape victims in other cultures, read Explore Other Cultures 14.3.

CHARACTERISTICS OF VICTIMS.   Any woman can be sexually assaulted, but some are especially vulnerable, such as adolescents and young women, those with disabilities, Black and Native American women, poor and homeless women, and those living in war zones (Abbey et al., 2010; Goodley, 2011; Jordan et al., 2010; Patwell, 2010). Moreover, as we saw earlier in this chapter, women who

---

GET INVOLVED 14.2
Gender and Rape Myths

Ask two female and two male acquaintances to indicate their degree of agreement with each of the following four statements about rape, from *strongly disagree* (1) to *strongly agree* (7). If possible, select participants from different ethnic groups.

_____**1.** Women often provoke rape.
_____**2.** Women enjoy rape.
_____**3.** Women frequently falsely claim that they have been raped.
_____**4.** Only men who are psychologically disturbed engage in rape.

WHAT DOES IT MEAN?

Sum the four ratings for each respondent. The scores can range from 4 to 28, with higher scores reflecting greater acceptance of rape myths. After scoring each person's answers, average the scores of the two females and those of the two males.

1. Did your male respondents express greater acceptance of rape myths than your female respondents did? If yes, explain. If no, indicate possible reasons why your respondents did not reflect the typically found gender difference.

2. If you tested men of different ethnicities, did you note any difference in their scores?

If yes, is this difference consistent with that presented in the text? Was there a difference between women respondents of different ethnicities?

3. Which of these four statements received the greatest degree of agreement from your respondents and which received the least agreement? Give possible reasons for these findings.

4. What do you think influences the development of these rape myths?

5. How do you think rape myth acceptance can be reduced?

EXPLORE OTHER CULTURES 14.3
Attitudes Toward Rape Victims Around the World

How are rape victims viewed in cultures outside the United States? Madhabika Nayak and her colleagues (2003) and researchers led by Colleen Ward (cited in Best, 2001) examined cross-cultural attitudes toward rape victims by interviewing university students from 17 countries. Relatively favorable attitudes were found in the United Kingdom, the United States, Germany, and New Zealand, whereas less favorable views were expressed in Turkey, Mexico, Zimbabwe, India, Japan, Kuwait, and Malaysia. Having read Chapters 2 and 3 about cross-cultural differences in gender-role attitudes, can you see a recurring pattern in these findings regarding attitudes toward rape victims? In those countries with more egalitarian views of women, attitudes toward rape victims are more positive, whereas rape victims are more likely to be stigmatized in countries where women's status is much lower than that of men. Some cultures have social and legal customs that sanction severe punishment of women in response to infractions of family "honor" (Henderson & Jeydel, 2010; Murthy et al., 2010b). For example, victims of rape may be subjected to severe punishments, including imprisonment, public flogging, and being stoned to death (Worth, 2010). Little distinction is made between forced and consensual sex. Men are rarely convicted in rape cases, but girls and women who report a rape are often charged with adultery, which is considered a crime more serious than murder (Burn, 2011). Each year, hundreds of girls or women die of "honor killings," often by male members of their own families, for perceived breaches of chastity (Calarco, 2011; Henderson & Jeydel, 2010; Murthy et al., 2010b). In Turkey, a girl who has allegedly dishonored the family may be pressured to commit suicide, in order to spare her family from having to murder her (Thacker, 2011).

are raped are more likely than nonvictimized women to have been sexually abused in childhood and/or adolescence (Anderson, 2010; T. D. Hill et al., 2010), possibly because early victimization can contribute to feelings of self-blame and powerlessness. Victims of intimate partner violence are also more likely than other women to suffer forced sexual activity.

ALCOHOL CONSUMPTION. There is considerable evidence that alcohol consumption by the perpetrator and the victim increases the risk of rape or attempted rape (Abbey et al., 2010; Jordan et al., 2010; McKenzie & Rozee, 2010; Ross et al., 2011; Ullman & Najdowski, 2011). In part, this is because alcohol impairs the perpetrator's judgment and lowers the victim's resistance. Furthermore, when men drink, they may be more likely to misperceive women's drinking as a sign of sexual interest (McKenzie & Rozee, 2010; Ullman & Najdowski, 2011).

Effects of Rape

The psychological impact of rape can be profound. Whether they are victims of acquaintance rape or stranger rape, survivors may be plagued by anxiety, self-blame, shame, humiliation, powerlessness, depression, and suicidal thoughts (Campbell et al., 2009; Diamond & Savin-Williams, 2009; Jordan et al., 2010; Weiss, 2009). Some symptoms, such as self-blame and powerlessness, may be more common among acquaintance victims. As shown in one college student's emotional reaction to rape by her resident advisor, "I wouldn't even admit it to myself until about 4 months later when the guilt and fear that had been eating at me became too much to hide and I came very close to a complete nervous breakdown. I tried to kill myself, but fortunately I chickened out at the last minute" (Warshaw, 1988, pp. 67–68). Women with a prior history of emotional and behavioral problems have greater difficulty than other women in recovering from rape (Campbell et al., 2009).

In addition, women who blame themselves for being sexually assaulted show poor recovery (Martin et al., 2011). Women who are victims of multiple sexual assaults also have more severe physical and emotional consequences than women who experience a single rape (Lundberg-Love & Waits, 2010).

Some rape survivors also develop physical health problems, such as chronic headaches, pain, fatigue, and sleep disturbances (Martin et al., 2011). Some may experience sexual problems, including diminished sexual activity, interest, and enjoyment (Ahrens et al., 2008; Alexander et al., 2010). Some rape survivors show increases in risky sexual behavior (Martin et al., 2011). Others abuse drugs and alcohol or attempt suicide (Campbell et al., 2009). Often, rape survivors undergo a "second rape," which refers to further victimization at the hands of insensitive medical, legal, and mental health personnel (Campbell & Patterson, 2011; Luce et al., 2010; Tillman et al., 2010). Placing unnecessary blame on rape survivors adds to the trauma of the original sexual assault and may hamper recovery.

Despite the many negative effects of rape, many survivors report positive life changes following sexual assault that help them cope with the event. For a closer look, see Learn About the Research 14.1.

Rape Prevention

Many rape education programs exist, most of them focusing on changing attitudes such as rape myths or increasing women's self-protection (Ahrens et al., 2008; Gidycz et al., 2011). Although education can help women learn how to communicate better with male partners or how to avoid

---

LEARN ABOUT THE RESEARCH 14.1
Positive Life Changes Following Sexual Assault

In the aftermath of traumatic events, some individuals may experience positive as well as negative life changes as a result of trying to come to terms with these events (Campbell et al., 2009; Martin et al., 2011; Vishnevsky et al., 2010; Wadsworth, 2010). Patricia Frazier and her colleagues (2005, 2006) did a longitudinal study of 171 women who experienced sexual assault, in order to assess factors that best predicted positive life changes during the women's recovery process. Positive life change was measured by asking participants to rate the extent to which specific aspects of their lives had changed since the assault. Items dealt with one's self (e.g., "My ability to take care of myself"); relationships (e.g., "My relationships with family"); life philosophy or spirituality (e.g., "My sense of purpose in life"); and empathy (e.g., "My concern for others

in my similar situation"). Participants rated each item on a 5-point scale ranging from "much worse now" to "much better now." The participants, who were between 16 and 52 years old (mean age, 27), filled out questionnaires at two weeks, two months, six months, and one year after the assault.

One factor that strongly related to positive change was social support, which, as we have seen, is related to good mental health. A second factor related to positive change, called "approach coping," involved viewing the stressful event differently and expressing emotions about it (as opposed to avoiding people and acting as if nothing had happened). In addition, those who showed positive life changes relied on their religious faith to cope, and perceived that they had control over their recovery process.

WHAT DOES IT MEAN?

1. Based on these results, what suggestions could you offer to a friend of yours who had just experienced sexual assault?

2. Do you think that these results would be similar for men who are survivors of sexual assault? Explain your answer.

high-risk situations, it is basically men's behaviors that must be changed if rape is to be prevented (Ahrens et al., 2008; Filipovic, 2008). Because attitudes supportive of rape and the sexual script are learned at a young age, rape education programs should begin early (Gidycz et al., 2011).

In addition to rape education, institutions must develop effective procedures for dealing with complaints. Women who report a rape must be assured that their claims will be fairly investigated and that if guilt is determined, the perpetrators will receive appropriate sanctions (Donatelle, 2012; Fisher et al., 2010).

Theories of Rape

How can rape be explained? Our examination focuses on three theories that posit different mechanisms to account for rape.

EVOLUTIONARY THEORY.   Evolutionary theory applies the principles of natural selection and its goal of reproductive survival to understand social behavior, including rape. According to this theory, rape evolved because it was a strategy males could use to ensure their genes would be passed on to future generations. From an evolutionary view, it is to males' reproductive advantage to mate often and with numerous partners. To support this view, evolutionary theorists note that forced copulations have been observed in a variety of animal species and that females of childbearing age are the most likely rape victims (Thornhill & Palmer, 2000).

Critics, however, contend that it is not appropriate to draw conclusions about rape by observing nonhuman species because human behavior is more complexly determined (Butler, 2008; Koss, 2003; Travis, 2003). Others question the theory's view that frequent copulation with multiple partners is reproductively effective for men. Natalie Angier (1999) argues that a continuous relationship with one woman might be as reproductively successful as promiscuous mating. Joan Roughgarden (2009) also notes that although the majority of rape victims are young women of childbearing age, one-third of all rapes are of females too young or old to reproduce. Furthermore, the fact that some men rape wives and partners with whom they also have had consensual sex and that most men do not rape are not consistent with this assumption that the purpose of rape is reproduction (de Waal, 2002). Finally, evolutionary theorists ignore instances of rape that are inconsistent with the theory, such as homosexual rape or rape in the context of war (Ahrens et al., 2008; Roughgarden, 2009).

FEMINIST THEORY.   A different perspective is offered by **feminist theory**, *which contends that rape is rooted in the longstanding and pervasive power imbalance between women and men* (Bent-Goodley et al., 2011). Men have greater legal, economic, and political power, which provides them with more power in interpersonal situations. Men use rape as one mechanism to control women and maintain their dominance.

Support for feminist theory at the societal level is provided by evidence that urban areas with greater gender equality in economic, legal, and political power have lower rape rates than do urban areas with less gender equality (Ullman & Najdowski, 2011). Moreover, a man's endorsement of male dominance and restricted rights for women is strongly connected to his acceptance of rape myths (Ahrens et al., 2008).

SOCIAL LEARNING THEORY.   Social learning theory provides a third perspective to the phenomenon of rape. As discussed in Chapter 3, this theory *contends that social behaviors are learned through observation and reinforcement. This includes learning both attitudes supportive of rape and sexually aggressive behaviors* (Sigal & Novitskie, 2010). The theory assumes, for example, that men can develop attitudes supportive of rape or sexually aggressive behaviors via media depictions of sexuality and violence. The theory further holds that men's sexual aggressiveness can be reinforced by the widespread acceptance of rape myths, which blame the victim and excuse the perpetrator, and by the traditional sexual script, which encourages males to be aggressive in sexual situations.

Both of these assumptions have received some support from research. Consistent with the hypothesized influence of observational learning, for example, studies have shown that experience with pornography is related to greater sexual aggressiveness (Knight & Sims-Knight, 2011). However, this relationship could reflect either an effect of pornography on sexual aggressiveness or the possibility that sexually aggressive men choose to view violent pornography. In support of the importance of reinforcement, men who more strongly accept rape myths tend to be more sexually aggressive (Suarez & Gadalla, 2010).

INTIMATE PARTNER VIOLENCE

> *I have had glasses thrown at me. I have been kicked in the abdomen, kicked off the bed, and hit while lying on the floor—while I was pregnant. I have been whipped, kicked, and thrown, picked up and thrown down again.* (Boston Women's Health Book Collective, 1998, p. 162)

> *I was pretty much in a cage . . . He didn't let me use the phone . . . didn't let me go out . . . took away all of my freedom.* (Zink & Sill, 2004, p. 33)

Intimate partner violence refers to *physical and psychological abuse committed by an intimate partner, that is, a spouse, romantic partner, or a former spouse/partner* (Campbell et al., 2011; DeKeseredy & Schwartz, 2011). It is a major social and public health problem with significant costs to women across all cultures, ethnicities, income levels, and sexual orientations (Basile & Black, 2011). Intimate partner violence ranges from the relatively mild **common couple violence**, which consist of *minor acts of aggression such as pushing, slapping, and shoving,* to **intimate terrorism**, *the systematic use of violence, threats, and isolation to dominate and control a partner* (Basile & Black, 2011). As with dating violence, women are somewhat more likely than men to engage in common couple violence, often in self-defense (DeKeseredy & Schwartz, 2011; Frieze & Chen, 2010; Tolman & Edleson, 2011). The vast majority of acts of intimate terrorism, illustrated by the opening vignette of this section, are perpetuated by men (Ansara & Hindin, 2010; Diamond et al., 2010; Reed et al., 2010). Psychological abuse, illustrated in the second vignette, includes overt attempts to dominate, isolate, control, and undermine self-esteem (Frieze & Chen, 2010). Psychological abuse may have as great an effect on women's physical and mental health as does physical violence because it involves emotional humiliation and the destruction of one's identity (Follingstad, 2009; Hill et al., 2009).

Incidence

Like rape, intimate partner violence is an underreported crime, but it is estimated that at least 6 to 25 percent of women are assaulted by their male partners in the United States each year (Burn, 2011). Men's attacks on women result in 2 million injuries and 1,200 deaths each year (Basile & Black, 2011). Between 30 and 50 percent of all murders of American women are committed by intimate partners compared to only 4 percent of men's murders (Aldarondo & Castro-Fernandez, 2011; Rothman et al., 2005). In one study, about half of women seeking health care at emergency departments or primary care clinics reported having experienced physical and/or emotional abuse at some point in their lives. One in four reported severe physical or sexual abuse. Only one-quarter of the women had ever been asked about abuse by a health care provider. Most, however, said they would reveal abuse if asked in a nonhurried, concerned manner (Kramer et al., 2004). Sadly, many doctors say that they don't ask such questions because of a lack of time, training, and easy access to services that help these patients (Marcus, 2008; Mitchell & Anglin, 2008).

Violence in lesbian and gay relationships occurs about as often as in heterosexual couples (Blosnich & Bossarte, 2009; Frieze & Chen, 2010). Similar to violence in heterosexual relationships, this abuse can be both physical and emotional (Diamond et al., 2010).

Role of Disability, Social Class, and Ethnicity

Disability, poverty, and ethnicity are all factors in intimate partner violence, once again demonstrating the influence of intersectionality (Burn, 2011). Women with disabilities experience abuse at a higher rate than able-bodied women, and their abusive relationships continue for a longer period of time (Curry et al., 2009; de Alwis, 2008; Fryers, 2010; Goodley, 2011; Hague et al., 2011). They are also abused by a greater number of people, including health care providers or attendants, in addition to partners or family members (Alexander et al., 2010; Campbell et al., 2011). Poorer women and those with less education report the highest rates of physical abuse (Bryant-Davis et al., 2009; Frieze & Chen, 2010; Goodman et al., 2009; Perilla et al., 2011; Taft et al., 2009; J. R. Williams et al., 2009). Black women are more likely than White women to be victims of domestic violence (U.S. Department of Health and Human Services, 2009), but they are more likely to fight back against sexual assault. In one study of poor, urban women (Fine & Weis, cited in Fine & Carney, 2001), abused Black women were more likely than abused White women to secure orders of protection, call the police, go to a shelter, throw the batterer out of the house, or report the incident to brothers and fathers who might confront the abuser.

The Asian American community has the lowest reported rates of intimate partner violence of any other ethnic group (Bryant-Davis et al., 2009), but this could be an underestimate of its actual occurrence. Asian Americans emphasize the family over the individual, the strong value placed on the male as the authority in the family, and the belief that family affairs must be kept private. These reasons may keep Asian American women from seeking assistance for their abuse (Ely, 2004).

Studies of domestic violence among Latinas/os in the United States have produced a mixed picture, although often their rates are comparable to those of Whites (Castañeda, 2008; Ellison et al., 2007). Methodological problems, such as lumping together all Latina/o subgroups and not considering the influence of acculturation into U.S. society, may be responsible for these inconsistencies.

Native American and Alaska Native women have the highest rate of intimate partner violence (Jordan et al., 2010). This may be related to both alcohol abuse and patriarchal beliefs introduced by the Westernization of native peoples (Evans-Campbell, 2008; Wahab & Olson, 2004). In addition, the forced removal from homes and disrupted family structures that resulted from European colonization may make native women particularly vulnerable to violence (Jordan et al., 2010).

Things are no better in other parts of the world, as you'll see in Explore Other Cultures 14.4.

Risk Factors

The need for power and control and the belief that men have the right to punish their female partners play an important role in men's intimate partner violence (Flood & Pease, 2009; Thapar-Björkert & Morgan, 2010). Alcohol and drug abuse by batterers in both heterosexual and same-sex relationships are also common (Campbell et al., 2011; Curry et al., 2009; Feingold et al., 2008; Li et al., 2010; Torpy, 2010b). Violent husbands are more likely than other husbands to display poor problem-solving and communication skills, high levels of anger and hostility, antisocial behavior, and low self-esteem. Occupational, economic, and marital stresses are also associated with intimate partner violence (Aldarondo & Castro-Fernandez, 2011; Anderson, 2010; Renzetti, 2011). Not surprisingly, male batterers and abused women are more likely than other men and women to

EXPLORE OTHER CULTURES 14.4
Intimate Partner Violence Around the World

Sadly, violence against women by their male partners occurs in all countries, (Burn, 2011; UNIFEM, 2010). Data from Australia, the United States, Canada, Israel, and South Africa, for example, show that 40 to 70 percent of female murder victims are killed by their partners (Burn, 2011; Kirk & Okazawa-Rey, 2009; "Violence Against Women," 2009). In addition, thousands of women each year are victims of dowry-related killings or are disfigured by acid thrown in their faces by rejected suitors in Bangladesh, Colombia, India, Nigeria, and Pakistan (Burn, 2011; Kirk & Okazawa-Rey, 2009). In sub-Saharan Africa and in the patriarchal societies of the Middle East and south Asia, both men and women often consider wife beating to be justified under certain circumstances, such as disobeying one's husband and neglecting one's children

(Dhaher et al., 2010; Kristof & WuDunn, 2009; Rani & Bonu, 2008). Furthermore, they blame women for the beating, believe that women benefit from the violence, and oppose assistance for battered women from governmental agencies (Btoush & Haj-Yahia, 2008).

To make matters worse, the criminal justice system may take crimes of violence against ethnic minority or immigrant women less seriously than those committed against majority women. For example, the longstanding ill treatment of the Roma (formerly called Gypsy) people in the Czech Republic and Croatia have made Roma women reluctant to report crimes of violence to the police. In some countries, the legal system downplays attacks on minority women, attributing them to the group's culture (UNIFEM, 2003).

have witnessed violence between their parents or experienced physical or sexual abuse in childhood (Djikanovic et al., 2010; Flood & Pease, 2009). This does not mean that all adults with a history of violence will be involved in an abusive relationship, or that all those involved in domestic violence have a history of family battering (Aldarondo & Castro-Fernandez, 2011). However, these findings do suggest that observing a parent commit violence gives boys the message that violence is a means for handling anger and conflict and influences the development of negative attitudes toward women. For women, the early experience of family violence can provide a similar message that aggression is a "normal" aspect of close relationships.

Effects of Intimate Partner Violence

The effects of abuse include a wide variety of long-term physical and psychological problems and reduced economic well-being (Strauss et al., 2010; UNIFEM, 2010). Health problems include physical injuries and reproductive difficulties. Abused women may also suffer psychological problems such as lower self-esteem, depression, anxiety, drug and alcohol abuse, sexual risk-taking behavior, eating disorders, PTSD, and suicide attempts (Chowdhary & Patel, 2010; Coker et al., 2011; Dutton, 2009; Jordan et al., 2010). Moreover, the health problems caused by physical and psychological abuse may keep women from obtaining or keeping employment, which can keep them financially dependent on the abuser (Coker et al., 2011; Martin et al., 2011). Children who observe parental violence also suffer psychological trauma (Cannon et al., 2010; Chan & Yeung, 2009; Graham-Bermann & Perkins, 2010), as illustrated by Susan's anguished comments at the beginning of the chapter.

Leaving the Abusive Relationship

Many people wonder why abused women don't leave their batterer. Two major barriers to leaving are financial dependence and fear of retaliation (Bell et al., 2009; Bostock et al., 2009; Kim & Gray, 2008; Lacey, 2010; Paludi, Wilmot et al., 2010). Abusers can interpret women's attempt to leave as a loss of control and their violence can accelerate. As one abused woman reported, "The very first time that I attempted to leave he tried to choke me with the sheets to the point where I turned blue" (Sorenson, 1996, p. 129). Many older women have stayed in abusive marriages because they were socialized to remain with their husbands regardless of circumstances (Zink et al., 2004). Women with disabilities may also be more likely than other women to stay in an abusive relationship, especially if their job or transportation opportunities are limited, or if their only alternative living arrangement is in an institution (Goodley, 2011; Olkin, 2008). Other women stay because cultural or religious beliefs forbid divorce (Donatelle, 2012). Immigrant women may be reluctant to inform authorities about domestic violence because of fear of deportation, discrimination, and anti-immigrant sentiment (Alexander et al., 2010; Frieze & Chen, 2010).

Theories of Intimate Partner Violence

Two theories presented as explanations of rape are also useful in understanding intimate partner violence. As discussed previously, feminist theory emphasizes gender power imbalance as a destructive factor in men's interactions with women. When applied to intimate partner violence, it contends that men use violence against women as a means to maintain their power and status (Sigal & Novitskie, 2010; White et al., 2011). Social learning theory posits that domestic violence is a learned behavior that can develop from observing violence within the family and from receiving reinforcement for aggressive acts (DeKeseredy & Schwartz, 2011).

Interventions

In the past 30 years, a body of laws and policies has developed nationally and globally concerning domestic violence. These include mandatory arrest of the abuser and orders of protection that prohibit the abuser from coming near or contacting the woman (Goodman & Epstein, 2011; Koss & White, 2008). The development of shelters, transitional housing programs, and other services for abused women have been other key interventions (Macy et al., 2010; Sullwan, 2011). Feminist therapy (discussed in Chapter 13) is a useful tool for helping to re-empower the battered woman. Programs also have been designed to treat the batterer either alone or with his partner. They deal with attitudes toward women and toward violence against women, as well as anger management (Bent-Goodley et al., 2011; Mitchell, 2009; Tolman & Edleson, 2011). Unfortunately, the effects of such programs in preventing further violence are modest (Bent-Goodley et al., 2011; Mitchell & Anglin, 2011).

ELDER ABUSE

> *A male caregiver of an elderly woman gains her trust and confidence and then steals from her.* (Nerenberg, 2008)

> *A woman withdraws large sums from her ailing great-aunt's bank account to pay for her own expenses, including cars, furniture, and jewelry.* (Edwards, 2007)

> *A crack-addicted man physically batters his elderly aunts if they do not give him money for his next fix. Eventually, they lose their savings and their home and are reduced to begging in the streets.* (Kleinfield, 2004)

Elder abuse refers to *physical, psychological, financial, and neglectful acts that harm the health or welfare of an older adult, and that occur within a relationship of trust* (Hildreth, 2009a; OWL, 2009) (see Table 14.1). Abuse of older people is a significant public health problem. An estimated 1 to 2 million older people in the United States experience moderate to severe abuse each year (Aciemo

TABLE 14.1   Types of Elder Abuse

Type of Abuse	Description
Physical and sexual abuse	Inflicting physical pain, sexually molesting, or confining the person against her or his will
Psychological abuse	Threatening, humiliating, insulting, and/or intimidating the person; forcing the person to do degrading things; treating the person like a child
Financial abuse	Destroying property or possessions, stealing the person's money, denying the person access to his or her money
Neglect	Depriving the person of items needed for daily living (food, warmth, shelter, glasses, dentures, money), inattention, isolation

Source: OWL (2009).

et al., 2010; Laumann et al., 2008; Hildreth, 2009a). Older Blacks have the highest rates of reported abuse. Latinos/as and Asian Americans are the least likely to report abuse, which may result in part from language barriers and from a reluctance to bring dishonor upon the family (Ruf, 2006). For a look at elder abuse in other countries, see Explore Other Cultures 14.5. Neglect and financial exploitation are the most commonly reported types of abuse (Bugental & Hehman, 2007). Sadly, a substantial number of older women have experienced more than one type of abuse (Fisher et al., 2011).

All states now have laws against elder mistreatment, with most mandating that abuse be reported. Yet studies estimate that only 1 in every 14 cases is reported (Amstadter et al., 2011; Dong et al., 2009; OWL, 2009). One obstacle is denial of the problem. In addition, older persons themselves may lack the opportunity or the physical and mental ability to report abuse. They often fear not being believed, reprisal, abandonment, and institutionalization. Also, victimized older people may wish to protect the abuser, who is most often a family member (Alexander et al., 2010; Brozowski & Hall, 2010; OWL, 2009).

EXPLORE OTHER CULTURES 14.5
A Global View of Elder Abuse

Unfortunately, elder abuse exists around the world (Dixon et al., 2010; Garre-Olmo et al., 2009). A recent cross-national study conducted in 11 European countries found a prevalence rate for elder abuse of 2 percent in Nordic countries, 10 percent in Germany, and 12 percent in Italy (Garre-Olmo et al., 2009). Recent interviews with older people in Argentina, Austria, Brazil, Canada, India, Kenya, Lebanon, and Sweden (World Health Organization, 2002) indicate that although forms of abuse vary across countries, the most common victims are the older poor, widows, and childless older women.

In Austria, India, Japan, Korea, Lebanon, and Taiwan, older women report that family conflict and jealousy lead to neglect and abuse by their daughters-in-law (Malley-Morrison, 2004; World Health Organization, 2002). In Kenya and Brazil, one serious form of abuse is the practice of abandoning older family members in hospitals, especially during times of drought, poor crop yields, or even holidays. A common theme across many cultures is a pervasive lack of respect for older people, whether in health, governmental, and commercial institutions or in personal interactions.

Who Is Abused and Who Abuses?

The typical victim of elder abuse is a woman over age 75, usually widowed or divorced. She often lives at home with adult caregivers but is isolated and fearful. Frequently, she is physically and/or mentally frail and may suffer from cognitive impairments (Aciemo et al., 2010; Amstadter et al., 2011; Karch & Nunn, 2011; OWL, 2009). Most elder abuse is committed by family members, including adult children and spouses. Paid household workers or caregivers may be abusive as well, as shown in the vignettes at the beginning of this section. The typical abuser is a middle-aged son of the victim, who may have mental, alcohol, or drug problems. Often, the abuser is the caregiver of the victim and may also be financially dependent upon the victim (Brozowski & Hall, 2010; Hildreth, 2009a; OWL, 2009; Williams et al., 2009).

The stress of providing care for an ill relative may contribute to the problem of elder abuse because the caregiver may be unprepared, unable, or unwilling to provide the necessary care (Alexander et al., 2010) and may express frustration by becoming abusive. However, one must be careful not to simply "blame the victim" for being abused. (Notice the parallel with inappropriately blaming a woman who has been raped.) The feminist perspective puts elder abuse in a larger social context. From this point of view, elder abuse is part of a spectrum of male violence against women (White & Frabutt, 2006) that reflects a social context in which men wield more power and dominance over women.

What Can Be Done?

Some of the options that are available to the younger abused woman—deciding to leave a relationship or going to a shelter—are impractical or virtually impossible for most abused older people. Awareness of the problem is the first step. One encouraging sign is that the United Nations now recognizes the need to eliminate violence against older people, especially women, around the world ("U.N. Offers," 2002). Education and training are essential to alert the general public and professional service providers to the prevalence of elder abuse and neglect (Gronda et al., 2010). Professionals must learn to recognize the symptoms of abuse, understand the victim's denial, and strengthen the victim's resolve to end the abuse. The public should be encouraged to report any known or suspected case of abuse (Hildreth, 2009a). New laws have been passed in recent years governing the treatment of victims, which focus on the need for safety, assistance in accessing the courts, and information about the progress of the proceedings. Support groups for victims help validate the victims' experiences and provide a sense of empowerment that may enable them to change the power structure of the abusive relationship (Barnett et al., 2005; Edwards, 2007; Nerenberg, 2008).

What can you do? See What You Can Do 14.2 for ways in which you can work to combat violence against women.

WHAT YOU CAN DO 14.2
Working to Combat Violence

1. Become a volunteer at your local domestic violence center.
2. Get involved with a "Take Back the Night" demonstration held every April during Sexual Assault Awareness Month. The event usually features a nighttime walk followed by a rally with speakers. Contact your college or university women's center or local NOW chapter for more information.

Source: Burn (2011).

Summary

SEXUAL HARASSMENT AT SCHOOL

- Reports of sexual harassment are increasing among junior and senior high school students.
- Girls are more likely than boys to be sexually harassed by their schoolmates and they are more upset by it.
- Schools are now legally obligated to protect students from severe and pervasive harassment by other students.
- More female than male students experience sexual harassment on campus. Most incidents involve subtle forms of harassment, and most are perpetrated by other students.
- Ethnic and sexual minority students are more likely to experience harassment than are other students.

SEXUAL HARASSMENT IN THE WORKPLACE

- It is estimated that up to half of employed women will experience sexual harassment. Sexist remarks and jokes are common forms of harassment; sexual coercion is relatively rare.
- Women in blue-collar occupations and the military are more likely to be targets of harassment than other women.
- This might be due to the high prevalence of both the male gender stereotype and male-related physical traits in these fields.
- According to sex-role spillover theory, sexual harassment occurs because men respond to females in the workplace as women rather than as workers. Power theory states that harassment is used by more powerful individuals either to gain sexual favors or to reinforce their position of greater power.
- Most targets of sexual harassment use informal strategies for dealing with the harassment, such as ignoring it or asking the harasser to stop. They rarely file formal complaints or seek legal redress.
- Numerous negative outcomes can stem from sexual harassment.

STALKING

- Stalking refers to unwanted and repeated actions toward an individual that induces fear or concern for safety.
- Most stalkers are male and most victims are female.
- Stalking can produce harmful psychological effects.

VIOLENCE AGAINST GIRLS

- The incidence of child sexual abuse may run as high as one in four girls and one in six boys. Most abuse is committed by a relative or family friend (usually male).
- Sexual abuse can have a devastating impact on the physical and mental health of children, both immediately and in the long term.
- School-based sexual-abuse prevention programs may help children avoid and report abuse. Psychotherapy can help abused children and women heal.
- Countries with strong preferences for boys show elevated rates of abortion, infanticide, and neglect of female children.
- Many girls and young women around the world have been lured into sexual slavery.

DATING VIOLENCE

- Substantial numbers of teenagers experience violence in their dating relationships. More males than females report being victims of such violence.

RAPE

- An estimated one-quarter of women experience rape, much of it perpetrated by acquaintances.
- Physical aggressiveness, hostility toward women, gender-stereotypical attitudes, and a history of family violence differentiate sexually aggressive men from other men.
- Alcohol consumption increases the risk of sexual coercion and rape.

- Rape victims can experience a variety of emotional and health problems.
- Evolutionary, feminist, and social learning theories attempt to account for rape. Although some support for all three has been reported, there are many criticisms of evolutionary theory.

INTIMATE PARTNER VIOLENCE

- Up to one in four women in the United States are victims of intimate partner violence each year.
- Intimate partner violence occurs in sexual minority and heterosexual relationships and across ethnic groups, although it is more frequent among Blacks than Whites.
- Major risk factors for both perpetrators and victims of intimate partner violence are a history of family violence and alcohol and drug abuse.
- Numerous physical and psychological problems can result from victimization, including physical injuries, reproductive difficulties, lower self-esteem, anxiety, and depression.
- Financial problems and fear of the perpetrator are the primary reasons for remaining in an abusive relationship.
- Feminist and social learning theories help explain intimate partner violence.

ELDER ABUSE

- Elder abuse can have physical, psychological, financial, and neglect dimensions. Between 1 and 2 million older adults in the United States are affected, but few cases are reported.
- The typical victim is a woman age 75 or older, who lives with a caregiver. The typical abuser is a middle-aged son who has mental, alcohol, or drug problems.
- The following are essential in order to combat elder abuse: educating professionals and the public; reporting abuse cases; passing victims' rights laws; and forming support groups.

Key Terms

sexual harassment in an educational setting *332*
sexual harassment in the workplace *335*
quid pro quo harassment *335*
hostile environment *335*
sexual coercion *336*
gender harassment *336*
unwanted sexual attention *336*
sex-role spillover theory *338*

power theory *338*
organizational tolerance *339*
internally focused responses *339*
externally focused responses *339*
stalking *339*
child sexual abuse *340*
incest *340*
human trafficking *343*
rape *345*
acquaintance rape *345*

sexual script *346*
rape myths *347*
evolutionary theory *350*
feminist theory *350*
social learning theory *350*
intimate partner violence *351*
common couple violence *351*
intimate terrorism *351*
elder abuse *354*

What Do You Think?

1. Some people have criticized the recent U.S. Supreme Court ruling that obligates schools to protect students from severe and pervasive sexual harassment by other students. Some argue that sexual taunting and even touching are normal rites of adolescence. Others contend that even such apparently innocent gestures as the exchange of Valentine's Day cards by first graders will now be classified as sexual harassment and thus forbidden. What is your position on this issue, and why?

2. Which of the recommended procedures for reducing sexual harassment on campus do you think would be particularly effective at your school? Can you think of other activities that might be beneficial on your campus?

3. Why are family members often the perpetrators of child sexual abuse? What actions can be taken to prevent such behaviors?

4. Using either the feminist or social learning theory as a framework, discuss societal changes that might lead to a reduction in both rape and intimate partner violence.

5. How can public awareness of elder abuse be increased?

If You Want to Learn More

Brownridge, D. A. (2009). *Violence against women: Vulnerable populations.* New York: Routledge.

Fisher, B. S., Daigle, L. E., & Cullen, F. T. (2010). *Unsafe in the ivory tower: The sexual victimization of college women.* Thousand Oaks, CA: Sage.

Greene, J. A. (2006). *Blue-collar women at work with men: Negotiating the hostile environment.* Westport, CT: Praeger.

Hattery, A. J. (2009). *Intimate partner violence.* Plymouth, UK: Rowman & Littlefield.

Horvath, M., & Brown, J. (Eds.). (2011). *Rape: Challenging contemporary thinking.* Devon, UK: Willan Publishing.

Howard, L. J. (2007). *The sexual harassment handbook.* Franklin Lakes, NJ: Career Press.

Johnson, H., Ollus, N., & Nevala, S. (2010). *Violence against women: An international perspective.* New York: Springer.

Kearl, H. (2010). *Stop street harassment: Making public places safe and welcoming for women.* Santa Barbara, CA: Praeger.

Meyer, E. J. (2009). *Gender bullying and harassment: Strategies to end sexism and homophobia in schools.* New York: Teachers College Press.

Mullen, P. E., Pathé, M., & Purcell, R. (2008). *Stalkers and their victims.* Cambridge, UK: Cambridge University Press.

Potter, H. (2008). *Battle cries: Black women and intimate partner abuse.* New York: New York University Press.

Renzetti, C. M., Edleson, J. L., & Bergen, R. K. (2011). *Sourcebook on violence against women* (2nd ed.). Thousand Oaks, CA: Sage.

Sandler, B. R., & Stonehill, H. (2005). *Student-to-student sexual harassment K-12: Strategies and solutions for educators to use in the classroom.* Lanham, MD: Rowman & Littlefield.

Shelley, L. (2010). *Human trafficking: A global perspective.* Cambridge, UK: Cambridge University Press.

Warner, S. (2009). *Women and child sexual abuse: Theory, research, and practice.* New York: Psychology Press.

Weisz, A. N., & Black, B. (2009). *Programs to reduce teen dating violence and sexual assault.* New York: Columbia University Press.

Websites

Education
American Association of University Women
http://www.aauw.org

Sexual Harassment
Feminist Majority Foundation: Sexual Harassment Hotline Resource List
http://www.feminist.org/911/harass.html

Violence Against Girls
Abuse/Incest Support
http://www.siawso.org/

Rape
National Clearinghouse on Marital and Date Rape
http://www.ncmdr.org/

Intimate Partner Violence
American Bar Association Commission on Domestic Violence
http://www.americanbar.org/groups/domestic_violence.html
National Center for Injury Prevention and Control
http://www.cdc.gov/ncipc
Family Violence Prevention Fund
http://endabuse.org
Same-Sex Domestic Violence
http://www.rainbowdomesticviolence.itgo.com/
State Reporting Requirements
http://endabuse.org/statereport/list.php3
Stop Abuse for Everyone (SAFE)
http://www.safe4all.org
U.S. Department of Justice
http://www.ovw.usdoj.gov/

Elder Abuse
National Center on Elder Abuse (NECA)
http://www.ncea.aoa.gov/ncearoot/Main_Site/index.aspx

CHAPTER 15

A Feminist Future
Goals, Actions, and Attitudes

Feminist Goals
  Goal One: Gender Equality
    in Organizational Power
  Goal Two: Gender
    Equality in Relationship
    Power
  Goal Three: Gender
    Equality in Power for All
    Groups of Women
  Goal Four: Greater
    Flexibility in the Social
    Construction of Gender
**Actions to Achieve These
Goals**
  Research and Teaching
  Socialization of Children
  Institutional Procedures
  Individual Actions
  Collective Action
Feminist Beliefs
  Feminist Identification
  Emergence of Feminist
    Beliefs
  Men and Feminism
Postscript

It has become customary for the three of us [friends taking Claire's Psychology of Women course] to discuss women's issues at a local coffee shop on Tuesday evenings, not just among ourselves, but our friends as well . . . I have never taken a class that has caused me to engage in so much conversation outside of the classroom. The biggest success of your class is that regardless of how people feel about a certain issue, your class is causing people to talk and more people are becoming aware of issues that wouldn't be discussed otherwise . . . I feel that my eyes have been opened to a world of issues that have always been right in front of me. (Julie, a 22-year-old senior)

We saw in Chapter 1 that science is not value free, and as the experience of Julie and her friends illustrates, neither is teaching. "The process of education is political" (Wyche & Crosby, 1996, p. 5); that is, both subject matter and teaching methods are influenced by the value system of the instructor and the academic community. Applying this to the field of psychology, Kimberly Kinsler and Sue Rosenberg Zalk (1996) contend that "the greatest value of psychology lies in the field's ability to reveal the psychological processes perpetuating social injustices and to correct the social systems that have an unjust impact on the quality of people's lives" (p. 35). Given this political dimension of teaching, we end this textbook with a look at feminist goals for the future.

In Chapter 1, we presented three feminist themes that have recurred throughout this book: the intersectionality and diversity of women's lives and experiences, gender differences in power, and the social construction of gender. In this chapter, we return to these themes and translate them into goals for the future, consider actions for achieving these aims, and, because these goals have their roots in feminist thought, explore the prevalence of feminist beliefs among North American women.

FEMINIST GOALS

Based on the themes in this book, we have chosen four feminist goals for the future. Do you have others that you would add?

Goal One: Gender Equality in Organizational Power

Despite legislation that prohibits gender discrimination in employment (Title VII of the Civil Rights Act of 1964) and educational programs (Title IX, 1972), gender differences in organizational and interpersonal power continue to limit women's advancement in the workplace. Antidiscrimination legislation alone cannot change attitudes, and discriminatory policies are hard to monitor. Therefore, as has been noted throughout this text, men, especially White men, continue to have greater access to economic and political resources than women do (Kahn & Ferguson, 2010). They continue to greatly outnumber women at high levels of management and in political office and own most of the wealth (Chapter 10).

To combat this inequity, we choose as our first goal for the future greater equality of organizational power. A strong commitment from an organization's top management can help create a culture that promotes the advancement of young women (Costello & Wight, 2003). As more and more women attain levels of power currently held by men, gender equality will begin to affect other areas. Women's accessibility to important mentors and social networks will increase, providing even more promotion opportunities for women. And because job level is one factor determining salaries, women's wages will rise and become more similar to those of men. The close association between sexual harassment and the power imbalance also suggests that a greater power equality will mean less harassment of women.

Goal Two: Gender Equality in Relationship Power

In addition to greater organizational power, men continue to hold more interpersonal power relative to women. For instance, they tend to have more control over a couple's activities on dates and more influence in marriage (Chapter 8). A second goal, therefore, is greater equality in relationship power. Women would benefit by having a greater voice in dating decision making and a more balanced division of household labor. The latter, in turn, could reduce women's role overload and interrole conflict. Furthermore, because both rape and domestic violence are due, at least in part, to male dominance, shared interpersonal power would go a long way in reducing intimate violence against women.

Goal Three: Gender Equality in Power for All Groups of Women

Women are disadvantaged due not only to the gender inequality of power but also to differences within genders that add extra burdens to the lives of many women. White women are advantaged compared to women of color; middle-class women have more power than working-class or poor women; heterosexual women are privileged in comparison to lesbian, bisexual, and transgender women; able-bodied women are more advantaged than women with disabilities; and younger women have more power than their older counterparts. We have seen that ethnic minority women and women with disabilities experience even greater wage inequities than White and able-bodied women (Chapter 10). Furthermore, women of color and sexual minority women experience more job discrimination and sexual harassment than White and heterosexual women (Chapters 10 and 14). Thus, a third power goal is to ensure that increases in female power benefit all women, regardless of ethnicity, class, ableness, sexual orientation, or age.

Goal Four: Greater Flexibility in the Social Construction of Gender

We have noted throughout the text that gender is socially constructed and that most gender behaviors and roles—such as career choice (Chapter 9), friendship behaviors (Chapter 8), and contribution to household labor (Chapter 11)—are shaped by interpersonal, societal, and cultural expectations and are not constrained by biological sex. In examining some of the mechanisms that influence this construction of gender, we explored stereotypes that reflect societal gender expectations (Chapter 3), theoretical perspectives about the mechanisms whereby children learn the behaviors and roles expected for their gender (Chapter 3), and parental shaping of the behaviors and interests of girls and boys (Chapter 4). We saw that it is not the biological nature of females and males that serves as the major foundation for people's view of gender or their gender-related activities and preferences, but their conception of what it means to be a female or a male in society today.

Additionally, we have seen that the imbalance of power also guides the social construction of gender (Lorber, 2010). People with more power, who are in dominant positions, are likely to acquire and use different traits and behaviors than people in subordinate positions. Individuals in high-status positions are more likely to display independence, a male gender-related trait that is difficult to embrace if one lacks access to necessary resources in the home, workplace, or social environment. People lacking powerful resources, on the other hand, are more likely to rely instead on emotional connections between people and, consequently, to develop female gender-related traits, such as compassion. Thus, females' and males' development of gender-related traits, behaviors, and roles is constructed via stereotype-based expectations; socialization by parents, peers, and others; and hierarchical status within society.

Unfortunately, a rigid construction of gender is damaging to human potential (Lorber, 2010). It hinders development of individuals' unique talents and interests by guiding them in directions dictated by the social constructs of their biological sex. Judith recalls her days as a new bride when she refused to allow her husband to share the housecleaning, although both she and her husband were employed full time. Her insistence was based on her traditional conception of the "wife" role, a perception that was constructed from television and magazine images and from the roles of many married couples at that time (the 1960s). Her "wife role" behaviors were not based on her own interests, her time availability, or her husband's desires, but solely on her construction of this role from the societal images and social behaviors she observed around her.

A fourth goal for women, then, is greater flexibility in the construction of gender. Flexibility can lead to an expansion in career options, more flexible decisions about work and family dilemmas, greater sexual equality, and numerous other reductions in gender-constrained behaviors that limit choices made by both women and men. Flexibility of gender-related behaviors and roles also has the potential to reduce the prevalence of sexual harassment and acquaintance rape (Chapter 14), both of which are fostered, at least in part, by traditional constructions of the behaviors of men and women. Further, it can enhance communication within heterosexual couples by freeing each partner from constraints expected for her or his gender.

ACTIONS TO ACHIEVE THESE GOALS

Research and Teaching

Research and teaching about the psychology of women can play a significant role in achieving feminist goals for several reasons. First, greater knowledge of gender differences in interpersonal and societal power can help clarify the role that power imbalance plays in women's lives. Understanding the extent to which male power influences rape and battering (Chapter 14), serves as the basis for the division of household labor (Chapter 11), and contributes to wage inequities (Chapter 10) means that both female and male students will be aware of the prevalence of male power. A reduction in male privilege cannot occur until people recognize that it exists (Hidalgo, 2011; Kahn & Ferguson, 2010; LeSavoy, 2011). Exposure to this issue within the classroom can increase awareness that can spark the motivation and action necessary for change. The more we (psychologists and students) understand the dynamics and the effects of power differentials, the better armed we are to reduce privilege and its negative consequences for the less powerful.

Second, research and teaching about the psychology of women enlighten people about the way they construct gender in their lives. Scientific investigation gives people a better understanding of the influences on this construction and of the effects their personal images of gender have on their experiences as females or males. Similarly, exploration of these issues in the classroom has the potential to transform. As both women and men learn about the social basis for gender behaviors and roles, they might feel freer to experiment and to make choices that are less traditional but more personally appropriate (Paludi et al., 2008).

Third, research and teaching about the experiences of diverse women can dispel myths and stereotypes that distort individuals' understanding and reduce tolerance. These activities also foster greater understanding, appreciation, and celebration of people's similarities and differences and can empower all females, not only those in the most privileged group. Although recent years have brought a greater inclusion of underrepresented groups in both research and educational curricula to achieve these diversity goals, the field must continue to expand the diversity of its research participants. A more representative body of knowledge can ensure that researchers, instructors, and students do not generalize from one narrow group of females, carrying the implicit message that people in this group are "normal" and any discrepant behaviors, attitudes, or roles on the part of other individuals are "abnormal" (Allen, 2009; Crabtree et al., 2009; LeSavoy, 2011).

Consideration of diverse women's experiences must include a broader scope of topics as well. Research and teaching must address previously underexamined issues, such as employment obstacles for poor women, dating concerns of women with disabilities, experiences of lesbian mothers, outcomes of living in an extended family, and achievement goals of working-class and poor young women. A broader conceptualization of research and teaching topics not only facilitates understanding but can also inform policy interventions. For example, although company-supplied day care might ease the work–family burden of women in white-collar and professional jobs, free temporary child care might be a better resource for women in poverty who are seeking job training. Similarly, principles guiding custody decisions for divorced heterosexual women might not apply to divorced lesbian women. It is only through an examination of questions relevant to all types of women that societal interventions can best address the diversity of women's needs.

Although there is less information available about ethnic minority women, working-class and poor women, women with disabilities, sexual minority women, and older women, it is essential that psychologists incorporate the knowledge base that does exist into their teaching (Basow, 2010a; Lott, 2010; Unger, 2010). This diversity focus in their teaching will better prepare students to function in a culturally pluralistic and global society (Crabtree et al., 2009). Focusing on diversity also helps demonstrate to students how culture, marginalization, and privilege have formed their own experiences (Kahn & Ferguson, 2010).

Socialization of Children

Another approach to developing greater flexibility in gender construction is the feminist socialization of children. Parents can bring up their children so that preferences and skills, rather than gender, are the defining characteristics that guide development. How can this be achieved? Read Learn About the Research 15.1 to examine Phyllis Katz's perspective on this topic.

What would be the outcomes of gender-flexible upbringing? First, it would expand the range of activities, behaviors, and roles from which the child and, later, the adult could choose.

LEARN ABOUT THE RESEARCH 15.1
Why and How Should We Raise Feminist Children?

Phyllis Katz (1996) asks what it means to raise a feminist child. One answer is the elimination of all gender-related traits, behaviors, and roles, that is, raising children so that gender is irrelevant. Katz contends, however, that this would not be possible. Children are exposed to influences beyond the home. Consequently, even if parents were to treat their daughters and sons identically, these children would continue to be exposed to other people for whom gender would be important.

Instead, Katz advocates raising children to be gender flexible, that is, to select activities and behaviors on the basis of "individual likes and skills rather than being bogged down by gender stereotypes" (1996, pp. 333–334). She notes that be-cause much gender learning takes place during the preschool years, several actions by the parents can play an important role. One is role modeling. For example, maternal employment and nontraditional division of household labor by parents can help develop less stereotypic expectations and behaviors in children. Furthermore, the kinds of activities and goals encouraged by the parents can be instrumental. As examples, discouragement of gender stereotypic activities, toys, and future aspirations can be effective. Also, Katz notes that limiting the amount of television their children can watch might be beneficial because there is some evidence that children who watch less television have less stereotypic conceptions of gender.

WHAT DOES IT MEAN?

1. Do you think that the development of gender flexibility is a positive goal? Explain your answer.

2. Katz suggests it might not be possible to eliminate all gender-stereotypic influences on children. Do you agree or disagree? Explain your answer.

3. Regardless of your own opinion about gender flexibility, use the knowledge you have gained from this course to suggest other factors besides parental behaviors that might facilitate its development in children and adolescents.

_____

Source: Katz (1996).

Instead of assuming, for example, that men make dating decisions, pay for dates, and initiate sex (Chapter 8), whichever dating partner was more comfortable with these behaviors could select them. Furthermore, these might vary depending on the circumstances. This, in turn, could lead to more egalitarian relationships because decision making and instrumental behaviors would not be relegated specifically to men. Similarly, women and men would make occupational choices on the basis of skills, interests, and personal needs without consideration of the gender appropriateness of the field (Chapter 10), a process that might lead to greater occupational prestige and salaries for women and to greater job satisfaction for both genders.

Second, given the higher status of the male role in North American society, gender flexibility would lead boys to develop a greater understanding and respect for behaviors and roles traditionally associated with females. If boys observe their fathers and other influential adult men performing traditional female behaviors, such as washing the dishes and caring for young children, and if boys are required to perform these chores, they will be more apt to view the traditional female role as worthy and dignified. The far-reaching implications are, of course, that when these boys grow up to be men, the values instilled in them in childhood will influence their own involvement in traditional female activities and increase their respect for others who perform such activities. This greater respect could, in turn, carry over to the workplace, where more familiarity with family-related activities might encourage the initiation and support of additional family-friendly policies.

Third, gender flexibility would minimize the extent to which people view and evaluate others on the basis of a rigid construction of gender. For example, girls who play sports would receive the same degree of encouragement as sports-oriented boys (Chapter 4) and women in blue-collar trades would be accepted rather than harassed by their coworkers (Chapter 14). People would evaluate mothers who voluntarily stay home to care for their children or those who elect to work full time in the same way as they would evaluate fathers in these roles. They would have the same reaction to women and men who are fiercely independent and to those who are highly dependent. That is, if children were brought up with a feminist perspective of equality, their impressions of others would be influenced by their behaviors and roles rather than by the perceived suitability of those behaviors for individuals of one gender or the other, and the choice of roles, for everyone, would be limitless.

Institutional Procedures

Another route for attaining feminist goals is for institutions to initiate practices that reduce gender inequality and that create hospitable environments for both women and men. In Chapters 10 and 11, we examined organizational procedures that improve working conditions for women (e.g., pay equity, affirmative action) or that facilitate balancing of family and work (e.g., flextime, child care assistance programs). Institutional initiatives can enhance the quality of life for women in other ways as well. Raising public awareness of women's issues on a community-wide basis, with stakeholders including educators, religious organizations, media, and health care institutions among others, is critical (APA Task Force, 2007; Paludi et al., 2008; Rios et al., 2010). For example, Bonnie Fisher and her colleagues (2011) propose several college campus interventions that can lower the risk of sexual victimization and assist women who have experienced it.

First, Fisher and her associates emphasize the importance of education in changing the traditional culture of the campus. They suggest that the curriculum should include an examination and reconceptualization of gender roles, prevention of substance abuse, and exploration of rape myths. This type of curriculum would expose students to problems inherent in traditional gender-related behaviors and roles, would make them more sensitive to the experiences and pressures of the other gender, and would make them aware of the nature of and influences on violence against women.

Second, the researchers state that female students must be protected against sexual predators. This can include measures such as escort services, key cards at residence halls, call boxes, extra lighting, and self-defense training.

Third, Fisher and her colleagues address ways that counseling and health care services on campus can more effectively treat women who have been victimized. They stress the importance of campus policy and health care providers having adequate training in treating the physical and mental health problems that arise from sexual victimization. These campus personnel must be sensitive to victims' needs and be able to offer effective medical treatment as well as appropriate referrals for psychological counseling or legal assistance.

Individual Actions

Many women seek to achieve success and better their own lives through individual efforts. In fact, consistent with a traditional North American value system that applauds individualism, many American women place greater emphasis on their own hard work in improving their lives than on women's collective efforts (Boxer, 1997; Konek et al., 1994). These women believe that women's personal effort and success today, more than changes in organizational or governmental policies and practices, will lead to better opportunities for future generations of women (Konek et al., 1994), and they are willing to work hard, assert their rights, seek out opportunities for advancement, and make sacrifices if necessary.

Collective Action

Contrary to the individual approach, many feminist psychologists contend that collective action is necessary in order to achieve significant improvement in women's lives (Kirk & Okazawa-Rey, 2010; Worell, 2001). This does not imply that women should not work hard to attain personal goals. However, it does mean that women, both individually and in groups, should strive to empower all women, not just themselves; they should advocate for social change, not just personal betterment. Furthermore, these collective efforts should address the concerns of diverse groups of women.

One woman who has made a difference in the lives of many other women is Catherine Hamlin, an Australian-born surgeon who has spent over 40 years in Ethiopia repairing fistulas, which are seriously ripped tissues resulting from female genital cutting. She and her husband founded a fistula hospital, which has treated thousands of women (Henderson & Jeydel, 2010; Kristof & WuDunn, 2009).

Two other wonderful examples of women who have made a difference are the winners of the Nobel Peace Prize in 2003 and 2004. The 2003 winner is Shirin Ebadi, an Iranian lawyer, judge, writer, and university lecturer who has spent three decades advancing human rights in her country. While many professional women left Iran after the 1979 Islamic revolution, she stayed and became one of Iran's outspoken advocates for the rights of women and children (Henderson & Jeydel, 2010). Wangari Maathai, the 2004 Nobel Peace Prize winner, is the first Black African woman to receive the award. She won for her work as the founder and leader of an organization that has fought deforestation of the land and has improved women's lives through education, family planning, and better nutrition (Henderson & Jeydel, 2010; Lorber, 2010).

Girls and women also work together in groups, taking up the banner of collective activism to advocate for social change. They are fighting for issues such as immigrant rights, increased spending on education, and taking on corporate sexist practices (Taft, 2010). One example of the latter type of activism is the work of a group of girls, ages 13 to 16, who protested against Abercrombie and Fitch (A&F) tee shirts printed with demeaning slogans such as "Who needs a brain when you have these?" The girls worked with the Women and Girls Foundation of Southern Pennsylvania

Wangari Maathai (left) and Shirin Ebadi (right), winners of the Nobel Peace Prize in 2004 and 2003, respectively, were honored for advancing human rights in their countries.

to organize a "girlcott" of A&F that drew national media attention and led A&F to withdraw the shirts from stores (APA Task Force, 2007). See What You Can Do 15.1 for ways you can become an advocate for change.

The feminist movement in the United States, a collective movement aimed at enhancing women's lives, was focused initially on the needs of White, middle-class, heterosexual, able-bodied women and has been criticized for failing to deal with unique problems faced by women of color, poor and working-class women, sexual minority women, and women with disabilities (Kinser, 2010; Lott, 2010; Reid, 2011; Russo & Landrine, 2010). In the words of a Black college instructor and administrator, "Until very recently I did not call myself a feminist . . . even academic feminism did not include me until the 1980s. Feminism in the United States was pretty monolithic, pretty homogeneous . . . and so until recently, America did not embrace my experiences" (Kmiec et al., 1996, p. 58).

Although all women have certain experiences in common by virtue of their gender, other factors like racism, classism, ageism, heterosexism, and ableism contribute to double and triple jeopardies experienced by women who are not in the privileged group (Hill Collins, 2008; Rojas, 2009). Fortunately, the efforts of women of color, poor women, older women, sexual minority women, and women with disabilities have gradually expanded the feminist movement's perspective, and participation by previously excluded groups has increased (C. Lewis, 2010; Lorber, 2010; Russo & Landrine, 2010). This expansion of goals and inclusive participation must continue to grow. Attempts to achieve gender equality should concurrently strive to eradicate inequalities based on ethnicity, class, sexual orientation, ableness, and age. Only the collective efforts of diverse groups of

WHAT YOU CAN DO 15.1
Become an Advocate

1. Volunteer to help a woman's organization in your community.
2. Go to Amnesty International's Website, http://www.amnesty.org, and take action to support a currently imprisoned women's rights activist.

EXPLORE OTHER CULTURES 15.1
Women's Movements Worldwide

Until recently, feminist academics from the Western world focused on the largely middle-class women's movements in the United States and Europe. However, women in the non-Western world, many of them poor, also have had a long history of battling for women's rights (Burn, 2011; Henderson & Jeydel, 2010; Kristof & WuDunn, 2009). Because cultures differ, the struggle does not always focus on the same set of issues. For example, family-planning agendas have helped to mobilize Western feminists but may be viewed skeptically by women in developing nations, where having many children confers status or provides a source of family labor ("Mother or Nothing," 2010; Shah & Batzer, 2010). The Afghan Women's Bill of Rights, crafted by a group of Afghan women in 2003, has as its first priority the guarantee of an education. Then come health care, personal security, and support of widows, with freedom of speech taking up fifth place. Even these basic rights are still in jeopardy in Afghanistan ("Afghan Women's Rights," 2003; Kristof & WuDunn, 2009). In addition to women's movements that exist in individual countries, there is also an international women's movement, sometimes called global feminism. This movement advocates the idea that all humans share the same rights, while at the same time it recognizes the diversity of women's lives and cultures. The global feminist movement is working to challenge violence against women, expand the education of girls, support women's reproductive and sexual freedom, increase women's political power, and champion women's access to health care and economic independence (Bose & Kim, 2009; Chowdhury, 2010; Moghadam, 2009; Murthy et al., 2010b). The United Nations has attempted to play a leadership role in this effort. In 1979, it issued a treaty known as the Convention on the Elimination of All Forms of Discrimination Against Women. Out of 193 nations, only 7 have not ratified the treaty. The nonratifying countries are Iran, Sudan, Somalia, three small Pacific islands—and the United States ("Human Rights Index," 2010). Why do you think the United States is the only developed nation to not ratify the treaty?

women working together for the elimination of all types of power inequality can provide a brighter future for all girls and women. For a look at women's movements worldwide, see Explore Other Cultures 15.1.

Given that some women ascribe to beliefs in equality but are not oriented toward working for change for others, how can these women's motivation for social activism be enhanced? Communication with other women, learning about the experiences and problems of other women, and exposure to varied situations that involve gender discrimination can broaden one's understanding of women's issues and encourage greater involvement in advocating for women's rights (Kirk & Okazawa-Rey, 2010). Taking women's studies courses, experiencing discrimination firsthand, and having a mother who is a feminist also are linked to students' participation in collective action (Liss et al., 2004).

The Internet has revolutionized the way women organize and act collectively. The use of e-mail, Websites, Listservs, search engines, and social media has improved communication for virtually all groups but has been especially important in linking women's groups, which tend to be small and often isolated from each other (Lee, 2004). One example of the effectiveness of the Internet in bringing women into the political process occurred when President George W. Bush cut off government funding to family planning programs outside the United States even if the money was not going to be used for abortion. *Los Angeles Times* writer Patt Morrison denounced the decision in her column and publicly made a donation to Planned Parenthood in Bush's name. The news spread rapidly via e-mail, and donations totaling half a million dollars poured into Planned Parenthood in the president's name (Lee, 2004).

GET INVOLVED 15.1
A Perfect Future Day

Imagine what you would like your life to be like 10 years in the future. Write a paragraph describing what your ideal typical day would be like. Also, ask one same-gender and two other-gender students to perform the same exercise.

WHAT DOES IT MEAN?

Read through the four descriptions and record similarities and differences about the following: (1) marital status, (2) presence of children, (3) if married, family responsibilities of each spouse, (4) employment status, (5) if employed, gender dominance of the occupation, and (6) leisure activities.

1. Do the descriptions written by the women differ from those written by the men in relation to these or any other topics? If yes, use information learned in this course to explain these differences.

2. Are there any current gender-based expectations about interpersonal or societal roles and behaviors that might hinder your own ideal life from becoming a reality? If yes, what kinds of changes do you think would reduce this impediment? Would you be interested in working for this change?

Source: Based on Kerr (1999).

Do feminist goals presented here for the future coincide with your perspectives and those of your acquaintances? Try Get Involved 15.1 to explore students' fantasies about their ideal futures.

FEMINIST BELIEFS

We began the text with a discussion of the meaning of feminism, and now we come full circle, back to this topic. Because the goals we have presented and many of the actions taken to achieve these goals are rooted in a feminist perspective, it is important to explore the prevalence and accuracy of feminist beliefs.

Although most North Americans believe that feminism has had a positive impact on women's attainment of greater economic, political, and legal opportunities, a relatively small number have argued that feminists are the root of numerous personal and social problems and are responsible for the decline of the "traditional" North American family (Faludi, 2007). Many feminists are, indeed, disturbed about the subordination of women within _patriarchal_ families where husbands hold the power and dictate the activities of wives and children (Coontz, 2011; Kirk & Okazawa-Rey, 2010), but they are supportive of egalitarian families in which husbands and wives share power and respect. It is untrue to say that most feminists oppose the notion of the family— they oppose the notion of an unequal family.

Another accusation made by some antifeminists is that feminists hate men. While it is true that many feminists object to male power that has oppressed women in the workplace, government, education, and the home (Tomlinson, 2010), an objection to male _privilege_ should not be confused with an objection to men per se.

Sadly, these antifeminist beliefs not only dangerously distort the truth but also discredit feminist ideology. Given that most North Americans are strongly profamily and that males have high status and respect within society, the depiction of feminists as antifamily male-bashers sets them up for ridicule and makes it easier to dismiss their beliefs as extremist (Tomlinson, 2010). What are your thoughts on feminism? Perform Get Involved 15.2 to reassess your views.

GET INVOLVED 15.2
How Do You View Feminism?

Answer the following questions without looking back at the answers you gave in Chapter 1. First, indicate which of the following categories best characterizes your identity as a feminist.

   a. consider myself a feminist and am currently involved in the Women's Movement

   b. consider myself a feminist but am not involved in the Women's Movement

   c. do not consider myself a feminist but agree with at least some of the objectives of feminism

   d. do not consider myself a feminist and disagree with the objectives of feminism.

   Second, on a scale from 1 (strongly disagree) to 6 (strongly agree), indicate the extent to which you disagree or agree with each of the following statements.

1. Women should be considered as seriously as men as candidates for the presidency of the United States.

2. Although women can be good leaders, men make better leaders.

3. A woman should have the same job opportunities as a man.

4. Men should respect women more than they currently do.

5. Many women in the workforce are taking jobs away from men who need the jobs more.

6. Doctors need to take women's health concerns more seriously.

7. Women have been treated unfairly on the basis of their gender throughout most of human history.

8. Women are already given equal opportunities with men in all important sectors of their lives.

9. Women in the United States are treated as second-class citizens.

10. Women can best overcome discrimination by doing the best they can at their jobs, not by wasting time with political activity.

WHAT DOES IT MEAN?

Before computing your score for the 10 items, reverse the points for statements 2, 5, 8, and 10. That is, for a rating of "1" (strongly disagree), give 6 points, for a rating of "2," give 5 points, and so on. Then sum the points for the 10 items. Note that higher scores reflect greater agreement with feminist beliefs.

1. Compare your feminist identification (Part I) here with your feminist identification at the

beginning of the course (see Get Involved 1.1). If there has been a change, explain why.

2. Compare your feminist beliefs at the two points in time. If there has been a change, explain why. What specific course material, if any, contributed to this change?

Source: Based on Morgan (1996).

Feminist Identification

Although support for the women's movement has increased steadily since the mid-1970s, the proportion of American women who identify themselves as feminists remains low (Houvouras & Carter, 2008; Rudman & Fairchild, 2007).

     According to nationwide polls and studies of college students (Breen & Karpinski, 2008; Duncan, 2010; Houvouras & Carter, 2008), only about 25 to 30 percent of American women label themselves as feminists, and the percentage of men is even lower. Furthermore, college women of color and working-class White women are less likely than middle-class White college women to label themselves as feminists (Aronson, 2003; Myaskovsky & Wittig, 1997). As stated earlier, the feminist movement has been dominated by White women, and some women of color feel that feminists do not have an interest in their unique experiences and concerns (Manago et al., 2009; White, 2010). Some women of color, therefore, have embraced women of color feminism, a form of feminism that, as we saw in Chapter 1, addresses racism and other issues of importance to ethnic minority females (O'Leary, 2011). Another problem for some women of color is the perception of conflict between the values embraced by their ethnic group and values associated with feminist ideology. For example, Latina women may feel torn between the more patriarchal belief system of their cultures and the feminist value of egalitarianism (Manago et al., 2009).

Interestingly, many women who reject the feminist label support the goals of feminism (Breen & Karpinski, 2008; Houvouras & Carter, 2008; Kanner & Anderson, 2010; Ramsey et al., 2007). Alyssa Zucker (2004; Bay-Cheng & Zucker, 2007) refers to this group of women as "egalitarians." How can these discrepancies between a feminist identification and views about feminist goals be explained? First, women may be concerned about negative images that some people attach to feminism and feminists. At a personal level, they might want to avoid a negative self-image, which they believe would result from identifying themselves with a term that has negative connotations. At a public level, they might fear the social disapproval that could follow from their identification as a feminist (Kanner & Anderson, 2010; Ramsey et al., 2007). One negative image, that of feminists as anti-male, was illustrated in Chapter 1 by a student's definition of feminist as "a big, bra-burning man-hater" (Houvouras & Carter, 2008). Still others equate feminism with being unfeminine and physically unattractive (Leaper & Arias, 2011; Rudman & Fairchild, 2007) using terms such as "militant," "violent," "fat," and "butch" (Houvouras & Carter, 2008). Given the perception that feminists are overly masculine, it is not surprising that women who rate themselves high in femininity are more likely to reject the "feminist" label than women who rate themselves high in masculinity (Toller et al., 2004). Along these same lines, college students respond more favorably to a profeminist message when it is presented by a feminine-appearing speaker than by a masculine-appearing speaker (Bullock & Fernald, 2003), a phenomenon referred to as "feminism lite."

A second reason that some women refuse to identify as feminists despite their agreement with many feminist goals is that they believe that gender equality has already been achieved (Houvouras & Carter, 2008). Illustrating this view, college women who believe that women are disadvantaged relative to men are more likely to participate in activities that enhance the status of women (e.g., talking about women's issues with others, attending talks on women's issues, joining protests). Women who perceive fewer gender differences in social conditions are less likely to be involved in activism (Foster, 1999).

A third reason some women do not label themselves as feminists is because they associate feminism with collective political activism, whereas they personally favor individual actions in everyday life as a way to achieve feminist goals. Recent research (Yoder et al., 2011) does, in fact, show that women who label themselves as feminists are more likely to engage in increased activism on behalf of women.

Emergence of Feminist Beliefs

During this class, I feel my eyes have been opened to what not just women in general, but ethnic, young, old, and disabled women go through every day. . . . Before I took this class, I thought I was aware of all the issues women face. Boy, was I wrong! (Shawna, a 21-year-old senior)

Before this course, I thought some women made too big a deal over women's rights issues. My eyes have been so opened, and now I am extremely sensitized to gender issues in society. I actively try to educate people on gender inequality of power and social construction of gender.

I am really going to try to raise very gender-flexible children. In a way, I feel like I stepped out of the dark into the light. (Jessica, a 25-year-old senior)

One important route to feminist consciousness is enrollment in women's studies courses (Case, 2007; Good & Moss-Racusin, 2010; Leaper & Arias, 2011; Paludi et al., 2008; Stake & Malkin, 2003). Women's studies programs (some are now called gender studies) have proliferated since the early 1970s, and about half of all universities in the United States currently offer a course on the psychology of women (Yoder, 2005). These courses help foster feminist goals by providing students with the knowledge to transform society (Case, 2007). Similar to the experiences of Shawna and Jessica (section-opening vignette), and Julie (chapter-opening vignette), studies have shown that women's studies courses are instrumental in decreasing gender-stereotypic attitudes (Bryant, 2003; Case, 2007) and increasing commitment to feminism (Katz et al., 2004; Nelson et al., 2008; Yoder et al., 2007). Furthermore, Jayne Stake and her colleagues (see Stake, 2007) have found that women's studies and gender studies courses can encourage activism. Their research shows that students who take such courses, compared to those who do not, become more active in feminist activities and make more changes in their own roles and/or ways of interacting with others. Moreover, these changes last over time. Exposure to feminism in other ways can also give rise to feminist identity. For example, feminists are more likely than other women to have feminists in their family of origin, such as their mother or sister (Nelson et al., 2008; Zucker, 2004). But even simply reading a paragraph containing positive statements about feminists increases the likelihood that women will identify themselves as feminist (Roy et al., 2007).

A second route toward feminism involves personal experiences women have that make them painfully aware that they live in a sexist society. For example, experiencing sexual harassment or rape is associated with increased support for feminism and women's rights activism (Ayres et al., 2009; Livosky et al., 2008; Nelson et al., 2008; Zucker, 2004). For some women, social or historical events such as the *Roe v. Wade* Supreme Court decision on abortion rights, attending NOW (National Organization for Women) meetings, or reading Betty Friedan's book *The Feminine Mystique* (1963) shaped their feminist identity (Coontz, 2011).

Whatever a woman's route to feminism, studies show that women who identify as feminists have greater psychological well-being than other women (Eisele & Stake, 2008; Saunders & Kashubeck-West, 2006; Yakushko, 2007). This may result from a sense of greater independence and personal empowerment on the part of feminist women.

To assess your own involvement in feminist activism, try Get Involved 15.3.

Men and Feminism

Various men's movements have developed in recent years, partly as a response to the women's movement. The mythopoetic movement started by Robert Bly (1990) emphasizes men reconnecting with each other through rituals and retreats. Two religiously based movements of the late 1990s are the Promise Keepers, a Christian fundamentalist group, and the Million Man March, a Black men's group. Both of these movements seek to bring men back into the family, certainly a desirable objective. However, the underlying theme is a return to the traditional roles of men as leaders and women as followers (Kimmel, 2001).

Other men work within a feminist framework as part of the profeminist movement, which supports equality of women and men in all spheres of life, both professional and personal (Kahn & Ferguson, 2010). Profeminist men have initiated a number of organizations including the National Organization for Men Against Sexism (Kimmel, 2001), as well as programs such as One in Four and Men Can Stop Rape, which focus on preventing sexual assault (Tarrant, 2009). One of the

GET INVOLVED 15.3
How Involved in Feminist Activism Are You?

Check each of the following nine activities you engaged in during the six months before the beginning of this semester. Then check each activity you engaged in during this semester.

Before

___ kept informed on women's rights issues
___ talked with others to influence their attitudes about women's rights issues
___ signed a petition related to women's rights
___ attended a march, rally, or protest related to women's rights
___ wrote letters to politicians or newspapers about women's rights issues
___ contributed money to a women's rights cause or to politicians who supported such causes
___ circulated a petition about a women's rights cause
___ worked for a phone bank, letter writing campaign, or political campaign in the cause of women's rights
___ participated in other activity related to women's rights

During

___
___

___
___

___

___

___

___

___

WHAT DOES IT MEAN?

1. Has there been an increase in your feminist activities due to this course? If yes, indicate some of the information you learned that contributed to this change.
2. Which of the following types of activities do you believe is the preferable route toward increased rights and opportunities for women: individual effort alone or individual effort combined with collective action? Explain your answer.

Source: Based on Stake et al. (1994).

most successful profeminist organizations is the White Ribbon Campaign, which began in Canada in 1991 in response to the mass killing of 14 women engineering students at the University of Montreal by a deranged man. The campaign, whose slogan is "Men, working to end men's violence against women," has now spread to over 55 countries (United Nations, 2007).

POSTSCRIPT

We end this exploration of women's lives with two cautionary notes. First, when thinking about the material in this text, keep in mind that the knowledge individuals have about the psychology of women is situated in a particular time in history. It is strongly connected to existing societal attitudes and to current political, economic, and legal events. As a result of economic and attitudinal changes in the last decades of the twentieth century and the first decade of the twenty-first century, for example, a major concern for many married mothers today is the balancing of work and family. However, this issue would have been largely irrelevant to stay-at-home mothers in the 1960s. We can expect that some of the information presented here will become obsolete over time. In fact, if women are successful in their efforts, if legislative initiatives and workplace policies address gender inequities in power and opportunities, and if gender roles become more flexible, some current problems, such as wage differentials and sexual harassment, will, we hope, be eliminated.

Second, as discussed in Chapter 1, teaching does not take place in an ideological vacuum. Even if not explicitly stated, a particular set of values underlies all scholarly research, textbooks, and course content, and this book is no exception. Our (authors of this text) feminist values served as the basis for our examination of the lives of girls and women. Regardless of your own commitment to these beliefs, we hope your exploration of the psychology of women has been an enriching experience and that you have achieved an increased understanding of the negative effects of male privilege, a greater appreciation of women's intersecting identities and diversity, and a greater awareness of the role that interpersonal and societal forces play in shaping gender-based attitudes, behaviors, and goals. And, we sincerely hope you apply what you have learned from this text and course to other academic interests, career pursuits, your own experiences, and perhaps to societal change.

Summary

FEMINIST GOALS

- Greater gender equality of organizational and interpersonal power would benefit women in several ways by increasing opportunities in the workplace, giving women a greater voice in dating relationships, creating a more equitable division of household labor, and reducing intimate violence. It is essential that increases in women's power benefit all women, regardless of ethnicity, class, disability/ability, sexual orientation, or age.
- The benefits of a flexible construction of gender include behavior and role choices that reflect individual preferences instead of social expectations, as well as a reduction in sexual harassment and acquaintance rape.

ACTIONS TO ACHIEVE THESE GOALS

- Several actions can facilitate the achievement of these goals including a diversity-oriented psychology of women that can inform about the role of male privilege and the constraints of rigid gender roles and enhance one's understanding of diversity and increase tolerance.
- Raising gender-flexible children would free people to make personally appropriate choices, rather than those based on gender-role expectations. Additionally, it would help foster greater appreciation of women's traditional roles and lessen the tendency to evaluate others on the basis of their conformity to gender expectations.
- Interventions by societal institutions, as well as the media, can address violence against women.
- Some women believe that they can enhance their own lives more through their individual efforts than as a result of collective action.
- Many feminists believe that improvement of the lives of women requires collective action. However, the feminist movement has been focused more on the lives of privileged women than on those who experience double and triple jeopardies stemming from racism, classism, ageism, homophobia, and/or ableism.

FEMINIST BELIEFS

- North Americans have mixed views about the value of feminism. Some believe it has helped women. Others believe that feminists are responsible for many personal and social problems.

- Only 25 percent of U.S. women label themselves as feminists. Some of the women who do not identify themselves as feminists support the goals of feminism. Reasons for this discrepancy include negative images of feminists, the assumption that women have already attained power equality, and the belief that feminism implies collective action.
- Women's studies courses tend to decrease students' gender-stereotypic attitudes and increase their commitment to feminism and activism.
- Various men's movements have developed in recent years, including the mythopoetic movement, Promise Keepers, Million Man March, and profeminism.

POSTSCRIPT

- Current knowledge about women's lives is situated in this historical period.
- This textbook is grounded in feminist values that emphasize women's intersecting identities and diversity, the importance of empowering girls and women, and the critical role of interpersonal and social forces in constructing gender.

What Do You Think?

1. The text presented greater equality of power and greater flexibility in the construction of gender as beneficial to girls and women. Do you think there are any disadvantages for females associated with these goals? In what ways would these goals benefit males? In what ways might they be detrimental to males?
2. Which one or more of the various strategies for improving women's lives do you think would be most effective? Explain your answer.

If You Want to Learn More

Abdulhadi, R. Alsultany, E., & Naber, N. (Eds.). (2011). *Arab and Arab-American feminisms: Gender, violence, and belonging.* Syracuse, NY: Syracuse University Press.

Bravo, E. (2007). *Taking on the big boys: Or why feminism is good for families, business, and the nation.* New York: Feminist Press.

Burn, S. M. (2011). *Women across cultures: A global perspective* (3rd ed.). New York: McGraw-Hill.

Collins, G. (2009). *When everything changed: The amazing journey of American women from 1960 to the present.* New York: Little, Brown and Company.

Ens, C. Z., & Sinacore, A. L. (Eds.). (2005). *Teaching and social justice: Integrating multicultural and feminist theories in the classroom.* Washington, DC: American Psychological Association.

Gillis, S., Howie, G., & Munford, R. (Eds.). (2007). *Third wave feminism: Expanded* (2nd ed.). New York: Palgrave Macmillan.

Henderson, S. L., & Jeydel, A. S. (2010). *Women and politics in a global world* (2nd ed.). New York: Oxford University Press.

Hewitt, N. A. (2010). *No permanent waves: Recasting the history of U.S. feminism.* Piscataway, NJ: Rutgers University Press.

Kirk, G., & Okazawa-Rey, M. (2010). *Women's lives: Multicultural perspectives* (5th ed.). Mountain View, CA: Mayfield.

Kristof, N. D., & WuDunn, S. (2009). *Half the sky: Turning oppression into opportunity for women worldwide.* New York: Alfred A. Knopf.

Lindio-McGovern, L., & Wallimann, I. (2009). *Globalization and Third World women: Exploitation, coping, and resistance.* Burlington, VT: Ashgate Publishing.

Murthy, P., & Smith, C. L. (2010). *Women's global health and human rights.* Sudbury, MA: Jones & Bartlett Publishers.

Paludi, M. A. (Ed.). (2010). *Feminism and women's rights worldwide* (Vols. 1–3). Santa Barbara, CA: Praeger.

Peterson, V. S., & Runyan, A. S. (2009). *Global gender issues in the new millennium* (3rd ed.). New York: Westview Press.

Rojas, M. (2009). *Women of color and feminism*. Berkeley, CA: Seal Press.

Seely, M. (2007). *Fight like a girl: How to be a fearless feminist*. New York: New York University Press.

Tarrant, S. (2009). *Men and feminism*. Berkeley, CA: Seal Press.

Valenti, J. (2007). *Full frontal feminism: A young woman's guide to why feminism matters*. Emeryville, CA: Seal Press.

White, A. M. (Ed.). (2010). *African Americans doing feminism: Putting theory into everyday practice*. Albany, NY: SUNY Press.

Websites

Feminism

feminist.com http://www.feminist.com/
Women of Color Web http://userpages.umbc.edu/~korenman/ wmst/lin ks_wc.htmI

Advocating for Change

Activist Web Sites for Women's Issues http://www.research.umbc.ed/~korenman/wmst/links_actv.html
The Ethnic Woman International http://www.thenewmagazinecity.com/woman-international.html

REFERENCES

AARP. (2001). *In the middle: A report on multicultural boomers coping with family and aging issues.* Washington, DC: Author.

AARP. (2003). *Lifestyles, dating and romance: A study of midlife singles.* Washington, DC: Author.

AARP. (2004, Winter). *The GIC Voice,* p. 11.

AARP. (2006). *Medicare at 40: Past accomplishments and future challenges.* Washington, DC: Author.

AAUW. (2001). *Hostile hallways: Bullying, teasing, and sexual harassment in school.* Washington, DC: Author.

AAUW. (2004). *Under the microscope.* Washington, DC: Author.

AAUW. (2006). *Mom's retirement security.* Washington, DC: Author.

AAUW. (2008a). *Pay equity: A simple matter of fairness.* Washington, DC: Author.

AAUW. (2008b). *Where the girls are: The facts about gender equity in education.* Washington, DC: Author.

AAUW. (2008c). *Women, retirement, and social security.* Washington, DC: Author.

AAUW. (2010). *Why so few? Women in science, technology, engineering, and mathematics.* Washington, DC: Author.

AAUW. (2011). *The simple truth about the gender pay gap.* Washington, DC: Author.

Abbey, A. D., Jacques-Tiura, A. J., & Parkhill, M. R. (2010). Sexual assault among diverse populations of women: Common ground, distinctive features, and unanswered questions. In H. Landrine & N. F. Russo (Eds.), *Handbook of diversity in feminist psychology* (pp. 391–425). New York: Springer.

Abela, J. R. Z., & Hankin, B. L. (2009). Cognitive vulnerability to depression in adolescents: A developmental psychopathology perspective. In S. Nolen-Hoeksema & L. M. Hilt (Eds.), *Handbook of depression in adolescents* (pp. 335–376). New York: Taylor & Francis.

Abortion. (2010, March 7). *Gallup.* Retrieved from http://www.gallup.com/poll/1576/abortion.aspx

Abrams, L. S., & Curran, L. (2009). "And you're telling me not to stress?" A grounded theory study of postpartum depression symptoms among low-income mothers. *Psychology of Women Quarterly, 33,* 351–362.

Acierno, R., et al. (2010). Prevalence and correlates of emotional, physical, sexual, and financial abuse and potential neglect in the United States: The national elder mistreatment study. *American Journal of Public Health, 100,* 292–297.

Acosta, R. V., & Carpenter, L. J. (2008). *Women in intercollegiate sport: A longitudinal, national study: Thirty-one-year-update.* West Brookfield, MA: Acosta/Carpenter.

Acosta, R. V., & Carpenter, L. J. (2010). *Women in intercollegiate sport: A longitudinal, national study: Thirty-three-year update.* West Brookfield, MA: Acosta/Carpenter.

Adams, H. L., & Phillips, L. (2009). Ethnic related variations from the Cass Model of Homosexual Identity formation: The experiences of two-spirit, lesbian and gay Native American. *Journal of Homosexuality, 56,* 959–976.

Adams, P. F., Lucas, J. W., & Barnes, P. M. (2008). *Summary health statistics for the U.S. Population: National Health Interview Survey, 2006.* NCHS Vital Health Statistics, 10(236). Washington, DC: U.S. Government Printing Office.

Adelmann, P. K. (1993). Psychological well-being and homemaker vs. Retiree identity among older women. *Sex Roles, 29,* 195–212.

Ader, D. N., & Johnson, S. B. (1994). Sample description, reporting, and analysis of sex in psychological research: A look at APA and APA division journals in 1990. *American Psychologist, 49,* 216–218.

Adkins, D. E., Wang, V., Dupre, M. E., van den Oord, E. J. C. G., & Elder, G. H., Jr. (2009). Structure and stress: Trajectories of depressive symptoms across adolescent and young adulthood. *Social Forces, 88,* 31–60.

Administration on aging. (2011). *A profile of older Americans.* Washington, DC: Author.

Afghan women's rights. (2003, September 24). *New York Times,* p. A26.

Africa's homeless widows. (2004, June 16). *New York Times,* p. A18.

Agahi, N., & Parker, M. G. (2008). Leisure activities and mortality. *Journal of Aging and Health, 20,* 855–871.

Aging and HIV. (2010, February). *Project Inform Perspective, 50,* 7–9.

Ahmed, S. B., et al. (2004). Gender bias in cardiovascular advertisements. *Journal of Evaluation in Clinical Practice, 10,* 531.

Ahnert, L., Pinquart, M., & Lamb, M. E. (2006). Security of children's relationships with nonparental care providers: A meta-analysis. *Child Development, 74,* 664–679.

Ahrens, C. E., Dean, K., Rozee, P. D., & McKenzie, M. (2008). Understanding and preventing rape. In F. L. Denmark & M. A. Paludi (Eds.), *Psychology of women: A handbook of issues and theories* (2nd ed., pp. 509–554). Westport, CT: Praeger.

Aisenbrey, S., Evertsson, M., & Grunow, D. (2009). Is there a career penalty for mothers' time out? A comparison of Germany, Sweden and the United States. *Social Forces, 88,* 573–606.

Aldarondo, E., & Castro-Fernandez, M. (2011). Risk and protective factors for domestic violence perpetration. In J. W. White, M. P. Koss, & A. E. Kazdin (Eds.), *Violence against women and children: Mapping the terrain* (Vol. 1, pp. 221–242). Washington, DC: American Psychological Association.

Aldwin, C. M., Yancura, L. A., & Boeninger, D. K. (2010). Coping across the life span. In M. E. Lamb & A. M. Freund (Eds.), *The handbook of life-span development: Social and emotional development* (Vol. 2, pp. 298–340). Hoboken, NJ: Wiley.

Aleman, K., & Doctor, R. (2010). Lesbianism and mental health. In D. Kohen (Ed.), *Oxford textbook of women and mental health* (pp. 42–48). New York: Oxford University Press.

Alexander, K. (2004, April 13). Grandma finds a job, looking after junior. *New York Times,* p. E2.

Alexander, L. L., LaRosa, J. H., Bader, H., Garfield, S., & Alexander, W. J. (2010). *New dimensions in women's health* (5th ed.). Sudbury, MA: Jones and Bartlett.

Alexandre, C. (2011). Childbirth, home versus hospital. In M. Z. Stange, C. K. Oyster, & J. E. Sloan (Eds.), *Encyclopedia of women in today's world* (Vol. 1, pp. 264–266). Newberry Park, CA: Sage.

Alfieri, T., Ruble, D. N., & Higgins, E. T. (1996). Gender stereotypes during adolescence: Developmental changes and the transition to junior high school. *Developmental Psychology, 32,* 1129–1137.

Ålgars, M., et al. (2009). The adult body: How age, gender, and body mass index are related to body image. *Journal of Aging and Health, 21,* 1112–1132.

Alhabib, S., Nur, U., & Jones, R. (2010). Domestic violence against women: Systematic review of prevalence studies. *Journal of Family Violence, 25,* 369–382.

Alink, L. R. A., et al. (2006). The early childhood aggression curve: Development of physical aggression in 10- to 50-month-old children. *Child Development, 77,* 954–966.

Allen, C. T., Swan, S. C., & Raghavan, C. (2009). Gender symmetry, sexism, and intimate partner violence. *Journal of Interpersonal Violence, 24,* 1816–1834.

Allen, K. R. (2009). Keeping the feminist in our teaching: Daring to make a difference. In S. Lloyd, A. Few, & K. Allen (Eds.), *Handbook of family feminist studies* (pp. 351–359). Thousand Oaks, CA: Sage.

Allen, K. R., & Chin-Sang, V. (1990). A lifetime of work: The context and meanings of leisure for aging black women. *Gerontologist, 30,* 734–740.

Allen, K. R., & Walker, A. J. (2009). Theorizing about families and aging from a feminist perspective. In V. Bengtson, M. Silverstein, N. M. Putney, & D. Gans (Eds.), *Handbook of theories of aging* (2nd ed., pp. 517–528). New York: Springer.

Allen, M. W. (2004). The role of laughter when discussing workplace barriers: Women in information technology jobs. *Sex Roles, 50,* 177–189.

Almond, B. (2010). *The monster within: The hidden side of motherhood.* Berkeley and Los Angeles, CA: University of California Press.

Alschuler, L. (2010). Cervical cancer. In V. Maizes & T. Low Dog (Eds.), *Integrative women's health* (pp. 335–347). New York: Oxford University Press.

Alterovitz, S. S., & Mendelsohn, G. A. (2009). Partner preferences across the life span: Online dating by older adults. *Psychology and Aging, 24,* 513–517.

Altman, L. K. (2006, August 13). Grandmothers from Africa rally for AIDS orphans. *New York Times,* p. YT10.

Altman, L. K. (2008, March 12). Sex infections found in quarter of teenage girls. *New York Times,* pp. A1, A17.

Altman, S. E., & Shankman, S. A. (2009). What is the association between obsessive-compulsive disorder and eating disorders? *Clinical Psychology Review, 29,* 638–646.

Amanatullah, E. T., & Morris, M. W. (2010). Negotiating gender roles: Gender differences in assertive negotiating are mediated by women's fear of backlash and attenuated when negotiating on behalf of others. *Journal of Personality and Social Psychology, 98,* 256–267.

Amaro, H., et al. (2002). Cultural influences on women's sexual health. In G. M. Wingood & R. J. DiClemente (Eds.), *Handbook of women's sexual and reproductive health* (pp. 71–92). New York: Kluwer Academic/Plenum.

Amato, P. R. (2000). The consequences of divorce for adults and children. *Journal of Marriage and the Family, 62,* 1269–1287.

Amato, P. R. (2005). The impact of family formation change on the cognitive, social, and emotional well-being of the next generation. *Future of Children, 15,* 75–96.

Amato, P. R. (2010). Research on divorce: Continuing trends and new developments. *Journal of Marriage and Family, 72,* 650–666.

Amato, P. R., & Cheadle, J. E. (2008). Parental divorce, marital conflict and children's behavior problems: A comparison of adopted and biological children. *Social Forces, 86,* 1139–1161.

Amato, P. R., & Kane, J. B. (2011). Life-course pathways and the psychosocial adjustment of young adult women. *Journal of Marriage and Family, 73,* 279–295.

Ambady, N., & Weisbuch, M. (2010). Nonverbal behavior. In S. T. Fiske, D. T. Gilbert, & G. Lindzey (Eds.), *Handbook of social psychology* (5th ed., Vol. 1, pp. 464–497). Hoboken, NJ: Wiley.

American Cancer Society. (2008). *Breast cancer resources.* Atlanta, GA: Author.

American Cancer Society. (2009). *Breast cancer facts & figures 2009–2010.* Atlanta, GA: Author. Retrieved from http://www .cancer.org/downloads/STT/F861009_final%209-08-09.pdf

American Cancer Society. (2010a). *Breast cancer.* Atlanta, GA: Author. Retrieved from http://documents.cancer.org/ 104.00/104.00.pdf

American Cancer Society. (2010b). *Cancer facts & figures 2010.* Atlanta, GA: Author.

American Cancer Society. (2010c). *Cervical cancer.* Atlanta, GA: Author.

American College of Obstetricians and Gynecologists. (2010). *Your pregnancy and childbirth: Month to month* (5th ed.). Washington, DC: Author.

American Heart Association. (2009). *American heart association complete guide to women's heart health: The go red for women way to well-being and vitality.* Dallas, TX: Author.

American Institute for Cancer Research. (2010, February 10). Fighting both cancer and heart disease: A similar approach. *Cancer Research Update,* (36). Retrieved from http://www.aicr .org/site/News2?page=NewsArticle&id=17953

American Psychiatric Association. (1994). *Diagnostic and statistical manual of mental disorders* (4th ed.). Washington, DC: Author.

American Psychological Association. (1975). Report of the task force on sex bias and sex-role stereotyping in psychotherapeutic practice. *American Psychologist, 30,* 1169–1175.

American Psychological Association. (2002). *Developing adolescents: A reference for professionals.* Washington, DC: Author.

American Psychological Association. (2004). Guidelines for psychological practice with older adults. *American Psychologist, 59,* 236–260.

American Psychological Association. (2006). *Women in the American Psychological Association 2006.* Washington, DC: Author.

American Psychological Association. (2007). Guidelines for psychological practice with girls and women. *American Psychologist, 62,* 949–979.

American Psychological Association. (2009). *Report of the APA task force on gender identity and gender variance.* Washington, DC: Author.

American Psychological Association. (2010). *Publication manual of the American Psychological Association* (6th ed.). Washington, DC: Author.

American Society of Clinical Oncology. (2009, November). *Women and lung cancer.* Alexandria, VA: Author. Retrieved from http:// www.cancer.net/

American Society of Plastic Surgeons. (2009). *2009 report of the 2008 statistics.* Arlington Heights, IL: Author.

Amnesty International USA. (2010). *Female genital mutilation/cutting.* New York: Author. Retrieved from http://www .amnestyusa.org/violence-against-women/stop-violence-against-women-svaw/female-genital-mutilation/page.do?id=1108226

Amstadter, A. B., Cisler, J. M., McCauley, J. L., Hernandez, M. A., Muzzy, W., & Acierno, R. (2011). Do incident and perpetrator characteristics of elder mistreatment differ by gender of the victim? Results from the national elder mistreatment study. *Journal of Elder Abuse & Neglect, 23,* 43–57.

Andersen, B. L., et al. (2008). Psychologic intervention improves survival for breast cancer patients. *Cancer, 113,* 3450–3458.

Anderson, E. R., & Mayes, L. C. (2010). Race/ethnicity and internalizing disorders in youth: A review. *Clinical Psychology Review, 30,* 338–348.

Anderson, J. (2007, April 25). Morgan Stanley to settle sex bias suit. *New York Times,* pp. C1, C18.

Anderson, K. L. (2010). Conflict, power, and violence in families. *Journal of Marriage and Family, 72,* 726–742.

Anderson, S. J., & Johnson, J. T. (2003). The who and when of "gender-blind" attitudes: Predictors of gender- role egalitarianism in two different domains. *Sex Roles, 49,* 527–532.

Anderson, V. N., Simpson-Taylor, D., & Herrmann, D. J. (2004). Gender, age, and rape-supportive rules. *Sex Roles, 50,* 77–90.

Anderson-Frye, E. (2009). Cross-cultural issues in body image among children and adolescents. In L. Smolak & J. K.

Thompson (Eds.), *Body image, eating disorders, and obesity in youth: Assessment, prevention, and treatment* (pp. 113–134). Washington, DC: American Psychological Association.

Andreasen, N. C. (2005). Vulnerability to mental illnesses: Gender makes a difference, and so does providing good psychiatric care. *American Journal of Psychiatry, 162,* 211–213.

Andreescu, T., Gallian, J. A., Kane, J. M., & Mertz, J. E. (2008). Cross-cultural analysis of students with exceptional talent in mathematical problem solving. *Notices of the American Mathematical Society, 55,* 1248–1260.

Angier, N. (1999, February 21). Men, women, sex and Darwin. *New York Times Magazine,* pp. 48–53.

Angier, N. (2001, April 10). A lifetime later, still in love with the lab. *New York Times,* pp. D1, D6.

Angier, N. (2002, November 5). The importance of grandma. *New York Times,* pp. D1, D4.

Angier, N. (2007, April 10). Birds do it. Bees do it. People seek the keys to it. *New York Times,* pp. D1, D4.

Ansara, D. L., & Hindin, M. J. (2010). Exploring gender differences in the patterns of intimate partner violence in Canada: A latent class approach. *Journal of Epidemiology and Community Health, 64,* 849–854.

Anschutz, D. J., Kanters, L. J. A., Van Strien, T., Vermulst, A. A., & Engels, R. C. M. E. (2009). Maternal behaviors and restrained eating and body dissatisfaction in young children. *International Journal of Eating Disorders, 42,* 54–61.

Ansehl, A., Katz, M. B., & Murthy, P. (2010). Society, exercise, and women. In P. Murthy & C. L. Smith (Eds.), *Women's global health and human rights* (pp. 451–460). Sudbury, MA: Jones and Bartlett.

Antonucci, T. C., Birditt, K. S., & Akiyama, H. (2009). Convoys of social relations: An interdisciplinary approach. In V. Bengtson, M. Silverstein, N. M. Putney, & D. Gans (Eds.), *Handbook of theories of aging* (2nd ed., pp. 247–260). New York: Springer.

Antonucci, T. C., Blieszner, R., & Denmark, F. L. (2010). Psychological perspectives on older women. In H. Landrine & N. F. Russo (Eds.), *Handbook of diversity in feminist psychology* (pp. 233–257). New York: Springer.

Antonucci, T. C., Fiori, K. L., Birditt, K., & Jackey, L. M. H. (2010). Convoys of social relations: Integrating life span and life-course perspectives. In M. E. Lamb & A. M. Freund (Eds.), *The handbook of life-span development: Social and emotional development* (Vol. 2, pp. 434–473). Hoboken, NJ: Wiley.

APA Task Force on the Sexualization of Girls. (2007). *Report on the APA task force on the sexualization of girls.* Washington, DC: American Psychological Association.

Apparala, M. L., Reifman, A., & Munsch, J. (2003). Cross-national comparison of attitudes toward fathers' and mothers' participation in household tasks and childcare. *Sex Roles, 48,* 189–203.

Arber, S. (2004). Gender, marital status, and ageing: Linking material, health, and social resources. *Journal of Aging Studies, 18,* 91–108.

Archer, J. (2004). Sex differences in aggression in real-world settings: A meta-analytic review. *Review of General Psychology, 8,* 291–322.

Archer, S. L. (1992). A feminist's approach to identity research. In G. R. Adams, T. P. Gullotta, & R. Montemayor (Eds.), *Adolescent identity formation* (pp. 25–49). Newberry Park, CA: Sage.

Armenta, B. E. (2010). Stereotype boost and stereotype threat effects: The moderating role of ethnic identification. *Cultural Diversity and Ethnic Minority Psychology, 16,* 94–98.

Armstrong, M. J. (2001). Ethnic minority women as they age. In J. D. Garner & S. O. Mercer (Eds.), *Women as they age* (2nd ed., pp. 97–114). New York: Haworth.

Arnett, J. J. (2008). The neglected 95%: Why American psychology needs to become less American. *American Psychologist, 63,* 602–614.

Arney, H. T. (2001, May 23). Friends, active social life help turn widow's life around. *Peoria Times-Observer,* p. A8.

Arnold, J. E., & Lang, U. A. (2007). Changing American home life: Trends in domestic leisure and storage among middle-class families. *Journal of Family and Economic Issues, 28,* 23–48.

Aronson, P. (2003). Feminists or "postfeminists"? Young women's attitudes toward feminism and gender relations. *Gender & Society, 17,* 903–922.

Aronson, P. (2008). The markers and meanings of growing up: Contemporary young women's transition from adolescence to adulthood. *Gender & Society, 22,* 56–82.

Årseth, A. K., Kroger, J., Martinussen, M., & Bakken, G. (2009). Intimacy status, attachment, separation-individuation patterns, and identity status in female university students. *Journal of Social and Personal Relationships, 26,* 697–712.

Asendorpf, J. B., Denissen, J. J. A., & van Aken, M. A. G. (2008). Inhibited and aggressive preschool children at 23 years of age: Personality and social transitions into adulthood. *Developmental Psychology, 44,* 997–1011.

Ashkinaze, C. (2005, Summer). A matter of opinion. *Ms.,* 17.

Ata, R. N., Ludden, A. B., & Lally, M. M. (2007). The effects of gender and family, friend, and media influences on eating behaviors and body image during adolescence. *Journal of Youth and Adolescence, 36,* 1024–1037.

Athenstaedt, U., Haas, E., & Schwab, S. (2004). Gender role self-concept and gender-typed communication behavior in mixed-sex and same-sex dyads. *Sex Roles, 50,* 37–52.

Attar-Schwartz, S., Tan, J.-P., Buchanan, A., Flouri, E., & Griggs, J. (2009). Grandparenting and adolescent adjustment in two-parent biological, lone-parent, and step-families. *Journal of Family Psychology, 23,* 67–75.

Attia, E., & Walsh, B. T. (2009). Behavioral management for anorexia nervosa. *New England Journal of Medicine, 360,* 500–5006.

Aubeeluck, A., & Maguire, M. (2002). The menstrual joy questionnaire alone can positively prime reporting of menstrual attitudes and symptoms. *Psychology of Women Quarterly, 26,* 160–162.

Aubin, S., & Heiman, J. R. (2004). Sexual dysfunction from a relationship perspective. In J. H. Harvey, A. Wenzel, & S. Sprecher (Eds.), *The handbook of sexuality in close relationships* (pp. 477–517). Mahwah, NJ: Erlbaum.

Aubrey, J. S. (2010). Looking good versus feeling good: An investigation of media frames of health advice and their effects on women's body-related self-perceptions. *Sex Roles, 63,* 50–63.

Aumann, K., & Galinsky, E. (2009). *The state of health in the American workforce: Does having an effective workplace matter?* New York: Families and Work Institute.

Aune, T., & Stiles, T. C. (2009). The effects of depression and stressful life events on the development and maintenance of syndromal social anxiety: Sex and age differences. *Journal of Clinical Child & Adolescent Psychology, 38,* 501–512.

Austen, S., & Ong, R. (2010). The employment transitions of midlife women: Health and care effects. *Ageing and Society, 30,* 207–227.

Auster, E. R. (2001). Professional women's midcareer satisfaction: Toward an explanatory framework. *Sex Roles, 44,* 719–750.

Ayala, C., Xie, J., McGruder, H. F., & Valderrama, A. L. (2008). Receipt of outpatient cardiac rehabilitation among heart attack survivors—United States, 2005. *Morbidity and Mortality Weekly Report, 57,* 89–94.

Ayers, B., Forshaw, M., & Hunter, M. S. (2010). The impact of attitudes towards the menopause on women's symptom experience: A systematic review. *Maturitas, 65,* 28–36.

Ayman, R., & Korabik, K. (2010). Leadership: Why gender and culture matter. *American Psychologist, 65,* 157–170.

Ayman, R., Korabik, K., & Morris, S. (2009). Is transformational leadership always perceived as effective? Male subordinates' devaluation of female transformational leaders. *Journal of Applied Social Psychology, 39,* 852–879.

Ayotte, B. J., Yang, F. M., & Jones, R. N. (2010). Physical health and depression: A dyadic study of chronic health conditions and depressive symptomatology in older adult couples. *Journal of Gerontology: Psychological Sciences, 65B,* 438–448.

Ayoub, N. C. (2004, April 2). Nota bene. *Chronicle of Higher Education,* p. A18.

Ayres, M. M., Friedman, C. K., & Leaper, C. (2009). Individual and situational factors related to young women's likelihood of confronting sexism in their everyday lives. *Sex Roles, 61,* 449–460.

Azar, B. (2011, January). Meet your 2011 president. *Monitor on Psychology,* pp. 64–66.

Azzam, H., & Kaljee, L. (2010). Vaccines and women: Cultural and structural issues for acceptability. In P. Murthy & C. L. Smith (Eds.), *Women's global health and human rights* (pp. 311–328). Sudbury, MA: Jones and Bartlett.

Babcock, L., & Laschever, S. (2008). *Ask for it: How women can use the power of negotiation to get what they really want.* New York: Bantam.

Bach, P. B. (2010). Postmenopausal hormone therapy and breast cancer: An uncertain trade-off. *Journal of the American Medical Association, 304,* 1719–1720.

Badger, K., Craft, R. C., & Jensen, L. (1998). Age and gender differences in value orientation among American adolescents. *Adolescence, 33,* 591–596.

Badgwell, B. D., et al. (2008). Mammography before diagnosis among women age 80 years and older with breast cancer. *Journal of Clinical Oncology, 26,* 2482–2488.

Baiardi, J., & Wolf, P. (2009). Loss and bereavement. In J. C. Urbancic & C. J. Groh (Eds.), *Women's mental health: A clinical guide for primary care providers* (pp. 473–495). Philadelphia, PA: Lippincott Williams & Wilkins.

Bailey, J. M., Pillard, R. C., Neale, M. C., & Agyei, Y. (1993). Heritable factors influence sexual orientation in women. *Archives of General Psychiatry, 48,* 1089–1096.

Baillargeon, R. H., et al. (2007). Gender differences in physical aggression: A prospective population-based survey of children before and after 2 years of age. *Developmental Psychology, 43,* 13–26.

Baird, C., Pancari, J. V., Lutz, P. J., & Baird, T. (2009). Addiction disorders. In J. C. Urbancic & C. J. Groh (Eds.), *Women's mental health: A clinical guide for primary care providers* (pp. 125–179). Philadelphia, PA: Lippincott Williams & Wilkins.

Bair-Merritt, M. H., Crowne, S. S., Thompson, D. A., Sibinga, E., Trent, M., & Campbell, J. (2010). Why do women use intimate partner violence? A systematic review of women's motivations. *Trauma, Violence & Abuse, 11,* 178–189.

Bairey Merz, C. N., et al. (2010). Proceedings from the scientific symposium: Sex differences in cardiovascular disease and implications for therapies. *Journal of Women's Health, 19,* 1059–1072.

Baker, C. N. (2005). Images of women's sexuality in advertisements: A content analysis of black- and white-oriented women's and men's magazines. *Sex Roles, 52,* 13–27.

Baker, C. N. (2008). *The women's movement against sexual harassment.* New York: Cambridge University Press.

Baker, D. M. (2003, August). *Childfree women's experience of gender.* Paper presented at the meeting of the American Psychology Association, Toronto.

Baker, J., & Milligan, K. (2010). Evidence from maternity leave expansions of the impact of maternal care on early child development. *Journal of Human Resources, 45,* 1–32.

Baker, L. (2010). In women's voices. In M. A. Paludi (Ed.), *Feminism and women's rights worldwide: Feminism as human rights* (Vol. 2, pp. 251–252). Santa Barbara, CA: Praeger.

Baker, L., & Gringart, E. (2009). Body image and self-esteem in older adulthood. *Aging and Society, 29,* 977–995.

Baker, L. A., & Mutchler, J. E. (2010). Poverty and maternal hardship in grandparent-headed households. *Journal of Marriage and Family, 72,* 947–962.

Baker, T. B., McFall, R. M., & Shoham, V. (2008). Current status and future prospects of clinical psychology toward a scientifically principled approach to mental and behavioral health care. *Psychological Science in the Public Interest, 9,* 67–103.

Baker-Sperry, L., & Grauerholz, L. (2011). The pervasiveness and persistence of the feminine beauty ideal in children's fairy tales. In J. Z. Spade & C. G. Valentine (Eds.), *The kaleidoscope of gender: Prisms, patterns, and possibilities* (3rd ed., pp. 185–192). Thousand Oaks, CA: Sage.

Bakirci, K. (2011). Sexual orientation-based violence: Outside United States. In M. Z. Stange, C. K. Oyster, & J. E. Sloan (Eds.), *Encyclopedia of women in today's world.* Newberry Park, CA: Sage.

Bakker, M. P., Ormel, J., Verhulst, F. C., & Oldehinkel, A. J. (2010). Peer stressors and gender differences in adolescents' mental health: The TRAILS study. *Journal of Adolescent Health, 46,* 444–450.

Ballou, M., & Hill, M. (2008). The context of therapy: Theory. In M. Ballou, M. Hill, & C. West (Eds.), *Feminist therapy theory and practice: A contemporary perspective* (pp. 1–8). New York: Springer.

Banerjee, N. (2001, August 10). Some "bullies" seek ways to soften up. *New York Times,* pp. C1, C2.

Banerjee, N. (2006, August 26). Clergywomen find hard path to bigger pulpit. *New York Times,* pp. A1, A11.

Bang, E., Hall, M. E. L., Anderson, T. L., & Willingham, M. M. (2005). Ethnicity, acculturation, and religiosity as predictors of female college students' role expectations. *Sex Roles, 53,* 231–237.

Banks, A., & Gartrell, N. K. (1995). Hormones and sexual orientation: A questionable link. *Journal of Homosexuality, 28,* 247–268.

Banks, M. E. (2010). Feminist psychology and women with disabilities: An emerging alliance. *Psychology of Women Quarterly, 34,* 431–442.

Banyard, V. L., Ward, S., Cohn, E. S., Plante, E. G., Moorhead, C., & Walsh, W. (2007). Unwanted sexual contact on campus: A comparison of women's and men's experiences. *Violence and Victims, 22,* 52–70.

Barash, D. P. (2002, May 24). Evolution, males, and violence. *Chronicle of Higher Education,* pp. B7–B9.

Barash, D. P., & Lipton, J. E. (2002). *Gender gap: The biology of male-female differences.* New York: Transaction.

Barefoot, J. C., et al. (2001). A longitudinal study of gender differences in depressive symptoms from age 50 to 80. *Psychology and Aging, 16,* 342–345.

Barefoot, J. C., et al. (2011). Recovery expectations and long-term prognosis of patients with coronary heart disease. *Archives of Internal Medicine, 171.* doi:10.1001/archinternmed.2011.41

Barker, E. T., & Bornstein, M. H. (2007, March). *Temporal ordering of body dissatisfaction and self-esteem across early adolescence.* Poster presented at the meeting of the Society for Research in Child Development, Boston.

Barlett, C. P., & Harris, R. J. (2008). The impact of body emphasizing video games on body image concerns in men and women. *Sex Roles, 59,* 586–601.

Barnes, B. (2010, November 21). Disney ties lots of hopes to lots of hair. *New York Times,* p. AR8.

Barnett, M. A., Scaramella, L. V., Neppl, T. K., Ontai, L. L., & Conger, R. D. (2010). Grandmother involvement as a protective factor for early childhood social adjustment. *Journal of Family Psychology, 24,* 635–645.

Barnett, O., Miller-Perrin, C. L., & Perrin, R. D. (2005). *Family violence across the lifespan: An introduction*. Thousand Oaks, CA: Sage Publications.

Barnett, R. C. (2007). Women, leadership, and the natural order. In B. Kellerman & D. L. Rhode (Eds.), *Women & leadership: The state of play and strategies for change* (pp. 149–173). San Francisco, CA: Jossey-Bass.

Barot, S. (2010, Spring). Past due: Emergency contraception in U.S. reproductive health programs overseas. *Guttmacher Policy Review, 13*(2), 8–11.

Barreto, M., Ryan, M. K., & Schmitt, M. T. (2009). Introduction: Is the glass ceiling still relevant in the 21st century? In M. Barreto, M. K. Ryan, & M. T. Schmitt (Eds.), *The glass ceiling in the 21st century: Understanding barriers to gender equality* (pp. 3–18). Washington, DC: American Psychological Association.

Barrett, S., & Ballou, M. (2008). The person of the client: Theory. In M. Ballou, M. Hill, & C. West (Eds.), *Feminist therapy theory and practice: A contemporary perspective* (pp. 39–54). New York: Springer.

Barrionuevo, A. (2010, July 16). Argentina approves gay marriage, a first for region. *New York Times*, p. A3.

Barrow, K. (2010, December 27). Difference is the norm on these dating sites. *New York Times*, p. D6.

Barry, L. C., Allore, H. G., Guo, Z., Bruce, M. L., & Gill, T. M. (2008). Higher burden of depression among older women. *Archives of General Psychiatry, 65*, 172–178.

Bartini, M. (2006). Gender role flexibility in early adolescence: Developmental change in attitudes, self-perception, and behaviors. *Sex Roles, 55*, 233–245.

Bartlett, T. (2002, April 5). The question of sex between professors and students. *Chronicle of Higher Education*, pp. A8, A9.

Bartlett, T. (2009, November 27). The puzzle of boys: Scholars and others debate what it means to grow up male in America. *Chronicle of Higher Education*, pp. B7–B9.

Bartoli, A. M., & Clark, M. D. (2006). The dating game: Similarities and differences in dating scripts among college students. *Sexuality & Culture, 10*, 54–80.

Barton, L. (2005, January 5). Celebrities distort girls' search for ideal shape. *Guardian (London)*, p. 7.

Basile, K. C., & Black, M. C. (2011). Intimate partner violence against women. In C. M. Renzetti, J. L. Edleson, & R. K. Bergen (Eds.), *Sourcebook on violence against women* (2nd ed., pp. 111–130). Thousand Oaks, CA: Sage.

Basow, S. A. (2008a). Gender socialization, or how long a way has baby come? In J. C. Chrisler, C. Golden, & P. D. Rozee (Eds.), *Lectures on the psychology of women* (pp. 80–95). New York: McGraw-Hill.

Basow, S. A. (2008b). Speaking in a "man's world": Gender differences in communication styles. In M. A. Paludi (Ed.), *The psychology of women at work: Challenges and solutions for our female workforce: Career liberation, history, and the new millennium* (Vol. 1, pp. 15–30). Westport, CT: Praeger.

Basow, S. A. (2010a). Changes in psychology of women and psychology of gender textbooks (1975–2010). *Sex Roles, 62*, 151–152.

Basow, S. A. (2010b). Women in education: Students and professors worldwide. In M. A. Paludi (Ed.), *Feminism and women's rights worldwide* (Vol. 1, pp. 43–62). Santa Barbara, CA: Praeger.

Basow, S. A., & Minieri, A. (2011). "You owe me a date": Effects of date cost, who pays, participant gender, and rape myth beliefs on perceptions of rape. *Journal of Interpersonal Violence, 26*, 479–449.

Bauer, P. J., Liebl, M., & Stennes, L. (1998). Pretty is to dress as brave is to suitcoat: Gender-based property-to-property inferences by 4-year-old children. *Merrill-Palmer Quarterly, 44*, 355–377.

Baum, K., Catalano, S., Rand, M., & Rose, K. (2009). *Stalking victimization in the United States*. Washington, DC: Bureau of Justice Statistics, U.S. Department of Justice.

Baumgarte, R., & Nelson, D. W. (2009). Preference for same- versus cross-sex friendships. *Journal of Applied Social Psychology, 39*, 901–917.

Bauminger, N., Finzi-Dottan, R., Chason, S., & Har-Even, D. (2008). Intimacy in adolescent friendship: The roles of attachment, coherence, and self-disclosure. *Journal of Social and Personal Relationships, 25*, 409–428.

Bauserman, R. (2002). Child adjustment in joint-custody versus sole-custody arrangements: A meta-analytic review. *Journal of Family Psychology, 16*, 91–102.

Baxter, J., Hewitt, B., & Haynes, M. (2008). Life course transitions and housework: Marriage, parenthood, and time on housework. *Journal of Marriage and Family, 70*, 259–272.

Bay-Cheng, L. Y., Robinson, A. D., & Zucker, A. N. (2009). Behavioral and relational contexts of adolescent desire, wanting, and pleasure: Undergraduate women's retrospective accounts. *Journal of Sex Research, 46*, 511–5524.

Bay-Cheng, L. Y., & Zucker, A. N. (2007). Feminism between the sheets: Sexual attitudes among feminists, nonfeminists, and egalitarians. *Psychology of Women Quarterly, 31*, 157–163.

Bazelon, E. (2009, February 1). 2 kids + 0 husbands = family: Many college-educated single mothers are setting up lives around other single mothers and all their children, with no role for men or romance. *New York Times Magazine*, pp. 30–35.

Bazzini, D. G., McIntosh, W. D., Smith, S. M., Cook, S., & Harris, C. (1997). The aging woman in popular film: Underrepresented, unattractive, unfriendly, and unintelligent. *Sex Roles, 36*, 531–543.

Beach, S., Schulz, R., Castle, N., & Rosen, J. (2010). Financial exploitation and psychological mistreatment among older adults: Differences between African Americans and non-African Americans in a population-based survey. *Gerontologist, 50*, 744–757.

Beals, K. P., & Peplau, L. A. (2005). Identity support, identity devaluation, and well-being among lesbians. *Psychology of Women Quarterly, 29*, 140–148.

Bean-Mayberry, B. A., Chang, C. H., McNeil, M. A., & Scholle, S. H. (2006). Ensuring high quality primary care for women: Predictors of success. *Women's Health Issues, 16*, 22–29.

Bearman, P. (2004, March). *Rules, behaviors, and networks that influence STD prevention among adolescents*. Paper presented at the meeting of the National STD Prevention Conference, Philadelphia.

Bearman, P. S., & Moody, J. (2004). Suicide and friendships among American adolescents. *American Journal of Public Health, 94*, 89–96.

Beaton, A. M., Tougas, F., & Joly, S. (1996). Neosexism among male managers: Is it a matter of numbers? *Journal of Applied Social Psychology, 26*, 2189–2203.

Beck, M. E., & Arnold, J. E. (2009). Gendered time use at home: An ethnographic examination of leisure time in middle-class families. *Leisure Studies, 28*, 121–142.

Becker, A. E., Fay, K., Gilman, S. E., & Striegel-Moore, R. (2007). Facets of acculturation and their diverse relations to body shape concern in Fiji. *International Journal of Eating Disorders, 40*, 42–50.

Becker, M. A., Levin, B. L., & Hanson, A. R. M. (2010). Public health and women's mental health. In B. L. Levin & M. A. Becker (Eds.), *A public health perspective of women's mental health* (pp. 3–10). New York: Springer.

Beckles, G. L., & Truman, B. I. (2011, January 14). Education and income—United States, 2005 and 2009. *Morbidity and Mortality Weekly Report, 60*(Suppl.), 13–17.

Beckman, L. J. (2006). Women's reproductive health: Issues, findings, and controversies. In J. Worell & C. D. Goodheart (Eds.), *Handbook of girls' and women's psychological health: Gender and well-being across the lifespan* (pp. 330–338). New York: Oxford University Press.

Bedford, V. H. (1995). Sibling relationships in middle and old age. In R. Blieszner & V. H. Bedford (Eds.), *Handbook of aging and the family* (pp. 201–222). Westport, CT: Greenwood.

Beers, M. H., & Jones, T. V. (2004). *The Merck manual of health and aging.* Whitehouse Station, NJ: Merck Research Laboratories.

Behforouz, H. L., & Chung, J. (2010). Poor, black, and female: The growing face of AIDS in the United States. In P. Murthy & C. L. Smith (Eds.), *Women's global health and human rights* (pp. 141–160). Sudbury, MA: Jones and Bartlett.

Behm-Morawitz, E., & Mastro, D. (2009). The effects of sexualization of female video game characters on gender stereotyping and female self-concept. *Sex Roles, 61,* 808–823.

Beilock, S. L., Gunderson, E. A., Ramirez, G., & Levine, S. C. (2010). Female teachers' math anxiety affects girls' math achievement. *Proceedings of the National Academy of Sciences, 107,* 1860–1863.

Beiner, T. M., & O'Connor, M. (2007). When an individual finds herself to be the victim of sex discrimination. In F. J. Crosby, M. S. Stockdale, & S. A. Ropp (Eds.), *Sex discrimination in the workplace* (pp. 19–56). Malden, MA: Blackwell.

Bekker, M. H. J., & van Assen, M. A. L. M. (2008). Autonomy-connectedness and gender. *Sex Roles, 59,* 532–544.

Belgrave, F. Z., & Allison, K. W. (2010). *African American psychology: From Africa to America* (2nd ed.). Thousand Oaks, CA: Sage.

Belkin, L. (2010, October 24). Calling Mr. Mom? *New York Times Magazine,* pp. 13–14.

Belknap, J. (2010). Rape: Too hard to report and too easy to discredit victims. *Violence Against Women, 16,* 1335–1344.

Bell, L. C. (2004). Psychoanalytic theories of gender. In A. H. Eagly, A. E. Beall, & R. J. Sternberg (Eds.), *The psychology of gender* (pp. 145–168). New York: Guilford.

Bell, M. E., Goodman, L. A., & Dutton, M. A. (2009). Variations in help-seeking, battered women's relationship course, emotional well-being, and experiences of abuse over time. *Psychology of Women Quarterly, 33,* 149–162.

Bellafante, G. (2005, May 8). Even in gay circles, women want the ring. *New York Times,* pp. ST1, ST7.

Belsky, J., Steinberg, L., Houts, R. M., & Halpern-Felsher, B. L. (2010). The development of reproductive strategy in females: Early maternal harshness → earlier menarche → increased sexual risk taking. *Developmental Psychology, 46,* 120–128.

Belsky, J., et al. (2007). Family rearing antecedents of pubertal timing. *Child Development, 78,* 1302–1321.

Bem, S. L. (1974). The measurement of psychological androgyny. *Journal of Consulting and Clinical Psychology, 42,* 155–162.

Bem, S. L. (1975). Sex role adaptability: One consequence of psychological androgyny. *Journal of Personality and Social Psychology, 31,* 634–643.

Bem, S. L. (1993). *The lenses of gender: Transforming the debate on sexual inequality.* New Haven, CT: Yale University Press.

Bem, S. L. (1998). *An unconventional family.* New Haven, CT: Yale University Press.

Bem, S. L. (2008). Transforming the debate on sexual inequality: From biological difference to institutionalized androcentrism. In J. C. Chrisler, C. Golden, & P. D. Rozee (Eds.), *Lectures on the psychology of women* (pp. 2–15). New York: McGraw-Hill.

Benedict, H. (2008, Fall). The scandal of military rape. *Ms.,* 41–45.

Benenson, J. F., et al. (2009). Males' greater tolerance of same-sex peers. *Psychological Science, 20,* 184–190.

Benenson, J. F., Morash, D., & Petrakos, H. (1998). Gender differences in emotional closeness between preschool children and their mothers. *Sex Roles, 38,* 975–985.

Benjamin, S. (2010). Gender and schooling. In B. Featherstone, C.-A. Hooper, J. Scourfield, & J. Taylor (Eds.), *Gender and child welfare in society* (pp. 95–120). Hoboken, NJ: Wiley.

Bennett, J. (2009, April 6). Tales of a modern diva. *Newsweek,* pp. 42–43.

Bennett, J., & Yabroff, J. (2008). Revenge of the nerdette. *Newsweek,* pp. 44–45.

Bennhold, K., Kulish, N., & Donadio, R. (2010, March 24). Abuse scandal's ripples spread across Europe. *New York Times,* p. A12.

Bent-Goodley, T. B., Rice, J., II., Williams, O. J., & Pope, M. (2011). Treatment for perpetrators of domestic violence. In M. P. Koss, J. W. White, & A. E. Kazdin (Eds.), *Violence against women and children: Navigating solutions* (Vol. 2, pp. 199–214). Washington, DC: American Psychological Association.

Bentley, C. G., Galliher, R. V., & Ferguson, T. J. (2007). Associations among aspects of interpersonal power and relationship functioning in adolescent romantic couples. *Sex Roles, 57,* 483–496.

Beral, V., et al. (2007). Ovarian cancer and hormone replacement therapy in the million women study. *Lancet, 369,* 1703–1710.

Berdahl, J. L. (2007). The sexual harassment of uppity women. *Journal of Applied Psychology, 92,* 425–437.

Berdahl, J. L., & Moore, C. (2006). Workplace harassment: Double jeopardy for minority women. *Journal of Applied Psychology, 91,* 426–436.

Berdahl, T. A. (2008). Racial/ethnic and gender differences in individual workplace injury risk trajectories: 1988–1998. *American Journal of Public Health, 98,* 2258–2263.

Berenbaum, S. A., Bryk, K. K., Nowak, N., Quigley, C. A., & Moffat, S. (2009). Fingers as a marker of prenatal androgen exposure. *Endocrinology, 150,* 5119–5124.

Berger, J. S., et al. (2009). Sex differences in mortality following acute coronary syndromes. *Journal of the American Medical Association, 302,* 874–882.

Berger, L. (2000, July 18). A new body politic: Learning to like the way we look. *New York Times,* p. D7.

Bergmann, B. R. (2011). Sex segregation in the blue-collar occupations: Women's choices or unremedied discrimination? Comment on England. *Gender & Society, 25,* 88–93.

Berk, L. E. (2009). *Child development* (8th ed.). Boston, MA: Allyn & Bacon.

Berk, L. E., Wholeben, B. M., & Bouchey, H. A. (1998). *Instructors resource manual for Berk, L. E. (1998): Development through the lifespan.* Boston, MA: Allyn & Bacon.

Berkowitz, R. L., Roberts, J., & Minkoff, H. (2006). Challenging the strategy of maternal age-based prenatal genetic counseling. *Journal of the American Medical Association, 295,* 1446–1448.

Berlau, D. J., Corrada, M. M., & Kawas, C. (2009). The prevalence of disability in the oldest-old is high and continues to increase with age: Findings from The 90+ Study. *International Journal of Geriatric Psychiatry, 24,* 1217–1225.

Bernard, S., & Correll, S. J. (2010). Normative discrimination and the motherhood penalty. *Gender & Society, 24,* 616–646.

Bernstein, B. L., Jacobson, R., & Russo, N. F. (2010). Mentoring women in science, technology, engineering, and mathematics fields. In C. A. Rayburn, F. L. Denmark, M. E. Reuder, & A. M. Austria (Eds.), *A handbook for women mentors: Transcending barriers of stereotype, race, and ethnicity* (pp. 43–63). Santa Barbara, CA: Praeger.

Bernstein, B. L., & Russo, N. F. (2008). Explaining too few women in STEM careers: A psychosocial perspective. In M. A. Paludi (Ed.), *The psychology of women at work: Challenges and solutions for our female workforce: Obstacles and the identity juggle* (Vol. 2, pp. 1–33). Westport, CT: Praeger.

Bernstein, N. (2002, August 14). Child-only cases grow on welfare. *New York Times*, pp. A1, A21.

Berry, G. L. (2007). Television, social roles, and marginality: Portrayals of the past and images for the future. In N. Pecora, J. P. Murray, & E. A. Wartella (Eds.), *Children and television: Fifty years of research* (pp. 85–107). Mahwah, NJ: Erlbaum.

Bersamin, M., Todd, M., Fisher, D. A., Hill, D. L., Grube, J. W., & Walker, S. (2008). Parenting practices and adolescent sexual behavior: A longitudinal study. *Journal of Marriage and Family, 70,* 97–112.

Bertakis, K. D. (2009). The influence of gender on the doctor-patient interaction. *Patient Education and Counseling, 76,* 356–360.

Bertakis, K. D., & Azari, R. (2007). Patient gender and physician practice style. *Journal of Women's Health, 16,* 859–868.

Bessenoff, G. R., & Del Priore, R. E. (2007). Women, weight, and age: Social comparison to magazine images across the lifespan. *Sex Roles, 56,* 215–222.

Best, D. L. (2001). Cross-cultural gender roles. In J. Worell (Ed.), *Encyclopedia of women and gender* (pp. 279–290). San Diego, CA: Academic Press.

Best, D. L. (2009). Another view of the gender-status relation. *Sex Roles, 61,* 341–351.

Best, D. L. (2010). Gender. In M. H. Bornstein (Ed.), *Handbook of cultural developmental science* (pp. 209–222). New York: Psychology Press.

Best, D. L., & Thomas, J. J. (2004). Cultural diversity and cross-cultural perspectives. In A. H. Eagly, A. E. Beall, & R. J. Sternberg (Eds.), *The psychology of gender* (pp. 296–327). New York: Guilford.

Betz, N. E. (2008). Women's career development. In F. L. Denmark & M. A. Paludi (Eds.), *Psychology of women: A handbook of issues and theories* (2nd ed., pp. 717–752). Westport, CT: Praeger.

Beumont, P. (2005, January 9). Alexander the Turkey? *Observer (London),* p. 22.

Beyer, S. (1997, June). *Gender differences in causal attributions of imagined performance on English, history, and math exams.* Paper presented at the meeting of the American Psychological Society, Washington, DC.

Beyer, S. (2006). Comparing gender differences in computer science and management information systems majors. In E. M. Trauth (Ed.), *Encyclopedia of gender and information technology* (pp. 109–115). Hershey, PA: Idea Group.

Beyers, W., & Seiffge-Krenke, I. (2010). Does identity precede intimacy? Testing Erikson's theory on romantic development in emerging adults of the 21st century. *Journal of Adolescent Research, 25,* 387–415.

Bianchi, S. M., Hotz, V. J., McGarry, K., & Seltzer, J. A. (2008). Intergenerational ties: Theories, trends, and challenges. In A. Booth, A. C. Crouter, S. M. Bianchi, & J. A. Seltzer (Eds.), *Intergenerational caregiving* (pp. 3–43). Washington, DC: Urban Institute Press.

Bianchi, S. M., & Milkie, M. A. (2010). Work and family research in the first decade of the 21st century. *Journal of Marriage and Family, 72,* 705–725.

Bianchi, S. M., & Wight, V. R. (2010). The long reach of the job: Employment and time for family. In K. Christensen & B. Schneider (Eds.), *Workplace flexibility: Realigning 20th-century jobs for a 21st-century workforce* (pp. 17–42). Ithaca, NY: Cornell University Press.

Biblarz, T. J., & Savci, E. (2010). Lesbian, gay, bisexual, and transgender families. *Journal of Marriage and Family, 72,* 480–497.

Biblarz, T. J., & Stacey, J. (2010). How does the gender of parents matter? *Journal of Marriage and Family, 72,* 3–22.

Biegel, S. (2010). *The right to be out: Sexual orientation and gender identity in America's public schools.* Minneapolis, MN: University of Minnesota Press.

Bierman, K. L., et al. (2004). Early disruptive behaviors associated with emerging antisocial behavior among girls. In M. Putallaz & K. L. Bierman (Eds.), *Aggression, antisocial behavior, and violence among girls: A developmental perspective* (pp. 137–161). New York: Guilford.

Biernat, M., Fuegen, K., & Kobrynowicz, D. (2010). Shifting standards and the inference of incompetence: Effects of formal and informal evaluation tools. *Personality and Social Psychology Bulletin, 36,* 855–868.

Bieschke, K. J., Paul, P. L., & Blasko, K. A. (2007). Review of empirical research focused on the experience of lesbian, gay, and bisexual clients in counseling and psychotherapy. In K. J. Bieschke, R. M. Perez, & K. A. DeBord (Eds.), *Handbook of counseling and psychotherapy with lesbian, gay, bisexual, and transgender clients* (2nd ed., pp. 293–316). Washington, DC: American Psychology Association.

Bieschke, K. J., & Toepfer-Hendey, E. (2006). Career counseling with lesbian clients. In W. B. Walsh & M. J. Heppner (Eds.), *Handbook of career counseling for women* (2nd ed., pp. 351–386). Mahwah, NJ: Erlbaum.

Billari, F. C., & Liefbroer, A. C. (2008). Intergenerational ties: What can be gained from an international perspective? In A. Booth, A. C. Crouter, S. M. Bianchi, & J. A. Seltzer (Eds.), *Intergenerational caregiving* (pp. 53–66). Washington, DC: Urban Institute Press.

Billing, Y. D. (2011). Are women in management victims of the phantom of the male norm? *Gender, Work and Organization, 18,* 298–317.

Billings, A. C., Halone, K. K., & Denham, B. E. (2002). "Man, that was a pretty shot": An analysis of gendered broadcast commentary surrounding the 2000 men's and women's NCAA final four basketball championships. *Mass Communication & Society, 5,* 295–315.

Binder, E. F., et al. (2008). Effects of exercise training on frailty in community-dwelling older adults: Results of a randomized, controlled trial. *Journal of the American Geriatrics Society, 50,* 1921–1928.

Binge drinking on college campuses. (2008). Washington, DC: Center for Science in the Public Interest.

Birchard, K. (2011, November 11). "Nosy" and observant, a neuroscientist continues her memorable career at 93. *Chronicle of Higher Education,* p. A26.

Birchler, G., & Fals-Stewart, W. (1998). Marriage and divorce. In M. Hersen & V. B. Van Hasselt (Eds.), *Handbook of clinical geropsychology* (pp. 449–467). New York: Plenum.

Bird, C. E., Lang, M. E., & Rieker, P. P. (2010). Changing gendered patterns of morbidity and mortality. In E. Kuhlmann & E. Annandale (Eds.), *Palgrave handbook of gender and healthcare* (pp. 125–141). London: Palgrave Macmillan.

Bird, C. E., & Rieker, P. P. (2008). *Gender and health: The effects of constrained choices and social policies.* New York: Cambridge University Press.

Bird, S., et al. (2009). The influence of the built environment and other factors on the physical activity of older women from different ethnic communities. *Journal of Women & Aging, 21,* 33–47.

Birenbaum, M., & Kraemer, R. (1995). Gender and ethnic- group differences in causal attributions for success and failure in mathematics and language examinations. *Journal of Cross-Cultural Psychology, 26,* 342–359.

Birnbaum, G. E., Cohen, O., & Wertheimer, V. (2007). Is it all about intimacy? Age, menopausal status, and women's sexuality. *Personal Relationships, 14,* 167–185.

Bisaga, K., Whitaker, A., Davies, M., Chuang, S., Feldman, J., & Walsh, B. T. (2005). Eating disorder and depressive symptoms in urban high school girls from different ethnic backgrounds. *Journal of Developmental & Behavioral Pediatrics, 26,* 257–266.

Bisagni, G. M., & Eckenrode, J. (1995). The role of work identity in women's adjustment to divorce. *American Journal of Orthopsychiatry, 65,* 574–583.

Bjorklund, B. R., & Bee, H. L. (2008). *The journey of adulthood* (6th ed.). Upper Saddle River, NJ: Prentice Hall.

Black, K. A., Marola, J. A., Littman, A. I., Chrisler, J. C., & Neace, W. P. (2009). Gender and form of cereal box characters: Different medium, same disparity. *Sex Roles, 60,* 882–889.

Black, M. C., Noonan, R., Leggs, M., Eaton, D., & Breiding, M. J. (2006). Physical dating violence among high school students—United States, 2003. *Morbidity and Mortality Weekly Report, 55,* 532–535.

Blackwell, G. L. (2010, Winter). A little help along the way. *American Association of Univeristy Women Outlook, 104*(1), 16–19.

Blagbrough, J. (2008). Child domestic labour: A modern form of slavery. *Children & Society, 22,* 179–190.

Blake, S. M., et al. (2003). Condom availability programs in Massachusetts high schools: Relationships with condom use and sexual behavior. *American Journal of Public Health, 93,* 955–962.

Blakemore, J. E. O. (2003). Children's beliefs about violating gender norms: Boys shouldn't look like girls, and girls shouldn't act like boys. *Sex Roles, 48,* 411–419.

Blakemore, J. E. O., Berenbaum, S. A., & Liben, L. S. (2009). *Gender development.* New York: Psychology Press.

Blakemore, J. E. O., & Centers, R. E. (2005). Characteristics of boys' and girls' toys. *Sex Roles, 53,* 619–633.

Blakemore, J. E. O., & Hill, C. A. (2008). The child gender socialization scale: A measure to compare traditional and feminist parents. *Sex Roles, 58,* 192–207.

Blank, L., Baxter, S. K., Payne, N., Guillaume, L. R., & Pilgrim, H. (2010). Systematic review and narrative synthesis of the effectiveness of contraceptive service interventions for young people, delivered in educational settings. *Journal of Pediatric and Adolescent Gynecology, 23,* 341–351.

Blascovich, J., & Mendes, W. B. (2010). Social psychophysiology and embodiment. In S. T. Fiske, D. T. Gilbert, & G. Lindzey (Eds.), *Handbook of social psychology* (5th ed., Vol. 1, pp. 194–227). Hoboken, NJ: Wiley.

Bleeker, M. M. (2003, April). *Children's attraction to math and science: The importance of parents' gender stereotypes and activities.* Paper presented at the meeting of the Society for Research in Child Development, Tampa, FL.

Blieszner, R., Vista, P. M., & Mancine, J. A. (1996). Diversity and dynamics in late-life mother-daughter relationships. *Journal of Women and Aging, 8*(3/4), 5–24.

Block, J. D. (2008). *Sex over 50.* New York: Penguin.

Blosnich, J. R., & Bossarte, R. M. (2009). Comparisons of intimate partner violence among partners in same-sex and opposite-sex relationships in the United States. *American Journal of Public Health, 99,* 2182–2184.

Bly, R. (1990). *Iron John.* Reading, MA: Addison-Wesley.

Bobel, C. (2010). *New blood: Third-wave feminism and the politics of menstruation.* Piscataway, NJ: Rutgers University Press.

Bobo, M., Hildreth, B. L., & Durodoye, B. (1998). Changing patterns in career choices among African-American, Hispanic, and Anglo children. *Professional School Counseling, 1,* 37–42.

Bocalini, D. S., Serra, A. J., dos Santos, L., Murad, N., & Levy, R. F. (2009). Strength training preserves the bone mineral density of postmenopausal women without hormone replacement therapy. *Journal of Aging and Health, 21,* 519–527.

The Body: The Complete HIV/AIDS Resource. (2008). *Older women and HIV/AIDS facts.* New York: Body Health Resources Corporation.

Boehmer, U., & Bowen, D. J. (2010). Breast and cervical cancer among diverse women. In H. Landrine & N. F. Russo (Eds.), *Handbook of diversity in feminist psychology* (pp. 311–333). New York: Springer.

Bogle, K. A. (2008). *Hooking up: Sex, dating, and relationships on campus.* New York: New York University Press.

Bohan, J. S. (2002). Sex differences and/in the self: Classic themes, feminist variations, postmodern challenges. *Psychology of Women Quarterly, 26,* 74–88.

Bond, M. A., et al. (2004). Gendered work conditions, health, and work outcomes. *Journal of Occupational Health Psychology, 9,* 28–45.

Bondurant, B., & Donat, P. L. N. (1999). Perceptions of women's sexual interest and acquaintance rape. *Psychology of Women Quarterly, 23,* 691–705.

Bongaarts, J., & Zimmer, Z. (2002). Living arrangements of older adults in the developing world: An analysis of demographic and health survey household surveys. *Journals of Gerontology Services B: Psychological Sciences and Social Sciences, 57,* S145–S157.

Bönte, M., et al. (2008). Women and men with coronary heart disease in three countries: Are they treated differently? *Women's Health Issues, 18,* 191–198.

Bookwala, J., & Fekete, E. (2009). The role of psychological resources in the affective well-being of never- married adults. *Journal of Social and Personal Relationships, 26,* 411–428.

Boonstra, H. D. (2009a, Winter). Advocates call for a new approach after the era of "abstinence-only" sex education. *Guttmacher Policy Review, 12*(1), 6–11.

Boonstra, H. D. (2009b, Fall). Worldwide, young people speak up for their sexual and reproductive health and rights, but U.S. policy lags. *Guttmacher Policy Review, 12*(4), 7–11.

Borck, C. (2011). Two-spirit. In M. Z. Stange, C. K. Oyster, & J. E. Sloan (Eds.), *Encyclopedia of women in today's world.* Newberry Park, CA: Sage.

Borkhoff, C. M., Hawker, G. A., Kreder, H. J., Glazier, R. H., Mahomed, N. N., & Wright, J. G. (2008). The effect of patients' sex on physicians' recommendations for total knee arthroplasty. *Canadian Medical Association Journal, 178,* 681–687.

Bornstein, M. H., et al. (2008). Mother-child emotional availability in ecological perspective: Three countries, two regions, two genders. *Developmental Psychology, 44,* 666–680.

Boroughs, M. S., Krawczyk, R., & Thompson, J. K. (2010). Body dysmorphic disorder among diverse racial/ethnic and sexual orientation groups: Prevalence estimates and associated factors. *Sex Roles, 63,* 725–737.

Borrayo, E. A., et al. (2009). Characteristics associated with mammography screening among both Hispanic and non-Hispanic white women. *Journal of Women's Health, 18,* 1585–1594.

Borzekowski, D. L., Schenk, S., Wilson, J. L., & Peebles, R. (2010). E-Ana and e-Mia: A content analysis of pro-eating disorder web sites. *American Journal of Public Health, 100,* 1526–1534.

Bos, H., & Sandfort, T. G. M. (2010). Children's gender identity in lesbian and heterosexual two-parent families. *Sex Roles, 62,* 114–126.

Bos, H. M. W., Sandfort, T. G. M., de Bruyn, E. H., & Hakvoort, E. M. (2008). Same-sex attraction, social relationships, psychosocial functioning, and school performance in early adolescence. *Developmental Psychology, 44,* 59–68.

Bosacki, S. L., & Moore, C. (2004). Preschoolers' understanding of simple and complex emotions: Links with gender and language. *Sex Roles, 50,* 659–675.

Bose, C. E., & Kim, M. (2009). *Global gender research: Transnational perspectives*. New York: Routledge.

Bostock, J., Plumpton, M., & Pratt, R. (2009). Domestic violence against women: Understanding social processes and women's experiences. *Journal of Community & Applied Social Psychology, 19*, 95–110.

The Boston Women's Health Book Collective. (1992). *The new our bodies, ourselves: A book by and for women*. New York: Touchstone.

The Boston Women's Health Book Collective. (1998). *Our bodies, ourselves for the new century: A book by and for women*. New York: Touchstone.

The Boston Women's Health Book Collective. (2008). *Our bodies ourselves: Pregnancy and birth*. New York: Touchstone.

Bostwick, W. B., Boyd, C. J., Hughes, T. L., & McCabe, S. E. (2010). Dimensions of sexual orientation and the prevalence of mood and anxiety disorders in the United States. *American Journal of Public Health, 100*, 468–475.

Bosworth, B., Burtless, G., & Sahm, C. (2001, August). *The trend in lifetime earnings inequality and its impact on the distribution of retirement income*. Chestnut Hill, MA: Center for Retirement Research at Boston College.

Botticello, A. L. (2009). A multilevel analysis of gender differences in psychological distress over time. *Journal of Research on Adolescence, 19*, 217–247.

Bound, J., Schoenbaum, M., & Waidmann, T. (1996). Race differences in labor force attachment and disability status. *Gerontologist, 36*, 311–321.

Bourne, E. J. (2010). *The anxiety and phobia workbook* (5th ed.). Oakland, CA: New Harbinger.

Boushey, H. (2009). The new breadwinners: Women now account for half of all jobs, with sweeping consequences for our nation's economy, society and future prosperity. In M. Shriver (Ed.), *The Shriver report: A woman's nation changes everything* (pp. 30–67). Washington, DC: Maria Shriver and the Center for American Progress.

Bowen, C. E., Noack, M. G., & Staudinger, U. M. (2011). Aging in the work context. In K. W. Schaie & S. L. Willis (Eds.), *Handbook of the psychology of aging* (7th ed., pp. 279–294). San Diego, CA: Academic Press.

Bowen, M. E., & González, H. M. (2010). Childhood socioeconomic position and disability in later life: Results of the health and retirement study. *American Journal of Public Health, 100*, S197–S203.

Bower, J. K., Schreiner, P. J., Sternfeld, B., & Lewis, C. E. (2009). Black-white differences in hysterectomy prevalence: The CARDIA study. *American Journal of Public Health, 99*, 300–307.

Bowleg, L. (2008a). The health risks of being Black, Latina, woman, and/or poor: Redefining women's health within the context of social inequality. In J. C. Chrisler, C. Golden, & P. D. Rozee (Eds.), *Lectures on the psychology of women* (pp. 204–219). New York: McGraw-Hill.

Bowleg, L. (2008b). When Black + lesbian + woman ≠ Black lesbian woman: The methodological challenges of qualitative and quantitative intersectionality research. *Sex Roles, 59*, 312–325.

Bowleg, L., Brooks, K., & Ritz, S. F. (2008). "Bringing home more than a paycheck": An exploratory analysis of Black lesbians' experiences of stress and coping in the workplace. *Journal of Lesbian Studies, 12*, 69–84.

Bowles, E. (2011). Bisexuality. In M. Z. Stange, C. K. Oyster, & J. E. Sloan (Eds.), *Encyclopedia of women in today's world* (Vol. 1, pp. 156–162). Newberry Park, CA: Sage.

Bowles, H. R., Babcock, L., & Lai, L. (2007). Social incentives for gender differences in the propensity to initiate negotiations: Sometimes it does hurt to ask. *Organizational Behavior and Human Decision Processes, 103*, 84–103.

Boxer, S. (1997, December 14). One casualty of the women's movement: Feminism. *New York Times*, p. WK3.

Boynton, P. (2003). Abiding by the rules: Instructing women in relationships. *Feminism & Psychology, 13*, 237–245.

Brabeck, M. M., & Brabeck, K. M. (2006). Women and relationships. In J. Worell & C. D. Goodheart (Eds.), *Handbook of girls' and women's psychological health: Gender and well-being across the lifespan* (pp. 208–217). New York: Oxford University Press.

Bradbury, T. N., & Karney, B. R. (2010). *Intimate relationships*. New York: W.W. Norton.

Bradshaw, C., Kahn, A. S., & Saville, B. K. (2010). To hook up or date: Which gender benefits? *Sex Roles, 62*, 661–669.

Bradsher, J. E. (2001). Older women and widowhood. In J. M. Coyle (Ed.), *Handbook on women and aging* (pp. 112–128). Westport, CT: Greenwood.

Brady, D., & Kall, D. (2008). Nearly universal, but somewhat distinct: The feminization of poverty in affluent Western democracies, 1969–2000. *Social Science Research, 37*, 976–1007.

Brake, D. L. (2010). *Getting in the game: Title IX and the women's sports revolution*. New York: New York University Press.

Branch, D. W., Gibson, M., & Silver, R. M. (2010). Recurrent miscarriage. *New England Journal of Medicine, 363*, 1740–1747.

Brauer, C. A., Coca-Perraillon, M., Cutler, D. M., & Rosen, A. B. (2009). Incidence and mortality of hip fractures in the United States. *Journal of the American Medical Association, 302*, 1573–1579.

Braun, V. (2010). Female genital cosmetic surgery: A critical review of current knowledge and contemporary debates. *Journal of Women's Health, 19*, 1393–1407.

Braveman, P. A., Cubbin, C., Egerter, S., Williams, D. R., & Pamuk, E. (2010). Socioeconomic disparities in health in the United States: What the pattern tells us. *American Journal of Public Health, 100*, S186–S196.

Brazile, D. (2007, Summer). The Imus effect. *Ms.*, 79.

Brazile, D. (2010, Winter). The global pandemic of rape. *Ms.*, 63.

Breedlove, S. M. (2010). Minireview: Organizational hypotheses: Instances of the fingerpost. *Endocrinology, 151*, 4116–4122.

Breen, A. B., & Karpinski, A. (2008). What's in a name? Two approaches to evaluating the label feminist. *Sex Roles, 58*, 299–310.

Breheny, M., & Stephens, C. (2009). A life of ease and immorality: Health professionals' constructions of mothering on welfare. *Journal of Community & Applied Social Psychology, 19*, 257–270.

Brehm, S. S. (2007, July/August). Some thoughts about women, leadership, and the future. *Monitor on Psychology, 38*, 5.

Brenner, B. R., Lyons, H. Z., & Fassinger, R. E. (2010). Can heterosexism harm organizations? Predicting the perceived organizational citizenship behaviors of gay and lesbian employees. *Career Development Quarterly, 58*, 318–331.

Brescoll, V., & LaFrance, M. (2004). The correlates and consequences of newspaper reports of research on sex differences. *Psychological Science, 15*, 515–520.

Brescoll, V. L., Dawson, E., & Uhlmann, E. L. (2010). Hard won and easily lost: The fragile status of leaders in gender-stereotype-incongruent occupations. *Psychological Science, 21*, 1640–1642.

Brescoll, V. L., & Uhlmann, E. L. (2008). Can an angry woman get ahead? Status conferral, gender, and expression of emotion in the workplace. *Psychological Science, 19*, 268–275.

Brewster, K. L., & Padavic, I. (2002). Change in gender ideology, 1977–1996: The contributions of intracohort change and population turnover. *Journal of Marriage and the Family, 62*, 477–487.

Bridges, J. S. (1993). Pink or blue: Gender-stereotypic perceptions of infants as conveyed by birth congratulations cards. *Psychology of Women Quarterly, 17,* 193–205.

Bridges, J. S., & Etaugh, C. (1995). College students' perceptions of mothers: Effects of maternal employment-childrearing pattern and motive for employment. *Sex Roles, 32,* 735–751.

Bridges, J. S., & Etaugh, C. (1996). Black and white college women's maternal employment outcome expectations and their desired timing of maternal employment. *Sex Roles, 35,* 543–562.

Bridges, J. S., & Orza, A. M. (1993). Effects of maternal employment-childrearing pattern on college students' perceptions of a mother and her child. *Psychology of Women Quarterly, 17,* 103–117.

Bridges, J. S., & Orza, A. M. (1996). Black and white employed mothers' role experiences. *Sex Roles, 35,* 377–385.

Bridges, L. J., Roe, A. E. C., Dunn, J., & O'Connor, T. G. (2007). Children's perspectives on their relationships with grandparents following parental separation: A longitudinal study. *Social Development, 16,* 539–554.

Bridges, M. (2003/2004, Winter). Poverty up, women still down. *Ms.,* p. 16.

Bridges, S. K., Lease, S. H., & Ellison, C. R. (2000, August). *Predicting women's sexual satisfaction: Implications for the new millennium.* Paper presented at the meeting of the American Psychological Association, Washington, DC.

Brier, N. (2008). Grief following miscarriage: A comprehensive review of the literature. *Journal of Women's Health, 17,* 451–464.

Briere, J., & Hodges, M. R. (2010). Assessing the effects of early and later childhood trauma in adults. In E. Vermetten, R. Lanius, & C. Pain (Eds.), *The impact of early life trauma on health and disease* (pp. 207–216). New York: Cambridge University Press.

Briggs, C. A., & Pepperell, J. L. (2009). *Women, girls, and addiction: Celebrating the feminine in counseling treatment and recovery.* New York: Routledge.

Briggs, E. C., Thompson, R., Ostrowski, S., & Lekwuawa, R. (2011). Psychological, health, behavioral, and economic impact of child maltreatment. In J. W. White, M. P. Koss, & A. E. Kazdin (Eds.), *Violence against women and children: Mapping the terrain* (Vol. 1, pp. 77–98). Washington, DC: American Psychological Association.

Brinkman, B. G., & Rickard, K. M. (2009). College students' descriptions of everyday gender prejudice. *Sex Roles, 61,* 461–475.

Brinkmann, A. O. (2009). Androgen physiology: Receptor and metabolic disorders. In R. McLachlan (Ed.), *Endocrinology of male reproduction.* South Dartmouth, MA: MDText.com, Inc. Retrieved from http://www.endotext.org/male/male3/maleframe3.htm

Brinton, E. A., Hopkins, P. N., & Sankaran, G. (2010). Cardiovascular disease in women: Risk factors and risk reduction. In P. Murthy & C. L. Smith (Eds.), *Women's global health and human rights* (pp. 161–176). Sudbury, MA: Jones and Bartlett.

Britain, D. R., Gyurcsik, N. C., McElroy, M., & Hillard, S. A. (2011). General and arthritis-specific barriers to moderate physical activity in women with arthritis. *Women's Health Issues, 21,* 57–63.

Britsch, B., Callahan, N., & Peterson, K. (2010, Winter). The power of partnerships. *AAUW Outlook, 104*(1), 12–15.

Broadbridge, A., & Hearn, J. (2008). Gender and management: New directions in research and continuing patterns in practice. *British Journal of Management, 19,* S38–S49.

Broderick, D. J., Birbilis, J. M., & Steger, M. (2008). Lesbians grieving the death of a partner: Recommendations for practice. *Journal of Lesbian Studies, 12,* 225–235.

Broderick, P. C., & Korteland, C. (2002). Coping style and depression in early adolescence: Relationships to gender, gender role, and implicit beliefs. *Sex Roles, 46,* 201–213.

Brody, J. E. (2001, August 21). Nutrition a key to better health for elderly. *New York Times,* p. D8.

Brody, J. E. (2004a, June 1). Abstinence-only: Does it work? *New York Times,* p. D7.

Brody, J. E. (2004b, May 11). The risks and demands of pregnancy after 20. *New York Times,* p. D8.

Brody, J. E. (2005, April 12). Women struggle for parity of the heart. *New York Times,* p. D7.

Brody, J. E. (2007, April 10). A lively libido isn't reserved for the young. *New York Times,* p. D5.

Brody, J. E. (2009a, March 31). A dip in the sex drive, tied to menopause. *New York Times,* p. D7.

Brody, J. E. (2009b, July 21). Much has changed in surrogate pregnancies. *New York Times,* p. D7.

Brody, J. E. (2010a, July 13). Blame's net catches lung cancer patients. *New York Times,* p. D7.

Brody, J. E. (2010b, March 2). Even more reasons to get a move on. *New York Times,* p. D7.

Brody, J. E. (2010c, June 15). Getting on with life after a partner dies. *New York Times,* p. D7.

Brody, J. E. (2010d, July 27). What do you lack? Probably vitamin D. *New York Times,* p. D7.

Brody, J. E. (2011, January 24). Long and short of calcium and vitamin D. *New York Times,* p. D7.

Brody, L. R., & Hall, J. A. (2008). Gender and emotion in context. In M. Lewis & J. M. Haviland-Jones (Eds.), *Handbook of emotions* (3rd ed., pp. 395–408). New York: Guilford.

Bromberger, J. T., et al. (2010). Longitudinal change in reproductive hormones and depressive symptoms across the menopausal transition: Results from the study of women's health across the nation (SWAN). *General Psychiatry, 67,* 598–607.

Bronstein, P. (2006). The family environment: Where gender role socialization begins. In J. Worell & C. D. Goodheart (Eds.), *Handbook of girls' and women's psychological health: Gender and well-being across the lifespan* (pp. 262–271). New York: Oxford University Press.

Brooks, A. T. (2010). Aesthetic anti-ageing surgery and technology: Women's friend or foe? *Sociology of Health & Illness, 32,* 238–257.

Brooks-Gunn, J., Han, W. -J., & Waldfogel, J. (2010). First-year maternal employment and child development in the first 7 years. *Monographs of the Society for Research in Child Development, 75*(2, Serial No. 296), 1–147.

Brougham, R. R., & Walsh, D. A. (2005). Goal expectations as predictors of retirement intentions. *International Journal of Aging and Human Development, 61,* 141–160.

Broverman, I. K., Broverman, D. M., Clarkson, F. E., Rosenkrantz, P. S., & Vogel, S. R. (1970). Sex-role stereotypes and clinical judgements of mental health. *Journal of Consulting Psychology, 34,* 1–7.

Brown, B. B., & Larson, J. (2009). Peer relationships in adolescence. In R. M. Lerner & L. Steinberg (Eds.), *Handbook of adolescent psychology* (3rd ed., Vol. 2, pp. 74–103). Hoboken, NJ: Wiley.

Brown, C. E. (2007, May). *Examining college women's body image using the body figure scale.* Poster presented at the annual meeting of the Midwestern Psychological Association, Chicago.

Brown, C. S., & Leaper, C. (2010). Latina and European American girls' experiences with academic sexism and their self-concepts in mathematics and science during adolescence. *Sex Roles, 63,* 860–870.

Brown, I., & Misra, J. (2003). The intersection of gender and race in the labor market. *Annual Review of Sociology, 29,* 487–513.

Brown, J. R., & O'Connor, G. T. (2010). Coronary heart disease and prevention in the United States. *New England Journal of Medicine, 362,* 2150–2153.

Brown, L. M. (2006, Spring). What about the boys? *Feminist Psychologist,* p. 5.

Brown, L. S. (2010). *Feminist therapy.* Washington, DC: American Psychological Association.

Brown, S. L., & Rinelli, L. N. (2010). Family structure, family processes, and adolescent smoking and drinking. *Journal of Research on Adolescence, 20,* 259–273.

Brown, S. L., Brown, R. M., House, J. S., & Smith, D. M. (2008). Coping with spousal loss: Potential buffering effects of self-reported helping behavior. *Personality and Social Psychology Bulletin, 34,* 849–861.

Brownlow, S., Rosamond, J. A., & Parker, J. A. (2003). Gender-linked linguistic behavior in television interviews. *Sex Roles, 49,* 121–132.

Brozowski, K., & Hall, D. R. (2010). Aging and risk: Physical and sexual abuse of elders in Canada. *Journal of Interpersonal Violence, 25,* 1183–1199.

Bruckmüller, S., & Branscombe, N. R. (2010). The glass cliff: Why and when women are selected as leader in crisis contexts. *British Journal of Social Psychology, 49,* 433–451.

Brumberg, J. J. (1997). *The body project: An intimate history of American girls.* New York: Random House.

Bryant, A. N. (2003). Changes in attitudes toward women's roles: Predicting gender-role traditionalism among college students. *Sex Roles, 48,* 131–142.

Bryant-Davis, T., Chung, H., & Tillman, S. (2009). From the margins to the center: Ethnic minority women and the mental health effects of sexual assault. *Trauma, Violence, & Abuse, 10,* 330–357.

Btoush, R., & Haj-Yahia, M. M. (2008). Attitudes of Jordanian society toward wife abuse. *Journal of Interpersonal Violence, 23,* 1531–1554.

Buchanan, E. M., Weinstein, L. C., & Hillson, C. (2009). Endometrial cancer. *American Family Physician, 80,* 1075–1080.

Buchanan, N. T., & West, C. M. (2010). Sexual harassment in the lives of women of color. In H. Landrine & N. F. Russo (Eds.), *Handbook of diversity in feminist psychology* (pp. 449–476). New York: Springer.

Buchanan, T., & Selmon, N. (2008). Race and gender differences in self-efficacy: Assessing the role of gender role attitudes and family background. *Sex Roles, 58,* 822–836.

Buchmann, C., DiPrete, T. A., & McDaniel, A. (2008). Gender inequalities in education. *Annual Review of Sociology, 34,* 319–337.

Buchmueller, T., & Carpenter, C. S. (2010). Disparities in health insurance coverage, access, and outcomes for individuals in same-sex versus different-sex relationships, 2000–2007. *American Journal of Public Health, 100,* 489–495.

Buchner, D. M. (2010). Promoting physical activity in older adults. *American Family Physician, 81,* 24.

Budig, M. J., & Hodges, M. J. (2010). Differences in disadvantage: Variation in the motherhood penalty across white women's earnings distribution. *American Sociological Review, 75,* 705–727.

Buijsse, B., Weikert, C., Drogan, D., Bergmann, M., & Boeing, H. (2010). Chocolate consumption in relation to blood pressure and risk of cardiovascular disease in German adults. *European Heart Journal, 31,* 1616–1623.

Bugental, D. B., & Hehman, J. A. (2007). Ageism: A review of research and policy implications. *Social Issues and Policy Review, 1,* 173–216.

Bukatko, D., & Shedd, J. (1999, April). *Children's evaluations of gender-stereotyped traits, activities and occupations.* Poster presented at the meeting of the Society for Research in Child Development, Albuquerque, NM.

Bulanda, J. R. (2011). Gender, marital power, and marital quality in later life. *Journal of Women & Aging, 23,* 3–22.

Buller, D. J. (2009). Four fallacies of pop evolutionary psychology. *Scientific American, 300,* 74–81.

Bullock, H. E., & Fernald, J. L. (2003). "Feminism?" Feminist identification, speaker appearance, and perceptions of feminist and antifeminist messengers. *Psychology of Women Quarterly, 27,* 291–299.

Bullock, H. E., Lott, B., & Wyche, K. F. (2010). "Making room at the table": Gender, ethnic, and class inequities. In H. Landrine & N. F. Russo (Eds.), *Handbook of diversity in feminist psychology* (pp. 479–499). New York: Springer.

Bulun, S. E. (2009). Endometriosis. *New England Journal of Medicine, 360,* 268–279.

Burchinal, M., Vandergrift, N., Pianta, R., & Mashburn, A. (2010). Threshold analysis of association between child care quality and child outcomes for low-income children in pre-kindergarten programs. *Early Childhood Research Quarterly, 25,* 166–176.

Burgess, E. O. (2004). Sexuality in midlife and later life couples. In J. H. Harvey, A. Wenzel, & S. Sprecher (Eds.), *The handbook of sexuality in close relationships* (pp. 437–454). Mahwah, NJ: Erlbaum.

Burgess, M. C. R., Stermer, S. P., & Burgess, S. R. (2007). Sex, lies, and video games: The portrayal of male and female characters on video game covers. *Sex Roles, 57,* 419–433.

Burn, S. M. (2011). *Women across cultures: A global perspective* (3rd ed.). New York: McGraw-Hill.

Burns, A., & Leonard, R. (2005). Chapters of our lives: Life narratives of midlife and older Australian women. *Sex Roles, 52,* 269–277.

Bursik, K. (1992). Perceptions of sexual harassment in an academic context. *Sex Roles, 27,* 401–412.

Burton, L. M., Bonilla-Silva, E., Ray, V., Buckelew, R., & Freeman, E. H. (2010). Critical race theories, colorism, and the decade's research on families of color. *Journal of Marriage and Family, 72,* 440–459.

Bush, V. B., Chambers, C. R., & Walpole, M. (Eds.). (2009). *From diplomas to doctorates: The success of Black women in higher education and its implications for equal educatoinal opportunities for all.* Sterling, VA: Stylus Publishing.

Bushman, B. J., & Huesmann, L. R. (2010). Aggression. In S. T. Fiske, D. T. Gilbert, & G. Lindzey (Eds.), *Handbook of social psychology* (5th ed., Vol. 2, pp. 833–863). Hoboken, NJ: Wiley.

Buss, D. M. (1994). *The evolution of desire: Strategies of human mating.* New York: Basic Books.

Busseri, M. A., Willoughby, T., Chalmers, H., & Bogaert, A. F. (2008). On the association between sexual attraction and adolescent risk behavior involvement: Examining mediation and moderation. *Developmental Psychology, 44,* 69–80.

Bussey, K., & Bandura, A. (2004). Social cognitive theory of gender development and functioning. In A. H. Eagly, A. E. Beall, & R. J. Sternberg (Eds.), *The psychology of gender* (2nd ed., pp. 92–119). New York: Guilford.

Butler, B. J. (2008). Psychiatric disorders in women. In A. L. Clouse & K. Sherif (Eds.), *Women's health in clinical practice: A handbook for primary care* (pp. 317–354). Totowa, NJ: Humana Press.

Butler, L. D., & Nolen-Hoeksema, S. (1994). Gender differences in responses to depressed mood in a college sample. *Sex Roles, 30,* 331–346.

Butler, R., & Lewis, M. I. (2002). *The new love and sex after 60.* New York: Ballantine.

Button, E. J., Chadalavada, B., & Palmer, R. L. (2009). Mortality and predictors of death in a cohort of patients presenting to an eating disorders service. *International Journal of Eating Disorders, 43,* 387–392.

Butts, S. F., & Seifer, D. B. (2010). Racial and ethnic differences in reproductive potential across the life cycle. *Fertility and Sterility, 93,* 681–690.

Buysse, J. M., & Embser-Herbert, M. S. (2004). Constructions of gender in sport: An analysis of intercollegiate media guide cover photographs. *Gender & Society, 18,* 66–81.

Bynum, L., et al. (2010, December 17). Adverse childhood experiences reported by adults-five states, 2009. *Morbidity and Mortality Weekly Report, 59,* 1609–1613.

Byrne, B. M. (2008). Testing for time-invariant and time-varying predictors of self-perceived ability in math, language arts, and science: A look at the gender factor. In H. M. G. Watt & J. S. Eccles (Eds.), *Gender and occupational outcomes: Longitudinal assessments of individual, social, and cultural influences* (pp. 145–170). Washington, DC: American Psychological Association.

Cabrera, N., Shannon, J., Mitchell, S. J., & West, J. (2009). Mexican American mothers' and fathers' prenatal attitudes and father prenatal involvement: Links to mother-infant interaction and father engagement. *Sex Roles, 60,* 510–526.

Cahill, L. (2005, May). His brain, her brain. *Scientific American, 292,* 40–47.

Cahn, N. R. (2009). *Test tube families: Why the fertility market needs legal regulation.* New York: New York University Press.

Caiazza, A., Shaw, A., & Werschkul, M. (2004). *The status of women in the states: Wide disparities by race, ethnicity, and region.* Washington, DC: Institute for Women's Policy Research.

Calarco, P. E. (2011). Honor killings. In M. Z. Stange, C. K. Oyster, & J. E. Sloan (Eds.), *Encyclopedia of women in today's world* (Vol. 2, pp. 721–722). Newberry Park, CA: Sage.

Calasanti, T. (2007). Bodacious berry, potency wood and the aging monster: Gender and age relations in anti-aging ads. *Social Forces, 86,* 335–355.

Calasanti, T. (2009). Theorizing feminist gerontology, sexuality, and beyond: An intersectional approach. In V. Bengtson, M. Silverstein, N. M. Putney, & D. Gans (Eds.), *Handbook of theories of aging* (2nd ed., pp. 471–485). New York: Springer.

Calasanti, T. (2010). Gender relations and applied research on aging. *Gerontologist, 50,* 720–734.

Calefati, J. (2009, March 11). The changing face of women's colleges. *U.S. News & World Report.* Retrieved from http://www.usnews.com

Calogero, R. M., Pina, A., Park, L. E., & Rahemtulla, Z. (2010). Objectification theory predicts college women's attitudes toward cosmetic surgery. *Sex Roles, 63,* 32–41.

Calogero, R. M., Tantleff-Dunn, S., & Thompson, J. K. (2011). *Self-objectification in women: Causes, consequences and counteractions.* Washington, DC: American Psychological Association.

Calogero, R. M., & Thompson, J. K. (2009). Sexual self-esteem in American and British college women: Relations with self-objectification and eating problems. *Sex Roles, 60,* 160–173.

Calvert, S. L., Kondla, T. A., Ertel, K. A., & Meisel, D. S. (2001). Young adults' perceptions and memories of a television woman hero. *Sex Roles, 45,* 31–52.

Cambron, M. J., Branum-Martin, L., Acitelli, L. K., & Stuebing, K. K. (2008). *What do we really know about gender differences in developmental self-esteem during adolescence?* Manuscript under review, University of Houston.

Cameron, D. (2007). *The myth of Mars and Venus: Do men and women really speak different languages?* Oxford, UK: Oxford University Press.

Camilli, G., Vargas, S., Ryan, S., & Barnett, W. S. (2010). Meta-analysis of the effects of early education interventions on cognitive and social development. *Teacher College Record, 112,* 579–620.

Campbell, A., Shirley, L., & Candy, J. (2004). A longitudinal study of gender-related cognition and behaviour. *Developmental Science, 7,* 1–9.

Campbell, A., Shirley, L., & Caygill, L. (2002). Sex-typed preferences in three domains: Do two-year-olds need cognitive variables? *British Journal of Psychology, 93,* 203–217.

Campbell, J. C., Alhusen, J., Draughon, J., Kub, J., & Walton-Moss, B. (2011). Vulnerability and protective factors for intimate partner violence. In J. W. White, M. P. Koss, & A. E. Kazdin (Eds.), *Violence against women and children: Mapping the terrain* (Vol. 1, pp. 243–264). Washington, DC: American Psychological Association.

Campbell, R., Dworkin, E., & Cabral, G. (2009). An ecological model of the impact of sexual assault on women's mental health. *Trauma, Violence, and Abuse, 10,* 225–246.

Campbell, R., & Patterson, D. (2011). Services for victims of sexual violence. In M. P. Koss, J. W. White, & A. E. Kazdin (Eds.), *Violence against women and children: Navigating solutions* (Vol. 2, pp. 95–114). Washington, DC: American Psychological Association.

Campbell, R., & Townsend, S. M. (2011). Defining the scope of sexual violence against women. In C. M. Renzetti, J. L. Edleson, & R. K. Bergen (Eds.), *Sourcebook on violence against women* (2nd ed., pp. 95–108). Thousand Oaks, CA: Sage.

Campbell, S. B., Spieker, S., Vandergrift, N., Belsky, J., Burchinal, M., & The NICHD Early Child Care Research Network. (2010). Predictors and sequelae of trajectories of physical aggression in school-age boys and girls. *Development and Psychopathology, 22,* 133–150.

Campbell, S. M., & Collaer, M. L. (2009). Stereotype threat and gender differences in performance on a novel visuospatial task. *Psychology of Women Quarterly, 33,* 437–444.

Campione, W. (2008). Employed women's well-being: The global and daily impact of work. *Journal of Family and Economic Issues, 29,* 346–361.

Canabal, M. E. (1995). Native Americans in higher education. *College Student Journal, 29,* 455–457.

Canetto, S. S. (2001). Older adult women: Issues, resources, and challenges. In R. K. Unger (Ed.), *Handbook of the psychology of women and gender* (pp. 183–197). New York: Wiley.

Canetto, S. S. (2003). Older adulthood. In L. Slater, J. H. Daniel, & A. E. Banks (Eds.), *The complete guide to mental health for women* (pp. 56–64). Boston, MA: Beacon Press.

Cann, A., & Vann, E. D. (1995). Implications of sex and gender differences for self: Perceived advantages and disadvantages of being the other gender. *Sex Roles, 33,* 531–541.

Cannon, E. A., Bonomi, A. E., Anderson, M. L., Rivara, F. P., & Thompson, R. S. (2010). Adult health and relationship outcomes among women with abuse experiences during childhood. *Violence and Victims, 25,* 291–305.

Caplan, P. J. (2008, Summer). Pathologizing your period. *Ms.,* 63–64.

Caplan, P. J., & Caplan, J. B. (2009). *Thinking critically about research on sex and gender* (3rd ed.). Boston, MA: Pearson.

Caprara, G. V., Barbaranelli, C., & Pastorelli, C. (2001). Prosocial behavior and aggression in childhood and pre-adolescence. In A. C. Bohart & D. J. Stipek (Eds.), *Constructive and destructive behavior: Implications for family, school, and society* (pp. 187–203). Washington, DC: American Psychological Association.

Caprile, M., & Pascual, A. S. (2011). The move towards the knowledge-based society: A gender approach. *Gender, Work and Organization, 18,* 48–72.

Card, N. A., Stucky, B. D., Sawalani, G. M., & Little, T. D. (2008). Direct and indirect aggression during childhood and adolescence: A meta-analytic review of gender differences, intercorrelations, and relations to maladjustment. *Child Development, 79,* 1185–1229.

Carli, L. L. (2010). Gender and group behavior. In J. C. Chrisler & D. R. McCreary (Eds.), *Handbook of gender research in psychology* (Vol. 2, pp. 337–358). New York: Springer.

Carli, L. L., & Bukatko, D. (2000). Gender, communication, and social-influence: A development perspective. In T. Eckes & H. M. Trautner (Eds.), *The developmental social psychology of gender* (pp. 295–332). Mahwah, NJ: Erlbaum.

Carlson, K. J., Eisenstat, S. A., & Ziporyn, T. (2004). *The new Harvard guide to women's health*. Cambridge, MA: Harvard University Press.

Carlson, S. A., Brooks, J. D., Brown, D. R., & Buchner, D. M. (2010). Racial/ethnic differences in perceived access, environmental barriers to use, and use of community parks. *Preventing Chronic Disease, 7.* Retrieved from http://www.cdc.gov/pcd/issues/2010/may/09_0150.htm

Carney, R. M., et al. (2009). History of depression and survival after acute myocardial infarction. *Psychosomatic Medicine, 71,* 253–259.

Carp, F. M. (2001). Retirement and women. In Coyle J. M (Ed.), *Handbook on women and aging* (pp. 112–128). Westport, CT: Greenwood.

Carpenter, C., & Gates, G. J. (2008). Gay and lesbian partnership: Evidence from California. *Demography, 45,* 573–590.

Carr, C. L. (2007). Where have all the tomboys gone? Women's accounts of gender in adolescence. *Sex Roles, 56,* 439–448.

Carr, D. (1997). The fulfillment of career dreams at midlife: Does it matter for women's mental health? *Journal of Health and Social Behavior, 38,* 331–344.

Carr, D. (2004). Gender, preloss marital dependence, and older adults' adjustment to widowhood. *Journal of Marriage and Family, 66,* 220–235.

Carr, D., & Ha, J.-H. (2006). Bereavement. In J. Worell & C. D. Goodheart (Eds.), *Handbook of girls' and women's psychological health: Gender and well-being across the lifespan* (pp. 397–405). New York: Oxford University Press.

Carr, P. B., & Steele, C. M. (2010). Stereotype threat affects financial decision making. *Psychological Science,* 1411–1416.

Carrell, S. E., Page, M. E., & West, J. E. (2009). *Sex and science: How professor gender gap perpetuates the gender gap.* Cambridge, MA: National Bureau of Economic Research.

Carter, B., & Elliott, S. (2004, May 26). MTV to start first network aimed at gays. *New York Times,* pp. C1, C8.

Carter, J. C., et al. (2010). Maintenance treatment for anorexia nervosa: A comparison of cognitive behavior therapy and treatment as usual. *International Journal of Eating Disorders, 42,* 202–207.

Carter, N. M., & Silva, C. (2010). *Pipeline's broken promise.* New York: Catalyst.

Carter-Edwards, L., et al. (2010). Body image and body satisfaction differ by race in overweight postpartum mothers. *Journal of Women's Health, 19,* 305–311.

Carvajal, D. (2011, March 7). The changing face of medical care. *New York Times.* Retrieved from http://www.nytimes.com/2011/03/08/world/europe/08iht-ffdocs08.html?_r=1&amp=&pagewanted=all

Carver, C. S., Scheier, M. F., & Segerstrom, S. C. (2010). Optimism. *Clinical Psychology Review, 30,* 879–889.

Carver, P. R., Egan, S. K., & Perry, D. G. (2004). Children who question their heterosexuality. *Developmental Psychology, 40,* 43–53.

Carver, P. R., Yunger, J. L., & Perry, D. G. (2003). Gender identity and adjustment in middle childhood. *Sex Roles, 49,* 95–109.

Case, K. A. (2007). Raising male privilege awareness and reducing sexism: An evaluation of diversity courses. *Psychology of Women Quarterly, 31,* 426–435.

Casey, M. B. (2002). Developmental perspectives on gender. In S. G. Kornstein & A. H. Clayton (Eds.), *Women's mental health: A comprehensive textbook* (pp. 499–514). New York: Guilford.

Cash, T. F., Morrow, J. A., Hrabosky, J. I., & Perry, A. A. (2004). How has body image changed? A cross-sectional investigation of college women and men from 1983 to 2001. *Journal of Consulting and Clinical Psychology, 72,* 1081–1089.

Cashdan, E. (1998). Smiles, speech, and body posture: How women and men display sociometric status and power. *Journal of Nonverbal Behavior, 22,* 209–228.

Casper, R. F., & Yonkers, K. A. (2010). *Epidemiology and pathogenesis of premenstrual syndrome and premenstrual dysphoric disorder.* Retrieved form http://www.uptodate.com/contents/epidemiology-and-pathogenesis-of-premenstrual-syndrome-and-premenstrual-dysphoric-disorder?source=see_link

Caspi, J. (Ed.). (2011). *Sibling development: Implications for mental health practitioners.* New York: Springer.

Castañeda, D. (1996). Gender issues among Latinas. In J. C. Chrisler, C. Golden, & P. D. Rozee (Eds.), *Lectures on the psychology of women* (pp. 167–181). New York: McGraw-Hill.

Castañeda, D. (2008). Gender issues among Latinas. In J. C. Chrisler, C. Golden, & P. D. Rozee (Eds.), *Lectures on the psychology of women* (pp. 250–267). New York: McGraw-Hill.

Castañeda, D., & Burns-Glover, A. L. (2008). Women's friendships and romantic relationships. In F. L. Denmark & M. A. Paludi (Eds.), *Psychology of women: A handbook of issues and theories* (2nd ed., pp. 332–350). Westport, CT: Praeger.

Castañeda, D., & Coates, B. E. (2008). Relationships with men. In M. A. Paludi (Ed.), *The psychology of women at work: Challenges and solutions for our female workforce: Obstacles and the identity juggle* (Vol. 2, pp. 125–147). Westport, CT: Praeger.

Casteñada, D., & Ulibarri, M. (2010). Women and sexuality: An international perspective. In M. A. Paludi (Ed.), *Feminism and women's rights worldwide: Feminism as human rights* (Vol. 2, pp. 81–100). Santa Barbara, CA: Praeger.

Castilla, E. J. (2008). Gender, race, and meritocracy in organizational careers. *American Journal of Sociology, 113,* 1479–1526.

Catalyst. (2010). *2010 Catalyst census: Fortune 500 women board of directors.* New York: Author.

Caughey, A. (2009). Preventive induction of labor: Can its use really lower the cesarean delivery rate? *Journal of Women's Health, 18,* 1743–1745.

Cavanaugh, J. C., & Blanchard-Fields, F. (2011). *Adult development and aging* (6th ed.). Belmont, CA: Wadsworth.

Cavazos-Rehg, P. A., et al. (2010). Understanding adolescent parenthood from a multisystemic perspective. *Journal of Adolescent Health, 46,* 525–531.

Cebula, R. J., & Coombs, C. K. (2008). Recent evidence on factors influencing the female labor force participation rate. *Journal of Labor Research, 29,* 272–284.

Ceci, S. J., & Williams, W. M. (Eds.). (2007). *Why aren't more women in science? Top researchers debate the evidence.* Washington, DC: American Psychological Association.

Ceci, S. J., & Williams, W. M. (2010). Sex differences in math-intensive fields. *Current Directions in Psychological Science, 19,* 275–279.

Center for American Progress/Work Life Law. (2010). *The three faces of work-family conflict: The poor, the professionals, and the missing middle.* Washington/San Francisco, DC/CA: Author.

Center for American Women and Politics. (2008). *Record number of women to serve in senate and house.* New Brunswick, NJ: Rutgers University.

Center for American Women and Politics. (2011). *Women in the U.S. Congress 2011.* New Brunswick, NJ: Rutgers University.

Center on Alcohol Marketing and Youth. (2010). *Youth exposure to alcohol advertising in national magazines, 2001–2008.* Baltimore, MD: Johns Hopkins University.

Centers for Disease Control and Prevention. (2000). *All the stages of our lives.* Atlanta, GA: Author.

Centers for Disease Control and Prevention. (2010a, December 17). Sexually transmitted diseases treatment guidelines, 2010. *Morbidity and Mortality Weekly Report, 59*(RR-12).

Centers for Disease Control and Prevention. (2010b). *Tobacco control state highlights, 2010*. Atlanta, GA: Author.

Centers for Disease Control and Prevention. (2010c). Vital signs: Current cigarette smoking among adults aged >18 years—United States, 2009. *Morbidity and Mortality Weekly Report, 59,* 1135–1140.

Centers for Disease Control and Prevention. (2011). Vital signs: Teen pregnancy—United States, 1991–2009. *Morbidity and Mortality Weekly Report, 60,* 414–420.

Cermele, J. A., Daniels, S., & Anderson, K. L. (2001). Defining normal: Constructions of race and gender in the *DSM-IV* casebook. *Feminism & Psychology, 11,* 229–247.

Chambers, P., Allan, G., Phillipson, C., & Ray, M. (2009). *Family practices in later life*. Bristol, UK: Policy Press.

Chan, K. S., Bird, C. E., Weiss, R., Duan, N., Meredith, L. S., & Sherbourne, C. D. (2006). Does patient-provider gender concordance affect mental health care received by primary care patients with major depression? *Women's Health Issues, 16,* 122–132.

Chan, P. S., et al. (2009). Racial differences in survival after in-hospital cardiac arrest. *Journal of the American Medical Association, 302,* 1195–1201.

Chan, Y. C., & Yeung, J. W.-K. (2009). Children living with violence within the family and its sequel: A meta-analysis from 1995–2006. *Aggression and Violent Behavior, 14,* 313–322.

Chandra, A., Mosher, W. D., & Copen, C. (2011). *Sexual behavior, sexual attraction, and sexual identity in the United States: Data from the 2006–2008 national survey of family growth*. Hyattsville, MD: National Center for Health Statistics.

Chang, J. T., et al. (2004). Interventions for the prevention of falls in older adults: Systematic review and meta-analysis of randomised clinical trials. *British Medical Journal, 328,* 680–683.

Chapleau, K. M., & Oswald, D. L. (2010). Power, sex, and rape myth acceptance: Testing two models of rape proclivity. *Journal of Sex Research, 47,* 66–78.

Chaplin, T. M., Cole, P. M., & Zahn-Waxler, C. (2005). Parental socialization of emotion expression: Gender differences and relations to child adjustment. *Emotion, 5,* 80–88.

Chapman, D. P., & Perry, G. S. (2008). Depression as a major component of public health for older adults. *Preventing Chronic Disease, 5*. Retrieved from http://www.cdc.gov/pcd/issues/2008/jan/07_0150.htm

Characteristics and health of caregivers and care recipients—North carolina, 2005. (2007). *Morbidity and Mortality Weekly Report, 56,* 529–532.

Charlebois, J. (2011). *Gender and the construction of dominant, hegemonic, and oppositional femininities*. Lanham, MD: Lexington Books.

Charles, M., & Bradley, K. (2009). Indulging our gendered selves? Sex segregation by field of study in 44 countries. *American Journal of Sociology, 114,* 924–976.

Charles, V. E., Polis, C. B., Sridhara, S. K., & Blum, R. W. (2008). Abortion and long-term mental health outcomes: A systematic review of the evidence. *Contraception, 79,* 436–450.

Charo, R. A. (2007). Politics, parents, and prophylaxis—mandating HPV vaccination in the United States. *New England Journal of Medicine, 356,* 1905–1908.

Chassin, L., Hussong, A., & Beltran, I. (2009). Adolescent substance use. In R. M. Lerner & L. Steinberg (Eds.), *Handbook of adolescent psychology* (3rd ed., Vol. 1, pp. 723–764). Hoboken, NJ: Wiley.

Chaudoir, S. P., & Quinn, D. M. (2010). Bystander sexism in the intergroup context: The impact of cat-calls on women's reactions toward men. *Sex Roles, 62,* 623–634.

Chaudron, L. H., & Caine, E. D. (2004). Suicide among women: A critical review. *Journal of the American Medical Women's Association, 59,* 125–134.

Chen, I. (2009). A clash of science and politics over PMS. *New York Times*. Retrieved from http://www.nytimes.com

Chen, L. H., Warner, M., Fingerhut, L., & Makuc, D. (2009, September). Injury episodes and circumstances: National Health Interview Survey, 1997–2007. *Vital and Health Statistics, 10*(241). Retrieved from http://www.cdc.gov/nchs/data/series/sr_10/sr10_241.pdf

Chen, P. W. (2010, May 6). Do women make better doctors? *New York Times*. Retrieved from http://www.nytimes.com/2010/05/06/health/06chen.html

Chen, X., & Wang, L. (2010). China. In M. H. Bornstein (Ed.), *Handbook of cultural developmental science* (pp. 429–444). New York: Psychology Press.

Chen, Y., & Ullman, S. E. (2010). Women's reporting of sexual and physical assaults to police in the national violence against women survey. *Violence Against Women, 16,* 262–279.

Cherlin, A. J. (2010). Demographic trends in the United States: A review of research in the 2000s. *Journal of Marriage and Family, 72,* 403–419.

Cherlin, A. J., & Krishnamurthy, P. (2004, May 9). What works for mom. *New York Times*, p. WK13.

Cherney, I. D. (2008). Mom, let me play more computer games: They improve my mental rotation skills. *Sex Roles, 59,* 776–786.

Cherney, I. D., & London, K. (2006). Gender-linked differences in the toys, television shows, computer games, and outdoor activities of 5- to 13-year-old children. *Sex Roles, 54,* 717–726.

Cherney, I. D., & Ryalls, B. O. (1999). Gender-linked differences in the incidental memory of children and adults. *Journal of Experimental Child Psychology, 72,* 305–328.

Cherry, A. L., Byers, L., & Dillon, M. (2009). A global perspective on teen pregnancy. In J. E. Ehiri (Ed.), *Maternal and child health: Global challenges, programs, and policies* (pp. 375–397). New York: Springer.

Cheryan, S., & Plaut, V. C. (2010). Explaining underrepresentation: A theory of precluded interest. *Sex Roles, 63,* 475–488.

Cheryan, S., Plaut, V. C., Davies, P. G., & Steele, C. M. (2009). Ambient belonging: How stereotypical cues impact gender participation in computer science. *Journal of Personality and Social Psychology, 97,* 1045–1060.

Cheung, F. M., & Halpern, D. F. (2010). Women at the top: Powerful leaders define success as work + family in a culture of gender. *American Psychologist, 65,* 182–193.

Chevarley, F. M., Thierry, J. M., Gill, C. J., Ryerson, A. B., & Nosek, M. A. (2006). Health, preventive health care, and health care access among women with disabilities in the 1994–1995 National Health Interview Survey, supplement on disability. *Women's Health Issues, 16,* 297–312.

Chiang, K.-C., Seman, L., Belza, B., & Tsai, J. H.-C. (2008). "It is our exercise family": Experiences of ethnic older adults in a group-based exercise program. *Preventing Chronic Disease, 5*. Retrieved from http://www.cdc.gov/pcd/issues/2008/jan/06_0170.htm

Chida, Y., Hamer, M., Wardle, J., & Steptoe, A. (2008). Do stress-related psychosocial factors contribute to cancer incidence and survival? *Nature Clinical Practice Oncology, 5,* 466–475.

Chida, Y., & Steptoe, A. (2008). Positive psychological well-being and mortality: A quantitative review of prospective observational studies. *Psychosomatic Medicine, 70,* 741–756.

Chida, Y., & Steptoe, A. (2009). The association of anger and hostility with future coronary heart disease. *Journal of the American College of Cardiology, 53,* 936–946.

Chin, J. L. (2010). Introduction to the special issue on diversity and leadership. *American Psychologist, 65,* 150–156.

Chisholm, J., & Greene, B. (2008). Women of color: Perspectives on "multiple identities" in psychological theory, research, and practice. In F. L. Denmark & M. A. Paludi (Eds.), *Psychology of women: A handbook of issues and theories* (2nd ed., pp. 40–69). Westport, CT: Praeger.

Cho, L., Hoogwerf, B., Huang, J., Brennan, D. M., & Hazen, S. L. (2008). Gender differences in utilization of effective cardiovascular secondary prevention: A Cleveland clinic prevention database study. *Journal of Women's Health, 17,* 515–521.

Chodorow, N. J. (1994). *Femininities, masculinities, sexualities: Freud and beyond.* Lexington, KY: University of Kentucky Press.

Choi, N. G. (2000). Determinants of engagement in paid work following social security benefit receipt among older women. *Journal of Women & Aging, 12,* 133–154.

Choma, B. L., Shove, C., Busseri, M. A., Sadava, S. W., & Hosker, A. (2009). Assessing the role of body image coping strategies as mediators or moderators of the links between self-objectification, body shame, and well-being. *Sex Roles, 61,* 699–713.

Chowdhary, N., & Patel, V. (2010). Gender-based violence and mental health. In D. Kohen (Ed.), *Oxford textbook of women and mental health* (pp. 7–16). Oxford, UK: Oxford University Press.

Chowdhury, A. K. (2010). Women's engagement: Essential to building the culture of peace. In P. Murthy & C. L. Smith (Eds.), *Women's global health and human rights* (pp. 495–498). Sudbury, MA: Jones and Bartlett.

Chrisler, J. C. (2007). Body image issues of women over 50. In V. Muhlbauer & J. C. Chrisler (Eds.), *Women over 50: Psychological perspectives* (pp. 6–25). New York: Springer.

Chrisler, J. C. (2008a). The menstrual cycle in a biopsychosocial context. In F. L. Denmark & M. A. Paludi (Eds.), *Psychology of women: A handbook of issues and theories* (2nd ed., pp. 400–439). Westport, CT: Praeger.

Chrisler, J. C. (2008b). PMS as a culture-bound syndrome. In J. C. Chrisler, C. Golden, & P. D. Rozee (Eds.), *Lectures on the psychology of women* (pp. 154–171). New York: McGraw-Hill.

Chrisler, J. C. (2008c). Presidential address: Fear of losing control: Power, perfectionism, and the psychology of women. *Psychology of Women Quarterly, 32,* 1–12.

Chrisler, J. C., & Almond, A. L. (2011). Menopause, medical aspects of. In M. Z. Stange, C. K. Oyster, & J. E. Sloan (Eds.), *Encyclopedia of women in today's world* (Vol. 2, pp. 923–925). Newberry Park, CA: Sage.

Chrisler, J. C., & Clapp, S. K. (2008). When the boss is a woman. In M. A. Paludi (Ed.), *The psychology of women at work: Challenges and solutions for our female workforce: Career liberation, history, and the new millennium* (Vol. 1, pp. 39–65). Westport, CT: Praeger.

Chrisler, J. C., & Garrett, C. (2010). Women's reproductive rights: An international perspective. In M. A. Paludi (Ed.), *Feminism and women's rights worldwide: Feminism as human rights* (Vol. 2, pp. 129–146). Santa Barbara, CA: Praeger.

Chrisler, J. C., Johnston, I. K., Champagne, N. M., & Preston, K. E. (1994). Menstrual joy: The construct and its consequences. *Psychology of Women Quarterly, 18,* 347–387.

Chrisler, J. C., & Rose, J. G. (2011). Premenstrual syndrome. In M. Z. Stange, C. K. Oyster, & J. E. Sloan (Eds.), *Encyclopedia of women in today's world.* Newberry Park, CA: Sage.

Chrisler, J. C., & Versace, J. (2011). Menopause, social aspects of. In M. Z. Stange, C. K. Oyster, & J. E. Sloan (Eds.), *Encyclopedia of women in today's world* (Vol. 2, pp. 925–927). Newberry Park, CA: Sage.

Christ, G. (2008, October 28). Mother gives birth to triplets for her daughter. *Daily Record.* Retrieved from http://www.the-daily-record.com/news/article/4453907

Christensen, K., & Schneider, B. (2010a). Conclusions: Solving the workplace/workforce mismatch. In K. Christensen & B. Schneider (Eds.), *Workplace flexibility: Realigning 20th-century jobs for a 21st-century workforce* (pp. 337–349). Ithaca, NY: Cornell University Press.

Christensen, K., & Schneider, B. (2010b). Introduction: Evidence of the worker and workplace mismatch. In K. Christensen & B. Schneider (Eds.), *Workplace flexibility: Realigning 20th-century jobs for a 21st-century workforce* (pp. 1–14). Ithaca, NY: Cornell University Press.

Christie-Mizell, C. A., & Peralta, R. L. (2009). The gender gap in alcohol consumption during late adolescence and young adulthood: Gendered attitudes and adult roles. *Journal of Health and Social Behavior, 50,* 410–426.

Chu, A. T., Pineda, A. S., DePrince, A. P., & Freyd, J. J. (2011). Vulnerability and protective factors for child abuse and maltreatment. In J. W. White, M. P. Koss, & A. E. Kazdin (Eds.), *Violence against women and children: Mapping the terrain* (Vol. 1, pp. 55–76). Washington, DC: American Psychological Association.

Chuang, S. S., & Su, Y. (2009). Says who? Decision-making and conflicts among Chinese-Canadian and mainland Chinese parents of young children. *Sex Roles, 60,* 527–536.

Chung, Y. B., Williams, W., & Dispenza, F. (2009). Validating work discrimination and coping strategy models for sexual minorities. *Career Development Quarterly, 58,* 162–170.

Church, H. A., & Lucey, J. W. (2010). Anxiety disorders in women. In D. Kohen (Ed.), *Oxford textbook of women and mental health* (pp. 83–92). Oxford, UK: Oxford University Press.

Ciairano, S., Liubicich, M. E., & Rabaglietti, E. (2010). The effects of a physical activity programme on the psychological wellbeing of older people in a residential care facility: An experimental study. *Ageing and Society, 30,* 609–626.

Ciambrone, D. (2003). *Women's experiences with HIV/AIDS: Mending fractured selves.* Binghamton, NY: Haworth Press.

Cicchetti, D., Rogosch, F. A., Gunnar, M. R., & Toth, S. L. (2010). The differential impacts of early physical and sexual abuse and internalizing problems on daytime cortisol rhythm in school-aged children. *Child Development, 81,* 252–269.

Cichy, K. E., Lefkowitz, E. S., & Fingerman, K. L. (2007). Generational differences in gender attitudes between parents and grown offspring. *Sex Roles, 57,* 825–836.

Cicirelli, V. G. (2010). Attachment relationships in old age. *Journal of Social and Personal Relationships, 27,* 191–199.

Clancy, C. M. (2000). Gender issues in women's health care. In M. B. Goldman & M. C. Hatch (Eds.), *Women & health* (pp. 50–64). New York: Academic Press.

Clark, C. R., et al. (2009). Addressing social determinants of health to improve access to early breast cancer detection: Results of the Boston REACH 2010 Breast and Cervical Cancer Coalition Women's Health demonstration project. *Journal of Women's Health, 18,* 677–690.

Clark, L., & Tiggemann, M. (2008). Sociocultural and individual psychological predictors of body image in young girls: A prospective study. *Developmental Psychology, 44,* 1124–1134.

Clark, M. D., & Carroll, M. H. (2008). Acquaintance rape scripts of women and men: Similarities and differences. *Sex Roles, 58,* 616–625.

Clark, R. A. (1998). A comparison of topics and objectives in a cross section of young men's and women's everyday conversations. In D. J. Canary & K. Dindia (Eds.), *Sex differences and similarities in communication: Critical essays and empirical investigations of sex and gender in interaction* (pp. 303–319). Mahwah, NJ: Erlbaum.

Clarke, A. Y., Adams, J., & Steinmetz, G. (2011). *The inequalities of love: College-educated Black women and the barriers to romance and family.* Durham, NC: Duke University Press.

Clarke, P. J., O'Malley, P. M., Johnston, L. D., Schulenberg, J. E., & Lantz, P. (2009). Differential trends in weight-related health behaviors among American young adults by gender, race/ethnicity, and socioeconomic status: 1984–2006. *American Journal of Public Health, 99,* 1893–1901.

Clarke-Stewart, A., & Miner, J. L. (2008). Effects of child and day care. In M. M. Haith & J. B. Benson (Eds.), *Encyclopedia of infant and early childhood development* (Vol. 1, pp. 268–278). San Diego, CA: Academic Press.

Clarren, R. (2005, Summer). The green motel. *Ms.*, 40–45.

Clayton, S., Garcia, A. L., & Crosby, F. J. (2010). Women in the workplace: Acknowledging difference in experience and policy. In H. Landrine & N. F. Russo (Eds.), *Handbook of diversity in feminist psychology* (pp. 559–581). New York: Springer.

Clearfield, M. W., & Nelson, N. M. (2006). Sex differences in mothers' speech and play behavior with 6-, 9-, and 14-month-old infants. *Sex Roles, 54,* 127–137.

Clements, C. M., & Ogle, R. L. (2009). Does acknowledgment as an assault victim impact postassault psychological symptoms and coping? *Journal of Interpersonal Violence, 24,* 1595–1614.

Clemetson, L. (2002, October 7). A neighborhood clinic helps fill the gap for Latinos without health care. *New York Times,* p. A12.

Closson, L. M. (2009). Aggressive and prosocial behaviors within early adolescent friendship cliques: What's status got to do with it? *Merrill-Palmer Quarterly, 55,* 406–435.

Clouse, A. L. (2008). Eating disorders. In A. L. Clouse & K. Sherif (Eds.), *Women's health in clinical practice: A handbook for primary care* (pp. 295–316). Totowa, NJ: Humana Press.

COACHE. (2010). *COACHE tenure-track faculty job satisfaction survey.* Cambridge, MA: Harvard University.

Coall, D. A., & Hertwig, R. (2011). Grandparental involvement: A relic of the past or a resource for the future? *Current Directions in Psychological Science, 20,* 93–98.

Cocchiara, F. K., & Bell, M. P. (2009). Gender and work stress: Unique stressors, unique responses. In C. L. Cooper, J. C. Quick, & M. J. Schabracq (Eds.), *International handbook of work and health psychology* (3rd ed., pp. 123–146). Malden, MA: Wiley.

Cohen, D. (Ed.). (2010). *Oxford textbook of women and mental health.* Oxford, UK: Oxford University Press.

Cohen, H. B. (2008). Premenstrual syndrome and premenstrual dysphoric disorder. In A. L. Clouse & K. Sherif (Eds.), *Women's health in clinical practice: A handbook for primary care* (pp. 19–28). Totowa, NJ: Humana Press.

Cohen, P., et al. (2003). Variations in patterns of developmental transitions in the emerging adulthood period. *Developmental Psychology, 39,* 657–669.

Cohen, P. N., & Huffman, M. L. (2003). Occupational segregation and the devaluation of women's work across U.S. labor markets. *Social Forces, 81,* 881–908.

Cohen, S. A. (2009). Facts and consequences: Legality, incidence and safety of abortion worldwide. *Guttmacher Policy Review, 12*(4), 2–6.

Cohen, S. A. (2010). Family planning and safe motherhood: Dollars and sense. *Guttmacher Policy Review, 13*(2), 12–16.

Coker, A. L., Williams, C. M., Follingstad, D. R., & Jordan, C. E. (2011). Psychological, reproductive and maternal health, behavioral, and economic impact of intimate partner violence. In J. W. White, M. P. Koss, & A. E. Kazdin (Eds.), *Violence against women and children: Mapping the terrain* (Vol. 1, pp. 265–284). Washington, DC: American Psychological Association.

Cole, E. (2010, Spring). Sex and politics: Keep your hands on my body. *Feminist Psychologist, 37*(2), 1–3.

Cole, E. R. (2009). Intersectionality and research in psychology. *American Psychologist, 64,* 170–180.

Cole, E. R., & Sabik, N. J. (2009). Repairing a broken mirror: Intersectional approaches to diverse women's perceptions of beauty and bodies. In M. T. Berger & K. Guidroz (Eds.), *The intersectional approach: Transforming the academy through race,* *class, and gender* (pp. 173–192). Chapel Hill, NC: University of North Carolina Press.

Cole, J. B., & Guy-Sheftall, B. (2003). *Gender talk: The struggle for women's equality in African American communities.* New York: Random House.

Cole, M. M. (2010). Endometriosis. In V. Maizes & T. Low Dog (Eds.), *Integrative women's health* (pp. 283–301). New York: Oxford University Press.

Coleman, J. M., & Franiuk, R. (2011). Perceptions of mothers and fathers who take temporary work leave. *Sex Roles, 64,* 311–323.

Colgan, F., Creegan, C., McKearney, A., & Wright, T. (2008). Lesbian workers: Personal strategies amid changing organizational responses to "sexual minorities" in UK workplaces. *Journal of Lesbian Studies, 12,* 31–45.

Colley, A., Berman, E., & Van Millingen, L. (2005). Age and gender differences in young people's perceptions of sport participants. *Journal of Applied Social Psychology, 35,* 1440–1454.

Collins, G. (2009). *When everything changed: The amazing journey of American women from 1960 to the present.* New York: Little, Brown.

Collins, W. A., & Steinberg, L. (2006). Adolescent development in interpersonal context. In W. Damon, R. M. Lerner (Series Eds.) & N. Eisenberg (Vol. Ed.), *Handbook of child psychology: Vol. 3. Social, emotional, and personality development* (6th ed., pp. 1003–1067). Hoboken, NJ: Wiley.

Colton, P. A., Olmsted, M. P., & Rodin, G. M. (2007). Eating disturbances in a school population of preteen girls: Assessment and screening. *International Journal of Eating Disorders, 40,* 435–440.

Coltrane, S., & Messineo, M. (2000). The perpetuation of subtle prejudice: Race and gender imagery in 1990s television advertising. *Sex Roles, 42,* 363–389.

Comas-Diaz, L. (2010a). Ethnocultural psychotherapy: Women of color's resilience and liberation. In M. A. Paludi (Ed.), *Feminism and women's rights worldwide: Mental and physical health* (Vol. 2, pp. 25–40). Santa Barbara, CA: Praeger.

Comas-Diaz, L. (2010b, Summer). Sin nombre: Female immigrants and the anti-immigration law. *Feminist Psychologist,* pp. 7, 14.

Comerford, L. (2011). Partner rights. In M. Z. Stange, C. K. Oyster, & J. E. Sloan (Eds.), *Encyclopedia of women in today's world.* Newberry Park, CA: Sage.

Commission on Women's Health. (2003). *The Commonwealth Fund Survey of women's health.* New York: Commonwealth Fund.

Commonwealth Fund. (1997). *In their own words: Adolescent girls discuss health and health care issues.* New York: Author.

Compas, B. E., & Luecken, L. (2002). Psychological adjustment to breast cancer. *Current Directions in Psychological Science, 11,* 111–114.

Concannon, T. W., et al. (2009). Elapsed time in emergency medical services for patients with cardiac complaints: Are some patients at greater risk for delay? *Circulation: Cardiovascular Quality and Outcomes, 2,* 9–15.

Conger, K. J., & Little, W. M. (2010). Sibling relationships during the transition to adulthood. *Child Development Perspectives, 4,* 87–94.

Conkle, A. (2010, February). Modern love: Scientific insights from 21st century dating. *Association for Psychological Science Observer, 23,* 12–16.

Connell, C. (2010). Doing, undoing, or redoing gender? Learning from the workplace experiences of transpeople. *Gender & Society, 24,* 31–55.

Conner, L. C., LeFauve, C. E., & Wallace, B. C. (2009). Ethnic and cultural correlates of addiction among diverse women. In K. T. Brady, S. E. Back, & S. F. Greenfield (Eds.), *Women and addiction: A comprehensive handbook* (pp. 453–474). New York: Guilford.

Connidis, I. A. (2010). *Family ties and aging* (2nd ed.), Thousand Oaks, CA: Pine Forge Press.

Connolly, J. A., & McIsaac, C. (2009). Romantic relationships in adolescence. In R. M. Lerner & L. Steinberg (Eds.), *Handbook of adolescent psychology* (3rd ed., Vol. 2, pp. 104–151). Hoboken, NJ: Wiley.

Conron, K. J., Mimiaga, M. J., & Landers, S. J. (2010). A population-based study of sexual orientation identity and gender differences in adult health. *American Journal of Public Health, 100,* 1953–1960.

Consedine, N. S., et al. (2004). Fear, anxiety, worry, and breast cancer screening behavior: A critical review. *Cancer Epidemiology, Biomarkers & Prevention, 13,* 501–510.

Conwell, Y., Duberstein, P. R., Hirsch, J. K., Conner, K. R., Eberly, S., & Caine, E. D. (2010). Health status and suicide in the second half of life. *International Journal of Geriatric Psychiatry, 25,* 371–379.

Cook, S. L., Gidycz, C. A., Koss, M. P., & Murphy, M. (2011). Emerging issues in the measurement of rape victimization. *Violence Against Women, 17,* 201–218.

Coomber, K., & King, R. M. (2008). The role of sisters in body image dissatisfaction and disordered eating. *Sex Roles, 59,* 81–93.

Coontz, S. (2008). Introduction to the second edition. In S. Coontz (Ed.), *American families: A multicultural reader* (2nd ed., pp. 1–22). New York: Taylor & Francis.

Coontz, S. (2011). *A strange stirring: "The feminine mystique" and American women at the dawn of the 1960's.* New York: Basic Books.

Cornelius, N., & Skinner, D. (2008). The careers of senior men and women—capabilities theory perspective. *British Journal of Management, 19,* S141–S149.

Cornwell, E. Y., & Waite, L. J. (2009). Social disconnectedness, perceived isolation, and health among older adults. *Journal of Health and Social Behavior, 50,* 31–48.

Corra, M., Carter, S. K., Carter, J. S., & Knox, D. (2009). Trends in marital happiness by gender and race, 1973 to 2006. *Journal of Family Issues, 30,* 1379–1404.

Correa-de-Araujo, R., Miller, E., Banthin, J. S., & Trinh, Y. (2005). Gender differences in drug use and expenditures in a privately insured population of older adults. *Journal of Women's Health, 14,* 73–80.

Correll, S. J., Benard, S., & Paik, I. (2007). Getting a job: Is there a motherhood penalty? *American Journal of Sociology, 112,* 1297–1338.

Corrigall, E. A., & Konrad, A. M. (2006). The relationship of job attribute preferences to employment, hours of paid work, and family responsibilities: An analysis comparing women and men. *Sex Roles, 54,* 95–111.

Corrigall, E. A., & Konrad, A. M. (2007). Gender role attitudes and careers: A longitudinal study. *Sex Roles, 56,* 847–855.

Cortina, L. M. (2004). Hispanic perspectives on sexual harassment and social support. *Personality and Social Psychology Bulletin, 30,* 570–584.

Cortina, L. M., & Magley, V. J. (2003). Raising voice, risking retaliation: Events following interpersonal mistreatment in the workplace. *Journal of Occupational Health Psychology, 8,* 247–265.

Costello, C. B., & Wight, V. R. (2003). Taking it from here: Policies for the twenty-first century. In C. B. Costello, V. R. Wight, & A. J. Stone (Eds.), *The American woman 2003–2004: Daughters of a revolution— Young women today* (pp. 127–142). New York: Palgrave Macmillan.

Costigan, C. L., Cauce, A. M., & Etchison, K. (2007). Changes in African American mother-daughter relationships during adolescence: Conflict, autonomy, and warmth. In B. J. R. Leadbeater & N. Way (Eds.), *Urban girls revisited: Building strengths* (pp. 177–201). New York: New York University Press.

Cote, L. R., & Bornstein, M. H. (2009). Child and mother play in three U.S. cultural groups: Comparisons and associations. *Journal of Family Psychology, 23,* 355–363.

Cotter, D., England, P., & Hermsen, J. (2008). Moms and jobs: Trends in mothers' employment and which mothers stay home. In S. Coontz (Ed.), *American families: A multicultural reader* (2nd ed., pp. 379–386). New York: Taylor & Francis.

Coulter, I., Jacobson, P., & Parker, L. E. (2000). Sharing the mantle of primary female care: Physicians, nurse practitioners, and physician assistants. *Journal of the American Medical Women's Association, 55,* 100–103.

Coursolle, K. M., Sweeney, M. M., Raymo, J. M., & Ho, J.-H. (2010). The association between retirement and emotional well-being: Does prior work-family conflict matter? *Journal of Gerontology: Social Sciences, 65B,* 609–620.

Cowley, G., & Murr, A. (2004, December 6). The new face of AIDS. *Newsweek,* pp. 76–79.

Cox, D. (2008). Intergenerational caregiving and exchange: Economic and evolutionary approaches. In A. Booth, A. C. Crouter, S. M. Bianchi, & J. A. Seltzer (Eds.), *Intergenerational caregiving* (pp. 81–125). Washington, DC: Urban Institute Press.

Cox, D. L., et al. (2006, August). *Just between us: Mother-daughter relationships in the context of U.S. beauty culture.* Paper presented at the annual meeting of the American Psychological Association, New Orleans, LA.

Coyle, S. B. (2009). Health-related quality of life of mothers: A review of the research. *Health Care for Women International, 30,* 484–506.

Coyne, S. M., Archer, J., & Eslea, M. (2006). "We're not friends anymore! unless . . .": The frequency and harmfulness of indirect, relational, and social aggression. *Aggressive Behavior, 32,* 294–307.

Cozzarelli, C., Wilkinson, A. V., & Tagler, M. J. (2001). Attitudes toward the poor and attributions for poverty. *Journal of Social Issues, 57,* 207–228.

Crabtree, R. D., Sapp, D. A., & Licona, A. C. (2009). Introduction: The passion and the praxis of feminist pedagogy. In R. D. Crabtree, D. A. Sapp, & A. C. Licona (Eds.), *Feminist pedagogy: Looking back to move forward* (pp. 1–20). Baltimore, MD: John Hopkins Press.

Craig, L., & Mullan, K. (2010). Parenthood, gender and work-family time in the United States, Australia, Italy, France and Denmark. *Journal of Marriage and Family, 72,* 1344–1361.

Craig, L., & Sawrikar, P. (2009). Work and family: How does the (gender) balance change as children grow? *Gender, Work & Organization, 16,* 687–709.

Craven, C. (2010). *Pushing for midwives: Homebirth mothers and the reproductive rights movement.* Philadelphia, PA: Temple University Press.

Crawford, M., & MacLeod, M. (1990). Gender in the college classroom: An assessment of the "chilly climate" for women. *Sex Roles, 23,* 101–122.

Crawley, S. L. (2011). Visible bodies, vicarious masculinity, and "the gender revolution": Comment on England. *Gender & Society, 25,* 108–112.

Crepaz, N., et al. (2009). The efficacy of HIV/STI behavioral interventions for African American females in the United States: A meta-analysis. *American Journal of Public Health, 99,* 2069–2078.

Crick, N. R., Murray-Close, D., Marks, P. E., & Mohajeri-Nelson, N. (2009). Aggression and peer relationships in school-age children: Relational and physical aggression in group and dyadic contexts. In K. H. Rubin, W. M. Bukowski, & B. Laursen (Eds.), *Handbook of peer interactions, relationships, and groups* (pp. 287–302). New York: Guilford.

Crimmons, E. M., & Beltrán-Sánchez, H. (2010). Mortality and morbidity trends: Is there compression of morbidity? *Journal of Gerontology: Social Sciences, 66B,* 75–86.

Crockett, L. J. (1991). Sex roles and sex-typing in adolescence. In R. M. Lerner, A. C. Petersen, & J. Brooks-Gunn (Eds.), *Encyclopedia of adolescence* (Vol. 2, pp. 1007–1017). New York: Garland.

Croghan, I. T., et al. (2009). The role of smoking in breast cancer development: An analysis of a Mayo clinic cohort. *Breast Journal, 15,* 489–495.

Crooks, C. V., Jaffe, P. G., Wolfe, D. A., Hughes, R., & Chiodo, D. (2011). School-based dating violence prevention. In C. M. Renzetti, J. L. Edleson, & R. K. Bergen (Eds.), *Sourcebook on violence against women* (2nd ed., pp. 327–346). Thousand Oaks, CA: Sage.

Crosby, A. E., Ortega, L., & Stevens, M. R. (2011, January 14). Suicides—United States, 1999–2007. *Morbidity and Mortality Weekly Report, 60*(Suppl.), 56–60.

Crosby, F. J. (1991). *Juggling: The unexpected advantages of balancing career and home for women and their families.* New York: Free Press.

Crosby, F. J. (2008). Sex discrimination at work. In J. C. Chrisler, C. Golden, & P. D. Rozee (Eds.), *Lectures on the psychology of women* (pp. 42–57). New York: McGraw-Hill.

Crosby, F. J., & Sabattini, L. (2006). Family and work balance. In J. Worell & C. D. Goodheart (Eds.), *Handbook of girls' and women's psychological health: Gender and well-being across the lifespan* (pp. 350–358). New York: Oxford University Press.

Crosnoe, R., & Cavanagh, S. E. (2010). Families with children and adolescents: A review, critique, and future agenda. *Journal of Marriage and Family, 72,* 594–611.

Croteau, J. M., Anderson, M. Z., & VanderWal, B. L. (2008). Models of workplace sexual identity disclosure and management: Reviewing and extending concepts. *Group & Organization Management, 33,* 532–565.

Croteau, J. M., Bieschke, K. J., Fassinger, R. E., & Manning, J. L. (2008). Counseling psychology and sexual orientation: History, selective trends, and future directions. In S. D. Brown & R. W. Lent (Eds.), *Hand-book of counseling psychology* (4th ed., pp. 194–211). New York: Wiley.

Crouter, A. C., Whiteman, S. D., McHale, S. M., & Osgood, D. W. (2007). Development of gender attitude traditionality across middle childhood and adolescence. *Child Development, 78,* 911–926.

Crowl, A. L., Ahn, S., & Baker, J. (2008). A meta-analysis of developmental outcomes for children of same-sex and heterosexual parents. *Journal of GLBT Family Studies, 4,* 385–407.

Crowley, K., Callanan, M. A., Tenenbaum, H. R., & Allen, E. (2001). Parents explain more often to boys than to girls during shared scientific thinking. *Psychological Science, 12,* 258–261.

Cuddy, A. J. C., Fiske, S. T., & Glick, P. (2004). When professionals become mothers, warmth doesn't cut the ice. *Journal of Social Issues, 60,* 701–718.

Cuijpers, P., Brännmark, J. G., & van Straten, A. (2008). Psychological treatment of postpartum depression: A meta-analysis. *Journal of Clinical Psychology, 64,* 103–118.

Cuijpers, P., van Straten, A., & Smit, F. (2006). Psychological treatment of late-life depression: A meta-analysis of randomized controlled trials. *International Journal of Geriatric Psychiatry, 21,* 1139–1149.

Cumming, G. (2011). *Understanding the new statistics: Effect sizes, confidence intervals, and meta-analysis.* New York: Routledge.

Cunningham, G. B. (2008). Creating and sustaining gender diversity in sport organizations. *Sex Roles, 58,* 136–145.

Cunningham, J., & Macan, T. (2007). Effects of applicant pregnancy on hiring decisions and interview ratings. *Sex Roles, 57,* 497–508.

Cunningham, M. (2001). The influence of parental attitudes and behaviors on children's attitudes toward gender and household labor in early adulthood. *Journal of Marriage and Family, 63,* 111–122.

Cunningham, M. (2008). Changing attitudes toward the male breadwinner, female homemaker family model: Influences of women's employment and education over the lifecourse. *Social Forces, 87,* 299–322.

Cunningham, M., Beutel, A. M., Barber, J. S., & Thornton, A. (2005). Reciprocal relationships between attitudes about gender and social contexts during young adulthood. *Social Science Research, 34,* 862–892.

Curry, M. A., et al. (2009). Development of measures of abuse among women with disabilities and the characteristics of their perpetrators. *Violence Against Women, 15,* 1001–1025.

Curtis, G., & Schuler, J. (2004). *Your pregnancy week by week* (5th ed.). Cambridge, MA: DaCapo Press.

Curtis, K. M. (2010, May 28). U.S. medical eligibility criteria for contraceptive use, 2010. *Morbidity and Mortality Weekly Report, 59,* 1–6.

Curtis, L. H., et al. (2004). Inappropriate prescribing for elderly Americans in a large outpatient population. *Archives of Internal Medicine, 164,* 1621–1625.

Cutajar, M. C., Mullen, P. E., Ogloff, J. R., Thomas, S. D., Wells, D. L., & Spataro, J. (2010). Schizophrenia and other psychotic disorders in a cohort of sexually abused children. *General Psychiatry, 67,* 1114–1119.

Cutler, D. M., & Lleras-Muney, A. (2008). Education and health: Evaluating theories and evidence. In R. F. Schoeni, J. S. House, G. A. Kaplan, & H. Pollack (Eds.), *Making Americans healthier: Social and economic policy as health policy* (pp. 29–60). New York: Russell Sage Foundation.

Cvencek, D., Meltzoff, A. N., & Greenwald, A. G. (2011). Math-gender stereotypes in elementary school children. *Child Development, 82,* 766–779.

Czajkowski, S. M., Arteaga, S., & Burg, M. M. (2012). Social support and coronary heart disease. In R. Alan & J. Fisher (Eds.), *Heart and mind: The practice of cardiac psychology* (2nd ed., pp. 169–195). Washington, DC: American Psychological Association.

Daar, J. F., & Brzyski, R. G. (2009, October 21). Genetic screening of sperm and oocyte donors: Ethical and policy implications. *Journal of the American Medical Association, 302,* 1702–1704.

Dailard, C. (2003). Marriage is no immunity from problems with planning pregnancies. *The Guttmacher Report on Public Policy,* 10–13.

Daley, A. (2009). Exercise and premenstrual symptomatology: A comprehensive review. *Journal of Women's Health, 18,* 895–899.

Dalla, R. L., Marchetti, A. M., Sechrest, E. A., & White, J. L. (2010). "All men here have the Peter Pan Syndrome—they don't want to grow up": Navajo adolescent mothers' intimate partner relationships—a 15-year perspective. *Violence Against Women, 16,* 743–763.

Dalleck, L. C., Allen, B. A., Hanson, B. A., Borresen, E. C., Erickson, M. E., & De Lap, S. L. (2009). Dose-response relationship between moderate-intensity exercise duration and coronary heart disease risk factors in postmenopausal women. *Journal of Women's Health, 18,* 105–113.

Dance, L. J. (2009). Racial, ethnic, and gender disparities in early school leaving (dropping out). In B. T. Dill & R. E. Zambrana (Eds.), *Emerging intersections: Race, class, and gender in theory, policy, and practice* (pp. 180–202). Piscataway, NJ: Rutgers University Press.

Daniels, E. A. (2009). Sex objects, athletes, and sexy athletes: How media representations of women athletes can impact adolescent girls and college women. *Journal of Adolescent Research, 24,* 399–422.

Danielsson, A.-K., Romelsjö, A., & Tengström, A. (2011). Heavy episodic drinking in early adolescence: Gender-specific risk and protective factors. *Substance Abuse & Misuse, 46,* 633–643.

Daniluk, J. C. (1998). *Women's sexuality across the life span: Challenging myths, creating meanings.* New York: Guilford.

Darby, A., Hay, P., Mond, J., Quirk, F., Buttner, P., & Kennedy, L. (2009). The rising prevalence of comorbidity obesity and eating disorder behaviors from 1995 to 2005. *International Journal of Eating Disorders, 42,* 104–108.

Dardenne, B., Dumont, M., & Bollier, T. (2007). Insidious dangers of benevolent sexism: Consequences for women's performance. *Journal of Personality and Social Psychology, 93,* 764–779.

Dare, J. S. (2010). Transitions in midlife women's lives: Contemporary experiences. *Health Care for Women International, 32,* 111–133.

Darlington, P. S., & Mulvaney, B. M. (2003). *Women, power, and ethnicity: Working toward reciprocal empowerment.* New York: Haworth.

Darroch, J. E., Frost, J. J., Singh, S., & the Study Team. (2001). *Teenage sexual and reproductive behavior in developed countries: Can more progress be made?* (Occasional Report No. 3). New York: Alan Guttmacher Institute.

Das, M. (2011). Gender role portrayals in Indian television ads. *Sex Roles, 64,* 208–222.

Daubman, K. A., Heatherington, L., & Ahn, A. (1992). Gender and the self-presentation of academic achievement. *Sex Roles, 27,* 187–204.

Daubman, K. A., & Sigall, H. (1997). Gender differences in perceptions of how others are affected by self-disclosure of achievement. *Sex Roles, 37,* 73–89.

Davé, S., Petersen, I., Sherr, L., & Nazareth, I. (2010). Incidence of maternal and paternal depression in primary care: A cohort study using a primary care database. *Archives of Pediatrics & Adolescent Medicine, 164,* 1038–1044.

Davenport, M. L. (2008). Moving toward an understanding of hormone replacement therapy in adolescent girls: Looking through the lens of Turner syndrome. *Annals of the New York Academy of Sciences, 1135,* 126–137.

Davey, A., & Szinovacz, M. E. (2004). Dimensions of marital quality and retirement. *Journal of Family Issues, 25,* 431–464.

David, H. P., & Lee, E. (2001). Abortion and its health effects. In J. Worell (Ed.), *Encyclopedia of women and gender* (pp. 1–14). San Diego, CA: Academic Press.

Davidson, D. (2011a). Doulas. In M. Z. Stange, C. K. Oyster, & J. E. Sloan (Eds.), *Encyclopedia of women in today's world* (Vol. 1, pp. 423–424). Newberry Park, CA: Sage.

Davidson, D. (2011b). Intersex. In M. Z. Stange, C. K. Oyster, & J. E. Sloan (Eds.), *Encyclopedia of women in today's world* (Vol. 2, pp. 766–767). Newberry Park, CA: Sage.

Davidson, D. (2011c). Reproductive cancers. In M. Z. Stange, C. K. Oyster, & J. E. Sloan (Eds.), *Encyclopedia of women in today's world.* Newberry Park, CA: Sage.

Davila, J. (2008). Depressive symptoms and adolescent romance: Theory, research, and implications. *Child Development Perspectives, 2,* 26–31.

Davis, C. L. (2011). Girl-friendly schools. In M. Z. Stange, C. K. Oyster, & J. E. Sloan (Eds.), *Encyclopedia of women in today's world* (Vol. 2, pp. 622–623). Newberry Park, CA: Sage.

Davis, K., Collins, K. S., & Schoen, C. (2000). Women's health and managed care. In M. B. Goldman & M. Hatch (Eds.), *Women and health* (pp. 55–63). New York: Academic Press.

Davis, K. E., Coker, A. L., & Sanderson, M. (2002). Physical and mental health effects of being stalked for men and women. *Violence and Victims, 17,* 429–443.

Davis, P. J. (1999). Gender differences in autobiographical memory for childhood emotional experiences. *Journal of Personality and Social Psychology, 76,* 498–510.

Davis, S. N., & Greenstein, T. N. (2009). Gender ideology: Components, predictors, and consequences. *Annual Review of Sociology, 35,* 87–105.

Davis, S. N., Greenstein, T. N., & Gerteisen Marks, J. P. (2007). Effects of union type on division of household labor: Do cohabiting men really perform more housework? *Journal of Family Issues, 28,* 1246–1272.

Davison, H. K., & Burke, M. J. (2000). Sex discrimination in simulated employment contexts: A meta-analytic investigation. *Journal of Vocational Behavior, 56,* 225–248.

Day, J. C., & Downs, B. (2009, April/May). *Opting-out: An exploration of labor force participation of new mothers.* Paper presented at the 2009 annual meeting of the Population Association of America, Detroit, MI.

de Alwis, R. d. S. (2008). *Disability rights, gender, and development: A resource tool for action.* Wellesley, MA: Wellesley College. Retrieved from http://www.wcwonline.org/pdf/free/UNRPDWCWExecutiveSummary.pdf

DeAngelis, T. (2010a). Mapping menopause. *Monitor on Psychology, 41,* 44–46.

DeAngelis, T. (2010b). Menopause, the makeover. *Monitor on Psychology, 41,* 41–43.

de Backer, C., Braeckman, J., & Farinpour, L. (2008). Mating intelligence in personal ads. In G. Geher & G. Miller (Eds.), *Mating intelligence: Sex, relationships, and the mind's reproductive system* (pp. 77–101). New York: Taylor & Francis.

DeBate, R., Blunt, H., & Becker, M. A. (2010). Eating disorders. In B. L. Levin & M. A. Becker (Eds.), *A public health perspective of women's mental health* (pp. 121–142). New York: Springer.

DeBate, R. D., Gabriel, K. P., Zwald, M., Huberty, J., & Zhang, Y. (2009). Changes in psychosocial factors and physical activity frequency among third- to eighth-grade girls who participated in a developmentally focused youth sport program: A preliminary study. *Journal of School Health, 79,* 474–484.

DeBraganza, N., & Hausenblas, H. A. (2010). Media exposure of the ideal physique on women's body dissatisfaction and mood: The moderating effects of ethnicity. *Journal of Black Studies, 40,* 700–716.

Dechamps, A., et al. (2010). Effects of exercise programs to prevent decline in health-related quality of life in highly deconditioned institutionalized elderly persons. *Archives of Internal Medicine, 170,* 162–169.

Deech, R., & Smajdor, A. (2007). *From IVF to immortality: Controversy in the era of reproductive technology.* Oxford, UK: Oxford University Press.

DeFour, D. C. (2008). Challenges for women of color. In M. A. Paludi (Ed.), *The psychology of women at work: Challenges and solutions for our female workforce: Obstacles and the identity juggle* (Vol. 2, pp. 109–119). Westport, CT: Praeger.

Defrancisco, V. P., & Palczewski, C. H. (2007). *Communicating gender diversity: A critical approach.* Newbury Park, CA: Sage.

DeGroot, J., & Fine, J. (2003). Integrating work and life: Young women forge new solutions. In C. B. Costello, V. R. Wight, & A. J. Stone (Eds.), *The American woman 2003–2004: Daughters of a revolution—Young women today* (pp. 127–142). New York: Palgrave Macmillan.

DeKeseredy, W. S., & Schwartz, M. D. (2011). Theoretical and definitional issues in violence against women. In C. M. Renzetti, J. L. Edleson, & R. K. Bergen (Eds.), *Sourcebook on violence against women* (2nd ed., pp. 3–20). Thousand Oaks, CA: Sage.

De Lisi, R., & Soundranayagam, L. (1990). The conceptual structure of sex role stereotypes in college students. *Sex Roles, 23,* 593–611.

DeLoach, C. P. (1989). Gender, career choice and occupational outcomes among college alumni with disabilities. *Journal of Applied Rehabilitation Counseling, 20,* 8–12.

DeLoache, J. S., Simcock, G., & Macari, S. (2007). Planes, trains, automobiles—and tea sets: Extremely intense interests in very young children. *Developmental Psychology, 43,* 1579–1586.

Delpisheh, A., Brabin, L., Attia, E., & Brabin, B. J. (2008). Pregnancy late in life: A hospital-based study of birth outcomes. *Journal of Women's Health, 17,* 965–970.

DeMaris, A. (2010). The 20-year trajectory of marital quality in enduring marriages: Does equity matter? *Journal of Social and Personal Relationships, 27,* 449–471.

Denissen, J. J. A., Zarrett, N. R., & Eccles, J. S. (2007). I like to do it, I'm able, and I know I am: Longitudinal couplings between domain-specific achievement, self-concept, and interest. *Child Development, 78,* 430–447.

Denizet-Lewis, B. (2004, May 30). Friends, friends with benefits and the benefits of the local mall. *New York Times Magazine,* pp. 30–35, 54–58.

Denmark, F. L. (1999). Enhancing the development of adolescent girls. In N. G. Johnson, M. C. Roberts, & J. Worell (Eds.), *Beyond appearance: A new look at adolescent girls* (pp. 337–404). Washington, DC: American Psychological Association.

Denmark, F. L., & Klara, M. D. (2007). Empowerment: A prime time for women over 50. In V. Muhlbauer & J. C. Chrisler (Eds.), *Women over 50: Psychological perspectives* (pp. 182–203). New York: Springer.

Denmark, F. L., Klara, M. D., Baron, E., & Cambareri-Fernandez, L. (2008). Historical development of the psychology of women. In F. L. Denmark & M. A. Paludi (Eds.), *Psychology of women: A handbook of issues and theories* (2nd ed., pp. 3–39). Westport, CT: Praeger.

Denmark, F. L., Rabinowitz, V., & Sechzer, J. (2000). *Engendering psychology.* Needham Heights, MA: Allyn & Bacon.

Denner, J., & Coyle, K. (2006). Condom use among sexually active Latina girls in alternative high schools. In B. J. R. Leadbeater & N. Way (Eds.), *Urban girls revisited: Building strengths* (pp. 281–300). New York: New York University Press.

Dennis, A., Henshaw, S. K., Joyce, T. J., Finer, L. B., & Blanchard, K. (2009). *The impact of laws requiring parental involvement for abortion: A literature review.* New York: Guttmacher Institute. Retrieved from http://www.guttmacher.org/pubs/ParentalInvolvementLaws.pdf

Dennis, C.-L., et al. (2009). Effect of peer support on prevention of postnatal depression among high risk women: Multisite randomized controlled trial [Online publication]. *British Medical Journal, 338.*

Denny, K. E. (2011). Gender in context, content, and approach: Comparing gender messages in girl scout and boy scout handbooks. *Gender and Society, 25,* 27–47.

DePaulo, B. (2006). *Singled out: How singles are stereotyped, stigmatized, and ignored, and still live happily ever after.* New York: St. Martin's Press.

DePaulo, B. (2009). *Fact sheet for unmarried and single Americans week.* Chicago, IL: Council on Contemporary Families.

DePaulo, B. M., Moran, R. F., & Trimberger, E. K. (2007, September 28). Make room for singles in teaching and research. *Chronicle of Higher Education,* pp. B44–B45.

DePaulo, B. M., & Morris, W. L. (2006). The unrecognized stereotyping and discrimination against singles. *Current Directions in Psychological Science, 15,* 251–254.

Depression & women. (2003, August). *National Women's Health Report, 25,* 1–4.

D'Erasmo, S. (2004, January 11). Lesbians on television: It's not easy being seen. *New York Times,* p. 1.

DeRose, L. M., & Brooks-Gunn, J. (2006). Transition into adolescence: The role of pubertal processes. In L. Balter & C. S.

Tamis-LeMonda (Eds.), *Child psychology: A handbook of contemporary issues* (2nd ed., pp. 385–414). New York: Taylor & Francis.

Desmond, R., & Danilewicz, A. (2010). Women are on, but not in, the news: Gender roles in local television news. *Sex Roles, 62,* 822–829.

DeSouza, E. R. (2008). Workplace incivility, sexual harassment, and racial micro-aggression: The interface of three literatures. In M. A. Paludi (Ed.), *The psychology of women at work: Challenges and solutions for our female workforce: Obstacles and the identity juggle* (Vol. 2, pp. 65–84). Westport, CT: Praeger.

Deutsch, F. M., & Saxon, S. E. (1998). Traditional ideologies, non-traditional lives. *Sex Roles, 38,* 331–362.

de Valk, H. A. G. (2008). Parental influence on work and family plans of adolescent of different ethnic backgrounds in The Netherlands. *Sex Roles, 59,* 738–751.

Devetter, F.-X. (2009). Gender differences in time availability: Evidence from France. *Gender, Work & Organization, 16,* 429–450.

Devi, G., Shin, E., Kim, E., & Lo, V. (2009). AMWA position statement on emergency contraception. *Journal of Women's Health, 18,* 1539–1540.

Devos, T., Blanco, K., Rico, F., & Dunn, R. (2008). The role of parenthood and college education in the self-concept of college students: Explicit and implicit assessments of gendered aspirations. *Sex Roles, 59,* 214–228.

De Vries, B., & Megathlin, D. (2009). The meaning of friendship for gay men and lesbians in the second half of life. *Journal of GLBT Family Studies, 5,* 82–98.

Dew, J., & Wilcox, W. B. (2011). If momma ain't happy: Explaining declines in marital satisfaction among new mothers. *Journal of Marriage and Family, 73,* 1–12.

de Waal, F. B. M. (2002). Evolutionary psychology: The wheat and the chaff. *Current Directions in Psychological Science, 11,* 187–191.

DeZolt, D. M., & Hull, S. H. (2001). Classroom and social climate. In J. Worell (Ed.), *Encyclopedia of women and gender* (pp. 257–264). San Diego, CA: Academic Press.

Dhaher, E. A., Mikolajczyk, R. T., Maxwell, A. E., & Krämer, A. (2010). Attitudes toward wife beating among Palestinian women of reproductive age from three cities in West Bank. *Journal of Interpersonal Violence, 25,* 518–537.

Diamond, L. M. (2003). What does sexual orientation orient? A biobehavioral model distinguishing romantic love and sexual desire. *Psychological Review, 110,* 173–192.

Diamond, L. M. (2007). A dynamical systems approach to the development and expression of female same-sex sexuality. *Perspectives on Psychological Science, 2,* 142–161.

Diamond, L. M. (2008). Female bisexuality from adolescence to adulthood: Results from a 10-year longitudinal study. *Developmental Psychology, 44,* 5–14.

Diamond, L. M., Fagundes, C. P., & Butterworth, M. R. (2010). Intimate relationships across the life span. In *The handbook of life-span development: Social and emotional development* (Vol. 2, pp. 379–433). Hoboken, NJ: Wiley.

Diamond, L. M., & Savin-Williams, R. C. (2009). Adolescent sexuality. In R. M. Lerner & L. Steinberg (Eds.), *Handbook of adolescent psychology* (3rd ed., Vol. 1, pp. 479–523). Hoboken, NJ: Wiley.

Diamond, M. (2009). Clinical implications of the organizational and activational effects of hormones. *Hormones and Behavior, 55,* 621–632.

Diamond, M. (2010). Intersexuality. In E. J. Haeberle (Ed.), Human sexuality: An encyclopedia. Retrieved from http://www.hawaii.edu/PCSS/biblio/articles/2010to2014/2010-intersexuality.html

DiClemente, R. J., et al. (2008). Psychosocial predictors of HIV-associated sexual behaviors and the efficacy of prevention interventions in adolescents at-risk for HIV infection: What works and what doesn't work? *Psychosomatic Medicine, 70,* 598–605.

Diekman, A. B., & Eagly, A. H. (1997, May). *Past, present, and future: Perceptions of change in women and men.* Paper presented at the meeting of the Midwestern Psychological Association, Chicago.

Diekman, A. B., Goodfriend, W., & Goodwin, S. (2004). Dynamic stereotypes of power: Perceptions of change and stability in gender hierarchies. *Sex Roles, 50,* 201–215.

Diekman, A. B., & Schneider, M. C. (2010). A social role theory perspective on gender gaps in political attitudes. *Psychology of Women Quarterly, 34,* 486–497.

Diener, E., Gohm, C. L., Suh, M., & Oishi, S. (2000). Similarity of the relation between marital status and subjective well-being across cultures. *Journal of Cross-Cultural Psychology, 31,* 419–436.

Dijkstra, J. K., Lindenberg, S., Verhulst, F. C., Ormel, J., & Veenstra, R. (2009). The relation between popularity and aggressive, destructive, and norm-breaking moderating effects of athletic abilities, physical attractiveness, and prosociality. *Journal of Research on Adolescence, 19,* 401–413.

Dill, B. T., & Zambrana, R. E. (2009a). Critical thinking about inequality: An emerging lens. In B. T. Dill & R. E. Zambrana (Eds.), *Emerging intersections: Race, class, and gender in theory, policy, and practice* (pp. 1–21). Piscataway, NJ: Rutgers University Press.

Dill, B. T., & Zambrana, R. E. (Eds.). (2009b). *Emerging intersections: Race, class and gender in theory, policy, and practice.* New Brunswick, NJ: Rutgers University Press.

Dill, K. E., & Thill, K. P. (2007). Video game characters and the socialization of gender roles: Young people's perceptions mirror sexist media depictions. *Sex Roles, 57,* 851–864.

Dillaway, H., Byrnes, M., Miller, S., & Rehan, S. (2008). Talking "among us": How women from different racial-ethnic groups define and discuss menopause. *Health Care for Women International, 29,* 766–781.

Dillaway, H., & Paré, E. (2008). Locating mothers: How cultural debates about stay-at-home versus working mothers define women and home. *Journal of Family Issues, 29,* 437–464.

Dilley, J. A., Simmons, K. W., Boysun, M. J., Pizacani, B. A., & Stark, M. J. (2010). Demonstrating the importance and feasibility of including sexual orientation in public health surveys: Health disparities in the Pacific Northwest. *American Journal of Public Health, 100,* 460–467.

Dillon, S. (2002, June 15). Women tell of priests' abusing them as girls. *New York Times,* p. A11.

Dingfelder, S. F. (2010, March). Ending an epidemic. *Monitor on Psychology, 41,* 33–35.

Disparities in diagnoses of HIV infection between Blacks/African Americans and other racial/ethnic populations—37 states, 2005–2008. (2011, February 4). *Morbidity and Mortality Weekly Report, 60,* 93–98.

Dittmann, M. (2003, March). Coping with cancer through social connection. *Monitor on Psychology, 41,* 24–26.

Dittmar, H., Halliwell, E., & Ive, S. (2006). Does Barbie make girls want to be thin? The effect of experimental exposure to images of dolls on the body image of 5- to 8-year-old girls. *Developmental Psychology, 42,* 283–292.

DiVall, S. A., & Radovick, S. (2008). Pubertal development and menarche. *Annals of the New York Academy of Sciences, 1135,* 19–28.

Dixon, J., et al. (2010). Defining elder mistreatment: Reflections on the United Kingdom study of abuse and neglect of older people. *Ageing and Society, 30,* 403–420.

Djikanovic, B., Jansen, H. A., & Otasevic, S. (2010). Factors associated with intimate partner violence against women in Serbia: A cross-sectional study. *Journal of Epidemiology and Community Health, 64,* 728–735.

Dockray, S., & Steptoe, A. (2010). Positive affect and psychobiological processes. *Neuroscience & Biobehavioral Reviews, 35,* 69–75.

Dodoo, F. N.-A., & Frost, A. E. (2008). Gender in African population research: The fertility/reproductive health example. *Annual Review of Sociology, 34,* 431–452.

Dodson, L., & Zincavage, R. M. (2007). "It's like a family": Caring labor, exploitation, and race in nursing homes. *Gender & Society, 21,* 905–928.

Doering, L. V., Cross, R., Magsarili, M. C., Howitt, L. Y., & Cowan, M. J. (2007). Utility of observer-rated and self-report instruments for detecting major depression in women after cardiac surgery: A pilot study. *American Journal of Critical Care, 16,* 260–269.

Dohm, F.-A., Brown, M., Cachelin, F. M., & Striegel-Moore, R. H. (2010). Ethnicity, disordered eating, and body image. In H. Landrine & N. F. Russo (Eds.), *Hand-book of diversity in feminist psychology* (pp. 285–309). New York: Springer.

Dohnt, H., & Tiggemann, M. (2006). The contribution of peer and media influences to the development of body satisfaction and self-esteem in young girls: A prospective study. *Developmental Psychology, 42,* 929–936.

Dolnick, S. (2011, February 18). Ethnic differences emerge in plastic surgery. *New York Times,* p. A17.

Dominus, S. (2002, September 29). Shabana is late for school. *New York Times Magazine,* pp. 42–47, 56, 62–63, 118–120.

Dominus, S. (2004, October 24). Growing up with mom and mom. *New York Times Magazine,* pp. 68–75, 84, 143–144.

Donaghue, N., & Smith, N. (2008). Not half bad: Self and others' judgements of body size and attractiveness across the life span. *Sex Roles, 58,* 875–882.

Donatelle, R. J. (2012). *Access to health* (12th ed.). San Francisco, CA: Benjamin Cummings.

Donatelle, R. J., & Davis, L. G. (1998). *Access to health* (5th ed.). Boston, MA: Allyn & Bacon.

Dong, X., et al. (2009). Elder self-neglect and abuse and mortality risk in a community-dwelling population. *Journal of the American Medical Association, 302,* 517–526.

Donohoe, M. (2005). Increase in obstacles to abortion: The American perspective in 2004. *Journal of the American Medical Women's Association, 60,* 16–25.

Donovan, R. A., Sillice, M., & Masdea, J. R. (2005, March). *Have things changed? Contemporary images of Black and White women.* Paper presented at the annual meeting of the American Psychological Association, Washington, DC.

Doress-Worters, P. B., & Siegal, D. L. (1994). *The new ourselves growing older.* New York: Simon & Schuster.

Dorfman, L. T., & Rubenstein, L. M. (1993). Paid and unpaid activities and retirement satisfaction among rural seniors. *Physical & Occupational Therapy in Geriatrics, 12,* 45–63.

Döring, N. (2000). Feminist views of cybersex: Victimization, liberation, and empowerment. *Cyberpsychology & Behavior, 3,* 863–884.

Dorius, C. R., & Wray-Lake, L. (2008). Expanding the horizon: New directions for the study of intergenerational care and exchange. In A. Booth, A. C. Crouter, S. M. Bianchi, & J. A. Seltzer (Eds.), *Intergenerational caregiving* (pp. 351–381). Washington, DC: Urban Institute Press.

Doss, B. D., Rhodes, G. K., Stanley, S. M., & Markman, H. J. (2009). The effect of the transition to parenthood on relationship quality: An 8-year prospective study. *Journal of Personality and Social Psychology, 96,* 601–619.

Douglas, S. J. (2010). *Enlightened sexism: The seductive message that feminism's work is done.* New York: Times Books.

Dovidio, J. F., & Gaertner, S. L. (2010). Intergroup bias. In S. T. Fiske, D. T. Gilbert, & G. Lindzey (Eds.), *Handbook of social psychology* (5th ed., Vol. 2, pp. 1084–1121). Hoboken, NJ: Wiley.

Dowd, J. J. (2007, August). *The grip of tradition: Hollywood film and the reproduction of women's place.* Paper presented at the meeting of the American Sociological Association, New York.

Dowling, W. (2001). Volunteerism among older women. In J. M. Coyle (Ed.), *Handbook on women and aging* (pp. 242–252). Westport, CT: Greenwood.

Downs, E., & Smith, S. L. (2010). Keeping abreast of hypersexuality: A video game character content analysis. *Sex Roles, 62,* 721–733.

Drago, R. W. (2007). *Striking a balance: Work, family, life.* Boston, MA: Dollars & Sense.

Drago, R. W. (2009). The parenting of infants: A time-use study. *Monthly Labor Review, 132,* 33–43.

Drew, J. A. R. (2009). Disability and the self-reliant family: Revisiting the literature on parents with disabilities. *Marriage & Family Review, 45,* 431–447.

Drew, P. (2011). Sex education, comprehensive. In M. Z. Stange, C. K. Oyster, & J. E. Sloan (Eds.), *Encyclopedia of women in today's world* (Vol. 3, pp. 1299–1301). Newberry Park, CA: Sage.

Duehr, E. E., & Bono, J. E. (2006). Men, women, and managers: Are stereotypes finally changing? *Personnel Psychology, 59,* 815–846.

Duff, J. L. (1996). *The best of friends: Exploring the moral domain of adolescent friendship.* Unpublished doctoral dissertation, Stanford University.

Duffy, J., Wareham, S., & Walsh, M. (2004). Psychological consequences for high school students of having been sexually harassed. *Sex Roles, 50,* 811–821.

Duff-McCall, K., & Schweinle, W. (2008). Leadership and women. In M. A. Paludi (Ed.), *The psychology of women at work: Challenges and solutions for our female workforce: Career liberation, history, and the new millennium* (Vol. 1, pp. 87–99). Westport, CT: Praeger.

Dugassa, B. F. (2009). Women's rights and women's health during HIV/AIDS epidemics: The experience of women in Sub-Saharan Africa. *Health Care for Women International, 30,* 690–706.

Dumas, J., Hancur-Bucci, C., Naylor, M., Sites, C., & Newhouse, P. (2008). Estrogen interacts with the cholinergic system to affect verbal memory in post-menopausal women: Evidence for the critical period hypothesis. *Hormones and Behavior, 53,* 159–169.

Duncan, L. E. (2010). Women's relationship to feminism: Effects of generation and feminist self-labeling. *Psychology of Women Quarterly, 34,* 498–507.

Dunifon, R., & Kowaleski-Jones, L. (2007). The influence of grandparents in single-mother families. *Journal of Marriage and Family, 69,* 465–481.

Dunkel, T. M., Davidson, D., & Qurashi, S. (2010). Body satisfaction and pressure to be thin in younger and older Muslim and non-Muslim women: The role of western and non-western dress preferences. *Body Image, 7,* 56–65.

Dupéré, V., Lacourse, É., Willms, J. D., Leventhal, T., & Tremblay, R. E. (2008). Neighborhood poverty and early transition to sexual activity in young adolescents: A developmental ecological approach. *Child Development, 79,* 1463–1476.

Dupre, M. E., & Meadows, S. O. (2007). Disaggregating the effects of marital trajectories on health. *Journal of Family Issues, 28,* 623–652.

Duquaine-Watson, J. (2011). Trafficking, women and children. In M. Z. Stange, C. K. Oyster, & J. E. Sloan (Eds.), *Encyclopedia of women in today's world.* Newberry Park, CA: Sage.

Dutton, M. A. (2009). Pathways linking intimate partner violence and posttraumatic disorder. *Trauma Violence, & Abuse, 10,* 211–224.

Duxbury, L., Higgins, C., & Schroeder, B. (2009). *Balancing paid work and caregiving responsibilities: A closer look at family caregivers in Canada.* Ottawa, ON: Human Resources and Skill Development Canada.

Duxbury, L., Lyons, S., & Higgins, C. (2008). Too much to do, and not enough time: An examination of role overload. In K. Korabik, D. Lero, & D. Whitehead (Eds.), *Handbook of work-family integration: Research, theory, and best practices* (pp. 125–139). San Diego, CA: Academic Press.

Dworkin, S. L., & Wachs, F. L. (2009). *Body panic: Gender, health, and the selling of fitness.* New York: New York University Press.

Dye, J. L. (2010). *Fertility of American women: 2008. Current Population Reports,* P20–563. Washington, DC: US Census Bureau.

Dykstra, P. A., & Hagestad, G. O. (2007a). Childlessness and parenthood in two centuries: Different roads—different maps? *Journal of Family Issues, 28,* 1518–1532.

Dykstra, P. A., & Hagestad, G. O. (2007b). Roads less taken: Developing a nuanced view of older adults without children. *Journal of Family Issues, 28,* 1275–1310.

Eagly, A. H. (2007). Female leadership advantage and disadvantage: Resolving the contradictions. *Psychology of Women Quarterly, 31,* 1–12.

Eagly, A. H. (2009, August). *The his and hers of prosocial behavior: An examination of the social psychology of gender.* Address delivered at the 117th annual meeting of the American Psychological Association, Toronto, ON.

Eagly, A. H., & Carli, L. L. (1981). Sex of researchers and sex-typed communications as determinants of sex differences in influenceability: A meta-analysis of social influence studies. *Psychological Bulletin, 90,* 1–20.

Eagly, A. H., & Carli, L. L. (2007). *Through the labyrinth: The truth about how women become leaders.* Boston, MA: Harvard Business School Press.

Eagly, A. H., & Chin, J. L. (2010). Diversity and leadership in a changing world. *American Psychologist, 65,* 216–224.

Eagly, A. H., Karau, S. J., & Makhijani, M. G. (1995). Gender and the effectiveness of leaders: A meta-analysis. *Psychological Bulletin, 117,* 125–145.

Eagly, A. H., Makhijani, M. G., & Klonsky, B. G. (1992). Gender and the evaluation of leaders: A meta-analysis. *Psychological Bulletin, 111,* 3–22.

Eagly, A. H., & Sczesny, S. (2009). Stereotypes about women, men, and leaders: Have times changed? In M. Barreto, M. K. Ryan, & M. T. Schmitt (Eds.), *The glass ceiling in the 21st century: Understanding barriers to gender equality* (pp. 19–47). Washington, DC: American Psychological Association.

Eagly, A. H., Wood, W., & Diekman, A. B. (2000). Social role theory of sex differences and similarities: A current appraisal. In T. Eckes & H. M. Trautner (Eds.), *The developmental social psychology of gender* (pp. 123–174). Mahwah, NJ: Erlbaum.

Eagly, A. H., Wood, W., & Johannesen-Schmidt, M. (2004). Social role theory of sex differences and similarities: Implications for the partner preferences of women and men. In A. H. Eagly, A. E. Beall, & R. J. Sternberg (Eds.), *The psychology of gender* (pp. 269–295). New York: Guilford.

Earnshaw, V. A., Pitpitan, E. V., & Chaudoir, S. R. (2011). Intended responses to rape as functions of attitudes, attributions of fault, and emotions. *Sex Roles, 64,* 382–393.

East, P. L. (2009). Adolescents' relationships with siblings. In R. M. Lerner & L. Steinberg (Eds.), *Handbook of adolescent psychology* (3rd ed., Vol. 2, pp. 43–73). Hoboken, NJ: Wiley.

East, P. L. (2010). Children's provision of family caregiving: Benefit or burden? *Child Development Perspectives, 4,* 55–61.

East, P. L., Khoo, S. T., & Reyes, B. T. (2006). Risk and protective factors predictive of adolescent pregnancy: A longitudinal, prospective study. *Applied Developmental Science, 10,* 188–199.

Easton, S., Coohey, C., O'leary, P., Zhang, Y., & Hua, L. (2011). The effect of childhood sexual abuse on psychosexual functioning during adulthood. *Journal of Family Violence, 26,* 41–50.

Eastwick, P. W., & Finkel, E. J. (2008). Sex differences in mate preferences revisited: Do people know what they initially desire in a romantic partner? *Journal of Personality and Social Psychology, 94,* 245–264.

Eaton, D. K., Davis, K. S., Barrios, L., Brener, N. D., & Noonan, R. K. (2007). Associations of dating violence victimization with lifetime participation, co- occurrence, and early initiation of risk behaviors among U.S. high school students. *Journal of Interpersonal Violence, 22,* 585–602.

Eaton, D. K., et al. (2010). Youth risk behavior surveillance—United States, 2009. *Morbidity and Mortality Weekly Report, 59*(SS-5), 1–142.

Ebenstein, A. (2010). The "missing girls" of China and the unintended consequences of the one child policy. *Journal of Human Resources, 45,* 87–115.

Eccles, J. S., Freedman-Doan, C., Frome, P., Jacobs, J., & Yoon, K. S. (2000). Gender-role socialization in the family: A longitudinal approach. In T. Eckes & H. M. Trautner (Eds.), *The developmental social psychology of gender* (pp. 333–360). Mahwah, NJ: Erlbaum.

Eccles, J. S., & Roeser, R. W. (1999). School and community influences on human development. In M. H. Bornstein & M. E. Lamb (Eds.), *Developmental psychology: An advanced textbook* (4th ed., pp. 503–554). Mahwah, NJ: Erlbaum.

Echaveste, M. (2009). Invisible yet essential: Immigrant women in America. In M. Shriver (Ed.), *The Shriver report: A woman's nation changes everything* (pp. 114–119). Washington, DC: Maria Shriver and the Center for American Progress.

Eckenrode, J. (2011). Primary prevention of child abuse and maltreatment. In M. P. Koss, J. W. White, & A. E. Kazdin (Eds.), *Violence against women and children: Navigating solutions* (Vol. 2, pp. 71–92). Washington, DC: American Psychological Association.

Eckert, P., & McConnell-Ginet, S. (2003). *Language and gender.* Cambridge, MA: Cambridge University Press.

Eddleman, J., Essien, L., & Pollak, L. (2003, Spring/Summer). Success strategies. *AAUW Outlook,* p. 25.

Edelman, J. S. (2010). *Menopause matters: Your guide to a long and healthy life.* Baltimore, MD: Johns Hopkins University Press.

Edin, K., & Kissane, R. J. (2010). Poverty and the American family: A decade in review. *Journal of Marriage and Family, 72,* 460–479.

Edward, J. (2010). The healthcare needs of gay and lesbian patients. In E. Kuhlmann & E. Annandale (Eds.), *The Palgrave handbook of gender and healthcare* (pp. 256–271). New York: Palgrave Macmillan.

Edwards, C. P., Knoche, L., & Kumru, A. (2001). Play patterns and gender. In J. Worell (Ed.), *Encyclopedia of women and gender* (pp. 809–815). San Diego, CA: Academic Press.

Edwards, M. (2007, July–August). Protecting the vulnerable. *AARP Bulletin,* pp. 18–19.

Edwards, M. R. (2007). An examination of employed mothers' work-family narratives and perceptions of husbands' support. *Marriage & Family Review, 42,* 59–89.

Edwards, P., & Sterne, M. J. (2008). *Intentional grandparenting: A contemporary guide.* Golden, CO: Fulcrum.

Edwards George, J. B., & Franko, D. L. (2010). Cultural issues in eating pathology and body image among children and adolescents. *Journal of Pediatric Psychology, 35,* 231–247.

Ehrensaft, D. (2008). Just Molly and me, and donor makes three: Lesbian motherhood in the age of assisted reproductive technology. *Journal of Lesbian Studies, 12,* 161–178.

Ehrlich, S. B., Levine, S. C., & Goldin-Meadow, S. (2005, April). *Early sex differences in spatial skill: The implications of spoken and gestured strategies.* Paper presented at the meeting of the Society for Research in Child Development, Atlanta, GA.

Eibach, R. P., & Ehrlinger, J. (2010). Reference points in men's and women's judgements of progress toward gender equality. *Sex Roles, 63,* 882–893.

Eisenberg, M. E., Neumark-Sztainer, D., & Story, M. (2003). Associations of weight-based teasing and emotional well-being among adolescents. *Archives of Pediatrics and Adolescent Medicine, 157,* 733–738.

Eisenberg, N., & Fabes, R. A. (1998). Prosocial development. In W. Damon (Series Ed.) & N. Eisenberg (Vol. Ed.), *Handbook of child psychology: Vol. 3. Social, emotional and personality development* (5th ed., pp. 701–778). New York: Wiley.

Eisenberg, N., Fabes, R. A., & Spinrad, T. L. (2006). Prosocial development. In W. Damon, R. M. Lerner (Series Eds.), & N. Eisenberg (Vol. Ed.), *Handbook of child psychology: Vol. 3. Social, emotional, and personality development* (6th ed., pp. 646–718). Hoboken, NJ: Wiley.

Eisenberg, N., Martin, C. L., & Fabes, R. A. (1996). Gender development and gender effects. In D. C. Berliner & R. C. Calfee (Eds.), *The handbook of educational psychology* (pp. 358–396). New York: Simon & Schuster.

Eisenberg, N., Morris, A. S., McDaniel, B., & Spinrad, T. L. (2009). Moral cognitions and prosocial responding in adolescence. In R. M. Lerner & L. Steinberg (Eds.), *Handbook of adolescent psychology* (3rd ed., Vol. 1, pp. 229–265). Hoboken, NJ: Wiley.

Eisenberg, N., Spinrad, T. L., & Sadovsky, A. (2008). Empathy-related responding in children. In M. Killen & J. G. Smetana (Eds.), *Handbook of moral development* (pp. 517–549). Mahwah, NJ: Erlbaum.

Eisenberg, S. (2010). Marking gender boundaries: Porn, piss, power tools. In J. Goodman (Ed.), *Global perspectives on gender & work* (pp. 417–431). Lanham, MD: Rowman & Littlefield.

El-Bassel, N., Caldeira, N. A., Ruglass, L. M., & Gilbert, L. (2009). Addressing the unique needs of African-American women in HIV prevention. *American Journal of Public Health, 99,* 996–1001.

Elder, J. (1997, June 22). Poll finds women are the healthsavvier sex, and the warier. *New York Times,* p. WH8.

Eliot, L. (2009). *Pink brain, blue brain: How small differences grow into troublesome gaps—and what we can do about it.* New York: Houghton Mifflin Harcourt.

Ellin, A. (2004a, October 17). Helping grandparents help the grandkids. *New York Times,* p. BU9.

Ellin, A. (2004b, February 29). When it comes to salary, many women don't push. *New York Times,* p. BU7.

Elliott, K., & Urquiza, A. (2006). Ethnicity, culture, and child maltreatment. *Journal of Social Issues, 62,* 787–809.

Ellis, B. J., & Essex, M. J. (2007). Family environments, adrenarche, and sexual maturation: A longitudinal test of a life history model. *Child Development, 78,* 1799–1817.

Ellis, L., et al. (2008). *Sex differences: Summarizing more than a century of scientific research.* New York: Taylor & Francis Group.

Ellison, C. G., Trinitapoli, J. A., Anderson, K. L., & Johnson, B. R. (2007). Race/ethnicity, religious involvement, and domestic violence. *Violence Against Women, 13,* 1094–1112.

Elo, I. T. (2009). Social class differentials in health and mortality: Patterns and explanations in comparative perspective. *Annual Review of Sociology, 35,* 553–572.

El-Sadr, W. M., Mayer, K. H., & Hodder, S. L. (2010). AIDS in America—forgotten but not gone. *New England Journal of Medicine, 362,* 967–970.

Elsawy, B., & Higgins, K. E. (2010). Physical activity guidelines for older adults. *American Family Physician, 81,* 55–59, 60–62.

Else-Quest, N. M., & Hyde, J. S. (2008, May). *Cross-national gender differences in mathematics performance: A meta-analysis.* Poster presented at the meeting of the Association for Psychological Science, Chicago.

Else-Quest, N. M., Hyde, J. S., Goldsmith, H. H., & Van Hulle, C. A. (2006). Gender differences in temperament: A meta-analysis. *Psychological Bulletin, 132,* 33–72.

Else-Quest, N. M., Hyde, J. S., & Linn, M. C. (2010). Cross-national patterns of gender differences in mathematics: A meta-analysis. *Psychological Bulletin, 136,* 103–127.

Elson, J. (2004). *Am I still a woman?* Philadelphia, PA: Temple University Press.

Elwert, F., & Christakis, N. A. (2008). Variation in the effect of widowhood on mortality by the causes of death of both spouses. *American Journal of Public Health, 98,* 2092–2098.

Ely, G. E. (2004). Domestic violence and immigrant communities in the United States: A review of women's unique needs and recommendations for social work practice and research. *Stress, Trauma and Crisis, 7,* 223–241.

Enander, V. (2010). "A fool to keep staying": Battered women labeling themselves stupid as an expression of gendered shame. *Violence Against Women, 16,* 5–31.

England, D. E., Descartes, L., & Collier-Meek, M. A. (2011). Gender role portrayal and the Disney princesses. *Sex Roles, 64,* 555–567.

England, P. (2010). The gender revolution: Uneven and stalled. *Gender & Society, 24,* 149–166.

England, P., & McClintock, E. A. (2009). The gendered double standard of aging in U.S. marriage markets. *Population and Development Review, 35,* 797–816.

England, P., Schafer, E. F., & Fogarty, A. C. K. (2007). Hooking up and forming romantic relationships on today's college campuses. In M. Kimmel (Ed.), *The gendered society reader* (pp. 531–547). New York: Oxford University Press.

Engle, J. (2003, April). *Fear of success revisited: A replication of Matina Horner's study 30 years later.* Paper presented at the annual meeting of the American Educational Research Association, Chicago, IL.

English, A., Hartmann, H., & Hayes, J. (2010, April). *Are women now half the labor force? The truth about women and equal participation in the labor force* (IWPR #C374). Washington, DC: Institute for Women's Policy Research.

Enns, C. Z., & Byars-Winston, A. M. (2010). Multicultural feminist therapy. In H. Landrine & N. F. Russo (Eds.), *Handbook of diversity in feminist psychology* (pp. 367–388). New York: Springer.

Epstein, E. E., Fischer-Elber, K., & Al-Otaiba, Z. (2007). Women, aging, and alcohol use disorders. *Journal of Women and Aging, 19,* 31–48.

Epstein, R. H. (2009, July 14). When eating disorders strike in midlife. *New York Times.* Retrieved from http://www.nytimes.com

Erbert, L. A., & Alemán, M. W. (2008). Taking the grand out of grandparent: Dialectical tensions in grandparent perceptions of surrogate parenting. *Journal of Social and Personal Relationships, 25,* 671–695.

Ericksen, J. A. (2008). *Taking charge of breast cancer.* Berkeley, CA: University of California Press.

Ericksen, J. A., & Schultheiss, D. E. (2009). Women pursuing careers in trades and construction. *Journal of Career Development, 36,* 68–89.

Erickson, K. I., et al. (2011). Exercise training increases size of hippocampus and improves memory. *Proceedings of the National Academy of Sciences.* doi:10.1073/pnas.1015950108

Erikson, E. H. (1968). *Identity: Youth and crisis.* New York: Norton.

Erikson, E. H. (1980). *Identity and the life cycle.* New York: Norton.

Ernst, E., Bergholdt, S., Jørgensen, J. S., & Andersen, C. Y. (2010). The first woman to give birth to two children following transplantation of frozen/thawed ovarian tissue. *Human Reproduction, 25,* 1280–1281.

Ertel, K. A., Glymour, M. M., & Berkman, L. F. (2009). Social networks and health: A life course perspective integrating observational and experimental evidence. *Journal of Social and Personal Relationships, 26,* 73–92.

Eschenbeck, H., Kohlmann, C. W., & Lohaus, A. (2007). Gender differences in coping strategies in children and adolescents. *Journal of Individual Differences, 28,* 18–26.

Eshbaugh, E. M., & Gute, G. (2008). Hookup and sexual regret among college women. *Journal of Social Psychology, 148,* 77–89.

ESHRE Task Force on Ethics and Law. (2010). Lifestyle-related factors and access to medically assisted reproduction. *Human Reproduction, 25,* 578–583.

Esmail, A. (2010). "Negotiating fairness": A study on how lesbian family members evaluate, construct, and maintain "fairness" with the division of household labor. *Journal of Homosexualiy, 57,* 591–609.

Espenshade, T. J., & Radford, A. W. (2009). *No longer separate, not yet equal: Race and class in elite college admission and campus life.* Princeton, NJ: Princeton University Press.

Estes, C. R., Jackson, L. L., & Castillo, D. N. (2010). Occupational injuries and deaths among younger workers—United States, 1998–2007. *Morbidity and Mortality Weekly Report, 59,* 449–455.

Estimated percentage of patients aged >45 years who received exercise counseling from their primary-care physicians, by sex and age group—National Ambulatory Medical Care Survey and National Hospital Ambulatory Medical Care Survey, United States, 2003–2005. (2007). *Morbidity and Mortality Weekly Report, 56,* 1142.

Etaugh, C. (2008). Women in the middle and later years. In F. L. Denmark & M. A. Paludi (Eds.), *Psychology of women: A handbook of issues and theories* (2nd ed., pp. 271–302). Westport, CT: Praeger.

Etaugh, C., Bridges, J. S., Cummings-Hill, M., & Cohen, J. (1999). "Names can never hurt me?" The effects of surname use on perceptions of married women. *Psychology of Women Quarterly, 23,* 819–823.

Etaugh, C., Campbell, P., Schwartz, N., Zurek, R., & Pasdach, T. (2007, May). *Four decades of gender stereotypes in children's picture books: Different patterns for children and adults.* Poster presented at the annual meeting of the Midwestern Psychological Association, Chicago, IL.

Etaugh, C., & Conrad, M. (2004, July). *Perceptions of parents choosing traditional or nontraditional roles and surnames.* Poster presented at the meeting of the American Psychological Association, Honolulu, HI.

Etaugh, C., & Duits, T. (1990). Development of gender discrimination: Role of stereotypic and counter-stereotypic gender cues. *Sex Roles, 23,* 215–222.

Etaugh, C., & Folger, D. (1998). Perceptions of parents whose work and parenting behaviors deviate from role expectations. *Sex Roles, 39,* 215–223.

Etaugh, C., & Fulton, A. (1995, June). *Perceptions of unmarried adults: Gender and sexual orientation (not social attractiveness) matter.* Paper presented at the meeting of the American Psychological Association, New York.

Etaugh, C., Grinnell, K., & Etaugh, A. (1989). Development of gender labeling: Effect of age of pictured children. *Sex Roles, 21,* 769–773.

Etaugh, C., Jones, N. A., & Patterson, K. (1995, August). *Gender comparisons and stereotypes: Changing views in introductory psychology textbooks.* Paper presented at the meeting of the American Psychological Association, New York.

Etaugh, C., Knoblauch, S., & Schwartz, N. (2010, April). *Women over 40: Invisible in psychology of women/gender textbooks?* Poster presented at the annual meeting of the Midwestern Psychological Association, Chicago, IL.

Etaugh, C., Levine, D., & Mennella, A. (1984). Development of sex biases in children: Forty years later. *Sex Roles, 10,* 913–924.

Etaugh, C., & Liss, M. B. (1992). Home, school, and playroom: Training grounds for adult gender roles. *Sex Roles, 26,* 129–146.

Etaugh, C., & Moss, C. (2001). Attitudes of employed women toward parents who choose full-time or part-time employment following their child's birth. *Sex Roles, 44,* 611–619.

Etaugh, C., & Nekolny, K. (1990). Effects of employment status and marital status on perceptions of mothers. *Sex Roles, 23,* 273–280.

Etaugh, C., & O'Brien, E. (2003, April). *Perceptions of parents' gender roles by preschoolers in traditional and egalitarian families.* Paper presented at the meeting of the Society for Research in Child Development, Tampa, FL.

Etaugh, C., & Poertner, P. (1991). Effects of occupational prestige, employment status, and mental status on perceptions of mothers. *Sex Roles, 24,* 345–353.

Etaugh, C., & Poertner, P. (1992). Perceptions of women: Influence of performance, marital, and parental variables. *Sex Roles, 26,* 311–321.

Etaugh, C., & Rathus, S. (1995). *The world of children.* Fort Worth, TX: Harcourt Brace.

Etaugh, C., & Roe, L. (2002, June). *"What's in a name?" Surname choice affects perceptions of women and men.* Poster presented at the meeting of the American Psychological Society, New Orleans.

Etaugh, C., Roe, L., & Zurek, R. (2003, July). *From "frogs and snails" to "Mr. Mom": Stereotypes of boys and men in children's books.* Poster presented at the European Congress of Psychology, Vienna.

Etgen, T., Sander, D., Huntgeburth, U., Poppert, H., Förstl, H., & Bickel, H. (2010). Physical activity and incident cognitive impairment in elderly persons. *Archives of Internal Medicine, 170,* 186–193.

Evans, C. D., & Diekman, A. B. (2009). On motivated role selection: Gender beliefs, distant goals, and career interest. *Psychology of Women Quarterly, 33,* 235–249.

Evans-Campbell, T. (2008). Historical trauma in American Indian/Native Alaska communities: A multilevel framework for exploring impacts on individuals, families, and communities. *Journal of Interpersonal Violence, 23,* 316–338.

Evens, R. R., Roy, J., Geiger, B. F., Werner, K. A., & Burnett, D. (2008). Ecological strategies to promote healthy body image among children. *Journal of School Health, 78,* 359–367.

Evenson, R. J., & Simon, R. W. (2005). Clarifying the relationship between parenthood and depression. *Journal of Health and Social Behavior, 46,* 341–358.

Ewing Lee, E. A., & Troop-Gordon, W. (2011). Peer processes and gender role development: Changes in gender atypicality related to negative peer treatment and children's friendships. *Sex Roles, 64,* 90–102.

Expósito, F., Herrera, M. C., Moya, M., & Glick, P. (2010). Don't rock the boat: Women's benevolent sexism predicts fears of marital violence. *Psychology of Women Quarterly, 34,* 36–42.

Eynon, N., Yamin, C., Ben-Sira, D., & Sagiv, M. (2009). Optimal health and function among the elderly: Lessening severity of ADL disability. *European Review of Aging and Physical Activity, 6,* 55–61.

Fabes, R. A., & Martin, C. L. (2003). *Exploring child development* (2nd ed.). Boston, MA: Allyn & Bacon.

Facts on American teens' sexual and reproductive health. (2010, January). New York: Guttmacher Institute. Retrieved from http://www.guttmacher.org/pubs/FB-ATSRH.html

Facts on induced abortion in the United States. (2010, May). New York: Guttmacher Institute.

Facts on induced abortion worldwide. (2009, October). New York: Guttmacher Institute.

Facts on sexually transmitted infections in the United States. (2009, June). New York: Guttmacher Institute. Retrieved from http://www.guttmacher.org/pubs/FIB_STI_US.html

Fahs, B. (2011). Menstruation. In M. Z. Stange, C. K. Oyster, & J. E. Sloan (Eds.), *Encyclopedia of women in today's world.* Newberry Park, CA: Sage.

Fairfield, H. (2009, March 1). Why is her paycheck smaller? *New York Times,* p. BU4.

Faller, K. C. (2011). Victim services for child abuse. In M. P. Koss, J. W. White, & A. E. Kazdin (Eds.), *Violence against women and children: Navigating solutions* (Vol. 2, pp. 11–26). Washington, DC: American Psychological Association.

Faludi, S. (2007). *The terror dream: Fear and fantasy in post-9/11 America.* New York: Metropolitan Books.

Family Caregiver Alliance. (2003). *Women and caregiving: Facts and figures* [Fact sheet]. San Francisco, CA: Author.

Fan, A. Z., Strine, T. W., Huang, Y., Murray, M. R., Musingo, S., Jiles, R., & Mokdad, A. H. (2009). Self-rated depression and physician-diagnosed depression and anxiety in Florida adults: Behavioral risk factor surveillance system, 2006. *Preventing Chronic Disease, 6.* Retrieved from http://cdc.gov/pcd/issues/2009/jan/07_0227.htm

Faraday-Brash, L. (2010). Working life as a house: A tale of floors, walls, and ceilings. In M. A. Paludi (Ed.), *Feminism and women's rights worldwide* (Vol. 1, pp. 65–84). Santa Barbara, CA: Praeger.

Fargo, J. D. (2009). Pathways to adult sexual revictimization: Direct and indirect behavioral risk factors across the lifespan. *Journal of Interpersonal Violence, 24,* 1771–1791.

Faris, R., & Felmlee, D. (2011). Status struggles: Network centrality and gender segregation in same- and cross-gender aggression. *American Sociological Review, 76,* 48–73.

Farmer, H. S. (2006). History of career counseling for women. In W. B. Walsh & M. J. Heppner (Eds.), *Handbook of career counseling for women* (2nd ed., pp. 1–44). Mahwah, NJ: Erlbaum.

Farr, D., & Degroult, N. (2008). Understanding the queer world of the L-esbian body: Using *Queer as Folk* and *The L Word* to address the construction of the lesbian body. *Journal of Lesbian Studies, 12,* 423–434.

Farr, R. H., Forssell, S. L., & Patterson, C. J. (2010a). Gay, lesbian, and heterosexual adoptive parents: Couple and relationship issues. *Journal of GLBT Family Studies, 6,* 199–213.

Farr, R. H., Forssel, S. L., & Patterson, C. J. (2010b). Parenting and child development in adoptive families: Does parental sexual orientation matter? *Applied Developmental Science, 14,* 164–178.

Farris, C., Treat, T. A., Viken, R. J., & McFall, R. M. (2008). Perceptual mechanisms that characterize gender differences in decoding women's sexual intent. *Psychological Science, 19,* 348–354.

Farquhar, C., Marjoribanks, J., Lethaby, A., Suckling, J. A., & Lamberts, Q. (2009). Long term hormone therapy for perimenopausal and postmenopausal women. *Cochrane Database of Systematic Reviews,* (2). Art. No.: CD004143.

Fassinger, R. E. (1995). From invisibility to integration: Lesbian identity in the workplace. *Career Development Quarterly, 44,* 148–167.

Fassinger, R. E. (2008). Workplace diversity and public policy: Challenges and opportunities for psychology. *American Psychologist, 63,* 252–268.

Fassinger, R. E., & Arseneau, J. R. (2008). Diverse women's sexualities. In F. L. Denmark & M. A. Paludi (Eds.), *Psychology of women: A handbook of issues and theories* (2nd ed., pp. 484–505). Westport, CT: Praeger.

Fassinger, R. E., & Asay, P. A. (2006). Career counseling for women in science, technology, engineering, and mathematics (STEM) fields. In W. B. Walsh & M. J. Heppner (Eds.), *Handbook of career counseling for women* (2nd ed., pp. 427–452). Mahwah, NJ: Erlbaum.

Fassinger, R. E., & Israel, T. (2010). Sanctioning sexuality within cultural contexts: Same-sex relationships for women of color. In H. Landrine & N. F. Russo (Eds.), *Handbook of diversity in feminist psychology* (pp. 211–231). New York: Springer.

Fassinger, R. E., Shullman, S. L., & Stevenson, M. R. (2010). Toward an affirmative lesbian, gay, bisexual, and transgender leadership paradigm. *American Psychologist, 65,* 201–215.

Fausto-Sterling, A. (2000, July/August). The five sexes, revisited. *Sciences, 40,* 18–23.

Fauth, R. C., & Brooks-Gunn, J. (2008). Are some neighborhoods better for child health than others? In R. F. Schoeni, J. S. House, G. A. Kaplan, & H. Pollack (Eds.), *Making Americans healthier: Social and economic policy as health policy* (pp. 344–376). New York: Russell Sage Foundation.

Featherstone, B. (2010). Engaging fathers—promoting gender equality? In B. Featherstone, G. A. Hooper, J. Scourfield, & J. Taylor (Eds.), *Gender and child welfare in society* (pp. 173–194). Malden, MA: Wiley.

February is black history month. (2004, February). *Women's Psych-E, 3*(2), 1.

Federal Bureau of Investigation. (2009). *Hate crime statistics, 2008.* Retrieved from http://www.fbi.gov/ucr/hc2008/

Federal Glass Ceiling Commission. (1995a, March). *Good for business: Making full use of the nation's human capital.* Washington, DC: Author.

Federal Glass Ceiling Commission. (1995b, November). *A solid investment: Making full use of the nation's human capital.* Washington, DC: Author.

Federal Interagency Forum on Aging-Related Statistics. (2009). *Older Americans 2008: Key indicators of well-being.* Washington, DC: Author.

Federal Interagency Forum on Child and Family Statistics. (2007). *American's children: Key national indicators of well-being, 2007.* Washington, DC: U.S. Government Printing Office.

Feijoo, A. (2009). Adolescent sexual health in Europe and the U.S.—Why the difference? *Advocates for Youth, 3,* 1–6.

Feigelson, H. S., et al. (2004). Weight gain, body mass index, hormone replacement therapy, and postmenopausal breast cancer in a large prospective study. *Cancer Epidemiology Biomarkers & Prevention, 13,* 220–224.

Feingold, A. (1988). Cognitive gender differences are disappearing. *American Psychologist, 43,* 95–103.

Feingold, A. (1993). Cognitive gender differences: A developmental perspective. *Sex Roles, 29,* 91–112.

Feingold, A., Kerr, D. C. R., & Capaldi, D. M. (2008). Associations of substance use problems with intimate partner violence for at-risk men in long-term relationships. *Journal of Family Psychology, 22,* 429–438.

Feingold, A., & Mazzella, R. (1998). Gender differences in body image are increasing. *Psychological Science, 9,* 32–37.

Felder, S. (2006). The gender longevity gap: Explaining the difference between singles and couples. *Journal of Population Economics, 19,* 543–557.

Feldman, S., Byles, J. E., & Beaumont, R. (2000). "Is anybody listening?" The experiences of widowhood for older Australian women. *Journal of Women & Aging, 12,* 155–176.

Felix, E. D., & McMahon, S. D. (2006). Gender and multiple forms of peer victimization: How do they influence adolescent psychosocial adjustment?*Violence and Victims, 21,* 707–724.

Felmlee, D., Orzechowicz, D., & Fortes, C. (2010). Fairy tales: Attraction and stereotypes in same-gender relationships. *Sex Roles, 62,* 226–240.

Female Athlete Triad Coalition. (2008–2010). *The female athlete triad.* University Park, PA: Author.

Feminist Women's Health Center. (2009). *The abortion pill: Medical abortion with mifepristone and misoprostol.* Yakima, WA: Author.

Feng, J., Spence, I., & Pratt, J. (2007). Playing an action video game reduces gender differences in spatial cognition. *Psychological Science, 18,* 850–855.

Fergusson, D. M., & Woodward, L. J. (2000). Educational, psychosocial, and sexual outcomes of girls with conduct problems in early adolescence. *Journal of Child Psychology and Psychiatry, 41,* 779–792.

Ferraro, S. (2006, December 26). Self-exams are passé? Believers beg to differ. *New York Times,* pp. D5, D8.

Ferree, M. M. (2010). Filling the glass: Gender perspectives on families. *Journal of Marriage and Family, 72,* 420–439.

Ferriman, K., Lubinski, D., & Benbow, C. P. (2009). Work preferences, life values, and personal views of top math/science graduate students and the profoundly gifted: Developmental changes and gender differences during emerging adulthood and parenthood. *Journal of Personality and Social Psychology, 97,* 517–532.

Ferro, C., Cermele, J., & Saltzman, A. (2008). Current perceptions of marital rape: Some good news and not-so-good news. *Journal of Interpersonal Violence, 23,* 764–779.

Fiedler, M. E. (Ed.). (2010). *Breaking through the stained glass ceiling: Women religious leaders in their own words.* New York: Seabury Books.

Field, D., & Weishaus, S. (1992). Marriage over half a century: A longitudinal study. In M. Bloom (Ed.), *Changing lives* (pp. 269–273). Columbia, SC: University of South Carolina Press.

Fielder, R. L., & Carey, M. P. (2010). Predictors and consequences of sexual "hookups" among college students: A short-term prospective study. *Archives of Sexual Behavior, 39,* 1105–1119.

Fields, J., & Casper, L. M. (2001). *America's families and living arrangements: March 2000.* Current Population Reports, P20-537. Washington, DC: U.S. Census Bureau.

Filipovic, J. (2008). Offensive feminism: The conservative gender norms that perpetuate rape culture, and how feminists can fight back. In J. Friedman & J. Valenti (Eds.), *Yes mean yes!: Visions of female sexual power & a world without rape* (pp. 13–28). Berkeley, CA: Seal Press.

Fine, M., & Carney, S. (2001). Women, gender, and the law: Toward a feminist rethinking of responsibility. In R. K. Unger (Ed.), *Handbook of the psychology of women and gender* (pp. 388–409). New York: Wiley.

Fincham, F. D., & Beach, S. R. (2010). Marriage in the new millennium: A decade in review. *Journal of Marriage and Family, 72,* 630–649.

Findlay, L. C., & Bowker, A. (2007). The link between competitive sport participation and self-concept in early adolescence: A consideration of gender and sport orientation. *Journal of Youth and Adolescence, 38,* 29–40.

Fine, C. (2010). *Delusions of gender: How our minds, society, and neurosexism create difference.* New York: W. W. Norton.

Fineran, S., & Gruber, J. (2008). Mental health impact of sexual harassment. In M. A. Paludi (Ed.), *The psychology of women at work: Challenges and solutions for our female workforce: Self, family, and social affects* (Vol. 3, pp. 89–107). Westport, CT: Praeger.

Fingerman, K. L. (2003). *Mothers and adult daughters: Mixed emotions, enduring bonds.* Amherst, NY: Prometheus.

Fingerman, K. L., & Birditt, K. S. (2011). Relationships between adults and their aging parents. In K. W. Schaie & S. L. Willis (Eds.), *Handbook of the psychology of aging* (7th ed., pp. 219–232). San Diego, CA: Academic Press.

Fingerman, K. L., & Charles, S. T. (2010). It takes two to tango: Why older people have the best relationships. *Current Directions in Psychological Science, 19,* 172–176.

Fingerman, K. L., Miller, L., Birditt, K., & Zarit, S. (2009). Giving to the good and the needy: Parental support of grown children. *Journal of Marriage and Family, 71,* 1220–1233.

Fingerman, K. L., Pitzer, L. M., Chan, W., Birditt, K., Franks, M. M., & Zarit, S. (2010). Who gets what and why? Help middle-aged adults provide to parents and grown children. *Journal of Gerontology: Social Sciences, 66B,* 87–98.

Fingerson, L. (2006). *Girls in power: Gender, body, and menstruation in adolescence.* Albany, NY: State University of New York Press.

Fink, J. S., & Kensicki, L. J. (2002). An imperceptible difference: Visual and textual constructions of femininity in sports illustrated and sports illustrated for women. *Mass Communication & Society, 5,* 317–339.

Finkel, E. J., & Eastwick, P. W. (2008). Speed-dating. *Current Directions in Psychological Science, 17,* 193–197.

Fischer, A. R., & Holz, K. B. (2010). Testing a model of women's personal sense of justice, control, well-being, and distress in the context of sexist discrimination. *Psychology of Women Quarterly, 3,* 297–310.

Fisher, B. S., Daigle, L. E., & Cullen, F. T. (2010). *Unsafe in the ivory tower: The sexual victimization of college women.* Thousand Oaks, CA: Sage.

Fisher, B. S., Zink, T., & Regan, S. L. (2011). Abuses against older women: Prevalence and health effects. *Journal of Interpersonal Violence, 26,* 254–268.

Fisher, L. L. (2010). *Sex, romance, and relationships: AARP survey of midlife and older adults.* Washington, DC: AARP.

Fisher-Thompson, D., Sausa, A. D., & Wright, T. F. (1995). Toy selection for children: Personality and toy request influences. *Sex Roles, 33,* 239–255.

Fiske, A., Wetherell, J. L., & Gatz, M. (2009). Depression in older adults. *Annual Review of Clinical Psychology, 5,* 363–389.

Fiske, S. T. (2010a). Interpersonal stratification: Status, power, and subordination. In S. T. Fiske, D. T. Gilbert, & G. Lindzey (Eds.), *Handbook of social psychology* (5th ed., Vol. 2, pp. 941–982). Hoboken, NJ: Wiley.

Fiske, S. T. (2010b). Venus and Mars of down to earth: Stereotypes and realities of gender differences. *Perspectives on Psychological Science, 5,* 688–692.

Fitzgerald, L., Collinsworth, L. L., & Harned, M. S. (2001). Sexual harassment. In J. Worell (Ed.), *Encyclopedia of women and gender* (pp. 991–1004). San Diego, CA: Academic Press.

Fitzgerald, L. F. (1996). Sexual harassment: The definition and measurement of a construct. In M. A. Paludi (Ed.), *Sexual harassment on college campuses: Abusing the ivory power* (pp. 25–47). Albany, NY: SUNY.

Fitzpatrick, M. J., & McPherson, B. J. (2010). Coloring within the lines: Gender stereotypes in contemporary coloring books. *Sex Roles, 62,* 127–137.

Fitzpatrick, T. R. (2009). The quality of dyadic relationships, leisure activities and health among older women. *Health Care for Women International, 30,* 1073–1092.

Fivush, R., Brotman, M. A., Buckner, J. P., & Goodman, S. H. (2000). Gender differences in parent-child emotion narratives. *Sex Roles, 42,* 233–253.

Flanagan, C. (1993). Gender and social class: Intersecting issues in women's achievement. *Educational Psychologist, 28,* 357–378.

Fleck, C. (2007, October). Women and a secure retirement: Two steps forward, one step back. *AARP Bulletin,* pp. 1–2.

Fleming, L. M., & Tobin, D. J. (2005). Popular child-rearing books: Where is daddy? *Psychology of Men & Masculinity, 6,* 18–24.

Fletcher, J. M., & Wolfe, B. L. (2009). Education and labor market consequences of teenage childbearing. *Journal of Human Resources, 44,* 303–325.

Flood, M., & Pease, B. (2009). Factors influencing attitudes to violence against women. *Trauma, Violence, & Abuse, 10,* 125–142.

Flook, L. (2011). Gender differences in adolescents' daily interpersonal events and well-being. *Child Development, 82,* 454–461.

Flores, G. (2006). Language barriers to health care in the United States. *New England Journal of Medicine, 355,* 229–231.

Flores, L., Navarro, R., & Ojeda, L. (2006). Career counseling with Latinas. In W. B. Walsh & M. J. Heppner (Eds.), *Handbook of career counseling with women* (2nd ed., pp. 271–314). Mahwah, NJ: Erlbaum.

Flouri, E., & Hawkes, D. (2008). Ambitious mothers-successful daughters: Mothers' early expectations for children's education and children's earnings and sense of control in adulthood. *British Journal of Educational Psychology, 78,* 411–433.

Flynn, K. A. (2008). In their own voices: Women who were sexually abused by members of the clergy. *Journal of Child Sexual Abuse, 17,* 216–237.

Fogg, P. (2003, April 18). The gap that won't go away: Women continue to lag behind men in pay; the reasons may have little to do with gender bias. *Chronicle of Higher Education,* pp. A12–A15.

Follingstad, D. R. (2009). Psychological aggression and women's mental health: The status of the field. *Trauma, Violence, and Abuse, 10,* 271–289.

Folta, S. C., Lichtenstein, A. H., Seguin, R. A., Goldberg, J. P., Kuder, J. F., & Nelson, M. E. (2009). The Strong Women—Healthy Hearts program: Reducing cardiovascular disease risk factors in rural sedentary, overweight, and obese midlife and older women. *American Journal of Public Health, 99,* 1271–1277.

Fontaine, N., et al. (2008). Girls' hyperactivity and physical aggression during childhood and adjustment problems in early adulthood: A 15-year longitudinal study. *Archives of General Psychiatry, 65,* 320–328.

Fontes, L. A., & McCloskey, K. A. (2011). Cultural issues in violence against women. In C. M. Renzetti, J. L. Edleson, & R. K. Bergen (Eds.), *Sourcebook on violence against women* (2nd ed., pp. 151–167). Thousand Oaks, CA: Sage.

Foody, J. M., et al. (2010). The office on women's health initiative to improve women's heart health: Program description, site characteristics, and lessons learned. *Journal of Women's Health, 19,* 507–516.

Forbes, G. B., Adams-Curtis, L. E., White, K. B., & Holmgren, K. M. (2003). The role of hostile and benevolent sexism in women's and men's perceptions of the menstruating woman. *Psychology of Women Quarterly, 27,* 58–63.

Forbes, G. B., & Frederick, D. A. (2008). The UCLA Body Project II: Breast and body dissatisfaction among African, Asian, European, and Hispanic American college women. *Sex Roles, 58,* 449–457.

Ford, E. S., et al. (2008). Gender differences in coronary heart disease and health-related quality of life: Findings from 10 states from the 2004 behavioral risk factor surveillance system. *Journal of Women's Health, 17,* 757–768.

Ford, M. (2009). *Navigating the land of if: Understanding infertility and exploring your options.* Berkeley, CA: Seal Press.

Forman, J. P., Stampfer, M. J., & Curhan, G. C. (2009). Diet and lifestyle risk factors associated with incident hypertension in women. *Journal of the American Medical Association, 302,* 401–411.

Fortenberry, J. D., Schick, V., Herbenick, D., Sanders, S. A., Dodge, B., & Reece, M. (2010). Sexual behaviors and condom use at last vaginal intercourse: A national sample of adolescents ages 14 to 17 years. *Journal of Sexual Medicine, 7,* 305–314.

Fortier, M. A., DiLillo, D., Messman-Moore, T. L., Peugh, J., DeNardi, K. A., & Gaffey, K. J. (2009). Severity of child sexual abuse and revictimization: The mediating role of coping and trauma symptoms. *Psychology of Women Quarterly, 33,* 308–320.

Foshee, V. A., Reyes, H. L., & Wyckoff, S. C. (2009). Approaches to preventing psychological, physical, and sexual partner abuse. In K. D. O'Leary & E. M. Woodin (Eds.), *Psychological and physical aggression in couples: Causes and interventions* (pp. 165–190). Washington, DC: American Psychological Association.

Foster, M. D. (1999). Acting out against gender discrimination: The effects of different social identities. *Sex Roles, 40,* 167–186.

Foster, S. (2011). Heads of state, female. In M. Z. Stange, C. K. Oyster, & J. E. Sloan (Eds.), *Encyclopedia of women in today's world* (Vol. 2, pp. 667–671). Newberry Park, CA: Sage.

Foster-Rosales, A. (2010). Maternal mortality: The eye of the storm. In P. Murthy & C. L. Smith (Eds.), *Women's global health and human rights* (pp. 279–286). Sudbury, MA: Jones and Bartlett.

Fouad, N. A., & Byars-Winston, A. M. (2005). Cultural context of career choice: Meta-analysis of race/ethnicity differences. *Career Development Quarterly, 53,* 223–233.

Fouad, N. A., & Kantamneni, N. (2008). Contextual factors in vocational psychology: Intersections of individual, group, and societal dimensions. In S. D. Brown & R. W. Lent (Eds.), *Handbook of counseling psychology* (4th ed., pp. 408–425). Hoboken, NJ: Wiley.

Fourcroy, J. (2010). A woman's sexuality. In P. Murthy & C. L. Smith (Eds.), *Women's global health and human rights* (pp. 461–472). Sudbury, MA: Jones and Bartlett.

Foust-Cummings, H., Sabattini, L., & Carter, N. (2008). *Women in technology: Maximizing talent, minimizing barriers.* New York: Catalyst.

Fouts, G., & Burggraf, K. (2000). Television situation comedies: Female weight, male negative comments, and audience reactions. *Sex Roles, 42,* 925–932.

Fowers, B. J., Applegate, B., Tredinnick, M., & Slusher, J. (1996). His and her individualisms? Sex bias and individualism in psychologists' responses to case vignettes. *Journal of Psychology, 130,* 159–174.

Fox, C. K., Barr-Anderson, D., Neumark-Sztainer, D., & Wall, M. (2010). Physical activity and sports team participation: Associations with academic outcomes in middle school and high school students. *Journal of School Health, 80,* 31–37.

Frank, A. (1995). *The diary of a young girl: The definitive edition.* New York: Bantam Books.

Frank, K. A., et al. (2008). The social dynamics of mathematics coursetaking in high school. *American Journal of Sociology, 113,* 1645–1696.

Frankel, L. P. (2004). *Nice girls don't get the corner office 101: Unconscious mistakes women make that sabotage their careers.* New York: Warner.

Franko, D. L., Becker, A. E., Thomas, J. J., & Herzog, D. B. (2007). Cross-ethnic differences in eating disorder symptoms and related distress. *International Journal of Eating Disorders, 40,* 156–164.

Frantz, D. (2000, November 3). Turkish women who see death as a way out. *New York Times,* p. A3.

Frasure, L. A., & Williams, L. F. (2009). Racial, ethnic, and gender disparities in political participation and civic engagement. In B. T. Dill & R. E. Zambrana (Eds.), *Emerging intersections: Race, class, and gender in theory, policy, and practice* (pp. 203–228). Piscataway, NJ: Rutgers University Press.

Frazier, P. A., & Kaler, M. E. (2006). Assessing the validity of self-reported stress-related growth. *Journal of Consulting and Clinical Psychology, 74,* 859–869.

Frazier, P. A., Mortensen, H., & Steward, J. (2005). Coping strategies as mediators of the relations among perceived control and distress in sexual assault survivors. *Journal of Counseling Psychology, 52,* 267–278.

Fredriksen-Goldsen, K. I., Kim, H.-J., Barkan, S. E., Balsam, K. F., & Mincer, S. L. (2010). Disparaties in health-related quality of life: A comparison of lesbians and bisexual women. *Journal of Public Health, 11,* 2255–2261.

Freeman, C. (2010). Myths of docile girls and matriarchs: Local profiles of global workers. In J. Goodman (Ed.), *Global perspectives on gender & work* (pp. 289–304). Lanham, MD: Rowman & Littlefield.

Freeman, E. W., et al. (2011). Efficacy of Escitalopram "Lexapro" for hot flashes in healthy menopausal women: A randomized controlled trial. *American Medical Association, 305,* 267–274.

Freizinger, M., Franko, D. L., Dacey, M., Okun, B., & Domar, A. D. (2010). The prevalence of eating disorders in infertile women. *Fertility and Sterility, 93,* 72–78.

Frenzel, A. C., Goetz, T., Pekrun, R., & Watt, H. M. G. (2010). Development of mathematics interest in adolescence: Influences of gender, family, and school context. *Journal of Research on Adolescence, 20,* 507–537.

Freud, S. (1925/1989). Some psychological consequences of the anatomical distinction between the sexes. In P. Gay (Ed.), *The Freud reader* (pp. 670–678). New York: Norton.

Freud, S. (1938). The transformation of puberty. In A. A. Brill (Ed. and Trans.), *The basic writings of Sigmund Freud* (pp. 604–629). New York: Random House.

Freyd, J. J., et al. (2005). The science of child sexual abuse. *Science, 308,* 501.

Fried, L. P., et al. (2004, March). A social model for health promotion for an aging population: Initial evidence on the experience corps model. *Journal of Urban Health, 81,* 64–78.

Friedan, B. (1963). *The feminine mystique.* New York: Norton.

Friedman, A. L., & Bloodgood, B. (2010). "Something we'd rather not talk about": Findings from CDC exploratory research on sexually transmitted disease communication with girls and women. *Journal of Women's Health, 19,* 1823–1831.

Friedman, R. A. (2009, December 8). Postpartum depression strikes fathers, too. *New York Times,* p. D6. Retrieved from http://www.nytimes.com

Friedman, S. R., & Weissbrod, C. S. (2005). Work and family commitment and decision making status among emerging adults. *Sex Roles, 53,* 317–325.

Frieze, I. H., & Chen, K. Y. (2010). Intimate partner violence: Perspectives from racial/ethnic groups in the United States. In H. Landrine & N. F. Russo (Eds.), *Handbook of diversity in feminist psychology* (pp. 427–447). New York: Springer.

Frieze, I. H., et al. (2003). Gender-role attitudes in university students in the United States, Slovenia, and Croatia. *Psychology of Women Quarterly, 27,* 256–261.

Frieze, I. H., & Li, M. Y. (2001). Gender, aggression, and prosocial behavior. In J. C. Chrisler & D. R. McCreary (Eds.), *Handbook of gender research in psychology* (Vol. 2, pp. 311–335). New York: Springer.

Frieze, I. H., Olson, J. E., & Murrell, A. L. (2011). Working beyond 65: Predictors of late retirement for women and men MBA's. *Journal of Women & Aging, 23,* 40–57.

Frisén, A., & Holmqvist, K. (2010). Factors associated with body dissatisfaction in 16-year-old boys and girls. *Sex Roles, 63,* 373–385.

Frith, K. T., Cheng, H., & Shaw, P. (2005). The construction of beauty: A cross-cultural analysis of women's magazine advertising. *Journal of Communication, 55,* 56–70.

Frone, M. R. (2003). Work-family balance. In J. C. Quick & L. E. Tetrick (Eds.), *Handbook of occupational health psychology* (pp. 143–162). Washington, DC: American Psychological Association.

Frost, J. J., Darroch, J. E., & Remez, L. (2008). Improving contraceptive use in the United States. *In brief* (1). New York: Guttmacher Institute.

Fryers, T. (2010). Women and disability. In P. Murthy & C. L. Smith (Eds.), *Women's global health and human rights* (pp. 353–370). Sudbury, MA: Jones and Bartlett.

Fuegen, K., Biernat, M., Haines, E., & Deaux, K. (2004). Mothers and fathers in the workplace: How gender and parental status influence judgments of job-related competence. *Journal of Social Issues, 60*, 737–754.

Fukkink, R. G., & Lont, A. (2007). Does training matter? A meta-analysis and review of caregiver training studies. *Early Childhood Research Quarterly, 22*, 294–311.

Fulcher, M. (2005, April). *Individual differences in children's occupational aspirations as a function of parental traditionality*. Poster presented at the meeting of the Society for Research in Child Development, Atlanta, GA.

Fulcher, M. (2011). Individual differences in children's occupational aspirations as a function of parental traditionality. *Sex Roles, 64*, 117–131.

Fulcher, M., Sutfin, E. L., & Patterson, C. J. (2003, April). *Parental sexual orientation, parental division of labor, and children's sex-typed occupational aspirations*. Paper presented at the meeting of the Society for Research in Child Development, Tampa, FL.

Fulcher, M., Sutfin, E. L., & Patterson, C. J. (2008). Individual differences in gender development: Associations with parental sexual orientation, attitudes, and division of labor. *Sex Roles, 58*, 330–341.

Fuller-Rowell, T. E., & Doan, S. N. (2010). The social costs of academic success across ethnic groups. *Child Development, 81*, 1696–1713.

Fulton, J. E. (2009). Physical activity: An investment that pays multiple health dividends. *Archives of Internal Medicine, 169*, 2124–2127.

Fumia, D. (2011). Lesbians. In M. Z. Stange, C. K. Oyster, & J. E. Sloan (Eds.), *Encyclopedia of women in today's world* (Vol. 2, pp. 844–847). Newberry Park, CA: Sage.

Furman, W. (2002). The emerging field of adolescent romantic relationships. *Current Directions in Psychological Science, 11*, 177–180.

Furnham, A., Crawshaw, J., & Rawles, R. (2006). Sex differences in self-estimates on two validated IQ test subscale scores. *Journal of Applied Social Psychology, 36*, 417–440.

Furnham, A., Reeves, E., & Budhani, S. (2002). Parents think their sons are brighter than their daughters: Sex differences in parental self-estimations and estimations of their children's multiple intelligences. *Journal of Genetic Psychology, 163*, 24–39.

Gager, C. T. (2008). What's fair is fair? Role of justice in family labor allocation decisions. *Marriage & Family Review, 44*, 511–545.

Gager, C. T., Sanchez, L. A., & Demaris, A. (2009). Whose time is it? The effect of employment and work/family stress on children's housework. *Journal of Family Issues, 30*, 1459–1485.

Gagné, L. (2010). Osteoporosis. In V. Maizes & T. Low Dog (Eds.), *Integrative women's health* (pp. 623–645). New York: Oxford University Press.

Gajendran, R. S., & Harrison, D. A. (2007). The good, the bad, and the unknown about telecommuting: Meta-analysis of psychological mediators and individual consequences. *Journal of Applied Psychology, 92*, 1524–1541.

Galambos, N. L. (2004). Gender and gender role development in adolescence. In R. M. Lerner & L. Steinberg (Eds.), *Handbook of adolescent psychology* (2nd ed., pp. 233–262). Hoboken, NJ: Wiley.

Galambos, N. L., Berenbaum, S. A., & McHale, S. M. (2009). Gender development in adolescence. In R. M. Lerner & L. Steinberg (Eds.), *Handbook of adolescent psychology* (3rd ed., Vol. 1, pp. 305–357). Hoboken, NJ: Wiley.

Galinsky, E. (2006). *The economic benefits of high- quality early childhood programs: What makes the difference?* Washington, DC: Committee for Economic Development.

Galinsky, E., Aumann, K., & Bond, J. T. (2009). *Times are changing: Gender and generation at work and at home.* New York: Families and Work Institute.

Galinsky, E., Bond, J. T., & Sakai, K. (2008). *2008 National study of employers.* New York: Families and Work Institute.

Galinsky, E., Sakai, K., Eby, S., Bond, J. T., & Wigton, T. (2010). Employer-provided workplace flexibility. In K. Christensen & B. Schneider (Eds.), *Workplace flexibility: Realigning 20th-century jobs for a 21st- century workforce* (pp. 131–156). Ithaca, NY: Cornell University Press.

Gallagher, K. E. (2008). What accounts for heterosexual women's negative emotional responses to lesbians? Examination of traditional gender role beliefs and sexual prejudice. *Sex Roles, 59*, 229–239.

Galliher, R. V., Rostosky, S. S., Welsh, D. P., & Kawaguchi, M. C. (1999). Power and psychological well-being in late adolescent romantic relationships. *Sex Roles, 40*, 689–710.

Gallup. (2010, March 7). *Abortion.* Retrieved from http://www.gallup.com/poll/1576/abortion.aspx

Galupo, M. P. (2007). Women's close friendships across sexual orientation: A comparative analysis of lesbian-heterosexual and bisexual-heterosexual women's friendships. *Sex Roles, 56*, 473–482.

Galupo, M. P. (2009). Cross-category friendships patterns: Comparison of heterosexual and sexual minority adults. *Journal of Social and Personal Relationships, 26*, 811–831.

Gangestad, S. W., et al. (2004). Women's preferences for male behavioral displays change across the menstrual cycle. *Psychological Science, 15*, 203–207.

Gangl, M., & Ziefle, A. (2009). Motherhood, labor force behavior, and women's careers: An empirical assessment of the wage penalty for motherhood in Britain, Germany, and the United States. *Demography, 46*, 341–369.

Gannon, L., Luchetta, T., Rhodes, K., Pardie, L., & Segrist, D. (1992). Sex bias in psychological research: Progress or complacency? *American Psychologist, 47*, 389–396.

Ganong, L. H., Coleman, M., Thompson, A., & Goodwin-Watkins, C. (1996). African American and European American college students' expectations for self and future partners. *Journal of Family Issues, 17*, 758–775.

Ganske, K. H., & Hebl, M. R. (2001). Once upon a time there was a math contest: Gender stereotyping and memory. *Teaching of Psychology, 28*, 266–268.

Garavalia, L. S., et al. (2007). Does health status differ between men and women in early recovery after myocardial infarction? *Journal of Women's Health, 16*, 93–101.

Garcia, F. A., et al. (2010). Progress and priorities in the health of women and girls: A decade of advances and challenges. *Journal of Women's Health, 19*, 671–680.

García Coll, C. T., & Pachter, L. (2002). Ethnic and minority parenting. In M. H. Bornstein (Ed.), *Handbook of parenting, Volume 4: Social conditions and applied parenting* (2nd ed., pp. 1–20). Mahwah, NJ: Lawrence Erlbaum.

Garland-Thomson, R. (2004). Integrating disability, transforming feminist theory. In B. G. Smith & B. Hutchison (Eds.), *Gendering disability* (pp. 73– 103). Piscataway, NJ: Rutgers University Press.

Garnets, L. D. (2008). Life as a lesbian: What does gender have to do with it? In J. C. Chrisler, C. Golden, & P. D. Rozee (Eds.), *Lectures on the psychology of women* (pp. 232–249). New York: McGraw-Hill.

Garre-Olmo, J., Planas-Pujol, X., López-Pousa, S., Juvinyà, D., Vilà, A., & Vilalta-Franch, J. (2009). Prevalence and risk factors of suspected elder abuse subtypes in people aged 75 and older. *Journal of the American Geriatrics Society, 57*, 815–822.

Garrett, B. E., Dube, S. R., Trosclair, A., Caraballo, R. S., & Pechacek, T. F. (2011). Cigarette smoking—United States, 1965–2008. *Morbidity and Mortality Weekly Report, 60*(Suppl.), 109–113.

Garrett, C. C., & Kirkman, M. (2009). Being an XY female: An analysis of accounts from the website of the androgen insensitivity syndrome support group. *Health Care for Women International, 30,* 428–446.

Gates, G. (2008). Diversity among same-sex couples and their children. In S. Coontz (Ed.), *American families: A multicultural reader* (2nd ed., pp. 394–399). New York: Taylor & Francis.

Gatta, M. (2009). Developing policy to address the lived experiences of working mothers. In B. T. Dill & R. E. Zambrana (Eds.), *Emerging intersections: Race, class, and gender in theory, policy, and practice* (pp. 101–122). Piscataway, NJ: Rutgers University Press.

Gavey, N., & McPhillips, K. (1999). Subject to romance: Heterosexual passivity as an obstacle to women initiating condom use. *Psychology of Women Quarterly, 23,* 349–367.

Gavin, L., et al. (2009). Sexual and reproductive health of persons aged 10–24 years—United States, 2002–2007. *Morbidity and Mortality Weekly Report, 58*(SS-6).

Geary, D. C. (2007). An evolutionary perspective on sex differences in mathematics and the sciences. In S. J. Ceci & W. M. Williams (Eds.), *Why aren't more women in science? Top researchers debate the evidence* (pp. 173–188). Washington, DC: American Psychological Association.

Geary, D. C. (2010). *Male, female: The evolution of human sex differences.* Washington, DC: American Psychological Association.

Gee, G. C., Pavalko, E. K., & Long, J. S. (2007). Age, cohort and perceived age discrimination: Using the life course to assess self-reported age discrimination. *Social Forces, 86,* 265–290.

Gelman, S. A., Taylor, M. G., & Nguyen, S. P. (2004). *Mother-child conversations about gender.* Boston, MA: Blackwell Publishing.

The gender wage gap by occupation (IWPR #C350a). (2010, April). Washington, DC: Institute for Women's Policy Research.

Gentile, B., Grabe, S., Dolan-Pascoe, B., Twenge, J. M., Wells, B. E., & Maitino, A. (2009). Gender differences in domain-specific self-esteem: A meta-analysis. *Review of General Psychology, 13,* 34–45.

Gentile, L., Kisber, S., Suvak, J., & West, C. (2008). The practice of psychotherapy: Theory. In M. Ballou, M. Hill, & C. West (Eds.), *Feminist therapy theory and practice: A contemporary perspective* (pp. 67–86). New York: Springer.

Genzlinger, N. (2004, January 20). An actress of a certain age eyes the beauty cult. *New York Times,* pp. B1, B5.

George, L. K. (2010). Still happy after all these years: Research frontiers on subjective well-being in later life. *Journal of Gerontology: Social Sciences, 65B,* 331–339.

Gerber, G. L. (2009). Status and the gender stereotyped personality traits: Toward an integration. *Sex Roles, 61,* 297–316.

Gergen, M. (2008). Positive aging for women. In J. C. Chrisler, C. Golden, & P. D. Rozee (Eds.), *Lectures on the psychology of women* (pp. 376–391). New York: McGraw-Hill.

Gergen, M. (2010). Qualitative inquiry on gender studies. In J. C. Chrisler & D. R. McCreary (Eds.), *Handbook of gender research in psychology: Gender research in general and experimental psychology* (Vol. 1, pp. 103–131). New York: Springer.

Gergen, M. M., & Gergen, K. J. (2006). Positive aging: Reconstructing the life course. In J. Worell & C. D. Goodheart (Eds.), *Handbook of girls' and women's psychological health: Gender and well-being across the lifespan* (pp. 416–426). New York: Oxford University Press.

Gershoff, E. T., et al. (2010). Parent discipline practices in an international sample: Associations with child behaviors and moderation by perceived normativeness. *Child Development, 81,* 487–502.

Gerson, K. (2002). Moral dilemmas, moral strategies, and the transformation of gender: Lessons from two generations of work and family change. *Gender & Society, 16,* 8–28.

Gerson, K. (2009). Changing lives, resistant institutions: A new generation negotiates gender, work and family change. *Sociological Forum, 24,* 735–753.

Gerson, K. (2010). *The unfinished revolution: How a generation is shaping family, work, and gender in America.* New York: Oxford University Press.

Gerstel, N., & Sarkisian, N. (2008). The color of family ties: Race, class, gender, and extended family involvement. In S. Coontz (Ed.), *American families: A multicultural reader* (2nd ed., pp. 447–453). New York: Taylor & Francis.

Gervais, S. J., Vescio, T. K., & Allen, J. (2011). What you see is what you get: The consequences of the objectifying gaze for women and men. *Psychology of Women Quarterly, 35,* 5–17.

Gholizadeh, L., & Davidson, P. (2008). More similarities than differences: An international comparison of CVD mortality and risk factors in women. *Health Care for Women International, 29,* 3–22.

Gibbons, J. L. (2000). Gender development in cross-cultural perspective. In T. Eckes & H. M. Trautner (Eds.), *The developmental social psychology of gender* (pp. 389–415). Mahwah, NJ: Erlbaum.

Gibbs, J. C., Basinger, K. S., Grime, R. L., & Snarey, J. R. (2007). Moral judgment development across cultures: Revisiting Kohlberg's universality claims. *Developmental Review, 27,* 443–500.

Gibbs, N. (2002, April 15). Making time for a baby. *Time,* pp. 49–54.

Gibson, H. B. (1996). Sexual functioning in later life. In R. T. Woods (Ed.), *Handbook of the clinical psychology of aging* (pp. 183–193). New York: Wiley.

Gidycz, C. A., Orchowski, L. M., & Edwards, K. M. (2011). Primary prevention of sexual violence. In M. P. Koss, J. W. White, & A. E. Kazdin (Eds.), *Violence against women and children: Navigating solutions* (Vol. 2, pp. 159–180). Washington, DC: American Psychological Association.

Giesbrecht, N. (1998). Gender patterns of psychosocial development. *Sex Roles, 39,* 463–478.

Giladi, A. (2010). Preventing abuse of young girls and women. In M. A. Paludi (Ed.), *Feminism and women's rights worldwide: Feminism as human rights* (Vol. 2, pp. 239–250). Santa Barbara, CA: Praeger.

Gilbert, L. A. (1994). Reclaiming and returning gender to context: Examples from studies of heterosexual dual-earner families. *Psychology of Women Quarterly, 18,* 539–558.

Gilbert, L. A., & Scher, M. (1999). *Gender and sex in counseling and psychotherapy.* Boston, MA: Allyn & Bacon.

Gilbert, L. A., & Rader, J. (2008). Work, family, and dual-earner couples: Implications for research and practice. In S. D. Brown & R. W. Lent (Eds.), *Handbook of counseling psychology* (4th ed., pp. 416–443). Hoboken, NJ: Wiley.

Gilbert, N. (2008). *A mother's work: How feminism, the market, and the policy shape family life.* New Haven, CT: Yale University Press.

Gilbert, S. (1999, August 3). For some children, it's an after-school pressure cooker. *New York Times,* p. D7.

Giles, J. W., & Heyman, G. D. (2005). Young children's beliefs about the relationship between gender and aggressive behavior. *Child Development, 76,* 107–121.

Gill, R. (2007). *Gender and the media.* Cambridge, UK: Polity Press.

Gillam, K., & Wooden, S. R. (2011). Post-princess models of gender: The new man in Disney. In M. Kimmel & A. Aronson (Eds.), *The gendered society reader* (4th ed., pp. 471–478). New York: Oxford University Press.

Gilligan, C. (1982). *In a different voice.* Cambridge, MA: Harvard University Press.

Gilligan, C. (1993). Joining the resistance: Psychology, politics, girls and women. In L. Weis & M. Fine (Eds.), Beyond silenced voices (pp. 143–168). Albany, NY: SUNY Press.

Gilligan, C. (1994). In a different voice: Women's conceptions of self and morality. In B. Puka (Ed.), Caring voices and women's moral frames: Gilligan's view (Moral development: A compendium (Vol. 6, pp. 1–37). New York: Garland.

Gilligan, C. (2002). Beyond pleasure. New York: Knopf.

Gilpatric, K. (2010). Violent female action characters in contemporary American cinema. Sex Roles, 62, 734–746.

Ginsberg, R. L., & Gray, J. J. (2006). The differential depiction of female athletes in judged and non-judged sport magazines. Body Image, 3, 365–373.

Girard, A. L., & Senn, C. Y. (2008). The role of the new "date rape drugs" in attributions about date rape. Journal of Interpersonal Violence, 23, 3–20.

Girls Scouts of America. (2010). Beauty redefined: Girls and body image. New York: Author.

Gironda, M. W., et al. (2010). Education and training of mandated reporters: Innovative models, overcoming challenges, and lessons learned. Journal of Elder Abuse & Neglect, 22, 340–364.

Girshick, L. B. (2008). Transgender voices: Beyond women and men. Lebanon, NH: University Press of New England.

Given, B., & Given, C. W. (2008). Older adults and cancer treatment. Cancer, 113, 3505–3511.

Glasser, C. L., Robnett, B., & Feliciano, C. (2009). Internet daters' body type preferences: Race-ethnic and gender differences. Sex Roles, 61, 14–33.

Glauber, R. (2008). Race and gender in families and at work: The fatherhood wage premium. Gender & Society, 22, 8–30.

Gleason, J. B., & Ely, R. (2002). Gender differences in language development. In A. McGillicuddy-DeLisi & R. DeLisi (Eds.), Biology, society, and behavior: The development of sex differences in cognition. Advances in applied developmental psychology (Vol. 21, pp. 127–154). Westport, CT: Ablex.

Glenn, D. (2004, April 30). A dangerous surplus of sons? Chronicle of Higher Education, pp. 14–18.

Glenn, E. N. (2010). Forced to care: Coercion and caregiving in America. Cambridge, MA: Harvard University Press.

Glick, P., & Fiske, S. T. (2007). Sex discrimination: The psychological approach. In F. J. Crosby, M. S. Stockdale, & S. A. Ropp (Eds.), Sex discrimination in the workplace (pp. 155–188). Malden, MA: Blackwell.

Glick, P., et al. (2000). Beyond prejudice as simple antipathy: Hostile and benevolent sexism across cultures. Journal of Personality and Social Psychology, 79, 763–775.

Glied, S. (1998). The diagnosis and treatment of mental health problems among older women. Journal of the American Medical Women's Association, 53, 187–191.

Glover, J. A., Galliher, R. V., & Lamere, T. G. (2009). Identity development and exploration among sexual minority adolescents: Examination of a multidimensional model. Journal of Homosexuality, 56, 77–101.

Glynn, K., Maclean, H., Forte, T., & Cohen, M. (2009). The association between role overload and women's mental health. Journal of Women's Health, 18, 217–223.

Gochfeld, M. (2010). Sex-gender research sensitivity and healthcare disparities. Journal of Women's Health, 19, 189–194.

Godfrey, J. R., & Low Dog, T. (2008). Toward optimal health: Menopause as a rite of passage. Journal of Women's Health, 17, 509–514.

Godfrey, J. R., & Nelson, M. E. (2009). Promoting physical activity in women. Journal of Women's Health, 18, 295–298.

Godfrey, J. R., & Studenski, S. A. (2010). Preventing falls and promoting mobility in older women. Journal of Women's Health, 19, 185–188.

Godfrey, J. R., & Warshaw, G. A. (2009). Considering the enhanced healthcare needs of women caregivers. Journal of Women's Health, 18, 1739–1742.

Goerge, R. M., Harden, A., & Lee, B. J. (2008). Consequences of teen childbearing for child abuse, neglect, and foster care placement. In S. D. Hoffman & R. Maynard (Eds.), Kids having kids: Economic costs and social consequences of teen pregnancy (2nd ed., pp. 257–288). Washington, DC: Urban Institute Press.

Goff, P. A., Thomas, M. A., & Jackson, M. C. (2008). "Ain't I a woman?": Towards an intersectional approach to person perception and group-based harms. Sex Roles, 59, 392–403.

Gold, M. A., et al. (2010). Associations between religiosity and sexual and contraceptive behaviors. Journal of Pediatric and Adolescent Gynecology, 23, 290–297.

Goldberg, A. E. (2010). Lesbian and gay parents and their children: Research on the family life cycle. Washington, DC: American Psychological Association.

Goldberg, A. E., & Perry-Jenkins, M. (2007). The division of labor and perceptions of parental roles: Lesbian couples across the transition to parenthood. Journal of Social and Personal Relationships, 24, 297–318.

Goldberg, C. (1999, May 16). Wellesley grads find delicate balance. Hartford Courant, p. G3.

Goldberg, W. A., & Lucas-Thompson, R. (2008). Effects of maternal and paternal employment. In M. M. Haith & J. B. Benson (Eds.), Encyclopedia of infant and early childhood development (Vol. 2, pp. 268–279). San Diego, CA: Academic Press.

Goldberg, W. A., Prause, J., Lucas-Thompson, R., & Himsel, A. (2008). Maternal employment and children's achievement in context: A meta-analysis of four decades of research. Psychological Bulletin, 134, 77–108.

Golden, C. (2008). The intersexed and the transgendered: Rethinking sex/gender. In J. C. Chrisler, C. Golden, & P. D. Rozee (Eds.), Lectures on the psychology of women (pp. 136–152). New York: McGraw-Hill.

Golden, J., et al. (2009). Loneliness, social support networks, mood and wellbeing in community-dwelling elderly. International Journal of Geriatric Psychiatry, 24, 694–700.

Goldfield, G. S., Moore, C., Henderson, K., Buchholz, A., Obeid, N., & Flament, M. F. (2010). Body dissatisfaction, dietary restraint, depression, and weight status in adolescents. Journal of School Health, 80, 186–192.

Goldin, C. (2006, March 15). Working it out. New York Times, p. A27.

Goldkind, S. F., Sahin, L., & Gallauresi, B. (2010). Enrolling pregnant women in research—lessons from the H1N1 influenza pandemic. New England Journal of Medicine, 362, 2241–2243.

Goldman, L. (2008). Coming out, coming in: Nurturing the wellbeing and inclusion of gay youth in mainstream society. New York: Routledge.

Goldner, M., & Drentea, P. (2009). Caring for the disabled: Applying different theoretical perspectives to understand racial and ethnic variations among families. Marriage & Family Review, 45, 499–518.

Goldstein, A. (2000, February 29). Breadwinning wives are on the rise. Hartford Courant, pp. A1, A7.

Goldston, D. B., Molock, S. D., Whitbeck, L. B., Murakami, J. L., Zayas, L. H., & Hall, G. C. N. (2008). Cultural considerations in adolescent suicide prevention and psychosocial treatment. American Psychologist, 63, 14–31.

Gollenberg, A. L., et al. (2010). Perceived stress and severity of perimenstrual symptoms: The biocycle study. Journal of Women's Health, 19, 959–967.

Golombok, S., Rust, J., Zervoulis, K., Croudace, T., Golding, J., & Hines, M. (2008). Developmental trajectories of sex-typed behavior in boys and girls: A longitudinal general population study of children aged 2.5-8 years. Child Development, 79, 1583–1593.

Golombok, S., et al. (2004). Families created through surrogacy arrangements: Parent-child relationships in the first year of life. *Developmental Psychology, 40,* 400–411.

Gomez, M. J., et al. (2001). Voces abriendo caminos (voices forging paths): A qualitative study of the career development of notable Latinas. *Journal of Counseling Psychology, 48,* 286–300.

Goñi-Legaz, S., Ollo-López, A., & Bayo-Moriones, A. (2010). The division of household labor in Spanish dual earner couples: Testing three theories. *Sex Roles, 63,* 515–529.

González, H. M., Vega, W. A., Williams, D. R., Tarraf, W., West, B. T., & Neighbors, H. W. (2010). Depression care in the United States: Too little for too few. *Archives of General Psychiatry, 67,* 37–46.

Gonzalez, O., Berry, J. T., McKnight-Eily, L. R., Strine, T., Edwards, V. J., & Lu, H. (2010). Current depression among adults—United States, 2006–2008. *Morbidity and Mortality Weekly Report, 59,* 1229–1235.

Good, C., Aronson, J., & Inzlicht, M. (2003). Improving adolescents' standardized test performance: An intervention to reduce the effects of stereotype threat. *Personality and Social Psychology Bulletin, 24,* 645–662.

Good, J. J., & Moss-Racusin, C. A. (2010). "But, that doesn't apply to me": Teaching college students to think about gender. *Psychology of Women Quarterly, 3,* 418–420.

Goodchilds, J. D. (2000, Summer). Afterword. *Journal of Social Issues.* Retrieved from http://www.findarticles.com/cf_dls/m0341/2_56/66419872/print.jhtml

Goode, E. (2000, May 19). Scientists find a particularly female response to stress. *New York Times,* p. A20.

Goode, E. (2003, June 22). How to talk to teenage girls about weight? Very carefully. *New York Times,* p. WH8.

Gooden, A. M., & Gooden, M. A. (2001). Gender representation in notable children's picture books: 1995–1999. *Sex Roles, 45,* 89–101.

Gooding, G. E., & Kreider, R. M. (2010). Women's marital naming choices in a nationally representative sample. *Journal of Family Issues, 31,* 681–701.

Goodley, D. (2011). *Disability studies: An interdisciplinary introduction.* Thousand Oaks, CA: Sage.

Goodman, L. A., & Epstein, D. (2011). The justice system response to domestic violence. In M. P. Koss, J. W. White, & A. E. Kazdin (Eds.), *Violence against women and children: Navigating solutions* (Vol. 2, pp. 215–236). Washigton, DC: American Psychological Association.

Goodman, L. A., Smyth, K. F., Borges, A. M., & Singer, R. (2009). When crises collide: How intimate partner violence and poverty intersect to shape women's mental health and coping? *Trauma, Violence, & Abuse, 10,* 306–329.

Goodwin, S. A., & Fiske, S. T. (2001). Power and gender: The double-edged sword of ambivalence. In R. K. Unger (Ed.), *Handbook of the psychology women and gender* (pp. 358–366). New York: Wiley.

Goodwin, S. C., & Spies, J. B. (2009). Uterine fibroid embolization. *New England Journal of Medicine, 361,* 690–697.

Gorchoff, S. M., John, O. P., & Helson, R. (2009). Contextualizing change in marital satisfaction during middle age. *Psychological Science, 18,* 1194–1200.

Gordon, R. A., Chase-Lansdale, P. L., & Brooks-Gunn, J. (2004). Extended households and the life course of young mothers: Understanding the associations using a sample of mothers with premature, low birth weight babies. *Child Development, 75,* 1013–1038.

Gorin, S. S., Gauthier, J., Hay, J., Miles, A., & Wardle, J. (2008). Cancer screening and aging: Research barriers and opportunities. *Cancer, 113,* 3493–3504.

Gornick, J. C. (2010). Limiting working time and supporting flexibility for employees: Public policy lessons from Europe. In K. Christensen & B. Schneider (Eds.), *Workplace flexibility: Realigning 20th-century jobs for a 21st-century workforce* (pp. 223–244). Ithaca, NY: Cornell University Press.

Gotlib, A. (2011). Computer games. In M. Z. Stange, C. K. Oyster, & J. E. Sloan (Eds.), *Encyclopedia of women in today's world* (Vol. 1, pp. 321–323). Newberry Park, CA: Sage.

Gould, L. (1990). X: A fabulous child's story. In A. G. Halberstadt & S. L. Ellyson (Eds.), *Social psychology readings: A century of research* (pp. 251–257). Boston, MA: McGraw-Hill.

Govil, S. R., Weidner, G., Merritt-Worden, T., & Ornish, D. (2009). Socioeconomic status and improvements in lifestyle, coronary risk factors, and quality of life: The multisite cardiac lifestyle intervention program. *American Journal of Public Health, 99,* 1263–1270.

Grabe, S., & Hyde, J. S. (2006). Ethnicity and body dissatisfaction among women in the United States: A meta-analysis. *Psychological Bulletin, 132,* 622–640.

Grabe, S., & Hyde, J. S. (2009). Body objectification, MTV, and psychological outcomes among female adolescents. *Journal of Applied Social Psychology, 39,* 2840–2858.

Grabe, S., Hyde, J. S., & Lindberg, S. M. (2007). Body objectification and depression in adolescents: The role of gender, shame, and rumination. *Psychology of Women Quarterly, 31,* 164–175.

Grabe, S., Ward, L. M., & Hyde, J. S. (2008). The role of the media in body image concerns among women: A meta-analysis of experimental and correlational studies. *Psychological Bulletin, 134,* 460–476.

Graber, J. A., & Brooks-Gunn, J. (2002). Adolescent girls' sexual development. In G. M. Wingood & R. J. DiClemente (Eds.), *Handbook of women's sexual and reproductive health* (pp. 21–42). New York: Kluwer Academic/Plenum.

Graber, J. A., & Sontag, L. M. (2009). Internalizing problems during adolescence. In R. M. Lerner & L. Steinberg (Eds.), *Handbook of adolescent psychology* (3rd ed., Vol. 1, pp. 642–682). Hoboken, NJ: Wiley.

Grace, S. L., Gravely-Witte, S., Kayaniyil, S., Brual, J., Suskin, N., & Stewart, D. E. (2009). A multisite examination of sex differences in cardiac rehabilitation barriers by participation status. *Journal of Women's Health, 18,* 209–216.

Grady, D. (2010, March 23). Caesarean births are at a high in U.S. *New York Times,* p. A13.

Graham-Bermann, S. A., & Perkins, S. (2010). Effects of early exposure and lifetime exposure to intimate partner violence (IPV) on child adjustment. *Violence and Victims, 25,* 427–439.

Grall, T. S. (2009, November). *Custodial mothers and fathers and their child support: 2007.* Consumer Income, P60-237. Washington, DC: U.S. Census Bureau.

Grandparents raising grandchildren. (2002, June). *AARP Bulletin,* p. 27.

Grann, V. R. (2010). Erasing barriers to minority participation in cancer research. *Journal of Women's Health, 19,* 837–838.

Grant, J. A., & Hundley, H. L. (2007). Myths of sex, love, and romance of older women in *Golden Girls.* In M.-L. Galician & D. L. Merskin (Eds.), *Critical thinking about sex, love, and romance in the mass media: Media literacy applications* (pp. 121–139). Mahwah, NJ: Erlbaum.

Grant, M. J., & Behrman, J. R. (2010). Gender gaps in educational attainment in less developed countries. *Population and Development Review, 36,* 71–89.

Gray, J. (1992). *Men are from Mars, women are from Venus.* New York: HarperCollins.

Gray-Little, B., & Hafdahl, A. R. (2000). Factors influencing racial comparisons of self-esteem: A quantitative review. *Psychological Bulletin, 126,* 26–54.

Green, T. L., & Darity, W. A. (2010). Under the skin: Using theories from biology and the social sciences to explore the mechanisms behind the Black-White health gap. *American Journal of Public Health, 100,* S36–S39.

Green, V. A., Bigler, R., & Catherwood, D. (2004). The variability and flexibility of gender-typed toy play: A close look at children's behavioral responses to counterstereotypic models. *Sex Roles, 51,* 371–386.

Greenberg, B. S., et al. (2003). Portrayals of overweight and obese individuals on commercial television. *American Journal of Public Health, 93,* 1342–1348.

Greene, B. (2010). Riding Trojan horses from symbolism to structural change: In feminist psychology, context matters. *Psychology of Women Quarterly, 34,* 443–457.

Greene, M. L., & Way, N. (2005). Self-esteem trajectories among ethnic minority adolescents: A growth curve analysis of the patterns and predictors of change. *Journal of Research on Adolescence, 15,* 151–178.

Greenfield, S. F., & Pirard, S. (2009). Gender-specific treatment for women with substance use disorders. In K. T. Brady, S. E. Back, & S. F. Greenfield (Eds.), *Women and addiction: A comprehensive handbook* (pp. 289–306). New York: Guilford.

Greenhaus, J. H., & Powell, G. N. (2006). When work and family are allies: A theory of work-family enrichment. *Academy of Management Review, 31,* 72–92.

Greenhouse, S. (2007). Manhattan store owner accused of underpaying and sexually harassing workers. In P. S. Rothenberg (Ed.), *Race, class, and gender in the United States: An integrated study* (7th ed., pp. 280–281). New York: Worth.

Greenhouse, S. (2010, August 25). Wal-Mart asks Supreme Court to hear bias suit. *New York Times,* p. B1.

Greenleaf, C., Boyer, E. M., & Petrie, T. A. (2009). High school sport participation and subsequent psychological well-being and physical activity: The mediating influences of body image, physical competence, and instrumentality. *Sex Roles, 61,* 714–726.

Greenstein, T. N. (2009). National context, family satisfaction, and fairness in the division of household labor. *Journal of Marriage and Family, 71,* 1039–1051.

Greenwood, D. N. (2007). Are female action heroes risky role models? Character identification, idealization, and viewer aggression. *Sex Roles, 57,* 725–732.

Greil, A. L., Slauson-Blevins, K., & McQuillan, J. (2010). The experience of infertility: A review of recent literature. *Sociology of Health & Illness, 32,* 140–162.

Grella, C. (2009). Treatment seeking and utilization. In K. T. Brady, S. E. Back, & S. F. Greenfield (Eds.), *Women and addiction: A comprehensive handbook* (pp. 387–322). New York: Guilford.

Greytak, E. A., Kosciw, J. G., & Diaz, E. M. (2009). *Harsh realities: The experiences of transgender youth in our nation's schools.* New York: Gay, Lesbian, and Straight Education Network.

Grimberg, A., Kutikov, J. K., & Cucchiara, A. J. (2005). Sex differences in patients referred for evaluation of poor growth. *Journal of Pediatrics, 146,* 212–216.

Grimmell, D., & Stern, G. S. (1992). The relationship between gender role ideals and psychological well-being. *Sex Roles, 27,* 487–497.

Grippo, K. P., & Hill, M. S. (2008). Self-objectification, habitual body monitoring, and body dissatisfaction in older European American women: Exploring age and feminism as moderators. *Body Image, 5,* 173–182.

Grogan, S. (2008). *Body image: Understanding body dissatisfaction in men, women and children* (2nd ed.). New York: Routledge.

Groh, C. J. (2009). Foundations of women's mental health. In J. C. Urbancic & C. J. Groh (Eds.), *Women's mental health: A clinical guide for primary care providers* (pp. 1–21). Philadelphia, PA: Lippincott Williams & Wilkins.

Groh, C. J., & Serowky, M. (2009). Sexuality and intimacy. In J. C. Urbancic & C. J. Groh (Eds.), *Women's mental health: A clinical guide for primary care providers* (pp. 412–450). Philadelphia, PA: Lippincott Williams & Wilkins.

Groh, C. J., Urbancic, J. C., LaGore, S. M., & Whall, A. (2009). Mental health issues for older women. In J. C. Urbancic & C. J. Groh (Eds.), *Women's mental health: A clinical guide for primary care providers* (pp. 313–349). Philadelphia, PA: Lippincott Williams & Wilkins.

Gross, H., & Pattison, H. (2007). *Sanctioning pregnancy: A psychological perspective on the paradoxes and culture of research.* New York: Routledge.

Gross, S. M., Ireys, H. T., & Kinsman, S. L. (2000). Young women with physical disabilities: Risk factors for symptoms of eating disorders. *Developmental and Behavioral Pediatrics, 21,* 87–96.

Grossardt, B. R., Bower, J. H., Geda, Y. E., Colligan, R. C., & Rocca, W. A. (2009). Pessimistic, anxious, and depressive personality traits predict all-cause mortality: The Mayo Clinic cohort study of personality and aging. *Psychosomatic Medicine, 71,* 491–500.

Grossbard, J. R., Lee, C. M., Neighbors, C., & Larimer, M. E. (2009). Body image concerns and contingent self-esteem in male and female college students. *Sex Roles, 60,* 198–207.

Grossman, A. H. (2006). Parent "reactions to transgender youth" gender nonconforming expression and identity. *Journal of Gay & Lesbian Social Services, 18,* 3–16.

Grossman, A. H., D'Augelli, A. R., & O'Connel, T. S. (2001). Being lesbian, gay, bisexual, and 60 or older in North America. *Journal of Gay & Lesbian Social Services, 13,* 23–40.

Grossman, A. J. (2007, December 2). To be safe, call the bride by her first name. *New York Times,* p. ST22.

Grossman, A. L., & Tucker, J. S. (1997). Gender differences and sexism in the knowledge and use of slang. *Sex Roles, 37,* 101–110.

Gruber, J., & Fineran, S. (2010). Bullying and sexual harrassment of adolescents. In M. A. Paludi (Ed.), *Feminism and women's rights worldwide: Mental and physical health* (Vol. 2, pp. 211–230). Santa Barbara, CA: Praeger.

Gruenfeld, D. H., & Tiedens, L. Z. (2010). Organizational preferences and their consequences. In S. T. Fiske, D. T. Gilbert, & G. Lindzey (Eds.), *Handbook of social psychology* (5th ed., Vol. 2, pp. 194–227). Hoboken, NJ: Wiley.

Guastello, D. D., & Guastello, S. J. (2003). Androgyny, gender role behavior, and emotional intelligence among college students and their parents. *Sex Roles, 49,* 663–673.

Guiaux, M., Van Tilburg, T., & Van Groenou, M. B. (2007). Changes in contact and support exchange in personal networks after widowhood. *Personal Relationships, 14,* 457–473.

Guidelines for psychotherapy with lesbian, gay, and bisexual clients. (2000). *American Psychologist, 55,* 1440–1451.

Guilmoto, C. Z. (2009). The sex ratio transition in Asia. *Population and Development Review, 35,* 519–549.

Guiso, L., Monte, F., Sapienza, P., & Zingales, L. (2008). Culture, gender, and math. *Science, 320,* 1164–1165.

Gulati, M., & Torkos, S. (2011). *Saving women's hearts: How you can prevent and reverse heart disease with natural and conventional strategies.* Missisauga, Ontario, Canada: John Wiley.

Güngör, G., & Biernat, M. (2009). Gender bias or motherhood disadvantage? Judgments of blue collar mothers and fathers in the workplace. *Sex Roles, 60,* 232–246.

Gupta, S. (2007). Autonomy, dependence, or display? The relationship between married women's earnings and housework. *Journal of Marriage and Family, 69,* 399–417.

Gutman, L. M., & Eccles, J. S. (2007). Stage-environment fit during adolescence: Trajectories of family relations and adolescent outcomes. *Developmental Psychology, 43,* 522–537.

Guttmacher Institute. (2010a). *Facts on American teens' sexual and reproductive health.* Washington, DC: Author.

Guttmacher Institute. (2010b, April). *Facts on satisfying the need for contraception in developing countries.* New York: Author.

Guttmacher Institute. (2010c). *Facts on the sexual and reproductive health of adolescent women in the developing world*. Washington, DC: Author.

Guttmacher Institute. (2011a). *Facts on American teens' sources of information about sex*. Washington, DC: Author.

Guttmacher Institute. (2011b). *Facts on induced abortion in the United States*. Washington, DC: Author.

Guttmacher Institute. (2011c). *State policies in brief: An overview of abortion laws*. Washington, DC: Author.

Guttmacher Institute. (2011d). *State policies in brief: Bans on "partial-birth" abortion*. Washington, DC: Author.

Gysbers, N. C., Heppner, M. J., & Johnston, J. A. (2009). *Career counseling: Contexts, processes, and techniques* (3rd ed.). Alexandria, VA: American Counseling Association.

Ha, J.-H. (2008). Changes in support from confidants, children, and friends following widowhood. *Journal of Marriage and Family, 70*, 306–318.

Haag, P. (1999). *Voices of a generation: Teenage girls on sex, schools, and self*. Washington, DC: American Association of University Women.

Haddad, E. A., & Schweinle, W. (2010). The feminine political persona: Queen Victoria, Ellen Johnson Sirleaf, and Michelle Bachelet. In M. A. Paludi (Ed.), *Feminism and women's rights worldwide* (Vol. 1, pp. 97–110). Santa Barbara, CA: Praeger.

Hafner, K. (2003, August 21). 3 women and 3 paths, 10 years later. *New York Times*, pp. E1, E7.

Hague, G., Thiara, R., & Mullender, B. (2011). Disabled women and domestic violence: Making the links, a national U.K. study. *Psychiatry, Psychology, and Law, 18*, 117–136.

Haider, S. J., & Loughran, D. S. (2010). Elderly labor supply: Work or play? In K. Christensen & B. Schneider (Eds.), *Workplace flexibility: Realigning 20th-century jobs for a 21st-century workforce* (pp. 110–127). Ithaca, NY: Cornell University Press.

Halbreich, U. (2005). The association between pregnancy processes, preterm delivery, low birth weight, and postpartum depressions—the need for interdisciplinary integration. *American Journal of Obstetrics and Gynecology, 193*, 1312–1322.

Hall, D. M. (2008). Feminist perspectives on the personal and political aspects of mothering. In J. C. Chrisler, C. Golden, & P. D. Rozee (Eds.), *Lectures on the psychology of women* (pp. 58–79). New York: McGraw-Hill.

Hall, J. A. (2006). How big are nonverbal sex difference? The case of smiling and nonverbal sensitivity. In K. Dindia & D. J. Canary (Eds.), *Sex differences and similarities in communication* (2nd ed., pp. 59–82). Mahwah, NJ: Erlbaum.

Hall, J. A., Park, N., Song, H., & Cody, M. J. (2010). Strategic misrepresentation in online dating: The effects of gender, self-monitoring, and personality traits. *Journal of Social and Personal Relationships, 27*, 117–135.

Hall, J. A., & Schmid Mast, M. (2008). Are women always more interpersonally sensitive than men? Impact of goals and content domain. *Personality and Social Psychology Bulletin, 34*, 144–155.

Hall, R. E. (2003, June). Eurocentric bias in women's psychology journals: Resistance to issues significant to people of color. *European Psychologist, 8*, 117–122.

Hall, R. L. (2007). On the move: Exercise, leisure activities, and midlife women. In V. Muhlbauer & J. C. Chrisler (Eds.), *Women over 50: Psychological perspectives* (pp. 79–94). New York: Springer.

Hall, R. L. (2008). Sweating it out: The good news and the bad news about women and sport. In J. C. Chrisler, C. Golden, & P. D. Rozee (Eds.), *Lectures on the psychology of women* (pp. 96–115). New York: McGraw-Hill.

Halleröd, B., & Gustafsson, J. E. (2011). A longitudinal analysis of the relationship between changes in socio-economic status and changes in health. *Social Science & Medicine, 72*, 116–123.

Halpern, D. F., Benbow, C. P., Geary, D. C., Gur, R. C., Hyde, J. S., & Gernsbacher, M. A. (2007). The science of sex differences in science and mathematics. *Psychological Science in the Public Interest, 8*, 1–51.

Halpern, D. F., & Cheung, F. M. (2008). *Women at the top: Powerful leaders tell us how to combine work and family*. Malden, MA: Wiley-Blackwell.

Halpern, D. F., Straight, C., & Stephenson, C. L. (2011). Beliefs about cognitive gender differences: Accurate for direction, underestimated for size. *Sex Roles, 64*, 336–347.

Hamby, S. (2008). The path of helpseeking: Perceptions of law enforcement among American Indian victims of sexual abuse. *Journal of Prevention & Intervention in the Community, 36*, 89–104.

Hamer, M., Kivimaki, M., Lahiri, A., Marmot, M. G., & Steptoe, A. (2010). Persistent cognitive depressive symptoms are associated with coronary artery calcification [Advanced online publication]. *Atherosclerosis*.

Hamer, M., Molloy, G. J., & Stamatakis, E. (2008). Psychological distress as a risk factor for cardiovascular events: Pathophysiology and behavioral mechanisms. *Journal of the American College of Cardiology, 52*, 2156–2162.

Hamilton, B. E., Martin, J. A., & Sutton, P. D. (2004). *Births: Preliminary data for 2003*. National Vital Statistics Reports, 53(9). Hyattsville, MD: National Center for Health Statistics.

Hamilton, B. E., Martin, J. A., & Ventura, S. J. (2009). *Births: Preliminary data for 2007*. National Vital Statistics Reports, 57(12). Hyattsville, MD: National Center for Health Statistics.

Hamilton, B. E., Martin, J. A., & Ventura, S. J. (2010). *Births: Preliminary data for 2009*. National Vital Statistics Reports, 59. Hyattsville, MD: National Center for Health Statistics.

Hamilton, L., & Armstrong, E. A. (2009). Gendered sexuality in young adulthood: Double binds and flawed options. *Gender & Society, 23*, 589–616.

Hamilton, M. C. (1991). Masculine bias in the attribution of personhood: People = male, male = people. *Psychology of Women Quarterly, 15*, 393–402.

Hammen, C. (2009). Stress exposure and stress generation in adolescent depression. In S. Nolen-Hoeksema & L. M. Hilt (Eds.), *Handbook of depression in adolescents* (pp. 305–333). New York: Taylor & Francis.

Hampson, E., & Moffat, S. D. (2004). The psychobiology of gender: Cognitive effects of reproductive hormones in the adult nervous system. In A. H. Eagly, A. E. Beall, & R. J. Sternberg (Eds.), *The psychology of gender* (pp. 38–64). New York: Guilford.

Hampton, T. (2008). Studies address racial and geographic disparities in breast cancer treatment. *Journal of the American Medical Society, 300*, 1641.

Hampton, T. (2010). Child marriage threatens girls' health. *Journal of the American Medical Association, 304*, 509–510.

Hank, K., & Buber, I. (2009). Grandparents caring for their grandchildren: Findings from the 2004 survey of health, ageing, and retirement in Europe. *Journal of Family Issues, 30*, 53–73.

Hankin, B. L. (2008). Rumination and depression in adolescence: Investigating symptom specificity in a multiwave prospective study. *Journal of Clinical Child & Adolescent Psychology, 37*, 701–713.

Hankin, B. L., Stone, L., & Wright, P. A. (2010). Corumination, interpersonal stress generation, and internalizing symptoms: Accumulating effects and transactional influences in a multiwave study of adolescents. *Development and Psychopathology, 22*, 217–235.

Hankinson, A. L., et al. (2010). Maintaining a high physical activity level over 20 years and weight gain. *Journal of the American Medical Association, 304*, 2603–2610.

Hannaford, P. C., Iversen, L., Macfarlane, T. V., Elliott, A. M., Angus, V., & Lee, A. J. (2010). Mortality among contraceptive pill users: Cohort evidence from Royal College of General Practitioners' Oral Contraception Study. *BMJ, 340,* c927.

Hanratty, B., Drever, F., Jacoby, A., & Whitehead, M. (2007). Retirement age caregivers and deprivation of area of residence in England and Wales. *European Journal of Aging, 4,* 35–43.

Hanson, K., & Wapner, S. (1994). Transition to retirement: Gender differences. *International Journal of Aging and Human Development, 39,* 189–208.

Hanson, S. L. (2007). Success in science among young African American women: The role of minority families. *Journal of Family Issues, 28,* 3–33.

Hant, M. A. (2011). Aging, attitudes toward. In M. Z. Stange, C. K. Oyster, & J. E. Sloan (Eds.), *Encyclopedia of women in today's world* (Vol. 1, pp. 46–48). Newberry Park, CA: Sage.

Hardie, J. H., & Lucas, A. (2010). Economic factors and relationship quality among young couples: Comparing cohabitation and marriage. *Journal of Marriage and Family, 72,* 1141–1154.

Hardin, M., Lynn, S., & Walsdorf, K. (2005). Challenge and conformity on "contested terrain": Images of women in four women's sport/fitness magazines. *Sex Roles, 53,* 105–117.

Hare-Mustin, R. T., & Marecek, J. (1990). On making a difference. In R. T. Hare-Mustin & J. Marecek (Eds.), *Making a difference: Psychology and the construction of gender* (pp. 1–21). New Haven, CT: Yale University Press.

Harel, Z. (2008). Dysmenorrhea in adolescents. *Annals of the New York Academy of Sciences, 1135,* 185–195.

Harmon, A. (2003, June 29). Online dating sheds its stigma as losers.com. *New York Times,* pp. YT1, YT21.

Harper, M., & Schoeman, W. J. (2003). Influences of gender as a basic-level category in person perception on the gender belief system. *Sex Roles, 49,* 517–526.

Harper, S. R., & Hurtado, S. (2007). Nine themes in campus racial climates and implications for institutional transformation. In S. R. Harper & L. D. Patton (Eds.), *Responding to the realities of race on campus. New directions for student services* (Vol. 120, pp. 7–24). San Francisco, CA: Jossey Bass.

Harriger, J. A., Calogero, R. M., Witherington, D. C., & Smith, J. E. (2010). Body size stereotyping and internalization of the thin ideal in preschool girls. *Sex Roles, 63,* 609–620.

Harrington, B., & Ladge, J. J. (2009). Got talent? It isn't hard to find: Recognizing and rewarding the value women create in the workplace. In M. Shriver (Ed.), *The Shriver report: A woman's nation changes everything* (pp. 198–231). Washington, DC: Maria Shriver and the Center for American Progress.

Harris, A. C. (1994). Ethnicity as a determinant of sex role identity: A replication study of item selection for the Bem Sex Role Inventory. *Sex Roles, 31,* 241–273.

Harris, G. (2010a, August 14). F.D.A. approves 5-day emergency contraceptive. *New York Times,* p. A1.

Harris, G. (2010b, June 18). Panel recommends approval of after-sex pill to prevent pregnancy. *New York Times,* p. A14.

Harris, J. N. (2008). A woman's world. . . . In J. Friedman & J. Valenti (Eds.), *Yes means yes!: Visions of female sexual power & a world without rape* (pp. 53–66). Berkeley, CA: Seal Press.

Harris, M. T. C. (2008). Aging women's journey toward wholeness: New visions and directions. *Health Care for Women International, 29,* 962–979.

Harris, R. J., & Firestone, J. M. (1998). Changes in predictors of gender role ideologies among women: A multivariate analysis. *Sex Roles, 38,* 239–252.

Harrison, M. S., & Thomas, K. M. (2009). The hidden prejudice in selection: A research investigation on skin color bias. *Journal of Applied Social Psychology, 39,* 134–168.

Harrocks, J., & House, A. (2010). Self-harm and suicide in women. In D. Kohen (Ed.), *Oxford textbook of women and mental health* (pp. 246–283). Oxford, UK: Oxford University Press.

Hart, J., & Fellabaum, J. (2008). Analyzing campus climate studies: Seeking to define and understand. *Journal of Diversity in Higher Education, 1,* 222–234.

Harter, S. (1990). Adolescent self and identity development. In S. S. Feldman & G. R. Elliot (Eds.), *At the threshold: The developing adolescent* (pp. 352–387). Cambridge, MA: Harvard University Press.

Harter, S. (1998). The development of self-representations. In W. Damon (Series Ed.) & N. Eisenberg (Vol. Ed.), *Handbook of child psychology: Vol. 3. Social, emotional and personality development* (5th ed., pp. 553–617). New York: Wiley.

Harter, S. (1999). *The construction of the self: A developmental perspective.* New York: Guilford.

Hartley, H., & Tiefer, L. (2003, Spring/Summer). Taking a biological turn: The push for a "female Viagra" and the push for medicalization of women's sexual problems. *Women's Studies Quarterly, 31,* 42–54.

Hartman, H., & Hartman, M. (2008). How undergraduate engineering students perceive women's (and men's) problems in science, math and engineering. *Sex Roles, 58,* 251–265.

Hartmann, H., English, A., & Hayes, J. (2010, February). *Women and men's employment and unemployment in the Great Recession* (IWPR #C373). Washington, DC: Institute for Women's Policy Research.

Hartmann, H., Rose, S. J., & Lovell, V. (2006). How much progress in closing the long-term earnings gap? In F. D. Blau, M. C. Brinton, & D. B. Grunsky (Eds.), *The declining significance of gender?* (pp. 125–155). New York: Russell Sage Foundation.

Hartmann, K. E., et al. (2004). Quality of life and sexual function after hysterectomy in women with preoperative pain and depression. *Obstetrics & Gynecology, 104,* 701–709.

Harvey, S. T., & Taylor, J. E. (2010). A meta-analysis of the effects of psychotherapy with sexually abused children and adolescents. *Clinical Psychology Review, 30,* 517–535.

Harvey Wingfield, A. (2009). Racializing the glass escalator: Reconsidering men's experiences with women's work. *Gender & Society, 23,* 5–26.

Harville, M. L., & Rienzi, B. M. (2000). Equal worth and gracious submission: Judeo-Christian attitudes toward employed women. *Psychology of Women Quarterly, 24,* 145–147.

Harwood, J., & Anderson, K. (2002). The presence and portrayal of social groups on prime-time television. *Communication Reports, 15,* 81–97.

Haskell, M. (1998, February 8). Where the old boy always get the girl. *New York Times,* p. AR11.

Haskell, M., & Harmetz, A. (1998, March-April). Star power. *Modern Maturity, 41,* 32–40.

Hattery, A. (2001). *Women, work, and family: Balancing and weaving.* Thousand Oaks, CA: Sage.

Hatzenbuehler, M. L., McLaughlin, K. A., Keyes, K. M., & Hasin, D. S. (2010). The impact of institutional discrimination on psychiatric disorders in lesbian, gay, and bisexual populations: A prospective study. *American Journal of Public Health, 100,* 452–459.

Hausmann, R., Tyson, L. D., & Zahidi, S. (2009). *The global gender gap report 2009.* Geneva, Switzerland: World Economic Forum.

Hawes, Z. C., Wellings, K., & Stephenson, J. (2010). First heterosexual intercourse in the United Kingdom: A review of the literature. *Journal of Sex Research, 47,* 137–152.

Hawkes, K. (2010). How grandmother effects plus individual variation in frailty shape fertility and morality: Guidance from human-chimpanzee comparisons. *Proceedings of the National Academy of Sciences, 107,* 8977–8984.

Hawkins, J. W., & Aber, C. S. (1993). Women in advertisements in medical journals. *Sex Roles, 28,* 233–244.

Hawkins, S. M., & Matzuk, M. M. (2008). The menstrual cycle: Basic biology. *Annals of the New York Academy of Sciences, 1135*, 10–18.

Haxton, C. L., & Harknett, K. (2009). Racial and gender differences in kin support: A mixed-methods study of African American and Hispanic couples. *Journal of Family Issues, 30*, 1019–1040.

Hayatbakhsh, M. R., Najman, J. M., McGee, T. R., Bor, W., & O'Callaghan, M. J. (2008). Early pubertal maturation in the prediction of early adult substance use: A prospective study. *Addiction, 104*, 59–66.

Hayden, S. (2011). Childlessness as choice. In M. Z. Stange, C. K. Oyster, & J. E. Sloan (Eds.), *Encyclopedia of women in today's world* (Vol. 1, pp. 274–276). Newberry Park, CA: Sage.

Hayes, J., Hartmann, H., & Lee, S. (2010). *Social security: Vital to retirement security for 35 million women and men* (IWPR #D487). Washington, DC: Institute for Women's Policy Research.

Hayslip, B., Jr., & Kaminski, P. (Eds.). (2008). *Parenting the custodial grandchild: Implications for clinical practice*. New York: Springer.

He, W., Sengupta, M., Velkoff, V. A., & DeBarros, K. A. (2005). *65+ in the United States: 2005*. Current Population Reports, P23-209. Washington, DC: U.S. Census Bureau.

Headlam, B. (2000, January 20). Barbie PC: Fashion over logic. *New York Times*, p. E4.

Heaphy, B. (2009). Choice and its limits in older lesbian and gay narratives of relational life. *Journal of GLBT Family Studies, 5*, 119–138.

Heath, G. W. (2009). Physical activity transitions and chronic disease. *American Journal of Lifestyles Medicine, 3*, 27S–31S.

Heatherington, L., et al. (1993). Two investigations of "female modesty" in achievement situations. *Sex Roles, 29*, 739–754.

Hébert, M., & Bergeron, M. (2007). Efficacy of a group intervention for adult women survivors of sexual abuse. *Journal of Sexual Abuse, 16*, 37–61.

Hebl, M. R., King, E. B., Glick, P., Singletary, S. L., & Kazama, S. (2007). Hostile and benevolent reactions toward pregnant women: Complementary interpersonal punishments and rewards that maintain traditional roles. *Journal of Applied Psychology, 92*, 1499–1511.

Heckert, T. M., et al. (2002). Gender differences in anticipated salary: Role of salary estimates for others, job characteristics, career paths, and job inputs. *Sex Roles, 47*, 139–151.

Hedberg, P., Brulin, C., & Aléx, L. (2009). Experiences of purpose in life when becoming and being a very old women. *Journal of Women & Aging, 21*, 125–137.

Heffner, L. J. (2004). Advanced maternal age—how old is too old? *New England Journal of Medicine, 351*, 1927–1929.

Hegewisch, A., Liepmann, H., Hayes, J., & Hartmann, H. (2010). *Separate and not equal? Gender segregation in the labor market and the gender wage gap* (IWPR #C377). Washington, DC: Institute for Women's Policy Research.

Hegewisch, A., & Luyri, H. (2010). *The Workforce Investment Act and women's progress: Does WIA funded training reinforce sex segregation in the labor market and the gender wage gap?* (IWPR #C372). Washington, DC: Institute for Women's Policy Research.

Heilman, M. E. (2001). Description and prescription: How gender stereotypes prevent women's ascent up the organizational ladder. *Journal of Social Issues, 57*, 657–674.

Heilman, M. E., & Okimoto, T. G. (2007). Why are women penalized for success at male tasks? The implied communality deficit. *Journal of Applied Psychology, 92*, 81–92.

Heilman, M. E., & Okimoto, T. G. (2008). Motherhood: A potential source of bias in employment decisions. *Journal of Applied Psychology, 93*, 189–198.

Heiman, J. R. (2008). Treating low sexual desire—new findings for testosterone in women. *New England Journal of Medicine, 359*, 2047–2049.

Heisig, J. P. (2011). Who does more housework: Rich or poor? A comparison of 33 countries. *American Sociological Review, 76*, 74–99.

Heiss, C., & Kelm, M. (2010). Chocolate consumption, blood pressure, and cardiovascular risk. *European Heart Journal, 31*, 1554–1556.

Heiss, G., et al. (2008). Health risks and benefits 3 years after stopping randomized treatment with estrogen and progestin. *Journal of the American Medical Association, 299*, 1036–1045.

Helgeson, V. (2005). *The psychology of gender* (2nd ed.). Upper Saddle River, NJ: Prentice Hall.

Hellerstein, J. K., & Morrill, M. S. (2011). Dads and daughters: The changing impact of fathers on women's occupational choices. *Journal of Human Resources, 46*, 333–372.

Helson, R. (1992). Women's difficult times and the rewriting of the life story. *Psychology of Women Quarterly, 16*, 331–347.

Hemmings, C. (2011). *Why stories matter: The political grammar of feminist theory*. Durham, NC: Duke University Press.

Henderson, C. E., Hayslip, B., Jr., Sanders, L. M., & Louden, L. (2009). Grandmother-grandchild relationship quality predicts psychological adjustment among youth from divorced families. *Journal of Family Issues, 30*, 1245–1264.

Henderson, D., & Tickamyer, A. (2009). The intersection of poverty discourses: Race, class, culture, and gender. In B. T. Dill & R. E. Zambrana (Eds.), *Emerging intersections: Race, class, and gender in theory, policy, and practice* (pp. 50–72). Piscataway, NJ: Rutgers University Press.

Henderson, S. L., & Jeydel, A. S. (2010). *Women and politics in a global world* (2nd ed.). New York: Oxford University Press.

Henderson-King, D., & Brooks, K. D. (2009). Materialism, sociocultural appearance messages, and paternal attitudes predict college women's attitudes about cosmetic surgery. *Psychology of Women Quarterly, 33*, 133–142.

Hendrick, C. L., & Reddy, D. M. (2007, May). *Predictors of sexual risk behavior in women*. Poster presented at the annual meeting of the Midwestern Psychological Association, Chicago.

Henig, R. M. (2004a, June 6). Sex without estrogen: Remedies for the midlife mind and body. *New York Times*, p. WH12.

Henig, R. M. (2010a, October 5). In vitro revelation. *New York Times*, p. 31.

Henig, R. M. (2010b, August 18). What is it about 20-somethings? *New York Times Magazine*, pp. 28–37, 46–47, 49.

Henley, N. M. (1995). Body politics revisited: What do we know today? In P. J. Kalbfleisch & M. J. Cody (Eds.), *Gender, power, and communication in human relationships* (pp. 27–61). Hillsdale, NJ: Erlbaum.

Henley, S. J., King, J. B., German, R. R., Richardson, L. C., & Plescia, M. (2010). Surveillance of screening- detected cancers (colon and rectum, breast, and cervix)—United States, 2004–2006. *Morbidity and Mortality Weekly Report, 59*(SS09), 1–25.

Henningsen, D. D. (2004). Flirting with meaning: An examination of miscommunication in flirting interactions. *Sex Roles, 50*, 481–489.

Henningsen, D. D., Henningsen, M. L. M., & Valde, K. S. (2006). Gender differences in perceptions of women's sexual interest during cross-sex interactions: An application and extension of cognitive valence theory. *Sex Roles, 54*, 821–829.

Henrici, J. M., Helmuth, A. S., Zlotnick, F., & Hayes, J. (2010). *Women in poverty during the Great Recession* (IWPR #D493). Washington, DC: Institute for Women's Policy Research.

Henz, U. (2009). Couples' provision of informal care for parents and parents-in-law: Far from sharing equally? *Ageing and Society, 29*, 369–395.

Henz, U. (2010). Parent care as unpaid family labor: How do spouses share? *Journal of Marriage and Family, 72*, 148–164.

Heo, J., Lee, Y., McCormick, B. P., & Pedersen, P. M. (2010). Daily experience of serious leisure, flow and subjective well-being of older adults. *Leisure Studies, 29*, 207–225.

Heo, M., Murphy, C. F., Fontaine, K. R., Bruce, M. L., & Alexopoulos, G. S. (2008). Population projection of US adults with lifetime experience of depressive disorder by age and sex from year 2005 to 2050. *International Journal of Geriatric Psychiatry, 23*, 1266–1270.

Hequembourg, A. L., & Brallier, S. A. (2009). An exploration of sexual minority stress across the lines of gender and sexual identity. *Journal of Homosexuality, 56*, 273–298.

Herbenick, D., Reece, M., Schick, V., Sanders, S. A., Dodge, B., & Fortenberry, J. D. (2010a). An event-level analysis of the sexual charateristics and composition among adults ages 18 to 59: Results from a national probability sample in the United States. *International Society for Sexual Medicine, 7*, 346–361.

Herbenick, D., Reece, M., Schick, V., Sanders, S. A., Dodge, B., & Fortenberry, J. D. (2010b). Sexual behavior in the United States: Results from a national probability sample of men and women ages 14–94. *International Society for Sexual Medicine, 7*, 255–265.

Herbenick, D., Reece, M., Schick, V., Sanders, S. A., Dodge, B., & Fortenberry, J. D. (2010c). Sexual behaviors, relationships, and perceived health status among adult women in the United States: Results from a national probability survey. *International Society for Sexual Medicine, 7*, 277–290.

Herbst, C. M., & Barnow, B. S. (2008). Close to home: A simultaneous equations model of the relationship between child care accessibility and female labor force participation. *Journal of Family and Economic Issues, 29*, 128–151.

Herd, P., House, J. S., & Schoeni, R. F. (2008). Income support policies and health among the elderly. In R. F. Schoeni, J. S. House, G. A. Kaplan, & H. Pollack (Eds.), *Making Americans healthier: Social and economic policy as health policy* (pp. 97–121). New York: Russell Sage Foundation.

Herek, G. M. (2009a). Hate crimes and stigma-related experiences among sexual minority adults in the United States: Prevalence estimates from a national probability sample. *Journal of Interpersonal Violence, 24*, 54–74.

Herek, G. M. (2009b). Sexual stigma and sexual prejudice in the United States: A conceptual framework. In D. A. Hope (Ed.), *Contemporary perspectives on lesbian, gay & bisexual identities: The 54th Nebraska symposium on motivation* (pp. 65–112). New York: Springer.

Herek, G. M. (2010). Sexual orientation differences as deficits: Science and stigma in the history of American psychology. *Perspectives on Psychological Science, 5*, 693–699.

Herek, G. M., & Garnets, L. (2007). Sexual orientation and mental health. *Annual Review of Clinical Psychology, 3*, 353–375.

Herman-Giddens, M. E., Kaplowitz, P. B., & Wasserman, R. (2004). Navigating the recent articles on girls' puberty in pediatrics: What do we know and where do we go from here? *Pediatrics, 113*, 911–917.

Herman-Giddens, M. E., et al. (1997). Secondary sexual characteristics and menses in young girls seen in office practice: A study from the pediatric research in office settings network. *Pediatrics, 99*, 505–512.

Herman-Stahl, M., et al. (2007). Serious psychological distress among parenting and nonparenting adults. *American Journal of Public Health, 97*, 2222–2229.

Heron, M. (2010). Deaths: Leading causes for 2006. *National Vital Statistics Reports, 58* (14). Hyattsville, MD: National Center for Health Statistics.

Herrera, A. P., Snipes, S. A., King, D. W., Torres-Vigil, I., Goldberg, D. S., & Weinberg, A. D. (2010). Disparate inclusion of older adults in clinical trials: Priorities and opportunities for policy and practice change. *American Journal of Public Health, 100*, S105–S112.

Herrera, V. M., Koss, M. P., Bailey, J., Yuan, N. P., & Lichter, E. L. (2006). Survivors of male violence: Research and training initiatives to facilitate recovery from depression and posttraumatic stress disorder. In J. Worell & C. D. Goodheart (Eds.), *Handbook of girls' and women's psychological health: Gender and well-being across the lifespan* (pp. 455–466). New York: Oxford University Press.

Hesse-Biber, S., Livingstone, S., Ramirez, D., Barko, E. B., & Johnson, A. L. (2010). Racial identity and body image among Black female college students attending predominately White colleges. *Sex Roles, 63*, 697–711.

Hessol, N. A., et al. (2009). Retention and attendance of women enrolled in a large prospective study of HIV-1 in the United States. *Journal of Women's Health, 18*, 1627–1637.

Hether, H. J., & Murphy, S. T. (2010). Sex roles in health storylines on prime time television: A content analysis. *Sex Roles, 62*, 810–821.

Hetherington, E. M. (2004, July). *Lessons learned and unlearned in thirty five years of studying families.* Paper presented at the meeting of the American Psychological Association, Honolulu.

Hetherington, E. M., & Kelly, J. (2002). *For better or for worse: Divorce reconsidered.* New York: Norton.

Hewlett, S. A. (2007). *Off-ramps and on-ramps: Keeping talented women on the road to success.* Boston, MA: Harvard Business School Press.

Hewlett, S. A. (2010). Keeping engaged parents on the road to success. In K. Christensen & B. Schneider (Eds.), *Workplace flexibility: Realigning 20th-century jobs for a 21st-century workforce* (pp. 95–109). Ithaca, NY: Cornell University Press.

Hewlett, S. A., Luce, C. B., & Servon, L. J. (2008). Stopping the exodus of women in science. *Harvard Business Review, 86*. doi:10.1225/F0806A

Heyl, A. R. (2004). The transition from career to retirement: Focus on well-being and financial considerations. *Journal of the American Medical Women's Association, 59*, 235–237.

Heymann, J., Earle, A., & Hayes, J. (2007). *The work, family, and equity index: How does the United States measure up?* Montreal, QC: Project on Global Working Families.

Hidalgo, T. R. (2011). Feminism, American. In M. Z. Stange, C. K. Oyster, & J. E. Sloan (Eds.), *Encyclopedia of women in today's world.* Newberry Park, CA: Sage.

Higginbotham, E. (2009). Entering a profession: Race, gender, and class in the lives of Black women attorneys. In B. T. Dill & R. E. Zambrana (Eds.), *Emerging intersections: Race, class, and gender in theory, policy, and practice* (pp. 22–49). Piscataway, NJ: Rutgers University Press.

Higginbotham, E., & Weber, L. (1996). Moving up with kin and community: Upward social mobility for Black and White women. In E. N. Chow, D. Wilkinson, & M. B. Zinn (Eds.), *Race, class, & gender: Common bonds, different voices* (pp. 125–148). Thousand Oaks, CA: Sage.

Higgins, C. A., Duxbury, L. E., & Lyons, S. T. (2010). Coping with overload and stress: Men and women in dual-earner families. *Journal of Marriage and Family, 72*, 847–859.

Hilbrecht, M., Zuzanek, J., & Mannell, R. C. (2008). Time use, time pressure, and gendered behavior in early and late adolescence. *Sex Roles, 58*, 342–357.

Hildreth, C. J. (2009a). Elder abuse. *Journal of the American Medical Association, 302*, 588.

Hildreth, C. J. (2009b). Risk factors for heart disease. *Journal of the American Medical Association, 301*, 2176.

Hildreth, C. J. (2009c). Uterine fibroids. *Journal of the American Medical Association, 301,* 122.

Hill, C., & Silva, E. (2005). *Drawing the line: Sexual harassment on campus.* Washington, DC: AAUW Educational Foundation.

Hill, E. J., Erickson, J. J., Holmes, E. K., & Ferris, M. (2010). Workplace flexibility, work hours, and work-life conflict: Finding an extra day or two. *Journal of Family Psychology, 24,* 349–358.

Hill, M., & Jeong, J. Y. (2008). Putting it all together: Theory. In M. Ballou, M. Hill, & C. West (Eds.), *Feminist therapy theory and practice: A contemporary perspective* (pp. 135–149). New York: Springer.

Hill, S. A. (2009). Cultural images and the health of African American women. *Gender & Society, 23,* 733–746.

Hill, T. D., Kaplan, L. M., French, M. T., & Johnson, R. J. (2010). Victimization in early life and mental health in adulthood: An examination of the mediating and moderating influences of psychosocial resources. *Journal of Health and Social Behavior, 51,* 48–63.

Hill, T. D., Schroeder, R. D., Bradley, C., Kaplan, L. M., & Angel, R. J. (2009). The long-term health consequences of relationship violence in adulthood: An examination of low-income women from Boston, Chicago, and San Antonio. *American Journal of Public Health, 99,* 1645–1650.

Hill Collins, P. (2008). *Black feminist thought: Knowledge, consciousness and the politics of empowerment.* New York: Taylor & Francis.

Hillard, P. J. A. (2008). Menstruation in adolescents: What's normal, what's not. *Annals of the New York Academy of Sciences, 1135,* 29–35.

Hillberg, T., Hamilton-Giachritsis, C., & Dixon, L. (2011). Review of meta analyses on the association between child sexual abuse and adult mental health difficulties: A systematic approach. *Trauma, Violence, & Abuse, 12,* 38–49.

Hilliard, L. J., & Liben, L. S. (2010). Differing levels of gender salience in preschool classrooms: Effects on children's gender attitudes and intergroup bias. *Child Development, 81,* 1787–1798.

Hillman, J. L., & Stricker, G. (1994). A linkage of knowledge and attitudes toward elderly sexuality: Not necessarily a uniform relationship. *Gerontologist, 34,* 256–260.

Hilt, L. M., & Nolen-Hoeksema, S. (2009). The emergence of gender differences in depression in adolescence. In S. Nolen-Hoeksema & L. M. Hilt (Eds.), *Handbook of depression in adolescents* (pp. 111–136). New York: Taylor & Francis.

Himmelstein, K. W., & Brückner, H. (2011). Criminal-justice and school sanctions against nonheterosexual youth: A national longitudinal study. *Pediatrics, 126,* 49–57.

Hines, M. (2010). Gendered behavior across the lifespan. In M. Lamb & A. Freund (Eds.), *The handbook of life-span development: Social and emotional development* (Vol. 2, pp. 341–378). Hoboken, NJ: Wiley.

Hinshaw, S. (2009). *The triple bind: Saving our teenage girls from today's pressures.* New York: Ballantine.

Hirschberger, G. S., Srivastava, S., Marsh, P., Cowan, C. P., & Cowan, P. A. (2009). Attachment, marital satisfaction, and divorce during the first fifteen years of parenthood. *Personal Relationships, 16,* 401–420.

Hirsh, C. E., & Kornrich, S. (2008). The context of discrimination: Workplace conditions, institutional environments, and sex and race discrimination charges. *American Journal of Sociology, 113,* 1394–1432.

Hitchcock, C. L. (2008). Elements of the menstrual suppression debate. *Health Care for Women International, 29,* 702–719.

Hochman, A. (2004, June). Don't panic. *Health,* pp. 99–103.

Hodges, M. J., & Budig, M. J. (2010). Who gets the daddy bonus? Organizational hegemonic masculinity and the impact of fatherhood on earnings. *Gender & Society, 24,* 717–745.

Hoeber, L. (2008). Gender equity for athletes: Multiple understandings of an organizational value. *Sex Roles, 58,* 58–71.

Hofferth, S. L., & Goldscheider, F. (2010). Family structure and the transition to early parenthood. *Demography, 47,* 415–437.

Hofferth, S. L., & Reid, L. (2002). Early childbearing and children's achievement and behavior over time. *Perspectives on Sexual and Reproductive Health, 34,* 41–49.

Hoffman, E. (2002, June). When couples clam up. *AARP Bulletin,* pp. 24–25.

Hoffman, L. W., & Youngblade, L. M. (2001, April). *Mothers' employment: Effects on families and children.* Paper presented at the meeting of the Society for Research in Child Development, Minneapolis, MN.

Hoffman, S. D. (2008a). Trends in fertility and sexual activity among U.S. teenagers. In S. D. Hoffman & R. A. Maynard (Eds.), *Kids having kids: Economic costs and social consequences of teen pregnancy* (pp. 25–50). Washington, DC: Urban Institute Press.

Hoffman, S. D. (2008b). Updated estimates of the consequences of teen childbearing for mothers. In S. D. Hoffman & R. A. Maynard (Eds.), *Kids having kids: Economic costs and social consequences of teen pregnancy* (2nd ed., pp. 74–118). Washington, DC: Urban Institute Press.

Hoffnung, M. (2004). Wanting it all: Career, marriage, and motherhood during college-educated women's 20s. *Sex Roles, 50,* 711–723.

Hogan, J. D., & Sexton, V. S. (1991). Women and the American Psychological Association. *Psychology of Women Quarterly, 15,* 623–634.

Hogg, M. A. (2010). Influence and leadership. In S. T. Fiske, D. T. Gilbert, & G. Lindzey (Eds.), *Handbook of social psychology* (5th ed., pp. 1166–1207). Hoboken, NJ: Wiley.

Hogue, M., Yoder, J. D., & Singleton, S. B. (2007). The gender wage gap: An explanation of men's elevated wage entitlement. *Sex Roles, 56,* 573–579.

Holahan, C. K., & Sears, R. R. (1995). *The gifted group in later maturity.* Stanford, CA: Stanford University Press.

Holcombe, E., Carrier, D., Manlove, J., & Ryan, S. (2008). *Contraceptive use patterns across teens' sexual relationships* (Child Trends Fact Sheet #2008–07). Retrieved from http://www.childtrends.org/Files//Child_Trends-2008_02_20_FS_ContraceptiveUse.pdf

Holick, M. F. (2007). Vitamin D deficiency. *New England Journal of Medicine, 357,* 266–281.

Hollander, D. (2008). Despite differences in legal status, abortion occurs at similar rates in developing and developed countries. *Perspectives on Sexual and Reproductive Health, 40,* 55–56.

Hollander, D. (2010). Body image predicts some risky sexual behaviors among teenage women. *Perspectives on Sexual and Reproductive Health, 42,* 67.

Hollingsworth, M. A., Tomlinson, M. J., & Fassinger, R. E. (1997, August). *Working it out: Career development among prominent lesbian women.* Paper presented at the meeting of the American Psychological Association, Chicago.

Holm-Denoma, J. M., Scaringi, V., Gordon, K. H., Van Orden, K. A., & Joiner, T. E., Jr. (2009). Eating disorder symptoms among undergraduate varsity athletes, club athletes, independent exercisers, and nonexercisers. *International Journal of Eating Disorders, 42,* 47–53.

Holmes, J., Powell-Griner, E., Lethbridge-Cejku, M., & Heyman, K. (2009). *Aging differently: Physical limitations among adults aged 50 years and over: United States, 2001–2007.* NCHS Data Brief, No. 20. Hyattsville, MD: National Center for Health Statistics.

Holroyd, S. (2002). Aging and elderly women. In S. G. Kornstein & A. H. Clayton (Eds.), *Women's mental health: A comprehensive textbook* (pp. 584–593). New York: Guilford.

Holtgraves, T. (2010). Social psychology and language: Words, utterances, and conversations. In S. T. Fiske, D. T. Gilbert, & G. Lindzey (Eds.), *Handbook of social psychology* (5th ed., Vol. 2, pp. 1386–1422). Hoboken, NJ: Wiley.

Holvino, E. (2008). Intersections: The simultaneity of race, gender and class in organization studies. *Gender, Work & Organization, 17,* 248–277.

Holzman, C., et al. (2009). Maternal weathering and risk of preterm delivery. *American Journal of Public Health, 99,* 1864–1871.

Honekopp, J., & Watson, S. (2010). Meta-analysis of digit ratio 2D:4D show greater sex difference in the right hand. *American Journal of Human Biology, 22,* 619–630.

Hoobler, J. M., Rospenda, K. M., Lemmon, G., & Rosa, J. A. (2010). A within-subject longitudinal study of the effects of positive job experiences and generalized workplace harassment on well-being. *Journal of Occupational Health Psychology, 15,* 434–451.

Hooghe, M., Claes, E., Harell, A., Quintelier, E., & Dejaeghere, Y. (2010). Anti-gay sentiment among adolescents in Belgium and Canada: A comparative investigation into the role of gender and religion. *Journal of Homosexuality, 57,* 384–400.

Hook, J. L. (2010). Gender inequality in the welfare state: Sex segregation in housework, 1965–2003. *American Journal of Sociology, 115,* 1480–1523.

Hook, M. K., & Bowman, S. (2008). Working for a living: The vocational decision making of lesbians. *Journal of Lesbian Studies, 12,* 85–95.

Hooks, B. (1990). Feminism: A transformational politic. In D. L. Rhode (Ed.), *Theoretical perspectives in sexual difference* (pp. 185–193). New Haven, CT: Yale University Press.

Hopcroft, R. L., & Bradley, D. B. (2007). The sex difference in depression across 29 countries. *Social Forces, 85,* 1483–1507.

Hopkins, A. B. (2007). Opposing views, strongly held. In F. J. Crosby, M. S. Stockdale, & S. A. Ropp (Eds.), *Sex discrimination in the workplace* (pp. 59–68). Malden, MA: Blackwell.

Hooper, C. (2010). *Mothers surviving child sexual abuse.* New York: Routledge.

Hornbacher, M. (1998). *Wasted: A memoir of anorexia and bulimia.* New York: Harper Perennial.

Horner, M. S. (1972). Toward an understanding of achievement-related conflicts in women. *Journal of Social Issues, 28,* 157–176.

Horney, K. (1926/1974). The flight from womanhood: The masculinity-complex in women as viewed by men and women. In J. Strouse (Ed.), *Women and analysis: Dialogues on psychoanalytic views of femininity* (pp. 171–186). New York: Viking.

Horowitz, J. E., Galst, J. P., & Elster, N. (2010). *Ethical dilemmas in fertility counseling.* Washington, DC: American Psychological Association.

Horrocks, J., & House, A. (2010). Self-harm and suicide in women. In D. Kohen (Ed.), *Oxford textbook of women and mental health* (pp. 246–283). Oxford, UK: Oxford University Press.

Hounsell, C. (2008). *The female factor 2008: Why women are at greater financial risk in retirement and how annuities can help.* Washington, DC: Americans for Secure Retirement.

Houser, M. L., Horan, S. M., & Furler, L. A. (2008). Dating in the fast lane: How communication predicts speed-dating success. *Journal of Social and Personal Relationships, 25,* 749–768.

Housman, J., & Dorman, S. (2005). The Alameda County study: A systematic, chronological review. *American Journal of Health Education, 36,* 302–308.

Houvouras, S., & Carter, J. S. (2008). The F word: College students' definition of a feminist. *Sociological Forum, 23,* 234–256.

Huang, H., & Coker, A. D. (2010). Examining issues affecting African American participation in research studies. *Journal of Black Studies, 40,* 619–636.

Huber, L. R. B., & Ersek, J. L. (2009). Contraceptive use among sexually active university students. *Journal of Women's Health, 18,* 1063–1070.

Hudson, T. (2010). Menopause. In V. Maizes & T. Low Dog (Eds.), *Integrative women's health* (pp. 366–384). New York: Oxford University Press.

Hughes, M. E., & Waite, L. J. (2009). Marital biography and health at mid-life. *Journal of Health and Social Behavior, 50,* 344–358.

Human Rights Campaign. (2011, July 6). Marriage equality & other relationship recognition laws. Retrieved from http://www.hrc.org/files/assets/resources/Relationship_Recognition_Laws_Map(1).pdf

Human Rights Index: United Nations Convention on the Elimination of All Forms of Discrimination Against Women. (2010). Iowa City, IA: University of Iowa Center for Human Rights.

Hummert, M. L. (2011). Age stereotypes and aging. In K. W. Schaie & S. L. Willis (Eds.), *Handbook of the psychology of aging* (7th ed., pp. 249–262). San Diego, CA: Academic Press.

Humphreys, T. (2007). Perceptions of sexual consent: The impact of relationship history and gender. *Journal of Sex Research, 44,* 307–315.

Hunnicutt, G. (2009). Varieties of patriarchy and violence against women: Resurrecting "patriarchy" as a theoretical tool. *Violence Against Women, 15,* 553–573.

Hunt, K., Adamson, J., & Galdas, P. (2010). Gender and help-seeking: Towards gender-comparative studies. In E. Kuhlmann & E. Annandale (Eds.), *The Palgrave handbook of gender and healthcare* (pp. 207–221). New York: Palgrave Macmillan.

Hunter, S. V. (2009). Beyond surviving: Gender differences in response to early sexual experiences with adults. *Journal of Family Issues, 30,* 391–412.

Hurd, L. C. (2011). *Facing age: Women growing older in an anti-aging culture.* Lanham, MD: Rowman & Littlefield.

Hurd, L. C., & Griffin, M. (2008). Visible and invisible ageing: Beauty work as a response to ageism. *Ageing and Society, 28,* 653–674.

Hurtado, A. (2010). Multiple lenses: Multicultural feminist theory. In H. Landrine & N. F. Russo (Eds.), *Handbook of diversity in feminist psychology* (pp. 29–54). New York: Springer.

Husser, E. K., & Roberto, K. A. (2009). Older women with cardiovascular disease: Perceptions of initial experiences and long-term influences on daily life. *Journal of Women & Aging, 21,* 3–18.

Hutchens, R., & Nolen, P. (2010). Will the real family-friendly employer please stand up: Who permits work hour reductions for childcare? In K. Christensen & B. Schneider (Eds.), *Workplace flexibility: Realigning 20th-century jobs for a 21st-century workforce* (pp. 157–177). Ithaca, NY: Cornell University Press.

Hutcherson, S. T., & Epkins, C. C. (2009). Differentiating parent- and peer-related interpersonal correlates of depressive symptoms and social anxiety in preadolescent girls. *Journal of Social and Personal Relationships, 26,* 875–897.

Huyck, M. H. (1995). Marriage and close relationships of the marital kind. In R. Blieszner & V. H. Bedford (Eds.), *Handbook of aging and the family* (pp. 181–200). Westport, CT: Greenwood.

Hvas, L. (2006). Menopausal women's positive experience of growing older. *Maturitas, 54,* 245–251.

Hyde, J. S. (2003). Issues for women in middle age. In L. Slater, J. H. Daniel, & A. E. Banks (Eds.), *The complete guide to mental health for women* (pp. 48–50). Boston, MA: Beacon Press.

Hyde, J. S. (2007). Women in science: Gender similarities in abilities and sociocultural forces. In S. J. Ceci & W. M. Williams (Eds.), *Why aren't more women in science? Top researchers debate the evidence* (pp. 131–145). Washington, DC: American Psychological Association.

Hyde, J. S., & Kling, K. C. (2001). Women, motivation, and achievement. *Psychology of Women Quarterly, 25*, 364–378.

Hyde, J. S., & McKindley, N. M. (1997). Gender differences in cognition: Results from meta-analyses. In P. J. Caplan, M. Crawford, J. S. Hyde, & J. T. E. Richardson (Eds.), *Gender differences in human cognition* (pp. 30–51). New York: Oxford University Press.

Hyde, J. S., & Mertz, J. E. (2009). Gender, culture, and mathematics performance. *Proceedings of the National Academy of Sciences, 106*, 8801–8807.

Iervolino, A. C., Hines, M., Golombok, S. E., Rust, J., & Plomin, R. (2005). Genetic and environmental influences on sex-typed behavior during the preschool years. *Child Development, 76*, 826–840.

Igars, M, Santtila, P., & Sandnabba, N. K. (2010). Conflicted gender identity, body dissatisfaction, and disordered eating in adult men and women. *Sex Roles, 63*, 118–125.

Im, E.-O. (2009). Ethnic differences in symptoms experienced during the menopausal transition. *Health Care for Women International, 30*, 339–355.

Im, E.-O., Liu, Y., Dormire, S., & Chee, W. (2008). Menopausal symptom experience: An online forum study. *Journal of Advanced Nursing, 62*, 541–550.

Imperato-McGinley, J. (2002). 5a-reductase-2 deficiency and complete androgen insensitivity: Lessons from nature. In S. A. Zderic, D. A. Canning, M. C. Carr, & H. M. Snyder (Eds.), *Pediatric gender assignment: A critical reappraisal* (pp. 121–134). New York: Plenum.

Impett, E. A., Henson, J. M., Breines, J. G., Schooler, D., & Tolman, D. L. (2011). Embodiment feels better: Girls' body objectification and well-being across adolescence. *Psychology of Women Quarterly, 35*, 46–58.

Inglehart, J. (2010). Medicaid expansion offers solutions, challenges. *Health Affairs, 29*, 230–232.

Institute for Women's Policy Research. (2007a, February). *Women and paid sick days: Crucial for family well-being* [Fact sheet]. Washington, DC: Author.

Institute for Women's Policy Research. (2007b, November). *The economic security of older women and men in the United States.* Washington, DC: Author.

Institute for Women's Policy Research. (2009). *The gender wage gap by occupation* (IWPR #C350a). Washington, DC: Author.

Institute for Women's Policy Research. (2010). *The gender wage gap: 2009* (IWPR #C350). Washington, DC: Author.

International Treatment Preparedness Coalition. (2009). *Failing women, failing children: HIV, vertical transmission and women's health.* Retrieved from http://www.itpcglobal.org/index. php?option=com_content&task=view&id=92&Itemid=108

Inter-Parliamentary Union. (2011). *Women in national parliaments.* Geneva, Switzerland: Author.

Irni, S. (2009). Cranky old women? Irritation, resistance and gender practices in work organizations. *Gender, Work & Organization, 16*, 667–683.

Irwin, T. W. (2009). Substance use disorders among sexual-minority women. In K. T. Brady, S. E. Back, & S. F. Greenfield (Eds.), *Women and addiction: A comprehensive handbook* (pp. 475–489). New York: Guilford.

Isbell, L. M., Swedish, K., & Gazan, D. B. (2005). Who says it's sexual harassment? The effects of gender and likelihood to sexually harass on legal judgments of sexual harassment. *Journal of Applied Social Psychology, 35*, 745–772.

IsHak, W. W., Bokarius, A., Jeffrey, J. K., Davis, M. C., & Bakhta, Y. (2010). Disorders of orgasm in women: A literature review of etiology and current treatments. *International Society for Sexual Medicine, 7*, 3254–3268.

Iwamasa, G. Y., Sorocco, K. H., & Koonce, D. A. (2002). Ethnicity and clinical psychology: A content analysis of the literature. *Clinical Psychology Review, 22*, 931–944.

Iyer, A. (2009). Increasing the representation and status of women in employment: The effectiveness of affirmative action. In M. Barreto, M. K. Ryan, & M. T. Schmitt (Eds.), *The glass ceiling in the 21st century: Understanding barriers to gender equality* (pp. 3–18). Washington, DC: American Psychological Association.

Jack, D. C. (2003). The anger of hope and the anger of despair: How anger relates to women's depression. In J. M. Stoppard & L. M. McMullen (Eds.), *Situating sadness: Women and depression in social context* (pp. 62–87). New York: New York University Press.

Jack, D. C., & Ali, A. (Eds.). (2010). *Silencing the self across cultures: Depression and gender in the social world.* New York: Oxford University Press.

Jackson, A. P., & Dorsey, M. R. (2009). *Achieving against the odds: African American professional women in higher education.* Bloomington, IN: AuthorHouse.

Jackson, D., Engstrom, E., & Emmers-Sommer, T. (2007). Think leader, think male and female: Sex vs. seating arrangement as leadership cues. *Sex Roles, 57*, 713–723.

Jackson, Y., & Warren, J. S. (2000). Appraisal, social support, and life events: Predicting outcome behavior in school-age children. *Child Development, 71*, 1441–1457.

Jacobs, A. (2009, April 5). Chinese hunger for sons fuels boys' abductions. *New York Times*, pp. Y1, Y8.

Jacobs, J. A., & Gerson, K. (2008). Work and American families: Diverse needs, common solutions. In S. Coontz (Ed.), *American families: A multicultural reader* (2nd ed., pp. 454–466). New York: Taylor & Francis.

Jacobs, R. J., & Kane, M. N. (2009). Theory-based policy development for HIV prevention in racial ethnic minority midlife and older women. *Journal of Women & Aging, 21*, 19–32.

Jacobs, R. J., & Thomlison, B. (2009). Self-silencing and age as risk factors for sexually acquired HIV in midlife and older women. *Journal of Aging and Health, 21*, 102–128.

Jacobson, C. M., & Gould, M. (2009). Suicide and nonsuicidal self-injurious behaviors among youth: Risk and protective factors. In S. Nolen-Hoeksema & L. M. Hilt (Eds.), *Handbook of depression in adolescents* (pp. 207–235). New York: Taylor & Francis.

Jacobson, J. (2006, July 7). Report disputes notion that boys' academic performance is in decline. *Chronicle of Higher Education*, p. A35.

Jadva, V., et al. (2003). Surrogacy: The experiences of surrogate mothers. *Human Reproduction, 18*, 2196–2204.

Jaffe, J., & Diamond, M. O. (2011). *Reproductive trauma: Psychotherapy with infertility and pregnancy loss.* Washington, DC: American Psychological Association.

Jaffee, S., & Hyde, J. S. (2000). Gender differences in moral orientation: A meta-analysis. *Psychological Bulletin, 126*, 703–726.

Jain, S., Buka, S. L., Subramanian, S. V., & Molnar, B. E. (2010). Neighborhood predictors of dating violence victimization and perpetration in young adulthood: A multilevel study. *American Journal of Public Health, 100*, 1737–1744.

James S. D. (2007, December 13). World's oldest mom says she is "seriously ill." Retrieved May 16, 2008, from http:// abcnews. go.com/pring?id=3991578

Jang, S. J., & Zippay, A. (2011). The juggling act: Managing work-life conflict and work-life balance. *Families in Society, 92*, 84–90.

Janssen, I., Craig, W. M., Boyce, W. F., & Pickett, W. (2004). Association between overweight and obesity with bullying behaviors in school-aged children. *Pediatrics, 113*, 1187–1194.

Jansz, J., & Martis, R. G. (2007). The Lara phenomenon: Powerful female characters in video games. *Sex Roles, 56,* 141–148.

Jardines, L. (2008). Breast disorders. In A. L. Clouse & K. Sherif (Eds.), *Women's health in clinical practice: A handbook for primary care* (pp. 213–250). Totowa, NJ: Humana Press.

Jefferson, D. L., & Stake, J. E. (2009). Appearance self-attitudes of African American and European American women: Media comparisons and internalization of beauty ideals. *Psychology of Women Quarterly, 33,* 396–409.

Jenkins, C. L. (2003). Widows and divorcees in later life. *Journal of Women & Aging, 15,* 1–6.

Jenkins, H., & Cassell, J. (2008). From quake girls to desperate housewives: A decade of gender and computer games. In Y. Kafai, C. Heeter, J. Denner, & J. Sun (Eds.), *Beyond Barbie and Mortal Kombat: New perspectives on gender and gaming* (pp. 5–20). Cambridge, MA: MIT Press.

Jepsen, E. K., Svagaard, T., Theele, M. I., McCullough, L., & Martinsen, E. W. (2009). Inpatient treatment for adult survivors of childhood sexual abuse: A preliminary outcome study. *Journal of Trauma & Dissociation, 10,* 315–333.

Jin, L., & Christakis, N. A. (2007, August). *Investigating the mechanism of marital mortality reduction: The transition to widowhood and quality of health care.* Paper presented at the meeting of the American Sociological Association, New York.

Jin, L., & Chrisatakis, N. A. (2009). Investigating the mechanisms of marital mortality reduction: The transition to widowhood and quality of health care. *Demography, 46,* 605–625.

John, D. H., & Ebbeck, V. (2008). Gender-differentiated associations among objectified body consciousness, self-conceptions and physical activity. *Sex Roles, 59,* 623–632.

Johnson, A. (2009, May). *Women in the history of psychology: The "classic history" and what we can learn from it.* Paper presented at the annual meeting of the Association for Psychological Science, San Francisco, CA.

Johnson, A. B., & Rodgers, J. L. (2006). The impact of having children on the lives of women: The effects of children questionnaire. *Journal of Applied Social Psychology, 36,* 2685–2714.

Johnson, C. L. (1994). Differential expectations and realities: Race, socioeconomic status, and health of the oldest old. *International Journal of Aging and Human Development, 38,* 13–27.

Johnson, D., & Scelfo, J. (2003, December 15). Sex, love and nursing homes. *Newsweek,* pp. 54–55.

Johnson, D. J., et al. (2003). Studying the effects of early child care experiences on the development of children of color in the United States: Toward a more inclusive research agenda. *Child Development, 74,* 1227–1244.

Johnson, J. L., Eaton, D. K., Pederson, L. L., & Lowry, R. (2009). Associations of trying to lose weight, weight control behaviors, and current cigarette use among US high school students. *Journal of School Health, 79,* 355–360.

Johnson, J. O., & Downs, B. (2005). *Maternity leave and employment patterns: 1961–2000.* Current Population Reports, P70-103. Washington, DC: U.S. Census Bureau.

Johnson, M. P. (2010). Langhinrichsen-Rohling's confirmation of the feminist analysis of intimate partner violence: Comment on "controversies involving gender and intimate partner violence in the United States." *Sex Roles, 62,* 212–219.

Johnson, R. D., Stone, D. L., & Phillips, T. N. (2008). Relations among ethnicity, gender, beliefs, attitudes, and intention to pursue a career in information technology. *Journal of Applied Social Psychology, 38,* 999–1022.

Johnson, S. M., & O'Connor, E. (2002). *The gay baby boom: The psychology of gay parenthood.* New York: New York University Press.

Johnson, T. D. (2008). *Maternity leave and employment patterns: 2001–2003* (Report No. P70-113). Washington, DC: U.S. Census Bureau.

Johnson, W., McGue, M., Krueger, R. F., & Bouchard, T. J., Jr. (2004). Marriage and personality: A genetic analysis. *Journal of Personality and Social Psychology, 86,* 285–294.

Johnston, D., & Swanson, D. (2003). Undermining mothers: A content analysis of the representations of mothers in magazines. *Mass Communication and Society, 6,* 243–265.

Johnston, L. D., O'Malley, P. M., Bachman, J. G., & Schulenberg, J. E. (2010a). *Demographic subgroup trends for various licit and illicit drugs, 1975–2009* (Monitoring the future occasional paper 73). Ann Arbor, MI: Institute for Social Research, University of Michigan.

Johnston, L. D., O'Malley, P. M., Bachman, J. G., & Schulenberg, J. E. (2010b). *Monitoring the future: National results on adolescent drug use: Overview of key findings, 2009.* Ann Arbor, MI: Institute for Social Research, University of Michigan.

Johnston, L. D., O'Malley, P. M., Bachman, J. G., & Schulenberg, J. E. (2011). *Monitoring the future: National results on adolescent drug use: Overview of key findings, 2010.* Ann Arbor, MI: Institute for Social Research, University of Michigan.

Jonason, P. K., & Fisher, T. D. (2009). The power of prestige: Why young men report having more sex partners than young women. *Sex Roles, 60,* 151–159.

Jones, D. C. (2004). Body image among adolescent girls and boys: A longitudinal study. *Developmental Psychology, 40,* 823–835.

Jones, D. J., O'Connel, C., Gound, M., Heller, L., & Forehand, R. (2004). Predictors of self-reported physical symptoms in low income, inner-city African American women: The role of optimism, depressive symptoms, and chronic illness. *Psychology of Women Quarterly, 28,* 112–121.

Jones, I., Heron, J., & Blackmore, E. R. (2010). Puerperal depression. In D. Kohen (Ed.), *Oxford textbook of women and mental health* (pp. 179–186). Oxford, UK: Oxford University Press.

Jones, R. (2008). *Looking younger: Makeovers that make you look as young as you feel.* Beverly, MA: Fair Winds Press.

Jones, R. K., Zolna, M. R. S., Henshaw, S. K., & Finer, L. B. (2008). Abortion in the United States: Incidence and access to services, 2005. *Perspectives on Sexual and Reproductive Health, 40,* 6–16.

Jones, S. (2007). Exercising agency, becoming a single mother: Decision-making processes of unmarried women. *Marriage & Family Review, 42,* 35–61.

Jones, S. M., & Dindia, K. (2004). A meta-analytic perspective on sex equity in the classroom. *Review of Educational Research, 74,* 443–471.

Jones, S. R. (2007). Working-poor mothers and middle-class others: Psychosocial considerations in home-school relations and research. *Anthropology & Education Quarterly, 38,* 159–177.

Jones-DeWeever, A. A. (2009). *Black girls in New York City: Untold strength & resilience.* Washington, DC: Institute for Women's Policy Research.

Jones-DeWeever, A. A., Dill, B. T., & Schram, S. (2009). Racial, ethnic, and gender disparities in the workforce, education, and training under welfare reform. In B. T. Dill & R. E. Zambrana (Eds.), *Emerging intersections: Race, class, and gender in theory, policy, and practice* (pp. 150–179). Piscataway, NJ: Rutgers University Press.

Jordan, C. E., Campbell, R., & Follingstad, D. (2010). Violence and women's mental health: The impact of physical, sexual, and psychological aggression. *Annual Review of Clinical Psychology, 6,* 1–22.

Jordan, J. V. (Ed.). (1997). *Women's growth in diversity: More writings from the stone center.* New York: Guilford.

Jordan, J. V., Banks, A. E., & Walker, M. (2003). Growth in connection: A relational-cultural model of growth. In L. Slater, J. H. Daniel, & A. E. Banks (Eds.), *The complete guide to mental health for women* (pp. 92–99). Boston, MA: Beacon Press.

Jordan-Young, R. M. (2010). *Brainstorm: The flaws in the science of sex differences.* Cambridge, MA: Harvard University Press.

Jose, A., O'Leary, D., & Moyer, A. (2010). Does premarital cohabitation predict subsequent marital stability and marital quality? A meta-analysis. *Journal of Marriage and Family, 72,* 105–116.

Josselson, R. (1996). *Revising herself: The story of women's identity from college to midlife.* New York: Oxford University Press.

Joutsenniemi, K., Martelin, T., Martikainen, P., Pirkola, S., & Koskinen, S. (2006). Living arrangements and mental health in Finland. *Journal of Epidemiology and Community Health, 60,* 468–475.

Joy, E. A., Van Hala, S., & Cooper, L. (2009). Health-related concerns of the female athlete: A lifespan approach. *American Family Physician, 79,* 489–495.

Juckett, G., & Rudolph-Watson, L. (2010). Recognizing mental illness in culture-bound syndromes. *American Family Physician, 81,* 206.

Judkins, B., & Presser, L. (2008). Division of eco-friendly household labor and the marital relationship. *Journal of Social and Personal Relationships, 25,* 923–941.

Jung, J., & Forbes, G. B. (2010). Body dissatisfaction and disordered eating: The globalization of western appearance ideals. In M. A. Paludi (Ed.), *Feminism and women's rights worldwide* (Vol. 1, pp. 161–186). Santa Barbara, CA: Praeger.

Jung, J., Forbes, G. B., & Lee, Y-j. (2009). Body dissatisfaction and disordered eating among early adolescents from Korea and the US. *Sex Roles, 61,* 42–54.

Jungheim, E. S., & Colditz, G. A. (2011). Short-term use of unopposed estrogen: A balance of inferred risks and benefits. *Journal of the American Medical Association, 305,* 1354–1355.

Juntunen, C. L., Barraclough, D. J., Broneck, C. L., Seibel, G. A., Winlow, S. A., & Morin, P. M. (2001). American Indian perspectives on the career journey. *Journal of Counseling Psychology, 48,* 274–285.

Kaestner, R., & Xu, X. (2010). Title IX, girls' sports participation, and adult female physical activity and weight. *Evaluation Review, 34,* 52–78.

Kagan, J. (2010). Emotions and temperament. In M. H. Bornstein (Ed.), *Handbook of cultural developmental science* (pp. 175–194). New York: Psychology Press.

Kahlenberg, R. (2011, March 17). Are admissions preferences for men OK? *Chronicle of Higher Education.* Retrieved from http://chronicle.com/blogs/innovations/are-admissions-preferences-for-men-okay/28909

Kahlenberg, S. G., & Hein, M. M. (2010). Progression on Nickelodeon? Gender-role stereotypes in toy commercials. *Sex Roles, 62,* 830–847.

Kahn, J. R., McGill, B. S., & Bianchi, S. M. (2011). Help to family and friends: Are there gender differences at older ages? *Journal of Marriage and Family, 73,* 77–92.

Kahn, J. S., & Ferguson, K. (2010). Men as allies in feminist pedagogy in the undergraduate psychology curriculum. *Women & Therapy, 33,* 121–139.

Kail, B. L., Quadagno, J., & Keene, J. R. (2009). The political economy perspective of aging. In V. Bengtson, M. Silverstien, N. M. Putney, & D. Gans (Eds.), *Handbook of theories of aging* (pp. 555–571). New York: Springer.

Kainen, A. (1995). Only your regrets. In B. Benatovich (Ed.), *What we know so far: Wisdom among women.* New York: St. Martin's Griffin.

Kajantie, E. (2008). Physiological stress response, estrogen, and the male-female mortality gap. *Current Directions in Psychological Science, 17,* 348–352.

Kalb, C., & Murr, A. (2006, May 15). Battling a black epidemic. *Newsweek,* pp. 42–48.

Kalil, A., & Kunz, J. (2002). Teenage childbearing, marital status, and depressive symptoms in later life. *Child Development, 73,* 1748–1760.

Kalil, A., Ziol-Guest, K. M., & Epstein, J. L. (2010). Nonstandard work and marital instability: Evidence from the national longitudinal survey of youth. *Journal of Marriage and Family, 72,* 1289–1300.

Kalmijn, M. (2007). Gender differences in the effects of divorce, widowhood and remarriage on intergenerational support: Does marriage protect fathers? *Social Forces, 85,* 1079–1104.

Kan, M. L., Cheng, Y. A., Landale, N. S., & McHale, S. M. (2010). Longitudinal predictors of change in number of sexual partners across adolescence and early adulthood. *Journal of Adolescent Health, 46,* 25–31.

Kane, E. W. (2000). Racial and ethnic variations in gender-related attitudes. *Annual Review of Sociology, 26,* 419–439.

Kane, E. W. (2006). "No way my boys are going to be like that!": Parents' responses to children's gender nonconformity. *Gender & Society, 20,* 149–176.

Kanner, M., & Anderson, K. J. (2010). The myth of the man-hating feminist. In M. A. Paludi (Ed.), *Feminism and women's rights worldwide* (Vol. 1, pp. 1–26). Santa Barbara, CA: Praeger.

Kanny, D., Liu, Y., & Brewer, R. D. (2011). Binge drinking—United States, 2009. *Morbidity and Mortality Weekly Report, 60*(Suppl.), 101–104.

Kanny, D., Liu, Y., Brewer, R. D., & Balluz, L. (2010). Vital signs: Binge drinking among high school students and adults—United States, 2009. *Morbidity and Mortality Weekly Report, 59,* 1–6.

Kantor, M. (2009). *Homophobia: The state of sexual bigotry today* (2nd ed.). Westport, CT: Praeger.

Kantrowitz, B. (2005, January 31). Sex and science. *Newsweek,* pp. 36–38.

Karch, D., & Nunn, K. C. (2011). Characteristics of elderly and other vulnerable adult victims of homicide by a caregiver: National violent death reporting system—17 US states, 2003–2007. *Journal of Interpersonal Violence, 26,* 137–157.

Karch, D. L., Dahlberg, L. L., & Patel, N. (2010). Surveillance for violent deaths—National violent death reporting system, 16 states, 2007. *Morbidity and Mortality Weekly Report, 59,* 1–50.

Kåreholt, I., Lennartsson, C., Gatz, M., & Parker, M. G. (2011). Baseline leisure time activity and cognition more than two decades later. *International Journal of Geriatric Psychiatry, 26,* 65–74.

Karlyn, K. R. (2011). *Unruly girls, unrepentant mothers: Redefining feminism on screen.* Austin, TX: University of Texas Press.

Karpel, A. (2010, June 6). "L Word" creator enters uncharted territory. *New York Times,* pp. AR22, AR24.

Karpiak, C. P., Buchanan, J. P., Hosey, M., & Smith, A. (2007). University students from single-sex and coeducational high schools: Differences in majors and attitudes at a Catholic university. *Psychology of Women Quarterly, 31,* 282–289.

Karraker, K., & Hartley, J. (2007, March). *Mothers' toy choices for their male and female toddlers.* Poster presented at the meeting of the Society for Research in Child Development, Boston, MA.

Karraker, K. H., Vogel, D. A., & Lake, M. A. (1995). Parents' gender-stereotyped perceptions of newborns: The eye of the beholder revisited. *Sex Roles, 33,* 687–701.

Karreman, A., van Tuijl, C., van Aken, M. A. G., & Deković, M. (2009). Predicting young children's externalizing problems: Interactions among effortful control, parenting, and child gender. *Merrill-Palmer Quarterly, 55,* 111–134.

Kasen, S., Chen, H., Sneed, J. R., & Cohen, P. (2010). Earlier stress exposure and subsequent major depression in aging women. *International Journal of Geriatric Psychiatry, 25,* 91–99.

Kashubeck-West, S., Mintz, L. B., & Weigold, I. (2005). Separating the effects of gender and weight-loss desire on body satisfaction and disordered eating behavior. *Sex Roles, 53,* 505–518.

Kates, E. (1996). Educational pathways out of poverty: Responding to the realities of women's lives. *American Journal of Orthopsychiatry, 66,* 548–556.

Kates, E. (2007). *Low income women's access to education?: A case-study of welfare recipients in Boston.* Boston, MA: Center for Women in Politics and Public Policy.

Katz, D. S., & Andronici, J. F. (2006, Fall). No more excuses! *Ms.,* 63–64.

Katz, J., Swindell, S., & Farrow, S. (2004). Effects of participation in a first women's studies course on collective self-esteem, gender-related attitudes, and emotional well-being. *Journal of Applied Social Psychology, 34,* 2179–2199.

Katz, P. A. (1996). Raising feminists. *Psychology of Women Quarterly, 20,* 323–340.

Katz, P. A., & Walsh, V. (1991). Modification of children's gender-stereotyped behavior. *Child Development, 62,* 338–351.

Kaufman, G., & Goldscheider, F. (2007). Do men "need" a spouse more than women? Perceptions of the importance of marriage for men and women. *Sociological Quarterly, 48,* 29–46.

Kaufman-Scarborough, C. (2004). Integrating consumer disabilities into models of information processing: Color-vision deficiencies and their effects on women's marketplace choices. In B. G. Smith & B. Hutchison (Eds.), *Gendering disability* (pp. 272–285). Piscataway, NJ: Rutgers University Press.

Kavan, M. G., Elsasser, G. N., & Barone, E. J. (2009). Generalized anxiety disorder: Practical assessment and management. *American Family Physician, 79,* 785–791.

Kawamura, S., & Brown, S. L. (2007, August). *Mattering and wives' perceived fairness of the division of household labor.* Paper presented at the meeting of the American Sociological Association, New York.

Keaveny, T. J., Inderrieden, E. J., & Toumanoff, P. G. (2007). Gender differences in pay of young management professionals in the United States: A comprehensive view. *Journal of Labor Research, 28,* 327–346.

Keel, P. K., Gravener, J. A., Joiner, T. E., Jr., & Haedt, A. A. (2010). Twenty-year follow-up of bulimia nervosa and related eating disorders not otherwise specified. *International Journal of Eating Disorders, 43,* 492–497.

Keel, P. K., & McCormick, L. (2010). Diagnosis, assessment, and treatment planning for anorexia nervosa. In C. M. Grilo & J. E. Mitchell (Eds.), *The treatment of eating disorders: A clinical handbook* (pp. 3–27). New York: Guilford.

Keene, J. R., & Prokos, A. H. (2008). Widowhood and the end of spousal care-giving: Relief or wear and tear? *Ageing and Society, 28,* 551–570.

Keltner, D., & Lerner, J. S. (2010). Emotion. In S. T. Fiske, D. T. Gilbert, & G. Lindzey (Eds.), *Handbook of social psychology* (5th ed., Vol. 1, pp. 317–352). Hoboken, NJ: Wiley.

Kemmler, W., von Stengel, S., Engelke, K., Häberle, L., & Kalender, W. A. (2010). Exercise effects on bone mineral density, falls, coronary risk factors, and health care costs in older women. *Archives of Internal Medicine, 170,* 179–185.

Kenfield, S. A., Stampfer, M. J., Rosner, B. A., & Colditz, G. A. (2008). Smoking and smoking cessation in relation to mortality in women. *Journal of the American Medical Association, 299,* 2037–2047.

Kenna, H. A., Ghezel, T., & Rasgon, N. L. (2010). Epidemiology of mental disorders in older women. In B. L. Levin & M. A. Becker (Eds.), *A public health perspective of women's mental health* (pp. 65–80). New York: Springer.

Kennedy, H. P. (2010). The problem of normal birth. *Journal of Midwifery & Women's Health, 55,* 199–201.

Kenney, C. T., & Bogle, R. (2009, May 2). *Mothers' gatekeeping of father involvement in married and cohabiting-couple families.* Paper presented at the annual meeting of the Population Association of America, Detroit, MI.

Kern, M. L., Reynolds, C. A., & Friedman, H. S. (2010). Predictors of physical activity patterns across adulthood: A growth curve analysis. *Personality and Social Psychology Bulletin, 36,* 1058–1072.

Kerr, B. (1999, March 5). When dreams differ: Male–female relations on campus. *Chronicle of Higher Education,* pp. 87, 88.

Kersting, K. (2003, May). Cognitive sex differences: A "political minefield." *Monitor on Psychology, 34,* 54–55.

Kessel, C., & Nelson, D. J. (2011). Statistical trends in women's participation in science: Commentary on Valla and Ceci. *Perspectives on Psychological Science, 6,* 147–149.

Kessler, E.-M., Schwender, C., & Bowen, C. E. (2010). The portrayal of older people's social participation on German prime-time TV advertisements. *Journal of Gerontology: Social Sciences, 65B,* 97–106.

Kessler, R. C., Berglund, P., Demler, O., Jin, R., & Walters, E. E. (2005). Lifetime prevalence and age-of-onset distributions of DSM-IV disorders in the National Comorbidity Survey Replication. *Archives of General Psychiatry, 62,* 593–602.

Khang, K., & Heller de Leon, C. (2006). *More than serving tea: Asian American women on expectations, relationships, leadership, and faith.* Downers Grove, IL: InterVarsity Press.

Khare, M. M., et al. (2009). A lifestyle approach to reducing cardiovascular risk factors in underserved women: Design and methods of the Illinois WISEWOMAN program. *Journal of Women's Health, 18,* 409–419.

Khosla, S. (2011). Is nitroglycerin a novel and inexpensive treatment for osteoporosis? *Journal of the American Medical Association, 305,* 826.

Kiang, L., Moreno, A. J., & Robinson, J. L. (2004). Maternal preconceptions about parenting predict child temperament, maternal sensitivity, and children's empathy. *Developmental Psychology, 40,* 1081–1092.

Kiefer, A. K., & Sekaquaptewa, D. (2007). Implicit stereotypes, gender identification, and math-related outcomes: A prospective study of female college students. *Psychological Science, 18,* 13–18.

Kiefer, A. K., & Shih, M. J. (2004, May). *Stereotype relevance and gender differences in performance attributions.* Poster presented at the meeting of American Psychological Society, Chicago.

Kiesner, J. (2009). Physical characteristics of the menstrual cycle and premenstrual depressive symptoms. *Psychological Science, 20,* 763–770.

Kilbourne, A., Switzer, G., Hyman, K., Crowley-Matoka, M., & Fine, M. (2006). Advancing health disparities research within the health care system: A conceptual framework. *American Journal of Public Health, 96,* 2113–2121.

Kilbourne, J. (2000). *Can't buy me love: How advertising changes the way we think and feel.* New York: Touchstone Books.

Kilianski, S. E. (2003). Explaining heterosexual men's attitudes toward women and gay men: The theory of exclusively masculine identity. *Psychology of Men & Masculinity, 4,* 37–56.

Kim, J., & Gray, K. A. (2008). Leave or stay? Battered women's decision after intimate partner violence. *Journal of Interpersonal Violence, 23,* 1465–1482.

Kim, J. E., & Moen, P. (2001). Moving into retirement: Preparation and transitions in late midlife. In M. Lachman (Ed.), *Handbook of midlife development* (pp. 487–527). New York: Wiley.

Kim, W. J., & Singh, T. (2004). Trends and dynamics of youth suicides in developing countries. *Lancet, 363,* 1090.

Kimerling, R., Alvarez, J., Pavao, J., Mack, K. P., Smith, M. W., & Baumrind, N. (2009). Unemployment among women: Examining the relationship of physical and psychological intimate partner violence and posttraumatic stress disorder. *Journal of Interpersonal Violence, 24,* 450–463.

Kimmel, D. G. (2002, August). *Ageism and implications for sexual orientation*. Paper presented at the American Psychological Association, Chicago.

Kimmel, E. B., & Crawford, M. (2001). Methods for studying gender. In J. Worell (Ed.), *Encyclopedia of women and gender* (pp. 749–758). San Diego: Academic Press.

Kimmel, M. (2001). Real men join the movement. In S. M. Shaw & J. Lee (Eds.), *Women's voices, feminist visions* (pp. 536–540). Mountain View, CA: Mayfield.

Kimmel, M. (2008). A war against boys? In S. Coontz (Ed.), *American families: A multicultural reader* (2nd ed., pp. 387–393). New York: Taylor & Francis.

Kimmel, M. (2009). Has a man's world become a woman's nation? In M. Shriver (Ed.), *The Shriver report: A woman's nation changes everything* (pp. 322–557). Washington, DC: Maria Shriver and the Center for American Progress.

Kimmel, M. (2011). Introduction. In M. Kimmel & A. Aronson (Eds.), *The gendered society reader* (4th ed., pp. 1–8). New York: Oxford University Press.

Kimura, D. (2007). "Underrepresentation" or misrepresentation? In S. J. Ceci & W. M. Williams (Eds.), *Why aren't more women in science? Top researchers debate the evidence* (pp. 39–46). Washington, DC: American Psychological Association.

King, C., & Olsen, P. R. (2002, August 18). Follow the herd? Not her. *New York Times*, p. BU13.

King, E. B., Hebl, M. R., George, J. M., & Matusik, S. F. (2010). Understanding tokenism: Antecedents and consequences of a psychological climate of gender inequity. *Journal of Management, 36*, 482–510.

King, J. E. (2010). *Gender equity in higher education: 2010*. Washington, DC: American Council on Education.

King, L. A., & King, D. W. (1990). Abbreviated measures of sex role egalitarian attitudes. *Sex Roles, 23*, 659–673.

Kinsella, K., & Velkoff, V. A. (2001). *An aging world: 2001* (U.S. Census Bureau, Series P95/01-1). Washington, DC: U.S. Government Printing Office.

Kinser, A. E. (2010). *Motherhood and feminism*. Berkeley, CA: Seal Press.

Kinsey, A. C., Pomeroy, W. B., Martin, C. E., & Gebhard, P. H. (1953). *Sexual behavior in the human female*. Philadelphia, PA: Saunders.

Kinsler, K., & Zalk, S. R. (1996). Teaching is a political act: Contextualizing gender and ethnic voices. In K. F. Wyche & F. J. Crosby (Eds.), *Women's ethnicities: Journeys through psychology* (pp. 27–48). Boulder, CO: Westview.

Kinzie, J., Thomas, A. D., Palmer, M. M., Umbach, P. D., & Kuh, G. D. (2007). Women students at coeducational and women's colleges: How do their experiences compare? *Journal of College Student Development, 48*, 145–165.

Kirk, G., & Okazawa-Rey, M. (2009). *Women's lives: Multicultural perspectives* (5th ed.). Mountain View, CA: Mayfield.

Kirmizioglu, Y., Doğan, O., Kuğu, N., & Akyüz, G. (2009). Prevalence of anxiety disorders among elderly people. *International Journal of Geriatric Psychiatry, 24*, 1026–1033.

Kissling, E. A. (2006). *Capitalizing on the curse: The business of menstruation*. Boulder, CO: Lynne Rienner.

Kite, M. E. (2001). Changing times, changing gender roles: Who do we want women and men to be? In R. K. Unger (Ed.), *Handbook of the psychology of women and gender* (pp. 215–227). New York: Wiley.

Kite, M. E., Deaux, K., & Haines, E. L. (2008). Gender stereotypes. In F. L. Denmark & M. A. Paludi (Eds.), *Psychology of women: A handbook of issues and theories* (2nd ed., pp. 205–236). Westport, CT: Praeger.

Kite, M. E., et al. (2001). Women psychologists in academe: Mixed progress, unwarranted complacency. *American Psychologist, 56*, 1080–1098.

Kitts, R. L. (2010). Barriers to optimal care between physicians and lesbian, gay, bisexual, transgender, and questioning adolescent patients. *Journal of Homosexuality, 57*, 730–747.

Kitzinger, C. (1999). Researching subjectivity and diversity: Q-methodology in feminist psychology. *Psychology of Women Quarterly, 23*, 267–276.

Kitzman, D. W., & Rich, M. W. (2010). Age disparities in heart failure research. *Journal of the American Medical Association, 304*, 1950–1951.

Klein, A. (2008, July). Finding order in disorder. *University Business, 42–44*.

Kleinfeld, J. (2009). No map to manhood: Male and female mindsets behind the college gender gap. *Gender Issues, 26*, 171–182.

Klimstra, T. A., Hale, W. W., III, Raaijmakers, Q. A. W., Branje, S. J. T., & Meeus, W. H. J. (2009). Maturation of personality in adolescence. *Journal of Personality and Social Psychology, 96*, 898–912.

Klimstra, T. A., Hale, W. W., III, Raaijmakers, Q. A. W., Branje, S. J. T., & Meeus, W. H. J. (2010). Identity formation in adolescence: Change or stability. *Journal of Youth and Adolescence, 39*, 150–162.

Kling, K. C., Hyde, J. S., Showers, C. J., & Buswell, B. N. (1999). Gender differences in self-esteem: A meta-analysis. *Psychological Bulletin, 125*, 470–500.

Klohnen, E. C., & Luo, S. (2003). Interpersonal attraction and personality: What is attractive—self similarity, ideal similarity, complementarity, or attachment security? *Journal of Personality and Social Psychology, 85*, 709–722.

Klonsky, E. D., & Moyer, A. (2008). Childhood sexual abuse and non-suicidal self-injury: Meta-analysis. *British Journal of Psychiatry, 192*, 166–170.

Kluck, A. S. (2010). Family influence on disordered eating: The role of body image dissatisfaction. *Body Image, 7*, 8–14.

Klumb, P. L., & Lampert, T. (2004). Women, work, and well-being 1950–2000: A review and methodological critique. *Social Science and Medicine, 58*, 1007–1024.

Klump, K. L., Bulik, C. M., Kaye, W. H., Treasure, J., & Tyson, E. (2009). Academy for eating disorders position paper: Eating disorders are serious mental illnesses. *International Journal of Eating Disorders, 42*, 97–103.

Klump, K. L., Burt, A., Spanos, A., McGue, M., Iacono, W. G., & Wade, T. D. (2010). Age differences in genetic and environmental influences on weight and shape concerns. *International Journal of Eating Disorders, 43*, 679–688.

Kmiec, J., Crosby, J. F., & Worell, J. (1996). Walking the talk: On stage and behind the scenes. In K. F. Wyche & F. J. Crosby (Eds.), *Women's ethnicities: Journeys through psychology* (pp. 49–61). Boulder, CO: Westview.

Knafo, A., & Plomin, R. (2006). Prosocial behavior from early to middle childhood: Genetic and environmental influences on stability and change. *Developmental Psychology, 42*, 771–786.

Knauss, C., Paxton, S. J., & Alsaker, F. (2008). Body dissatisfaction in adolescent boys and girls: Objectified body consciousness, internalization of the media body ideal and perceived pressure from media. *Sex Roles, 59*, 633–643.

Knight, G. P., Roosa, M. W., & Umaña-Taylor, A. J. (2009). *Studying ethnic minority and economically disadvantaged populations: Methodological challenges and best practices*. Washington, DC: American Psychological Association.

Knight, J. L., & Giuliano, T. A. (2001). He's a Laker; she's a "Looker": The consequences of gender-stereotypical portrayals of male and female athletes by the print media. *Sex Roles, 45*, 217–229.

Knight, R. A., & Sims-Knight, J. (2011). Risk factors for sexual violence. In J. W. White, M. P. Koss, & A. E. Kazdin (Eds.), *Violence against women and children: Mapping the terrain* (Vol. 1, pp. 125–150). Washington, DC: American Psychological Association.

Knightley, P. (1999, September 20). Grandma led two lives. *New York Times*, p. A21.

Knudsen, K., & Wærness, K. (2008). National context and spouses' housework in 34 countries. *European Sociological Review, 24*, 97–113.

Koball, H. L., Moiduddin, E., Henderson, J., Goesling, B., & Besculides, M. (2010). What do we know about the link between marriage and health? *Journal of Family Issues, 31*, 1019–1040.

Kobrynowicz, D., & Branscombe, N. R. (1997). Who considers themselves victims of discrimination? Individual difference predictors of perceived gender discrimination in women and men. *Psychology of Women Quarterly, 21*, 347–363.

Kogan, M. D., et al. (2010). Underinsurance among children in the United States. *New England Journal of Medicine, 363*, 841–851.

Koh, H. K., Oppenheimer, S. C., Massin-Short, S. B., Emmons, K. M., Geller, A. C., & Viswanath, K. (2010). Translating research evidence into practice to reduce health disparities: A social determinants approach. *American Journal of Public Health, 100*, S72–S80.

Kohatsu, W. (2010). Nutrition. In V. Maizes & T. Low Dog (Eds.), *Integrative women's health* (pp. 7–29). New York: Oxford University Press.

Kohlberg, L. (1966). A cognitive-developmental analysis of children's sex-role concepts and attitudes. In E. E. Maccoby (Ed.), *The development of sex differences* (pp. 82–173). Stanford, CA: Stanford University Press.

Kohlberg, L., & Puka, B. (1994). *Kohlberg's original study of moral development*. New York: Garland.

Kolata, G. (2002, September 25). Abortion pill slow to win users among women and their doctors. *New York Times*, p. A1.

Kolata, G. (2007). *Rethinking thin: The new science of weight loss— and the myths and realities of dieting*. New York: Picador.

Kolata, G. (2010, November 30). Report questions need for 2 diet supplements. *New York Times*, p. A1.

Kolata, G., & Moss, M. (2002, February 11). X-ray vision in hindsight: Science, politics and the mammogram. *New York Times*, p. A23.

Kolb, D., & McGinn, K. (2009). Beyond gender and negotiation to gendered negotiations. *Negotiation and Conflict Management Research, 2*, 1–16.

Kominos, V. A. (2010). Cardiovascular health. In V. Maizes & T. Low Dog (Eds.), *Integrative women's health* (pp. 588–622). New York: Oxford University Press.

Konek, C. W., Kitch, S. L., & Shore, E. R. (1994). The future of women and careers: Issues and challenges. In C. W. Konek & S. L. Kitch (Eds.), *Women and careers: Issues and challenges* (pp. 234–248). Thousand Oaks, CA: Sage.

Konkel, K. E. (2010). HIV. In V. Maizes & T. Low Dog (Eds.), *Integrative women's health* (pp. 521–534). New York: Oxford University Press.

Konrad, A. M. (2003). Family demands and job attribute preferences: A 4-year longitudinal study of women and men. *Sex Roles, 49*, 35–46.

Konrad, A. M., Ritchie, J. E., Lieb, P., & Corrigall, E. (2000). Sex differences and similarities in job attribute preferences: A meta-analysis. *Psychological Bulletin, 126*, 593–641.

Kontula, O., & Haavio-Mannila, E. (2009). The impact of aging on human sexual activity and sexual desire. *Journal of Sex Research, 46*, 46–56.

Koput, K. W., & Gutek, B. A. (2011). *Gender stratification in the IT industry: Sex, status, and social capital*. Northampton, MA: Edward Elgar Publishing.

Koropeckyj-Cox, T., & Call, V. R. (2007). Characteristics of older childless persons and parents: Cross-national comparisons. *Journal of Family Issues, 28*, 1362–1414.

Koropeckyj-Cox, T., Romano, V., & Moras, A. (2007). Through the lenses of gender, race, and class: Students' perceptions of childless/childfree individuals and couples. *Sex Roles, 56*, 415–428.

Kosciulek, J. F. (2009). Empowering individuals with disabilities through career counseling. In N. C. Gysbers, M. J. Heppner, & J. A. Johnston (Eds.), *Career counseling: Contexts, processes, and techniques* (3rd ed., pp. 125–136). Alexandria, VA: American Counseling Association.

Kosciw, J. G., Diaz, E. M., & Greytak, E. A. (2008). *The 2007 national school climate survey: Key findings on the experiences of lesbian, gay, bisexual and transgender youth in our nation's schools*. New York: Gay, Lesbian and Straight Education Network.

Koss, M. P. (2003). Evolutionary models of why men rape: Acknowledging the complexities. In C. B. Travis (Ed.), *Evolution, gender, and rape* (pp. 191–205). Cambridge, MA: MIT Press.

Koss, M. P., & White, J. W. (2008). National and global agendas on violence against women: Historical perspective and consensus. *American Journal of Orthopsychiatry, 78*, 386–393.

Koss, M. P., White, J. W., & Kazdin, A. E. (2011). Violence against women and children: Perspectives and next steps. In M. P. Koss, J. W. White, & A. E. Kazdin (Eds.), *Violence against women and children: Navigating solutions* (Vol. 2, pp. 261–306). Washington, DC: American Psychological Association.

Kossek, E. E., & Lambert, S. J. (2005). *Work and life integration: Organizational, cultural, and individual perspectives*. Mahwah, NJ: Erlbaum.

Kostiainen, E., Martelin, T., Kestilä, L., Martikainen, P., & Koskinen, S. (2009). Employee, partner, and mother: Woman's three roles and their implications for health. *Journal of Family Issues, 30*, 1122–1150.

Krahé, B., & Krause, C. (2010). Presenting thin media models affects women's choice of diet or normal snacks. *Psychology of Women Quarterly, 3*, 349–355.

Kramer, A., Lorenzon, D., & Mueller, G. (2004, January/February). Prevalence of intimate partner violence and health implications for women using emergency departments and primary care clinics. *Women's Health Issues, 14*, 19–29.

Kraus, M. W., Côté, S., & Keltner, D. (2010). Social class, contextualism, and empathic accuracy. *Psychological Science, 21*, 1716–1723.

Krieger, N., Chen, J. T., & Waterman, P. D. (2010). Decline in US breast cancer rates after the women's health initiative: Socioeconomic and racial/ethnic differentials. *American Journal of Public Health, 100*, S132–S139.

Kreiger, T. C. (2005, April). *Gender-atypical behavior in young children and its relation to social adjustment*. Poster presented at the meeting of the Society for Research in Child Development, Atlanta, GA.

Kristof, N. D., & WuDunn, S. (2009). *Half the sky: Turning oppression into opportunity for women worldwide*. New York: Alfred A. Knopf.

Kroenke, C. H., Kubzansky, L. D., Schernhammer, E. S., Holmes, M. D., & Kawachi, I. (2006). Social networks, social support, and survival after breast cancer diagnosis. *Journal of Clinical Oncology, 24*, 1105–1111.

Kroenke, C. H., et al. (2004). Functional impact of breast cancer by age at diagnosis. *Journal of Clinical Oncology, 22*, 1849–1856.

Kronenfeld, L. W., Reba-Harrelson, L., Von Holle, A., Reyes, M. L., & Bulik, C. M. (2010). Ethnic and racial differences in body size perception and satisfaction. *Body Image, 7*, 131–136.

Kronish, I. M., Rieckmann, N., Schwartz, J. E., Schwartz, D. R., & Davidson, K. W. (2009). Is depression after an acute coronary syndrome simply a marker of known prognostic factors for mortality? *Psychosomatic Medicine, 71,* 697–703.

Krumrei, E., Coit, C., Martin, S., Fogo, W., & Mahoney, A. (2007). Post-divorce adjustment and social relationships: A meta-analytic review. *Journal of Divorce and Remarriage, 46,* 145–166.

Krupp, C. (2008). *How not to look old.* New York: Springboard Press.

Kuchment, A. (2006, January 30). Beating back the blues. *Newsweek,* p. 62.

Kuhlmann, E., & Annandale, E. (2010). Bringing gender to the heart of health policy, practice and research. In E. Kuhlmann & E. Annandale (Eds.), *The Palgrave handbook of gender and healthcare* (pp. 1–18). New York: Palgrave Macmillan.

Kuhn, J. (2005, Winter). Feminism and childbirth (part 2 of 2). *Feminist Psychologist,* p. 5.

Kuhn, M. (1991). *No stone unturned.* New York: Ballatine Books.

Kulik, L. (2010). Women's experiences with volunteering: A comparative analysis by stages of the life cycle. *Journal of Applied Social Psychology, 40,* 360–388.

Kulik, L., & Havusha-Morgenstern, H. (2011). Does cohabitation matter? Differences in initial marital adjustment among women who cohabited and those who did not. *Families in Society, 92,* 120–127.

Kumra, S., & Vinnicombe, S. (2008). A study of the promotion to partner process in a professional services firm: How women are disadvantaged. *British Journal of Management, 19,* S65–S74.

Kunstman, J. W., & Maner, J. K. (2011). Sexual overperception: Power, mating motives, and biases in social judgment. *Journal of Personality and Social Psychology, 100,* 282–294.

Kuperberg, A., & Stone, P. (2008). The media depiction of women who opt out. *Gender & Society, 22,* 497–517.

Kurdek, L. A. (2008). Change in relationship quality for partners from lesbian, gay male, and heterosexual couples. *Journal of Family Psychology, 22,* 701–711.

Kurtz-Costes, B., Rowley, S. J., Harris-Britt, A., & Woods, T. A. (2008). Gender stereotypes about mathematics and science and self-perceptions of ability in late childhood and early adolescence. *Merrill-Palmer Quarterly, 54,* 386–409.

Kuyper, L., & Fokkema, T. (2009). Loneliness among older lesbian, gay, and bisexual adults: The role of minority stress. *Archives of Sexual Behavior, 39,* 1171–1180.

Kvaavik, E., Batty, G. D., Ursin, G., Huxley, R., & Gale, C. R. (2010). Influence of individual and combined health behaviors on total and cause-specific mortality in men and women: The United Kingdom health and lifestyle survey. *Archives of Internal Medicine, 170,* 711–718.

Kwon, P., & Hugelshofer, D. S. (2010). The protective role of hope for lesbian, gay, and bisexual individuals facing a hostile workplace climate. *Journal of Gay & Lesbian Mental Health, 14,* 3–18.

Lacey, K. K. (2010). When is it enough for me to leave? Black and Hispanic women's response to violent relationships. *Journal of Family Violence, 25,* 669–677.

Lachance-Grzela, M., & Bouchard, G. (2010). Why do women do the lion's share of the housework? A decade of research. *Sex Roles, 63,* 767–780.

Lachs, M. (2010). *Treat me, not my age.* New York: Penguin.

Ladge, J. J., Greenberg, D., & Clair, J. A. (2011). What to expect when she's expecting: Work family and identity integration challenges and opportunities of "soon-to-be" working professional mothers. In S. Kaiser, M. J. Ringlstetter, D. R. Eikhof, & M. Pina e Cunha (Eds.), *International perspectives on the work-life integration of professionals* (pp. 143–155). Berlin Heidelberg: Springer-Verlag.

LaFrance, M. (2001). Gender and social interaction. In R. K. Unger (Ed.), *Handbook of the psychology of women and gender* (pp. 245–255). New York: Wiley.

LaFrance, M., Hecht, M. A., & Paluck, E. L. (2003). The contingent smile: A meta-analysis of sex differences in smiling. *Psychological Bulletin, 129,* 305–334.

LaFraniere, S. (2005, February 18). AIDS and custom leave African families nothing. *New York Times,* pp. A1, A6.

LaFraniere, S. (2009, April 11). Study shows extent of gender imbalance in China. *New York Times,* p. A5.

LaFromboise, T. D., Heyde, A. M., & Ozer, E. J. (1990). Changing and diverse roles of women in American Indian cultures. *Sex Roles, 22,* 455–476.

Lai, Y., & Hynie, M. (2011). A tale of two standards: An examination of young adults' endorsement of gendered and ageist sexual double standards. *Sex Roles, 64,* 360–371.

Lakoff, R. T. (1990). *Talking power: The politics of language.* New York: Basic Books.

Lalor, K., & McElvaney, R. (2010). Child sexual abuse, links to later sexual exploitation/high-risk sexual behavior, and prevention treatment programs. *Trauma, Violence, & Abuse, 11,* 159–177.

Lam, L. C. W., et al. (2009). Modality of physical exercise and cognitive function in Hong Kong older Chinese community. *International Journal of Geriatric Psychiatry, 24,* 48–53.

Lamb, S. (2006). *Packaging girlhood: Rescuing our daughters from marketers' schemes.* New York: St. Martin's Press.

Lamb, S. (2010). Toward a sexual ethics curriculum: Bringing philosophy and society to bear on individual development. *Harvard Educational Review, 80,* 81–105.

Lambdin, J. R., et al. (2003). The animal 5 male hypothesis: Children's and adults' beliefs about the sex of non-sex specific stuffed animals. *Sex Roles, 48,* 471–482.

Landesman, P. (2004, January 25). The girls next door. *New York Times Magazine,* pp. 30–39, 66–67, 72–75.

Lane, M., & Etaugh, C. (2001, July). *Is stereotyping of females declining in children's books? It depends on the measure you use.* Poster presented at the meeting of the Seventh European Congress of Psychology, London.

Laner, M. R., & Ventrone, N. A. (1998). Egalitarian daters/ traditionalist dates. *Journal of Family Issues, 19,* 468–477.

Lang, M. M., & Risman, B. J. (2006). Blending into equality: Family diversity and gender convergence. In K. Davis, M. Evans, & J. Lorber (Eds.), *Handbook of gender and women's studies* (pp. 287–303). London: SAGE Publications.

Langhinrichsen-Rohling, J. (2010a). Controversies involving gender and intimate partner violence in the United States. *Sex Roles, 62,* 179–193.

Langhinrichsen-Rohling, J. (2010b). Controversies involving gender and intimate partner violence: Response to commentators. *Sex Roles, 62,* 221–225.

Langhout, R. D., Bergman, M. E., Cortina, L. M., Fitzgerald, L. F., Drasgow, F., & Williams, J. H. (2005). Sexual harassment severity: Assessing situational and personal determinants and outcomes. *Journal of Applied Social Psychology, 35,* 975–1007.

Langhout, R. D., & Mitchell, C. A. (2008). Engaging contexts: Drawing the link between student and teacher experiences of the hidden curriculum. *Journal of Community & Applied Social Psychology, 18,* 593–614.

Lansford, J. E. (2009). Parental divorce and children's adjustment. *Perspectives on Psychological Science, 4,* 140–152.

Lansford, J. E., Yu, T., Erath, S. A., Pettit, G. S., Bates, J. E., & Dodge, K. A. (2010). Development precursors of number of sexual partners from ages 16 to 22. *Journal of Research on Adolescence, 20,* 651–677.

Lapchick, R. (2010). *The 2009 racial and gender report card: College sport.* Orlando, FL: Institute for Diversity and Ethics in Sport.

Lareau, A., & Weininger, E. (2008). Time, work, and family life: Reconceptualizing gendered time patterns through the case of children's organized activities. *Sociological Forum, 23*, 419–454.

Larker, J. (2010). *Gender inequality: Feminist theory and politics* (4th ed.). New York: Oxford University Press.

L'Armand, K., et al. (2002, June). *Faculty-student romances: Effects of respondent gender and student status on judgments.* Poster presented at the meeting of the American Psychological Society, New Orleans.

Larose, S., Ratelle, C. F., Guay, F., Senécal, C., Harvey, M., & Drouin, E. (2008). A sociomotivational analysis of gender effects on persistence in science and technology: A 5-year longitudinal study. In H. M. G. Watt & J. S. Eccles (Eds.), *Gender and occupational outcomes: Longitudinal assessments of individual, social, and cultural influences* (pp. 171–192). Washington, DC: American Psychological Association.

Larson, S. C., Bergkvist, L., & Wolk, A. (2009). Glycemic load, glycemic index and breast cancer risk in a prospective cohort of Swedish women. *International Journal of Cancer, 125*, 153–157.

Lasswell, M. (2002). Marriage and family. In S. G. Kornstein & A. H. Clayton (Eds.), *Women's mental health: A comprehensive textbook* (pp. 515–526). New York: Guilford.

Latzer, Y., Lavee, Y., & Gal, S. (2009). Marital and parent child relationships in families with daughters who have eating disorders. *Journal of Family Issues, 30*, 1201–1220.

Laumann, E. O., Das, A., & Waite, L. J. (2008). Sexual dysfunction among older adults: Prevalence and risk factors from a nationally representative U.S. probability sample of men and women 57–85 years of age. *Journal of Sexual Medicine, 5*, 2300–2311.

Laumann, E. O., Leitsch, S. A., & Waite, L. J. (2008). Elder mistreatment in the United States: Prevalence estimates from a nationally representative study. *Journal of Gerontology, 63B*, S248–S254.

Laumann, E. O., et al. (2004). *The sexual organization of the city.* Chicago, IL: University of Chicago Press.

Laumann, E. O., & Mahay, J. (2002). The social organization of women's sexuality. In G. M. Wingood & R. J. DiClemente (Eds.), *Handbook of women's sexual and reproductive health* (pp. 43–70). New York: Kluwer Academic/Plenum.

Laumann, E. O., Paik, A., & Rosen, R. C. (1999). Sexual dysfunction in the United States: Prevalence and predictors. *Journal of the American Medical Association, 281*, 537–544.

Laursen, B., & Collins, W. A. (2009). Parent-child relationships during adolescence. In R. M. Lerner & L. Steinberg (Eds.), *Handbook of adolescent psychology* (3rd ed., Vol. 2, pp. 3–42). Hoboken, NJ: Wiley.

Lauzen, M. M. (2003). *The celluloid ceiling: Behind-the-scenes and on-screen employment of women in the top 250 films of 2002.* Retrieved from MoviesByWomen.com

Lauzen, M. M., Doxier, D. M., & Horan, N. (2008). Constructing gender stereotypes through social roles in prime-time television. *Journal of Broadcasting & Electronic Media, 52*, 200–214.

Lauzen, M. M., & Dozier, D. M. (2002). You look mahvelous: An examination of gender and appearance comments in the 1999–2000 prime-time season. *Sex Roles, 46*, 429–437.

Lavie, C. J., & Milani, R. (2009). Secondary coronary prevention in women: It starts with cardiac rehabilitation, exercise, and fitness. *Journal of Women's Health, 18*, 1115–1117.

Lawrence, E., Cobb, R. J., Rothman, A. D., Rothman, M. T., & Bradbury, T. N. (2008). Marital satisfaction across the transition to parenthood. *Journal of Family Psychology, 22*, 41–50.

Lawrence, E., Nylen, K., & Cobb, R. J. (2007). Prenatal expectations and marital satisfaction over the transition to parenthood. *Journal of Family Psychology, 21*, 155–164.

Laws, lies and the abortion debate. (2010, March 10). *New York Times*, p. A26.

Lawton, C. A., Blakemore, J. E. O., & Vartanian, L. R. (2003). The new meaning of Ms.: Single, but too old for miss. *Psychology of Women Quarterly, 27*, 215–220.

Lax, J. R., & Phillips, J. H. (2009). Gay rights in the states: Public opinion and policy responsiveness. *American Political Science Review, 103*, 367–386.

Leach, C. R., & Schoenberg, N. E. (2007). The vicious cycle of inadequate early detection: A complementary study on barriers to cervical cancer screening among middle-aged and older women. *Preventing Chronic Disease, 4*. Retrieved from http://www.cdc.gov/pcd/issues/2007/oct/06_0189.htm

Leach, C. R., Schoenberg, N. E., & Hatcher, J. (2011). Factors associated with participation in cancer prevention and control studies among rural Appalachian women. *Family & Community Health, 34*, 119–125.

Leach, P., et al. (2006). Child care before 6 months of age: A qualitative study of mothers' decisions and feelings about employment and non-maternal care. *Infant and Child Development, 15*, 471–502.

Leaper, C. (2000). The social construction and socialization of gender during development. In P. H. Miller & E. K. Scholnick (Eds.), *Toward a feminist developmental psychology* (pp. 127–152). Florence, KY: Taylor & Francis/Routledge.

Leaper, C. (2002). Parenting girls and boys. In M. H. Bornstein (Ed.), *Handbook of parenting* (2nd ed., pp. 189–225). Mahwah, NJ: Erlbaum.

Leaper, C. (2004, July). Gender-related variations in affiliative and assertive speech: Meta-analyses. Paper presented at the American Psychological Association Convention, Honolulu.

Leaper, C., & Arias, D. M. (2011). College women's feminist identity: A multidimensional analysis with implications for coping with sexism. *Sex Roles, 64*, 475–490.

Leaper, C., & Ayers, M. M. (2007). A meta-analytic review of gender, variations in adults' language use: Talkativeness, affiliative speech, and assertive speech. *Personality and Social Psychology Review, 11*, 328–363.

Leaper, C., & Brown, C. S. (2008). Perceived experiences with sexism among adolescent girls. *Child Development, 79*, 685–704.

Leaper, C., & Friedman, C. K. (2007). The socialization of gender. In J. E. Grusec & P. D. Hastings (Eds.), *Handbook of socialization: Theory and research* (pp. 561–587). New York: Guilford.

Leaper, C., & Robnett, R. D. (2011). Women are more likely than men to use tentative language, aren't they? A meta-analysis testing for gender differences and moderators. *Psychology of Women Quarterly, 35*, 129–142.

Leaper, C., & Smith, T. E. (2004). A meta-analytic review of gender variations in children's language use: Talkativeness, affiliative speech, and assertive speech. *Developmental Psychology, 40*, 993–1027.

Leary, W. E. (1998, September 29). Older people enjoy sex, survey says. *New York Times*, p. B16.

Leathwood, C., & Read, B. (2009). *Gender and the changing face of higher education: A feminized future?* Berkshire, UK: Open University Press.

Lebensohn, P. (2010). Physical activity. In V. Maizes & T. Low Dog (Eds.), *Integrative women's health* (pp. 47–64). New York: Oxford University Press.

Lee, C., & Gramotnev, H. (2007). Life transitions and mental health in a national cohort of young Australian women. *Developmental Psychology, 43*, 877–888.

Lee, I. (2007). Dose-response relation between physical activity and fitness. *Journal of the American Medical Association, 297*, 2137–2138.

Lee, I.-M., Djoussé, L., Sesso, H. D., Wang, L., & Buring, J. E. (2010). Physical activity and weight gain prevention. *Journal of the American Medical Association, 303*, 1173–1179.

Lee, J. (2008). "A kotex and a smile": Mothers and daughters at menarche. *Journal of Family Issues, 29,* 1325–1347.

Lee, J. (2009). Bodies at menarche: Stories of shame, concealment, and sexual maturation. *Sex Roles, 60,* 615–627.

Lee, J. 8. (2007, May 10). The incredible flying granny nanny. *New York Times,* pp. El, E7.

Lee, L., Howes, C., & Chamberlain, B. (2007). Ethnic heterogeneity of social networks and cross-ethnic friendships of elementary school boys and girls. *Merrill-Palmer Quarterly, 53,* 325–346.

Lee, S. (2004). The new girls network: Women, technology, and feminism. In V. Labaton & D. L. Martin (Eds.), *The fire this time* (pp. 84–104). New York: Anchor Books.

Lee, S. (2007). *Keeping moms on the job: The impacts of health insurance and child care on job retention and mobility among low-income mothers.* Washington, DC: Institute for Women's Policy Research.

Lee, T. L., Fiske, S. T., & Glick, P. (2010). Next gen ambivalent sexism: Converging correlates, causality in context, and converse causality, and introduction to the special issue. *Sex Roles, 62,* 395–404.

Lee, Y., & Park, K. (2008). Does physical activity moderate the association between depressive symptoms and disability in older adults? *International Journal of Geriatric Psychiatry, 23,* 249–256.

Leeb, R. T., & Rejskind, F. G. (2004). Here's looking at you, kid! A longitudinal study of perceived gender differences in mutual gaze behavior in young infants. *Sex Roles, 50,* 1–14.

Lefkowitz, E. S., & Fingerman, K. L. (2003). Positive and negative emotional feelings and behaviors in mother-daughter ties in late life. *Journal of Family Psychology, 17*(4), 607–617.

Lefkowitz, E. S., & Zeldow, P. B. (2006). Masculinity and femininity predict optimal mental health: A belated test of the androgyny hypothesis. *Journal of Personality Assessment, 87,* 95–101.

Lehavot, K., Walters, K., & Simoni, J. (2009). Abuse, mastery, and health among lesbian, bisexual, and two-spirit American Indian and Alaska Native women. *Cultural Diversity and Ethnic Minority Psychology, 15,* 275–284.

Lehr, S. (2001a). The anomalous female and the ubiquitous male. In S. Lehr (Ed.), *Beauty, brains, and brawn: The construction of gender in children's literature* (pp. 193–207). Portsmouth, NH: Heinemann.

Lehr, S. (Ed.). (2001b). *Beauty, brains, and brawn: The construction of gender in children's literature.* Portsmouth, NH: Heinemann.

Lehti, A. H., Johansson, E. E., Bengs, C., Danielsson, U., & Hammarström, A. (2010). "The Western gaze"—an analysis of medical research publications concerning the expressions of depression, focusing on ethnicity and gender. *Health Care for Women International, 31,* 100–112.

Leibson-Hawkins, B. (2004). *I'm too young to have breast cancer.* Washington, DC: Regnery Publishing.

Leicht, K. T. (2008). Broken down by race and gender? Sociological explanations of new sources of earnings inequality. *Annual Review of Sociology, 34,* 237–255.

Leitner, M. J., & Leitner, S. F. (2004). *Leisure in later life* (3rd ed.). Binghamton, NY: Haworth.

Leland, J. (2004, March 23). He's retired, she's working, they're not happy. *New York Times,* pp. A1, A18.

Leman, P. J., Ahmed, S., & Ozarow, L. (2005). Gender, gender relations, and the social dynamics of children's conversations. *Developmental Psychology, 41,* 64–74.

Leman, P. J., & Lam, V. L. (2008). The influence of race and gender on children's conversations and playmate choices. *Child Development, 79,* 1329–1343.

Lemieux, S. R., & Byers, E. S. (2008). The sexual well-being of women who have experienced child sexual abuse. *Psychology of Women Quarterly, 32,* 126–144.

Lemme, B. H. (2006). *Development in adulthood* (4th ed.). Boston, MA: Allyn & Bacon.

Lengua, L. J., & Stormshok, E. A. (2000). Gender, gender roles, and personality: Gender differences in the prediction of coping and psychological symptoms. *Sex Roles, 42,* 787–819.

LePage-Lees, P. (1997). Struggling with a nontraditional past: Academically successful women from disadvantaged backgrounds discuss their relationship with "disadvantage." *Psychology of Women Quarterly, 21,* 365–385.

Lerner, J. S., Castellino, D. R., Lolli, E., & Wan, S. (2002). Children, families and work: Research findings and implications for policies and programs. In R. M. Lerner, F. Jacobs, & D. Wertlieb (Eds.), *Handbook of applied developmental science* (Vol. 1, pp. 281–304). Thousand Oaks, CA: Sage.

Lerner, S. (2010). *The war on moms: On life in a family-unfriendly nation.* Hoboken, NJ: Wiley.

Lerner-Veva, L., Boyko, V., Blumstein, T., & Benyamini, Y. (2010). The impact of education, cultural background, and lifestyle on symptoms of the menopausal transition: The women's health at midlife study. *Journal of Women's Health, 19,* 975–985.

LeSavoy, B. (2011). Women's studies. In M. Z. Stange, C. K. Oyster, & J. E. Sloan (Eds.), *Encyclopedia of women in today's world.* Newberry Park, CA: Sage.

Lesbian teacher loses job after wedding. (2010, November 12). Retrieved November 12, 2010, from upi.com: http://www.upi.com/Top_News/US/2010/11/12/Lesbian-teacher-loses-job-after-wedding/UPI-20521289581171/

Leskinen, E. A., Cortina, L. M., Kabat, D. B. (2011). Gender harassment: Broadening our understanding of sex-based harassment at work. *Law and Human Behavior, 35,* 25–39.

Lester, D., & Yang, B. (1998). *Suicide and homicide in the twentieth century: Changes over time.* Commack, AL: Nova Science.

Levant, R., Richmond, K., Cook, S., House, A. T., & Aupont, M. (2007). The femininity ideology scale: Factor structure, reliability, convergent and discriminant validity, and social contextual variation. *Sex Roles, 57,* 373–383.

Levesque, M. J., Nave, C. S., & Lowe, C. A. (2006). Toward and understanding of gender differences in inferring sexual interest. *Psychology of Women Quarterly, 30,* 150–158.

Levine, A. D. (2010). Self-regulation, compensation, and the ethical recruitment of oocyte donors. *Hastings Center Report, 40,* 25–36.

Levine, M. (2004, June 1). Tell the doctor all your problems, but keep it to less than a minute. *New York Times,* p. F6.

Levine, M. P., & Smolak, L. (2009). Recent developments and promising directions in the prevention of negative body image and disordered eating in children and adolscents. In L. Smolak & J. K. Thompson (Eds.), *Body image, eating disorders, and obesity in youth: Assessment, prevention, and treatment* (pp. 215–240). Washington, DC: American Psychological Association.

Levison, S. P., & Straumanis, J. (2002, September/October). FIPSE: Changing medical education forever. *Change,* pp. 19–26.

Levy, B. (2009). Stereotype embodiment: A psychological approach to aging. *Current Directions in Psychological Science, 18,* 332–336.

Levy, G. D., Zimmerman, B., Barber, J., Martin, N., & Malone, C. (1998, May). *Preverbal awareness of gender roles in toddlers.* Poster presented at the meeting of the American Psychological Society, Washington, DC.

Lew, A. S., Allen, R., Papouchis, N., & Ritzler, B. (1998). Achievement orientation and fear of success in Asian American college students. *Journal of Clinical Psychology, 54,* 97–108.

Lewin, J. (2010). Depression in women. In D. Kohen (Ed.), *Oxford textbook of women and mental health* (pp. 93–101). Oxford, UK: Oxford University Press.

Lewin, T. (2010, January 27). After long decline, teenage pregnancy rates rise. *New York Times*, p. A14.

Lewis, C. (2010). Meeting the leadership challenges of women with disabilities: Mobility International USA. In G. Kirk & M. Okazawa-Rey (Eds.), *Women's lives: Multicultural perspectives* (5th ed., pp. 621–624). Boston, MA: McGraw-Hill.

Lewis, J. (2010). *Work-family balance, gender and policy*. Northampton, MA: Elgar.

Li, Q., Kirby, R. S., Sigler, R. T., Hwang, S.-S., LaGory, M. E., & Goldenberg, R. L. (2010). A multilevel analysis of individual, household, and neighborhood correlates of intimate partner violence among low-income pregnant women in Jefferson County, Alabama. *American Journal of Public Health, 100*, 531–539.

Liao, L.-M., Michala, L., & Creighton, S. M. (2009). Labial surgery for well women: A review of the literature. *BJOG, 117*, 20–25.

Liben, L., & Christensen, A. E. (2011). Spatial development: Evolving approaches to enduring questions. In V. Gaswami (Ed.), *The Wiley-Blackwell handbook of childhood development* (2nd ed., pp. 446–472). West Sussex, UK: Wiley-Blackwell.

Liben, L. S., et al. (2002). The effects of sex steroids on spatial performance: A review and an experimental clinical investigation. *Developmental Psychology, 38*, 236–253.

Lichtenstein, A. H., Rasmussen, H., Yu, W. W., Epstein, S. R., & Russell, R. M. (2008). Modified MyPyramid for older adults. *Journal of Nutrition, 138*, 78–82.

Liechty, T., & Yarnal, C. M. (2010). Older women's body image: A lifecourse perspective. *Ageing and Society, 30*, 1197–1218.

Lien, L., Haavet, O. R., & Dalgard, F. (2010). Do mental health and behavioural problems of early menarche persist into late adolescence? A three year follow-up study among adolescent girls in Oslo, Norway. *Social Science & Medicine, 71*, 529–533.

Liljestrand, J., & Gryboski, K. (2002). Women at risk of maternal mortality. In E. Murphy (Ed.), *Reproductive health and rights: Reaching the hardly reached* (pp. 121–128). Washington, DC: Program for Appropriate Technology in Health.

Lindau, S. T., & Gavrilova, N. (2010). Sex, health, and years of sexually active life gained due to good health: Evidence from two US population based cross sectional surveys of aging. *BMJ, 340*, c810.

Lindberg, L. D., Santelli, J. S., & Singh, S. (2006). Changes in formal sex education: 1995–2002. *Perspectives on Sexual and Reproductive Health, 38*, 182–189.

Lindberg, S. M., Grabe, S., & Hyde, J. S. (2007). Gender, pubertal development, and peer sexual harassment predict objectified body consciousness in early adolescence. *Journal of Research on Adolescence, 17*, 723–742.

Lindberg, S. M., Hyde, J. S., & Hirsch, L. M. (2008). Gender and mother-child interactions during mathematics homework: The importance of individual differences. *Merrill-Palmer Quarterly, 54*, 232–255.

Lindberg, S., Hyde, J., Petersen, J., & Linn, M. (2010). New trends in gender and mathematics performance: A meta-analysis. *Psychological Bulletin, 136*, 1123–1135.

Lindgren, K. P., Parkhill, M. R., George, W. H., & Hendershot, C. S. (2008). Gender differences in perceptions of sexual intent: A qualitative review and integration. *Psychology of Women Quarterly, 32*, 423–439.

Lindner, K. (2004). Images of women in general interest and fashion magazine advertisements from 1955 to 2002. *Sex Roles, 51*, 409–421.

Lindsey, E. W., & Mize, J. (2001). Contextual differences in parent-child play: Implications for children's gender role development. *Sex Roles, 44*, 155–176.

Linn, M. C., & Petersen, A. C. (1985). Emergence and characterization of sex differences in spatial ability: A meta-analysis. *Child Development, 56*, 1479–1498.

Linsk, N., Mason, S., Fendrich, M., Bass, M., Prubhughate, P., & Brown, A. (2009). No matter what I do they still want their family: Stressors for African American grandparents and other relatives. *Journal of Family Social Work, 12*, 25–43.

Lipka, S. (2007, April 2). At 35th-anniversary conference, backer of Title IX discuss challenges to women's sports. *Chronicle of Higher Education Today's News*. Retrieved from http://chronicle.com/daily/2007/04/2007040203n.htm

Lipka, S. (2010, March 16). Support for gay marriage is greater among college freshmen than Americans at large. *Chronicle of Higher Education*. Retrieved from http://chronicle.com/article/College-Freshmen-Approve-of/64685/

Lipkin, E. (2009). *Girls' studies*. Berkeley, CA: Seal Press.

Lippa, R. A. (2005). *Gender, nature, and nurture* (2nd ed.). Mahwah, NJ: Erlbaum.

Lippa, R. A. (2008). Sex differences and sexual orientation differences in personality: Findings from the BBC Internet survey. *Archives of Sexual Behavior, 37*, 173–187.

Lips, H. M. (1997). *Sex and gender: An introduction* (3rd ed.). Mountain View, CA: Mayfield.

Lips, H. M. (2010). Stalking a moving target: Thirty years of summarizing a changing field for changing students. *Sex Roles, 62*, 159–165.

Lips, H. M., & Lawson, K. (2009). Work values, gender, and expectations about work commitment and pay: Laying the groundwork for the "motherhood penalty"? *Sex Roles, 61*, 667–676.

Liptak, A., & Greenhouse, S. (2010, December 7). Supreme Court agrees to hear Wal-Mart appeal. *New York Times*, p. B1.

Liss, M., Crawford, M., & Popp, D. (2004). Predictors and correlates of collective action. *Sex Roles, 50*, 771–779.

Little, M. V. (2005). Getting your financial priorities straight. *Journal of the American Medical Women's Association, 60*, 9–10.

Littlefield, G. D., et al. (2000). Common themes in long-term lesbian relationships. *Family Therapy, 27*, 71–79.

Littleton, H., Axsom, D., & Grills-Taquechel, A. (2009). Sexual assault victims' acknowledgment status and revictimization risk. *Psychology of Women Quarterly, 33*, 34–42.

Liu, H. (2009). Till death do us part: Marital status and U.S. mortality trends, 1986–2000. *Journal of Marriage and Family, 71*, 1158–1173.

Liu, H., & Umberson, D. J. (2008). The times they are a changin': Marital status and health differentials from 1972 to 2003. *Journal of Health and Social Behavior, 49*, 239–253.

Liu-Ambrose, T., Nagamatsu, L. S., Graf, P., Beattie, B. L., Ashe, M. C., & Handy, T. C. (2010). Resistance training and executive functions: A 12-month randomized controlled trial. *Archives of Internal Medicine, 170*, 170–178.

Livengood, J. L. (2010). *Exploring predictors of perceptions of mothers and children in various work/family situations*. Unpublished master's thesis, Kansas State Univeristy, Manhattan, KS.

Livingston, G., & Cohen, D. (2010). *The new demography of American motherhood*. Washington, DC: Pew Research Center.

Livingston, G., & Parker, K. (2010). *Since the start of the great recession, more children raised by grandparents*. Washington, DC: Pew Research Center.

Livosky, M., Pettijohn, T. F., II., & Capo, J. R. (2008). *Reducing sexist attitudes by completing a psychology of gender course*. Poster presented at the meeting of the Association for Psychological Science, Chicago, IL.

Lloyd, C. B., Grant, M., & Ritchie, A. (2008). Gender differences in time use among adolescents in developing countries: Implications of rising school enrollment rates. *Journal of Research on Adolescence, 18*, 99–120.

Lloyd-Jones, D., et al. (2009). Heart disease and stroke statistics 2010 update. A report from the American Heart Association. *Circulation, 121*, 948–954.

Lo Sasso, A. T., Richards, M. R., Chou, C.-F., & Gerber, S. E. (2011). The $16,819 pay gap for newly trained physicians: The unexplained trend of men earning more than women. *Health Affairs, 30,* 193–201.

Lock, J., LeGrange, D., Agras, W. S., Moye, A., Bryson, S. W., & Jo, B. (2010). Randomized clinical trial comparing family-based treatment with adolescent-focused individual therapy for adolescents with anorexia nervosa. *Archives of General Psychiatry, 67,* 1025–1032.

Lockwood, G., Rosenthal, P., & Budjnaovcanin, A. (2011). A quantitative and qualitative analysis of sexual harassment claims 1995–2005. *Industrial Relations Journal, 42,* 86–103.

Logan, J. E., Smith, S. G., & Stevens, M. R. (2011, January 14). Homicides—United States, 1999–2007. *Morbidity and Mortality Weekly Report, 60*(Suppl.), 67–70.

Logan, T. K., & Walker, R. (2009). Partner stalking: Psychological dominance or "business as usual"? *Trauma, Violence, & Abuse, 10,* 247–270.

Logan, T. K., & Walker, R. (2010). Toward a deeper understanding of the harms caused by partner stalking. *Violence and Victims, 25,* 450–455.

Logan, T. K., Walker, R., & Hunt, G. (2009). Understanding human trafficking in the United States. *Trauma, Violence, & Abuse, 10,* 3–30.

Logel, C., Walton, G. W., Spencer, S. J., Iserman, E. C., von Hippel, W., & Bell, A. E. (2009). Interacting with sexist men triggers social identity threat among female engineers. *Journal of Personality and Social Psychology, 96,* 1089–1103.

Logsdon-Conradsen, S. (2011). Pregnancy. In M. Z. Stange, C. K. Oyster, & J. E. Sloan (Eds.), *Encyclopedia of women in today's world.* Newberry Park, CA: Sage.

Lonborg, S. D., & Hackett, G. (2006). Career assessment and counseling for women. In W. B. Walsh & M. J. Heppner (Eds.), *Handbook of career counseling for women* (2nd ed., pp. 103–166). Mahwah, NJ: Erlbaum.

London, K., Bruck, M., Ceci, S. J., & Shuman, D. W. (2007). Disclosure of child sexual abuse: A review of the contemporary empirical literature. In M.-E. Pipe, M. E. Lamb, Y. Orbach, & A.-C. Cederborg (Eds.), *Child sexual abuse: Disclosure, delay, and denial* (pp. 11–40). Mahwah, NJ: Erlbaum.

Long, C. (2009). "I don't know who to blame": HIV-positive South African women navigating heterosexual infection. *Psychology of Women Quarterly, 33,* 321–333.

Lonsway, K. A., Cortina, L. M., & Magley, V. J. (2008). Sexual harassment mythology: Definition, conceptualization, and measurement. *Sex Roles, 58,* 599–615.

Lorber, J. (2010). *Gender inequality: Feminist theories and politics* (4th ed.). New York: Oxford University Press.

Lott, B. (2010). *Multiculturalism and diversity: A social psychological perspective.* Malden, MA: Wiley-Blackwell.

Lott, B., & Bullock, H. E. (2001, Summer). Who are the poor? *Journal of Social Issues, 57,* 189–206.

Lott, B., & Bullock, H. (2010). Social class and women's lives. *Psychology of Women Quarterly, 3,* 421–422.

Lott, B., & Maluso, D. (2001). Gender development: Social learning. In J. Worell (Ed.), *Encyclopedia of women and gender* (pp. 537–549). San Diego, CA: Academic Press.

Loughran, D. S., & Zissimopoulos, J. M. (2009). Why wait? The effect of marriage and childbearing on the wages of men and women. *Journal of Human Resources, 44,* 326–349.

Lovas, G. S. (2005). Gender and patterns of emotional availability in mother-toddler and father-toddler dyads. *Infant Mental Health Journal, 26,* 327–353.

Love, S., & Mills, D. J. (2010). Breast cancer. In V. Maizes & T. Low Dog (Eds.), *Integrative women's health* (pp. 348–365). New York: Oxford University Press.

Love, S. M. (2010). *Dr. Susan Love's breast book* (5th ed). Philadelphia, PA: Da Capo Press.

Lovejoy, M., & Stone, P. (2011). Opting back in: The influence of time at home on professional women's career redirection after opting out. *Gender, Work and Organization.* doi:10.111 1/j.1468-0432.2010.00550

Lovell, V., O'Neill, E., & Olsen, S. (2007, August). *Maternity leave in the United States: Paid parental leave is still not standard, even among the best U.S. employers* [Fact sheet]. Washington, DC: Institute for Women's Policy Research.

Low Dog, T., & Maizes, V. (2010). Women's health: An epilogue. In V. Maizes & T. Low Dog (Eds.), *Integrative women's health* (pp. 660–670). New York: Oxford University Press.

Lowe, M. R., Bunell, D. W., Neeren, A. M., Chernyak, Y., & Greberman, L. (2010). Evaluating the real-world effectiveness of cognitive-behavior therapy efficacy research on eating disorders: A case study from a community-based clinical setting. *International Journal of Eating Disorders, 44,* 9–18.

Luanaigh, C. O., & Lawlor, B. A. (2008). Loneliness and the health of older people. *International Journal of Geriatric Psychiatry, 23,* 1213–1221.

Lucas, R. E., Clark, A. E., Georgellis, Y., & Diener, E. (2003). Reexamining adaptation and the set point model of happiness: Reactions to changes in marital status. *Journal of Personality and Social Psychology, 84,* 527–539.

Lucas-Thompson, R. G., Goldberg, W. A., & Prause, J. (2010). Maternal work early in the lives of children and its distal associations with achievement and behavior problems: A meta-analysis. *Psychological Bulletin, 135,* 915–942.

Luce, H., Schrager, S., & Gilchrist, V. (2010). Sexual assault of women. *American Family Physician, 81,* 489–495, 496.

Luciano, L. (2003). The economics of young women today. In C. B. Costello, V. R. Wight, & A. J. Stone (Eds.), *The American woman 2003–2004: Daughters of a revolution—Young women today* (pp. 143–163). New York: Palgrave Macmillan.

Luft, R. E. (2009). Intersectionality and the risk of flattening difference: Gender and race logics, and the strategic use of anti-racist singularity. In M. T. Berger & K. Guidroz (Eds.), *The intersectional approach: Transforming the academy through race, class, and gender* (pp. 100–117). Chapel Hill, NC: University of North Carolina Press.

Luijendijk, H. J., et al. (2008). Incidence and recurrence of late-life depression. *Archives of General Psychiatry, 65,* 1394–1401.

Lummis, M., & Stevenson, H. W. (1990). Gender differences in beliefs and achievement: A cross-cultural study. *Developmental Psychology, 26,* 254–563.

Lumpkin, J. R. (2008). Grandparents in a parental or near-parental role. *Journal of Family Issues, 29,* 357–372.

Lundberg-Love, P., & Faulkner, D. L. (2008). Stress and health. In M. A. Paludi (Ed.), *The psychology of women at work: Challenges and solutions for our female workforce: Self, family, and social affects* (Vol. 3, pp. 59–83). Westport, CT: Praeger.

Lundberg-Love, P., & Waits, B. (2010). Women and sexual violence: Emotional, physical, behavioral, and organizational responses. In M. A. Paludi (Ed.), *Feminism and women's rights worldwide: Mental and physical health* (Vol. 2, pp. 41–64). Santa Barbara, CA: Praeger.

Lussier, G., Deater-Deckard, K., Dunn, J., & Davies, L. (2002). Support across two generations: Children's closeness to grandparents following parental divorce and remarriage. *Journal of Family Psychology, 16,* 363–376.

Luthar, H. K., & Luthar, V. K. (2007). A theoretical framework explaining cross-cultural sexual harassment: Integrating Hofstede and Schwartz. *Journal of Labor Research, 28,* 169–188.

Lydon-Rochelle, M. T. (2004). Minimal intervention—nurse-midwives in the United States. *New England Journal of Medicine, 351,* 1929–1931.

Lykes, M. B., Coquillon, E., & Rabenstein, K. L. (2010). Theoretical and methodological challenges in participatory community-based research. In H. Landrine & N. F. Russo (Eds.), *Handbook of diversity in feminist psychology* (pp. 55–82). New York: Springer.

Lyness, K. S., Thompson, C. A., Francesco, A. M., & Judiesch, M. K. (1999). Work and pregnancy: Individual and organizational factors influencing organizational commitment, timing of maternity leave, and return to work. *Sex Roles, 41,* 485–508.

Lyons, H. Z., Brenner, B. R., & Lipman, J. (2010). Patterns of career and identity interference for lesbian, gay, and bisexual young adults. *Journal of Homosexuality, 57,* 503–524.

Maas, C. D., Fleming, C. B., Herrenkohl, T. I., & Catalano, R. F. (2010). Childhood predictors of teen dating violence victimization. *Violence and Victims, 25,* 131–149.

Mabry, M. (2007). *Twice as good: Condoleezza Rice and her path to power.* New York: Modern Times.

MacCallum, F., Golombok, S., & Brinsden, P. (2007). Parenting and child development in families with a child conceived through embryo donation. *Journal of Family Psychology, 21,* 278–287.

Maccoby, E. E. (1998). *The two sexes: Growing up apart, coming together.* Cambridge, MA: Harvard University Press.

Maccoby, E. E., & Jacklin, C. N. (1974). *The psychology of sex differences.* Stanford, CA: Stanford University Press.

Macdonald, C. L. (2010). *Shadow mothers: Nannies, au pairs, and the micropolitics of mothering.* Berkeley: University of California Press.

MacDorman, M. F., Menacker, F., & Declercq, E. (2010). *Trends and characteristics of home and other out-of-hospital births in the United States, 1990–2006. National Vital Statistics Reports, 58*(11). Hyattsville, MD: National Center for Health Statistics.

MacGeorge, E. L., et al. (2004). The myth of gender cultures: Similarities outweigh differences in men's and women's provision of and responses to supportive communication. *Sex Roles, 50,* 143–175.

Mackenzie, E. R., & Rakel, B. (2010). Healthy aging: The whole woman approach. In V. Maizes & T. Low Dog (Eds.), *Integrative women's health* (pp. 646–659). New York: Oxford University Press.

Mackey, E. R., & La Greca, A. M. (2008). Does this make me look fat? Peer crowd and peer contributions to adolescent girls' weight control behaviors. *Journal of Youth and Adolescence, 37,* 1097–1110.

Macy, R. J., Giattina, M. C., Parish, S. L., & Crosby, C. (2010). Domestic violence and sexual assault services: Historical concerns and contemporary challenges. *Journal of Interpersonal Violence, 25,* 3–32.

Magai, C., Consedine, N., Neugut, A. I., & Hershman, D. L. (2007). Common psychosocial factors underlying breast cancer screening and breast cancer treatment adherence: A conceptual review and synthesis. *Journal of Women's Health, 16,* 11–23.

Mager, J. & Helgeson, J. G. (2011). Fifty years of advertising images: Some changing perspectives on role portrayals along with enduring consistencies. *Sex Roles, 64,* 238–252.

Magley, V. J., Gallus, J. A., & Bunk, J. A. (2010). The gendered nature of workplace mistreatment. In J. C. Chrisler & D. R. McCreary (Eds.), *Handbook of gender research in psychology* (Vol. 2, pp. 423–441). New York: Springer.

Magley, V. J., & Shupe, E. I. (2005). Self-labeling sexual harassment. *Sex Roles, 53,* 173–189.

Maguen, S., & Shipherd, J. C. (2010). Suicide risk among transgender individuals. *Psychology & Sexuality, 1,* 34–43.

Maine, D., & Chavkin, W. (2002, Summer). Maternal mortality: Global similarities and differences. *Journal of the Medical Women's Association, 57,* 127–130.

Maine, M., McGilley, B. H., & Bunnell, D. (Eds.). (2010). *Treatment of eating disorders: Bridging the research-practice gap.* London, UK: Elsevier.

Mainiero, L. A., Gibson, D. E., & Sullivan, S. E. (2008). Retrospective analysis of gender differences in reaction to media coverage of crisis events: New insights on the justice and care orientations. *Sex Roles, 58,* 556–566.

Majerovitz, S. D. (2006). Physical health and illness in older women. In J. Worell & C. D. Goodheart (Eds.), *Handbook of girls' and women's psychological health: Gender and well-being across the lifespan* (pp. 379–387). New York: Oxford University Press.

Major, B., Appelbaum, M., Beckman, L., Dutton, M. A., Russo, N. F., & West, C. (2009). Abortion and mental health: Evaluating the evidence. *American Psychologist, 64,* 863–890.

Major, B., Cozzarelli, C., Cooper, L., Zubek, J., Richards, C., Wilhite, M., & Gramzow, R. H. (2000). Psychological responses of women after first-trimester abortion. *Archives of General Psychiatry, 57,* 777–784.

Makela, L. (2011). A narrative approach to pregnancy-related discrimination and leader-follower relationships. *Gender, Work and Organization.* doi:10.1111/j.1468-0432.2010.00544

Malanchuk, O., & Eccles, J. S. (2006). Self-esteem. In J. Worell & C. D. Goodheart (Eds.), *Handbook of girls' and women's psychological health: Gender and well-being across the life span* (pp. 149–156). New York: Oxford University Press.

Malcolmson, K. A., & Sinclair, L. (2007). The Ms. stereotype revisited: Implicit and explicit facets. *Psychology of Women Quarterly, 31,* 305–310.

Malley-Morrison, K. (Ed.). (2004). *International perspectives on family violence and abuse.* Mahwah, NJ: Erlbaum.

Malson, H., & Burns, M. (Eds.). (2009). *Critical feminist approaches to eating dis/orders.* New York: Routledge.

Manago, A. M., Brown, C. S., & Leaper, C. (2009). Feminist identity among Latina adolescents. *Journal of Adolescent Research, 24,* 750–776.

Manganello, J. A. (2008). Teens, dating violence, and media use: A review of the literature and conceptual model for future research. *Trauma, Violence, & Abuse, 9,* 3–18.

Mangweth-Matzek, B., et al. (2006). Never too old for eating disorders or body dissatisfaction: A community study of elderly women. *International Journal of Eating Disorders, 39,* 583–586.

Maniglio, R. (2009). The impact of child sexual abuse on health: A systematic review of reviews. *Clinical Psychology Review, 29,* 647–657.

Manlove, J., Ikramullah, E., Mincieli, L., Holcombe, E., & Danish, S. (2009). Trends in sexual experience, contraceptive use, and teenage childbearing: 1992–2002. *Journal of Adolescent Health, 44,* 413–423.

Manlove, J., Logan, C., Moore, K. A., & Ikramullah, E. (2008). Pathways from family religiosity to adolescent sexual activity and contraceptive use. *Perspectives on Sexual and Reproductive Health, 40,* 105–117.

Manlove, J., Ryan, S., & Franzetta, K. (2003). Patterns of contraceptive use within teenagers' first sexual relationships. Perspectives on Sexual and Reproductive Health, 35, 246–255.

Mannheim Research Institute for the Economics of Aging. (2005). *Health, ageing, and retirement in Europe.* Mannheim, Germany: Author.

Manning, W. D., Flanigan, C. M., Giordano, P. C., & Longmore, M. A. (2009). Relationship dynamics and consistency of condom use among adolescents. *Perspectives on Sexual and Reproductive Health, 41,* 181–190.

Mannino, C. A., & Deutsch, F. M. (2007). Changing the division of household labor: A negotiated process between partners. *Sex Roles, 56,* 309–324.

Mansfield, K. C. (2011). Single-sex education. In M. Z. Stange, C. K. Oyster, & J. E. Sloan (Eds.), *Encyclopedia of women in today's world.* Newberry Park, CA: Sage.

Manthorpe, J., & Iliffe, S. (2010). Suicide in later life: Public health and practitioner perspectives. *International Journal of Geriatric Psychiatry, 25,* 1230–1238.

Manuel, T., & Zambrana, R. E. (2009). Exploring the intersections of race, ethnicity, and class on maternity leave decisions: Implications for public policy. In B. T. Dill & R. E. Zambrana (Eds.), *Emerging intersections: Race, class, and gender in theory, policy, and practice* (pp. 123–149). Piscataway, NJ: Rutgers University Press.

Manzoli, L., Villari, P., Pirone, G. M., & Boccia, A. (2007). Marital status and mortality in the elderly: A systematic review and meta-analysis. *Social Science & Medicine, 64,* 77–94.

Marano, H. E. (1997, July 1). Puberty may start at 6 as hormones surge. *New York Times,* pp. B9, B12.

March of Dimes. (2009). *Pregnancy after 35.* White Plains, NY: Author. Retrieved from http://www.marchofdimes.com/professionals/14332_1155.asp

Marcus, E. N. (2008, May 20). Screening for abuse may be key to ending it. *New York Times,* p. F5.

Marecek, J., Crawford, M., & Popp, D. (2004). On the construction of gender, sex, and sexualities. In A. H. Eagly, A. E. Beall, & R. J. Sternberg (Eds.), *The psychology of gender* (2nd ed., pp. 192–216). New York: Guilford.

Mares, M.-L., & Fitzpatrick, M. A. (2004). Communication in close relationships of older people. In J. F. Nussbaum & J. Coupland (Eds.), *Handbook of communication and aging research* (2nd ed., pp. 231–250). Mahwah, NJ: Erlbaum.

Markey, C. N., & Markey, P. M. (2009). Correlates of young women's interest in obtaining cosmetic surgery. *Sex Roles, 61,* 158–166.

Markovic, M., Manderson, L., & Warren, N. (2008). Pragmatic narratives of hysterectomy among Australian women. *Sex Roles, 58,* 467–476.

Marks, S. R., & Leslie, L. A. (2008). Intersectionality and work-family studies. In S. Coontz (Ed.), *American families: A multicultural reader* (2nd ed., pp. 245–257). New York: Taylor & Francis.

Markson, E. W., & Taylor, C. A. (1993). Real versus reel world: Older women and the academy awards. In N. D. Davis, E. Cole, & E. Rothblum (Eds.), *Faces of women and aging* (pp. 157–175). New York: Harrington Park Press.

Markward, M., & Yegidis, B. (2011). *Evidence-based practice with women: Toward effective social work practice with low-income women.* Thousand Oaks, CA: Sage.

Marlino, D., & Wilson, F. (2006). Career expectations and goals of Latina adolescents: Results from a nationwide study. In J. Denner & B. L. Guzmán (Eds.), *Latina girls: Voices of adolescent strength in the United States* (pp. 123–137). New York: New York University Press.

Marriage and the transition to parenthood. (2010). In T. N. Bradbury & B. R. Karney (Eds.), *Intimate relationships* (pp. 576–578). New York: W. W. Norton & Company, Inc.

Marsh, P. A., & Keith, T. M. (2011). Addiction and substance abuse. In M. Z. Stange, C. K. Oyster, & J. E. Sloan (Eds.), *Encyclopedia of women in today's world* (Vol. 1, pp. 20–23). Newberry Park, CA: Sage.

Marshal, M. P., Friedman, M. S., Stall, R., & Thompson, A. L. (2009). Individual trajectories of substance use in lesbian, gay and bisexual youth and heterosexual youth. *Addiction, 104,* 974–981.

Marshall, N. L., & Barnett, R. C. (1993). Work-family strains and gains among two-earner couples. *Journal of Community Psychology, 21,* 64–78.

Martijn, C., Smeets, E., Jansen, A., Hoeymans, N., & Schoemaker, C. (2009). Don't get the message: The effect of a warning text before visiting a proanorexia website. *International Journal of Eating Disorders, 42,* 139–145.

Martin, C. L. (1995). Stereotypes about children with traditional and nontraditional gender roles. *Sex Roles, 33,* 727–751.

Martin, C. L., & Dinella, L. M. (2001). Gender development: Gender schema theory. In J. Worell (Ed.), *Encyclopedia of women and gender* (pp. 507–521). San Diego, CA: Academic Press.

Martin, C. L., & Ruble, D. N. (2010). Patterns of gender development. *Annual Review of Psychology, 61,* 353–381.

Martin, C. L., Ruble, D. N., & Szkrybalo, J. (2002). Cognitive theories of early gender development. *Psychological Bulletin, 128,* 903–933.

Martin, J. L., & Ross, H. S. (2005). Sibling aggression: Sex differences and parents' reactions. *International Journal of Behavioral Development, 29,* 129–138.

Martin, J. A., et al. (2009). *Births: Final data for 2006. National Vital Statistics Reports, 57*(7). Hyattsville, MD: National Center for Health Statistics.

Martin, J. A., et al. (2011). *Births: Final data for 2009.* National Vital Statistics Reports, 60(1). Hyattsville, MD: National Center for Health Statistics.

Martin, J. L. (2008a). Gendered violence on campus: Unpacking bullying, harassment, and stalking. In M. A. Paludi (Ed.), *Understanding and preventing campus violence* (pp. 3–26). Westport, CT: Praeger.

Martin, J. L. (2008b). Shifting the load: Personality factors and women in the workplace. In M. A. Paludi (Ed.), *The psychology of women at work: Challenges and solutions for our female workforce: Career liberation, history, and the new millennium* (Vol. 1, pp. 153–200). Westport, CT: Praeger.

Martin, J. L. (2010). Gender differences: The arguments regarding abilities. In M. A. Paludi (Ed.), *Feminism and women's rights worldwide* (Vol. 1, pp. 27–42). Santa Barbara, CA: Praeger.

Martin, K. A., & Kazyak, E. (2009). Hetero-romantic love and heterosexiness in children's G-rated films. *Gender & Society, 23,* 315–336.

Martin, K. A., & Luke, K. (2010). Gender differences in the ABC's of the birds and the bees: What mothers teach young children about sexuality and reproduction. *Sex Roles, 62,* 278–291.

Martin, M. O., Mullis, I. V., & Foy, P. (2009). *TIMSS 2007 international mathematics report.* Boston, MA: Boston College.

Martin, N., Williams, D. C., Harrison, K., & Ratan, R. A. (2009). A content analysis of female body imagery in video games. *Sex Roles, 61,* 824–836.

Martin, S. E. (2010). "Outsider within" the station house: The impact of race and gender on Black women police. In J. Goodman (Ed.), *Global perspectives on gender & work* (pp. 260–277). Lanham, MD: Rowman & Littlefield.

Martin, S. L., Macy, R. J., & Young, S. K. (2011). The impact of sexual violence against women: Health and economic consequences. In J. White, M. P. Koss, & A. Kazdin (Eds.), *Violence against women and children* (Vol. 1, pp. 173–195). Washington, DC: American Psychological Association.

Martinengo, G. J., Jacob, J. I., & Hill, E. J. (2010). Gender and the work-family interface: Exploring differences across the family life course. *Journal of Family Issues, 31,* 1363–1390.

Martinez, S. (2005). Women's intrinsic and extrinsic motivations for working. In B. Schneider & L. J. Waite (Eds.), *Being together, working apart: Dual-career families and the work-life balance* (pp. 79–101). Cambridge, MA: Cambridge University Press.

Martire, L. M., & Parris Stephens, M. A. (2003). Juggling parent care and employment responsibilities: The dilemmas of adult daughter caregivers in the workforce. *Sex Roles, 48*, 167–173.

Marton, K. (2004, May 10). A worldwide gender gap. *Newsweek*, p. 94.

Martsolf, D. S., & Draucker, C. B. (2005). Psychotherapy approaches for adult survivors of childhood sexual abuse: An integrative review of outcomes research. *Mental Health Nursing: Journal of the Psychiatric Nurses Association, 26*, 801–825.

Marván, M. L., Islas, M., Vela, L., Chrisler, J. C., & Warren, E. A. (2008). Stereotypes of women in different stages of their reproductive life: Data from Mexico and the United States. *Health Care for Women International, 29*, 673–687.

Maserejian, N. N., Link, C. L., Lutfey, K. L., Marceau, L. D., & McKinlay, J. B. (2009). Disparities in physicians' interpretations of heart disease symptoms by patient gender: Results of a video vignette factorial experiment. *Journal of Women's Health, 18*, 1661–1667.

Masser, B., Grass, K., & Nesic, M. (2007). "We like you, but we don't want you"—the impact of pregnancy in the workplace. *Sex Roles, 57*, 703–712.

Massey, E. K., Gebhardt, W. A., & Garnefski, N. (2008). Adolescent goal content and pursuit: A review of the literature from the past 16 years. *Developmental Review, 28*, 421–460.

Massoni, K. (2004). Modeling work: Occupational messages in Seventeen magazine. *Gender & Society, 18*, 47–65.

Mastro, D. E., & Greenberg, B. S. (2000, Fall). The portrayal of racial minorities on prime time television. *Journal of Broadcasting & Electronic Media*, 690–703.

Masuy, A. J. (2009). Effect of caring for an older person on women's lifetime participation in work. *Ageing and Society, 29*, 745–763.

Mather, S. (2008). Women and coronary heart disease. In A. L. Clouse & K. Sherif (Eds.), *Women's health in clinical practice: A handbook for primary care* (pp. 71–96). Totowa, NJ: Humana Press.

Mathias, M. B. (2008). Religion and women at work. In M. A. Paludi (Ed.), *The psychology of women at work: Challenges and solutions for our female workforce: Self, family, and social affects* (Vol. 3, pp. 109–141). Westport, CT: Praeger.

Matlin, M. W. (2001, May). *Wise and wonderful . . . or wrinkled and wretched: How psychologists and the rest of the world view older women.* Invited address presented at the Midwestern Psychological Association, Chicago, IL.

Matlin, M. W. (2003). From menarche to menopause: Misconceptions about women's reproductive lives. *Psychology Science, 45*, 106–122.

Mattis, J. S. (2002). Religion and spirituality in the meaning-making and coping experiences of African American women: A qualitative analysis. *Psychology of Women Quarterly, 26*, 309–321.

Maume, D. J. (2008). Gender differences in providing urgent childcare among dual-earner parents. *Social Forces, 87*, 273–297.

Mauthner, N. S. (2002). *The darkest days of my life: Stories of postpartum depression.* Cambridge, MA and London: Harvard University Press.

Mavin, S. (2008). Queen bees, wannabees and afraid to bees: No more "best enemies" for women in management? *British Journal of Management, 19*, S75–S84.

Maxwell, J., Belser, J. W., & David, D. (2007). *A health handbook for women with disabilities.* Berkeley, CA: Hesperian.

Maxwell, M., et al. (2010). Life beyond the eating disorder: Education, relationships, and reproduction. *International Journal of Eating Disorders, 44*, 225–232.

Mayer, K. H., Bradford, J. B., Makadon, H. J., Stall, R., Goldhammer, H., & Landers, S. (2008). Sexual and gender

minority health: What we know and what needs to be done. *American Journal of Public Health, 98*, 989–995.

Maynard, R., & Hoffman, S. D., (2008). The costs of adolescent childbearing. In S. D. Hoffman & R. Maynard (Eds.), *Kids having kids: Economic costs and social consequences of teen pregnancy* (2nd ed., pp. 359–402). Washington, DC: Urban Institute Press.

Mazzeo, S. E., Mitchell, K. S., & Williams, L. J. (2008). Anxiety, alexithymia, and depression as mediators of the association between childhood abuse and eating disordered behavior in African American and European American women. *Psychology of Women Quarterly, 32*, 267–280.

McAdams, D. P., & Cox, K. S. (2010). Self and identity across the life span. In M. E. Lamb & A. M. Freund (Eds.), *The handbook of life-span development: Social and emotional development* (Vol. 2, pp. 158–207). Hoboken, NJ: Wiley.

McCabe, S. E., Bostwick, W. B., Hughes, T. L., West, B. T., & Boyd, C. J. (2010). The relationship between discrimination and substance use disorders among lesbians, gay, and bisexual adults in the United States. *American Journal of Public Health, 100*, 1946–1952.

McCabe, S. E., Hughes, T. L., Bostwick, W. B., West, B. T., & Boyd, C. J. (2009). Sexual orientation, substance use behaviors and substance dependence in the United States. *Addiction, 104*, 1333–1345.

McCloskey, C., & Mintz, L. (2006). A culturally oriented approach for career counseling with Native American women. In W. B. Walsh & M. J. Heppner (Eds.), *Handbook of career counseling with women* (2nd ed., pp. 315–350). Mahwah, NJ: Erlbaum.

McConnell, A. R., & Fazio, R. H. (1996). Women as men and people: Effects of gender-marked language. *Personality & Social Psychology Bulletin, 22*, 1004–1013.

McDaniel, A., DiPrete, T. A., Buchmann, C., & Shwed, U. (in press). The Black gender gap in educational attainment: Historical trends and racial comparisons. *Demography.*

McDonald, P., Dear, K., & Backstrom, S. (2008). Expecting the worst: Circumstances surrounding pregnancy discrimination at work and progress to formal redress. *Industrial Relations Journal, 39*, 229–247.

McDonald, S., & Mair, C. A. (2010). Social capital across the life course: Age and gendered patterns of network resources. *Sociological Forum, 25*, 335–359.

McDonnell, K. (2010). Income of the elderly population age 65 and over, 2008. *Employee Benefit Research Institute Notes, 31*(6), 2–7.

McDougall, P., & Hymel, S. (2007). Same-gender versus cross-gender friendship conceptions: Similar or different? *Merrill-Palmer Quarterly, 53*, 347–380.

McDowell, M. A., Brody, D. J., & Hughes, J. P. (2007). Has age at menarche changed? Results from the national health and nutrition examination survey (NHANES) 1999–2004. *Journal of Adolescent Health, 40*, 227–231.

McFarlane, J., et al. (2010). Connecting the dots of heart disease, poor mental health, and abuse to understand gender disparities and promote women's health: A prospective cohort analysis. *Health Care for Women International, 31*, 313–326.

McGlone, M. S., & Aronson, J. (2006). Stereotype threat, identity salience, and spatial reasoning. *Journal of Applied Developmental Psychology, 27*, 486–493.

McGorty, E. K., Iyer, S. N., & Hunt, J. S. (2003, May). *The effect of patient sex on medical decision-making: A meta-analysis.* Paper presented at the meeting of the Midwestern Psychological Association, Chicago, IL.

McHale, S. M., Bissell, J., & Kim, J.-Y. (2009). Sibling relationship, family, and genetic factors in sibling similarity in sexual risk. *Journal of Family Psychology, 23*, 562–572.

McHale, S. M., & Crouter, A. C. (2008). Families as nonshared environments for siblings. In A. Booth, A. C. Crouter, S. M. Bianchi, & J. A. Seltzer (Eds.), *Intergenerational caregiving* (pp. 243–255). Washington, DC: Urban Institute Press.

McHale, S. M., Crouter, A. C., & Tucker, C. J. (1999). Family context and gender role socialization in middle childhood comparing girls to boys and sisters to brothers. *Child Development, 70,* 990–1004.

McHale, S. M., Crouter, A. C., & Tucker, C. J. (2001). Free-time activities in middle childhood: Links with adjustment in early adolescence. *Child Development, 72,* 1764–1778.

McHale, S. M., Kim, J.-Y., Dotterer, A. M., Crouter, A. C., & Booth, A. (2009). The development of gendered interests in personality qualities from middle childhood through adolescence: A biosocial analysis. *Child Development, 80,* 482–495.

McHale, S. M., Kim, J.-Y., Whiteman, S., & Crouter, A. C. (2004). Links between sex-typed time use in middle childhood and gender development in early adolescence. *Developmental Psychology, 40,* 868–881.

McHale, S. M., Shanahan, L., Updegraff, K. A., Crouter, A. C., & Booth, A. (2004). Developmental and individual differences in girls' sex-typed activities in middle childhood and adolescence. *Child Development, 75,* 1575–1593.

McHugh, M. C. (2007). Women and sex at midlife: Desire, dysfunction, and diversity. In V. Muhlbauer & J. C. Chrisler (Eds.), *Women over 50: Psychological perspectives* (pp. 26–52). New York: Springer.

McHugh, M. C. (2008). A feminist approach to agoraphobia: Challenging traditional views of women at home. In J. C. Chrisler, C. Golden, & P. D. Rozee (Eds.), *Lectures on the psychology of women* (pp. 392–417). New York: McGraw-Hill.

McIntyre, M. H., & Edwards, C. P. (2009). The early development of gender differences. *Annual Review of Anthropology, 38,* 83–97.

McIntyre, S. H., Newburn-Cook, C. V., O'Brien, B., & Demianczuk, N. N. (2009). Effect of older maternal age on the risk of spontaneous preterm labor: A population-based study. *Health Care for Women International, 30,* 670–689.

McKelvey, M. W., & McKenry, P. C. (2000). The psychosocial well-being of Black and White mothers following marital dissolution. *Psychology of Women Quarterly, 24,* 4–14.

McKenzie, M., & Rozee, P. (2010). Rape: A global perspective. In M. A. Paludi (Ed.), *Feminism and women's rights worldwide: Feminism as human rights* (Vol. 2, pp. 177–208). Santa Barbara, CA: Praeger.

McKibbin, W. F., Shackelford, T. K., Goetz, A. T., & Starratt, V. G. (2008). Why do men rape? An evolutionary psychological perspective. *Review of General Psychology, 12,* 86–97.

McKinley, N. M. (2006). The developmental and cultural contexts of objectified body consciousness: A longitudinal analysis of two cohorts of women. *Developmental Psychology, 42,* 679–687.

McLanahan, S., & Percheski, C. (2008). Family structure and the reproduction of inequalities. *Annual Review of Sociology, 34,* 257–276.

McLaren, S. (2009). Sense of belonging to the general and lesbian communities as predictors of depression among lesbians. *Journal of Homosexuality, 56,* 1–13.

McLaughlin, D., Adams, J., Vagenas, D., & Dobson, A. (2011). Factors which enhance or inhibit social support: A mixed-methods analysis of social networks in older women. *Ageing & Society, 31,* 18–33.

McLaughlin, K. A., Hatzenbuehler, M. L., & Keyes, K. M. (2010). Responses to discrimination and psychiatric disorders among black, hispanic, female, and lesbian, gay and bisexual individuals. *American Journal of Public Health, 100,* 1477–1484.

McLean, C. P., & Anderson, E. R. (2009). Brave men and timid women? A review of the gender differences in fear and anxiety. *Clinical Psychology Review, 29,* 496–505.

McLean, K. C., & Breen, A. V. (2009). Processes and content of narrative identity development in adolescence: Gender and well-being. *Developmental Psychology, 45,* 702–710.

McLean, S. A., Paxton, S. J., & Wertheim, E. H. (2010). Factors associated with body dissatisfaction and disordered eating in women in midlife. *International Journal of Eating Disorders, 43,* 527–536.

McNair, R., Szalacha, L. A., & Hughes, T. L. (2011). Health status, health service use, and satisfaction according to sexual identity of young Australian women. *Women's Health Issues, 21,* 40–47.

McPherson, B. J., Fitzpatrick, M. J., Armenta, M. I., Dale, J. A., & Miller, T. E. (2007, August). *Coloring within the lines: Gender stereotypes in children's coloring books.* Poster presented at the annual meeting of the American Psychological Association, San Francisco, CA.

McQuaide, S. (1998). Women at midlife. *Social Work, 43,* 21–31.

McTiernan, A. (2010). Physical activity, weight, diet, and breast cancer risk reduction. *Archives of Internal Medicine, 170,* 1792–1793.

Mead, S. (2006). *The evidence suggests otherwise: The truth about boys and girls.* Washington, DC: Education Sector.

Meadows, S. O. (2007). Evidence of parallel pathways: Gender similarity in the impact of social support on adolescent depression and delinquency. *Social Forces, 85,* 1143–1167.

Meana, M. (2010). Elucidating women's (hetero)sexual desire: Definitional challenges and content expansion. *Journal of Sex Research, 47,* 104–122.

Mechakra-Tahiri, S., Zunzunegui, M. V., Préville, M., & Dubé, M. (2009). Social relationships and depression among people 65 years and over living in rural and urban areas of Quebec. *International Journal of Geriatric Psychiatry, 24,* 1226–1236.

Media Awareness Network. (2010). *Media portrayal of girls and women.* Ottawa, ON: Author.

Mednick, M., & Thomas, V. (2008). Women and achievement. In F. L. Denmark & M. A. Paludi (Eds.), *Psychology of women: A handbook of issues and theories* (2nd ed., pp. 625–651). Westport, CT: Praeger.

Meece, J. L., & Scantlebury, K. (2006). Gender and schooling: Progress and persistent barriers. In J. Worell & C. D. Goodheart (Eds.), *Handbook of girls' and women's psychological health: Gender and well-being across the lifespan* (pp. 283–291). New York: Oxford University Press.

Meekosha, H. (2010, Fall). The complex balancing act of choice, autonomy, valued life, and rights: Bringing a feminist disability perspective to bioethics. *International Journal of Feminist Approaches to Bioethics, 3,* 1–8.

Meem, D. T., Gibson, M. A., & Alexander, J. F. (2010). *Finding out: An introduction to LGBT studies.* Thousand Oaks, CA: Sage.

Mehler, P. S. (2011). Medical complications of bulimia nervosa and their treatments. *International Journal of Eating Disorders, 44,* 95–104.

Mehler, P. S., & MacKenzie, T. D. (2009). Treatment of osteopenia and osteoporosis in anorexia nervosa: A systematic review of the literature. *International Journal of Eating Disorders, 42,* 195–201.

Mehta, C. M., & Strough, J. N. (2009). Sex segregation in friendships and normative contexts across the life span. *Developmental Review, 29,* 201–220.

Mehta, C. M., & Strough, J. N. (2010). Gender segratation and gender-typing in adolescence. *Sex Roles, 63,* 251–263.

Meier, A. M. (2007). Adolescent first sex and subsequent mental health. *American Journal of Sociology, 112,* 1811–1847.

Meier, A., Hull, K. E., & Ortyl, T. A. (2009). Young adult relationship values at the intersection of gender and sexuality. *Journal of Marriage and Family, 71,* 510–525.

Melendez de Santa Ana, T. (2008, September/October). Opening up the superintendency. *Leadership Magazine, 38*. Retrieved from http://www.acsa.org/FunctionalMenuCategories/Media/LeadershipMagazine/2008-archives/LeadershipCurrentIssue/OpeningtheSuperintedency.aspx

Mello, Z. R. (2008). Gender variation in development trajectories of educational and occupational expectations and attainment from adolescence to adulthood. *Developmental Psychology, 44*, 1069–1080.

Mellor, D., Fuller-Tyszkiewicz, M., McCabe, M. P., & Ricciardelli, L. A. (2010). Body image and self-esteem across age and gender: A short-term longitudinal study. *Sex Roles, 63*, 672–681.

Menacker, F., & Hamilton, B. E. (2010). *Recent trends in cesarean delivery in the United States. NCHS Data Brief, (35).* Hyattsville, MD: National Center for Health Statistics.

Mendle, J., et al. (2009). Associations between father absence and age of first sexual intercourse. *Child Development, 80*, 1463–1480.

Mendle, J., Turkheimer, E., & Emery, R. E. (2007). Detrimental psychological outcomes associated with early pubertal timing in adolescent girls. *Developmental Review, 27*, 151–171.

Mendelsohn, D. M., & Perry-Jenkins, M. (2007, March). *Relationship between parental sex-role ideologies and children's gender-typed attitudes.* Poster presented at the meeting of the Society for Research in Child Development, Boston, MA.

Menec, V. H. (2003). The relation between everyday activities and successful aging: A 6-year longitudinal study. *Journal of Gerontology: Social Sciences, 58B*, S74–S82.

Menzel, J. E., Schaefer, L. M., Burke, N. L., Mayhew, L. L., Brannick, M. T., & Thompson, J. K. (2010). Appearance-related teasing, body dissatisfaction, and disordered eating: A meta-analysis. *Body Image, 7*, 261–270.

Mercer, S. O., Garner, J. D., & Findley, J. (2001). Older women: A global view. In J. D. Garner & S. O. Mercer (Eds.), *Women as they age* (2nd ed., pp. 13–32). New York: Haworth.

Mercurio, A. E., & Landry, L. J. (2008). Self-objectification and well-being: The impact of self-objectification on women's overall sense of self-worth and life satisfaction. *Sex Roles, 58*, 458–466.

Merkin, D. (2004, May 2). Keeping the forces of decrepitude at bay. *New York Times*, pp. 64–67, 96–98.

Merline, A. C., et al. (2004). Substance use among adults 35 years of age: Prevalence, adulthood predictors, and impact of adolescent substance use. *American Journal of Public Health, 94*, 95–103.

Merz, C. N. B., et al. (2010). Proceedings from the scientific symposium: Sex differences in cardiovascular disease and implications for therapies. *Journal of Women's Health, 19*, 1059–1072.

Messersmith, E. E., Garrett, J. L., Davis-Kean, P. E., Malanchuk, O., & Eccles, J. S. (2008). Career development from adolescence through emerging adulthood: Insights from information technology occupations. *Journal of Adolescent Research, 23*, 206–227.

Messner, M. A., Duncan, M. C., & Jensen, K. (1993). Separating the men from the girls: The gendered language of televised sports. *Gender & Society, 7*, 121–137.

MetLife. (2010a). *The MetLife study of working caregivers and employer health care costs.* New York: Author.

MetLife. (2010b). *What today's woman needs to know and do: The new retirement journey.* New York: Author.

MetLife Mature Market Institute & the Lesbian and Gay Aging Issues Network of the American Society on Aging. (2010). Out and aging: The MetLife study of lesbian and gay baby boomers. *Journal of GLBT Family Studies, 6*, 40–57.

Metzl, J. M. (2003, Fall). Selling sanity through gender. *Ms.*, pp. 40–45.

Meyer, D. (2011). Sexual orientation-based social discrimination: United States. In M. Z. Stange, C. K. Oyster, & J. E. Sloan (Eds.), *Encyclopedia of women in today's world* (Vol. 3, pp. 1328–1330). Newberry Park, CA: Sage.

Meyer, E. J. (2009). *Gender, bullying, and harassment: Strategies to end sexism and homophobia in schools.* New York: Teachers College.

Meyer, I. H., & Wilson, P. A. (2009). Sampling lesbian, gay, and bisexual populations. *Journal of Counseling Psychology, 56*, 23–31.

Meyer, J. L., Gold, M. A., & Haggerty, C. L. (2011). Advance provision of emergency contraception among adolescent and young women: A systematic review of literature. *Journal of Pediatric and Adolescent Gynecology, 24*, 2–9.

Meyer, M. H., & Herd, P. (2007). *Market friendly or family friendly? The state and gender inequality in old age.* New York: Russell Sage Foundation.

Mezulis, A. H., Abramson, L. Y., Hyde, J. S., & Hankin, B. L. (2004). Is there a universal positivity bias in attributions? A meta-analytic review of individual, developmental, and cultural differences in the self-serving attributional bias. *Psychological Bulletin, 130*, 711–747.

Michael, S. T., Crowther, M. R., Schmid, B., & Allen, R. S. (2003). Widowhood and spirituality: Coping responses. *Journal of Women & Aging, 15*, 145–166.

Michael, Y. L., Berkman, L. F., Colditz, G. A., & Kawachi, I. (2001). Living arrangements, social integration, and change in functional health status. *American Journal of Epidemiology, 153*, 123–131.

Michaud, S. L., & Warner, R. M. (1997). Gender differences in self-reported response to troubles talk. *Sex Roles, 37*, 527–540.

Michelfelder, A. J. (2009). Soy: A complete source of protein. *American Family Physician, 79*, 43–47.

Mignon, S. I., Faiia, M. M., Myers, P. L., & Rubington, E. (2009). *Substance use and abuse: Exploring alcohol and drug issues.* Boulder, CO: Lynne Rienner.

Mihesuah, D. A. (2004). *American Indians: Stereotypes & realities.* Atlanta, GA: Clarity Press.

Milar, K. S. (2000). The first generation of women psychologists and the psychology of women. *American Psychologist, 55*, 616–620.

Milar, K. S. (2010, February). Overcoming "sentimental rot." *Monitor on Psychology, 41*, 26–27.

Milburn, S. S., Carney, D. R., & Ramirez, A. M. (2001). Even in modern media the picture is still the same: A content analysis of clipart images. *Sex Roles, 44*, 277–294.

Miles-Cohen, S. E., Keita, G. P., Twose, G. H. J., & Houston, S. J. (2010). Beyond mentoring: Opening doors and systems. In C. A. Rayburn, F. L. Denmark, M. E. Reuder, & A. M. Austria (Eds.), *A handbook for women mentors: Transcending barriers of stereotype, race, and ethnicity* (pp. 233–248). Santa Barbara, CA: Praeger.

Milke, M. A., Raley, S. B., & Bianchi, S. M. (2009). Taking on the second shift: Time allocations and time pressures of U.S. parents with preschoolers. *Social Forces, 88*, 487–517.

Milkie, M. M. (2011). Social and cultural resources for and constraints on new mothers' marriages. *Journal of Marriage and Family, 73*, 18–22.

Miller, A. K., Canales, E. J., Amacker, A. M., Backstrom, T. L., & Gidycz, C. A. (2011). Stigma-threat motivated nondisclosure of sexual assault and sexual revictimization: A prospective analysis. *Psychology of Women Quarterly, 35*, 119–128.

Miller, C. C. (2010, April 18). Out of the loop in Silicone Valley: In the wide-open world of tech, why so few women? *New York Times*, pp. BU1, BU8, BU9.

Miller, C. F., Trautner, H. M., & Ruble, D. N. (2006). The role of gender stereotypes in children's preferences and behavior. In L. Batter & C. S. Tamis-LeMonda (Eds.), *Child psychology: A handbook of contemporary issues* (2nd ed., pp. 293–323). New York: Psychology Press.

Miller, D. (2010). Premenstrual syndrome. In V. Maizes & T. Low Dog (Eds.), *Integrative women's health* (pp. 165–187). New York: Oxford University Press.

Miller, E., Jordan, B., Levenson, R., & Silverman, J. G. (2010). Reproductive coercion: Connecting the dots between partner violence and unintended pregnancy. *Contraception, 81,* 457–459.

Miller, F. P., Vandome, A. F., & McBrewster, J. (Eds.). (2009). Sex education. Beau-Bassin, Mauritius: Alphascript Publishing.

Miller, J., & Knudsen, D. D. (2007). *Family abuse and violence: A social problems perspective.* Lanham, MD: AltaMira Press.

Miller, J. B. (2008). How change happens: Controlling images, mutuality, and power. *Women & Therapy, 31,* 109–127.

Miller, K., Helmuth, A. S., & Farabee-Siers, R. (2009). *The need for paid parental leave for federal employees: Adapting to a changing workforce.* Washington, DC: Institute for Women's Policy Research.

Miller, L. (2011). Physical abuse in a college setting: A study of perceptions and participation in abusive dating relationships. *Journal of Family Violence, 26,* 71–80.

Miller, M. K., & Summers, A. (2007). Gender differences in video game characters' roles, appearances, and attire as portrayed in video game magazines. *Sex Roles, 57,* 733–742.

Miller, M. M., & James, L. E. (2009). Is the generic pronoun he still comprehended as excluding women? *American Journal of Psychology, 4,* 483–496.

Miller, Y. D., & Brown, W. J. (2005). Determinants of active leisure for women with young children—an "ethic of care" prevails. *Sport & Leisure Management, 27,* 405–420.

Miller-Day, M. A. (2004). *Communication among grandmothers, mothers, and adult daughters.* Mahwah, NJ: Erlbaum.

Milletich, R., Kelley, M., Doane, A., & Pearson, M. (2010). Exposure to interparental violence and childhood physical and emotional abuse as related to physical aggression in undergraduate dating relationships. *Journal of Family Violence, 25,* 627–637.

Mills, M., & Taht, K. (2010). Nonstandard work schedules and partnership quality: Quantitative and qualitative findings. *Journal of Marriage and Family, 72,* 860–875.

Milner, A., & DeLeo, D. (2010). Suicide research and prevention in developing countries in Asia and the Pacific. *Bulletin of the World Health Organization, 88,* 795–796.

Mindiola, T., Niemann, Y. F., & Rodríguez, N. (2002). *Brown-black relations and stereotypes.* Austin, TX: University of Texas Press.

Miner, J. L., & Clarke-Stewart, K. A. (2008). Trajectories of externalizing behavior from age 2 to age 9: Relations with gender, temperament, ethnicity, parenting, and rater. *Developmental Psychology, 44,* 771–786.

Minnotte, K. L., Cook, A., & Minnotte, M. C. (2010). Occupation and industry sex segregation, gender, and workplace support: The use of flexible scheduling policies. *Journal of Family Issues, 31,* 656–680.

Minto, C., Woodhouse, C., Ransley, P., & Creighton, S. (2003). The effect of clitoral surgery on sexual outcome in individuals who have intersex conditions with ambiguous genitalia: A cross-sectional study. *Lancet, 361,* 1252–1257.

Misa, T. J. (2010). *Gender codes: Women and men in the computing professions.* Hoboken, NJ: Wiley.

Mischel, W. (1966). A social-learning view of sex differences in behavior. In E. E. Maccoby (Ed.), *The development of sex differences* (pp. 56–81). Stanford, CA: Stanford University Press.

Misra, M. (2008). Long-term skeletal effects of eating disorders with onset in adolescence. *Annals of the New York Academy of Sciences, 1135,* 212–218.

MIT. (2011). *A report on the status of women faculty in the schools of science and engineering at MIT, 2011.* Cambridge, MA: Author.

Mitchell, B. A., & Lovegreen, L. D. (2009). The empty nest syndrome in midlife families: A multimethod exploration of parental gender differences and cultural dynamics. *Journal of Family Issues, 30,* 1651–1670.

Mitchell, C. (2009). *Intimate partner violence: A health-based perspective.* New York: Oxford University Press.

Mitchell, C., & Anglin, D. (2008). Intimate partner violence. In A. L. Clouse & K. Sherif (Eds.), *Women's health in clinical practice: A handbook for primary care* (pp. 355–384). Totowa, NJ: Humana Press.

Mitchell, K. S., & Mazzeo, S. E. (2009). Evaluation of a structural model of objectification theory and eating disorder symptomatology among European American and African American undergraduate women. *Psychology of Women Quarterly, 33,* 384–395.

Mitchell, V., & Green, R.-J. (2008). Different storks for different folks: Gay and lesbian parents' experiences with alternative insemination and surrogacy. *Journal of GLBT Family Studies, 3,* 81–104.

Mitnick, D. M., Heyman, R. E., & Slep, A. M. (2009). Changes in relationship satisfaction across the transition to parenthood: A meta-analysis. *Journal of Family Psychology, 23,* 848–852.

Mobily, K. E. (1992). Leisure, lifestyle, and lifespan. In M. L. Teague & R. D. MacNeil (Eds.), *Aging and leisure: Vitality in later life* (2nd ed., pp. 179–206). Dubuque, IA: Brown & Benchmark.

Moe, A. (2009). Are males always better than females in mental rotation? Exploring a gender belief explanation. *Learning and Individual Differences, 19,* 21–27.

Moen, P., Huang, Q., Plassmann, V., & Dentinger, E. (2006). Deciding the future: Do dual-earner couples plan together for retirement? *American Behavioral Scientist, 49,* 1–22.

Moen, P., Kim, J. E., & Hofmeister, H. (2001). Couples' work/retirement transitions, gender, and mental quality. *Social Psychology Quarterly, 64,* 55–71.

Moghadam, V. (2009). *Globalization and social movements: Islamism, feminism, and the global justice movement.* Lanham, MD: Rowman & Littlefield.

Moilanen, K. L., Crockett, L. J., Raffaelli, M., & Jones, B. L. (2010). Trajectories of sexual risk from middle adolescence to early adulthood. *Journal of Research on Adolescence, 20,* 114–139.

Molnar, B. E., Browne, A., Cerda, M., & Buka, S. L. (2005). Violent behavior by girls reporting violent victimization. *Archives of Pediatrics & Adolescent Medicine, 159,* 731–739.

Monahan, K. (2010). Themes of adult sibling sexual abuse survivors in later life: An initial exploration. *Clinical Social Work Journal, 38,* 361–369.

Monda, K. L., Ballantyne, C. M., & North, K. E. (2009). Longitudinal impact of physical activity on lipid profiles in middle-aged adults: The atherosclerosis risk in communities study. *Journal of Lipid Research, 50,* 1685–1691.

Mondschein, E. R., Adolph, K. E., & Tamis-LeMonda, C. S. (2000). Gender bias in mothers' expectations about infant crawling. *Journal of Experimental Child Psychology, 77,* 304–316.

Mongeau, P. A., Carey, C. M., & Williams, M. L. M. (1998). First date initiation and enactment: An expectancy violation approach. In D. J. Canary & K. Dindia (Eds.), *Sex differences and similarities in communication: Critical essays and empirical investigations of sex and gender in interaction* (pp. 413–426). Mahwah, NJ: Erlbaum.

Monin, J. K., Clark, M. S., & Lemay, E. P. (2008). Communal responsiveness in relationships with female versus male family members. *Sex Roles, 59,* 176–188.

Monsour, M. (2002). *Women and men as friends: Relationships across the life span in the 21st century.* Mahwah, NJ: Erlbaum.

Moonesinghe, R., Zhu, J., & Truman, B. I. (2011, January 14). Health insurance coverage—United States, 2004 and 2008. *Morbidity and Mortality Weekly Report, 60*(Suppl.), 35–37.

Moore, A. (2010). From victim to empowered survivor: Feminist therapy with survivors of rape and sexual assault. In M. A. Paludi (Ed.), *Feminism and women's rights worldwide: Mental and physical health* (Vol. 2). Santa Barbara, CA: Praeger.

Moore, D. (2007). Self perceptions and social misconceptions: The implications of gender traits for locus of control and life satisfaction. *Sex Roles, 56,* 767–780.

Moore, D. (Ed.). (2009). *Women's health for life.* New York: DK Publishing.

Moore, D. S., & Johnson, S. P. (2008). Mental rotation in human infants: A sex difference. *Psychological Science, 19,* 1063–1066.

Moore, S. E. H. (2008). Gender and the "new paradigm" of health. *Sociology Compass, 2,* 268–280.

Moos, R. (1985). *Premenstrual symptoms: A manual and overview of research with the menstrual distress questionnaire.* Stanford, CA: Stanford University.

Moradi, B. (2010). Addressing gender and cultural diversity in body image: Objectification theory as a framework for integrating theories and grounding research. *Sex Roles, 63,* 138–148.

Moradi, B., & DeBlaere, C. (2010). Women's experiences of sexist discrimination: Review of research and directions for centralizing race, ethnicity, and culture. In H. Landrine & N. F. Russo (Eds.), *Handbook of diversity in feminist psychology* (pp. 173–210). New York: Springer.

Moradi, B., & Huang, Y.-P. (2008). Objectification theory and psychology of women: A decade of advances and future directions. *Psychology of Women Quarterly, 32,* 377–398.

Moreau, R., & Yousafzai, S. (2004, October 11). "Living dead" no more. *Newsweek,* p. 37.

Moreman, R. D. (2008). Best friends: The role of confidants in older women's health. *Journal of Women & Aging, 20,* 149–167.

Morgan, B. L. (1996). Putting the feminism into feminism scales: Introduction of a liberal feminist attitude and ideology scale (LFAIS). *Sex Roles, 34,* 359–390.

Morgan, P., & Gruber, J. (2008). Sexual harassment and male dominance: Toward an ecological approach. In M. A. Paludi (Ed.), *The psychology of women at work: Challenges and solutions for our female workforce: Obstacles and the identity juggle* (Vol. 2, pp. 85–107). Westport, CT: Praeger.

Morgan, P., & Gruber, J. E. (2011). Sexual harassment: Violence prevention at work and in schools. In C. M. Renzetti, J. L. Edleson, & R. K. Bergen (Eds.), *Sourcebook on violence against women* (2nd ed., pp. 75–92). Thousand Oaks, CA: Sage.

Morr Serewicz, M.C. & Gale, E. (2008). First-date scripts: Gender roles, context, and relationship. *Sex Roles, 58,* 149–164.

Morris, E. W. (2007). "Ladies" or "loudies"? Perceptions and experiences of Black girls in classrooms. *Youth & Society, 38,* 490–515.

Morrison, G. Z. (2010). Two separate worlds: Students of color at a predominantly White university. *Journal of Black Studies, 40,* 987–1015.

Morrison, M. A., Morrison, T. G., & Sager, C. L. (2004, May). Does body satisfaction differ between gay men and lesbian women and heterosexual men and women? *Body Image, 1,* 127–138.

Morrison, T. G., Speakman, C., & Ryan, T. A. (2009). Irish university students' support for the human rights of lesbian women and gay men. *Journal of Homosexuality, 56,* 387–400.

Morrongiello, B. A., & Dawber, T. (2000). Mothers' responses to sons and daughters engaging in injury-risk behaviors on a playground: Implications for sex differences in injury rates. *Journal of Experimental Child Psychology, 76,* 89–103.

Morrongiello, B. A., & Hogg, K. (2004). Mothers' reactions to children misbehaving in ways that can lead to injury: Implications for gender differences in children's risk taking and injuries. *Sex Roles, 50,* 103–118.

Morrow-Howell, N. (2010). Volunteering in later life: Research frontiers. *Journal of Gerontology: Social Sciences, 65B,* 461–469.

Mortenson, J. (2011a). Lesbian adoption. In M. Z. Stange, C. K. Oyster, & J. E. Sloan (Eds.), *Encyclopedia of women in today's world* (Vol. 2, pp. 839–842). Newberry Park, CA: Sage.

Mortenson, J. (2011b). Midwifery. In M. Z. Stange, C. K. Oyster, & J. E. Sloan (Eds.), *Encyclopedia of women in today's world* (Vol. 2, pp. 951–954). Newberry Park, CA: Sage.

Morton, T. A., Postmes, T., Haslam, S. A., & Hornsey, M. J. (2009). Theorizing gender in the face of social change: Is there anything essential about essentialism? *Journal of Personality and Social Psychology, 96,* 653–664.

Mosack, K. E., Randolph, M. E., Dickson-Gomez, J., Abbott, M., Smith, E., & Weeks, M. R. (2010). Sexual risk-taking among high-risk urban women with and without histories of childhood sexual abuse: Mediating effects of contextual factors. *Journal of Child Sexual Abuse, 19,* 43–61.

Mosca, L., Ferris, A., Fabunmi, R., & Robertson, R. M. (2004). Tracking women's awareness of heart disease: An American Heart Association national study. *Circulation, 109,* 573–579.

Mosca, L., Mochari-Greenberger, H., Dolor, R. J., Newby, L. K., & Robb, K. J. (2010). Twelve-year follow-up of American women's awareness of cardiovascular disease risk and barriers to heart health [Advance online publication]. *Circulation: Cardiovascular Quality and Outcomes, 3.*

Moser, D. K., Dracup, K., & Wu, J. (2012). Cardiac denial and delay in treatment for myocardial infarction. In R. Alan & J. Fisher (Eds.), *Heart and mind: The practice of cardiac psychology* (2nd ed., pp. 305–326). Washington, DC: American Psychological Association.

Mosher, W. D., Chandra, A., & Jones, J. (2005). *Sexual behavior and selected health measures: Men and women 15–44 years of age, United States, 2002.* Advance Data from Vital and Health Statistics, 362. Hyattsville, MD: National Center for Health Statistics.

Mosher, W. D., & Jones, J. (2010). *Use of contraception in the United States: 1982–2008. NCHS Vital Health Statistics, 23*(29). Hyattsville, MD: *National Center for Health Statistics.*

Moskowitz, D. A., Rieger, G., & Roloff, M. E. (2010). Heterosexual attitudes toward same-sex marriage. *Journal of Homosexuality, 57,* 325–336.

Moss, N. W. (2008, October 21). A planet of pain, where no words are quite right. *New York Times,* p. D5.

Mother or nothing: The agony of infertility. (2010). *Bulletin of the World Health Organization, 88,* 881–882.

Mottarella, K. E., Fritzsche, B. A., Whitten, S. N., & Bedsole, D. (2009). Exploration of "good mother" stereotypes in the college environment. *Sex Roles, 60,* 223–231.

Moynihan, R., & Mintzes, B. (2010). *Sex, lies and pharmaceuticals: How drug companies plan to profit from female sexual dysfunction.* Vancouver, BC: Greystone Books.

Muehlenhard, C. L. (2011). Examining stereotypes about token resistance to sex. *Psychology of Women Quarterly, 35,* 676–683.

Muehlenhard, C. L., & Rodgers, C. S. (1998). Token resistance to sex: New perspectives on an old stereotype. *Psychology of Women Quarterly, 22,* 443–463.

Mueller, A. S., Pearson, J., Muller, C., Frank, K., & Turner, A. (2010). Sizing up peers: Adolescent girls' weight control and social comparison in the school context. *Journal of Health and Social Behavior, 51,* 64–78.

Muennig, P., Fiscella, K., Tancredi, D., & Franks, P. (2010). The relative health burden of selected social and behavioral risk factors in the United States: Implications for policy. *American Journal of Public Health, 100,* 1758–1764.

Muise, A., & Desmarais, S. (2010). Women's perceptions and use of "anti-aging" products. *Sex Roles, 63,* 126–137.

Mukherjee, J. S., Farmer, D. B., & Farmer, P. E. (2010). The AIDS pandemic and women's rights. In P. Murthy & C. L. Smith (Eds.), *Women's global health and human rights* (pp. 129–140). Sudbury, MA: Jones and Bartlett.

Mulac, A. (1998). The gender-linked language effect: Do language differences really make a difference? In D. J. Canary & K. Dindia (Eds.), *Sex differences and similarities in communication: Critical essays and empirical investigations of sex and gender in interaction* (pp. 127–153). Mahwah, NJ: Erlbaum.

Mulac, A., et al. (1998). "Uh-huh. What's that all about?" Differing interpretations of conversational backchannels and questions as sources of miscommunication across gender boundaries. *Communication Research, 25,* 641–668.

Mullis, I. V. S., Martin, M. O., Kennedy, A. M., & Foy, P. (2007). *IEA's progress in international reading literacy study in primary schools in 40 countries.* Boston, MA: Boston College.

Munk-Olsen, T., Laursen, T., Pedersen, C. B., Lidegaard, O., & Mortensen, P. B. (2011). Induced first-trimester abortion and risk of mental disorder. *New England Journal of Medicine, 364,* 332–339.

Muñoz, L. R., et al. (2010). Awareness of heart disease among female college students. *Journal of Women's Health, 19,* 2253–2259.

Munson, L. J., Miner, A. G., & Hulin, C. (2001). Labeling sexual harassment in the military: An extension and replication. *Journal of Applied Psychology, 86,* 293–303.

Murray, B. (1998, October). Survey reveals concerns of today's girls. *APA Monitor, 29,* 12.

Murray, D. P. (2011). Advertising, portrayal of women in. In M. Z. Stange, C. K. Oyster, & J. E. Sloan (Eds.), *Encyclopedia of women in today's world* (Vol. 1, pp. 36–39). Newberry Park, CA: Sage.

Murray, T., & Steil, J. (2000, August). *Construction of gender: Comparing children of traditional vs. egalitarian families.* Poster presented at the meeting of the American Psychological Association, Washington, DC.

Murray-Close, D., & Ostrov, J. M. (2009). A longitudinal study of forms and functions of aggressive behavior in early childhood. *Child Development, 80,* 828–842.

Murrell, A. J., Frieze, I. H., & Frost, J. L. (1991). Aspiring to careers in male- and female-dominated professions: A study of black and white college women. *Psychology of Women Quarterly, 15,* 103–126.

Murthy, P., Persaud, R. D., & Toda, M. (2010a). Human trafficking: A modern plague. In P. Murthy & C. L. Smith (Eds.), *Women's global health and human rights* (pp. 59–72). Sudbury, MA: Jones and Bartlett.

Murthy, P., Upadhyay, U. D., & Nwadinobi, E. (2010b). Violence against women and the girl-child: A silent global pandemic. In P. Murthy & C. L. Smith (Eds.), *Women's global health and human rights* (pp. 11–24). Sudbury, MA: Jones and Bartlett.

Muss, H. B., et al. (2009). Adjuvant chemotherapy in older women with early-stage breast cancer. *New England Journal of Medicine, 360,* 2055–2065.

Mustanski, B. S., et al. (2004). Genetic and environmental influences on pubertal development: Longitudinal data from Finnish twins at ages 11 and 14. *Developmental Psychology, 40,* 1188–1198.

Mustanski, B. S., Garofalo, R., & Emerson, E. M. (2010). Mental health disorders, psychological distress, and suicidality in a diverse sample of lesbian, gay, bisexual, and transgender youths. *American Journal of Public Health, 12,* 2426–2432.

Mutchler, J. E., & Baker, L. A. (2009). The implications of grandparent coresidence for economic hardship among children in mother-only families. *Journal of Family Issues, 30,* 1576–1597.

Muzio, C. (1996). Lesbians choosing children: Creating families, creating narratives. In J. Laird & R.-J. Green (Eds.), *Lesbians and gays in couples and families* (pp. 358–369). San Francisco, CA: Jossey-Bass.

Myaskovsky, L., & Wittig, M. A. (1997). Predictors of feminist social identity among college women. *Sex Roles, 37,* 861–883.

Myers, K., & Raymond, L. (2010). Elementary school girls and heteronormativity: The girl project. *Gender & Society, 24,* 167–188.

Myint, P. K., Luben, R. N., Wareham, N. J., Bingham, S. A., & Khaw, K.-T. (2009). Combined effect of health behaviors and risk of first ever stroke in 20,040 men and women over 11 years' follow-up in Norfolk cohort of European prospective investigation of cancer (EPIC Norfolk): Prospective population study. *BMJ, 338,* b349.

Nabi, H., Kivimaki, M., De Vogli, R., Marmot, M. G., & Singh-Manoux, A. (2008). Positive and negative affect and risk of coronary heart disease: Whitehall II prospective cohort study. *BMJ, 337,* 32–36.

Nadal, K. L. (2010). Gender microaggressions: Implications for mental health. In M. A. Paludi (Ed.), *Feminism and women's rights worldwide: Mental and physical health* (Vol. 2, pp. 155–176). Santa Barbara, CA: Praeger.

Nadeem, E., & Romo, L. F. (2008). Low-income Latina mothers' expectations for their pregnant daughters' autonomy and interdependence. *Journal of Research on Adolescence, 18,* 15–238.

Nagoshi, J. L., Adams, K. A., Terrell, H. K., Hill, E. D., Brzuzy, S., & Nagoshi, C. T. (2008). Gender differences in correlates of homophobia and transphobia. *Sex Roles, 59,* 521–531.

Nagy, G., Garrett, J., Trautwein, U., Cortina., K. S., Baumert, J., & Eccles, J. S. (2008). Gendered high school course selection as a precursor of gendered careers: The mediating role of self-concept and intrinsic value. In H. M. G. Watt & J. S. Eccles (Eds.), *Gender and occupational outcomes: Longitudinal assessments of individual, social, and cultural influences* (pp. 115–144). Washington, DC: American Psychological Association.

Nagy, G., Watt, H. M. G., Eccles, J. S., Trautwein, U., Lüdtke, O., & Baumert, J. (2010). The development of students' mathematics self-concept in relation to gender: Different countries, different trajectories? *Journal of Research on Adolescence, 20,* 482–506.

Najdowski, C. J., & Ullman, S. E. (2009). PTSD symptoms and self-rated recovery among adult sexual assault survivors: The effects of traumatic life events and psychosocial variables. *Psychology of Women Quarterly, 33,* 43–53.

Nalebuff, R. K. (Ed.). (2009). *My little red book.* New York: Twelve.

Nanda, S. (2011). Multiple genders among North American Indians. In J. Z. Spade & C. G. Valentine (Eds.), *The kaleidoscope of gender: Prisms, patterns, and possibilities* (3rd ed., pp. 47–54). Thousand Oaks, CA: Sage.

Nario-Redmond, M. R. (2010). Cultural stereotypes of disabled and non-disabled men and women: Consensus for global category representations and diagnostic domains. *British Journal of Social Psychology, 49,* 471–488.

Nassif, A., & Gunter, B. (2008). Gender representation in television advertisements in Britain and Saudi Arabia. *Sex Roles, 58,* 752–760.

The Nation: Student demographics. (2010, August 27). *Chronicle of Higher Education,* pp. 25–32.

National Academies of Sciences Committee on Science, Engineering and Public Policy (COSEPUP) and Policy and Global Affairs (PGA). (2007). *Beyond bias and barriers: Fulfilling the potential of women in academic science and engineering.* Washington, DC: Author.

National Alliance for Caregiving. (2009). *Caregiving in the U.S.* Bethesda, MD: Author.

National Campaign to Prevent Teen Pregnancy. (2003). *With one voice 2003: America's adults and teens sound off about teen pregnancy.* Washington, DC: Author.

National Center for Health Statistics. (2004). *Health, United States, 2004 with chartbook on trends in the health of Americans.* Hyattsville, MD: Author.

National Center for Health Statistics. (2007). *Health, United States, 2007.* Hyattsville, MD: Author.

National Center for Health Statistics. (2011). *Health, United States, 2010.* Hyattsville, MD: Author.

National Center for Victims of Crime. (2008). *Child sexual abuse.* Washington, DC: Author.

National Institute of Child Health and Human Development (NICHD) Early Child Care Research Network. (2006). Childcare effect sizes for the NICHD study of early child care and youth development. *American Psychologist, 61,* 99–116.

National Institute on Aging. (2007). *Growing older in America: The health and retirement study.* Washington, DC: Author.

National Institute on Aging. (2009). *HIV, AIDS, and older people.* Gaithersburg, MD: Author.

National Institute on Alcohol Abuse and Alcoholism. (2008). *Alcohol: A women's health issue.* Rockville, MD: Author.

National Institute on Drug Abuse. (2009). *NIDA InfoFacts: Steroids (anabolic-androgenic).* Washington, DC: Author.

National Institutes of Health Osteoporosis and Related Bone Diseases National Resource Center. (2009). *Osteoporosis overview.* Washington, DC: Author. Retrieved from http://www.niams.nih.gov/health_Info/Bone/Osteoporosis/

National Osteoporosis Foundation. (2010). *Clinician's guide to prevention and treatment of osteoporosis.* Washington, DC: Author.

National Science Foundation. (2008). *Science and engineering indications 2008.* Washington, DC: Author.

National Women's Health Information Center. (2005). *Lesbian health.* Washington, DC: Author.

National Women's Health Information Center. (2011). *Lesbian and bisexual health.* Washington, DC: Author.

Natsuaki, M. N., Biehl, M. C., & Ge, X. (2009). Trajectories of depressed mood from early adolescence to young adulthood: The effects of pubertal timing and adolescent dating. *Journal of Research on Adolescence, 19,* 47–74.

Navarro, M. (2002, May 16). Trying to get beyond the role of the maid. *New York Times,* pp. B1, B4.

Navarro, M. (2006, May 25). Families add 3rd generation to households. *New York Times,* pp. A1, A22.

Navarro, R. L., Worthington, R. L., Hart, J., & Khairallah, T. (2009). Liberal and conservative political ideology, experiences of harassment, and perceptions of campus climate. *Journal of Diversity in Higher Education, 2,* 78–90.

Nayak, M. B., Byrne, C. A., Martin, M. K., & Abraham, A. G. (2003). Attitudes toward violence against women: A cross-nation study. *Sex Roles, 49,* 333–342.

Neff, K. D., & Terry-Schmitt, L. N. (2002). Youths' attributions for power-related gender attributes: Nature, nurture, or God? *Cognitive Development, 17,* 1185–1202.

Neff, L. A., & Karney, B. R. (2005). Gender differences in social support: A question of skill or responsiveness? *Journal of Personality & Social Psychology, 88,* 79–90.

Neiterman, E. (2007, August). *When pregnant body becomes visible . . .* Paper presented at the meeting of the American Sociological Association, New York.

Nelson, D. A., Hart, C. H., Keister, E. K., & Piassetskaia, K. (2010). Russia. In M. H. Bornstein (Ed.), *Handbook of cultural developmental science* (pp. 175–194). New York: Psychology Press.

Nelson, J. A., et al. (2008). Identity in action: Predictors of feminist self-identification and collective action. *Sex Roles, 58,* 721–728.

Nelson, M. K. (2010). *Parenting out of control: Anxious parents in uncertain times.* New York: New York University Press.

Nelson, M. R., & Paek, H.-J. (2005). Cross-cultural differences in sexual advertising content in a transnational women's magazine. *Sex Roles, 53,* 371–383.

Nerenberg, L. (2008). *Elder abuse prevention: Emerging trends and promising strategies.* New York: Springer.

Nesbitt, M. N., & Penn, N. E. (2000). Gender stereotypes after thirty years: A replication of Rosencrantz et al. (1968). *Psychological Reports, 87,* 493–511.

Netburn, D. (2002, May 26). Young, carefree, and hooked on sunlamps. *New York Times,* pp. ST1, ST7.

Neuendorf, K. A., Gore, T. D., Dalessandro, A., Janstova, P., & Snyder-Suhy, S. (2010). Shaken and stirred: A content analysis of women's portrayals in James Bond films. *Sex Roles, 62,* 747–761.

Newcombe, N. S. (2007). Taking science seriously: Straight thinking about spatial sex differences. In S. J. Ceci & W. M. Williams (Eds.), *Why aren't more women in science? Top researchers debate the evidence* (pp. 69–77). Washington, DC: American Psychological Association.

Newcombe, N. S. (2009, June). *Women hate maps, men won't ask for directions: Fact or myth?* Paper presented at the annual meeting of the Association for Psychological Science, San Francisco, CA.

Newcombe, N. S., et al. (2009). Psychology's role in mathematics and science education. *American Psychologist, 64,* 538–550.

Newcombe, P. A., van den Eynde, J., Hafner, D., & Jolly, L. (2008). Attributions of responsibility for rape: Differences across familiarity of situation, gender, and acceptance of rape myths. *Journal of Applied Social Psychology, 38,* 1736–1754.

Newman, A. A. (2007, December 31). A guide to embracing life as a single (without the resignation, that is). *New York Times,* p. C4.

Newman, M. L., Groom, C. J., Handelman, L. D., & Pennebaker, J. W. (2008). Gender differences in language use: An analysis of 14,000 text samples. *Discourse Processes, 45,* 211–236.

Newtson, R. L., & Keith, P. M. (2001). Single women in later life. In J. M. Coyle (Ed.), *Handbook on women and aging* (pp. 385–399). Westport, CT: Greenwood.

Ng, J., et al. (2010). Self-reported delays in receipt of health care among women with diabetes and cardiovascular conditions. *Women's Health Issues, 20,* 316–322.

Nguyen, H.-H. D., & Ryan, A. M. (2008). Does stereotype threat affect performance of minorities and women? A meta-analysis of experimental evidence. *Journal of Applied Psychology, 93,* 1314–1334.

Niemann, Y. F., Jennings, L., Rozelle, R. M., Baxter, J. C., & Sullivan, E. (1994). Use of free responses and cluster analysis to determine stereotypes of eight groups. *Personality and Social Psychology Bulletin, 20,* 379–390.

Nierman, A. J., Thompson, S. C., Bryan, A., & Mahaffey, A. L. (2007). Gender role beliefs and attitudes toward lesbians and gay men in Chile and the U.S. *Sex Roles, 57,* 61–67.

Nieuwenhoven, L., & Klinge, I. (2010). Scientific excellence in applying sex- and gender-sensitive methods in biomedical and health research. *Journal of Women's Health, 19,* 313–321.

Nishina, A., & Juvonen, J. (2005). Daily sports of witnessing and experiencing peer harassment in middle school. *Child Development, 76,* 435–450.

Nix-Stevenson, D. (2011). Womanism. In M. Z. Stange, C. K. Oyster, & J. E. Sloan (Eds.), *Encyclopedia of women in today's world.* Newberry Park, CA: Sage.

Nolan, S. A., Buckner, J. P., Marzabadi, C. H., & Kuck, V. J. (2008). Training and mentoring of chemists: A study of gender disparity. *Sex Roles, 58,* 235–250.

Nolen-Hoeksema, S. (2002). Gender differences in depression. In I. Gotlib & C. Hammen (Eds.), *Handbook of depression* (pp. 492–509). New York: Guilford.

Nolen-Hoeksema, S. (2007, May). *Lost in thought: Rumination and depression*. Poster presented at the annual meeting of the Association for Psychological Science, Washington, DC.

Nolen-Hoeksema, S., Larson, J., & Grayson, C. (1999). Explaining the gender difference in depressive symptoms. *Journal of Personality and Social Psychology, 77*, 1061–1072.

Nolen-Hoeksema, S., Wisco, B. E., & Lyubomirsky, S. (2008). Rethinking rumination. *Perspectives on Psychological Science, 3*, 400–424.

Nomaguchi, K. M. (2006). Maternal employment, nonparental care, mother–child interactions, and child outcomes during preschool years. *Journal of Marriage and Family, 68*, 1341–1369.

Noonan, R. K., & Charles, D. (2009). Developing teen dating violence prevention strategies: Formative research with middle school youth. *Violence Against Women, 15*, 1087–1105.

Nordberg, J. (2010, September 20). Afghan boys are prized, so girls live the part. *New York Times*, p. A1.

Nori, R., Mercuri, N., Giusberti, F., Bensi, L., & Gambetti, E. (2009). Influences of gender role socialization and anxiety on spatial cognitive style. *American Journal of Psychology, 4*, 497–505.

Norris, P., & Inglehart, R. (2004, Spring). It's the women, stupid. *Ms.*, pp. 47–49.

North American Menopause Society. (2003). *Menopause guidebook.* Cleveland, OH: Author.

North American Menopause Society. (2008, November). Super stats: 10 menopause-related facts & figures. *Menopause Flashes.* Retrieved from http://www.regardinghealth.com/nam/RHO/2008/11/Article.aspx?mkEMC=44420

North American Menopause Society. (2009, May). The heat is on: 5 fixes for hot flashes. *Menopause Flashes.* Retrieved from http://www.regardinghealth.com/nam/RHO/2009/05/Article.aspx?bmkEMC=50464

North American Menopause Society. (2011). *Sexual health and menopause.* Mayfield Hts, OH: Author.

Northrup, C. (2010). *Women's bodies, women's wisdom.* New York: Bantam.

Nosek, B. A.-A., et al. (2009). National differences in gender-science stereotypes predict national sex differences in science and math achievement. *Proceedings of the National Academy of Sciences, 106*, 10593–10597.

Nosek, M. A. (2010). Feminism and disability: Synchronous agendas in conflict. In H. Landrine & N. F. Russo (Eds.), *Handbook of diversity in feminist psychology* (pp. 501–533). New York: Springer.

Nosek, M., Kennedy, H. P., Beyene, Y., Taylor, D., Gilliss, C., & Lee, K. (2010). The effects of perceived stress and attitudes toward menopause and aging on symptoms of menopause. *Journal of Midwifery and Womens Health, 55*, 328–334.

Novak, M. (2008). *Issues in aging* (2nd ed.). Boston, MA: Allyn & Bacon.

Novartis deal to settle bias claim. (2010, July 15). *New York Times*, p. B2.

Novotney, A. (2010, February). Members elect Vasquez as APA's next president. *Monitor on Psychology*, 60–61.

Nowell, A., & Hedges, L. V. (1998). Trends in gender differences in academic achievement from 1960 to 1994: An analysis of differences in mean, variance, and extreme scores. *Sex Roles, 39*, 21–43.

Nussbaum, M. C. (2010). Women's education: A global challenge. In J. Goodman (Ed.), *Global perspectives on gender & work* (pp. 508–517). Lanham, MD: Rowman & Littlefield.

Nutt, R. L., & Brooks, G. R. (2008). Psychology of gender. In S. D. Brown & R. W. Lent (Eds.), *Handbook of counseling psychology* (4th ed., pp. 176–193). Hoboken, NJ: Wiley.

Nyad, D. (2004, August 15). The rise of the buff bunny. *New York Times*, p. ST7.

Obradović, J., & Hipwell, A. (2010). Psychopathology and social competence during the transition to adolescence: The role of family adversity and pubertal development. *Development and Psychopathology, 22*, 621–634.

O'Brien, E. (2005). *Medicaid's coverage of nursing home costs: Asset shelter for the wealthy or essential safety net?* Washington, DC: Georgetown University Health Policy Institute. Retrieved from http://ltc.georgetown.edu/pdfs/nursinghomecosts.pdf

O'Brien, K. E., Biga, A., Kessler, S. R., & Allen, T. D. (2010). A meta-analytic investigation of gender differences in mentoring. *Journal of Management, 36*, 537–554.

O'Brien, K., Friedman, S. C., Tipton, L. C., & Linn, S. G. (2000). Attachment, separation, and women's vocational development: A longitudinal analysis. *Journal of Counseling Psychology, 47*, 301–315.

O'Brien, T. L. (2006, March 19). Why do so few women reach the top of big law firms? *New York Times*, pp. BU1, BU4.

O'Byrne, R., Hansen, S., & Rapley, M. (2008). If a girl doesn't say "no" . . . : Young men, rape and claims of "insufficient knowledge." *Journal of Community & Applied Social Psychology, 18*, 168–193.

O'Connor, A. (2009, March 31). Heart attack symptoms differ according to sex. *New York Times*, p. D5.

Odoi-Agyarko, K. (2010). FGM—the clinician's perspective. In P. Murthy & C. L. Smith (Eds.), *Women's global health and human rights* (pp. 473–482). Sudbury, MA: Jones and Bartlett.

OECD Programme for International Student Assessment. (2009). *Equally prepared for life? How 15-year-old boys and girls perform in school.* Paris: Author.

Offer, S., & Schneider, B. (2010). Multitasking among working families: A strategy for dealing with the time squeeze. In K. Christensen & B. Schneider (Eds.), *Workplace flexibility: Realigning 20th-century jobs for a 21st-century workforce* (pp. 43–56). Ithaca, NY: Cornell University Press.

Office of Dietary Supplements, National Institutes of Health. (2009). *Dietary supplement fact sheet: Calcium.* Bethesda, MD: Author. Retrieved from http://dietary-supplements.info.nih.gov/factsheets/calcium.asp

Office on Women's Health. (2007). *Frequently asked questions: Health insurance and women.* Washington, DC: Author. Retrieved from http://www.womenshealth.gov/faq/health-insurance-women.cfm

Office on Women's Health. (2009a). *Action steps for improving women's mental health.* Washington, DC: Author.

Office on Women's Health. (2009b). *Menstruation and the menstrual cycle.* Washington, DC: Author. Retrieved from http://www.womenshealth.gov/faq/menstruation.cfm

Ofstedal, M. B., Reidy, E., & Knodel, J. (2003, November). *Gender differences in economic support and well-being of older Asians* (Report No. 03-540). Population Studies Center at the Institute for Social Research, University of Michigan.

O'Grady, M., & Lori, J. R. (2009). Reproductive issues. In J. C. Urbancic & C. J. Groh (Eds.), *Women's mental health: A clinical guide for primary care providers* (pp. 386–411). Philadelphia, PA: Lippincott Williams & Wilkins.

Ojeda, L., & Flores, L. Y. (2008). The influence of gender, generation level, parents' education level, and perceived barriers on the educational aspirations of Mexican American high school students. *Career Development Quarterly, 57*, 84–95.

Okimoto, T. G., & Brescoll, V. L. (2010). The price of power: Power seeking and backlash against female politicians. *Personality and Social Psychology Bulletin, 36*, 923–936.

Okun, K., August, K. J., Rook, K. S., & Newson, J. T. (2010). Does volunteering moderate the relationship between functional limitations and mortality. *Social Science & Medicine, 71,* 1662–1668.

O'Leary, A., & Kornbluh, K. (2009). Family friendly for all families: Workers and caregivers need government policies that reflect today's realities. In M. Shriver (Ed.), *The Shriver report: A woman's nation changes everything* (pp. 74–109). Washington, DC: Maria Shriver and the Center for American Progress.

O'Leary, C. M., Nassar, N., Zubrick, S. R., Kurinczuk, J. J., Stanley, F., & Bower, C. (2009). Evidence of a complex association between dose, pattern and timing of prenatal alcohol exposure and child behavior problems. *Addiction, 105,* 74–86.

O'Leary, P. (2011). Feminism on college campuses. In M. Z. Stange, C. K. Oyster, & J. E. Sloan (Eds.), *Encyclopedia of women in today's world* (pp. 535–537). Newberry Park, CA: Sage.

O'Leary, P., Coohey, C., & Easton, S. D. (2010). The effect of severe child sexual abuse and disclosure on mental health during adulthood. *Journal of Child Sexual Abuse, 19,* 275–289.

Olff, M., Langeland, W., Draijer, N., & Gersons, B. P. R. (2007). Gender differences in posttraumatic stress disorder. *Psychological Bulletin, 133,* 183–204.

Olfson, M., Cherry, D. K., & Lewis-Fernández, R. (2009). Racial differences in visit duration of outpatient psychiatric visits. *Archives of General Psychiatry, 66,* 214–221.

Olkin, R. (2008). Women with disabilities. In J. C. Chrisler, C. Golden, & P. D. Rozee (Eds.), *Lectures on the psychology of women* (pp. 190–203). New York: McGraw-Hill.

Olkin, R. (2010). The three Rs of supervising graduate psychology students with disabilities: Reading, writing, and reasonable accommodations. *Women & Therapy, 33,* 73–84.

Olsen, J. P., Parra, G. R., & Bennett, S. A. (2010). Predicting violence in romantic relationships during adolescence and emerging adulthood: A critical review of the mechanisms by which familial and peer influences operate. *Clinical Psychology Review, 30,* 411–422.

Olson, E. (2006, June 1). Widowers are eager for another whirl. *New York Times,* p. E2.

Olson, J. E., et al. (2007). Beliefs in equality for women and men as related to economic factors in Central and Eastern Europe and the United States. *Sex Roles, 56,* 297–308.

Olson, K. R., & Dweck, C. S. (2008). A blueprint for social cognitive development. *Perspectives on Psychological Science, 3,* 193–202.

Olson, S. L., & Ceballo, R. E. (1996). Emotional well-being and parenting behavior among low-income single mothers: Social support and ethnicity as contexts of adjustment. In K. F. Wyche & F. J. Crosby (Eds.), *Women's ethnicities: Journeys through psychology* (pp. 105–123). Boulder, CO: Westview.

Ong, A. D. (2010). Pathways linking positive emotion and health in later life. *Current Directions in Psychological Science, 19,* 358–362.

Onishi, N. (2002, October 3). Globalization of beauty makes slimness trendy. *New York Times,* p. A4.

Ong, A. D. (2010). Pathways linking positive emotion and health in later life. *Current Directions in Psychological Science, 19,* 358–362.

Opie, K., & Power, C. (2008). Grandmothering and female coalitions: A basis for matrilineal priority? In N. J. Allen, H. Callan, R. Dunbar, & W. James (Eds.), *Early human kinship: From sex to reproduction* (pp. 168–186). Malden, MA: Blackwell.

Orbuch, T. L., & Custer, L. (1995). The social context of married women's work and its impact on Black husbands and White husbands. *Journal of Marriage and the Family, 57,* 333–345.

Orenstein, P. (2007, July 15). Your gamete, myself. *New York Times,* pp. 34–41, 58, 63.

Orenstein, P. (2011). *Cinderella ate my daughter: Dispatches from the front lines of the new girlie-girl culture.* New York: Harper Collins.

Oringanje, C., Meremikwu, M. M., Eko, H., Esu, E., Meremikwu, A., & Ehiri, J. E. (2009). Interventions for preventing unintended pregnancies among adolescents. *Cochrane Database of Systematic Reviews.* (Art No. CD005215).

Orman, S. (2010). *Women and money: Owning the power to control your destiny.* New York: Spiegel & Grau.

Ormerod, A. J., Collinsworth, L. L., & Perry, L. A. (2008). Critical climate: Relations among sexual harassment, climate, and outcomes for high school girls and boys. *Psychology of Women Quarterly, 32,* 113–125.

Orringer, K., & Gahagan, S. (2010). Adolescent girls define menstruation: A multiethnic exploratory study. *Health Care for Women International, 31,* 831–847.

Ortega, L. A. G., & Karch, D. (2010). Precipitating circumstances of suicide among women of reproductive age in 16 U.S. states, 2003–2007. *Journal of Women's Health, 19,* 5–7.

Orth, U., Robins, R. W., & Roberts, B. W. (2008). Low self-esteem prospectively predicts depression in adolescence and young adulthood. *Journal of Personality and Social Psychology, 95,* 695–708.

Orth, U., Trzesniewski, K. H., & Robins, R. W. (2010). Self-esteem development from young adulthood to old age: A cohort-sequential longitudinal study. *Journal of Personality and Social Psychology, 98,* 645–658.

Orth-Gomér, K. (2009). Are social relations less health protective in women than in men? Social relations, gender, and cardiovascular health. *Journal of Social and Personal Relationships, 26,* 63–71.

Osborne, J. M. (2008). *The career development of Black female chief nurse executives.* FIU electronic theses and dissertations paper 208, Florida International University, Miami, FL.

Osborne, L., Miller, K., & Farabee-Siers, R. (2008). *Pedagogical methods for improving women's participation and success in engineering education: A review of recent literature.* Washington, DC: Institute for Women's Policy Research.

Ostrov, J. M., & Godleski, S. A. (2010). Toward an integrated gender-linked model of aggression subtypes in early and middle childhood. *Psychological Review, 117,* 233–242.

Oswald, D. L., & Harvey, R. D. (2003). A q-methodological study of women's subjective perspectives on mathematics. *Sex Roles, 49,* 133–142.

Oswald, R. F., Fonseca, C. A., & Hardesty, J. L. (2010). Lesbian mothers' counseling experiences in the context of intimate partner violence. *Psychology of Women Quarterly, 3,* 286–296.

Oswald, R. F., & Masciadrelli, B. P. (2008). Generative ritual among nonmetropolitan lesbians and gay men: Promoting social inclusion. *Journal of Marriage and Family, 70,* 1060–1073.

Otis, M. D., Riggle, E. D. B., & Rostosky, S. S. (2006). Impact of mental health on perceptions of relationship satisfaction and quality among female same-sex couples. *Journal of Lesbian Studies, 10,* 267–283.

O'Toole, C. J. (2004). The sexist inheritance of the disability movement. In B. G. Smith & B. Hutchison (Eds.), *Gendering disability* (pp. 294–300). Piscataway, NJ: Rutgers University Press.

Out of the shadows: Women and lung cancer. (2010). *Women's Health Policy and Advocacy Program.* Boston, MA: Brigham and Women's Hospital.

Ovarian Cancer National Alliance. (2010). *About ovarian cancer.* Washington, DC: Author. Retrieved from http://www.ovariancancer.org/about-ovarian-cancer/3

Overstreet, N. M., Quinn, D. M., & Agocha, V. B. (2010). Beyond thinness: The influence of a curvaceous body ideal on body dissatisfaction in black and white women. *Sex Roles, 63,* 91–103.

Owen, J. L., Rhoades, G. K., Stanley, S. M., & Fincham, F. D. (2010). "Hooking up" among college students: Demograhic and psychosocial correlates. *Archives of Sexual Behavior, 39,* 653–663.

OWL. (2006). *Women and long-term care: Where will I live, and who will take care of me?* Washington, DC: Author.

OWL. (2007). *Give 'em health revisited: Medicare for all.* Washington, DC: Author.

OWL. (2009). *Elder abuse: A women's issue. Mother's day report 2009.* Washington, DC: Author.

OWL. (2010). *End-of-life choices: Who decides?* Washington, DC: Author.

Ozer, E. M., & Irwin, C. E., Jr. (2009). Adolescent and young adult health: From basic health status to clinical interventions. In R. M. Lerner & L. Steinberg (Eds.), *Handbook of adolescent psychology* (3rd ed., Vol. 1, pp. 618–641). Hoboken, NJ: Wiley.

Packard, E. (2005, December). From basic research to health-care messages. *Monitor on Psychology, 36,* 84–85.

Padavic, I., & Reskin, B. F. (2002). *Women and men at work* (2nd ed.). Thousand Oaks, CA: Sage.

Padgett, D. (1999). Aging minority women. In L. A. Peplau, S. C. DeBro, R. C. Veniegas, & P. L. Taylor (Eds.), *Gender, culture and ethnicity: Current research about women and men* (pp. 173–181). Mountain View, CA: Mayfield.

Padilla-Walker, L. M., Harper, J. M., & Jensen, A. C. (2010). Self-regulation as a mediator between sibling relationship quality and early adolescents' positive and negative outcomes. *Journal of Family Psychology, 4,* 419–428.

Padilla-Walker, L. M., Nelson, L. J., Carroll, J. S., & Jensen, A. C. (2009). More than a just a game: Video game and internet use during emerging adulthood. *Journal of Youth and Adolescence, 39,* 103–113.

Paek, H.-J., Nelson, M. R., & Vilela, A. M. (2011). Examination of gender-role portrayals in television adversiting across seven countries. *Sex Roles, 64,* 192–207.

Paludi, M. A. (2008a). Introduction. In M. A. Paludi (Ed.), *The psychology of women at work: Challenges and solutions for our female workforce* (Vol. 1, pp. xi–xviii). Westport, CT: Praeger.

Paludi, M. A. (2008b). *Understanding and preventing campus violence.* Westport, CT: Praeger.

Paludi, M. A. (2010). Introduction. In M. A. Paludi (Ed.), *The psychology of women at work: Challenges and solutions for our female workforce* (Vol 1, pp. xi–xviii). Westport, CT: Praeger.

Paludi, M. A., Denmark, F. L., & DeFour, D. C. (2008). The psychology of women course as a "catalyst for change" for campus violence. In M. A. Paludi (Ed.), *Understanding and preventing campus violence* (pp. 103–111). Westport, CT: Praeger.

Paludi, M. A., Martin, J. L., Paludi, J. C., Boggess, S. M., Hicks, K., & Speach, L. (2010). Pay equity as justice: United States and international perspectives. In M. A. Paludi (Ed.), *Feminism and women's rights worldwide: Feminism as human rights* (Vol. 2, pp. 147–176). Santa Barbara, CA: Praeger.

Paludi, M., Martin, J., Stern, T., & DeFour, D. C. (2010). Promises and pitfalls of mentoring women in business and academia. In C. A. Rayburn, F. L. Denmark, M. E. Reuder, & A. M. Austria (Eds.), *A handbook for women mentors: Transcending barriers of stereotype, race, and ethnicity* (pp. 79–108). Santa Barbara, CA: Praeger.

Paludi, M. A., Wilmot, J., & Speach, L. (2010). Intimate partner violence as a workplace concern: Impact on women's emotional and physical well-being and careers. In M. A. Paludi (Ed.), *Feminism and women's rights worldwide: Mental and physical health* (Vol. 2, pp. 103–138). Santa Barbara, CA: Praeger.

Pan, G. (2008, Fall/Winter). The Internet and women: Shaping a new society. *AAUW Outlook,* 7–9.

Pankake, A. (2011). Women's colleges. In M. Z. Stange, C. K. Oyster, & J. E. Sloan (Eds.), *Encyclopedia of women in today's world* (Vol. 4, pp. 1566–1568). Newberry Park, CA: Sage.

Panter, A. T., Daye, C. E., Allen, W. R., Wightman, L. F., & Deo, M. (2008). Everyday discrimination in a national sample of incoming law students. *Journal of Diversity in Higher Education, 1,* 67–79.

Papalia, D. (2005). *A child's world: Infancy through adolescence* (10th ed.). New York: McGraw-Hill.

Paradise, S. A. (1993). Older never married women: A cross cultural investigation. In N. D. Davis, E. Cole, & E. Rothblum (Eds.), *Faces of women and aging* (pp. 129–139). New York: Harrington Park Press.

Paras, M. L., et al. (2009). Sexual abuse and lifetime diagnosis of somatic disorders: A systematic review and meta-analysis. *Journal of the American Medical Association, 302,* 550–561.

Parera, N., & Surís, J. C. (2004). Having a good relationship with their mother: A protective factor against sexual risk behavior among adolescent females? *Journal of Pediatric and Adolescent Gynecology, 17,* 267–271.

Park, E. (2009). Gender as a moderator in the association of body weight to smoking and mental health. *American Journal of Public Health, 99,* 146–151.

Park, L. E., DiRaddo, A. M., & Calogero, R. M. (2009). Sociocultural influence and appearance-based rejection sensitivity among college students. *Psychology of Women Quarterly, 33,* 108–119.

Parke, R. D., & Buriel, R. (2006). Socialization in the family: Ethnic and ecological perspectives. In W. Damon, R. M. Lerner (Series Eds.), & N. Eisenberg (Vol. Ed.), *Handbook of child psychology: Vol. 3. Social, emotional, and personality development* (6th ed., pp. 429–504). Hoboken, NJ: Wiley.

Parker, A. (2011, February 16). Lawsuit says military is rife with sexual abuse. *New York Times,* p. A18.

Parker, E. M., & Short, S. E. (2009). Grandmother coresidence, maternal orphans, and school enrollment in Sub-Saharan Africa. *Journal of Family Issues, 30,* 813–836.

Parker, H. M., & Fink, J. S. (2008). The effect of sport commentator framing on viewer attitudes. *Sex Roles, 58,* 116–126.

Parker, R. G. (2007). Sexuality, health, and human rights. *American Journal of Public Health, 97,* 972–973.

Parker, W. H., et al. (2009). Ovarian conservation at the time of hysterectomy and long-term health outcomes in the nurses' health study. *Obstetrics & Gynecology, 62,* 1027–1037.

Parker-Pope, T. (2008, June 23). Many normal-weight teens feel fat. *New York Times.* Retrieved from http://www.nytimes.com

Parker-Pope, T. (2009a, January 20). Your nest is empty? Enjoy each other. *New York Times,* p. D5.

Parker-Pope, T. (2009b, May 11). The troubling allure of eating disorder books. *New York Times.* Retrieved from http://www.nytimes.com

Parker-Pope, T. (2010). *For better: The science of a good marriage.* New York: Dutton.

Parker-Pope, T. (2011, March 28). An older generation falls prey to eating disorders. *New York Times,* p. D6.

Parkes, A., Henderson, M., Wight, D., & Nixon, C. (2011). Is parenting associated with teenagers' early sexual risk-taking, autonomy and relationship with sex partners? *Perspectives on Sexual and Reproductive Health, 43,* 30–40.

Parks, C. A., Hughes, T. L., & Matthews, A. K. (2004). Race/ethnicity and sexual orientation: Intersecting identities. *Cultural Diversity and Ethnic Minority Psychology, 10,* 241–254.

Parks, J. B., & Robertson, M. A. (2004). Attitudes toward women mediate the gender effect on attitudes toward sexist language. *Psychology of Women Quarterly, 28,* 233–239.

Parks, S. (2010). *Fierce angels: The strong Black woman in American life and culture.* New York: Ballantine Books.

Parmley, M., & Cunningham, J. G. (2008). Children's gender-emotion stereotypes in the relationship of anger to sadness and fear. *Sex Roles, 58,* 358–370.

Parrott, D. J., & Gallagher, K. E. (2008). What accounts for heterosexual women's negative emotional responses to lesbians?: Examination of traditional gender role beliefs and sexual prejudice. *Sex Roles, 59,* 229–239.

Parsons, K. (2010, Spring). Feminist reflections on miscarriage, in light of abortion. *International Journal of Feminist Approaches to Bioethics, 3,* 1–22.

Pascoe, E. A., & Smart Richman, L. (2009). Perceived discrimination and health: A meta-analytic review. *Psychological Bulletin, 135,* 531–554.

Patrick, J. H., & Goedereis, E. A. (2009). The importance of context and the gain-loss dynamic for understanding grandparent caregivers. In K. Shifren (Ed.), *How caregiving affects development: Psychological implications for child, adolescent, and adult caregivers* (pp. 169–190). Washington, DC: American Psychological Association.

Patterson, C. J. (2000). Family relationships of lesbians and gay men. *Journal of Marriage and the Family, 62,* 1052–1069.

Patterson, C. J. (2006). Children of lesbian and gay parents. *Current Directions in Psychological Science, 15,* 241–244.

Patterson, C. J. (2009). Children of lesbian and gay parents: Psychology, law, and policy. *American Psychologist, 64,* 725–736.

Patwell, M. (2010). Women with disabilities in education: The United States and the Americans with Disabilities Act. In P. Murthy & C. L. Smith (Eds.), *Women's global health and human rights* (pp. 371–382). Sudbury, MA: Jones and Bartlett.

Paul, P. (2010, October 8). The playround gets even tougher. *New York Times,* p. ST12.

Paulson, J. F., & Bazemore, S. D. (2010). Prenatal and postpartum depression in fathers and its association with maternal depression: A meta-analysis. *Journal of the American Medical Association, 303,* 1961–1969.

Paykel, J. M. (2010). Pregnancy and lactation. In V. Maizes & T. Low Dog (Eds.), *Integrative women's health* (pp. 201–232). New York: Oxford University Press.

Pazol, K., Gamble, S. B., Parker, W. Y., Cook, D. A., Zane, S. B., & Hamdan, S. (2009, November 27). Abortion surveillance—United States, 2006. *Morbidity and Mortality Weekly Report, 58*(SS-8), 1–35.

Pazol, K., et al. (2011). Abortion surveillance—United States, 2007. *Morbidity and Mortality Weekly Report, 60*(SS1), 1–39.

Peacock, P. (1998). Marital rape. In R. K. Bergen (Ed.), *Issues in intimate violence* (pp. 225–235). Thousand Oaks, CA: Sage.

Pearce, S. C., Clifford, E. J., & Tandon, T. (2011). *Immigration and women: Understanding the American experience.* New York: New York University Press.

Pearson, J., Crissey, S. R., & Riegle-Crumb, C. (2009). Gendered fields: Sports and advanced course taking in high school. *Sex Roles, 61,* 519–535.

Pecora, N., Murray, J. P., & Wartella, E. A. (2007). *Children and television: Fifty years of research.* Mahwah, NJ: Erlbaum.

Pedersen, D. E., Minnotte, K. L., Kiger, G., & Mannon, S. E. (2008). Workplace policy and environment, family role quality, and positive family-to-work spillover. *Journal of Family and Economic Issues, 30,* 80–89.

Pellegrini, A. D. (2001). A longitudinal study of heterosexual relationships, aggression, and sexual harassment during the transition from primary school through middle school. *Applied Developmental Psychology, 22,* 119–133.

Penner, A. M. (2008). Gender differences in extreme mathematical achievement: An international perspective on biological and social factors. *American Journal of Sociology, 114,* S138–170.

Peplau, L. A. (1998). Lesbian and gay relationships. In D. L. Anselmi & A. L. Law (Eds.), *Questions of gender: Perspectives & paradoxes* (pp. 505–519). Boston: McGraw-Hill.

Peplau, L. A. (2002, August). *Venus and Mars in the laboratory: Current research on gender and sexuality.* Paper presented at the meeting of the American Psychological Association, Chicago, IL.

Peplau, L. A., & Fingerhut, A. W. (2004). The paradox of the lesbian worker. *Journal of Social Issues, 60,* 719–735.

Pepler, D., Jiang, D., Craig, W., & Connolly, J. (2008). Developmental trajectories of bullying and associated factors. *Child Development, 79,* 325–338.

Percheski, C. (2008). Opting out? Cohort differences in professional women's employment rates from 1960–2005. *American Sociological Review, 73,* 497–517.

Pérez, M. Z. (2008). When sexual autonomy isn't enough: Sexual violence against immigrant women in the United States. In J. Friedman & J. Valenti (Eds.), *Yes means yes!: Visions of female sexual power & a world without rape* (pp. 141–150). Berkeley, CA: Seal Press.

Pérez-Peña, R. (2004, March 15). Use of midwives, a childbirth phenomenon, fades in city. *New York Times,* p. A21.

Perilla, J. L., Lippy, C., Rosales, A., & Serrata, J. V. (2011). Prevalence of domestic violence. In J. W. White, M. P. Koss, & A. E. Kazdin (Eds.), *Violence against women and children: Mapping the terrain* (Vol. 1, pp. 199–220). Washington, DC: American Psychological Association.

Perkins, K. P. (1992). Psychosocial implications of women and retirement. *Social Work, 37,* 526–532.

Perlez, J. (2003, July 14). For these transvestites, still more role changes. *New York Times,* p. A4.

Perrin, E. M., Boone-Heinonen, J., Field, A. E., Coyne-Beasly, T., & Gordon-Larsen, P. (2009). Perception of overweight and self-esteem during adolescence. *International Journal of Eating Disorders, 43,* 447–454.

Perron, J. L. (2010). Uterine fibroids. In V. Maizes & T. Low Dog (Eds.), *Integrative women's health* (pp. 319–334). New York: Oxford University Press.

Perrone, K. M., Wright, S. L., & Jackson, Z. V. (2009). Traditional and nontraditional gender roles and work-family interface for men and women. *Journal of Career Development, 36,* 8–24.

Perry, J., & Vance, K. S. (2010). Possible selves among urban youths of color: An exploration of peer beliefs and gender differences. *Career Development Quarterly, 58,* 257–269.

Perry-Jenkins, F., Goldberg, A. E., Pierce, C. P., & Sayer, A. G. (2007). Shift work, role overload, and the transition to parenthood. *Journal of Marriage and Family, 69,* 123–138.

Perry-Jenkins, M., & Claxton, A. (2009). Feminist visions for rethinking work and family connections. In S. Lloyd, A. Few, & K. Allen (Eds.), *Handbook of family feminist studies* (pp. 121–133). Thousand Oaks, CA: Sage.

Perry-Jenkins, M., Seery, B., & Crouter, A. C. (1992). Linkages between women's provider-role attitudes, psychological well-being, and family relationships. *Psychology of Women Quarterly, 16,* 311–329.

Perz, J., & Ussher, J. M. (2008). "The horror of this living decay": Women's negotiation and resistance of medical discourses around menopause and midlife. *Women's Studies International Forum, 31,* 293–299.

Peter, T. (2009). Exploring taboos: Comparing male- and female-perpetrated child sexual abuse. *Journal of Interpersonal Violence, 24,* 1111–1128.

Peters, R. D., et al. (2010). The better beginnings, better futures project: Findings from grade 3 to grade 9. *Monographs of the Society for Research in Child Development, 75*(3, Serial No. 297).

Petersen, J. L., & Hyde, J. S. (2010). A meta-analytic review of research on gender differences in sexuality, 1993–2007. *Psychological Bulletin, 136,* 21–38.

Peterson, E., & Yancy, C. W. (2009). Eliminating racial and ethnic disparities in cardiac care. *New England Journal of Medicine, 360,* 1172–1174.

Peterson, M. M. (2005). Assisted reproductive technologies and equity of access issues. *Journal of Medical Ethics, 31,* 280–285.

Peterson, Z. D., & Muehlenhard, C. L. (2011). A match-and-motivation model of how women label their nonconsensual sexual experiences. *Psychology of Women Quarterly, 35,* 558–570.

Petrie, T. A., Greenleaf, C., & Martin, S. (2010). Biopsychosocial and physical correlates of middle school boys' and girls' body satisfaction. *Sex Roles, 63,* 631–644.

Pettinati, H. M., & Plebani, J. G. (2009). Depression and substance use disorders in women. In K. T. Brady, S. E. Back, & S. F. Greenfield (Eds.), *Women and addiction: A comprehensive handbook* (pp. 193–208). New York: Guilford.

Pew Research Center. (2007a). *As marriage and parenthood drift apart, public is concerned about social impact.* Washington, DC: Author.

Pew Research Center. (2007b). *Modern marriage.* Washington, DC: Author.

Pew Research Center. (2009, October 9). *Most still oppose same-sex marriage: Majority continues to support civil unions.* Washington, DC: Author.

Pew Research Center. (2010a). *Millennials: A portrait of generation next.* Washington, DC: Author.

Pew Research Center. (2010b). *Women, men and the new economics of marriage.* Washington, DC: Author.

Pew Research Center. (2010c). *The return of the multi-generational family.* Washington, DC: Author.

Pfaff, L. A., & Associates. (1999). *Five-year study shows gender differences in leadership skills.* Kalamazoo, MI: Authors.

Phares, T. M., et al. (2004, July). Surveillance for disparities in maternal health-related behaviors—selected states, pregnancy risk assessment monitoring system (PRAMS), 2000–2001. *Surveillance Summaries. Morbidity and Mortality Weekly Report, 53*(SS-4), 1–13.

Physicians Committee for Responsible Medicine. (2007). *Using foods against menstrual pain.* Washington, DC: Author.

Pianta, R. C., Barnett, W. S., Burchinal, M., & Thornburg, K. R. (2009). The effects of preschool education: What we know, how public policy is or is not aligned with the evidence base, and what we need to know. *Psychological Science in the Public Interest, 10,* 49–88.

Pierce, W. D., Sydie, R. A., Stratkotter, R., & Krull, C. (2003). Social concepts and judgments: A semantic differential analysis of the concepts feminist, man, and woman. *Psychology of Women Quarterly, 27,* 338–346.

Pike, K. M., Carter, J. C., & Olinsted, M. P. (2010). Cognitive-behavioral therapy for anorexia nervosa. In C. M. Grilo & J. E. Mitchell (Eds.), *The treatment of eating disorders: A clinical handbook* (pp. 83–107). New York: Guilford.

Piller, C. (1998, September). Women avoiding computer field as gender gap goes high tech. *Hartford Courant,* pp. A12–A13.

Pina, A., Gannon, T. A., & Saunders, B. (2009). An overview of the literature on sexual harassment: Perpetrator, theory, and treatment issues. *Aggression and Violent Behavior, 14,* 126–138.

Pinquart, M., & Silbereisen, R. K. (2010). European Union. In M. H. Bornstein (Ed.), *Handbook of cultural developmental science* (pp. 341–358). New York: Psychology Press.

Pinquart, M., & Sörensen, S. (2006). Gender differences in caregiver stressors, social resources, and health: An updated meta-analysis. *Journal of Gerontology, 61B*(1), 33–45.

Pinto, K. M., & Coltrane, S. (2009). Divisions of labor in Mexican origin and Anglo families: Structure and culture. *Sex Roles, 60,* 482–495.

Pittman, L. D. (2007). Grandmothers' involvement among young adolescents growing up in poverty. *Journal of Research on Adolescence, 17,* 89–116.

Plach, S. K. (2008). Psychological well-being in women with heart failure: Can social roles make a difference? *Health Care for Women International, 29,* 54–75.

Plante, L. A. (2009, Spring). Mommy, what did you do in the industrial revolution? Meditations on the rising cesarean rate. *International Journal of Feminist Approaches to Bioethics, 2,* 140–147.

Plassman, B. L., Williams, J. W., Jr., Burke, J. R., Holsinger, T., & Benjamin, S. (2010). Systematic review: Factors associated with risk for and possible prevention of cognitive decline in later life. *Annals of Internal Medicine, 153,* 182–193.

Plawecki, K. L., Evans, E. M., Mojtahedi, M. C., McAuley, E., & Capman-Novakofski, K. (2009). Assessing calcium intake in postmenopausal women. *Preventing Chronic Disease, 6.* Retrieved from http://www.cdc.gov/pcd/issues/2009/oct/08_0197.htm

Plec, E. (2011). Mankiller, Wilma. In M. Z. Stange, C. K. Oyster, & J. E. Sloan (Eds.), *Encyclopedia of women in today's world* (Vol. 2, pp. 893–894). Newberry Park, CA: Sage.

Plöderl, M., & Fartacek, R. (2009). Childhood gender nonconformity and harassment as predictors of suicidality among gay, lesbian, bisexual, and heterosexual Austrians. *Archives of Sexual Behavior, 38,* 400–410.

Plucker, J. A. (1996). Secondary science and mathematics teachers and gender equity: Attitudes and attempted interventions. *Journal of Research in Science Teaching, 33*(7), 737–751.

Polimeni, A.-M., Austin, B., & Kavanagh, A. M. (2009). Sexual orientation and weight, body image, and weight control practices among young Australian women. *Journal of Women's Health, 18,* 355–362.

Poltera, J. (2011). Abortion, ethical issues of. In M. Z. Stange, C. K. Oyster, & J. E. Sloan (Eds.), *Encyclopedia of women in today's world* (Vol. 1, pp. 6–9). Newberry Park, CA: Sage.

Polycystic ovary syndrome. (2010). *Journal of Midwifery & Women's Health, 55,* 477.

Pomerleau, A., Bolduc, D., Malcuit, G., & Cossette, L. (1990). Pink or blue: Environmental gender stereotypes in the first two years of life. *Sex Roles, 22,* 359–367.

Poortman, A.-R., & van der Lippe, T. (2009). Attitudes toward housework and child care and the gendered division of labor. *Journal of Marriage and Family, 71,* 526–541.

Popenoe, D., & Whitehead, B. D. (1999). *The state of our unions: The social health of marriage in America.* New Brunswick, NJ: National Marriage Project at Rutgers University.

Popp, D., et al. (2003). Gender, race, and speech style stereotypes. *Sex Roles, 48,* 317–325.

Porter, P. (2008). "Westernizing" women's risks? Breast cancer in lower-income countries. *New England Journal of Medicine, 358,* 213–216.

Porter, T., & Gavin, H. (2010). Infanticide and neonaticide: A review of 40 years of research literature on incidence and causes. *Trauma, Violence, & Abuse, 11,* 99–112.

Post, L. A., Biroscak, B. J., & Barboza, G. (2011). Prevalence of sexual violence. In J. W. White, M. P. Koss, & A. E. Kazdin (Eds.), *Violence against women and children: Mapping the terrain* (Vol. 1, pp. 101–124). Washington, DC: American Psychological Association.

Potter, D. (2010). Psychosocial well-being and the relationship between divorce and childrens' academic achievement. *Journal of Marriage and Family, 72,* 933–946.

Potter, J., Bouyer, J., Trussell, J., & Moreau, C. (2009). Premenstrual syndrome prevalence and fluctuation over time: Results from a French population-based survey. *Journal of Women's Health, 18,* 31–39.

Poulin, F., & Chan, A. (2010). Friendship stability and change in childhood and adolescence [Advance online publication]. *Developmental Review.*

Poulin, F., & Pedersen, S. (2007). Developmental changes in gender composition of friendship networks in adolescent girls and boys. *Developmental Psychology, 43,* 1484–1496.

Poulin-Dubois, D., Serbin, L. A., Eichstedt, J. A., Sen, M. G., & Beissel, C. F. (2002). Men don't put on make-up: Toddlers' knowledge of the gender stereotyping of household activities. *Social Development, 11,* 166–181.

Powell, B., Bolzendahl, C., Geist, C., & Steelman, L. C. (2010). *Counted out: Same-sex relations and Americans' definitions of family.* New York: Russell Sage.

Powell, G. N., & Greenhaus, J. H. (2010). Sex, gender, and decisions at the family → work interface. *Journal of Management, 36,* 1011–1039.

Powell, L. M., Slater, S., Chaloupka, F. J., & Harper, D. (2006). Availability of physical activity—related facilities and neighborhood demographic and socioeconomic characteristics: A national study. *American Journal of Public Health, 96,* 1676–1680.

Powlishta, K. K. (2001, April). *Own-sex favoritism and gender-role development.* Poster presented at the meeting of the Society for Research in Child Development, Minneapolis, MN.

Powlishta, K. K., Sen, M. G., Serbin, L. A., Poulin-Dubois, D., & Eichstedt, J. A. (2001). From infancy through middle childhood: The role of cognitive and social factors in becoming gendered. In R. K. Unger (Ed.), *Handbook of the psychology of women and gender* (pp. 116–132). New York: Wiley.

Pozner, J. L. (2004, Fall). The unreal world. *Ms.,* pp. 50–53.

Pratto, F., & Walker, A. (2004). The bases of gendered power. In A. H. Eagly, A. E. Beall, & R. J. Sternberg (Eds.), *The psychology of gender* (pp. 242–268). New York: Guilford.

Pregler, J., et al. (2009). The heart truth professional education campaign on women and heart disease: Needs assessment and evaluation results. *Journal of Women's Health, 18,* 1541–1547.

Prejean, J., Satcher, A. J., Durant, T., Hu, X., & Lee, L. M. (2006). Racial/ethnic disparities in diagnosis of HIV/AIDS—33 states, 2001–2004. *Morbidity and Mortality Weekly Report, 55,* 121–125.

Prentice, K. (2008, February). When a caregiver needs care. *Heart Insight,* pp. 17–19.

Press, J., Fagan, J., & Bernd, E. (2006). Child care, work, and depressive symptoms among low-income mothers. *Journal of Family Issues, 27,* 609–632.

Press, R., Carrasquillo, O., Sciacca, R. R., & Giardina, E.-G. V. (2008). Racial/ethnic disparities in time to follow-up after an abnormal mammogram. *Journal of Women's Health, 17,* 923–930.

Prevalence of self-reported physically active adults—United States, 2007. (2008, December 5). *Morbidity and Mortality Weekly Report, 57,* 1297–1300.

Priebe, G., & Svedin, C. G. (2009). Prevalence, characteristics, and associations of sexual abuse with sociodemographics and consensual sex in a population-based sample of Swedish adolescents. *Journal of Child Sexual Abuse, 18,* 19–39.

Prieler, M., Kohlbacher, F., Hagiwara, S., & Arima, A. (2011). Gender representation of older people in Japanese television advertisements. *Sex Roles, 64,* 405–415.

Primm, A. B., et al. (2010). The role of public health in addressing racial and ethnic disparities in mental health and mental illness. *Preventing Chronic Disease, 7.* Retrieved from http://www.cdc.gov/pcd/issues/2010/jan/09_0125.htm

Prinstein, M. J., & La Greca, A. M. (2004). Childhood peer rejection and aggression as predictors of adolescent girls' externalizing and health risk behaviors: A 6-year longitudinal study. *Journal of Consulting and Clinical Psychology, 72,* 103–112.

Pronk, R. E., & Zimmer-Gembeck, M. J. (2010). It's "mean," but what does it mean to adolescents? Relational aggression described by victims, aggressors, and their peers. *Journal of Adolescent Research, 25,* 175–204.

Propp, K. (2003). Pregnancy as a life passage. In L. Slater, J. H. Daniel, & A. E. Banks (Eds.), *The complete guide to mental health for women* (pp. 6–9). Boston, MA: Beacon Press.

Proulx, C. M., & Helms, H. M. (2008). Mothers' and fathers' perceptions of change and continuity in their relationships with young adult sons and daughters. *Journal of Family Issues, 29,* 234–261.

Proulx, C. M., Helms, H. M., & Buehler, C. (2007). Marital quality and personal well-being: A meta- analysis. *Journal of Marriage and Family, 69,* 576–593.

Pruchno, R. A. (1999). Raising grandchildren: The experiences of Black and White grandmothers. *Gerontologist, 39,* 209–221.

Pruchno, R. A., Wilson-Genderson, M., & Cartwright, F. (2010). A two-factor model of successful aging. *Journal of Gerontology: Psychological Sciences, 65B,* 671–679.

Pruthi, S. (2010). *Women's health encyclopedia: An integrated approach to wellness for every season of a woman's life.* London, UK: Marshall Editions Ltd.

Pryor, J. H., Hurtado, S., Saenz, V. B., Lindholm, J. A., Korn, W. S., & Mahoney, K. M. (2005). *The American freshman: National norms for fall 2005.* Los Angeles, CA: Higher Education Research Institute, UCLA.

Putman, F. W. (2003). Ten-year research update review: Child sexual abuse. *Journal of the American Academy of Child & Adolescent Psychiatry, 42,* 269–278.

Puts, D. A., McDaniel, M. A., Jordan, C. L., & Breedlove, S. M. (2008). Spatial ability and prenatal adrogens: Meta-analyses of congential adrenal hyperplasia and digit ratio (2D:4D) studies. *Archives of Sexual Behavior, 37,* 100–111.

QuickStats: Percentage of adults aged ≥20 years who said they tried to lose weight during the preceding 12 months, by age group and sex—National health and nutrition examination survey, United States, 2005–2006. (2008, October 24). *Morbidity and Mortality Weekly Report, 57,* 1155.

QuickStats: Percentage of adults aged ≥25 years who reported regular leisure-time physical activity, by education level—National Health Interview Survey, United States, 1997 and 2007. (2009, March 20). *Morbidity and Mortality Weekly Report, 58,* 261.

QuickStats: Percentage of adults aged ≥18 years who looked up health information on the Internet, by age group and sex—National Health Interview Survey, United States, January–September 2009. (2010a, April 23). *Morbidity and Mortality Weekly Report, 59,* 461.

QuickStats: Percentage of women aged ≥18 years who had a Papanicolaou (Pap) smear test during the preceding 3 years, by age group and poverty status—National Health Interview Survey, United States, 2008. (2010b, April 16). *Morbidity and Mortality Weekly Report, 59,* 431.

QuickStats: Percentage of adults aged 25–44 years reporting fair or poor health, by sex—National Health Interview Survey, United States, 1999–2009. (2011, February 25). *Morbidity and Mortality Weekly Report, 60,* 216.

Quinlan, K., Bowleg, L., & Ritz, S. F. (2008). Virtually invisible women: Women with disabilities in mainstream psychological theory and research. *Review of Disability Studies: An International Journal, 4,* 4–17.

Quinn, J. B. (2001, February 17). Investing women aren't emotionally impaired. *Peoria Journal Star,* p. C2.

Quinn, P. C., & Liben, L. S. (2008). A sex difference in mental rotation in young infants. *Psychological Science, 19,* 1067–1070.

Rabasca, L. (2000, October). The Internet and computer games reinforce the gender gap. *Monitor on Psychology,* pp. 32–33.

Rabin, R. C. (2009, April 24). Smoking may have role in breast cancer after all, a science panel says. *New York Times,* p. A14.

Rabin, R. C. (2010a, October 10). Grown-up, but still irresponsible. *New York Times,* p. WK2.

Rabin, R. C. (2010b, November 23). Hazards: Work stress raises women's heart risk, study says. *New York Times,* p. D6.

Raffaelli, M., & Ontai, L. L. (2004). Gender socialization in Latino/a families: Results from two retrospective studies. *Sex Roles, 50,* 287–299.

Raiford, J. L., Wingood, G. M., & Diclemente, R. J. (2007). Prevalence, incidence, and predictors of dating violence: A longitudinal study of African American female adolescents. *Journal of Women's Health, 16,* 822–832.

Raj, A., Gomez, C., & Silverman, J. G. (2008). Driven to a fiery death—the tragedy of self-immolation in Afghanistan. *New England Journal of Medicine, 358,* 2201–2203.

Raley, G. (2008). Avenue to adulthood: Teenage pregnancy and the meaning of motherhood in poor communities. In S. Coontz (Ed.), *American families: A multicultural reader* (2nd ed., pp. 338–350). New York: Taylor & Francis.

Raley, S., & Bianchi, S. (2006). Sons, daughters, and family processes: Does gender of children matter? *Annual Review of Sociology, 32,* 401–421.

Ramaswami, A., Dreher, G. F., Bretz, R., & Wiethoff, C. (2010). Gender, mentoring, and career success: The importance of organizational context. *Personnel Psychology, 63,* 385–405.

Ramisetty-Mikler, S., Caetano, R., & McGrath, C. (2007). Sexual aggression among White, Black, and Hispanic couples in the U.S.: Alcohol use, physical assault and psychological aggression as its correlates. *American Journal of Drug and Alcohol Abuse, 33,* 31–43.

Ramsey, L. R., et al. (2007). Thinking of others: Feminist identification and the perception of others' beliefs. *Sex Roles, 56,* 611–616.

Range, L. M. (2006). Women and suicide. In J. Worell & C. D. Goodheart (Eds.), *Handbook of girls' and women's psychological health: Gender and well-being across the lifespan* (pp. 129–136). New York: Oxford University Press.

Rani, M., & Bonu, S. (2008). Attitudes toward wife beating: A cross-country study in Asia. *Journal of Interpersonal Violence, 24,* 1371–1397.

Rankin, L. E., & Eagly, A. H. (2008). Is his heroism hailed and hers hidden? Women, men, and the social construction of heroism. *Psychology of Women Quarterly, 32,* 414–422.

Rankin, S., Blumenfeld, W. J., Weber, G. N., & Frazer, S. (2010). *State of higher education for lesbian, gay, bisexual and transgender people.* Charlotte, NC: Campus Pride.

Rape, Abuse & Incest National Network. (2009). *Who are the victims?* Washington, DC: Author.

Rathus, S., Nevid, J., & Fichner-Rathus, L. (2008). *Human sexuality in a world of diversity* (6th ed.). Boston: Allyn & Bacon.

Rathus, S., Nevid, J., & Fichner-Rathus, L. (2010). *Human sexuality in a world of diversity* (8th ed.). Upper Saddle River, NJ: Prentice Hall.

Räty, H., & Kasanen, K. (2010). A seven-year follow-up study on parents' expectations of their children's further education. *Journal of Applied Social Psychology, 40,* 2711–2735.

Rawlins, W. K. (2004). Friendships in later life. In J. F. Nussbaum & J. Coupland (Eds.), *Handbook of communication and aging research* (2nd ed., pp. 273–304). Mahwah, NJ: Erlbaum.

Ray, O. (2004). How the mind hurts and heals the body. *American Psychologist, 59,* 29–40.

Ray, R., Gornick, J. C., & Schmitt, J. (2009). *Parental leave policies in 21 countries: Assessing generosity and gender equality.* Washington, DC: Center for Economic and Policy Research.

Rayburn, C. A., Denmark, F. L., Reuder, M. E., & Austria, A. M. (2010). Conclusion. In C. A. Rayburn, F. L. Denmark, M. E. Reuder, & A. M. Austria (Eds.), *A handbook for women mentors: Transcending barriers of stereotype, race, and ethnicity* (pp. 275–277). Santa Barbara, CA: Praeger.

Read, M. M. (2009). Midlife lesbian lifeworlds: Narrative theory and sexual identity. In P. L. Hammack & B. J. Cohler (Eds.), *The story of sexual identity: Narrative perspectives on the gay and lesbian life course* (pp. 347–374). New York: Oxford University Press.

Read, S., & Grundy, E. (2011). Fertility history and quality of life in older women and men. *Ageing & Society, 31,* 125–145.

Rebar, R. W., & DeCherney, A. H. (2004). Assisted reproductive technology in the United States. *New England Journal of Medicine, 350,* 1603–1604.

Reczek, C., Elliott, S., & Umberson, D. (2009). Commitment without marriage: Union formation among long-term same-sex couples. *Journal of Family Issues, 30,* 738–756.

Redberg, R. F. (2007). Disparities in use of implantable cardioverter-defibrillators: Moving beyond process measures to outcomes data. *Journal of the American Medical Association, 298,* 1564–1566.

Reece, M., Herbenick, D., Schick, V., Sanders, S. A., Dodge, B., & Fortenberry, J. D. (2010). Sexual behaviors, relationships, and perceived health among adult men in the United States: Results from a national probability sample. *International Society for Sexual Medicine, 7,* 291–304.

Reed, E., Raj, A., Miller, E., & Silverman, J. G. (2010). Losing the "gender" in gender-based violence: The missteps of research on dating and intimate partner violence. *Violence Against Women, 16,* 348–354.

Reed, S. C., & Evans, S. M. (2009). Research design and methodology in studies of women and addiction. In K. T. Brady, S. E. Back, & S. F. Greenfield (Eds.), *Women and addiction: A comprehensive handbook* (pp. 14–34). New York: Guilford.

Reeder, H. M. (2003). The effect of gender role orientation on same- and cross-sex friendship formation. *Sex Roles, 49,* 143–152.

Reeves, J. B., & Darville, R. L. (1994). Social contact patterns and satisfaction with retirement of women in dual-career/earner families. *International Journal of Aging and Human Development, 39,* 163–175.

Regan, P. C. (2008). *The mating game: A primer on love, sex, and marriage.* Thousand Oaks, CA: Sage Publications.

Regan, P. C., & Cachelin, F. M. (2006). Binge eating and purging in a multi-ethnic community sample. *International Journal of Eating Disorders, 39,* 523–526.

Regnerus, M., & Uecker, J. (2011). *Premarital sex in America: How young Americans meet, mate and think about marrying.* New York: Oxford University Press.

Reibis, R. K., Bestehorn, K., Pittrow, D., Jannowitz, C., Wegscheider, K., & Völler, H. (2009). Elevated risk profile of women in secondary prevention of coronary artery disease: A 6-year survey of 117,913 patients. *Journal of Women's Health, 18,* 1123–1131.

Reichert, F. F., Barros, A. J. D., Domingues, M. R., & Hallal, P. C. (2007). The role of perceived personal barriers to engagement in leisure-time physical activity. *American Journal of Public Health, 97*, 515–519.

Reichert, T., & Carpenter, C. (2004). An update on sex in magazine advertising: 1983–2003. *Journalism and Mass Communication Quarterly, 81*, 823–837.

Reichert, T., & Lambiase, J. J. (Eds.). (2005). *Sex in consumer culture: The erotic content of media and marketing.* Mahwah, NJ: Erlbaum.

Reid, P. T. (1999). Poor women in psychological research: Shut up and shut out. In L. A. Peplau, S. C. DeBro, R. C. Veniegas, & P. L. Taylor (Eds.), *Gender, culture and ethnicity: Current research about women and men* (pp. 336–352). Mountain View, CA: Mayfield.

Reid, P. T. (2011). Revisiting "Poor women: Shut up and shut out." *Psychology of Women Quarterly, 35*, 189–192.

Reid, P. T., Cooper, S. M., & Banks, K. H. (2008). Girls to women: Developmental theory, research, and issues. In F. L. Denmark & M. A. Paludi (Eds.), *Psychology of women: A handbook of issues and theories* (2nd ed., pp. 237–270). Westport, CT: Praeger.

Reid, P. T., & Kelly, E. (1994). Research on women of color: From ignorance to awareness. *Psychology of Women Quarterly, 18*, 477–486.

Reid, P. T., & Zalk, S. R. (2001). Academic environments: Gender and ethnicity in higher education. In J. Worell (Ed.), *Encyclopedia of women and gender* (pp. 29–42). San Diego, CA: Academic Press.

Reid, R. O., Friedberg, M. W., Adams, J. L., McGlynn, E. A., & Mehrotra, A. (2010). Associations between physician characteristics and quality of care. *Archives of Internal Medicine, 170*, 1442–1449.

Reiner, W. G., & Gearhart, J. P. (2004). Discordant sexual identity in some genetic males with cloacal exstrophy assigned to female sex at birth. *New England Journal of Medicine, 350*, 333–341.

Renk, K. (2007). Disorders of conduct in young children: Developmental considerations, diagnoses, and other characteristics. *Developmental Review, 28*, 316–341.

Renzetti, C. M. (2011). Economic issues and intimate partner violence. In C. M. Renzetti, J. Edleson, & R. K. Bergen (Eds.), *Sourcebook on violence against women* (2nd ed., pp. 171–187). Thousand Oaks, CA: Sage.

Reskin, B. (2010). Unconsciousness raising. In J. Goodman (Ed.), *Global perspectives on gender & work* (pp. 385–390). Lanham, MD: Rowman & Littlefield.

Revenson, T. A. (2001). Chronic illness adjustment. In J. Worell (Ed.), *Encyclopedia of women and gender* (pp. 245–255). San Diego, CA: Academic Press.

Reviere, R. (2011). Suicide rates. In M. Z. Stange, C. K. Oyster, & J. E. Sloan (Eds.), *Encyclopedia of women in today's world* (Vol. 3, pp. 1416–1417). Newberry Park, CA: Sage.

Revisiting our roots. (2010, Winter). *Psychology of Black Women Newsletter, 4–5*, 8. Retrieved from http://issuu.com/psychology_of_black_women/docs/winter_2010

Reyes, C. J. (2008). Exploring the relations among the nature of the abuse, perceived parental support, and child's self-concept and trauma symptoms among sexually abused children. *Journal of Child Sexual Abuse, 17*, 51–70.

Reynolds, J. (2008). *The single woman: A discursive analysis.* Clifton, NJ: Psychology Press.

Reynolds, J., Wetherell, M., & Taylor, S. (2007). Choice and chance: Negotiating agency in narrative of singleness. *Sociological Review, 55*, 331–351.

Reynolds-Dobbs, W., Thomas, K. M., & Harrison, M. S. (2008). From mammy to superwoman: Images that hinder Black women's career development. *Journal of Career Development, 35*, 129–150.

Rezvani, S. (2010). *The next generation of women leaders: What you need to lead but won't learn in business school.* Santa Barbara, CA: Praeger.

Rhoades, G. K., Stanley, S. M., & Markman, H. J. (2009). Couples' reasons for cohabitation: Associations with individual well-being and relationship quality. *Journal of Family Issues, 30*, 233–258.

Rhoads, S. E., Webber, L., & Van Vleet, D. (2010, June 20). The emotional costs of hooking up. *Chronicle of Higher Education.* Retrieved from http://chronicle.com/article/The-Emotional-Costs-of-Hooking/65960/

Rhodes, J. E., Davis, A. A., Prescott, L. R., & Spencer, R. (2007). Caring connections: Mentoring relationships in the lives of urban girls. In B. J. R. Leadbeater & N. Way (Eds.), *Urban girls revisited: Building strengths* (pp. 142–156). New York: New York University Press.

Riall, T. S., Townsend, C. M., Kuo, Y.-F., Freeman, J. L., & Goodwin, J. S. (2010). Dissecting racial disparities in the treatment of patients with locoregional pancreatic cancer: A 2-step process. *Cancer, 116*, 930–939.

Ricci, E., Cipriani, S., Chiaffarino, F., Malvezzi, M., & Parazzini, F. (2010). Soy isoflavones and bone mineral density in perimenopausal and postmenopausal western women: A systematic review and meta-analysis of randomized controlled trials. *Journal of Women's Health, 19*, 1609–1617.

Ricciardelli, L. A., McCabe, M. P., Mussap, A. J., & Holt, K. E. (2009). Body image in preadolescent boys. In L. Smolak & J. K. Thompson (Eds.), *Body image, eating disorders, and obesity in youth: Assessment, prevention, and treatment* (pp. 77–96). Washington, DC: American Psychological Association.

Rice, J., & Russo, N. F. (2010). International perspectives on women and mental health. In M. A. Paludi (Ed.), *Feminism and women's rights worldwide: Mental and physical health* (Vol. 2, pp. 1–24). Santa Barbara, CA: Praeger.

Rice, J. K., & Else-Quest, N. (2006). The mixed messages of motherhood. In J. Worell & C. D. Goodheart (Eds.), *Handbook of girls' and women's psychological health: Gender and well-being across the lifespan* (pp. 339–349). New York: Oxford University Press.

Richards, A. (2008). *Opting in: Having a child without losing yourself.* New York: Farrar, Straus and Giroux.

Richards, J. E., Risser, J. M., Padgett, P. M., Rehman, H. U., Wolverton, M. L., & Arafat, R. R. (2008). Condom use among high-risk heterosexual women with concurrent sexual partnerships, Houston, Texas, USA. *International Journal of STD & AIDS, 19*, 768–771.

Richards, M. A., & Oinonen, K. A. (2010, 2011). Age at menarche is associated with divergent alcohol use patterns in early adolescence and early adulthood. *Journal of Adolescence, 33*.

Richardson, L. C., Rim, S. H., & Plescia, M. (2010, July 6). Vital signs: Breast cancer screening among women aged 50–74 years—United States, 2008. *Morbidity and Mortality Weekly Report, 59*, 6–9.

Ridgeway, C. L., & England, P. (2007). Sociological approaches to sex discrimination in employment. In F. J. Crosby, M. S. Stockdale, & S. A. Ropp (Eds.), *Sex discrimination in the workplace* (pp. 189–212). Malden, MA: Blackwell.

Ridgeway, C. L. (2011). Framed before we know it: How gender shapes social relations. In M. Kimmel & A. Aronson (Eds.), *The gendered society reader* (4th ed., pp. 190–200). New York: Oxford University Press.

Rife, J. C. (2001). Middle-aged and older women in the work force. In J. M. Coyle (Ed.), *Handbook on women and aging* (pp. 93–111). Westport, CT: Greenwood.

Riggio, H. R., & Desrochers, S. (2005). The influence of maternal employment on the work and family attitudes of young adults. In D. F. Halpern & S. E. Murphy (Eds.), *From work-family balance to work- family interaction: Changing the metaphor* (pp. 177–196). Mahwah, NJ: Erlbaum.

Riggio, H. R., & Desrochers, S. J. (2006). Relations with young adults' work and family expectations and self-efficacy. *American Behavioral Scientist, 49,* 1328–1353.

Riggle, E. D. B., Rostosky, S. S., & Danner, F. (2009). LGB identity and eudaimonic well being in midlife. *Journal of Homosexuality, 56,* 789–798.

Riley, S., Rodham, K., & Gavin, J. (2009). Doing weight: Pro-ana and recovery identities in cyberspace. *Journal of Community & Applied Social Psychology, 19,* 348–359.

Rintala, D. H., et al. (1997). Dating issues for women with physical disabilities. *Sexuality and Disability, 15,* 219–242.

Rios, D., Stewart, A. J., & Winter, D. G. (2010). "Thinking she could be the next president": Why identifying with the curriculum matters. *Psychology of Women Quarterly, 3,* 328–338.

Risman, B. J., & Seale, E. (2009). Betwixt and between: Gender contradictions among middle schoolers. In B. J. Risman (Ed.), *Families as they really are* (pp. 340–361). New York: Norton.

Roark, A. C. (2009, July 13). With friends aplenty, many widows choose singlehood. *New York Times.* Retrieved from http://newoldage.blogs.nytimes.com/2009/07/13/with-friends-aplenty-many-widows-choose-singlehood/

Robbins, C. L., & Padavic, I. (2007). Structural influences on racial and ethnic disparities in women's health care. *Sociology Compass, 1,* 682–700.

Roberts, D. F., Henriksen, L., & Foehr, U. G. (2009). Adolescence, adolescents, and media. In R. M. Lerner & L. Steinberg (Eds.), *Handbook of adolescent psychology* (3rd ed., Vol. 2, pp. 314–344). Hoboken, NJ: Wiley.

Roberts, S. (2009, November 24). Economy is forcing young adults back home in big numbers, survey finds. *New York Times,* p. A16.

Robins, R. W., & Trzesniewski, K. H. (2005). Self-esteem development across the lifespan. *Current Directions in Psychological Science, 14,* 158–162.

Robinson, B. K., & Hunter, E. (2008). Is mom still doing it all? Reexamining depictions of family work in popular advertising. *Journal of Family Issues, 29,* 465–486.

Robinson, G., & Nelson, B. M. (2010). Pursuing upward mobility: African American professional women reflect on their journey. *Journal of Black Studies, 40,* 1168–1188.

Robinson, J. D., Skill, T., & Turner, J. W. (2004). Media usage patterns and portrayals of seniors. In J. F. Nussbaum & J. Coupland (Eds.), *Handbook of communication and aging research* (2nd ed., pp. 423–450). Mahwah, NJ: Erlbaum.

Roche, J., Gilvarry, E., & Day, E. (2010). Women and alcohol. In D. Kohen (Ed.), *Oxford textbook of women and mental health* (pp. 201–207). Oxford, UK: Oxford University Press.

Roche, K. M., & Leventhal, T. (2009). Beyond neighborhood poverty: Family management, neighborhood disorder, and adolescents' early sexual onset. *Journal of Family Psychology, 23,* 819–827.

Roche, K. M., et al. (2005). Parenting influences on early sex initiation among adolescents. *Journal of Family Issues, 26,* 32–54.

Rodgers, R. F., Faure, K., & Chabrol, H. (2009). Gender differences in parental influences on adolescent body dissatisfaction and disordered eating. *Sex Roles, 61,* 837–849.

Rodríguez-Muñoz, A., Moreno-Jiménez, B., Vergel, A. I. S., & Hernádez, E. G. (2010). Post-traumatic symptoms among victims of workplace bullying: Exploring gender differences and shattered assumptions. *Journal of Applied Social Psychology, 40,* 2616–2635.

Roehling, P. V., Jarvis, L. H., & Swope, H. E. (2005). Variations in negative work-family spillover among White, Black, and Hispanic American men and women. *Journal of Family Issues, 26,* 840–865.

Roett, M. A., & Evans, P. (2009). Ovarian cancer: An overview. *American Family Physician, 80,* 609–616.

Roffman, E. (2008). Ethics and activism: Theory— identity politics, conscious acts, and ethical aspirations. In M. Ballou, M. Hill, & C. West (Eds.), *Feminist therapy theory and practice: A contemporary perspective* (pp. 109–125). New York: Springer.

Rogers, S. J., & DeBoer, D. D. (2001). Changes in wives' income: Effects in marital happiness, psychological well-being, and the risk of divorce. *Journal of Marriage and Family, 63,* 458–472.

Rogríguez, M., Valentine, J. M., Son, J. B., & Muhammad, M. (2009). Intimate partner violence and barriers to mental health care for ethnically diverse populations of women. *Trauma, Violence, & Abuse, 10,* 358–374.

Rogstad, K. E. (Ed.). (2011). *ABC of sexually transmitted infections* (6th ed.). New York: Wiley.

Röhner, J., & Schütz, A. (2011). Psychological disorders by gender, rates of. In M. Z. Stange, C. K. Oyster, & J. E. Sloan (Eds.), *Encyclopedia of women in today's world* (Vol. 3, pp. 1180–1181). Newberry Park, CA: Sage.

Rojas, M. (2009). *Women of color and feminism.* Berkeley, CA: Seal Press.

Rolfe, A. (2008). You've got to grow up when you've got a kid: Marginalized young women's accounts of motherhood. *Journal of Community & Applied Social Psychology, 18,* 299–314.

Rolfe, D. E., Yoshida, K., Renwick, R., & Bailey, C. (2009). Negotiating participation: How women living with disabilities address barriers to exercise. *Health Care for Women International, 30,* 743–766.

Romaine, S. (1999). *Communicating gender.* Mahwah, NJ: Erlbaum.

Rondon, M. B. (2010). A gender perspective is fundamental to improve women's health. *Journal of Women's Health, 19,* 1949–1950.

Rood, L., Roelofs, J., Bögels, S. M., Nolen-Hoeksema, S., & Schouten, E. (2009). The influence of emotion-focused rumination and distraction on depressive symptoms in non-clinical youth: A meta-analytic review. *Clinical Psychology Review, 29,* 607–616.

Rook, K. S. (2009). Gaps in social support resources in later life: An adaptational challenge in need of further research. *Journal of Social and Personal Relationships, 26,* 103–112.

Rose, A. J., & Rudolph, K. D. (2006). A review of sex differences in peer relationship processes: Potential trade-offs for the emotional and behavioral development of girls and boys. *Psychological Bulletin, 132,* 98–131.

Rose, A. J., & Smith, R. L. (2009). Sex differences in peer relationships. In K. H. Rubin, W. M. Bukowski, & B. Laursen (Eds.), *Handbook of peer interactions, relationships, and groups* (pp. 379–393). New York: Guilford.

Rose, A. J., Swenson, L. P., & Waller, E. M. (2004). Overt and relational aggression and perceived popularity: Developmental differences in concurrent and prospective relations. *Developmental Psychology, 40,* 378–387.

Rose, S. (2000, Summer). Heterosexism and the study of women's romantic and friend relationships. *Journal of Social Issues, 56,* 315–328.

Rose, S., & Frieze, I. H. (1993). Young singles contemporary dating scripts. *Sex Roles, 28,* 499–509.

Rose, S. J., & Hartmann, H. I. (2008). *Still a man's labor market: The long-term earnings gap.* Washington, DC: Institute for Women's Policy Research.

Rose, S. M. (2007). Enjoying the returns: Women's friendships after 50. In V. Muhlbauer & J. C. Chrisler (Eds.), *Women over 50: Psychological perspectives* (pp. 112–130). New York: Springer.

Rose, S. M., & Zand, D. (2002). Lesbian dating and courtship from young adulthood to midlife. In S. M. Rose (Ed.), *Lesbian love and relationships* (pp. 85–109). Binghamton, NY: Harrington Park Press.

Rosen, R. S., & the Committee on Adolescence. (2010). Identification and management of eating disorders in children and adolescents. *Pediatrics, 126,* 1240–1253.

Rosenfeld, A. G. (2006). State of the heart: Building science to improve women's cardiovascular health. *American Journal of Critical Care, 15,* 556–566.

Rosenfeld, D. (2009). Heteronormativity and homonormativity as practical and moral resources: The case of lesbian and gay elders. *Gender & Society, 23,* 617–638.

Rosenthal, L., & Levy, S. R. (2010). Understanding women's risk for HIV infection using social dominance theory and the four bases of gendered power. *Psychology of Women Quarterly, 34,* 21–35.

Rosin, H. (2010, July/August). The end of men. *Atlantic, 306*(1), 56–72. Retrieved from http://www.theatlantic.com/magazine/archive/2010/07/the-end-of-men/8135/

Rospenda, K. M., Richman, J. A., & Shannon, C. A. (2009). Prevalence and mental health correlates of harassment and discrimination in the workplace: Results from a national study. *Journal of Interpersonal Violence, 24,* 819–884.

Ross, J. M., & Babcock, J. C. (2010). Gender and intimate partner violence in the United States: Confronting the controversies. *Sex Roles, 62,* 194–200.

Ross, L. T., Kolars, C. L., Krahn, D. D., Gomberg, E. S., Clark, G., & Niehaus, A. (2011). Nonconsensual sexual experiences and alcohol consumption among women entering college. *Journal of Interpersonal Violence, 26,* 299–413.

Rossi, A. S. (2004). The menopausal transition and aging processes. In O. G. Brim, C. D. Ryff, & R. C. Kessler (Eds.), *How healthy are we? A national study of well-being at midlife* (pp. 153–201). Chicago, IL: University of Chicago Press.

Rothblum, E. D. (2002). Gay and lesbian body images. In T. F. Cash & T. Pruzinsky (Eds.), *Body images: A handbook of theory, research, and clinical practice* (pp. 257–265). New York: Guilford Publications.

Rothblum, E. D. (2007, May). *Same-sex couples in legalized relationships: I do, or do I?* Paper presented at the annual meeting of the Association for Psychological Science, Washington, DC.

Rothblum, E. D., Balsam, K. F., & Solomon, S. E. (2008). Comparison of same-sex couples who were married in Massachusetts, had domestic partnerships in California, or had civil unions in Vermont. *Journal of Family Issues, 29,* 48–78.

Rothman, E. F., Hemenway, D., Miller, M., & Azrael, D. (2005). Batterers' use of guns to threaten intimate partners. *Journal of the American Medical Women's Association, 60,* 62–68.

Roughgarden, J. (2009). *Evolution's rainbow: Diversity, gender, and sexuality in nature and people.* Berkeley, CA: University of California Press.

Rowland, D. T. (2007). Historical trends in childlessness. *Journal of Family Issues, 28,* 1311–1337.

Roy, B., Diez-Roux, A. V., Seeman, T., Ranjit, N., Shea, S., & Cushman, M. (2010). Association of optimism and pessimism with inflammation and hemostasis in the multi-ethnic study of atherosclerosis (MESA). *Psychosomatic Medicine, 72,* 134–140.

Roy, R. E., Weibust, K. S., & Miller, C. T. (2007). Effects of stereotypes about feminists on feminist self-identification. *Psychology of Women Quarterly, 31,* 146–156.

Royo-Vela, M., Aldas-Manzano, J., Küster, I., & Vila, N. (2008). Adaptation of marketing activities to cultural and social context: Gender role portrayals and sexism in Spanish commercials. *Sex Roles, 58,* 379–390.

Rubin, A. G., Gold, M. A., & Primack, B. A. (2009). Associations between depressive symptoms and sexual risk behaviors in a diverse sample of female adolescents. *Journal of Pediatric and Adolescent Gynecology, 23,* 306–312.

Rubin, K. H., Bukowski, W. M., & Parker, J. G. (2006). Peer interactions, relationships, and groups. In W. Damon, R. M. Lerner (Series Eds.), & N. Eisenberg (Vol. Ed.), *Handbook of child psychology: Vol. 3. Social, emotional, and personality development* (6th ed., pp. 571–645). Hoboken, NJ: Wiley.

Rubin, K. H., Cheah, C., & Menzer, M. M. (2010). Peers. In M. H. Bornstein (Ed.), *Handbook of cultural developmental science* (pp. 223–238). New York: Psychology Press.

Rubin, M. S., Colen, C. G., & Link, B. G. (2009). Examination of inequalities in HIV/AIDS mortality in the United States from a fundamental cause perspective. *American Journal of Public Health, 100,* 1053–1059.

Rubin, R. M., & White-Means, S. I. (2009). Informal caregiving: Dilemmas of sandwiched caregivers. *Journal of Family and Economic Issues, 30,* 252–267.

Rubinstein, R. L. (1994). Adaptation to retirement among the never married, childless, divorced, gay and lesbian, and widowed. In A. Monk (Ed.), *The Columbia retirement handbook* (pp. 448–461). New York: Columbia University Press.

Ruble, D. N., & Martin, C. L. (1998). Gender development. In W. Damon (Series Ed.) & N. Eisenberg (Vol. Ed.), *Handbook of child psychology. Vol. 3. Social, emotional and personality development* (5th ed., pp. 933–1016). New York: Wiley.

Ruble, D. N., Taylor, L. J., Cyphers, L., Greulich, F. K., Lurye, L. E., & Shrout, P. E. (2007). The role of gender constancy in early gender development. *Child Development, 78,* 1121–1136.

Rudman, L. A., & Fairchild, K. (2007). The F word: Is feminism incompatible with beauty and romance? *Psychology of Women Quarterly, 31,* 125–136.

Rúdólfsdóttir, A., & Morgan, P. (2009). Alcohol is my friend': Young middle class women discuss their relationship with alcohol. *Journal of Community & Applied Social Psychology, 19,* 492–505.

Rudolph, K. D. (2009). The interpersonal context of adolescent depression. In S. Nolen-Hoeksema & L. M. Hilt (Eds.), *Handbook of depression in adolescents* (pp. 377–418). New York: Taylor & Francis.

Rudolph, K. D., Ladd, G., & Dinella, L. (2007). Gender differences in the interpersonal consequences on early-onset depressive symptoms. *Merrill-Palmer Quarterly, 53,* 461–488.

Rudolph, K. D., & Troop-Gordon, W. (2010). Personal-accentuation and contextual-amplification models of pubertal timing: Predicting youth depression. *Development and Psychopathology, 22,* 433–451.

Rueger, S. Y., Malecki, C. K., & Demaray, M. K. (2008). Relationship between multiple sources of perceived social support and psychological and academic in early adolescence: Comparisons across gender. *Journal of Youth and Adolescence, 39,* 47–61.

Ruf, P. (2006). Understanding elder abuse in minority populations. In R. Summers & A. Hoffman (Eds.), *Elder abuse: A public health persepective* (pp. 51–64). Washington, DC: American Public Health Association.

Ruggles, S., & Heggeness, M. (2008). Intergenerational coresidence in developing countries. *Population and Development Review, 34,* 253–281.

Ruiz, S. A., & Silverstein, M. (2007). Relationships with grandparents and the emotional well-being of late adolescent and young adult grandchildren. *Journal of Social Issues, 63,* 793–808.

Runowicz, C. D. (2007). Molecular screening for cervical cancer—time to give up Pap tests? *New England Journal of Medicine, 357,* 1650–1653.

Rural Center for AIDS/STD Prevention. (2009). *Tearing down fences: HIV/STD prevention in rural America.* Bloomington, IN: Author.

Ruspini, E. (2011). Stereotypes of women. In M. Z. Stange, C. K. Oyster, & J. E. Sloan (Eds.), *Encyclopedia of women in today's world* (Vol. 3, pp. 1398–1401). Newberry Park, CA: Sage.

Russell, D. E. H. (2001). Femicide: An international speakout. In D. E. H. Russell & R. A. Harmes (Eds.), *Femicide in global perspective* (pp. 128–137). New York: Teachers College Press.

Russell, J. E. A. (2006). Career counseling for women in management: Career counseling with lesbian clients. In W. B. Walsh & M. J. Heppner (Eds.), *Handbook of career counseling for women* (2nd ed., pp. 453–512). Mahwah, NJ: Erlbaum.

Russell, S. T., Kosciq, J., Horn, S., & Saewyc, E. (2010). Safe schools policy for LGBTQ students. *Social Policy Report, 24*(4), 3–17.

Russell, S. T., & Seif, H. (2002). Bisexual female adolescents: A critical analysis of past research, and results from a national survey. *Journal of Bisexuality, 2,* 73–94.

Russo, N. F. (1979). Overview: Roles, fertility and the motherhood mandate. *Psychology of Women Quarterly, 4,* 7–15.

Russo, N. F. (2010). Diversity and women's mental health. In H. Landrine & N. F. Russo (Eds.), *Handbook of diversity in feminist psychology* (pp. 261–284). New York: Springer.

Russo, N. F., & Landrine, H. (2010). Overview: Diversity in feminist psychology. In H. Landrine & N. F. Russo (Eds.), *Handbook of diversity in feminist psychology* (pp. 3–27). New York: Springer.

Russo, N. F., & Tartaro, J. (2008). Women and mental health. In F. L. Denmark & M. A. Paludi (Eds.), *Psychology of women: A handbook of issues and theories* (2nd ed., pp. 440–483). Westport, CT: Praeger.

Rust, J., et al. (2000). The role of brothers and sisters in the development of preschool children. *Journal of Experimental Child Psychology, 77,* 292–303.

Rust, P. C. (2001). Too many and not enough: The meanings of bisexual identities. *Journal of Bisexuality, 1,* 33–68.

Rust, P. C. R. (2009). Bisexuality in a house of mirrors: Multiple reflections, multiple identities. In P. L. Hammack & B. J. Cohler (Eds.), *The story of sexual identity: Narrative perspectives on the gay and lesbian life course* (pp. 107–129). New York: Oxford University Press.

Rutherford, A., Vaughn-Blount, K., & Ball, L. C. (2010). Responsible opposition, disruptive voices: Science, social change, and the history of feminist psychology. *Psychology of Women Quarterly, 34,* 460–473.

Rutherford, A., & Yoder, J. D. (2011). Thirty-five years and counting: Feminist psychology in PWQ, a job for the long hand. *Psychology of Women Quarterly, 35,* 171–174.

Rutledge, T., Vaccarino, V., Shaw, L. J., & Bairey Merz, C. N. (2012). Gender differences in psychosocial risk factors and cardiovascular disease. In R. Alan & J. Fisher (Eds.), *Heart and mind: The practice of cardiac psychology* (2nd ed., pp. 327–352). Washington, DC: American Psychological Association.

Rutledge, T., et al. (2009). Comorbid depression and anxiety symptoms as predictors of cardiovascular events: Results from the NHLBI-sponsored women's ischemia syndrome evaluation (WISE) study. *Psychosomatic Medicine, 71,* 958–964.

Ryan, M. K., Haslam, S. A., Hersby, M. D., Kulich, C., & Wilson-Kovacs, M. D. (2009). The stress of working on the edge: Implications of glass cliffs for both women and organizations. In M. Barreto, M. K. Ryan, & M. T. Schmitt (Eds.), *The glass ceiling in the 21st century: Understanding barriers to gender equality* (pp. 153–169). Washington, DC: American Psychological Association.

Ryan, S., Franzetta, K., & Manlove, J. (2007). Knowledge, perceptions, and motivations for contraception: Influence on teens' contraceptive consistency. *Youth & Society, 39,* 182–208.

Rydell, R. J., Shiffrin, R. M., Boucher, K. L., Van Loo, K., & Rydell, M. T. (2010). Stereotype threat prevents perceptual learning. *Preceedings of the National Academy of Sciences, 107,* 14042–14047.

Ryle, R. (2011). *Questioning gender: A sociological exploration.* Thousand Oaks, CA: Pine Forge Press.

Saad, L. (2010, May). *Four moral issues sharply divide Americans.* Princeton, NJ: Gallup, Inc.

Sabattini, L., & Crosby, F. J. (2009). Ceilings and walls: Work-life and "family-friendly" policies. In M. Barreto, M. K. Ryan, & M. T. Schmitt (Eds.), *The glass ceiling in the 21st century: Understanding barriers to gender equality* (pp. 201–223). Washington, DC: American Psychological Association.

Sabattini, L., & Dinolfo, S. (2010). *Unwritten rules: Why doing a good job might not be enough.* New York: Catalyst.

Sachs-Ericsson, N., & Ciarlo, J. A. (2000). Gender, social roles, and mental health: An epidemiological perspective. *Sex Roles, 43,* 605–628.

Sadker, D., & Zittleman, K. (2009). *Still failing at fairness: How gender bias cheats girls and boys in school and what we can do about it.* New York: Scribner.

Sadker, M., & Sadker, D. (1994). *Failing at fairness: How America's schools cheat girls.* New York: Scribner.

Sadler, C., et al. (2010). Lifestyle factors, hormonal contraception, and prementrual symptoms: The United Kingdom Southampton women's survey. *Journal of Women's Health, 19,* 391–396.

Safran, M. A., et al. (2009). Mental health disparities. *American Journal of Public Health, 99,* 1962–1966.

Saftlas, A. F., et al. (2000). Racial disparity in pregnancy-related mortality associated with live birth: Can established risk factors explain it? *American Journal of Epidemiology, 152,* 413–419.

Sai, F. T. (2010). Women's health in a multicultural world: Challenges and progress in Africa. In P. Murthy & C. L. Smith (Eds.), *Women's global health and human rights* (pp. 499–508). Sudbury, MA: Jones and Bartlett.

Salafia, E. H. B., Gondoli, D. M., Corning, A. F., Bucchianeri, M. M., & Godinez, N. M. (2008). Longitudinal examination of maternal psychological control and adolescents' self-competence as predictors of bulimic symptoms among boys and girls. *International Journal of Eating Disorders, 42,* 422–428.

Salazar, L. F., et al. (2009). Applying ecological perspectives to adolescent sexual health in the United States: Rhetoric or reality? *Health Education Research, 25,* 552–562.

Salomone, R. (2007, February 16). A place for women's colleges. *Chronicle of Higher Education,* p. B20.

Sammel, M. D., Freeman, E. W., Liu, Z., Lin, H., & Guo, W. (2009). Factors that influence entry into stages of the menopausal transition. *Menopause, 16,* 1218–1227.

Sanchez, M. (2010). Older women's access to health and human rights. In P. Murthy & C. L. Smith (Eds.), *Women's global health and human rights* (pp. 393–408). Sudbury, MA: Jones and Bartlett.

Sanchez-Hucles, J. V. (2003). Intimate relationships. In L. Slater, J. H. Daniel, & A. E. Banks (Eds.), *The complete guide to mental health for women* (pp. 104–120). Boston, MA: Beacon Press.

Sanci, L., et al. (2008). Childhood sexual abuse and eating disorders in females. *Archives of Pediatrics and Adolescent Medicine, 162,* 261–267.

Sandall, J., Devane, D., Soltani, H., & Hatem, M. (2010). Improving quality and safety in maternity care: The contribution of midwife-led care. *Journal of Midwifery & Women's Health, 55,* 255–261.

Sandelowski, M., Barroso, J., & Voils, C. I. (2009). Gender, race/ethnicity and social class in research reports on stigma in HIV-positive women. *Health Care for Women International, 30,* 273–288.

Sander, L. (2011, March 4). In the game, but rarely No. 1. *Chronicle of Higher Education,* pp. A1, A15.

Sanders, S. A., Reece, M., Herbenick, D., Schick, V., Dodge, B., & Fortenberry, J. D. (2010). Condom use during most recent vaginal intercourse event among a probability sample of adults in the United States. *Journal of Sexual Medicine, 7,* 362–373.

Sandhu, H., Adams, A., Singleton, L., Clark-Carter, D., & Kidd, J. (2009). The impact of gender dyads on doctor-patient communication: A systematic review. *Patient Education and Counseling, 76,* 348–355.

Sanmartin, C., et al. (2004). *Joint Canada/United States survey of health, 2002-03* (Catalogue 82M0022-XIE). Canada: Centers for Disease Control and Prevention and Statistics.

Santelli, J. S., Orr, M., Lindberg, L. D., & Diaz, D. C. (2009). Changing behavioral risk for pregnancy among high school students in the United States, 1991–2007. *Journal of Adolescent Health, 45,* 25–32.

Sardadvar, K. (2011). Household division of labor. In M. Z. Stange, C. K. Oyster, & J. E. Sloan (Eds.), *Encyclopedia of women in today's world* (Vol. 2, pp. 726–728). Newberry Park, CA: Sage.

Sargent, J., Stein, K., & Rosen, D. (2009). Eating disorders. In J. C. Urbancic & C. J. Groh (Eds.), *Women's mental health: A clinical guide for primary care providers* (pp. 180–224). Philadelphia, PA: Lippincott Williams & Wilkins.

Sarkisian, N., & Gerstel, N. (2008). Till marriage do us part: Adult children's relationships with their parents. *Journal of Marriage and Family, 70,* 360–376.

Sarwer, D. B., Infield, A. L., & Crerand, C. E. (2009). Plastic surgery for children and adults. In L. Smolak & J. K. Thompson (Ed.), *Body image, eating disorders, and obesity in youth: Assessment, prevention, and treatment* (pp. 303–326). Washington, DC: American Psychological Association.

Sasaki, T., Hazen, N. L., & Swann, W. B., Jr. (2010). The supermom trap: Do involved dads erode moms' self-competence? *Personal Relationships, 17,* 71–79.

Sassler, S. (2010). Partnering across the life course: Sex, relationships, and mate selection. *Journal of Marriage and Family, 72,* 557–575.

Saul, S. (2009a, December 13). Building a baby, with few ground rules. *New York Times,* p. A1.

Saul, S. (2009b, October 11). The gift of life, and its price. *New York Times,* pp. A1, A24–A25.

Saunders, K. J., & Kashubeck-West, S. (2006). The relations among feminist identity development, gender-role orientation, and psychological well-being in women. *Psychology of Women Quarterly, 30,* 199–211.

Sava, S., McCaffrey, A., & Yurgelun-Todd, D. A. (2009). Gender, cognition and addiction. In K. T. Brady, S. E. Back, & S. F. Greenfield (Eds.), *Women and addiction: A comprehensive handbook* (pp. 133–146). New York: Guilford.

Savin-Williams, R. C. (2006). Who's gay? Does it matter? *Current Directions in Psychological Science, 15,* 40–44.

Sawchuk, D. (2009). The raging grannies: Defying stereotypes and embracing aging through activism. *Journal of Women & Aging, 21,* 171–185.

Sax, L. (2010). *Girls on the edge: The four factors driving the new crisis for girls: Sexual identity, the cyberbubble, obsessions, environmental toxins.* New York: Basic Books.

Sax, L. J. (2008). *The gender gap in college: Maximizing the developmental potential of women and men.* San Francisco, CA: Jossey-Bass.

Sax, L. J., & Bryant, A. N. (2006). The impact of college on sex-atypical career choices of men and women. *Journal of Vocational Behavior, 68,* 52–63.

Sayal, K., Heron, J., Golding, J., & Emond, A. (2007). Prenatal alcohol exposure and gender differences in childhood mental health problems: A longitudinal population-based study. *Pediatrics, 119,* 426–434.

Sayer, L. C. (2005). Gender, time, and inequality: Trends in women's and men's paid work, unpaid work, and free time. *Social Forces, 84,* 285–303.

Sbarra, D. A., & Nietert, P. J. (2009). Divorce and death: Forty years of the Charleston heart study. *Psychological Science, 20,* 107–113.

Scarborough, E. (2005, Winter). Constructing a women's history of psychology. *Feminist Psychologist,* p. 6.

Scarborough, E. (2010, September). Understanding the animal mind. *Monitor on Psychology, 41,* 28–29.

Schachner, D. A., Shaver, P. R., & Gillath, O. (2008). Attachment style and long-term singlehood. *Personal Relationships, 15,* 479–491.

Schalet, A. (2010). Sexual subjectivity revisited: The significance of relationships in Dutch and American girls' experiences of sexuality. *Gender & Society, 24,* 304–329.

Scheckler, R. K. (2011). Computer science, women in. In M. Z. Stange, C. K. Oyster, & J. E. Sloan (Eds.), *Encyclopedia of women in today's world* (Vol. 1, pp. 323–326). Newberry Park, CA: Sage.

Schellenbach, C. J., Strader, K., Pernice-Duca, F., & Key-Carniak, M. (2010). Building strengths and resilience among at-risk mothers and their children: A community- based prevention partnership. In R. D. Peters, B. Leadbeater, & R. J. McMahon (Eds.), *Resilience in children, families, and communities: Linking context to practice and policy* (pp. 101–116). New York: Kluwer Academic/Plenum.

Schick, V., et al. (2010). Sexual behaviors, condom use, and sexual health of Americans over 50: Implications for sexual health promotion for older adults. *International Society for Sexual Medicine, 7,* 315–329.

Schiebinger, L., & Gilmartin, S. K. (2010, January–February). Housework is and academic issue. *Academe, 96,* 39–44.

Schiffman, M., & Wacholder, S. (2009). From India to the world—a better way to prevent cervical cancer. *New England Journal of Medicine, 360,* 1453–1455.

Schilt, K., & Westbrook, L. (2009). Doing gender, doing heteronormativity: "Gender normals," transgender people, and the social maintenance of heterosexuality. *Gender & Society, 23,* 440–464.

Schmader, T. (2010). Stereotype threat deconstructed. *Current Directions in Psychological Science, 19,* 14–18.

Schmitt, M. T., Branscombe, N. R., Kobrynowicz, D., & Owen, S. (2002). Perceiving discrimination against one's gender group has different implications for well-being in women and men. *Personality and Social Psychology Bulletin, 28,* 197–210.

Schmitt, M. T., Spoor, J. R., Danaher, K., & Branscombe, N. R. (2009). Rose-colored glasses: How tokenism and comparisons with the past reduce the visibility of gender inequality. In M. Barreto, M. K. Ryan, & M. T. Schmitt (Eds.), *The glass ceiling in the 21st century: Understanding barriers to gender equality* (pp. 49–71). Washington, DC: American Psychological Association.

Schmittdiel, J. A., Traylor, A., Uratsu, C. S., Mangione, C. M., Ferrara, A., & Subramanian, U. (2009). The association of patient-physician gender concordance with cardiovascular disease risk factor control and treatment in diabetes. *Journal of Women's Health, 18,* 2065–2070.

Schneider, C., & Segre, T. (2009). Green tea: Potential health benefits. *American Family Physician, 79,* 591–594.

Schnurr, M. P., Lohman, B. J., & Kaura, S. A. (2010). Variation in late adolescents' reports of dating violence perpetration: A dyadic analysis. *Violence and Victims, 25,* 84–100.

Schoen, R., et al. (2002). Women's employment, marital happiness, and divorce. *Social Forces, 81,* 643–662.

Schoenberg, N. E., Peters, J. C., & Drew, E. M. (2003). Unraveling the mysteries of timing: Women's perceptions about time to treatment for cardiac symptoms. *Social Science & Medicine, 56,* 271–284.

Schoenfeld, R., Lehmann, W., & Leplow, B. (2010). Effects of age and sex in mental rotation and spatial learning from virtual environments. *Journal of Individual Differences, 31,* 78–82.

Schoevers, R. A., Geerlings, M. I., Deeg, D. J. H., Holwerda, T. J., Jonker, C., & Beekman, A. T. F. (2009). Depression and excess mortality: Evidence for a dose response relation in community living elderly. *International Journal of Geriatric Psychiatry, 24,* 169–176.

Scholtz, S., Hill, L. S., & Lacey, H. (2010). Eating disorders in older women: Does late onset anorexia nervosa exist? *International Journal of Eating Disorders, 43,* 393–397.

Schooler, D. (2008). Real women have curves: A longitudinal investigation of TV and the body image development of Latina adolescents. *Journal of Adolescent Research, 23,* 132–153.

Schoon, I., Ross, A., & Martin, P. (2007). Science related careers: Aspirations and outcomes in two British cohort studies. *Equal Opportunities International, 26,* 129–143.

Schuette, C., & Killen, M. (2009). Children's evaluations of gender-stereotypic household activities in the family context. *Early Education and Development, 20,* 693–712.

Schulman, A. (2003). Female sexuality. In L. Slater, J. H. Daniel, & A. E. Banks (Eds.), *The complete guide to mental health for women* (pp. 82–91). Boston, MA: Beacon Press.

Schultz, K. S., & Wang, M. (2011). Psychological perspectives on the changing nature of retirement. *American Psychologist, 66,* 170–179.

Schultz, R. M., & Beals, K. P. (2010). Sexual minority women: Sources and outcomes of stigmatization. In M. A. Paludi (Ed.), *Feminism and women's rights worldwide* (Vol. 1, pp. 125–148). Santa Barbara, CA: Praeger.

Schuppe, J. (2007). Women in the State Police: Trouble in the ranks. In P. S. Rothenberg (Ed.), *Race, class, and gender in the United States: An integrated study* (7th ed., pp. 274–277). New York: Worth.

Schur, L. (2004). Is there still a "double handicap"? Economic, social, and political disparities experienced by women with disabilities. In B. G. Smith & B. Hutchison (Eds.), *Gendering disability* (pp. 253–271). Piscataway, NJ: Rutgers University Press.

Schur, L., Kruse, D., Blasi, J., & Blanck, P. (2009). Is disability disabling in all workplaces? Workplace disparities and corporate culture. *Industrial Relations, 48,* 381–406.

Schüz, B., Wurm, S., Warner, L. M., & Tesch-Römer, C. (2009). Health and subjective well-being in later adulthood: Different health states—different needs? *Applied Psychology: Health and Well-Being, 1,* 23–45.

Schwartz, G. M., & Campagna, J. (2008). New meaning for the emotional state of the elderly, from a leisure standpoint. *Leisure Studies, 27,* 207–211.

Schwartz, J. (2010). Investigating differences in public support for gay rights issues. *Journal of Homosexuality, 57,* 748–759.

Schwartz, J. (2011). Whose voices are heard? Gender, sexual orientation, and newspaper sources. *Sex Roles, 64,* 265–275.

Schwartz, P. (2007). *Prime: Adventures and advice on sex, love, and the sensual years.* New York: HarperCollins.

Schwartz, S. H., & Rubel-Lifschitz, T. (2009). Cross-national variation in the size of sex differences in values: Effects of gender equality. *Journal of Personality and Social Psychology, 97,* 171–185.

Scott, L. S. (2009). *Two is enough: A couple's guide to living childless by choice.* Berkeley, CA: Seal Press.

Scully, J. L., Baldwin-Ragaven, L., & Fitzpatrick, P. (2010). *Feminist bioethics at the center, on the margins.* Baltimore, MD: Johns Hopkins University Press.

Sear, R., & Mace, R. (2008). Who keeps children alive? A review of the effects of kin on child survival. *Evolution and Human Behavior, 29,* 1–18.

Sears, K. L., Intrieri, R. C., & Papini, D. R. (2011). Sexual harassment and psychosocial maturity outcomes among young adults recalling their first adolescent work experiences. *Sex Roles, 64,* 491–505.

Sechrist, G. B. (2010). Making attributions to and plans to confront gender discrimination: The role of optimism. *Journal of Applied Social Psychology, 40,* 1678–1707.

Sechzer, J., & Rabinowitz, V. C. (2008). Feminist perspectives on research methods. In F. L. Denmark & M. A. Paludi (Eds.), *Psychology of women: A handbook of issues and theories* (2nd ed., pp. 93–141). Westport, CT: Praeger.

Seedat, S., et al. (2009). Cross-national associations between gender and mental disorders in the World Health Organization world mental health surveys. *Archives of General Psychiatry, 66,* 785–795.

Seedyk, E., & deLaet, M. (2005). Women, games, and women's games. *Phi Kappa Phi Forum, 85*(2), 25–28.

Seem, S. R., & Clark, M. D. (2006). Healthy women, healthy men, and healthy adults: An evaluation of gender role stereotypes in the twenty-first century. *Sex Roles, 55,* 247–258.

Seeman, M. V. (2009). Mechanisms of sex difference: A historical perspective. *Journal of Women's Health, 18,* 861–866.

Seeman, T. E., Merkin, S. S., Crimmins, E. M., & Karlamangla, A. S. (2010). Disability trends among older Americans: National health and nutrition examination surveys, 1988–1994 and 1999–2004. *American Journal of Public Health, 100,* 100–107.

Segal, D. L., Honn Qualls, S., & Smyer, M. A. (2011). *Aging and mental health* (2nd ed.). Malden, MA: Wiley.

Seiden, O. J., & Bilett, J. L. (2007). *Sex in the golden years: The best sex ever.* Parker, CO: Thornton.

Seidman, I., & Pokorak, J. J. (2011). Justice responses to sexual violence. In M. P. Koss, J. W. White, & A. E. Kazdin (Eds.), *Violence against women and children: Navigating solutions* (Vol. 2, pp. 137–158). Washington, DC: American Psychological Association.

Seitz, V., & Apfel, N. (2010). Creating effective school-based interventions for pregnant teenagers. In R. D. Peters, B. Leadbeater, & R. J. McMahon (Eds.), *Resilience in children, families and communities: Linking context to practice and policy* (pp. 65–82). New York: Kluwer Academic/Plenum.

Sellers, S. A. (2008). *Native American women's studies: A primer.* New York: Peter Lang.

Selwyn, N. (2007). Hi-tech = Guy-tech? An exploration of undergraduate students' gendered perceptions of information and communication technologies. *Sex Roles, 56,* 525–536.

Sen, A. K. (2010). More than 100 million women are missing. In P. Murthy & C. L. Smith (Eds.), *Women's global health and human rights* (pp. 99–112). Sudbury, MA: Jones and Bartlett.

Sengupta, R. (2006). Reading representations of Black, East Asian, and White women in magazines for adolescent girls. *Sex Roles, 54,* 799–808.

Serbin, L. A., Powlishta, K. K., & Gulko, J. (1993). The development of sex-typing in middle childhood. *Monographs of the Society for Research in Child Development, 58,* 1–95. (Serial No. 232).

Serbin, L. A., et al. (2001). Gender stereotyping in infancy: Visual preferences for knowledge of gender-stereotyped toys in the second year. *International Journal of Behavioral Development, 25,* 7–15.

Serbin, L. A., et al. (2004). When aggressive girls become mothers: Problems in parenting, health, and development across two generations. In M. Putallaz & K. L. Bierman (Eds.), *Aggression, antisocial behavior, and violence among girls: A developmental perspective* (pp. 262–288). New York: Guilford.

Settersten, R. A., Jr., & Trauten, M. E. (2009). The new terrain of old age: Hallmarks, freedoms, and risks. In V. Bengtson, M.

Silverstein, N. M. Putney, & D. Gans (Eds.), *Handbook of theories of aging* (2nd ed., pp. 455–469). New York: Springer.

Settles, I. H., Cortina, L. M., Stewart, A. J., & Malley, J. (2007). Voice matters: Buffering the impact of a negative climate for women in science. *Psychology of Women Quarterly, 31,* 270–281.

Settles, I. H., Pratt-Hyatt, J. S., & Buchanan, N. T. (2008). Through the lens of race: Black and White women's perceptions of womanhood. *Psychology of Women Quarterly, 32,* 454–468.

Shacklock, K., Brunetto, Y., & Nelson, S. (2009). The different variables that affect older males' and females' intentions to continue working. *Asia Pacific Journal of Human Resources, 47,* 79–101.

Shah, K., & Batzer, F. (2010, Fall). Infertility in the developing world: The conbined role for feminists and disability rights proponents. *International Journal of Feminist Approaches to Bioethics, 3,* 109–125.

Shakespeare-Finch, J., & De Dassel, T. (2009). Exploring posttraumatic outcomes as a function of childhood sexual abuse. *Journal of Child Sexual Abuse, 18,* 623–640.

Shakin, M., Shakin, D., & Sternglanz, S. H. (1985). Infant clothing: Sex labeling for strangers. *Sex Roles, 12,* 955–964.

Shankar, A., McMunn, A., & Steptoe, A. (2010). Health-related behaviors in older adults relationships with socioeconomic status. *American Journal of Preventative Medicine, 38,* 39–46.

Shanok, A. F., & Miller, L. (2007). Stepping up to motherhood among inner-city teens. *Psychology of Women Quarterly, 31,* 252–261.

Shapiro, J. R., & Neuberg, S. L. (2007). From stereotype threat to stereotype threats: Implications of a multi-threat framework for causes, moderators, mediators, consequences, and interventions. *Personality and Social Psychology Review, 11,* 107–130.

Share, T. L., & Mintz, L. B. (2002). Differences between lesbians and heterosexual women in disordered eating and related attitudes. *Journal of Homosexuality, 42,* 89–106.

Sharp, E. A., & Ganong, L. (2007). Living in the gray: Women's experiences of missing the marital transition. *Journal of Marriage and Family, 69,* 831–844.

Sharp, E. A., & Ispa, J. M. (2009). Inner-city single black mothers' gender-related childrearing expectations and goals. *Sex Roles, 60,* 656–668.

Shaw, B. A., Liang, J., Krause, N., Gallant, M., & McGeever, K. (2010). Age differences and social stratification in the long-term trajectories of leisure-time physical activity. *Journal of Gerontology: Social Sciences, 65B,* 756–766.

Shaw, L. J., et al. (2008). Importance of socioeconomic status as a predictor of cardiovascular outcome and costs of care in women with suspected myocardial ischemia. Results from the national institutes of health, national heart, lung and blood institute-sponsored women's ischemia syndrome evaluation (WISE). *Journal of Women's Health, 17,* 1081–1092.

Sheehan, N. W., & Petrovic, K. (2008). Grandparents and their adult grandchildren: Recurring themes from the literature. *Marriage & Family Review, 44,* 99–124.

Sheehy, G. (2007). *Sex and the seasoned woman: Pursuing the passionate life.* New York: Ballantine.

Sheldon, K. M. (2007). Gender differences in preferences for singles ads that proclaim extrinsic versus intrinsic values. *Sex Roles, 57,* 119–128.

Shellenbarger, S. (2004). *The breaking point: How female midlife crisis is transforming today's women.* New York: Holt.

Shellenbarger, S. (2008, March 20). In search of wedded bliss: What research can tell us. *Wall Street Journal,* p. D1.

Shelley, L. (2010). *Human trafficking: A global perspective.* Cambridge, UK: Cambridge University Press.

Shelton, N. (2011). Pospartum depression. In M. Z. Stange, C. K. Oyster, & J. E. Sloan (Eds.), *Encyclopedia of women in today's world* (Vol. 3, pp. 1126–1129). Newberry Park, CA: Sage.

Shepela, S. T., & Levesque, L. L. (1998). Poisoned waters: Sexual harassment and the college climate. *Sex Roles, 38,* 589–611.

Sherman, S. R. (2001). Images of middle-aged and older women: Historical, cultural, and personal. In J. M. Coyle (Ed.), *Handbook on women and aging* (pp. 14–28). Westport, CT: Greenwood.

Sherrill, A. (2010). *Women in management: Female managers' representation, characteristics, and pay (GAO-10-1046T, 111th Cong., 1).*

Shinn, L. K., & O'Brien, M. (2008). Parent-child conversational styles in middle childhood: Gender and social class differences. *Sex Roles, 59,* 61–67.

Shipherd, J. C., Green, K. E., & Abramovitz, S. (2010). Transgender clients: Identifying and minimizing barriers to mental health treatment. *Journal of Gay & Lesbian Mental Health, 14,* 94–108.

Shirtcliff, E. A., Dahl, R. E., & Pollak, S. D. (2009). Pubertal development: Correspondence between hormonal and physical development. *Child Development, 80,* 327–337.

Short, M. B., & Rosenthal, S. L. (2008). Psychosocial development and puberty. *Annals of the New York Academy of Sciences, 1135,* 36–42.

Shulte, M. T., Ramo, D., & Brown, S. A. (2010). Gender differences in factors influencing alcohol use and drinking progression among adolescents. *Clinical Psychology Review, 29,* 535–547.

Sices, L., et al. (2004). How do primary care physicians manage children with possible developmental delays? A national survey with an experimental design. *Pediatrics, 113,* 274–282.

Sidener, J. (2004, September 27). Digital dating: A growing number of seniors are looking for love online. *Peoria Journal Star,* pp. C5, C6.

Siebenbruner, J., Zimmer-Gembeck, M. J., & Egeland, B. (2007). Sexual partners and contraceptive use: A 16-year prospective study predicting abstinence and risk behavior. *Journal of Research on Adolescence, 17,* 179–206.

Sigal, J. (2008). Stalking as a form of campus violence: Case studies. In M. A. Paludi (Ed.), *Understanding and preventing campus violence* (pp. 99–102). Westport, CT: Praeger.

Sigal, J., et al. (2005). Cross-cultural reactions to academic sexual harassment: Effects of individualist vs. collectivist culture and gender of participants. *Sex Roles, 52,* 201–215.

Sigal, J., & Wnuk-Novitskie, D. (2010). Cross-cultural violence against women and girls: From dating to intimate partner violence. In M. A. Paludi (Ed.), *Feminism and women's rights worldwide: Mental and physical health* (Vol. 2, pp. 65–102). Santa Barbara, CA: Praeger.

Signorielli, N., & Bacue, A. (1999). Recognition and respect: A content analysis of prime-time television characters across the decades. *Sex Roles, 40,* 527–544.

Silver, R. B., Measelle, J. R., & Stice, E. (2007, March). *Developmental trajectories of antisocial behavior in adolescent females: Trajectory classes, predictors, and outcomes.* Poster presented at the meeting of the Society for Research in Child Development, Boston, MA.

Silverstein, M. (2008). Do bioevolutionary forces shape intergenerational transfers? Detecting evidence in contemporary survey data. In A. Booth, A. C. Crouter, S. M. Bianchi, & J. A. Seltzer (Eds.), *Intergenerational caregiving* (pp. 127–144). Washington, DC: Urban Institute Press.

Silverstein, M., & Giarrusso, R. (2010). Aging and family life: A decade review. *Journal of Marriage and Family, 72,* 1039–1058.

Sim, L. A., Homme, J. H., Lteif, A. N., Vande Voort, J. L., Schak, K. M., & Ellingson, J. (2009). Family functioning and maternal distress in adolescent girls with anorexia nervosa. *International Journal of Eating Disorders, 42,* 531–539.

Simkhada, P. (2008). Life histories and survival strategies amongst sexually trafficked girls in Nepal. *Children & Society, 22,* 235–248.

Simkin, P., Whalley, J., Keppler, A., Durham, J., & Bolding, A. (2010). *Pregnancy, childbirth and the newborn: The complete guide* (4th ed.). Minnetonka, MN: Meadowbrook Press.

Simmons, R. G., & Blyth, D. A. (1987). *Moving into adolescence: The impact of pubertal change and school context.* Hawthorne, NY: Aldine de Gruyter.

Simon, R. W. (2008). The joys of parenthood, reconsidered. *Contexts, 7,* 40–45.

Simon, R. W., & Nath, L. E. (2004). Gender and emotion in the United States: Do men and women differ in self-reports of feelings and expressive behavior? *American Journal of Sociology, 109,* 1137–1176.

Simon, V. A., Aikins, J. W., & Prinstein, M. J. (2008). Romantic partner selection and socialization during early adolescence. *Child Development, 79,* 1676–1692.

Simoni, J. M., Evans-Campbell, T., Andrasik, M. P., Lehavot, K., Valencia-Garcia, D., & Walters, K. L. (2010). HIV/AIDS among women of color and sexual minority women. In H. Landrine & N. F. Russo (Eds.), *Handbook of diversity in feminist psychology* (pp. 335–365). New York: Springer.

Simons, R. L. (1996). The effect of divorce on adult and child adjustment. In R. L. Simons, et al. (Eds.), *Understanding differences between divorced and intact families: Stress, interaction, and child outcome* (pp. 3–20). Thousand Oaks, CA: Sage.

Simpkins, S. D., Davis-Kean, P. E., & Eccles, J. S. (2005). Parents' socializing behavior and children's participation in math, science, and computer out-of-school activities. *Applied Developmental Science, 9,* 14–30.

Simpson, R. (2011). Singletons/single by choice. In M. Z. Stange, C. K. Oyster, & J. E. Sloan (Eds.), *Encyclopedia of women in today's world (1356–1357).* Newberry Park, CA: Sage.

Singer, N. (2007, October 4). Is the "mom job" really necessary? *New York Times,* pp. E1, E3.

Singer, N. (2010, June 27). Sex and the single drug. *New York Times,* p. BU3.

Singer, N., & Wilson, D. (2009, December 13). Menopause, as brought to you by big pharma. *New York Times,* pp. BU1–BU2.

Sinha, R., Cross, A. J., Graubard, B. I., Leitzmann, M. F., & Schatzkin, A. (2009). Meat intake and mortality: A prospective study of over half a million people. *Archives of Internal Medicine, 169,* 562–571.

Sinno, S. M., & Killen, M. (2009). Moms at work and dads at home: Children's evaluations of parental roles. *Developmental Science, 13,* 16–29.

Skerrett, P. J., & Willett, W. C. (2010). Essentials of healthy eating: A guide. *Journal of Midwifery & Women's Health, 55,* 492–501.

Skodova, Z., et al. (2008). Socioeconomic differences in psychosocial factors contributing to coronary heart disease: A review. *Journal of Clinical Psychology in Medical Settings, 15,* 204–213.

Skoe, E. E. A., Cumberland, A., Eisenberg, N., Hansen, K., & Perry, J. (2002). The influences of sex and gender-idle identity on moral cognition and prosocial personality traits. *Sex Roles, 46,* 295–309.

Slagle, R. A., & Yep, G. A. (2007). Taming brain: Sex, love, and romance in *Queer* as *Folk.* In M.-L. Galician & D. L. Merskin (Eds.), *Critical thinking about sex, love, and romance in the mass media: Media literacy applications* (pp. 189–202). Mahwah, NJ: Erlbaum.

Slater, A., & Tiggemann, M. (2010). Body image and disordered eating in adolescent girls and boys: A test of objectification theory. *Sex Roles, 63,* 42–49.

Slevec, J., & Tiggemann, M. (2010). Attitudes toward cosmetic surgery in middle-aged women: Body image, aging anxiety, and the media. *Psychology of Women Quarterly, 34,* 65–74.

Slevin, K. F. (2010). "If I had lots of money . . . I'd have a body makeover:" Managing the aging body. *Social Forces, 88,* 1003–1020.

Slon, S. (2008). *Alcohol use and abuse.* Boston, MA: Harvard Medical School.

Smetana, J. G., & Daddis, C. (2002). Domain-specific antecedents of parental psychological control and monitoring: The role of parenting beliefs and practices. *Child Development, 73,* 563–580.

Smetana, J. G., Metzger, A., & Campione-Barr, N. (2004). African American late adolescents' relationships with parents: Developmental transitions and longitudinal patterns. *Child Development, 75,* 932–947.

Smirles, K. E. (2004). Attributions of responsibility in cases of sexual harassment: The person and the situation. *Journal of Applied Social Psychology, 34,* 342–365.

Smith, A. (2007). Sexual violence as a tool of genocide. In P. S. Rothenberg (Ed.), *Race, class, and gender in the United States: An integrated study* (7th ed., pp. 673–683). New York: Worth.

Smith, C. A. (2008). Women, weight, and body image. In J. C. Chrisler, C. Golden, & P. D. Rozee (Eds.), *Lectures on the psychology of women* (pp. 116–135). New York: McGraw-Hill.

Smith, C. A., & Stillman, S. (2002). What do women want? The effects of gender and sexual orientation on the desirability of physical attributes in the personal ads of women. *Sex Roles, 46,* 337–342.

Smith, C. L. (2010). Shadows on the sunshine of women's global health and human rights: The global gag rule, Tuskegee and HIV studies, tobacco marketing, torture and forced sterilization. In P. Murthy & C. L. Smith (Eds.), *Women's global health and human rights* (pp. 73–82). Sudbury, MA: Jones and Bartlett.

Smith, C. S. (2011). Psychotropic medications. In M. S. Stange, C. K. Oyster, & J. E. Sloan (Eds.), *Encyclopedia of women in today's world* (Vol. 3, pp. 1184–1185). Newberry Park, CA: Sage.

Smith, C. S., & Li-Ching, H. (2011). Megan's law. In M. Z. Stange, C. K. Oyster, & J. E. Sloan (Eds.), *Encyclopedia of women in today's world* (Vol. 2, pp. 920–922). Newberry Park, CA: Sage.

Smith, D. (2005, January 16). Brown: Let women lead Africa out of poverty. *Sunday Times (London),* p. 8.

Smith, G., Mysak, K., & Michael, S. (2008). Sexual double standards and sexually transmitted illnesses: Social rejection and stigmatization of women. *Sex Roles, 58,* 391–401.

Smith, J. L. (2006). The interplay among stereotypes, performance-avoidance goals, and women's math performance expectations. *Sex Roles, 54,* 287–296.

Smith, K. P., & Christakis, N. A. (2009). Association between widowhood and risk of diagnosis with a sexually transmitted infection in older adults. *American Journal of Public Health, 99,* 2055–2062.

Smith, S. J., Axelton, A. M., & Saucier, D. A. (2009). The effects of contact on sexual prejudice: A meta-analysis. *Sex Roles, 61,* 178–191.

Smith, S. L., Kennard, C., & Granados, A. D. (2009). Sexy socialization: Today's media and the next generation of women. In M. Shriver (Ed.), *The Shriver report: A woman's nation changes everything* (pp. 310–317). Washington, DC: Maria Shriver and the Center for American Progress.

Smith, S. L., Pieper, K. M., Granados, A., & Choueiti, M. (2010). Assessing gender-related portrayals in top-grossing G-rated films. *Sex Roles, 62,* 774–786.

Smits, A., Van Gaalen, R. I., & Mulder, C. H. (2010). Parent-child coresidence: Who moves in with whom and for whose needs? *Journal of Marriage and Family, 72,* 1022–1033.

Smock, P. J., & Greenland, F. R. (2010). Diversity in pathways to parenthood: Patterns, implications, and emerging research directions. *Journal of Marriage and Family, 72,* 576–593.

Smolak, L. (2009). Risk factors in the development of body image, eating problems, and obesity. In L. Smolak & J. K. Thompson (Eds.), *Body image, eating disorders, and obesity in youth: Assessment, prevention, and treatment* (pp. 135–156). Washington, DC: American Psychological Association.

Smolak, L., & Munstertieger, B. F. (2002). The relationship of gender and voice to depression and eating disorders. *Psychology of Women Quarterly, 26,* 234–241.

Smolak, L., & Thompson, J. K. (Eds.). (2009). *Body image, eating disorders, and obesity in youth: Assessment, prevention, and treatment.* Washington, DC: American Psychological Association.

Smolderen, K. G., et al. (2010). Health care insurance, financial concerns in accessing care, and delays to hospital presentation in acute myocardial infarction. *Journal of the American Medical Association, 303,* 1392–1400.

Snell, M. B. (2002, November/December). Good going. *Sierra,* pp. 26–27.

Snowden, M., Steinman, L., & Frederick, J. (2008). Treating depression in older adults: Challenges to implementing the recommendations of an expert panel. *Preventing Chronic Disease, 5.* Retrieved from http://www.cdc.gov/pcd/issues/2008/jan/07_0154.htm

Snyder, N. M. (1994). Career women and motherhood: Child care dilemmas and choices. In C. W. Konek & S. L. Kitch (Eds.), *Women and careers: Issues and challenges* (pp. 155–172). Thousand Oaks, CA: Sage.

Snyder, T. D., & Dillow, S. A. (2010). *Digest of education statistics 2009.* Washington, DC: National Center for Education Statistics.

Sobchack, V. (2009). Scary women: Cinema, surgery, and special effects. In C. J. Heyes & M. Jones (Eds.), *Cosmetic surgery: A feminist primer* (pp. 79–95). Burlington, VT: Ashgate.

Social Security Administration. (2009). *What every woman should know* (SSA Publication No. 05-10127). Washington, DC: Author.

Society of Actuaries. (2010). *Key findings and issues: The impact of retirement risk on women.* Schaumburg, IL: Author.

Solberg, J. (2010). Sexual harassment laws' impact on women. In M. A. Paludi (Ed.), *Feminism and women's rights worldwide: Feminism as human rights* (Vol. 2, pp. 209–238). Santa Barbara, CA: Praeger.

Solomon, C. (2005, July 17). Mean girls. *New York Times,* p. AR4.

Son, J., Yarnal, C., & Kerstetter, D. (2010). Engendering social capital through a leisure club for middle-aged and older women: Implications for individual and community health and well-being. *Leisure Studies, 29,* 67–83.

Sonfield, A. (2010). Contraception: An integral component of preventive care for women. *Guttmacher Policy Review, 13*(2), 2–7.

Sonnert, G., & Holton, G. (1996). Career patterns of women and men in the sciences. *American Scientist, 84,* 63–71.

Sontag, S. (1997). The double standard of aging. In M. Pearsall (Ed.), *The other within us: Feminist exploration of women and aging* (pp. 19–24). Boulder, CO: Westview Press.

Soons, J. P., & Kalmijn, M. (2009). Is marriage more than cohabitation? Well-being differences in 30 European countries. *Journal of Marriage and Family, 71,* 1141–1157.

Sorenson, S. B. (1996). Violence against women: Examining ethnic differences and commonalities. *Evaluation Review, 20,* 123–145.

Spade, J. Z., & Valentine, C. G. (Eds.). (2011). *The kaleidoscope of gender: Prisms, patterns, and possibilities* (3rd ed.). Thousand Oaks, CA: Sage.

Speer, S. A., & Stokoe, E., (Eds.). (2011). *Conversation and gender.* Cambridge, UK: Cambridge University Press.

Spelke, E. S. (2005). Sex differences in intrinsic aptitude for mathematics and science? A critical review. *American Psychologist, 60,* 950–958.

Spence, J. T., & Buckner, C. E. (2000). Instrumental and expressive traits, trait stereotypes, and sexist attitudes: What do they signify? *Psychology of Women Quarterly, 24,* 44–62.

Spence, J. T., & Helmreich, R. L. (1978). *Masculinity & femininity: Their psychological dimensions, correlates, & antecedents.* Austin, TX: University of Texas Press.

Spencer, J. M., et al. (2002). Self-esteem as a predictor of initiation of coitus in early adolescents. *Pediatrics, 109,* 581–584.

Sperry, S., Roehrig, M., & Thompson, J. K. (2009). Treatment of eating disorders in childhood and adolescence. In L. Smolak & J. K. Thompson (Eds.), *Body image, eating disorders, and obesity in youth: Assessment, prevention, and treatment* (pp. 261–280). Washington, DC: American Psychological Association.

Spiegel, D. (2011). Mind matters in cancer survival. *Journal of the American Medical Association, 305,* 502.

Spitzberg, B. H., & Cupach, W. R. (2007). The state of the art of stalking: Taking stock of the emerging literature. *Aggression and Violent Behavior, 12,* 64–86.

Spitzer, R. L., et al. (Eds.). (1994). *DSM-IV casebook.* Washington, DC: American Psychiatric Association.

Sprecher, S., Fehr, B., & Zimmerman, C. (2007). Expectation for mood enhancement as a result of helping: The effects of gender and compassionate love. *Sex Roles, 56,* 543–549.

Sprecher, S., & Felmlee, D. (1997). The balance of power in romantic heterosexual couples over time from "his" and "her" perspectives. *Sex Roles, 37,* 361–379.

Sprecher, S., Schwartz, P., Harvey, J., & Hatfield, E. (2008). TheBusinessofLove.com: Relationship initiation at internet matchmaking services. In S. Sprecher, A. Wenzel, & J. Harvey (Eds.), *Handbook of relationship initiation* (pp. 249–268). New York: Psychology Press.

Springen, K., & Seibert, S. (2005, January 17). Artful aging. *Newsweek,* pp. 57–65.

Springer, K. W. (2010). The race and class privilege of motherhood: New York Times presentations of pregnant drug-using women. *Sociological Forum, 25,* 476–499.

Spurgeon, D. (2007). Gender gap persists in treatment of Canadians after heart attack and stroke. *British Medical Journal, 334,* 280.

Srivastava, S., John, O. P., Gosling, S. D., & Potter, J. (2003). Development of personality in early and middle adulthood: Set like plaster or persistent change? *Journal of Personality and Social Psychology, 84,* 1041–1053.

Sroufe, L. A., Bennett, C., Englund, M., Urban, J., & Shulman, S. (1993). The significance of gender boundaries in preadolescence: Contemporary correlates and antecedents of boundary violation and maintenance. *Child Development, 64,* 455–466.

St. John, P. D., Montgomery, P. R., & Tyas, S. L. (2009). Alcohol misuse, gender and depressive symptoms in community-dwelling seniors. *International Journal of Geriatric Psychiatry, 24,* 369–375.

St. John, W. (2002, May 20). The talk of the book world still can't sell. *New York Times,* pp. A1, A16.

St. Rose, A. (2010, Winter). Why so few? Women in science, technology, engineering, and mathematics. *AAUW Outlook, 104*(1), 8–11.

Stacey, J., & Biblarz, T. J. (2001). (How) does the sexual orientation of parents matter? *American Sociological Review, 66,* 159–183.

Staff, J., Messersmith, E. E., & Schulenberg, J. E. (2009). Adolescents and the world of work. In R. M. Lerner & L. Steinberg (Eds.), *Handbook of adolescent psychology* (3rd ed., Vol. 2, pp. 270–313). Hoboken, NJ: Wiley.

Stake, J. E. (1997). Integrating expressiveness and instrumentality in real-life settings: A new perspective on the benefits of androgyny. *Sex Roles, 37,* 541–564.

Stake, J. E. (2007). Predictors of change in feminist activism through women's and gender studies. *Sex Roles, 57,* 43–54.

Stake, J. E., & Malkin, C. (2003). Students' quality of experience and perceptions of intolerance and bias in the women's and gender studies classroom. *Psychology of Women Quarterly, 27*, 174–185.

Stake, J. E., Roades, L., Rose, S., Ellis, L., & West, C. (1994). The women's studies experience: Impetus for feminist activism. *Sex Roles, 18*, 17–24.

Stake, J. E., & Rose, S. (1994). The long-term impact of women's studies on students' personal lives and political activism. *Psychology of Women Quarterly, 18*, 403–412.

Stankiewicz, J. M., & Rosselli, F. (2008). Women as sex objects and victims in print advertisements. *Sex Roles, 58*, 579–589.

Stanley, A. (2002, January 13). For women, to soar is rare, to fall is human. *New York Times*, pp. BU1, BU10.

Stanley, D., & Freysinger, V. J. (1995). The impact of age, health, and sex on the frequency of older adult's leisure activity participation: A longitudinal study. *Activities, Adaptation & Aging, 19*, 31–42.

Stanley, S. M., Rhoades, G. K., Amato, P. R., Markman, H. J., & Johnson, C. A. (2010). The timing of cohabitation and engagement: Impact on first and second marriages. *Journal of Marriage and Family, 72*, 906–918.

Stanley, S. M., Rhoades, G. K., & Fincham, F. D. (2011). Understanding romantic relationships among emerging adults: The significant roles of cohabitation and ambiguity. In F. D. Fincham & M. Cui (Eds.), *Romantic relationships in emerging adulthood* (pp. 234–251). New York: Cambridge University Press.

Stanton, A. L. (1995). Psychology of women's health: Barriers and pathways to knowledge. In A. L. Stanton & S. J. Gallant (Eds.), *The psychology of women's health: Progress and challenges in research and application* (pp. 3–21). Washington, DC: American Psychological Association.

Stark, E. (2010). Do violent acts equal abuse? Resolving the gender parity/asymmetry dilemma. *Sex Roles, 62*, 201–211.

The State of the Kid: 2009 survey results. (2009). *Highlights Magazine*. Columbus, OH: Author.

Statistics Canada. (2006, November 27). *Readiness to learn at school among five-year-old children in Canada.* Retrieved from http://www.statcan.ca/english/research/89-599-MIE/89-599-MIE2006004.pdf

Staudinger, U. M., & Bowen, C. E. (2010). Life-span perspectives on positive personality development in adulthood and old age. In M. E. Lamb & A. M. Freund (Eds.), *The handbook of life-span development: Social and emotional development* (Vol. 2, pp. 254–297). Hoboken, NJ: Wiley.

Steele, C. M., Spencer, S. J., & Aronson, J. (2002). Contending with group image: The psychology of stereotype and social identity threat. In M. P. Zanna (Ed.), *Advances in experimental social psychology, 34*, 379–440.

Steele, J., James, J. B., & Barnett, R. C. (2002). Learning in a man's world: Examining the perceptions of undergraduate women in male-dominated academic areas. *Psychology of Women Quarterly, 26*, 46–50.

Steffens, M. C., & Jelenec, P. (2011). Separating implicit gender stereotypes regarding math and language: Implicit ability stereotypes and self-serving for boys and men, but not for girls and women. *Sex Roles, 64*, 324–335.

Steinberg, J. R., & Finer, L. B. (2011). Examining the association of abortion history and current mental health: A reanalysis of the national comorbidity survey using a common-risk-factors model. *Social Science & Medicine, 72*, 72–82.

Steinberg, J. R., True, M., & Russo, N. F. (2008). Work and family roles: Selected issues. In F. L. Denmark & M. A. Paludi (Eds.), *Psychology of women: A handbook of issues and theories* (2nd ed., pp. 652–700). Westport, CT: Praeger.

Steinmayr, R., & Spinath, B. (2009). What explains boys stronger confidence in their intelligence? *Sex Roles, 61*, 736–749.

Stephan, Y., Boiché, J., & Le Scanff, C. (2010). Motivation and physical activity behaviors among older women: A self-determination perspective. *Psychology of Women Quarterly, 3*, 339–348.

Stephens, J., Moore, B., Galyon, A., Wright, C., & Brinthaupt, T. (2007, May). *BMI, fitness, and body image dissatisfaction in young children.* Poster presented at the annual meeting of the Midwestern Psychological Association, Chicago, IL.

Stephens, M. A. P., Franks, M. M., Martire, L. M., Norton, T. R., & Atienza, A. A. (2009). Women at midlife: Stress and rewards of balancing parent care with employment and other family roles. In K. Shifren (Ed.), *How caregiving affects development: Psychological implications for child, adolescent, and adult caregivers* (pp. 147–167). Washington, DC: American Psychological Association.

Stephens, M. B. (2009). Cardiac rehabilitation. *American Family Physician, 80*, 955–959.

Stephenson, J. (2010). Human trafficking in Europe. *Journal of the American Medical Association, 304*, 513.

Stepp, L. S. (2007). *Unhooked: How young women pursue sex, delay love and lose at both.* New York: Penguin.

Stern, M., & Karraker, K. H. (1989). Sex stereotyping of infants: A review of gender labeling studies. *Sex Roles, 20*, 501–521.

Stern, T. (2008). Self-esteem and high-achieving women. In M. A. Paludi (Ed.), *The psychology of women at work: Challenges and solutions for our female workforce: Self, family, and social affects* (Vol. 3, pp. 25–53). Westport, CT: Praeger.

Stevens, L. M. (2010). Postpartum depression. *Journal of the American Medical Association, 304*, 1736.

Stevens, L. M., Lynm, C., & Glass, R. M. (2010). Postpartum depression. *Journal of the American Medical Association, 304*, 1736.

Stevens, P., & Galvao, L. (2007). He won't use condoms: HIV-infected women's struggles in primary relationships with serodiscordant partners. *American Journal of Public Health, 97*, 1015–1022.

Stevenson, B. (2010, February). *Beyond the classroom: Using Title IX to measure the return to high school sports* (National Bureau of Economic Research, Working Paper 15728). Retrieved from http://www.nber.org/papers/w15728

Stevenson, B., & Isen, A. (2010). *Who's getting married? Education and marriage today and in the past.* Chicago, IL: Council on Contemporary Families.

Stewart, A. J., & Ostrove, J. M. (1998). Women's personality in middle age: Gender history, and midcourse corrections. *American Psychologist, 53*, 1185–1194.

Stewart, A. J., & Vandewater, E. A. (1999). "If I had it to do over again . . .": Midlife review, midcourse corrections, and women's well-being in midlife. *Journal of Personality and Social Psychology, 76*, 270–283.

Stewart, S. H., Gavric, D., & Collins, P. (2009). Women, girls and alcohol. In K. T. Brady, S. E. Back, & S. F. Greenfield (Eds.), *Women and addiction: A comprehensive handbook* (pp. 341–359). New York: Guilford.

Stinson, D. A., et al. (2008). The cost of lower self-esteem: Testing a self- and social-bonds model of health. *Journal of Personality and Social Psychology, 94*, 412–428.

Stockdale, M. S., & Bhattacharya, G. (2009). Sexual harassment and the glass ceiling. In M. Barreto, M. K. Ryan, & M. T. Schmitt (Eds.), *The glass ceiling in the 21st century: Understanding barriers to gender equality* (pp. 171–199). Washington, DC: American Psychological Association.

Stohs, J. H. (2000). Multicultural women's experience of household labor, conflicts, and equity. *Sex Roles, 42*, 339–361.

Stolberg, S. G. (2010, December 22). Obama signs away "Don't ask, don't tell." *New York Times.* Retrieved from http://www.nytimes.com

Stone, A. A., Schwartz, J. E., Broderick, J. E., & Deaton, A. (2010). A snapshot of the age distribution of psychological well-being in the United States [Advance online publication]. *Proceedings of the National Academy of Sciences.*

Stoner, C. C., Gallatti, N., Dugan, A. E., & Cole, P. M. (2005, April). *Anger expression, expressive language & gender in 18-month-olds.* Poster presented at the meeting of the Society for Research in Child Development, Atlanta, GA.

Stotzer, R. L. (2009). Violence against transgender people: A review of United States data. *Aggression and Violent Behavior, 14,* 170–179.

Strahan, E. J., Lafrance, A., Wilson, A. E., Ethier, N., Spencer, S. J., & Zanna, M. P. (2008). Victoria's dirty secret: How sociocultural norms influence adolescent girls and women. *Personality and Social Psychology Bulletin, 34,* 288–301.

Straus, H., et al. (2009). Intimate partner violence and functional health status: Associations with severity, danger, and self-advocacy behaviors. *Journal of Women's Health, 18,* 625–742.

Strauss, R. S. (2000). Childhood obesity and self-esteem. *Pediatrics, 105*(1), e15.

Strauss, S. (2008). Aggressive men and witchy women: The double standard. In M. A. Paludi (Ed.), *The psychology of women at work: Challenges and solutions for our female workforce: Self, family, and social affects* (Vol. 3, pp. 1–20). Westport, CT: Praeger.

Strauss, W., Strand, M., & Paludi, M. A. (2010). Feminist and women's rights organizations worldwide. In M. A. Paludi (Ed.), *Feminism and women's rights worldwide: Mental and physical health* (Vol. 2, pp. 253–262). Santa Barbara, CA: Praeger.

Street, A. E., Stafford, J., & Bruce, T. A. (2003, Winter). Sexual harassment. *PTSD Research Quarterly, 14,* 1–7.

Street, S., Kimmel, E. B., & Kromrey, J. D. (1995). Revisiting university student gender role perceptions. *Sex Roles, 33,* 183–201.

Street, S., Kromrey, J. D., & Kimmel, E. (1995). University faculty gender roles perceptions. *Sex Roles, 32,* 407–422.

Stricker, R., Eberhart, R., Chevallier, M. C., Quinn, F. A., Bischof, P., & Stricker, R. (2006). Establishment of detailed reference values for luteinizing hormone, follicle stimulating hormone, estradiol, and progesterone during different phases of the menstrual cycle on the Abbott ARCHITECT analyzer. *Clinical Chemistry and Laboratory Medicine, 44,* 883–887.

Stringhini, S., et al. (2010). Association of socioeconomic position with health behaviors and mortality. *Journal of the American Medical Association, 303,* 1159–1166.

Strong, T. H. (2000). *Expecting trouble: The myth of prenatal care in America.* New York: New York University Press.

Stross, R. (2008, November 16). What has driven women out of computer science? *New York Times,* p. BU4.

Stubbs, M. L. (2008). Cultural perceptions and practices around menarche and adolescent menstruation in the United States. *Annals of the New York Academy of Sciences, 1135,* 58–66.

Stuenkel, C. P. (2005). A strategy for working families: Highlevel commodification of household services. In B. Schneider & L. J. Waite (Eds.), *Being together, working apart: Dual-career families and the work-life balance* (pp. 252–272). Cambridge, MA: Cambridge University Press.

Stuhlmacher, A. F. (2009, May 1). *Gender differences in negotiation: The impact of context.* Invited address, annual meeting of the Midwestern Psychological Association, Chicago.

Štulhofer, A., & Rimac, I. (2009). Determinants of homonegativity in Europe. *Journal of Sex Research, 46,* 24–32.

Su, R., Rounds, J., & Armstrong, P. I. (2009). Men and things, women and people: A meta-analysis of sex differences in interests. *Psychological Bulletin, 135,* 859–884.

Suarez, E., & Gadalla, T. M. (2010). Stop blaming the victim: A meta-analysis on rape myths. *Journal of Interpersonal Violence, 25,* 2010–2035.

Sue, D. W. (2010). *Microaggressions in everyday life: Race, gender, and sexual orientation.* New York: Wiley.

Sue, D. W., Lin, A. I., Torino, G. C., Capodilupo, C. M., & Rivera, D. P. (2009). Racial microaggressions and difficult dialogues on race in the classroom. *Cultural Diversity and Ethnic Minority Psychology, 15,* 183–190.

Suellentrop, K. K. (2011). *What works 2011–2012: Curriculum-based programs that help prevent teen pregnancy.* Washington, DC: The National Campaign to Prevent Teen and Unplanned Pregnancy.

Sulik, S. M., & Heath, C. B. (Eds.). (2010). *Primary care procedures in women's health.* New York: Springer.

Sullivan, C. M. (2011). Victim services for domestic violence. In M. P. Koss, J. W. White, & A. E. Kazdin (Eds.), *Violence against women and children: Navigating solutions* (Vol. 2, pp. 183–198). Washington, DC: American Psychological Association.

Sumberg, E. (2007, January 21). Starting over: Many grandparents raising children for second time. *Peoria Journal Star,* pp. A1, A14.

Summers-Effler, E. (2004). Little girls in women's bodies: Social interaction and the strategizing of early breast development. *Sex Roles, 51,* 29–44.

Sun, Q., Townsend, M. K., Okereke, O. I., Franco, O. H., Hu, F. B., & Grodstein, F. (2010). Physical activity at midlife in relation to successful survival in women at age 70 years or older. *Archives of Internal Medicine, 170,* 194–201.

Sunderam, S., et al. (2009, June 12). Assisted reproductive technology surveillance—United States, 2006. Surveillance summaries. *Morbidity and Mortality Weekly Report, 58*(SS-5), 1–25.

Susman, E. J., & Dorn, L. D. (2009). Puberty: Its role in development. In R. M. Lerner & L. Steinberg (Eds.), *Handbook of adolescent psychology* (3rd ed., Vol. 1, pp. 116–151). Hoboken, NJ: Wiley.

Susman, E. J., et al. (2010). Longitudinal development of secondary sexual characteristics in girls and boys between ages 9½ and 15½ years. *Archives of Pediatric Adolescent Medicine, 164,* 166–173.

Susman, E. J., & Rogol, A. (2004). Puberty and psychological development. In R. M. Lerner & L. Steinberg (Eds.), *Handbook of adolescent psychology* (2nd ed., pp. 15–44). Hoboken, NJ: Wiley.

Susskind, J. E. (2003). Children's perception of gender-based illusory correlations: Enhancing preexisting relationships between gender and behavior. *Sex Roles, 48,* 483–494.

Susskind, J. E., Hodges, C., Carter, B., & Witmack, C. (2005, April). *Cooties: Distinguishing gender-based in-group favoritism from out-group derogation.* Poster presented at the meeting of the Society for Research in Child Development, Atlanta, GA.

Sutfin, E. L., Fulcher, M., Bowles, R. P., & Patterson, C. J. (2008). How lesbian and heterosexual parents convey attitudes about gender to their children: The role of gendered environments. *Sex Roles, 58,* 501–513.

Swaby, A. N., & Morgan, K. A. D. (2009). The relationship between childhood sexual abuse and sexual dysfunction in Jamaican adults. *Journal of Child Sexual Abuse, 18,* 247–266.

Swahn, M. H., Simon, T. R., Arias, I., & Bossarte, R. M. (2008). Measuring sex differences in violence victimization and perpetration within date and same-sex peer relationships. *Journal of Interpersonal Violence, 23,* 1120–1138.

Swami, V., Coles, R., Wilson, E., Salem, N., Wyrozumska, K., & Furnham, A. (2010). Oppressive beliefs at play: Associations among beauty ideals and practices and individual differences in sexism, objectification of others, and media exposure. *Psychology of Women Quarterly, 3,* 365–379.

Swami, V., et al. (2010). The attractive female body weight and female body dissatisfaction in 26 countries across 10 world regions: Results of the International Body Project I. *Personality and Social Psychology Bulletin, 36,* 309–325.

Swanbrow, D. (2007, January). Time, money and who does the laundry. *Research Update*. Ann Arbor, MI: University of Michigan, Institute for Social Research.

Swanson, K. M., Chen, H.-T., Graham, J. C., Wojnar, D. M., & Petras, A. (2009). Resolution of depression and grief during the first year after miscarriage: A randomized controlled clinical trial of couples-focused interventions. *Journal of Women's Health, 18,* 1245–1257.

Swartz, T. T. (2009). Intergenerational family relations in adulthood: Patterns, variations, and implications in the contemporary United States. *Annual Review of Sociology, 35,* 191–212.

Swearer, S. M., Turner, R. K., Givens, J. E., & Pollack, W. S. (2008). "You're so gay!": Do different forms of bullying matter for adolescent males? *School Psychology Review, 37,* 160–173.

Swearingen-Hilker, N., & Yoder, J. D. (2002). Understanding the context of unbalanced domestic contributions: The influence of perceiver's attitudes, target's gender, and presentational format. *Sex Roles, 46,* 91–98.

Sweeney, C. (2008, February 28). Skin deep: Never too young for that first pedicure. *New York Times,* p. G3.

Sweeney, M. M. (2010). Remarriage and stepfamilies: Strategic sites for family scholarship in the 21st century. *Journal of Marriage and Family, 72,* 667–684.

Swim, J. K., Aikin, K. J., Hall, W. S., & Hunter, B. A. (1995). Sexism and racism: Old-fashioned and modern prejudices. *Journal of Personality and Social Psychology, 68,* 199–214.

Swim, J. K., Becker, J. C., Lee, E., & Pruitt, E.-R. (2010). Sexism reloaded: Worldwide evidence for its endorsement, expression, and emergence in multiple contexts. In H. Landrine & N. F. Russo (Eds.), *Handbook of diversity in feminist psychology* (pp. 137–171). New York: Springer.

Swim, J. K., Eyssell, K. M., Murdoch, E. Q., & Ferguson, M. J. (2010). Self-silencing to sexism. *Society for the Psychological Study of Social Issues, 66,* 493–507.

Swim, J. K., & Hyers, L. L. (2008). Sexism. In T. D. Nelson (Ed.), *Handbook of prejudice, stereotyping, and discrimination* (pp. 407–430). Philadelphia, PA: Psychology Press.

Swim, J. K., Mallett, R., & Stangor, C. (2004). Understanding subtle sexism: Detection and use of sexist language. *Sex Roles, 51,* 117–128.

Swim, J. K., Scott, E., Sechrist, G. B., Campbell, B., & Stangor, C. (2003). The role of intent and harm in judgments of prejudice. *Journal of Personality and Social Psychology, 84,* 944–959.

Switzer, J. Y. (1990). The impact of generic word choices: An empirical investigation of age- and sex-related differences. *Sex Roles, 22,* 69–82.

Sybert, V. P., & McCauley, E. (2004). Turner's syndrome. *New England Journal of Medicine, 351,* 1227–1238.

Syltevik, L. J. (2010). Sense and sensibility: Cohabitation in "cohabitation land." *Sociological Review, 58,* 444–462.

Szinovacz, M. (1991). Women and retirement. In B. B. Hess & E. W. Markson (Eds.), *Growing old in America* (4th ed., pp. 293–303). New Brunswick, NJ: Transaction.

Szinovacz, M. E., & Davey, A. (2008). The division of parent care between spouses. *Aging and Society, 28,* 571–597.

Szymanski, D. M., & Owens, G. P. (2008). Do coping styles moderate or mediate the relationship between internalized heterosexism and sexual minority women's psychological distress? *Psychology of Women Quarterly, 32,* 95–104.

Tafalla, R. J. (2007). Gender differences in cardiovascular reactivity and game performance relate to sensory modality in violent video game play. *Journal of Applied Social Psychology, 37,* 2008–2023.

Taft, C. T., Bryant-Davis, T., Woodward, H. E., Tillman, S., & Torres, S. E. (2009). Intimate partner violence against African American women: An examination of the socio-cultural context. *Aggression and Violent Behavior, 14,* 50–58.

Taft, J. K. (2010). *Rebel girls: Youth activism & social change across the Americas.* New York: NYU Press.

Talley, A. E., Sher, K. J., & Littlefield, A. K. (2010). Sexual orientation and substance use trajectories in emerging adulthood. *Addiction, 105,* 1235–1245.

Tamis-LeMonda, C. S., Kalman, R. K., & Yoshikawa, H. (2009). Father involvement in immigrant family and ethnically diverse families from the prenatal period to the second year: Prediction and mediating mechanisms. *Sex Roles, 60,* 496–509.

Tamis-LeMonda, C. S., Shannon, J. D., Cabrera, N. J., & Lamb, M. E. (2004). Fathers and mothers at play with their 2- and 3-year olds: Contributions to language and cognitive development. *Child Development, 75,* 1806–1819.

Tan, J.-P., Buchanan, A., Flouri, E., Attar-Schwartz, S., & Griggs, J. (2010). Filling the parenting gap? Grandparent involvement with U.K. adolescents. *Journal of Family Issues, 31,* 992–1015.

Tang, F., Choi, E., & Morrow-Howell, N. (2010). Organizational support and volunteering benefits for older adults [Advance online publication]. *Gerontologist.*

Tapia, A. (2008). *Women in leadership at a crossroads: Why current best practices will not be enough to shatter the glass ceiling.* Lincolnville, IL: Hewitt Associates.

Tarrant, S. (2009). *Men and feminism.* Berkeley, CA: Seal Press.

Tasker, F. (2010). Same-sex parenting and child development: Reviewing the contribution of parental gender. *Journal of Marriage and Family, 72,* 35–40.

Tasker, F. L. (2005). Lesbian mothers, gay fathers, and their children: A review. *Journal of Developmental and Behavioral Pediatrics, 26,* 224–240.

Tassone, S. A., & Landherr, K. M. (2009). *Hands off my belly! The pregnant woman's survival guide to myths, mothers, and moods.* Amherst, NY: Prometheus Books.

Tavernise, S. (2011, January 18). Parenting by gays more common in the South, census shows. *New York Times,* p. A1.

Taylor, C. J. (2010). Occupational sex composition and the gendered availability of workplace support. *Gender & Society, 24,* 189–212.

Taylor, D. (2007). Employment preferences and salary expectations of students in science and engineering. *BioScience, 57,* 175–185.

Taylor, J. L. (2009). Midlife impacts of adolescent parenthood. *Journal of Family Issues, 30,* 484–510.

Taylor, K. L., et al. (2003). Psychological adjustment among African American breast cancer patients: One-year follow-up results of a randomized psychoeducational group intervention. *Health Psychology, 22,* 316–323.

Taylor, N. L. (2011). "Guys, she's humongous!": Gender and weight-based teasing in adolescence. *Journal of Adolescent Research, 26,* 178–199.

Taylor, P. L., Tucker, M. B., & Mitchell-Kernan, C. (1999). Ethnic variations in perceptions of men's provider role. *Psychology of Women Quarterly, 23,* 741–761.

Taylor, S. E. (2010). Health. In S. T. Fiske, D. T. Gilbert, & G. Lindzey (Eds.), *Handbook of social psychology* (5th ed., Vol. 1, pp. 698–723). Hoboken, NJ: John Wiley & Sons.

Taylor, S. E., et al. (2000). Biobehavioral responses to stress in females: Tend-and-befriend, not fight-or-flight. *Psychological Review, 107,* 411–429.

Taylor, U. Y. (2010). Black feminisms and human agency. In *No permanent waves: Recasting the history of U.S. feminism* (pp. 61–76). Piscataway, NJ: Rutgers University Press.

Teachman, J. (2010). Wives' economic resources and risk of divorce. *Journal of Family Issues, 31,* 1305–1323.

Teasdale, B., & Bradley-Engen, M. S. (2010). Adolescent same-sex attraction and mental health: The role of stress and support. *Journal of Homosexuality, 57,* 287–309.

Teig, S., & Susskind, J. E. (2008). Truck driver or nurse? The impact of gender roles and occupational status on children's occupational preferences. *Sex Roles, 58*, 848–863.

Teitelman, A. M., Seloilwe, E. S., & Campbell, J. C. (2009). Voices from the frontlines: The epidemics of HIV/AIDS and violence among women and girls. *Health Care for Women International, 30*, 184–194.

Temkin, J., & Krahé, B. (2008). *Sexual assault and the justice gap: A question of attitude*. Oxford, England: Hart Publishing.

Templeton, K. (2010). Women's musculoskeletal health. In P. Murthy & C. L. Smith (Eds.), *Women's global health and human rights* (pp. 223–236). Sudbury, MA: Jones and Bartlett.

Tenenbaum, H. R., & Leaper, C. (2002). Are parents' gender schemas related to their children's gender-related cognitions? A meta-analysis. *Developmental Psychology, 38*, 615–630.

Tenenbaum, H. R., & Leaper, C. (2003). Parent–child conversations about science: The socialization of gender inequities. *Developmental Psychology, 39*, 34–47.

Tenenbaum, H. R., Snow, C. E., Roach, K. A., & Kurland, B. (2005). Talking and reading science: Longitudinal data on sex differences in mother–child conversations in low-income families. *Applied Developmental Psychology, 26*, 1–19.

Terlecki, M. S., & Newcombe, N. S. (2005). How important is the digital divide? The relation of computer and videogame usage to gender differences in mental rotation ability. *Sex Roles, 53*, 433–441.

Terlecki, M. S., Newcombe, N. S., & Little, M. (2008). Durable and generalized effects of spatial effects on mental rotation: Gender differences in growth patterns. *Applied Cognitive Psychology, 22*, 996–1013.

Terzian, M., Hamilton, K., & Ling, T. (2011). *What works for acting-out (externalizing) behavior: Lessons from experimental evaluations of social interventions*. Washington, DC: Child Trends.

Teten, A. L., Ball, B., Valle, L. A., Noonan, R., & Rosenbluth, B. (2009). Considerations for the definition, measurement, consequences, and prevention of dating violence victimization among adolescent girls. *Journal of Women's Health, 18*, 923–927.

Thacker, D. G. (2011). Honor suicides. In M. Z. Stange, C. K. Oyster, & J. E. Sloan (Eds.), *Encyclopedia of women in today's world* (Vol. 2, pp. 722–723). Newberry Park, CA: Sage.

Thacker, H. L. (2009). *The Cleveland Clinic guide to menopause*. New York: Kaplan.

Thapar-Björkert, S., & Morgan, K. J. (2010). "But sometimes I think . . . they put themselves in the situation": Exploring blame and responsibility in interpersonal violence. *Violence Against Women, 16*, 32–59.

This year's freshmen at 4-year colleges: A statistical profile. (2005, February 4). *Chronicle of Higher Education*, p. A33.

Thomas, A. J., Hacker, J. D., & Hoxha, D. (2011). Gendered racial identity of Black young women. *Sex Roles, 64*, 530–554.

Thomas, J. J., & Daubman, K. A. (2001). The relationship between friendship quality and self-esteem in adolescent girls and boys. *Sex Roles, 45*, 53–65.

Thomas, J. L., Sperry, L., & Yarbrough, M. S. (2000). Grandparents as parents: Research findings and policy recommendations. *Child Psychiatry and Human Development, 31*, 3–22.

Thomas, P. A. (2010). Is it better to give or to receive? Social support and the well-being of older adults. *Journal of Gerontology: Social Sciences, 65B*, 351–357.

Thomas, S. (2011). Fetal alcohol spectrum disorders. In M. Z. Stange, C. K. Oyster & J. E. Sloan (Eds.), *Encyclopedia of women in today's world*. Newberry Park, CA: Sage.

Thompson, B. (2010). Multiracial feminism: Recasting the chronology of second wave feminism. In N. A. Hewitt (Ed.), *No permanent waves: Recasting the history of U.S. feminism* (pp. 39–60). Piscataway, NJ: Rutgers University Press.

Thompson, E. M., & Morgan, E. M. (2008). "Mostly straight" young women: Variations in sexual behavior and identity development. *Developmental Psychology, 44*, 15–21.

Thompson, G. (1999, March 30). New clinics seek patients among lesbians, who often shun health care. *New York Times*, p. 25.

Thompson, K. M. (2009). Sibling incest: A model for group practice with adult female victims of brother-sister incest. *Journal of Family Violence, 24*, 531–537.

Thompson, M. P., Light, L. S. (2011). Examining gender differences in risk factors for suicide attempts made 1 and 7 years later in a nationally representative sample. *Journal of Adolescent Health, 48*, 391–397.

Thorne, B. (1993). *Gender play: Girls and boys in school*. New Brunswick, NJ: Rutgers University Press.

Thornhill, R., & Palmer, C. T. (2000). *A natural history of rape: Biological bases of sexual coercion*. Cambridge, MA: MIT Press.

Thrane, C. (2000). Men, women, and leisure time: Scandinavian evidence of gender inequality. *Sport & Leisure Management, 22*, 109–122.

Thurston, R. C., & Kubzansky, L. D. (2009). Women, loneliness, and incident coronary heart disease. *Psychosomatic Medicine, 71*, 836–842.

Tichenor, V. (2005). Maintaining men's dominance: Negotiating identity and power when she earns more. *Sex Roles, 53*, 191–205.

Tiefer, L. (2008). Sexual problems. In A. L. Clouse & K. Sherif (Eds.), *Women's health in clinical practice: A handbook for primary care* (pp. 97–104). Totowa, NJ: Humana Press.

Tiegs, T. J., Perrin, P. B., Kaly, P. W., & Heesacker, M. (2007). My place or yours? An inductive approach to sexuality and gender role conformity. *Sex Roles, 56*, 449–456.

Tiggemann, M., & Miller, J. (2010). The internet and adolescent girls' weight satisfaction and drive for thinness. *Sex Roles, 63*, 79–90.

Tiggemann, M., & Polivy, J. (2010). Upward and downward: Social comparison processing of thin idealized media images. *Psychology of Women Quarterly, 3*, 356–364.

Tillman, S., Bryant-Davis, T., Smith, K., & Marks, A. (2010). Shattering silence: Exploring barriers to disclosure for African American sexual assault survivors. *Trauma, Violence, & Abuse, 11*, 59–70.

Timmerman, G. (2003). Sexual harassment of adolescents perpetrated by teachers and by peers: An exploration of the dynamics of power, culture, and gender in secondary schools. *Sex Roles, 48*, 231–244.

Tindle, H. A., et al. (2009). Optimism, cynical hostility, and incidence coronary heart disease and mortality in the women's health initiative. *Circulation, 120*, 656–662.

Titze, C., Heil, M., & Jansen, P. (2008). Gender differences in the Mental Rotations Test (MRT) are not due to task complexity. *Journal of Individual Differences, 29*, 130–133.

Tobacco company marketing to kids. (2011). Washington, DC: Campaign for Tobacco-Free Kids.

Tobach, E. (2001). Development of sex and gender: Biochemistry, physiology, and experience. In J. Worell (Ed.), *Encyclopedia of women and gender* (pp. 315–332). San Diego, CA: Academic Press.

Toller, P. W., Suter, E. A., & Trautman, T. C. (2004). Gender role identity and attitudes toward feminism. *Sex Roles, 51*, 85–90.

Tolman, D. L. (2002). *Dilemmas of desire: Teenage girls talk about sexuality*. Cambridge, MA: Harvard University Press.

Tolman, D. L., Striepe, M. I., & O'Sullivan, L. F. (2003). How do we define sexual health for women? In L. Slater, J. H. Daniel, & A. E. Banks (Eds.), *The complete guide to mental health for women* (pp. 74–81). Boston, MA: Beacon Press.

Tolman, R. M., & Edleson, J. L. (2011). Intervening with men for violence prevention. In C. M. Renzetti, J. L. Edleson, & R. K. Bergen (Eds.), *Sourcebook on violence against women* (2nd ed., pp. 351–367). Thousand Oaks, CA: Sage.

Tolomio, S., Ermolai, A., Lalli, A., & Zaccaria, M. (2010). The effect of a multicomponent dual-modality exercise program targeting osteoporosis on bone health status and physical function capacity of postmenopausal women. *Journal of Women & Aging, 22*, 241–254.

Tomey, K., Sowers, M. R., Harlow, S., Jannausch, M., Zheng, H., & Bromberger, J. (2010). Physical functioning among midlife women: Associations with trajectory of depressive symptoms. *Social Science & Medicine, 71*, 1259–1267.

Tomlinson, B. (2010). *Feminism and affect at the scene of argument: Beyond the trope of the angry feminist.* Philadelphia, PA: Temple University Press.

Topa, G., Moriano, J. A., Depolo, M., Alcover, C.-M., & Morales, J. F. (2009). Antecedents and consequences of retirement planning and decision-making: A meta-analysis and model. *Journal of Vocational Behavior, 75*, 38–55.

Torges, C. M., Stewart, A. J., & Miner-Rubino, K. (2005). Personality after the prime of life: Men and women coming to terms with regrets. *Journal of Research in Personality, 39*, 148–165.

Torpy, J. (2009). Coronary heart disease risk factors. *Journal of the American Medical Association, 302*, 2388.

Torpy, J. (2010a). Depression. *Journal of the American Medical Association, 303*, 1994.

Torpy, J. (2010b). Intimate partner violence. *Journal of the American Medical Association, 304*, 596.

Torpy, J. M. (2007). Women's sexual concerns after menopause. *Journal of the American Medical Association, 297*, 664.

Torpy, J. M. (2011). Generalized anxiety disorder. *Journal of the American Medical Association , 305*, 522.

Torrez, D. J. (2001). The health of older women: A diverse experience. In J. M. Coyle (Ed.), *Handbook on women and aging* (pp. 131–148). Westport, CT: Greenwood.

Tougas, F., Brown, R., Beaton, A. M., & Joly, S. (1995). Neosexism: Plus ça change, plus c'est pareil. *Personality and Social Psychology Bulletin, 21*, 842–849.

Toussaint, D. (2003, September/October). Outward bound. *Bride's*, p. 346.

Townsend, T. G. (2008). Protecting our daughters: Intersection of race, class and gender in African American mothers' socialization of their daughters' heterosexuality. *Sex Roles, 59*, 429–442.

Townsend, T. G., Thomas, A. J., Neilands, T. B., & Jackson, T. R. (2010). I'm no Jezebel; I am young, gifted, and Black: Identity, sexuality, and Black girls. *Psychology of Women Quarterly, 3*, 273–285.

Tracy, J. K., & Junginger, J. (2007). Correlates of lesbian sexual functioning. *Journal of Women's Health, 16*, 499–509.

Tracy, J. K., Lydecker, A. D., & Ireland, L. (2010). Barriers to cervical cancer screening among lesbians. *Journal of Women's Health, 19*, 229–237.

Trautner, H. M., Ruble, D. N., Cyphers, L., Kirsten, B., Behrendt, R., & Hartmann, P. (2005). Rigidity and flexibility of gender stereotypes in childhood: Developmental or differential? *Infant and Child Development, 14*, 365–381.

Travis, C. B. (2003). Theory and data on rape and evolution. In C. B. Travis (Ed.), *Evolution, gender, and rape* (pp. 207–220). Cambridge, MA: The MIT Press.

Travis, C. B., & Compton, J. D. (2001). Feminism and health in the decade of behavior. *Psychology of Women Quarterly, 25*, 312–323.

Travis, C. B., Gross, L. J., & Johnson, B. A. (2009). Tracking the gender pay gap: A case study. *Psychology of Women Quarterly, 33*, 410–418.

Treas, J., & Tai, T.-O. (2007, August). *Long apron strings of working mothers: Maternal employment, occupational attainments, and housework in cross-national perspective.* Paper presented at the meeting of the American Sociological Association, New York.

Treas, J., & Widmer, E. D. (2000). Married women's employment over the life course: Attitudes in cross-national perspective. *Social Forces, 78*, 1409–1436.

Trimberger, E. K. (2005). *The new single woman.* Boston, MA: Beacon Press.

Trivers, K. F., Stewart, S. L., Peipins, L., Rim, S. H., & White, M. C. (2009). Expanding the public health research agenda for ovarian cancer. *Journal of Women's Health, 18*, 1299–1305.

Troxel, W. M., Matthews, K. A., Gallo, L. C., & Kuller, L. H. (2005). Marital quality and occurrence of the metabolic syndrome in women. *Archives of Internal Medicine, 165*, 1022–1027.

Trzesniewski, K. H., Donnellan, M. B., Moffitt, T. E., Robins, R. W., Poulton, R., & Caspi, A. (2006). Low self-esteem during adolescence predicts poor health, criminal behavior, and limited economic prospects during adulthood. *Developmental Psychology, 42*, 381–390.

Tucker, C. M., & Herman, K. C. (2002). Using culturally sensitive theories and research to meet the academic needs of low-income African-American children. *American Psychologist, 57*, 762–773.

Tudge, J. (2008). *The everyday lives of young children: Culture, class, and child rearing in diverse societies.* New York: Cambridge University Press.

Tuggle, C. A., Huffman, S., & Rosengard, D. S. (2002). A descriptive analysis of NBC's coverage of the 2000 Summer Olympics. *Mass Communication & Society, 5*, 361–375.

Tuller, D. (2010, May 11). Payment offers to egg donors prompt scrutiny. *New York Times*, p. D5.

Turchik, J. A., & Wilson, S. M. (2010). Sexual assault in the U.S. military: A review of the literature and recommendations for the future. *Aggression and Violent Behavior, 15*, 267–277.

Turell, S. C., & Herrmann, M. M. (2008). "Family" support for family violence: Exploring community support systems for lesbian and bisexual women who have experienced abuse. *Journal of Lesbian Studies, 12*, 207–220.

Turiel, E. (2006). The development of morality. In W. Damon, R. M. Lerner (Series Eds.), & N. Eisenberg (Vol. Ed.), *Handbook of child psychology: Vol. 3. Social, emotional, and personality development* (6th ed., pp. 789–857). Hoboken, NJ: Wiley.

Turjanski, N. (2010). Postnatal depression. In D. Kohen (Ed.), *Oxford textbook of women and mental health* (pp. 169–178). Oxford, UK: Oxford University Press.

Turner, J. S. (2011). Sex and the spectacle of music videos: An examination of the portrayal of race and sexuality in music videos. *Sex Roles, 64*, 173–191.

Tuval-Mashiach, R., Walsh, S., Harel, S., & Shulman, S. (2008). Romantic fantasies, cross-gender friendships, and romantic experiences in adolescence. *Journal of Adolescent Research, 23*, 471–487.

Twenge, J. M. (1997). Changes in masculine and feminine traits over time: A meta-analysis. *Sex Roles, 36*, 305–325.

Twenge, J. M. (2001). Changes in women's assertiveness in response to status and roles: A cross-temporal meta-analysis, 1931–1993. *Journal of Personality and Social Psychology, 81*, 133–145.

Twenge, J. M. (2009). Status and gender: The paradox of progress in an age of narcissism. *Sex Roles, 61*, 338–340.

Twenge, J. M., & Crocker, J. (2002). Race and self-esteem: Meta-analyses comparing Whites, Blacks, Hispanics, Asians and American Indians and comment on Gray-Little and Hafdahl (2000). *Psychological Bulletin, 128*, 371–408.

Tyler, K. A., & Johnson, K. A. (2006). A longitudinal study of the effects of early abuse on later victimization among highrisk adolescents. *Violence and Victims, 21*, 287–306.

Tylka, T. K., & Sabik, N. J. (2010). Integrating social comparison theory and self-esteem within objectification theory to predict women's disordered eating. *Sex Roles, 63*, 18–31.

Tyre, P. (2008). *The trouble with boys: A surprising report card on our sons, their problems at school, and what parents and educators must do.* New York: Crown.

Tyre, P., & Pierce, E. (2003, September 14). Ma, I'll be at the spa. *Newsweek*, p. 10.

Tzuriel, D., & Egozi, G. (2010). Gender differences in spatial ability of young children: The effects of training and processing strategies. *Child Development, 81*, 1417–1430.

Uchino, B. N. (2009). Understanding the links between social support and physical health: A life-span perspective with emphasis on the separability of perceived and received support. *Perspectives on Psychological Science, 4*, 236–255.

Uchitelle, L. (2001, June 26). Women forced to delay retirement. *New York Times*, p. A1.

Uecker, J. E. (2008). Religion, pledging, and the premarital sexual behavior of married young adults. *Journal of Marriage and Family, 70*, 728–744.

Ueno, K., Gayman, M. D., Wright, E. R., & Quantz, S. D. (2009). Friends' sexual orientation, relational quality, and mental health among gay, lesbian, and bisexual youth. *Personal Relationships, 16*, 659–670.

Ueno, K., & McWilliams, S. (2010). Gender-typed behaviors and school adjustment. *Sex Roles, 63*, 580–591.

Uhlmann, E. L., & Cohen, G. L. (2005). Constructed criteria: Redefining merit to justify discrimination. *Psychological Science, 16*, 474–480.

Ui, M., & Matsui, Y. (2008). Japanese adults' sex role attitudes and judgment criteria concerning gender equality: The diversity of gender egalitarianism. *Sex Roles, 58*, 412–422.

Ulker, A. (2008). Wealth holdings and portfolio allocation of the elderly: The role of marital history. *Journal of Family and Economic Issues, 30*, 90–108.

Ullman, S. E. (2007). Relationship to perpetrator, disclosure, social reactions, and PTSD symptoms in child sexual abuse survivors. *Journal of Child Sexual Abuse, 16*, 19–36.

Ullman, S. E., & Najdowski, C. J. (2010). Understanding alcohol-related sexual assaults: Characteristics and consequences. *Violence and Victims, 25*, 29–44.

Ullman, S. E., & Najdowski, C. J. (2011). Vulnerability and protective factors for sexual assault. In J. W. White, M. P. Koss, & A. E. Kazdin (Eds.), *Violence against women and children: Mapping the terrain* (Vol. 1, pp. 151–172). Washington, DC: American Psychological Association.

Ullman, S. E., Najdowski, C. J., & Filipas, H. H. (2009). Child sexual abuse, post-traumatic stress disorder, and substance use: Predictors of revictimization in adult sexual assault survivors. *Journal of Child Sexual Abuse, 18*, 367–385.

Umberson, D., Pudrovska, T., & Reczek, C. (2010). Parenthood, childlessness, and well-being: A life course perspective. *Journal of Marriage and Family, 72*, 612–629.

U.N. offers action plan for a world aging rapidly. (2002, April 14). *New York Times*, p. YNE5.

UNAIDS. (2009). *AIDS epidemic update: December 2009.* Geneva, Switzerland: Author.

UNAIDS. (2010). *2010 global report.* Geneva, Switzerland: Author.

Understanding and coping with sexual behavior problems in children. (2010). Los Angeles/Durham, CA/NC: National Child Traumatic Stress Network.

Underwood, M. K., & Rosen, L. H. (2009). Gender, peer relations, and challenges for girlfriends and boyfriends coming together in adolescence. *Psychology of Women Quarterly, 33*, 16–20.

Unger, J. B., & Seeman, T. E. (2000). Successful aging. In M. B. Goldman & M. C. Hatch (Eds.), *Women & health* (pp. 1238–1251). New York: Academic Press.

Unger, R. K. (2010). Leave no text behind: Teaching the psychology of women during the emergence of second wave feminism. *Sex Roles, 62*, 153–158.

Unger, R. K. (2011). Through the looking glass once more. *Psychology of Women Quarterly, 35*, 180–182.

UNICEF. (2000). Domestic violence against women and girls. *Innocenti Digest, 6*, 1–29.

UNICEF. (2007). *The state of the world's children 2008: Child survival.* New York: Author.

UNICEF. (2008). *Progress for children: A report card on maternal mortality.* New York: Author.

UNICEF. (2011). *The state of the world's children: Adolescence, an age of opportunity.* New York: Author.

UNIFEM. (2003). *Not a minute more: Ending violence against women.* New York: Author.

UNIFEM. (2008). *Who answers to women? Gender and accountability.* New York: Author.

UNIFEM. (2010). *Gender justice: Key to achieving the millennium development goals.* New York: Author.

United Nations. (2007, March). *Ending impunity for violence against women and girls.* New York: Author.

United Nations Children's Fund. (2007). *The millennium development goals report 2007.* New York: Author.

United Nations Office on Drugs and Crime. (2009). *Trafficking in persons: Analysis on Europe.* Vienna: Author.

Unützer, J. (2007). Late-life depression. *New England Journal of Medicine, 357*, 2269–2276.

Upadhyay, U. D., & Murthy, P. (2010). Sexual and reproductive health: Women's health is society's wealth. In P. Murthy & C. L. Smith (Eds.), *Women's global health and human rights* (pp. 237–250). Sudbury, MA: Jones and Bartlett.

Urbancic, J. C. (2009). Depressive disorders. In J. C. Urbancic & C. J. Groh (Eds.), *Women's mental health: A clinical guide for primary care providers* (pp. 22–57). Philadelphia, PA: Lippincott Williams & Wilkins.

Urbancic, J. C., & Moser, C. (2009). Anxiety disorders. In J. C. Urbancic & C. J. Groh (Eds.), *Women's mental health: A clinical guide for primary care providers* (pp. 58–86). Philadelphia, PA: Lippincott Williams & Wilkins.

U.S. Bureau of Labor Statistics. (2010a, June 22). *American time use survey—2009 results* (USDL-10-0855). Washington, DC: Author.

U.S. Bureau of Labor Statistics. (2010b, June). *Highlights of women's earnings in 2009* (Report 1025). Washington, DC: Author.

U.S. Census Bureau. (2003). *Educational attainment in the United States: March 2001 and March 2002.* Current Population Reports. Washington, DC: Author.

U.S. Census Bureau. (2007). *Marriage and divorce: 2004.* Washington, DC: Author.

U.S. Census Bureau. (2008, January 2). *Women's history month: March 2008* (CB08-FF.03). Washington, DC: Author.

U.S. Census Bureau. (2009, March). *Current population survey.* Washington, DC: Author.

U.S. Census Bureau. (2010a). *Educational attainment in the United States: 2008.* Washington, DC: Author.

U.S. Census Bureau. (2010b). *Mother's day: May 9, 2010* (CB10-FF.09). Washington, DC: Author.

U.S. Census Bureau. (2010c). *Statistical abstract of the United States: 2010* (129th ed.). Washington, DC: U.S. Government Printing Office.

U.S. Census Bureau. (2010d). *Grandparents day 2010: Sept 12* (CB10-FF.16). Washington, DC: Author.

U.S. Census Bureau. (2011). *Mother's day: May 8, 2011* (CB11-FF.07). Washington, DC: Author.

U.S. Census Bureau, International Database. (1997, 1995). Retrieved from http://www.census.gov/International/Aging Statistics.htm

U.S. Department of Commerce. (2011). *Women in America: Indicators of social and economic well-being.* Washington, DC: Author.

U.S. Department of Education. (2007a). *The condition of education 2007.* Washington, DC: Author.

U.S. Department of Education. (2007b). *The nation's report card: Writing 2007.* Washington, DC: Author.

U.S. Department of Health and Human Services. (2009). *Women's health USA 2009.* Rockville, MD: Author. Retrieved from http://mchb.hrsa.gov/whusa09/

U.S. Department of Health and Human Services. (2010). *Health behaviors of adults: United States, 2005–2007.* NCHS *Vital and Health Statistics, 10*(245). Hyattsville, MD: National Center for Health Statistics.

U.S. Department of Justice. (2009). *2008 Crime in the United States.* Washington, DC: Author.

U.S. Department of Labor. (n.d.). *Affirmative action at OFCCP: A sound policy and a good investment.* Employment Standards Administration, Office of Federal Contract Compliance Programs. Washington, DC: Author.

Utter, J., Neumark-Sztainer, D., Wall, M., & Story, M. (2003). Reading magazine articles about dieting and associated weight control behaviors among adolescents. *Journal of Adolescent Health, 32,* 78–82.

Vaccaro, A. (2010). What lies beneath seemingly positive campus climate results: Institutional sexism, symbolic racism and male hostility toward equity initiatives. *Journal of Equity and Excellence in Education, 43,* 202–215.

Valkenburg, P. M., & Peter, J. (2007). Preadolescents' and adolescents' online communication and their closeness to friends. *Developmental Psychology, 43,* 267–277.

Valla, J. M., & Ceci, S. J. (2011). Can sex differences in science be tied to the long reach of prenatal hormones? Brain organization theory, digit ratio (2D/4D), and sex differences in preferences and cognition. *Perspectives on Psychological Science, 6,* 134–146.

Vallance, D. (2011). Yates, Andrea. In M. Z. Stange, C. K. Oyster, & J. E. Sloan (Eds.), *Encyclopedia of women in today's world* (Vol. 4, pp. 1599–1600). Newberry Park, CA: Sage.

Valls-Fernández, F., & Martinez-Vicente, J. M. (2007). Gender stereotypes in Spanish television commercials. *Sex Roles, 56,* 691–699.

van Dam, R. M., Li, T., Spiegelman, D., Franco, O. H., & Hu, F. B. (2008). Combined impact of lifestyle factors on mortality: Prospective cohort study in U.S. women. *BMJ, 337,* a1440.

Van de gaer, E., Pustjens, H., Van Damme, J., & De Munter, A. (2009). School engagement and language achievement: A longitudinal study of gender differences across secondary school. *Merrill-Palmer Quarterly, 55,* 373–405.

Van de Velde, S., Bracke, P., & Levecque, K. (2010). Gender differences in depression in 23 European countries: Cross-national variation in the gender gap in depression. *Social Services & Medicine, 71,* 305–313.

Van den Berg, P., Neumark-Sztainer, D., Hannan, P. J., & Haines, J. (2007). Is dieting advice from magazines helpful or harmful? Five-year associations with weight-control behaviors and psychological outcomes in adolescents. *Pediatrics, 119,* e30–e37.

Van den Hoonaard, D. K. (2011). *The widowed self: The older woman's journey through widowhood.* Waterloo, Ontario: Wilfrid Laurier University Press.

Van Evra, J. (2004). *Television and child development* (3rd ed.). Mahwah, NJ: Erlbaum.

Van Gelderen, L., Gartrell, N., Bos, H., & Hermanns, J. (2009). Stigmatization and resilience in adolescent children of lesbian mothers. *Journal of GLBT Family Studies, 5,* 268–279.

Van Home, B. S., Wiemann, C. M., Berenson, A. B., Horwitz, I. B., & Volk, R. J. (2009). Multilevel predictors of inconsistent condom use among adolescent mothers. *American Journal of Public Health, 99,* S417–S424.

Van Steirteghem, A., Bonduelle, M., & Liebaers, I. (2010, February 22). *What we know of the health of children conceived by assisted reproductive technology.* Paper presented at the annual meeting of the American Association for the Advancement of Science, San Diego, CA.

Van Willigen, M., & Drentea, P. (2001). Benefits of equitable relationships: The impact of sense of fairness, household division of labor, and decision making power on perceived social support. *Sex Roles, 44,* 571–597.

Vandell, D. L., Belsky, J., Burchinal, M., Steinberg, L., & Vandergrift, N. (2010). Do effects of early child care extend to age 15 years? Results from the NICHD study of early child care and youth development. *Child Development, 81,* 737–756.

Vandermaelen, A., et al. (2009). Optimal management of HIV-infected women during pregnancy and delivery: An audit of compliance with recommendations. *Journal of Women's Health, 18,* 1881–1887.

Vanfraussen, K., Ponjaert-Kristoffersen, I., & Brewaeys, A. (2003). Family functioning in lesbian families created by donor insemination. *American Journal of Orthopsychiatry, 73,* 78–90.

Vasilyeva, M. (2010). Spatial development. In R. M. Lerner (Ed.), *The handbook of life-span development* (pp. 720–753). Hoboken, NJ: Wiley.

Vasquez, M. J. T., & de las Fuentes, C. (1999). American-born Asian, African, Latina, and American Indian adolescent girls: Challenges and strengths. In N. G. Johnson, M. C. Roberts, & J. Worell (Eds.), *Beyond appearance: A new look at adolescent girls* (pp. 151–173). Washington, DC: American Psychological Association.

Vaughan, C. A., & Halpern, C. T. (2010). Gender differences in depressive symptoms during adolescence: The contributions of weight-related concerns and behaviors. *Journal of Research on Adolescence, 20,* 389–419.

Veloski, C. (2008). Osteoporosis. In A. L. Clouse & K. Sherif (Eds.), *Women's health in clinical practice: A handbook for primary care* (pp. 47–70). Totowa, NJ: Humana Press.

Veniegas, R. C., & Conley, T. D. (2000). Biological research on women's sexual orientations: Evaluating the scientific evidence. *Journal of Social Issues, 56,* 267–282.

Ventura, S. J., Abma, J. C., Mosher, W. D., & Henshaw, S. K. (2009). *Estimated pregnancy rates for the United States, 1990–2005: An update.* National Vital Statistics Reports, 58(4). Hyattsville, MD: National Center for Health Statistics.

Ventura, S. J., Mathews, T. J., Hamilton, B. E., Sutton, P. D., & Abma, J. C. (2011, January 14). Adolescent pregnancy and childbirth—United States, 1991–2008. *Morbidity and Mortality Weekly Report, 60*(Suppl.), 105–108.

Vézina, J., & Hébert, M. (2007). Risk factors for victimization in romantic relationships of young women: A review of empirical studies and implications for prevention. *Trauma, Violence, & Abuse, 8,* 33–66.

Villarosa, L. (2002, June 4). At elders' home, each day is valentine's day. *New York Times,* pp. D6, D10.

Villarosa, L. (2003, December 23). More teenagers say no to sex, but experts aren't sure why. *New York Times,* pp. D6, D8.

Vincent, W., Peterson, J. L., & Parrott, D. J. (2009). Differences in African American and White women's attitudes toward lesbians and gay men. *Sex Roles, 61,* 599–606.

Vinson, C., Mollen, D., & Smith, N. G. (2010). Perceptions of childfree women: The role of perceivers' and targets' ethnicity. *Journal of Community & Applied Social Psychology, 20,* 426–432.

Violence against women. (2009, April). Words to action: Newsletter on violence against women New York: United Nations.

Violence against women: An urgent public health priority. (2011). *Bulletin of the World Health Organization, 89,* 2–3.

Vishnevsky, T., Cann, A., Calhoun, L. G., Tedeschi, R. G., & Demakis, G. J. (2010). Gender differences in self-reported posttraumatic growth: A meta-analysis. *Psychology of Women Quarterly, 34,* 110–120.

Viswanathan, H. (2010). Being a woman in rural India. In P. Murthy & C. L. Smith (Eds.), *Women's global health and human rights* (pp. 509–518). Sudbury, MA: Jones and Bartlett.

von Soest, T., & Wichstrøm, L. (2009). Gender differences in the development of dieting from adolescence to early adulthood: A longitudinal study. *Journal of Research on Adolescence, 19,* 509–529.

Vona-Davis, L., & Rose, D. P. (2009). The influence of socioeconomic disparities on breast cancer tumor biology and prognosis: A review. *Journal of Women's Health, 18,* 883–893.

Voorpostel, M., van der Lippe, T., Dykstra, P. A., & Flap, H. (2007). Similar or different? The importance of similarities and differences for support between siblings. *Journal of Family Issues, 28,* 1026–1053.

Votruba-Drzal, E., Coley, R. L., Maldonado-Carreño, C., Li-Grining, C. P., & Chase-Lansdale, P. L. (2010). Child care and the development of behavior problems among economically disadvantaged children in middle childhood. *Child Development, 81,* 1460–1474.

Voyer, D., Voyer, S., & Bryden, M. P. (1995). Magnitude of sex differences in spatial abilities: A meta-analysis and consideration of critical variables. *Psychological Bulletin, 117,* 250–270.

Vuoksimaa, E., et al. (2010). Having a male co-twin masculinizes mental rotation performance in females. *Psychological Science, 21,* 1069–1071.

Vyver, E., Steinegger, C., & Katzman, D. K. (2008). Eating disorders and menstrual dysfunction in adolescents. *Annals of the New York Academy of Sciences, 1135,* 253–264.

Wadler, J. (2009, May 14). Caught in the safety net. *New York Times,* pp. D1, D6.

Wadsworth, S. M. M. (2010). Family risk and resilience in the context of war and terrorism. *Journal of Marriage and Family, 72,* 537–556.

The WAGE Project. (2007). The wage gap and its costs. In P. S. Rothenberg (Ed.), *Race, class, and gender in the United States: An integrated study* (7th ed., pp. 373–378). New York: Worth.

Wahab, S., & Olson, L. (2004). Intimate partner violence and sexual assault in Native American communities. *Trauma, Violence, & Abuse, 5,* 353–366.

Wai, J., Cacchio, M., Putallaz, M., & Makel, M. C. (2010). Sex differences in the right tail of cognitive abilities: A 30 year examination. *Intelligence, INTELL-00579,* 1–12.

Wainright, J. L., & Patterson, C. J. (2008). Peer relations among adolescents with female same-sex parents. *Developmental Psychology, 44,* 117–126.

Waits, B. L., & Lundberg-Love, P. (2008). The impact of campus violence on college students. In M. A. Paludi (Ed.), *Understanding and preventing campus violence* (pp. 51–70). Westport, CT: Praeger.

Walby, S. (2011). Is the knowledge society gendered? *Gender, Work and Organization, 18,* 1–29.

Waldrop, A. E. (2009). Violence and victimization among women with substance use disorders. In K. T. Brady, S. E. Back, & S. F. Greenfield (Eds.), *Women and addiction: A comprehensive handbook* (pp. 493–499). New York: Guilford.

Walker, E. L. (2011). *Complete without kids: An insider's guide to childfree living by choice or by chance.* Austin, TX: Greenleaf Book Group.

Walker, H., Grant, D., Meadows, M., & Cook, I. (2007). Women's experiences and perceptions of age discrimination in employment: Implications for research and policy. *Social Policy & Society, 6,* 37–48.

Walker, L. J. (2006). Gender and morality. In M. Killen & J. G. Smetana (Eds.), *Handbook of moral development* (pp. 93–115). Mahwah, NJ: Erlbaum.

Walker, R. B., & Luszcz, M. A. (2009). The health and relationship dynamics of late-life couples: A systematic review of the literature. *Ageing and Society, 29,* 455–480.

Wallace, S. P., Cochran, S. D., Durazo, E. M., & Ford, C. L. (2011, March). *The health of aging lesbian, gay, and bisexual adults in California.* Los Angeles, CA: UCLA Center for Health Policy Research.

Wallis, C. (2011). Performing gender: A content analysis of gender display in music videos. *Sex Roles, 64,* 160–172.

Walsh, J. L., Ward, L. M., Caruthers, A., & Merriwether, A. (2011). Awkward or amazing: Gender and age trends in first intercourse experience. *Psychology of Women Quarterly, 35,* 59–71.

Walsh, K., Blaustein, M., Knight, W. G., Spinazzola, J., & van der Kolk, B. A. (2007). Resiliency factors in the relation between childhood sexual abuse and adulthood sexual assault in college-age women. *Journal of Child Sexual Abuse, 16,* 1–17.

Walsh, K., Fortier, M. A., & DiLillo, D. (2010). Adult coping with childhood sexual abuse: A theoretical and empirical review. *Aggression and Violent Behavior, 15,* 1–13.

Walsh, R. (2011). Life style and mental health. *American Psychologist.* doi: 10.1037/a0021769

Walsh, W. A., Dawson, J., & Mattingly, M. J. (2010). How are we measuring resilience following childhood maltreatment? Is the research adequate and consistent? What is the impact on research, practice, and policy? *Trauma, Violence, & Abuse, 11,* 27–41.

Walsh, W. B., & Heppner, M. J. (Eds.). (2006). *Handbook of career counseling for women* (2nd ed.). Mahwah, NJ: Erlbaum.

Walsh-Bowers, R. (1999). Fundamentalism in psychological science: The publication manual as bible. *Psychology of Women Quarterly, 23,* 375–392.

Walter, C. A. (2003). *The loss of a life partner: Narratives of the bereaved.* New York: Columbia University Press.

Walton, G. M., & Spencer, S. J. (2009). Latent ability: Grades and test scores systematically underestimate the intellectual ability of negatively stereotyped students. *Psychological Science, 20,* 1132–1139.

Wang, M., Henkens, K., & van Solinge, H. (2011). Retirement adjustment: A review of theoretical and empirical advancements. *American Psychologist, 66,* 204–213.

Wang, M., & Shultz, K. S. (2010). Employee retirement: A review and recommendations for future investigation. *Journal of Management, 36,* 172–206.

Wang, P., & Walumbwa, F. O. (2007). Family-friendly programs, organizational commitment, and work withdrawal: The moderating role of transformational leadership. *Personnel Psychology, 60,* 397–427.

Wang, Q., & Pomerantz, E. M. (2009). The motivational landscape of early adolescence in the United States and China: A longitudinal investigation. *Child Development, 80,* 1272–1287.

Wangby, M., Bergman, L. R., & Magnusson, D. (1999). Development of adjustment problems in girls: What syndromes emerge? *Child Development, 70,* 678–699.

Want, S. C., Vickers, K., & Amos, J. (2009). The influence of television programs on appearance satisfaction: Making and mitigating social comparisons to "friends." *Sex Roles, 60,* 642–655.

Ward, L. M. (2002). Does television exposure affect emerging adults' attitudes and assumptions about sexual relationships? Correlational and experimental confirmation. *Journal of Youth and Adolescence, 31,* 1–15.

Ward, L. M. (2007, March). A longitudinal study of media use and gender role beliefs among Black and White 6th graders. In L. M. Ward (Chair), *Television's role in the gender and sexual socialization of Black adolescents.* Paper symposium conducted at the meeting of the Society for Research in Child Development, Boston.

Ward, L. M., Hansbrough, E., & Walker, E. (2005). Contributions of music video exposure to black adolescents' gender and sexual schemas. *Journal of Adolescent Research, 20,* 143–166.

Ward, L. M., & Harrison, K. (2005). The impact of media use on girls' beliefs about gender roles, their bodies, and sexual relationships: A research synthesis. In E. Cole & J. H. Daniel (Eds.), *Featuring females: Feminist analyses of media* (pp. 3–24). Washington, DC: American Psychological Association.

Wareham, S., Fowler, K., & Pike, A. (2007). Determinants of depression severity and duration in Canadian adults: The moderating effects of gender and social support. *Journal of Applied Social Psychology, 37,* 2951–2979.

Warner, J. (2009). The choice myth. *New York Times.* Retrieved from http://opinionator.blogs.nytimes.com/2009/10/08/the-opt-out-myth/?cp=1&sq=the%20choice%20myth&st=cse

Warner, S. (2009). *Women and child sexual abuse: Theory, research, and practice.* New York: Psychology Press.

Warren, C. S., Schoen, A., & Schafer, K. J. (2010). Media internalization and social comparison as predictors of eating pathology among Latino adolescents: The moderating effect of gender and generational status. *Sex Roles, 63,* 712–724.

Warren, J. T., Harvey, S. M., & Henderson, J. T. (2010). Do depression and low self-esteem follow abortion among adolescents? Evidence from a national study. *Perspectives on Sexual Reproductive Health, 42,* 230–235.

Warren, M. P., & Chua, A. T. (2008). Exercise-induced amenorrhea and bone health in the adolescent athlete. *Annals of the New York Academy of Sciences, 1135,* 244–252.

Warshaw, R. (1988). *I never called it rape: The Ms. report on recognizing, fighting, and surviving date and acquaintance rape.* New York: Harper & Row.

Wartik, N. (2002, June 23). Hurting more, helped less? *New York Times,* pp. WH1, WH6, WH7.

Washington, D. L., & Bird, C. E. (2002). Sex differences in disease presentation in the emergency department. *Annuals of Emergency Medicine, 40,* 461–463.

Wasserman, G. A., McReynolds, L. S., Ko, S. J., Katz, L. M., & Carpenter, J. R. (2005). Gender differences in psychiatric disorders at juvenile probation intake. *American Journal of Public Health, 95,* 131–137.

Watamura, S. E., Morrissey, T. W., Phillips, D. A., McCartney, K., & Bub, K. (2011). Double jeopardy: Poorer social-emotional outcomes for children in the NICHD SECCYD experiencing home and child-care environments that confer risk. *Child Development, 82,* 48–65.

Waterman, A. S. (1999). Identity, the identity statuses, and identity status development: A contemporary statement. *Developmental Review, 19,* 591–621.

Watson, E. (1995). Comfort. In B. Benatovich (Ed.), *What we know so far: Wisdom among women.* New York: St. Martin's Griffin.

Watson, H. J., Raykos, B. C., Street, H., Fursland, A., & Nathan, P. R. (2011). Mediators between perfectionism and eating disorder psychopathology: Shape and weight overevaluation and conditional goal-setting. *International Journal of Eating Disorders, 44,* 142–149.

Watt, H. M. G. (2004). Development of adolescents' self-perceptions, values, and task perceptions according to gender and domain in 7th-through 11th-grade Australian students. *Child Development, 75,* 1556–1574.

Watt, H. M. G. (2008). Gender and occupational outcomes: An introduction. In H. M. G. Watt & J. S. Eccles (Eds.), *Gender and occupational outcomes: Longitudinal assessments of individual, social, and cultural influences* (pp. 3–24). Washington, DC: American Psychological Association.

Waxman, S. (2005, February 21). "Simpsons" animates gay nuptials, and a debate. *New York Times,* p. A17.

Wayne, J. H., & Cordeiro, B. L. (2003). Who is a good organizational citizen? Social perception of male and female employees who use family leave. *Sex Roles, 49,* 233–246.

Weaver, H. N. (2009). The colonial context of violence: Reflections on violence in the lives of Native American women. *Journal of Interpersonal Violence, 24,* 1552–1563.

Webster, M., Jr., & Rashotte, L. S. (2009). Fixed roles and situated actions. *Sex Roles, 61,* 325–337.

Weger, H., Jr., & Emmett, M. E. (2009). Romantic intent, relationship uncertainty, and relationship maintenance in young adults' cross-sex friendships. *Journal of Social and Personal Relationships, 26,* 964–988.

Wegman, H. L., & Stetler, C. (2009). A meta-analytic review of the effects of childhood abuse on medical outcomes in adulthood. *Psychosomatic Medicine, 71,* 805–812.

Weichold, K., Silbereisen, R. K., & Schmitt-Rodermund, E. (2003). Short-term and long-term consequences of early versus late physical maturation in adolescents. In C. Hayward (Ed.), *Gender differences at puberty* (pp. 241–276). Cambridge, MA: Cambridge University Press.

Weigt, J. M., & Solomon, C. R. (2008). Work-family management among low-wage service workers and assistant professors in the USA: A comparative intersectional analysis. *Gender, Work and Organization, 15,* 621–649.

Weinberg, D. H. (2004). *Evidence from census 2000 about earnings by detailed occupation for men and women.* Washington, DC: U.S. Census Bureau.

Weinberg, M. S., Williams, C. J., & Pryor, D. W. (1994). *Dual attraction: Understanding bisexuality.* New York: Oxford University Press.

Weinberger, N., & Stein, K. (2007, March). *The role of gender and gender composition on early competitive game playing.* Poster presented at the meeting of the Society for Research in Child Development, Boston, MA.

Weinstock, J. S. (2009). (My) stories of lesbian friendship. In P. L. Hammack & B. J. Cohler (Eds.), *The story of sexual identity: Narrative perspectives on the gay and lesbian life course* (pp. 177–205). New York: Oxford University Press.

Weisgram, E. S., & Bigler, R. S. (2006). Girls and science careers: The role of altruistic values and attitudes about scientific tasks. *Journal of Applied Developmental Psychology, 27,* 326–348.

Weisgram, E. S., Bigler, R. S., & Liben, L. S. (2010). Gender, values, and occupational interests among children, adolescents, and adults. *Child Development, 81,* 778–796.

Weiss, K. G. (2009). "Boys will be boys" and other gendered accounts: An exploration of victims' excuses and justifications for unwanted sexual contact and coercion. *Violence Against Women, 15,* 810–834.

Weiss, M. C., & Weiss, E. T. (2010). *Living well beyond breast cancer: A survivor's guide for when treatment ends and the rest of your life begins.* New York: Three Rivers Press.

Weitz, R. (2010). *The sociology of health, illness, and health care: A critical approach.* Boston, MA: Wadsworth.

Weitzer, R., & Kubrin, C. E. (2011). Misogyny in rap music: A content analysis of prevalence and meanings. In M. Kimmel

& A. Aronson (Eds.), *The gendered society reader* (4th ed., pp. 453–470). New York: Oxford University Press.

Wellesley Centers for Women. (2009, Spring). *Overcoming persistent inequities: Educational disparities among women in Massachusetts.* Wellesley, MA: Author.

Wellman, N. S., Kamp, B., Kirk-Sanchez, N. J., & Johnson, P. M. (2007). Eat better & move more: A community-based program designed to improve diets and increase physical activity among older Americans. *American Journal of Public Health, 97,* 710–717.

Welsh, A. (2010). On the perils of living dangerously in the slasher horror film: Gender differences in the association between sexual activity and survival. *Sex Roles, 62,* 762–773.

Welton, A. J., et al. (2009). Health related quality of life after combined hormone replacement therapy: Randomised controlled trial. *BMJ, 337,* a1190.

Wenger, G. C., Melkas, T., & Knipscheer, K. C. (2007). Social embeddedness and late-life parenthood: Community activity, close ties, and support networks. *Journal of Family Issues, 28,* 1419–1456.

Wentzel, K. R., Filisetti, L., & Looney, L. (2007). Adolescent prosocial behavior: The role of self-processes and contextual cues. *Child Development, 78,* 895–910.

Wenzel, A. (2010). *Anxiety in childbearing women: Diagnosis and treatment.* Washington, DC: American Psychological Association.

Werhun, C. (2011). Sexual orientation: Scientific theories of causation. In M. Z. Stange, C. K. Oyster, & J. E. Sloan (Eds.), *Encyclopedia of women in today's world.* Newberry Park, CA: Sage.

Werner, E. E. (2010). Resilience research: Past, present, and future. In R. D. Peters, B. Leadbeater, & R. J. McMahon (Eds.), *Resilience in children, families and communities: Linking context to practice and policy* (pp. 3–12). New York: Kluwer Academic/Plenum.

Werner, E. E., & Smith, R. S. (2001). *Journeys from childhood to midlife: Risk, resilience and recovery.* Ithaca, NY: Cornell University Press.

Wertheim, E. H., Paxton, S. J., & Blaney, S. (2009). Body image in girls. In L. Smolak & J. K. Thompson (Eds.), *Body image, eating disorders, and obesity in youth: Assessment, prevention, and treatment* (pp. 47–76). Washington, DC: American Psychological Association.

Wessler, S. L., & De Andrade, L. L. (2006). Slurs, sterotypes, and student interventions: Examining the dynamics, impact, and prevention of harassment in middle and high school. *Journal of Social Issues, 62,* 511–532.

West, B., & Gandhi, S. (2006). Reporting abuse: A study of the perceptions of people with disabilities (PWD) regarding abuse directed at PWD. *Disability Studies Quarterly, 26*(1). Retrieved from http://www.dsq-sds.org/article/view/650/827

Weyerer, S., et al. (2009). At-risk alcohol drinking in primary care patients aged 75 years and older. *International Journal of Geriatric Psychiatry, 24,* 1376–1385.

Whaley, R. B. (2001). The paradoxical relationship between gender inequality and rape: Toward a refined theory. *Gender & Society, 15,* 529–553.

Whang, W., et al. (2009). Depression and risk of sudden cardiac death and coronary heart disease in women. *Journal of the American College of Cardiology, 53,* 950–958.

Whealin, J. M., Zinzow, H. M., Salstrom, S. A., & Jackson, J. L. (2007). Sex differences in the experience of unwanted sexual attention and behaviors during childhood. *Journal of Child Sexual Abuse, 16,* 41–58.

Wheeler, M. (2011, Winter). Saving the girl child. *Ms.,* 24.

Whelan, P. (2010). Abortion rates and universal health care. *New England Journal of Medicine, 362,* e45(1)–e45(3).

Whiffen, V. E. (2001). Depression. In J. Worell (Ed.), *Encyclopedia of women and gender* (pp. 303–314). San Diego, CA: Academic Press.

Whipple, V. (2006). *Lesbian widows: Invisible grief.* New York: Harrington.

Whisman, M. A., & Snyder, D. K. (2007). Sexual infidelity in a national survey of American women: Differences in prevalence and correlates as a function of method of assessment. *Journal of Family Psychology, 21,* 147–154.

Whiston, S. C., & Keller, B. K. (2004). The influences of the family of origin on career development: A review and analysis. *Counseling Psychologist, 32,* 493–568.

Whitbourne, S. K., Sneed, J. R., & Sayer, A. (2009). Psychosocial development from college through midlife: A 34-year sequential study. *Developmental Psychology, 45,* 1328–1340.

White, A. A., III. (2011). *Seeing patients: Unconscious bias in health care.* Cambridge, MA: Harvard University Press.

White, A. M. (Ed.). (2010). *African Americans doing feminism: Putting theory into everyday practice.* Albany, NY: SUNY Press.

White, J. W. (2011). *Taking sides: Clashing views in gender* (5th ed.). New York: McGraw-Hill.

White, J. W., & Frabutt, J. M. (2006). Violence against girls and women: An integrative developmental prespective. In J. Worell & C. D. Goodheart (Eds.), *Handbook of girls' and women's psychological health: Gender and well-being across the lifespan* (pp. 85–93). New York: Oxford University Press.

White, J. W., Koss, M. P., & Kazdin, A. E. (2011). Conclusions and next steps. In J. W. White, M. P. Koss, & A. E. Kazdin (Eds.), *Violence against women and children: Mapping the terrain* (Vol. 1, pp. 287–310). Washington, DC: American Psychological Association.

White, J. W., & Kowalski, R. M. (1994). Deconstructing the myth of the nonaggressive woman: A feminist analysis. *Psychology of Women Quarterly, 18,* 487–508.

Whitehead, B. D., & Popenoe, D. (2008). *Life without children: The social retreat from children and how it is changing America.* Piscataway, NJ: The National Marriage Project, Rutgers.

Whitley, B. E., Jr. (2007, May). *Religiosity and anti-gay prejudice: A meta-analysis.* Poster presented at the annual meeting of the Association for Psychological Science, Washington, DC.

Whitley, B. E., Jr., Childs, C. E., & Collins, J. B. (2011). Differences in Black and White American college students' attitudes toward lesbians and gay men. *Sex Roles, 64,* 299–310.

Whitley, H. P., & Lindsey, W. (2009). Sex-based differences in drug activity. *American Family Physician, 80,* 1254–1258.

Whitmire, R. (2007, July 20). The latest way to discriminate against women. *Chronicle of Higher Education,* p. B16.

Whitmire, R. (2010). *Why boys fail: Saving our sons from an educational system that's leaving them behind.* New York: AMACOM.

Whooley, M. A., et al. (2008). Depressive symptoms, health behaviors, and risk of cardiovascular events in patients with coronary heart disease. *Journal of the American Medical Association, 300,* 2379–2388.

Wiederman, M. W. (2005). The gendered nature of sexual scripts. *Family Journal: Counseling and Therapy for Couples and Families, 13,* 496–502.

Wigfield, A., Eccles, J. S., Schiefele, U., Roeser, R. W., & Davis-Kean, P. (2006). Development of achievement motivation. In W. Damon, R. M. Lerner (Series Eds.), & N. Eisenberg (Vol. Ed.), *Handbook of child psychology: Vol. 3. Social, emotional, and personality development* (6th ed., pp. 933–1002). Hoboken, NJ: Wiley.

Wijeysundera, H. C., et al. (2010). Association of temporal trends in risk factors and treatment uptake with coronary heart disease mortality, 1994–2005. *Journal of the American Medical Association, 303,* 1841–1847.

Wilbourn, M. P., & Kee, D. W. (2010). Henry the nurse is a doctor too: Implicitly examining children's gender stereotypes for male and female occupational roles. *Sex Roles, 62,* 670–683.

Wilbur, J., et al. (2009). Neighborhood characteristics, adherence to walking, and depressive symptoms in midlife African American women. *Journal of Women's Health, 18,* 1201–1210.

Wilcox, S., et al. (2003a). The effects of widowhood on physical and mental health, health behaviors, and health outcomes: The women's health initiative. *Health Psychology, 22,* 513–522.

Wilcox, S., et al. (2003b). Psychosocial and perceived environmental correlates of physical activity in rural and older African American and white women. *Journals of Gerontology, 58,* P329–P337.

Wilcox, W. B., & Nock, S. L. (2007). "Her" marriage after the revolutions. *Sociological Forum, 22,* 104–111.

Wilkinson, J. A., & Ferraro, K. F. (2002). Thirty years of ageism research. In T. D. Nelson (Ed.), *Ageism: Stereotyping and prejudice against older persons* (pp. 339–358). Cambridge, MA: MIT Press.

Wilkinson, L., & Pearson, J. (2009). School culture and the well-being of same-sex-attracted youth. *Gender & Society, 23,* 542–568.

Williams, C. L. (2010). The glass escalator: Hidden advantages for men in the "female" professions. In J. Goodman (Ed.), *Global perspectives on gender & work* (pp. 195–211). Lanham, MD: Rowman & Littlefield.

Williams, D., Martins, N., Consalvo, M., & Ivory, J. D. (2009). The virtual census: Representations of gender, race and age in video games. *New Media & Society, 11,* 815–834.

Williams, J. C. (2010). The odd disconnect: Our family-hostile public policy. In K. Christensen & B. Schneider (Eds.), *Workplace flexibility: Realigning 20th-century jobs for a 21st-century workforce* (pp. 196–219). Ithaca, NY: Cornell University Press.

Williams, J. C., & Boushey, H. (2010). *The three faces of work-family conflict: The poor, the professionals, and the missing middle.* San Francisco, CA: Center for American Progress.

Williams, J. E., & Best, D. L. (1990). *Measuring sex stereotypes: A multination study.* Newbury Park, CA: Sage.

Williams, J. R., Baty, M. L., Gonzalez-Guarda, R. M., Nash, K. R., & Campbell, J. C. (2009). Trauma and violence. In J. C. Urbancic & C. J. Groh (Eds.), *Women's mental health: A clinical guide for primary care providers* (pp. 350–385). Philadelphia, PA: Lippincott Williams & Wilkins.

Williams, J. R., Ghandour, R. M., & Kub, J. E. (2008). Female perpetration of violence in heterosexual intimate relationships: Adolescence through adulthood. *Trauma, Violence, & Abuse, 9,* 227–249.

Williams, M. J., Paluck, E. L., & Spencer-Rodgers, J. (2010). The masculinity of money: Automatic stereotypes predict gender differences in estimated salaries. *Psychology of Women Quarterly, 34,* 7–20.

Williams, T., & Williams, K. (2010). Self-efficacy and performance in mathematics: Reciprocal determinism in 33 nations. *Journal of Educational Psychology, 102,* 453–466.

Williamson, J., & Pahor, M. (2010). Evidence regarding the benefits of physical exercise. *Archives of Internal Medicine, 170,* 124–125.

Willness, C. R., Steel, P., & Lee, K. (2007). A meta-analysis of the antecedents and consequences of workplace sexual harassment. *Personnel Psychology, 60,* 127–162.

Willoughby, T. (2008). A short-term longitudinal study of internet and computer game use by adolescent boys and girls: Prevalence, frequency of use, and psychosocial predictors. *Developmental Psychology, 44,* 195–204.

Wilper, A. P., Woolhandler, S., Lasser, K. E., McCormick, D., Bor, D. H., & Himmelstein, D. U. (2009). Health insurance and mortality in US adults. *American Journal of Public Health, 99,* 2289–2295.

Wilsnack, R. W., Wilsnack, S. C., Kristjanson, A. F., Vogeltanz-Holm, N. D., & Gmel, G. (2009). Gender and alcohol consumption: Patterns from the multinational GENACIS project. *Addiction, 104,* 1487–1500.

Wilson, G. T., Wilfley, D. E., Agras, W. S., & Bryson, S. W. (2010). Psychological treatments of binge eating disorder. *Archives of General Psychiatry, 67,* 94–101.

Wilson, H. W., & Widom, C. S. (2008). An examination of risky sexual behavior and HIV in victims of child abuse and neglect: A 30-year follow-up. *Health Psychology, 27,* 149–158.

Wilson, J. (2011). Sexually transmitted infection in pregnancy. In K. E. Rogstad (Ed.), *ABC of sexually transmitted infections* (6th ed., pp. 59–63). New York: Wiley.

Wilson, R. (2004a, January 23). Louts in the lab. *Chronicle of Higher Education,* pp. A7–A9.

Wilson, R. (2004b, December 3). Where the elite teach, it's still a man's world. *Chronicle of Higher Education,* pp. A8–A14.

Wilson, R. (2007a, January 27). The new gender divide. *Chronicle of Higher Education,* pp. A36–A39.

Wilson, R. (2007b, May 4). Where have all the women gone? *Chronicle of Higher Education,* pp. A40–A44.

Winfield, L. (2005). *Straight talk about gays in the workplace* (3rd ed.). Binghamton, NY: Haworth.

Wingert, P., & Kantrowitz, B. (2009). *The menopause book.* New York: Workman.

Winkle-Wagner, R. (2009). *The unchosen me: Race, gender, and identity among Black women in College.* Baltimore, MD: Johns Hopkins Press.

Winn, J., & Heeter, C. (2009). Gaming, gender, and time: Who makes time to play? *Sex Roles, 61,* 1–13.

Winterich, J. A. (2003). Sex, menopause, and culture: Sexual orientation and the meaning of menopause for women's sex lives. *Gender & Society, 17,* 627–642.

Wiseman, R. (2009). Queen bees and wannabes: Helping your daughter survivie cliques, gossip, boyfriends, and the new realities of girl world (2nd ed). New York: Three Rivers Press.

WISER. (2006). *Social security reform.* Washington, DC: Author.

WISER. (2007). *What today's woman needs to know: A retirement journey.* Washington, DC: Author.

WISER. (2008). *Seven life-defining financial decisions.* Washington, DC: Author.

WISER. (2000–2010). *Women & pensions: An overview.* Washington, DC: Author.

WISER. (2011, Spring). The national deficit and the debt? Why is social security part of the debate? *WISERWoman, 1,* 4.

Witten, T. M. (2008). Transgender bodies, identities, and health-care: Effects of perceived and actual violence and abuse. In J. J. Kronenfeld (Ed.), *Research in the sociology of healthcare: Inequalities and disparities in health care and health—Concerns of patients* (Vol. 25, pp. 225–249). Oxford, England: Elsevier.

Witten, T. M. (2009). Graceful exits: Intersection of aging, transgender identities, and the family-community. *Journal of GLBT Family Studies, 5,* 36–62.

Wolf, J. (2011). *Is breast best? Taking on the breastfeeding experts and the new high stakes of motherhood.* New York: NYU Press.

Wolfe, D. A., Crooks, C. C., Chiodo, D., & Jaffe, P. (2009). Child maltreatment, bullying, gender-based harassment, and adolescent dating violence: Making the connections. *Psychology of Women Quarterly, 33,* 21–24.

Wolf-Wendel, L. E., Baker, B., & Morphew, C. (2000). Dollars and $ense: Institutional resources and the baccalaureate origins of women doctorates. *Journal of Higher Education, 71,* 165–189.

Wolitzky-Taylor, et al. (2010). Has adolescent suicidality decreased in the United States? Data from two national samples of adolescents interviewed in 1995 and 2005. *Journal of Clinical Child & Adolescent Psychology, 39,* 64–76.

Woman named Mohegan tribal chief. (2010, March 5). *Washington Times.* Retrieved from http://www.washingtontimes.com/news/2010/mar/05/woman-named-mohegan-chief/

Women and heart health: From prevention to intervention. (2005, February). *National Women's Health Report, 27*(1), 1–4.

Women can have multiple orgasms. (2007, April 10). *New York Times,* p. D6.

WomenHeart. (2011). *Women and heart disease fact sheet.* Washington, DC: Author.

Women's College Coalition. (2008). *What matters in college after college: A comparative alumnae research study.* West Hartford, CT: Author.

Women's rights are human rights: US ratification of the Convention on the Elimination of All Forms of Discrimination Against Women (CEDAW). (2010). *Hearing before the Committee on the Judiciary, United States Senate. 111th Cong., 1.*

Women's Sports Foundation. (2009). *Her life depends on it II: Sport, physical activity, and the health and well-being of American girls and women.* East Meadow, NY: Author.

Wong, J. Y., & Earl, J. K. (2009). Towards an integrated model of individual, psychosocial, and organizational predictors of retirement adjustment. *Journal of Vocational Behavior, 75,* 1–13.

Wood, J. T. (1994). *Gendered lives: Communication, gender, and culture.* Belmont, CA: Wadsworth.

Wood, W., & Eagly, A. H. (2010). Gender. In S. T. Fiske, D. T. Gilbert, & G. Lindzey (Eds.), *Handbook of social psychology* (5th ed., Vol. 1, pp. 629–667). Hoboken, NJ: Wiley.

Woodhill, B. M., & Samuels, C. A. (2003). Positive and negative androgyny and their relationship with psychological health and well-being. *Sex Roles, 48,* 555–565.

Woods, K. C., & Buchanan, N. T. (2008). Sexual harassment in the workplace. In M. A. Paludi (Ed.), *The psychology of women at work: Challenges and solutions for our female workforce: Vol. 1. Career liberation, history, and the new millennium* (pp. 119–132). Westport, CT: Praeger.

Woods, K. C., & Buchanan, N. T. (2010). Discrimination, harassment, and women's physical and mental health. In M. A. Paludi (Ed.), *Feminism and women's rights worldwide: Mental and physical health* (Vol. 2, pp. 235–252). Santa Barbara, CA: Praeger.

Woods, N. F., Mitchell, E. S., & Smith-Di Julio, K. (2010). Sexual desire during the menopausal transition and early postmenopause: Observations from the Seattle midlife women's health study. *Journal of Women's Health, 19,* 209–218.

Woodzicka, J. A., & LaFrance, M. (2005). The effects of subtle sexual harassment on women's performance in a job interview. *Sex Roles, 53,* 67–77.

Woolf, S. E., & Maisto, S. A. (2008). Gender differences in condom use behavior? The role of power and partner type. *Sex Roles, 58,* 689–701.

Woolven, L. (2008). *The smart woman's guide to PMS and pain-free periods.* New York: Wiley.

Worell, J. (2001). Feminist interventions: Accountability beyond symptom reduction. *Psychology of Women Quarterly, 25,* 335–343.

Worell, J., & Etaugh, C. (1994). Transforming theory and research with women: Themes and variations. *Psychology of Women Quarterly, 18,* 443–450.

Worell, J., & Johnson, D. M. (2001). Feminist approaches to psychotherapy. In J. Worell (Ed.), *Encyclopedia of women and gender* (pp. 425–437). San Diego, CA: Academic Press.

World Health Organization. (2002). *World report on violence and health.* Geneva: Author.

World Health Organization. (2009). *World health statistics 2009.* Geneva, Switzerland: Author. Retrieved from http://www.who.int/whosis/whostat/EN_WHS09_Full.pdf//

World Health Organization. (2010a). *Gender, women and primary health care renewal: A discussion paper.* Geneva, Switzerland: Author.

World Health Organization. (2010b). *World no tobacco day 2010.* Geneva, Switzerland: Author. Retrieved from http://www.who.int/tobacco

Worth, R. F. (2010, August 22). Crime (sex) and punishment (stoning). *New York Times,* pp. WK1, WK4.

Wrench, J. S., & Knapp, J. L. (2008). The effects of body image perceptions and sociocommunicative orientations on self-esteem, depression, and identification and involvement in the gay community. *Journal of Homosexuality, 55,* 471–503.

Wright, L., & Cassidy, T. (2009, April). *Family structure and environment in psychological adjustment.* Paper presented at the meeting of the British Psychological Society, Brighton, England.

Wroolie, T., & Holcomb, M. (2010). Menopause. In B. L. Levin & M. A. Becker (Eds.), *A public health perspective of women's mental health* (pp. 143–164). New York: Springer.

Wurtele, S. K. (2009). Preventing sexual abuse of children in the twenty-first century: Preparing for challenges and opportunities. *Journal of Child Sexual Abuse, 18,* 1–18.

Wyche, K. F., & Crosby, F. J. (Eds.). (1996). *Women's ethnicities: Journeys through psychology.* Boulder, CO: Westview.

Wylie, S. A., Corliss, H. L., Boulanger, V., Prokop, L. A., & Austin, S. B. (2010). Socially assigned gender nonconformity: A measure for use in surveillance and investigation of health disparities. *Sex Roles, 63,* 264–276.

Xinran, (2011). *Message from an unknown Chinese mother: Stories of love and loss.* New York: Scribner.

Xu, J., Kochanek, J. D., Murphy, S. L., & Tejada-Vera, B. (2010). *Deaths: Final data for 2007. National Vital Statistics Reports, 58,* 1–37. Washington, DC: U.S. Department of Health and Human Services, National Center for Health Statistics.

Xu, Q., Anderson, D., & Courtney, M. (2010). A longitudinal study of the relationship between lifestyle and mental health among midlife and older women in Australia: Findings from the healthy aging of women study. *Health Care for Women International, 31,* 1082–1096.

Xue, F., Willett, W. C., Rosner, B. A., Hankinson, S. E., & Michels, K. B. (2011). Cigarette smoking and the incidence of breast cancer. *Archive of Internal Medicine, 171,* 125–133.

Yabroff, J. (2007, October 1). Mothers to blame. *Newsweek,* p. 86.

Yagil, D., Karnieli-Miller, O., Eisikovits, Z., & Enosh, G. (2006). Is that a "no"? The interpretation of responses to unwanted sexual attention. *Sex Roles, 54,* 251–260.

Yaish, M., & Stier, H. (2009). Gender inequality in job authority: A cross-national comparison of 26 countries. *Work and Occupations, 36,* 434–366.

Yakushko, O. (2007). Do feminist women feel better about their lives? Examining patterns of feminist identity development and women's subjective well-being. *Sex Roles, 57,* 223–234.

Yan, F. A., Howard, D. E., Beck, K. H., Shattuck, T., & Hallmark-Kerr, M. (2010). Psychosocial correlates of physical dating violence victimization among Latino early adolescents. *Journal of Interpersonal Violence, 25,* 808–831.

Yang, Z., & Gaydos, L. M. (2010). Reasons for and challenges of recent increases in teen birth rates: A study of family planning service policies and demographic changes at the state level. *Journal of Adolescent Health, 46,* 517–524.

Yankaskas, B. C., et al. (2010). Barriers to adherence to screening mammography among women with disabilities. *American Journal of Public Health, 100,* 947–953.

Yao, M. Z., Mahood, C., & Linz, D. (2010). Sexual priming, gender stereotyping, and likelihood to sexually harass: Examining the cognitive effects of playing a sexually-explicit video game. *Sex Roles, 62,* 77–88.

Yardley, J. (2004, December 21). Rural exodus for work fractures Chinese family. *New York Times,* pp. A1–A8.

Yeater, E. A., Lenberg, K. L., Avina, C., Rinehart, J. K., & O'Donohue, W. (2008). When social situations take a turn for the worse: Situational and interpersonal risk factors for sexual aggression. *Sex Roles, 59,* 151–163.

Yeretssian, G., et al. (2009). Gender differences in expression of the human caspase-12 long variant determines susceptibility to *Listeria monocytogenes* infection. *Proceedings of the National Academy of Sciences, 106,* 9016–9020.

Yeung, D. Y. L., Tang, C. S., & Lee, A. (2005). Psychosocial and cultural factors influencing expectations of menarche: A study on Chinese premenarcheal teenage girls. *Journal of Adolescent Research, 20,* 118–135.

Yoder, J. D. (2005, Summer). Reflections on the place of the *Psychology of Women* course in psychology's curriculum. *Feminist Psychologist,* pp. 18–19.

Yoder, J. D. (2010). Does "making a difference" still make a difference? A textbook author's reflections. *Sex Roles, 62,* 173–178.

Yoder, J. D., & Aniakudo, P. (1999). "Outsider within" the firehouse: Subordination and difference in the social interactions of African American women fire-fighters. In L. A. Peplau, S. C. DeBro, R. C. Veniegas, & P. L. Taylor (Eds.), *Gender, culture and ethnicity: Current research about women and men* (pp. 135–152). Mountain View, CA: Mayfield.

Yoder, J. D., Fischer, A. R., Kahn, A. S., & Groden, J. (2007). Changes in students' explanations for gender differences after taking a psychology of women class: More constructionist and less essentialist. *Psychology of Women Quarterly, 31,* 415–425.

Yoder, J. D., Tobias, A., & Snell, A. F. (2011). When declaring "I am a feminist" matters: Labeling is linked to activism. *Sex Roles, 64,* 9–18.

Yoon, D. P., & Lee, E. O. (2004). Religiousness/spirituality and subjective well-being among rural elderly Whites, African Americans, and Native Americans. *Journal of Human Behavior in the Social Environment, 10,* 191–211.

Young, J. R. (2003, September 12). Sexual assault of female Air Force Academy cadets is much more common than reported, survey finds. *Chronicle of Higher Education, 50,* A31.

Yu, L., & Xie, D. (2010). Multidimensional gender identity and psychological adjustment in middle childhood: A study in China. *Sex Roles, 62,* 100–113.

Yuan, A. S. V. (2007a). Gender differences in the relationship of puberty with adolescents' depressive symptoms: Do body perceptions matter? *Sex Roles, 57,* 69–80.

Yuan, A. S. V. (2007b). Perceived age discrimination and mental health. *Social Forces, 86,* 265–290.

Yunger, J. L., Carver, P. R., & Perry, D. G. (2004). Does gender identity influence children's psychological well-being? *Developmental Psychology, 40,* 572–582.

Zabin, L. S., & Cardona, K. M. (2002). Adolescent pregnancy. In G. M. Wingood & R. J. DiClemente (Eds.), *Handbook of women's sexual and reproductive health* (pp. 231–253). New York: Kluwer Academic/Plenum.

Zager, K., & Rubenstein, A. (2002). *The inside story on teen girls.* Washington, DC: American Psychological Association.

Zahn-Waxler, C., Shirtcliff, E. A., & Marceau, K. (2008). Disorders of childhood and adolescence: Gender and psychopathology. *Annual Review of Clinical Psychology, 4,* 275–303.

Zalk, S. R. (1991, Fall). Task force report response of mainstream journals to feminist submissions. *Psychology of Women: Newsletter,* pp. 10–12.

Zambrana, R. E., & MacDonald, V.-M. (2009). Staggered inequalities in access to higher education by gender, race, and ethnicity. In B. T. Dill & R. E. Zambrana (Eds.), *Emerging intersections: Race, class, and gender in theory, policy, and practice* (pp. 73–100). Piscataway, NJ: Rutgers University Press.

Zaritsky, E., & Dibble, S. L. (2010). Risk factors for reproductive and breast cancers among older lesbians. *Journal of Women's Health, 19,* 125–131.

Zavos, H. M., Gregory, A. M., Lau, J. F., & Eley, T. C. (2011). New behavior-genetic approaches to depression in childhood and adolescence: Gene-environment interplay and the role of cognitions. In T. J. Strauman, P. R. Costanzo, & J. Garber (Eds.), *Depression in adolescent girls: Science and prevention* (pp. 35–63). New York: Guilford.

Zenilman, J. M., & Shahmanesh, M. (Eds.). (2012). *Sexually transmitted infections: Diagnosis, management, and treatment.* Sudbury, MA: Jones & Bartlett.

Zerbe, K. J. (2008). *Integrated treatment of eating disorders: Beyond the body betrayed.* New York: W. W. Norton.

Zernike, K. (2003, December 16). Teenagers want more advice from parents on sex, study says. *New York Times,* p. A32.

Zhang, S., Schmader, T., & Forbes, C. (2009). The effects of gender stereotypes on women's career choice: Opening the glass door. In M. Barreto, M. K. Ryan, & M. T. Schmitt (Eds.), *The glass ceiling in the 21st century: Understanding barriers to gender equality* (pp. 125–150). Washington, DC: American Psychological Association.

Zhang, Y., Dixon, T. L., & Conrad, K. (2010). Female body image as a function of themes in rap music videos: A content analysis. *Sex Roles, 62,* 787–797.

Zhou, Q., Hofer, C., Eisenberg, N., Reiser, M., Spinrad, T. L., & Fabes, R. A. (2007). The developmental trajectories of attention focusing, attentional and behavioral persistence, and externalizing problems during school-age years. *Developmental Psychology, 43,* 369–385.

Zhou, Q., et al. (2002). The relations of parental warmth and positive expressiveness to children's empathy-related responding and social functioning: A longitudinal study. *Child Development, 73,* 893–915.

Zichy, S. (2007). *Career match: Connecting who you are with what you love to do.* New York: AMACOM.

Zilberman, M. L. (2009). Substance abuse across the lifespan in women. In K. T. Brady, S. E. Back, & S. F. Greenfield (Eds.), *Women and addiction: A comprehensive handbook* (pp. 3–13). New York: Guilford.

Zimmer-Gembeck, M. J., & Helfand, M. (2008). Ten years of longitudinal research on U.S. adolescent sexual behavior: Developmental correlates of sexual intercourse, and the importance of age, gender and ethnic background. *Developmental Review, 28,* 153–224.

Zimmerman, E. (2009, November 22). Expecting a baby, but not the stereotypes. *New York Times,* p. BU10.

Zink, T., Jacobson, C. J., Regan, S., & Pabst, S. (2004). Hidden victims: The healthcare needs and experiences of older women in abusive relationships. *Journal of Women's Health, 13,* 898–908.

Zink, T., & Sill, M. (2004). Intimate partner violence and job instability. *Journal of the American Medical Women's Association, 59,* 32–35.

Zinn, M. B., & Wells, B. (2008). Diversity within Latino families: New lessons for family social science. In S. Coontz (Ed.), *American families: A multicultural reader* (2nd ed., pp. 222–244). New York: Taylor & Francis.

Ziv-Gal, A., & Flaws, J. A. (2010). Factors that may influence the experience of hot flushes by healthy middle-aged women. *Journal of Women's Health, 19,* 1905–1910.

Zosuls, K. M., Lurye, L. E., & Ruble, D. N. (2008). Gender: Identity, awareness, and stereotyping. In M. M. Haith & J. B. Benson (Eds.), *Encyclopedia of infant and early childhood development* (Vol. 2, pp. 1–12). San Diego, CA: Academic Press.

Zosuls, K. M., Ruble, D. N., Tamis-LeMonda, C. S., Shrout, P. E., Bornstein, M. H., & Greulich, F. K. (2009). The acquisition of gender labels in infancy: Implications for gender-typed play. *Developmental Psychology, 45*, 688–701.

Zucker, A. N. (2004). Disavowing social identities: What it means when women say, "I'm not a feminist, but . . ." *Psychology of Women Quarterly, 28*, 423–435.

Zucker, A. N., Ostrove, J. M., & Stewart, A. (2002). College-educated women's personality development in adulthood: Perceptions and age differences. *Psychology and Aging, 17*, 236–244.

Zucker, A. N., & Stewart, A. J. (2007). Growing up and growing older: Feminism as a context for women's lives. *Psychology of Women Quarterly, 31*, 137–145.

Zucker, K. J. (2001). Biological influences on psychosocial differentiation. In R. K. Unger (Ed.), *Handbook of the psychology of women and gender* (pp. 101–115). New York: Wiley.

Zucker, K. J. (2008). On the "natural history" of gender identity disorder in children. *Journal of American Academy of Child and Adolescent Psychiatry, 47*, 1361–1363.

Zucker, N. L., Losh, M., Bulik, C. M., LaBar, K. S., Piven, J., & Pelphrey, K. A. (2007). Anorexia nervosa and autism spectrum disorders: Guided investigation of social cognitive endophenotypes. *Psychological Bulletin, 133*, 976–1006.

Zurbriggen, E. L. (2010). Rape, war and the socialization of masculinity: Why our refusal to give up war ensures that rape cannot be eradicated. *Psychology of Women Quarterly, 34*, 538–549.

NAME INDEX

A

AARP, 178, 196, 199, 281
Abbey, A., 347, 348
Abela, J., 320
Abrams, L., 162
Acosta, R. V., 77
Adams, H.L., 52
Adams, P. F., 302
Adelmann, P. K., 244
Ader, D. N., 9
Adkins, E., 318
Agahi, N., 300
Ahmed, S. B., 278
Ahnert, L., 265
Ahrens, C. E., 345, 346, 349, 350
Aisenbrey, S., 267
Aldarondo, E., 351, 352, 353
Aldwin, C., 187, 194
Alexander, K., 196
Alexander, L., 137, 139, 144, 151, 154,
    156, 160, 162, 167, 223, 277, 279,
    280, 281, 284, 287, 288, 292, 298,
    300, 302, 312, 325, 349, 352, 354,
    355, 356
Alexandre, C., 159
Alfieri, T., 75
Algars, M., 97
Alhabib, S., 340
Alink, L. R. A., 101
Allen, C. T., 344
Allen, K. R., 245, 273, 363
Allen, M. W., 228
Allison, K., 190
Almond, B., 166, 167, 188
Alschuler, L., 287
Altman, L. K., 198
Altman, S. E., 314
Amanatullah, E. T., 234
Amaro, H., 130
Amato, P. R., 183, 184, 255
Ambady., N., 108
American Association of University Women,
    112, 113, 117, 205, 212, 224, 232, 233,
    234, 239, 248, 250, 332, 333
American Cancer Society, 137, 279, 287,
    293, 294, 295, 296, 297, 298
American College of Obstretrians and
    Gynecologists, 155, 156, 160
American Heart Association, 290, 292, 293
American Institute for Cancer Research,
    294
American Psychiatric Association, 125
American Psychological Association, 6, 13,
    26, 49, 52, 88, 311, 323, 325, 326,
    327
American Psychological Association Task
    Force on the Sexualization of Girls.,
    33, 38, 39, 40, 95, 135, 365, 367
Andersen, B. L., 297
Anderson, E. R., 103, 317, 318
Anderson, J., 228

Anderson, K. L., 205, 348, 352
Anderson, S. J., 65
Anderson, V. N., 346
Anderson-Frye, E., 94, 315
Andreasen, N. C., 311
Andreescu, T., 113
Andronici, J. F., 234
Angier, N., 124, 197. 350
Anasara, D. L., 351
Aniakudo, P., 337
Anschutz, D. J., 95
Ansehl, A., 304, 305
Antonucci, T., 26, 137, 180, 186, 324,
    325
Apparala, M. L., 66
Arber, S., 173
Archer, J., 101
Archer, S. L., 90
Armenta, B.E., 117
Armstrong, E., 134
Armstrong, M. J., 195
Arney, H. T., 186
Arnold, J.E., 260
Aronson, P., 91, 117, 371
Arseneau, J. R., 123, 125, 131
Arseth, A. K., 90
Asay, P. A., 212
Asendorpf, J. B., 101
Ashkinaze, C., 226
Ata, R. N., 95
Athenstaedt, U., 105, 106
Attar-Schwartz, S., 197
Attia, E., 312, 313
Aubeeluck, A., 146
Aubin, S., 138
Aubrey, J. S., 95
Aumann, K., 180, 255, 298
Aune, T., 318
Austen, S., 243, 260
Auster, E. R., 236
Ayala, C., 293
Ayers, B., 166, 167
Ayers, M. M., 105, 108
Ayman, R., 229
Ayotte, B. J., 321
Ayoub, N.C., 288
Ayres, M. M., 335, 372
Azar, B., 6
Azari, R., 317

B

Babcock, L., 233, 234 241
Bach, P., 167, 168
Bacue, A., 35, 37
Badger, K., 93
Badgwell, B. D., 277
Baiardi, J., 186, 187
Bailey, J. M., 132
Baillargeon, R. H., 101
Baird, C., 315
Bairey Merz, C. N., 277, 278, 290, 292

Baker, C. N., 40, 336
Baker, D. M., 165
Baker, J., 265
Baker, L., 175
Baker, L. A., 197, 198
Baker, T. B., 314
Baker-Sperry, L., 40
Bakirci, K., 130
Bakker, M., 319
Ballou, M., 328
Bandura, A., 57
Banerjee, N., 225, 229
Bang, E., 66
Banks, A., 54
Banks, M. E., 27, 124, 174, 223
Banyard, V. L., 335
Barash, D. P., 188
Barefoot, J. C., 311, 324
Barker, E. T., 91
Barlett, C. P., 115
Barnes, B., 39
Barnett, M. A., 197
Barnett, O., 340, 356
Barnett, R. C., 256, 264
Barot, S., 151
Barreto, M., 150
Barrett, S., 328
Barrionuevo, A., 132
Barrow, K., 178
Barry, L., 324
Bartini, M., 93
Bartlett, T., 335
Bartoli, A., 177
Barton, L., 94
Basile, K., 351
Basow, S. A., 8, 38, 80, 81, 84, 93, 105,
    108, 175, 205, 332, 364
Batzer, F., 154, 368
Bauer, P. J., 75
Baum, K., 339, 340
Baumgarte, R., 173
Bauserman, R., 183
Baxter, J., 259
Bay-Cheng, L. Y., 135, 371
Bazelon, E., 185, 189
Bazemore, S., 162
Bazzini, D. G., 35
Beals, K. P., 323
Bean-Mayberry, B. A., 278
Bearman, P., 149
Bearman, P. S., 322
Beaton, A., 230
Beck, M., 260
Becker, A. E., 314, 315
Becker, J. C., 31
Becker, M., 310
Beckles, G., 206
Beckman, L. J., 164
Bedford, V. H., 194
Bee, H., 302
Beers, M. H., 139, 281, 322

Behforouz, H., 284
Behm-Morawitz, E., 39
Beilock, S., 114
Beiner, T. M., 339
Bekker, M. H., 103
Belgrave, F., 190
Belkin, L., 267
Belknap, J., 246
Bell, L. C., 56
Bell, M., 353
Bellafante, G., 181
Belsky, J., 87, 88
Bem, S. L., 7, 43, 56, 58, 59, 60, 62, 63
Benedict, H., 337
Benenson, J. F., 103, 173
Benjamin, S., 205
Bennett, J., 116
Bennhold, K., 341
Bent-Goodley, T., 350
Bentley, C. G., 344
Berdahl, J. L., 299, 336, 337
Berenbaum, S. A., 133
Berger, J., 290
Berger, L., 95
Berk, L. E., 37, 74
Berkowitz, R. L., 160
Berlau, D., 302
Bernard, S., 235
Berstein, B., 227, 228, 229
Bernstein, N., 198
Berry, G. L., 34
Bersamin, M., 135
Bertakis, K. D., 278, 317
Bessenoff, G. R., 35
Best, D. L., 14, 54, 65, 75, 76, 81, 348
Betz, N. E., 75, 113, 207, 208, 212, 213, 217
Beyer, S., 116, 216
Beyers, W., 91
Bianchi, S. M., 81, 195, 259, 260, 262, 263
Biblarz, T. J., 190, 191, 259
Bierman, K. L., 311
Biernat, M., 230
Bieschke, K., 217. 323
Bigler, R. S., 211
Bilett, J. L., 136, 140
Billari, F., 195
Billing, Y., 229
Billings, A. C., 39
Birchard, K., 238
Bird, C. E., 277, 298, 305
Birenbaum, M., 136
Bisaga, K., 96
Bisagni, G. M., 184
Bjorklund, B., 302
Black, K.A., 33
Black, M. C., 344, 351
Blackwell, G. L., 118
Blagbrough, J., 343
Blake, S. M., 149
Blakemore, J. E. O., 2, 3, 50, 51, 59, 75, 76, 77, 78, 80, 81, 83, 102, 103, 117, 172, 311
Blank, L., 149

Blascovich, J., 117
Bleeker, M., 115
Blieszner, R., 194
Block, J., 136, 137, 139, 140, 141
Blosnich, J., 352
Bly, R., 372
Bobel, C., 88, 145, 148
Bobo, M., 75
Bocalini, D., 290
Boehmer, U., 279, 280, 287, 297
Bogle, K., 134, 141
Bogle, R., 261
Bohan, J., 2
Bond, M., 229, 236
Bondurant, B., 346
Bongaarts, J., 195
Bono, J., 229
Bönte, M., 292
Book, A., 101
Bookwala, J., 185
Boonstra, H., 149, 153, 285
Borck, C., 52
Bordo, S., 35, 98
Borkhoff, C. M., 278
Bornstein, M. H., 78, 83, 91
Boroughs, M., 92
Borrayo, E., 279, 296
Borzekowski, D., 312
Bos, H., 191, 323
Bosacki, S., 103
Bose, E., 368
Bossarte, R., 352
Boston Women's Health Book Collective, 129, 143, 154, 155, 156, 159, 160, 162, 170, 185, 188, 351
Bostwick, W., 323
Bosworth, B., 232
Botticello, A., 318
Bound, J., 243
Bourne, E., 317
Boushey, H., 213, 223, 233, 239, 255, 256, 262
Bowen, C., 26, 246
Bowen, D., 279, 280, 287, 297
Bowen, M., 301
Bower, J., 288
Bowker, A., 77
Bowleg, L., 131, 277, 337
Bowles, E., 129
Bowles, H. 234
Bowman, S., 212, 217
Boxer, S., 366
Boynton, P., 177
Brabeck, K. M., 174, 188
Brabeck, M. M., 174, 188
Bradbury, T., 180, 192
Bradley, K., 3
Bradshaw, C., 134
Bradsher, J. E., 186
Brady, D., 190
Brake, D., 77
Brallier, S., 129
Branch, D., 156
Branscombe, N. R., 30, 227
Brauer, C., 288
Braun, V., 175

Brazile, D., 33, 337
Breedlove, S., 133
Breen, A. B., 370, 371
Breen, A., V., 91
Breheny, M., 189
Brehm, S. S., 6
Brenner, B., 237, 238
Brescoll, V. L., 13, 229
Brewster, K. L., 66
Bridges, J. S., 41, 65, 213, 214, 256, 257, 262
Bridges, L. J., 196
Bridges, M., 246
Bridges, S. K., 28
Brier, N., 156
Briere, J., 341
Briggs, C., 317
Briggs, E., 340, 341
Brinkman, B., 335
Brinkmann, A., 53
Brinton, E., 167, 290
Britain, D., 246, 305
Britsch, B., 118
Broadbridge, A., 226
Broderick, D., 187
Broderick, P. C., 311
Brody, J. E., 136, 137, 149, 160, 163, 164, 185, 289, 290, 292, 274, 298, 304, 305
Brody, L. R., 103, 108
Bronstein, P., 80
Brooks, A. T., 35
Brooks, K. D., 95
Brooks-Gunn, J., 89, 256
Broughman, R., 243
Broverman, I. K., 325
Brown, B. B., 101, 172
Brown, C. S., 30, 117
Brown, J., 291
Brown, L., 310, 325, 327, 328
Brown, L. M., 205
Brown, S., 261, 316
Brown, W., 260
Brownlow, S., 106
Brozowski, K., 355, 356
Bruckmüller, S., 227
Bruckner, H., 131
Brumberg, J. J., 94
Bryant, A. N., 66, 372
Bryant-Davis, T., 345, 352
Brzyski, R., 163
Btoush, R., 353
Buber, I., 196
Buchanan, T., 91, 92, 216, 265, 336, 337, 338
Buchmueller, T., 280
Buchanan, C., 287
Buchner, D., 246, 304
Budig, M., 235
Bugental, D. B., 26, 355
Buijsse, B. 291
Bukatko, D., 75, 105
Bulanda, J., 180
Bullock, H. E., 10, 279, 371
Bulun, S., 286
Burchinal, M. R., 265

Burgess, C., 115
Burgess, E. O., 138, 139
Burggraf, K., 39, 95
Buriel, R., 83, 265
Burke, M. J., 228
Burn, S. M., 18, 129, 130, 132, 152, 154,
    155, 190, 206, 207, 225, 229, 231,
    233, 234, 235, 261, 262, 267, 285,
    336, 338, 339, 343, 348, 351, 356,
    368
Burns, A., 271
Burns, E. A., 172, 173
Burns, M., 314, 325
Bursik, K., 333
Burton, L. M., 17
Bush, V., 208
Busman, B. J., 101, 102
Buss, D. M., 175
Busseri, M. A., 323
Bussey, K., 57
Butler, B., 315, 316, 318, 320
Butler, L. D., 137, 139, 311, 350
Butler, R., 140
Button, L., 312
Butts, S., 86, 164, 166
Buysse, J. M., 38
Byars-Winston, A. M., 16, 211, 327
Byers, E. S., 341
Byrne, B. M., 216
Bynum, L., 340

C

Cabrera, N., 29
Cachelin, F. M., 96
Cahill, L., 319
Cahn, N., 164
Caine, E. D., 321, 322
Calarco, P., 348
Calasanti, T., 35, 174, 247, 249, 250
Calefati, J., 210
Call, V., 195
Calogero, R. M., 94, 95
Calvert, S. L., 38
Cambron, M. J., 91
Cameron, D., 105
Camilli, G., 265
Campagna, J., 244
Campbell, A., 73, 74
Campbell, R., 345, 348, 349, 350, 351,
    352
Campbell, S. B., 101
Campbell, S. M., 117
Camplone, W., 236
Canabal, M. E., 208
Canetto, S. S., 173, 242, 247, 324
Cann, A., 67, 68
Cannon, E., 353
Caplan, J. B., 2, 3, 7, 12, 13, 101
Caplan, P. J., 2, 3, 7, 12, 13, 101, 148
Caprara, G. V., 102
Caprile, M., 231
Card, N. A., 101
Carey, M., 134
Carli, L. L., 102, 103, 105, 229, 231, 234,
    259
Carlson, K., 305

Carlson, S., 304
Carney, S., 292, 352
Carp, F. M., 244
Carpenter, C., 39, 181, 280
Carpenter, L. J., 77
Carvajal, D., 278
Carr, C. L., 77, 93
Carr, D., 186, 187, 271
Carr, P., 251
Carrell, S. E., 118, 212
Carroll, M. H., 346
Carter, B., 37
Carter, J. S., 3, 370, 371
Carter, N., 227
Carter-Edwards, L., 96
Carver, P. R., 93, 132
Case, K. A., 372
Casey, M. B., 56, 59
Cash, T. F., 94
Cashdan, E., 105
Casper, L. M., 186
Casper, R., 147
Caspi, J., 83, 84
Cassell, J., 116
Castañeda, D., 66, 126, 131, 173, 352
Castilla, E., 234
Castro-Fernandez, M., 351, 352, 353
Catalyst, 226
Caughey, A., 159
Cavanagh, S., 224, 265, 269
Cavanaugh, J. C., 179, 246, 299
Ceci, S. J., 12, 111, 112, 113, 114, 212
Ceballo, R., 190
Cebula, R., 223
Center for American Women and Politics,
    226
Center on Alcohol Marketing and Youth,
    316
Centers for Disease Control and Prevention,
    134, 148, 158, 282, 283, 300
Centers, R. E., 77
Cermele, J. A., 326
Chambers, P., 186, 187, 194, 195, 196
Chan, A., 78, 172
Chan, K. S., 291, 317
Chan, Y., 353
Chandra, A., 129, 133
Chapleau, K., 347
Chaplin, T. M., 102
Charlebois, J., 18, 268
Charles, D., 344
Charles, M., 3, 26, 152
Charo, R., 287
Chassin, L., 300, 317
Chaudoir, S. P., 338
Chaudron, L. H., 321, 322
Chavkin, W., 155
Cheadle, J., 183
Chen, I., 148
Chen, P., 278, 299
Chen, X., 172
Chen, Y., 346, 351, 352, 354
Cherlin, A. J., 179, 180, 181, 192, 264
Cherney, I. D., 59, 77, 109, 112, 115
Cheryan, S., 212
Cheung, F., 227, 235, 268

Chevarley, F. M., 302
Chida, Y., 292
Chiang, K., 305
Chin, J., 226, 229, 230, 231
Chin-Sang, V., 245
Chisholm, J., 26, 27
Chittister, J., 26
Cho, L., 293
Chodorow, N. J., 3
Choi, N. G., 238
Choma, B. L., 94
Chowdhary, A., 368
Chowdhury, N., 340, 353
Chrisler, J. C., 8, 18, 34, 35, 86, 88, 124,
    144, 145, 146, 147, 148, 161. 166,
    167, 168, 231, 270
Christ, G., 164
Christakis, N. A., 180, 186, 187, 286
Christensen, A. E., 112, 267, 268
Christensen, K., 223, 225
Chu, A., 341
Chuang, S. S., 29
Chug, A., 314
Chung, J., 284
Chung, Y., 237
Church, H., 318
Ciarlo, J., 263
Ciambrone, D., 285, 286
Cicchetti, D., 341
Cichy, K. E., 66
Cicirelli, V., 186, 187
Clancy, C. M., 278
Clapp, S., 231
Clark, C., 279, 296
Clark, L., 94
Clark, M. D., 177, 326, 346
Clark, R. A., 107
Clarke, A., 213
Clarke, P., 304
Clarke-Stewart, K. A., 101, 265
Clarren, R., 336
Claxton, A., 10
Clayton, S., 226, 236
Clearfield, M. W., 83, 109
Clements, C., 346
Clemetson, L., 279
Closson, L. M., 101
Clouse, A., 314
COACHE, 228
Cocchiara, F., 262
Cohen, D., 188
Cohen, H., 148
Cohen, P., 185
Cohen, P. N., 229, 233
Cohen, S. A., 152, 155
Coker, A. D., 10, 11
Coker, A. L., 353
Colditz, G., 167
Cole, E. R., 16, 34, 35, 131
Cole, J. B., 132
Cole, M., 286
Coleman, J. M., 28, 256
Colgan, F., 217
Coll, C. G., 190
Collaer, M., 117
Colley, A., 76, 77

Collins, G., 189
Collins, W. A., 135, 172, 194
Colton, P. A., 94, 259, 261
Coltrane, S., 34
Comas-Diaz, L., 279, 327
Comerford, L., 180
Commission on Women's Health, 278
Commonwealth Fund, 88, 95, 172
Compas, B. E., 297
Concannon, T., 292
Compton, J. D., 304, 305
Conger, K., 183, 194
Conkle, A., 174, 178
Conley, T. D., 132
Connell, C., 49
Conner, L., 317
Connidis, T., 138, 165, 174, 179, 180, 182,
    184, 186, 187, 194, 195, 196, 197,
    198, 260
Connolly, J., 177
Conrad, M., 29, 213
Conron, K., 280
Considine, N. S., 296
Conwell, Y., 322
Cook, S., 345, 346
Coomber, K., 95
Coombs, C., 223
Coontz, S., 369, 372
Cordeiro, B. L., 267
Cornelius, N., 259
Cornwell, E., 183, 310
Corra, M., 180
Correa-de-Araujo, R., 278
Correll, S. J., 228, 235
Corrigall, E. A., 65
Cortina, L. M., 219
Costello, C. B., 361
Costigan, C. L., 92
Cote, L. R. 77
Cotter, D., 223, 256
Coulter, I., 278
Coursolle, K., 244
Cowley, G., 285
Cox, D. L., 95
Coyle, K., 148
Coyle, S., 188
Coyne, S. M., 101
Cozzarelli, C., 26
Crabtree, R. D., 13, 363, 364
Craig, L., 259, 267, 268
Crawford, M., 4, 216
Crawley, S. L., 337, 338
Crepaz, N., 281
Crick, N. R., 101
Crimmons, E., 302
Crocker, J., 91
Crockett, L. J., 93
Croghan, I., 294
Crooks, C., 344
Crosby, F. J., 228, 240, 264, 267, 321,
    360
Crosnoe, R., 224, 265, 269
Croteau, J., 217, 237, 323
Crouter, A. C., 75, 78, 81, 84, 93
Crowley, K., 116
Cuddy, A., 235, 298

Cuijpers, P., 163, 321
Cumming, G., 6, 14
Cunningham, G. B., 77
Cunningham, J., 156
Cunningham, J. G., 75, 103
Cunningham, M., 66, 216, 265
Cupach, W., 340
Curran, L., 162
Curry, M., 352
Curtis, K., 149
Curtis, L. H., 154, 278
Custer, L., 266
Cutler, D., 301
Crencek, D., 114
Cutajar, M., 342
Cvencek, D., 114
Czajkowski, S., 292

D

Daan, J., 163
D'Erasmo, S., 36
Daddis, C., 83
Dailard, C., 148
Daley, A., 148
Dalla, R., 190
Dalleck, L., 304
Danilewicz, A., 38
Daniluk, J. C., 97, 135
Darby, A., 312
Dardenne, B., 31
Dare, J., 166
Darity, W., 302
Darroch, J. E., 157
Darville, R. L., 244
Das, M., 33, 38
Daubman, K. A., 216
Dave, S., 5, 162
Davenport, M. L., 51
Davey, E. H., 244, 260
David, H. P., 152
Davidson, D., 51, 160, 287
Davila, J., 319
Davis, A., 206
Davis, K., 281
Davis, P. J., 104
Davis, S. N., 65, 66, 230, 262, 265
Davison, H. K., 228
Dawber, T., 83
Day, J., 256
de Alwis, 352
De Andrade, L. L., 332
de Backer, C., 174
de Laet, M., 115
de las Fuentes, C., 91
de Valk, H., 65
de Waal, F. B. M., 350
DeAngelis, T., 166
DeBate, R. D., 77, 312, 313, 314
DeBlaere, C., 30
DeBoer, D. D., 266
DeBraganza, N., 96
Dechamps, A., 305
DeCherney, A. H., 163
DeFour, D., 230
Deech, R., 161, 162

DeFrancisco, V. P., 12, 13, 36, 43, 44, 45,
    105, 108
DeGroot, J., 259
DeGroult, N., 97
DeKeseredy, W., 351, 354
DeLeo, D., 322
Del Priore, R. E., 35
Delaney, J., 147
DeLoach, C. P., 211
DeLoache, J. S., 77
Delpisheh, A., 160
DeMaris, A., 180
Denissen, J. J. A., 114
Denizet-Lewis, B., 133
Denmark, F. L., 6, 7, 18, 56, 91, 229, 338
Denner, J., 148
Dennis, A., 151
Dennis, C., 163
Denny, K. E., 39
DePaulo, B. M., 184, 185
DeRose, L. M., 89
Desmarais, S., 175
Desmond, R., 38
DeSouza, E., 337, 338
Desrochers, S. J., 65, 83, 265
Deutsch, F. M., 261, 262, 269
DeVetter, F., 259
Devi, F., 149, 150, 151
De Vries, B., 174
de Waal, F., 350
Dew, T., 180
DeZolt, D. M., 84
Dhaher, E., 353
Diamond, L. M., 123, 125, 128, 129, 134,
    135, 149, 158, 180, 181, 182, 183,
    348, 351, 352
Diamond, M., 51, 53, 156
Dibbles, S., 280
DiClemente, R. J., 149
Diekman, A. B., 28
Diener, E., 180
Dijkstra, J. K., 101
Dill, B. T., 16, 18
Dill, K. E., 115
Dillaway, H., 167, 188, 270
Dilley, J., 264, 280, 323
Dillon, S., 341
Dillow, S. A., 113, 204, 206, 211
Dindia, K., 84
Dinella, L. M., 59
Dingfelder, S., 344
Dinolgo, S., 227
Dittmann, M., 298
Dittmar, H., 95
DiVall, S. A., 86
Dixon, C., 355
Doan, S. N., 92
Doctor, R., 323
Dodoo, F., 285
Dodson, L., 233
Doering, L. V., 293
Dohm, F., 96, 97, 312
Dohnt, H., 94
Dolnick. S., 175
Dominus, S., 191, 207
Donaghue, N., 175

Donat, P., 346
Donatelle, R. J., 122, 123, 124, 133, 144, 145, 146, 147, 150, 151, 155, 281, 283, 285, 287,290, 291, 292, 293, 300, 304, 312, 317, 325, 346, 350, 354
Dong, X., 355
Donohoe, M., 152
Donovan, R. A., 26
Doress-Worters, P. B., 121, 137, 138, 140, 185, 187, 194, 199, 243, 246, 247
Dorfman, L. T., 243
Döring, N., 133, 134
Dorius, C., 195, 197
Dorn, L. D., 86, 89
Dorsey, N., 217, 218
Doss, B., 180, 188
Douglas, S. J., 37, 38, 189
Dovidio, J. F., 28
Dowd, J. J., 37
Dowling, W., 246
Downs, B., 223, 256, 257
Downs, E., 115
Dozier, D. M., 39
Drago, R., 189, 259, 262
Draucker, C., 342
Drentea, P., 195, 199, 261
Drew, J.,191
Drew, P., 158
Duehr, E., 229
Dugussa, B., 285
Duff, J. L., 172
Duff-McCall, K., 231
Duffy, J., 332
Duits, T., 73
Dumas, J., 168
Duncan, L., 370
Dunifon, R., 197
Dunkel, T., 315
Dupere, V., 135
Dupre, M., 180
Duquaine-Watson, J., 343
Dutton, M., 353
Duxbury, L., 260, 262, 263
Dweck, C. S., 57
Dworkin, S. L., 39, 40
Dye, J., 189
Dykstra, P. A., 165, 185

E

Eagly, A. H., 2, 14, 18, 23, 24, 28, 30, 102, 103, 225, 226, 229, 230, 231, 234, 259
Earl, J., 244
Earnshaw, V., 347
East, P. L., 81, 135
Easton, S., 341
Eastwick, P. W., 174, 178
Eaton, D. K., 96, 133, 300, 304, 316, 317, 318, 321, 344
Eberhardt, J. L., 240
Echaveste, M., 225
Eccles, J. S., 91, 115, 118
Eckenrode, J., 184, 342
Eckert, P., 105
Eddleman, J., 228, 234

Edelman, J., 164, 167, 168
Edin, K., 319
Edleson, J., 351, 354
Edwards, C. P., 78, 102
Edwards, P., 198
Edwards, George, J. B., 96
Edwards, M., 268
Edwards, V., 344, 354, 356
Egozi, G., 110, 112
Ehrensaft, D., 190
Ehrlich, S. B., 111
Ehrlinger, J., 230
Eibach, R., 230
Eisele, H., 372
Eisenberg, M., 95
Eisenberg, N., 75, 79, 83, 84, 102, 103, 336
El-Bassel, N., 284
Elder, J., 282
Eliot, L., 51, 52, 101
Ellin, A., 198, 214, 234, 299
Elliot, S., 37
Elliott, K., 341
Ellis, B. J., 87
Ellis, L., 87
Ellison, C., 352
Elo, I., 301
El-Sadr, W., 284
Elsawy, B., 304
Else-Quest, N. W., 103, 112, 113, 184
Elson, J., 288
Elwert, F., 185
Ely, R., 83, 103, 105
Embser-Herbert, M. S., 38
Emmett, M., 173
Enander, V., 45
England, P., 3, 35, 39, 134, 185, 223, 225, 229
Engle, J., 215
English, A., 223, 242
Enns, C. Z. 16, 327
Epkins, C., 319
Epstein, C. F., 312, 354
Epstein, E., 317
Erbert, L., 198
Ericksen, J., 297
Ericksen, J. A., 336
Erikson, E. H., 90
Erikson, K., 304
Ernst, E., 161
Ersek, J., 149
Ertel, K., 300
Eschenbeck, H., 310
Eshbaugh, E., 134
ESHRE Task Force, 163
Esmail., A., 181
Espenshade, T., 205
Essex, M. J., 87
Estes, C., 299
Etaugh, C., 6, 15, 26, 28, 29, 34, 37, 38, 65, 73, 74, 75, 76, 77, 80, 81, 83, 112, 128, 136, 160, 183, 184, 185, 186, 187, 189, 193, 195, 196, 213, 214, 238, 239, 243, 244
Etgen, T., 304
Ewing Lee, E. A., 84

Evans, C., 211, 212
Evans, P., 287
Evans, S., 315
Evens, R. R., 94
Evenson, R. J., 263
Exposito, F., 31
Eynon, N., 304

F

Fabes, R. A., 31, 83, 85
Fahs, B., 87, 145, 146
Fairchild, K., 370, 371
Fairfield, H., 234
Faludi, S., 369
Family Caregiver Alliance, 243
Fan, A., 318
Faraday-Brash, L., 234
Faris, R., 101
Fargo, J., 341
Farmer, H. S., 212
Farquhar, C., 167, 168
Farr, D., 97, 182
Farris, C., 175, 346
Fartacek, R., 131, 323
Fassinger, R. E., 27, 123, 125, 131, 212, 217, 237, 238, 323
Faulkner, D., 268
Fausto-Sterling, A., 52
Fazio, R. H., 43
Federal Bureau of Investigation, 131
Federal Glass Ceiling Commission, 230, 240
Federal Interagency Forum, 158, 185, 195, 248, 265, 296, 302
Feingold, A., 94, 111, 352
Fekete, E., 185
Felder, S., 180
Feldman, S., 187
Felix, E. D., 332
Felmlee, D. H., 101, 174, 177
Female Athlete Triad Coalition, 314
Feminist Women's Health Center, 152
Feng, J., 112
Fergusson, D. M., 312
Fergusson, K., 361, 363, 364
Fernald, J. C., 371
Ferraro, K. F., 35, 278
Ferraro, S., 295
Ferree, M. M., 16
Ferriman, K., 219
Ferro, C., 345, 347
Fiedler, M., 226
Fielder, R., 134
Fields, J., 186
Filipovic, J., 350
Fincham, F., 180
Findlay, L. C., 77
Fine, C., 50, 104, 112, 228
Fine, J., 259
Fine, M., 7, 12, 352
Finer, L., 152
Fineran, S., 332, 338
Fingerhut, A. W., 217
Fingerman, K. L., 26, 171, 192, 194
Fingerson, L., 146
Fink, J. S., 38, 39
Finkel, E. J., 174, 178

Firestone, J. M., 65
Fisher, B., 345, 346, 350, 355, 365
Fisher, L. L., 123, 124, 137, 138
Fisher, T. D., 125
Fisher-Thompson, D., 81
Fiske, S. T., 12, 26, 30, 31, 32, 42, 44, 65, 228, 240, 321
Fitzgerald, L. F., 335
Fitzpatrick, M. A., 135, 244
Fitzpatrick, M. J., 33
Fitzpatrick, T., 300
Fivush, R., 103
Flanagan, C., 218
Flaws, J., 166
Fleck, C., 247
Fleming, L. M., 188
Fletcher, J., 158
Flood, M.., 344, 347, 352, 353
Flook, L., 318
Flores, G., 279
Flores, L., 217, 218
Flouri, E., 218
Flynn, K.A., 341
Fogg, P., 222, 234
Fokkema, T., 182, 323
Folger, D., 256
Follingstad, D., 351
Folta, S., 291
Fontaine, N., 8, 311
Fontes, L., 342, 343
Foody, J., 277
Forbes, G. B., 94, 96, 146, 314
Ford, E., 293
Ford, M., 163
Forman, J., 291
Fortenberry, J., 147, 290
Fortier, M. A., 341
Foshee, V. A., 344
Foster, M. D., 371
Foster, S., 226
Foster-Rosales, A., 155
Fouad, N. A., 210, 217
Fourcroy, J., 154
Foust-Cummings, H., 227, 228
Fouts, G., 39, 95
Fowers, B. J., 326
Fox, C., K., 77
Franiuk, R., 28, 256
Frank, A., 85, 86
Frank, K., 204
Frankel, L. P., 234
Franko, D. L., 96
Frantz, D., 322
Frazier, P., 349
Frederick, D. A., 96
Fredriksen-Goldsen, K., 323
Freeman, E., 34, 168, 235
Freizinger, M., 163, 312
Frenzel, A. C., 114
Freud, S., 54, 123, 132
Freyd, J. J., 341
Freysinger, V. J., 245
Fried, L. P., 246
Friedan, B., 7, 372
Friedman, A., 283, 284
Friedman, C. K., 74, 77, 78, 83

Friedman, R., 162
Friedman, S. R., 213
Frieze, I. H., 101, 102, 177, 178, 243, 351, 352, 354
Frisen, A., 94, 95
Frith, K. T., 39
Frome, P. M., 211, 219
Frone, M. R., 268
Frost, A., 285
Frost, J., 150
Fryers, T., 352
Fuegen, K., 256
Fukkink, R. G., 265
Fulcher, M., 75, 191
Fuller-Rowell., T., E., 92
Fulton, A., 128
Fulton, J., 304
Fumia, D., 130
Furman, W., 344
Furnham, A., 115, 216

G

Gadalla, T., 347, 351
Gaertner, S. L., 28
Gagne, L., 288, 290
Gajendran, R. S., 268
Galambos, N. L., 58, 75, 77, 78, 83, 91, 93, 94, 102, 114, 194, 318
Gale, E., 177
Galinsky, E., 180, 255, 258, 265, 268, 298
Gallagher, K., 130
Galliher, R. V., 177
Gallup, 151
Galupo, M. P., 173
Galvao, L., 149, 152
Gangestad, S. W., 174
Gangl, M., 235
Gannon, L., 122
Ganong, L. H., 184, 211
Ganske, K. H., 59
Garavalia, L. S., 293
Garcia, F., 277
Garnets, L. D., 10, 131
Garre-Olmo, J., 355
Garrett, B., 300
Garrett, C. C., 52, 124
Gartrell, N. K., 54
Gates, G., 181, 190
Gavey, N., 149
Gavin, H., 343, 341, 344, 356
Gavin, L., 285
Gavrilova, N., 137, 138, 139, 140
Gearhart, J. P., 53
Geary, D. C., 115
Gee, G., 239
Gelman, S. A., 81
Gentile, L., 91, 94, 328
Genzlinger, N., 35
George, W., 324
Gerber, G., 23
Gergen, K. J., 173
Gergen, M., 10, 173
Gershoff, E. T., 101
Gerson, K., 242, 255, 257, 265,
Gerstel, N., 190, 194
Gervais, S. J., 117

Giarusso, R., 186, 198, 199, 260
Gibbs, N., 104, 160
Gidycz, C. A., 342, 349, 350
Giesbrecht, N., 91
Gilbert, L. A., 13, 85, 243
Gilbert, N., 250
Gilbert, S., 165, 179
Giles, J. W., 101
Gill, R., 34, 35, 37, 38, 39, 40
Gillam, K., 38, 39
Gilligan, C., 3, 4, 90, 92, 104
Gilmartin, S., 259
Gilpatrick, K., 38
Ginsberg, R. L., 39
Girard, A., L., 12
Girl Scouts, 95
Girschick, L. B., 52
Giuliano, T. A., 39
Given, B., 277
Given, C., 277
Glasser, C., 174
Glauber, R., 235
Gleason, J. B., 83, 103, 105
Glenn, D., 260, 343
Glick, P., 30, 31, 32, 65
Glied, S., 321
Glover, J., 217
Glynn, K., 262
Gochfelld, M., 277
Godfrey, J. R., 166, 198, 260, 299, 304
Godleski, S., 11, 101
Goedereis, E. 187, 198
Goerge, R., 158
Gold, M., 135
Goldberg, A. E., 181, 182, 190, 191, 237, 259, 265
Goldberg, C., 210
Golden, C., 51
Golden, J., 310
Goldfield, G., S., 94
Goldin, C., 256
Goldman, M. B., 131
Goldner, M., 195, 199
Goldscheider, F., 135, 179
Goldstein, A., 259
Gollenberg, A., 148
Golombok, S., 77, 164, 192
Gomez, M. J., 218
Gonzalez, H., 301, 318, 327
Good, C., 117
Good, J. J., 372
Goodchilds, J. D., 137
Goode, E., 95, 310
Gooden, A. M., 34
Gooden, M. A., 34
Gooding, G. E., 29, 30
Goodley, D., 223, 302, 347, 352
Goodman, M., 352, 354
Goodwin, S. A., 31
Goodwin, S. C., 288
Gordon, R. A., 197
Gorin, S., 279, 290
Gornick, J., 267
Gottlib, A., 115
Govil, S., 291
Grabe, S., 39, 40, 94, 96, 319

Graber, J. A., 89
Grace, S., 293
Grady, D., 159, 167
Graham-Bermann, S., 353
Gramotnev, H., 183
Grann, V., 277
Grant, J. A., 26
Grant, M., 206
Grauerholz, L., 40
Gray, J., 104, 106, 107
Gray, J. J., 39
Gray, K., 353
Gray-Little, B., 91
Green, R.-J., 190
Green, T., 302
Green, V. A., 77
Greenberg, B. S., 34, 40
Greene, B., 27, 328
Greene, M. L., 91
Greenfield, S., 317
Greenhaus, J. H., 262, 264
Greenhouse, S., 228, 336
Greenland, F., 163, 179
Greenleaf, C., 77
Greenstein, T. N., 65, 66, 230, 260, 261, 262, 265
Greenwood, D. N., 38
Greil, A., 163
Grella, C., 317
Greytak, E., 131
Grimberg, A., 279
Grimmell, D., 62
Gringart, E., 175
Grogan, S., 94, 96
Groh, C. J., 124, 277, 279, 280, 283, 321, 322
Gronda, H., 356
Gross, H., 156, 161, 164
Gross, S. M., 313
Grossardt, B., 311
Grossman, A. H., 131, 182
Grossman, A. J., 29
Grossman, A. L., 45
Gruber, J., 332, 335, 338
Gruenfeld, D., 225
Grundy, E., 165
Gryboski, K., 155
Guastello, D. D., 61
Guastello, S. J., 61
Guilmoto, C., 343
Gulati, M., 290, 291, 292, 293
Güngür, G., 235
Gunter, B., 37
Gupta, S., 261
Gustafsson, J., 301
Gute, G., 134
Gutek, B., 212, 228
Guttmacher Institute, 133, 134, 148, 149, 151, 152, 153, 157
Guy-Sheftall, B., 131
Gysbers, N., 212

H

Ha, J.-H., 186, 187
Haavio-Mannila, E., 137
Haag, P., 157

Hackett, G., 212
Haddad, E., 231
Hafdahl, A. R., 91
Hafner, K., 223
Hagestad, G., 165, 185
Hague, G., 352
Haider, S., 238
Haj-Yahia, M. M., 353
Halbreich, U., 155
Hall, D. M., 165, 188
Hall, D. R., 355, 356
Hall, J. A., 103, 108, 174
Hall, R. E., 10
Hall, R. L., 76, 77, 173
Hallerod, B., 301
Halpern., C. T., 91, 94, 319
Halpern, D. F., 24, 108, 109, 110, 111, 227, 235, 268
Hamby, S. L., 345
Hamilton, B. E., 157, 159, 160
Hamilton, E., 134
Hamilton, L., 134
Hamilton, M. C., 42
Hammen, C., 319
Hammond, C. B., 440
Hampson, E., 111
Hampton, T., 153, 297
Hank, K., 196
Hankin, B. L., 319, 320
Hankinson, A., 303
Hannaford, P., 287
Hanratty, B., 260
Hanson, S., 217, 218, 245
Hant, M. A., 35
Hardie, J., 180, 181
Hardin, M., 39
Harel, Z., 144, 145
Hare-Mustin, R. T., 3, 7
Harknett, K., 196
Harmetz, A., 35
Harmon, A., 178
Harper, M., 61
Harriger, J. A., 94
Harrington, B., 268
Harris, A. C., 25, 39
Harris, G., 151
Harris, M., 166
Harris, R. J., 65, 115
Harrison, D. A., 268
Harrison, K., 85
Harrison, M. S., 40
Harter, S., 90, 92
Hartley, J., 81
Hartman, H., 118, 212, 259
Hartman, M., 115, 212
Harvey, R., 114
Harvey, S., 342
Harvey-Wingfield, A., 226
Harville, M. L., 66
Hartwig, R., 197
Haskell, M., 35
Hattery, A., 262
Hatzenbuehler, M., 131, 323
Hausenblas, H. A., 96
Hausmann, R., 155, 206, 207
Havusha-Morgenstern, H., 181
Hawes, Z., 135

Hawkes, D., 218
Hawkes, K., 197
Hawkins, S., 144
Haxton, C., 196
Hayatabkhsh, M. R., 89
Hayden, S., 165
Hayes, J., 247, 248
He, W., 195, 302
Headlam, B., 115
Heaphy, B., 174
Hearn, J., 226
Heath, C., 151, 152, 287, 304
Heatherington, L., 216
Hébert, M., 342, 344
Hebl, M. R., 59, 156
Heckert, T. M., 214, 219
Hedberg, P., 325
Hedges, L. V., 109
Heeter, C., 115
Heffner, L. J., 163
Heggeness, M., 195
Hehman, J. A., 26, 355
Heilman, M. E., 229, 235
Heiman, J.R., 126, 138
Heiman, S. R., 138
Hein, M. M., 38
Heisig, J., 259
Heiss, C., 291
Heiss, G., 167
Helfand, M., 133, 134, 135
Helgeson, V. S., 38, 322
Hellerstein, J., 217
Helmreich, R. L., 60, 61
Helms, H., 192
Helson, R., 271
Hemmings, C., 4
Henderson, D., 10
Henderson, S., 151, 154, 155, 336, 348, 366, 368
Henderson-King, D., 95
Hendrick, C. L., 135, 341, 343
Henig, R. M., 135, 163, 193
Henley, N. M., 108
Henningsen, D. D., 175, 176
Henrici, J., 247
Henz, V., 260
Heo, M., 244, 318
Heppner, M. J., 240
Hequembourg, A., 129
Herbenick, D., 124, 128, 138
Herbst, C., 265
Herd, P., 232, 233, 260, 281, 301, 302
Herek, G. M., 27, 130, 131, 323
Herman, K. C., 8
Herman-Giddens, M. E., 86
Herman-Stahl, M., 324
Heron, M. P., 302
Herrera, V. M., 277, 340, 342
Hesse-Biber, S., 13, 96
Hessol, N., 284
Hether, H. J., 33
Hetherington, E. M., 183, 184
Hewlett, S. A., 230, 233, 270
Heyl, A. R., 243
Heyman, G. D., 101
Heymann, J., 267
Hidalgo, T. R., 363

Higginbotham, E., 213, 217, 218
Higgins, C., 270
Higgins, K., 304
Hilbrecht, M., 93, 115
Hildreth, C., 286, 292, 354, 355, 356
Hill, C., 332, 335
Hill Collins, P., 4
Hill, E., 268
Hill, M., 328
Hill, T. D., 341, 348
Hillard, P. J., 86, 367
Hillberg, T., 341
Hilliard, L. J., 59
Hillman, J. L., 139
Himmelstein, K., 131
Hindin, M. J., 351
Hines, M., 51, 52, 53, 54, 56, 73, 77, 78,
    83, 101, 102, 108, 109, 110, 111, 112,
    113, 115, 132, 135
Hipwell, A., 311
Hirschberger, G., 180
Hodges, M., 235, 341
Hoeber, L., 77
Hofferth, S. L., 135, 158
Hoffman, E., 251
Hoffman, L.W., 63, 83, 265
Hoffman, S. D., 133, 158
Hoffnung, M., 204, 213
Hogan, J. D., 7
Hogg, K., 83
Hogg, M. A., 103
Hogue, M., 234
Holcomb, M. 137, 164, 165, 166, 167
Holcombe, E., 149
Hollander, D., 96
Holmes, S., 302
Holmqvist, K., 94, 95
Holm-Denoma, J., 314
Holtgraves, T., 42, 43
Holton, G., 212
Holvino, E., 257
Holzman, C., 160
Honekopp, J., 133
Hoobler, J. M., 338
Hooghe, M., 130, 131
Hook, J. L., 259, 261
Hook, M. K., 212, 217
hooks, b., 18
Hooper, C., 341
Hopkins, A. B., 30, 230
Hornbacher, M., 313
Horner, M. S., 215
Horney, K., 3
Horowitz, J., 164
Hounsell, C., 250
Houvouras, S., 370, 371
Houser, M., 178
Huang, H., 10, 11
Huang, Y., 94
Huber, L., 149
Hudson, T., 168
Huesmann, L. R., 101, 102
Huffman, M. L., 233
Hugelshofer, D., 237
Hughes, M., 180, 185
Hull, S. H., 84
Hunt, K., 300

Hunter, E., 37
Hummert, M., 26
Humphreys, T., 346
Hundley, H. L., 26
Hunter, S., 341
Hurd Clark, L., 26, 34, 35, 174, 175
Hurtado, A., 10, 16
Husser, E., 293
Hutchens, R., 268
Hutcherson, S., 319
Huyck, M. H., 182
Hvas, L., 166
Hyde, J. S., 40, 96, 104, 109, 112, 113,
    123, 124, 130, 131, 215, 242, 266
Hyers, L., 30
Hymel, S., 172
Hynie, M., 137

I

Iervolino, A. C., 80
Iglehart, J. K., 281
Iliffe, S., 322
Im, E., 164, 166
Imperato-McGinley, J., 53
Impett, E. A., 91
Inglehart, R., 65
Institute for Women's Policy Research, 231,
    232, 261
Inter-Parliamentary Union, 226
Irwin, C., 318, 324
Isbell, L. M., 333
IsHak, W., 126
Ispa, J. M., 92
Israel, T., 131
Iwamasa, G. Y., 327
Iyer, A., 240

J

Jack, D. C., 319
Jacklin, C. N., 14
Jackson, A., 217, 218
Jackson, D., 229
Jackson, L. A., 310
Jacobs, A., 343
Jacobs, J., 242
Jacobs, R., 286
Jacobson, J., 205
Jadva, V., 164
Jaffe, J., 156
Jaffe, S., 104
Jain, S., 344
James, L. E., 43
James, S. D., 161
Jang, S., 262, 263, 267, 268
Janssen, I., 95
Jansz, J., 115
Jelenec, P., 114
Jenkins, C. L., 184
Jenkins, H., 116
Jeong, J., 228
Jepsen, E., 342
Jeydel, A., 151, 154, 155, 206, 207, 227,
    235, 242, 247, 250, 285, 336, 343,
    348, 366, 368
Jin, L., 180, 187
Johns, M., 150

Johnson, A., 4
Johnson, A. B., 188
Johnson, C. L., 325
Johnson, D., 135, 196
Johnson, D. M., 326
Johnson, J. L., 300
Johnson, J. O., 223, 267
Johnson, J. T., 65
Johnson, R. D., 116
Johnson, S. B., 9
Johnson, S. M., 191
Johnson, W., 180
Johnston, D. D., 189
Johnston, L., 316, 317
Jonason, P., K., 125
Jones, D. C., 95
Jones, D. J., 311
Jones, I., 162
Jones, J., 150
Jones, R. K., 151
Jones, S. M., 84, 185
Jones, T. V., 139, 281, 322
Jones-DeWeever, A. A., 92, 232
Jordan, C., 340, 347, 348, 352, 353
Jordan, J. V., 92
Jordan-Young, R. M. 50, 53, 54, 111, 128,
    132
Jose, A., 180, 181
Josselson, R., 90
Joutsenniemi, K., 180
Juckett, G., 327
Judkins, P., 259
Jung, J. 94, 314
Jungheim, E., 167
Juntunen, C. L., 217
Juvonen, J., 332

K

Kaestner, R., 77
Kagan, J., 103
Kahlenberg, R., 205
Kahlenberg, S. G., 38
Kahn, J., 192, 198
Kahn, J. S., 361, 363, 364, 372
Kail, B., 242
Kainen, A., 324
Kajantie, E., 299
Kalb, C., 284
Kalil, A., 158, 269
Kall, D., 190
Kalmijn, M., 181, 194
Kan, M. 135
Kane, J. B., 255
Kane, E. W., 25, 65, 68, 83, 255
Kane, M., 286
Kanner, M., 371
Kanny, D., 316
Kanner, M., 205
Kantamneni, N., 217
Kantor, M., 130, 323
Kantrowitz, B., 117, 164, 165, 166, 167
Karch, D., 322, 356
Käreholt, I., 304
Karlyn, K., 188
Karney, B. R., 179, 180, 192,
Karpiak, C. P., 66
Karpel, A., 36

Karpinski, A., 370, 371
Karraker, K. H., 27, 80, 81
Karreman, A., 311
Kasanen, K., 109, 115
Kasen, S., 319
Kashubeck-West, S., 94, 372
Kates, E., 209
Katz, D. S., 234
Katz, J., 372
Katz, P. A., 76, 364
Kaufman, G., 179
Kavan, M., 318
Kawamura, S., 261
Kazyak, E., 34, 39
Keaveny, T., 233
Keel, P. K., 312, 313, 315
Keene, J., 186
Keith, P. M., 185
Keith, T., 317
Keller, B. K., 218
Kelly, E., 9, 10
Kelly, J., 183, 184
Kelm, M., 291
Keltner, D. 108
Kemmler, W., 290, 304,
Kenfield, S. A., 291
Kenna, H., 322, 324
Kennedy, H. 159
Kenney, C., 261
Kensicki, L. J., 38, 39
Kern, M., 304
Kerpelman, J., 217
Kerr, B., 369
Kersting, K., 108
Kessel, C., 211
Kessler, E., 34, 317
Khang, K., 26
Khare, M., 301
Khosla, S., 290
Kiang, L., 102
Kiefer, A. K., 114, 216
Kiesner, J., 148
Kilbourne, A., 279
Killen, M., 265
Kilianski, S. E., 68
Killen, M., 83
Kim, J. E., 353
Kim, M., 368
Kim, W. J., 77, 322
Kimmel, D. G., 174, 205
Kimmel, E., 4, 16, 18, 25
Kimmel, M., 259, 372
Kimura, D., 115
King, C., 222, 226, 235
King, D. W., 64
King, J. E., 204, 205
King, L. A., 64
King, R. M., 95
Kinsella, K., 249
Kinser, A. E., 3, 16, 188, 189, 271, 367
Kinsey, A. C., 123
Kinsler, K., 361
Kinzie, J., 210
Kirk, G., 4, 36, 353, 366, 368
Kirkman, M., 52, 369
Kirmizioglu, Y.,318
Kissane, R., 319

Kissling, E. A., 88, 146
Kite, M. E., 23, 28, 68, 239, 280
Kitts, R., 323
Kitzinger, C., 114
Kitzman, D., 277
Klara, M. D., 18
Klein, A., 314
Kleinfeld, J., 204
Kleinfield, N. R., 354
Klimstra, T. A., 91, 93
Kling, K. C., 91, 215
Klinge, I., 277
Klohnen, E. C., 174
Klonsky, E., 341
Kluck, A. S., 95
Klumb, P. L., 271
Klump, K., 313
Kmiec, J., 367
Knafo, A., 02
Knapp, J. L., 97
Knight, J. L., 39
Knight, R., 351
Knightley, P., 43
Knudsen, K., 259
Koball, H., 180
Kobrynowicz, D., 30
Kogan, M., 279
Koh, H., 301
Kohatsu, W., 305
Kohlberg, L., 57, 58, 104
Kolata, G., 94, 152, 305
Kolb, D., 228
Kominos, V., 290, 291, 292
Konek, C. W., 240, 366
Konkel, K., 284
Konrad, A. M., 65, 219
Kontula, O., 137
Kooijmans, J., 343
Koput, K., 212, 228
Korabik, K., 229
Kornbluh, K., 250, 255, 268
Kornrich, S., 225
Koropeckyj-Cox, T., 165, 195
Korteland, C., 311
Kosciulek, J., 212
Kosciw, J., 131
Koss, M. P., 345, 350, 354
Kostianen, E., 264
Kowaleski-Jones, L., 197
Kowalski, R. M., 102
Kraemer, R., 216
Krahé, B., 95, 346
Kramer, A., 351
Kraus, M. W., 108
Krause, C., 95
Kreider, R. M., 29, 30
Kreiger, T. C., 84
Krieger, N., 294
Krishnamurthy, P., 264
Kristof, N. D., 153, 154, 206, 207, 235,
     322, 343, 353, 366, 368
Kroenke, C. H., 297
Kromrey, J. D., 25
Kronenfeld, L. W., 96
Kronish, I., 292
Krumrei, E., 183
Kubrin, C. E., 39

Kubzansky, L., 292
Kuchment, A., 321
Kuhlmann, E., 277
Kuhn, J., 160
Kuhn, M., 323
Kulik, L., 181, 246
Kumra, S., 229
Kunstman, J., 338
Kunz, J., 158
Kuperberg, A., 256
Kurdek, L., 182
Kurtz-Costes, B., 114
Kuyper, L., 182, 323
Kvaavik, E., 299, 303
Kwon, P., 237

L
L'Armand, K., 335
Lacey, K., 353
Lachance-Grzela, M., 261, 262
Lachs, M., 279
Ladge, J., 188, 268
LaFrance, M., 13, 106, 108, 338
LaFraniere, F., 249, 342, 343
LaFromboise, T. D., 218
LaGreca, A. M., 95, 311
Lai, Y., 137
Lakoff, R., 12
Lalor, K., 341
Lam, L. 304
Lam, V. L., 105
Lamb, S., 33, 149
Lambdin, J. R., 42
Lambiase, J. J., 40
Lampert, T., 271
Landesman, P., 343
Landherr, K., 154, 156, 160
Landrine, H., 9, 367
Landry, L. J., 91
Lane, M., 34
Laner, M. R., 177
Lang, M. M., 259, 260
Lang, U. A., 260
Langhout, R. D., 205, 338
Lansford, J., 134, 135, 183
Lapchick, R., 77
Lareau, A., 259
Larose, S., 217
LaRossa, R., 37
Larson, J., 172
Larson, S., 294
Laschever, S., 233, 234, 241
Lasswell, M., 180
Latzer, Y., 314
Laumann, E. O., 125, 126, 178
Lauzen, M. M., 33, 34, 35, 37, 39
Lavie, A., 290
Lawlor, D. A., 324
Lawrence, E., 180, 188
Lawson, K., 235
Lawton, C. A., 29
Lax, J., 131
Leach, C. R., 259, 277, 287
Leaper, C., 25, 30, 74, 77, 78, 80, 83, 106,
     108, 109, 116, 117, 371, 372
Leary, W. E., 138
Leathwood, C., 205, 206, 228

Lebenson, P., 304
Lee, A., 88, 89
Lee, C., 183
Lee, E., 152
Lee, E. O., 325
Lee, I., 303, 304
Lee, J., 196
Lee, L., 78, 172
Lee, S., 224, 227, 368
Lee, T. L., 31
Lee, Y., 304
Leeb, R. T., 108
Lefkowitz, E. S., 62
Lehr, S., 39
Lehti, A., 327
Leibson-Hawkins, B., 297
Leicht, K., 225
Leitner, M. J., 138, 139, 245, 246
Leitner, S. F., 138, 139, 245, 246
Leland, J., 243
Leman, P. J., 105
Lemieux, S. R., 341
Lemme, B., 180, 244
Lengua, L. J., 319
Leonard, R., 271, 325
LePage-Lees, P., 209
Lerner, J. S., 108
Lerner, S., 265, 268, 269
Lerner-Veva, L., 167
Laskinen, E., 338
LeSavoy, B., 363
Lester, D., 322
Leung, S. A., 211
Levant, R. F., 65
Leventhal, T., 135
Levesque, L. L., 334
Levesque, M. J., 176
Levine, A., 173
Levine, M., 300
Levine, S. C., 26
Levy, G. D., 74
Levy, S., 284
Lew, A., 208, 209
Lewin, T., 158, 318, 319
Lewis, M. I., 137, 139, 140
Li, C., 217
Li, Q., 102, 352
Liao, L., 175
Liben, L. S., 59, 111, 112
Li Ching, H., 342
Lichtenstein, A. H., 305
Liechty, T., 175
Liefbroet, A., 195
Lien, L., 90
Light, L., 322
Liljestrand, J., 155
Lindau, S. T., 137, 138, 139, 140
Lindberg, L. D., 89, 112, 114, 115, 158
Lindgren, K. P., 175, 176
Lindner, K., 38
Lindsey, E., 80
Lindsey, W., 277, 302, 316
Linn, M. C., 110
Linsk, N., 198
Lipka, S., 77, 130
Lipkin, E., 34, 39
Lippa, R. A., 53, 109, 217

Lips, H. M., 8, 156, 235
Liptak, A., 228
Liss, M. B., 75, 77, 81, 368
Little, M. V., 251
Little, W., 194
Littlefield, G. D., 182
Littleton, H., 346
Liu, H., 180
Liu-Ambrose, T., 304
Livengood, J., 256
Livingston, G., 188, 196
Lleras-Mooney, A., 301
Lloyd, C., 81
Lloyd-Jones, D. M., 291, 293
Lockwood, G., 338
Logan, J., 300
Logan, T. K., 339, 340, 343
Logel, C., 117
Logsdon-Conradsen, S., 135, 153, 155, 158
Lonborg, S., 212
London, K., 77, 109, 115
Londsway, K. A., 333, 338
Lont, A., 265
Lorber, J., 4, 18, 146, 154, 235, 362, 366, 367
Lori, J., 166
Lo Sasso, A., 232
Lott, B., 10, 17, 18, 27, 84, 279, 327, 364, 367
Loughran, D., 238
Lovas, G. S., 83
Love, S., 294, 295, 297
Lovell, V., 267
Low Dog, T., 167, 170, 277, 279
Lowe, M., 314
Lucas, R. E., 180, 181, 186
Lucas-Thompson, R., 265
Luce, H., 349
Luciano, L., 232
Luecken, L., 297
Luijendijk, H., 324
Luke, K., 83
Lummis, M., 109, 115
Lumpkin, J., 197, 198
Lundberg-Love, P., 268, 349
Luo, S., 174
Lussier, G., 196
Lydon-Rochelle, M. T., 160
Lykes, M., 13
Lyness, K. S., 267
Lyons, H., 217

M

Maas, C., 344
Mabry, M., 230
Macan, T., 155
Maccoby, E. E., 14, 79, 93, 177
Macy, R., 364
MacDonald, C., 189, 208
MacDonald, V., 208
MacDorman, M., 160
MacGeorge, E. L., 106, 107
MacKenzie, T., 314
Mackey, E., 95
MacLeod, M., 216
Magai, C., 296
Mager, J., 38
Magley, V. J., 337, 338, 339
Maguire, M., 146

Mahay, J., 125
Maine, D., 155
Mainiero, L. A., 104
Mair, C., 244
Maisto, S., 149
Maizes, V., 170, 277, 279
Majerovitz, S. D., 325
Major, B., 152
Mäkela, L, 156
Malanchuk, O., 91
Malcolmson, K. A., 29
Malkin, C., 372
Malson, H., 314
Maluso, D., 84
Manago, A., 371
Maniglio, R., 341
Manlove, J., 135, 149, 158
Mannheim Research Institute, 302
Manning, W. D., 148
Manthorpe, J., 322
Manuel, J., 267
Manzoli, L., 186, 187
Marano, H. E., 86
March of Dimes, 160
Marcus, E. N., 352
Marecek, J., 3, 7
Mares, M. L., 137, 244
Markovic, M., 288
Markson, E. W., 35
Markward, M., 319, 327
Marsh, P., 317
Marshall, N., 264
Martijn, C., 312
Martin, C. L., 27, 57, 59, 75, 77, 85, 111
Martin, J. A., 27, 159, 160
Martin, J. L., 102, 217, 339, 340
Martin, K., 34, 39, 83
Martin, M. O., 113
Martin, N., 115
Martinengo, G., 263
Martin, S. E., 337, 349, 353
Martinez, S., 236
Martínez-Vicente, J. M., 37, 38
Martire, L. M., 264
Martis, R. G., 115
Marton, K., 285
Martsolf, D., 342
Marvan, M., 166
Masciadrelli, B., 174
Maserejian, N., 292
Masser, B., 156
Massey, E., 204, 210
Massoni, K., 38
Mastro, D. E., 34, 39
Masui, A., 260
Mather, S., 291
Matlin, M. W., 26, 146
Matsui, Y., 65, 82
Mattis, J. S., 325
Matzuk, M., 144
Maume, D., 259
Mauthner, N., 162
Mavin, S., 236
Maxwell, J, 124, 191, 312
Maxwell, M., 166
Mayer, K. H., 280

Mayes, L., 318
Mazzella, R., 194
Mazzeo, S., 314
McAdams, D., 271
McCabe, S., 323
McCauley, E., 51, 53
McClintock, E., 35, 185
McCormick, L., 312, 313, 315
McCloskey, C., 218
McCloskey, K., 342, 343
McConnell, A. R., 43
McConnell-Ginet, S., 105
McDonald, P., 156
McDonald, S., 244
McDonnell, K., 248
McDougall, P., 173
McDowell, M. A., 86
McElvaney, R., 341
McGinn, K., 228
McGlone, M. S., 117
McHale, S. M., 77, 78, 81, 135
McHugh, M. C., 139
McIntyre, M., 78, 102, 160
McIsaac, C., 177
McKelvey, M. W., 183
McKenry, P. C., 183
McKenzie, M., 337, 342, 348
McKibbin, W., 9
McKinley, N., 312
McLanahan, S. S., 183
McLaren, S., 323
McLean, C., 103, 317
McLean, K., 91
McLean, S., 174
McLaughlin, D., 300, 310, 319, 327
McLoyd, V. C., 338
McNair, R., 280, 323
McPherson, B. J., 33, 38
McPhillips, K., 149
McTiernan, A., 294
McWilliams, S., 323
Mead, S., 205
Meadows, S., 118
Mechacra-Tahiri, S., 310
Media Awareness Network, 33, 38, 94
Mednick, M. T., 216
Meece, J. L., 34, 84
Meekosha, H., 156
Meem, D., 16, 36, 51, 52, 126, 129, 133
Megalethin, D., 114
Mehta, C., 78, 172, 173
Meier, A. M., 135, 174
Melendez de Santa Ana, T., 226
Mello, Z. R., 204
Mellor, D., 174
Menacker, F., 159
Mendelsohn, D. M., 80
Mendelsohn, G. A., 174
Mendes, W., 117
Mendle, J., 56, 88, 89
Menec, V., 303
Menzel, J., 95
Mercer, S. O., 195, 249,
Mercurio, A. E., 91
Merline, A. C., 317
Merskin, D., 175

Mertz, J., 113
Messersmith, E., 116
Messineo, M., 34
Messner, M., 44
METLIFE, 182
Metzl, J. M., 278
Meyer, D., 132
Meyer, J., 151
Meyer, M., 232, 233, 237, 260, 281, 302
Mezulis, A. H., 215, 216
Michael, S. T., 186
Michael, Y. L., 195
Michaud, S., 106, 107
Michelfelder, A., 168
Mignon, S., 316, 317, 323
Mihesuah, D., 66
Milani, R., 290
Milar, K. S., 4
Milburn, S. S., 33
Miles-Cohen, S., 228
Milkie, M. A., 188, 259, 260, 262, 263
Miller, C. C., 212
Miller, C. E., 74
Miller, D., 144, 147, 148, 149
Miller, E., 344
Miller, J., 95
Miller, J. B., 3
Miller, K., 257
Miller, L., 190
Miller, M. K., 115
Miller, M. M., 43
Miller-Day, M. A., 194
Milner, A., 322
Mindiola, T., 26
Miner, J. L., 101
Minieri, A., 175
Minnote, K., 267
Minto, C., 51
Mintz, L., 97, 218
Mintzes, B., 126
Miotto, K., 449
Misa, T., 116
Mischel, W., 56
Misra, M., 288
Mitchell, C., 352, 353
Mitchell, D., 163
Mitchell, K., 314
Mitchell, V., 190
Mize, J., 80
Mobily, K. E., 244
Moe, A., 112
Moen, P., 242, 243, 244
Moffat, S. C., 11
Moghadam, V., 368
Molnar, B. E., 312
Monahan, K., 340
Monda, K., 291
Mondschein, E. R., 76
Mongeau, P. A., 175
Monin, J., 23
Monsour, M., 173
Moody, J., 322
Moonesinghe, R., 279
Moore, A., 328
Moore, C., 103
Moore, D., 62

Moore, S. E., 277, 285, 291, 302, 305, 337
Moradi, B., 30, 94
Moreau, R., 322
Moreman, R. D., 173
Morgan, B. L., 370
Morgan, E. M., 128
Morgan, K., 312, 352
Morgan, P., 316, 332, 335, 336
Morr Serewicz, M., 177
Morrill, M., 217
Morris, B. R., 132, 398
Morris, E. W., 84
Morris, M., 234
Morris, W. L., 184
Morrison, G., 208
Morrison, M. A., 97
Morrison, T. G., 131
Morrongiello, B. A., 83
Morrow-Howell, M., 246
Mortenson, J., 160
Mosca, L., 277, 290
Moser, D., 292
Moser, S., 318
Mosher, C. E., 129, 150
Moskowitz, D., 130
Moss, C., 256
Moss, N. W., 156
Mottarella, K., 256, 258
Moyer, A., 341
Moynihan, R., 126
Muehlenhard, C. L., 346
Mueller, A., 95
Muennig, P., 279
Muise, A., 175
Mukherjee, J., 285
Mulac, A., 106
Mullis, I. V., 109
Munk-Olsen, I., 152
Muñoz, L., 290
Munson, L. J., 338
Munstertieger, B. F., 92
Murphy, S. T., 33
Murr, A., 284, 285
Murray, D. P., 39
Murray, T., 83, 91
Murray-Close, D., 101
Murrell, A. J., 212
Murthy, P., 152, 282, 343, 348
Muss, H., 277
Mustanski, B. S., 88, 323
Mutchler, J., 196, 197, 198
Muzio, C., 171
Myers, K., 177
Myint, P., 291

N
Nabi, H., 292
Nadal, K., 228, 335
Nadeem, E., 196
Nagoshi, J. L., 131
Nagy, G., 113, 216
Najdowski, C., 9, 348, 380
Nanda, S., 52
Nassif, A., 37
Nath, L. E., 103

National Academies of Sciences, 117
National Alliance for Caregiving, 198
National Campaign to Prevent Teen
    Pregnancy, 157
National Center for Health Statistics, 279,
    299, 300, 301
National Center for Victims of Crime, 340
National Institute of Child Health and
    Human Development, 360, 361
National Institute of Mental Health, 407
National Institutes of Health, 289
National Institute on Aging, 246, 286, 302
National Institute on Alcohol Abuse and
    Alcoholism, 288, 289, 290, 317
National Institute on Drug Abuse, 317
National Osteoporosis Foundation, 288,
    289, 290
National Science Foundation, 113
National Women's Health Information
    Center, 280
Natsuaki, M., 89
Navarro, M., 34, 197
Nayak, M. B., 348
Neff, K. D., 67
Neff, L. A., 179
Neiterman, E., 156
Nekolny, K., 28
Nelson, B., 218
Nelson, D., 172, 173, 211
Nelson, J. A., 372
Nelson, M. E., 304
Nelson, M. K., 188
Nelson, M. R., 39
Nelson, N. M., 83, 109
Nerenberg, I., 354, 356
Nesbitt, M. N., 23
Netburn, D., 94
Neuberg, S., 117
Neuendorf, K., 39
Newcombe, N. S., 111, 112, 115, 212, 265
Newcombe, P., 347
Newman, A. A., 185
Newman, M. L., 107
Newtson, R. L., 185
Ng, J., 278, 292
Nguyen, H., 117
NICHD Early Child Care Research
    Network, 265
Niemann, Y. F., 26
Nierman, A. J., 65
Nietert, P., 180
Nieuwenhoven, L., 277
Nix-Stevenson, D., 4
Nolan, S., 227
Nolen, P., 268
Nolen-Hoeksema, S., 319
Nomaguchi, K. M., 265
Noonan, R., 344
Nordberg, J., 207
Nori, R., 112
North American Menopause Society, 161,
    165, 166, 167, 168
Northrup, C., 145, 159
Nosek, M. A., 27, 115, 124, 166, 174, 206,
    223, 302
Novak, M., 246

Novitskie, D., 344, 350, 354
Nowell, A., 109
Nunes, K. L., 441
Nunn, K., 356
Nussbaum, M., 207
Nutti, R., 327
Nyad, D., 317

O

Oakley, D., 417
Oates, M. R., 205
Obradovic, J., 311
O'Brien, E., 83, 281
O'Brien, K., 218, 225, 227
O'Brien, M., 105
O'Byrne, R., 346
O'Connor, E., 191
O'Connor, G., 291, 292
O'Connor, M., 339
Odoi-Agyarko, R., 154
OECD, 109
Offer, S., 260
Office on Women's Health, 145, 281, 310
Ofstedal, M. B., 195
O'Grady, M., 166
Ogle, R., 346
Oinonon, K., 89
Okazawa-Rey, M., 4, 36, 353, 365, 369
Okimoto, T. G., 229, 235
Okun, K., 246
O'Leary, A., 250, 255, 268, 316
O'Leary, P., 342, 371
Olff, M., 341
Olkin, R., 179, 183, 184, 191, 206, 318,
    354
Olsen, J., 344
Olsen, P. R., 222
Olson, E., 186
Olson, J. E., 65
Olson, L., 352
Olson, K. R., 57
Olson, S. L., 190
Ong, R., 243, 260, 311
Onishi, N., 215
Ontai, L. L., 93
Opi, E., 197
Orbuch, T. L., 266
Orenstein, P., 95, 163
Oringanje, C., 158
Orman, S., 249
Ormerod, A. J., 332
Orringer, K., 88
Ortega, L., 322
Orth, U., 91, 324
Orza, A. M., 338
Osborne, L., 118, 218
Ostrove, J., 11, 101
Oswald, D., 114, 347
Oswald, R., 174
Ovarian Cancer National Alliance, 168, 287
Overstreet, N., 96
Owen, J., 134
Owens, G. P., 130
OWL, 182, 187, 195, 198, 247, 250, 280,
    281, 354, 355, 356
Ozer, E., 318

P

Pachter, L., 190
Packard, E., 293
Padavic, I., 66, 223, 234
Padgett, D., 193
Padilla-Walker, L., 83, 115
Paek, H.-J., 33, 38, 39
Pahor, M., 304
Palczewski, C., 12, 13, 36, 43, 44, 45, 105,
    108
Palmer, C. T., 9, 350
Paludi, M. A., 75, 268, 335, 336, 353, 363,
    365, 372
Pan, G., 116
Pankake, A., 210
Papalia, D., 151
Paradise, S. A., 185
Paras, M., 341
Paré, E., 188, 270
Parera, N., 135
Park, E., 300
Park, K., 304
Parke, R. D., 83, 265
Parker, E., 198
Parker, H. M., 38
Parker, K., 196
Parker, R. G., 52
Parker, W., 288
Parker-Pope, T., 94, 124, 180, 312
Parkes, A., 5, 135
Parks, C. A., 131
Parmley, M., 75, 103
Parsons, K., 156
Pascoe, E., 319
Pascual, A., 231
Patel, V., 340, 353
Patrick, J., 197, 198
Patterson, C. J., 132, 182, 191
Patterson, D., 349
Pattison, H., 156, 161, 164
Patwell, M., 223, 347
Paul, P., 95
Paulson, J., 162
Paykel, J., 154, 160
Pazol, K., 151, 152
Peacock, P., 345
Pearce, S., 343
Pearson, J., 77, 323
Pease, B., 344, 347, 352, 353
Pecora, N., 40
Pedersen, D., 267
Pedersen, S., 89
Pellegrini, A. D., 79
Penn, N. E., 23
Penner, A. M., 113
Peplau, L. A., 124, 125, 217
Pepler, D., 101
Pepperell, J., 317
Percheski, C., 183, 256
Pérez, M., 343
Pérez-Pêna, R., 160
Perkins, S., 353
Perilla, J., 352
Perlez, J., 52
Perrin, E. M., 94, 96

Perron, J., 286
Perrone, K., 262
Perry, J., 204, 211
Perry-Jenkins, M., 10, 80, 259, 266, 269
Perz, J., 166
Peter, J., 172
Peter, T., 341
Peterman, L. M., 448
Peters, R., 265
Petersen, A. C., 110
Peterson, J. E., 279
Peterson, J. L., 123, 124, 130, 131
Peterson, J. Z., 346
Peterson, K. A., 161, 162
Petravic, K., 196
Petrie, T. A., 94
Pettinati, H., 317
Pew Research Center, 130, 131, 151, 157,
    165, 179, 180, 181, 182, 183, 184,
    185, 188, 195, 257, 265
Pfaff and Associates, 231
Phares, V., 158
Phillips, J. H., 131
Phillips, L., 52
Physicians Committee, 145
Pianta, R., 265
Piaweek, K., 305
Piller, C., 331
Pina, A., 336
Pinquart, M., 172, 260
Pinto, K., 259, 261
Pirard, S., 317
Pittman, L.D., 196
Plante, L., 159
Plebani, C., 317
Plassman, B., 304
Plaut, V., 212
Plec, E., 66
Plöderl, M., 131, 323
Plomin, R., 102
Plucker, J.A., 117
Poertner, P., 28
Pokorak, J., 345
Poline, J., 95
Polimeni, A., 97
Poltery, J., 152
Poortman, A., 261, 262
Pomerantz, E., 204
Pomerleau, A., 80
Popenoe, D., 91
Popp, D., 104
Porter, P., 294
Porter, T., 343
Posner, R.B., 40
Post, L., 345
Potter, D., 183
Potter, J., 148
Poulin, F., 78, 89, 172
Poulin-Dubois, D., 74
Powell, B., 190
Powell, G.N., 262, 264
Powell, L.M., 304
Power, C., 197
Powlishta, K.K., 58, 73
Pregler, J., 292
Prejean, J., 286
Prentice, K., 293

Press, J., 259, 279
Presser, L., 259
Priebe, G., 341
Prieler, M., 34
Primm, A., 327
Prinstein, M.J., 311
Prokos, A., 186
Pronk, R.E., 84
Propp, K., 153
Proulx, C.M., 180, 192
Pruchno, R.A., 198, 302
Pruthi, S., 145, 150, 151, 154, 159, 279,
    283, 288, 290, 291, 305, 313
Puts, D.A., 111

Q

Quinlan, K., 10, 11
Quinn, D., 338
Quinn, J.B., 251
Quinn, P.C., 111

R

Rabasca, L., 115
Rabin, R., 286, 292
Rabinowitz, V.C., 8, 13
Rader, J., 179
Radford, A., 205
Radovick, S., 86
Rafaelli, M., 93
Raiford, J.L., 344
Raj, A., 322
Rakel, B. 303
Raley, S., 81, 157
Ramaswami, A., 227
Ramisetty-Mikler, S., 346
Ramsey, L.R., 371
Range, L., 322
Rani, M., 353
Rankin, L. E., 102
Rankin, S., 131
Rape, Abuse, and Incest National Network, 345
Rashotte, L., 23
Rathus, S., 76, 80, 86, 87, 112, 122, 123,
    124, 125, 126, 136, 137, 138, 150,
    151, 283, 285, 340, 342
Ratner, E., 294
Räty, H., 109, 115
Rawlins, W., 173
Ray, O., 297
Ray, R., 267
Rayburn, C., 227
Raymond, L., 177
Read, B., 205, 206, 228
Read, J., 139
Read, M., 182, 237, 323
Read, S., 165
Rebar, R.W., 163
Reczek, C., 181
Redberg, R.F., 293
Reddy, D.M., 135, 341
Reed, E., 351
Reed, S., 315
Reeder, H.M., 173
Reeves, J.B., 244
Regan, P.C., 183
Reece, M., 124
Regan, P.C., 96

Regnerus, M. 134, 149, 179
Reibis, R., 290
Reichert, F.F., 304, 305
Reichert, T., 39, 40
Reid, L., 158
Reid, P.T., 8, 9, 10, 80, 88, 210, 367
Reid, R., 278
Reiner, W.G., 53
Rejeskind, F.G., 108
Renk, K., 311
Renzetti, C., 352
Reskin, B.F.,223, 231, 234
Revenson, T.A., 297
Reviere, R., 322
Reyes, C., 342
Reynolds, J., 184
Rezvani, S., 229
Rhoades, G., 134, 180
Rhode, D.L., 91, 92
Riall, T., 279
Ricci, E., 168
Ricciardelli, L. A., 94
Rice, J.K., 184, 278
Rich, M., 277
Richards, A., 189
Richards, J., 149
Richards, M.A., 89
Richardson, L., 296
Rickard, K., 335
Ridgeway, C.L., 229
Rienzi, B.M., 66
Rieker, P., 277
Rife, J.C., 239
Riggio, H.R., 65, 83, 265
Riggle, E., 323
Riley, S., 312
Rimac, I., 130
Rinelli, L., 316
Rintala, D.H., 176
Rios, D., 365
Risman, B.J., 68, 259
Roberto, K.A., 293
Roberts, D.F., 95
Roberts, S., 193
Robin, L., 158
Robins, R.W., 279, 324
Robinson, B.K., 37
Robinson, G., 218
Robinson, J.D., 35
Robnett, R.D., 105
Roche, J., 135
Roche, K., 135, 315, 316
Rodgers, C.S., 346
Rodgers, R.F., 95
Rodriguez-Munoz, A., 338
Roe, L., 29
Roehling, P., 263
Roeser, R.W., 118
Roett, M., 287
Roffman, E., 328
Rogers, J., 188
Rogers, S.J., 266
Rogol, A., 89
Rogstad, K., 281, 282
Röhner, J., 311
Rojas, M., 367
Rolfe, A., 189

Rolfe, D., 304
Romaine, S., 42, 44
Romo, L., 196
Rondon, M., 277, 310
Rood, L., 319
Rook, K.S., 186
Rose, A.J., 310
Rose, D., 294
Rose, S.M., 101, 172, 174, 177, 178
Rosen, L., 176
Rosen, R., 314
Rosenfeld, A., 293
Rosenfeld, D., 131
Rosenthal, L., 284
Rosenthal, S.L., 88, 89
Rosin, H., 205
Rospenda, K.M., 336, 337
Ross, H.S., 102
Ross, L., 348
Rosselli, F., 39
Rossi, A.S., 166
Rothblum, E.D., 97, 181, 182
Rothman, E.F., 351
Roughgarden, J., 49, 52, 53, 350
Rowland, D., 165
Roy, B., 311
Roy, R.E., 372
Royo-Vela, M., 37
Rozee, P., 337, 343, 348
Rubel-Lifschitz, T., 219
Rubenstein, A., 133
Rubenstein, L.M., 244
Rubin, A., 135
Rubin, K.H., 84
Rubin, M., 284
Rubin, R., 260
Ruble, D.N., 58, 75, 111
Rudman, L.A., 370, 371
Rudolfsdottir, A., 316
Rudolph, K.D., 89, 172, 310, 311, 318, 319
Rudolph-Watson, L., 327
Rueger, S., 172
Ruf, P., 355
Ruggles, S., 195
Ruiz, S.A., 197
Runowicz, C.D., 287
Rural Center, 284, 285
Ruspini, E., 23
Russell, D.E.H., 332
Russell, J.E.A., 240
Russell, S.T., 128, 131
Russo, N.F., 9, 62, 189, 228, 229, 278, 310,
    311, 318, 319, 320, 326, 327, 367
Rust, J., 84
Rust, P.C., 129
Rutherford, A., 7, 8
Rutledge, T., 290, 291, 292, 293, 311
Ryan, A.M., 117, 149
Ryan, M., 227
Ryalls, B.O., 59
Rydell, R.J., 117
Ryle, R., 49

S

Saad, L., 131
Sabattini, L., 227, 264, 267
Sabik, N.J., 34, 35, 94

Sachs-Ericsson, N., 263
Sadker, D., 84, 92
Sadker, M. 84
Sadler, C. 148
Safran, M., 327
Saftlas, A., 155
Sai, F., 153, 155
Salafia, E., 314
Salazar, L., 149
Salomone, R., 210
Sammel, M., 164
Samuels, C.A., 62
Sanchez, M., 301, 302
Sanchez-Hucles, J., 173
Sanci, L., 314
Sandall, J., 160
Sandelowski, M., 284
Sander, L., 77
Sanders, S., 148
Sandfort, T., 191
Sandhu, H., 278
Sanmartin, C., 302
Sardadvar, K., 260
Sargent, J., 313, 314, 315
Sarkisian, N., 190, 194
Sasaki, T., 259, 262
Sassler, S., 176, 185
Saul, S., 163, 164
Saunders, K.J., 372
Savci, E., 190, 259
Savin-Williams, R.C., 123, 129, 135, 149,
    158, 348
Sawchuk, D., 246
Sawrikar, P., 267, 268
Sax, L., 204, 217
Saxon, S.E., 269
Sayal, K., 316
Sayer, L., 260
Sbarra, D., 180
Scantlebury, K., 34, 84
Scarborough, E., 6
Schachner, D., 185
Schalet, A., 135
Scheckler, R.K., 116
Schellenbach, C., 158
Scher, M., 85
Schick, V., 139, 286
Schiebinger, L., 259
Schilt, R., 52, 128
Schmader, T., 117
Schmid Mast, M., 108
Schmitt, M.T., 226, 229
Schmittdiel, J., 278
Schneider, B., 223, 225, 260, 267, 268
Schneider, C., 292
Schneider, M.C., 28
Schnurr, M., 344
Schoeman, W.J., 61
Schoen, R., 266
Schoenberg, N.E., 287
Schoenfeld, R., 110
Scholtz, S., 312
Schooler, D., 95
Schoon, I., 218
Schuette, C., 83
Schuler, J., 154
Schulman, A., 122

Schultheiss, D., 336
Schultze, M., 316
Schultz, K., 242, 243, 244
Schultz, R., 323
Schuppe, J., 336
Schur, L., 206, 232
Schutz, A., 311
Schuz, B., 298
Schwartz, G., 244
Schwartz, J., 38, 131
Schwartz, M., 351, 354
Schwartz, S., 219
Schweinle, W., 231
Scott, L., 165
Sczesny, 23, 24, 225
Sear, R., 197
Searle, E., 68
Sears, K.L., 337
Sears-Roberts Alterovitz, S., 174
Sechrist, G., 311
Sechzer, J., 8, 13
Seedat, S., 317
Seedyk, E., 115
Seem, S.R., 326
Seeman, T.E., 299, 302, 303
Segal, D., 322
Segre, T., 292
Seiden, O.J., 140
Seidman, I., 345
Seif, H., 128
Seifer, D.B., 86, 164, 166
Seiffge-Krenke, L., 91
Seitz, V., 158
Sekaquaptewa, D., 114
Sellers, S.A., 52, 66
Selmon, N., 91, 92, 216, 265
Selwyn, N., 212
Sen, A., 301, 343
Sengupta, R., 34
Senn, C.Y., 12
Serbin, L.A., 75, 76, 77, 312
Serowky, M., 124, 126
Settles, I.H., 92, 236, 283
Sexton, V.S., 5
Shacklock, K., 242
Shah, K., 154, 368
Shakin, D., 80
Shanok, A.F., 190
Shamanesh, M., 283
Shankar, A., 301
Shankman, S., 314
Shapiro, J.R., 117
Share, T.L., 97
Sharp, E.A., 92, 184
Shaw, L., 244, 247
Shedd, J., 75
Sheehan, N., 196
Sheldon, K.M., 174
Shellenbarger, S., 183, 266, 271
Shelley, L., 343
Shelton, N., 162, 163
Shepela, S.T., 334
Sherman, S.R., 26, 239
Shih, M.J., 216
Shinn, L.K., 104
Shipherd, J., 323
Shirtcliff, E.A., 86

Short, M.B., 88, 89
Short, S., 198
Shupe, E.I., 337, 338
Sices, L., 109
Sidener, J., 179
Siebenbruner, J., 135
Siebert, S., 243
Siegal, D.L., 121, 137, 138, 140, 185, 187, 194, 199, 243, 246, 247
Sigal, J., 216, 333, 339, 344, 350, 354
Signorielli, N., 35, 37
Silberreisen, R., 172
Sill, M., 351
Silva, C., 227
Silva, E., 332, 335
Silver, R.B., 312
Silverstein, M., 186, 196, 197, 198, 260
Simkhada, P., 343
Simkin, P., 154, 155, 159, 305
Simmons, R.G., 90
Sim, L., 314
Simmons, R. G., 115
Simmons, T., 233, 251
Simon, L. J., 360
Simon, R. W., 103, 165, 177, 188, 263
Simoni, J., 284
Simpkins, S. D., 115
Sinclair, L., 29
Singer, N., 126, 166, 175
Singh, T., 322
Sinha, R., 305
Sinno, S., 265
Skerrett, P., 305
Skinner, D., 259
Skoe, E., 104
Slagle, R., 36
Slater, A., 94
Slevin, K. F., 97
Slon, S., 316
Smart Richman, L., 319
Smetana, J. G., 83
Smith, A., 66
Smith, C. A., 94, 174
Smith, C. L., 300, 317
Smith, C. S., 342
Smith, D., 206
Smith, G., 123, 134
Smith, J. L., 216
Smith, K., 286
Smith, N., 175
Smith, R. L., 172
Smith, R. S., 197
Smith, S. L., 33, 34, 37, 39, 115
Smits, A., 193
Smock, P., 163, 179
Smolak, L., 92, 94
Snell, M. B., 303
Snyder, T. D., 113
Sobchack, V., 35
Society of Actuaries, 248
Solberg, J., 335, 339
Solomon, C., 38
Son, J., 246
Sonfield, A., 158
Sonnert, G., 216
Sontag, L., 318
Sontag, S., 35

Soons, J., 181
Spade, J., 16
Speer, S., 105
Spelke, E. S., 115
Spence, J. T., 60, 61
Spencer, J. M., 135
Spencer, S. J., 117
Sperry, S., 314
Spiegel, D., 297
Spies, J., 288
Spitzberg, B., 340
Spitzer, B. L., 326
Sprecher, S., 102, 177
Spinath, B., 216
Springen, K., 243
Springer, K., 189
Srivastava, S., 324
Sroufe, L. A., 79
St. John, W., 160, 315
St. Rose, A., 118
Stacey, J., 191
Staff, J., 219
Stake, J. E., 63
Stankiewicz, J. M., 39
Stanley, A., 222
Stanley, S., 180, 181, 245
Stanton, A. L., 276
Statistics Canada, 109
Staudinger, U., 26
Steele, C. M., 117
Steele, J., 212, 251
Steffens, M. C., 114
Steil, J. M., 83
Stein, K., 78
Steinberg, J. R., 23, 152, 264, 268
Steinberg, L., 135
Steinmayr, R., 216
Stephan, Y., 305
Stephens, J., 94
Stephens, M. A., 263, 234
Stephens, M. B., 293
Stepp, L., 134
Stern, G. S., 62
Stern, M., 80
Stern, T., 91
Sterne, E. M., 198
Stetler, C., 342
Stevens, L., 162
Stevens, P., 149, 152
Stevenson, B., 77
Stevenson, H. W., 109, 115
Stewart, A. J., 271, 272, 273, 316, 317
Stier, H., 226
Stiles, T., 318
Stillman, S., 174
Stinson, D. A., 94
Stockdale, M., 337, 338
Stohs, J. H., 261
Stokoe, E., 105
Stone, P., 256, 324
Stoner, C. C., 109
Stormshok, E., 319
Stotzer, R., 323
Strahan, E., 95
Straumanis, J., 278
Strauss, R. S., 92
Strauss, S., 229

Strauss, W., 353
Street, A. E., 336
Stricker, G., 139
Strickland, B. R., 3
Stringhini, S., 301
Strong, T. H., 160
Stross, S., 212
Strough, J., 78, 172, 173
Stubbs, M., 88
Studenski, S., 304
Stuhlmacher, A., 233
Stueve, A., 171
Stulhofer, A., 130
Su, R., 211, 219
Su, Y., 9
Suarez, E., 347, 351
Sue, D. W., 208, 228
Suellentropp, K., 158
Sulik, S., 151, 152, 158
Sullivan, C. M., 354
Sumberg, E., 198
Summers, A., 1115
Summers-Effler, E., 89
Sun, Q., 303
Sunderam, S., 163
Suris, J., 135
Susman, E. J., 86, 89
Susskind, J. E., 59, 73, 75
Sutfin, E. L., 83
Svedin, C., 341
Swaby, A., 342
Swanson, D. H., 189
Swanson, K., 156
Swartz, T., 193, 194, 195, 198
Swearer, S., 68
Swearingen-Hilker, N., 262
Sweeney, C., 95
Sweeney, M., 186
Swim, J. K., 30, 31, 32, 45, 67, 94, 97
Switzer, J. Y., 43
Sybert, V. P., 51, 53
Syltevik, L., 180
Szinovacz, M. E., 244
Szymanski, D. M., 130

T

Tafalla, R. J., 115
Taft, C., 352
Taft, J., 366
Taht, K., 269
Tai, T.-O., 265
Talley, A., 323
Tamis-Lemonda, C., 29, 109
Tan, J., 196
Tang, F., 246
Tapia, A., 229
Tarrant, S., 372
Tartaro, J., 62, 318, 319, 320, 326, 327
Tasker, F. L., 191, 192
Tassone, S., 154, 156, 160
Tavernise, J., 190
Taylor, C. A., 35
Taylor, C. J., 228
Taylor, D., 214
Taylor, J.E., 342
Taylor, J. L., 158
Taylor, N. L., 95

Teachman, J., 264, 266
Teasdale, B., 323
Teig, S., 75
Teitelman, A., 282
Temkin, J., 346
Templeton, K., 209, 305
Tenenbaum, H. R., 80, 116
Terlecki, M. S., 112
Terry-Schmitt, L. N., 67
Terzian, M., 311
Teten, A., 344
Thacker, D., 358
Thacker, H., 166, 167, 168
Thaper-Björkert, S., 342
Thill, K. P., 115
Thomas, A. J., 92
Thomas, J. J., 65, 76
Thomas, J. L., 198
Thomas, K., 40
Thomas, P., 194, 310
Thomas, V., 216
Thomlinson, B., 286
Thompson, E. M., 128
Thompson, G., 280
Thompson, K. M., 340
Thompson, M., 322
Thorne, B., 75
Thornhill, R., 9, 350
Thurston, R., 292
Tichenor, V., 261
Tickamyer, A., 10, 125, 126, 127
Tiedemann, J., 147
Tiedens, L., 225
Tiegs, T. J., 135
Tiggemann, M., 94, 95
Tillman, M. S., 345, 349
Timmerman, G., 332
Titze, C., 110
Tobach, E., 50
Tobin, D. J., 188
Toepfer-Hendey, E., 217
Toller, P. W., 371
Tolman, D. L., 125, 135
Tolman, R., 351, 354
Tolomio, S., 290
Tomlinson, B., 369
Topa, G., 243
Torges, C., 271
Torkas, S., 291, 292, 293
Torpy, J. M., 136, 291, 318, 352
Toth, E., 147
Tougas, F., 32
Toussaint, D., 37
Townsend, S., 345
Townsend, T. G., 40, 92
Tracy, J., 280
Trautner, H. M., 75
Travis, C. B., 304, 305
Treas, J., 65, 257, 265
Trimberger, E. K., 184
Trivers, K., 287
Troop-Gordon, W., 84, 89, 311
Troxel, W. M., 292
Trzesniewski, K. H., 91, 206, 324
Tucker, C. J., 78
Tucker, C. M., 8
Tucker, J. S., 45

Tudge, J., 81
Tuggle, C. A., 38
Tuller, D., 163
Turchik, J. A., 337
Turiel, E., 104
Turjanski, N., 163
Twenge, J. M., 23, 60, 61, 62, 68, 91
Tyler, K. A., 135
Tylka, T., 94
Tyre, P., 95
Tzuriel, D., 110, 112

U

U.S. Bureau of Labor Statistics, 259, 260
U.S. Census Bureau, 23, 38, 79, 182, 184,
     185, 189, 190, 195, 196, 197, 198, 204,
     223, 224, 225, 226, 232, 233, 238, 249
U.S. Department of Commerce, 165, 179, 231
U.S. Department of Education, 109
U.S. Department of Health and Human
     Services (USDHHS), 281, 291, 304,
     315, 324, 327, 352
U.S. Department of Justice, 311
U.S. Department of Labor, 232, 240
Uchino, B., 300
Uchitelle, L., 251
Uecker, J., 134, 135, 149, 179
Ueno, K., 173, 323
Ui, M., 65
Ulibari, M., 126
Ullman, S., 9, 343, 346, 350
Umberson, D., 180, 198
UNAIDS, 283, 285
Underwood, M., 176
Unger, J. B., 303
Unger, R. K., 7, 9, 13, 364
UNICEF, 153, 155, 206, 384
UNIFEM, 155, 206
United Nations, 373
United Nations Childrens' Fund, 285
United Nations Office on Drugs and Crime,
     343
Upadhyay, U., 152
Upton, M., 147
Urquiza, A., 341
Ussher, J., 166
Utter, J., 95

V

Vaccaro, A., 207, 228
Valentine, C., 16
Valian, V., 143, 144
Valkenburg, P. M., 172
Valla, J., 12, 111
Vallance, D., 162
Valls-Fernández, F., 37, 38
Van Assen, M., 103
Vance, K., 204, 211
vanDam, R., 303
Van de gaer, E., 109
Vandell, D., 265
Van den Berg, P., 95
van den Hoonard, D., 186, 187
Van der Lippe, T., 261, 262
Vandermaelen, A., 284
Van de Velde, S., 318

Vandewater, E. A., 264, 271, 272
Van Evra, J., 34, 35, 41, 85
vanGelderen, L., 191
Van Home, B., 149
Van Willigen, M., 261
Vanfraussen, K., 191
Vann, E. D., 67, 68
van Steirteghem, A., 163
Vasilyeva, M., 111, 112
Vasquez, M., 6, 91
Vaughan, C. A., 91, 94
Veloski, C. 290
Veniegas, R. C., 132
Ventura, S. J., 158
Vézina, J., 344
Villarosa, L., 121, 139
Vincent, W., 131
Vinson, C., 165
Vishnevsky, T., 349
Viswanathan, H., 343
Vona-Davis, L., 294
Voorpostal, M., 194
Votruba-Drzal, E., 265
Voyer, D., 109, 111
Vuoksimaa, E., 111

W

Wadler, J., 193
Wadsworth, S., 349
WAGE Project, 232
Wahab, S., 352
Wai, J., 109, 112
Wainright, J. L., 191
Waits, B., 349
Walby, S., 233
Walker, A., 17, 273
Walker, E., 165
Walker, H., 239
Walker, L., 104
Walker, M., 21
Walker, R., 339, 340
Wallace, S., 280, 323
Wallis, C., 39
Walsh, B., 312, 313
Walsh, D., 243
Walsh, J., 133, 135
Walsh, K., 341
Walsh, R., 304
Walsh, V., 76
Walsh, W. B., 221, 240, 241
Walsh-Bowers, R., 6
Walter, C., 185, 187
Walton, G., 117
Walumbwa, F., 268
Wang, L., 172
Wang, M., 242, 243, 244
Wang, P., 268
Wang, Q., 204
Wangby, M., 312
Ward, C., 348
Ward, L., 40, 85
Wareham, S., 310
Warner, J., 256
Warner, R., 106, 107
Warner, S., 342, 359
Warren, C., 152
Warren, J. S., 310

Warren, J. T., 152
Warren, M., 314
Warshaw, G., 198, 260, 299
Warshaw, R., 348
Wartik, N., 278
Washington, D., 292
Wasserman, G., 311
Watamura, S., 265
Waterman, A., 91
Watson, E., 324
Watson, S., 133
Watt, H., 113, 216, 221
Waxman, S., 37
Wayne, J., 267
Weaver, H., 66
Webster, M., 23
Weger, H., 173
Wegman, H., 342
Weichold, K., 90
Weigt, J., 268
Weinberg, D., 233
Weinberg, M., 181
Weinberger, N., 78
Weinstock, J., 173, 174
Weisgram, E., 211
Weiss, K., 346, 347, 348
Weitz, R., 99, 279, 301
Weitzer, R., 39
Wellman, N., 305
Wells, B., 17
Welsh, A., 39
Welton, A., 167
Wenger, G., 185
Wentzel, K., 103
Wenzel, A., 155
Werhun, C., 132, 133
Werner, E., 197
Wertheim, E., 94
Wessler, S., 332
West, C., 337, 338
Weyerer, S., 315
Whaley, R., 9
Whang, W., 292
Whealin, J., 341
Wheeler, M., 343
Whelan, P., 151
Whiffen, V., 162
Whipple, V., 187
Whiston, S., 218
Whitbourne, S., 172
White, A. A., 277, 278
White A. M., 371, 376
White, J., 18, 21, 71, 101, 102, 341, 344, 354, 356
Whitehead, B., 91
Whitehead, D., 275
Whitley, B., 131
Whitley, H., 277, 302, 316
Whitmire, R., 205
Whooley, M., 292
Widmer, E., 327
Widom, C., 341
Wiederman, M., 346
Wigfield, A., 216, 217
Wijeysundera, H., 291

Wilbourn, M., 75
Wilbur, J., 319
Wight, V., 259, 260, 361
Wilcox, S., 186
Wilcox, W., 180
Wilkinson, J., 35, 278
Wilkinson, L., 323
Williams, C., 226
Williams, D., 34, 115
Williams, J. C., 255, 268
Williams, J. E., 24, 76
Williams, J. R., 344, 352, 356
Williams, K., 113
Williams, M., 214
Williams, N., 159
Williams, R., 473
Williams, T., 113
Williams, W., 112, 113
Williamson, J., 304
Willness, C., 338
Willoughby, T., 115
Wilper, A., 279
Wilsnack, R., 315
Wilson, D., 166
Wilson, F., 218
Wilson, G., 314
Wilson, H., 341
Wilson, J., 284
Wilson, P., 237
Wilson, R., 205, 207, 228
Wilson, S., 337
Winfield, L., 237
Wingert, P., 164, 165, 166, 167
Winkle-Wagner, R., 208, 221
Winn, J., 115
Winterich, J., 136
Wiseman, R., 101
WISER, 247, 248, 249, 250, 251
Witten, T., 174, 182
Wittig, M., 371
Wolf, J., 188
Wolf, P., 186, 187
Wolfe, B., 158
Wolfe, D., 344
Wolf-Wendel, L., 210
Wolitzky-Taylor, K., 321
WomenHeart, 277
Women's College Coalition, 210
Women's Sports Foundation, 77
Wong, J., 244
Wood, J., 44
Wood, W., 2, 18, 28, 30, 102, 175, 226, 229
Woodhill, B., 62,
Woods, K., 336, 337, 338
Woods, N., 136
Woodward, L. J., 171, 397
Woodzicka, J., 338
Woolf, S., 149
Wollven, L., 144
Worell, J., 15, 326, 327, 330, 366
World Health Organization, 39, 154, 300, 301, 343, 355
Worth, R., 348
Wrench, J., 97
Wright, L., 84

Wroolie, T., 136, 137, 164, 165, 166, 167
Wurtele, S., 342
Wyche, K., 360
Wylie, S., 131

X

Xie, D., 80
Xinran, 343
Xu, J., 299
Xu, Q., 324
Xu, X., 77
Xue, F., 294

Y

Yabroff, J., 116, 188
Yagil, D., 339
Yaish, M., 226
Yakushko, O., 372
Yan, F., 344
Yang, B., 322
Yang, Z., 149
Yankaskas, B., 279
Yao, M., 33, 39, 115
Yardley, J., 198
Yates, A., 162, 188
Yeretssian, G., 299
Yeung, D., 88
Yeung, J., 353
Yoder, J., 8, 262, 337, 371, 372
Yoon, D., 325
Young, J., 337
Youngblade, L., 63, 83, 265
Yousafzai, S., 322
Yu, L., 80
Yuan, A., 89, 94, 239
Yunger, J., 84, 93

Z

Zabin, L., 134
Zager, K., 133
Zahn-Waxler, C., 318
Zalk, S., 10, 210, 361
Zambrana, R., 16, 18, 21, 208, 267
Zand, D., 177
Zaritsky, E., 280
Zavos, H., 319
Zenilman, J., 283
Zerbe, K., 312
Zernike, K., 185
Zhang, Y., 39, 117
Zhou, Q., 82, 311
Zilberman, M., 316
Zichy, S., 266
Zimmer, Z., 195
Zimmer-Gembeck, M., 133, 134, 135
Zimmerman, E., 156
Zink, T., 351, 354
Zinn, M., 17
Ziv-Gal, A., 166
Zosuls, K., 73, 74, 79
Zucker, A., 271, 371, 372
Zucker, K., 49, 53
Zucker, N., 312
Zurbriggen, E., 347

SUBJECT INDEX

A

Ableism, 27
Acquired immunodeficiency syndrome
  (AIDS), 283–286
Abortion, 151–152
  attitudes toward, 151
  consequences of, 152
  incidence, 151–152
  methods, 152
Abuse of children. *See* Child sexual abuse.
Abuse of women
  dating violence, 344
  intimate partner violence, 351
  elder abuse, 355
Achievement level, 214–219
Achievement motivation
  attributions for own success or failure,
    215
  confidence in own achievement, 216
  definition of, 214
  fear of success, 215
Activities of daily living (ADLs), 302
Adolescence
  body image and, 93–97
  contraception, 148–149
  dating, 176–177
  eating disorders, 312–313
  friendship during, 172
  gender intensification, 92–93
  growth spurt, 89
  identity formation in, 90–91
  maturation, 89–90
  menarche, 86–89
  pregnancy, 157–158
  psychosocial development, 90–97
  puberty, 85–90
  self-esteem, 91–92
  sexual activity during, 133–134
  sexually transmitted infections,
    281–285
  substance abuse, 315–317
  suicide, 321–322
Advocate, 246
Affiliative interruption, 105
Affirmative action, 240
Age
  breast cancer and, 294
  heart disease and, 290
Ageism, 26
Agency, 23
  stereotypes in the media, 38–39
Agoraphobia, 318
Aggression, 101–102
Alcohol
  abuse, 315–317
  breast cancer and, 294
  consequences, 316
  ethnicity, 315
  heart disease and, 292
  incidence, 315–316

intimate partner violence, and,
    352
  osteoporosis and, 289
  rape and, 348
  risk factors, 316
  sexual activity and, 135
  treatment, 316–317
Alpha bias, 2
Ambivalent sexism, 31–33
American Psychological Association,
  women in leadership roles, 5–8
Androgen-insensitivity syndrome, 52
Androgens, 50
Androgyny
  definition, 60
  evaluation of concept, 62–63
  psychological adjustment, 62
Anorexia nervosa, 312
Anxiety disorders, 317–318
Acquaintance rape, 345
Aromatase inhibitors, 297
Asian Americans
  academic values, 208–209
  alcohol use, 315
  body image and, 96
  career aspirations, 211
  degrees attained, 204–206
  divorce, 183
  elder caregiving, 199
  employment rates, 223
  gender stereotypes, 26
  illegal drug use, 317
  intimate partner violence, 352
  living with relatives, 195
  marriage of, 179
  menopause attitudes, and, 167
  mortality rates for, 301–302
  osteoporosis, 289
  perception of family and employment
    roles, 261
  poverty, 248
  raising grandchildren, 198
  rape, 345
  single mothers, 189
  teen pregnancy, 157
  wages, 231–232
Association for Women in Psychology, 8
Attractiveness
  disabilities and, 174
  media emphasis on, 39–40
  in romantic relationships, 174–175
Augmented families, 190
Authoritarianism and gender attitudes, 67

B

Backlash effect, 30
Balancing family and work, 255–273
Barriers hindering women's
    advancement, 227–231
Battering. *See* Domestic violence.

BEM Sex Role Inventory (BSRI), 60
Benevolent sexism, 31–32
Beta bias, 2
Biases
  in research, 8–13
  in publications, 12–13
Binge drinking, 316
Binge eating disorder, 313
Birth control pills, 149, 150, 287,
    292
Bisexuals, 129
Bisphosphonates, 290
Blacks
  abortion, 151–152
  academic environment, 208
  adolescent friendships, 172
  AIDS and, 283–284
  alcohol use by, 315
  body image and, 96
  breast cancer, 294
  career aspirations, 211, 217–218
  cervical cancer, 287
  degrees attained, 204, 206
  divorce and, 183
  elder caregiving, 199
  employment rates, 223
  fibroid tumors, 286
  gender attitudes, 65
  gender stereotypes and, 25–26
  healthcare and, 271
  heart disease, 291
  high blood pressure, 291
  hysterectomy, 288
  illegal drugs and, 317
  intimate partner violence, 352
  lesbian women of color, 131
  living with relatives, 195
  marriage of, 179
  menarche, 86
  menopause attitudes and, 167
  mortality rates for, 301–302
  occupational choices, 225
  older women, 325
  pension income, 250
  perception of family and employment
    roles, 261
  poverty, 248
  raising grandchildren, 198
  rape, 345
  retirement, 243–244
  self-esteem in adolescence,
    91–92
  sexual harassment and, 337
  sexually transmitted diseases and,
    281–284
  sexual problems, 126
  single motherhood, 189
  suicide, 321
  teen pregnancy, 157
  wages, 231–232

Body image, 93–97
  ethnic differences in, 96–97
  gender differences in, 94
  lesbians and, 97
Boy crisis, 205
Brain differentiation, 50–51
Brain size, 7
BRCA-1 and BRCA-2 genes, 294
Breast cancer, 293–298
Bulimia nervosa, 313

C

Calcium, 289, 305
Career aspirations, 211–212
Career counseling, 212
Cancer
  breast, 293–298
  cervical, 287
  endometrial (uterine), 287
  lung, 398, 300
  ovarian, 287
Caregiving
  of elderly, 198–199
Castration anxiety, 54
Cervical cancer, 287
Cesarean section, 159
Child sexual abuse, 340
  consequences of, 341–342
  incidence of, 340–341
  prevention, 342
  treatment, 342
Childbirth. *See also* Pregnancy.
  after age 35, 160
  cesarean section, 159
  doula, 160
  family-centered approach to, 160
  Lamaze method, 159–160
  in later life, 161–162
  methods of, 159–160
  nurse-midwives, 160
  and postpartum distress, 162–163
  stages of pregnancy, 159
Childfree, 165
Children
  adult, 194–195
  effects of mother's employment on, 265
  feminist socialization of, 364–265
Children's literature
  sexist stereotypes in, 38–40
  underrepresentation of females, 34
Chilly campus climate, 207
Chlamydia, 282–283
Chromosomes, 50
Classism, 4
Clitoris, 122
Common couple violence, 351
Cognitive abilities, 108–118
Cognitive developmental theory, 55–58
Cohabitation, 180–181
Communication style, 104–108
Communion, 23, 38–39
Communal orientation, 105
Computers, 115–116
Congenital adrenal hyperplasia (CAH), 52–54

Contraception, 148–151
  adolescents and, 148–149
  methods, 149–151
Corpus callosum, 7
Corumination, 319
Cosmetic surgery, 175
Counselor self-disclosure, 328
Cybersex, 133

D

Dating
  during adolescence, 176–177
  online sites, 178
  recent trends in, 178–179
  scripts, 177
  violence and, 344
  women with disabilities and, 176
Depression
  gender differences in, 318
  heart disease and, 292
  in adolescence, 318–319
  in adulthood, 318
  in older adults, 321
  postpartum, 162
  theories of, 319–320
Diabetes, 291
Diagnostic and Statistical Manual
  of Mental Disorders, 326
Diet. *See* Nutrition.
Differences approach, 2–3
Disabilities, women with
  ableism, 27
  career aspirations and, 211
  dating issues for women with, 176
  divorce, 183
  eating disorders, 313
  employment rates, 223
  health care, 280
  higher education and, 208
  in later life, 302–303
  intimate partner violence, 352
  perceived attractiveness, 174
  physical campus environment and, 206
  research on, 9–10
  sexuality and, 124
  stereotypes of, 27
Discrimination
  against sexual minorities, 131–132
  age, 239
  in the workplace, 228–229, 234–235
Division of family labor, 258–262
Divorce, 182–184
Domestic violence
  definition of, 351
  disability and, 352
  effects of, 353
  ethnic and global comparisons, 353
  incidence, 351–352
  intervention, 354
  risk factors, 352–353
  theories of, 354
Double standard
  of aging, 35
  sexual, 126–135
Doula, 160

Drawing conclusions
  meta-analysis, 14–16
  narrative approach, 14
Dual entitlement, 250
Durable power of attorney, 249
Dysmenorrhea, 144
Dyspareunia, 126

E

Eating disorders, 312–315
  anorexia nervosa, 312–313
  binge eating disorder, 313
  bulimia nervosa, 313
  causes of, 313–314
  female athlete triad and, 314
  treatment, 314–315
Economic issues in later life, 247–251
Education
  attainment of, 204–207
  campus climate, 207–210
  goals, 204
  level, and gender attitudes, 66
  sexual harassment in school, 332–335
  single-sex schools, 209–210
Effacement, 159
Effect size, 16
Egalitarian gender attitude, 64
Elder abuse, 355
Electra complex, 55
Emotionality, 103–104
Emotions
  during motherhood, 188
  in pregnancy, 155
Empathy, 103
Employment. 222–253. *See also* Work.
Empty nest period, 192
Endometriosis, 163, 286
Enhancement hypothesis of multiple
  roles, 264
Equal Pay Act, 232
Eriksen, Erik, 4, 90
Essentialism, 3
Estrogen, 50, 144, 145, 164, 166,
  167, 168, 290. *See also* Hormone
  replacement therapy, Progesterone.
Ethnicity
  abortion and, 151–152
  AIDS and, 283–284
  and alcohol, 315
  academic environment and, 208
  attitudes toward menopause
    and, 167
  body image and, 96–97
  breast cancer and, 294
  cervical cancer and, 287
  collectivistic values and, 208–209
  defined, 17
  degrees attained and, 206
  feminism and, 371
  gender attitudes and, 65–66
  gender stereotypes and, 26
  and health care, 279
  intimate partner violence, 352
  and lesbianism, 131
  mental health therapy issues and, 327
  mortality rates and, 301–302

occupational choices, 225
rape and, 345
self-esteem and, 91–92
sexual dysfunction and, 126
sexual harassment and, 337
sexually transmitted infections, 281, 284
single motherhood and, 189
wage differentials and, 231–232
workplace segregation and, 233
Evolutionary theory of rape, 350
Exercise. *See* Physical activity.
Excitement phase, of sexual response cycle, 122
Extended families, 190
External genitalia, 50–51
Externalizing disorders, 311–312
External female anatomy, 122–123
Externally focused responses, 339

F

Family
augmented, 190
coordinating work and, 262–270
division of household labor, 329–333
extended, 190
midlife transition in roles, 270–273
solutions to family-work balancing challenges, 262–270
Father. *See also* Family.
household responsibilities, 258–259
Fatherhood wage premium, 235
Fear of success, 215
Fee-for-service insurance, 281
Female
athlete triad, 314
genital cutting, 154
orgasmic disorder, 126
Feminism
beliefs, 369–373
definition, 3, 4
liberal feminism, 4
cultural feminism, 3, 4
goals of, 361–369
men and, 372–373
socialist feminism, 4
radical feminism, 4
women of color feminism, 4
women's studies courses and, 363–364
Feminist identification, 370–371
Feminist research methods, 13–14
Feminist theory
of intimate partner violence, 354
of rape, 350
Feminist therapy, 327
Femininity, 60
Feminization of poverty, 190
Fetal alcohol effect, 316
Fetal alcohol syndrome, 316
Fibroid embolization, 288
Fibroid tumors, 286
5 alpha-reductase deficiency, 53
Field dependence and independence, 12
Flextime, 268
Follicular phase, 144

Freud, Sigmund, 7, 54–56
psychosexual stages of development, 54–56
Friends with benefits, 134
Friendships
in adolescence, 172
in adulthood, 172–173
gender differences in, 172–173
lesbian, 128
of older women, 173–174

G

Gay man, 128
Gender
attitudes, 49, 63–68
children's knowledge of, 73–76
constancy, 57–58
definition of, 2
distinction between sex and, 2
in English language, 42–45
identity, 49
in the media, 33–41
self concept, 49–50
social construction of, 18–19
Gender bias
in diagnosis of psychological disorders, 325–326
in psychotherapy, 326–327
Gender-biased language, 13
Gender comparisons. *See also* Gender differences.
aggression, 101–102
alcohol abuse, 315
attitudes, 63–68
attribution patterns, 275
brain, 7
cognitive abilities, 108–118
communication style, 104–108
computer usage, 115–116
depression, 318
double standard of sexuality, 126, 135
educational attainment and, 204, 206
educational values, 204
emotionality, 103–104
empathy, 103
exercise, 304
friendships, 172–173
health care and health services, 356–357
health insurance, 280–281
importance of physical attractiveness, 174–175
influenceability, 102–103
leisure activities, 244–245
mathematics ability, 112–118
mental health, 324
moral reasoning, 3, 104
motor skills, 76–77
physical performance and sports, 76–77
prosocial behavior, 102
retirement, 242–244
salary expectations, 214
self-esteem during adolescence, 91–92
substance abuse, 317

verbal ability, 109
video game usage, 115–116
visual-spatial ability, 109–112
Gender development
influences on, 80–85
media, 85
parents, 80–83
peers, 84
school, 84
siblings, 83–84
Gender differences. *See also* Gender comparisons.
body image and, 93–97
division of household labor, 258–259
friendships, 172–173
heart disease and, 290
in illness, 302
job satisfaction, 236–237
in leadership and job advancement, 225–231
in lung cancer, 298
in mortality, 298–299
nonverbal communication, 108
in occupational distribution, 233
in power, 17–18
in puberty, 89
in salaries, 231–235
sexual activity and, 124–125
sexual attitudes and, 123–124
in suicide, 321–322
verbal communication, 104–107
Gender harassment, 336
Gender identity, 73–74
Gender intensification, 92–93
Gender paradox, 298
Gender-related activities and interests, 76–79
Gender-related traits, 60–63
changes in, over time, 60–62
psychological adjustment and, 62
social behaviors and personality traits, 100–104
Gender roles, 2
Gender schema theory, 55, 58–59
Gender segregation, 78–79
Gender stereotypes
as a barrier to advancement, 229–230
of children, 27
of children in single parent homes, 83
children's knowledge of, 73–76
development of, 74–76
in English language, 42–45
and ethnicity, 25–26
of occupations, 75
portrayed by media, 33–41
Gender typing
definition of, 54
media and, 33–41
theories of, 54–59
Generalized anxiety disorder, 318
Genital herpes, 283
Genital warts, 283
Glass ceiling, 226
Glass cliff, 227
Glass escalator, 226

Global perspectives
  AIDS epidemic, 285
  benevolent sexism, 32
  economic status of older women, 249
  education, gender differences in, 206
  educational climate under Taliban, 207
  elder abuse, 355
  employment of married women,
    attitudes toward, 257
  female genital cutting, 154
  gender attitudes, 65
  gender stereotypes development of, 76
  grandmothers, 197
  health of women, 301
  human trafficking, 343
  infanticide, 342–343
  intimate partner violence, 353
  living arrangements, older women, 195
  mate selection, 175
  mathematics achievement, 113
  menopause, 166
  multiple genders, 52
  parental leave policies, 267
  pregnancy-related deaths, 155
  rape victims, attitudes toward, 348
  reproductive lives, 153
  research on gender, 14
  sexual minorities, 130
  suicide, gender differences in, 322
  thinness, cultural pressure for, 315
  women's movements, 368
  working conditions, girls and women,
    235
Gonadal development, 50
Gonorrhea, 282–283
Grandmothers, 196–198
Group pressure conformity studies, 103

H

Harassment. *See* Sexual harassment.
Health insurance, 280–281
Health services and care
  for sexual minorities, 280
  physician-patient relationship, 278
  type and quality, 278–279
  women of color, 279
Heart disease, 290–293
Hepatitis B, 283
Herceptin, 297
Heterosexism, 130
High blood pressure. *See* Hypertension.
Higher education
  campus climate, 207–210
  degrees received by women, 206, 211
  ethnicity and, 208, 209
  poor and working class women and, 209
Homophobia, 130–132
Honor killings, 348
Hook-up, 134
Hopkins vs. Price Waterhouse, 30, 230
Hormone replacement therapy, 167
  alternatives to standard, 168
  definition of, 167
  benefits, 168
  risks and side effects, 168
Hostile environment, 335

Hostile sexism, 31–33
Hot flashes, 164
Household labor
  division of gender differences in,
    258–259
  explanations of, 261–262
  women's perceptions of, 260–261
Human capital perspective, 233
Human papilloma virus, 282–283
Human trafficking, 343
HIV, 283–286
Hypertension, 291
Hysterectomy, 288

I

Identification, 54
Identity formation
  in adolescence, 90–91
Identity labels, 29–30
In vitro fertilization, 163
Incest, 340
Individuation, 90
Infanticide, 342–343
Infertility, 163–164
Infibulation, 154
Influenceability, 102–103
Inhibited sexual desire, 125
Instrumental activities of daily living
    (IADLs), 302
Insurance. *See* Health insurance.
Intellectual ability, 108
Internal reproductive organs, 50–51
Internalizing disorders, 311
Internally focused response, 339
Interrole conflict, 262
Interruption of speech
  affiliative, 105
  intrusive, 105
Intersectionality, 16, 17
Intersexuality, 51–54
Intimate partner violence. *See* Domestic
    violence.
Intimate terrorism, 351
In vitro fertilization, 163

J

Job satisfaction, 236–238
Job-related characteristics and career
    choice, 219

K

Kinkeepers, 194

L

Labia majora, 122
Labia minora, 122
Labor force participation rates of women,
    223–224
Laissez-faire leadership, 231
Lamaze method, 159
Language
  Gender bias in research, 13
  gender representation in, 42–45
  practices based on normative male,
    42–43
  negative female terms, 44–45

Lateralization, 111–112
Latinas
  academic values, 208
  AIDS and, 284
  alcohol use by, 315
  body image and, 96
  cervical cancer, 287
  degrees attained, 204, 206
  divorce, 183
  elder caregiving, 199
  gender attitudes, 65–66
  gender stereotypes, 25–26
  healthcare and, 279
  heart disease, 291
  illegal drugs and, 317
  intimate partner violence, 352
  living with relatives, 195
  marriage of, 179
  media and, 34
  menarche, 86
  menopause attitudes and, 167
  mortality rates for, 301–302
  occupational choices, 225
  perception of work and family roles,
    261
  poverty, 248
  raising grandchildren, 198
  rape, 345
  self-esteem in adolescence, 91
  sexual harassment, 336
  sexual problems, 126
  single motherhood, 189
  teen pregnancy, 157
  wages, 231–232
Leadership
  discrimination, 228–229
  effectiveness, 231
  glass ceiling, 226
  ingroup favoritism, 230
  mentors, 227–228
  perceived threat, 230–231
  positions, 226–227
  stereotypes, 229–230
Leadership style
  Laissez-faire, 231
  transformational vs. transactional
    style, 231
Leisure activities in retirement, 244–247
Leisure time, 260
Lesbians
  attitudes toward, 130–131
  body image and, 97
  career selection, 217
  definition of, 128
  discrimination against, 131–132
  friendships, 173–174
  health and healthcare, 280
  intimate partner violence, 352
  job satisfaction, 237–238
  loss of partner, 187
  in media, 36–37,
  mental health of, 323–324
  as mothers, 190–191
  relationships, 181–182
  research on, 10
  same-sex spousal rights, 132

sexual harassment and, 337
stereotypes of, 27
STIs and, 283
women of color, 131
Living arrangements of elderly, 195
Lumpectomy, 297
Lung cancer, 298
Luteal phase, 144

M

Male as normative, 42–43
Mammogram, 295
Managed care, 281
Marriage
  rates, 179
  same sex, 132
  satisfaction with, 179–180
Masculine generic language, 42–43
Masculinity, 60
Mastectomy, 297
Mate selection across cultures, 175
Maternal employment
  attitudes toward, 255–258
  effects on children, 265
  effects on spouse, partner, 266
Maternal wall, 227
Maternity blues, 162
Mathematics ability, 112–118
  Achievement, 112–113
  attitudes toward mathematics,
    113–114
  and mathematics self-efficacy, 113
  parents' influence on, 115–116
  stereotype threat, 117
  teachers' influence on, 116–118
Maturation, effects of early and late,
  89–90
Media
  attractiveness emphasized in, 39–40
  ethnic women in, 34
  gender representation in, 33–41
  ingroup favoritism, 230
  invisibility of older women in, 34–35
  lesbians and gays in, 36–37
  sexuality in, 39–40
  thinness emphasized in, 39–40
Medicaid, 281
Medicare, 280
Menarche, 86–88
Menopause
  attitudes toward, 166
  definition of, 164
  hormone replacement and, 167–168
  physical symptoms, 164–166
  psychological reaction to, 166
Menstrual joy, 146
Menstruation, 7, 140–148
  menarche, 86–88
  attitudes toward, 144–146
  menstrual cycle, 144
  menstrual pain, 144–145
Mental health
  childhood and adolescence, 311–312
  gender differences in, 310
  older women, 324–325
  and optimism, 311

of sexual minority women, 323–324
  and social support, 310
Mental rotation, 110–111
Meta-analysis, 14–16
Mentoring, 227
Microaggressions, 208
Midlife
  double standard of aging, 35
  menopause, 164–168
  satisfaction with life roles, 271–272
  sexuality and, 136–137
  transitions, 270–273
Miscarriage 156
Modeling. *See* Observational learning.
Modern sexism, 31
Modified radical mastectomy, 297
Mons pubis, 122
Moral reasoning, 3, 104
Morbidity, 298
Mortality, 298
  female-male gap, 298–299
  leading causes of death, 301
  social class and ethnic differences,
    300, 301
Motherhood
  Empty nest period, 191–193
  lesbians and, 190–191
  mandate, 189
  single women, 189–190
  stereotypes of, 188–189
  surrogate, 163
  wage penalty, 235
  women with disabilities and, 191
Motor skills, 76
Mullerian ducts, 50–51
Mullerian inhibiting substance, 51
Multiple genders, 32
Myomectomy, 288

N

Narrative approach, 14
Native Americans
  academic environment and, 208
  alcohol use, 315
  body image and, 96–97
  cervical cancer, 287
  degrees attained, 204, 206
  gender attitudes, 66
  heart disease, 291
  illegal drug use, 317
  intimate partner violence, 352
  mortality rates for, 301, 302
  multiple genders, 52
  raising grandchildren, 198
  rape, 345
  single motherhood, 189
  suicide, 321
  teen pregnancy, 157
  wages, 294
  women leaders, 66
Negative terms for females, 44–45
Never-married women. *See* Single women.
Nonportability, 250
Nontraditional gender attitude, 64
Nonverbal communication gender
  comparisons, 108

Nurse-midwives, 160
Nutrition
  in breast cancer, 294
  in heart disease, 291–292
  needs throughout life, 305
  in osteoporosis, 290

O

Observational learning, 56
Occupational choices, 224–225
Occupations. *See also* Employment, Work.
Oedipus complex, 54
Older women
  adult children and, 194
  advocate/activist, 246–247
  and AIDS, 285–286
  attitudes toward, 26
  earnings of, 232
  exercise, 303–305
  friendships, 173–174
  grandchildren of, 196–198
  health services, 277
  health insurance, 280–281
  leisure activities of, 244–247
  living arrangements of, 195
  in media, 34–35
  mental health of, 324–325
  pensions, 250–251
  in poverty, 247–248
  research on, 10
  retirement, 242–251
  sexuality of, 137–140
  siblings of, 194
  Social Security benefits, 248–249
  vital older women, 324–325
  as volunteers, 246
  widowhood, 185–187
  work and, 238–239
Optimism, 311
Organizational tolerance, 339
Orgasm, 123
Orgasmic phase, of sexual response
  cycle, 123
Orgasmic platform, 123
Osteoporosis, 288–290
Ovarian cancer, 287
Ovulation, 144

P

Panic disorder, 318
Pap smear, 287
Paradox of contended female worker, 236
Parallel terms, 44
Parental leave, 266–267
Parents and gender development, 80–83
Patriarchy, 4
Patronizing behavior, 228
Pay equity, 239
Peers and gender development, 84
Penis envy, 54
Pension plans, 250–251
Perimenopause, 164
Personal Attributes Questionnaire
  (PAQ), 60, 61
Persuasion studies, 102
Phobias, 318

Physical activity, 289, 291, 294, 303–305
Physical attractiveness. *See* Attractiveness.
Physical health in later life, 381–383
Phyto-estrogens, 168
Plateau phase, of sexual response cycle, 123
Play
    gender differences, 77–79
    parental influence on, 80–81
    rough-and-tumble, 78
Population, 9
Postpartum depression, 162
Postpartum psychosis, 162
Poverty, 247–248
Power
    gender differences in, 17–18
    interpersonal, 17
    in lesbian relationships, 181
    organizational, 17, 361
    power-over, 17
    power-to, 18
    rape and, 446–447
    in relationships, 361
    sexual harassment and, 338
    theory of, 338
    touch and, 108
Pregnancy. *See also* Abortion, Childbirth.
    death related to, 55
    physical changes during, 154–155
    psychological changes during, 155
    reactions to pregnant women, 156
    women with disabilities, 156
Premenstrual dysphoric disorder, 147
Premenstrual syndrome (PMS), 147
    definition of, 147
    treatment, 148
Prenatal development
    androgens, 50
    brain differentiation, 51
    estrogens, 50
    external genitalia, 51
    gonadal development, 50
    internal reproductive organs, 50–51
    sex differentiation, 49–51
Primary sex characteristics, 86
Progesterone/progestin, 144–145, 167
Prostaglandins, 145
Prosocial behavior, 102
Psychoanalytic theory, 54–56
Psychological disorders, diagnosis and treatment, 325–328
Psychology of women
    history of, 7–8
    research and teaching, 363–364
Psychosocial development 90–97
Psychotherapy
    feminist therapy, 327–328
    gender bias, 326–327
    poor women and women of color, issues for, 327
    traditional therapies, 327
Puberty, 85–90
    early and late maturation, 89–90
    events of menarche, 86–89
    gender differences in, 89
    stages of, 87

Q

Quid pro quo harassment, 335

R

Race
    defined, 17
Racism, 4
Radical mastectomy, 297
Raloxifene, 290
Rape
    acquaintance rape, 345
    alcohol consumption and, 348
    attitudes toward, 348
    characteristics of rapists, 346–347
    characteristics of victims, 347–348
    definition of, 345
    effects of, 348–349
    evolutionary theory of, 350
    feminist theory of, 350
    incidence, 345
    myths, 347
    prevention of, 349–350
    social learning theory of, 350
Reach to Recovery program, 137
Reinforcement and punishment, 56
Relational aggression, 104
Relationships in later life, 193–199
Religious beliefs and gender attitudes, 66
Reproductive functioning in midlife and beyond, 164–168
Reproductive health of women globally, 153
Reproductive system disorders, 286–288
Research
    bias in, 8–13
    feminist methods, 13–14
    women's contribution, 6
Resolution phase, of sexual response cycle, 123
Retirement, 242–251
    adjustment to, 243–244
    decision to retire, 242–243
    economic planning for, 248–251
Roe vs. Wade, 151
Role models, 56
Role overload, 262
Role strain, 262
Romantic relationships, 174–179
Rough-and-tumble play, 78
Ruminative style, 319

S

Salary
    discrimination in, 234–235
    expectations, 214
    fatherhood wage premium, 235
    negotiations, 233–234
    reasons for differences in, 232–235
    gender differences in, 231–236
    motherhood wage penalty, 235
Sample, 9
Sandwich generation, 260
Savings and investments, 251
Scarcity hypothesis of multiple roles, 262
Secondary sex characteristics, 86
Secular trend, 86

Selection effect, 181
Self-efficacy, 113, 217
Self-esteem
    in adolescence 91–92
    and ethnicity, 91–92
Self-objectification, 94
Self-serving attributional bias, 215
Sex. *See also* Gender.
    definition of, 2
    distinction between gender and, 2
Sexism. *See also* Discrimination.
    ambivalent sexism, 31–32
    attitude changes, 31
    benevolent sexism, 31–33
    definition of, 4
    experiences with, 30
    hostile sexism, 31–33
    modern sexism, 31–32
Sex roles, 2
Sex Role Egalitarianism Scale, 64
Sex-role spillover theory, 338
Sexual abuse of children, 340
Sexual arousal disorder, 126
Sexual attitudes, 123–124
    double standard, 123, 135
Sexual behaviors, 124–125
Sexual coercion, 336
Sexual desire, 135–136
Sexual harassment
    in blue-collar occupations, 336
    college students and, 333–335
    consequences of, 338
    explanations of, 338–339
    hostile environment, 335
    incidence, 335–336
    in elementary and secondary school, 332
    in the military, 337
    offender characteristics, 337–338
    quid pro quo harassment, 335
    target characteristics related to, 337
    women's responses to, 335, 339
    in the workplace, 335
Sexual interest, perception of, 175–176
Sexual minorities. *See* Lesbians, Gay Men, Bisexuals, Transgender Individuals.
Sexuality
    adolescent sexual behavior, 133–136
    female sexual anatomy, 122–123
    gender differences, 123–125
    in later life, 137–139
    media portrayal of, 39
    midlife and, 136–137
    orgasm, 123
    sexual response cycle, 122–123
    wive's employment and sexual satisfaction, 266
Sexually transmitted infections, (STIs), 281–286
    acquired immunodeficiency syndrome, 283–286
    Chlamydia, 282–284
    gender differences, 282
    gonorrhea, 282–283
    HIV, 283–286
    human papillomavirus, 282–283
    risk factors in, 282–283

Sexual orientation, 49, 128–133
  and career development, 217
  explanations of, 132
  and gender stereotypes, 27
Sexual orientation hypothesis, 68
Sexual problems/dysfunction, 125–127
  female orgasmic disorder, 126
  inhibited sexual desire, 125
  New view, 126–127
  painful intercourse, 126
  sexual arousal disorder, 126
  vaginismus, 126
Sexual response cycle, 122–123
Sexual script, 346
Shifting standards, 230
Siblings, 83–84, 194
Similarities approach, 2
Simple mastectomy, 297
Single-sex schools, 209–210
Single women
  attitudes toward, 184–185
  as mothers, 189–190
  never-married, 184–185
Skip-generation parent, 197
Slimness, emphasis on, 39–40, 94–96
Smoking, 144, 166, 291, 294, 298, 300
Social categorization, 27–28
Social class. *See also* Ethnicity.
  and academic environment, 209
  and breast cancer, 294
  and friendships, 173
  and gender attitudes, 66
  and gender stereotypes, 26–27
  and mortality, 301
  and postpartum depression, 162
  and sexual dysfunction, 126–127
  and therapy, 327
Social cognitive theory, 57
Social construction of gender, 18–19
Socialization, 82
Social learning theory, 55–57
  of rape, 350
Social role theory, 28–29
Social Security, 248–250
Social status hypothesis, 68
Social support and mental health, 310
Soy products, 168
Specific phobia, 318
Spending down, 71
Sports, 76–77
Spotlighting, 42–43
Stalking, 339
Statistical significance, 12
Stereotypes
  of disabled women, 27
  of employed women, 229–230
  of ethnic minority women, 8, 26
  of females and males, 23–30
  of girls and boys, 27
  of lesbians, 27
  of older women, 26
  of poor women, 26–27
Stereotype threat, 117, 208
Sticky floor, 227
Substance abuse, 315–317
Suicide, 321–322
Surname choice, 29–30

Surrogate motherhood, 163
Syphilis, 282–283
Sweatshops, 235

T

Tag-team parenting, 269
Tamoxifen, 297
Teenage pregnancy, 157–158
  consequences of, 158
  prevention of, 158
  rate of, 157
Telescoping, 315
Television, as gender-typed socializing
  agent, 33–41
Tend and befriend, 310
Testosterone, 51
Therapy. *See* Psychotherapy.
Title of address, stereotypes based on,
  29–30
Title IX of the Education Amendments
  Act, 77
Token woman, 226
Toys. *See also* Play.
  gender differences in preferences, 77–78
  visual spatial skills and, 112
Traditional gender attitude, 64
Transformational leader, 231
Transactional leader, 231
Transgender individuals, 49, 128
Trichimoniasis, 283
Turner syndrome, 51–53
Type A personality, 292

U

Undifferentiation, 60
Unwanted sexual
  attention, 336
Uterine cancer, 287

V

Vacuum aspiration, 157
Vagina, 122
Vaginismus, 126
Vasocongestion, 122
Verbal ability, 108
Verbal communication, 104–107
Vesting, 250
Violence. *See* Abuse of women, Child
  sexual abuse, Dating.
Visual-spatial abilities, 109–112
  explanations of, 111–112
  mental rotation, 110–111
  spatial perception, 110–111
  spatial visualization, 110–111
Vital older women, 324–325
Vitamin D, 289, 305
Vulva, 122

W

Wages. *See* Salary.
Wage discrimination, 234
White Ribbon Campaign, 373
Whites
  abortion, 151–152
  AIDS and, 284

adolescent friendships, 172
alcohol use, 315
breast cancer and, 294
career aspirations, 211
degrees attained, 204, 206
divorce and, 183
elder caregiving, 199
employment rates, 223
heart disease, 291
illegal drugs and, 317
intimate partner violence, 352
living with relatives, 195
marriage of, 179
menarche, 86
menopause attitudes, 167
mortality rates for, 301–302
occupational choices, 225
osteoporosis, 289
pension income, 250
perception of family and employment
  roles, 261
poverty, 248
raising grandchildren, 198
rape, 345
research on, 10
retirement, 243–244
single motherhood, 189
suicide, 321
teen pregnancy, 157
wages, 231–232
Widowhood, 185–187
Wolffian ducts, 50–51
Women-as-problem bias, 185
Women of color. *See also* Ethnicity.
  academic environment for,
    208–209
  eating disorders, 312
  feminism, 4
  and health care, 278–279
  research on, 10–11
  therapy issues, 327
  underrepresentation in media, 34
Women psychologists, 4–8
Women's magazines
  emphasis on appearance, 39
  gender-based social roles in, 38
  older women in, 35
Women's movements, 366–368
Women studies courses, 363–364
Work. *See also* Employment,
  Jobs, Maternal Employment,
  Occupations.
  balancing family and, 262–270
  discrimination in advancement,
    228–229
  employment rates, 223–224
  family expectations and, 213
  in later life, 238–239
  parental leave, 266–267
  salaries, 231–235
  work-related goals, 210–214
Working-class and poor women. *See also*
  Social class.
  academic environment for, 209
  research on, 10
  stereotypes of, 26–27
  therapy issues for, 327

PHOTO CREDITS